Capi Allowance in Canada

2nd Edition

www.cch.ca ®

A WoltersKluwer Company

CCH CANADIAN LIMITED
90 Sheppard Avenue East, Suite 300
Toronto, ON M2N 6X1
Telephone: (416) 224-2248 Toll Free: 1-800-268-4522
Fax: (416) 224-2243 Toll Free: 1-800-461-4131
www.cch.ca

Published by CCH Canadian Limited

Edited by: Rose Filice

Library and Archives Canada Cataloguing in Publication

Capital cost allowance in Canada. — 2nd ed.

Previously published under title: Canadian capital cost allowance guide.

Includes index.
ISBN 1-55367-511-8

1. Depreciation allowances — Law and legislation — Canada.

KE5810.C36 2005   343.7105′234   C2005-904647-3   KF6397.ZA2C36 2005

Typeset by CCH Canadian Limited.
Printed in Canada.

FOREWORD

CAPITAL COST ALLOWANCE IN CANADA (formerly the CANADIAN CAPITAL COST ALLOWANCE GUIDE) is designed for handy reference and provides you with the answers to all your capital cost allowance questions.

The book is divided into two parts: Part I is commentary, arranged by subject, which explains the law in easy-to-understand language; Part II sets out in full text the law, regulations, Interpretation Bulletins and Information Circulars relating to capital cost allowances for income tax purposes.

This new edition reflects all relevant amendments to the *Income Tax Act*, the *Income Tax Application Rules, 1971*, and the Income Tax Regulations up to September 15, 2005. Proposed amendments to the Act are incorporated in boxes immediately below the provisions affected. Similarly, draft regulations have been incorporated throughout the relevant portions of the Income Tax Regulations.

As in previous editions, CAPITAL COST ALLOWANCE IN CANADA discusses the various features of the capital cost allowance system by topic. A comprehensive Table of Contents, an Alphabetical Table of Capital Cost Allowance Rates, and a detailed Topical Index make information easy to find. Extensive Reference Tables provide a speedy method of locating Interpretation Bulletins, Information Circulars, and sections of the Act and regulations reproduced in the book.

It should be noted that proposals, amendments, and rulings affecting income tax law are issued so frequently and in such volume that no bound book can remain up-to-date for long. Only electronic or loose leaf reporting can keep up with the changes. Those who wish to be informed of the latest amendments in the law and its application may want to subscribe to CCH's CANADIAN TAX REPORTER or CANADA INCOME TAX GUIDE.

CCH Canadian Limited

iii

TABLE OF CONTENTS

This Table lists the main topics in this division.

Part II — The Law

PART I

COMMENTARY

INTRODUCTION

¶50

General

In order to arrive at a figure for taxable income, under Canadian income tax law a taxpayer reduces the revenue figure for the taxation year by amounts incurred for expenses related to the earning of that revenue that are allowed under the *Income Tax Act*. Paragraph 18(1)(*b*) of the *Income Tax Act* specifically rules out the deduction of "an outlay, loss or replacement of capital, a payment on account of capital or an allowance in respect of depreciation, obsolescence or depletion except as expressly permitted". It must therefore be understood that any allowance made for depreciation or in respect of the capital cost of assets must be "expressly permitted". Paragraph 20(1)(*a*) of the *Income Tax Act* provides express permission to deduct those allowances which are allowed by regulation in respect of the capital cost of the taxpayer's property. Note that paragraph 20(1)(*a*) simply contains the enabling legislation. The details of the operation of the capital cost allowance system, based on the declining balance principle, are given in Part XI of the Income Tax Regulations, reproduced at ¶1780 *et seq.*

Paragraph 20(1)(*b*) provides for the deductibility of certain business expenditures which are neither current in nature nor in respect of the capital cost of property. These expenditures relate to such items as goodwill and the cost of incorporation, and similar types of intangibles. See ¶725 *et seq.*

¶55

Depreciation and Capital Cost Allowances Distinguished

Under the *Income War Tax Act* of 1917, the Act that first introduced income tax in Canada, capital cost allowance was related to the wear and tear of assets used to earn income, and therefore was called "depreciation" allowance. This allowance was left to the discretion of the Minister, who not only decided the rates of depreciation, but also determined whether any allowance would be made. The system in use at the time was the "straight-line" system under which a fixed rate of depreciation was applied to the original cost of each depreciable asset each year, so that a set amount was deducted for depreciation each year, as long as the depreciable asset continued to earn income, until the original cost of the asset had been recovered.

The *Income War Tax Act* persisted until the *Income Tax Act* (Chapter 52, Statutes of Canada, 1948) came into force at the beginning of the 1949 taxation year. Since then, a system termed the "diminishing balance" or "declining balance" system has existed. Under this system, the allowance in respect of the capital cost of assets is not necessarily dependent on wear and tear of the asset, and is termed "capital cost allowance", rather than "depreciation allowance", since it is based on the cost of the asset to the taxpayer and computed according to the declining balance system. In the case of timber limits and industrial mineral mines, the allowance is based on the amount of the raw material taken out of the asset.

"Depreciable property" is defined to mean property acquired by the taxpayer in respect of which the taxpayer has been allowed or, if the taxpayer owned the property at the end of the year, would, except for the available-for-use rules, be entitled to a deduction under the regulations relating to capital cost allowances. The present system allows deductions in respect of a broader group of assets than did the old, but land has never been considered depreciable under either system.

Intangibles or "nothings" are not "capital property" or "depreciable property", but are instead "eligible capital property". Part of the cost of goodwill or other intangibles may be amortized in a manner not unlike capital cost allowances. See Part I, Chapter 10 for a discussion of these types of property.

CHAPTER 1

THE CAPITAL COST ALLOWANCE SYSTEM

¶100

Capital Cost Allowance as a "Right"

Under paragraph 20(1)(a) of the *Income Tax Act* (the "Act"), a taxpayer has a positive right to deduct such allowance in respect of the capital cost of assets as is allowed by regulation. Part XI of the Income Tax Regulations and Schedule II set out the various classes of property on which capital cost allowance ("CCA") may be claimed, based on the declining balance system and the maximum rate applicable to each. Schedule III relates to leasehold interests, while Schedules IV, V, and VI

3 ¶100

relate to capital cost allowance in respect of the exhaustion of an asset such as wood assets, a timber limit, or an industrial mineral mine. Part XVII of the regulations permits taxpayers who use assets in a farming or fishing business to use the straight-line method for assets acquired prior to 1972. If the Part XVII method is not adopted in respect of an asset, Part XI of the regulations must be followed with rates of capital cost allowance as established by Schedule II.

Note that it is not necessary for the taxpayer to claim the maximum or any amount of capital cost allowance in any taxation year. Regulation $1100(1)(a)$, which sets out the rates of capital cost allowances, states that "the following deductions are allowed in computing a taxpayer's income for each taxation year", equal to "such amount as he may claim in respect of property" of the classes described in Schedule II, but not exceeding the stipulated rates.

Under certain circumstances, the Canada Revenue Agency (the "CRA") will accept a request from a taxpayer to revise capital cost allowance claims for previous taxation years. See Information Circular 84-1, "Revision of Capital Cost Allowance Claims and Other Permissive Deductions", at ¶3500.

¶105

Basis for Allowance

The present capital cost allowance system is based on the declining balance method for most classes, rather than the straight-line method. Under the declining balance system, a fixed maximum rate of allowance is established for most of the classes of assets set out in Schedule II of the Income Tax Regulations, and the rate is applied to the undepreciated cost of the assets of each class at the end of the taxation year. The amount of the deduction in the first year of claim on an asset is generally one-half the prescribed percentage of the cost of the asset. In all subsequent years, it is the full prescribed percentage of the balance remaining after subtracting the amount of the previous year's deduction from the cost of the asset. See the alphabetical table of current capital cost allowance rates at ¶620.

Under this system, all the assets of one class must be grouped together and a uniform rate applied to the class. If there are additions to the class during the year, the rate is applied to the undepreciated cost of all the assets of the class as of the end of the taxation year, with an adjustment for one-half of net additions (see ¶140). If a taxpayer disposes of some of the assets of a class before the end of the year, the taxpayer must deduct from the total undepreciated cost of the class the proceeds of disposition up to the amount of the original capital cost of the asset disposed of.

If and when all assets of a class are disposed of, the taxpayer's position will depend on whether the proceeds of the disposition exceeded or were less than the undepreciated capital cost. Any excess has to be included in the taxpayer's income as recapture (see ¶180 *et seq.*). Where the proceeds are less than the undepreciated cost, the taxpayer can deduct the difference as a "terminal loss" (see ¶215 *et seq.*). If the proceeds of disposition exceed the capital cost of the property to the taxpayer, the amount recovered in excess of the capital cost is considered to be a capital gain.

Additions of certain property cannot be pooled and are required to be put into a separate class. See ¶245 for further commentary on separate classes.

¶110

Who May Deduct Capital Cost Allowance

Capital cost allowance may be deducted by a taxpayer in computing the taxpayer's income from a business or property, or, in certain circumstances, in computing the taxpayer's income from employment. A deduction from employment income is allowed where the taxpayer is entitled under paragraph $8(1)(j)$ to deduct capital cost allowance on a motor vehicle or an aircraft that is used in the performance of the taxpayer's duties of employment.

The taxpayer must own or have a leasehold interest in the asset (see Class 13 at ¶420), and the asset must have been acquired for the purpose of gaining or producing income. In *Wardean Drilling Limited*, 69 DTC 5194, the Exchequer Court set out that a purchaser has acquired property for purposes of claiming capital cost allowance when title has passed, assuming that the assets exist at that time, or when the purchaser has all the incidents of title, such as possession, use and risk, although legal title may remain in the vendor as security for the purchase price, pursuant to commercial practice under conditional sales agreements. In *Hickman Motors*, 97 DTC 5363 (S.C.C.), the taxpayer with a calendar year end wound up one of its operating subsidiaries and acquired the subsidiary's assets on December 28, 1984. The assets were sold on January 2, 1985. The Supreme Court of Canada held that they were business assets that were used to earn income and, therefore, the taxpayer was entitled to claim capital cost allowance on them for its taxation year ending December 31, 1984. It was irrelevant that the amount of income earned by the assets during the five days they were held by the taxpayer was very small and it did not matter that the taxpayer may have intended to transfer the assets to another subsidiary. In *Saskatoon Community Broadcasting Co. Ltd. v. M.N.R.*, 58 DTC 491 (T.A.B.), the taxpayer was unable to deduct capital cost allowance on a broadcasting gondola built by the taxpayer for use at an arena and which was the property of the arena rather than the taxpayer. In *Yorkton Broadcasting Co. Ltd. v. M.N.R.*, 87

DTC 165 (T.C.C.), the taxpayer was denied capital cost allowance in a taxation year on an airplane that was not acquired before the year-end, and the capital cost allowance claim on another airplane was reduced because the asset was used for business activities only 40% of the time.

In the case of leased property, the legal nature of the contract will determine if the property is owned by the lessor or whether the contract is a sale. The CRA's position on lease-option agreements and sale-leaseback agreements is set out in Technical News No. 21, dated June 14, 2001:

> ... [I]t is our view that the determination of whether a contract is a lease or sale is based on the legal relationship created by the terms of the agreement, rather than on any attempt to ascertain the underlying economic reality. Therefore, in the absence of sham, it is our view that a lease is a lease and a sale is a sale. However, notwithstanding the legal relationship, GAAR may be used to assess cases in which there is an avoidance transaction that results in a misuse or an abuse of provisions of the Act.

In Technical Interpretation No. 2004-0100771E5, dated November 22, 2004, the CRA commented that in its view, there can be only one owner of a property and "whether the transaction is a lease or a sale, only one party is entitled to the capital cost allowance claim and any related investment tax credits". In certain circumstances, the lessee may be able to claim capital cost allowance on the property. See comments concerning lease-option agreements and sale-leaseback agreements at ¶195 and the election by a lessee to treat a lease as a loan at ¶270.

Capital cost allowance on property owned by a partnership is calculated at the partnership level rather than by each partner. Most references to a "taxpayer" in this commentary can apply equally to partnerships. See also ¶295 *et seq.*

¶115

Property Eligible for Capital Cost Allowance and Exclusions

As mentioned above, capital cost allowance is only deductible on property specified in the Income Tax Regulations which is acquired for the purpose of producing income. Any property not included in the regulations is not eligible. In addition, there are certain assets which are specifically excluded by the regulations. These are mainly found in Regulation 1102 (¶2004 *et seq.*), but additional exclusions can be found in Classes 8 (¶2454), 13 (¶2466), and 14 (¶2468).

Whether or not property is acquired by the taxpayer for the purpose of gaining or producing income is a question of fact. In *Electrical Industries (Western) Ltd. v. M.N.R.*, 90 DTC 1842 (T.C.C.), the taxpayer supplied fixed assets to its wholly-owned subsidiary rent-free. The taxpayer was allowed to claim capital cost allowance on these assets because they were acquired for the purpose of producing income, even though, due to the financial straits of the subsidiary, no rent was earned on these assets. See Interpretation Bulletin IT-128R, "Capital Cost Allowance — Depreciable Property", at ¶3115.

¶117 Property Excluded from Capital Cost Allowance

Regulations 1102(1) to (3) specify certain types of property in respect of which capital cost allowance may not be taken. Property denied a deduction for capital cost allowance includes:

(1) *Deductible property.* The exclusion of property, the cost of which is deductible in computing the taxpayer's income, recognizes the fact that in order to claim capital cost allowance, the outlay must be a capital expenditure. Therefore, if an expenditure is deductible under a general or specific provision of the Act, no capital cost allowance will be claimed. Examples of this include landscaping costs, deductible under paragraph $20(1)(aa)$; expenses to investigate the suitability of a site for a building, deductible under paragraph $20(1)(dd)$; and amounts paid by a taxpayer for the purpose of making a service connection of electricity, gas, water, etc. to the taxpayer's place of business, deductible under paragraph $20(1)(ee)$. One type of expenditure that causes difficulty when determining if an amount is to be expensed or capitalized and depreciated is repairs and maintenance. Minor repairs are deducted as incurred; however, major repairs which extend an asset's useful life will be capitalized and be eligible for capital cost allowance. In *Pugliese v. M.N.R.* (1987), 88 DTC 1762 (T.C.C.), repairs to rental properties in the form of a new furnace and new roof were considered to be for the enduring benefit of the taxpayer and, therefore, were required to be capitalized rather than expensed in the year. See Interpretation Bulletin IT-128R, "Capital Cost Allowance — Depreciable Property", at ¶3115, for further discussion of the treatment of repairs and maintenance expenditures.

(2) *Property, the cost of which qualifies as "Canadian Renewable and Conservation Expense".* These expenses are described in Regulation 1219 and are included in the calculation of Canadian exploration expenses under subsection 66.1(6). See also the discussion at ¶567.

(3) *Inventory.* Assets that are purchased by a taxpayer for the purpose of resale are included in the taxpayer's inventory. Such assets are not eligible for capital cost allowance. See Interpretation Bulletin IT-102R2, "Conversion of Property, Other Than Real Property, From or To Inventory", at ¶3107.

(4) *Non-income earning property.* Property not acquired for the purpose of gaining or producing income is excluded from claiming capital cost allowance. It would appear that the assets need not be actually used in the taxpayer's business; however, there must be a connection between the use of the asset and the producing of income. The amount of income

earned was addressed by the Supreme Court of Canada in *Hickman Motors*, 97 DTC 5363, where it was decided that CCA could be claimed for assets that were owned for only five days at the end of the year. In *Clapham v. M.N.R.* (1969), 70 DTC 1012 (T.A.B.), a motel owner was not allowed a deduction for capital cost allowance where the owner's motel was rented at less than its fair rental value and was therefore demonstrably not acquired for the purpose of gaining or producing income. In *Bolus-Revelas-Bolus Ltd.*, 71 DTC 5153 (Ex. Ct.), the company that ran a gift shop and leased property could not claim capital cost allowance on two amusement park rides that were in storage.

(5) *Scientific research and experimental development expenditures.* Property acquired by an expenditure allowed as a deduction for scientific research and experimental development ("SR&ED") under section 37 is not eligible for capital cost allowance. It is deductible under a special provision in section 37.

(6) *Certain antiques, objects of art, etc.* This refers to a print, etching, drawing, or similar work of art, as well as a tapestry or carpet, unless any of these items were created by a Canadian. Items such as an engraving, lithograph, map made before 1900, or piece of antique furniture that was more than 100 years old and cost over $1,000 when acquired are also prohibited from having capital cost allowance claimed on them.

(7) *Recreational property.* The exclusion relates to property that is a yacht, camp, lodge, golf course, or a facility or club, the main purpose of which is to provide dining, recreational, or sporting facilities, unless the taxpayer is in the business of providing such property for hire.

(8) *Land.* Land is not depreciable. The classes of property described in Schedule II are deemed not to include the land upon which a property described therein was constructed or is situated. In certain circumstances (described in ¶195), land may be deemed to be depreciable property, but no capital cost allowance may be claimed on it.

(9) *Non-resident-owned property.* Regulation 1102(3) provides that where the taxpayer is a non-resident person, property owned outside Canada is not taken into account for capital cost allowance purposes. This is consistent with the general treatment of non-resident persons under the Act.

(10) *Property of a life insurer.* The property of a life insurer used by it or held by it in the course of carrying on an insurance business outside Canada is not eligible for a deduction.

(11) *Property that is linefill contained in a pipeline.*

¶117

¶120

How is Capital Cost Allowance Calculated?

The capital cost allowances that may be claimed under Regulation $1100(1)(a)$ are based on the undepreciated capital cost to the taxpayer of property of a class. In these instances, capital cost allowance will be calculated on the declining balance method. This is determined by taking the undepreciated capital cost of the class at the beginning of the year, adding the capital cost of any additions during the year (subject to the half-year rule outlined at ¶140), subtracting the proceeds of any dispositions, and multiplying the remainder by the specified rate of the class. Adjustments must also be made to the calculation for any assets acquired but not put into use in the year. The maximum rates allowed for these classes are set out in Regulation $1100(1)(a)$. Provisions for accelerated or additional allowances and the determination for certain classes, where the rates are subject to transitional rules or determined based on other than the declining balance method, are described in Regulation $1100(1)$.

The calculation of the capital cost allowance claim in the year of acquisition of property may best be illustrated by an example.

Example: Calculating Capital Cost Allowance

Assumptions:	Opening undepreciated capital cost for Class 8 assets . . .	$ 100
	Acquisitions during the year.	70
	Proceeds from disposals during the year.	20

Opening undepreciated capital cost		$100
Additions in the year	$70	
Disposals in the year	(20)	
	$50(a)	____
Half-year rule:		
50% of (a)		$ 25
Undepreciated capital cost before capital cost allowance claim . .		$125(b)
Capital cost allowance: 20% of (b)		(25)
		100
Add: Capital cost deferred		
50% of (a)		25
Undepreciated capital cost at end of year.		$125

Certain classes of assets are not subject to the declining balance method. The capital cost allowance on these assets is either determined on the straight-line method (a certain portion of the original capital cost is deducted each year) or by a rate determined by the consumption of the asset. Schedule III and Regulation $1100(1)(b)$ determine the deduction in respect of Class 13; Regulation $1100(1)(c)$ in respect of Class 14; Schedule IV and Regulation $1100(1)(f)$ in respect of Class 15; Schedule V and Regulation $1100(1)(g)$ in respect of industrial mineral mines; and Schedule VI and Regulation $1100(1)(e)$ in respect of timber limits.

Capital cost allowance is a permissive deduction. In a taxation year the taxpayer may claim any amount from zero up to the prescribed maximum. In certain circumstances, a taxpayer may wish to defer claiming all or a portion of the eligible capital cost allowance in a given year. For example, a taxpayer may wish to create enough income to allow a loss carryover to be used or an investment tax credit to be claimed. Any amount not taken will just result in a higher opening undepreciated capital cost in the next year. For classes such as Class 13, where the capital cost allowance deduction is not determined by the undepreciated capital cost, the deferral may not affect the CCA claim for the next year.

Book Depreciation

The method of computing capital cost allowance is independent of the taxpayer's book depreciation. As the two methods can differ substantially, it is quite possible that the amount of depreciation shown in a taxpayer's books will vary considerably from the amount of capital cost allowance taken for tax purposes. In addition, various circumstances (such as "rollovers") can produce different capital costs for tax purposes. Accordingly, the undepreciated balance of assets on the taxpayer's books may not coincide at all with the undepreciated capital cost outstanding for tax purposes.

¶125

Restrictions on Capital Cost Allowance — General

Available-for-Use Rules

Effective for the 1989 and subsequent taxation years, capital cost allowance may only be claimed when the asset to which it relates becomes "available for use". The "available-for-use" rules are discussed in detail at ¶135.

Half-Year Rule

Regulations $1100(1)(b)$, (t), (ta), (v), and Regulation $1100(2)$ have the effect of limiting the capital cost allowance that may be claimed on depreciable assets acquired during the taxation year and after November 12, 1981. In most instances, the half-year rule applies to net additions (that is, disposals in the year are deducted from the year's additions), and half of the net amount is subtracted from the undepreciated capital cost balance at the end of the year before calculating that year's capital cost allowance. The undepreciated capital cost balance carried forward to the next year is not affected by the 50% reduction. See ¶140 for further commentary on the half-year rule.

Short Taxation Years

Capital cost allowance is required to be prorated for taxation years that are shorter than 12 months (Regulation 1100(3)). See ¶145.

Passenger Vehicles

The capital cost of passenger vehicles for purposes of calculating capital cost allowance is limited to a prescribed amount ($30,000 for 2001 to 2005) plus applicable federal and provincial sales taxes. See ¶250.

Rental Property

Regulations 1100(11) to (14) prevent certain taxpayers (mainly individuals) from using the capital cost allowance on rental real estate to shelter other income from tax. See ¶255.

Leasing Property

Regulations 1100(15) to (20) limit the aggregate capital cost allowance on "leasing property", discussed at ¶260, to the net income for the year from renting, leasing, or earning royalties from the leasing properties, and Regulations 1100(1.1) to (1.3) limit capital cost allowance on "specified leasing property". See ¶265.

Certified Films and Video Tapes

Regulations 1100(21) to (22) limit the aggregate capital cost allowance that may be claimed on certified films and video tapes where there is a revenue guarantee or a convertible debt obligation with respect to such films or tapes.

Change of Control

Where a corporation, or a partnership of which the corporation is a majority interest partner, acquires depreciable property (other than property acquired from persons related to the corporation throughout the period) within a 12-month period ending before a change of control, and the property is not used in a business carried on by the corporation or partnership before that period, the capital cost of the property will not be included in computing the undepreciated capital cost until after the change of control. See ¶275.

¶130

Determining Date of Ownership or Interest

Capital cost allowance may only be claimed on assets owned by the taxpayer, or in which the taxpayer has a leasehold interest at the end of the taxation year. However, see ¶215 concerning a loss on certain transfers where the transferor may continue to claim a portion of CCA. For assets acquired after 1989, there are two important dates for the taxpayer to determine. The first is the date of acquisition, which is the date on which the cost is credited to the capital cost allowance class. The second is the date on which the asset is available for use, which is the date that determines when capital cost allowance may be claimed. Often these dates will coincide.

¶133 Date of Acquisition

The acquisition date is important because by crediting an asset to the capital cost allowance class, the taxpayer may defer recapture or a terminal loss in a year even if capital cost allowance may not yet be claimed on that asset. In addition, the date that an asset is acquired often determines which class the asset will fall into.

Generally speaking, a taxpayer will be considered to have acquired a depreciable property at the earlier of:

(a) the date on which the taxpayer obtains title to it; and

(b) the date on which the taxpayer has all the incidents of title, such as possession, use, and risk, even though legal title remains with the vendor as security for the purchase price.

The purchaser must have a right in the asset itself and not merely rights under a contract, of which the asset is subject, to acquire it in the future. In *M.N.R. v. Wardean Drilling Ltd.*, 69 DTC 5194 (Ex. Ct.), all the contracts for the purchase of a drilling rig and equipment were completed in a taxation year, but the taxpayer was not allowed to claim CCA in that year since it was stipulated in the contract that title was to pass on the date of shipment which was the following year. In *Borstad Welding Supplies (1972) Ltd.*, 93 DTC 5457 (F.C.T.D.), the taxpayer entered into an agreement to sell gas cylinders over five years on the basis of one-fifth of the number of cylinders per year. Although the Minister argued that the incidents of possession, use and risk were transferred to the acquiring company at the time of the agreement, the Court held that the disposition occurred over the course of five years, as set out in the agreement, not at the time the agreement was signed. The company selling the cylinders could claim capital cost allowance on the cylinders to which it retained title.

Where a depreciable asset is under construction at the end of the taxation year and progress payments have been made to the contractor, the taxpayer is considered to have acquired the asset to the extent of the total amount of the progress payments made at the end of the taxation year, provided the taxpayer has title to the property while it is under construction. Thus, the total amount of the progress payments made in such a case will be added to the undepreciated capital cost of the class. If the asset is a piece of machinery or an airplane, for example, and is not being built on the taxpayer's premises, it would appear to be necessary for the taxpayer to prove that he or she has title to the asset under construction in order to be deemed to have acquired it.

The asset under construction must of course be an asset which is being built for the purpose of producing income for the taxpayer, even though it may not produce income in the taxation year or years while it is under construction. See also Interpretation Bulletin IT-285R2, "Capital Cost Allowance — General Comments", at ¶3175.

Special rules are in effect when a corporation or partnership acquires depreciable property prior to a change in control of a corporation (see ¶275).

¶135   Available-for-Use Rules

The "available-for-use" rules set out in subsections 13(26) to (32) determine the earliest taxation year in which certain expenses and credits may be claimed for property acquired after 1989. These expenses and credits include capital cost allowance ("CCA"), scientific research and experimental development ("SR&ED") expenses, and investment tax credits ("ITCs"). Generally, under this rule, taxpayers may begin deducting CCA and SR&ED expenditures and claiming ITCs at the earliest of:

(a) the time when the related property is "available for use" for the purpose of earning income; and

(b) the second taxation year after the date the property was acquired by the taxpayer.

An asset that has not otherwise become available for use, becomes available for use immediately before it is disposed of by the taxpayer.

Rollovers are provided for certain (primarily non-arm's length) transfers of property. Capital cost allowance claims subject to the maximum two-year ("rolling start") rule are exempted from the half-year rule (¶140). The available-for-use rules do not apply to certified productions in Class 10(w).

Buildings

A building will be considered to be available for use at the earliest of:

(a) the time at which all or substantially all of the building (generally taken by the CRA to mean 90% or more) is used by the taxpayer for its intended purpose;

(b) the time at which construction is complete;

(c) the start of the first taxation year commencing more than 357 days after the end of the taxation year during which the property was acquired (the two-year "rolling start" rule);

(d) the time immediately before the property is disposed of by the taxpayer (note that the disposition of a property will not cause it to be available for use for the purpose of claiming an investment tax credit); and

(e) where the property is a replacement property for property which has been involuntarily disposed of, but which was acquired before 1990 or had otherwise become available for use, the time at which the replacement property is acquired.

For the purposes of available-for-use rules only, a renovation, alteration or addition to a building will be considered to be a separate building.

Property Other than Buildings

A property other than a building will be considered to be available for use at the earliest of:

(a) the time at which the property is first used for the purpose of earning income;

(b) the start of the first taxation year commencing more than 357 days after the end of the taxation year during which the property was acquired (the two-year "rolling start" rule); i.e., if the property is acquired in Year 1 but is not used to earn income in Years 1 or 2, capital cost allowance can be claimed in Year 3 with no half-year rule application;

(c) the time immediately before the property is disposed of by the taxpayer (note that disposition of a property will not cause it to be available for use for the purpose of claiming the investment tax credit);

(d) the time at which the property has been delivered or made available to the taxpayer and is capable of producing a saleable product or performing a saleable service;

(e) in the case of air or water pollution abatement equipment, the time at which the property is installed and is capable of operating;

¶135

(f) in the case of certain public corporations and their subsidiaries, the time at which the property commences to be depreciable for accounting purposes;

(g) in the case of property acquired for use in a farming or fishing business, the time at which the property is delivered and is capable of operation;

(h) in the case of certain transportation equipment in respect of which various permits, licences and certificates may be required, the time at which the permits, licences and certificates have been acquired;

(i) in the case of spare parts, the time at which the property for which the spare part may be required is available for use;

(j) in the case of certain offshore production facilities, the time at which the concrete gravity base structure deballasts and lifts the topside facilities (such as oil rigs); and

(k) where the property is a replacement property for property which has been involuntarily disposed of, but which was acquired before 1990 or had otherwise become available for use, the time at which the replacement property is acquired.

Long-Term Project Rule

A special elective rule is provided in subsection 13(29) for property, including buildings other than rental buildings, acquired for use in a long-term project, to have expenditures incurred in the course of a project be considered available for use prior to the project's actual completion date. The election must be filed with the taxpayer's income tax return for the taxation year commencing more than 357 days after the end of the year in which the project commences. Regulation 600 provides that an election under subsection 13(29) is a prescribed election for purposes of paragraphs 220(3.2)(*a*) and (*b*) so that the Minister of Revenue may extend the time for making such an election or grant permission to amend or revoke such an election.

Under subsection 13(29), the general available-for-use rules will be applied to all expenditures incurred in the first two years of the project. However, in the third and subsequent years of the project, the long-term project rule, if elected, will apply to allow a doubling-up of amounts claimed under the rolling start rule to determine an additional amount that is available for use. For example, in Year 3 of a project for which this election is made, the additional amount that would be considered to have become available for use is the lesser of:

(a) the part of the project that is acquired in Year 3 less amounts of Year 3 property that have otherwise become available for use under any rule; and

¶135

(b) the project property acquired in Year 1 that has not become available for use under other rules except for this election or the rolling start rule, less any prior claims made under this election.

The capital cost allowance claims for these expenditures claimed under the long-term project rule are subject to the half-year rule.

The application of the long-term project rule is set out in a government illustration from the explanatory notes to subsection 13(29):

Example: Long-Term Project Rule

A \$160 million industrial project commences in Year 1 and is completed and put in use to earn income in Year 6. It is assumed that none of the property incorporated in the project will be otherwise available for use until the project is completed (other than property which becomes available for use during the construction period by reason of this rule or by reason of the two-year rolling start rule). The taxpayer elects in Year 3 of the project to have the long-term project rule apply. The application of subsection 13(29) in these circumstances is shown below.

		Addition to UCC		Current year expenditures	
Year	Expenditures	Long-term project	Rolling start	Other	Deferred
1	10	0	n/a		10
2	20	0	n/a		20
3	70	$10^{(1)}$	$10^{(2)}$		60
4	50	$20^{(3)}$	$20^{(4)}$		30
5	5	$35^{(5)}$	$60^{(6)}$		0
6	5	0	—	$5^{(7)}$	0
Totals	160	65	90	5	

Notes

(1) Lesser of 70 (Year 3 expenditure not available for use before the end of that year) and $10 - 0 = 10$ (Year 1 expenditures less amounts previously determined to be available for use under this rule) $=10$

(2) Year 1 expenditures available for use under the rolling start rule (not subject to the half-year convention).

(3) Lesser of $120 - 10 = 110$ (Year 3 and 4 expenditures not available for use before the end of the year) and $30 - 10 = 20$ (aggregate of Year 1 and 2 expenditures less amount calculated under (1) above) $= 20$

(4) Year 2 expenditures available for use under the rolling start rule (not subject to the half-year convention).

(5) Lesser of 125 (aggregate of Year 3, 4, and 5 expenditures) less $10 + 20 + 60$ (portion of Year 3, 4, and 5 expenditures already available for use at the end of the year) $= 35$ (Year 3, 4, and 5 expenditures not available for use before the end of the year) and 100 (aggregate of Year 1, 2, and 3 expenditures) less 30 (aggregate of amounts calculated under (1) and (3) above) $= 70$ $= 35$

(6) The remainder of Year 3 expenditures available for use under the rolling start rule.

(7) Year 6 expenditures available for use when the project is put in use (paragraph $13(27)(a)$ of the Act) during the sixth year.

¶135

Rollovers

Rollovers are provided for non-arm's length transfers of property. In these cases and in the case of a butterfly reorganization, as long as the property was available for use by the transferor (other than as a result of the disposition), it will be considered to be available for use at the earlier of the time it is acquired by the transferee, or if applicable, at a time prescribed in the regulations. As well, there is a continuity of ownership relief in determining the application of the rolling start rule and the long-term project election. Under these circumstances the acquirer is deemed to have acquired the depreciable property at the time it was acquired by the transferor.

Anti-Avoidance Provision

An anti-avoidance provision in subsection 13(32) deals with the situation where a taxpayer leases depreciable property from a non-arm's length person before the property would be considered to be available for use if the taxpayer had acquired it. In this case, the lease payments that would otherwise be deductible by the taxpayer are deemed to be a leasehold interest Class 13 asset. Capital cost allowance is therefore allowed on these lease payments only after the property becomes available for use.

¶140

The Half-Year Rule

Regulation 1100(2) limits the claim for capital cost allowance in respect of depreciable assets acquired during the year (after November 12, 1981) to one-half the normal rate. This is achieved by providing for a notional reduction in the undepreciated capital cost of property in the class equal to one-half the net additions (i.e., cost of additions net of proceeds of disposals). The capital cost allowance rates specified in Regulation 1100(1)(a) are then applied to this notionally reduced balance. In the event that the disposals for the year exceed additions, there is no 50% reduction of this negative amount.

This rule applies to both the cost of depreciable property that was acquired or that became available for use in the year, and the increase in undepreciated capital cost arising on the repayment of any government assistance or inducement payment after the disposition of a depreciable property if the assistance or inducement had previously reduced the cost of the assets.

The half-year rule does not apply to property that becomes available for use, and thus eligible for capital cost allowance, under the two-year rolling start rule.

Example: Half-Year Rule

A Ltd. constructed a piece of machinery for its manufacturing business which operates on a calendar year fiscal period. A Ltd. spent $25,000 on the machinery in 2000, $60,000 in 2001 and $25,000 in June 2002. The machinery was put into use in September 2002. In 2000 and 2001, no capital cost allowance was claimed on the machinery due to the available-for-use rule. In 2002, capital cost allowance would be permitted as follows:

	Class 43 30%
Additions from 2000	$ 25,000
2001	$ 60,000
2002	$ 25,000
	$110,000
Less: one-half net additions	$(42,500)^{(1)}$
	$ 67,500
CCA claimed	(20,250)
	$ 47,250
Add: Capital cost deferred	42,500
Undepreciated capital cost January 1, 2003	$ 89,750

(1) The $60,000 from 2001 which was put into use in 2002 and the $25,000 from 2002 are subject to the half-year rule. The $25,000 from 2000 became available for use on January 1, 2002 under the rolling start rule and therefore is not subject to the half-year rule.

¶141 Exceptions to the Half-Year Rule

Excluded Property

The following assets are excluded from the application of Regulation 1100(2):

(a) Canadian vessels — Regulation 1100(1)(*v*);

(b) certified productions acquired after 1987 — paragraph (*w*) of Class 10;

(c) Class 12 assets *other than* the following specific assets included in:

(i) Class 12 by virtue of paragraph (*d*), a jig, die, mould, or last;

(ii) paragraph (*j*), the cutting or shaping part of a machine;

(iii) paragraph (m), a motion picture film or television commercial message;

(iv) paragraph (n), a certified feature film or production other than one included in paragraph (w) of Class 10 as noted above;

(v) paragraph (o), computer software; and

(vi) paragraph (r), video tapes acquired for the purpose of renting;

(d) Class 13 assets — leasehold interests;

(e) Class 14 assets — franchise or licences for a limited period);

(f) Class 15 property acquired for cutting and removing merchantable timber or a timber resource;

(g) Class 23 assets — leasehold interests and buildings relating to Expo 67 and Expo 86;

(h) Class 24, 27, and 34 assets — pollution control and energy conservation equipment;

(i) Class 29 manufacturing equipment acquired before 1988;

(j) property that is a "specified leasing property" of a principal business leasing corporation at the end of the year in which it was acquired;

(k) leased property that has actually been acquired that previously had been the subject of an election under section 16.1 of the Act (commentary at ¶270) which permits a lessor and lessee to jointly elect to have a lease treated as a purchase and loan; and

(l) property that has become available for use in the year under the two-year rolling start rule.

Despite these exceptions, other regulations produce similar results as the half-year rule for Canadian vessels in Class 7 (Regulation 1100(1)(v)); Class 13 assets, leasehold interests (Regulation 1100(1)(b)); and assets in Classes 24, 27, 29, and 34 (Regulations 1100(1)(t) and (ta)). See the discussion under these specific classes for the calculation of capital cost allowance.

Transitional Relief from the Half-Year Rule

Regulation 1100(2.1) provides transitional relief from the half-year rule in certain circumstances. Specifically, the general half-year rule as well as the separate ones mentioned above that apply to Canadian vessels, leasehold interests, and assets in Classes 24, 27, 29, and 34 will not apply where a taxpayer acquires property after November 12, 1981 and before 1983 where certain conditions relating to the acquisition apply. In these circumstances, the taxpayer is treated as though he or she acquired the

¶141

property under the previous regime and is therefore entitled to a full claim.

In addition, property acquired in these circumstances is deemed to be "designated property" for the purposes of Regulations $1100(1)(t)$ and (ta). Those regulations govern the capital cost allowance that may be claimed in respect of property included in Classes 24, 27, 29 and 34 (accelerated write-off classes). Where property is designated property, the half-year rule does not apply to reduce the accelerated write-off in the year of acquisition.

Non-Arm's Length Transactions

In addition to the transitional rules described above for properties which were in the process of being acquired prior to November 13, 1981, Regulation 1100(2.2) provides that the half-year rule for property acquisitions will not apply in certain non-arm's length situations. In particular, where property is acquired in the course of a divisive corporate reorganization (a so-called "butterfly transaction") that complies with paragraph $55(3)(b)$, or where property is acquired from a person with whom the taxpayer does not deal at arm's length, the half-year rule will not apply if one of the following conditions are met:

(a) the property was depreciable property of the vendor who owned it continuously during the period from a day that is at least 364 days before the end of the taxpayer's taxation year in which the vendor acquired the property to the day it was acquired by the taxpayer;

(b) the property was depreciable property of the vendor who owned it continuously during the period from November 12, 1981 to the day it was acquired by the taxpayer;

(c) the transitional relief provided by Regulation 1100(2.1) (described above) applied to the vendor on the vendor's original acquisition of the property; or

(d) the non-arm's length transaction rules found in Regulation 1100(2.2) applied to the vendor on the vendor's original acquisition of the property.

(For these purposes, however, Regulation $1100(2.2)(e)$ provides that a person who does not deal at arm's length does not include a person who is deemed not to deal at arm's length by virtue only of certain rights or option agreements as described in paragraph $251(5)(b)$ of the Act.)

Property acquired in these circumstances is not subject to the half-year rule, and is deemed to be "designated property" for the purposes of Regulation $1100(1)(ta)$ which governs the allowable claim in respect of properties included in Classes 24, 27, 29, and 34 (accelerated write-off classes). Where property is designated property, the allowable claim is not reduced in the year of acquisition.

¶141

Property in Classes 24, 27, 29, or 34 that is acquired in a non-arm's length or butterfly transfer is deemed to have been acquired at the beginning of the transferee's first taxation year beginning after it was acquired by the transferor. This allows a catch-up claim of capital cost allowance by the transferee if the transferor has not claimed the full amount in the preceding years. For example, if a taxpayer held a Class 34 asset for three years but claimed no CCA on it and then transferred it in a non-arm's length transaction, the transferee could claim 100% CCA in the year of acquisition.

For property acquired before June 18, 1987, Regulation 1100(2.2) applied to exempt the application of the half-year rule where property was acquired pursuant to certain specified rollover provisions of the Act, including transfers of property pursuant to section 85, corporate amalgamations pursuant to section 87, and windings-up of 90% or more owned Canadian subsidiaries pursuant to section 88. Regulation 1100(2.2) was amended for property acquired after June 17, 1987 to block perceived abuses where rollover provisions of the Act were applicable in what were essentially arm's length transactions.

Regulation 1102(20) is an anti-avoidance measure and applies where taxpayers who would otherwise be dealing at arm's length undertake a transaction or series of transactions so as to be considered not to be dealing at arm's length and therefore avoid the application of the half-year rule. Regulation 1102(20) will deem the taxpayers to deal at arm's length with respect to the acquisition of the particular property. Regulation 1102(20) is also applicable for the purposes of Regulations 1100(19), leasing property; 1101(1ad), separate classes for rental properties; and 1102(14), property of a prescribed class acquired by way of a transfer.

Regulation 1100(2.21) provides that where a taxpayer is deemed to have disposed of and acquired or reacquired a property, the taxpayer will be deemed to have acquired the property from a person with whom the taxpayer was not dealing at arm's length. Thus, in such circumstances, the half-year rule would not apply to the taxpayer upon the deemed acquisition or reacquisition of the property.

Regulation 1100(2.3) provides that if the half-year rule does not apply to the purchaser in one of the transactions described above, then the vendor would not net the proceeds against the current year's additions which are subject to the half-year rule. This effectively increases the vendor's net additions subject to the half-year rule.

¶145

Short Taxation Years

Regulation 1100(3) provides that if a taxation year is less than 12 months in duration, the amount of capital cost allowance that may be claimed for depreciable property used in a business is prorated. In such a situation, the capital cost allowance permitted will be the proportion of the maximum amount otherwise allowable that the number of days in the taxation year is of 365.

Under section 35 of the *Interpretation Act*, "month" is defined to mean a calendar month. The proration of CCA applies to the amount which would be computed under the half-year rule in Regulation 1100(2) (¶140), and with some exceptions to the additional allowances under Regulation 1100(1).

Example:

C Ltd. incorporated and started business on May 1, 2003. It has a December 31 fiscal year-end. During the first year, C Ltd. purchased $30,000 worth of computer equipment for use in its business. The capital cost allowance claim on this equipment in 2003 is as follows:

	Class 10 30%
2003 Additions	$30,000
Minus: one-half net additions	$15,000
	$15,000
CCA claim: 30% $\times$ 15,000 $\times \frac{245}{365}$	(3,021)
	$11,979
Add: capital cost deferred	15,000
Undepreciated capital cost January 1, 2004	$26,979

¶147   Where Proration Not Required

Capital cost allowance is not prorated for assets in certain classes. In most cases the allowances for these assets are based on income or units extracted so they would presumably be less in a short taxation year without being prorated.

Certain Allowances

The following allowances are not prorated:

(a) the allowances for Class 14 (patents, franchises, etc.) under Regulation 1100(1)(*c*);

(b) the allowances for timber limits and cutting rights under Regulation 1100(1)(*e*);

(c) the allowances for Class 15 (woods assets) under Regulation 1100(1)(*f*);

(d) the allowances for industrial mineral mines under Regulation 1100(1)(g);

(e) the additional allowance with respect to certified productions described in paragraph (w) of Class 10 under Regulation 1100(1)(l);

(f) the additional allowance with respect to Canadian film or video productions under Regulation 1100(1)(m);

(g) the additional allowances for mining assets in Classes 28 and 41 under Regulations 1100(1)(w), (x), (y), and (ya); and

(h) the allowances for Year 2000 computer hardware and software under Regulations 1100(1)(zg) and (zh).

The allowances respecting patents and franchises will vary in any event according to the length of the taxation year. Allowances respecting timber limits, woods assets, and industrial mineral mines will vary according to the number of units of timber cut or mineral mined in the taxation year. The additional allowances in respect of certified productions and mining assets are limited by income which presumably will be reduced in a short taxation year in any event.

Income from Property

Where income-producing property is acquired by an individual taxpayer, provided that the income is from property and not from business, the taxation year will be a full 12 months since income from property is reported on a calendar year basis. As decided in *Walsh and Micay*, 65 DTC 5293 (Ex. Ct.), the provision of janitorial services, heat, stoves, refrigerators, etc. resulting from ownership of apartment buildings is a function normally performed by a landlord, and rentals received for these services are income from property rather than from business. The taxpayers were allowed to claim capital cost allowance on the buildings for the full year rather than for the 61 days that they owned them.

Employees

Where an individual starts a job part way through the year which entitles the individual as an employee to claim capital cost allowance on an automobile or aircraft, the individual will not have to prorate the capital cost allowance based on the length of the taxation year. The automobile is subject to the half-year rule in the year of acquisition.

Business Income

Where an individual taxpayer's income includes income from a business whose fiscal period does not coincide with the calendar year, the reference to taxation year for purposes of capital cost allowance claims is a reference to the fiscal period of the business. Capital cost allowance must be computed according to the fiscal year of the business, and the

¶147

allowance which the taxpayer may claim will be the capital cost allowance taken for the business in the fiscal year which ended in the individual taxpayer's taxation year. In Technical Interpretation No. 2001-0070105, dated April 18, 2001, the CRA confirmed that where an individual begins carrying on a business in the middle of the year, the reference to taxation year in Regulation 1100(3) refers to the fiscal period of the business, and in the case of a short fiscal period, the capital cost allowance is prorated.

Terminal Loss

Notwithstanding the fact that the taxation year may be less than 12 months in duration, the taxpayer is still entitled to a deduction for a terminal loss on disposition of all assets of a class in the taxation year.

¶150
Meaning of "Capital Cost"

The provisions of the *Income Tax Act* and the regulations refer in many instances to the "capital cost" of depreciable property. Unfortunately, there is no definition of "capital cost" in the Act or regulations. Usually it is the amount actually expended by the taxpayer for a capital asset. Capital cost is the *cost* of the asset and not its value. It includes freight, installation, duties, and other "laid down" costs. Contingent liabilities are not considered to be part of the cost of the asset. If the taxpayer is constructing or modifying a depreciable asset, the cost will include any allocable labour, materials, or overhead.

Capital cost is calculated net of any amounts received, be they inducements, grants, or tax credits (see ¶155). In addition, subsection 13(7.1) provides that the capital cost of a depreciable asset is to be reduced by the forgiven amount applied against the capital cost of the asset when a debt is settled. This adjustment applies to taxation years that end after February 21, 1994 and is a result of the debt forgiveness rules in subsection 80(5). If a capital asset is purchased with foreign currency, the cost will be translated into Canadian dollars using the rate of exchange at the time of acquisition. See Interpretation Bulletin IT-285R2, "Capital Cost Allowance — General Comments", at ¶3175.

To be considered a capital cost, an expenditure must bring into existence an advantage for the enduring benefit of the taxpayer. See the discussion at ¶115 concerning expenditures not eligible for CCA. See also ¶160 for a description of the term "undepreciated capital cost".

Some provisions of the Act contain special rules for establishing the capital cost under certain circumstances. One example is in the case of a passenger vehicle costing over a certain set limit (see ¶250). Where an asset is acquired from a person with whom the taxpayer is not dealing at arm's length, at an amount greater than the fair market value of the asset, paragraph 69(1)(*a*) of the Act provides that the taxpayer is deemed to have acquired it at fair market value. In *CIT Financial Ltd.*, 2004 DTC 6573, the Federal Court of Appeal reduced by $20 million the capital cost of software acquired in a non-arm's length transaction, resulting in reduced capital cost allowance claims.

Subsection 13(7) provides for the determination of the capital cost of property in circumstances involving a change of use or an acquisition from a non-arm's length party (see the commentary at ¶200 or ¶205). When an asset is acquired under certain rollover provisions, a taxpayer's capital cost may be deemed to be something other than its actual cost. For example, paragraph 85(1)(*e*) provides that where depreciable property is transferred to a corporation pursuant to a rollover under section 85, the corporation's cost of the property is the least of three specified amounts. Paragraph 87(2)(*d*) deals with amalgamations and provides rules for determining the capital cost of depreciable property to the amalgamated corporation. Paragraphs 88(1)(*c*) and (*f*) provide for determination of capital cost on the winding-up of a corporation. See also ¶281 which outlines the special rules for determining capital cost on the transfer of property between spouses.

Subsection 13(33) provides rules for the determination of the capital cost of an asset when a trade-in is involved. Subsection 13(33) sets out that where a taxpayer acquires depreciable property after November 1992 using a trade-in as part of the consideration, the portion of the cost of the depreciable property that relates to the trade-in cannot exceed the fair market value of the property traded in. These amendments were implemented after the decision in *Zeiben v. M.N.R.*, 91 DTC 886 (T.C.C.). In this case, the taxpayer traded in a tractor that had a fair market value of approximately $45,000 for a new tractor listed at $125,000. The contract showed that the taxpayer purchased the new tractor with a trade-in of the old tractor valued at $104,500 and a cash payment of $20,500. The dealer testified that the cash price of the new tractor was about $63,000. The Court held that the trade-in value could stand since the contract was agreed between arm's length parties, both had recorded the transaction in this manner, and there was no basis for setting it aside.

¶155

Government Assistance, Debt Forgiveness, Tax Credits, and Other Inducements

¶156   Government Assistance

Where a taxpayer receives (or is entitled to receive) government assistance in respect of the acquisition of depreciable property, subsection 13(7.1) provides that the capital cost of that property prior to its disposition, for all purposes of the Act, is reduced by the amount of this assistance. For example, if A Ltd. acquires Class 8 machinery in 2001 at an actual cost of $1,000, and receives a partially forgivable loan from a government in the amount of $600, the capital cost of the machinery is deemed to be $400. A Ltd. may therefore claim capital cost allowance for 2001 on $400 (subject to the half-year rule).

Where the taxpayer repays part of the government assistance pursuant to an obligation to do so prior to the disposition of the property, the amount repaid is added to the capital cost of the property. Continuing the above example, if A Ltd. repaid $100 of the loan in 2002, its capital cost of the machinery would increase to $500. It should be noted, however, that the increase in capital cost on account of repayment generates capital cost allowance only in the year of repayment and in subsequent years. Thus, the maximum capital cost allowance available to A Ltd. in 2001 would be $40 (20% of ($400 × ½)) after giving effect to the half-year rule. Assuming A Ltd. claimed this full amount in 2001, it could claim $92 in 2002 (20% of [$400 − $40 + $100]). Similarly, if a taxpayer has not received, and is not entitled to receive, any assistance in the year in which the depreciable property is acquired, the taxpayer may claim capital cost allowance based on the cost of the property to the taxpayer without making any adjustment for assistance. The amount of assistance that the taxpayer receives or is entitled to receive in a subsequent year is deducted from the capital cost of the property for that and subsequent years, but not for any year prior to that in which the assistance is made.

The government assistance which requires this type of adjustment to capital cost may be received from the federal, provincial, or municipal government, or from any other public authority. It may be in the form of a grant, subsidy, forgivable loan, deduction from tax, investment allowance, or in any other form. Reference should be made to items C and D in the definition of undepreciated capital cost in subsection 13(21) in respect of assistance repaid or assistance received (or entitled to be received) after the disposition of the property (see ¶160 for commentary).

Government or non-government assistance that the taxpayer has received, or is entitled to receive, in respect of SR&ED expenditures is excluded from subsection 13(7.1) since these types of assistance reduce the pool of SR&ED expenditures under subsection 37(1) of the Act. Grants received under a prescribed program of the federal government which are included in income under paragraphs 12(1)(u) or 56(1)(s) are not treated as government assistance (the Canadian Home Insulation Program and the Canada Oil Substitution Program are prescribed programs). Depletion allowance, which is deductible under section 65, can be earned in some cases by acquiring depreciable property (e.g., mining machinery). Depletion allowance is not, however, regarded as government assistance.

Subsection 13(7.2) requires that a trust or partnership reduce the capital cost of depreciable property where any form of government assistance or tax credit is received in respect of such property held or acquired

¶156

by the trust or partnership by a taxpayer who is a beneficiary of the trust or a member of the partnership.

The reduction in capital cost on account of government assistance applies for all purposes of the Act. Thus, for example, if depreciable property costing $5,000 is acquired with a grant of $2,000, its capital cost is deemed to be $3,000. Under the definition of adjusted cost base in section 54, the taxpayer's adjusted cost base of the property would also be $3,000. If the property was later sold for $4,000, the taxpayer would realize a capital gain.

Subsection 13(7.1) also provides a reduction in capital cost where necessary under section 80. Generally, where a taxpayer has a commercial debt obligation which is forgiven, the provisions of section 80 apply. Where applicable, subsection 80(5) may apply to reduce the capital cost of the taxpayer's depreciable property. The reduction is limited to the undepreciated capital cost of the class to which the property belongs.

¶157 Tax Credits

Investment Tax Credit

The investment tax credit provided for in subsection 127(5) and defined in subsection 127(9) is calculated as a percentage of the capital cost of certain property. This credit is regarded as government assistance and must therefore be deducted in computing the capital cost of the property acquired to earn it. The reduction in capital cost does not have to be made until after the taxpayer has actually deducted the investment tax credit, rather than at the time the taxpayer may be entitled to deduct it.

The capital cost as otherwise determined under subsection 13(7.1) is reduced by the amount of the investment tax credit deducted in any preceding taxation year. Since the assistance is not considered to be received until the credit is claimed, if the property is disposed of prior to the claim, then the capital cost is not reduced. Rather, pursuant to item I in the definition of undepreciated capital cost in subsection 13(21) (see ¶160), the undepreciated capital cost of the class to which the property belonged is reduced. The result of not claiming an investment tax credit prior to the disposition of the related asset is to convert proceeds equal to the investment tax credit from capital gains to recaptured depreciation.

The use of the investment tax credit to reduce the liability of a co-operative corporation in respect of taxes withheld on patronage dividends is provided for under subsection 127(6) and will be considered government assistance, thereby requiring a deduction by the co-operative corporation of the investment tax credit so taken in computing the capital cost of the property acquired.

GST Credits and Rebates on Depreciable Property

Under the federal Goods and Services Tax (GST), which was implemented January 1, 1991 under the authority of the *Excise Tax Act*, most businesses pay GST on their expenditures for goods and services, and recover the amount paid (under the GST system and not the income tax system) as either an "input tax credit" or rebate of GST.

Working through the rules, the GST payable by the acquirer of depreciable capital property is initially included in capital cost under general principles of accounting and is therefore eligible for capital cost allowance. However, subsection 248(16) deems the GST input tax credit or rebate to be government assistance and therefore the credit or rebate reduces the capital cost of the depreciable property under subsection 13(7.1). The GST credits and rebates flow through the capital cost allowance system, although timing differences may result in CCA being claimed on GST in one taxation year, and then the capital cost of the asset being reduced in the following year when the rebate is received or the credit is claimed.

Subsections 248(16) and (17) contain rules governing the timing of these adjustments. Where GST paid on depreciable property is claimed as a GST input tax credit in the same GST reporting period in which it is paid, it is considered received when the related GST was paid or payable. This will be a convenience in most accounting systems, since it means the GST can be effectively ignored for income tax purposes, being offset by the related input tax credit at the same time it might become eligible for depreciation. Where a GST input tax credit is claimed in a different period from that in which the related GST was paid, the notional government assistance arises at the end of the GST reporting period for which the input tax credit is claimed. Where a GST rebate rather than a GST input tax credit is claimed on depreciable property, the notional government assistance arises at the time the rebate amount is received or credited.

Where a GST input tax credit related to depreciable property is recalculated and reduced or reversed, subsection 248(18) provides that the amount becomes assistance repaid, and therefore adds to capital cost under paragraph 13(7.1)(*d*).

Technical amendments to subsections 248(16) to (18) have not been enacted into law at the time of writing, but for taxation years commencing after December 20, 2002, it is proposed that the rules governing the time at which GST credits or rebates must be recognized be amended to provide the following three alternatives:

(1) *General rule for large businesses.* An input tax credit of a taxpayer who is a GST filer with a GST threshold amount of $500,000 or more (as determined under subsection 249(1) of the *Excise Tax Act* and so in general, a company that must report GST quarterly or monthly) for the fiscal year of the taxpayer that includes the earlier of the time that the GST in respect of the input tax credit was paid or became payable, is

¶157

considered to have been received at the time the related GST was paid or became payable, even though the input tax credit is claimed in a later GST reporting period. However, this is the case only if the taxpayer claims the input tax credit at least 120 days before the taxation year in which the GST was paid or became payable becomes statute-barred for income tax purposes. In general, this requires big businesses to write down cost for income tax purposes for GST input tax credits as soon as the expenditure generating the potential credit is made, regardless of when the credits are actually claimed or received.

(2) *General rule for small businesses.* An input tax credit is considered to be received at the end of the reporting period in which it is claimed if the first rule does not apply and the taxpayer's threshold amount (as determined under subsection 249(1) of the *Excise Tax Act*) is less than $500,000 for the fiscal year of the taxpayer that includes the earlier of the time that the GST in respect of the input tax credit was paid or became payable.

(3) *Fallback rule.* If neither of the first two rules applies, the input tax credit is considered to have been received on the last day of the taxpayer's earliest taxation year (i) that begins after the taxation year that includes the earlier of the time that the GST in respect of the input tax credit was paid, and the time that it became payable, and (ii) for which the normal reassessment period for the taxpayer ends at least 120 days after the time at which the input tax credit was claimed. This would seem to apply most commonly to situations where the first rule did not apply because of a (very) late claim for input tax credit.

Special rules govern GST on automobiles and aircraft acquired by individuals or partnerships. Where the individual or partnership is registered and therefore eligible for GST credits, but business-use of the automobile or airplane is less than 90%, GST credits are prorated. The input tax credit is calculated by reference to the capital cost allowance on the vehicle which is deducted in proportion to business-use. In this situation, in order to ensure correct timing between input tax credit entitlement and the CCA adjustment, subsection 248(17) deems the input tax credit to have been received in the taxation year or fiscal period following that in which the GST is considered to have been paid for purposes of determining the credit. For taxation years of registrants ending after March 1991, a registrant taxpayer may not claim an input tax credit in respect of a passenger vehicle or aircraft if, for the taxation year for which the capital cost allowance is computed, the vehicle or aircraft was at any time made available by the registrant to an individual, giving rise to a taxable benefit under paragraph 6(1)(*e*) or subsection 15(1).

¶157

Example: GST Input Tax Credit

A self-employed individual, who is registered for GST, purchases a vehicle in 2001 costing $38,000 plus $2,660 GST and $3,040 provincial sales tax (PST). The vehicle is used 70% for the business.

(a) The vehicle is included in Class 10.1 at an amount of $34,500, in accordance with the amount permitted by Regulation 7307(1); ($30,000 plus $2,100 (GST on $30,000) plus $2,400 (PST on $30,000)).

The 2001 CCA claim is calculated as follows:

$$\$34,500 \times \tfrac{1}{2} \times 30\% = \$5,175 \times 70\% = \$3,622$$

(b) The individual will claim an input tax credit for the vehicle, which is deemed by subsection 248(17) to have been received in 2002, i.e., the taxation year following that in which the GST is considered to have been paid. The capital cost of the vehicle is reduced in 2002 by the amount of the input tax credit.

The GST input tax credit is calculated as follows:

$$\$3,622 \times \tfrac{7}{107} = \$237$$

(c) Assume the business-use of the vehicle drops to 40% in 2002.

The CCA claim in 2002 is calculated as follows:

$$(\$34,500 - \$237 - \$5,175) \times 30\% \times 40\% = \$3,491.$$

The individual may claim a GST input tax credit based on the 2002 CCA claim calculated as follows:

$$\$3,491 \times \tfrac{7}{107} = \$228.$$

QST Credits

In 1992, Quebec introduced a sales tax regime similar to GST. However, the tax base for Quebec sales tax (QST) is not identical to federal GST, and input tax credits are available for some business assets purchased but not for others. Where there are no input tax credits permitted on specific assets, it seems that QST paid on assets purchased is simply part of the cost of those assets for income tax purposes, as with any other provincial sales tax.

Where QST is recovered through input tax credits claimed for the tax component of assets purchased, previously there was no statutory guidance as to the treatment of these tax recoveries parallel to that for GST, as described above. Technical amendments to the Act introduce subsections 248(16.1), (17.1) and (17.3), which include provisions to deem QST input tax credits to be government assistance and impose timing rules for the recognition of those credits which parallels the federal rules for GST. These amendments are to be effective for taxation years commencing after February 27, 2004. Under these new rules, for capital cost allowance purposes the results for QST and GST should be the same.

¶157

¶158   Other Inducements and Reimbursements

In addition to government grants, subsidies, and other assistance, a taxpayer may receive an inducement or reimbursement from another source. Such amounts received are required by paragraph $12(1)(x)$ to be included in the taxpayer's income. If the inducement or reimbursement relates to depreciable property, subsection 13(7.4) provides that rather than including the amount of the inducement, contribution, reimbursement, or allowance in income, the taxpayer may elect to reduce the capital cost of the depreciable property acquired in the year that the inducement is received or in any of the three immediately preceding years or the following year. The taxpayer must file the election on or before the day which the taxpayer is required to file the tax return for the year during which the inducement was received or the following year if the property was acquired in the following year. It should be noted that the election under subsection 13(7.4) is a prescribed election under Regulation 600. As a result, pursuant to paragraphs $220(3.2)(a)$ and (b) of the Act, the Minister may extend the time for making such an election or may grant permission to amend or revoke the election if the taxpayer applies within 10 calendar years from the applicable taxation year.

Under subsection 13(7.4), the elected amount by which the capital cost of the depreciable property can be reduced cannot exceed the least of:

(a) the amount received by the taxpayer;

(b) the capital cost of the property as otherwise determined; and

(c) nil, where the taxpayer has disposed of the property before the year.

Subsection 13(7.4) also provides for an increase in the capital cost of the property in the event that the taxpayer repays all or a portion of the inducement in respect of which the taxpayer previously elected to reduce his or her capital cost of the property. The addition to the taxpayer's cost can only be made if the taxpayer holds the related property at the time of payment. See the definition of undepreciated capital cost in subsection 13(21), commented on at ¶160, for the treatment of a repayment that occurs after the disposition of property.

¶160

Undepreciated Capital Cost

The capital cost allowances that may be claimed under Regulation $1100(1)(a)$ are based upon the undepreciated capital cost to the taxpayer of property of a class as of the end of the taxation year. The term "undepreciated capital cost" to a taxpayer of depreciable property of a prescribed class is defined in subsection 13(21) to mean, at any time, the sum of five positive components less the sum of eight negative components.

Positive Components

(1) *Capital cost of assets acquired for the class.* The basic positive component is the capital cost to the taxpayer of the assets acquired for the class (item A of the formula in the definition of undepreciated capital cost). This calculation is made on a cumulative basis and thus includes the cost of all assets acquired at any time in the past, including assets that have previously been disposed of. See ¶150 for a discussion of the capital cost of depreciable property. The onus is on the taxpayer to demonstrate what the capital cost of a property is when the Minister disputes the taxpayer's contention (see *Zavadiuk v. M.N.R.*, 67 DTC 5298 (Ex. Ct.)).

(2) *Amount of recapture.* The second positive component of undepreciated capital cost is the amount of any recapture included in income for a previous taxation year (item B of the formula in the definition of undepreciated capital cost). For example, if the undepreciated capital cost of a particular class on the last day of a year shows a negative balance of $1,000, this $1,000 will be included in computing income for that year. The amount so included is added in computing the undepreciated capital cost of the class on the first day of the next year so that in the absence of other factors the pool will be nil at this time. See ¶180 for further discussion on recapture.

(3) *Portion of assistance repaid on disposal of property.* The third positive component of undepreciated capital cost is the portion of any assistance repaid subsequent to the disposal of a property on which assistance was received to the extent that if the amount of the assistance had been repaid prior to the disposition of the property, it would have been included in the capital cost of the property (item C of the formula in the definition of undepreciated capital cost; see also subsection 13(7.1) at ¶155). This provision corrects timing difficulties where the taxpayer no longer owns a property, and the payments would otherwise not form part of the capital cost of the property.

(4) *Portion of inducement, contribution, allowance, or assistance repaid on disposition of property.* The fourth positive component of undepreciated capital cost is the portion of any inducement, contribution, allowance, or assistance that is repaid by the taxpayer after the disposition of a property to the extent that such amount would have been added to the capital cost of the property under subsection 13(7.4) had the repayment been made before the disposition of the property (item D of the formula in the definition of undepreciated capital cost). Under subsection 13(7.4), if the amount of the inducement, contribution, allowance, or assistance is repaid prior to the disposition of the property, such amount can be added to the capital cost of the property and is, thereafter, eligible for capital cost allowance claims (see ¶155). Like the provision in (3) above, this provision corrects timing difficulties where the taxpayer no

¶160

longer owns a property and the payments would otherwise not form part of the capital cost of the property.

(5) *Amounts paid for countervailing or anti-dumping duty.* The fifth positive component of the undepreciated capital cost of a class is the total of all amounts paid as or on account of an existing or proposed countervailing or anti-dumping duty in respect of depreciable capital property of the class. This measure applies after February 23, 1998.

Negative Components

(1) *Total depreciation.* In computing the undepreciated capital cost of a class at any time, the taxpayer is required to deduct the "total depreciation" allowed for previous taxation years (item E of the formula in the definition of undepreciated capital cost). This expression is defined in subsection 13(21) to mean all capital cost allowance taken in respect of the class for preceding years, plus any terminal loss allowed under subsection 20(16) or that would have been allowed but for the exclusion in subsection 20(16.1). Where the property in the class is a passenger vehicle costing in excess of $20,000 or the prescribed limit, terminal loss is denied under subsection 20(16.1). For taxation years ending after December 20, 2002, it is proposed that subsection 20(16.1) applies to deny a terminal loss to a limited period franchise, concession or licence that is a former business property for which the taxpayer has elected replacement property treatment under subsection 13(4.2). In both these cases, the denied terminal loss would be included in the definition of total depreciation.

(2) *Amounts under debt forgiveness rules.* Where a taxpayer has had a commercial debt obligation forgiven without full payment, section 80 may apply to reduce the undepreciated capital cost of the taxpayer's depreciable property.

(3) *Proceeds of disposition or capital cost.* Where a property of the class has been disposed of (except where the property is a timber resource property), the undepreciated capital cost of the class is reduced by the lesser of the proceeds of disposition of that property (less any costs of disposition) and its capital cost (item F of the formula in the definition of undepreciated capital cost). The effect of this rule is to limit recapture to any recovery of capital cost allowance up to the capital cost of the property, any gain on the disposition being treated as a capital gain. See ¶165 concerning the meaning of disposition.

(4) *Full proceeds of disposition for timber resource property.* Where the property disposed of is a timber resource property (Class 33), the undepreciated capital cost of the class is reduced by the full proceeds of disposition for that property (less any costs of disposition) (item G of the formula in the definition of undepreciated capital cost). Under this rule, recapture applies not only to the capital cost allowance claimed in respect of a timber resource property, but to any proceeds in excess of the

¶160

original cost. This excess is thus included in income in full instead of being treated as a capital gain.

(5) *Certain mining income.* If the taxpayer has brought a new mine into production between November 7, 1969 and December 31, 1973, the taxpayer may elect under section 28 of the *Income Tax Application Rules* to exempt certain income of the mine from tax. Ordinarily, such an election precludes the taxpayer from claiming accelerated capital cost allowance under Regulations $1100(1)(w)$ and (x) on the Class 28 property acquired in respect of that mine. Under Regulation 1100A, the taxpayer may further elect to take accelerated capital cost allowance, but must then reduce the undepreciated capital cost of his or her Class 28 property by the income exempted from tax by reason of the election under ITAR 28 (item H of the formula in the definition of undepreciated capital cost).

(6) *Investment tax credit claimed.* To the extent that an investment tax credit is claimed after the property is disposed of, the undepreciated capital cost of the class to which that property was allocated is reduced by the investment tax credit claimed (item I of the formula in the definition of undepreciated capital cost).

(7) *Assistance received.* Where assistance is received in respect of a specific property after the disposition of such property, to the extent that such assistance would have reduced the cost of the property under paragraph $13(7.1)(f)$ if received prior to its disposal (see ¶155), the assistance reduces the undepreciated capital cost of the class (item J of the formula in the definition of "undepreciated capital cost" in subsection $13(21)$).

(8) *Refunds of countervailing or anti-dumping duties paid.* Where an amount is received in respect of a refund of countervailing or anti-dumping duties paid in respect of depreciable capital property of the class, that amount is subtracted from the undepreciated capital cost of the class if it was previously added to the undepreciated capital cost of the class. This measure applies after February 23, 1998.

Resulting Balance

If the total of the positive and negative components is positive and there are assets still physically in the class, then capital cost allowance is calculated on the year-end balance of undepreciated capital cost. If the balance is positive but there are no assets in the class, then a terminal loss results. (See ¶167.) If the total of the negative elements of the undepreciated capital cost calculation exceeds the total of the positive elements at the year end, the negative balance must be recaptured and included in income for that year. Unlike a terminal loss, recapture may arise if there are assets remaining in the class at year end. It is the balance of the undepreciated capital cost of the class at the end of the taxation year, after taking into account all the positive and negative components, that will trigger recapture. See ¶167.

¶160

CHAPTER 2

DISPOSITIONS, EXCHANGES, AND TRANSFERS OF PROPERTY

Disposition of Depreciable Property .... ¶165

Uncollectible Proceeds of Disposition .... ¶175

Recapture of Capital Cost Allowance .... ¶180

Exchanges of Property .... ¶190

Lease-Option Arrangements .... ¶195

Change in Use of Assets................................... ¶200

Non-Arm's Length Transfers of Depreciable Property .... ¶205

Deemed Dispositions of Depreciable Property Upon a Change
    of Control or Change in Tax Status .... ¶210

Terminal Loss .... ¶215

¶165

Disposition of Depreciable Property

Paragraph (*a*) of the definition of "disposition" in subsection 248(1) includes any transaction or event entitling a taxpayer to proceeds of disposition of property. By using the word "include", the definition does not rule out circumstances where no proceeds arise (see *Wilfred Dowbiggin v. M.N.R.*, 66 DTC 97 (T.A.B.)). See Interpretation Bulletin IT-460, "Dispositions — Absence of Consideration", at ¶3237.

When a disposition occurs, the proceeds of disposition must be deducted from the undepreciated capital cost of the particular class. If the

¶165

proceeds exceed the capital cost of the asset, then only the portion equal to the capital cost will be deducted from the class. The proceeds in excess of capital cost will normally be treated as a capital gain. Capital losses cannot arise on depreciable property. One-half of the capital gain is taxable. See ¶170 for the rules concerning the disposition of depreciable property owned on December 31, 1971.

¶166   Proceeds of Disposition

"Proceeds of disposition" is defined in subsection 13(21) and is usually the sale price, net of commissions or other expenses of sale, received by the transferor. Proceeds of disposition can also include:

(a) compensation for property damaged, expropriated, injuriously affected, or unlawfully taken;

(b) proceeds of an insurance policy paid on destruction or loss of property;

(c) that part of insurance proceeds paid on damage to property which is not spent on repairing the damage within a reasonable time; and

(d) proceeds of sale of mortgaged property by way of foreclosure.

Special rules in subsections 20(4) and (5) provide for a deduction from income where any portion of the proceeds of disposition of depreciable property becomes uncollectible (see ¶175).

All proceeds of an insurance policy in respect of destruction of or damage to depreciable property will be treated as proceeds of disposition of the property except in the case of insurance proceeds paid in respect of damage to property, that are used to repair the damage within a reasonable time after it occurs. In such cases, the amount payable to the taxpayer is directly included in income under paragraph $12(1)(f)$. In this situation, the amount to be included in the taxpayer's income in a particular year will be equal to the amount of the insurance proceeds expended in that year on repairing the damage which is deductible under the general rules in section 18. Thus, in effect, the amount included in income will offset the amount deducted as an expense in the year for repairing the property. Any part of the proceeds of an insurance policy in respect of damage to property that is not used to repair property within a reasonable time after the damage is treated as proceeds of disposition of depreciable property.

Special rules are provided in subsection 44(2) for determining the time of disposition of capital property that has been stolen, destroyed, or expropriated, and the time when the proceeds of disposition are considered to have become receivable. In general, these rules recognize that on dispositions of this kind, the proceeds are seldom received or even determined until some considerable time after the taxpayer ceases to have use of the property. The disposition is deemed to have taken place and the proceeds are deemed to have become receivable on the earliest of the following five specified days:

(1) the day when the taxpayer agrees to the *full* compensation for the stolen, destroyed, or expropriated property; if the taxpayer agrees to a certain minimum amount and actually receives that pending final agreement as to the full compensation, it would appear that the taxpayer would not regard the initial amount as proceeds until the full amount has been agreed upon;

(2) the day when the taxpayer's compensation is finally determined by a court or other competent tribunal;

(3) where the taxpayer has not agreed on full compensation and the matter has not been taken before a court or tribunal within two years of the loss, destruction, or expropriation of the property, the day that is two years after the loss, destruction, or expropriation;

(4) if the taxpayer ceases to be resident in Canada or dies and as a result is deemed to have disposed of his or her property, the day of such cessation of residence or death; and

(5) where the taxpayer is a corporation, other than a taxable Canadian corporation all of whose shares are owned by a second taxable Canadian corporation, and the taxpayer winds up, the day of such winding-up.

Where property of a taxpayer is foreclosed or sold under a mortgage, the amount of such proceeds is the amount by which the taxpayer's liability to a mortgagee has been reduced as a result. Any amount which the taxpayer may receive, following such a sale, is included in the proceeds.

Special Rules

Special rules are provided in subsection 13(21.1) for the joint disposition of land and buildings. These rules essentially ensure that any loss on the sale of the building will be reduced by any gain on the land. This prevents the taxpayer from claiming a fully deductible income loss when the corresponding capital gain is only partly taxable. See ¶225.

See also Interpretation Bulletins IT-170R, "Sale of Property — When Included in Income Computation", at ¶3130; IT-220R2, "Capital Cost Allowance — Proceeds of Disposition of Depreciable Property", at ¶3155; and IT-418, "Capital Cost Allowance — Partial Dispositions of Property", at ¶3220.

¶167   Recapture and Terminal Loss

Recapture

Recapture arises when the deduction of proceeds of disposition of a property from a class leads to a negative undepreciated capital cost. This negative undepreciated capital cost must be added to the taxpayer's income in the year it arises. Recapture can be avoided by acquiring new assets belonging to that class before the end of the year. This may not be possible if the assets are required to be placed in a separate class. The acquisition of certain business "replacement" property or replacement property for involuntary dispositions can also eliminate recapture. See ¶180 for further commentary on recapture.

Terminal Loss

Where all the assets of a particular class are disposed of and no assets of that class are on hand at the end of the year, the taxpayer is required to deduct an amount for the year equal to the undepreciated capital cost of property of the class as of the end of the taxation year. This deduction under subsection 20(16) is usually referred to as a "terminal loss". See further commentary on terminal losses at ¶215.

Example 1:   Recapture and Terminal Loss

The following is an illustration of the working of the system of capital cost allowances when the asset disposed of is the only asset of its class.

	Case 1	*Case 2*	*Case 3*
Capital cost of property of prescribed class	$ 5,000	$ 5,000	$ 5,000
Capital cost allowance taken	1,500	1,500	1,500
Undepreciated capital cost	$ 3,500	$ 3,500	$ 3,500
Amount realized on disposition	2,500	4,000	6,000
Recapture	—	500	1,500
Terminal loss	1,000	—	—
Capital gain.	—	—	1,000

¶170   Disposition of Depreciable Property Owned on December 31, 1971

Prior to 1972, the disposition of depreciable property could trigger recapture when the proceeds of disposition exceeded the undepreciated capital cost of property involved. However, if the proceeds of disposition exceeded the capital cost of the asset involved, the excess constituted a non-taxable capital gain. With the introduction of tax on capital gains in 1972, it is necessary to determine the amount of capital gain involved in a disposition of depreciable property that was owned on December 31, 1971, since capital gains accruing to December 31, 1971 remain non-taxable.

If the capital cost of the property was greater than either the actual proceeds of disposition or the value on Valuation Day of the property, no special calculation is required and the proceeds of disposition for tax purposes will be the actual proceeds of disposition (unless the disposition is by way of a gift or is to a spouse). For publicly traded shares and securities, Valuation Day is December 22, 1971, and for all other property, it is December 31, 1971.

Where the capital cost to a taxpayer of any depreciable property of a prescribed class acquired by the taxpayer before 1972, and owned from December 31, 1971 until the time the taxpayer disposes of it, is less than the fair market value of the property on Valuation Day, and less than the proceeds of disposition, the following two transitional provisions under ITAR 20(1) apply.

(1) For the purpose of the provisions relating to capital gains and losses, recapture, and capital cost allowances, the proceeds of disposition are deemed to be the capital cost plus the excess of the actual proceeds over the Valuation Day value.

Example:

Capital cost of a building	$ 50,000
Valuation Day value	70,000
Ultimate proceeds of sale	80,000

The taxpayer's proceeds of disposition will be deemed to be $50,000 + (80,000 − 70,000) or $60,000. The taxpayer will be subject to full recapture and will have a capital gain of $10,000. If the ultimate proceeds of sale had been $65,000, i.e., less than the fair market value of the property on Valuation Day, but greater than its capital cost, the proceeds of disposition would be deemed to be $50,000. The taxpayer would be subject to full recapture, but would have no capital gain or loss.

---

(2) If the property is transferred in one or more non-arm's length transactions, each non-arm's length purchaser, for purposes of calculating capital cost allowance, capital gains, and recapture, is deemed to have incurred a capital cost equal to the proceeds the vendor is deemed to have received under rule (1) above. Upon a subsequent disposition, the transferee calculates the proceeds under rule (1) above as if the transferee had owned the property since December 31, 1971.

Example:

Assume:

Capital cost to taxpayer A of a depreciable property acquired before 1972	$6,500
Fair market value of the property on Valuation Day	$7,200
Selling price of property in 1973	$7,800

¶170

Results on sale in 1973:

A's deemed proceeds of disposition: $6,500 + ($7,800 − $7,200) = $7,100

A's capital gain for taxation purposes:

$7,100 − $6,500 = $600

If the purchaser was dealing at arm's length with A, the purchaser's capital cost would be $7,800, but if the purchaser of A's property was the purchaser's son B (or any other person not dealing at arm's length with A), then B's capital cost for capital cost allowance purposes is the deemed proceeds of $7,100.

Assume:

B subsequently disposes of the property for $9,000

B's deemed proceeds: $6,500 + ($9,000 − $7,200) = $8,300

B's capital gain for tax purposes: $8,300 − $7,100 = $1,200

The overall gain can be broken down into:

Gain accrued to A prior to Valuation Day, not taxable . . . . $ 700

Gain in A's hands 600

Gain in B's hands 1,200

Overall gain:

($9,000 − $6,500) $2,500

The transitional provisions under ITAR 20(1) are not applicable to transfers of depreciable property to a spouse or a trust to which subsections 70(6) or 73(1) apply, or to a transfer of farm property from a farmer to his or her child to which subsection 70(9) applies. The spouse, trust, or child assumes the position of the transferor when the property is actually disposed of. There is also special treatment in the case of the following transfers of property:

(a) dispositions of capital property to a corporation by a person or partnership and the winding-up of a partnership (subsections 85(1), (2), and (3));

(b) amalgamations after 1971 (subsection 87(2));

(c) contributions to a partnership (subsection 97(3));

(d) distributions on dissolution of a partnership (subsections 98(3) and (5));

(e) distributions in satisfaction of a capital interest in a trust (subsection 107(2));

(f) winding-up of a corporation (section 88); and

(g) deemed dispositions on death (subsection 70(5)).

Where a taxpayer acquires depreciable property under any of the above forms of tax-free rollovers after 1971 from a person who owned it

¶170

from December 31, 1971, the transitional rules deem the taxpayer to have acquired the property before 1972 and to have owned it continuously from December 31, 1971, so that the rules may be applicable on a subsequent disposition by the taxpayer.

If property owned on December 31, 1971 is used in farming or fishing and the taxpayer has continuously taken capital cost allowances on the straight-line basis, the taxpayer is not subject to recapture of depreciation on the sale of the property.

Property that was acquired prior to 1949 is not subject to recapture on the normal capital cost allowance taken prior to 1949.

¶175

Uncollectible Proceeds of Disposition

Subsection 20(4) provides that a taxpayer may claim a deduction in computing his or her income if the taxpayer has disposed of depreciable property, other than a timber resource property or a passenger vehicle having a cost in excess of a prescribed amount (see the chart at ¶252), and any portion of the proceeds of disposition becomes a bad debt. The amount deductible is the lesser of:

(a) the amount of the bad debt; and

(b) the amount by which the capital cost to the taxpayer of the property disposed of exceeds the amount realized on the disposition.

This is consistent with amounts up to the capital cost of depreciable property being on income account and amounts in excess of capital cost being on capital account.

Subsection 20(5) provides that in certain circumstances, a taxpayer may claim a deduction from income for a loss suffered on the sale of an agreement for sale, or of a mortgage or hypothec on land that has been taken back as part of the proceeds of disposition of depreciable property (other than a timber resource property) sold in a previous year. Similar to the bad debt mentioned above, the amount of the deduction will be the lesser of:

(a) the amount by which the principal amount outstanding on the agreement, mortgage or hypothec at the time of sale exceeds the sale price; and

(b) such excess in (a) minus any capital gain realized by the taxpayer on the disposal of the depreciable property.

Thus, where a taxpayer has realized a capital gain on the sale of depreciable property, any loss incurred on the subsequent sale of a mortgage taken back as part consideration is deductible only to the extent that it exceeds the capital gain.

Although a timber resource property is a depreciable property, gains are treated on income account. Subsection 20(4.1) provides that if a taxpayer has disposed of a timber resource property and any portion of the proceeds has become a bad debt, the full amount of the bad debt may be deducted from income. Similarly, subsection 20(5.1) provides that a taxpayer may claim a deduction from income of the full amount of a loss suffered on the sale to an arm's length person of an agreement for sale, mortgage, or hypothec on land that has been taken back as part of the proceeds of disposition of a timber resource property. No limitation is imposed on the amounts deductible under subsections 20(4.1) or (5.1) because the full amount by which the proceeds of disposition exceeded the undepreciated capital cost of the property would have been included in computing income. See ¶185 regarding the disposition of timber resource properties.

¶180

Recapture of Capital Cost Allowance

Section 13 establishes the so-called "recapture" principle under which the capital cost allowance deducted over the years by a taxpayer under paragraph 20(1)(a) may be wholly or partially brought back into the taxpayer's income in a later year. The basic rule upon which section 13 is founded is that the deduction to which a taxpayer is entitled under paragraph 20(1)(a) in respect of the taxpayer's capital cost of particular depreciable property cannot in the long run exceed the actual decline in value of the property. For example, if the taxpayer acquires depreciable property at a cost of $10,000, and some years later sells it for $4,000, the maximum deduction allowable in computing income is $6,000. If the capital cost allowance actually claimed was $7,000, the taxpayer would be obliged to include $1,000 in income.

Recapture applies only to capital cost allowance previously claimed, not to a realization of an amount in excess of the original cost of the property. Continuing the above example, if the property was sold for $12,000, all capital cost allowance claimed would be recaptured, but the excess of selling price over original cost (i.e., $2,000) would be treated as a capital gain. The one exception to this rule is the case where the property in question is a timber resource property. For property of this kind, any gain over original cost is subject to recapture and thus full income inclusion instead of capital gains treatment.

The converse of the recapture principle is the terminal loss allowed by subsection 20(16). The purpose of this provision is to recognize a case where the capital cost allowance claimed on a property has been less than its actual decline in value. For example, if property costing $10,000 is sold for $4,000, but only $5,000 of capital cost allowance has been claimed and there are no assets remaining in the class, the other $1,000 may be deductible under subsection 20(16). See ¶215.

The key element in both the capital cost allowance system and the recapture principle is the "undepreciated capital cost" of a class of property at any time. This term is defined in subsection 13(21) and is discussed at ¶160. Where the undepreciated capital cost of the class at the year-end is negative because of CCA claims, proceeds of disposition and other negative components exceeding capital cost and any other positive components, subsection 13(1) requires this negative balance to be recaptured and included in income for that taxation year, notwithstanding that the property may not have been disposed of by the year-end. A nil balance in the undepreciated capital cost of the class will then be carried forward for the class for the next year.

Example: Undepreciated Capital Cost

Assume that X Ltd. acquired the following Class 8 properties in 1996:

		Cost
Property A		$ 500
Property B		750
Property C		1,250
Capital cost of class		$2,500

Capital cost allowance was claimed in 1996 to 2000 totalling $1,300. In 2001 property B is sold for $600 and property C is sold for $800.

The undepreciated capital cost of the class at the end of 2001 is therefore:

Capital cost of properties	$2,500
Capital cost allowance claimed	(1,300)
Proceeds of disposition	(1,400)
	$ (200)

Under subsection 13(1), X Ltd. would be required to include $200 in computing 2001 income, and the balance in Class 8 at the beginning of 2002 would be nil.

If the undepreciated capital cost of a class becomes negative at some point during the taxation year (for example, because all or a substantial portion of the assets in the class have been sold for amounts that recover some part of the capital cost allowance previously claimed), recapture can be avoided through the acquisition of further properties of that class before the end of the taxation year. Under subsection 13(1), recapture arises only if the undepreciated capital cost of the class is negative at the year-end. If, before the year-end, positive elements can be injected through further acquisitions sufficient to offset any negative balance that might have temporarily arisen during the year, the negative balance will not exist at year-end and no recapture will arise that year.

Recapture can be averted by the acquisition of assets of that class before year-end even if no capital cost allowance may be claimed on the assets because they are not "available for use". The capital cost of the asset is still credited to the class.

On occasion, an asset may not be included in the same class as a similar asset because of a change in class rules. Where this occurs, special rules may still permit the deferral of recapture. See ¶235.

In some situations, the recapture rules do not automatically apply to a negative undepreciated capital cost ("UCC") balance at year-end. Subsection 13(2) precludes recapture from arising on the disposition of a passenger vehicle having a cost in excess of $20,000 or the prescribed limit (see ¶250 and the chart at ¶252). Subsection 13(4) provides special rules for the deferral of recapture on property disposed of involuntarily, or in some cases, voluntarily (¶190). For further commentary on recapture, see Interpretation Bulletin IT-478R2, "Capital Cost Allowance — Recapture and Terminal Loss", at ¶3265.

Example: Recapture

The following illustrates the working of the system of capital cost allowances where the assets disposed of are simply part of the property of a particular class held by the taxpayer:

	Case 1	Case 2	Case 3	Case 4
Total assets of class — Capital cost	$100,000	$100,000	$100,000	$100,000
Accumulated capital cost allowances	80,000	80,000	80,000	50,000
Undepreciated capital cost of property of class immediately before disposition	20,000	20,000	20,000	50,000
Dispositions of property included in group:				
Capital cost	30,000	30,000	30,000	10,000
Proceeds	15,000	25,000	35,000	25,000
Amount deducted from undepreciated capital cost of property of class*	15,000	25,000	30,000	10,000
Capital gain	nil	nil	5,000	15,000
Amount recaptured	nil	5,000	10,000	nil
Undepreciated capital cost of assets remaining in class	5,000	nil	nil	40,000

* The definition of "undepreciated capital cost" restricts the deduction to the lesser of (a) proceeds of disposition and (b) capital cost.

¶180

¶185   Disposition of Timber Resource Properties

A "timber resource property" as defined in subsection 13(21) is a Class 33 property eligible for capital cost allowance at 15%. When a taxpayer disposes of a timber resource property, the definition of "undepreciated capital cost" in subsection 13(21) requires that the undepreciated capital cost of the class to which the timber resource property belongs be reduced by the full amount of the proceeds of disposition. This rule applies even where the proceeds exceed the original capital cost of the timber resource property. Accordingly, recapture may arise not only in respect of the capital cost allowance claimed but on any amount realized in excess of original cost. Ordinarily, any such excess realized on a disposition of depreciable property is treated as a capital gain. Subparagraph 39(1)(a)(iv) specifically provides that capital gains and losses cannot be realized or incurred on timber resource properties. See Interpretation Bulletin IT-481, "Timber Resource Property and Timber Limits", at ¶3270. It should be noted that where the proceeds of disposition of a timber resource property include a debt which is later disposed of at a loss or established to have become bad, subsections 20(5.1) or 20(4.1), respectively, may apply to allow a deduction in computing income. See ¶175.

¶190

Exchanges of Property

Where a taxpayer has depreciable property which has been stolen, expropriated or destroyed, a "disposition" is deemed to have occurred. This may give rise to recapture of capital cost allowance, notwithstanding that the taxpayer intends to replace the property. Subsection 13(4) allows a taxpayer to elect to defer recognition of recapture of capital cost allowance where qualified property has been disposed of in those particular circumstances. A similar election is available under subsection 44(1) in respect of any capital gain arising from the same disposition. By virtue of subsection 44(4), an election under either subsection 13(4) or 44(1) will be deemed to also be an election under the other subsection.

The election is available in respect of depreciable property of a prescribed class or a timber resource property where the proceeds arise as a result of certain involuntary dispositions, or in respect of any disposition of property described as "former business property". In order to qualify for the election, a "replacement property", as defined in subsection 13(4.1), must be acquired in respect of involuntary dispositions, before the end of the second taxation year and, in respect of a voluntary disposition of a former business property, before the end of the first taxation year, following the year in which the proceeds of disposition became receivable. Where the replacement property is acquired after the prescribed time limits, no deferral of recaptured income will be allowed in respect of that disposition. The reference to a time of acquisition refers to the time of actual acquisition, rather than to the time a property is considered to be available for use.

If the disposition of the former property and the acquisition of the replacement property occur in the same year, the election is made by reporting the income tax consequences of the transaction on the basis that subsection 13(4) applied. If the replacement property is acquired in a year subsequent to the disposition, a letter should be filed with the tax return for the year in which the property is replaced. The letter would include a request for an amendment to the recapture calculation of the previous year. If the property is replaced in a year prior to the disposition, a letter outlining the particulars should be filed in the year the replacement property is acquired. As set out in IT-259R4, in these circumstances, the election will also be accepted in the year of the disposition of the former property. Regulation 600 provides that the Minister may extend the time for making an election under subsection 13(4), or may grant permission to amend or revoke such an election.

Where the election is made, the proceeds of disposition may be reduced by the amount that otherwise would be the recapture of capital cost allowance. Consequently, recapture will not be income in the year, but instead will reduce the undepreciated capital cost of whichever class of property the replacement property falls into. Where the replacement property is of the same class as the property disposed of, the result is the same as if the replacement property had been acquired at the same time as the proceeds of disposition of the former property reduced the undepreciated capital cost of the class.

Where the cost of the replacement property is less than the amount of recapture of capital cost allowance otherwise determined, the net difference will remain as recapture by virtue of the limitation in subparagraph 13(4)(c)(ii). See Interpretation Bulletin IT-259R4, "Exchanges of Property", at ¶3158.

Where the replacement property is in a different class than the property that has been disposed of, the undepreciated capital cost of the class of the former property is first reduced to nil, and then any reduced proceeds still remaining reduce the undepreciated capital cost of the new class. If the disposition of the old property and the acquisition of the new property occur in the same year, and the replacement property is placed in a different class only because of its date of acquisition (i.e., Class 3 and Class 1 buildings), an alternative election under Regulation 1103(2d), described at ¶235, is available.

¶190

Example: Exchanges of Property

Capital cost of former property	$ 45,000
Undepreciated capital cost of former property	$ 35,000(1)
Proceeds	$ 40,000(2)
Recapture otherwise determined ((2) – (1))	$ 5,000(3)
Cost of replacement property	$ 42,000(4)
Restated proceeds: Proceeds minus lesser of: (i) recapture and (ii) cost of replacement property ((2) – (3))	$ 35,000(5)
Recaptured CCA ((5) – (1))	nil

The recognition of recapture is deferred by the acquisition of the replacement property. The capital cost of the replacement property is thus deemed to be reduced by proceeds of disposition equal to the reduction in recapture.

Cost of replacement property	$ 42,000
Less: Deemed proceeds of disposition (equal to reduction above)	5,000
Undepreciated capital cost of replacement property before CCA	$ 37,000

¶191   Involuntary Dispositions

The types of proceeds covered by the rollover on involuntary dispositions are described in the definition of "proceeds of disposition" in subsection 13(21). These are compensation for stolen or destroyed property, including proceeds of insurance and compensation for property that is expropriated, or the selling price of property sold to an expropriating authority after notice of expropriation has been given. Under subsection 44(2), the proceeds in these circumstances will be deemed to have become receivable at the earliest of five specified days as described at ¶166. For involuntary dispositions, the replacement property must be acquired before the end of the second taxation year following the year when the original property is considered to have been disposed of under these rules. For dispositions occurring in taxation years ending on or after December 20, 2000, amendments are proposed to the permitted replacement period to accommodate short taxation years, so that the replacement property must be acquired before the later of the end of the second taxation year following the year when the original property is considered to have been disposed of, and 24 months after the end of the taxation year in which the involuntary disposition occurred.

Where the replacement property is acquired before the compensation for the former property becomes receivable, subparagraph $13(4)(d)(ii)$ provides that any amount otherwise included in recapture in the year when the compensation does become receivable is considered to be proceeds of disposition in respect of the class applicable to the replacement property, so that the taxpayer's right to claim future capital cost allowance in respect of the replacement property is reduced, but no immediate recapture occurs. The replacement property must still be owned at the time the former property is disposed of in order for the deferral of recapture to apply.

Where the replacement property is acquired in a year subsequent to the disposition, the taxpayer may often face a dilemma in reporting income for the year of disposition. Where it is known that a replacement property is or will be acquired within the prescribed time limits, it may be possible to file on the basis that a rollover will be available. In any other case, it would appear to be necessary to file an amended return for the initial year, which would delete the recapture already reported.

¶192   Voluntary Dispositions

Subsection $13(4)$ also applies to voluntary dispositions of what is described as "former business property", where a replacement property is acquired before the end of the subsequent taxation year. For dispositions occurring in taxation years ending on or after December 20, 2001, amendments are proposed to the permitted replacement period to accomodate short taxation years so that the replacement property must be acquired before the later of the end of the taxation year following the year when the original property is considered to have been disposed of, and 12 months after the end of the taxation year in which the disposition occurred.

The term "former business property" is defined in subsection $248(1)$ as real property, or an interest therein, that is capital property used primarily for the purpose of earning business income. It does not include a rental property, land related to the rental property, such as parking areas, driveways, yards, or gardens, or a leasehold interest in such property. "Rental property", for the purposes of this definition, does not include property that is leased under an agreement whereby the lessee will use the property to carry on the business of selling or promoting the sale of the taxpayer's goods or services, e.g., a gasoline service station or franchise restaurant. Real property rented to a related party may qualify as a former business property, provided it was used in the related party's business (i.e., was not a rental property in that person's hands). It would appear that the purpose of allowing a rollover for a former business property is to permit a business to change location or facilities without creating recapture of capital cost allowance which might otherwise arise.

Proposed amendments to the definition of "former business property" will extend the replacement property rules to apply to franchises, concessions or limited period licences (i.e., certain Class 14 properties) in certain circumstances. The election for these properties is made under proposed subsection 13(4.2). To qualify for the election under subsection 13(4.2), a franchise, concession or limited period licence must be wholly attributable to a business carried on in a fixed place, and must have been disposed of directly by the transferor to the transferee, or if the property by the transferor was terminated, the transferee must acquire a similar property in respect of the same fixed place from another person. The rules under proposed subsections 13(4.2) and (4.3) for the replacement of franchises, concessions and licences apply to dispositions (or terminations) of franchises, concessions and limited period licences that occur after December 20, 2002.

An "interest in real property" is defined in subsection 248(4) to include a leasehold interest in real property, but does not include an interest as security only derived by virtue of a mortgage, hypothec, agreement for sale, or similar obligation.

¶193 Replacement Property

The expression "replacement property" used in subsection 13(4) is defined in subsection 13(4.1). In order to qualify as replacement property, it must be depreciable property acquired for the same or a similar use as the use to which the taxpayer or a person related to the taxpayer, put the former property. It should be noted that the replacement property need not be property of the same class as the former property in order to meet the requirements of subsection 13(4.1). If the former property was used for earning business income by the taxpayer or a related person, the replacement property must be acquired for earning income from the same or a similar business by the taxpayer or a related person as that for which the former property was used. It appears that the related person acquiring replacement property need not be the same related person as that disposing of former property. Whether property is acquired for the same or a similar use or whether a business is the same or a similar business will be a question of fact. Paragraphs 16 and 17 of IT-259R4 (see ¶3158) set out the CRA's views on the term "same or similar use". In addition, CRA Technical News No. 25 notes that a property acquired under a business expansion may not qualify as a replacement property if there is not a causal connection between the properties, but again this is fact specific.

Where the former property was "taxable Canadian property" as defined in subsection 248(1), the replacement property must also be taxable Canadian property. Taxable Canadian property is essentially Canadian real property or any capital property used in carrying on business in Canada. It also includes Canadian resource and timber resource properties, and a number of other items, which, however, are intangible and would not normally seem subject to involuntary disposition. This rule previously applied only to non-residents, but was extended to Canadian residents effective for dispositions after April 2, 1990.

For a disposition that occurs in a taxation year ending after 1997, there is a further stipulation that if the former property was a taxable Canadian property of the taxpayer other than a treaty-protected property, the replacement property must also be a taxable Canadian property other than a treaty-protected property. This rule is intended to prevent the replacement of a non-treaty-protected capital property (the disposition of which could be taxable in Canada) with a treaty-protected property (the disposition of which would not be taxable in Canada). A treaty-protected property is a property the gain from the disposition of which would be exempt from tax because of an income tax treaty between Canada and another country.

Typically, a non-resident's capital property forming part of the business property of a permanent establishment in Canada would be considered taxable Canadian property other than a treaty-protected property (in other words, its disposition by the non-resident would be taxable in Canada). Essentially, this appears to mean that buildings located in Canada, or capital property used in carrying on a business through a permanent establishment in Canada, must be replaced with property with such a Canadian location and use. If the non-resident is resident in a non-treaty country, any capital property used in carrying on a business in Canada would be a taxable Canadian property other than a treaty-protected property.

¶195

Lease-Option Arrangements

Subsections 13(5.2) and (5.3) provide statutory rules which deal with the situation where a taxpayer originally leases property, acquires that property pursuant to an option contained in the lease, and later disposes of that property. These rules operate to ensure that a portion of amounts paid as rent for the property and deducted from income will be recaptured where the property, or an option thereon, is sold at more than the actual cost of the property or the option.

Rather than purchase a depreciable asset or real property, a taxpayer may lease that property for a number of years and, at the termination of the lease, purchase the property pursuant to an option contained in the lease. This purchase may be at a price agreed upon at the beginning of the lease. In most cases, all the rental payments for the use of the property will have been deducted for income tax purposes in the year incurred. A subsequent sale of the property would, but for subsection 13(5.2), result in a capital gain to the extent that the proceeds of sale exceeded the exercise price of the option and there would be no income inclusion with respect to the previously deducted rent.

The CRA's current position is that the determination of whether a contract is a lease or sale should be based on the legal relationship created under the terms of an agreement. This position is set out in CRA Technical News No. 21, dated June 14, 2001. This document cancelled IT-233R which set out the CRA's previous position.

In general, subsection 13(5.2) applies where a taxpayer has acquired a depreciable property or real property for a cost or capital cost less than fair market value from a lessor, and has paid rent for the use of that property which has been deducted in computing taxable income. The fair market value of the property is determined at the time the property is acquired by the taxpayer and is to be determined without taking into consideration any option on the property. Thus, subsection 13(5.2) could apply in cases where the lease is not treated as a sale for income tax purposes but where, when the option to purchase is exercised, the fair market value of the property is in excess of the option exercise price. Subsection 13(5.2) also applies where a party who does not deal at arm's length with the taxpayer has rented a property and subsequently the taxpayer acquires that property at an amount less than its then fair market value.

Subsection 13(5.3) applies where a taxpayer disposes of a capital property which is an option to acquire either depreciable property or real property where the property has been rented by the taxpayer or a non-arm's length party and the rent has been deductible from income. Where the option is sold (rather than exercised with a subsequent sale of the property such that subsection 13(5.2) would apply), subsection 13(5.3) provides that the proceeds of disposition less the cost of the option are to be included in income as recaptured income.

The purpose behind subsection 13(5.3) is to prevent the taxpayer from avoiding subsection 13(5.2) by disposing of the option and including any excess as capital gains rather than recapture.

Under subsection 13(5.2), for the purposes of recapture and the claiming of capital cost allowance, the taxpayer is deemed, at the time of the exercise of the option, to acquire the property at a cost that is equal to the lesser of:

(a) the fair market value of the property at the time of the exercise of the option (determined without taking into consideration any option on that property); and

(b) the actual cost of the property at the time of the exercise of the option, plus all previous payments on account of rent for the use of that property.

For these purposes, rental payments include rental payments made by persons with whom the taxpayer was not dealing at arm's length. However, rental payments made to a person with whom the taxpayer does not deal at arm's length are not included for the purposes of (b). If the taxpayer acquiring the property is a corporation which was not in existence at the time when rental payments were made by a non-arm's length party, that corporation, for the purposes of subsections 13(5.2) and (5.3),

¶195

will be deemed to have been in existence at the time the rental payments were made and not to have been dealing at arm's length with the previous lessor. In most cases, the lesser amount will be the fair market value of the property at the time the property is acquired. The limitation in (b) above ensures that subsection 13(5.2) will operate only to the extent of previously deductible rental payments.

To the extent that the actual cost of the property is less than the deemed cost determined as described above, that difference is added to the total of the depreciation previously allowed to the taxpayer with respect to the capital cost allowance class to which the property belongs. Consequently, any proceeds of disposition up to (but not exceeding) the deemed cost of the property will reduce the undepreciated capital cost of the class to which the property belongs, whereas, if subsection 13(5.2) did not apply, only proceeds of disposition up to the actual cost would reduce the undepreciated capital cost of the class. For example, if the deemed cost of depreciable property under subsection 13(5.2) is $200, and the option price or actual cost is $50, the taxpayer is deemed to have claimed $150 of capital cost allowance, and this amount will be subject to potential inclusion in income as recapture of capital cost allowance.

Where the property leased and then acquired is not otherwise depreciable property, for example, land, that property is deemed to be depreciable property of a separate prescribed class, specifically Class 36. To the extent that the deemed cost under subsection 13(5.2) is greater than the actual cost, recaptured depreciation could result on the subsequent sale of the land, rather than a capital gain. The fact that the land is deemed to be property of a prescribed class does not, however, entitle the taxpayer to claim capital cost allowance on that property. By virtue of Class 36 and Regulation 1101(5g), each Class 36 property will form a separate class, thus recaptured depreciation will be calculated on an asset by asset basis, rather than on a pool basis.

Example: Lease-Option Arrangements

S Ltd. entered into an arm's length lease agreement with T Ltd. requiring annual rental payments of $2,000 in land and $8,000 for the building on the land. S Ltd. had the option at the end of the 5 years of acquiring the land for $5,000 and the building for $5,000. At the time the option is exercised, the fair market value of the land is $30,000 and the building is $20,000. In Year 6, the land and building are sold for $21,000 and $29,000, respectively.

		Land	*Building*
		$	$
Cost of exercising the option	(A)	5,000	5,000
Deemed cost			
Lesser of:			
(a) fair market value		30,000	20,000

¶195

		Land	Building
		$	$
(b) aggregate of all expenditures made on the lease, including cost		15,000	45,000
Lesser value = deemed cost	(B)	15,000	20,000
Depreciation deemed to have been allowed (which is potentially subject to recapture) ((B) – (A))	(C)	10,000	15,000
On sale in Year 6			
Proceeds		21,000	29,000
Deemed cost	(B)	15,000	20,000
Capital gain		6,000	9,000
Recaptured depreciation.	(C)	10,000	15,000*

* If the taxpayer owns more than one building, the recapture of depreciation will not be immediately recognized. Instead, the proceeds up to the amount of deemed cost will reduce the undepreciated capital cost of the remaining buildings of the same class. However, the land will form a separate class for these purposes.

Subsection 13(5.4) supplements the provisions of subsections 13(5.2) and (5.3). It is intended to operate so that the amounts paid for the use of, or right to use a depreciable property, will be taken into account in determining any recapture. The provisions in subsection 13(5.4) are applicable where a taxpayer, or a person with whom the taxpayer was not dealing at arm's length, disposes of a property for which a deduction in respect of an outlay or expense was made or incurred for the use of or right to use the property. The outlay or expense involved is generally rent.

A situation when subsection 13(5.4) might apply is where a taxpayer leases land to a third party who, in turn, constructs a building on the land and leases the building back to the taxpayer. Under this sort of arrangement, the taxpayer may, as a matter of law, acquire ownership of the building once it is constructed since the taxpayer is the owner of the land. This ownership interest is, of course, subject to the leasehold interest of the third party which has constructed the building. This type of arrangement is commonly referred to as a "lease-leaseback" arrangement.

Where rental payments are incurred after the taxpayer acquired the depreciable property, then the deductible payments will, within limits, be added to the capital cost of the property and will be considered to be depreciation (capital cost allowance) allowed to the taxpayer before the disposition. The amount that is added to the capital cost of the depreciable property is the lesser of (i) the total amount of the deductible outlays or expenses incurred prior to the disposition, and (ii) the fair market value of the depreciable property at the earlier of the expiry of the last period in respect of which the deductible outlay or expense was made

¶195

or incurred, or the time of disposition of the property. Therefore, upon subsequent disposition of the property, the amount of the deductible outlays will be included in the income of the taxpayer as recapture. Deductible lease cancellation payments are excluded from the amount that may be recaptured. An exception to the rules in subsection 13(5.4) is provided where the depreciable property is disposed of in a non-arm's length transaction, and the purchaser is subject to the provisions of subsection 13(5.2).

Example: Subsection 13(5.4)

As an example of how the provisions in subsection 13(5.4) might apply, consider the following hypothetical situation.

Facts:

(1) The taxpayer owns land and leases the land to a builder for ten years.

(2) The builder develops the land and leases the building to the taxpayer for 10 years at $1,000 per month with a right to acquire the building at the end of 10 years for $100,000.

(3) Fair market value of the building after 10 years is $250,000.

(4) The building is sold in year 12 for $300,000.

For the purposes of determining recapture, the amount added to the capital cost of the property would be as follows:

Lesser of:

(a) Total lease payments (10×12×$1,000) $120,000

(b) (i) Fair market value of the building at the expiration period to which the lease payments applied; $250,000

   less

   (ii) Capital cost of the building   100,000

                                       Excess $150,000

In this situation, the taxpayer would have a deemed capital cost of the building of $220,000 ($100,000 + $120,000) and, assuming no capital cost allowance was claimed after the end of the lease, an undepreciated capital cost of $100,000. The sale of the building for $300,000 would result in recapture of $120,000 being the full amount of the previously deductible rental payments, plus a capital gain of $80,000. A sale of the building at $200,000 would result in recapture of $100,000 only.

¶195

¶200

Change in Use of Assets

Subsection 13(7) deals with various factual circumstances involving the change in use of depreciable property and provides rules for the computation of capital cost and proceeds of disposition at the time the use changes:

(a) business assets converted to non-business use;

(b) non-business assets converted to business use;

(c) assets used partly for business and partly for non-business purposes;

(d) changes in proportion of use of a capital asset;

(e) non-arm's length transfers of depreciable property; and

(f) deemed dispositions of depreciable property upon a change of control or a change in status from taxable to exempt or vice versa.

Each of these rules is discussed below.

In the case of *Hewlett Packard (Canada) Ltd. v. The Queen* (2003 DTC 1324 (T.C.C.), overturned by 2004 DTC 6498 (F.C.A.)), the Minister argued that by receiving a new fleet of automobiles, there was a change in use for the old fleet of vehicles that was being turned over to Ford Canada. The Tax Court decided that the time period during which the old fleet was being readied to be returned to Ford Canada did not constitute a period during which there was a change in use of the vehicles from a business use. As long as the vehicles were not put to another use, the fact that they were still being held and were redundant because of the arrival of the new fleet, did not result in a change in use. The Federal Court of Appeal overturned the Tax Court's decision on the timing of the disposition of the old fleet, but agreed with the analysis and decision regarding change in use.

¶201 Business Assets Converted to Non-Business Use

Paragraph 13(7)(*a*) provides that where a taxpayer acquired a property to gain or produce income from it or to use it in a business and later begins to use the property for another purpose, the taxpayer is deemed to dispose of the property at the time of the change and to reacquire it immediately thereafter. The proceeds of disposition are deemed to be the fair market value of the property at that time. This means that where the property is a depreciable property, the undepreciated capital cost of the class to which the property belongs will be reduced by the lesser of this fair market value and the cost of the property. Future capital cost allowance will therefore be reduced and recapture may arise. The cost of the reacquired property is also the fair market value at the time of the deemed disposition. Note that there is a companion rule for capital gains purposes in subsection 45(1) that will deem a disposition of the property at the time of the conversion and require recognition of any increase from cost to fair market value at that time.

A common example of the application of paragraph $13(7)(a)$ is the case where an individual acquires a house for rental purposes and some time later begins to live in it. On the change in use, the individual would be deemed to dispose of the house at its fair market value. Assuming that the house is the only property in the class, the individual would usually be subject to recapture or be entitled to a terminal loss.

¶202   Non-Business Assets Converted to Business Use

Paragraph $13(7)(b)$ deals with the converse of the situation described above. Where a taxpayer acquires property for some purpose other than the earning of income, and later converts the property to an income earning use, the taxpayer is deemed to have acquired the property for a specified amount. If the fair market value of the property at the time of the change in use is less than the cost of the property to the taxpayer, as determined without reference to paragraphs $13(7)(a)$ or (b) or subparagraph $13(7)(d)(ii)$, then the specified amount is the fair market value. However, where the cost of the property to the taxpayer is less than its fair market value at the time of the change in use, the specified amount will be limited to the aggregate of the actual cost of the property to the taxpayer and $1/2$ of the excess of the property's fair market value over such cost, to the extent that a capital gains exemption was not claimed in relation to such excess. (For taxation years ending before February 28, 2000, the fraction $1/2$ should be read as $3/4$. For taxation years beginning after February 28, 2000 and ending before October 17, 2000, the fraction is $2/3$. When a taxation period of the taxpayer includes either February 28, 2000 or October 17, 2000, the fraction should be the fraction referred to by the transitional rules to paragraph $38(a)$.)

The specified amount constitutes the capital cost of the property for capital cost allowance purposes. Note that there is a companion rule for capital gains purposes in subsection 45(1) that will deem a disposition of the property at the time of the conversion and require recognition of any increase from cost to fair market value at that time. Note that applicable after 1992, subsection 70(13) provides that for certain purposes regarding deemed proceeds of disposition, the capital cost of depreciable property to a taxpayer at the time of the taxpayer's death is to be determined without the change in use adjustment.

The limitations imposed on the "step-up" in cost limit capital cost for CCA purposes to cost plus any capital gain recognized by the taxpayer on the change in use. The taxpayer cannot take advantage of the spread between the capital gain (only one-half of which is included in income) and CCA based on full fair market value. The reduction in cost for any capital gains deduction claimed is to prevent the taxpayer from claiming capital cost allowance on any capital gain which has not been subject to tax by virtue of the capital gains exemption.

Where a conversion is made of an asset wholly devoted to a non-income purpose to an income-earning purpose, the taxpayer can elect under subsection 45(2) not to have the change-of-use rules apply. This would prevent capital cost allowance being claimed, but permit deferral of capital gain recognition.

Example: Change in Use — Personal to Business

M purchased a yacht in 2001 for personal use at a cost of $25,000. In 2003, M changed the use and carried on a business of renting the yacht. The fair market value at the time the property became an income-producing asset was $30,000. Assume that M does not elect out of the change-of-use rules.

Deemed proceeds of disposition	$30,000
Less: Adjusted cost base	25,000
Capital gain	$ 5,000
Taxable capital gain	$ 2,500

For capital cost allowance purposes, the income earning asset is deemed to be acquired at a specified amount calculated as the lesser of:

(i) FMV at time of change in use $30,000

(ii) the total of

    (A) the actual cost of yacht $25,000

    (B) the FMV at time of change $30,000

        Less: actual cost . . $25,000

        Plus: two times capital gains exemption* in respect of change in use

        (2 × Nil) . . .   Nil   25,000

                    $ 5,000

    $\frac{1}{2}$ of excess ($5,000 × $\frac{1}{2}$)   2,500

                               $27,500

For capital cost allowance purposes, the capital cost of the yacht in 2003 is $27,500.

*The capital gains exemption for general property was eliminated in 1994 with special phase-out rules.

¶202

¶203   Assets Used Partly for Business and Partly for Non-Business Purposes

Paragraph $13(7)(c)$ provides for the allocation of the cost of a property where the property is used in part for income-earning purposes and in part for some other purpose.

For example, an independent sales agent might acquire an automobile which is used 75% for business and 25% for transportation of a personal nature. In these circumstances, paragraph $13(7)(c)$ provides that the taxpayer is deemed to have acquired for business purposes that proportion of the property that the business-use is of the total use, and the taxpayer's cost is deemed to be the same proportion of total cost. When the taxpayer disposes of the property, the proceeds of disposition are allocated in this same proportion. Thus, if the sales agent's automobile cost $16,000, the capital cost for capital cost allowance purposes would be $12,000. If, after claiming $10,000 of capital cost allowance, the taxpayer sold the automobile for $8,000, $6,000 (75%) of the proceeds would reduce the undepreciated capital cost of the class. Assuming that there is no other property in the class, recapture of $4,000 would arise.

Whether property is being used for a purpose other than earning income is a question of fact to be determined by the court. (See *Goderich Manufacturing Co. Ltd. v. M.N.R.*, 53 DTC 152 (T.A.B.).)

Changes in the Proportion of Use of a Capital Asset

Paragraph $13(7)(d)$ contains rules that are applicable if the proportion of the use which is made of any particular property for the purpose of earning income is increased or decreased by a taxpayer.

Subparagraph $13(7)(d)(i)$ contains the rule that is applicable where there is an increase in the use of the property for the purpose of earning income. This paragraph provides that in the case of such an increase, the taxpayer will be deemed to have acquired depreciable property at the time of the increase.

The capital cost of the depreciable property so deemed to be acquired will be the same proportion of a specified amount that the increase in the use of earning income is of the entire use for all purposes.

The specified amount will be the fair market value of the property at the time of the change in the proportion of use of the capital asset, if that value is less than the cost of the property to a taxpayer. If, however, the fair market value of the property at the time of the change in the proportion of use exceeds the cost of the property to the taxpayer, then the specified amount is the aggregate of:

(a) the actual cost of the property to the taxpayer; and

(b) after February 27, 2000, $\frac{1}{2}$ of the excess of the property's fair market value over such cost, to the extent that a capital gains exemption was not claimed in relation to such excess. (Note that the capital gains exemption for general property was eliminated in 1994, with special phase-out rules.)

(For taxation periods of a taxpayer ending before February 28, 2000, the fraction $\frac{1}{2}$ should be read as $\frac{3}{4}$. For taxation periods beginning after February 28, 2000 and ending before October 17, 2000, the fraction should be read as $\frac{2}{3}$. When a taxation period of the taxpayer includes either February 28, 2000 or October 17, 2000, the fraction should be the fraction referred to by the transitional rules to paragraph 38(a).)

This rule may be expressed in the following formula:

$$
\begin{array}{c}
\text{Capital} \\
\text{cost of} \\
\text{depre-} \\
\text{ciable} \\
\text{prop-} \\
\text{erty} \\
\text{to be} \\
\text{acquired}
\end{array}
=
\left\{
\begin{array}{c}
\text{Present} \\
\text{proportion} \\
\text{of property} \\
\text{used to} \\
\text{earn income}
\end{array}
\quad \text{Minus} \quad
\begin{array}{c}
\text{Former} \\
\text{proportion} \\
\text{of property} \\
\text{used to} \\
\text{earn income}
\end{array}
\right\}
\times
\begin{array}{c}
\text{Specified} \\
\text{amount}
\end{array}
$$

This capital cost will be added to the undepreciated capital cost of property of the class and will accordingly increase the amount on which the taxpayer may claim capital cost allowance. Subsection 45(1) provides rules for capital gains consequences where there is a change in proportional use. As the allocation changes, there are deemed dispositions or acquisitions of non-business property, and corresponding deemed acquisitions or dispositions of depreciable property.

Example 1: Personal and Business Use Combined

Assume that a doctor acquired a brick house for the sum of $150,000 in 2001 and used 20% of it for an office and the balance as a residence. Assume also that this is the doctor's only asset in that class.

Under paragraph 13(7)(c), the doctor's capital cost of depreciable property of the class will be $30,000

For the taxation years 2001 to 2003 the doctor claims capital cost allowances of . . . . $ 2,800

Undepreciated capital cost at the end of the 2003 taxation year. $27,200

Assume that during the 2004 taxation year, the office space is increased from 20% to 35% of the house (an increase of 15% of the entire house) and the fair market value of the house at that time is $170,000.

Capital cost of depreciable property deemed to have been acquired will be

$\frac{15}{100} \times (\$150,000 + \frac{1}{2} \times (\$170,000 - \$150,000))$ 24,000

Undepreciated capital cost upon which capital cost allowances may be calculated. $51,200

¶203

Note that the half-year rule would appear to apply to the CCA claim on the addition arising from this change in use. Therefore, in 2004, the CCA claim would be calculated as 4% × ($27,200 + ($\frac{1}{2}$ × $24,000)).

For capital gain/loss purposes, there is a disposition in 2004 with proceeds equal to $170,000 × 15% = $25,500. From this is subtracted the cost base times the change in use, $150,000 × 15% = $22,500, giving rise to a capital gain on the personal use portion of the house of $3,000.

In the above example, the increase in use is in the physical proportion of the property which is used for earning income. Other standards of measurement, however, will apply in other circumstances, as for example, mileage travelled, or the time during the year in which the asset is used to earn income.

Subparagraph 13(7)(d)(ii) contains the rule that is applicable where there is a decrease in the use of property for the purpose of earning income. Under this provision, the taxpayer will be deemed to have disposed of depreciable property at the time of the decrease. The proceeds of this disposition are deemed to be an amount equal to the same proportion of the fair market value of the property at the time of the decrease, which the decrease in the use for earning income is of the entire use for all purposes. This rule may be expressed in the following formula:

$$\text{Deemed proceeds of disposition} = \left\{ \begin{array}{l} \text{Former proportion of property used to earn income} \end{array} \text{ Minus } \begin{array}{l} \text{Present proportion of property used to earn income} \end{array} \right\} \times \begin{array}{l} \text{Fair market value of entire property} \end{array}$$

The undepreciated capital cost to the taxpayer of property of that class (as defined in subsection 13(21)) will be reduced by the lesser of:

(a) the proceeds of disposition as determined under subparagraph 13(7)(d)(ii); and

(b) the capital cost of the property to the taxpayer. This will accordingly decrease the amount that the taxpayer may claim as capital cost allowance. If the proceeds of disposition exceed the undepreciated capital cost of property of the class so that the balance of the class is negative at the year-end, recapture will arise under subsection 13(1).

Example 2:　Personal and Business Use Combined

Assume that a doctor acquired a brick house for the sum of $150,000 in 2001 and used 20% of it for an office and the balance as a residence. Assume also that this is the doctor's only asset in that class.

¶203

Under paragraph $13(7)(c)$, the doctor's capital cost of depreciable property of the class will be $30,000

For the taxation years 2001 to 2003, the doctor claims capital cost allowances of . . . . $ 2,800

Undepreciated capital cost at the end of the 2003 taxation year $27,200

Assume that during the 2004 taxation year, the office space is decreased from 20% to 15% (a decrease of 5% of the entire house) and the fair market value of the house at that time is $170,000).

Deduct from "undepreciated capital cost" the lesser of

(a) proceeds of disposition of property deemed to be disposed of $5/100 \times $170,000 . . . . $ 8,500

(b) capital cost of property disposed of $5/100 \times$ $150,000 . . . . 7,500 (7,500)

Undepreciated capital cost upon which capital cost allowance may be calculated $19,700

There would be a capital gain on the deemed disposition of the business-use of the house of $1,000 ($8,500 − $7,500).

¶205

Non-Arm's Length Transfers of Depreciable Property

If depreciable property is acquired from a person with whom the taxpayer is not dealing at arm's length, there are special rules to determine the capital cost of the property to the taxpayer. These rules do not apply to a transfer arising as a consequence of the death of the transferor. Paragraph $13(7)(e)$ contains different sets of rules that apply in each of three particular circumstances to adjust the capital costs of the property, as discussed below.

¶206   Resident Transferor

Subparagraph $13(7)(e)(i)$ applies if two conditions are met:

(a) the transferor is an individual resident in Canada or a partnership of which any member was either an individual resident in Canada or another partnership; and

(b) the otherwise determined cost of the property to the transferee exceeds the cost (or capital cost for depreciable property) of the property to the transferor.

In such case, the transferee's capital cost of the property is deemed to be equal to the aggregate of the cost (or capital cost) of the property to

¶206

the transferor and $\frac{1}{2}$ of the amount by which the transferor's proceeds of disposition exceeds the capital cost of the property to the extent that a capital gains exemption related to the gain was not claimed under section 110.6. For taxation periods beginning after February 28, 2000 and ending before October 17, 2000, the fraction should be read as $\frac{2}{3}$. When a taxation period of the taxpayer includes either February 28, 2000 or October 17, 2000, the fraction should be the fraction referred to by the transitional rules to paragraph 38(a). The deemed capital cost is relevant for purposes of capital cost allowance and recapture calculations.

Note that the capital gains exemption for general property was eliminated in 1994 with special phase-out rules. Under subsection 110.6(19), an individual could make an election which resulted in a deemed disposition of his or her capital property as of February 22, 1994. The election was the last chance for individuals to claim the ordinary $100,000 capital gains exemption. Paragraph 13(7)(e.1) ensures that an individual's capital cost in the property in such a case is limited to its pre-disposition capital cost. Where the property subject to the election was real property, the portion of the gain not eligible for the capital gains exemption was not taxed immediately, and does not form part of the cost basis of the property immediately after the deemed disposition. As such, that amount is also excluded from the property's capital cost immediately after the deemed disposition.

¶207　Non-Resident Transferor

Subparagraph 13(7)(e)(ii) is identical to subparagraph 13(7)(e)(i), except that:

(a) it applies if the transferor is a person or partnership other than the type referred to in subparagraph 13(7)(e)(i); and

(b) the deemed capital cost of the property is not affected by the capital gains exemption since the exemption will not be available to the transferor.

¶208　Future Recapture

Subparagraph 13(7)(e)(iii) applies if the transferor's cost (or capital cost) exceeds the transferee's capital cost, as otherwise determined, which would occur, for example, when the fair market is less than the transferor's cost. In such cases, the transferee is deemed to acquire the property at the transferor's cost (or capital cost) and to have claimed the difference as capital cost allowance. As a result, the transferee inherits the transferor's position with respect to the potential recapture on a subsequent disposition.

It should be noted that subsection 13(7.3) provides that two corporations shall be deemed not to be related to each other simply because they are controlled by the same trustee, liquidator of a succession, or executor, and it is established that:

(a) the trustee, liquidator or executor acquired control of the companies as a result of the death of an individual; and

(b) control of the two companies was not acquired as a result of one or more trusts or estates created by the same individual or two or more individuals not dealing with each other at arm's length.

¶209 Prescribed Class of Property Acquired By Transfer

Regulation 1102(14) applies where a taxpayer acquires depreciable property of a prescribed class or separate prescribed class from a non-arm's length person or in connection with a divisive corporate reorganization (a so-called "butterfly transaction") that meets the requirements of paragraph 55(3)(*b*) of the Act. In such circumstances, the property is required to be included in the same prescribed class or separate class by the purchaser as it was by the vendor.

Regulation 1102(14) was amended applicable generally with respect to property acquired after June 17, 1987. For property acquired prior to June 18, 1987, Regulation 1102(14) also applied with respect to property acquired pursuant to certain specified rollover provisions of the Act.

Regulation 1102(20) acts as an anti-avoidance measure where taxpayers who would otherwise be dealing at arm's length undertake a transaction, or series of transactions, so as to be considered not to be dealing at arm's length and therefore come within the ambit of Regulation 1102(14). Regulation 1102(20) will deem the taxpayers to be dealing at arm's length with respect to the acquisition of the particular property. Regulation 1102(20) is also applicable for the purposes of Regulations 1100(2.2), 1100(19), and 1101(1ad).

Regulation 1102(14.1) provides that where, after May 25, 1976, a taxpayer acquires property from a non-arm's length person who owned the property before May 26, 1976, the property will continue to be included in the same class as it was to the vendor.

¶210

Deemed Dispositions of Depreciable Property Upon a Change of Control or Change in Tax Status

Where a corporation has a year-end resulting from an acquisition of control by a person or group of persons, paragraph 111(4)(*e*) permits the corporation to elect a deemed disposition of any capital property immediately before the year-end and a deemed reacquisition of such property immediately thereafter. The elected proceeds can be anywhere between the adjusted cost base and the fair market value of the property. Any property so elected to have been disposed of is deemed by paragraph $111(4)(e)$ to have been reacquired at a capital cost equal to the amount elected. However, for capital cost allowance and recapture purposes, paragraph $13(7)(f)$ provides that the capital cost of property that is depreciable property (other than a timber resource property) will be limited to the aggregate of the capital cost to the corporation at the time of disposition, and one-half of the amount, if any, by which the corporation's proceeds of disposition exceed the capital cost of the property at the time of disposition. For taxation periods of a taxpayer ending before February 28, 2000, the fraction $\frac{1}{2}$ should be read as $\frac{3}{4}$. For taxation periods beginning after February 28, 2000 and ending before October 17, 2000, the fraction should be read as $\frac{2}{3}$. When a taxation period of the taxpayer includes either February 28, 2000 or October 17, 2000, the fraction should be the fraction referred to by the transitional rules to paragraph $38(a)$.

Paragraph $149(10)(b)$ deems a corporation to have disposed of each type of property for fair market value upon becoming or ceasing to be exempt from tax under Part I, and to have reacquired such property immediately thereafter at a cost equal to its fair market value. Prior to April 27, 1995, if the capital cost of a depreciable property at the time of the deemed disposition exceeded the property's then fair market value, any difference was deemed to have been capital cost allowance previously claimed. However, if the fair market value of the property at the time of the deemed disposition exceeded its capital cost at that time, paragraph $13(7)(f)$ provided that, for capital cost allowance and recapture purposes, the capital cost of the depreciable property (other than a timber resource property) following the deemed reacquisition would be the aggregate of the capital cost to the corporation at the time of the deemed disposition and the amount that was three-quarters of the difference between the fair market value and the capital cost of the property.

¶215

Terminal Loss

In addition to capital cost allowance determined under paragraph $20(1)(a)$, which is a permissive deduction, subsection 20(16) provides that a taxpayer *must* deduct the unclaimed balance in a particular capital cost class where the taxpayer owns no assets of that class at the end of the taxation year. The amount to be deducted is the "undepreciated capital cost" of that class, as defined in subsection 13(21) (see ¶160). This deduction is commonly referred to as a "terminal loss". After the terminal loss is claimed, the undepreciated capital cost balance of that class is brought to nil.

The amount deducted as a terminal loss is included in the definition of "total depreciation" in subsection 13(21). As a result, it is also included in the variable "E" deduction in the formula used to calculate "undepreciated capital cost allowance" in subsection 13(21).

Under subsection 20(16), the terminal loss deduction is mandatory in the year in which the last asset of a class is disposed of, unless the taxpayer acquires additional assets of that class before the end of the year. In certain cases, a particular asset will fall into a separate class and consequently it will not be possible to postpone recognition of a terminal loss by acquiring a similar asset. This result occurs, for example, with real estate rental property costing $50,000 or more. See ¶245 for commentary on assets that are placed in a separate class.

Each passenger vehicle costing over the prescribed limit ($30,000 for 2001 to 2005; see the table at ¶252) is placed in a separate class, however subsection 20(16.1) prevents a taxpayer from deducting a terminal loss in respect of such a passenger vehicle. Similarly, as stated in ¶180, there is no recapture in respect of such vehicles. See ¶250 for commentary on capital cost allowance restrictions for passenger vehicles costing over the prescribed limit, as well as the special half-year allowance permitted for such vehicles in the year of disposition.

See also Interpretation Bulletin IT-478R2, "Capital Cost Allowance — Recapture and Terminal Loss", at ¶3265.

Stop-Loss Rule

Certain restrictions exist on the ability to claim terminal losses in non-arm's length transactions pursuant to subsections 13(21.1) (see ¶225) and 13(21.2). For dispositions occurring after November 30, 1999 (subject to certain grandfathering rules for dispositions made prior to July 1, 2000), subsection 13(21.2) denies the deduction of a terminal loss on the disposition of a depreciable property of a prescribed class by any person or partnership (transferor) where either the transferor or a person affiliated with the transferor owns the property or a right to acquire the property 30 days after the disposition. For dispositions occurring after April 26, 1995 (subject to certain grandfathering rules for dispositions made before 1996), subsection 13(21.2) applied to dispositions by a corporation, trust or partnership, but not to those of an individual. Prior to April 27, 1996, subsection 85(5.1) applied to deny a terminal loss in certain circumstances. Note that where a property was disposed of after April 26, 1995 and before June 20, 1996, the transferor may elect to treat the notional depreciable property created on the transfer to be in a *separate* class that is identical to the class of the property that was disposed of. The election must be made in writing before the end of September 1998. Where subsection 13(21.2) does not apply because of these transitional rules, the stop-loss rule found in former subsection 85(5.1) may apply.

The stop-loss rule in subsection 13(21.2) applies when:

(a) a corporation, trust, partnership or individual (transferor) disposes of a depreciable property of a particular prescribed class;

¶215

(b) the amount that would otherwise be the proceeds of disposition of the property is less than the lesser of: (i) the capital cost of the property, and (ii) the proportion of the undepreciated capital cost of the class of the property that the value of the property is of the value of all properties in the class immediately before the disposition; and

(c) on the 30th day after the disposition, either the transferor or a person affiliated with the transferor owns the property or a right to acquire the property (other than a right, as security only, under a mortgage, an agreement for sale, or similar obligation).

Any denied terminal loss under subsection 13(21.2) is in effect "frozen", and is subsequently allowed to the transferor upon the earliest of certain triggering events described below.

"Affiliated persons" is defined in section 251.1. Affiliated persons include, for example, a corporation and the person controlling the corporation (controller), the corporation and the controller's spouse, the corporation and another corporation controlled by the controller, and the corporation and another corporation controlled by someone affiliated with the controller.

The stop-loss rule does not apply to certain dispositions, namely those set out in paragraphs (c) to (g) of the definition of "superficial loss" found in section 54. The dispositions of property specifically excluded from the application of subsection 13(21.2) are:

(a) a deemed disposition of a loan or deposit ceasing to be an eligible loan of an international banking centre business (paragraph 33.1(11)(a);

(b) a deemed disposition that occurs when a taxpayer acquires a property for some purpose and later uses it for the purpose of gaining or producing income, or vice versa (subsection 45(1));

(c) a deemed disposition of a bad debt or a share, under the provisions of section 50;

(d) a deemed disposition upon the death of a taxpayer (section 70);

(e) a deemed disposition by a trust under subsection 104(4);

(f) a deemed disposition when a taxpayer becomes, or ceases to be, resident in Canada;

(g) a disposition under the mutual fund reorganization rules of paragraph 132.2(1)(f);

(h) a deemed disposition where a life insurer changes the use of the property (subsection 138(11.3));

¶215

(i) certain dispositions under the mark-to-market rules applicable to securities held by financial institutions, under subsection 142.5(2) and paragraph 142.6(1)(*b*);

(j) a deemed disposition of assets by an employee profit sharing plan under subsections 144(4.1) or (4.2);

(k) a deemed disposition where a corporation ceases to be exempt from Part I tax (subsection 149(10));

(l) the expiration of an option;

(m) a disposition of a debt obligation where the resulting loss was denied under paragraph 40(2)(*e*.1);

(n) a disposition of a property by a corporation whose control is acquired within 30 days after the disposition; and

(o) a disposition of a property by a person that becomes or ceases to be exempt from tax under Part I within 30 days after the disposition.

Subsection 13(21.2) does not appear to have application when a depreciable property becomes the property of a corporation upon an amalgamation of the corporation with another corporation, namely because the amalgamation does not give rise to a disposition of property by a predecessor corporation. Subsection 13(21.2) does not apply to a winding-up of a subsidiary into a parent corporation that is subject to the rollover provisions of subsection 88(1) (see paragraph 88(1)(*d*.1)).

The Effect of the Application of the Stop-Loss Rule

In general terms, subsection 13(21.2) provides the following results where it applies (in those circumstances described in the commentary above). First of all, sections 85 and 97 (rollover provisions for transfers of property to corporations and partnerships, respectively) do not apply to the disposition of the property.

For the purposes of subsection 13(21.2), section 20, and the capital cost allowance provisions as they apply to the transferor for taxation years ending after the disposition of the property (the transferred property), the disposition is deemed to take place at the lesser of: (a) the capital cost of the transferred property, and (b) the proportion of the UCC of the class of the property that the value of the property is of the value of all properties in the class immediately before the disposition (the latter amount referred to as the property's "tax cost"). In other words, instead of allowing the disposition to take place at the lower proceeds otherwise determined, and which might lead to a terminal loss (for example, where the transferred property is the only one in the class and the fair market value is less than both the capital cost and the tax cost of the property to the transferor), the proceeds of disposition are adjusted upwards so that a loss is not allowed. The proceeds of disposition are adjusted upwards by the amount by which the lesser of the property's capital cost and its tax

¶215

cost exceeds the proceeds otherwise determined. The excess is added back as a capital cost of a notional depreciable property of the same class and is deemed to have been acquired by the transferor before the taxation year that includes the disposition (therefore the half-year rule does not apply to the notional property). The transferor can continue to claim CCA in respect of the notional depreciable property. The notional depreciable property is deemed to have become available for use to the transferor at the time at which the transferred property becomes available for use to the subsequent owner (subparagraph 13(21.2)(e)(iv)).

The notional depreciable property is deemed to be owned by the transferor until immediately before the earliest of the following triggering events:

(a) a subsequent disposition of the transferred property so that neither the transferor nor an affiliated person of the transferor owns the property, provided that neither owns the property or a right to acquire the property throughout the 30-day period after that subsequent disposition;

(b) a change in use of the transferred property, where it is not used by the transferor or an affiliated person for the purpose of earning income, and is used for another purpose;

(c) upon the transferor becoming a non-resident, or if the transferor is a corporation, upon the corporation becoming or ceasing to be exempt from Part I tax;

(d) where the transferor is a corporation, immediately before the acquisition of control of the transferor by a person or group of persons; or

(e) a winding-up of the transferor, except where it is wound up into a parent corporation pursuant to subsection 88(1).

These "triggering events" are set out in subparagraph 13(21.2)(e)(iii). As noted, upon the occurrence of the earliest of these events, the transferor is no longer deemed to own the notional depreciable property. Therefore, if the transferor does not own any other depreciable property in the same class, it can claim a terminal loss, which will normally equal the previously denied terminal loss minus any CCA claimed in the interim in respect of the notional depreciable property. Under paragraph 13(21.2)(g), the subsequent owner of the transferred property (the affiliated person owning the property on the 30th day following the disposition of the property by the transferor) inherits the transferor's capital cost of the property, and is deemed to have claimed CCA on the amount of such capital cost in excess of its fair market value at the time of the disposition.

¶215

Example:

Corporation A owns one depreciable property of a particular prescribed class. In January 2000, immediately before it transfers the property to Corporation B at its fair market value of $500, the capital cost of the property to Corporation A is $1,000 and the UCC of the class is $800. Corporation B continues to own the property on the 30th day after the transfer, and for the rest of 2000. Corporation B is affiliated with Corporation A. Corporation A continues to carry on its business. Corporation B uses the depreciable property in its business.

Both Corporations A and B have taxation years ending with the calendar year.

In January 2001, Corporation B disposes of the property to a person not affiliated with Corporation A, and who owns the property throughout 2001.

The results to Corporations A and B under subsection 13(21.2) are as follows.

In its 2000 taxation year, Corporation A is deemed to have disposed of the depreciable property at the lower of its capital cost and the UCC. Therefore, it is deemed to have disposed of the property for $800, and not $500 which is the proceeds otherwise determined. Corporation A is denied the terminal loss of $300 that otherwise would have applied in 2000 ($800 − $500).

Corporation A is deemed to have acquired a notional depreciable property of the same class immediately before 2000 at a capital cost equal to the denied loss of $300, so that Corporation A can continue to claim CCA on that amount in 2000. In its 2001 taxation year, when the triggering event occurs (the disposition of the property to the non-affiliated person), Corporation A is allowed a terminal loss equal to the amount of the previously denied loss ($300) minus the amount of CCA, if any, claimed in respect of the notional property in 2000 (and assuming it has no other properties in the class at the end of 2001).

The capital cost of the property to Corporation B is deemed to be $1,000 (Corporation A's capital cost of the property). The amount by which $1,000 exceeds the property's fair market value at the time of disposition ($500) is deemed to have been deducted by Corporation B in previous taxation years. Therefore, the net amount of $500 is added to the UCC of the class of property to Corporation B.

If the transferor of the transferred property is a partnership that otherwise ceases to exist before one of the triggering events occurs, paragraph 13(21.2)(*f*) deems the partnership to continue to exist, and the members of the partnership to continue to be members, until immediately after the triggering event occurs. Therefore, any terminal loss previously denied on the transfer of the property is allowed at the time of the triggering event and is in turn flowed out to the former partners in the regular manner accorded to partnership income and loss. Note, however, that the provision does not deem the former partnership to continue to carry on a business. Therefore, it does not appear that CCA can be claimed by the partnership and flowed out as deductions/losses to the former partners in the interim taxation years (if any) between the disposition of the property by the partnership and the triggering event.

¶215

¶220   Assets Destroyed, Stolen, Lost, or Obsolete

A disposal is considered to occur where depreciable property has been abandoned, scrapped, stolen, or destroyed, even though no proceeds may be received. Where no actual or deemed proceeds are received, but the CRA is satisfied that there has been a disposition, a value of nil is to be used for the proceeds. See Interpretation Bulletin IT-460, "Disposition — Absence of Consideration", at ¶3237. Accordingly, a terminal loss would be claimed if all of the assets in the class were destroyed or lost.

Where one or more, but not all of the depreciable assets of a particular class are destroyed during the year (e.g., by fire), are lost, or otherwise taken out of production, the terminal loss provision of subsection 20(16) would not operate since not all of the assets of the class will have been disposed of. If not all of the assets of the class are affected, the taxpayer should be entitled to continue taking capital cost allowance on the undepreciated capital cost of the assets of the class, including the cost of the lost, destroyed or obsolete items. See ¶165 for comments on the loss or destruction of property where insurance proceeds are received.

¶225   Disposition of a Building

Subsection 13(21.1) will apply to reduce the terminal loss that would otherwise be realized under subsection 20(16) on a sale of a building where the proceeds of disposition of the building (otherwise determined) are less than the lesser of the undepreciated capital cost and the capital cost of the building. In these circumstances, subsection 13(21.1) will operate to decrease the undepreciated capital cost of the class by more than the actual proceeds of disposition allocable to the building. Subsection 13(21.1) will only apply if the taxpayer disposes of a building which is depreciable property and the land subjacent or contiguous to the building was owned by the taxpayer or a person with whom the taxpayer did not deal at arm's length. Subsection 13(21.1) applies whether or not the subjacent or contiguous land is disposed of. It should be noted that subsection 13(21.1) will apply if *at any time* preceding the disposition of the building, the taxpayer, or a person with whom the taxpayer was not dealing at arm's length, owned subjacent or contiguous land.

Without this provision, it could be advantageous for a vendor to tear down an existing building and sell the land as vacant in cases where the purchaser was not interested in the existing building but rather wished to redevelop the land. By doing this, the vendor could avoid the recapture of capital cost allowance in respect of the building, trigger a terminal loss on the building, and take the overall profit on the transaction as a capital gain on the land. The taxable capital gain would be offset in whole or in part by the terminal loss. Subsection 13(21.1) eliminates this form of tax avoidance and treats the vendor as if the building had been sold for its fair market value.

Subsection 13(21.1) applies, in general terms, to take the amount by which the undepreciated capital cost of the building exceeds the proceeds of disposition of the building otherwise determined and applies this amount first to reduce the capital gain that would otherwise be realized on the land. If the land is not disposed of in the same year as the building, in effect one-half of the excess of the undepreciated capital cost of the building over its proceeds of disposition is recognized as a terminal loss or, if there are other assets in the class, the undepreciated capital cost of the class is reduced by the actual proceeds plus one-half of that excess. Subsection 13(21.1) applies to both the situation where the building and the land are sold in the same year and where the building is sold alone.

It should be noted that the rules in subsection 13(21.1) operate before the stop-loss rule in subsection 13(21.2) described at ¶215 is applied. Also, subsections 13(21.1) and (21.2) are ignored for purposes of the adjustments to proceeds of disposition of the building set out in paragraphs 13(21.1)(a) and (b), described below.

Sale of Land and Building in the Same Year

Paragraph 13(21.1)(a) allocates the aggregate proceeds of disposition between land and building when both the building and the land subjacent to it and/or the land immediately contiguous to and necessary for the use of the building are sold in the same year. As noted above, it is not necessary that the taxpayer who disposes of the building also be the one who disposes of the land; it is sufficient to attract the application of subsection 13(21.1) if the land is disposed of in that year by a person who does not deal at arm's length with the taxpayer who disposed of the building. The year referred to is the taxation year of the person who disposes of the building. If the land is not disposed of in the same year as the building and that land is owned by the same person who disposed of the building or by a non-arm's length party, paragraph 13(21.1)(b) will apply (see below).

Where the parcel of land that is sold is larger than is necessary for the use of the building, it would appear necessary to treat the parcel as two parcels of land with subsection 13(21.1) applying to determine the proceeds of disposition only of the portion of the land which is necessary to the use of the building. For these purposes, it will be necessary to allocate the total fair market value of the land and the total adjusted cost base of the land between the portion of the land that is necessary for the use of the building and the portion which is not so necessary.

Paragraph 13(21.1)(a) outlines the method whereby the deemed proceeds of disposition of the building are determined. The proceeds of disposition of the building are deemed to be the lesser of:

(a) the amount calculated under subparagraph 13(21.1)(a)(i); and

(b) the amount calculated under subparagraph 13(21.1)(a)(ii).

¶225

The remainder of the actual proceeds of disposition of the building and land are deemed to be the proceeds of disposition of the land.

In the most common circumstances, subparagraph $13(21.1)(a)(ii)$ will operate to deem the proceeds of disposition of the building to equal the cost amount of the building. However, if the fair market value of the building immediately before the disposition is greater than the lesser of that cost amount and the capital cost of the building, the proceeds of disposition of the building will be deemed to equal that fair market value. This could happen when a building having significant value is torn down before selling the land. "Cost amount of a building" is defined in subsection $248(1)$ to mean the undepreciated capital cost of the class to which the building belongs if there is only one building in the class. Where there is more than one building in the class, the cost amount of a particular building is that portion of the undepreciated capital cost of that class that the original cost of that particular building is of the aggregate of the original costs of all buildings in that class.

In some cases, the lesser amount will be that calculated under subparagraph $13(21.1)(a)(i)$. This would occur where the aggregate of the fair market value of the building and the land exceeds the lesser of the fair market value and the cost of the land. Where there has been a disposition of the subject land within the three-year period preceding the disposition of the building by the taxpayer or a person with whom the taxpayer was not dealing at arm's length, to the taxpayer or to another person with whom the taxpayer was not dealing at arm's length, the cost amount of the land for purposes of clause $13(21.1)(a)(i)(B)$ is reduced by any capital gains in that period. Capital gains for this purpose are determined without reference to reserve adjustments pursuant to subparagraphs $40(1)(a)(ii)$ and (iii).

Subparagraph $13(21.1)(a)(i)$ will operate to fix the proceeds of disposition of the building where the excess of the undepreciated capital cost of the building over its fair market value is greater than the capital gain that would otherwise be realized on the land if the proceeds of disposition were determined without reference to subsection $13(21.1)$. Under these circumstances a terminal loss may still arise, although it would be reduced from the amount that would otherwise have been computed without reference to subsection $13(21.1)$.

Sale of Building Only

Paragraph $13(21.1)(b)$ applies where a building is disposed of but the related land is not disposed of in the same year. As noted above, the land subjacent to the building or contiguous to the building and necessary to its use must have been owned previously by the taxpayer who disposed of the building or a non-arm's length party. In these circumstances, the proceeds of disposition of the building are deemed to be the proceeds of disposition of the building otherwise determined, plus one-half of the difference between those proceeds of disposition and the greater of:

(a) the cost amount (undepreciated capital cost) of the building; and

¶225

(b) the fair market value of the building immediately before the disposition.

The calculation of deemed proceeds parallels the changes in the capital gains inclusion rate as implemented in section 38. For example, for taxation years ending after February 27, 2000, one-half the difference is added to the proceeds as otherwise determined; for taxation years that include February 28, 2000 or October 17, 2000, or began after February 28, 2000 and ended before October 17, 2000, the one-half rate is to be read as "the fraction determined when the fraction in 38(a) that applies to the taxpayer for the year is subtracted from 1". This change tracks the reduction in capital gains rates in 2000 from three-quarters to two-thirds to one-half. In most cases, the proceeds of disposition of the building otherwise determined will be the fair market value of the building when the building is sold. However, where a building is torn down, the proceeds of disposition of the building may be nil while the building may have had a significant fair market value before it was torn down.

The effect of paragraph 13(21.1)(b) is to allow as a terminal loss only one-half of the difference between the fair market value of the building and its undepreciated capital cost. If there are additional assets in the class, the undepreciated capital cost of the class is reduced by not only the actual proceeds of disposition, but also by an additional amount of one-half that difference. Effectively, the loss on the disposition of the building is treated as a capital loss and therefore the fluctuating capital gains inclusion rates must be considered to achieve the correct income inclusion or adjustment to the undepreciated capital cost of the class.

Examples of Allocation of Proceeds Between Land and Building

For the following examples, it is assumed that the building is the only asset in the class and that subsection 13(21.1) operates to reduce what would otherwise be a terminal loss. If there were other buildings in the class, the amount referred to as a terminal loss which is disallowed or denied would instead be a greater than usual reduction in the undepreciated capital cost of the class, which would have the effect of reducing the amount of capital cost allowance that would otherwise be available in the future. It is also assumed that the land related to the building is owned by the same person who owned the building and that no previous non-arm's length dispositions of the land were made. Furthermore, the capital cost of the building is assumed to be greater than its cost amount. Dispositions are considered to occur at a time when the one-half inclusion rate applies.

Example: **Sale of Land and Building**

Building		*Land*	
UCC	$30,000	ACB........	$100,000
FMV	$20,000	FMV	$150,000

¶225

The total proceeds of the land and building are $170,000. But for subsection 13(21.1), a terminal loss of $10,000 would be realized on the building. A capital gain of $50,000 would be realized on the land with one-half of that amount ($25,000) being included in income. There would be a net income inclusion of $15,000 after deducting the terminal loss. The deemed proceeds of disposition of the building will be the lesser of:

(a) aggregate fair market values $170,000

    minus the lesser of:

        ACB land $100,000

        FMV land 150,000   100,000

                                         $ 70,000

  and

(b) greater of:

        FMV building........................ $ 20,000

        UCC building........................ 30,000 $ 30,000

The deemed proceeds of disposition of the building are $30,000 such that no terminal loss arises. The proceeds of disposition of the land are deemed to be $140,000 ($170,000 – $30,000). A capital gain of $40,000 is realized and one-half of this amount ($20,000) is included in income. The terminal loss is denied and is instead applied to reduce the capital gain on the land. The same result would occur if the vendor tears down the building and sells the vacant land in the same year.

Example: Sale of Building Only

Building

    UCC $70,000

    FMV $20,000

If the taxpayer sold the building alone for $20,000 (combined possibly with a lease of the land), a terminal loss of $50,000 would otherwise result. However, paragraph 13(21.1)(*b*) deems the proceeds of disposition to be the aggregate of:

(a) proceeds otherwise determined........................ $20,000

and:

(b) ½ of the greater of:

       (i) UCC building...................... $70,000

       (ii) FMV building 20,000

    minus: amount in (a): ½ ($70,000 − $20,000) 25,000

                                        $45,000

The proceeds of disposition of the building are deemed to be $45,000, and a terminal loss of $25,000 is realized.

¶225

CHAPTER 3

INCLUSIONS IN, TRANSFERS BETWEEN, AND SEPARATE CLASSES

Additions and Alterations to Property .... ¶230

Inclusions In and Transfers Between Classes .... ¶235

Transferred and Misclassified Property .... ¶240

Separate Classes .... ¶245

¶230
Additions and Alterations to Property

Generally, the cost of additions or alterations of a capital nature made to depreciable property will be added to the undepreciated capital cost of the class in which the depreciable property is contained. However, in some instances, the class in which depreciable property is contained will depend on the date of acquisition of that property.

Regulation 1102(19) provides that if the original property would have been in a different class if acquired at the time the addition or alteration is made, the addition or alteration becomes property of that different class (the "present class"), rather than the class in which the original depreciable property is contained, unless special provision is made in Part XI of the regulations or Schedule II. For example, most buildings acquired after 1987 are placed in Class 1, while buildings of the same type acquired before 1988 are included in Class 3. The cost of additions or alterations to a Class 3 building made after 1987 would fall within Class 1 but for paragraph (k) of Class 3, which provides that additions or alterations up to an aggregate cost of the lesser of:

(a) $500,000, and

(b) 25% of the cost of the building and any additions or alterations, made to such a building prior to 1988

will be included in Class 3. Additions or alterations in excess of this amount would be included in Class 1. See Interpretation Bulletin IT-79R3, "Capital Cost Allowance — Buildings or Other Structures", at ¶3105.

<h1 style="text-align:center">¶235</h1>

Inclusions In and Transfers Between Classes

The rules in Regulation 1103 allow a taxpayer, under certain conditions, to elect to transfer assets from one class to another. The main advantage of electing under the provisions in Regulation 1103 is the deferral of recapture by permitting proceeds in excess of the undepreciated capital cost of one class to be credited to another class. As well, by grouping assets that would otherwise be in several different classes into one class, the taxpayer's capital cost allowance calculation is simplified.

Regulation 1103(2d) is a general rule and applies in a year where a taxpayer disposes of property of a former class and, before the end of the year, acquires property that is included in a different class. If the newly acquired property is included in a different class only by reason of its date of acquisition, and provided the present class is not a separate prescribed class described in Regulation 1101 (other than separate classes for railway cars described in Regulation 1101(5d)), then the taxpayer may elect to transfer the old property to the present class. In this way, recapture that could otherwise result may be deferred. The election is made by attaching a letter to the taxpayer's return for the year in which the disposition occurs. The transfer is deemed to occur prior to the disposition. The election under Regulation 1103(2d) is a prescribed election under Regulation 600. As a result, pursuant to paragraphs 220(3.2)(a) and (b) of the Act, the Minister may extend the time for making such an election, or may grant permission to amend or revoke the election if the taxpayer applies within 10 calendar years from the applicable taxation year.

Under Regulation 1103(1), a taxpayer may elect to include in Class 1 of Schedule II all properties acquired for the purpose of gaining or producing income from the same business, which would otherwise be included in Classes 2 to 10 and Classes 11 and 12 of Schedule II. Thus, the taxpayer would adopt one general classification for several of the assets used in one business. The rate applicable to assets in Class 1 of Schedule II is 4%, while the rate applicable to assets in Classes 2 to 10 and 11 and 12 ranges from 5% (Class 3) to 100% (Class 12). Such an election would simplify the taxpayer's CCA calculation and might defer recapture of CCA which might otherwise be included in income on the sale of some of the assets. For example, if plant and machinery are fully or nearly fully depreciated, and the building in which they are housed has a substantial undepreciated capital cost, it may be desirable to make an election under Regulation 1103(1) to avoid recapture of CCA upon sales of plant or machinery.

Under Regulation 1103(2), a taxpayer whose chief depreciable properties are included in Classes 2, 4, or 17 of Schedule II may elect that any other property acquired before May 26, 1976, for the purpose of gaining or producing income from the same business, shall be included in Classes 2, 4, or 17, as the case may be.

Elections under Regulations 1103(1) or (2) as described above are to be made by way of a registered letter addressed to the Tax Services Office where the taxpayer customarily files returns. The elections under Regulation 1103(1) and (2) are prescribed under Regulation 600. As a result, pursuant to paragraphs $220(3.2)(a)$ and (b) of the Act, the Minister may extend the time for making such an election or may grant permission to amend or revoke the election if the taxpayer applies within 10 calendar years from the applicable taxation year.

Regulation 1103(2a) provides that a taxpayer may elect to include in Class 8 all Class 19 or Class 21 property owned by the taxpayer at the commencement of the year. The election primarily affects the treatment of machinery and equipment that qualified for accelerated capital cost allowances many years ago. Class 19 assets include certain machinery and equipment acquired between 1963 and 1967, and Class 21 includes similar assets and also machinery used in an approved project prior to 1971.

Regulation 1103(2b) permits a taxpayer to elect to include in Class 37 (amusement parks) all of the taxpayer's property that is described in Class 37 but which would not otherwise be included because the property was acquired before the date upon which Class 37 became effective (February 26, 1982).

A number of asset classifications were changed effective May 26, 1976. Where, by reason of these changes, property acquired before and after the change is in different classes, Regulation 1101(2c) permits the taxpayer to elect to put all the property in one class or the other. This election must be made in the year of acquisition or the subsequent year.

Regulation 1103(2e) is a transitional provision introduced to implement some of the June 18, 1987 tax reform proposals to reduce the rate of capital cost allowance on certain properties used in manufacturing and processing from a straight-line fast write-off over three years, to a 30% declining balance rate. Assets such as powered industrial lift trucks, portable tools acquired to earn short-term rental income, general-purpose electronic data processing equipment, and systems software that were acquired in 1988 or 1989 and were included in Class 40, are to be transferred to Class 10 at the start of the first taxation year of the taxpayer commencing after 1989. Note that this transfer must occur for taxation

¶235

years beginning in 1990, i.e., the taxpayer does not have a choice whether or not to elect.

Class 20 includes property that was acquired after December 5, 1963 and before April 1, 1967 that would otherwise be included in Classes 3 or 6. Regulation 1103(2f) provides that a taxpayer may elect to include in Class 1, 3, or 6 all Class 20 property owned by the taxpayer at the commencement of the year. This election is available for the 1988 and subsequent taxation years.

A taxpayer may elect to place rapidly depreciating electronic equipment costing over $1,000 that is in Class 8 or Class 10, and that is acquired after April 26, 1993, into a separate class. This is designed to trigger a terminal loss when the property is disposed of, recognizing that such equipment often becomes obsolete and is disposed of before it is fully written off for tax purposes. See ¶245 for a more detailed description of the type of property eligible for this election. Regulation 1103(2g) provides that any undepreciated capital cost remaining in each separate class five years after a property became available for use, is to be transferred into the regular Class 8 or Class 10 pool after the beginning of that fifth taxation year. Note that all property in the separate class gets transferred at that time. Regulation 1103(2g) also applies to Class 43 manufacturing assets that, pursuant to Regulation 1101(5s), are included in a separate class. Any undepreciated capital cost ("UCC") balance remaining after five years, in each separate class created pursuant to this measure, must be transferred into the general Class 43.

Patents or the right to use patented information with a limited or unlimited life, acquired after April 26, 1993, are included in Class 44 (25% declining balance). Regulation 1103(2h) provides that the taxpayer may elect that the patents not be included in Class 44. In this case, a patent or right for a limited period will be included in Class 14, and a patent or right for an unlimited period will be eligible capital property.

Draft Regulation 1103(2i) provides an election in respect of railway cars and railway suspension devices that are acquired after February 27, 2000, described in proposed paragraph (h) of Class 7. Under the election, a taxpayer may include these railway assets in Class 35 (7% CCA rate) rather than Class 7 (15% CCA rate). Such property only qualifies to be placed in Class 35 under this election if the property would have been eligible for an additional 6% CCA allowance under Regulations 1100(1)(z.1a) and 1101(5d), or Regulations 1100(1)(z.1c) and 1101(5d.2) if Class 35 had applied to the property. This election may be useful for a taxpayer because although property to which Regulation 1103(2i) applies is eligible for a combined CCA rate of 13% (7% + 6%), rather than the 15% CCA rate available to Class 7 property, such property is "exempt property" for the purposes of the specified leasing property rules in Regulation 1100(1.13).

An election under Regulation 1103 is to be made by a letter attached to the taxpayer's return on income for the year. As noted above, Regula-

¶235

tion 1103(5) provides that an election under Regulations 1103(1) or (2) must be made by way of a registered letter addressed to the Tax Services Office where the taxpayer customarily files returns. To be effective, any of the elections allowed pursuant to Regulation 1103 must be made not later than on or before the day which the taxpayer is required by section 150 of the Act to file a return of income for the year, although, as noted above, the time for making an election under Regulation 1103(1), (2) or (2d) may be extended pursuant to Regulation 600 and subsection 220(3.2) of the Act.

An election made under Regulation 1103 shall be effective from the first day of the taxation year in which it is made and shall continue to be effective for all subsequent years. It will not affect assets acquired after the end of the taxation year. With the exception of an election under Regulation 1103(1), (2) or (2d), as described above, where the Minister may grant permission to amend or revoke the election, the elections made under Regulation 1103 are irrevocable.

¶240

Transferred and Misclassified Property

Special rules are provided in subsections 13(5) and (5.1) for determining the undepreciated capital cost of depreciable property that is transferred from one prescribed class to another. Their effect is that the undepreciated capital cost to the taxpayer of depreciable property of the former class is adjusted so that it becomes the amount it would have been if the transferred property had never been in that class. The undepreciated capital cost of the property of the class to which the transfer is made is also adjusted by adding to it the capital cost of the transferred property, and deducting the capital cost allowances that have been allowed in respect of the property while it was included in the former class.

A transfer from one class to another is necessary in a variety of situations. Such circumstances include an election under Regulation 1103 as described in ¶235 above, an amendment in the Act or regulations requiring certain types of assets to be included in another class, misclassified property, or, as described in subsection 13(5.1), a conversion of property from a leasehold interest to a freehold interest.

In order to accomplish a transfer from one class to another, the following steps must be followed:

(1) Under paragraph 13(5)(a), the capital cost of the property being transferred is deducted from the former class and added to the other class.

(2) Under paragraph 13(5)(*b*), the greater of the following amounts is included in computing the depreciation allowed to the taxpayer in respect of the other class, and is deducted in respect of the former class:

(a) the excess, if any, of the capital cost of the transferred property over the undepreciated capital cost of the former class; and

(b) the aggregate of all amounts that have been claimed on the property as capital cost allowance, using the effective rate of the former class.

When a taxpayer converts a leasehold interest in an asset into a freehold interest (e.g., buying a building which had previously been leased), under subsection 13(5.1) the leasehold interest is deemed to have been disposed of for proceeds equal to the undepreciated capital cost of the leasehold interest. The original capital cost of the leasehold interest is added to the freehold's relevant capital cost allowance class, and the capital cost allowance claimed to date on the leasehold interest is added to the total depreciation allowed with respect to the freehold class. Thus, what may have been a terminal loss before the implementation of this provision, is now deductible as capital cost allowance on the freehold interest. See Interpretation Bulletin IT-464R, "Capital Cost Allowance — Leasehold Interests", at ¶3240.

Where a taxpayer misclassifies depreciable property or fails to reclassify the depreciable property after an amendment to the regulations, subsection 13(6) permits the Minister to assess the situation as if the depreciable property had been properly included in the incorrect class for the years prior to the Minister's direction.

Where an amount in respect of depreciable property of a prescribed class has been added to the capital cost of depreciable property of another class, the Minister may direct, by virtue of subsection 13(6), that the property be deemed to have been properly included as property of the former class prior to the commencement of the particular taxation year, and to have been transferred to the other class at the commencement of that year. The Minister may make such direction with respect to any of the taxation years in which an assessment or reassessment may be made under subsection 152(4). However, the Minister may only make such a direction if the taxpayer has not disposed of the property. According to Interpretation Bulletin IT-190R2, "Capital Cost Allowance — Transferred and Misclassified Property" (see ¶3145), where the taxpayer has already disposed of depreciable property previously misclassified, the proceeds of disposition shall remain as a credit to that class.

¶240

Example 1: Transfer of Property to Different Class

F transfers to Class 9 (25%) property having an original capital cost of $10,000 and which has up to now been included by F in Class 8 (20%). Assume that the property was purchased 2 years previously and that maximum capital cost allowance for assets in Class 8 has been claimed. Assume also that the total undepreciated capital cost of Class 8 immediately before the transfer was $100,000.

	Effect on	
	Class 8	*Class 9*
Total undepreciated capital cost immediately before transfer	$100,000	nil
Capital cost of property transferred to Class 9 . .	(10,000)	$10,000

(a) Amount to be added to the capital cost to the taxpayer of the depreciable property of the former class (i.e., Class 8), the greater of:

   (i) Capital cost to the taxpayer of the transferred property $ 10,000

        Less the undepreciated capital cost of the depreciable property of the former class before the transfer   100,000

        Excess of capital cost of transferred property over undepreciated capital cost of former class . . . .   nil

  (ii) The total of the capital cost allowances which have been allowed, using the prescribed rate in the former class, in respect of the transferred property . . . . . . $ 2,800   2,800

(b) Amount added to the total depreciation allowed to the taxpayer for property of the other class — greater of (i) or (ii) above . . .   (2,800)

Undepreciated capital cost after transfer	$ 92,800	$ 7,200

Example 2: Transfer of Property to Different Class

F transfers to Class 9 (25%) property having an original capital cost of $150,000 and which has up to now been included by F in Class 8 (20%). Assume that the property was purchased two years previously and that maximum capital cost allowance for assets in Class 8 has been claimed. Assume also that the total undepreciated capital cost of Class 8 immediately before the transfer was $50,000.

¶240

		Effect on	
		Class 8	*Class 9*
Total undepreciated capital cost immediately before transfer		$ 50,000	nil
Capital cost of all property transferred to Class 9		(150,000)	$150,000
(a) Amount to be added to the capital cost to the taxpayer of the depreciable property of the former class (i.e., Class 8) — the greater of:			
(i) Capital cost to the taxpayer of the transferred property	$150,000		
Less the undepreciated capital cost of the depreciable property of the former class before the transfer	50,000		
Excess of capital cost of transferred property over undepreciated capital cost of former class	$100,000		
(ii) The total of the capital cost allowances which have been allowed, using the prescribed rates for Class 8 in respect of the transferred property	$ 42,000	$100,000	
(b) Amount added to the total depreciation allowed to the taxpayer for property of the other class — greater of (i) or (ii) above . .			(100,000)
Undepreciated capital cost after transfer		nil	$ 50,000

¶245

Separate Classes

Regulation 1101 sets out the circumstances whereby separate classes of properties are to be established for purposes of capital cost allowance, recapture, and terminal loss. The establishment of a separate class for an asset affects the timing of the recognition of recapture or a terminal loss on the disposition of the property. Under the usual pool method, recapture or a terminal loss may be deferred by adding more assets into the class. This option is not available when dealing with a separate class. The establishment of a separate class for an asset will not affect the rate at which capital cost allowance is claimed. The rate for each separate class is the rate prescribed for the class in which the properties would otherwise be included. A separate class may be established for a property under various circumstances.

¶247 Types of Assets Required To Be Included in a Separate Class

(1) *Properties of one class used for more than one purpose.* Where a property was acquired for the purpose of gaining or producing income from a business, and a similar property was acquired for gaining or producing income from a different business or from property, Regulation 1101(1) provides that separate capital cost allowance classes are to be established for the properties even though they would otherwise have been included in only one class. For example, a taxpayer might acquire two brick buildings, one for use in a manufacturing business and one to be rented to other persons. Both buildings are Class 1 assets but separate classes must be established. Capital cost allowance for both assets would be claimed at the same 4% rate.

The question of identity or separateness of two or more businesses may be one of degree and usually will be resolved on facts of each case. For example, in *M.N.R. v. Trudeau*, 62 DTC 1109 (Ex. Ct.), the operation by the taxpayer of a rooming house and a hotel with a tavern was held to amount to the carrying on of two different businesses. Regulation 1101(1) does not apply to establish separate classes for properties, each of which has been acquired solely for the purpose of producing income from the property. In *M.N.R. v. Midwest Hotel Co. Ltd.*, 72 DTC 6440 (S.C.C.), affirming 70 DTC 6316 (Ex. Ct.), which reversed 70 DTC 1220 (T.A.B.), the validity of Regulation 1101(1) was upheld, thereby reversing a series of decisions by the Tax Appeal Board.

Where the taxpayer is a life insurer, separate classes are established for property used by the life insurer in its non-life insurance business and in its life insurance business.

Where, at the end of 1971, more than one property of a taxpayer who was a member of a partnership is described in the same class, and one of the properties can reasonably be regarded to be the interest of the taxpayer in a depreciable property that is partnership property of the partnership, a separate class is prescribed for the depreciable property. Regulation 1102(1a) provides that property described under Part XI of the regulations or in Schedule II is deemed not to include any property that is an interest of a taxpayer in depreciable property that is partnership property of the partnership.

In addition to separate businesses, there are several types of property for which a separate class is required for each asset in the class. For certain other assets, the taxpayer may elect that they be included in a separate class (see ¶248).

(2) *Rental property — less than $50,000.* Where the taxpayer is not a life insurance corporation nor a principal business corporation or part-

nership, as described in ¶255, and owns property that is rental property and similar property that is not rental property, the rental property is to be placed in a separate class. This provision applies to rental properties other than those acquired at a cost of more than $50,000 which individually form a separate class as described in "(3) *Rental Property — $50,000 or More*" below.

Similarly, Regulation 1101(5c) establishes a separate class for leasing property where a taxpayer, other than a principal business corporation or partnership, owns property that is leasing property and similar property that is not leasing property. See also "(15) *Specified Leasing Property*" below.

(3) *Rental property — $50,000 or more*. Each rental property, as defined in Regulation 1100(14), acquired after 1971 and costing not less than $50,000, will, subject to Regulation 1101(5h) (see (4) below), form a separate capital cost allowance class. A separate class must also be established for each multiple unit residential building ("MURB") in Class 31 or 32 that costs not less than $50,000. Rental properties acquired prior to 1972 or after 1972, at a cost of less than $50,000, will form a single class for CCA purposes. See Interpretation Bulletin IT-274R, "Rental Properties — Capital Cost of $50,000 or More", at ¶3165.

Where a rental property is acquired in a non-arm's length transaction, or in connection with a divisive corporate reorganization (a so-called "butterfly transaction") that complies with paragraph 55(3)(*b*) of the Act, Regulation 1101(1ad) will apply to exempt the purchaser from the requirement to include the property in a separate class if it was not required to be included in a separate class by the transferor. For example, if the transferor had originally acquired the property before 1972, or if the capital cost to the transferor was less than $50,000, the purchaser would not be required to include the property in a separate class if it is acquired from a non-arm's length vendor or in connection with a butterfly transaction. For property acquired before June 18, 1987, Regulation 1101(1ad) applied to exempt the application of the separate class rule where a rental property was acquired pursuant to certain specified rollover provisions of the Act, including transfers of property pursuant to section 85, corporate amalgamations pursuant to section 87, and windings-up of 90% or more owned Canadian subsidiaries pursuant to section 88. Regulation 1102(20) is an anti-avoidance measure for transfers under which Regulation 1101(1ad) may apply. Where taxpayers who would otherwise be dealing at arm's length undertake a transaction or series of transactions so as to be considered not to be dealing at arm's length and therefore avoid the application of the separate class rule for rental properties, Regulation 1102(20) will deem the taxpayers to deal at arm's length with respect to the acquisition of the particular property.

(4) *Leasehold interests*. Under Regulation 1101(5h), all the leasehold interests in buildings, which would otherwise be Class 1, 3 or 6, will form a separate class if the leasehold interests are described in Regulation

¶247

1100(13). Regulation 1100(13) describes leasehold interests in buildings that are leased by a taxpayer, including an insurance corporation and a principal business corporation or partnership to a person who owns the land on which the building is situated, or to a person who has an interest in that land or an option in respect thereof.

(5) *Passenger vehicles.* Each passenger vehicle costing over a prescribed amount set out in Regulation 7307(1) ($30,000 for 2001 to 2005) is included in a separate class for Class 10.1 assets. See ¶250.

(6) *Limited-period franchise, concession or licence.* Under draft Regulation 1101(1ag), after December 20, 2002, each property in respect of which the taxpayer has elected under proposed subsection 13(4.2) concerning replacement property is included in a separate class. Generally, this includes a limited-period franchise, concession or licence that is in Class 14.

(7) *Vessels.* A separate class is established for vessels that meet the requirements of Canadian vessels as described in Regulation 1101(2a). See Class 7 assets at ¶390 for further discussion. Regulation 1101(2b) prescribes a separate class for Class 7 vessels that are offshore drilling vessels. Note that offshore exploration and drilling vessels acquired after 1987 are included in Class 41(*b*) (25% CCA rate) with no separate class requirement.

Class 7 vessels and attachments that are described in Regulations 1101(2a) and (2b) are eligible for additional capital cost allowance (over and above the 15% rate in Class 7) as set out in Regulations 1100(1)(*v*) and (*va*) (see ¶390). Draft Regulation 1101(2c) provides that Regulations 1101(2a) and (2b) do not apply to such vessels and attachments to vessels that are financed with a benefit under the Structured Financing Facility Program administered by Industry Canada. An amendment to paragraph (*b*) of Class 41 excludes from Class 41 property described in draft Regulation 1101(2c). Instead, the Class 41 vessels and attachments built under the Structured Financing Facility Program are included in Class 7 (15%).

(8) *Timber limits.* Each timber limit or right to cut timber owned by a taxpayer, other than a timber resource property, is placed in a separate class.

(9) *Mines.* The regulations provide for additional capital cost allowance for property of new or expanded mines in Class 28 or Class 41(*a*), (*a*.1) or (*a*.2) at a rate equal to the rate at which the mine or group of mines earn income. All Class 28 or 41 property relating to a certain mine or a certain group of mines is put in a class separate from any such property relating to another mine or another group of mines. The purpose of the division of Class 28 and Class 41 assets into separate classes is to match the additional allowance on particular mining assets to the income of the mine or group of mines to which they relate.

¶247

(10) *Industrial mineral mines.* Where a taxpayer has more than one industrial mineral mine or more than one right to remove minerals from such a mine or both, each mine or right is deemed to be a separate class of property.

(11) *Telecommunications spacecraft.* A separate class is established for each telecommunications spacecraft described in Class 10(f.2) or Class 30.

(12) *Railway property.* Regulations 1101(5d) to (5f) provide that separate classes be established for railway property in Classes 1, 3 and 35. The separate classes enable additional allowances to be calculated based on the various types of property and the date they are acquired. See the commentary at ¶360 for Class 1 railway assets, ¶370 for Class 3 railway trestles, and ¶525 for Class 35 railway cars and suspension devices.

(13) *Certified productions.* All certified productions acquired after 1987 and before March 1996, described in Class 10(w), are to be put into a separate class.

(14) *Canadian film or video productions.* Regulation 1101(5k.1) requires all Canadian film or video productions in Class 10(x) in respect of which a Canadian film or video production tax credit under subsection 125.4(3) of the Act has been received by the corporation or a related corporation to be in a separate class. These productions are defined in Regulation 1106(4). As with the certified productions described above, all of a taxpayer's Class 10(x) assets are to be in one class, separate from the other Class 10 assets.

(15) *Specified leasing property.* A separate class is established for specified leasing property, including any additions or alterations to the property included in the same class. See item (d) in ¶248 below.

(16) *Specified energy property.* Regulation 1100(25) defines "specified energy property". Such property is included in Class 34 or 43.1 depending on the date it was acquired. Regulation 1101(5m) provides that a separate class is established for a specified energy property. See ¶520 and ¶567.

(17) *Class 36 property.* A separate class is established for property such as land that is deemed to be depreciable property in Class 36. See ¶195 for commentary on lease option arrangements that give rise to an asset being included in Class 36.

(18) *Computer software tax shelter property.* Regulation 1101(5r) requires that all computer software tax shelter properties in a prescribed class are to be in a separate class. Therefore, if one or more computer software tax shelter properties are in Class 12 with other types of Class 12 assets, they would be in a separate class of Class 12 assets. If the taxpayer also had a computer software tax shelter property that was in Class 10 (systems software), this property would be a separate Class 10 item.

¶247

¶248 Types of Assets that *May* Be Included in a Separate Class

Assets which the taxpayer may *elect* to put into a separate class include the following:

(a) Each Class 2 pipeline, including extensions or conversions costing not less than $10 million, that was commenced after 1984 and completed after September 1, 1985.

(b) Earth moving equipment acquired after 1987 and included in Class 38.

(c) Outdoor advertising signs in Class 8(*l*) acquired after 1987.

(d) Property of a principal business corporation or partnership that is exempt for purposes of the specified leasing property rules.

(e) Rapidly depreciating electronic equipment in Class 8 or Class 10(*f*) costing over $1,000 and acquired after April 26, 1993. This equipment includes computer software, photocopiers, fax machines, electronic telephone equipment including related ancillary equipment, and general-purpose electronic data processing equipment and systems software therefor. However, for property acquired after 2004, draft amendments to Regulation 1101(5p) provide that this election applies only to Class 8 property that is computer software, photocopiers or electronic communication office equipment such as a fax or telephone equipment, and not to Class 10 property. General-purpose electronic data processing equipment and systems software for that equipment acquired after March 22, 2004 is described in Class 45 (45% CCA rate) and is not eligible for this election.

(f) Manufacturing or processing property described in paragraph (*a*) of Class 43, acquired after February 27, 2000, for a cost of at least $1,000 (draft Regulation 1101(5s)).

(g) New combustion turbines (including associated burners and compressors) that generate electricity, described in subparagraph (*a*.1)(i) of Class 17, and are acquired after February 27, 2000 (draft Regulation 1101(5t)).

For the exempt property in (d) to (g) above, the taxpayer may elect to put one or more of such properties into one or more separate classes. Each property need not go into its own separate class. In order to elect to establish a separate class for property, the taxpayer is to attach a letter to the tax return for the year in which the property or properties are acquired.

Note that for assets described in (a) to (d) above, Regulation 1101(5j) provides that the separate class election is effective from the first day of the taxation year in which the election is made, and continues for all subsequent taxation years. For the electronic equipment in (e) and the manufacturing or processing property in (f), Regulation 1103(2g) provides that any such property for which an election has been made, remaining in a separate class five years after the property became available for use, is to be transferred into the regular Class 8, Class 10 or Class 43 pool, as the case may be. Therefore, the property may be depreciated in a separate class for five years beginning when the first property in the class becomes available for use. Immediately after the end of the fifth taxation year in which some capital cost allowance could be claimed in the class, the class as a whole merges into Class 8, 10, or 43, as the case may be.

For the assets described in (e) above, it appears that one cannot aggregate the values of Class 8 equipment to achieve the $1,000 threshold. With respect to computers, the reference to ancillary data processing equipment seems to make it clear that the regulation allows one separate Class 10 for a computer and all peripheral equipment acquired in the year (before 2005), as long as the aggregate value is at least $1,000. It also appears that one cannot aggregate the assets described in (f) to achieve the $1,000 threshold.

The 2005 Budget proposes to increase the CCA rate to 15% for new combustion turbine engines acquired on or after February 23, 2005, and cancel the separate class election set out in (g) above. To accommodate this transition, it is proposed that taxpayers may elect to have combustion turbines acquired before 2006 that would otherwise be eligible for the higher rate included in Class 17 and therefore eligible for the separate class election.

¶248

CHAPTER 4

RESTRICTIONS ON CAPITAL COST ALLOWANCE

¶250

Passenger Vehicles

¶251 Definitions

"Passenger vehicle" is defined in subsection 248(1) of the Act generally as an automobile acquired or leased after June 17, 1987.

The term "automobile" refers to a motor vehicle designed or adapted to carry individuals on highways or streets and which has a seating capacity of not more than a driver and eight passengers. Specifically *excluded* from the definition of "automobile" in subsection 248(1) of the Act are the following vehicles:

(a) an ambulance;

(b) an emergency-response vehicle that is clearly marked and used in connection with or in the course of an individual's office or employment with a fire department, police, or an emergency medical response or ambulance service;

(c) a taxi;

(d) a bus;

(e) a hearse;

(f) a vehicle acquired to be sold, rented, or leased in the course of carrying on a business of selling, renting, or leasing motor vehicles;

(g) a van or pickup truck that:

(i) has a seating capacity of not more than the driver and two passengers and which, in the year it is acquired or leased, is used primarily for the transportation of goods or equipment in the course of producing income;

(ii) all or substantially all the use of which is for the transportation of goods, equipment or passengers in the course of producing income in the year it is acquired or leased; or

(iii) for taxation years beginning after 2002, a pickup truck that is used primarily for the transportation of goods, equipment or passengers in the course of producing income at a remote work location that is at least 30 kilometres from the nearest urban community, with a population of at least 40,000.

Administratively, the CRA considers the word "primarily" to mean more that 50% and the term "all or substantially all" to mean 90% or more, although these percentages have been disputed in the courts. See, for example, *Pronovost*, 2003 DTC 720 (T.C.C.).

See Interpretation Bulletins IT-521R, "Motor Vehicle Expenses Claimed by Self-Employed Individuals", and IT-522R, "Vehicle and Other Travelling Expenses — Employees", at ¶3295 and ¶3300 respectively.

¶252   Restrictions on Capital Cost Allowance

A passenger vehicle that costs over $20,000 or a prescribed amount is included in Class 10.1 instead of Class 10, which is the other class for automotive equipment. The prescribed amount for passenger vehicles is outlined in Regulation 7307(1). For vehicles acquired from 2001 to 2005, the prescribed amount is $30,000. For previous years, the prescribed amounts were $27,000 for 2000; $26,000 for 1998 and 1999; $25,000 for 1997; and $24,000 before 1997. From 1991 onwards, applicable federal and provincial sales taxes are added to the prescribed figure. See the chart reproduced at the end of ¶252.

The capital cost allowance rate for Class 10.1 is 30%, the same as for Class 10. Capital cost allowance is claimed in the normal way, but only on the prescribed amount. As provided by paragraph $13(7)(g)$, the cost of the vehicle in excess of the prescribed amount is not eligible for capital cost allowance. Class 10.1 assets are subject to the half-year rule in the year of acquisition.

The following situation outlines the capital cost allowance rules for an automobile purchased at an amount above the prescribed amount: An automobile used to earn income is acquired in January 2004 at a cost of $38,000 + $2,660 (GST) + $3,040 (PST at 8%) for a total cost of $43,700. The automobile is included in Class 10.1 in a separate class at an amount of $34,500 ($30,000 + $2,100 (GST) + $2,400 (PST at 8%)). In 2004, CCA is claimed, subject to the half-year rule, as follows: $34,500 × ½ × 30% = $5,175. No CCA may be claimed on the excess of actual cost over the Class 10.1 threshold ($43,700 − $34,500 = $9,200).

The following illustration outlines the capital cost allowance rules for an automobile purchased at an amount below the prescribed amount: An automobile used to earn income is acquired in January 2004 at a cost of $28,000 + $1,960 (GST) + $2,240 (PST at 8%) for a total cost of $32,200. The automobile is included in Class 10, not Class 10.1, and not in a separate class since the cost of the vehicle, excluding federal and provincial sales taxes, is less than $30,000. The capital cost of the Class 10 vehicle is $32,200. In 2004, CCA is claimed, subject to the half-year rule, as follows: $32,200 + ½ × 30% = $4,830.

This limitation with respect to the depreciable capital cost for passenger vehicles applies for taxation years that commence after June 17, 1987 and end after 1987. Automobiles that have been included in Class 10 in error, and should be in Class 10.1, must be transferred to Class 10.1 (see ¶240).

Additions to the Vehicle

Additions to the vehicle (for example, options purchased after title to the passenger vehicle has been assumed) would be subject to the limitation as if installed at the time of purchase, since any additions would form part of the capital cost of the vehicle and thereby be subject to this limitation.

Separate Classes, Recapture, and Terminal Loss

Each passenger vehicle described in Class 10.1 is put into a separate class. As a result, when each vehicle is disposed of there will generally be a negative or positive balance left in the CCA class which would normally give rise to recapture or a terminal loss. However, subsection 13(2) provides that such vehicles are not subject to recapture on disposition. Similarly, subsection 20(16.1) provides that no terminal loss may be claimed in respect of such a passenger vehicle. On disposition, the balance in the class is set to nil without an income inclusion from recapture or deduction from a terminal loss. However, when a Class 10.1 vehicle is disposed of, Regulation 1100(2.5) provides that in the year of disposition only, the taxpayer may claim a half-year of CCA on the vehicle. The taxpayer need not acquire another vehicle of any kind in order to claim this one time capital cost allowance in the year of disposition.

Automobiles costing less than the prescribed amount and other motor vehicles that do not meet the definition of "automobile" continue to be included in Class 10. These Class 10 vehicles are subject to normal recapture and terminal loss rules.

Transfer of Vehicle to Non-Arm's Length Person

Paragraph 13(7)(*h*) is intended to prevent the prescribed limit on the depreciable capital cost of a passenger vehicle from being circumvented by means of a transfer of the vehicle between parties not at arm's length. To accomplish this, the capital cost of a vehicle transferred between non-arm's length persons is limited to the least of:

¶252

(a) the fair market value of the vehicle at the time of the transfer;

(b) the cost amount to the vendor ("cost amount" is defined in subsection 248(1) as the *pro rata* share of the UCC of the class determined with reference to the capital cost of the assets in the class); and

(c) the prescribed limit (i.e., for 2001 to 2005, $30,000 plus federal and provincial sales taxes, or such other amount as set out by Regulation 7307(1)).

Therefore, it will not be possible to increase the depreciable base through a non-arm's length transfer, even if its fair market value is greater than its proportionate UCC.

Joint Ownership Arrangements

A further anti-avoidance rule ensures that joint ownership arrangements designed to circumvent the capital cost limitation in paragraph 13(7)(*g*) will limit the capital cost of motor vehicles to the prescribed limit. Specifically, section 67.4 will ensure that the total capital cost available as a deduction to all owners cannot exceed the maximum amount that would be allowed to one owner.

Example: Passenger Vehicles

In 2004, T acquired two automobiles to be used in T's business, one for $35,000, including applicable sales taxes, and one for $18,000, including applicable sales taxes. This same year, T disposed of a Class 10.1 passenger vehicle with a 2004 opening undepreciated capital cost of $8,500 for proceeds of $5,000. T has other assets in Class 10 which have a 2004 opening undepreciated capital cost of $12,000.

The 2004 capital cost allowance would be calculated as follows:

	Class 10 *30%*	*Class 10.1* *30%*	
		A	B
Opening UCC balance	$12,000	$8,500	
Additions.	18,000		$34,500*
Disposals		(5,000)	
Less ½ net additions	(9,000)		(17,250)
	$21,000	$3,500**	$17,250
CCA at 30%	6,300	$1,275***	5,175
	$14,700		$12,075
Plus deferred capital cost	9,000		17,250
Closing UCC balance	$23,700	nil	$29,325

---

* The maximum allowed for CCA purposes in 2004 is $30,000 plus federal and provincial sales taxes on $30,000 (assumed 15%). Note that this amount will vary depending on the provincial sales tax rate. Note too that the new passenger vehicle is placed in a separate Class 10.1 class.

** The terminal loss is denied.

*** The half-year rule on the sale of Class 10.1 assets allows a CCA claim of 30% of ($8,500 × ½). This could have been claimed even if T had not acquired another Class 10.1 vehicle.

¶252

Example: Automobile Rates and Limits

The following rates and limits are prescribed in sections 7305.1 to 7307 of the Income Tax Regulations. In recent years, the Department of Finance has been adjusting the amounts by News Release issued at the end of the calendar year.

See the definitions of "automobile" and "passenger vehicle" in subsection 248(1).

Operating expense benefit - per kilometre [1]	Jan. 1/96-Dec. 31/96	Jan. 1/97-Dec. 31/99	Jan. 1/00-Dec. 31/00	Jan. 1/01-Dec. 31/02	Jan. 1/03-Dec. 31/04	Jan. 1/05-Dec. 31/05
Employees	13¢	14¢	15¢	16¢	17¢	20¢
Employees employed principally in selling or leasing automobiles	10¢	11¢	12¢	13¢	14¢	17¢

Reasonable allowance per kilometre [2] Deductible by employer where tax-free allowance paid to employee:	Jan. 1/96-Dec. 31/96	Jan. 1/97-Dec. 31/99	Jan. 1/00-Dec. 31/00	Jan. 1/01-Dec. 31/02	Jan. 1/03-Dec. 31/04	Jan. 1/05-Dec. 31/05
All Provinces*	33¢/27¢	35¢/29¢	37¢/31¢	41¢/35¢	42¢/36¢	45¢/39¢
Nunavut, Yukon and Northwest Territories*	37¢/31¢	39¢/33¢	41¢/35¢	45¢/39¢	46¢/40¢	49¢/43¢

	Jan. 1/97-Dec. 31/97	Jan. 1/98-Dec. 31/99	Jan. 1/00-Dec. 31/00	Jan. 1/01-Dec. 31/02	Jan. 1/03-Dec. 31/04	Jan. 1/05-Dec. 31/05
Cost of passenger vehicle [3]	$25,000**	$26,000**	$27,000**	$30,000**	$30,000**	$30,000**
Prescribed monthly interest [4]	$250	$250	$250	$300	$300	$300
Monthly lease amount [5]	$550**	$650**	$700**	$800**	$800**	$800**

* The first number applies to the first 5,000 kilometres driven in the year. The second number applies to subsequent kilometres driven in the year.

** Applicable federal and provincial sales taxes are added to these figures to calculate the ceiling amount.

[1] Reg. 7305.1; prescribed for s. 6(1)(k)(v).
[2] Reg. 7306; prescribed for s. 18(1)(r).
[3] Reg. 7307(1); prescribed for ss. 13(2), 13(7)(g), 13(7)(b)(iii), 20(4), 20(16.1), the description of B in 67.3(d) and 85(1)(e.4)(i).
[4] Reg. 7307(2); prescribed for the description of A in s. 67.2.
[5] Reg. 7307(3); prescribed for the description of A in s. 67.3(c).

¶252

¶255

Rental Property

¶256   Definitions

"Rental property" is defined in Regulation 1100(14) to mean a building or a leasehold interest in real property if the leasehold interest is property of Class 1, 3, 6, or 13, owned by the taxpayer or partnership, and used in the taxation year principally for the purpose of gaining or producing gross revenue that is rent. The definition excludes a property leased to a lessee who undertakes to use the property to carry on the business of selling or promoting the sale of the taxpayer's goods or services. Therefore, property leased in connection with a franchise agreement would be excluded from rental property. For taxation years prior to 1994, "rental property" does not include a building that is a multiple-unit residential building ("MURB") as described in Class 31 or 32. In *Gulf Canada Resources Limited*, 93 DTC 5345 (F.C.T.D.), it was held that the building that was used partly by the taxpayer, partly by a subsidiary (at reduced rent and without a lease), and 45% by unrelated tenants, was not a rental property within the definition of Regulation 1100(14).

¶257   Restrictions on Capital Cost Allowance

Regulations 1100(11) to (14.2) provide that, in most circumstances, a taxpayer or partnership may not deduct capital cost allowance in respect of rental property to the full extent otherwise allowed by the rates set out in Schedule II. The purpose of this restriction is to prevent certain taxpayers from using CCA to produce a loss from rental property which would reduce or shelter other income that would otherwise be subject to tax.

Regulation 1100(11) establishes the limitation on capital cost allowance that may be deducted in respect of rental properties by a taxpayer or partnership which does not fall within the exemption in Regulation 1100(12) (described below). The aggregate of CCA deductions in respect of classes of property which include rental property may not exceed the net rental income of the taxpayer from rental properties (before deducting CCA). This net rental income is determined by adding together the rental income from properties owned directly (before CCA) and the taxpayer's share of rental income of a partnership, and then deducting rental losses from properties owned directly and the taxpayer's share of rental losses of a partnership. In the case of a taxpayer who just owns rental property directly, the incomes and losses (before CCA) from the rental properties must be netted to determine the aggregate CCA that may be claimed in respect of classes of property which include rental properties. Assuming that the taxpayer has net rental income from rental properties, the taxpayer may then deduct CCA to the extent of such net income, even if the deducting of this CCA will produce a loss with respect to a particular rental property. Therefore, the restriction is on the aggregate of the income from all the rental properties owned by the taxpayer, even though they are in separate classes, not on each individual property.

Capital cost allowance in respect of partnership property is deducted by the partnership in determining the income or loss that is allocated to the partners. Unless all the members of the partnership are the types of corporations described in Regulation 1100(12)(a), the partnership is subject to the limitations set out in Regulation 1100(11). Thus, the partnership may deduct CCA in respect of rental properties only to the extent that its income from rental properties exceeds its losses from rental properties. Therefore, CCA may not be deducted to produce an overall loss to the partnership from rental properties. Where a loss arises before deducting CCA, the partner's share is then taken into account in determining the net income of the taxpayer from rental properties for the purpose of determining the CCA that may be claimed by the taxpayer in respect of rental property owned directly.

Exemptions from Restrictions

Under Regulation 1100(12), the restriction in Regulation 1100(11) on the amount of capital cost allowance that may be deducted in respect of rental properties does not apply, except in limited circumstances, to:

(a) a life insurance corporation;

(b) a corporation whose principal business throughout the year was the leasing, rental, development, or sale, or any combination thereof, of real property owned by it; or

(c) a partnership, each member of which was a corporation described in (a) or (b).

The Canada Revenue Agency's view as to the meaning of the term "principal business" is set out in Interpretation Bulletin IT-371 at ¶3215. See also *Satin Finish Hardwood Flooring (Ontario) Limited*, 97 DTC 287 (T.C.C.), where the real estate operations were deemed to be the principal business of the taxpayer who also carried on a manufacturing business.

Regulation 1100(13) provides that insurance corporations and principal business corporations (and partnerships thereof) will in some cases (such as with respect to certain lease-leaseback agreements) be subject to the Regulation 1100(11) CCA restrictions. The restrictions will apply if the corporation or partnership holds a leasehold interest in a building which was treated as Class 1, 3 or 6 property by virtue of Regulation 1102(5), and that building was leased by the taxpayer or partnership to the owner of the land on which the building was situated, or to a person who had an interest in that land or an option in respect thereof.

If each member of a partnership is a life insurance corporation or a principal business corporation as defined in Regulation 1100(12), the partnership will not be subject to the restrictions of Regulation 1100(11)

¶257

in claiming capital cost allowance unless Regulation 1100(13) applies (see above). In some circumstances, doubt may exist as to whether one partner qualifies for the exemption under Regulation 1100(12) and the parties may wish to establish a joint venture, such that it is not a partnership. A partnership is essentially the relationship among persons carrying on business in common with a view to profit. Thus, if parties own rental property as tenants in common and do not carry on business in common, their relationship may not be that of partnership and the party that qualifies for the exemption under Regulation 1100(12) will not be restricted in claiming CCA in respect of its interest in the rental property.

¶258   Separate Classes

In addition to the capital cost allowance restrictions in Regulation 1100(11), Regulation 1101 provides that separate classes be established for rental property. Where a taxpayer, other than a corporation or a partnership that is exempt from the CCA restrictions as described in Regulation 1100(12), owns property that is rental property and similar property that would be in the same class that is not rental property, Regulation 1101(1ae) provides that a separate class is to be established for the rental property. Similarly, Regulation 1101(5h) places leasehold interests in real property, which are described in Regulation 1100(13), into a separate class. As well, Regulation 1101(1ac) provides that each rental property of a taxpayer acquired after 1971, costing $50,000 or more, is to be in a separate class. Regulation 1101(5b) stipulates that a separate class is also established for each MURB in Class 31 or 32 costing not less than $50,000. Regulation 1101(1ac) will not operate to place each rental property costing not less than $50,000 in a separate class if the property was acquired in a non-arm's length transaction or a divisive corporate reorganization (a "butterfly transaction") that meets the requirements of paragraph 55(3)(*b*), and it had not been required to be included in a separate class by the transferor. The establishment of separate classes prevents the deferral of recapture.

See ¶245 for further discussion of separate classes. Also see Interpretation Bulletins IT-195R4, "Rental Property — Capital Cost Allowance Restrictions", at ¶3147; IT-274R, "Rental Properties — Capital Cost of $50,000 or More", at ¶3165; and IT-304R2, "Condominiums", at ¶3180.

¶258

Example: Rental Property

J owns two rental properties. A summary of J's 2004 rental operation is as follows:

	Building A	Building B
Rent	$17,000	$15,000
Allowable expenses other than CCA	15,200	16,000
Net rental income (loss) before claiming CCA	$ 1,800	$(1,000)

J can claim $800 of capital cost allowance for the year. The income of Building A is combined with the loss of Building B to determine the net income for reduction by capital cost allowance.

2004	Building A	Building B
Opening UCC balance	$100,000	$75,000
Less: CCA claim (maximum allowed)		800
	$100,000	$74,200

Capital cost allowance may be claimed on either of the buildings in separate classes even if it increases the rental loss from that particular building. If J sold Building A in 2005, the capital cost allowance claimed on it could be recaptured. J therefore claimed the 2004 capital cost allowance on Building B.

¶260

Leasing Property

¶261 Definitions

"Leasing property" of a taxpayer or partnership is defined in Regulation 1100(17) as depreciable property of a taxpayer or a partnership which is used principally to earn rent, royalty or leasing revenue *other than*:

(a) a rental property;

(b) a computer software tax shelter property (defined in Regulation 1100(20.2));

(c) a certified production acquired after 1987 or before March 1996 (paragraph (*w*) of Class 10); or

(d) a certified feature film or certified production referred to in paragraph (*n*) of Class 12.

The definition excludes properties leased in the ordinary course of selling goods or rendering services under an agreement by which the lessee undertakes to use the property to carry on the business of selling or promoting the sale of the taxpayer's (or partnership's) goods or services. For taxation years prior to 1994, "leasing property" does not include a multiple-unit residential building described in Class 31 or 32 (as well as furniture, fixtures, or equipment, if any, located within and ancillary thereto).

The depreciable property may be movable or immovable and must be used in the year principally for the purpose of gaining or producing gross revenue that is rent, royalty, or leasing revenue. In *McCoy*, 2003 DTC 660 (T.C.C.), the profits of the joint venture in which the partnership expected to share were profits from trading futures contracts and could not be called rent royalty or leasing revenue. As a result, the software acquired was not leasing property as defined in Regulation 1100(17). In *Mackay et al.*, 89 DTC 515 (T.C.C.), the taxpayer acquired a yacht and leased it to a family member who was responsible for the maintenance of the yacht and arranging charters. The yacht was found to be leasing property and the capital cost allowance claim was restricted accordingly. Regulation 1100(17.1) provides that if the depreciable property is not used for any purpose in the year in which it is acquired and its first subsequent use satisfies this principal-purpose test, the property is deemed to have satisfied the principal-purpose test in the taxation year in which it was acquired.

For more commentary on leasing property, see Interpretation Bulletin IT-443, "Leasing Property — Capital Cost Allowance Restrictions", at ¶3232.

¶262 Restrictions on Capital Cost Allowance

Regulation 1100(15) provides that the aggregate capital cost allowance in respect of a prescribed class of "leasing property" is limited to the net income for the year from renting, leasing, or earning royalties from leasing properties. This rule is designed to prevent taxpayers from claiming CCA to increase or create a loss on leasing properties which could be used to shelter other unrelated income. Regulation 1101(5c) establishes a separate class for leasing property (except in the case of a principal business leasing corporation or partnership described in Regulation 1100(16), see below).

Exemptions from Restrictions

Regulation 1100(16) provides that corporations (including corporate partnerships) whose principal business is the renting or leasing of leasing property (including property that would be leasing property but for Regulation 1100(18), (19) or (20)), or the renting or leasing of such property combined with the sale and service of property of the same general type and description, are not subject to the leasing property rules in cases where their gross revenue in the year from such sources amounts to at least 90% of their gross revenue from all sources. This exemption from the leasing property rules applies for a given taxation year, where the stated conditions are met throughout the year.

Regulation 1100(18) exempts any property acquired before May 26, 1976 from the leasing property rules, subject to some transitional rules for agreements entered into before that time. However, Regulation 1100(18) does not exempt an addition or improvement made after May 26, 1976 to such a property from the leasing property rules, so that the addition may be leasing property.

Regulation 1100(20) also provides an exemption from the leasing property rules in certain circumstances where a property that would otherwise be a leasing property is acquired by a corporation or partnership as a replacement property (within the meaning of subsection 13(4) of the Act, see ¶190). Where the property replaced was not a leasing property by virtue of Regulation 1100(18) (i.e., because it was acquired before May 26, 1976), 1100(19) (pertaining to certain rollover provisions discussed below), or 1100(20), then the replacement property will be deemed not to be a leasing property. A series of replacements under this rule will continue to be exempt as long as the replacement property rules in subsection 13(4) apply to each replacement.

Regulation 1100(19) provides an exemption from the leasing property rules in circumstances where a property that would otherwise be a leasing property is acquired from a non-arm's length person or in connection with a divisive corporate reorganization (a so-called "butterfly transaction") that meets the requirements of paragraph 55(3)(*b*). Property acquired in such circumstances will be exempt where the property was not leasing property to the transferor by virtue of Regulation 1100(18) (i.e., because it was acquired before May 26, 1976) or 1100(20) (i.e., because it was acquired as a replacement property in circumstances described above). For property acquired prior to June 18, 1987, Regulation 1100(19) applied with respect to property acquired pursuant to certain specified rollover provisions of the Act, including transfers of property pursuant to section 85, property transferred by a partner to a Canadian partnership or vice versa pursuant to subsections 97(2) and 98(3), corporate amalgamations pursuant to section 87, and windings-up of 90% or more owned Canadian subsidiaries pursuant to section 88. For purposes of Regulation 1100(19), Regulation 1102(20) is an anti-avoidance measure where taxpayers who would otherwise be dealing at arm's length undertake a transaction or series of transactions so as to be considered not to be dealing at arm's length and, therefore, avoid the application of the leasing property rules. Regulation 1102(20) will deem the taxpayers to deal at arm's length with respect to the acquisition of the particular property.

¶262

¶263

Specified Leasing Property

The "specified leasing property" rules in Regulations 1100(1.1) to (1.3) were introduced as a result of the government's growing concern that non-taxpaying entities were using leasing arrangements as a means of after-tax financing. These regulations are intended to discourage non-taxpaying entities from structuring an asset acquisition with borrowed funds as a lease, and trading their capital cost allowance deductions to lessors for reduced lease payments. Although the Income Tax Regulations already contain a number of provisions that restrict the claiming of capital cost allowance on leasing properties to the amount of income earned from renting or leasing such properties (see commentary on Regulations 1100(15) to (20) at ¶260), these provisions do not extend to a corporation whose principal business is the renting or leasing of such properties (referred to as a principal business leasing corporation). Regulations 1100(1.1) to (1.3) apply to all lessors that make arm's length leases of specified leasing property (defined below) for periods of greater than one year. The restrictions apply to leases entered into after 10:00 p.m., Eastern Daylight Saving Time, April 26, 1989, other than leases entered into pursuant to a prior written agreement which has not been substantially modified.

In general, the application of Regulations 1100(1.1) to (1.3) to a lease of specified leasing property restricts the available capital cost allowance deductions to the lessor by treating the lease as a loan and the lease payments as blended payments of principal and interest. The amount of capital cost allowance that the lessor may deduct is then restricted to the notional amount of principal received or receivable. In other words, the specified leasing property rules attempt to notionally unwind the lease transaction by treating the lease as a purchase of the leased assets by the lessee, financed by the lessor. These rules do not affect the lessee's position, but see ¶270.

¶264 Definitions

Specified Leasing Property

The definition of "specified leasing property" is found in Regulation 1100(1.11). In general terms, "specified leasing property" is defined as depreciable property, other than exempt property, that is principally used to earn rental or leasing revenue where the depreciable property is subject to an arm's length lease of more than one year, and the fair market value of all the properties subject to the lease is, in aggregate, greater than $25,000.

However, specified leasing property will not include intangible property, such as systems software or other software referred to in

Class 12(o), nor will it include certified feature films or certified productions in Class 10(w) or Class 12(n) of Schedule II of the regulations.

Exempt Property

"Exempt property", as defined in Regulation 1100(1.13)(a), includes assets that are commonly leased which, in the government's view, do not provide any scope for abuse since the capital cost allowance rate on these assets approximates actual depreciation. Specifically, "exempt property" means:

(a) general-purpose office furniture and equipment in Class 8, or general-purpose electronic and ancillary data processing equipment in Class 10(f) or Class 45, other than any individual asset having a capital cost in excess of $1 million;

(b) furniture, appliances, television or radio receivers, telephones, furnaces, hot water heaters, and other similar properties designed for residential use;

(c) motor vehicles, including automobiles, ambulances, funeral vehicles, taxis, rental vehicles, vans and light duty trucks, trucks or tractors designed for use on highways, including trailers designed to be hauled by these trucks or tractors;

(d) buildings and component parts (e.g., electric wiring, plumbing, sprinkler systems, air conditioning and heating equipment, etc.) other than, under certain conditions, a building leased to a tax-exempt person (see below);

(e) vessel mooring space; and

(f) Class 35 property, which includes a railway car acquired after May 25, 1976, or a rail suspension device designed to carry trailers that are designed for both highways and railway tracks.

A building leased after February 2, 1990 primarily to a tax-exempt person (under section 149 of the Act), a person who uses the building to earn tax-exempt income, or a government or public authority who formerly owned the building, other than for an ownership period of less than one year or only during construction, does not qualify as exempt property. This latter restriction is intended to curtail the use of sale leaseback transactions of assets that have appreciated in value involving tax-exempt entities. It should be noted that in the case of a building that is not exempt property, the lease term in order to qualify as specified leasing property is three years rather than one year.

In addition to the above, where a property is owned by two or more persons or by a partnership, Regulation 1100(1.13)(a) deems each person's or each partner's capital cost in respect of the property to be the full capital cost to the person or the partnership for purposes of the $1 million threshold in the "exempt property" definition.

¶264

¶265　Restrictions on Capital Cost Allowance

The rules which govern the amount of capital cost allowance available to a lessor in respect of a specified leasing property are found in Regulation 1100(1.1). In general, Regulation 1100(1.1) operates to treat a lease of specified leasing property as a loan and the lease payments as blended payments of principal and interest, with the amount of capital cost allowance that the lessor may deduct being restricted to the notional amount of principal received or receivable on the loan.

The amount of capital cost allowance deductible in respect of a specified leasing property is the lesser of the two amounts in Regulations $1100(1.1)(a)$ and (b).

The first limit in Regulation $1100(1.1)(a)$ determines, in general terms, the cumulative amount of notional principal repayments that would have been received in a year or a preceding year by the lessor if the lease is considered to be a loan made by the lessor to the lessee. The amount of capital cost allowance is then restricted to this cumulative amount of notional principal repayments, less the actual amount of capital cost allowance claimed in prior years.

More specifically, Regulation $1100(1.1)(a)(i)$ calculates the return of principal that would be received by the lessor in the year and all preceding years after the property last became a specified leasing property. For this purpose, the lessor's return of principal is calculated as though the lessor had made a loan to the lessee at the interest rate prescribed by Regulation 4302 that is in effect at the earlier of the time the lessor last entered into an agreement to lease the property, and the time the property last became a specified leasing property. The principal amount of the loan is equal to the fair market value of the property at the time it last became a specified leasing property. The lease payments are treated as blended payments of principal and interest on the loan and are deemed to be applied by Regulation $1100(1.1)(a)(C)$, in order of priority, on account of interest, on account of interest on unpaid interest, and finally on account of principal. Note that interest on the notional loan is computed on a semi-annual compounding basis.

Where the lease provides for floating lease payments which vary according to prevailing interest rates, the lessor may elect, in respect of all the property that is subject to that lease, to have Regulation 4302 apply at the beginning of the period for which the interest is being calculated. This election must be made by the lessor in the lessor's income tax return for the taxation year in which the lease was entered into.

Where a property of the lessor is converted to a specified leasing property part way through a taxation year, Regulation $1100(1.1)(a)(ii)$ provides that the notional capital cost allowance that would otherwise be available to the lessor will be added to the lessor's return of principal for purposes of computing the capital cost allowance restriction. The notional amount of capital cost allowance that is added back is computed on the basis that the property had been transferred to a separate class at the later of the beginning of the year and the time the property was acquired. As well, the part of the year prior to the conversion is considered to be a separate taxation year. The computation of this notional capital cost allowance is subject to the half-year rule (¶140) and Regulation 1100(3), which requires a proration of the capital cost allowance claim, in respect of certain classes, for short taxation years, i.e., less than 12 months (see ¶145).

Finally, the cumulative notional principal is reduced pursuant to Regulation 1100(1.1)(*a*)(iii) by the actual capital cost allowance claimed by the lessor in preceding years in respect of the property after it last became a specified leasing property.

Regulation 1100(1.1)(*b*) provides the other parameter that may limit the capital cost allowance claim available in respect of a specified leasing property. This second restriction is the amount by which the cumulative amount of capital cost allowance the lessor could have claimed in respect of a specified leasing property in the year, and all preceding taxation years in which the lessor owned the property, exceeds the actual amount of capital cost allowance claimed by the lessor in respect of the property. This cumulative maximum capital cost allowance entitlement is computed on the assumption that Regulation 1100(1.1) and, in the case of a lessor that is not a principal business leasing corporation, Regulations 1100(11) and (15) (capital cost allowance restrictions on rental properties and leasing properties) had not applied for the relevant taxation years. Furthermore, the half-year rule will not apply for purposes of this computation to a property acquired by a principal business leasing corporation if it is a specified leasing property at the end of the year in which it is acquired.

Regulation 1100(1.14) permits a taxpayer that is a principal business leasing corporation (see ¶260 for commentary on Regulation 1100(16) that defines "principal business leasing corporation") to elect that all of its property that is the subject of leases be deemed not to be exempt property, and that the aggregate fair market value of all the property that is the subject of each such lease be deemed to have been, at the time the lease was entered into, in excess of $25,000. In other words, a principal business leasing corporation may elect to have the specified leasing property rules apply to all the property leased by it, including exempt property and property that is subject to a lease where the aggregate fair market value of all the property subject to that lease does not exceed $25,000. The election is made by the taxpayer in the taxpayer's tax return for a taxation year and will apply to all leases entered into in that taxation year and all subsequent taxation years.

It should be noted that Regulations 1100(11) and (15) do not apply for the purposes of the calculation in Regulation 1100(1.1)(*b*). These regulations will continue to apply to restrict capital cost allowance claims by a taxpayer, other than a principal business leasing corporation, to the

¶265

taxpayer's rental or leasing income from the property for the relevant year.

The following example illustrates in general the computations under Regulations 1100(1.1)(a) and (b).

Example: Specified Leasing Property Rules

Taxpayer A, the lessor, leases a specified leasing property to B. The class rate for the property is 20%. The fair market value (FMV) of the property that is being leased is $100,000. The annual leasing payments are $13,140. Under the rules, the $13,140 payment is considered a blended payment of interest and principal. The interest is determined by the formula: FMV × prescribed interest rate. Assuming the prescribed interest rate is 10%, and ignoring the compounding, the interest portion is $100,000 × 10% = $10,000. What remains of the $13,140 payment, $3,140, is deemed amortization. This is compared to CCA available under normal rules ($100,000 × 20% × half-year rule = $10,000), and the lesser ($3,140) is the maximum CCA for the year.

In the following year, the interest formula will be applied to an unamortized balance of $96,860, giving notional interest of $9,686. Subtracting this from the $13,140 payment leaves a notional amortization of $3,454. However, return of principal is considered to be cumulative, with actual claims deducted, so the actual calculation is last year's return of principal ($3,140) plus this year's ($3,454) minus last year's actual claim ($3,140). Accordingly, the limitation under this part of the formula will be $3,454. The "ordinary" cumulative CCA will be ($90,000 × 20% = $18,000), plus $10,000 from last year, less $3,140 actually claimed from last year, or $24,860. The current year claim is the lesser of these, $3,454.

The prescribed interest rate is determined at the time the lease is entered into or, if an agreement to lease is made before the commencement of the lease, at the time of the agreement. If the lease contains a floating interest rate, the lessor may elect to use the rate prescribed at the beginning of the period for which each calculation is made. This election can be made lease by lease, but must be made once and for all in the first year of the lease. The prescribed interest rate will not be the usual quarterly rate, but will be adjusted monthly to be one point above the government rate on certain bonds for the preceding month.

Where property otherwise ordinarily depreciable in a year is leased during the year and is subject to these rules, ordinary depreciation prorated for the portion of the year prior to the lease may be added to depreciation under the rules to determine capital cost allowance for the year.

The specified leasing property rules will cease to apply to the lessor when the property ceases to be specified leasing property to the lessor at the end of any taxation year. The normal rules concerning recapture and terminal losses provided for in the Act and the regulations will apply when the lessor disposes of the property.

¶265

The interest rates applicable with respect to the specified leasing rules are calculated under Regulation 4302 as one percentage point greater than the long-term Government of Canada bond rate for the last Wednesday of the month before the immediately preceding month. The long-term Government of Canada bond rate is published by the Bank of Canada at http://www.bankofcanada.ca/en/rates/bonds.html. The monthly prescribed rates for leasing rules are posted on the CRA Web site at http://www.cra-arc.gc.ca/tax/individuals/faq/lease-e.html.

¶267   Separate Classes

Regulation 1101(5n) provides that a separate class is to be established for each specified leasing property for that year and all subsequent taxation years.

A taxpayer that is a principal business leasing corporation may make a separate class election under Regulation 1101(5o) in respect of one or more properties of a prescribed class that are exempt properties. The effect of this election, which is on a class-by-class basis, is to group all exempt properties of a certain class together as a separate class. The election is made by the taxpayer in the income tax return for the taxation year in which the property or properties (of the particular class) is acquired. This election may be advantageous to a taxpayer with one exempt property of a particular class as well as other properties of the same class, none of which is an exempt property or a specified leasing property. In this case, the election will be beneficial if a terminal loss will result when the exempt property is disposed of since the election places the exempt property into a separate class. Conversely, the election will not be beneficial if recapture is expected on the disposition of the exempt property, since in the absence of the election, the undepreciated capital cost balance of the other assets will protect against recapture.

¶268   Anti-Avoidance

Several anti-avoidance provisions were introduced in connection with the specified leasing property regulations to prevent or minimize the circumvention of these rules.

Regulations 1100(1.13)(b)(i) and (ii) deem a property to be subject to a lease for a term of greater than one year if the property has in fact been leased to the lessee or a related person for more than one year, or where the lessor knew or ought to have known that the lessee or related person would have leased the property for more than one year. This anti-avoidance provision is intended to prevent taxpayers from circumventing the rules by structuring what would otherwise be a long-term lease into a series of short-term leases so as to have the leased property fall outside the definition of "specified leasing property" by virtue of the lease having a short lease term (i.e., not more than one year). The test in subparagraph (ii) is a reasonableness test which turns on whether the lessor knew, or ought to have known, that the lessee would lease the property for more than one year. Presumably, factors such as the nature of the asset, the nature of the lessor's business, and the other terms of the lease must be weighed together to determine whether this anti-avoidance rule will apply. Regulation 1100(1.3) provides that, in the case of a building, the reference to one year in Regulation 1100(1.13)(*b*) is to be read as three years.

Regulation 1100(1.13)(*c*) contains an anti-avoidance rule aimed at taxpayers who structure separate leases, each in respect of property with a fair market value of less than $25,000, in order to be excluded from the specified leasing property rules by virtue of Regulation 1100(1.11)(*c*). This anti-avoidance provision will apply where it is reasonable to conclude that one of the main reasons for the existence of the separate leases is to avoid the application of the specified leasing property rules. If applied, each of the separate leases shall be deemed to be a lease of property that had, at the time the lease was entered into, a fair market value in excess of $25,000. As with Regulation 1100(1.13)(*b*)(ii), the test in Regulation 1100(1.11)(*c*) is based on reasonableness. However, the test may arguably be more restrictive in scope than the reasonableness test found in subparagraph (*b*)(ii) since it is only necessary to establish that avoidance of the specified leasing property rules is one of the main reasons for the separate existence of the leases.

It should also be noted that these anti-avoidance rules do not affect the fair market value determination of a property for any other purpose, including the determination of the principal amount of the notional loan under Regulation 1100(1.1)(*a*)(i)(A).

¶269 Changes to the Lease, Lessor, or Leased Property

Regulations 1100(1.15) to (1.2) provide a series of rules which apply when property subject to a lease is sold or altered in any manner, and in situations where the terms of the lease are amended.

Sale of Leased Property

Regulation 1100(1.15) provides that where a taxpayer acquires, from an arm's length person, property that is the subject of a lease with a remaining term of more than one year, the taxpayer shall be deemed to have entered into a lease of the property at the time of acquisition for a term of more than one year. Consequently, where the property is specified leasing property, the specified leasing property rules will apply to the acquirer (i.e., the new lessor). Regulation 1100(1.3) provides that, in the case of a building, the reference to one year in Regulation 1100(1.15) is to be read as three years.

The fair market value of the property at the time the taxpayer acquired it, and the prescribed interest rate in effect at that time, will be used to determine the capital cost allowance restrictions in Regulation

1100(1.1). Regulation 1100(1.16) provides an exception to this rule where the taxpayer acquires a property that was specified leasing property of the vendor in a non-arm's length transaction or by virtue of an amalgamation under subsection 87(1) of the Act. In this case, the taxpayer shall be treated as being the same person and a continuation of the vendor. In other words, the taxpayer will step into the same position as the vendor in respect of the property acquired for purposes of the specified leasing property rules, and any future income tax implications in respect of the property (i.e., recapture or terminal loss).

Replacement of Leased Property

Regulation 1100(1.17) provides rules that apply where a leased property is replaced with a similar property by the lessor for the remaining term of the lease (of the original leased property) and the lease payments remain unchanged. In this case, the replacement property is deemed to have been leased by the taxpayer to the lessee at the same time and for the same term as the original property, and the original property is deemed no longer to be the subject of the lease. The attributes of the original property, such as its fair market value at the time of inception of the lease and the amounts received or receivable in respect of the original property, will be assumed by the replacement property for the purpose of determining whether the replacement property is a specified leasing property, and for the purpose of determining the return of principal applicable to the replacement property under Regulation $1100(1.1)(a)$. However, the replacement property will not assume the attributes of the original property for purposes of Regulation $1100(1.1)(b)$ (the alternative limitation on the available deduction) wherein the amount by which the total capital cost allowance that could have been claimed in respect of the property in earlier years exceeds the total capital cost allowance claimed in respect of the property.

Breakdown of Leased Property

Regulation 1100(1.18) sets out a rule which applies during the time when no lease payments are received or receivable by a lessor as a consequence of a breakdown of the leased property. In this case, the amount or amounts that would have been received or receivable by the lessor is deemed to have been received or receivable by the lessor. The implication of this provision is that amounts deemed to have been received or receivable as lease payments will be relevant for the purpose of determining the lessor's return of principal under Regulation 1100(1.1) and, in turn, affect the amount of capital cost allowance that the lessor is entitled to claim in a particular taxation year.

Additions or Alterations to Leased Property

Where an addition or alteration is made to a leased property and the rent is increased as a consequence of the addition or alteration, Regulation 1100(1.19) will apply to deem the taxpayer to have leased the "addi-

¶269

tional property" to the lessee at the time the addition or alteration is made. Moreover, if the term of the original property lease was greater than one year, the term of the additional property lease will be deemed to be greater than one year, and the prescribed rate for the additional property lease will be deemed to equal the prescribed rate in effect for the original property. Regulation 1100(1.3) provides that, in the case of a building, the reference to one year in Regulation 1100(1.19) is to be read as three years.

In effect, Regulation 1100(1.19) results in the additional property being deemed to have the same attributes as the original property for the purpose of determining whether it is a specified leasing property, and also provides for an increase in the principal balance of the loan attributable to the original property by an amount equal to the fair market value of the additional property. In determining the application of the specified leasing property rules, the $25,000 threshold in Regulation 1100(1.11)(c) will not apply to the additional property.

Renegotiation of Lease

Regulation 1100(1.2) provides rules that apply where a lease is renegotiated in a *bona fide* manner and, as a result, the lease payment is changed. In this case, the original lease will be deemed to have ended and a new lease will be deemed to have been entered into at that time. In addition, Regulation 1100(1.13)(b), which sets out the anti-avoidance rule to prevent situations where taxpayers structure a long-term lease into a series of short-term leases, will not apply to deem the lease period to be greater than one year (or three years in the case of certain leases of buildings). For this exception to apply, however, the renegotiation must be *bona fide*, which presumably requires the process of renegotiation and the eventual results of the negotiation to be fair and representative of economic circumstances.

¶270

Election To Treat Lease as Loan

Unlike the position of the lessor under the specified leasing property rules (outlined in ¶263), whereby the lessor is required to treat certain leases as loans, a lessee may elect to have a lease treated as a purchase and a loan. This election must be made by both the lessor and the lessee in prescribed form (T2145) with their returns of income in the taxation year that the lease is first entered into. Note that this election does not affect the lessor's tax position in any way, although it is likely that the lessor will be subject to the specified leasing property rules anyway. The involvement of the lessor in filing the election is to ensure that the parties agree on the fair market value of the property. Section 16.1 of the Act sets out the elective scheme of rules which apply to treat a lease as a loan for purposes only of the lessee's taxation.

The election is available only with respect to leased tangible property, other than prescribed property, that would otherwise have been depreciable property. The property must be leased from a person with whom the lessee was dealing at arm's length who is resident in Canada (excluding tax exempt entities for leases entered into after 3:30 p.m. Eastern Daylight Savings Time on August 18, 1998), or one who carries on business through a permanent establishment in Canada, provided that the property is used in connection with that establishment and the income from that business is taxable in Canada. For purposes of this provision, a permanent establishment is prescribed by Regulation 8201. As well, the lease must be for a term of more than one year. The exclusion of short-term leases recognizes that short-term leases are not normally used as a means of after-tax financing.

Regulation 8200 defines "prescribed property" that is not eligible to be elected upon as:

(a) tangible property that is the subject of a lease where the fair market value of the property at the time the lease was entered into was not in excess of $25,000;

(b) intangible property; and

(c) property that is exempt property under the specified leasing property rules (see ¶263).

If the election is filed, paragraphs $16.1(1)(a)$, (b), and (c) deem the lessee to have acquired the property at its fair market value and to have borrowed an equivalent amount from the lessor for the purpose of acquiring the property. The reference to the purpose for the borrowing is relevant since it assists in establishing the deductibility of interest on the deemed loan. Under paragraph $16.1(1)(d)$, interest will be deemed to accrue on the principal amount of the deemed loan from the time that the lease is entered into, at the prescribed rate in effect at that time, and will be calculated assuming that it compounds semi-annually, not in advance.

Under Regulation 4302, the rate of interest applicable for a particular month is one percentage point greater than the long-term Government of Canada bond rate for the month before the immediately preceding month. This rate is published by the Bank of Canada at http://www.bankofcanada.ca/en/rates/bonds.html. The monthly prescribed rates for leasing rules are posted on the CRA Web site at http://www.cra-arc.gc.ca/tax/individuals/faq/lease-e.html.

Paragraph $16.1(1)(e)$ provides a hierarchy for determining the nature of rental payments which are considered to be blended payments of principal and interest. Payments under a lease are considered to be, in order, payments of interest, interest on unpaid interest and finally principal. Any payment in excess of these amounts is considered to be an amount paid or payable on account of interest. In such case, the amount is also deemed to be paid or payable on account of a legal obligation to pay interest in

¶270

respect of the year on borrowed money. This latter deeming provision assists in establishing the deductibility of the deemed interest.

Paragraph 16.1(1)(*f*) provides a set of rules which apply on the expiration, cancellation or assignment of the lease, as well as when the subject property is sublet. In such case, the lessee is deemed to have disposed of the property for a specified amount unless subsection 16.1(4) applies (i.e., when property is transferred by reason of an amalgamation or wind-up governed by subsections 87(1) or 88(1), respectively). The specified proceeds of disposition under paragraph 16.1(1)(*f*) are calculated as the amount, if any, by which the aggregate of:

(a) the deemed principal amount of the original deemed loan (i.e., the fair market value of the property at the inception of the lease); plus

(b) any consideration received or receivable by the lessee for cancelling, assigning or subletting;

exceeds the aggregate of:

(c) all deemed principal repayments; plus

(d) all amounts paid or payable by the lessee for the cancellation, assignment, or subletting of the property.

Paragraph 16.1(1)(*g*) deems all amounts paid for the use of, or right to use, the property to have been deducted as such in computing income for purposes of subsections 13(5.2) and (5.3). These subsections apply when a taxpayer acquires or disposes of previously leased property. See ¶210 for a detailed discussion.

Paragraph 16.1(1)(*h*) applies to any amount paid or payable by or on behalf of a lessee for granting or assigning a lease that would otherwise be treated as the cost of a leasehold interest. Such amounts are deemed to have been paid or payable for the use of the property over the remaining term of its lease. Thus, such amounts will be governed by paragraph 16.1(1)(*e*) and treated as payments of interest or principal.

Paragraph 16.1(1)(*i*) applies if an election under section 16.1 is made and the owner ceases to be resident in Canada and no longer holds the property in connection with a business carried on through a permanent establishment in Canada (as defined by regulation). In such case, the lease is deemed to have been cancelled and thus the rules on disposition in paragraph 16.1(1)(*f*) will apply.

Example: Section 16.1 Election

An asset with a fair market value of $50,000 is leased by X from an arm's length party. The prescribed interest rate at the commencement of the lease is 13%. The annual lease cost to X is $6,800 and the asset is subject to a 30% CCA rate on a declining basis. The following example illustrates the effect of a section 16.1 election made by the lessor and X.

¶270

Year	Lease Payment	Principal Repaid	Interest	Principal Outstanding	UCC	CCA
0	—	—	—	$50,000	$50,000	—
1	$ 6,800	$ 300	$ 6,500	49,700	42,500	$ 7,500
2	6,800	339	6,461	49,361	29,750	12,750
3	6,800	383	6,417	48,978	20,825	8,925
4	6,800	433	6,367	48,545	14,578	6,248
5	6,800	489	6,311	48,056	10,204	4,373
6	6,800	553	6,247	47,503	7,143	3,061
7	6,800	625	6,175	46,878	5,000	2,143
8	6,800	706	6,094	46,172	3,500	1,500
9	6,800	798	6,002	45,374	2,450	1,050
10	6,800	901	5,899	44,473	1,715	735
	$68,000	$5,527	$62,473	$44,473	$ 1,715	$48,285

X would be entitled to deduct both the notional interest and the capital cost allowance each year. At the end of the 10 year lease, X will be deemed to have disposed of the asset for the remaining principal amount which is $44,473. If the asset was the only property in the class, X would be subject to recapture of $42,758 ($44,473 (proceeds) − $1,715 (UCC)). The total deduction allowed to X with respect to the asset over the term of the lease would be $68,000 ($62,473 (interest) + $48,285 (CCA) − $42,758 (recapture)). Property subject to an election under section 16.1 is not required to be placed in a separate class. Therefore, the deemed disposition at the end of the lease term does not necessarily result in recapture, but would reduce the UCC balance in the class.

If the original lease provides that the rent varies in accordance with prevailing interest rates, the lessee can elect to use the prescribed rate of interest in effect at the time the interest is being calculated. The election under section 16.1 must be made in respect of all property under the lease, and must be made on Form T2145 and filed with the tax return for the year in which the lease is entered into.

Subsection 16.1(2) applies when a lessee who has made a subsection 16.1(1) election assigns a lease or sublets property to another person ("assignee"). In such case, subsection 16.1(1) ceases to apply from that time. Further, the lessee and the assignee may jointly elect (on Form T2146) to have the provisions of section 16.1 apply to the assignee. In effect, subsection 16.1(1) will apply as if the assignee had leased the property from the owner for a term of more than one year. Subsection 16.1(2) does not apply to assignments or sublets governed by subsection 16.1(3) or (4).

Subsection 16.1(3) applies to property governed by a subsection 16.1(1) election which is assigned or sublet to a non-arm's length party. In this case, the assignee is deemed to be the same person as the original lessee, i.e., the assignee takes over the lessee's position with respect to

¶270

subsection 16.1(1), except that the assignee will have a deemed cost of the property equal to the original deemed principal amount (i.e., fair market value at inception), less any deemed principal repayments by the lessee.

Subsection 16.1(4) applies when a lease which is governed by subsection 16.1(1) is assigned by a corporation to a non-arm's length corporation as a consequence of a subsection 87(1) or 88(1) amalgamation or wind-up. In such case, the assignee is deemed to be the same corporation as and a continuation of the first corporation. Thus, the assignee inherits the lessee's tax position with respect to the lease.

Subsection 16.1(5) applies when a lessor provides to a lessee a similar property to replace the original property which was the subject of the lease, and the amount payable by the lessee for the replacement property is the same as the amount payable for the original property. In this case, subsection 16.1(5) deems the replacement property to be the same property as the original property. As a result, the substitution of the original property with a similar property will not affect the subsection 16.1(1) election made by the lessor and the lessee with respect to the lease for the original property. However, if the rent payable for the replacement property is different than the rent payable for the original property, subsection 16.1(7) (discussed below) will deem the original lease to have expired and a new lease to have been entered into at the time the replacement property is provided by the lessor.

Similarly, subsection 16.1(6) applies when an addition or alteration is made to a property subject to a lease for which the lessee has made an election under subsection 16.1(1), and the rent payable by the lessee for the property is increased as a result of the addition or alteration. In this case, subsection 16.1(6) will deem the lessee to have leased the additional property at that time under a lease for a term of greater than one year, and will deem the lessor and the lessee to have made a subsection 16.1(1) election in respect of the lease of the additional property. In effect, the lessee will be deemed to have acquired the additional property at its fair market value and to have increased the outstanding principal amount of the earlier deemed loan (i.e., the deemed loan in respect of the original subject property before the addition or alteration) by the fair market value of the additional property. The prescribed rate of interest for the additional property will be the same as the prescribed rate in effect for the original property lease.

Subsection 16.1(7) applies when there is a *bona fide* renegotiation in the terms of a lease and, as a result of such renegotiation, the rent payable for the leased property is altered. In this case, the original lease is deemed to have expired and the renegotiated lease will be deemed to be a new lease entered into between the lessor and the lessee at that time. This subsection will not apply if the change in the rental payment is the result of an addition or alteration to the property that is subject to subsection 16.1(6).

¶270

¶275

Change of Control of Corporation or Partnership

Subsection 13(24) is intended to prevent a loss corporation transferring its depreciable property to a profitable corporation in the 12-month period prior to the loss corporation acquiring control of the profitable corporation. It would also apply to acquisition of depreciable property by the profitable corporation from third parties where the property is acquired in contemplation of the acquisition of control.

This subsection provides that, for the purpose of the definition of "undepreciated capital cost" and for investment tax credit and refundable investment tax credit purposes, any depreciable property acquired by the corporation in the 12 months prior to the corporation being acquired by another person or group of persons will be deemed not to have been acquired at that time but, instead, to have been acquired immediately after the acquisition of control. Accordingly, capital cost allowance will not be available for the taxation year which ends immediately prior to the acquisition of control. This rule will not apply if the property was owned by the corporation or a person or persons affiliated with the corporation for the period beginning immediately before the 12-month period prior to the acquisition of control, and ending upon the acquisition of the property by the corporation. For purposes of determining affiliated persons for the rules in subsection 13(24), the reference to "control" means legal (*de jure*) control, not control in fact (*de facto*).

The provisions of subsection 13(24) also apply to acquisitions of depreciable property by a partnership in the 12-month period preceding the acquisition of control of a corporation that is a "majority interest partner", as defined by subsection 248(1).

If any property to which this subsection applies is disposed of prior to the acquisition of control, it is deemed to have been acquired immediately before the disposition.

Subsection 13(25) provides special rules in the event a corporation was incorporated in the 12-month period preceding an acquisition of its control. In that case, it is deemed, for that portion of the 12-month period that precedes its incorporation, to have been in existence and affiliated with any person with whom it was affiliated throughout the portion of the 12-month period subsequent to its incorporation. This subsection is intended to make the exception for acquisitions from affiliated persons available to newly incorporated companies.

CHAPTER 5

TRANSFERS INTER VIVOS AND ON DEATH

¶280

Transfers *Inter Vivos*

¶281 Transfers to Spouses and Common-Law Partners, Former Spouses and Common-Law Partners, and Qualifying Trusts

Section 73 provides an exception to the general rule that a taxpayer who disposes of a capital property must recognize the accrued gain or loss thereon at the time of disposition. Section 73 allows a taxpayer to accomplish an *inter vivos* tax-free "rollover" with respect to capital property where the taxpayer transfers it to the taxpayer's spouse or common-law partner, the taxpayer's former spouse or common-law partner in settlement of rights arising out of the marriage or common-law relationship, or to a trust specified in paragraph 73(1.01)(c). The specifics of the rollover are discussed in more detail below. The transferor may elect out of the rollover, in which case the proceeds of disposition will be those proceeds otherwise determined for the purposes of the Act.

Assuming that the transferor does not elect out of the rollover, it applies automatically so that the realization of any accrued gain, recapture, or terminal loss in respect of a depreciable property will be postponed until the transferee disposes of the property. However, owing to the attribution rules in sections 74.1 to 74.5, the gains and losses realized by the transferee may be attributed to the transferor if the transferee is the transferor's spouse or common-law partner, or a trust for the benefit of the spouse or common-law partner.

The following conditions must be satisfied in order for the rollover to apply:

(1) The property must be capital property;

(2) Both the transferor and the transferee must be resident in Canada at the time of the transfer; and

(3) The transferee must be either:

(a) the transferor's spouse or common-law partner,

(b) the transferor's former spouse or common-law partner and the transfer of the property is in settlement of rights arising out of the marriage or common-law partnership,

(c) a transferee trust that fulfills the conditions described in more detail below.

The first type of trust that qualifies as a transferee for the purposes of the rollover is commonly referred to as a spousal trust or common-law partner trust. This type of trust provides that only the transferor's spouse or common-law partner who is the beneficiary of the trust is entitled to receive all of the income of the trust, and no person other than the spouse or common-law partner may receive or obtain any income or capital of the trust, during the lifetime of the spouse or common-law partner. The term "income" for these purposes is defined in subsection 108(3) and generally means income for trust law purposes.

Two other types of trusts that qualify for the rollover are as follows. Both types of trusts must have been created after 1999 by an individual/ transferor who was at least 65 years of age when the trust was created, and the trust must be for the benefit of the transferor (an "*alter ego* trust"), or the joint benefit of the transferor and the transferor's spouse or common-law partner (a "joint partner trust"). In the case of an *alter ego* trust, the transferor must be entitled to all of the income of the trust that arises before the transferor's death, and no other person may receive or obtain any of the income or capital of the trust before the transferor's death. In the case of a joint partner trust, the transferor or the spouse or common-law partner must be entitled to all of the income of the trust, and no other person may receive or obtain any of the income or capital of the trust, before the later of the death of the transferor and the death of the spouse or common-law partner. See subparagraphs 73(1.01)(*c*)(ii) and (iii) and subsection 73(1.02).

If the above circumstances exist, subsection 73(1) applies automatically unless an election is made by the transferor that the provision not apply (the transferor may elect in his or her income tax return for the year in which the property is transferred that the provisions of subsection

¶281

73(1) not apply). When such an election is made, the proceeds of disposition will normally be the fair market value of the transferred property, since the transferee will normally be a non-arm's length person. In this regard, paragraph 251(1)(b) states that a taxpayer and a personal trust are deemed not to be dealing at arm's length if the taxpayer, or any person not dealing at arm's length with the taxpayer, is beneficially interested in the trust. Therefore, for example, a transfer to a spousal trust, common-law partner trust, or joint partner trust will be a transfer to a non-arm's length person. Furthermore, since the transferor will be affiliated with his or her spouse or common-law partner or such a trust (see paragraphs 251.1(1)(a) and (g)), any potential terminal loss on the transfer of depreciable property will be denied (or at least deferred) under the stop-loss rules of subsection 13(21.2) if the transferee continues to own the property 30 days after the transfer; subsection 13(21.2) is discussed in Chapter 2 at ¶215.

Assuming the election is not made, subparagraph 73(1)(a)(i) provides that where the transferred capital property is depreciable property of a prescribed class, the proceeds of disposition of the transferor are deemed to be that part of the undepreciated capital cost ("UCC") of the class to which the particular property belongs that the fair market value of the property immediately before the time of transfer is of the fair market value of all properties in the class at the time. The transferee (individual or trust) is deemed to acquire the property for this same amount. Subparagraph 73(1)(a)(ii) provides that if the capital property is not depreciable property of a prescribed class, the transferor is deemed to dispose of the property at his adjusted cost base at the time of transfer. The transferee is deemed to acquire the property for this same amount.

If, in the case of depreciable capital property, the capital cost of the property to the transferor exceeds the amount for which the transferee is deemed to acquire the property as described above, subsection 73(2) provides that for the purposes of sections 13 and 20 and the regulations under paragraph 20(1)(a), the capital cost of the property to the transferee is deemed to be the capital cost to the transferor. The amount of the excess is deemed to have been allowed to the transferee as capital cost allowance in years prior to the transfer. The effect of this treatment is to ensure that any built-in recapture that accrued to the time of the transfer is not, on a subsequent disposition of the property, treated as a capital gain.

A transfer of depreciable property to a non-arm's length person other than the transferor's spouse or common-law partner or qualifying trust is generally deemed to take place at the fair market value of the property, subject to the stop-loss rules of subsection 13(21.2); see ¶205 and ¶215. An exception to this general rule applies to depreciable farm property of a class, which can be rolled over to a child of the transferor; see ¶282 below.

¶281

Example: Rollover — Transfer to Spouse

Mr. A has a property in class 8 (his only property in that class) and transfers it to his spouse. Mr. A does not elect to exclude the rollover treatment provided in subsection 73(1).

Capital cost to Mr. A	$100,000
Undepreciated capital cost	60,000
Deemed proceeds to Mr. A	60,000
Acquisition price to spouse	60,000
Deemed capital cost to spouse	100,000
Deemed allowed to spouse as CCA ($100,000 − $60,000)	40,000
UCC to spouse	60,000

If the spouse sells the property for $105,000 she would realize a capital gain of $5,000 and recapture of $40,000. Under subsections 74.1 and 74.2, the capital gain and recapture would be attributed to the transferor, Mr. A, if he were still alive, resident in Canada and married to the spouse. In this way, the recapture and capital gains are postponed on the transfer to the spouse and realized later.

¶282   Transfers of Farm Property

Subsection 73(3) provides for an *inter vivos* rollover of farm land, depreciable property of a prescribed class used in farming, and eligible capital property in respect of a farming business from a taxpayer to the taxpayer's child without the necessity of realizing accrued gains or losses on that land or property.

In order for the rollover under subsection 73(3) to apply, the following conditions must be satisfied:

(1) The subject matter of the transfer must be land in Canada, depreciable property in Canada of a prescribed class, or eligible capital property in respect of a business carried on in Canada by the transferor which, before the transfer, was used principally in a farming business in which the taxpayer, the taxpayer's spouse or common-law partner or any of the taxpayer's children was actively engaged on a regular and continuous basis. (In the case of property used in the operation of a woodlot, these "actively engaged" and "regular and continuous" requirements are not necessary; it is sufficient that the taxpayer, spouse or child was engaged to the extent required by a prescribed forest management plan.) Neither the land, the depreciable property nor the eligible capital property need be used in farming after the transfer.

(2) The transferor must transfer the particular land, depreciable property, or the eligible capital property to a child who is resident in Canada immediately before the transfer. The word "child" is given an expanded meaning by paragraph 70(10)(a) to include a grandchild and a

great-grandchild. Note that the transferor need not be resident in Canada at any time during the transaction.

For the purposes of subsection 73(3), subsection 70(9.8) may deem property owned by a taxpayer to be used in the business of farming if the property is used by a "family farm corporation" or "family farm partnership" in the course of carrying on a farming business in Canada. The taxpayer, the taxpayer's spouse, or the taxpayer's child must have an interest in the corporation or partnership which uses the property in a farming business.

The term "farming" is defined in subsection 248(1) to include a number of activities which might not otherwise be considered as farming.

Subsection 70(9.6) permits such farming assets transferred to a child under subsection 73(3) to be transferred back to a parent on the death of the child on a tax-free or partially tax-free basis.

Depreciable Property of a Prescribed Class

If the subject matter of the transfer consists of depreciable farm property of a prescribed class, the proceeds of disposition deemed to be received by the transferor is determined by applying three mutually exclusive rules set out in paragraph 73(3)(a). To apply these rules it is necessary to ascertain first the "proceeds of disposition otherwise determined". Ordinarily, in a non-arm's length transaction, such proceeds would be the fair market value of the property (section 69). Paragraph 73(3)(c) provides, however, that section 69 does not apply for these purposes, and it appears from the provisions of the three rules discussed below that "proceeds of disposition otherwise determined" is intended to mean the consideration (if any) given by the child on transfer.

The three rules are as follows:

(1) If the consideration given by the child for the depreciable property exceeds the greater of both (a) its fair market value, and (b) its proportionate (based on fair market value) UCC, the proceeds of disposition of the transferor are deemed to be the greater of (a) and (b).

(2) If the consideration given by the child is less than the lesser of (a) the fair market value of the property, and (b) its proportionate UCC, the transferor's proceeds are deemed to be the lesser of (a) and (b).

(3) In any other case, the transferor is deemed to receive proceeds equal to the consideration given by the child.

The third rule effectively provides that where the actual consideration given by the child on the transfer falls between the fair market value and the proportionate UCC of the property, or is equal to either such amount, the actual consideration forms the transferor's proceeds of disposition.

¶282

Under paragraph $73(3)(d)$, the child is deemed to acquire the property for the same amount deemed to be the child's parent's proceeds of disposition. If the capital cost to the parent exceeds the amount at which the child is so deemed to acquire the depreciable property, paragraph $73(3)(e)$ provides that, for the purposes of sections 13 and 20 of the Act and regulations made under paragraph $20(1)(a)$, the child's capital cost is the parent's capital cost and any such excess is deemed to have been allowed the child as capital cost allowance in an earlier year. The effect of this treatment is to ensure that any recapture that accrued to the time of the transfer is not, on a subsequent disposition of the property, treated as a capital gain (see also the example in the box below).

The general effect of subsection $73(3)$ is to permit a rollover of the depreciable property and a postponement of recapture or terminal loss. However, because of the flexibility available in fixing the value at which the depreciable property passes to the child, it would be possible for the parent to realize some recapture on the transfer. If the parent has losses otherwise available in the year, this may be desirable.

The only depreciable property eligible for rollover under subsection $73(3)$ is depreciable property of a prescribed class. Farm property being depreciated on a straight-line basis (as allowed by Part XVII of the regulations, see ¶630) is not depreciable property of a prescribed class. Where a farmer disposes of such property to his or her child, the farmer will be deemed to receive proceeds equal to its fair market value (section 69). There will be no recapture because of ITAR 20(2), and no capital loss because of subparagraph $39(1)(b)(i)$. The farmer may, however, realize a capital gain.

Example: Transfer of Farm Property

Farmer A owns some farm machinery and wishes to transfer it to her son, B. The capital cost to A was $25,000 and the undepreciated capital cost is $15,000. The fair market value of the machinery is $18,000. Farmer A also has some business losses in the year of $3,000.

If A sells the machinery to B for $18,000 (perhaps taking back a promissory note), the following results:

Deemed proceeds to A	$18,000
Recapture to A	3,000
Income of A (recaptured amount − business loss)	0
Capital cost to B	25,000
Deemed taken by B as CCA ($25,000 − $18,000)	7,000
UCC of B	18,000

If B were to sell the machinery for its fair market value, B would suffer no recapture. A incurs the recapture and in the circumstances can use it to her advantage.

If the machinery were sold to B for $15,000, A would incur no recapture, but on a sale by B, B would do so. Since A has losses to be used up (and assuming B

¶282

does not) it appears preferable to sell the machinery for $18,000. A sale for less than $15,000 (A's UCC) will not result in a terminal loss for A because of subparagraph $73(3)(a)(iii)$, which fixes A's proceeds of disposition to at least $15,000.

¶285

Transfers on Death

¶286 General

Subsection $70(5)$ provides a series of rules which apply on the death of a taxpayer to deem the realization of all accrued gains and losses on capital properties owned by the taxpayer immediately before death.

Dispositions in 1992 or Earlier

Where death occurred in 1992 or earlier years, there was an exception to the general rule that all capital property is deemed to be disposed of at fair market value on the date of death. Where the deceased owned depreciable property of a prescribed class immediately before death, the deceased taxpayer was deemed to have disposed of it and to have received proceeds of disposition of an amount half-way between the fair market value of the property immediately prior to death, and the undepreciated capital cost thereof to the deceased at that time.

The person who acquired a depreciable property of a prescribed class of the taxpayer by virtue of the taxpayer's death, acquired it at a cost of that portion of the proceeds of disposition deemed to be received by the deceased for all properties of that class that the fair market value of the property in question was of the fair market value of all properties in that class.

Where the capital cost of depreciable property to the deceased exceeded the amount deemed to be the cost to the beneficiary, the beneficiary's capital cost was deemed to be the deceased's capital cost, and any such excess was deemed to have been allowed to the beneficiary as a deduction in respect of capital cost allowance in years prior to the beneficiary acquiring the property.

The result of these provisions was that recapture of capital cost allowance and terminal losses were reduced for the deceased below what they would have been had the depreciable property been disposed of for its fair market value during life. The amounts of these reductions were passed on to the beneficiary and were realized by the beneficiary when the property was ultimately disposed of.

Dispositions after 1992

For dispositions occurring after 1992, paragraph $70(5)(a)$ provides that a taxpayer who dies in a taxation year is deemed to have disposed, immediately before his or her death, of each capital property (including depreciable property) that was owned by the taxpayer immediately prior to his or her death, for proceeds of disposition equal to the fair market value of such property. Since the property is deemed to have been disposed of prior to death, if the taxpayer is a sole proprietor, capital cost allowance may not be claimed at the time of death, but terminal losses are allowed. Paragraph $70(5)(b)$ provides that a person who, as a consequence of the deceased taxpayer's death, has acquired any such property is deemed to have acquired it for a cost equal to its fair market value at the time of the deemed disposition.

If the capital cost of the depreciable property to the deceased exceeded its fair market value immediately before the death, paragraph $70(5)(c)$ provides that for the purposes of sections 13 and 20 and the regulations under paragraph $20(1)(a)$, the capital cost of the property to the person acquiring the property is deemed to be equal to the capital cost to the deceased. The amount of the excess is deemed to have been allowed to the recipient as capital cost allowance in a previous year. The effect of this treatment is to ensure that any built-in recapture that accrued to the time of the death is not, on a subsequent disposition of the property by the recipient, treated as a capital gain.

For dispositions after 1992, subsection 70(13) provides special rules for purposes of determining capital cost of depreciable property of a deceased taxpayer for deemed dispositions in section 70. Where the capital cost of the deceased taxpayer was previously adjusted as a result of the change-in-use rules outlined in ¶200, the capital cost is to be readjusted for purposes of determining the proceeds of disposition on death. If the taxpayer had acquired the depreciable property entirely for non-income-producing purposes, and later started using it for income-producing purposes, the adjustment required under the change-in-use rules is computed as if only the proportion of the fair market value at the time of change was required to be considered.

Where the proportion of business-use of an asset which had been used both for business and personal use increased, the change-in-use rules in ¶200 are to be applied as if the only applicable rule was the one which prorates the increase according to the fair market value at the time of change by the increase in use.

As well, where the deceased had acquired the depreciable property in a non-arm's length transaction under the rules described in ¶205, the adjustments to the deceased's cost as described in paragraph $13(7)(e)$ are not applied to reduce the cost.

Special rules are in effect for dispositions occurring after 1992 where the property of the deceased is a building and the land on which it is

¶286

situated, and the proceeds of disposition on death are redistributed in accordance with subsection 13(21.1) (see ¶225 for commentary on this subsection). Subsection 13(21.1) will apply to redistribute the proceeds of distribution between land and building to reduce any terminal loss on the building to the extent of any capital gain on the land. In these circumstances where the capital cost of the building to the deceased exceeds the deceased's proceeds of disposition of the building as determined by subsection 13(21.1), paragraph 70(5)(*d*) provides that the capital cost of the building to the recipient is deemed to be the capital cost to the deceased. The difference between the capital cost and the deceased's proceeds of disposition is deemed to be capital cost allowance previously claimed by the recipient. The cost to the recipient of the land is deemed to be the deceased's proceeds of disposition established under subsection 13(21.1).

¶287   Bequests to Spouse or Spouse Trust

Where the depreciable property of the deceased is distributed to the deceased's spouse or spouse trust (or common-law partner or common-law partner trust), subsection 70(6) provides an exception to the rules set out in subsection 70(5). This exception is commonly referred to as the "spousal rollover". The following three criteria must be met for this exception to apply:

(1) The deceased must have been resident in Canada immediately before death.

(2) Property of the deceased to which subsection 70(5) would otherwise apply must have been transferred or distributed on or after the death to one or the other (or both) of the following:

(a) the spouse (or common-law partner) of the deceased who was also resident in Canada immediately prior to the death of the deceased; or

(b) a trust created by the will of the deceased under the terms of which the spouse (or common-law partner) is entitled to receive all income during life, and no other person may, during the spouse's life, receive or have the use of any income or capital; such a trust is usually referred to as a "spouse trust"; the trust must be resident in Canada immediately after the property vests indefeasibly in the trust.

(3) The property in question must become vested indefeasibly in the spouse or spouse trust within 36 months after the death. The vesting period can be extended where the legal representative applies in writing to the Minister within the 36-month period and the Minister considers that a longer period is reasonable in the circumstances.

If these criteria are met, the following rules apply:

(1) Paragraphs 70(5)(*a*) and (*b*) do not apply to the property.

¶287

(2) Instead, the deceased is deemed to have disposed of each depreciable property of a prescribed class immediately prior to death for proceeds of disposition equal to the lesser of:

(a) capital cost; or

(b) the cost amount to the taxpayer immediately before the death.

"Cost amount" is that proportion of undepreciated capital cost of the class of property that the capital cost to the deceased taxpayer of the property of the class is of the capital cost of all property of the class (essentially, a *pro rata* UCC). Where a particular property is not depreciable property of a prescribed class, the proceeds of disposition are the adjusted cost base to the deceased immediately before death.

The spouse or the trust receives the property at a cost equal to these proceeds of disposition. Since the disposition of property of a prescribed class effectively occurs at the lesser of cost or *pro rata* UCC, there should be no possibility of recapture or capital gain. Where the cost to the deceased (capital cost) exceeds proceeds of disposition (lesser of cost and UCC), the difference is considered prior capital cost allowance allowed to the recipient spouse or trust. This means that the recipient spouse or trust under these rules also takes over the prior depreciation of the deceased where, as is usually the case, cost exceeds undepreciated capital cost. The rule ensures an inheritance by the recipient of ordinary tax characteristics, including potential recapture (on a subsequent disposition) where capital cost exceeds UCC.

Subsection 70(6.2) provides that the legal representative of the deceased taxpayer can elect, on an asset by asset basis, not to have the rollover rules to a spouse or a spouse trust apply; this might be done to ensure a full utilization of losses, or the capital gains exemption (if available to the deceased). The election must be made in the return for the deceased's year of death.

For dispositions occurring after 1992, subsection 70(14) provides that the legal representative of the deceased may elect the order in which the various depreciable properties of a prescribed class are considered to have been disposed of.

¶288   Farm Property

Under the usual rules of subsection 70(5), any gain on a farm accrued to the death of its owner would be included in computing the owner's income for the year of death. To encourage the children of farmers to operate the family farm after their parent's death, subsections 70(9) and (9.1) provide special rules under which a family farm may be passed from one generation to the next without immediate tax liability for accrued gains in its value. Similar rules apply under subsections 70(9.2) and (9.3) for the transfer of shares of a family farm corporation or an interest in a family farm partnership. Subsection 70(9.6) permits a re-transfer of such property to a parent on a rollover basis in the event of the death of the child.

Under subsection 70(9), a taxpayer may transfer farmland and depreciable farm property to his or her child at death without the tax consequences of a deemed realization under subsection 70(5). Similarly, under subsection 70(9.1), if a taxpayer has transferred farm and depreciable farm property to an *inter vivos* or testamentary trust for the taxpayer's spouse, the trust will not be considered to dispose of these properties for fair market value on the death of the spouse (as it ordinarily would under subsections 104(4) and (5)) if the property or a replacement property on which the trust has made an election under subsection 13(4) or 44(1) passes on the spouse's death to a child of the taxpayer. In all cases, tax on any accrued gains is postponed until the child disposes of the farm or the depreciable farm property.

Both subsections 70(9) and (9.1) allow a partial rollover to be elected. For an elected partial rollover to be available, all the conditions necessary to obtaining a full rollover must be met.

Rollover Directly to Child

The rollover to a child on the taxpayer's death (under subsection 70(9)) applies if:

(a) the deceased taxpayer owned land in Canada or depreciable property in Canada of a prescribed class;

(b) subsection 70(5) would otherwise apply to the land or depreciable property on the death of the deceased;

(c) before the taxpayer's death, the property in question was used principally in a farming business in which the taxpayer, the taxpayer's spouse or common-law partner or any of the taxpayer's children were actively engaged on a regular and continuous basis. Under the extended definition of "child" in subsection 70(1), a child for these purposes includes a grandchild and a great-grandchild. Note that, in the case of property used in the operation of a woodlot (for transfers after December 10, 2001), the "actively engaged" and "regular and continuous" requirements are not necessary; it is sufficient that the relevant person (the taxpayer, the taxpayer's spouse or child, etc.) be engaged to the extent required by a prescribed forest management plan;

(d) on or after the taxpayer's death the property in question was transferred or distributed to a child of the taxpayer as a consequence of death;

(e) the particular child was resident in Canada immediately before the taxpayer's death; and

(f) within 36 months of death, the property becomes indefeasibly vested in the child. The vesting period can be extended where the

¶288

legal representative applies in writing to the Minister within the 36-month period, and the Minister considers that a longer period is reasonable in the circumstances.

If these criteria are met, subsection 70(9) will apply automatically and permit a tax-free rollover of farmland and depreciable farm property of a prescribed class to the deceased taxpayer's child, unless an election is made to obtain only a partial rollover. Under a full rollover:

(1) Paragraphs 70(5)(*a*) and (*b*) do not apply to the property. That is, the deceased is not deemed to dispose of the property at fair market value and to realize accrued gains and losses.

(2) Instead, the deceased is deemed to dispose of the properties immediately prior to death for special proceeds of disposition. Where the property is depreciable property of a prescribed class, the proceeds of disposition for dispositions after 1992 are deemed to be the lesser of the deceased's capital cost and cost amount. Where the property is land that is described in Class 36 (see ¶195), it is transferred as depreciable property. For land that is not described in Class 36, the proceeds of disposition are deemed to be the adjusted cost base of the land to the deceased immediately before death. Basically, no capital gain, capital loss, recapture, or terminal loss arises in the income of the deceased.

The child who acquires the land or depreciable property is deemed to acquire it at a cost equal to the proceeds of disposition deemed to have been received by the deceased.

(3) Where the capital cost of particular depreciable property to the deceased exceeds the amount deemed to be the cost thereof to the child, the child is deemed to take over his or her parent's capital cost, and to have claimed as capital cost allowance in the past the amount of any such excess. The effect of this rule is to ensure that any recapture that accrued to the time of the deceased's death is not, on a subsequent disposition of the property by the child, treated as a capital gain.

Rollover Through Spouse Trust to Child

The rollover to a child from a spouse or common-law partner trust (under subsection 70(9.1)) applies if:

(a) the deceased taxpayer owned land in Canada or depreciable property in Canada of a prescribed class;

(b) this land or property has been placed in an *inter vivos* or testamentary spouse or common-law partner trust as described in subsection 73(1) or 70(6);

(c) immediately prior to the *spouse's* death (or the common-law partner's death, as the case may be) the property, or a replacement property on which the trust made an election under subsection 13(4) or 44(1), was used in the business of farming (apparently by any person);

¶288

(d) on the death of the spouse and as a consequence of that death, the property was transferred or distributed to a child of the taxpayer and became indefeasibly vested in the child; and

(e) the particular child was resident in Canada immediately before the spouse's death.

If these conditions are met, subsection 70(9.1) allows a rollover on the death of the spouse unless an election is made to obtain only a partial rollover. It will be appreciated, of course, that the original transfer to the spouse trust could also have been made on a tax-free rollover basis. Under a full rollover on the spouse's death:

(1) Subsections 104(4) and (5) do not apply on the death of the spouse. Ordinarily, capital property of a spouse trust (such as farmland) is deemed to be disposed of on the spouse's death under subsection 104(4) and depreciable property is deemed to be disposed of under subsection 104(5) at fair market value.

(2) The trust is deemed to dispose of the farmland and depreciable farm property for special proceeds. In the case of land, the proceeds are the adjusted cost base of the land to the trust. Thus, no capital gain or loss may arise. In the case of depreciable property, the proceeds for dispositions after 1992 are the lesser of the trust's capital cost and cost amount. Thus, no capital gain, recapture, or terminal loss would arise. The child acquiring this land or property on the death of the spouse does so at a cost equal to these proceeds of disposition to the trust. The rollover also applies where the rollover is replacement property for the property originally transferred to the trust. See ¶190.

(3) Where the child acquires depreciable property of a prescribed class on the death of the spouse, and its capital cost to the trust exceeds its deemed cost to the child, the child will assume the position of the trust for capital cost allowance and recapture purposes. The child's capital cost is deemed to be the capital cost to the trust, and the child is deemed to have claimed as capital cost allowance any excess of the capital cost to the trust over the undepreciated capital cost at the death of the spouse.

Elective Partial Rollover

Both subsections 70(9) and (9.1) provide for an election which can be made by the legal representatives of the deceased or the spouse trust, respectively. The election must be made in the return of income of the deceased for the year of death, or the return of income of the spouse trust for the year in which the spouse died. The effect of such an election is that the provisions of paragraphs 70(9)(*b*) or 70(9.1)(*b*), which provide for a deemed disposition at amounts which will produce an automatic complete rollover (as described above), are replaced by alternative rules. Under these alternative rules, the land and depreciable property are deemed to have been disposed of for proceeds equal to such amount as is elected. The elected amount which may be chosen is subject to certain restric-

¶288

tions. In the case of land, the elected amount must be between the adjusted cost base of the land and its fair market value. In the case of depreciable property, the elected amount must be between or equal to one of the following two amounts:

(a) the lesser of:

(i) the cost amount of the property, and

(ii) the capital cost of the property; and

(b) the fair market value of the property.

The cost amount of a particular property is determined on the basis of a portion of the undepreciated capital cost of the class to which the property belongs, based on the relative capital cost of that property compared to the capital cost of all property in that class.

If an elected amount is chosen which is outside the permitted range, the elected amount will automatically be adjusted to the amount which is at the nearest end of the permitted range.

For dispositions after 1992, similar rules as discussed above with respect to subsection 70(5) apply, where the deceased is deemed to dispose of a building and land on which it is situated. The proceeds are to be redistributed in accordance with subsection 13(21.1) (see ¶225). As well, the rules regarding adjustment to cost under subsection 70(13) discussed above (at ¶286) also apply to farm property.

Under the full rollover rules in subsections 70(9) and (9.1), no capital gains, capital losses, recapture of capital cost allowance or terminal losses will be realized, even though these may be inherent in the value of the property. The elections available permit selective realization of such gains, losses, recapture and terminal losses as the circumstances may warrant. It may be desirable to elect amounts which will result in capital gains or recapture where the deceased or spouse trust had losses available from other sources or from prior years to apply against these income inclusions, or where the deceased had a remaining capital gains exemption (in the case of land). Similarly, it may be desirable to elect amounts which will result in capital losses or terminal losses which can be applied against income of the deceased or the spouse trust.

The restrictions on the amount which may be elected to be the proceeds of disposition of a particular property are intended to ensure that the capital gains, capital losses, recapture or terminal losses generated by the use of the elected amount will not be greater than would have arisen had the property been disposed of for fair market value, and to ensure that only gains or capture will be realized, or only losses or terminal losses will be realized, if these are justified by the fair market value.

It should be noted that if the election permitted by subsection 70(9) or (9.1) is made, an elected amount must be designated with respect to each property that would otherwise be given automatic rollover treatment

¶288

under the ordinary rules in those subsections, even if it is intended to avoid the automatic rollover on less than all the property.

As with the ordinary rollover provisions under subsections 70(9) and (9.1), the elected amount which is the proceeds of disposition to the deceased or the spouse trust becomes the cost of the property to the child.

If the farming business is carried on through a corporation or a partnership, a rollover in respect of the shares or interest in the partnership may be available in similar circumstances under subsections 70(9.2) and (9.3).

Rollovers for depreciable farm property apply only to depreciable property *of a prescribed class*. Property on which a farmer is claiming capital cost allowance on the straight-line basis (as allowed by Part XVII of the regulations) is not depreciable property of a prescribed class and neither subsection 70(9) nor (9.1) would apply to it. If the farmer owned this property at death, the farmer would be deemed to dispose of it under paragraph 70(5)(*a*). Similarly, if it was held by a spouse trust, the trust would be deemed to dispose of it on the death of the spouse under subsection 104(5). No recapture would arise in either case because of ITAR 20(2), but tax on any accrued capital gains would be payable. Capital gains accrued to December 31, 1971 would escape tax under ITAR 20(1).

¶288

CHAPTER 6

TRUSTS AND PARTNERSHIPS

¶290

Trusts

As a result of amendments to subsection 104(13), for taxation years of trusts commencing after 1987 a beneficiary is no longer able, by virtue of this subsection, to include in income amounts payable to him or her which would be trust income if no deduction were taken for capital cost allowance under paragraph 20(1)(a), or for terminal loss under subsection 20(16). Prior to these amendments these amounts were included in a beneficiary's income. The beneficiary could then deduct capital cost allowance and terminal loss from the beneficiary's income, to the extent that the trust made a determination under subsection 104(16) to "flow out" these deductions to its beneficiaries. Because of the amendments, subsection 104(16) is no longer needed and has been repealed. The result is that capital cost allowance and terminal loss can no longer be "flowed out" to trust beneficiaries, but as noted below, the same net effect can still be achieved under subsection 104(13.1).

Deductions for capital cost allowance, terminal loss and depletion allowance must now be made at the trust level. If a trust is required to pay out all of its income to beneficiaries prior to making any deductions for these amounts, then the trust will not have any income against which to make these deductions. However, a trust in this situation can take advantage of subsection 104(6) to deduct from its income less than the full amount payable to its beneficiaries. The capital cost allowance and terminal loss can then be applied against the amount payable to the beneficiaries which the trust has not deducted in computing its income.

In turn, this latter amount is not included in the beneficiary's income if an election is made under subsection 104(13.1). The net result is that the capital cost allowance or terminal loss claimed by the trust effectively shelters income that is received by the beneficiaries.

If the trust is a commercial trust, the amount distributed, but not included in the beneficiary's income by virtue of the subsection 104(13.1) election, reduces the adjusted cost base of the beneficiary's interest in the trust pursuant to subparagraph 53(2)(*h*)(i.1). Therefore, such amount may form part of the beneficiary's capital gain on a subsequent disposition of the interest.

On a distribution in satisfaction of all or part of a capital interest in a personal or prescribed trust, subsection 107(2) provides that the following rules apply:

(1) The trust is deemed to dispose of the property which it distributes for proceeds of disposition equal to its "cost amount" to the trust. The cost amount of properties of various kinds is defined in subsection 248(1). For example, if the property is depreciable property of a prescribed class, its cost amount is its *pro rata* portion of the undepreciated capital cost of the class; if it is another type of capital property, the cost amount is the adjusted cost base. In this way, the trust realizes no capital gain or loss, has no recapture or terminal loss, and includes nothing in its income on the distribution.

(2) The beneficiary to whom the property is distributed acquires it at the trust's cost amount of the property plus an additional amount in certain cases. Where the beneficiary's adjusted cost base of the capital interest otherwise determined (generally, the beneficiary's actual or "hard" cost of the interest) exceeds his or her "cost amount" of the capital interest (as defined in subsection 108(1)), the beneficiary's cost of the property is increased by an amount equal to:

(a) in the case of capital property other than depreciable property, or eligible capital property in respect of a business of the trust, the whole of this excess; and

(b) in the case of any other type of property, including depreciable capital property, 50% of this excess.

Where there is no such addition, the beneficiary takes the property over at the trust's cost amount and assumes the obligation to eventually account for accrued gains or losses and recapture or terminal losses which accrued while the trust held the property. For example, where the capital interest was acquired gratuitously, such as on the creation of the trust or otherwise under the terms of the trust, the beneficiary's adjusted cost base otherwise determined will be nil, and the above-noted addition will not apply.

¶290

The addition to the cost of the distributed property to the capital beneficiary is intended to deal with situations where the beneficiary acquired the capital interest from another beneficiary (original beneficiary), and therefore had an actual or "hard" cost of the interest otherwise determined in excess of the cost amount of the distributed property. In this case, the beneficiary will have its cost of the distributed property increased in the manner described above.

(3) The beneficiary is deemed to dispose of the appropriate part of his or her capital interest for proceeds of disposition equal to the cost of the properties he or she acquires (computed using rule (2) above), except that for this purpose, regardless of the type of property distributed, the cost thereof is deemed to have been increased by the whole of any excess in the adjusted cost base of the beneficiary's capital interest in the trust otherwise determined over the cost amount of the capital interest. If the beneficiary is obliged to assume a debt or other obligation to pay an amount as a condition of the distribution, such debt or amount is deducted in arriving at his or her proceeds of disposition. To determine whether the beneficiary has a capital gain or loss on this disposition, if the trust is a personal or prescribed trust, subsection 107(1) must be applied. In the case of a capital interest in a personal or prescribed trust acquired at no cost, the beneficiary realizes no capital gain or loss on distribution. In cases where value was paid for the capital interest, no capital gain may result but the distribution may give rise to a capital loss if any debts are assumed as a condition of the distribution of property. Capital gains or losses may be realized on subsequent dispositions of the distributed property.

(4) Where depreciable property is distributed in satisfaction of a capital interest, and the trust's capital cost of it exceeds the cost at which by paragraph 107(2)(b) the beneficiary is deemed to acquire it, special rules apply which in general place the beneficiary in the trust's position for claiming capital cost allowance and recognizing recapture or terminal losses. In particular, paragraph 107(2)(d) provides that, for the purposes of sections 13 and 20 of the Act and the regulations made under paragraph 20(1)(a) respecting capital cost allowance, the beneficiary's capital cost is deemed to be the trust's capital cost. The beneficiary is considered to have claimed as capital cost allowance any excess of the trust's capital cost over the cost at which the beneficiary is deemed to acquire the asset.

Note that the rollover provisions of subsection 107(2) do not apply if subsection 107(2.1) applies to the distribution of the property in consideration for all or part of the beneficiary's capital interest in the trust. Subsection 107(2.1) applies in the following circumstances: Where either the trust or the beneficiary elect out of the rollover (subsections 107(2.001) and (2.002), respectively); where a spousal or common-law partner trust distributes the property to a person other than the spouse or common-law partner while the latter is alive (subsection 107(4)); where the trust is subject to subsection 75(2) and distributes the property to someone other than the person who contributed the property to the trust

¶290

or the spouse or common-law partner of such person, while the person is alive; or if the distribution is to a non-resident (subsection 107(5)). Where subsection 107(2.1) applies, the property is not distributed on a rollover basis. Instead, the trust is deemed to have disposed of the property for proceeds equal to its fair market value at the time of distribution and the beneficiary's cost is also deemed to be that fair market value. Thus, if the property is depreciable property, the trust may realize recapture and/or a capital gain, or a terminal loss. However, if the beneficiary is affiliated with the trust after the distribution of the property, for example, if the beneficiary is a "majority-interest beneficiary" of the trust after the distribution (see section 251.1), the stop-loss rule of subsection 13(21.2) may apply to deny any potential terminal loss; subsection 13(21.2) is discussed in Chapter 2 at ¶215.

¶291   Deemed Disposition of Assets

Subsection 70(5) provides that upon death, persons are deemed to dispose of their capital properties and, as a result, accrued unrealized capital gains will usually be subject to tax. To prevent persons from circumventing these provisions by settling their property upon trusts of prolonged duration, subsections 104(4), (5), and (5.2) provide that the trust itself is deemed to dispose of certain properties periodically. The properties covered by this deemed disposition are capital property (both depreciable and non-depreciable), Canadian and foreign resource properties and land inventory of the trust. On the deemed disposition, the trust may realize ordinary income and losses, capital gains and losses, and recapture. Unless the deemed disposition applies on the death of the beneficiary spouse or common-law partner (in the case of a spouse or common-law partner trust), or on the death of the settlor (in the case of an *alter ego* trust), the first possible date on which the rule applies is normally 21 years after the creation of the trust. Deemed dispositions of the trust's assets will continue to occur every 21 years after the initial application of the rule.

At each disposition time the trust is deemed by subsection 104(5) to dispose of all depreciable property of each prescribed class for proceeds equal to fair market value (if the deemed disposition occurred after 1992), and to have reacquired the property generally at a capital cost ("deemed capital cost") equal to the same amount. On the deemed disposition the trust may realize capital gains or recapture. No capital loss may be realized on a disposition of depreciable property (paragraph 39(1)(*b*)). A terminal loss cannot occur on the deemed disposition under subsection 20(16) because the trust continues to own the property at the time of the deemed disposition and there is no deemed year-end.

Example: Disposition under subsection 104(5)

	Case I	Case II	Case III
Capital cost of class 8 property......	$50,000	$50,000	$ 50,000
Undepreciated Capital Cost	35,000	35,000	35,000
Fair Market Value.................	45,000	70,000	30,000
Deemed Proceeds.................	45,000	70,000	30,000
Recapture	10,000	15,000	nil
Capital gain.....................	nil	20,000	nil
Denied Terminal loss	nil	nil	5,000

The terminal loss in Case III is not allowed under subsection 20(16) because the trust continues to own the property after the deemed disposition occurs.

If the original capital cost of the depreciable property to the trust immediately prior to the application of the deemed disposition rule is greater than the deemed capital cost, paragraph $104(5)(a)$ provides that for the purposes of sections 13 and 20, and the capital cost allowance regulations made under paragraph $20(1)(a)$, the capital cost of the property is the original capital cost, and the trust is deemed to have claimed the excess as capital cost allowance in the earlier years. If, for example, the trust disposes of the property in Case I (in the example above) for proceeds of disposition of $50,000 after the application of the rule, $5,000 will be treated as recaptured depreciation and not as a capital gain.

Paragraph $104(5)(b)$ provides that subsection 13(1) is read so as to add into income in a particular taxation year the amount of recaptured depreciation which results at the time that the depreciable property is deemed to be disposed of, rather than including the excess which remains at the end of the taxation year. Therefore, for example, recapture cannot be avoided as a consequence of the trust being deemed to reacquire its property immediately after the application of the rule. Paragraph $104(5)(c)$ provides that recaptured depreciation which results from a deemed disposition under that section is to be treated as an inclusion under section 13 for a prior taxation year for the purpose of computing any excess under subsection 13(1) at the end of the year in which the deemed disposition takes place.

Where farm land, depreciable property of a prescribed class that is used in the farming business in Canada, shares of the capital stock of a family farm corporation, or an interest in a family farm partnership has or have been transferred to the children of a settlor of a qualifying spousal or common-law partner trust on the death of the spouse or common-law partner, subsections 104(4) and (5) will not operate to deem a disposition and reacquisition at fair market value on the spouse's death, since specific

¶291

rollovers are available in these circumstances under subsections 70(9.1) and (9.3).

The deemed disposition rule in subsection 104(5) does not apply to depreciable property that is not of a prescribed class. For example, it does not apply to depreciable property used in connection with a farming or a fishing business as described in Part XVII of the regulations (see ¶630).

¶295

Partnerships

Capital cost allowance in respect of depreciable property is claimed at the partnership level in the computation of the partnership income, and is not directly claimed by the partners themselves. Investment tax credits earned by a partnership on expenditures in its fiscal period are allocated to partners to the extent that may reasonably be considered to represent the partners' shares (subsection 127(8)). The investment tax credits so earned reduce the capital cost of related property in the partnership at the end of the fiscal period in which they are earned, regardless of when (if ever) they are used by the partners (subsection 127(12)).

¶296 Transfers of Property to Partnership

Property transfers to a partnership from partners or from persons who are partners immediately after the transfer, are deemed to have taken place at the fair market value of the property at the time of transfer pursuant to subsection 97(1). Accordingly, on formation of a partnership or on admittance to an existing partnership, the new partner is deemed to have disposed of the property introduced into the partnership at its fair market value and the partnership is deemed to have acquired the property at that value. If the partnership and the partner are affiliated after the transfer, say, if the partner is a "majority interest partner" (see the definition in subsection 248(1) and section 251.1), the various stop-loss rules may apply to deny the immediate recognition of accrued losses (e.g., subsection 13(21.2), which may apply to transfers of depreciable property and which is discussed in Chapter 2 at ¶215).

In order to avoid the tax imposed on what in fact may be an unrealized gain, a rollover is provided under subsection 97(2) in the case of a Canadian partnership whereby all partners jointly elect in prescribed form and within prescribed time to have an "elected amount" deemed to be the proceeds of disposition of the property to the partners, and the same amount deemed to be the cost of the property acquired by the partnership.

The prescribed form for making an election under subsection 97(2) is T2059. The election is to be filed within the time set out in subsection 96(4), but may be filed at a later time as permitted by subsection 96(5) if a penalty is paid. The filing deadline pursuant to subsection 96(4) is the earliest of the tax-filing date for the partner/transferor and each member of the partnership for the taxation year in which the transfer takes place. The filing extension under subsection 96(5) is limited to three years after that date. If the election is not filed within this extended time, none can be made except with the consent of the Minister (subsection 96(5.1)).

The joint election will permit property to be transferred to a Canadian partnership on a fully or partially tax-deferred basis as desired. Generally, the election is used to fully defer tax by transferring the properties at tax values or cost amounts (e.g., adjusted cost base, undepreciated capital cost). In this case, the tax values of the properties are allocated to the consideration received (forming its cost base) and the partnership assumes the transferee's tax position in respect of the properties.

Example: Transfer of Property to Partnership under Subsection 97(2)

Assume the following:

	Original cost	Tax values	Fair market value	Elected amount
Inventory	$ 300	$ 300	$ 400	$ 300
Building	20,000	12,000	15,000	12,000
Land	10,000	10,000	30,000	10,000
			45,400	22,300

Further, assume that the only consideration received was a partnership interest with a value equal to the combined fair market value of the property transferred.

The elected amount was selected for each property so that the transferee would not realize any income, recapture or capital gains. The adjusted cost base of the partnership interest will be $22,300 (equal to the total of the elected amounts, and also the tax values of the transferred property) as determined by paragraph 97(2)(b).

The partnership will be deemed to have acquired the property at the elected amounts and will use these for computing its taxable income in the future. Pursuant to subsection 97(4), the partnership will be deemed to have the same original cost of $20,000 for the building as the transferor and to have previously claimed capital cost allowance of $8,000 being the difference between cost and the elected amount (i.e., the undepreciated capital cost). The partnership, therefore, inherits the transferor's position regarding future recapture and/or capital gains on the building.

As an alternative, the transferee could have received property other than a partnership interest (such as cash or debt, referred to as hard consideration) as part of the consideration. The tax-deferred status of the transfer is preserved in this case, provided this form of consideration does not exceed the elected amounts. In this example, the transferor could, for example, receive $22,300 of debt and a partnership interest valued at $23,100 for total consideration equal to the value of the property transferred ($45,400). The adjusted cost base of the partnership interest would be nil since the entire elected amount would be absorbed by the debt consideration.

¶296

The basic parameters for the elected amount under the joint election of subsection 97(2) are established by paragraphs 85(1)(*b*) and (*c*) which provide the upper and lower limits for the elected amount. Paragraph 85(1)(*c*) will automatically reduce an excessive elected amount to the fair market value of the transferred property and so prevent any artificial increase in the transferee's cost base of the property. This, for example, prevents a taxpayer with unused losses from effectively transferring them to another taxpayer. This could otherwise be done by transferring, for example, inventory or depreciable property at an artificially high value to a partnership with a taxable person that is earning taxable income in an attempt to shelter that income with the "stepped-up" basis for the transferred property.

Correspondingly, paragraph 85(1)(*b*) will generally increase an initial elected amount to the fair market value of the hard consideration received if the initial elected amount is less than this value. This prevents a taxpayer from immediately realizing value (as opposed to the deferred value of a partnership interest) for the transferred property in excess of the taxpayer's proceeds of disposition (elected amount).

Paragraph 85(1)(*e*) contains provisions to ensure that an artificial loss is not created on a transfer of depreciable property. To accomplish this an initial elected amount is automatically adjusted to the least of:

(a) the undepreciated capital cost of all property in the class;

(b) the cost of the property; and

(c) the fair market value of the property.

Separate reference to the cost of the particular property transferred and the particular class's undepreciated capital cost of the business is required to reflect the fact that the undepreciated capital cost may represent several properties, some or all of which are transferred.

Paragraph 85(1)(*e.1*) provides special ordering rules applicable when the undepreciated capital cost represents more than one property. Paragraph 85(1)(*e*) refers to an amount that may represent several properties (undepreciated capital cost of a class). Since an elected amount must be determined for each property, a simultaneous disposition could create difficulties. For example, the undepreciated capital cost of a class is otherwise unchanged by the disposition of each individual property so that at some point the undepreciated capital cost of the class can become the minimum for the elected amount, resulting in recaptured depreciation.

¶296

Example: Transfer of Class 8 Properties

Consider two Class 8 properties:

	Property A	*Property B*
Cost of property	$2,000	$5,000
Fair market value	1,000	6,000
Undepreciated capital cost of class	$4,000	

In the case of non-depreciable property, an elected amount of $4,000 would establish a tax-deferred transfer. However, in the absence of an ordering for the disposition of depreciable property, the undepreciated capital cost of the class will remain at $4,000 for both dispositions, so that the minimum amount that could be elected would be $1,000 for property A (its value) and $4,000 (the undepreciated capital cost of the class) for property B. The combined $5,000 proceeds of disposition would result in $1,000 of recaptured depreciation. Paragraph 85(1)(e.1) alleviates this problem by allowing the transferor to determine the order of disposition. (The Minister can designate the order if the taxpayer fails to do so.) Extending the example, the transferor could designate property A as the first disposed of (at an elected amount of $1,000), reducing the undepreciated capital cost of the class to $3,000 so that this amount could be used as the minimum elected amount for property B.

As a practical matter, the Canada Revenue Agency has stated that this ordering does not need to be filed with a subsection 85(1) election, but should be retained by the taxpayer for examination in cases where all the assets of a class are transferred. Presumably this policy will be extended to transfers under subsection 97(2).

Although the provisions of subsections 97(2) and 85(1) can result in the realization of an inherent terminal loss, subsection 13(21.1) (discussed at ¶225) can result in a denial of this loss in the case of a building if the transferor or a non-arm's length person owned the related land. Furthermore, the terminal loss in respect of any property may be denied under subsection 13(21.2) if the taxpayer and the partnership are "affiliated persons" (subsection 251.1(1)), which will be the case, for example, if the taxpayer is a majority interest partner of the partnership. Subsection 13(21.2) is discussed at ¶215.

¶297 Potential Recapture of Depreciation

Depreciable property transferred to a partnership at an amount agreed upon by all partners, as reported in a prescribed election form, will carry with it into the partnership the potential recapture of depreciation not recaptured by the transferring partner at that time. Where a partner transfers such property to a partnership for an amount less than the partner's capital cost, the partnership will be deemed to have acquired the property at an amount equal to the capital cost of the property to the partner and to have previously claimed the difference as capital cost allowance, so that there may be recaptured depreciation realized on a future sale (subsection 97(4)).

Subsection 97(4) does not apply to a taxpayer who, under subsection 98.1(1), is deemed to have retained a continuing partnership interest in the partnership because the taxpayer still has a right to receive property from the partnership. Such a taxpayer is not regarded as a partner for the purposes of subsection 97(4). If such a taxpayer sold depreciable property to the partnership, the taxpayer's proceeds and the partnership's cost would be the actual amount paid and received.

¶298   Disposition of Assets by Partnership

No rules corresponding to the rules on transfers of assets to partnerships apply on transfers of assets from a partnership to its members during its existence, probably for the reason that, if assets could move both into and out of partnerships without tax consequences, persons could effect tax-free exchanges of assets through the medium of a partnership.

Accordingly, the general rule under subsection 98(2) provides that where a partnership disposes of property to a partner, the disposition is deemed to take place at fair market value, subject to subsections 98(3) and (5) and 85(3), discussed below. The fair market disposition under subsection 98(2) may be subject to adjustments under paragraph $13(7)(e)$ (see ¶205) or subsection 13(21.1) (see ¶225). Furthermore, if the partner is affiliated with the partnership after the disposition, for example, if the partnership continues in existence and the partner is a "majority interest partner", the various stop-loss rules may apply to deny the immediate recognition of accrued losses (e.g., subsection 13(21.2), which may apply to dispositions of depreciable property and which is discussed at ¶215).

If all property of the partnership has been distributed to the partners, the partnership is no longer deemed to exist under subsection 98(1). If the property has been distributed in such a manner that each partner received his or her individual share of the property, such as specific accounts receivable allocated to each partner, inventory distributed in separate lots to each, or marketable securities divided amongst them, the fair market value applies to the property distributed.

Notwithstanding the general rule in subsection 98(2), rollovers are available to defer taxation in the following four situations:

(1) If a Canadian partnership has ceased to exist and all its property has been distributed to persons who were partners immediately before that time in such a manner that, immediately after the distribution, each such person has an undivided interest in each property distributed, the former partners have the right under subsection 98(3) to elect that fair market values do not apply. Each person's individual interest in a property must equal that person's undivided interest in each other such property (that person's "percentage").

¶298

(2) Where a Canadian partnership has ceased to exist but the business is carried on by a sole proprietor, subsection 98(5) provides an automatic rollover at tax values of property which continues in the business.

(3) Subsection 98(6) effectively permits a rollover from one Canadian partnership to another if all new partnership members were old partnership members; old partnership members can be shed but not added under this provision.

(4) Subsections 85(2) and (3) effectively permit the incorporation of a partnership on a rollover basis provided all partners (and the corporation) jointly elect.

Where property is distributed to persons who were partners so that subsection 98(3) applies, if the adjusted cost base of a partner's interest in the partnership exceeds the aggregate of the partner's percentage of the cost amounts of the partnership's properties (which would theoretically result in a capital loss to the partner at that time if the partner were permitted to recognize it for tax purposes) the excess can be designated by the partner and increase the cost to him or her of capital property received from the partnership (other than depreciable property) (paragraph 98(3)(b)). This write up of the cost base of capital property in the partner's hands is known colloquially as a "cost bump". (A similar rule applies to rollovers under subsection 98(5).) However, the designation of such excess to each property is subject to the following two rules:

(a) the amount designated cannot be more than the excess of the partner's percentage of the fair market value of the property at that time over the partner's percentage of the property's "cost amount"; and

(b) the amount designated cannot be more than the excess of the partner's adjusted cost base of the partner's interest over the aggregate of the partner's percentage of the "cost amounts" of all of the distributed properties (paragraph 98(3)(c)).

As noted, the "cost bump" does not apply to depreciable property. However, prior to December 5, 1985, one-half the excess of the partner's cost base of his or her partnership interest over the cost amount of property acquired could be used to increase the cost to the partner of depreciable property or property other than capital property. This provision formerly contained in paragraph 98(3)(d) was repealed because it was used in a manner considered abusive as part of the so-called "little Egypt bump". Partners and partnership property pre-dating December 5, 1985 are still entitled to utilize the much broader partnership bump rules under a transitional provision. The effect of this transitional rule is that, where it applies, a partner who qualifies for a bump in the cost base of property may allocate the amount of the bump not only to non-depreciable capital property, but also to depreciable capital property and non-capital property such as inventory and eligible capital property. The choice of

¶298

property to which or among which the allocation will be made is entirely within the discretion of each partner eligible for a bump. Where an allocation is made to property other than capital property, only half of the amount allocated will increase the cost of such property. That is to say, it requires $2 of allocation of excess cost to achieve a $1 bump in the cost of property other than capital property.

Allocations to depreciable and non-capital property subject to a subsection 98(3) election may be made under the transitional rules after December 4, 1985, only by a partner who acquired his or her (or its) partnership interest before December 5, 1985, or acquired it under a written agreement entered into before that date, or acquired it in a non-arm's length transaction from a person who held it before that date. It does appear possible for transitional protection to flow through a chain of non-arm's length transactions, provided there is no intervening arm's length acquisition.

If the partner is a corporation, allocations under the transitional rule can only be made if the corporation has not undergone a change of control since December 4, 1985.

In addition to the limitation on which partners can allocate a cost bump to other than capital property, the transitional rule only permits such an allocation to depreciable and non-capital property held by the partnership prior to December 5, 1985.

It follows from these rules that where a subsection 98(3) election is made, some partners making the election may be eligible for transitional rule protection while others will not. As well, not all non-capital property will be eligible for cost bump even to qualifying partners.

¶299   Problems of Recapture of Depreciation on Termination of Partnership

As noted above, if a partnership terminates and the partnership's property is distributed to the former partners so that each former partner has an undivided interest in the property (the partner's "percentage"), the rollover under subsection 98(3) can apply if the partners jointly elect that it apply. In order to preserve the potential tax on recaptured depreciation in respect of depreciable property distributed, the following additional rules are applicable to the former partner (paragraph 98(3)(*e*)):

(a) the former partner's capital cost of his or her interest in the depreciable property shall be deemed to be an amount equal to his or her percentage of the capital cost of that property to the partnership; and

(b) the excess of this deemed capital cost over the deemed proceeds (if any) shall be deemed to have been allowed to the former partner as capital cost allowance deductions in earlier years and, accordingly, may be subject to recapture in his or her hands upon a subsequent disposition.

Example: Recapture of Depreciation

Depreciable property — capital cost to partnership		$ 10,000
— total capital cost allowance claimed by partnership.		8,000
Undepreciated capital cost (cost amount) to partnership		$ 2,000
Partners' calculated percentage — based on cost	40%	60%
Partners' deemed capital cost (40% and 60% of $10,000) . . .	$4,000	$ 6,000
Partners' deemed cost of interest in property (40% and 60% of cost amount of $2,000)	800	1,200
Excess — deemed previous capital cost allowance to partner	$3,200	$ 4,800

The two partners would remain subject to a potential recapture totalling $8,000 which is the total depreciation deducted by the partnership.

If the depreciable property is transferred to a partner under subsection 98(2) (e.g., no joint election by partners under subsection 98(3)), the fair market value rule could result in partial or full recapture to the partnership, but the partner's cost would be the fair market value of the depreciable property at that time. If, for instance, the original cost of certain depreciable property to the partnership had been $1,000, and at the time of its transfer to the partner its fair market value had been $750 and its undepreciated capital cost $500, under subsection 98(2) the partnership's proceeds and the partner's cost would be $750. The partnership would have recaptured $250 of depreciation previously claimed (excess of $750 proceeds over $500 undepreciated capital cost), but the partner could realize a potential capital gain if the partner later sold the property for more than $750, even though the original cost to the partnership was $1,000. This partial recapture by the partnership is in contrast to the complete flow through of accrued recapture to the transferee of depreciable property under the following situations:

(a) Acquisition of depreciable property by partnership from partners (whether majority interest partners or not) — subsection 97(4) provides for complete flow through to partnership.

(b) Distribution of depreciable property by partnership to partners on cessation of partnership and joint election by all partners — paragraph 98(3)(*e*) provides for full flow through to partners.

(c) Continuance of partnership business as sole proprietorship by one partner — paragraph 98(5)(*e*) prescribes complete flow through to this partner.

¶299

(d) Transfer of partnership assets to a Canadian corporation — subsection 85(5) provides for complete flow through to the corporation.

In a non-arm's length disposition of depreciable property by a partnership to which subsection 98(2), rather than 98(3), is applicable, and the deemed fair market value proceeds of disposition exceed the capital cost of the property to the partnership, the partner's capital cost will be deemed to be equal to the capital cost of the partnership plus one-half of the aforementioned excess. This assumes that paragraph 13(7)(*e*) (see ¶205) overrides the general rule in subsection 98(2) by virtue of its notwithstanding clause. In addition, subsection 13(21.1) may operate to adjust the capital cost of land and building, although this is less clear in the absence of a similar notwithstanding clause.

Example: Operation of Subsection 98(3) Election

The effect of an election under subsection 98(3) on the partners of a two-person partnership can be illustrated as follows:

Partnership property immediately before cessation:		*Cost amount*	*Fair market value*
Cash		$ 3,000	$ 3,000
Capital property — other than depreciable property:			
Adjusted cost base		10,000	14,000
Depreciable property			
Cost	$25,000		
Total capital cost allowance claimed	13,000		
Undepreciated capital cost		12,000	18,000
Total		$25,000	$35,000

Partners' percentage interest in partnership and their adjusted cost base (assumed):

	Percentage interest	*Adjusted cost base*
A	40%	$ 8,000
B	60%	24,000

¶299

Calculation of partners' deemed proceeds of disposition (paragraph $98(3)(a)$):

Greater of:		*Partner A*	*Partner B*	*Total*
I.	Adjusted cost base	$ 8,000	$24,000	$32,000
	and			
II.	Money received	$ 1,200	$ 1,800	$ 3,000
	Aggregate percentage of cost amounts to partnership of capital property			
	Non-depreciable	4,000	6,000	10,000
	Depreciable	4,800	7,200	12,000
		$10,000	$15,000	$25,000
	Deemed proceeds (greater of I and II)	$10,000 (II)	$24,000 (I)	
	Realized capital gain	$ 2,000	nil	

Partner A realizes a capital gain of $2,000 on cessation of the partnership. The cost to Partner A of the properties acquired is as follows:

Cash		$ 1,200
Capital property		
Non-depreciable		4,000
Depreciable		
Cost 40% of $25,000	$10,000	
Deemed previous capital cost allowance	5,200	4,800
Total		$10,000

Partner A therefore remains subject to a potential recapture in respect of part or all of the $5,200 deemed capital cost allowance taken on the depreciable capital property, and also may be taxable at the time Partner A sells the non-depreciable capital property.

Partner B for tax purposes has no gain or loss on cessation of the partnership. However, since Partner B's adjusted cost base of his partnership interest exceeds the share of the aggregate of "cost amounts" by $9,000 ($24,000 less $15,000), Partner B is entitled to designate the allocation of the excess to the non-depreciable capital property received from the partnership.

Paragraph $98(3)(c)$ — Designated amount cannot exceed:

(a) Non-depreciable capital property:

Percentage of fair market value (60% of $14,000)	$8,400
Minus percentage of cost amount (60% of $10,000)	6,000
Excess	$2,400

and

(b) Excess of adjusted cost base over aggregate of percentage of all cost amounts $9,000

¶299

Partner B will be entitled to designate that $2,400 of the $9,000 excess be added to the "cost amount" of the non-depreciable capital property and Partner B's cost will be deemed to be $8,400. If Partner B sells the property at the time of cessation for its fair market value, Partner B will not realize a gain; if the sale is deferred, Partner B would be taxable only on any increase in value which takes place after obtaining the property from the partnership.

The provisions of subsection 98(3) are relatively complex. They are necessary to defer the taxation of capital gains (in most instances) and the deductibility of capital losses. These provisions are also necessary to ensure the potential recapture of depreciation in the partners' hands, since the fair market value rule in subsection 98(2) (which otherwise imputes fair market value as proceeds of disposition to the partnership) is, in effect, waived on the transfer of property to the partners on the cessation of the partnership (paragraph 98(3)(*f*)).

¶299

CHAPTER 7

CLASSES

¶350
Regulation 1100(1)(a)

¶352 Classes of Property Listed in Regulation 1100(1)(a)

Under Regulation 1100(1)(a), provision is made for deductions in respect of property of each of Classes 1 to 12, 16, 17, 18, 22, 23, 25, 26, 28, 30, 31, 32, 33, 35, 37, 41, 42, 43, 43.1 and 44 (and by draft regulation, Classes 45 and 46) in Schedule II. The allowable rate of capital cost allowance is set out for each of these classes, expressed as a percentage of the undepreciated capital cost of property of the class to the taxpayer as at the end of the taxation year. These percentages range from 4% to 100%. It may be noted that Class 8 in Schedule II is an omnibus class relating to property that is a tangible capital asset not included in any other class in the schedule (and not excluded elsewhere in the regulations); the rate prescribed in Class 8 is 20%.

The types of assets on which CCA may not be taken are enumerated in Regulations 1102(1) to (3), in Class 8 and some other classes of Schedule II. See the commentary at ¶115 for these exclusions. Note that Schedule II is reproduced in full at ¶2420 *et seq.*

Similar assets may sometimes fall into different classes depending on the date they are acquired. One example of this is assets used in manufacturing or processing in Canada. These can be included in Class 29, 39 or 43, and in some instances Class 10 or 40, depending on the acquisition date. Note that for purposes of determining the class in which the asset is included, the relevant date is the date of acquisition, not the date on which the asset becomes available for use (see ¶130).

¶355   Classes of Property *Not* Listed in Regulation 1100(1)(*a*)

Classes 13, 14 and 15 refer to leaseholds, patents, and woods assets, respectively. Capital cost allowance on properties in these classes is calculated according to a special formula in each case. See ¶420 (leaseholds), ¶425 (patents), and ¶430 (woods assets).

Classes 19, 20 and 21 provide for capital cost allowance on assets acquired during the 1960s on the straight-line method, essentially, at rates greatly in excess of the rates at which capital cost allowance is generally allowed by the declining balance method. See ¶450, ¶455 and ¶460, respectively.

In order to give tax incentives to particular segments of industry, special provision may be made for an accelerated write-off of assets. Thus, Regulations 1100(1)(*t*) and (*ta*) provided for the fast write-off of equipment in Classes 24, 27, 29 and 34. See ¶475, ¶490, ¶500 and ¶520, respectively. As well, additional allowances may be claimed over and above the rate for the class for certain types of assets. For example, Regulation 1100(1)(*va*) provides for an additional 15% on top of the regular 15% for offshore drilling vessels in Class 7. See ¶390.

Special rules are provided with respect to property that was leased by a taxpayer and then acquired at a cost of less than fair market value. Class 36 includes such property which is deemed to be depreciable property under these special rules but is not eligible for capital cost allowance. See ¶195 and ¶430.

Classes 38, 39 and 40 provide for capital cost allowance expressed as a percentage of undepreciated capital cost. The rates were phased in from 1988 to 1991. See ¶540, ¶545 and ¶550, respectively.

¶359

Rates and Inclusions

¶360   Class 1 (4%) — Buildings and Railway Assets, etc.

There are five general categories of assets that are included in Class 1 (4%). These are as follows:

(1) certain structures having to do with water or the diversion of water, including a bridge, canal, culvert or dam, and a jetty or mole acquired before May 25, 1976 (a jetty or mole acquired after May 25, 1976 is included in Class 3);

(2) certain surface constructions such as roads, parking areas and runways acquired before May 26, 1976, and subways or tunnels acquired after May 25, 1976 (surface constructions acquired after May 25, 1976 are included in Class 17);

(3) certain railway equipment acquired after May 25, 1976;

(4) most buildings and component parts acquired after 1987, subject to certain grandfathering provisions; and

(5) certain assets acquired after 1987 and before February 27, 2000 that are categorized as public utility equipment, including electrical generating equipment, distributing equipment and plants for producers or distributors of electrical energy, water and heat, as well as certain assets for the production or distribution of gas, subject to recent budget proposals (see below).

Assets in Class 1, along with assets in Classes 2, 3, 6 and 8 were previously eligible for an additional allowance for property that was certified by the Minister of Supply and Services. This additional allowance was intended to promote expenditures in the defence industry sector. The additional capital cost allowance was permitted under former Regulations $1100(1)(j)$ and (k), which were revoked in May 1995.

Under Regulation 1103(1), a taxpayer may elect to include in Class 1 all properties acquired for the purpose of gaining or producing income from the same business that would otherwise be included in Classes 2 to 10, 11 and 12.

Buildings and Component Parts

The term "building" has a wide range, covering any structure with walls and a roof affording protection and shelter. The term "structure" has been defined by the courts to include anything of substantial size that is built up from component parts and intended to remain permanently on a permanent foundation. Any component parts that ordinarily go with the building when it is bought or sold or which relate to the functioning of the building must be included in the building class. See Interpretation Bulletin IT-79R3, "Capital Cost Allowance — Buildings or Other Structures", at ¶3105.

In general, most buildings are included in Class 1, 3 or 6. Buildings of the construction described in paragraph (a) of Class 6 will qualify whenever constructed if they are used in a farming or fishing business or if they have no footings or base support below ground level. If the building has base support below ground level and is not used in a farming or fishing business, it will be included in Class 6 only if it was acquired before 1979

¶360

or if acquired after 1978 and has met the tests as to the installation of footings prior to 1979, the existence of an agreement to acquire and/or the commencement of construction (as set out in subparagraphs (a)(ix) and (x)) are satisfied. Buildings of the construction described in paragraph (a) of Class 6 which are acquired after 1978 and which do not meet the tests will fall either within Class 1 or 3, depending on the date of acquisition.

Buildings and component parts are included in Class 1 or 3 only if not included in any other class. The classification of buildings was changed from Class 3 (5%) to Class 1 (4%) to implement the June 18, 1987 tax reform proposals to reduce the CCA rate on buildings acquired after 1987, subject to certain grandfathering provisions. Buildings that are not included in any other class will be included in Class 3 if acquired before 1988, as will buildings acquired before 1990 if acquired pursuant to an obligation in writing entered into by the taxpayer before June 18, 1987, or if under construction by or on behalf of the taxpayer on June 18, 1987. A component part of a building that was under construction on June 18, 1987 will also be included in Class 3 if acquired before 1990.

Buildings that are not included in Class 6 and do not meet the date of acquisition tests for inclusion in Class 3 will fall within Class 1. In general, this will include buildings and component parts acquired after 1987 (subject to the grandfathering provisions discussed above).

There can be a number of occasions when doubt may arise as to whether an asset is a "building or other structure" and should therefore be included in Class 1, 3 or 6, or whether it is not included in the descriptions of those classes or any other class and may therefore be included in Class 8. To address a concern that certain buildings, structures or component parts that could be included in Class 8 (20%) could be required to be included in Class 1, a proposed amendment to paragraph (q) of Class 1 clarifies that property described in paragraphs (a) to (e) of Class 8 (buildings and other structures used in manufacturing and processing or farming) is excluded from Class 1, applicable to property acquired after 1987.

In the 1970s and 1980s, a building that would otherwise have been in Class 3 or 6 may have been in Class 31 or 32 if it qualified as a multiple-unit residential building. See the commentary at ¶510.

Class 20 and Regulation 1100(1)(p) together allow a taxpayer a deduction in computing income of 20%, on the straight-line method, of the capital cost of certain buildings acquired after December 5, 1963 and before April 1, 1967 that would otherwise have been included in Classes 3 or 6.

Under Regulation 1103(2f), a taxpayer may elect to transfer all Class 20 assets to Class 1, 3 or 6.

¶360

Additions and Alterations to Buildings

Additions and alterations to existing buildings may be included in Class 1, 3 or 6, depending on what class the building itself is included in and when the addition or alteration is made.

For buildings that are in Class 20, additions or alterations will be in Class 1, 3 or 6 depending on what class the building would otherwise be included in and the time the addition or alteration is made.

If the Class 20 building would otherwise have been included in Class 6, and the addition or alteration was made after March 31, 1967 and before 1979, or after 1978 pursuant to the terms of an agreement in writing entered into before 1979, then the addition or alteration would be included in Class 6.

If the Class 20 building would otherwise have been included in Class 3, and the addition or alteration was made after March 31, 1967 and before 1988, then the addition or alteration would be included in Class 3.

Additions and alterations to buildings that are included in Class 6 by virtue of subparagraph (a)(vi) (used in farming or fishing) or subparagraph (a)(vii) (has no footings or other base support below ground level) will be included in Class 6 regardless of when the addition or alteration is made.

Additions and alterations made after 1978 to a building described in subparagraph (a)(viii) of Class 6 (acquired before 1979 and not described in subparagraph (a)(vi) or (vii)) would be in Class 6 to the extent that the aggregate cost of all such additions and alterations to the building does not exceed $100,000.

Additions and alterations made after 1987 to a building included in whole or in part in Class 3, Class 6 by virtue of subparagraph (a)(viii), or in Class 20 would either be included in Class 3 or 1. The portion of such additions or alterations that may be included in Class 3 is prescribed in paragraph (k) of Class 3, which extends to all such additions or alterations made after 1987 other than those described in paragraph (k) of Class 6. That provision permits certain additions and alterations to be included in Class 6 to a maximum of $100,000 as described in the immediately preceding paragraph.

For additions or alterations made after 1987 that are not included in Class 6 by virtue of paragraph (k) thereof, the amount that may be included in Class 3 is limited to the lesser of:

(a) $500,000; and

(b) 25% of the capital cost of the building and any additions or alterations thereto included in Class 3, 6 or 20. For this purpose, the capital cost of the buildings and additions included in Class 3, 6 or 20 is determined without reference to amounts added pursuant to this provision.

¶360

Example: Buildings

A taxpayer acquired a building of frame construction in 1975 for $1.6 million. The building is not used in farming or fishing and has footings and other base support below ground level so that it is included in Class 6 by virtue of subparagraph (a)(viii). In 2000, additions costing $600,000 are made to the building. These additions will be included in the following classes:

Class 6

$100,000 is included in Class 6 pursuant to paragraph (k) of that class.

Class 3

$425,000 is included in Class 3 by virtue of paragraph (k) of that class. That amount is calculated as the lesser of:

(i) $500,000; and

(ii) 25% of the aggregate of:

— the capital cost of the buildings $1,600,000

— additions or alterations included in Class 6 by virtue of paragraph (k) thereof 100,000

$1,700,000

25% × $1,700,000 = $425,000

Class 1

The balance of the addition of $75,000 is included in Class 1.

Condominiums

Where a unit in a condominium includes land, the usual allocation of cost between land and building must be made; the allocation agreed to by the parties in an arm's length transaction is given considerable weight. A taxpayer's entire holdings in a building (exclusive of land) within a particular condominium building constitutes "a building" for capital cost allowance purposes. Two or more units owned by the taxpayer within the same building are regarded as a single property, with a single capital cost. See Interpretation Bulletin IT-304R2, "Condominiums", at ¶3180.

Railway Assets

Railway assets can fall within any of Class 1, 3, 4, 6, 7, 8, 10, 28, 35 or 41. They are eligible for normal capital cost allowance and, in some instances, additional straight-line or declining balance allowances. Some of these additional allowances are described below. See Class 35 at ¶525 for a discussion of the additional allowance for railway cars.

Regulation 1102(10) applies for the purpose of section 36 of the Act. In general, section 36 requires that certain expenditures incurred by railway companies in respect of the repair, replacement, alteration or renovation of depreciable property be capitalized rather than expensed for tax purposes. Regulation 1102(10) provides that such property falls into the class in Schedule II in which it would be included if it had been acquired at the time the expenditure was incurred, and that if the expenditure was incurred before May 26, 1976, the property is a Class 4 asset.

Additional Allowance — Railway Operations

Regulation 1100(1)(zc) provides an additional capital cost allowance deduction of 6% on a straight-line basis in respect of most new railway system assets acquired after April 10, 1978 and before 1988 which are used or situated in Canada, and owned by a taxpayer who owns and operates a railway as a common carrier. The additional deduction is available in respect of the year of acquisition and the four taxation years following the year of acquisition.

The designated property in respect of which the additional deduction is available could fall within any of Class 1, 3, 6, 8, 10, 28 or 35.

Additional Allowance — Railway Track and Related Property

Regulation 1100(1)(za) with Regulation 1101(5e) permit additional CCA on railway track and related property acquired after March 31, 1977 and before 1988. Most railway track and related property (such as ballast, ties, signal equipment, bridges, culverts and tunnels) is usually in Class 1 (4%). Under Regulation 1101(5e), property of this kind acquired during the aforementioned period is placed in a separate class and is eligible for additional CCA of another 4%. Where the taxpayer is a common carrier that owns and operates the railway, Regulation 1100(1)($za.$1) provides an additional allowance of 6% for the same type of property acquired after December 6, 1991. Regulation 1101(5e.1) provides that a separate class be established for such property eligible for the additional allowance.

A trestle is ordinarily in Class 3 where the rate is 5%. Under Regulation 1101(5f), a railway trestle acquired during the period March 31, 1977 to December 31, 1987 is placed in a separate class and is eligible for additional CCA of 3%. For trestles in Class 3 acquired after December 6, 1991, Regulation 1101(5e.2) provides that a separate class be established where the taxpayer is a common carrier that owns and operates a railway. The assets in this separate class are eligible for an additional allowance of 5% under Regulation 1100(1)($za.$2).

Each of these additional allowances is determined after applying the notional reduction under Regulation 1100(2) (half-year rule) (see ¶140).

Railway track and related property acquired after March 31, 1977 for the purpose of gaining or producing income from a mine (e.g., a spur line to the mine site) qualifies as Class 10 property where the rate is 30%. If the track and equipment is acquired before the mine comes into production, it qualifies as Class 41 (25%) if acquired after 1987, and Class 28 (30%) prior to 1988.

¶360

Railway Sidings

Regulation 1100(8) allows a deduction of 4% on the declining balance of the capital expenditure incurred by a taxpayer in respect of construction of a railway siding to the taxpayer's property or place of business. The expenditure must be incurred pursuant to a contract or arrangement with an operator of a railway system under which the railway siding does not become the taxpayer's property.

Equipment in the Nature of a Public Utility

Certain equipment in the nature of public utility equipment, including pipelines, is included in Class 1 if acquired after 1987, subject to certain grandfathering rules, draft legislation, and recent budget proposals.

Such properties acquired before 1988 are included in Class 2 with a CCA rate of 6%. In addition, such properties acquired before 1990 qualify for inclusion in Class 2 if acquired pursuant to an obligation in writing entered into before June 18, 1987, or if the property was under construction by or on behalf of the taxpayer on June 18, 1987. Such property that is a fixed and integral part of a building, plant or other structure under construction on June 18, 1987 also qualifies for inclusion in Class 2.

A draft amendment to Class 17 provides that certain assets including electrical generating equipment, distributing equipment and plants for producers or distributors of electrical energy, water, and heat, acquired after February 27, 2000, are included in Class 17 which has a CCA rate of 8% (see ¶440).

In addition, the 2005 Federal Budget announced increases in the CCA rate for certain assets for the distribution of gas and electrical energy. The Budget proposes to increase the CCA rate for transmission pipelines for petroleum, natural gas or related hydrocarbons from the 4% Class 1 rate to 8%, effective for assets acquired on or after February 23, 2005. As well, the CCA rate for transmission and distribution equipment and structures (not including buildings) of a distributor of electrical energy is also to be increased to 8%. These changes are meant to better reflect the useful life of these assets. The proposed changes will not affect gas or oil well equipment and pipelines determined to be exhausted within 15 years of operation, or distribution pipelines that distribute gas to consumers, which will continue to be included in Class 1 at the 4% CCA rate.

¶365   Class 2 (6%) — Public Utility Equipment

The property in Class 2 (6%) is public utility equipment, including pipelines. No assets acquired after 1987 (subject to certain grandfathering provisions) are included in Class 2. Assets acquired after 1987 that would otherwise be in Class 2 are included in Class 1 with a CCA rate of 4%, or for certain assets acquired after February 27, 2000, Class 17 with a rate of 8%.

The grandfathering provisions allow the public utility equipment to be included in Class 2 if it is acquired before 1990, pursuant to an obligation in writing entered into before June 18, 1987, or if the property was under construction by or on behalf of the taxpayer on June 18, 1987. Such property that is a fixed and integral part of a building, plant or other structure under construction on June 18, 1987 will also qualify for inclusion in Class 2.

The taxpayer may elect under Regulation 1101(5)(*i*) to place certain Class 2 pipelines, including extensions or conversions, costing $10 million or more in a separate class. See Interpretation Bulletin IT-482R, "Pipelines", at ¶3275.

Under Regulation 1103(2), a taxpayer whose chief depreciable properties are included in Class 2, may elect to include in Class 2 any other property acquired before May 26, 1976 for the purpose of gaining or producing income from the same business.

¶370 Class 3 (5%) — Buildings and Other Structures, Railway Trestles, Wire and Cable

Class 3 assets include any buildings or other structures not included in any other class and that are acquired before 1988, or before 1990 if certain grandfathering provisions are met. Refer to the commentary on Class 1 (see ¶360) for a discussion of buildings and other structures. For a complete listing of Class 3 assets, see ¶2424. Capital cost allowance on buildings, structures and component parts is discussed in Interpretation Bulletin IT-79R3, "Capital Cost Allowance — Buildings or Other Structures", at ¶3105.

Class 3 assets also include a jetty and mole, acquired after May 25, 1976, and a breakwater, dock or wharf. A jetty or a mole, acquired before May 26, 1976, is included in Class 1 with a capital cost allowance rate of 4%. Note that Class 3 includes a breakwater, a dock, a wharf or a windmill unless it is included in another class. If a windmill is used to produce electrical energy, it may qualify as a Class 34 or 43.1 asset.

Telephone, telegraph or data communication equipment acquired after May 25, 1976 and before February 23, 2005 that is wire or cable is included in Class 3. (Fibre-optic cable is included in Class 42 with a 12% rate.) The 2005 Federal Budget proposed to increase the CCA rate to 12% for wire and cable used for telephone, telegraph or data communication that is not fibre-optic cable, for such assets acquired after February 22, 2005 and which have not been used or acquired for use prior to February 23, 2005. Class 3 also includes equipment that is ancillary to the wire and cable as well as supporting equipment for fibre-optic cable. (See commentary on Class 42 (¶560) concerning an election for the inclusion of fibre-optic cable in Class 42.) Telephone, telegraph or data communication switching equipment is included in Class 17.

¶370

Railway trestles are Class 3 assets. Certain trestles are deemed to be in a separate class. See the commentary on Class 1 (¶360) for a description of this and the additional allowances that are available on trestles.

Additional Allowance in Respect of Grain Storage Facilities and Grain Elevators

Under the provisions of Regulation 1100(1)(*sb*), additional capital cost allowances are available in respect of grain elevators and grain drying storage facilities included in Classes 3, 6 or 8 that were acquired within a specified period. The specified period is the taxation year or one of the three immediately preceding taxation years that was after April 1, 1972 and before August 1, 1974. The assets include:

(1) a grain elevator certified by the Minister of Agriculture;

(2) an addition to a grain elevator described in (1) above;

(3) fixed machinery installed in a grain elevator or an addition described in (1) or (2) above;

(4) machinery for drying grain on a farm; and

(5) a building or other structure for storing grain on a farm.

The additional allowances are the lesser of:

(a) for Class 3 property, 22% of capital cost; for Class 6 property, 20% of capital cost; and for Class 8 property, 14% of the capital cost of property referred to in items (3) or (5) above, and 14% of the lesser of $15,000 and the capital cost of the property referred to in item (4) above; and

(b) the undepreciated capital cost of the class.

¶375   Class 4 (6%) — Railway Systems

Class 4 includes a tramway or trolley bus system, except for property that is included in Class 10, 13 or 14. A railway system or part thereof acquired before May 26, 1976 is also included in Class 4. Such property acquired after May 25, 1976 is included in Class 1. See the commentary at ¶360.

Under Regulation 1103(2), a taxpayer whose chief depreciable properties are included in Class 4, may elect to include in Class 4 any other property acquired before May 26, 1976 for the purpose of gaining or producing income from the same business.

¶380   Class 5 (10%) — Pulp Mills, etc.

Class 5 of Schedule II was amended in 1963 to exclude property described in Class 5 that was acquired after the end of the taxpayer's 1962 taxation year. Such property includes chemical and ground wood pulp mills and integrated mills producing chemical or ground wood pulp, including buildings, machinery and equipment. Capital cost allowance at the Class 5 rate may still be claimed for such property acquired before the taxpayer's 1963 taxation year. The text of Class 5 is reproduced at ¶2428.

¶385 Class 6 (10%) — Buildings, etc.

The assets included in Class 6 are mainly certain kinds of buildings. These may be frame, log, stucco on frame, galvanized iron or corrugated metal and are discussed in the commentary on Class 1 (see ¶360). Other types of property such as a fence, a greenhouse, an oil or water storage tank, and a wooden wharf are also included in Class 6 (see ¶2430). Note, however, that a greenhouse constructed with a replaceable flexible plastic cover on a rigid frame is a Class 8 asset.

¶390 Class 7 (15%) — Vessels, etc.

Class 7 assets include boats and vessels as well as the furniture, fixtures and equipment (other than radiocommunication equipment) attached to the vessel. Not included in Class 7 are a vessel that qualifies as a separate prescribed class under Regulation 1101(2a) and a vessel that is included in Class 41.

The term "vessel" is defined in subsection 13(21) to have the same meaning as a vessel as defined in the *Canadian Shipping Act*. Under that Act, "vessel" means "any ship or boat or any other description of vessel used or designed to be used in navigation".

A separate class is prescribed under Regulation 1101(2a) for each vessel including the furniture, fixtures, and radiocommunication and other equipment attached to it, that was constructed and registered in Canada and had not been used for any purpose prior to being acquired by the taxpayer. Such vessels are eligible for a special allowance. Costs of a conversion (as defined in subsection 13(21)) or major alteration to a vessel also form a separate class (as provided in subsection 13(14)) and are eligible for the special capital cost allowance. Regulation 1100(1)(v) provides the amount of CCA that may be claimed in respect of the capital cost of these Canadian vessels or conversion cost not exceeding $33\frac{1}{3}\%$ of the capital cost of qualifying vessels or conversion cost. This $33\frac{1}{3}\%$ claim is restricted to $16\frac{2}{3}\%$ in the year of acquisition. For vessels acquired prior to July 14, 1990, the accelerated capital cost allowance was available only if the Minister of Industry, Trade and Commerce certified that all the conditions regarding the vessel had been met. This requirement was removed for vessels acquired after July 13, 1990.

Each fishing vessel, described in Regulation 1101(2), is deemed to be in a separate class.

Under Regulation 1101(2b), a separate class is prescribed for all Class 7 vessels (including their furniture, fittings, and radiocommunication and other equipment) which meet one of the following two tests:

(1) the vessel must have been acquired after May 25, 1976 and must be designed principally for the purpose of determining the existence, location, extent, or quality of accumulations of petroleum or natural gas (other than mineral resources, i.e., petroleum or natural gas contained in tar sands, oil sands, or oil shale) or for the purpose of drilling oil or gas wells; or

(2) the vessel must have been acquired after May 17, 1979 and must have been designed principally for the purpose of determining the existence, location, extent or quality of mineral resources, i.e., deposits of base or precious metals, etc.

Under Regulation 1100(1)(*va*), these vessels are eligible for an additional 15% capital cost allowance calculated before the basic deduction under Class 7.

The additional deduction under Regulation 1100(1)(*va*), and the regular allowance under Regulation 1100(1)(*a*), are both computed on the undepreciated capital cost before any other deduction under Regulation 1100(1). The impact of the additional allowance is, therefore, to increase the effective rate on a Class 7 asset to 30% of the undepreciated capital cost. By virtue of Regulation 1100(2), both of these allowances are subject to the half-year rule (outlined in ¶140) in the year of acquisition.

An offshore drilling vessel acquired after December 31, 1987, or after December 31, 1989 if acquired pursuant to a written agreement entered into before June 18, 1987, becomes a Class 41 rather than a Class 7 asset, and the extra 15% allowance no longer applies. This shifts the effective depreciation rate down from 30% to 25%, subject to the half-year rule. However, an offshore drilling vessel can be included in a separate class and depreciated at $33\frac{1}{3}\%$ if it meets the criteria of a Canadian vessel described in Regulation 1101(2a).

Under draft amendments released in 2001, certain railway property acquired after February 27, 2000 is also included in Class 7. These assets include railway cars, railway locomotives (other than automotive railway cars), and railway suspension devices designed to carry trailers. Draft Regulation 1103(2i) provides an election to include certain leased railway cars and railway suspension devices in Class 35 (7% CCA rate) under certain circumstances. Under this election, taxpayers may be eligible to deduct an additional allowance of 6% in respect of such railway property and not have the specified leasing property rules apply to the railway property.

See Interpretation Bulletin IT-267R2, "Capital Cost Allowance — Vessels", at ¶3160.

¶390

¶395   Class 8 (20%) — Machinery and Equipment, Miscellaneous Assets

Class 8 includes a variety of assets ranging from machinery and equipment and certain storage buildings to a rapid transit car used within a metropolitan area, an outdoor advertising sign, and a greenhouse with a flexible plastic cover. Class 8 is also a "catch-all" class of assets since paragraph (i) states that, subject to the items enumerated in subparagraphs (i) to (xi), Class 8 includes "a tangible capital asset that is not included in another class in this Schedule". The text of Class 8 is reproduced at ¶2454.

Under draft regulations, data network infrastructure equipment acquired after March 22, 2004, that would otherwise be included in Class 8, is included in Class 46, with a 30% CCA rate for such equipment (see ¶580). Data network infrastructure equipment includes infrastructure equipment that supports advanced telecommunications applications such as e-mail, Web searching and hosting, instant messaging, audio- and video-over-IP (Internet Protocol), switches, multiplexers, routers, hubs, modems and domain name servers that are used to control, transfer, modulate and direct data. It does not include office equipment such as telephones, cell phones or fax machines, equipment such as Web servers that are currently considered to be computer equipment, or property such as wires, cables or structures.

Regulation 1101(5p) provides that a taxpayer may elect to place in one or more separate classes rapidly depreciating equipment, acquired after April 26, 1993, in Class 8. The Class 8 property eligible for separate class treatment is computer software, a photocopier and electronic communications office equipment such as a fax machine or telephone. Regulation 1103(2g) provides that any undepreciated capital cost remaining in each separate class five years after the end of the taxation year in which a property of the class became available for use, is to be transferred into the regular Class 8 pool after the beginning of that fifth taxation year. Regulation 1101(5p) also applies to certain Class 10 computer equipment acquired before 2005. See ¶405.

Under certain circumstances, a taxpayer may elect to include Class 19 or 21 property under Class 8. This election is provided for by Regulation 1103(2a). For further commentary on this election, see ¶235.

Certain machinery and equipment in Class 8, acquired after December 3, 1970 and before April 1, 1972, qualified for CCA on 115% of its capital cost. See commentary on Class 1 at ¶360 for further discussion of this incentive. See commentary on Class 3 at ¶370 concerning the additional allowance available under Regulation 1100(1)(*sb*) for machinery used for storing or drying grain in the 1970s.

Since certain equipment related to pipelines, including petroleum pumping equipment and natural gas compression equipment, is not specifically included in any of the CCA classes, this equipment is generally included in Class 8 as property not included in any other class. To standardize the CCA treatment of such equipment, the 2005 Federal Budget proposed to establish a 15% CCA rate for pumping and compression equipment, and equipment ancillary to it, related to transmission pipelines for petroleum, natural gas or related hydrocarbons, for such equipment purchased after February 22, 2005. As well, the Budget proposed that a separate class election be introduced for transmission pipelines and related pumping and compression equipment. These proposed changes do not apply to gas or oil-well equipment (Class 41) or buildings or other structures.

See Interpretation Bulletin IT-472, "Capital Cost Allowance — Class 8 Property", at ¶3250.

¶400   Class 9 (25%) — Radio and TV Equipment

Class 9 includes aircraft (including furniture, fittings, or equipment attached thereto or a spare part therefor) acquired after May 25, 1976. An aircraft acquired before May 26, 1976 is written off at a higher rate of 40% under Class 16. See the commentary on Class 10 below concerning aircraft.

The properties enumerated in paragraphs (a) to (f) of Class 9 (see ¶2456) are restricted to properties acquired before May 26, 1976. Such property as electrical generating equipment and radio transmission equipment acquired after May 25, 1976 is included in Class 8, which provides a lower rate of capital cost allowance.

¶405   Class 10 (30%)

Class 10 includes a wide variety of assets that are not included in any other class. These include general-purpose data processing equipment and systems software acquired before March 23, 2004 (or before 2005 if the taxpayer elects) and automotive equipment such as cars, trucks, trailers, portable rental tools and stable equipment. Certain automobiles that would otherwise be in Class 10 are included in Class 10.1.

Up to 1987, most resource extraction assets were included in Class 10, eligible for a 30% CCA rate. As part of the June 18, 1987 tax reform measures, resource extraction assets acquired after 1987 (or after 1989 if transitional relief is available) are required to be included in Class 41 (¶555), for which a 25% CCA rate is allowed. The particular properties required to be included in Class 41 are those that would otherwise be included in Class 10 by virtue of paragraphs $(f.1)$, (g), (j), (k), (l), (m), (r), (t) or (u). However, such assets acquired after 1987 and before 1990 will continue to be included in Class 10 if acquired pursuant to an obligation in writing entered into before June 18, 1987, or if under construction by or on behalf of the taxpayer on June 18, 1987. Machinery or equipment that is a fixed and integral part of such property under construction on June 18, 1987 will also qualify for the transitional relief.

Certain properties otherwise included in Class 10 which were acquired after November 7, 1969 and before 1988 (or 1990 if transitional relief is available), for use in connection with a new or expanded mine, are excluded from Class 10 and included in Class 28. These assets include mining buildings, mills, smelters, on-site office buildings, some electrical plants, mine machinery and equipment. Railway assets described in paragraph (m) acquired prior to the mine coming into production will also be in Class 28 if they meet the other requirements thereof. The basic purpose for dividing mining assets between Classes 10 and 28 is to provide for an accelerated capital cost allowance for Class 28 property.

Such properties acquired after the dates noted above (i.e., generally 1987, and in cases where transitional relief is available, 1989) will be included in Class $41(a)$ (instead of Class 28) and will continue to be eligible for an accelerated rate of capital cost allowance.

A contractor's movable equipment is included in Class $10(h)$. For a discussion of capital cost allowance in respect of a contractor's movable equipment, see Interpretation Bulletin IT-306R2 at ¶3185.

A certified production that is acquired after 1987 and before March 1996 (other than one that is subject to grandfathering rules) is included in Class $10(w)$. A certified production acquired before 1988 is included in Class $12(n)$. After 1994, the special capital cost allowance treatment for certified productions was discontinued and replaced by a tax credit set out in section 125.4 of the Act. After 1994, a Canadian film or video production is included in Class $10(x)$.

General data processing equipment and systems software acquired after March 22, 2004 is included in Class 45 with a CCA rate of 45% (released in draft at the time of writing). Such property includes general-purpose electronic data processing equipment and systems software for that equipment, including ancillary data processing equipment, but not including property that is principally or is used principally as electronic process control or monitor equipment and systems software, electronic communications control equipment and systems software, or data handling equipment (other than data handling equipment that is ancillary to general-purpose electronic data processing equipment). Computer equipment included in Class 45 does not qualify for the separate class election under Regulation 1101(5p).

Regulation 1101(5p) provides that a taxpayer may elect to place in one or more separate classes rapidly depreciating equipment, acquired after April 26, 1993, in Class 8 or 10. The Class 10 property eligible for separate class treatment is general-purpose electronic data processing equipment and systems software acquired before 2005. Regulation 1103(2g) provides that any undepreciated capital cost remaining in each separate class five years after the end of the taxation year in which a

¶405

property of the class became available for use, is to be transferred into the regular Class 10 pool after the beginning of that fifth taxation year.

Regulation 1100(1)(zg) provides that a taxpayer may elect to claim accelerated CCA (to a maximum of $50,000) for computer hardware and systems software acquired between January 1, 1998 and October 31, 1999 to replace property acquired before 1998 that was not Year 2000 compliant. Under Regulation 1100(1)(zg), the taxpayer could claim 85% of eligible property included in paragraph (*f*) of Class 10. When combined with the regular CCA (30% x ½ for half-year rule), 100% of the property could be written off in the year of acquisition. The $50,000 maximum must be shared by an associated group and is reduced by any accelerated CCA claimed on computer software under Regulation 1100(1)(zh) (see ¶415 for Class 12 assets). The accelerated CCA cannot be claimed by a large corporation (as defined in subsection 225.1(8)).

Generating Equipment

Regulation 1102(8) includes in Class 10 plant and equipment generating or distributing electrical energy where at least 80% of the output (for the distributor's 1948 and 1949 taxation years or the first two taxation years, whichever period is the later) of the producer or distributor was sold to a mine, smelter, metal refinery or ore mill. Regulation 1102(9) applies similarly to equipment used in the taxpayer's own mine, smelter, metal refinery or ore mill. In both cases, the property must have been acquired before 1988, or before 1990 if the grandfathering provisions apply, in order to be included in Class 10. Such properties acquired after 1987 or 1989, as applicable, are included in Class 41, for which a capital cost allowance rate of 25% is prescribed.

Automobiles and Aircraft

Automobiles or aircraft used to earn income from business or property are eligible for capital cost allowance at the rate of 30% of the automobile's (Class 10) and 25% of the aircraft's (Class 9) undepreciated capital cost. If a taxpayer is required to use his or her car or aircraft to fulfil the duties of employment, the taxpayer may claim capital cost allowance at the same rates. Only that portion of the depreciation incurred in the course of employment or relating to business-use is deductible, so that if, for example, the undepreciated capital cost of the automobile or aircraft is $4,800 and the automobile or aircraft is used 75% for purposes of the employment, the capital cost allowance will be calculated as follows: 30% of $4,800 = $1,440; 75% of $1,440 = $1,080. These assets are subject to normal recapture and terminal loss rules. Paragraph 24 of IT-522R (¶3300) notes, however, that the terminal loss provisions do not apply to employees.

Automobiles acquired after June 17, 1987 are defined as "passenger vehicles". Passenger vehicles costing more than a threshold amount are included in Class 10.1 (see the commentary at ¶407). See Class 16 (¶435)

¶405

regarding automobiles acquired after November 12, 1981 for short-term rentals or leases, and regarding large trucks and tractors acquired after December 6, 1991.

¶407 Class 10.1 (30%) — Passenger Vehicles

Automobiles acquired after June 17, 1987 are defined in subsection 248(1) as "passenger vehicles". Passenger vehicles that cost over a prescribed amount are included in Class 10.1 instead of Class 10. The capital cost allowance rate for Class 10.1 is also 30%; however, CCA may only be taken on the cost of the vehicle up to a maximum of the prescribed amount. Automobiles costing less than that amount continue to be included in Class 10.

The prescribed amount for passenger vehicles is outlined in Regulation 7307(1). These amounts are adjusted periodically, usually in the late fall of the preceding year. From 1991 onwards, applicable federal and provincial sales taxes are added to the prescribed figure. For vehicles acquired from 2001 to 2005, the prescribed amount is $30,000, plus applicable sales taxes. See the table reproduced in ¶250 for the prescribed amounts for prior years.

Each vehicle included in Class 10.1 is to be in a separate class. Capital cost allowance is claimed in the normal way based on the maximum threshold amount, subject to the half-year rule in the year of acquisition. These vehicles are not subject to recapture or terminal loss, but in the year such a vehicle is disposed of, Regulation 1100(2.5) provides that the taxpayer may claim a half-year of capital cost allowance on the vehicle.

If a passenger vehicle is acquired from a person with whom the taxpayer does not deal at arm's length, the capital cost to the taxpayer is limited to the least of the fair market value of the vehicle at the time of the transfer, the cost amount to the person from whom it was acquired, and the prescribed amount. Therefore, the depreciable limit for passenger vehicles cannot be circumvented through non-arm's length transfers.

For further commentary on passenger vehicles, see ¶250.

¶410 Class 11 (35%) — Outdoor Advertising Signs or Boards

Class 11 includes an outdoor advertising poster panel or bulletin board acquired before 1988 (or before 1990 pursuant to agreements in writing entered into before June 18, 1987, or for assets under construction on that date). Such assets acquired after this date are in Class 8 (20%). Class 11 also includes an electrical advertising sign owned by the manufacturer, acquired before May 26, 1976.

¶410

¶415   Class 12 (100%)

The text of Class 12 is reproduced at ¶2464. As described in Regulation 1100(2)(a)(iii), certain Class 12 assets are exempt from the half-year rule (¶140). These are assets in Class 12(a) to (c), (e) to (i), (k), (l), and (p) to (s). These assets can be written off 100% in the year they are acquired and available for use. Class 12 assets that are not exempt from the half-year rule can be written off over two years.

Many of the Class 12 assets are small items with a relatively short life such as a library book, chinaware, and kitchen utensils. Tools costing less than $200 may be depreciated at 100% in the year of purchase. If the tools cost $200 or over, they will be depreciable at 20% in Class 8. See Interpretation Bulletin IT-422, "Definition of Tools", at ¶3225.

Class 12(s) includes electronic point-of-sale equipment used in retail businesses in Canada acquired after August 8, 1989 and before 1993. This allowed retailers a 100% write-off for equipment acquired to handle the Goods and Services Tax implemented in 1991.

Computer software other than systems software is a Class 12 asset and is subject to the half-year rule. See below.

A "television commercial message" referred to in Class 12(m) is defined in Regulation 1104(2) as being a commercial message as defined in the Television Broadcasting Regulations made under the *Broadcasting Act*. Section 2 of the Television Broadcasting Regulations defines a "commercial message" as "an advertisement intended to sell or promote goods, services, natural resources or activities and includes an advertisement that mentions or displays in a list of prizes the name of the person selling or promoting these goods, services, natural resources or activities". Films or video tapes that qualify under this definition are eligible for CCA of 100%, but are subject to the half-year rule in the year of acquisition.

Regulation 1104(2) defines a "certified feature film" prescribed under Class 12(n) and a "certified production" for purposes of Classes 12(n) and 10(w). In general, such properties acquired prior to 1988 qualify as Class 12(n) assets, and those acquired after 1987 and before 1995 qualify as Class 10(w) assets for CCA purposes. Prior to 1995, certified feature films and certified productions were excluded from the application of leasing property rules under Regulation 1100(15). Furthermore, the half-year rule did not apply to certified productions in Class 10(w). An additional allowance was also available for property in Class 10(w) by virtue of Regulation 1100(1)(l). After 1994, the special capital cost allowance treatment for certified productions was discontinued and replaced by a tax credit set out in section 125.4 of the Act. See ¶405.

¶415

Computer Software

Computer software assets can fall within any of Classes 8, 10, 12, 29, 39, 40, 43, 45 or 46. Computer software is defined in Regulation 1104(2) as including systems software and a right or licence to use computer software. Computer software that is not systems software is included in Class 12, with 100% write-off, subject to the half-year rule in the year of acquisition.

Regulation 1100(1)(zh) provides that a taxpayer may elect to claim accelerated CCA (to a maximum of $50,000) for computer software acquired between January 1, 1998 and October 31, 1999 to replace property acquired before 1998 that is not Year 2000 compliant. Under Regulation 1100(1)(zh), the taxpayer may claim 50% of eligible property included in paragraph (o) of Class 12. When combined with the regular CCA (50% x ½ for half-year rule), 100% of the property is written off in the year of acquisition. The $50,000 maximum must be shared by an associated group and is reduced by any accelerated CCA claimed on computer hardware or systems software under Regulation 1100(1)(zg) (see ¶405). The accelerated CCA cannot be claimed by a large corporation.

"Systems software" is defined in Regulation 1104(2) to mean a combination of programs, documentation and data that allow the hardware to function in the use of other computer programs. This includes, for example, an operating system that enables application software to be run. Systems software is included in:

(1) Class 8 (20%) (¶395) if it is used principally as electronic process control or monitor equipment, or electronic communications control equipment or data handling equipment not ancillary to general-purpose electronic data processing equipment;

(2) Class 10(f) (30%) (¶405), unless it is used for the purposes described in (1), in which case it is Class 8;

(3) Class 29 (¶500) if it was acquired prior to 1988 (subject to grandfathering provisions) and it qualifies as manufacturing and processing equipment. Systems software acquired before 1988 that would otherwise be in either Class 8 or 10 is included in Class 29 if it is used for manufacturing and processing;

(4) Class 39 (¶545) if it was acquired after 1987 and before February 26, 1992 and it qualifies as manufacturing and processing equipment. The systems software in this case is that which would otherwise be included in Class 8 (see (1) above), except for the fact that it is used in manufacturing and processing;

(5) Class 40 (¶550) if it was acquired after 1987 and before 1990 and it qualifies as manufacturing and processing equipment. The systems software in this case is general purpose software which would otherwise be in Class 10 (see (2) above), except for the fact that it is used in

¶415

manufacturing and processing. The software in Class 40 is to be transferred to Class 10 for taxation years commencing after 1989;

(6) Class 43 (30%) (¶565) if it was acquired after February 25, 1992 and is software that would otherwise be included in Class 8, except for the fact that it is used in manufacturing and processing; and

(7) Class 45 (45%) (¶575) if it is general-purpose electronic data processing equipment and systems software therefor, including ancillary data processing equipment, acquired after March 22, 2004.

Data network infrastructure equipment acquired after March 22, 2004 is included in Class 46 (¶580) with a 30% CCA rate.

A taxpayer may elect to place computer software costing over $1,000 that is acquired after April 26, 1993 and included in Class 8 or, if acquired before 2005, Class 10(*f*), into a separate class. This will not change the rate of depreciation, but could give rise to a terminal loss because of the rapid obsolescence of computer software. See ¶248 for additional commentary on this rule.

¶420   Class 13 — Leasehold Interests

Class 13 consists of property that is a leasehold interest, except an interest in minerals, petroleum, natural gas, other related hydrocarbons, timber and related property, Expo 67 or Expo 86 leasehold interests (Class 23), and that part of a leasehold interest that is included in another class by reason of Regulations 1102(5) and (5.1). Property acquired by a taxpayer after December 23, 1991 that would, if it had been acquired by a person with whom the taxpayer was not dealing at arm's length at the time it was acquired by the taxpayer, be a leasehold interest of that non-arm's length person, subject to the exceptions mentioned above, is included in Class 13 by the taxpayer. Therefore, leasehold improvements can be depreciated by the person who acquires them even though that taxpayer does not actually hold the lease, as long as the person that does hold the lease is not dealing at arm's length with the taxpayer.

A leasehold interest is the interest of a tenant in any leased tangible property. A tenant who leases property acquires a leasehold interest in that property regardless of whether or not any capital cost is incurred in respect of that interest. However, a depreciable property is not considered to have been acquired until a capital cost has been incurred in respect of that property.

The capital cost of a leasehold interest of Class 13 property includes:

(a) an amount that a tenant expends in respect of improvements or alterations to a leased property that are capital in nature, other than improvements or alterations that are included as a building or structure; and

¶420

(b) an amount that a tenant expends to obtain or extend a lease or sublease, or pays to the landlord to permit the sublease of the property.

Regulations 1102(5) and (5.1) deal with the classification of amounts expended by leaseholders on buildings or other structures, or alterations to leasehold properties which substantially change their nature or character of the lease property. It is provided, in effect, that the part of the leasehold interest which results from such expenditures is excluded from Class 13 of Schedule II, and is included in the words "a building or other structure" where they appear in other classes of the schedule, typically Class 1, 3 or 6. Regulation 1102(5.1) provides that leasehold improvements which must be assigned to a building class and which are acquired after December 23, 1991 can be depreciated by the person who acquires them, even if the actual lessee is a non-arm's length person rather than the person who acquired the leasehold improvements. That is, suppose Ms. A leases a building personally and her wholly-owned company builds an addition for its use. The company may depreciate the cost of the addition in Class 1 (since it had no prior building), even though it has no leasehold interest to which the expenditures can attach.

The allowance permitted in respect of a particular leasehold property under Regulation 1100(1)(*b*) is determined by Schedule III of the regulations. This allowance must be the lesser of:

(a) the prorated portion of the capital cost of such interest, i.e., the lesser of:

(i) one-fifth of the capital cost thereof, and

(ii) the amount arrived at by dividing the capital cost thereof to the taxpayer by the number of 12-month periods, to a maximum of 40, which the lease has to run; and

(b) the undepreciated capital cost thereof at the end of the taxation year before claiming any allowance.

In the year of acquisition of a leasehold interest (other than a property described in subparagraph 1100(2)(*a*)(v), specified leasing property of a principal business leasing corporation; subparagraph 1100(2)(*a*)(vi), property acquired for which an election had previously been made to treat a lease as a loan; or subparagraph 1100(2)(*a*)(vii), property that has become available for use under the two-year rolling start rule), this allowance is restricted to half the normal claim pursuant to Regulation 1100(1)(*b*).

Where a taxpayer has acquired a leasehold interest that would, if it had been acquired by a person with whom the taxpayer was not dealing at arm's length at the time it was acquired by the taxpayer, be a Class 13 asset of that person, paragraph 4 of Schedule III provides that the terms and conditions of the leasehold interest for the taxpayer shall be deemed

¶420

to be the same that would have applied in respect of the non-arm's length person had that person acquired the property.

For the purpose of determining the capital cost of a leasehold property, any part of such cost incurred before the taxation year in which the property was acquired is deemed to have been incurred in the year in which the property was acquired. Where a tenant has the right to renew the lease for an additional term, or for more than one additional term, the lease is deemed to expire at the end of the term next succeeding the term in which the capital cost was incurred.

As a corollary to the provision that the capital cost allowance on leasehold property must be the lesser of the prorated portion of the capital cost of a particular property, or the undepreciated capital cost before any deduction under Regulation 1100, paragraph 3(d) of Schedule III provides that the prorated portion is nil if the capital cost does not exceed the aggregate of:

(a) the allowances deducted in previous years in respect of that leasehold property; and

(b) the proceeds of disposition, if any, of part or all of that property.

Furthermore, where at the end of a taxation year the undepreciated capital cost of all the leasehold properties is nil, the prorated portion of the capital cost for all subsequent years is deemed to be nil (Schedule III, paragraph 3(e)).

Throughout Schedule III, the words "prorated portion of the *part* of the capital cost of a particular leasehold interest" are used. This terminology recognizes the fact that a leasehold interest of a given amount may actually be represented by one or more outlays of a capital nature incurred at different times during the life of the lease, and provides that each component part must be depreciated in accordance with the provisions of Regulation 1100(1)(b). This point is further illustrated in Example 2 below.

Schedule III, paragraph 2(b), provides that the prorating of the capital cost of the leasehold interest should be done by dividing such cost by the number of *12-month periods* (not exceeding 40 such periods), commencing with the beginning of the taxation year in which the cost was incurred, and ending with the day the lease is to terminate.

¶420

Example: Schedule III

X acquired a leasehold interest running for the period from August 1, 2001 to November 30, 2005 at a cost of $6,400. X's fiscal year ends December 31.

The annual amounts of capital cost allowances would be computed as follows:

Year ended	Under Schedule III
2001	$ 640
2002	1,280
2003	1,280
2004	1,280
2005	1,280
2006	640
	$6,400

If the leasehold interest was the only asset in the pool and the lease terminated prior to the end of 2005, then the balance of the undepreciated capital cost could be written off in the fifth year as a terminal loss pursuant to subsection 20(16).

It is important to remember that under subsection 20(16), in most instances, where a taxpayer disposes of all the property of a prescribed class (including Class 13) and has no property of that class at the end of the taxation year, the taxpayer is allowed a deduction equal to the amount that would otherwise be the undepreciated capital cost of property of that class at the expiration of the taxation year. If a lease expires and is not renewed, the leasehold property will pass from the tenant to the owner, and if the tenant does not acquire other leasehold property before the end of the taxation year, the tenant may, in the last year of the lease, claim the full balance of the cost that has not previously been written off. Consequently, in these circumstances the deduction claimable under subsection 20(16) may exceed the limits imposed by Regulation 1100(1)(b).

A simple example of this may occur in the case of a two-year lease. In the first year, the taxpayer is restricted under Regulation 1100(1)(b) to deducting a tenth of the capital cost of the leasehold improvements in Class 13, but in the second year of the lease the taxpayer may deduct the remaining nine-tenths of the cost by reason of subsection 20(16).

Where a taxation year is less than 12 months, Regulation 1100(3) provides that the claim for the year is proportionately reduced. The amount of any claim which is reduced is deferred until after the end of the lease, or claimed as a terminal loss in the final year of the lease.

¶420

For a detailed discussion of leasehold interests, refer to Interpretation Bulletin IT-464R, "Capital Cost Allowance — Leasehold Interests", at ¶3240.

Example 1:   Leasehold Interests

On January 1, 1991, a taxpayer acquired a leasehold interest at a cost of $150,000 under a lease which ran to December 31, 2000 and which gave the tenant an option to renew (which the taxpayer duly exercised) for a further five years. In 2003, the tenant sold part of this leasehold interest, which was the only asset in the class, for $26,000.

Original capital cost $150,000

Amounts deducted as CCA for the years
1991 to 2002 under Reg. $1100(1)(b)$ =

$$12 \times \frac{\$150,000}{15} - \tfrac{1}{2} \times \frac{\$150,000}{15} = \quad \text{. . . . .} \quad \underline{115,000}$$

Undepreciated capital cost, January 1, 2003 . . . . $ 35,000

Less: Proceeds of disposal . . . . $\underline{26,000}$

Balance . . . . $ 9,000

Less: CCA under Schedule III . . . . $\underline{9,000}$

Undepreciated capital cost, December 31, 2003 . . . . $\underline{\underline{\text{nil}}}$

It should be noted that since the undepreciated capital cost for the years 2004 and 2005 is nil, no capital cost allowances can be claimed for those years.

Example 2:   Leasehold Interests

The terms of the lease agreement are the same as in Example 1 above. In 2003, the tenant incurred an expenditure of $24,000 for the purpose of improving the leasehold property.

Original capital cost $150,000

Amounts deducted as CCA for the years
1991 to 2002 under Reg. $1100(1)(b)$ =

$$12 \times \frac{\$150,000}{15} - \tfrac{1}{2} \times \frac{\$150,000}{15} = \quad \text{. . . . .} \quad \underline{115,000}$$

Undepreciated capital cost, January 1, 2003 . . . . $ 35,000

Add: Capital cost of improvements in 2003 . . . . $\underline{24,000}$

$ 59,000

Less: Capital cost allowances in 2003 —

$\frac{1}{15}$ of original capital cost of $150,000 = ... $10,000

$\frac{1}{5}$ of capital cost of improvements of $24,000 × 50% $\underline{2,400}$ $\underline{12,400}$

Undepreciated capital cost, December 31, 2003 . . . . $ 46,600

Less: CCA in 2004 (same as in 2003 above, except no 50% reduction for acquisitions) . . . . $\underline{14,800}$

¶420

Undepreciated capital cost, December 31, 2004		$ 31,800
Less: Capital cost allowances in 2005 — Balance of original cost ($150,000 − $135,000) = ...	$15,000	
Balance of cost of improvements ($24,000 − $7,200) under sec. 20(16)	16,800	31,800
Undepreciated capital cost, December 31, 2005		nil

The amounts of $2,400 in 2003 and $4,800 in 2004 are the maximum amounts permitted under the provisions of Regulation 1100(1)(*b*) and, in particular, under paragraph 2(*a*) of Schedule III to the regulations. Consequently, although at the time when the improvements were made, the lease had only three more years to run, the taxpayer could only claim $\frac{1}{5}$ of the cost incurred in that year and not $\frac{1}{3}$. The taxpayer is permitted, however, in 2005 to claim terminal allowance on the undepreciated balance under subsection 20(16) when the lease finally expires, provided that it is not renewable or that another leasehold interest is not acquired before the end of that year.

Example 3: Leasehold Interests

Assume that company X, which has a fiscal year ending on December 31, enters into the following four leases:

A. (i) Term of lease is from November 30, 1991 to December 31, 1998 (85 months).

   (ii) Capital cost of leasehold improvements is $16,000.

   (iii) "Period" as per Schedule III, paragraph 2(*b*), is January 1, 1991 to December 31, 1998 — 96 months or 8 years.

   (iv) CCA claimable:

1991	$ 1,000
1992–1998 (7 × 2,000)	14,000
1999	1,000
	$16,000

B. (i) Term of lease is January 1, 1992 to June 30, 1996 with three-year renewal clause (90 months).

   (ii) Capital cost of leasehold improvements — $21,000 incurred in November and December 1991.

   (iii) "Period" as per Schedule III, paragraph (2)(*b*) — 7 years.

   (iv) CCA claimable (see Schedule III, paragraph (3)(*a*)):

1991	nil
1992	$ 1,500
1993–1998 (6 × 3,000)	18,000
1999	1,500
	$21,000

C. (i) Term of lease is November 30, 1991 to December 31, 1993 (25 months).

   (ii) Capital cost incurred in 1991 — $5,000.

   (iii) "Period" per Schedule III, paragraph (2)(*b*) — 36 months or 3 years.

¶420

(iv) CCA claimable:

Maximum one-fifth of cost (see Schedule III, paragraph $(2)(a)$)

1991	$ 500
1992–1995 (4 × $1,000)	4,000
1996	500
	$ 5,000

Since leases A and B continue after termination of lease C, no terminal loss can be claimed.

D. (i) Term of lease July 1, 1993 to July 1, 1998 (60 months).

(ii) Capital cost — $15,000.

(iii) "Period" — 60 months or 5 years.

(iv) CCA claimable:

1993	$ 1,500
1994–1998 (4 × $3,000)	12,000
1999	1,500
	$15,000

Case I. Assume that in March 1993 part of lease A was sold for $9,000 and all of lease B was sold for $21,000 and that the Minister agreed to a change of year-end effective on June 30, 1993.

Case II. Assume that there was no change of year-end.

The attached CCA schedules show the computations under I and II.

		Leasehold Improvements				
		A	*B*	*C*	*D*	*Total*
		$	$	$	$	$
I.	Additions	16,000	—	5,000	—	21,000
	Less: Capital cost allowance 1991	(1,000)	—	(500)	—	(1,500)
	Undepreciated capital cost December 31, 1991	15000	—	4,500	—	19,500
	Additions	—	21,000	—	—	21,000
	Less: Capital cost allowance 1992	(2,000)	(1.500)	(1,000)	—	(4,500)
	Undepreciated capital cost December 31, 1992	13,000	19,500	3,500	—	36,000
	Additions	—	—	—	—	—
	Disposals	(9000)	(21,000)	—	—	(30,000)
		4,000	(1,500)	3,500	—	6,000
	Less: Capital cost allowance 1993[1]	(1,000)	—	(500)	—	(1,500)

¶420

Undepreciated capital cost June 30, 1993 ..	3,000	(1,500)	3,000	—	4,500
Additions: July 1, 1993 ...	—	—	—	15,000	15,000
Less: Capital cost allowance 1994	(2,000)	—	(1,000)	(1,500)	(4,500)
Undepreciated capital cost June 30, 1994 ..	1,000	(1,500)	2,000	13,500	15,000

[1] Prorated for short fiscal period.

Leasehold Improvements

	A	B	C	D	Total
	$	$	$	$	$
II. Undepreciated capital cost					
December 31, 1992	13,000	19,500	3,500	—	36,000
Additions	—	—	—	15,000	15,000
Disposals	(9,000)	(21,000)	—	—	(30,000)
	4,000	(1,500)	3,500	15,000	21,000
Less: Capital cost allowance 1993	(2,000)	—	(1,000)	(1,500)	(4,500)
Undepreciated capital cost December 31, 1993	2,000	(1,500)	2,500	13,500	16,500
Additions and disposals ..	—	—	—	—	—
Less: Capital cost allowance 1994	(2,000)	—	(1,000)	(3,000)	(6,000)
Undepreciated capital cost December 31, 1994	—	(1,500)	1,500	10,500	10,500
Additions and disposals ..	—	—	—	—	—
Less: Capital cost allowance 1995	—	—	(1,000)	(3,000)	(4,000)
Undepreciated capital cost December 31, 1995	—	(1,500)	500	7,500	6,500
Additions and disposals ..	—	—	—	—	—
Less: Capital cost allowance 1996	—	—	(500)	(3,000)	(3,500)
Undepreciated capital cost December 31, 1996	—	(1,500)	—	4,500	3,000
Less: Capital cost allowance 1997	—	—	—	(3,000)	(3,000)

¶420

Undepreciated capital cost December 31, 1997	—	(1,500)	—	1,500	—
Less: Capital cost allowance 1998	—	—	—	—	—
Undepreciated capital cost December 31, 1998	—	(1,500)	—	1,500	—

¶425   Class 14 — Patents, Copyrights, Franchises, Concessions, etc.

Property which is a patent, franchise, concession or licence for a limited period in respect of property is included in Class 14. *Excluded* from this provision are:

(a) a franchise (except a franchise for distributing gas to consumers or a licence to export gas from Canada or from a province), concession or licence in respect of minerals, petroleum, natural gas, other related hydrocarbons or timber, property relating to such products, or a right to explore for, drill for, take or remove such products;

(b) leasehold interests;

(c) a property included in Class 23 (a leasehold or licence in respect of land granted under an agreement with the Canadian Corporation for the 1967 World Exhibition or the Expo 86 Corporation);

(d) a licence to use computer software; and

(e) a patent or right to use patented information for a limited or unlimited period, acquired after April 26, 1993, that is included in Class 44.

Licences to use computer software for commercial exploitation are Class 12 property. See ¶415 for comments on classes for systems software. If an owner of a copyright sells to a third person the right to use the copyright for a limited period, such right becomes, in the hands of that third person, a licence or a concession, the cost of which is depreciable as a Class 14 asset under the provisions of Regulation 1100(1)(c).

The amount claimed for a Class 14 asset under Regulation 1100(1)(c) may not exceed the aggregate of the amounts for the year obtained by apportioning the capital cost to the taxpayer of each property equally over the life of the property remaining at the time the cost was incurred. This particular class of assets is depreciated on the straight-line method of depreciation, rather than on the declining balance system. The half-year rule (see ¶140) for the year in which assets are acquired does not apply to this class of assets. However, the Canada Revenue Agency's position is that the cost of an asset in Class 14 should be apportioned over the life of the asset on a *per diem* basis.

There is a special formula governed by Regulation 1100(9) for capital cost allowances in respect of patents, the cost of which is determined by reference to the use of the patent. Instead of the normal deduction allowed under Regulation 1100(1)(c) described above, the taxpayer may deduct the lesser of:

(a) the capital cost determined by reference to the use of the patent in the year *plus* the normal allowance claimed under Regulation 1100(1)(c) on that portion of the capital cost not determined by use; and

(b) the undepreciated cost to the taxpayer as of the end of the taxation year of property of the class, before making any deduction under this provision for that year.

To be a Class 14 asset, the patent, franchise, concession or licence must be for a limited period. Where a franchise, concession or licence is for an indefinite period, no capital cost allowance is permitted. However, the cost may be an eligible capital expenditure; see ¶725 *et seq.* See Interpretation Bulletin IT-477, "Capital Cost Allowance — Patents, Franchises, Concessions and Licences", at ¶3260.

A patent or the right to use patented information for a limited or unlimited period, acquired after April 26, 1993, is included in Class 44 at 25% (see ¶570). However, Regulation 1103(2h) provides that a taxpayer may elect not to include such property in Class 44. If the taxpayer so elects, the patent would be included in Class 14 if it is for a limited period, and an eligible capital expenditure if it is for an unlimited period. The election must be made in the year the property is acquired by a letter attached to the tax return for that year.

Proposed subsections 13(4.2) and (4.3) and a proposed amendment to the definition of "former business property" in subsection 248(1) allow for the replacement property rules in subsection 13(4) to apply to replacements of franchises, concessions or limited period licences (i.e., certain Class 14 properties) in certain circumstances. See ¶193, Replacement Property.

¶430   Class 15 — Woods Assets

Under Regulation 1100(1)(*f*), provision is made for deductions in respect of the capital cost of property of Class 15. This class consists of depreciable property that was acquired for the purpose of cutting and removing merchantable timber from a timber limit, and will be of no further use to the taxpayer after all merchantable timber has been removed from the limit. It is provided under Regulation 1102(7) that, for the purposes of Regulation 1100(1)(*f*), capital cost includes the amount expended by a taxpayer on river improvements for the purposes of facilitating the removal of timber from a timber limit.

The taxpayer may elect not to include a property in the class, but it appears that this election will be in effect for that property for all future years. The taxpayer may presumably claim an allowance on any property with respect to which the taxpayer makes such an election at the normal rates which would be applicable to the property if Class 15 were not in Schedule II.

Property identical to that described in Class 15 is also included in paragraph (n) of Class 10 to which the CCA rate of 30% is applicable. A taxpayer who elects to claim CCA under paragraph (n) of Class 10 will have to include all such property under that class. On the other hand, if the taxpayer chooses to take advantage of Class 15, the taxpayer need not place *all* such property under Class 15. Having selected Class 15, the taxpayer is free to exclude some of the property from being claimed under that class and may place it — if otherwise applicable — in another class, excepting, of course, paragraph (n) of Class 10. Thus, the taxpayer may elect, for example, to claim CCA on certain property under paragraph (o) of Class 10 (mechanical equipment for logging operations), rather than under Class 15, under which the taxpayer has placed his or her other assets. However, once such election has been made, the property included by the taxpayer under any other class cannot be included in Class 15.

The maximum amount that may be claimed in respect of the capital cost of property of Class 15 is determined in accordance with Schedule IV (¶2544). Under Schedule IV, the amount that may be deducted in respect of such property is an amount computed on the basis of a rate per cord, board foot, or cubic metre cut in the taxation year. If all the property of the class is used in connection with one timber limit or a section thereof, the rate per cord, board foot, or cubic metre is determined by dividing the undepreciated capital cost of the property by the number of cords, board feet, or cubic metres of timber in the limit or section thereof as at the commencement of the taxation year. Where different parts of the property of the class are used in connection with different timber limits or sections thereof, separate rates are computed for each part of the property as though each part of the property were the taxpayer's only property of that class. Since the property will be of no further use after the limit is exhausted, such as buildings and river improvements, unless the CCA is clearly related to the life of the limit, the taxpayer might be unable to recover the whole of his or her capital costs. The amount of the CCA is related to the number of units taken from the limit rather than to a predetermined percentage of capital cost. Under Schedule IV, the same rate of CCA will continue from year to year unless there is a cruise that indicates a change in the quantity of timber recoverable from the limit, or unless there are additions to or deletions from the capital cost of the woods assets. The half-year rule is not applicable to Class 15, nor is the capital cost allowance prorated in short years.

¶435 Class 16 (40%) — Large Trucks, Taxicabs, Rental Cars, Video and Pinball Games

Large trucks and tractors with a gross vehicle weight rating in excess of 11,788 kilograms that are acquired after December 6, 1991 are included in Class 16. These trucks and tractors must be used by the taxpayer, or a person with whom the taxpayer does not deal at arm's length, primarily for hauling freight. Other assets listed in Class 16 include: aircraft and aircraft fittings and equipment acquired before May 26, 1976; taxicabs acquired after May 25, 1976; automobiles acquired after November 12, 1981 for short-term rentals or leases (including vehicles otherwise excluded from the definition of automobile under paragraph (d) of the definition in subsection 248(1)); and coin-operated video games or pinball machines acquired after February 15, 1984.

An aircraft (including furniture, fittings, or equipment attached thereto, or a spare part therefor) acquired after May 25, 1976 is subject to a lower rate of 25% under Class 9.

Regulation 1100(2.4) was introduced as a result of the change in classification of rented or leased automobiles acquired after November 12, 1981 from Class 10 to Class 16. In order that taxpayers affected by this change be given the same tax treatment under the half-year rule as other taxpayers, any Class 10 dispositions of property which would have been considered Class 16, if acquired after November 12, 1981, will for purposes of the half-year rule in Regulation 1100(2) be considered to be dispositions of Class 16 assets. This regulation applies only for purposes of computing capital cost allowance, not for purposes of recapture. For the purposes of recapture, the property remains in Class 10, unless the taxpayer makes an election under Regulation 1103(2d) to transfer the Class 10 asset to Class 16.

¶440 Class 17 (8%) — Telegraph or Telephone Systems, Surface Construction

Class 17 incorporates property of a telephone or telegraph system as well as roads, sidewalks, airplane runways, parking areas, storage areas or similar surface construction acquired after May 25, 1976. Class 17 property is normally subject to an 8% rate of depreciation calculated on the undepreciated capital cost of the assets.

A road, sidewalk, airplane runway, parking area, storage area or similar surface construction, acquired before May 26, 1976, is included in Class 1 with a 4% rate of capital cost allowance. For additional telephone, telegraph or data communication equipment, acquired after May 25, 1976, see Classes 3 and 8, and for radio transmission equipment, see Class 9.

Under Regulation 1103(2), a taxpayer whose chief depreciable properties are included in Class 17, may elect to include in Class 17 any other property acquired before May 26, 1976 for the purpose of gaining or producing income from the same business.

Draft amendments add paragraph (a.1) to Class 17 to include property (other than a building or other structure) acquired after February 27, 2000 that is:

- new electrical generating equipment (except for equipment described in paragraphs (*f*) to (*h*) of Class 8); or

- new production and distribution equipment of a water or steam distributor that is used for heating or cooling (including pipe used to collect or distribute an energy transfer medium, but excluding equipment or pipe used to distribute water that is for consumption, disposal or treatment).

The 2005 Federal Budget proposes to increase the CCA rate for combustion turbine engines that generate electricity from 8% under Class 17, to 15% for such property acquired after February 22, 2005. The separate class election available under Regulation 1101(5t) for combustion turbines included in Class 17 will be eliminated for assets acquired after 2006. In addition, the specified energy property rules are to be expanded to include combustion turbine engines.

¶445 Class 18 (60%) — Motion Picture Films Acquired Before May 26, 1976

Class 18 includes motion picture films acquired before May 26, 1976, except television commercials and certified feature films. Commercials and certified feature films are Class 12 property and are subject to a rate of 100%. Other films acquired after May 25, 1976 are Class 10 assets. See the commentary at ¶415.

¶450 Class 19 — Accelerated Allowances

Class 19 was added to give accelerated capital cost allowances to some Canadian resident individuals and corporations. It applies to property that would otherwise be in Class 8, principally machinery and equipment. The property must have been acquired between June 14, 1963 and December 31, 1967 for use in Canada in a business (other than the operation of a gas or oil well, logging, mining or construction or any combination thereof) carried on by the taxpayer that, for the year of acquisition or the first year of business, whichever was later, derived at least two-thirds of its gross revenues from the sale of goods processed or manufactured in Canada, rent from such goods, or the sale of advertisements in a newspaper or magazine produced by the business. Class 19 and Regulation 1100(1)(*n*) allow the taxpayer a deduction of 50% of the capital cost of the asset.

Regulation 1103(2a) permits a taxpayer to elect to include in Class 8 all Class 19 or 21 property owned at the commencement of the year. The election is exercised by attaching a letter to that effect to the return for the taxation year concerned.

¶445

¶455 Class 20 — Buildings

Class 20 includes property that was acquired after December 5, 1963 and before April 1, 1967 that would otherwise be included in Class 3 or 6. Under Class 20, a taxpayer is permitted to deduct 20%, on a straight-line basis, of the capital cost of a new building, or a substantial extension to an existing building, in a designated area. Under Regulation 1103(2f), a taxpayer may elect to transfer all Class 20 assets to Classes 1, 3 or 6. See the commentary on Class 1 (at ¶360) for a discussion of capital cost allowance on buildings.

¶460 Class 21 — Straight-Line Depreciation

Class 21 and Regulation $1100(1)(q)$ together allow a taxpayer a deduction in computing income of 50%, on the straight-line method, of the capital cost of property that would otherwise be included in Class 8 or 19 that is:

(a) previously unused and acquired after December 5, 1963 and before April 1, 1967, to be used in a business that was certified by the Minister of Industry to be a new manufacturing or processing business in a designated area; or

(b) property whose capital cost was included in the approved capital cost for the purpose of a development grant under the *Area Development Incentives Act*. This Act is applicable to a facility or expanded facility brought into commercial production on or before March 31, 1971.

Regulation 1103(2a) permits a taxpayer to elect to include in Class 8 all Class 19 or 21 property owned at the commencement of a taxation year. The election is exercised by attaching a letter to that effect to the return for the taxation year concerned.

¶465 Class 22 — Fast Write-Off, Contractor's Movable Equipment

Class 22 provides capital cost allowance at 50% for certain equipment that would otherwise usually be treated as contractor's movable equipment under Class 10 where the rate is only 30%. The fast write-off applies only to property acquired before 1988, or before 1990 pursuant to an obligation in writing entered into by the taxpayer before June 18, 1987, or where the property was under construction by or on behalf of the taxpayer on June 18, 1987. Property acquired after those dates that would otherwise qualify for inclusion in Class 22 is required to be included in Class 38, which allows a capital cost allowance rate of 30%. A discussion of the types of property qualifying for inclusion in Class 22 is included with the commentary on Class 38 (¶540). See Interpretation Bulletin IT-469R, "Capital Cost Allowance — Earth-Moving Equipment", at ¶3245.

¶470   Class 23 (100%) — Property Acquired for World Exhibitions

Under the provisions of Regulation 1100(1)(a), the allowable rate of capital cost allowance for property falling within Class 23 is 100%.

Paragraph (a) of Class 23 requires that a lease must have been granted by the Canadian Corporation for the 1967 World Exhibition, and that the leasehold interest must expire no later than June 15, 1968. Under paragraph (b) the buildings must be of a temporary nature, and they are required to be removed no later than June 15, 1968.

Paragraphs (c) and (d) make similar provisions for leasehold interests and licences granted by the Expo 86 Corporation. Such interests or licences must expire no later than January 31, 1987, and buildings or other structures are required to be removed no later than that date.

¶475   Class 24 — Water Pollution Control Equipment

Class 24 permits a taxpayer to claim accelerated capital cost allowance in respect of water pollution control equipment. It was announced on February 22, 1994 that Classes 24 and 27 (air pollution equipment) are no longer available for property acquired after December 31, 1998. Pollution control equipment acquired after 1998 will mostly go into Class 1, 2, 3, 6, 8 or 43, depending on its description and use. The calculation of the three-year accelerated capital cost allowance provided for in Regulation 1100(1)(ta) is the same for assets in Classes 24, 27, 29 and 34. Generally, the maximum capital cost allowance that may be claimed in the year of acquisition is 25% of the original cost. The balance of the capital cost allowance is claimed over the following two years — 50% in Year 2 and 25% in Year 3. Assets in these classes that were acquired before November 13, 1981 were written off over two years. Transitional rules in Regulation 1100(1)(t) are in effect for property acquired around this period. Pollution control equipment designed to upgrade pre-1974 facilities must be acquired before 1999 in order to qualify for the accelerated write-off.

In respect of property acquired after April 26, 1965 and before January 1, 1971, the accelerated allowance applies to property that falls within Class 24(a) and which would otherwise be included in Class 2 (certain generating and distributing equipment, water, gas or oil pipelines), Classes 3 or 6 (buildings and similar structures) and Class 8 (assets not included in other classes) of Schedule II.

The water pollution control property described in paragraph (b) of Class 24 is that which was acquired after 1970 and before 1999, which would otherwise be included in another class of Schedule II and which has not been included in another class by the taxpayer. The property must be new when acquired and must be used primarily for the prevention, reduction, or elimination of pollution of inland, coastal or boundary water of

Canada, or of any lake, river, stream, watercourse, pond, swamp or well in Canada, which is caused by:

(a) operations carried on at a site where the taxpayer has carried on operations prior to 1974;

(b) the operation of a building or plant, the construction of which commenced, or an agreement in writing for the construction of which was entered into by the taxpayer, prior to 1974; or

(c) the operation of transportation or other movable equipment by the taxpayer in Canada from a time prior to 1974.

Paragraph (b) of Class 24 also includes property acquired after May 8, 1972 and before 1999 by a taxpayer whose business includes preventing, reducing or eliminating water pollution that is caused primarily by the operations referred to in that provision which are carried on by other taxpayers. In addition, this class includes property acquired after May 8, 1972 and before 1999 by a corporation whose principal business is financing the sale price of merchandise or services, lending money or leasing property, or any combination of these activities, if the property is to be leased to a taxpayer to be used in an operation of the kind referred to in this class in preventing, reducing or eliminating water pollution. Property of this kind will qualify if it is to be leased either to a taxpayer who carries on the operations causing the pollution, or a taxpayer whose business includes the preventing, reducing or eliminating of such pollution by other taxpayers under the conditions referred to above.

In order to qualify for the accelerated allowance, the property must, upon application by the taxpayer, have been accepted by the Minister of the Environment as property the primary purpose of which is the prevention, reduction or elimination of water pollution of the kind referred to in paragraph (b) of Class 24 and described above. The eligibility of such property, once established, can flow through corporate amalgamations and wind-ups.

¶480   Class 25 (100%) — Tax-Exempt Entities

Class 25 applies to certain corporations, commissions and associations, as well as their wholly-owned subsidiary corporations, where at least 90% of the shares or capital of such a corporation, commission or association is owned by Her Majesty in Right of Canada, a province or a Canadian municipality. Such otherwise tax-exempt entities, that were taxable because of the existence of a right or option to purchase their shares, may be entitled to an accelerated write-off of capital cost allowance at 100% for certain pre-1974 depreciable properties.

¶485   Class 26 (5%) — Catalysts and Heavy Water

Class 26 assets include catalysts and deuterium enriched water (commonly known as "heavy water") acquired after May 22, 1979. Such property is depreciable at a rate of 5%.

¶490   Class 27 — Air Pollution Control Equipment

The air pollution control equipment described in Class 27 is eligible for an accelerated allowance over three years of the capital cost of the property similar to that available for assets in Class 24 described above. It was announced on February 22, 1994 that Classes 24 (water pollution equipment) and 27 are no longer available for property acquired after December 31, 1998. Pollution control equipment acquired after 1998 will mostly go into Class 1, 2, 3, 6, 8 or 43, depending on its description and use. The property is that which was acquired after March 12, 1970 and before 1999, which would otherwise be included in another class of Schedule II, and which has not been included in another class by the taxpayer. The property must be new when acquired and must be acquired primarily for the purpose of removing particulate, toxic or injurious materials from smoke or gas to prevent the discharge of part or all of the smoke, gas or other air pollutant that is, or would be, discharged into the atmosphere as a result of:

(a) operations carried on at a site where the taxpayer has carried on operations prior to 1974;

(b) the operation of a building or plant, the construction of which commenced, or an agreement in writing for the construction of which was entered into by the taxpayer, prior to 1974; or

(c) the operation of transportation or other movable equipment by the taxpayer in Canada prior to 1974.

Pollution control equipment designed to upgrade pre-1974 facilities must be acquired before 1999 in order to qualify for the accelerated write-off.

Class 27 also includes property acquired after May 8, 1972 and before 1999 by a taxpayer whose business includes preventing, reducing or eliminating air pollution that is caused primarily by the operations referred to in that provision which are carried on by other taxpayers. In addition, this class includes property acquired after May 8, 1972 and before 1999 by a corporation whose principal business is financing the sale price of merchandise or services, lending money or leasing property, or any combination of these activities, if the property is to be leased to a taxpayer to be used in an operation of the kind referred to in this class in preventing, reducing or eliminating air pollution. Property of this kind will qualify if it is to be leased either to the taxpayer which carries on the operations causing the pollution, or a taxpayer whose business includes the preventing, reducing or eliminating of such pollution by other taxpayers under the conditions referred to above.

¶485

In order to qualify for the accelerated allowance, the property must, upon application by the taxpayer, have been accepted by the Minister of the Environment as property the primary purpose of which is the prevention, reduction or elimination of air pollution in the manner described above. The eligibility of such property, once established, can flow through corporate amalgamations and wind-ups.

Regulation $1100(1)(ta)$ provides that the maximum CCA available for a Class 27 asset is 25% in the year of acquisition, 50% the next year and 25% in Year 3. It will be noted that the accelerated allowance applies to the capital cost of the asset and not to the undepreciated capital cost. In other words, the allowance is computed on a straight-line basis. Since the prorating provisions in Regulation 1100(3) for taxation years of less than 12 months do extend to pollution control equipment, it is necessary for a taxpayer whose fiscal year is less than 12 months to prorate the accelerated allowance.

¶495 Class 28 — Mine Buildings, Machinery and Equipment

Class 28 property consists of certain mine buildings, machinery and equipment which would otherwise be in Class 10 but were acquired to be used in connection with a new mine or a major expansion of an existing mine. Property included in Class 28 is eligible for a 30% rate of capital cost allowance; however, Regulations $1100(1)(w)$ and (x) provide for an additional allowance to the extent of the income from the mine.

As a result of the tax reform measures tabled on June 18, 1987, the basic CCA rate for resource extraction assets was reduced from 30% to 25%. This was accomplished by introducing Class 41 (¶555) with a basic CCA rate of 25%, which generally includes all resource extraction assets acquired after 1987. The additional allowance for assets that would have qualified for inclusion in Class 28, but are now required to be included in Class 41, has been retained in Regulations $1100(1)(y)$ and (ya).

To qualify for inclusion in Class 28, the property must have been acquired after November 7, 1969 and generally before 1988, although certain property acquired before 1990 will be included in Class 28 if it was acquired pursuant to an obligation in writing entered into by the taxpayer before June 18, 1987, or was under construction by or on behalf of the taxpayer on June 18, 1987. In addition, machinery or equipment acquired before 1990 that is a fixed and integral part of property under construction on June 18, 1987 will also qualify.

Except for the date of acquisition, the requirements for inclusion of property in Class 28 are identical to the requirements for inclusion in Class $41(a)$. These requirements are discussed in detail in the commentary pertaining to Class 41 (¶555), as are the additional allowances available for Class 28 assets pursuant to Regulations $1100(1)(w)$ and (x).

¶500 Class 29 — Manufacturing and Processing Machinery and Equipment

Machinery and equipment used in Canadian manufacturing and processing that were acquired before January 1, 1988 are included in Class 29 and may be written off over three years in the same way as for assets in Classes 24, 27 and 34. The Class 29 fast write-off has been eliminated for property acquired after that date. Such property acquired between January 1, 1988 and February 25, 1992 inclusive is included in Class 39 at 25% (see ¶545). Manufacturing and processing machinery and equipment acquired after February 25, 1992 is included in Class 43 at 30% (see ¶565).

Property eligible for the fast write-off in Class 29 must meet three tests. The first two tests are also relevant for assets acquired after 1997 since the descriptions for Classes 39 and 43 refer to assets that, except for the date of acquisition, would otherwise have been included in Class 29. First, it must be used by the taxpayer directly or indirectly in Canada primarily in the manufacture or processing of goods for sale or lease. Property will also qualify if it is to be leased, in the ordinary course of business in Canada, to a lessee who will use the property primarily in the manufacture or processing of goods for sale or lease, if the lessor is a corporation whose principal business is:

(a) leasing property;

(b) manufacturing property that it sells or leases;

(c) the lending of money;

(d) the factoring of accounts receivable or other obligations representing the sale price of merchandise or services; or

(e) selling or servicing a type or property that it also leases, or any combination thereof.

Second, it must be property that would otherwise be included in Class 8 (except railway rolling stock or property described in Class 8(*j*) radiocommunication equipment), an oil or water storage tank, a powered industrial lift truck, certain small electrical generating equipment described in Class 9, rental tools described in Class 10(*b*), or general-purpose electronic data processing equipment and systems software described in Class 10(*f*).

Third, the property must be acquired after May 8, 1972, or if manufactured by the taxpayer, the manufacture must be completed after May 8, 1972. Additionally, the property must be acquired by the taxpayer before 1988, or before 1990 if it was acquired pursuant to a written obligation entered into before June 18, 1987. Transitional rules govern in the circumstance of assets under construction at June 18, 1987, or large projects commenced prior to that date.

Subsection 13(10) provides that a taxpayer who acquires prescribed property after December 3, 1970 and before April 1, 1972 for use in a prescribed manufacturing or processing business carried on by the taxpayer shall be deemed to have acquired the property at a capital cost equal to 115% of the amount that would otherwise have been its capital cost to the taxpayer.

Property prescribed for purposes of subsection 13(10) is set out in Regulation 1102(15)(*a*) and includes:

(a) buildings in Class 3 or 6 of Schedule II; or

(b) machinery and equipment in Class 8 of Schedule II (general machinery or equipment not included in any other class).

As a result of the tax reform measures tabled on June 18, 1987, many of the pre-existing tax incentives to the manufacturing sector, such as the business investment tax credit, the manufacturing and processing tax rate reduction to small Canadian companies, and the fast write-off of production machinery by virtue of Class 29, were either removed or significantly altered. The elimination of the fast write-off Class 29 property was accomplished by introducing Class 39 for manufacturing assets purchased after 1987 and before February 26, 1992. Class 39 assets bear a basic declining balance rate of 25%; however, transitional rules phase the rate down to that level starting at 40% for 1988, 35% for 1989, 30% for 1990, and 25% thereafter.

Except for the date of acquisition, and three specific deletions, the requirements for inclusion of property in Class 29 are identical to the requirements for inclusion in Classes 39 and 43(*a*). The Class 29 assets which are not included in Class 39 or 43 are powered industrial lift trucks, Class 10(*b*) portable tools acquired for earning short-term rental income, and Class 10(*f*) general-purpose electronic data processing equipment and systems software. Such assets are described in Class 40 for 1988 and 1989, and Class 10 thereafter. Class 40 is not in effect for taxation years beginning in 1990 and beyond and so all the assets in that class are transferred to Class 10 for taxation years beginning after 1989.

A taxpayer that has no manufacturing and processing profits because of the definition of manufacturing and processing profits (section 125.1) might still have Class 29 assets eligible for fast write-off. On the other hand, a taxpayer might have manufacturing and processing profits, but not all of its Class 8 assets (i.e., office equipment) would be eligible for the fast write-off because their primary use was not in the manufacturing or processing of goods for sale or lease.

Meaning of "Primarily" and "Manufacturing or Processing"

"Primarily" and "manufacturing or processing" are not defined in the *Income Tax Act*, but see Interpretation Bulletin IT-147R3, "Capital Cost Allowance — Accelerated Write-Off of Manufacturing and Processing

¶500

Machinery and Equipment" (¶3125), for the Canada Revenue Agency's interpretation.

The CRA uses the benchmark for "primarily" as being more than 50%. Court decisions indicate that it refers to first in rank or order of importance — i.e., not the majority but rather the largest of the activities carried on. In the case of a property which has only two uses, the majority use will govern. In *Mother's Pizza Parlour (London) Limited and Mother's Pizza Parlour Limited v. M.N.R.*, 88 DTC 6397 (F.C.A.), it was held that when different parts of the same building are used for two different purposes, such as the processing of food and the consumption of food, the most important factor in determining the purpose for which the building is primarily used is the amount of space in the building that is used for each one of those two purposes. In *Burger King Restaurants of Canada Inc. v. The Queen*, 2000 DTC 6061, the Federal Court of Appeal held that the processing areas in the taxpayer's buildings occupied less than 50% of the total areas of the buildings, so that such buildings were not being used "primarily" for the purpose of processing. In the judgment, however, the Court did state the following:

> In accordance with *Mother's Pizza*, use of the space in the buildings is the most important consideration in determining the use primarily made of the buildings. However, that does not exclude other considerations and we are prepared to assume, without deciding, that in a case such as this, a qualitative assessment is also relevant. See *Gulf Canada Resources Limited v. The Queen* (93 DTC 5345 (F.C.T.D.)).

> However, the qualitative evidence must be sufficiently persuasive and must be capable of being analysed in such a way as to cause the Court to displace the result of the quantitative space test.

In *Cintas Canada Limited v. The Queen*, 99 DTC 926, the Tax Court of Canada decided that the taxpayer's uniform rental business and dry-cleaning business involved the "manufacturing or processing of goods for sale or lease in Canada". The Court cited *Federal Farms Ltd. v. M.N.R.*, 66 DTC 5068 (Ex. Ct.), affirmed by the Supreme Court of Canada without reasons, 67 DTC 5311, as the leading case in determining the meaning of the term "processing" for the purposes of manufacturing and processing credit. In that case, Mr. Justice Cattanach of the Exchequer Court held that the term "processed" was to be given its common or ordinary meaning.

Regulation 1104(9) expressly *excludes* from the meaning of "manufacturing or processing" the following activities:

(a) farming and fishing;

(b) logging;

(c) construction;

(d) operating a gas or oil well;

(e) extracting minerals from a mineral resource;

¶500

(f) processing ore from a mineral resource to the prime metal stage or its equivalent;

(g) producing industrial minerals (other than sulphur produced by processing natural gas);

(h) producing or processing electrical energy or steam for sale;

(i) processing natural gas as part of the business of selling or distributing gas in the course of operating a public utility;

(j) processing in Canada heavy crude oil recovered from a natural reservoir in Canada to a stage not beyond the crude oil stage or its equivalent; or

(k) Canadian field processing.

¶505 Class 30 (40%) — Telecommunications Spacecraft

Class 30 of Schedule II contains property that is an unmanned telecommunication spacecraft designed to orbit above the earth. The CCA rate for Class 30 property is 40%. Such properties are included in Class 30 only if acquired before 1988, or before 1990 if acquired pursuant to an agreement in writing entered into before June 18, 1987, or if the property was under construction on June 18, 1987. Such properties acquired after 1987 and not eligible for "grandfathering" relief are included in Class 10(f.2), which has a capital cost allowance rate of 30%. Regulation 1101(5a) establishes a separate class for each such spacecraft for CCA purposes.

¶510 Classes 31 and 32 (5% and 10%) — Multiple-Unit Residential Buildings

Classes 31 and 32 encompass multiple-unit residential buildings ("MURBs"). These are buildings which would otherwise come within Class 3 or 6, and which meet the additional requirements discussed below for inclusion in Class 31 or 32. Such buildings qualify as MURBs if they are acquired by the taxpayer prior to June 18, 1987 subject to grandfathering provisions for obligations in writing entered into before June 18, 1987, or pursuant to a prospectus or similar filing document filed with a public authority before June 18, 1987. Buildings acquired after June 17, 1987 that do not meet these "grandfathering" tests are included in Class 1. Regulation 1101(5b) provides that each MURB with a capital cost of $50,000 or more is to be included in a separate class. See also the commentary on Class 1 at ¶360.

For taxation years up to and including 1993, MURBs included in Class 31 or 32 were not subject to the rental property restrictions in Regulation 1100(11) that prohibit the deduction of capital cost allowance where such deduction would create or increase a loss from rental properties in the year. Consequently, until 1994, capital cost allowance could be claimed in respect of such properties to create or increase a loss that could be used to "shelter" other income.

Class 31 MURBs

A building qualifies as a Class 31 (5%) MURB if:

(a) in respect of a building that would otherwise be included in Class 3, a certificate has been issued by Canada Mortgage and Housing Corporation (CMHC) (formerly Central Mortgage and Housing Corporation) certifying that the installation of footings or other base support had commenced either after November 18, 1974 and before January 1, 1980, or after October 28, 1980 and before January 1, 1982. Where the installation of footings or other base support commenced during the period January 1, 1980 to October 28, 1980, the building would not qualify;

(b) in respect of a building that would otherwise be included in Class 6, a certificate has been issued by CMHC certifying that the installation of footings or other base support had commenced after 1977 and before 1979;

(c) the certificate referred to in both (a) and (b) above certifies that according to the plans and specifications for the building, not less than 80% of the floor space will be used in providing self-contained domestic establishments and related parking, recreation, service and storage areas;

(d) actual experience with the building shows that not more than 20% of the floor space is used for purposes other than those referred to in (c);

(e) the certificate referred to in both (a) and (b) above has been issued on or before the later of December 31, 1981, and the day that is 18 months after the day on which the installation of footings or other base support of the building was commenced; and

(f) the construction of the building proceeds, after 1982, without undue delay, taking into consideration acts of God, labour disputes, fire, accidents or unusual delay by common carriers or suppliers of material or equipment.

In addition to these requirements, the building must have been acquired before June 18, 1987, subject to the grandfathering provisions discussed above.

Class 32 MURBs

A building qualifies as a Class 32 (10%) MURB if:

(a) it was acquired before 1980 and would otherwise be included in Class 6. In general, buildings of the construction described in para-

¶510

graph (a) of Class 6 only qualify for inclusion in Class 6 if acquired before 1979. However, for the purposes of Class 32, a building is considered to qualify for inclusion in Class 6 if acquired before 1980;

(b) a certificate has been issued by Central Mortgage and Housing Corporation certifying that the installation of footings or other base support had commenced after November 18, 1974 and before 1978;

(c) the CMHC certificate certifies that according to the plans and specifications for the building, not less than 80% of the floor space will be used in providing self-contained domestic establishments and related parking, recreation, service and storage areas; and

(d) actual experience with the building shows that not more than 20% of the floor space is used for purposes other than those referred to in (c).

Separate Classes

Under Regulation 1101(5b), each MURB costing not less than $50,000 forms a separate class of property. Thus, on a sale of such a building, there may be a recapture of capital cost allowance notwithstanding that the taxpayer owns other multiple-unit residential buildings. MURBs costing less than $50,000 will form a single class of Class 31 or 32 properties.

¶515   Class 33 (15%) — Timber Resource Property

Effective after May 6, 1974, timber resource property is included in Class 33 and capital cost allowance is claimed at 15% per year. Subsection 13(21) defines a "timber resource property" in terms of an "original right" and the extension or renewal of that right or a right acquired in substitution for such an original right. An original right is a right or licence to cut or remove timber from a limit or area in Canada originally acquired after May 6, 1974. At the time of the original acquisition it must be reasonably regarded that either:

(a) the taxpayer acquired, directly or indirectly, the right to extend or renew the right, or to acquire another such right or licence in substitution; or

(b) in the ordinary course of events, the taxpayer may expect to be able to extend or renew the original right or to acquire another such right or licence in substitution therefor.

A right or licence to cut or remove timber from a limit or area in Canada that may reasonably be regarded as an extension or renewal, or one of a series of extensions or renewals, of an original right, or as having been acquired in substitution for an original right, or as one of a series of substitutions, will also constitute timber resource property. If the right or licence in question can be considered to be an extension or renewal of, or to have been acquired in substitution for a right or licence which was originally acquired prior to May 7, 1974, such a right or licence will also constitute timber resource property. The right to or expectation of a single renewal, extension or substitution will be sufficient to constitute the original right and the renewal, extension or substitution of timber resource property. Since substitutions are included in the definition, the fact that the right arising after the termination of the original right is on terms which are substantially different from those of the original right would not prevent both rights from being timber resource property if one can reasonably be regarded as having been acquired in substitution for the other.

Where the right to cut timber constitutes timber resource property, a disposition will not give rise to a capital gain (subsection 39(1)), but rather the full amount by which the proceeds of disposition exceed the undepreciated capital cost of the class will be included in income (see the comment at ¶185). There is no separate class requirement for timber resource properties.

See Interpretation Bulletin IT-481, "Timber Resource Property and Timber Limits (Consolidated)", at ¶3270 and the discussion on timber limits at ¶605.

¶520   Class 34 — Energy Conservation Equipment

Equipment used for the production or distribution of heat and the generation of electricity or steam, acquired after May 25, 1976 and before February 22, 1994, which meets the prescribed criteria relating to efficient use for fuels or utilization of waste materials, and is so certified by either the Minister of Industry, Trade and Commerce (before December 11, 1979) or by the Minister of Energy, Mines and Resources (or as renamed, the Minister of Natural Resources), may be depreciated over three years on the basis of 25% the first year, 50% in Year 2, and 25% in Year 3. This accelerated depreciation is the same as for property in Classes 24, 27 and 29.

Additions to Class 34 were terminated for property acquired after February 21, 1994. There is transitional relief for property acquired pursuant to a written agreement entered into by the taxpayer before February 22, 1994, for property that was under construction before February 22, 1994, and for property acquired to satisfy a legally binding obligation entered into before February 22, 1994 to sell electricity to a public power utility in Canada. Assets that would be Class 34 except that they are acquired after February 21, 1994 are included in Class 43.1 and written off at a 30% rate. The requirement that the equipment be certified by the Minister of Energy, Mines and Resources is eliminated for these assets acquired after February 21, 1994.

It is to be noted that, insofar as property used for the production of heat is concerned, the definition of "eligible property" was expanded as of December 11, 1979. Before that date, only property designed to produce heat derived primarily from the consumption of wood wastes or municipal wastes was eligible for certification, while, on or after that date, property designed to produce heat derived primarily from the consumption of natural gas, coal, coal gas, lignite, peat, wood wastes, or municipal wastes was eligible for certification.

Certain other energy conservation equipment certified by the Minister of Energy, Mines and Resources is also Class 34 property. This includes active solar heating equipment, heat recovery equipment, and small-scale hydro-electric projects with a maximum generating capacity of 15 megawatts (acquired after December 10, 1979), as well as fixed-location wind-driven turbines and equipment ancillary thereto (acquired after February 25, 1986).

Regulations 1100(24) to (29) restrict the capital cost allowance claim on Class 34 and 43.1 assets for passive investors. Under Regulation 1100(24), the capital cost allowance that may be claimed by a passive investor in Class 34 or 43.1 "specified energy property" is limited to the amount of the investor's income from such property. "Specified energy property" is defined under Regulation 1100(25) as Class 34 or 43.1 property acquired after February 9, 1988, other than property used by the owner in carrying on a business in Canada (other than the business of selling the product of the property), or to earn Canadian income from other Canadian property. The restriction does not apply to corporations, the principal business of which is the sale, distribution or production of energy, or partnerships of such corporations, and for corporations whose principal business is manufacturing or leasing such property to qualified users. Effective for taxation years ending after March 6, 1996, these exceptions were extended to corporations whose principal businesses are mining or manufacturing and processing. The exceptions permit principal business corporations to claim capital cost allowance on Class 34/43.1 property against income from all sources. Grandfathering provisions outlined in Regulation 1100(27) (¶1930) apply to certain specified property acquired after February 9, 1988 and before 1990.

Regulation 1101(5m) requires that each specified energy property be placed in a separate class.

¶525   Class 35 (7%) — Railway Cars

Class 35 assets include railway cars acquired after May 25, 1976, and rail suspension devices designed to carry trailers that are designed to be hauled on both highways and railway tracks. The rail suspension devices must be acquired after December 23, 1991 other than such property acquired before 1993 pursuant to a written agreement entered into by the taxpayer before December 24, 1991, or that was under construction on December 23, 1991.

Separate classes are prescribed under Regulation 1101(5d) for railway cars included in Class 35 that are owned by a taxpayer and rented, leased or used by the taxpayer in Canada, other than those owned by a corporation that owns or operates a railway as a common carrier, or a corporation associated with such a corporation. Separate classes are prescribed for:

(1) railway cars acquired by the taxpayer before February 3, 1990, other than those acquired for rent or lease to another person;

(2) railway cars acquired by the taxpayer after February 2, 1990, other than those acquired for rent or lease to another person;

(3) railway cars acquired by the taxpayer before April 27, 1989 for rent or lease to another person; and

(4) railway cars acquired by the taxpayer after April 26, 1989 for rent or lease to another person.

For railway cars described under category (1), Regulation $1100(1)(z)$ permits a taxpayer to claim an additional allowance not exceeding 8% of the undepreciated capital cost to the taxpayer of such properties. Regulation $1100(1)(z.1a)$ provides a reduced 6% additional allowance for railway cars falling into categories (2) and (4). Railway cars that otherwise fall within category (2) will continue to qualify for the 8% allowance if they were acquired pursuant to an agreement in writing entered into before February 3, 1990, or if they were under construction by or on behalf of the taxpayer before February 3, 1990. For railway cars in category (3), the additional allowance is reduced by $1/3$% each year. For 1990, the applicable percentage is $7^2/3$%, for 1991 $7^1/3$%, for 1992 7%, for 1993 $6^2/3$%, and for 1994 $6^1/3$%. The 6% rate will apply for the 1995 and subsequent taxation years.

Regulation 1101(5d.1) prescribes a separate class for Class 35 assets acquired after December 6, 1991 by a taxpayer that was at that time a common carrier that owned and operated a railway. The assets in this separate class are eligible for an additional allowance of 3% on undepreciated capital cost as prescribed by Regulation $1100(1)(z.1b)$. A proposed amendment to Regulation 1101(5d.1) restricts its application to Class 35 assets acquired before February 28, 2000. New Regulation 1101(5d.2) prescribes a separate class for Class 35 assets acquired after February 27, 2000 by a taxpayer that was at that time a common carrier that owned and operated a railway. The assets in this separate class are eligible for an additional allowance of 6% on undepreciated capital cost as prescribed by Regulation $1100(1)(z.1c)$. The half-year rule in Regulation 1100(2), outlined in ¶140, applies when calculating any of these Class 35 additional allowances.

Draft Regulation 1103(2i) allows a taxpayer to elect to include in Class 35, rather than Class 7, railway assets that are described in paragraph (h) of Class 7, acquired after February 27, 2000, which would be eligible for an additional 6% allowance under Regulations $1100(1)(z.1a)$ and 1101(5d), or Regulations $1100(1)(z.1c)$ and 1101(5d.2), if Class 35

¶525

applied to the property. Property to which Regulation 1103(2i) applies is eligible for a combined allowance of 13% (7% + 6%), rather than an allowance of 15% under Class 7, but is exempt property for purposes of the specified leasing property rules in Regulation 1100(1.13).

As discussed in ¶360, Regulation 1100(1)(zc) provides an additional capital cost allowance deduction of 6% straight-line for new railway system assets acquired after April 10, 1978 and before 1988. The assets must be used or situated in Canada and owned by a taxpayer who owns and operates the railway as a common carrier. The additional deduction which applies to railway cars in Class 35 is available in the year of acquisition and the four taxation years following the year of acquisition.

For commentary on other types of railway assets see the commentary for Class 1 at ¶360.

¶530 Class 36 — Deemed Depreciable Property

Property deemed to be depreciable property by virtue of paragraph 13(5.2)(c) of the Act is included in Class 36. Under Regulation 1101(5g), each property in Class 36 is deemed to be a separate class. Under subsection 13(5.2) (see commentary at ¶195), certain rules apply if a taxpayer deducts the rental charges for the use of depreciable property or real property and later acquires that property at a cost of less than fair market value. The taxpayer is deemed to have acquired the property at a certain cost, and the difference between the deemed cost and the actual cost is deemed to have been allowed to the taxpayer as depreciation in respect of the class to which the property belongs. If the property would not otherwise be depreciable property (for example, because it was land), paragraph 13(5.2)(c) deems the property to be depreciable property of a separate prescribed class — Class 36.

As a result of these provisions, to the extent that the deemed cost is greater than the actual cost, recaptured depreciation up to the amount of the taxpayer's deemed cost rather than a capital gain could result on the subsequent sale of the property. The fact that real property is deemed to be property of a prescribed class does not, however, entitle the taxpayer to claim capital cost allowance on that property.

¶535 Class 37 (15%) — Amusement Park Property

Capital cost allowance at a maximum rate of 15% may be claimed in respect of the undepreciated capital cost of the property used in connection with an amusement park. An "amusement park" is defined in Regulation 1104(12) to mean a park open to the public where amusements, rides, and audio-visual attractions are permanently situated.

Under Regulation 1103(2b), a taxpayer may elect to include in Class 37 all property described in Class 37 notwithstanding the fact that the property was acquired before the date upon which Class 37 became effective (February 26, 1982).

¶540   Class 38 — Earth-Moving Equipment

Class 38 was introduced to implement the June 18, 1987 tax reform proposals to reduce the CCA rate for certain earth-moving equipment from 50% to 30%. The rate reduction was phased in (set out in Regulation 1100(1)(zd)) so that the rate for Class 38 was 40% for 1988, 35% for 1989, and 30% thereafter. These phase-in percentages applied for purposes of calculating the CCA claim in the calendar years in question; for fiscal periods ending on a date other than December 31, the relevant percentage was applied based on the number of days in the particular calendar year falling in the fiscal period.

Such property is included in Class 38 if it is acquired after 1988 subject to grandfathering rules for obligations entered into before June 18, 1987.

To be classified as Class 38 property, the property must be "power-operated movable equipment" and must be designed for the purpose of excavating, moving, placing or compacting earth, rock, concrete or asphalt. The words "power-operated" indicate that the equipment must be driven or handled either by its own motor or by a separate but closely associated source of power, such as a tractor in the case of earth-moving equipment, or a compressor in the case of a rock drill. Where the source of power is also movable and is designed for the purpose of operating the equipment, it too may qualify as Class 38 property.

"Movable" equipment denotes equipment that is designed to be moved on its own wheels or treads or to be carried. A compressed air drill used for excavating rock and a concrete bucket moved by a crane in the course of placing concrete would be in the latter group.

Equipment need not be designed exclusively or even primarily for the purposes set out in Class 38 in order to come within that class. It was held in the case of *Guay Inc. v. The Queen*, 74 DTC 6328 (F.C.T.D.), that a mobile crane which had many uses was Class 22 property (the description of which, except for the date of acquisition, is identical to the description of property included in Class 38) because one of the uses to which it could be put was excavation. Similarly, in *L&R Asphalt Ltd.*, 89 DTC 266 (T.C.C.), it was found that the equipment need not be designed exclusively for the particular purpose outlined in the class, nor be self-propelled.

Interpretation Bulletin IT-469R sets out that the following properties are not included in Class 38, even though they may fit the description:

(a) vessels, including dredges, equipment forming part of a marine railway, and any other property included in Class 7;

(b) property forming part of a railway included in Class 4;

(c) logging equipment included in Class 10 by virtue of paragraph (*n*) or (*o*) of that class;

(d) mining equipment and other property used in connection with a mine included in Class 41 that would otherwise be included in Class 28 or 10 by virtue of paragraph (k), (l), (m) or (r) of that class; and

(e) power-operated movable equipment designed principally for natural resource exploration and included in Class 41 or 10 by virtue of paragraph (t) thereof.

Regulation 1101(5l) provides that a taxpayer may elect to include particular properties that are in Class 38 in separate classes. It was noted in the June 18, 1987 White Paper on Tax Reform that the optional separate class treatment would be beneficial where the depreciation provided by the basic write-off rate is insufficient for particular assets due to special circumstances relating to their location or use since a terminal loss would presumably result upon the disposition of the property. However, it should also be noted that in circumstances where the depreciation provided by the basic write-off rate exceeds the economic depreciation, making the separate class election would presumably trigger recapture of CCA upon disposition.

To be effective, the election must be made on or before the day upon which the taxpayer is required by section 150 of the Act to file a tax return for the year in which the particular property was acquired. The election is made by attaching a letter to the return, and is effective from the first day of the taxation year in respect of which the election is made and for all subsequent taxation years. See Interpretation Bulletin IT-469R, "Capital Cost Allowance — Earth-Moving Equipment", at ¶3245.

¶545　Class 39 — Manufacturing Assets

Class 39 was introduced to implement the June 18, 1987 tax reform proposals to reduce the CCA rate for manufacturing assets from the former straight-line fast write-off over three years in Class 29, to a declining balance rate of 25%. Class 39 assets bear a basic declining balance rate of 25%; however, transitional rules in Regulation 1100(1)(ze) phase the rate down to that level starting at 40% for 1988, 35% for 1989, 30% for 1990, and 25% thereafter. These phase-in percentages apply for purposes of calculating the CCA claim in the years in question. For fiscal periods ending on a date other than December 31, the relevant percentage is applied based on the number of days in the particular calendar year falling in the fiscal period.

In order to qualify for inclusion in Class 39, property must satisfy three tests: (1) a use test, (2) an asset test, and (3) a time of acquisition test. These tests are described below.

Use Test

First, the property must be used by the taxpayer directly or indirectly in Canada primarily in the manufacture or processing of goods for sale or lease. Property will also qualify if it is to be leased, in the ordinary course of business in Canada, to a lessee who will use the property primarily in the manufacture or processing of goods for sale or lease if the lessor is a corporation whose principal business is one or a combination of any of the following:

(a) leasing of property;

(b) manufacturing property that it sells or leases;

(c) the lending of money;

(d) the factoring of accounts receivable, or other obligations representing the sale price of merchandise or services; or

(e) selling or servicing a type of property that it also leases.

For a discussion on the meaning of "primarily" and "manufacturing or processing", see the commentary on Class 29 at ¶500.

Asset Test

Second, it must be property that would otherwise be included in Class 8 (except railway rolling stock or property described in paragraph (*j*) of Class 8, radiocommunication equipment), an oil or water storage tank, or certain small electrical generating equipment described in Class 9. The types of property qualifying for Class 39 are essentially the same as that which previously qualified for Class 29, with the specific exclusions of powered industrial lift trucks, rental tools described in paragraph (*b*) of Class 10, and EDP equipment and systems software described in paragraph (*f*) of Class 10.

Time of Acquisition Test

Third, the property must be acquired after 1987 and before February 26, 1992. Some properties meeting the first two tests and acquired after 1987 and before 1990 continue to qualify for inclusion in Class 29 by virtue of the transitional rules thereto. Property that would otherwise be Class 39 property, except that it was acquired after February 25, 1992, is included in Class 43 (30%). See Interpretation Bulletin IT-147R3, "Capital Cost Allowance — Accelerated Write-Off of Manufacturing and Processing Machinery and Equipment", at ¶3125.

¶550　Class 40 — Manufacturing Assets

Class 40 was introduced to implement the June 18, 1987 tax reform proposals to reduce the CCA rate for manufacturing assets from the former straight-line fast write-off over three years, to a declining balance rate of 30% for three specific types of assets not eligible for Class 39.

In order to qualify for inclusion in Class 40, property must have been acquired after 1987 and before 1990 and be one of the following assets used primarily in the manufacturing or processing of goods for sale or lease in Canada:

(a) a powered industrial lift truck;

(b) a portable tool acquired for the purpose of earning rental income for short terms, such as hourly, daily, weekly or monthly, except a property described in Class 12; or

(c) general-purpose electronic data processing equipment and systems software therefor.

Class 40 property is eligible for a declining balance rate of 30%; however, transitional rules in Regulation 1100(1)(*zf*) phase the rate down to that level starting at 40% for 1988, 35% for 1989, and 30% thereafter. These phase-in percentages apply for purposes of calculating the CCA claim in the years in question; for fiscal periods ending on a date other than December 31, the relevant percentage is applied based on the number of days in the particular calendar year falling in the fiscal period.

An unusual feature of Class 40 is that it merely provides a transition for the three types of manufacturing and processing property outlined above from the Class 29 straight-line rates to the 30% declining balance rate allowed in Class 10, and it disappears for 1990 and beyond. Regulation 1103(2e) provides that all properties in Class 40 must be transferred to Class 10 at the commencement of the first taxation year of the taxpayer commencing after 1989.

For a discussion on the meaning of "primarily" and "manufacturing or processing", see the commentary on Class 29 at ¶500. See also Interpretation Bulletin IT-147R3, "Capital Cost Allowance — Accelerated Write-Off of Manufacturing and Processing Machinery and Equipment", at ¶3125.

¶555   Class 41 (25%) — Resource Extraction Assets

Class 41 was introduced to implement the June 18, 1987 tax reform proposals to reduce the CCA rate for resource extraction assets from 30% to 25%.

Certain assets acquired for the purpose of gaining or producing income from a new mine or in connection with a major expansion of an existing mine were previously included in Class 28. The CCA rate for Class 28 property is 30%, and an additional allowance is available up to the income of the mine. Such property is now included in Class 41(*a*), and although the capital cost allowance rate generally allowable is reduced to 25%, the additional allowance up to the income of the mine is retained. Paragraph (*a*.1) allows for accelerated CCA up to the income of the mine for the amount of Class 41 acquisitions that become available for use in respect of a mine in a year, in excess of 5% of the gross revenue from the mine for the year. Paragraph (*a*.2) of Class 41 permits oil sands *in situ* projects to be treated as mines for CCA purposes. It provides a "major expansion" test for *in situ* projects, analogous to the test in Class 28, to determine eligibility for accelerated CCA.

Most resource extraction assets previously included in Class 10 and eligible for a 30% capital cost allowance rate are now included in Class 41(b). A proposed amendment to paragraph (b) excludes from Class 41 property described in new Regulation 1101(2c). As a result, vessels and attachments to vessels that are financed with a benefit under the Structured Financing Facility Program administered by Industry Canada are not eligible for Class 41.

Property will generally be included in Class 41 if it is acquired after 1987. However, transitional rules provide that property acquired before 1990 will not be included in Class 41 if it was acquired pursuant to an obligation in writing entered into before June 18, 1987, or if it was under construction by or on behalf of the taxpayer on June 18, 1987. In addition, property that is machinery or equipment and that is a fixed and integral part of property under construction on June 18, 1987 will be grandfathered if acquired before 1990. Grandfathered property will be included in Class 10 or 28, as the case may be, and will qualify for the higher 30% rate.

Property Included in Class 41(a)

Class 41(a) includes property that would otherwise be included in Class 28 but that was acquired after 1987, or after 1989 if the grandfathering provisions discussed above are applicable. Apart from the timing of the acquisition of the assets, the requirements for inclusion in Class 41(a) are identical to the requirements for inclusion in Class 28.

Class 28 property (and therefore Class 41(a) property) must be situated in Canada and acquired for the purpose of gaining or producing income from one or more mines that either came into production or were the subject of major expansion after November 7, 1969. In the case of a new mine, the property must have been acquired before the coming into production of the mine in reasonable commercial quantities. In the case of a major expansion, the property must have been acquired before the completion of the expansion and must also have been acquired in the course of, and principally for the purposes of, the major expansion. The term "mine" as used here is defined in Regulations 1104(7) and (8). Draft Regulation 1104(8.1) clarifies that the term "production" in the definitions and in Class 41(a) means production in reasonable commercial quantities.

The actual assets included in Class 28 or 41(a) are described in paragraphs (g), (k), (l), (m) and (r) of Class 10. Paragraph (g) includes mining buildings or structures otherwise included in Class 1, 3 or 6. Paragraph (k) includes mining machinery and equipment or a structure that would otherwise be included in Class 8. Paragraph (l) describes certain social capital that provides service to a mine or mining community. Paragraph (m) includes railway track and other related property

¶555

used by the mine. However, assets that would otherwise be included in paragraph (m) of Class 10 only qualify for inclusion in Class 28 or $41(a)$ if acquired in connection with a new mine, and not if acquired in connection with a major expansion of an existing mine (however, see the description of Class $41(b)$ below which includes Class 10 assets). Paragraph (r) includes electrical generating equipment allocated to Class 10 by Regulation 1102(8) or (9).

Class $41(a.1)$ was added to permit accelerated CCA for Class 41 acquisitions that become available for use in respect of a mine in a year, in excess of 5% of the gross revenues from the mine for the year.

Class $41(a.1)$ provides that a portion of the capital cost of property purchased after March 6, 1999 may qualify for accelerated CCA, provided the property would, but for Class 41, be included in Class 10 because of paragraph (g), (k) or (l) of that Class, or that is included in Class 41 because of Regulation 1102(8) or (9). Eligible property includes property acquired by the taxpayer principally for the purpose of gaining or producing income from one or more mines that are operated by the taxpayer and situated in Canada, that became available for use for the purpose of subsection 13(26) of the Act in a taxation year, and had not previously been used for any purpose by any person or partnership with whom the taxpayer was not dealing at arm's length.

The portion eligible for accelerated CCA is based on a percentage formula. The percentage is determined by calculating the excess of the capital cost of the property which became available for use during the year over 5% of the gross revenue from the mine or mines, as the case may be (determined in accordance with Regulations 1104(5) and (5.1)), divided by the capital cost of the property which became available for use during the year. The eligible portion is prorated for short taxation years.

Class $41(a.2)$ permits oil sands *in situ* projects to be treated as mines for CCA purposes. Capital property eligible for Class 41 inclusion must meet the *major mine expansion* test for *in situ* projects, which is analogous to the test in Class 28. Eligible property is property that would, but for Class 41, be included in Class 10 because of paragraph (g), (k) or (l) of that Class or that is included in Class 41 because of Regulation 1102(8) or (9). In addition, the property must be acquired by the taxpayer in a taxation year principally for the purpose of gaining or producing income from one or more mines, each of which is one or more wells operated by the taxpayer from the extraction of material from a deposit of bituminous sands or oil shales, operated by the taxpayer and situated in Canada. The property must be the subject of a major expansion after March 6, 1996. To constitute a major expansion, Class $41(a.2)(ii)$ requires that the design capacity of the mine, measured in barrels of oil that are not beyond the crude oil stage or its equivalent, be increased by 25%. The property must be acquired after March 6, 1996 and before the completion of the expansion and in the course of and principally for the purposes of the expansion.

¶555

Property that is included in Class 41 because of Regulation 1102(8) or (9), other than property described in paragraph (a) or $(a.2)$ or the portion described in paragraph $(a.1)$, will also be eligible for accelerated depreciation.

Class 41(a), 41($a.1$) and 41($a.2$) Property Placed in Separate Classes

Where there are several properties in Class $41(a)$ and they have been acquired in connection with more than one mine, Regulations 1101(4c) and (4d) divide these properties into separate classes depending upon the mines in connection with which the properties were acquired. These rules are similar to the rules in Regulations 1101(4a) and (4b) for dividing Class 28 assets into separate classes. Properties in Class $41(a)$, $41(a.1)$ and $41(a.2)$ are eligible for accelerated capital cost allowance to the extent that the relevant mine produces income. The purpose of the division of such properties into separate classes, therefore, is to relate the accelerated allowance on particular mining assets to the income of the mine or mines to which they relate.

Regulation 1101(4c) deals with a case where the taxpayer has more than one mine and acquires different Class $41(a)$, $41(a.1)$ and $41(a.2)$ properties for each mine. For example, the taxpayer may have Mine No. 1 which is coming into production and Mine No. 2 which is undergoing a major expansion. If the taxpayer builds a smelter to be used for Mine No. 1 and acquires some machinery to be used at Mine No. 2, both properties would be Class $41(a)$, but the smelter and the machinery would be placed in separate classes. Regulation 1101(4d) deals with the case where the taxpayer has more than one Class $41(a)$ property and several mines and uses individual properties for select groups of mines. A property used to gain or produce income from several mines is in a separate class from property used in connection with another mine or group of mines, and is also separated from property used at only one of the mines in the same group. Suppose, for example, that a taxpayer has Mines Nos. 1, 2, 3, and 4, and acquires property A to use at Mines No. 1 and No. 2, property B to use at Mine No. 1 alone, and property C to use at Mines No. 3 and No. 4. In these circumstances, properties A, B and C are placed in separate classes of Class $41(a)$. Similarly, Regulations 1101(4a) and (4b) prescribe separate classes for properties included in Class 28 in the same way as Regulations 1101(4c) and (4d) for properties included in Class $41(a)$.

Additional Allowance on Class 41(a), 41($a.1$) and 41($a.2$) and Class 28 Property

Regulations 1100(1)(w) and (x) provide for additional CCA for property in Class 28, while Regulations 1100(1)(y) and (ya) provide for an additional CCA for property in Class $41(a)$, $41(a.1)$ and $41(a.2)$. Regulation 1100(1)(w) deals with Class 28 property relating to a single mine, while Regulation 1100(1)(x) deals with Class 28 property relating to more than one. Similarly, Regulations 1100(1)(y) and (ya) deal with

¶555

Class $41(a)$, $41(a.1)$ and $41(a.2)$ property relating to one mine and to more than one mine respectively.

The additional allowances apply only where the property is included in a separate class pursuant to Regulations 1101(4a) and (4b) (for Class 28 property) or 1101(4c) and (4d) (for Class $41(a)$, $41(a.1)$ and $41(a.2)$ property). There appears to be a technical deficiency in the wording of Regulations 1101(4a) and (4b) such that if there was only one property in Class 28, or if all the properties in Class 28 related to only a single mine, the regulations would not operate to prescribe a separate class for that property or those properties. Consequently, it would appear that the additional allowances provided for in Regulations $1100(1)(w)$ and (x) would not be available. That result, however, is apparently not intended; where the taxpayer has only a single Class 28 property or only a single mine, the accelerated allowance should be available.

The additional allowances available pursuant to Regulations $1100(1)(w)$ to (ya) each allow a claim to the extent of the lesser of the taxpayer's income from the particular mine, or mines, as the case may be, and the undepreciated capital cost of the separate prescribed class. In each case, for the purposes of determining the additional allowance, the income of the mine is computed before making any deduction under paragraph $20(1)(v.1)$ (resource allowance), section 65 (depletion allowance), sections 66, 66.1 and 66.2 (resource deductions), and section 66.7 (successor resource deductions) of the Act, and ITAR 29 which deals generally with pre-1972 exploration and development expenses.

Regulations $1100(1)(w)$ to (ya) also prescribe an order for determining the accelerated claim in respect of the separate prescribed classes as follows:

(a) first, to the extent of the undepreciated capital cost of Class 28 assets for which a separate class is prescribed by Regulation 1101(4a). These are Class 28 assets acquired for the purpose of gaining or producing income from only one mine;

(b) next, to the extent of the undepreciated capital cost of Class $41(a)$, $41(a.1)$ and $41(a.2)$ assets for which a separate class is prescribed by Regulation 1101(4c). These are Class $41(a)$ assets acquired for the purpose of gaining or producing income from only one mine;

(c) next, to the extent of the undepreciated capital cost of Class 28 assets for which a separate class is prescribed by Regulation 1101(4b). These are Class 28 assets acquired for the purpose of gaining or producing income from more than one mine; and

(d) finally, to the extent of the undepreciated capital cost of Class $41(a)$ assets for which a separate class is prescribed by Regulation 1101(4d). These are Class $41(a)$, $41(a.1)$ and $41(a.2)$

¶555

assets acquired for the purpose of gaining or producing income from more than one mine.

In computing the additional allowance, the half-year rule (¶140) must be taken into account only for the additional amount allowed pursuant to Regulations $1100(1)(w)$ and (x) pertaining to Class 28 assets. The half-year rule is not taken into account in determining the additional allowance available in respect of Class $41(a)$, $41(a.1)$ and $41(a.2)$ assets pursuant to Regulations $1100(1)(y)$ and (ya).

For purposes of these provisions, "income from a mine" is defined in Regulation 1104(5) to include income reasonably attributable to the processing of mineral ores from the taxpayer's own resources up to the prime metal stage or its equivalent, and the production (other than production from a well) of crude oil from bituminous sand, oil sand or oil shale. Effective March 31, 1977, the income also includes income attributable to the transportation of output over a railway spur line owned by the taxpayer and acquired after that date. Where Class 28 or $41(a)$ property is acquired in connection with a major expansion of a mine, it is understood that the income of that mine against which the additional allowance may be claimed is the total income, not merely the income attributable to the expansion.

The term "mine" is defined in Regulation 1104(7) to include a well for the extraction of minerals from a deposit of bituminous sands, oil shales, calcium chloride, sylvite or halite, as well as a pit for the extraction of kaolin or tar sands ore. Regulation 1104(7) excludes from the term "mine" any oil well or gas well, sand pit, gravel pit, clay pit, shale pit, peat bog, peat deposit or stone quarry (other than a kaolin pit or deposit of bituminous sands or oil shales).

Property Included in Class 41(*b*)

Class $41(b)$ was introduced to implement the June 18, 1987 tax reform measures to reduce the CCA rate for resource extraction assets from 30% to 25%. Property included in Class $41(b)$ is property that would otherwise be included in certain paragraphs of Class 10 and that was acquired after 1987. However, such property acquired after 1987 but before 1990 will continue to be included in Class 10 if acquired pursuant to an obligation in writing entered into by the taxpayer before June 18, 1987, or if it was under construction by or on behalf of the taxpayer on June 18, 1987. Machinery and equipment that is a fixed and integral part of such a property under construction on June 18, 1987 would also qualify for transitional relief.

The particular properties included in Class $41(b)$ are properties that would otherwise be included in Class 10 by virtue of paragraphs $(f.1)$ (a designated underground storage cost), (g) (mine buildings), (j) (oil or gas well equipment), (k) (mining structures, machinery and equipment), (l) (social or townsite assets related to a mine), (m) (railway track, machinery and equipment related to a mine), (r) (electrical generating

¶555

equipment used in mining), (t) (exploration equipment), and (u) (heavy crude oil processing equipment). Also, drillships and offshore platforms used in exploration or drilling oil or gas wells, that are acquired after 1987 subject to transitional rules discussed above, are included in Class 41(b). Offshore drilling vessels that are acquired before 1988 are included in Class 7.

A proposed amendment to Class 41(b) excludes from Class 41 property described in draft Regulation 1101(2c) (i.e., vessels that are financed with a benefit under the Structured Financing Facility Program administered by Industry Canada). Draft Regulation 1101(2c) provides that the separate classes in Regulations 1101(2a) and (2b) for vessels and attachments do not apply if the Minister of Industry agreed to a structured financing facility. As a result, the maximum allowance applicable to such property is 15% under Class 7, and an additional allowance under Regulations 1100(1)(v) and (va) will not be available.

¶560   Class 42 (12%) — Fibre-Optic Cable

Class 42 of Schedule II contains property that is fibre-optic cable acquired by a taxpayer after December 23, 1991, other than property acquired pursuant to a written agreement entered into by the taxpayer before December 24, 1991. A taxpayer may elect that Class 42 applies to fibre-optic cable acquired at any time in its first taxation year ending after December 23, 1991. The election is made in a letter filed with the tax return for the taxpayer's first taxation year ending after December 23, 1991, or in a letter filed with the Minister of National Revenue on or before August 8, 1994. The supporting equipment for the fibre-optic cable such as a pole, mast, tower, etc., is included in Class 3.

¶565   Class 43 (30%) — Manufacturing and Processing Assets

Class 43 was introduced to increase the CCA rate for manufacturing assets to 30% from 25% in Class 39. Class 43(a) of Schedule II includes machinery and equipment used in Canadian manufacturing and processing acquired after February 25, 1992. These are assets that would otherwise be in Class 39 except for the date of acquisition.

As with Class 39, Class 43(a) includes property that would otherwise be included in Class 8 (except railway rolling stock or property described in paragraph (j) of Class 8, radiocommunication equipment), an oil or water storage tank, or certain small electrical generating equipment described in Class 9. The types of property qualifying for Class 43 are essentially the same as those which previously qualified for Class 29, with the specific exclusion of powered industrial lift trucks, rental tools described in paragraph (b) of Class 10, and EDP equipment and systems software described in paragraph (f) of Class 10. See Class 39 (¶545) and

Class 29 (¶500) for commentary on the use to which the asset must be put in order to qualify as a Class 43 asset.

Class 43(b) includes assets acquired after February 25, 1992 that are used in the processing of foreign ore. This property is described in paragraph (k) of Class 10 and would otherwise be included in Class 41 (¶555). At the time of its acquisition, it must reasonably be expected that this equipment is to be used entirely in Canada and primarily for the processing of foreign ore. The taxpayer may elect to put such assets in Class 41 (25%) even if acquired after February 25, 1992.

¶567　Class 43.1 (30%) — Energy Conservation Equipment

Class 43.1 replaces the three-year write-off in Class 34 for energy conservation equipment acquired after February 21, 1994, and is extended to a wider variety of properties. Class 43.1 generally includes equipment used to produce heat and electricity from alternative or renewable energy sources and provides an accelerated capital cost allowance rate of 30%.

Energy conservation assets in Class 43.1 include active solar energy equipment; heat recovery equipment; mini-hydro facilities; fixed-location wind-driven turbines; fixed-location photovoltaic equipment used to generate electricity from solar energy; above-ground geothermal energy equipment used to generate electricity; above-ground equipment used to collect landfill or digester gas; and equipment used to generate heat from the consumption of wood waste, municipal waste, landfill gas, or digester gas if the heat energy produced is used directly in an industrial process.

Class 43.1(a) to (c) includes properties that would otherwise be included in Class 1, 2 or 8, acquired after February 21, 1994, that is electrical generating equipment, equipment that generates both electrical energy and heat energy, and heat recovery equipment, as well as ancillary equipment or additions to such equipment where the equipment is part of an operating system used by the taxpayer or the lessee of the taxpayer for:

(a) generating electrical energy or a combination of electrical and heat energy using only fossil fuel, wood waste, municipal waste, landfill gas, digester gas (bio-oil, for property acquired after February 18, 2003), or any combination of these fuels; or

(b) subject to other conditions, generating electrical energy using only a combination of natural gas and waste heat from one or more natural gas compression or pumping systems located on a natural gas pipeline.

Under draft regulations, Class 43.1 also includes qualifying electrical generating equipment acquired after February 27, 2000 that would otherwise be Class 17 property because of subparagraph (a.1)(i) of Class 17 (¶440).

¶567

Certain electrical generating plant and equipment acquired to provide power for a mine, ore mill, smelter, metal refinery or combination thereof, that would qualify to be Class 43.1 property is included in Class 41. Regulations 1102(8) and (9) provide that a taxpayer may elect to put such generating or distributing equipment acquired after February 21, 1994 in Class 43.1 instead of Class 41. Regulation 1103(4) provides that this election is effective from the first day of the taxation year in which the election is made.

Class 43.1(b) includes certain acquisitions of used equipment acquired after June 26, 1996. Previously, only new equipment was eligible for Class 43.1. Paragraph (b) relaxes this restriction to accommodate used equipment that was included in Class 34 or 43.1 of the vendor (or would have been so included if the vendor made an election to do so under Regulation 1102(8)(d) or 1102(9)(d)), if it remains at the same site in Canada and was acquired not more than five years after it became available for use. Under Regulation 1102(21), the cost of any used Class 34 or 43.1 equipment that can be included under Class 43.1 by the purchaser cannot exceed the original capital cost of the equipment when first placed in service.

Under Class 43.1(c), effective after February 16, 1999, electrical generating equipment using solution gas that would otherwise be flared during the production of crude oil is eligible for Class 43.1 treatment. Solution gas is excluded from the definition of fossil fuel for the purposes of the heat rate calculation for such electrical generation systems. Regulation 1104(13) defines "solution gas" and "fossil fuel" (as well as several other terms) for purposes of Class 43.1. Regulations 1104(14) and (15) provide that if generating equipment in Class 43.1 is not operating properly because of a deficiency, failing or shutdown that is beyond the scope of the taxpayer, or because of a failure of property owned by another person that is required by the taxpayer's system to operate properly, e.g., a "steam host", the taxpayer's Class 43.1 property will be deemed to be operating in the manner required. The taxpayer must make reasonable efforts to resolve the problem in a reasonable time, and in the case of the failure of property owned by someone else that is necessary to the taxpayer's generating system, the failure of the property must not have been able to have been foreseen by the taxpayer to occur within five years after the taxpayer's system became operational.

Paragraphs (d) and (e) of Class 43.1 also include (among other things) a range of renewable energy generation equipment, including wind turbines, small hydroelectric facilities, active solar heating equipment, fixed location photovoltaic equipment and geothermal energy equipment.

The Federal Budget of February 23, 2005 proposed to add the following items to Class 43.1:

- equipment used to produce biogas (which is primarily methane) from the anaerobic digestion of manure;

¶567

- specified distribution equipment of a taxpayer that is part of a district energy system used by the taxpayer (or a lessee) primarily to provide district heating or cooling through the use of heat produced by electrical cogeneration equipment that meets the requirements of Class 43.1;

- fuel cells use hydrogen to generate electricity, or electricity and heat. The Budget proposed that certain fixed-location fuel cells and ancillary fuel reformation and electrolysis equipment will now be eligible for Class 43.1 treatment. In order to qualify:

— the fuel cells must have a peak capacity of not less than 3 kilowatts of electrical output,

— the fuel cells must be part of a system that includes fuel reformation equipment or electrolysis equipment,

— where the fuel cells use hydrogen generated from ancillary fuel reformation equipment that uses fossil fuel, the fuel cell system will be required to satisfy the existing 6000 BTU per kilowatt-hour heat rate calculation, and

— where the fuel cells of a taxpayer use hydrogen generated by ancillary electrolysis equipment, the electrolysis equipment must use solar energy, wind energy conversion or hydroelectric energy equipment of the taxpayer;

- changes to provide incentives for the use of bio-oil. Bio-oil is created through a thermo-chemical conversion process that uses biomass that is wood waste or other plant residues. Equipment of a taxpayer that is used in a system to convert biomass into bio-oil will now be eligible for Class 43.1 if this bio-oil is used by the taxpayer (or a lessee) primarily to generate electricity or electricity and heat. Bio-oil is considered to be a neutral energy source with respect to greenhouse gases; and

- changes to extend eligibility for Class 43.1 to certain equipment used primarily to generate heat energy for use in a taxpayer's greenhouse operation. Qualifying equipment will include active solar heating equipment and equipment used to generate heat energy from the consumption of wood waste, municipal waste, landfill gas or digester gas.

The 2005 Federal Budget also carved out a limited subset of Class 43.1 assets to be included in an unnamed new class. New class assets must be acquired after February 23, 2005 and before 2012. New class assets are allowed a capital cost allowance rate of 50% (on the usual declining balance basis and subject, presumably, to the half-year rule). Capital cost allowance on this class will also be subject to the "specified energy property" rules (see ¶540).

¶567

The Budget description of assets eligible for the new class is as follows:

- Cogeneration systems (also called combined heat and power or CHP systems) that produce heat and power simultaneously by capturing the waste heat from the electrical generation process and using it for another purpose, such as manufacturing or space heating. Cogeneration equipment is currently eligible for Class 43.1 (30%) treatment if it converts approximately 57% or more of the energy value of the input fossil fuel into electricity and usable heat. In formal terms, this requires a system to use no more than 6000 British Thermal Units ("BTUs") of fossil fuel per kilowatt-hour of electricity produced on an annual basis. (The energy content of specified waste fuels, such as wood waste, municipal waste, bio-oil and biogas, is not counted for the purposes of this heat rate calculation.) The Budget proposed that cogeneration equipment that would otherwise be included in Class 43.1 will be included in the new class entitled to a 50% CCA rate if the equipment is part of a high-efficiency cogeneration system with an annual heat rate from fossil fuel that does not exceed 4750 BTUs per kilowatt-hour of electricity production. This corresponds to a total system efficiency of approximately 72%. To be eligible for the new class, the equipment must be acquired on or after February 23, 2005 and before 2012. Systems eligible for Class 43.1 treatment that exceed the 4750 BTU threshold will still qualify for the current 30% CCA rate.

- The Budget proposed that renewable energy generation equipment that would otherwise be included in Class 43.1 (including wind turbines, small hydroelectric facilities, active solar heating equipment, fixed location photovoltaic equipment and geothermal energy equipment) will be eligible for the new 50% CCA rate class. To be eligible for the new class, the equipment must be acquired on or after February 23, 2005 and before 2012.

- District or community energy systems transfer heat between a central generation plant and a group or district of buildings by continuously circulating steam, hot water or cold water through a system of underground pipes. The 2005 Budget proposed to extend eligibility for Class 43.1 to specified distribution equipment of a taxpayer that is part of a district energy system used by the taxpayer (or a lessee) primarily to provide district heating or cooling through the use of heat produced by electrical cogeneration equipment that meets the requirements of Class 43.1, including the heat rate requirements. Eligible components of a taxpayer's system will be pipes, pumps, chillers, meters and control equipment and heat exchangers attached to the main distribution line of the district energy system. Assets forming part of the internal heat and cooling system of the host building will not be eligible. This change will apply to eligible equipment acquired on or after February 23, 2005. Where the distri-

¶567

bution assets are acquired on or after February 23, 2005 and before 2012, and they carry heat produced by cogeneration equipment acquired during that period that qualifies for the new 50% CCA rate class, the distribution assets will also qualify for the new class.

- Class 43.1 (30%) CCA treatment will be extended to equipment used to produce biogas (which is primarily methane) from the anaerobic digestion of manure. Eligible equipment will be property of a taxpayer that is part of a system that is used by the taxpayer (or a lessee) primarily to produce, store and use biogas primarily for the production by the taxpayer (or the lessee) of heat for use in an industrial process, or electricity, and that is an anaerobic digester reactor, a buffer tank, biogas piping, a biogas storage tank, biogas scrubbing equipment, or generation equipment. Collection equipment, buildings and other structures, and equipment used to process the residue after digestion or to treat recovered liquids, will not be included. This change will apply to eligible equipment acquired on or after February 23, 2005. Further, such eligible equipment acquired before 2012 will be included in the new 50% CCA rate class.

Canadian Renewable and Conservation Expenses (CRCE)

Canadian Renewable and Conservation Expenses (CRCE) (described in Regulation 1219) form a category of intangible expenses associated with the preparatory phase of renewable energy and energy conservation projects. (These are projects for which the equipment is likely to be described in Class 43.1). CRCE expenditures are deemed to be Canadian Exploration Expenses (CEE) (described in subsection 66.1(6) of the Act) and form a pool of expenses which can be written off to the extent chosen up to 100% in a year and which can be syndicated to investors through flow-through share mechanisms.

Eligible expenses are defined from time to time by the Department of Natural Resources in a *Technical Guide to Canadian Renewable and Conservation Expenses.* According to the Natural Resources Canada Web site, the *Class 43.1 Technical Guide and Technical Guide to Canadian Renewable and Conservation Expenses (CRCE)* is available from the following address. Also, a written prior opinion can be obtained by writing to:

Class 34/43.1 Secretariat
Industrial Programs Division
Natural Resources Canada
580 Booth Street, 18th Floor
Ottawa, ON K1A 0E4
Tel.: (613) 996-0890
Fax: (613) 992-3161

¶567

On July 26, 2002, the government announced that it would extend to CRCE expenses incurred after that date the "look-back" rule under which companies can renounce expenses to be incurred in the coming year, subject to a transaction tax. Moreover, the government would expand its regulations and definitions in respect of wind turbines which qualify for CRCE treatment, so that more than one test turbine may qualify in respect of a taxpayer's wind farm project. The change regarding wind turbines is effective for expenses incurred after July 26, 2002, but the taxpayer may elect to have the revised regulations apply retroactively to expenditures incurred after December 5, 1996. The election is to be made in writing to the CRA within 90 days of formal publication of the amended regulations, which occurred on September 21, 2005 so the 90th day thereafter would be December 20, 2005.

Specified Energy Property Restrictions

The provisions in Regulations 1100(24) and (25) that restrict the capital cost allowance claim for passive investors with respect to specified energy property apply to energy conservation equipment in Class 43.1 as well (see ¶540).

Under these rules, deductions in a year for Class 34 or 43.1 and for certain additional property, as noted below, cannot exceed income for the year from that property (see ¶540). Exceptions are permitted for property acquired to be used by the owner primarily for its own business (other than selling the product of that property) or to earn Canadian income from other Canadian property. For example, a full Class 43.1 deduction from all sources of income is available to a farmer buying a windmill for supplementary farm energy. Exceptions are also permitted for corporations whose principal business is the sale, distribution or production of energy in any form, or partnerships of such corporations, and for corporations whose principal business is manufacturing or leasing such property to qualified users. Effective for taxation years ending after March 6, 1996, these exceptions were extended to corporations whose principal businesses are mining or manufacturing and processing. The exceptions permit principal business corporations to claim capital cost allowance on Class 34/43.1 property against income from all sources. These restrictions are effective for taxation years ending after February 9, 1988, subject to transitional protection for later acquisitions pursuant to agreements in place before that time of property approved at the time. For property acquired after February 23, 2005, the specified energy property rules will also apply to property in the new 50% version of Class 43.1, to combustion turbines which carry a 15% capital cost allowance rate, and to electricity transmission assets which carry an 8% capital cost allowance rate.

¶570   Class 44 (25%) — Patents

A patent or the right to use patented information for a limited or unlimited period, that is acquired after April 26, 1993, is included in Class 44 (25%). A patent acquired prior to April 27, 1993 that is for a limited period is a Class 14 asset (see ¶425). This is depreciated on a straight-line basis over the life of the patent. A patent for an unlimited period acquired before this date is an eligible capital expenditure (see ¶727).

Regulation 1103(2h) provides that a taxpayer may elect not to include patents acquired after April 26, 1993 in Class 44. If this election is made, then the patent would be included in Class 14 if for a limited period or as an eligible capital expenditure if for an unlimited period. The election must be made in the year the patent is acquired by a letter attached to the tax return for the year.

Patents in Class 44 are written off at a 25% declining balance. Regulation 1100(9.1) provides a special formula for a Class 44 patent where the cost of the patent is dependent on its use. Under these circumstances, the taxpayer deducts the lesser of:

(a) the capital cost determined by reference to the use of the patent in the year *plus* the normal allowance at 25% claimed on that portion of the capital cost not determined by use; and

(b) the undepreciated capital cost to the taxpayer as of the end of the taxation year of the property of the class before making a claim for the current year.

¶575 Class 45 (45%) — General-Purpose Electronic Data Processing Equipment

The 2004 Federal Budget contained a proposal to increase the capital cost allowance rate for certain general-purpose electronic data processing equipment from 30% to 45%. This proposal was implemented through new Class 45, which includes general-data processing equipment and systems software acquired after March 22, 2004. Such equipment was previously included in Class 10 (¶405).

Assets included in Class 45 include general-purpose electronic data processing equipment and systems software for that equipment, including ancillary data processing equipment, but not including property that is principally or is used principally as electronic process control or monitor equipment and related systems software; electronic communications control equipment and related software; or data handling equipment (unless it is ancillary to general-purpose electronic data processing equipment). The specified leasing property rule exemption for computers is extended to computer equipment included in Class 45, other than individual items with a capital cost in excess of $1 million. Computer equipment included in Class 45 does not qualify for the separate class election under Regulation 1101(5p) (see ¶405). For further information on computer software, see ¶415.

¶580 Class 46 (30%) — Data Network Infrastructure Equipment

The 2004 Federal Budget contained a proposal to increase the capital cost allowance rate for data infrastructure equipment from 20% to 30%. This proposal was implemented through new Class 46, which includes data network infrastructure equipment and systems software for that equipment, acquired after March 22, 2004, which would otherwise be included in Class 8(*i*) (¶395).

Under draft legislation, data network infrastructure equipment is defined in Regulation 1104(2) and includes infrastructure equipment that supports advanced telecommunications applications such as e-mail, Web searching and hosting, instant messaging, audio- and video-over-IP (Internet Protocol), switches, multiplexers, routers, hubs, modems and domain name servers that are used to control, transfer, modulate and direct data. It does not include office equipment such as telephones, cell phones or fax machines, equipment such as Web servers that are currently considered to be computer equipment, or property such as wires, cables or structures. For further information on computer software, see ¶415.

¶600

Capital Cost Allowance on Assets Not Allocated to Classes

Assets that are timber limits or industrial mineral mines are not allocated to a class in Schedule II of the regulations. In spite of that, capital cost allowance in respect of timber limits and industrial mineral mines is dealt with in Part XI of the regulations. The reason for this is presumably that the allowance in respect of timber limits and mines is linked to capital cost, as is the case with the allowance in respect of the other classes of property dealt with in Part XI. This appears to have been confirmed in *M.N.R. v. Highway Sawmills Ltd.*, 66 DTC 5116 (S.C.C.), affirming 65 DTC 5080 (Ex. Ct.), reversing 63 DTC 453 (T.A.B.).

Capital cost allowance on these assets is calculated based on usage, and so it is not subject to proration for short years.

¶605 Timber Limits and Cutting Rights

Under Regulation 1100(1)(*e*), provision is made for deductions in respect of the capital cost of timber limits or rights to cut timber from limits, except a timber resource property. The deductions may not exceed the amounts calculated under Schedule VI. See Interpretation Bulletin IT-481, "Timber Resource Property and Timber Limits", at ¶3270. See also the discussion at ¶515.

A timber limit is not defined in the Act, but is a property that would be a timber resource property except for the fact that it was acquired before May 7, 1974. Interpretation Bulletin IT-481 sets out that even though a property may otherwise qualify as a timber resource property, a timber limit that is owned by a corporation and acquired by a taxpayer in the course of a reorganization set out in Regulation $1102(14)(a)$, or from a non-arm's length party described in Regulation $1102(14)(d)$ is also a timber limit to the taxpayer acquiring the property. Capital cost allowance for a timber limit is set out in Regulation $1100(1)(e)$, and Schedule VI (see ¶605).

Timber Limit Deduction

Under Schedule VI, the amount that may be deducted in respect of a timber limit is *the lesser* of:

(a) the undepreciated cost of the timber limit (as of the end of the year and before making any deductions under this provision); and

(b) the aggregate of:

(i) an amount computed on the basis of a rate per cord, board foot, or cubic metre cut in the year, and

(ii) certain allowances in respect of survey and cruise expenses.

The computation of the rate per cord, board foot, or cubic metre will depend on whether or not the taxpayer has been granted an allowance in respect of the timber limit for a previous taxation year. Where such an allowance has not been granted, the rate is an amount determined as follows: the aggregate of the residual value of the timber limit and the survey expenses included in its capital cost are deducted from the capital cost of the limit and the result is divided by the quantity of timber in the limit or by the quantity of timber that the taxpayer has a right to cut. Where an allowance has been granted in respect of the limit in a previous taxation year, the rate is ascertained in two ways, depending on the circumstances. If it has been established that the quantity of timber in the limit or the limit's capital cost is in fact substantially different from that used for the computation of the rate in the previous year, the rate will be determined by deducting the residual value of the timber limit from its undepreciated cost as of the commencement of the year and dividing the result by the estimated quantity of timber that is in the limit or that the taxpayer has the right to cut at the commencement of the year. In the other alternative, i.e., where there is no difference as above, the rate will be that employed to determine the allowance for the most recent year for which the allowance was granted. "Residual value" is defined in Schedule VI as being the estimated value of the property if the merchantable timber were removed.

¶605

Survey and Cruise Expenses

The allowance in respect of the survey and cruise expenses is the lesser of:

(a) one-tenth of the amount expended by the taxpayer after the commencement of the taxpayer's 1949 taxation year for surveys, cruises or preparation of prints, maps and plans for the purpose of obtaining a licence or a right to cut timber (provided that the expense was included in the capital cost of the limit); and

(b) the amount as described above under (a), minus any amounts deducted in previous years.

Alternatively, instead of the allowances described above, a taxpayer may elect to claim an amount that is the lesser of:

(a) $100; and

(b) the amount received by the taxpayer in the taxation year from the sale of timber.

Note that the survey expenses dealt with in Schedule VI are expenditures that are part of the capital cost of a particular limit. If capital expenditures are incurred which do not result in the acquisition of a depreciable property, they are not covered by the regulations in respect of capital cost allowances. It should also be noted that under Regulation 1101(3), a timber limit or a right to cut timber from a limit is deemed to be a separate class of property, and where a taxpayer has more than one timber limit or rights to cut timber from more than one limit, each limit or right is deemed to be a separate class of property.

¶610 Industrial Mineral Mines

Under Regulation 1100(1)(*g*), provision is made for a deduction as calculated in Schedule V in respect of the capital cost of industrial mineral mines, or a right to remove industrial minerals from an industrial mineral mine. Regulation 1101(4) deems each mine and right to be a separate property.

Interpretation Bulletin IT-492, "Capital Cost Allowance — Industrial Mineral Mines" (at ¶3285), describes an "industrial mineral" as a non-metallic mineral capable of being used in industry, and gives the word "mineral" its ordinary meaning of "any chemical or compound occurring naturally as a product of inorganic processes". Regulation 1104(3) defines "industrial mineral mine" to include a peat bog or deposit of peat but not a mineral resource. Schedule V defines "residual value" to mean the estimated value of the property if all commercially mineable material were removed.

The capital cost allowance claimed on an industrial mineral mine cannot exceed the lesser of an amount computed on the basis of a rate per unit of mineral mined in the taxation year, or the undepreciated capital cost of the mine or right to the taxpayer as of the end of the taxation year. No adjustment of the rate is provided for when a taxpayer fails to claim the maximum capital cost allowance in any year.

The rate per unit mined for a taxation year is calculated in one of two ways. If there has been no capital cost allowance granted in previous years, the rate is determined by dividing the capital cost of the mine or right, less its residual value, by a specified number of units in the case of a right to remove only that specified number of units, or in any other case, by the total estimated number of commercially mineable units.

If the taxpayer had a previous allowance in respect of the mine or right, the rate applied is the rate used to determine the most recent allowance granted, unless it can be established that the capital cost or the number of units remaining to be mined in the year of the most recent allowance were substantially different from the amounts used in determining the rate. In the latter case, a new rate is determined by dividing the undepreciated capital cost of the mine or right, less residual value, by the specified number of units that the taxpayer had a right to remove, or by the estimated remaining commercially mineable units. All of these amounts are measured at the commencement of the year.

Instead of claiming capital cost allowance under this section, the taxpayer may elect to deduct the lesser of $100 or the proceeds received from the sale of minerals.

The claims discussed above are in respect of mines themselves. Equipment for mining is likely to be classified in Class 10, 28, or 41.

¶620

Alphabetical Table of Current Capital Cost Allowance Rates

The assets specifically covered in the classes in ¶360 to ¶570 above are listed alphabetically below. Note that under Class 8, tangible capital assets which are not otherwise listed in any other class and not specifically excluded are subject to the 20% rate. Note also that the classes of property described below do not include land upon which such property was constructed or is situated and that the rates listed are *maximum rates*. The taxpayer is not allowed to deduct more than indicated, however, the taxpayer is not prevented from deducting less or nothing at all. See footnotes at the end of the table.

Item	Rate	Class
Access roads and trails for the protection of standing timber	30%	10
Air conditioning equipment — same rate as building[1]		
Aircraft[16]	25%	9
furniture and fittings . . .	25%	9
hangars[1]	10%	6
Airplane runways[16]	8%	17
Amusement park components (including fences, bridges, canals, stalls, tractors, etc.)	15%	37
land improvements[40] . . .	15%	37
Apparel, used for earning rental income[1,26]	100%	12
Asphalt surface, storage yard[16]	8%	17
Assets, tangible capital[1,2]	20%	8
used primarily in manufacturing and processing[10,15]		29, 39, 40, 43
Automobiles[1]	30%	10
acquired after June 17, 1987 in excess of prescribed amount (Reg. 7307(1))[1,7]	30%	10.1
for lease or rental[22]	40%	16
Automotive equipment[1] . .	30%	10
designed for and used in amusement parks . .	15%	37
Bar code scanners — see Cash registers		
Billboards		
acquired before 1988 . . .	35%	11
acquired after 1987[10] . .	20%	8
Boats — see Vessels		
Boilers		
heating use — same rate as building		
used primarily in manufacturing or processing[10,15]		29, 39, 43

Item	Rate	Class
Books of lending libraries[26]	100%	12
Breakwaters		
wooden	10%	6
other	5%	3
Bridges[1]	4%	1
Buildings[1]		
addition or alteration — same class as buildings[13]		
amusement park stalls	15%	37
brick, stone, cement, etc., acquired before 1988	5%	3
brick, stone, cement, etc., acquired after 1987	4%	1
component parts — generally same class as building (see individual items)		
farm ensilage storage . .	20%	8
foundation excavation — same rate as building		
frame, log, stucco on frame, galvanized iron or corrugated metal[25]	10%	6
kiln, tank, vat used in manufacturing and processing	20%	8
mining (except refineries and office buildings not at mine)	30%	10
multiple-unit residential[7,18]	5%	31
frame, log, stucco, commenced before 1978 . .	10%	32
portable camp	30%	10
rental property[7]		
storage of fresh fruits and vegetables	20%	8
Buses	30%	10

¶620

Item	Rate	Class
Cable TV converters and descramblers (acquired after Aug. 31, 1984)	30%	10
Cables — telephone, telegraph or data communication		
acquired before Feb. 23, 2005	5%	3
acquired after Feb. 22, 2005^{35}	12%	
fibre optic^{29}	12%	42
Calculator	20%	8
Canals^1	4%	1
Canoes	15%	7
Capital tangible assets^{1,2}	20%	8
used primarily in manufacturing and processing^{10,15}		29, 39, 40, 43
Cash registers	20%	8
electronic, to record multiple sales taxes^3	100%	12
Catalyst^{21}	5%	26
Cattle	nil	—
Chinaware^{26}	100%	12
Cold storage structures . . .	20%	8
Computer hardware and systems software^{15,30}		
acquired before Mar. 23, 2004	30%	10
acquired after Mar. 22, 2004	45%	45
Computer software^{10,16,24,30}	100%	12
Concessions		14
Concrete mixing plant	20%	8
Contractors' movable equipment	30%	10
heavy, acquired before 1988^5	50%	22
heavy, acquired after 1987^{5,10}	30%	38
Conversion cost — see Vessels		
Copyrights		14

Item	Rate	Class
Costume and accessories for earning rental income^{1,26}	100%	12
Culverts^{1,10}	4%	1
Cutlery^{26}	100%	12
Cutting part of a machine^{1,27}	100%	12
Dairy plant and equipment	20%	8
Dams^1	4%	1
Data communication equipment — wire and cable		
acquired before Feb. 23, 2005	5%	3
acquired after Feb. 22, 2005^{35}	12%	
Data communication switching equipment^{16}	8%	17
Dental instruments (costing less than $200)^{1,16,26}	100%	12
Deuterium enriched water^{21}	5%	26
Dies^{1,27}	100%	12
Display fixtures (window)	20%	8
Distribution equipment for gas, heat, electrical energy, or water^4		
acquired before 1988 . . .	6%	2
acquired after 1987	4%	1
for heat or water, acquired after Feb. 27, 2000	8%	17
of a district energy system, acquired after Feb. 22, 2005 and before 2012^{35}	50%	
Docks^1	5%	3
Drive-in theatre property	30%	10
Electrical advertising signs^{10,16}	20%	8
Electrical generating and distributing equipment^{4,6,10}		

¶620

Item	Rate	Class
acquired before 1988 ...	6%	2
acquired after 1987	4%	1
acquired after Feb. 27, 2000 for generation[10]	8%	17
acquired after Feb. 22, 2005 for transmission[7,34,35]	8%	
combustion turbines acquired after Feb. 22, 2005[7,34,35] ..	15%	
energy efficient generating equipment	30%	43.1
Electrical power plants		
acquired before 1988[4] ..	6%	2
acquired after 1987	4%	1
not more than 15 kilowatts[16]	20%	8
not more than 15 megawatts[19]	50%	34
energy efficient, acquired after Feb. 21, 1994	30%	43.1
Electric wiring — same rate as building		
Electronic communications equipment including fax machines and telephone equipment[10]	20%	8
Electronic data processing equipment[1,15,16,30]		
applications or sales tax point of sale software[3]	100%	12
used primarily in manufacturing and processing[15]		10, 29, 40
Electronic data processing equipment — data network infrastructure and systems software		
acquired before March 23, 2004[10]	20%	8
acquired after March 22, 2004	30%	46
Electronic data processing equipment — general purpose and systems software		

Item	Rate	Class
acquired before March 23, 2004[10]	30%	10
acquired after March 22, 2004	45%	45
Elevators — same rate as building		
Energy conservation equipment[19]	50%	34
acquired after Feb. 21, 1994	30%	43.1
Equipment (see specific types)		
if not specifically mentioned[2]	20%	8
manufacturing and processing[10,15]		29, 39, 40, 43
Escalators — same rate as building		
Farming and fishing assets[39]		
Fences[1]	10%	6
Fibre-optic cable[29]	12%	42
Films, motion pictures		
Canadian production[7,37]	30%	10
certified production[37] ..	100%	12
certified production acquired after 1987 and before March 1996[7,37]	30%	10
other productions[16,37] ..	30%	10
television commercials..	100%	12
Franchises		14
Furniture (not otherwise listed)[15]	20%	8
Gas manufacturing and distributing equipment, plants and pipelines[4,8]		
acquired before 1988[10]	6%	2
acquired after 1987	4%	1
transmission pipelines acquired after Feb. 22, 2005[33,35] ...	8%	
Gas pumping and compression equipment		

¶620

Item	Rate	Class	Item	Rate	Class
acquired before Feb. 23, 2005	20%	8	Heavy water^{21}	5%	26
			Herbs	nil	—
acquired after Feb. 22, 2005^{33,35}	15%		Horses	nil	—
Gas well equipment			Instruments, dental or medical (under $200)^{1,16,26}	100%	12
acquired after 1987	25%	41			
acquired before 1988	30%	10	Jetties^{16}	5%	3
Generating equipment and plant of producer or distributor of electrical energy^{4,6}			wood	10%	6
			Jigs^{1,27}	100%	12
			Kitchen utensils (costing less than $200)^{1,16,26}	100%	12
acquired before 1988	6%	2	Land	nil	—
acquired after 1987	4%	1	deemed depreciable^{7}	nil	36
acquired after Feb. 27, 2000	8%	17	Lasts^{1,37}	100%	12
energy efficient	30%	43.1	Leasehold interest		13
Glass tableware^{1,26}	100%	12	Lending library books^{1,26}	100%	12
Grain drying machinery^{11}	20%	8	Licences		14
Grain storage facilities — see buildings^{11}			Lighting fixture — same rate as building		
Greenhouses^{1}	10%	6	Linen^{1,26}	100%	12
rigid frame with plastic cover	20%	8	Logging mechanical equipment	30%	10
Hangars^{1}	10%	6	Machinery and equipment		
Harness equipment^{1}	30%	10	additional capital cost allowance on grain elevators^{11}	14%	8
Heating equipment					
distribution plant, acquired before 1988	6%	2	not specifically listed^{2}	20%	8
distribution plant, acquired after 1987	4%	1	used primarily in manufacturing and processing^{10,15}		29, 39, 40, 43
general — same rate as building			Marine railways	15%	7
solar or energy efficient, acquired before Feb. 21, 1994^{19}	50%	34	Medical instruments (costing less than $200)^{1,16,26}	100%	12
solar or energy efficient, acquired after Feb. 21, 1994	30%	43.1	Metric scales^{1,20}	20%	8
			Mine shafts (sunk after mine in production)^{1,26}	100%	12
Heat production equipment and pipeline^{19}	50%	34	Mining equipment	30%	10
Heat recovery equipment^{19}	50%	34	Mining equipment, new or expanded mines^{7,14}		
			acquired before 1988	30%	28
acquired after Feb. 21, 1994	30%	43.1	acquired after 1987	25%	41

¶620

Item	Rate	Class	Item	Rate	Class
acquired after Feb. 25, 1992 for processing foreign ore unless Class 41 elected	30%	43		25%	44
			Patterns ^{1,27}	100%	12
Moles ^{1,16}	5%	3	Photocopy machines ^{10,15,30}	20%	8
Motion picture drive-in theatres	30%	10	Pinball machines — see Video games		
Motion picture films — see Films			Pipelines		
Moulds ^{1,27}	100%	12	acquired before 1988 ^{8,10}	6%	2
Multiple-unit residential buildings ^{7,18}	5%, 10%	31, 32	acquired after 1987	4%	1
Office equipment ^{30}	20%	8	Plumbing — same rate as building		
Offshore drilling platforms			Pollution control equipment ^{12}		
acquired before 1988	30%	10	air, certified, acquired before 1999	50%	27
acquired after 1987	25%	41	water, certified, acquired before 1999	50%	24
Offshore drilling vessels ^{7,16,17}			uncertified, used in M&P ^{10}	25%, 30%	39, 43
acquired before 1988	15%	7	not specifically listed — Class 1, 2, 6 or 8, depending on type of asset		
acquired after 1987	25%	41			
Oil pipelines			Portable construction camp buildings	30%	10
acquired before 1988 ^{8,10}	6%	2	Portable electrical generating equipment ^{16}	20%	8
acquired after 1987	4%	1	Portable equipment used for temporary rentals ^{15}	30%	10
acquired after Feb. 22, 2005 — transmission ^{33,35}	8%		Portable tools ^{1,15,16}	30%	10
Oil pumping and compression equipment			Power operated movable equipment ^{5,15}		
acquired before Feb. 23, 2005	20%	8	acquired before 1988	50%	22
acquired after Feb. 22, 2005 ^{33,35}	15%		acquired after 1987	30%	38
Oil storage tanks ^{1,15}	10%	6	Power plants — see Electrical power plants		
used primarily in manufacturing and processing ^{15}		29, 39, 43	Production equipment of distributor of heat (including structures)		
Oil well equipment ^{1}			acquired before 1988 ^{4}	6%	2
acquired before 1988	30%	10	acquired after 1987	4%	1
acquired after 1987	25%	41	acquired after Feb. 27, 2000	8%	17
acquired after 1987	20%	8			
Overburden removal cost, designated ^{1,26}	100%	12	Radar equipment ^{16}	20%	8
Parking area ^{16}	8%	17			
Patents		14			

¶620

Item	Rate	Class
Radio communication equipment (excluding satellites)[16]	20%	8
Radium	nil	—
Railway car and rail suspension devices[1,7,16,31]		
acquired before Feb. 28, 2000[31]	7%	35
acquired after Feb. 27, 2000[31]	15%	7
Railway locomotive excluding automotive railway car[16]	10%	6
Railway, marine	15%	7
Railway system or a part thereof designed to run on rail or track	6%	4
Railway track or grading[1,7,31]	4%	1
Railway traffic control or signalling equipment[1,7,16,31]	4%	1
Railway trestle[7,31]	5%	3
Rapid transit car[41]	20%	8
Refrigeration equipment	20%	8
Renewable energy generation equipment[7,34]		
acquired before Feb. 23, 2005	30%	43.1
acquired after Feb. 22, 2005 and before 2012[35]	50%	
bio-oil, fuel cell and heat energy equipment acquired after Feb. 18, 2003[36]	30%	43.1
Rental property[7]		
Roads[1,16]	8%	17
acquired in relation to a mine	25%	41
forestry (may be depreciated with timber limit)	30%	10
oil and gas mining temporary access[42]		
Roller rink floors	30%	10

Item	Rate	Class
Rowboats	15%	7
Sales tax calculation equipment[3]	100%	12
Satellites[7]		
acquired after 1987	30%	10
acquired before 1988	40%	30
Scales, metric — see Metric scales		
Scanners, bar codes[3]	100%	12
Scows	15%	7
Shafts, mine (sunk after mine in production)[1,26]	100%	12
Shaping part of a machine[1,27]	100%	12
Ships, including ships under construction	15%	7
Shrubs	nil	—
Sidewalks[16]	8%	17
Sleighs[1]	30%	10
Solar heating equipment[19]		
acquired before Feb. 21, 1994	50%	34
acquired after Feb. 21, 1994	30%	43.1
Spacecraft (telecommunication)[7]		
acquired before 1988	40%	30
acquired after 1987	30%	10
Spare parts for an aircraft[16]	25%	9
Sprinkler systems — same rate as building		
Stable equipment[1]	30%	10
Steam generating equipment[19]	50%	34
Storage area[16]	8%	17
Storage tanks, oil or water[1]	10%	6
direct manufacturing use[15]		29, 39, 43
Subway or tunnel[1,16]	4%	1
Swimming pool	10%	6

¶620

Item	Rate	Class
Systems software — general purpose electronic data processing equipment [1,16,30]		
acquired after Mar. 22, 2004	45%	45
acquired before Mar. 23, 2004 [10]	30%	10
primary manufacturing purpose [15]		10, 29, 40
Tableware, glass [1,26]	100%	12
Tangible capital assets [1,2]	20%	8
Tank cars, railway [1,7,16]	7%	35
Tanks, oil and water storage [1]	10%	6
used primarily in manufacturing and processing [15]		29, 39, 43
Taxicabs [16]	40%	16
Telecommunication spacecraft [7]		
acquired before 1988	40%	30
acquired after 1987	30%	10
Telegraph and telephone equipment, wires and cables [16]		
acquired before Feb. 23, 2005 [1,16]	5%	3
new and acquired after Feb. 22, 2005 [35]	12%	
poles and masts [1,16]	5%	3
fibre-optic cable [29]	12%	42
Telephone or telegraph communication non-electronic switching equipment [16]	8%	17
Telephone system (purchased) [30]	20%	8
Television aerial [16]	20%	8
Television commercials	100%	12
Timber cutting and removing equipment	30%	10, 15
Timber limits — see Sched. VI of the Income Tax Regulations [7]	30%	
Timber resource property	15%	33

Item	Rate	Class
Tools (under $200) [16,26]	100%	12
Tools (over $200) [15]	20%	8
Tractors [1]	30%	10
for hauling freight [28]	40%	16
Trailers [1,38]	30%	10
Tramways [4,9]	6%	4
Trees	nil	—
Trestles [1,31]	5%	3
Trolley bus system [4]	6%	4
Trucks, automotive [1]	30%	10
for hauling freight [28]	40%	16
Tunnel [1,16,31]	4%	1
Uniforms [1,26]	100%	12
Vessels [7,17]	15%	7
acquired after Nov. 12, 1981	$16^{2/3}$%	
acquired before Nov. 13, 1981	$33^{1/3}$%	
furniture, fittings and spare engines	15%	7
offshore drilling after 1987 [32]	25%	41
Video cassettes [23]	100%	12
Video games (coin operated) acquired after Feb. 15, 1984	40%	16
Video laser disks and digital video disks acquired after December 12, 1995 [23]	100%	12
Video tapes [1,16]	30%	10
television commercial	100%	12
Wagons [1]	30%	10
Water pipelines		
acquired before 1988 [10]	6%	2
acquired after 1987	4%	1
Water pollution control equipment — see Pollution control equipment		
Water storage tanks [1]	10%	6
primary manufacturing purpose [15]		

¶620

Item	Rate	Class	Item	Rate	Class
Water distribution plant and equipment[4]			Wind energy conversion system[19]		
acquired before 1988 . . .	6%	2	acquired before Feb. 21, 1994	50%	34
acquired after 1987	4%	1	acquired after Feb. 21, 1994	30%	43.1
Well equipment, oil or gas (for use above ground)			Windmills[1,43]	5%	3
acquired after 1987	25%	41	Wiring, electric — same rate as building		
acquired before 1988 . . .	30%	10			
Wharves[1]	5%	3			
wooden[1]	10%	6			

Notes:

[1] Unless included in another class of assets subject to a different rate.

[2] Not applicable to land, animals, herbs, trees, shrubs or similar growing things, gas wells, mines, oil wells, radium, rights of way, timber limits, tramway track or certain vessels.

[3] Electronic bar code scanners, electronic cash registers designed to calculate and record sales taxes imposed by multiple jurisdictions, software to allow multiple sales tax calculation, and related equipment acquired after August 8, 1989 and before 1993 for use in a retail business in Canada will be permitted a 100% write-off with no half-year rule.

[4] Except property included in Class 10, 13, 14, 26 or 28. For distributors of gas, not including a property acquired to produce or distribute gas normally distributed in portable containers, to process natural gas before its delivery to a gas distribution system and to produce oxygen or nitrogen.

[5] Designed for the purpose of excavating, moving, placing or compacting earth, rock, concrete or asphalt.

[6] Electrical generating equipment may be allocated to one of the following different classes: Class 1, if large and acquired by a producer; Class 2, if acquired before 1988; Class 8, if small; Class 9, if acquired before May 26, 1976 and not owned by a producer; or Class 17, if new and acquired after February 27, 2000 (with certain exclusions). Energy-efficient equipment may be in Class 34, if acquired before February 22, 1994, or 43.1, if acquired after February 21, 1994. Only a detailed reading of the classes can determine the appropriate one; see Schedule II of the Income Tax Regulations. If used in manufacturing and processing, see note 15.

[7] Separate classes may be required for each asset, including: certain rental properties costing $50,000 or more (effective January 1, 1972); certain automobiles in Class 10.1; certain vessels, including Canadian vessels and off-shore drilling vessels; all Class 28 or 41 property relating to a particular mine or group of mines; railway property in Class 1, 3 or 35; and land deemed to be depreciable property in Class 36. Certified productions and certain Canadian film or video productions in Class 10 are to be put in separate classes from other Class 10 assets. See Regulation 1101 for the provisions regarding separate classes.

[8] Unless, in the case of a pipeline for oil or natural gas, the Minister is satisfied that the main source of supply for the business is likely to be exhausted within 15 years; such pipelines, not being specifically listed, fall under the general rate of 20% (Class 8).

[9] Tramway tracks: 100% on cessation of tramcar operation.

[10] Separate class elections may be available for certain assets or groups of assets, including: Class 2 pipelines, commenced after 1984 and completed after September 1, 1985, costing at least $10 million; earth-moving equipment in Class 38 acquired after 1987; outdoor advertising signs in Class 8(*l*); and certain electronic equipment in Class 8 or 10 (including computer software, photocopiers, fax machines, electronic telephone equipment, and general purpose electronic data processing equipment and systems software). Certain Class 43 manufacturing and processing assets costing more than $1,000 may also be eligible for a separate class election after February 27, 2000; however, where the property is still on hand after five years, it must be merged into the general Class 43 UCC pool. See Regulation 1101 for the provisions regarding separate classes.

[11] A grain elevator or addition to a grain elevator situated in "Eastern Canada", acquired after April 1, 1972 and before August 1, 1974, is entitled to an additional allowance equal to the lesser of: 22% (Class 3), 20% (Class 6), or 14% (Class 8) of the lesser of $15,000 and the capital cost; or the undepreciated capital cost at the end of the taxation year before the allowance. New grain drying equipment for a farm acquired after July 31, 1968 and before January 1, 1970 or after April 1, 1972 but before August 1, 1974 may be depreciated at the rate equal to the lesser of 14% of the capital cost or $15,000.

¶620

[12] Certified pollution control equipment in Class 24 or 27 is depreciated 25/50/25 over three years for additions made before 1999. If not certified, the equipment may be Class 8, 39 or 43 if used primarily in manufacturing, or Class 1, 3 or 6, depending on its nature.

[13] An addition or alteration to a building originally placed in Class 3, 6 or 20, but which would no longer be in that class under current rules, may be added to the old class within certain dollar and transitional rule limitations. See IT-79R3 and Regulation 1102(19).

[14] Includes buildings, other than office buildings not situated on mining property, structures, machinery, equipment and houses, schools, hospitals, sidewalks, roads, sewers, etc., necessary to establish community facilities for the operation of a mine. Qualifying assets are included in a special class for each mine. The full amount of undepreciated capital cost up to the amount of income from a mine may be claimed, or at least 30% of the undepreciated balance. Additional allowances on property for new or expanded mines may be claimed up to the income from the new facility; acquisitions that become available for use in the year, in excess of 5% of gross revenue from the mine, also qualify for the additional allowance, for property acquired after March 6, 1996.

[15] Specified property used primarily in manufacturing and processing may be allocated to one of the following classes: Class 29 (25%/50%/25% straight line), if acquired after November 12, 1981 and before 1988; Class 39 (25%, see Reg. 1100(1)(*ze*) for transitional rates), if acquired after 1987 and before February 26, 1992; and Class 43 (30%), if acquired after February 25, 1992. Specified property includes property that would otherwise be in Class 8, an oil or water storage tank, a powered industrial lift truck, portable tools acquired for rental purposes, certain general purpose electronic data processing equipment and systems software, or electrical generating equipment described in Class 9 (see note 6). Powered industrial lift trucks, portable tools acquired for rental purposes, and general purpose electronic data processing equipment and systems software are excluded from Class 39 and 43. These items are included in Class 40 (30%, see Reg. 1100(1)(*zf*) for transitional rates), if acquired in 1988 or 1989, and after that, they are transferred to Class 10 (30%).

[16] Acquired after May 25, 1976. Property of this type acquired before May 26, 1976 may be in a different class. See Schedule II of the Income Tax Regulations.

[17] Accelerated capital cost allowances are provided on certain prescribed vessels and conversion costs. Additional capital cost allowances (not exceeding 15% of undepreciated capital cost) are provided in respect of offshore drilling vessels in Class 7 by Regs. 1100(1)(*va*) and 1101(2*b*).

[18] Buildings acquired before June 18, 1987 that would otherwise be included in Class 3 or 6 and in respect of which a certificate is issued by the Canada Mortgage and Housing Corporation.

[19] Property must be certified and must have been acquired after May 25, 1976 and before February 21, 1994. Such assets acquired after this date are eligible for a CCA at 30% in Class 43.1.

[20] Class 12 for metric scales or scales designed for ready conversion to metric weighing acquired after March 31, 1977 and before 1984. The scale must be for use in a retail business and must have a weighing capacity of no more than 100 kilograms.

[21] The heavy water must be acquired after May 22, 1979. Prior to May 23, 1979, a catalyst was depreciable at 1%.

[22] Automobiles acquired after November 12, 1981 for lease or rental other than to any one person for more than 30 days in a 12-month period.

[23] Items must be acquired for the purpose of renting to any one person for no more than 7 days in any 30-day period.

[24] Computer software in Class 12 is subject to the half-year rule. Systems software is in Class 10.

[25] Building must be used in farming or fishing business, or be unsupported below the ground.

[26] The half-year rule does not apply to this item. It may be written off in full in the year of acquisition.

[27] The half-year rule applies to assets of this description acquired after December 31, 1987. Prior acquisitions could be written off at 100% in the year of acquisition.

[28] Trucks or tractors acquired after December 6, 1991 that have a gross vehicle weight rating in excess of 11,788 kg.

[29] Acquired after December 23, 1991. See the history note for Class 42 for the election that can be made.

[30] May be eligible for a separate class. Up to $50,000 of computer expenditures (hardware and software combined) may be eligible for 100% deduction in year of acquisition if acquired by a small or medium-sized business in the period January 1, 1998 to October 31, 1999 to deal with Year 2000 problems.

[31] Railway equipment may be subject to additional allowances over and above the class rate. Railway system or parts allocated to Class 4 if acquired after the end of the taxpayer's 1958 taxation year and before May 26, 1976. Railway locomotives, railway cars and railway suspension devices acquired after February 27, 2000, are eligible for Class 7 (15%) depreciation rather than a combined rate of 10% or 13% (7% + additional allowance of 3% or 6%) previously available. Leased assets are included in Class 7 (15%) only if the lessor elects specified leasing property treatment.

¶620

[32] After November 7, 2001, Class 41 for offshore drilling vessels will not be available if the Minister of Industry has agreed to a structured financing facility. In such a case, the maximum CCA rate applicable to the vessel and its attachments will be 15% under Class 7.

[33] Applicable only to new transmission pipelines. Taxpayers may elect, in the year the pipelines are acquired, to place them in a separate CCA class.

[34] Specified energy property rules applicable. Includes high efficiency cogeneration equipment which is used in combined heat and power (CHP) systems, capturing waste heat from an electrical generation process and using it for manufacturing or space heating. Renewable energy generation equipment includes wind turbines, small hydroelectric facilities, active solar heating equipment, fixed location photovoltaic equipment, geothermal energy equipment and biogas production equipment.

[35] Rate set out in 2005 Federal Budget. The CCA class for this item has not yet been announced.

[36] The bio-oil must be used to generate electricity or electricity and heat. The fuel cell must have a minimum electrical output peak capacity and use hydrogen generated from fuel reformation or electrolysis equipment; if electrolysis equipment is used, it must use solar, wind or hydroelectric energy. Other equipment must generate heat energy from the consumption of wood waste, municipal waste, landfill gas, digester gas or bio-oil, and be used directly in a greenhouse or industrial process.

[37] Additional allowance and separate class treatment available in certain circumstances. For 1995 and subsequent taxation years, the accelerated capital cost allowance incentive for Canadian-owned film or video productions was replaced by a Canadian Film or Video Production Tax Credit under the *Income Tax Act*; for taxation years ending after October 1997, other film or video productions may qualify for the Film or Video Production Services Tax Credit.

[38] Includes trailers designed for use on both highways and railway tracks.

[39] A straight-line method may be used for assets acquired before 1972 and used in a farming or fishing business.

[40] This item excludes landscaping costs deductible under paragraph 20(1)(*aa*) of the Act.

[41] Used for public transportation within a metropolitan area and not part of a railway system.

[42] Temporary access roads in the oil and gas mining sectors may qualify as Canadian exploration or development expenses.

[43] Not to be confused with wind energy conversion systems included in Class 43.1.

¶620

CHAPTER 8

FARMING AND FISHING ASSETS

Special capital cost allowance rules are provided for taxpayers engaged in the business of farming or fishing for assets acquired prior to January 1, 1972.

¶630
Methods of Computing Capital Cost Allowance

In the past, taxpayers engaged in farming or fishing were allowed to choose between the Part XI method of claiming capital cost allowance in the Regulations, and the Part XVII "straight-line" method, which applied only to depreciable assets used in the business of farming or fishing. Under the Part XI method, which is used by all other taxpayers, assets of a similar type are pooled for capital cost allowance purposes. Any recovered capital cost allowance on the pool is included in income, and a terminal loss on the pool is allowed as a deduction. Under the Part XVII method, each asset is treated separately for capital cost allowance purposes. Recovered capital cost allowance is not taxable and a loss on disposal is not deductible.

With the introduction of capital gains tax in 1972, the Part XVII method has been phased out. Depreciable assets acquired after December 31, 1971 for use in farming and fishing are subject to depreciation for tax purposes only through the Part XI method of claiming capital cost allowance.

Taxpayers who were entitled to claim straight-line depreciation under Part XVII on property owned at December 31, 1971 may continue to depreciate that property on the same basis in subsequent years. Any capital cost allowance on that property, whether claimed before or after December 31, 1971, is not subject to tax if recovered on disposal of the property, provided the taxpayer has not at any time elected to claim depreciation under the Part XI method.

¶635

Property Acquired before 1972

Prior to 1972, taxpayers in the business of farming or fishing were entitled to elect an optional method of calculating capital cost allowances and if they elected to use this optional method in those years, they may continue to use it now, but only for the assets which they acquired prior to January 1, 1972. This optional method is known as the Part XVII method.

Both the Part XI and Part XVII methods are modified somewhat when a taxpayer is a member of a partnership — see Chapter 6 for a discussion on partnerships.

The major features of the Part XVII method of computing capital cost allowances, and differences from the Part XI method, are as follows:

(1) Annual allowance rates are generally lower than under the Part XI method. A table of Part XVII rates for certain specific assets follows. See also Information Circular 86-5R, Part XVII — Capital Cost Allowance, Farming and Fishing (archived by the CRA), and CRA Guides T4003, Farming Income, and T4004, Fishing Income. See ¶620 for an alphabetical table of Part XI rates for certain assets.

Depreciable Property	Part XVII Rate
Aircraft — acquired before May 26, 1976	15%
Aircraft — acquired after May 25, 1976	—
Automobiles	15%
Bee equipment	10%
Binders	10%
Boats and component parts	$7^1/_2$%
Breakwaters — Cement or stone	$2^1/_2$%
— Wood	5%
Brooders	10%
Buildings and component parts	
— Wood, galvanized or portable	5%
— Other	$2^1/_2$%
Buildings — Fruit and vegetable storage, acquired after Feb. 19, 1973	—
Casing, cribwork for waterwells	10%
Chain saws	10%
Cleaners — Grain or seed	10%
Combines — Drawn	10%
— Self-propelled	15%
Coolers — Milk	10%

¶635

Depreciable Property	Part XVII Rate
Corn binders	10%
Cream separators	10%
Cultivators	10%
Cutting boxes	10%
Dams — Cement, stone or earth	$2^1/_2$%
— Wood	5%
Discs	10%
Diggers — All types	10%
Docks — Cement, steel or stone	$2^1/_2$%
— Wood	5%
Drills — All types	10%
Dugouts, dikes and lagoons	5%
Electric light plants and batteries (not exceeding 15 kw)	
— acquired before May 26, 1976	15%
— acquired after May 25, 1976	—
Electric motors	10%
Elevators	10%
Engines — Stationary	10%
Fences — All types	5%
Forage harvesters — Drawn	10%
— Self-propelled	15%
Graders — Fruit or vegetable	10%
Grain drying equipment	10%
Grain loaders	10%
Grain separators	10%
Grain storage buildings	
— Wood, galvanized steel	5%
— Other	$2^1/_2$%
Greenhouses	5%
Grinders	10%
Harnesses	10%
Harrows	10%
Hay balers, hay bines and stookers	
— Drawn	10%
— Self-propelled	15%
Hay loaders	10%
Hydraulic and power take-off attachments	10%
Ice machines	10%
Incubators	10%
Irrigation equipment — Overhead	10%
Irrigation ponds	5%
Manure spreaders	10%
Milking machines	10%
Mixers	10%
Mowers	10%
Nets (see Note)	10%
Office equipment	10%
Outboard motors	15%
Piping — Permanent	10%
Planters — All types	10%
Ploughs	10%
Power block — (Purse-seine)	$7^1/_2$%
Pumps	10%

¶635

Depreciable Property	*Part XVII* *Rate*
Radio or radio equipment	
— acquired before May 26, 1976	15%
— acquired after May 25, 1976	—
Rakes	10%
Roads — Paved	$2\frac{1}{2}$%
— Unpaved (¶1710)	
Rollers	10%
Silo fillers	10%
Sleighs	15%
Sprayers	10%
Stable cleaners	10%
Stalk cutters	10%
Surface areas, paved or concrete	$2\frac{1}{2}$%
Swathers — Drawn	10%
— Self-propelled	15%
Tile drainage acquired before the 1965 taxation year (fully deductible after 1964)	10%
Tillers — All types	10%
Threshers	10%
Tools — under $200	100%
— $200 and over	10%
Tractors	15%
Trailers	15%
Trucks	15%
Wagons	15%
Water towers	5%
Weirs	5%
Weirs (fish)	10%
Welding equipment	10%
Well equipment	10%
Wharves — Cement, steel or stone	$2\frac{1}{2}$%
— Wood	5%
Windchargers	10%
Windmills	10%

Buildings acquired after February 19, 1973 for preserving farm ensilage or storing fresh fruit and vegetables of the grower in controlled temperature and humidity conditions are included in Part XI, Class 8.

NOTE: As an alternative to capital cost allowance on nets, the loss in value may be claimed as an expense, as shown in the following example:

Value of nets, traps, twine, etc., on hand at beginning of period		$ 750
Add: Cost of nets and traps purchased	$200	
Cost of twine and other net and trap materials purchased	125	325
Sub-total		$1,075
Deduct: Value of nets, traps, twine, etc., on hand at end of period	$700	
Proceeds from sale and insurance of nets, traps, twine, etc.	150	850
Loss on nets and traps claimed as expense		$ 225

¶635

Further points on Part XVII method:

(2) The annual allowance rates are applied each year to the original cost of the assets, rather than to the undepreciated balance of cost at the year end.

(3) In the year an asset is disposed of, the allowance may be claimed for the number of months in which the asset was owned. For example, an asset owned for five months of the year will qualify for an allowance of $5/12$ of the normal full year allowance. Under Part XI, when an asset is disposed of during the year, the allowance is based on the balance remaining in the class at the end of the year.

(4) Under Part XVII, no recapture or terminal loss will result when an asset is disposed of. If assets are sold for more than both their original cost and their value on December 31, 1971, the profit may be subject to tax as a capital gain. Under the Part XI method, in addition to capital gains, recapture or a terminal loss may arise on the disposal of an asset.

If the Part XVII method, applicable only to taxpayers in the business of farming or fishing, was adopted originally, a change can be made to the Part XI method at any time in a subsequent year.

Taxpayers in the business of farming or fishing who continue to use the Part XVII method for assets acquired before 1972 will be required to maintain two separate capital cost allowance schedules, one for calculations made under Part XVII and one for calculations made under Part XI. The Part XVII schedule will include only those assets purchased up to the end of 1971, the Part XI schedule will include assets purchased in 1972 and subsequent years.

Under both methods, capital cost allowance is an optional deduction — any amount up to the maximum allowance may be claimed; deferral of claims will leave a larger pool for future calculations.

¶655

Transfer of Farm Property to Child

Regardless of which method of depreciation is used, where farmland and/or depreciable farm property is transferred or distributed to a farmer's child *inter vivos* or as a consequence of death, and the particular child is resident in Canada, the property can be rolled over without triggering accrued gains or losses. See ¶282 and ¶288 for the rules surrounding such transfers. For purposes of these rollovers, subsection 70(10) and 73(6) provide that the term "child" includes a grandchild and great-grandchild.

CHAPTER 9

CAPITALIZING COST OF BORROWED MONEY

¶700

Subsection 21(1) allows a taxpayer who has acquired depreciable property in a particular taxation year to elect to capitalize any borrowing expenses referable to that property for which the taxpayer would ordinarily be entitled to a deduction for that year under paragraphs $20(1)(c)$, (d), (e), or $(e.1)$. Where the taxpayer elects under subsection 21(1), a deduction may not be claimed under any of paragraphs $20(1)(c)$, (d), (e), or $(e.1)$ for the year in respect of the borrowing expenses specified in the election. Instead, the expenses otherwise deductible are added to the taxpayer's capital cost of the property. An election under subsection 21(1) will not be allowed, however, where subsection 18(3.1) concerning construction period soft costs would require that the interest be added to the capital cost of depreciable property.

Not all applicable borrowing expenses in respect of a particular property need to be elected upon. The taxpayer can deduct some of them in the usual manner and elect to capitalize the remainder. Where the taxpayer acquires more than one property of a particular class, the taxpayer may elect in respect of the borrowing expenses of some properties and choose to make no election on the expenses of the others.

Where an election is made under subsection 21(1) in respect of the year in which the property is acquired, any borrowing expenses referable to that property for the preceding three years may also be capitalized. For example, if the taxpayer was having a plant constructed over several years, the taxpayer might incur standby fees in the early years which could then be capitalized when the plant became the property of the taxpayer. Subsection 21(5) requires the Minister to reassess the preceding three years to give effect to an election in respect of them.

Subsection 21(1) applies only to borrowing expenses incurred in the year the property is acquired (and to the three preceding years). A further election is required under subsection 21(3) if the taxpayer wishes to capitalize expenses incurred in years subsequent to the year the property is acquired. However, the taxpayer must elect in respect of each successive year after the property is acquired (or be required to capitalize costs under subsection 18(3.1)) in order to be entitled to elect under subsection 21(3) for further years. Furthermore, while an election under subsection 21(3) may be made with respect to all or any portion of the borrowing expenses of the year to which the election relates, an election on only a portion precludes any election in a subsequent year.

CHAPTER 10

TREATMENT OF GOODWILL AND OTHER "ELIGIBLE CAPITAL EXPENDITURES"

¶725

Introduction

Prior to the 1972 taxation year, the cost of certain types of intangible properties was not recognized under the Act. Goodwill, customer lists and similar intangible properties were often referred to as "nothings". For the 1972 and subsequent taxation years, certain intangible capital property that does not qualify for capital cost allowance deductions is accorded special treatment that is very similar to the capital cost allowance system. Such intangible capital property will qualify as "eligible capital property" (section 54) if the cost of acquisition qualifies as an "eligible capital expenditure" under the definition in subsection 14(5). Three-quarters of the eligible capital expenditure is added to the "cumulative eligible capital" (subsection 14(5)) of the taxpayer and under paragraph 20(1)(b) the taxpayer is permitted a deduction from business income of up to 7% of the taxpayer's cumulative eligible capital at the end of the year.

Although the mechanics of amortizing eligible capital expenditures are similar to those for claiming capital cost allowance on depreciable property (including the pool concept of accumulating costs and proceeds of sale and the declining balance method of claiming deductions), the deduction under paragraph $20(1)(b)$ is not capital cost allowance. The capital cost allowance provisions of paragraph $20(1)(a)$ and the assortment of regulations made thereunder do not apply.

If a taxpayer is carrying on more than one business, the taxpayer may have more than one cumulative eligible capital pool. The taxpayer may deduct 7% of each pool in computing income under paragraph $20(1)(b)$. When the aggregate deductions from the cumulative eligible capital balance exceed the aggregate additions as of the end of a year, there will be an inclusion in income under subsection 14(1), similar to the recapture of capital cost allowance.

¶727
Eligible Capital Expenditures

¶728   Capital Expenditures That Qualify

The term "eligible capital expenditure" is defined in subsection 14(5). Only expenditures made after 1971 which are on capital account and made for the purpose of gaining or producing income from a business may be eligible capital expenditures. The concept of eligible capital expenditure embraces goodwill and other intangible capital expenses which under the former Act were usually referred to as "capital nothings". That is, they were not deductible currently because they were on capital account and could not be amortized for tax purposes because they did not come within one of the capital cost allowance classes. As noted earlier, under paragraph $20(1)(b)$, ³⁄₄ of expenses of this kind may be amortized for tax purposes at a rate of 7% *per annum* on the declining balance basis.

In general terms, the definition of eligible capital expenditure provides that the expenditure must meet the following criteria:

- the expenditure must be made for the purpose of gaining or producing income from a business (other than exempt income);

- it must be on account of a capital asset which does not fall into any prescribed class of depreciable property;

- it must not be in respect of tangible property or intangible property that is depreciable property or whose cost is otherwise deductible under the Act; and

- its deduction cannot be prohibited under any provision of the Act other than paragraph 18(1)(*b*) (which otherwise restricts the deduction of capital amounts).

Where an eligible capital expenditure is made in respect of the acquisition of an eligible capital property from a non-arm's length vendor who has claimed a capital gains exemption in respect of the disposition (e.g., if it was a qualified farm property), subsection 14(3) provides that the eligible capital expenditure of the purchaser is reduced to reflect the exemption claimed by the vendor. This corresponds with the treatment of non-arm's length transfers of depreciable property and is applicable to dispositions of property after 1987. However, the deemed reduction will not apply in cases where the property was acquired by the taxpayer as a consequence of the death of the transferor and is, in other cases, reversed to the extent that the taxpayer has received proceeds of disposition for the property in excess of that deemed eligible capital expenditure in a subsequent arm's length transaction.

See Interpretation Bulletins IT-123R6, "Transactions Involving Eligible Capital Property", at ¶3111, and IT-143R3, "Meaning of Eligible Capital Expenditure", at ¶3120.

¶729 Capital Expenditures That Do Not Qualify

The following items do not qualify as eligible capital expenditures:

(a) amounts which are wholly or partially non-deductible by some other provision of the Act, or capital expenditures, the deduction of which is prohibited;

(b) outlays which are incurred for the purpose of gaining or producing exempt income;

(c) cost of tangible property;

(d) cost of intangible property that qualifies as depreciable property (goodwill is not defined to be depreciable property);

(e) property for which any deduction is permitted or would be permitted if business income were sufficient to make the amount entirely deductible;

(f) an interest in or a right to acquire property described in items (c), (d), and (e);

(g) an amount paid or payable to a creditor or on redemption of a debt security;

(h) an amount paid by a corporation to a person as a shareholder; and

(i) the cost of an interest in a trust or partnership or of any share or other security or an interest therein.

¶733

Deductions — Cumulative Eligible Capital

Although the mechanics of amortizing eligible capital expenditures are very similar to those for claiming capital cost allowances on capital assets, including the use of a "pool" system for accumulating costs and proceeds of disposal, and the use of a declining balance in calculating deductions, the deductions permitted in respect of a taxpayer's cumulative eligible capital are not capital cost allowances. Where the deductions from the cumulative eligible capital pool exceed the additions at the end of a year, the negative balance is included in income or deemed to be a taxable capital gain (see subsection 14(1), discussed in the next section).

A formula is provided in subsection 14(5) for calculating the cumulative eligible capital in respect of a business which may be briefly described as being the aggregate of:

(a) $\frac{3}{4}$ of the eligible capital expenditures previously made in respect of the business; and

(b) $\frac{3}{2}$ of amounts previously included in income under paragraph 14(1)(b), which is discussed in the next section (this variable was amended effective for taxation years after February 27, 2000 to gross up the amount to be included consequential to the change in inclusion rates. The amount is grossed up by $\frac{3}{2}$ (or $\frac{9}{8}$ if the taxation year ends after February 27, 2000 but before October 18, 2000));

less the aggregate of:

(c) amounts previously deducted under paragraph 20(1)(b) as cumulative eligible capital in respect of the business;

(d) $\frac{3}{4}$ of amounts receivable by the taxpayer for consideration given by the taxpayer where the nature of the consideration is such that if the taxpayer had made a payment after 1971 to acquire such consideration, it would have been an eligible capital expenditure. This is reduced by $\frac{3}{4}$ of the outlays and expenses made for the purpose of the sale. The amount deducted in this manner from cumulative eligible capital is referred to as an "eligible capital amount" and, in effect, represents $\frac{3}{4}$ of the net proceeds of disposition of eligible capital property; and

(e) reductions in the cumulative eligible capital required under subsection 80(7) where a debt is forgiven. The reduction is basically equal to $\frac{3}{4}$ of the foreign debt amount remaining after the application of other debt forgiveness rules.

For acquisitions of eligible capital property from a non-arm's length transferor after December 20, 2002, a proposed amendment reduces the cumulative eligible capital balance by the non-taxable portion of the transferor's gain on its disposition of the property (more particularly, by $\frac{1}{2}$ of

¶733

the amount required to be included in the transferor's income in respect of the transfer under either paragraph $14(1)(b)$ or $38(a)$). See amount "A" in the definition of "cumulative eligible capital".

Effective after October 7, 2003, amounts received or receivable by a taxpayer in respect of a restrictive covenant and included in income under subsection 56.4(2) do not serve to reduce the taxpayer's cumulative eligible capital account. However, subsection 56.4(2) does not apply if the amount received or receivable is otherwise considered an eligible capital amount (see above), if the taxpayer and the payer of the amount elect in prescribed form (paragraph $56.4(3)(b)$), in which case $\frac{3}{4}$ of the amount is subtracted from the taxpayer's cumulative eligible capital account in the manner described above.

Cumulative eligible capital is somewhat analogous to the undepreciated capital cost of depreciable property. It consists of the balance remaining when $\frac{3}{4}$ of a taxpayer's eligible capital expenditures are reduced by $\frac{3}{4}$ of eligible capital amounts (which are net of disposal costs) receivable and amounts previously deducted through the amortization of the balance. As noted, the amortization rate under paragraph $20(1)(b)$ is 7% of the cumulative eligible capital balance at the end of the relevant taxation year.

The three-quarters inclusion rate for the addition of the cost of the property and the deduction of the proceeds was not affected by the 2000 Budget change to the capital gains inclusion rate, and is effective for taxation years of corporations commencing after June 1988, and for fiscal periods of other taxpayers commencing after 1987. Prior to amendments introduced in 1988, $\frac{1}{2}$ of eligible capital expenditures were added to a taxpayer's cumulative eligible capital, and $\frac{1}{2}$ of eligible capital amounts were deducted therefrom. At the time that the $\frac{3}{4}$ inclusion rate became effective, the taxpayer's existing eligible capital was increased by $\frac{1}{2}$ to reflect the new inclusion rate.

If a taxpayer is carrying on more than one business, the cumulative eligible capital for each business must be calculated separately.

¶734

Negative Balance in Cumulative Eligible Capital Account

In general terms, under subsection 14(1) a taxpayer is required to include in its income from a business for a year the amount by which the negative components of the cumulative eligible capital in respect of that business exceed the positive components in respect of that business as at the end of the taxation year. This may occur, for example, where the taxpayer's proceeds of disposition from a sale of its eligible capital property exceed the cost of the property to the taxpayer.

The negative amount giving rise to the income inclusion (negative components in excess of positive components) may be comprised of two components — a recapture of amounts previously deducted in respect of the eligible capital property under paragraph $20(1)(b)$ (paragraph $14(1)(a)$), and any additional amount, which is treated like a capital gain (paragraph $14(1)(b)$). Thus, the provision provides results similar to that seen on a disposition of depreciable property at a gain, where the disposition can result in a recapture of previously claimed capital cost allowance and a capital gain.

In the case of an individual disposing of eligible capital property in respect of qualified farm property, the amount included as ordinary income under paragraph $14(1)(a)$ is, as noted, limited to the aggregate of amounts previously deducted under paragraph $20(1)(b)$. Such amount is essentially a recapture of previous deductions. Any excess of the negative cumulative eligible capital balance (the excess) is deemed to be a capital gain of the taxpayer, eligible for the enhanced $500,000 capital gains exemption available for qualified farm property (see also subsection $14(1.1)$).

Specific amendments to section 14 were put in place to ensure that the inclusion in income under paragraph $14(1)(b)$ in respect of the portion of a negative balance in the cumulative eligible capital pool attributable to proceeds received on a disposition of eligible capital property in excess of the cost of the property is computed at a rate equivalent to that imposed on capital gains. Accordingly, an adjustment is required to correspond to the three rates and periods that apply to capital gains realized in 2000 (see amount "B" in the definition of "cumulative eligible capital" in subsection $14(5)$).

As noted earlier, the inclusion rate of $\frac{3}{4}$ applies for additions of eligible capital expenditures to the cumulative eligible capital balance, and similarly a $\frac{3}{4}$ rate applies for deductions from the balance in respect of proceeds received on a disposition of eligible capital property. Thus, subsection $14(1)$, which effectively brings a negative cumulative eligible capital balance into income, provides:

- the inclusion in income for recapture of deductions previously claimed under paragraph $20(1)(b)$ (paragraph $14(1)(a)$); and

- the inclusion in income under paragraph $14(1)(b)$ relating to proceeds of disposition to $\frac{2}{3}$ for taxation years that end after February 27, 2000, with a transitional $\frac{8}{9}$ rate for taxation years that end after February 27, 2000 and before October 18, 2000. The application of these rates to the $\frac{3}{4}$ rate applicable to proceeds of disposition of eligible capital property credited to the cumulative eligible capital balance will yield the appropriate percentages for income inclusions: for example, $\frac{2}{3} \times \frac{3}{4} = \frac{1}{2}$ for taxation years that end after October 18, 2000.

¶734

Example:

Facts

- X had a cumulative eligible capital balance of $900,000 at the beginning of 2005, which reflected $100,000 of amounts previously deducted under paragraph $20(1)(b)$ (i.e., the original balance was $1 million, reflecting $1,333,333 million in eligible capital expenditures).

- In January 2005, X disposes of eligible capital property for proceeds of $4 million.

Calculation

$14(1)$ total "excess" (i.e., the negative pool balance)
= ($\frac{3}{4}$ × 4 million proceeds) + 100,000 (previous deduction) − 1 million (original balance)
= 2.1 million

$14(1)(a)$ inclusion (recapture of previous deduction under paragraph $20(1)(b)$)
= 100,000

$14(1)(b)$ inclusion (proceeds in excess of original cost, treated like capital gain)
= $\frac{2}{3}$ × (2.1 million − 100,000)
= $\frac{2}{3}$ × 2 million
= 1,333,333

Note that the $1,333,333 inclusion equals $\frac{1}{2}$ of the amount by which the proceeds of disposition ($4 million) exceed the original cost of the eligible capital expenditures ($1,333,333), or $2,666,667. As noted, this portion of the gain is effectively treated like a capital gain, as only $\frac{1}{2}$ of the gain is included in income.

Election under Subsection 14(1.01)

Applicable for taxation years that end after February 27, 2000, subsection 14(1.01) permits a taxpayer, on a disposition of an eligible capital property for proceeds in excess of its cost, to elect to effectively remove the property from the cumulative eligible capital pool and instead recognize a capital gain on the disposition as if the property were a non-depreciable capital property. This election might be made, for example, if a taxpayer has available capital losses to apply against the capital gain. The election, which can be used to recognize only gains, is not available for goodwill. Furthermore, it is available only if the cost of the property (in particular, the eligible capital expenditure in respect of the property) can be determined. A proposed amendment further provides that the election is not available for property acquired on a corporate rollover under subsection 85(1) or (2) if it was acquired from a non-arm's length person for whom the property had no determinable cost (draft paragraph $14(1.03)(b)$).

For dispositions of eligible capital property after December 20, 2002, draft subsection 14(1.02) provides a similar election to that in subsection 14(1.01) for property acquired before 1972, basically where the property, had it been acquired after 1971, would have qualified for the subsection

¶734

14(1.01) election. In such case, the adjusted cost base of the property is deemed to be nil and the proceeds of disposition are determined under subsection 21(1) of the *Income Tax Application Rules*.

¶735
Replacement Property

At the taxpayer's option, any income inclusion arising from the disposition of eligible capital property may be deferred. This parallels the deferral of recapture of depreciation on voluntary dispositions of capital property. Subsection 14(6) provides that any amount otherwise included as an eligible capital amount upon the disposition of eligible capital property in the year the proceeds have become payable, i.e., the initial year, is not to be included for that year if, within one year after the end of the initial year, the taxpayer acquires a replacement property and elects in the return for that year (the year the taxpayer acquires the replacement property) to adopt this treatment.

Under draft legislation, the specified time frame to acquire a replacement property and defer inclusion of a negative balance in a taxpayer's cumulative eligible capital account is adjusted to accommodate short taxation years. The time period in which the taxpayer can acquire the replacement property is extended from the end of the taxation year subsequent to the year of disposition, to the later of: (a) the end of that subsequent taxation year, and (b) 12 months after the end of the taxation year of disposition. This change is to apply to dispositions of eligible capital property occurring in taxation years that end on or after December 20, 2001.

Where an eligible capital property is disposed of in a particular year, this year becomes the "initial year". The taxpayer is allowed until the end of the following taxation year (or, under draft legislation, 12 months after the initial year) to acquire a replacement property and, having done so, is entitled to elect to exclude the eligible capital amount from the calculation of cumulative eligible capital for the initial year.

Replacement property is defined in subsection 14(7) as eligible capital property acquired for the same or similar use as the use of the former property. As well, the replacement property must be acquired for the purpose of gaining or producing income from the same or similar business as that in which the former property was used.

¶737
Cessation of Business

Subsection 24(1) allows a taxpayer to deduct the balance in the cumulative eligible capital pool of a business in the first taxation year in which the taxpayer has ceased to carry on the business and has disposed of all of the eligible capital property, other than property of no value held in respect of the business. The deduction is analogous to the terminal loss deduction in respect of depreciable property. This deduction is not permitted where the taxpayer is an individual, and the taxpayer's spouse or a corporation controlled directly or indirectly by the taxpayer carries on the business after the taxpayer has ceased to do so and acquires all of the eligible capital property in respect of the business. In this situation, the individual who has ceased business will no longer have cumulative eligible capital in respect of that business, but the spouse or corporation carrying on the business will effectively take over the balance of the cumulative eligible capital (subsection 24(2)).

Where, as a result of the death of a taxpayer and, as a consequence of the taxpayer's death, another person (the beneficiary) acquires a property that was eligible capital property of the taxpayer for the business that was carried on by the taxpayer until death, the taxpayer is deemed to have disposed of the property immediately before death. The deemed proceeds of disposition are $4/3$ of the proportion of any positive balance in the pool that the fair market value of the property is of the total fair market value of all the eligible capital property of the taxpayer for the business. The eligible capital amount for the property is then determined by multiplying the deemed proceeds by $3/4$. If the beneficiary continues to carry on the business, the result is essentially the same as that achieved by the rollover that occurs where the taxpayer's spouse/common-law partner or corporation carries on the business. However, the rollover in the case of a beneficiary carrying on the business is calculated on each particular property rather than for the entire eligible capital pool.

In certain circumstances, where the taxpayer was a member of a partnership that has been dissolved, the taxpayer may deduct an amount equal to that former member's portion of the amount that would have been deductible by the partnership had it not ceased to exist (subsection 24(3)).

If the taxpayer is a corporation, trust or partnership, the subsection 24(1) deduction may be denied, or at least deferred, if the eligible capital property is disposed of to an affiliated person. However, during the period of deferral, the taxpayer may continue to deduct amounts under paragraph 20(1)(*b*) on account of the cumulative eligible capital. See subsection 14(12).

¶739

Transfer of Goodwill to Canadian Corporation

An individual, corporation, trust, or partnership may dispose of certain types of property to a taxable Canadian corporation without immediate tax consequences. Section 85 of the Act provides an elective procedure whereby the disposing party and the corporation file a joint election in which they elect an amount that will be deemed to be the disposing party's proceeds of disposition and the corporation's cost of the property.

For example, where the election applies to a transfer of all of the eligible capital property of a business, an aggregate elected amount of $4/3$ of the taxpayer's positive cumulative eligible capital account will result in no tax payable for the taxpayer ($3/4$ of such amount will be deducted in computing the cumulative eligible capital balance). The transferee corporation will effectively inherit the taxpayer's cumulative eligible capital account. An election at more than $4/3$ of the cumulative eligible capital amount would result in an income inclusion for the taxpayer under paragraph 14(1) (see the earlier discussion at ¶734). The elected amount for each property cannot exceed the fair market value of the property, and cannot be less than the lesser of $4/3$ of the cumulative eligible capital in respect of the business, the cost of the transferred property, and the fair market value of the property (the limits are described in paragraph 85(1)(d)).

If all of the eligible capital property of an individual transferor's business is transferred to the corporation, the deduction under subsection 24(1) may be denied for the individual (see "Cessation of Business" at ¶737 above). If the transferor is a corporation, trust or partnership and is affiliated with the transferee corporation, the stop-loss rules in subsection 14(12) may apply to deny and defer any resulting deduction under subsection 24(1).

¶741

Deemed Proceeds of Disposition

In the case of a deemed disposition of eligible capital property, subsection 14(2) provides that any deemed proceeds of disposition are considered to have become payable at the time the deemed disposition occurs.

There are several sections in the Act which deem proceeds of disposition to have been received, such as:

- gifts and transfers for inadequate consideration (section 69);

- transfers to a controlled corporation (section 85);

- winding-up of a subsidiary (section 88);

- transfer of property to a partnership (section 97);

- distribution of property by a partnership (section 98); and

- distribution of property by a trust (sections 107 and 107.1).

PART II

THE LAW

CHAPTER 11

INCOME TAX ACT

Reproduced below are the relevant sections of the *Income Tax Act* current to date of publication. Amendments pending at that time appear in boxes immediately below the provisions affected.

[¶1200]

SECTION 13:

(1) Recaptured depreciation. Where, at the end of a taxation year, the total of the amounts determined for E to J in the definition "undepreciated capital cost" in subsection (21) in respect of a taxpayer's depreciable property of a particular prescribed class exceeds the total of the amounts determined for A to D in that definition in respect thereof, the excess shall be included in computing the taxpayer's income for the year.

Pending Amendment

Non-Resident Trusts, Foreign Investment Entities, and Technical Amendments (July 18, 2005)
Subsection 13(1) of the Act is replaced by the following:

SECTION 13:

(1) Recaptured depreciation. If, at the end of a taxation year, the total of the amounts determined for E to K in the definition "undepreciated capital cost" in subsection (21) in respect of a taxpayer's depreciable property of a particular prescribed class exceeds the total of the amounts determined for A to D.1 in that definition in respect of that property, the excess shall be included in computing the taxpayer's income of the year.

Applicable: To taxation years that end after February 23, 1998.

Explanatory Note:
Recaptured Depreciation

Subsection 13(1) of the Act provides for the inclusion in a taxpayer's income of recaptured capital cost allowance when the taxpayer's proceeds of disposition of depreciable property of a prescribed class exceeds the undepreciated capital cost (UCC) of the property.

Subsection 13(1) is amended to add a reference to new descriptions D.1 and K of the definition "undepreciated capital cost" in subsection 13(21). Those descriptions provide for an addition to the UCC of a class of certain countervailing duties paid in respect of property of the class ("D.1") and a corresponding reduction for any refunds of those amounts ("K").

This amendment applies to taxation years that end after February 23, 1998, and corrects a technical deficiency.

Editorial Note: Subsection 13(1) includes in income the negative balance of the undepreciated capital cost (UCC) in respect of a class of depreciable property, if any, at the end of a taxation year. In general terms, the inclusion is normally meant to reflect previously deducted depreciation to the extent it is "recaptured" on a sale of depreciable property (for example, where the sole property in a class is sold for proceeds in excess of the UCC). The amount included under subsection 13(1) is added to the UCC balance at the beginning of the next taxation year (see amount B in the UCC definition in subsection 13(21)).

[¶1204]

(2) Idem. Notwithstanding subsection (1), where an excess amount is determined under that subsection at the end of a taxation year in respect of a passenger vehicle having a cost to a taxpayer in excess of $20,000 or such other amount as may be prescribed, that excess amount shall not be included in computing the taxpayer's income for the year but shall be deemed, for the purposes of B in the definition "undepreciated capital cost" in subsection (21), to be an amount included in the taxpayer's income for the year by reason of this section.

[¶1208]

(3) "Taxation year", "year" and "income" of individual. Where a taxpayer is an individual whose income for a taxation year includes income from a business the fiscal period of which does not coincide with the calendar year and depreciable property acquired for the purpose of gaining or producing income from the business has been disposed of,

(a) for greater certainty, each reference in subsections (1) and (2) to a "taxation year" and "year" shall be read as a reference to a "fiscal period"; and

(b) a reference in subsection (1) to "the income" shall be read as a reference to "the income from the business".

[¶1212]

(4) Exchanges of property. Where an amount in respect of the disposition in a taxation year (in this subsection referred to as the "initial year") of depreciable property (in this section referred to as the "former property") of a prescribed class of a taxpayer would, but for this subsection, be the amount determined for F or G in the definition "undepreciated capital cost" in subsection (21) in respect of the disposition of the former property that is either

(a) property the proceeds of disposition of which were proceeds referred to in paragraph (b), (c) or (d) of the definition "proceeds of disposition" in subsection (21), or

(b) a property that was, immediately before the disposition, a former business property of the taxpayer,

and the taxpayer so elects under this subsection in the taxpayer's return of income for the taxation year in which the taxpayer acquires a depreciable property of a prescribed class of the taxpayer that is a replacement property for the taxpayer's former property,

(c) the amount otherwise determined for F or G in the definition "undepreciated capital cost" in subsection (21) in respect of the disposition of the former property shall be reduced by the lesser of

(i) the amount, if any, by which the amount otherwise determined for F or G in that definition exceeds the undepreciated capital cost to the taxpayer of property of the prescribed class to which the former property belonged at the time immediately before the time that the former property was disposed of, and

(ii) the amount that has been used by the taxpayer to acquire

(A) where the former property is referred to in paragraph (a), before the end of the second taxation year following the initial year, or

(B) in any other case, before the end of the first taxation year following the initial year,

¶1212

a replacement property of a prescribed class that has not been disposed of by the taxpayer before the time at which the taxpayer disposed of the former property, and

---

Pending Amendment

Non-Resident Trusts, Foreign Investment Entities, and Technical Amendments (July 18, 2005)

Subparagraph $13(4)(c)(ii)$ of the Act is replaced by the following:

(ii) the amount that has been used by the taxpayer to acquire

(A) if the former property is described in paragraph (a), before the later of the end of the second taxation year following the initial year and 24 months after the end of the initial year, or

(B) in any other case, before the later of the end of the first taxation year following the initial year and 12 months after the end of the initial year,

a replacement property of a prescribed class that has not been disposed of by the taxpayer before the time at which the taxpayer disposed of the former property, and

---

Applicable: In respect of dispositions that occur in taxation years that end on or after December 20, 2000, except that for those dispositions that occur in taxation years that end before December 20, 2001, clause $13(4)(c)(ii)(B)$ is to be read as follows:

" (B) in any other case, before the end of the first taxation year following the initial year, "

Explanatory Note:

Exchanges of Property

Subsection 13(4) of the Act allows a taxpayer, who is required under subsection 13(1) to include in income recaptured depreciation resulting from the disposition of certain depreciable property, to elect to defer tax on the recapture to the extent that the taxpayer reinvests the proceeds of disposition in a replacement property within a certain period of time, namely

● in the case of certain involuntary dispositions, e .g., theft or expropriation, before the end of the taxpayer's second taxation year that begins after the property was disposed of, or

● in other situations, before the end of the taxpayer's first taxation year that begins after the property was disposed of.

Subparagraph $13(4)(c)(ii)$ is amended to accommodate taxation years that are shorter than 12 months, by providing that the periods for acquiring replacement property end at the later of the times mentioned above and

● in the case of involuntary dispositions, within 24 months after the end of the taxation year in which the property was disposed of, or

● in other situations, within 12 months after the end of the taxation year in which the property was disposed of.

These amendments apply, in the case of involuntary dispositions, in respect of dispositions that occur in taxation years that end on or after December 20, 2000, and in any other case, in respect of dispositions that occur in taxation years that end on or after December 20, 2001.

¶1212

(d) the amount of the reduction determined under paragraph (c) shall be deemed to be proceeds of disposition of a depreciable property of the taxpayer that had a capital cost equal to that amount and that was property of the same class as the replacement property, from a disposition made on the later of

(i) the time the replacement property was acquired by the taxpayer, and

(ii) the time the former property was disposed of by the taxpayer.

[¶1216]

(4.1) Replacement for a former property.   For the purposes of subsection (4), a particular depreciable property of a prescribed class of a taxpayer is a replacement for a former property of the taxpayer if

(a) it is reasonable to conclude that the property was acquired by the taxpayer to replace the former property;

(a.1) it was acquired by the taxpayer and used by the taxpayer or a person related to the taxpayer for a use that is the same as or similar to the use to which the taxpayer or a person related to the taxpayer put the former property;

(b) where the former property was used by the taxpayer or a person related to the taxpayer for the purpose of gaining or producing income from a business, the particular depreciable property was acquired for the purpose of gaining or producing income from that or a similar business or for use by a person related to the taxpayer for such a purpose;

(c) where the former property was a taxable Canadian property of the taxpayer, the particular depreciable property is a taxable Canadian property of the taxpayer; and

(d) where the former property was a taxable Canadian property (other than treaty-protected property) of the taxpayer, the particular depreciable property is a taxable Canadian property (other than treaty-protected property) of the taxpayer.

Pending Amendment

Non-Resident Trusts, Foreign Investment Entities, and Technical Amendments (July 18, 2005)

Section 13 of the Act is amended by adding the following after subsection (4.1):

(4.2) Election — limited period franchise, concession or license. Subsection (4.3) applies in circumstances where

(a) a taxpayer (in this subsection and subsection (4.3) referred to as the "transferor") has, pursuant to a written agreement with a person or partnership (in this subsection and subsection (4.3) referred to as the "transferee"), at any time disposed of or terminated a former property that is a franchise, concession or licence for a limited period that is wholly attributable to the carrying on of a business at a fixed place;

(b) the transferee acquired the former property from the transferor or, on the termination, acquired a similar property in respect of the same fixed place from another person or partnership; and

(c) the transferor and the transferee jointly elect in their returns of income for their taxation years that include that time to have subsection (4.3) apply in respect of the acquisition and the disposition or termination.

(4.3) Effect of election. Where this subsection applies in respect of an acquisition and a disposition or termination,

(a) if the transferee acquired a similar property referred to in paragraph (4.2)(b), the transferee is deemed to have also acquired the former property at the time that the former property was terminated and to own the former property until the transferee no longer owns the similar property;

(b) if the transferee acquired the former property referred to in paragraph (4.2)(b), the transferee is deemed to own the former property until such time as the transferee owns neither the former property nor a similar property in respect of the same fixed place to which the former property related;

(c) for the purpose of calculating the amount deductible under paragraph 20(1)(a) in respect of the former property in computing the transferee's income, the life of the former property remaining on its acquisition by the transferee is deemed to be equal to the period that was the life of the former property remaining on its acquisition by the transferor; and

(d) any amount that would, if this Act were read without reference to this subsection, be an eligible capital amount to the transferor or an eligible capital expenditure to the transferee in respect of the disposition or termination of the former property by the transferor is deemed to be

(i) neither an eligible capital amount nor an eligible capital expenditure,

(ii) an amount required to be included in computing the capital cost to the transferee of the former property, and

(iii) an amount required to be included in computing the proceeds of disposition to the transferor in respect of a disposition of the former property.

Applicable: In respect of dispositions and terminations that occur after December 20, 2002.

Explanatory Note:

Election — Limited Period Franchise, Concession or License

Subsection 14(6) of the Act permits a taxpayer to defer tax otherwise arising on the disposition of an eligible capital property, to the extent that the taxpayer reinvests the proceeds of disposition in a replacement property within a certain period of time. A franchise, concession or license with an indefinite term may be such an eligible capital property. However, such a property with a defined term will generally be a depreciable property included in Class 14 of Schedule II of the Regulations and will not be eligible for similar replacement treatment under subsection 13(4) of the Act because such a property is not a "former business property" as defined in subsection 248(1) of the Act. Further, the replacement property provisions for depreciable property generally apply only to immoveable property.

New subsections 13(4.2) and (4.3) of the Act are added, concurrent with the amendment of the definition "former business property", to allow a taxpayer (the "transferor") to use the replacement property rules under subsection 13(4) in respect of the disposition or termination of a property that is the subject of a joint election with the purchaser (the "transferee") of the property.

¶1216

New subsection 13(4.2) describes the circumstances under which the transferor and the transferee may make a joint election. Property eligible for the election is a "former property" described in subsection 13(4) that is a franchise, concession or license for a limited period that is wholly attributable to the carrying on of a business at a fixed place. The election may be made where the property is disposed of directly by the transferor to the transferee or where the property of the transferor is terminated and the transferee acquires a similar property in respect of the same fixed place from another person. Both parties must elect in their returns of income for their respective taxation years that include the year of the disposition or termination.

New subsection 13(4.3) provides rules that apply when an election has been made under subsection 13(4.2). If the transferee acquires the property disposed of by the transferor (the "former property"), the transferee is deemed to own that property until such time as the transferee owns neither the former property nor a similar property in respect of the same fixed place to which the former property related. If the transferee instead acquires a similar property in respect of the same fixed place (i.e., the life of the former property was terminated), the transferee is deemed to have also acquired the former property and to continue to own it until the transferee no longer owns the similar property.

In either case, for the purpose of claiming a deduction by the transferee under paragraph $20(1)(a)$ of the Act, the life of the former property in the hands of the transferee is deemed to be the term remaining at the time the transferor originally acquired the property. For instance, a license with a 20-year life when it was originally acquired by the transferor, but with 5 years remaining at the time of the transfer, would be considered to have a 20 year life in the hands of the transferee for the purposes of claiming a deduction under paragraph $20(1)(a)$.

There may be circumstances where, but for an election under subsection 13(4.2), a portion of the consideration given by a transferee upon the sale of a limited period franchise, license or concession might reasonably be considered to be an eligible capital amount to the transferor and an eligible capital expenditure to the transferee. For instance, a portion of the consideration may reasonably relate to the preferred status that the transferee may receive in obtaining a new property at the end of the term. Where an election under subsection 13(4.2) is made, subsection 13(4.3) provides that such an amount will be neither an eligible capital amount to the transferor, nor an eligible capital expenditure to the transferee, but will instead be included in the cost to the transferee and proceeds of disposition of the transferor of the former property.

In this regard, it is also proposed that section 1101 of the Regulations be amended, applicable after December 20, 2002, by adding the following after subsection (1af):

(1ag) If more than one property of a taxpayer is described in the same class in Schedule II, and one or more of the properties is a property in respect of which the taxpayer is a transferee that has elected under subsection 13(4.2) of the Act, a separate class is prescribed for each such property of the taxpayer that would otherwise be included in the same class.

If, subsequent to the acquisition of the former property by the transferee, the life of the former property expires and a similar property in respect of the same fixed place is not acquired by the transferee, the transferee may, under subsection 20(16) of the Act, be entitled to a terminal loss in respect of the former property. Refer to the commentary to new paragraph $20(16.1)(b)$ of the Act regarding limitations in respect of the deduction of such a terminal loss.

New subsections 13(4.2) and (4.3) apply in respect of dispositions and terminations that occur after December 20, 2002.

Example 1

Ms. Mubarak is a franchisee with 5 years remaining of a 20-year agreement. The original cost was $60,000, and the undepreciated capital cost ("UCC") is $15,000. The agreement is transferable, so she agrees to sell the franchise to Mr. Grando at its fair market value of $85,000. Ms. Mubarak will, in the same taxation year, purchase from Ms.

¶1216

Vincent a replacement franchise that has 15 years remaining of a 20-year term, for $100,000.

But for the making of an election under subsection 13(4.2), Ms. Mubarak would have a capital gain of $25,000 (i.e., $85,000 – $60,000) and a UCC balance of $55,000 (i.e., $15,000 + $100,000 – $60,000) before deducting any capital cost allowance for the year. The adjusted cost base ("ACB") of her replacement franchise would be $100,000. Mr. Grando would have acquired a Class 14 property with an ACB and capital cost of $85,000, depreciable over 5 years.

If Ms. Mubarak and Mr. Grando jointly elect under subsection 13(4.2), Ms. Mubarak may elect under subsections 13(4) and 44(1) to defer the capital gain, such that the ACB and capital cost of the replacement franchise will be deemed to be $75,000 (i.e., $100,000 less the $25,000 deferred capital gain). Furthermore, Ms. Mubarak's UCC balance for Class 14 will be $30,000 (i.e., an increase equivalent to the $100,000 cost of the replacement franchise less the $85,000 proceeds from the former property), to be amortized over the remaining 15-year term. In this regard, note that the term for amortizing Ms. Mubarak's replacement franchise is unaffected by her and Mr. Grando's joint election in respect of the former property. Mr. Grando, on the other hand, will be required to amortize his $85,000 cost of the former property over 20 years, which was the term of the former property when it was first acquired by Ms. Mubarak.

If Mr. Grando does not enter into a new agreement with the franchisor after the 5-year period, he will be eligible for a terminal loss (even if there are other Class 14 assets, because the $85,000 property will be in a "separate class"). However, a terminal loss will not be available if a person dealing non-arm's length with Mr. Grando, at any time before the time that is 24 months after the expiry of the old agreement, enters into a new franchise agreement in respect of the same fixed place.

Example 2

Consider the same example, except that the original franchise agreement of Ms. Mubarak (the former property) is not transferable, but instead must be terminated and renewed with the franchisor. Suppose that it is renewed by Mr. Grando for a period of 12 years, with an additional amount of $120,000 paid by Mr. Grando to the franchisor for the new agreement.

In this case it is arguable that, for Mr. Grando, the $85,000 payment to Ms. Mubarak is, absent an election under subsection 13(4.2), an eligible capital expenditure by Mr. Grando. That is, Mr. Grando will pay a separate amount of $120,000 to the franchisor for a Class 14 asset, but the $85,000 payment to Ms. Mubarak is, in effect, incurred to acquire the right to renew the franchise, not to acquire a Class 14 property. Ms. Mubarak has likewise received proceeds of disposition of an eligible capital property (i.e., an "eligible capital amount", $3/4$ of which would reduce her CEC balance), not proceeds of disposition of a Class 14 property. Absent an election under subsection 13(4.2), Ms. Mubarak would not be entitled to acquire a replacement eligible capital property, but could be entitled to claim a terminal loss on the termination of the original franchise agreement (if she had no other Class 14 assets on hand at the end of the taxation year of disposition). Subsection 14(1) would apply to the eligible capital amount received by Ms. Mubarak.

The $120,000 cost of the new agreement to Mr. Grando, paid to the franchisor, could be written off by Mr. Grando over its 12-year term.

If Ms. Mubarak and Mr. Grando jointly elect under subsection 13(4.2), no part of the proceeds of disposition for the former property will be an eligible capital amount or an eligible capital expenditure. The results are the same as in Example 1, except that Mr. Grando will now have two Class 14 properties:

● the new franchise agreement, the $120,000 cost of which may be written off by him over its 12-year term; and

● the former property, deemed to have been acquired by him and included in a separate class, the $85,000 cost of which may be written off by him over its deemed 20-year term.

¶1216

Example 3

Consider again Example 1, but suppose that the replacement franchise, purchased by Ms. Mubarak from Ms. Vincent, is itself the subject of a joint election by them under subsection 13(4.2). Ms. Mubarak is required to amortize her $30,000 UCC (see Example 1) over the original 20-year term of Ms. Vincent, not over its remaining 15 years.

[¶1220]

(5) Reclassification of property. Where one or more depreciable properties of a taxpayer that were included in a prescribed class (in this subsection referred to as the "old class") become included at any time (in this subsection referred to as the "transfer time") in another prescribed class (in this subsection referred to as the "new class"), for the purpose of determining at any subsequent time the undepreciated capital cost to the taxpayer of depreciable property of the old class and the new class

(a) the value of A in the definition "undepreciated capital cost" in subsection (21) shall be determined as if each of those depreciable properties were

(i) properties of the new class acquired before the subsequent time, and

(ii) never included in the old class; and

(b) there shall be deducted in computing the total depreciation allowed to the taxpayer for property of the old class before the subsequent time, and added in computing the total depreciation allowed to the taxpayer for property of the new class before the subsequent time, the greater of

(i) the amount determined by the formula

$$A - B$$

where

A   is the total of all amounts each of which is the capital cost to the taxpayer of each of those depreciable properties, and

B   is the undepreciated capital cost to the taxpayer of depreciable property of the old class at the transfer time, and

(ii) the total of all amounts each of which is an amount that would have been deducted under paragraph $20(1)(a)$ in respect of a depreciable property that is one of those properties in computing the taxpayer's income for a taxation year that ended before the transfer time and at the end of which the property was included in the old class if

(A) the property had been the only property included in a separate prescribed class, and

(B) the rate allowed by the regulations made for the purpose of paragraph $20(1)(a)$ in respect of that separate class had been the effective rate that was used by the taxpayer to calculate a deduction under that paragraph in respect of the old class for the year.

[¶1224]

(5.1) Rules applicable. Where at any time in a taxation year a taxpayer acquires a particular property in respect of which, immediately before that time, the taxpayer had a leasehold interest that was included in a prescribed class, for the purposes of this section, section 20 and any regulations made under paragraph $20(1)(a)$, the following rules apply:

(a) the leasehold interest shall be deemed to have been disposed of by the taxpayer at that time for proceeds of disposition equal to the amount, if any, by which

(i) the capital cost immediately before that time of the leasehold interest

exceeds

(ii) the total of all amounts claimed by the taxpayer in respect of the leasehold interest and deductible under paragraph $20(1)(a)$ in computing the taxpayer's income in previous taxation years;

(b) the particular property shall be deemed to be depreciable property of a prescribed class of the taxpayer acquired by the taxpayer at that time and there shall be added to the capital cost to the taxpayer of the property an amount equal to the capital cost referred to in subparagraph (a)(i); and

(c) the total referred to in subparagraph (a)(ii) shall be added to the total depreciation allowed to the taxpayer before that time in respect of the class to which the particular property belongs.

[¶1228]

(5.2) Idem. Where, at any time, a taxpayer has acquired a capital property that is depreciable property or real property in respect of which, before that time, the taxpayer or any person with whom the taxpayer was not dealing at arm's length was entitled to a deduction in computing income in respect of any amount paid or payable for the use of, or the right to use, the depreciable property or real property and the cost or the capital cost (determined without reference to this subsection) at that time of the property to the taxpayer is less than the fair market value thereof at that time determined without reference to any option with respect to that property, for the purposes of this section, section 20 and any regulations made under paragraph $20(1)(a)$, the following rules apply:

Pending Amendment

Non-Resident Trusts, Foreign Investment Entities, and Technical Amendments (July 18, 2005)

The portion of subsection 13(5.2) of the Act before paragraph (a) is replaced by the following:

(5.2) Idem. Where, at any time, a taxpayer has acquired a capital property that is depreciable property or real or immovable property in respect of which, before that

---

time, the taxpayer or any person with whom the taxpayer was not dealing at arm's length was entitled to a deduction in computing income in respect of any amount paid or payable for the use of, or the right to use, the property and the cost or the capital cost (determined without reference to this subsection) at that time of the property to the taxpayer is less than the fair market value thereof at that time determined without reference to any option with respect to that property, for the purposes of this section, section 20 and any regulations made under paragraph $20(1)(a)$, the following rules apply:

Applicable: Royal Assent.

Explanatory Note:

Amendments Related to Bijuralism

As part of the harmonization of federal legislation, the Government has undertaken to review all its legislation where provincial private law concepts are found in order to reflect appropriately the common law and the civil law, in both official languages.

As part of this harmonization initiative, federal tax legislation is being reviewed. Several changes to the legislation have already been implemented, namely by way of the *Income Tax Amendments Act*, 2000, S.C. 2001, c. 17. The proposed amendments continue this harmonization initiative.

This Part proposes amendments to the *Income Tax Act* concerning the concepts of "joint and several liability" / "solidary liability", "tangible property" / "corporeal property", "intangible property" / "incorporeal property", "personal property" / "movable property", "real property" / "immovable property", "interest" / "right" which are further described below. The proposed amendments are not intended to change the current application of the amended provisions; they purport to reflect the concepts and terminology of the common law and the civil law in both official languages. They will come into force on Royal Assent to this Bill.

Joint and Several Liability and Solidary Liability

The French version of the current tax legislation uses the term "*solidairement*", which is appropriate for both civil law and common law. Therefore, the French version does not need to be amended.

In the English version of the current tax legislation, only the term "jointly and severally" is used. This term is maintained for common law purposes. The term "jointly and severally" is no longer adequate in civil law in English and has been replaced with the term "solidarily". Therefore, it is appropriate to add the term "solidarily" in the English version in order to reflect the civil law.

Tangible and Corporeal Property

In the French version of the current tax legislation, only the civil law terminology "*bien corporel*" is used. In the English version, only the common law term "tangible property" is used.

In the French version of the legislation, it is appropriate to add the term "*bien tangible*" in order to reflect the common law.

In the English version of the legislation, it is appropriate to add the term "corporeal property" in order to reflect the civil law.

Intangible and Incorporeal Property

In the French version of the current tax legislation, only the civil law terminology "*bien incorporel*" is used. In the English version, only the common law term "intangible property" is used.

In the French version of the legislation, it is appropriate to add the term "*bien intangible*" in order to reflect the common law. Where it is appropriate to do so, the shared elements of the relevant terms are combined in the phrase "*bien incorporel ou intangible*", which refers to both systems of law.

¶1228

In the English version of the legislation, it is appropriate to add the term "incorporeal property" in order to reflect the civil law. Where it is appropriate to do so, the shared elements of the relevant terms are combined in the phrase "intangible or incorporeal property", which refers to both systems of law.

Personal Property and Movable Property

In the French version of the current tax legislation, only the civil law terminology "*bien meuble*" is used. In the English version, the terms "personal property" and "chattels" are used to reflect the common law.

It is therefore appropriate to add in the French version a reference to the term "*bien personnel*" in order to reflect the common law. Where it is appropriate to do so, the shared elements of the relevant terms are combined in the phrase "*bien meuble ou personnel*", which refers to both systems of law.

In the English version of the legislation, the term "movable" is added in order to reflect the civil law. Where it is appropriate to do so, the shared elements are combined in the phrase "personal or movable property", which refers to both systems of law.

Real Property and Immovable Property

In the French version of the current tax legislation, only the civil law terminology "*bien immeuble*" is used. In the English version, only the common law concept of "real property" is used.

It is therefore appropriate to add a reference, in the French version, to the term "*bien réel*" in order to reflect the common law. Where it is appropriate to do so, the shared elements of the relevant terms are combined in the phrase "*bien immeuble ou réel*", which refers to both systems of law.

In the English version of the legislation, the term "immovable" is added in order to reflect the civil law. Where it is appropriate to do so, the shared elements of the relevant terms are combined in the phrase "real or immovable property", which refers to both systems of law.

Interest and Right

Generally, in the current tax legislation, the common law term "interest" and the civil law term "*droit*" are used to refer to the relationship that exists between a person and property. At common law, it is possible to have a right or an interest in property; an interest in property necessarily involves rights in property while the reverse is not always true.

For purposes of the civil law, it is appropriate to limit the application of the term "*droit*" in the French version to the civil law, unless otherwise provided. In the English version, it is appropriate to add a reference to the concept of "right" in order to address the civil law audience and to similarly limit the application of this term to the civil law, unless otherwise provided.

The term "interest" is a common law concept that is translated into French by the term "*intérêt*". It is therefore appropriate to add a reference to the concept of "*intérêt*" in the French version in order to address the common law audience.

(*a*) the property shall be deemed to have been acquired by the taxpayer at that time at a cost equal to the lesser of

(i) the fair market value of the property at that time determined without reference to any option with respect to that property, and

(ii) the total of the cost or the capital cost (determined without reference to this subsection) of the property to the taxpayer and all amounts (other than amounts paid or payable to a person with whom the taxpayer was not dealing at arm's length) each of which is an

¶1228

outlay or expense made or incurred by the taxpayer or by a person with whom the taxpayer was not dealing at arm's length at any time for the use of, or the right to use, the property,

and for the purposes of this paragraph and subsection (5.3), where a particular corporation has been incorporated or otherwise formed after the time any other corporation with which the particular corporation would not have been dealing at arm's length had the particular corporation been in existence before that time, the particular corporation shall be deemed to have been in existence from the time of the formation of the other corporation and to have been not dealing at arm's length with the other corporation;

(b) the amount by which the cost to the taxpayer of the property determined under paragraph (a) exceeds the cost or the capital cost thereof (determined without reference to this subsection) shall be added to the total depreciation allowed to the taxpayer before that time in respect of the prescribed class to which the property belongs; and

(c) where the property would, but for this paragraph, not be depreciable property of the taxpayer, it shall be deemed to be depreciable property of a separate prescribed class of the taxpayer.

[¶1232]

(5.3) Idem. Where, at any time in a taxation year, a taxpayer has disposed of a capital property that is an option with respect to depreciable property or real property in respect of which the taxpayer or any person with whom the taxpayer was not dealing at arm's length was entitled to a deduction in computing income in respect of any amount paid for the use of, or the right to use, the depreciable property or real property, for the purposes of this section, the amount, if any, by which the proceeds of disposition to the taxpayer of the option exceed the taxpayer's cost in respect thereof shall be deemed to be an excess referred to in subsection (1) in respect of the taxpayer for the year.

Pending Amendment

Non-Resident Trusts, Foreign Investment Entities, and Technical Amendments (July 18, 2005)

Subsection 13(5.3) of the Act is replaced by the following:

(5.3) Idem. Where, at any time in a taxation year, a taxpayer has disposed of a capital property that is an option with respect to depreciable property or real or immovable property in respect of which the taxpayer or any person with whom the taxpayer was not dealing at arm's length was entitled to a deduction in computing income in respect of any amount paid for the use of, or the right to use, the property, for the purposes of this section, the amount, if any, by which the proceeds of disposition to the taxpayer of the option exceed the taxpayer's cost in respect thereof shall be deemed to be an excess referred to in subsection (1) in respect of the taxpayer for the year.

Applicable: Royal Assent.

Explanatory Note: [See the Explanatory Note re amendments related to bijuralism following the amendment to subsection 13(5.2).]

[¶1236]

(5.4) Idem.   Where, before the time of disposition of a capital property that was depreciable property of a taxpayer, the taxpayer, or any person with whom the taxpayer was not dealing at arm's length, was entitled to a deduction in computing income in respect of any outlay or expense made or incurred for the use of, or the right to use, during a period of time, that capital property (other than an outlay or expense made or incurred by the taxpayer or a person with whom the taxpayer was not dealing at arm's length before the acquisition of the property), except where the taxpayer disposed of the property to a person with whom the taxpayer was not dealing at arm's length and that person was subject to the provisions of subsection (5.2) with respect to the acquisition by that person of the property, the following rules apply:

(a) an amount equal to the lesser of

(i) the total of all amounts (other than amounts paid or payable to the taxpayer or a person with whom the taxpayer was not dealing at arm's length) each of which was a deductible outlay or expense made or incurred before the time of disposition by the taxpayer, or by a person with whom the taxpayer was not dealing at arm's length, for the use of, or the right to use, during the period of time, the property, and

(ii) the amount, if any, by which the fair market value of the property at the earlier of

(A) the expiration of the last period of time in respect of which the deductible outlay or expense referred to in subparagraph (i) was made or incurred, and

(B) the time of the disposition

exceeds the capital cost to the taxpayer of the property immediately before that time

shall, immediately before the time of the disposition, be added to the capital cost of the property to the person who owned the property at that time; and

(b) the amount added to the capital cost to the taxpayer of the property pursuant to paragraph (a) shall be added immediately before the time of the disposition to the total depreciation allowed to the taxpayer before that time in respect of the prescribed class to which the property belongs.

[¶1240]

(5.5) Lease cancellation payment. For the purposes of subsection (5.4), an amount deductible by a taxpayer under paragraph $20(1)(z)$ or $(z.1)$ in respect of a cancellation of a lease of property shall, for greater certainty, be deemed not to be an outlay or expense that was made or incurred by the taxpayer for the use of, or the right to use, the property.

[¶1244]

(6) Misclassified property. Where, in calculating the amount of a deduction allowed to a taxpayer under subsection 20(16) or regulations made for the purposes of paragraph $20(1)(a)$ in respect of depreciable property of the taxpayer of a prescribed class (in this subsection referred to as the "particular class"), there has been added to the capital cost to the taxpayer of depreciable property of the particular class the capital cost of depreciable property (in this subsection referred to as "added property") of another prescribed class, for the purposes of this section, section 20 and any regulations made for the purposes of paragraph $20(1)(a)$, the added property shall, if the Minister so directs with respect to any taxation year for which, under subsection 152(4), the Minister may make any reassessment or additional assessment or assess tax, interest or penalties under this Part, be deemed to have been property of the particular class and not of the other class at all times before the beginning of the year and, except to the extent that the added property or any part thereof has been disposed of by the taxpayer before the beginning of the year, to have been transferred from the particular class to the other class at the beginning of the year.

[¶1248]

(7) Rules applicable. Subject to subsection 70(13), for the purposes of paragraphs $8(1)(j)$ and (p), this section, section 20 and any regulations made for the purpose of paragraph $20(1)(a)$,

[¶1250]

(a) where a taxpayer, having acquired property for the purpose of gaining or producing income, has begun at a later time to use it for some other purpose, the taxpayer shall be deemed to have disposed of it at that later time for proceeds of disposition equal to its fair market value at that time and to have reacquired it immediately thereafter at a cost equal to that fair market value;

[¶1252]

(b) where a taxpayer, having acquired property for some other purpose, has begun at a later time to use it for the purpose of gaining or producing income, the taxpayer shall be deemed to have acquired it at that later time at a capital cost to the taxpayer equal to the lesser of

(i) the fair market value of the property at that later time, and

(ii) the total of

(A) the cost to the taxpayer of the property at that later time determined without reference to this paragraph, paragraph (a) and subparagraph (d)(ii), and

(B) $\frac{1}{2}$ of the amount, if any, by which

(I) the fair market value of the property at that later time

exceeds the total of

(II) the cost to the taxpayer of the property as determined under clause (A), and

(III) twice the amount deducted by the taxpayer under section 110.6 in respect of the amount, if any, by which the fair market value of the property at that later time exceeds the cost to the taxpayer of the property as determined under clause (A);

[¶1254]

(c) where property has, since it was acquired by a taxpayer, been regularly used in part for the purpose of gaining or producing income and in part for some other purpose, the taxpayer shall be deemed to have acquired, for the purpose of gaining or producing income, the proportion of the property that the use regularly made of the property for gaining or producing income is of the whole use regularly made of the property at a capital cost to the taxpayer equal to the same proportion of the capital cost to the taxpayer of the whole property and, if the property has, in such a case, been disposed of, the proceeds of disposition of the proportion of the property deemed to have been acquired for gaining or producing income shall be deemed to be the same proportion of the proceeds of disposition of the whole property;

[¶1256]

(d) where, at any time after a taxpayer has acquired property, there has been a change in the relation between the use regularly made by the taxpayer of the property for gaining or producing income and the use regularly made of the property for other purposes,

(i) if the use regularly made by the taxpayer of the property for the purpose of gaining or producing income has increased, the taxpayer shall be deemed to have acquired at that time depreciable property of that class at a capital cost equal to the total of

(A) the proportion of the lesser of

(I) its fair market value at that time, and

(II) its cost to the taxpayer at that time determined without reference to this subparagraph, subparagraph (ii) and paragraph (a)

that the amount of the increase in the use regularly made by the taxpayer of the property for that purpose is of the whole of the use regularly made of the property, and

(B) $\frac{1}{2}$ of the amount, if any, by which

(I) the amount deemed under subparagraph $45(1)(c)(ii)$ to be the taxpayer's proceeds of disposition of the property in respect of the change

exceeds the total of

(II) that proportion of the cost to the taxpayer of the property as determined under subclause (A)(II) that the amount of the increase in the use regularly made by the taxpayer of the property for that purpose is of the whole of the use regularly made of the property, and

(III) twice the amount deducted by the taxpayer under section 110.6 in respect of the amount, if any, by which the amount determined under subclause (I) exceeds the amount determined under subclause (II), and

(ii) if the use regularly made of the property for the purpose of gaining or producing income has decreased, the taxpayer shall be deemed to have disposed at that time of depreciable property of that class and the proceeds of disposition shall be deemed to be an amount equal to the proportion of the fair market value of the property as of that time that the amount of the decrease in the use regularly made by the taxpayer of the property for that purpose is of the whole use regularly made of the property;

[¶1258]

(e) notwithstanding any other provision of this Act except subsection 70(13), where at a particular time a person or partnership (in this paragraph referred to as the "taxpayer") has, directly or indirectly, in any manner whatever, acquired (otherwise than as a consequence of the death of the transferor) a depreciable property (other than a timber resource property) of a prescribed class from a person or partnership with whom the taxpayer did not deal at arm's length (in this paragraph referred to as the "transferor") and, immediately before the transfer, the property was a capital property of the transferor,

(i) where the transferor was an individual resident in Canada or a partnership any member of which was either an individual resident in Canada or another partnership and the cost of the property to the taxpayer at the particular time determined without reference to this paragraph exceeds the cost, or where the property was depreciable property, the capital cost of the property to the transferor immediately before the transferor disposed of it, the capital cost of the property to the taxpayer at the particular time shall be deemed to be the amount that is equal to the total of

(A) the cost or capital cost, as the case may be, of the property to the transferor immediately before the particular time, and

(B) $\frac{1}{2}$ of the amount, if any, by which

¶1258

(I) the transferor's proceeds of disposition of the property

exceed the total of

(II) the cost or capital cost, as the case may be, to the transferor immediately before the particular time,

(III) twice the amount deducted by any person under section 110.6 in respect of the amount, if any, by which the amount determined under subclause (I) exceeds the amount determined under subclause (II), and

(IV) the amount, if any, required by subsection 110.6(21) to be deducted in computing the capital cost to the taxpayer of the property at that time

and, for the purposes of paragraph (b) and subparagraph $(d)(i)$, the cost of the property to the taxpayer shall be deemed to be the same amount,

(ii) where the transferor was neither an individual resident in Canada nor a partnership any member of which was either an individual resident in Canada or another partnership and the cost of the property to the taxpayer at the particular time determined without reference to this paragraph exceeds the cost, or where the property was depreciable property, the capital cost of the property to the transferor immediately before the transferor disposed of it, the capital cost of the property to the taxpayer at that time shall be deemed to be the amount that is equal to the total of

(A) the cost or capital cost, as the case may be, of the property to the transferor immediately before the particular time, and

(B) $\frac{1}{2}$ of the amount, if any, by which the transferor's proceeds of disposition of the property exceed the cost or capital cost, as the case may be, to the transferor immediately before the particular time

and, for the purposes of paragraph (b) and subparagraph $(d)(i)$, the cost of the property to the taxpayer shall be deemed to be the same amount, and

(iii) where the cost or capital cost, as the case may be, of the property to the transferor immediately before the transferor disposed of it exceeds the capital cost of the property to the taxpayer at that time determined without reference to this paragraph, the capital cost of the property to the taxpayer at that time shall be deemed to be the amount that was the cost or capital cost, as the case may be, of the property to the transferor immediately before the transferor disposed of it and the excess shall be deemed to have been allowed to the taxpayer in respect of the property under regulations made under paragraph $20(1)(a)$ in computing the taxpayer's income for taxation years ending before the acquisition of the property by the taxpayer;

¶1258

[¶1259]

(*e*.1) where a taxpayer is deemed by paragraph 110.6(19)(*a*) to have disposed of and reacquired a property that immediately before the disposition was a depreciable property, the taxpayer shall be deemed to have acquired the property from himself, herself or itself and, in so having acquired the property, not to have been dealing with himself, herself or itself at arm's length;

[¶1260]

(*f*) where a corporation is deemed under paragraph 111(4)(*e*) to have disposed of and reacquired depreciable property (other than a timber resource property), the capital cost to the corporation of the property at the time of the reacquisition is deemed to be the amount that is equal to the total of

(i) the capital cost to the corporation of the property at the time of the disposition, and

(ii) $\frac{1}{2}$ of the amount, if any, by which the corporation's proceeds of disposition of the property exceed the capital cost to the corporation of the property at the time of the disposition;

[¶1262]

(*g*) where the cost to a taxpayer of a passenger vehicle exceeds $20,000 or such other amount as is prescribed, the capital cost to the taxpayer of the vehicle shall be deemed to be $20,000 or that other prescribed amount, as the case may be; and

[¶1264]

(*h*) notwithstanding paragraph (*g*), where a passenger vehicle is acquired by a taxpayer at any time from a person with whom the taxpayer does not deal at arm's length, the capital cost at that time to the taxpayer of the vehicle shall be deemed to be the least of

(i) the fair market value of the vehicle at that time,

(ii) the amount that immediately before that time was the cost amount to that person of the vehicle, and

(iii) $20,000 or such other amount as is prescribed.

[¶1270]

(7.1) Deemed capital cost of certain property. For the purposes of this Act, where section 80 applied to reduce the capital cost to a taxpayer of a depreciable property or a taxpayer deducted an amount under subsection 127(5) or (6) in respect of a depreciable property or received or is entitled to receive assistance from a government, municipality or other public authority in respect of, or for the acquisition of, depreciable property, whether as a grant, subsidy, forgivable loan, deduction from tax, investment allowance or as any other form of assistance other than

(a) an amount described in paragraph 37(1)(d),

(b) an amount deducted as an allowance under section 65, or

($b.1$) an amount included in income by virtue of paragraph 12(1)(u) or 56(1)(s),

the capital cost of the property to the taxpayer at any particular time shall be deemed to be the amount, if any, by which the total of

(c) the capital cost of the property to the taxpayer, determined without reference to this subsection, subsection (7.4) and section 80, and

(d) such part, if any, of the assistance as has been repaid by the taxpayer, pursuant to an obligation to repay all or any part of that assistance, in respect of that property before the disposition thereof by the taxpayer and before the particular time

exceeds the total of

(e) where the property was acquired in a taxation year ending before the particular time, all amounts deducted under subsection 127(5) or (6) by the taxpayer for a taxation year ending before the particular time,

(f) the amount of assistance the taxpayer has received or is entitled, before the particular time, to receive, and

(g) all amounts by which the capital cost of the property to the taxpayer is required because of section 80 to be reduced at or before that time,

in respect of that property before the disposition thereof by the taxpayer.

[¶1274]

(7.2) Receipt of public assistance. For the purposes of subsection (7.1), where at any time a taxpayer who is a beneficiary of a trust or a member of a partnership has received or is entitled to receive assistance from a government, municipality or other public authority whether as a grant, subsidy, forgivable loan, deduction from tax, investment allowance or as any other form of assistance, the amount of the assistance that may reasonably be considered to be in respect of, or for the acquisition of, depreciable property of the trust or partnership shall be deemed to have been received at that time by the trust or partnership, as the case may be, as assistance from the government, municipality or other public authority for the acquisition of depreciable property.

[¶1278]

(7.3) Control of corporations by one trustee. For the purposes of paragraph (7)(e), where at a particular time one corporation would, but for this subsection, be related to another corporation by reason of both corporations being controlled by the same executor, liquidator of a succession or trustee and it is established that

(a) the executor, liquidator or trustee did not acquire control of the corporations as a result of one or more estates or trusts created by the same individual or by two or more individuals not dealing with each other at arm's length, and

(b) the estate or trust under which the executor, liquidator or trustee acquired control of each of the corporations arose only on the death of the individual creating the estate or trust,

the two corporations are deemed not to be related to each other at the particular time.

[¶1282]

(7.4) Deemed capital cost.   Notwithstanding subsection (7.1), where a taxpayer has in a taxation year received an amount that would, but for this subsection, be included in the taxpayer's income under paragraph $12(1)(x)$ in respect of the cost of a depreciable property acquired by the taxpayer in the year, in the three taxation years immediately preceding the year or in the taxation year immediately following the year and the taxpayer elects under this subsection on or before the day on or before which the taxpayer is required to file the taxpayer's return of income under this Part for the year, or, where the property is acquired in the taxation year immediately following the year, for that following year, the capital cost of the property to the taxpayer shall be deemed to be the amount by which the total of

(a) the capital cost of the property to the taxpayer otherwise determined, applying the provisions of subsection (7.1), where necessary, and

(b) such part, if any, of the amount received by the taxpayer as has been repaid by the taxpayer pursuant to a legal obligation to repay all or any part of that amount, in respect of that property and before the disposition thereof by the taxpayer, and as may reasonably be considered to be in respect of the amount elected under this subsection in respect of the property

exceeds the amount elected by the taxpayer under this subsection, but in no case shall the amount elected under this subsection exceed the least of

(c) the amount so received by the taxpayer,

(d) the capital cost of the property to the taxpayer otherwise determined, and

(e) where the taxpayer has disposed of the property before the year, nil.

[¶1284]

(7.5) Deemed capital cost.   For the purposes of this Act,

(a) where a taxpayer, to acquire a property prescribed in respect of the taxpayer, is required under the terms of a contract made after March 6, 1996 to make a payment to Her Majesty in right of Canada or a province or to a Canadian municipality in respect of costs incurred or to be incurred by the recipient of the payment

(i) the taxpayer is deemed to have acquired the property at a capital cost equal to the portion of that payment made by the taxpayer that can reasonably be regarded as being in respect of those costs, and

(ii) the time of acquisition of the property by the taxpayer is deemed to be the later of the time the payment is made and the time at which those costs are incurred;

(b) where

(i) at any time after March 6, 1996 a taxpayer incurs a cost on account of capital for the building of, for the right to use or in respect of, a prescribed property, and

(ii) the amount of the cost would, if this paragraph did not apply, not be included in the capital cost to the taxpayer of depreciable property of a prescribed class,

the taxpayer is deemed to have acquired the property at that time at a capital cost equal to the amount of the cost;

(c) where a taxpayer acquires an intangible property as a consequence of making a payment to which paragraph (a) applies or incurring a cost to which paragraph (b) applies,

(i) the property referred to in paragraph (a) or (b) is deemed to include the intangible property, and

(ii) the portion of the capital cost referred to in paragraph (a) or (b) that applies to the intangible property is deemed to be the amount determined by the formula

$$A \times B/C$$

where

A   is the lesser of the amount of the payment made or cost incurred and the amount determined for C,

B   is the fair market value of the intangible property at the time the payment was made or the cost was incurred, and

C   is the fair market value at the time the payment was made or the cost was incurred of all intangible properties acquired as a consequence of making the payment or incurring the cost; and

---

Pending Amendment

Non-Resident Trusts, Foreign Investment Entities, and Technical Amendments (July 18, 2005)

Paragraph 13(7.5)(c) of the Act is replaced by the following:

(c) where a taxpayer acquires an intangible property, or for civil law an incorporeal property, as a consequence of making a payment to which paragraph (a) applies or incurring a cost to which paragraph (b) applies,

¶1284

(i) the property referred to in paragraph (a) or (b) is deemed to include the intangible or incorporeal property, and

(ii) the portion of the capital cost referred to in paragraph (a) or (b) that applies to the intangible or incorporeal property is deemed to be the amount determined by the formula

$$A \times B/C$$

where

A   is the lesser of the amount of the payment made or cost incurred and the amount determined for C,

B   is the fair market value of the intangible or incorporeal property at the time the payment was made or the cost was incurred, and

C   is the fair market value at the time the payment was made or the cost was incurred of all intangible or incorporeal properties acquired as a consequence of making the payment or incurring the cost; and

Applicable: Royal Assent.

Explanatory Note: [See the Explanatory Note re amendments related to bijuralism following the amendment to subsection 13(5.2).]

(d) any property deemed by paragraph (a) or (b) to have been acquired at any time by a taxpayer as a consequence of making a payment or incurring a cost

(i) is deemed to have been acquired for the purpose for which the payment was made or the cost was incurred, and

(ii) is deemed to be owned by the taxpayer at any subsequent time that the taxpayer benefits from the property.

[¶1286]

(8) Disposition after ceasing business. Notwithstanding subsections (3) and 11(2), where a taxpayer, after ceasing to carry on a business, has disposed of depreciable property of the taxpayer of a prescribed class that was acquired by the taxpayer for the purpose of gaining or producing income from the business and that was not subsequently used by the taxpayer for some other purpose, in applying subsection (1) or (2), each reference therein to a "taxation year" and "year" shall not be read as a reference to a "fiscal period".

[¶1290]

(9) Meaning of "gaining or producing income". In applying paragraphs $(7)(a)$ to (d) in respect of a non-resident taxpayer, a reference to "gaining or producing income" in relation to a business shall be read as a reference to gaining or producing income from a business wholly carried on in Canada or such part of a business as is wholly carried on in Canada.

[¶1294]

(10) Deemed capital cost. For the purposes of this Act, where a taxpayer has, after December 3, 1970 and before April 1, 1972, acquired prescribed property

(a) for use in a prescribed manufacturing or processing business carried on by the taxpayer, and

(b) that was not used for any purpose whatever before it was acquired by the taxpayer,

the taxpayer shall be deemed to have acquired that property at a capital cost to the taxpayer equal to 115% of the amount that, but for this subsection and section 21, would have been the capital cost to the taxpayer of that property.

[¶1300]

(11) Deduction in respect of property used in performance of duties. Any amount deducted under subparagraph $8(1)(j)(ii)$ or $(p)(ii)$ of this Act or subsection 11(11) of the *Income Tax Act*, chapter 52 of the Statutes of Canada, 1948, shall be deemed, for the purposes of this section to have been deducted under regulations made under paragraph $20(1)(a)$.

[¶1304]

(12) Application of para. 20(1)(cc). Where, in computing the income of a taxpayer for a taxation year, an amount has been deducted under paragraph $20(1)(cc)$ or the taxpayer has elected under subsection 20(9) to make a deduction in respect of an amount that would otherwise have been deductible under that paragraph, the amount shall, if it was a payment on account of the capital cost of depreciable property, be deemed to have been allowed to the taxpayer in respect of the property under regulations made under paragraph $20(1)(a)$ in computing the income of the taxpayer

(a) for the year, or

(b) for the year in which the property was acquired,

whichever is the later.

[¶1308]

(13) Deduction under *Canadian Vessel Construction Assistance Act*. Where a deduction has been made under the *Canadian Vessel Construction Assistance Act* for any taxation year, subsection (1) is applicable in respect of the prescribed class created by that Act or any other prescribed class to which the vessel may have been transferred.

[¶1312]

(14) Conversion cost. For the purposes of this section, section 20 and any regulations made under paragraph $20(1)(a)$, a vessel in respect of which any conversion cost is incurred after March 23, 1967 shall, to the extent of the conversion cost, be deemed to be included in a separate prescribed class.

[¶1316]

(15) Where s. (1) and subdivision c do not apply. Where a vessel owned by a taxpayer on January 1, 1966 or constructed pursuant to a construction contract entered into by the taxpayer prior to 1966 and not completed by that date was disposed of by the taxpayer before 1974,

(a) subsection (1) and subdivision c do not apply to the proceeds of disposition

(i) if an amount at least equal to the proceeds of disposition was used by the taxpayer, before May, 1974 and during the taxation year of the taxpayer in which the vessel was disposed of or within 4 months after the end of that taxation year, under conditions satisfactory to the appropriate minister, either for replacement or to incur any conversion cost with respect to a vessel owned by the taxpayer, or

(ii) if the appropriate minister certified that the taxpayer had, on satisfactory terms, deposited

(A) on or before the day on which the taxpayer was required to file a return of the taxpayer's income for the taxation year in which the vessel was disposed of, or

(B) on or before such day subsequent to the day referred to in clause (A) as the appropriate minister specified in respect of the taxpayer,

an amount at least equal to the tax that would, but for this subsection, have been payable by the taxpayer under this Part in respect of the proceeds of disposition, or satisfactory security therefor, as a guarantee that the proceeds of disposition would be used before 1975 for replacement; and

(b) if within the time specified for the filing of a return of the taxpayer's income for the taxation year in which the vessel was disposed of

(i) the taxpayer elected to have the vessel constituted a prescribed class, or

(ii) where any conversion cost in respect of the vessel was included in a separate prescribed class, the taxpayer elected to have the vessel transferred to that class,

the vessel shall be deemed to have been so transferred immediately before the disposition thereof, but this paragraph does not apply unless the proceeds of disposition of the vessel exceed the amount that would be the undepreciated capital cost of property of the class to which it would be so transferred.

[¶1320]

(16) Election concerning vessel. Where a vessel owned by a taxpayer is disposed of by the taxpayer, the taxpayer may, if subsection (15) does not apply to the proceeds of disposition or if the taxpayer did not make an election under paragraph (15)(*b*) in respect of the vessel, within the time specified for the filing of a return of the taxpayer's income for the taxation year in which the vessel was disposed of, elect to have the proceeds that would be included in computing the taxpayer's income for the year under this Part treated as proceeds of disposition of property of another prescribed class that includes a vessel owned by the taxpayer.

[¶1324]

(17) Separate prescribed class concerning vessel. Where a separate prescribed class has been constituted either under this Act or the *Canadian Vessel Construction Assistance Act* by reason of the conversion of a vessel owned by a taxpayer and the vessel is disposed of by the taxpayer, if no election in respect of the vessel was made under paragraph (15)(*b*), the separate prescribed class constituted by reason of the conversion shall be deemed to have been transferred to the class in which the vessel was included immediately before the disposition thereof.

[¶1328]

(18) Reassessments. Notwithstanding any other provision of this Act, where a taxpayer has

(*a*) used an amount as described in paragraph (4)(*c*), or

(*b*) made an election under paragraph (15)(*b*) in respect of a vessel and the proceeds of disposition of the vessel were used before 1975 for replacement under conditions satisfactory to the appropriate minister,

such reassessments of tax, interest or penalties shall be made as are necessary to give effect to subsections (4) and (15).

[¶1330]

(18.1) Ascertainment of certain property. For the purpose of determining whether property meets the criteria set out in the Regulations in respect of prescribed energy conservation property, the Technical Guide to Class 43.1, as amended from time to time and published by the Department of Natural Resources, shall apply conclusively with respect to engineering and scientific matters.

[¶1332]

(19) Disposition of deposit. All or any part of a deposit made under subparagraph (15)(*a*)(ii) or under the *Canadian Vessel Construction Assistance Act* may be paid out to or on behalf of any person who, under conditions satisfactory to the appropriate minister and as a replacement for the vessel disposed of, acquires a vessel before 1975

(a) that was constructed in Canada and is registered in Canada or is registered under conditions satisfactory to the appropriate minister in any country or territory to which the British Commonwealth Merchant Shipping Agreement, signed at London on December 10, 1931, applies, and

(b) in respect of the capital cost of which no allowance has been made to any other taxpayer under this Act or the *Canadian Vessel Construction Assistance Act,*

or incurs any conversion cost with respect to a vessel owned by that person that is registered in Canada or is registered under conditions satisfactory to the appropriate minister in any country or territory to which the agreement referred to in paragraph (a) applies, but the ratio of the amount paid out to the amount of the deposit shall not exceed the ratio of the capital cost to that person of the vessel or the conversion cost to that person of the vessel, as the case may be, to the proceeds of disposition of the vessel disposed of, and any deposit or part of a deposit not so paid out before July 1, 1975 or not paid out pursuant to subsection (20) shall be paid to the Receiver General and form part of the Consolidated Revenue Fund.

[¶1336]

(20) Idem. Notwithstanding any other provision of this section, where a taxpayer made a deposit under subparagraph (15)(a)(ii) and the proceeds of disposition in respect of which the deposit was made were not used by any person before 1975 under conditions satisfactory to the appropriate minister as a replacement for the vessel disposed of,

(a) to acquire a vessel described in paragraphs (19)(a) and (b), or

(b) to incur any conversion cost with respect to a vessel owned by that person that is registered in Canada or is registered under conditions satisfactory to the appropriate minister in any country or territory to which the agreement referred to in paragraph (19)(a) applies,

the appropriate minister may refund to the taxpayer the deposit, or the part thereof not paid out to the taxpayer under subsection (19), as the case may be, in which case there shall be added, in computing the income of the taxpayer for the taxation year of the taxpayer in which the vessel was disposed of, that proportion of the amount that would have been included in computing the income for the year under this Part had the deposit not been made under subparagraph (15)(a)(ii) that the portion of the proceeds of disposition not so used before 1975 as such a replacement is of the proceeds of disposition, and, notwithstanding any other provision of this Act, such reassessments of tax, interest or penalties shall be made as are necessary to give effect to this subsection.

[¶1340]

(21) Definitions. In this section,

[¶1341]

"appropriate minister" — "appropriate minister" means the Canadian Maritime Commission, the Minister of Industry, Trade and Commerce, the Minister of Regional Industrial Expansion, the Minister of Industry, Science and Technology or the Minister of Industry or any other minister or body that was or is legally authorized to perform the act referred to in the provision in which this expression occurs at the time the act was or is performed;

[¶1342]

"conversion" — "conversion", in respect of a vessel, means a conversion or major alteration in Canada by a taxpayer;

[¶1343]

"conversion cost" — "conversion cost", in respect of a vessel, means the cost of a conversion;

[¶1344]

"depreciable property" — "depreciable property" of a taxpayer as of any time in a taxation year means property acquired by the taxpayer in respect of which the taxpayer has been allowed, or would, if the taxpayer owned the property at the end of the year and this Act were read without reference to subsection (26), be entitled to, a deduction under paragraph $20(1)(a)$ in computing income for that year or a preceding taxation year;

[¶1348]

"proceeds of disposition" — "proceeds of disposition" of property includes

(a) the sale price of property that has been sold,

(b) compensation for property unlawfully taken,

(c) compensation for property destroyed and any amount payable under a policy of insurance in respect of loss or destruction of property,

(d) compensation for property taken under statutory authority or the sale price of property sold to a person by whom notice of an intention to take it under statutory authority was given,

(e) compensation for property injuriously affected, whether lawfully or unlawfully or under statutory authority or otherwise,

(f) compensation for property damaged and any amount payable under a policy of insurance in respect of damage to property, except to the extent that the compensation or amount, as the case may be, has within a reasonable time after the damage been expended on repairing the damage,

(g) an amount by which the liability of a taxpayer to a mortgagee or hypothecary creditor is reduced as a result of the sale of mortgaged or hypothecated property under a provision of the mortgage or hypothec, plus any amount received by the taxpayer out of the proceeds of the sale, and

(h) any amount included because of section 79 in computing a taxpayer's proceeds of disposition of the property;

[¶1350]

"timber resource property" — "timber resource property" of a taxpayer means

(a) a right or licence to cut or remove timber from a limit or area in Canada (in this definition referred to as an "original right") if

(i) that original right was acquired by the taxpayer (other than in the manner referred to in paragraph (b)) after May 6, 1974, and

(ii) at the time of the acquisition of the original right

(A) the taxpayer may reasonably be regarded as having acquired, directly or indirectly, the right to extend or renew that original right or to acquire another such right or licence in substitution therefor, or

(B) in the ordinary course of events, the taxpayer may reasonably expect to be able to extend or renew that original right or to acquire another such right or licence in substitution therefor, or

(b) any right or licence owned by the taxpayer to cut or remove timber from a limit or area in Canada if that right or licence may reasonably be regarded

(i) as an extension or renewal of or as one of a series of extensions or renewals of an original right of the taxpayer, or

(ii) as having been acquired in substitution for or as one of a series of substitutions for an original right of the taxpayer or any renewal or extension thereof;

[¶1352]

"total depreciation" — "total depreciation" allowed to a taxpayer before any time for property of a prescribed class means the total of all amounts each of which is an amount deducted by the taxpayer under paragraph 20(1)(a) in respect of property of that class or an amount deducted under subsection 20(16), or that would have been so deducted but for subsection 20(16.1), in computing the taxpayer's income for taxation years ending before that time;

[¶1354]

"undepreciated capital cost" — "undepreciated capital cost" to a taxpayer of depreciable property of a prescribed class as of any time means the amount determined by the formula

$$(A + B + C + D + D.1) -$$
$$(E + E.1 + F + G + H + I + J + K)$$

where

A   is the total of all amounts each of which is the capital cost to the taxpayer of a depreciable property of the class acquired before that time,

B   is the total of all amounts included in the taxpayer's income under this section for a taxation year ending before that time, to the extent that those amounts relate to depreciable property of the class,

C   is the total of all amounts each of which is such part of any assistance as has been repaid by the taxpayer, pursuant to an obligation to repay all or any part of that assistance, in respect of a depreciable property of the class subsequent to the disposition thereof by the taxpayer that would have been included in an amount determined under paragraph (7.1)(*d*) had the repayment been made before the disposition,

D   is the total of all amounts each of which is an amount repaid in respect of a property of the class subsequent to the disposition thereof by the taxpayer that would have been an amount described in paragraph (7.4)(*b*) had the repayment been made before the disposition,

D.1 is the total of all amounts each of which is an amount paid by the taxpayer before that time as or on account of an existing or proposed countervailing or anti-dumping duty in respect of depreciable property of the class,

E   is the total depreciation allowed to the taxpayer for property of the class before that time,

E.1 is the total of all amounts each of which is an amount by which the undepreciated capital cost to the taxpayer of depreciable property of that class is required (otherwise than because of a reduction in the capital cost to the taxpayer of depreciable property) to be reduced at or before that time because of subsection 80(5),

F   is the total of all amounts each of which is an amount in respect of a disposition before that time of property (other than a timber resource property) of the taxpayer of the class, and is the lesser of

  (*a*) the proceeds of disposition of the property minus any outlays and expenses to the extent that they were made or incurred by the taxpayer for the purpose of making the disposition, and

  (*b*) the capital cost to the taxpayer of the property,

G   is the total of all amounts each of which is the proceeds of disposition before that time of a timber resource property of the taxpayer of the class minus any outlays and expenses to the extent that they were made or incurred by the taxpayer for the purpose of making the disposition,

H   is, where the property of the class was acquired by the taxpayer for the purpose of gaining or producing income from a mine and the taxpayer so elects in prescribed manner and within a prescribed time in respect of that property, the amount equal to that portion of the income derived from the operation of the mine that is, by virtue of the provisions of the *Income Tax Application Rules* relating to income from the operation of new mines, not included in computing income of the taxpayer or any other person,

I   is the total of all amounts deducted under subsection 127(5) or (6), in respect of a depreciable property of the class of the taxpayer, in computing the taxpayers' tax payable for a taxation year ending before that time and subsequent to the disposition of that property by the taxpayer,

J   is the total of all amounts of assistance that the taxpayer received or was entitled to receive before that time, in respect of or for the acquisition of a depreciable property of the class of the taxpayer subsequent to the disposition of that property by the taxpayer, that would have been included in an amount determined under paragraph (7.1)(*f*) had the assistance been received before the disposition; and

K   is the total of all amounts each of which is an amount received by the taxpayer before that time in respect of a refund of an amount added to the undepreciated capital cost of depreciable property of the class because of the description of D.1;

[¶1356]

"vessel" — "vessel" means a vessel as defined in the *Canada Shipping Act.*

[¶1360]

(21.1) Disposition of building.   Notwithstanding subsection (7) and the definition "proceeds of disposition" in section 54, where at any particular time in a taxation year a taxpayer disposes of a building of a prescribed class and the proceeds of disposition of the building determined without reference to this subsection and subsection (21.2) are less than the lesser of the cost amount and the capital cost to the taxpayer of the building immediately before the disposition, for the purposes of paragraph (*a*) of the description of F in the definition "undepreciated capital cost" in subsection (21) and subdivision c,

(*a*) where in the year the taxpayer or a person with whom the taxpayer does not deal at arm's length disposes of land subjacent to, or immediately contiguous to and necessary for the use of, the building, the proceeds of disposition of the building are deemed to be the lesser of

(i) the amount, if any, by which

(A) the total of the fair market value of the building at the particular time and the fair market value of the land immediately before its disposition

exceeds

(B) the lesser of the fair market value of the land immediately before its disposition and the amount, if any, by which the cost amount to the vendor of the land (determined without reference to this subsection) exceeds the total of the capital gains (determined without reference to subparagraphs $40(1)(a)(ii)$ and (iii)) in respect of dispositions of the land within 3 years before the particular time by the taxpayer or by a person with whom the taxpayer was not dealing at arm's length to the taxpayer or to another person with whom the taxpayer was not dealing at arm's length, and

(ii) the greater of

(A) the fair market value of the building at the particular time, and

(B) the lesser of the cost amount and the capital cost to the taxpayer of the building immediately before its disposition,

and, notwithstanding any other provision of this Act, the proceeds of disposition of the land are deemed to be the amount, if any, by which

(iii) the total of the proceeds of disposition of the building and of the land determined without reference to this subsection and subsection (21.2)

exceeds

(iv) the proceeds of disposition of the building as determined under this paragraph,

and the cost to the purchaser of the land shall be determined without reference to this subsection; and

(b) where paragraph (a) does not apply with respect to the disposition and, at any time before the disposition, the taxpayer or a person with whom the taxpayer did not deal at arm's length owned the land subjacent to, or immediately contiguous to and necessary for the use of, the building, the proceeds of disposition of the building are deemed to be an amount equal to the total of

(i) the proceeds of disposition of the building determined without reference to this subsection and subsection (21.2), and

(ii) $\frac{1}{2}$ of the amount by which the greater of

(A) the cost amount to the taxpayer of the building, and

(B) the fair market value of the building

¶1360

immediately before its disposition exceeds the proceeds of disposition referred to in subparagraph (i).

[¶1362]

(21.2) Loss on certain transfers.   Where

(a) a person or partnership (in this subsection referred to as the "transferor") disposes at a particular time (otherwise than in a disposition described in any of paragraphs (c) to (g) of the definition "superficial loss" in section 54) of a depreciable property of a particular prescribed class of the transferor,

(b) the lesser of

(i) the capital cost to the transferor of the transferred property, and

(ii) the proportion of the undepreciated capital cost to the transferor of all property of the particular class immediately before that time that

(A) the fair market value of the transferred property at that time

is of

(B) the fair market value of all property of the particular class immediately before that time

exceeds the amount that would otherwise be the transferor's proceeds of disposition of the transferred property at the particular time, and

(c) on the 30th day after the particular time, a person or partnership (in this subsection referred to as the "subsequent owner") who is the transferor or a person affiliated with the transferor owns or has a right to acquire the transferred property (other than a right, as security only, derived from a mortgage, hypothec, agreement for sale or similar obligation),

the following rules apply:

(d) sections 85 and 97 do not apply to the disposition,

(e) for the purposes of applying this section and section 20 and any regulations made for the purpose of paragraph 20(1)(a) to the transferor for taxation years that end after the particular time,

(i) the transferor is deemed to have disposed of the transferred property for proceeds equal to the lesser of the amounts determined under subparagraphs (b)(i) and (ii) with respect to the transferred property,

(ii) where two or more properties of a prescribed class of the transferor are disposed of at the same time, subparagraph (i) applies as if each property so disposed of had been separately disposed of in the order designated by the transferor or, if the transferor does not designate an order, in the order designated by the Minister,

¶1362

(iii) the transferor is deemed to own a property that was acquired before the beginning of the taxation year that includes the particular time at a capital cost equal to the amount of the excess described in paragraph (b), and that is property of the particular class, until the time that is immediately before the first time, after the particular time,

(A) at which a 30-day period begins throughout which neither the transferor nor a person affiliated with the transferor owns or has a right to acquire the transferred property (other than a right, as security only, derived from a mortgage, hypothec, agreement for sale or similar obligation),

(B) at which the transferred property is not used by the transferor or a person affiliated with the transferor for the purpose of earning income and is used for another purpose,

(C) at which the transferred property would, if it were owned by the transferor, be deemed by section 128.1 or subsection 149(10) to have been disposed of by the transferor,

(D) that is immediately before control of the transferor is acquired by a person or group of persons, where the transferor is a corporation, or

(E) at which the winding-up of the transferor begins (other than a winding-up to which subsection 88(1) applies), where the transferor is a corporation, and

(iv) the property described in subparagraph (iii) is considered to have become available for use by the transferor at the time at which the transferred property is considered to have become available for use by the subsequent owner,

(f) for the purposes of subparagraphs (e)(iii) and (iv), where a partnership otherwise ceases to exist at any time after the particular time, the partnership is deemed not to have ceased to exist, and each person who was a member of the partnership immediately before the partnership would, but for this paragraph, have ceased to exist is deemed to remain a member of the partnership, until the time that is immediately after the first time described in clauses (e)(iii)(A) to (E), and

(g) for the purposes of applying this section and section 20 and any regulations made for the purpose of paragraph 20(1)(a) to the subsequent owner,

(i) the subsequent owner's capital cost of the transferred property is deemed to be the amount that was the transferor's capital cost of the transferred property, and

(ii) the amount by which the transferor's capital cost of the transferred property exceeds its fair market value at the particular time is deemed to have been deducted under paragraph 20(1)(a) by the subsequent owner in respect of property of that class in computing income for taxation years that ended before the particular time.

¶1362

[¶1364]

(22) Deduction for insurer. For the purposes of E in the definition "undepreciated capital cost" in subsection (21), an insurer shall be deemed to have been allowed a deduction for depreciation for property of a prescribed class under paragraph $20(1)(a)$ in computing income for taxation years before its 1977 taxation year equal to the total of

(a) the amount determined, immediately after the end of its 1976 taxation year, for E in that definition, with respect to property of the particular prescribed class of the insurer (determined without reference to this subsection),

(b) the lesser of

(i) the amount of its 1975-76 excess capital cost allowance with respect to property of the particular prescribed class of the insurer, and

(ii) that proportion of the amount, if any, by which its 1975 branch accounting election deficiency exceeds the amount determined under subparagraph $138(4.1)(d)(ii)$ that

(A) the amount of its 1975-76 excess capital cost allowance with respect to property of the particular prescribed class of the insurer

is of

(B) the total of all its 1975-76 excess capital cost allowances with respect to properties of a prescribed class of the insurer, and

(c) the lesser of

(i) the amount, if any, by which

(A) the undepreciated capital cost of property of the particular prescribed class of the insurer immediately after the end of its 1976 taxation year (determined without reference to this subsection),

exceeds

(B) the amount determined under paragraph (b) in respect of property of the particular prescribed class of the insurer, and

(ii) that proportion of the amount, if any, by which its 1975 branch accounting election deficiency exceeds the total of

(A) the amount determined under subparagraph $138(4.1)(d)(ii)$,

(B) the total of all amounts determined under paragraph (b) with respect to property of a prescribed class of the insurer,

(C) the total described in subclause $138(4.1)(a)(ii)(B)(IV)$,

(D) the amount determined under subparagraph $138(4.1)(b)(ii)$, and

(E) the amount determined under subparagraph $138(4.1)(a)(ii)$

that

(F) the undepreciated capital cost of property of the particular pre-scribed class of the insurer immediately after the end of its 1976 taxation year (determined without reference to this subsection),

is of

(G) the total of all amounts each of which is the undepreciated capital cost of property of a prescribed class of the insurer immedi-ately after the end of its 1976 taxation year (determined without reference to this subsection).

[¶1370]

(23) Deduction for life insurer.   For the purposes of E in the defini-tion "undepreciated capital cost" in subsection (21), a life insurer shall be deemed to have been allowed a deduction for depreciation for property of a prescribed class under paragraph $20(1)(a)$ in computing income for taxation years before its 1978 taxation year equal to the total of

(a) the amount determined immediately after the end of its 1977 taxa-tion year for E in that definition, with respect to property of the particular prescribed class of the insurer (determined without refer-ence to this subsection), and

(b) the amount, if any, by which

(i) the total of all maximum amounts the insurer was entitled to claim with respect to property of the particular prescribed class of the insurer in taxation years ending before 1978 and after 1968

exceeds

(ii) the amount determined under paragraph (a).

[¶1372]

(23.1) Application of s. 138(12).   The definitions in subsection 138(12) apply to this section.

[¶1374]

(24) Acquisition of control.   Where control of a corporation has been acquired at any time by a person or group of persons and, within the 12-month period that ended immediately before that time, the corporation or a partnership of which it was a majority interest partner acquired depreciable property (other than property that was owned by the corporation or partnership or by a person that would, if section 251.1 were read without reference to the definition "con-trolled" in subsection 251.1(2) [(sic) Editor's note: should read 251.1(3)], be affiliated with the corporation throughout the period that began immediately before the 12-month period began and ended at the time the property was acquired by the corporation or partnership) that was not used, or acquired for use, by the corporation or partnership in a business that was carried on by it immediately before the 12-month period began,

(a) for the purposes of the description of A in the definition "undepreciated capital cost" in subsection (21) and of sections 127 and 127.1, the property is, subject to paragraph (b), deemed not to have been acquired by the corporation or partnership before that time and to have been acquired by it immediately after that time; and

(b) where the property was disposed of by it before that time and was not reacquired by it before that time, for the purpose of the description of A in that definition, the property is deemed to have been acquired by the corporation or partnership immediately before the property was disposed of.

[¶1380]

(25) Early change of control. For the purpose of subsection (24), where a corporation referred to in that subsection was incorporated or otherwise formed in the 12-month period referred to in that subsection, the corporation is deemed to have been, throughout the period that began immediately before the 12-month period and ended immediately after it was incorporated or otherwise formed,

(a) in existence; and

(b) affiliated with every person with whom it was affiliated (otherwise than because of a right referred to in paragraph 251(5)(b)) throughout the period that began when it was incorporated or otherwise formed and ended immediately before its control is acquired.

[¶1381]

(26) Restriction on deduction before available for use. In applying the definition "undepreciated capital cost" in subsection (21) for the purpose of paragraph 20(1)(a) and any regulations made for the purpose of that paragraph, in computing a taxpayer's income for a taxation year from a business or property, no amount shall be included in calculating the undepreciated capital cost to the taxpayer of depreciable property of a prescribed class in respect of the capital cost to the taxpayer of a property of that class (other than property that is a certified production, as defined by regulations made for the purpose of paragraph 20(1)(a)) before the time the property is considered to have become available for use by the taxpayer.

[¶1382]

(27) Interpretation — available for use. For the purposes of subsection (26) and subject to subsection (29), property (other than a building or part thereof) acquired by a taxpayer shall be considered to have become available for use by the taxpayer at the earliest of

(a) the time the property is first used by the taxpayer for the purpose of earning income,

(b) the time that is immediately after the beginning of the first taxation year of the taxpayer that begins more than 357 days after the end of the taxation year of the taxpayer in which the property was acquired by the taxpayer,

(c) the time that is immediately before the disposition of the property by the taxpayer,

(d) the time the property

(i) is delivered to the taxpayer, or to a person or partnership (in this paragraph referred to as the "other person") that will use the property for the benefit of the taxpayer, or, where the property is not of a type that is deliverable, is made available to the taxpayer or the other person, and

(ii) is capable, either alone or in combination with other property in the possession at that time of the taxpayer or the other person, of being used by or for the benefit of the taxpayer or the other person to produce a commercially saleable product or to perform a commercially saleable service, including an intermediate product or service that is used or consumed, or to be used or consumed, by or for the benefit of the taxpayer or the other person in producing or performing any such product or service,

(e) in the case of property acquired by the taxpayer for the prevention, reduction or elimination of air or water pollution created by operations carried on by the taxpayer or that would be created by such operations if the property had not been acquired, the time at which the property is installed and capable of performing the function for which it was acquired,

(f) in the case of property acquired by

(i) a corporation a class of shares of the capital stock of which is listed on a prescribed stock exchange,

(ii) a corporation that is a public corporation because of an election made under subparagraph (b)(i) of the definition "public corporation" in subsection 89(1) or a designation made by the Minister in a notice to the corporation under subparagraph (b)(ii) of that definition, or

(iii) a subsidiary wholly-owned corporation of a corporation described in subparagraph (i) or (ii),

the end of the taxation year for which depreciation in respect of the property is first deducted in computing the earnings of the corporation in accordance with generally accepted accounting principles and for the purpose of the financial statements of the corporation for the year presented to its shareholders,

(g) in the case of property acquired by the taxpayer in the course of carrying on a business of farming or fishing, the time at which the property has been delivered to the taxpayer and is capable of performing the function for which it was acquired,

¶1382

(h) in the case of property of a taxpayer that is a motor vehicle, trailer, trolley bus, aircraft or vessel for which one or more permits, certificates or licences evidencing that the property may be operated by the taxpayer in accordance with any laws regulating the use of such property are required to be obtained, the time all those permits, certificates or licences have been obtained,

(i) in the case of property that is a spare part intended to replace a part of another property of the taxpayer if required due to a breakdown of that other property, the time the other property became available for use by the taxpayer,

(j) in the case of a concrete gravity base structure and topside modules intended to be used at an oil production facility in a commercial discovery area (within the meaning assigned by section 2 of the *Canada Petroleum Resources Act*) on which the drilling of the first well that indicated the discovery began before March 5, 1982, in an offshore region prescribed for the purposes of subsection 127(9), the time the gravity base structure deballasts and lifts the assembled topside modules, and

(k) where the property is (within the meaning assigned by subsection (4.1)) a replacement for a former property described in paragraph (4)(a) that was acquired before 1990 or that became available for use at or before the time the replacement property is acquired, the time the replacement property is acquired,

and, for the purposes of paragraph (f), where depreciation is calculated by reference to a portion of the cost of the property, only that portion of the property shall be considered to have become available for use at the end of the taxation year referred to in that paragraph.

[¶1383]

(28) Idem. For the purposes of subsection (26) and subject to subsection (29), property that is a building or part thereof of a taxpayer shall be considered to have become available for use by the taxpayer at the earliest of

(a) the time all or substantially all of the building is first used by the taxpayer for the purpose for which it was acquired,

(b) the time the construction of the building is complete,

(c) the time that is immediately after the beginning of the taxpayer's first taxation year that begins more than 357 days after the end of the taxpayer's taxation year in which the property was acquired by the taxpayer,

(d) the time that is immediately before the disposition of the property by the taxpayer, and

(e) where the property is (within the meaning assigned by subsection (4.1)) a replacement for a former property described in paragraph (4)(a) that was acquired before 1990 or that became available for use at or before the time the replacement property is acquired, the time the replacement property is acquired,

and, for the purpose of this subsection, a renovation, alteration or addition to a particular building shall be considered to be a building separate from the particular building.

[¶1384]

(29) Idem. For the purposes of subsection (26), where a taxpayer acquires property (other than a building that is used or is to be used by the taxpayer principally for the purpose of gaining or producing gross revenue that is rent) in the taxpayer's first taxation year (in this subsection referred to as the "particular year") that begins more than 357 days after the end of the taxpayer's taxation year in which the taxpayer first acquired property after 1989, that is part of a project of the taxpayer, or in a taxation year subsequent to the particular year, and at the end of any taxation year (in this subsection referred to as the "inclusion year") of the taxpayer

(a) the property can reasonably be considered to be part of the project, and

(b) the property has not otherwise become available for use,

if the taxpayer so elects in prescribed form filed with the taxpayer's return of income under this Part for the particular year, that particular portion of the property the capital cost of which does not exceed the amount, if any, by which

(c) the total of all amounts each of which is the capital cost to the taxpayer of a depreciable property (other than a building that is used or is to be used by the taxpayer principally for the purpose of gaining or producing gross revenue that is rent) that is part of the project, that was acquired by the taxpayer after 1989 and before the end of the taxpayer's last taxation year that ends more than 357 days before the beginning of the inclusion year and that has not become available for use at or before the end of the inclusion year (except where the property has first become available for use before the end of the inclusion year because of this subsection or paragraph (27)(b) or (28)(c))

exceeds

(d) the total of all amounts each of which is the capital cost to the taxpayer of a depreciable property, other than the particular portion of the property, that is part of the project to the extent that the property is considered, because of this subsection, to have become available for use before the end of the inclusion year

shall be considered to have become available for use immediately before the end of the inclusion year.

[¶1385]

(30) Transfers of property. Notwithstanding subsections (27) to (29), for the purpose of subsection (26), property of a taxpayer shall be deemed to have become available for use by the taxpayer at the earlier of the time the property was acquired by the taxpayer and, if applicable, a prescribed time, where

(a) the property was acquired

(i) from a person with whom the taxpayer was not dealing at arm's length (otherwise than because of a right referred to in paragraph $251(5)(b)$) at the time the property was acquired by the taxpayer, or

(ii) in the course of a reorganization in respect of which, if a dividend were received by a corporation in the course of the reorganization, subsection $55(2)$ would not apply to the dividend because of paragraph $55(3)(b)$; and

(b) before the property was acquired by the taxpayer, it became available for use (determined without reference to paragraphs $(27)(c)$ and $(28)(d)$) by the person from whom it was acquired.

[¶1386]

(31) Idem. For the purposes of paragraphs $(27)(b)$ and $(28)(c)$ and subsection (29), where a property of a taxpayer was acquired from a person (in this subsection referred to as "the transferor")

(a) with whom the taxpayer was, at the time the taxpayer acquired the property, not dealing at arm's length (otherwise than because of a right referred to in paragraph $251(5)(b)$), or

(b) in the course of a reorganization in respect of which, if a dividend were received by a corporation in the course of the reorganization, subsection $55(2)$ would not apply to the dividend because of the application of paragraph $55(3)(b)$,

the taxpayer shall be deemed to have acquired the property at the time it was acquired by the transferor.

[¶1387]

(32) Leased property. Where a taxpayer has leased property that is depreciable property of a person with whom the taxpayer does not deal at arm's length, the amount, if any, by which

(a) the total of all amounts paid or payable by the taxpayer for the use of, or the right to use, the property in a particular taxation year and before the time the property would have been considered to have become available for use by the taxpayer if the taxpayer had acquired the property, and that, but for this subsection, would be deductible in computing the taxpayer's income for any taxation year

exceeds

(b) the total of all amounts received or receivable by the taxpayer for the use of, or the right to use, the property in the particular taxation year and before that time and that are included in the income of the taxpayer for any taxation year shall be deemed to be a cost to the taxpayer of a property included in Class 13 in Schedule II to the Income Tax Regulations and not to be an amount paid or payable for the use of, or the right to use, the property.

[¶1388]

(33) Consideration given for depreciable property. For greater certainty, where a person acquires a depreciable property for consideration that can reasonably be considered to include a transfer of property, the portion of the cost to the person of the depreciable property attributable to the transfer shall not exceed the fair market value of the transferred property.

[¶1389]

(34) Deductible expenses. Notwithstanding paragraph $1102(1)(a)$ of the Regulations, for taxation years that end after 1987 and before December 6, 1996, the classes of property prescribed for the purpose of paragraph $20(1)(a)$ are deemed to include property of a taxpayer that, if the Act were read without reference to sections 66 to 66.4, would be included in one of the classes.

[¶1390]

SECTION 14:

(1) Eligible capital property — inclusion in income from business. Where, at the end of a taxation year, the total of all amounts each of which is an amount determined, in respect of a business of a taxpayer, for E in the definition "cumulative eligible capital" in subsection (5) (in this section referred to as an "eligible capital amount") or for F in that definition exceeds the total of all amounts determined for A to D in that definition in respect of the business (which excess is in this subsection referred to as "the excess"), there shall be included in computing the taxpayer's income from the business for the year the total of

(a) the amount, if any, that is the lesser of

(i) the excess, and

(ii) the amount determined for F in the definition "cumulative eligible capital" in subsection (5) at the end of the year in respect of the business, and

(b) the amount, if any, determined by the formula

$$\tfrac{2}{3} \times (A - B - C - D)$$

where

A   is the excess,

B   is the amount determined for F in the definition "cumulative eligible capital" in subsection (5) at the end of the year in respect of the business,

C   is ½ of the amount determined for Q in the definition "cumulative eligible capital" in subsection (5) at the end of the year in respect of the business, and

D   is the amount claimed by the taxpayer, not exceeding the taxpayer's exempt gains balance for the year in respect of the business.

[¶1391]

(1.01) Election re capital gain.   Where, at any time in a taxation year, a taxpayer disposes of an eligible capital property (other than goodwill) in respect of a business, the cost of the property to the taxpayer can be determined, the proceeds of the disposition (in this subsection referred to as the "actual proceeds") exceed that cost, the taxpayer's exempt gains balance in respect of the business for the year is nil and the taxpayer so elects under this subsection in the taxpayer's return of income for the year,

(a) for the purposes of subsection (5), the proceeds of disposition of the property are deemed to be equal to that cost;

(b) the taxpayer is deemed to have disposed at that time of a capital property that had at that time an adjusted cost base to the taxpayer equal to that cost, for proceeds of disposition equal to the actual proceeds; and

---

Pending Amendment

Non-Resident Trusts, Foreign Investment Entities, and Technical Amendments (July 18, 2005)

The portion of subsection 14(1.01) of the Act before paragraph (c) is replaced by the following:

(1.01) Election re capital gain.   A taxpayer may, in the taxpayer's return of income for a taxation year, or with an election under subsection 83(2) filed on or before the taxpayer's filing-due date for the taxation year, elect that the following rules apply to a disposition made at any time in the year of an eligible capital property in respect of a business, if the taxpayer's actual proceeds of the disposition exceed the taxpayer's eligible capital expenditure in respect of the acquisition of the property, that eligible capital expenditure can be determined and, for taxpayers who are individuals, the taxpayer's exempt gains balance in respect of the business for the taxation year is nil:

(a) for the purpose of subsection (5) other than the description of A in the definition "cumulative eligible capital", the proceeds of disposition of the property are deemed to be equal to the amount of that eligible capital expenditure;

(b) the taxpayer is deemed to have disposed at that time of a capital property that had, immediately before that time, an adjusted cost base to the taxpayer equal to the amount of that eligible capital expenditure, for proceeds of disposition equal to the actual proceeds; and

Applicable: To dispositions of eligible capital property that occur in taxation years that end after February 27, 2000, except that, in its application to those dispositions of eligible capital property that occur before December 21, 2002, the portion of subsection 14(1.01) of the Act before paragraph (c) is to be read as follows:
   " (1.01) A taxpayer may, in the taxpayer's return of income for a taxation year, elect that the following rules apply to a disposition made at any time in the taxation year of an eligible capital property (other than goodwill) in respect of a business, if the taxpayer's actual pro-

ceeds of the disposition exceed the taxpayer's cost of the property, that cost can be determined and, for taxpayers who are individuals, the taxpayer's exempt gains balance in respect of the business for the taxation year is nil:

(a) for the purposes of subsection (5), the proceeds of disposition of the property are deemed to be equal to that cost;

(b) the taxpayer is deemed to have disposed at that time of a capital property that had, immediately before that time, an adjusted cost base to the taxpayer equal to that cost, for proceeds of disposition equal to the actual proceeds; and "

Explanatory Note:

Election re Capital Gain

Subsection 14(1.01) of the Act permits a taxpayer to elect, in the taxpayer's return of income for a taxation year, to report a capital gain on the disposition of an eligible capital property in respect of which the taxpayer can identify the cost of the particular property. Where the taxpayer has so elected, the taxpayer is deemed to have disposed of a capital property with an adjusted cost base equal to that cost, for proceeds of disposition equal to the actual proceeds of the eligible capital property. Paragraph 14(1.01)(a) removes the property from the cumulative eligible capital pool by coincidentally deeming the proceeds of disposition of the eligible capital property to be equal to its original cost.

Subsection 14(1.01) is amended to clarify that it is the eligible capital expenditure by the taxpayer to acquire the eligible capital property that must be verifiable.

The amended provision will allow a taxpayer to elect in the taxpayer's return of income for the taxation year of the disposition, or with an election under subsection 83(2) of the Act. This allows a taxpayer to consider the resulting capital gain when making a capital dividend election.

The amendments generally apply to dispositions of eligible capital property that occur on or after December 20, 2002.

(c) where the eligible capital property is at that time a qualified farm property (within the meaning assigned by subsection 110.6(1)) of the taxpayer, the capital property deemed by paragraph (b) to have been disposed of by the taxpayer is deemed to have been at that time a qualified farm property of the taxpayer.

Pending Amendment

Non-Resident Trusts, Foreign Investment Entities, and Technical Amendments (July 18, 2005)

Section 14 of the Act is amended by adding the following after subsection (1.01):

(1.02) Election re property acquired with pre-1972 outlays or expenditures. If at any time in a taxation year a taxpayer has disposed of an eligible capital property in respect of which an outlay or expenditure to acquire the property was made before 1972 (which outlay or expenditure would have been an eligible capital expenditure if it had been made or incurred as a result of a transaction that occurred after 1971), the taxpayer's actual proceeds of the disposition exceed the total of those outlays or expenditures, that total can be determined, subsection 21(1) of the *Income Tax Application Rules* applies in respect of the disposition and, for taxpayers who are individuals, the taxpayer's exempt gains balance in respect of the business for the taxation year is nil, the taxpayer may, in the taxpayer's return of income for the taxation year, or with an election under subsection 83(2) filed on or before the taxpayer's filing-due date for the taxation year, elect that the following rules apply:

¶1391

(*a*) for the purpose of subsection (5) other than the description of A in the definition "cumulative eligible capital", the proceeds of disposition of the property are deemed to be nil;

(*b*) the taxpayer is deemed to have disposed at that time of a capital property that had, immediately before that time, an adjusted cost base to the taxpayer equal to nil, for proceeds of disposition equal to the amount determined, in respect of the disposition, under subsection 21(1) of the *Income Tax Application Rules*; and

(*c*) if the eligible capital property is at that time a qualified farm property (within the meaning assigned by subsection 110.6(1)) of the taxpayer, the capital property deemed by paragraph (*b*) to have been disposed of by the taxpayer is deemed to have been at that time a qualified farm property of the taxpayer.

Applicable: To dispositions of eligible capital property that occur after December 20, 2002.

(1.03) Non-application of ss. (1.01) and (1.02). Subsections (1.01) and (1.02) do not apply to a disposition by a taxpayer of a property

(*a*) that is goodwill; or

(*b*) that was acquired by the taxpayer

(i) in circumstances where an election was made under subsection 85(1) or (2) and the amount agreed on in that election in respect of the property was less than the fair market value of the property at the time it was so acquired, and

(ii) from a person or partnership with whom the taxpayer did not deal at arm's length and for whom the eligible capital expenditure in respect of the acquisition of the property cannot be determined.

Applicable: To dispositions of eligible capital property that occur after December 20, 2002, except that, in its application to those dispositions that occur on or before February 27, 2004, it is to be read without reference to its paragraph (*b*).

Explanatory Note:

Election re Property Acquired with pre-1972 Outlays or Expenditures

Amended subsection 14(1.01) of the Act does not allow a taxpayer to elect under that subsection in respect of a property acquired prior to 1972. New subsection 14(1.02) of the Act is added to allow a taxpayer to make a similar election in respect of property that would, if an outlay or expenditure were made after 1971 to acquire the property, be eligible for the election under subsection 14(1.01). For the purposes of calculating the capital gain to the taxpayer under this election, the adjusted cost base of such property is deemed to be nil and the proceeds of disposition would be determined under subsection 21(1) of the *Income Tax Application Rules*.

New subsection 14(1.02) applies to dispositions of eligible capital property that occur after December 20, 2002.

Non-application of Subsections (1.01) and (1.02)

New subsection 14(1.03) of the Act is added, concurrently with the amendment of subsection 14(1.01) of the Act and the addition of new subsection 14(1.02) of the Act, to preclude a taxpayer from making an election under those subsections in respect of eligible capital property that is goodwill. Subsection 14(1.03) also precludes an election by a corporation under those subsections for property acquired in circumstances where an election was made under subsection 85(1) or (2) of the Act, if the amount agreed on as the corporation's cost under those subsections was less than the fair market value of the property at the time it was so acquired. However, this rule only applies in circumstances where the corporation is dealing at non-arm's length with the transferor of the property and the eligible capital expenditure of the transferor to acquire the property cannot be determined. The exclusion from electing for property acquired in a rollover prevents the conversion of property with no determinable cost into property with a cost that is determinable for tax purposes.

¶1391

New subsection 14(1.03) applies generally to dispositions of eligible capital property that occur after February 27, 2004, and in particular to dispositions of goodwill that occur after December 20, 2002.

[¶1392]

(1.1) Deemed taxable capital gain. For the purposes of section 110.6 and paragraph 3(*b*) as it applies for the purposes of that section, an amount included under paragraph (1)(*b*) in computing a taxpayer's income for a particular taxation year from a business is deemed to be a taxable capital gain of the taxpayer for the year from the disposition in the year of qualified farm property to the extent of the lesser of

(*a*) the amount included under paragraph (1)(*b*) in computing the taxpayer's income for the particular year from the business, and

(*b*) the amount determined by the formula

$$A - B$$

where

A is the amount by which the total of

(i) $3/4$ of the total of all amounts each of which is the taxpayer's proceeds from a disposition in a preceding taxation year that began after 1987 and ended before February 28, 2000 of eligible capital property in respect of the business that, at the time of the disposition, was a qualified farm property (within the meaning assigned by subsection 110.6(1)) of the taxpayer,

(ii) $2/3$ of the total of all amounts each of which is the taxpayer's proceeds from a disposition in the particular year or a preceding taxation year that ended after February 27, 2000 and before October 18, 2000 of eligible capital property in respect of the business that, at the time of the disposition, was a qualified farm property (within the meaning assigned by subsection 110.6(1)) of the taxpayer, and

(iii) $1/2$ of the total of all amounts each of which is the taxpayer's proceeds from a disposition in the particular year or a preceding taxation year that ended after October 17, 2000 of eligible capital property in respect of the business that, at the time of the disposition, was a qualified farm property (within the meaning assigned by subsection 110.6(1)) of the taxpayer

exceeds the total of

(iv) $3/4$ of the total of all amounts each of which is

(A) an eligible capital expenditure of the taxpayer in respect of the business that was made or incurred in respect of a qualified farm property disposed of by the taxpayer in a preceding taxation year that began after 1987 and ended before February 28, 2000, or

(B) an outlay or expense of the taxpayer that was not deductible in computing the taxpayer's income and that was made or incurred for the purpose of making a disposition referred to in clause (A),

(v) $2/3$ of the total of all amounts each of which is

(A) an eligible capital expenditure of the taxpayer in respect of the business that was made or incurred in respect of a qualified farm property disposed of by the taxpayer in the particular year or a preceding taxation year that ended after February 27, 2000 and before October 18, 2000, or

(B) an outlay or expense of the taxpayer that was not deductible in computing the taxpayer's income and that was made or incurred for the purpose of making a disposition referred to in clause (A), and

(vi) $1/2$ of the total of all amounts each of which is

(A) an eligible capital expenditure of the taxpayer in respect of the business that was made or incurred in respect of a qualified farm property disposed of by the taxpayer in the particular year or a preceding taxation year that ended after October 17, 2000, or

(B) an outlay or expense of the taxpayer that was not deductible in computing the taxpayer's income and that was made or incurred for the purpose of making a disposition referred to in clause (A), and

B   is the total of all amounts each of which is

(i) that portion of an amount deemed by subparagraph $(1)(a)(v)$ (as it applied in respect of the business to fiscal periods that began after 1987 and ended before February 23, 1994) to be a taxable capital gain of the taxpayer that can reasonably be attributed to a disposition of a qualified farm property of the taxpayer, or

(ii) an amount deemed by this section to be a taxable capital gain of the taxpayer for a taxation year preceding the particular year from the disposition of qualified farm property of the taxpayer.

[¶1393]

(2) Amount deemed payable.   Where any amount is, by any provision of this Act, deemed to be a taxpayer's proceeds of disposition of any property disposed of by the taxpayer at any time, for the purposes of this section, that amount shall be deemed to have become payable to the taxpayer at that time.

[¶1394]

(3) Acquisition of eligible capital property.   Notwithstanding any other provision of this Act, where at any particular time a person or partnership (in this subsection referred to as the "taxpayer") has, directly or indirectly, in any manner whatever, acquired an eligible capital property in respect of a business from a person or partnership with which the taxpayer did not deal at arm's length (in this subsection referred to as the "transferor") and the property was an eligible capital property of the transferor (other than property acquired by the taxpayer as a consequence of the death of the transferor), the eligible capital expenditure of the taxpayer in respect of the business is, in respect of that acquisition, deemed to be equal to $^4/_3$ of the amount, if any, by which

(a) the amount determined for E in the definition "cumulative eligible capital" in subsection (5) in respect of the disposition of the property by the transferor

---

Pending Amendment

Non-Resident Trusts, Foreign Investment Entities, and Technical Amendments (July 18, 2005)

Paragraph 14(3)(a) of the Act is replaced by the following:

(a) the amount determined for E in the definition "cumulative eligible capital" in subsection (5) in respect of the disposition of the property by the transferor or, if the property is the subject of an election under subsection (1.01) or (1.02) by the transferor, $^3/_4$ of the actual proceeds referred to in that subsection,

Applicable:　To taxation years that end after February 27, 2000.

Explanatory Note:

Acquisition of Eligible Capital Property

Subsection 14(3) of the Act provides rules regarding non-arm's length transfers of eligible capital property. The provision prevents the deduction, under paragraph 20(1)(b) of the Act, of the portion of the purchaser's cost that is reflected in a capital gains exemption claimed by the vendor under section 110.6 of the Act. Absent any claim by the vendor of a capital gains exemption under subsection 110.6, the eligible capital expenditure to the purchaser generally equals the proceeds of disposition of the vendor. That is, the eligible capital expenditure of the purchaser equals $^4/_3$ of the amount determined in respect of the vendor under the description of E in the formula in the definition "cumulative eligible capital" in subsection 14(5) of the Act.

Paragraph 14(3)(a) is amended, for taxation years that end after February 27, 2000, to ensure that, if the eligible capital property is the subject of an election by the vendor under subsection 14(1.01) or (1.02) of the Act, the eligible capital expenditure of the purchaser will, subject to the adjustments in subsection 14(3) for deductions under section 110.6, equal the actual proceeds of disposition to the vendor.

---

exceeds the total of

(b) the total of all amounts that can reasonably be considered to have been claimed as deductions under section 110.6 for taxation years that ended before February 28, 2000 by any person with whom the taxpayer was not dealing at arm's length in respect of the disposition of the property by the transferor, or any other disposition of the property before the particular time,

¶1394

(*b*.1) $^9/_8$ of the total of all amounts that can reasonably be considered to have been claimed as deductions under section 110.6 for taxation years that ended after February 27, 2000 and before October 18, 2000 by any person with whom the taxpayer was not dealing at arm's length in respect of the disposition of the property by the transferor, or any other disposition of the property before the particular time, and

(*b*.2) $^3/_2$ of the total of all amounts that can reasonably be considered to have been claimed as deductions under section 110.6 for taxation years that end after October 17, 2000 by any person with whom the taxpayer was not dealing at arm's length in respect of the disposition of the property by the transferor, or any other disposition of the property before the particular time,

except that, where the taxpayer disposes of the property after the particular time, the amount of the eligible capital expenditure deemed by this subsection to be made by the taxpayer in respect of the property shall be determined at any time after the disposition as if the total of the amounts determined under paragraphs (*b*), (*b*.1) and (*b*.2) in respect of the disposition were the lesser of

(*c*) the amount otherwise so determined, and

(*d*) the amount, if any, by which

(i) the amount determined under paragraph (*a*) in respect of the disposition of the property by the transferor

exceeds

(ii) the amount determined for E in the definition "cumulative eligible capital" in subsection (5) in respect of the disposition of the property by the taxpayer.

[¶1396]

(4) References to "taxation year" or "year". Where a taxpayer is an individual and the taxpayer's income for a taxation year includes income from a business the fiscal period of which does not coincide with the calendar year, for greater certainty a reference in this section to a "taxation year" or "year" shall be read as a reference to a "fiscal period" or "period".

[¶1398]

(5) Definitions. In this section,

[¶1399]

"adjustment time" — "adjustment time" of a taxpayer in respect of a business is

(*a*) in the case of a corporation formed as a result of an amalgamation occurring after June 30, 1988, the time immediately before the amalgamation,

(b) in the case of any other corporation, the time immediately after the commencement of its first taxation year commencing after June 30, 1988, and

(c) for any other taxpayer, the time immediately after the commencement of the taxpayer's first fiscal period commencing after 1987 in respect of the business;

[¶1400]

"cumulative eligible capital" — "cumulative eligible capital" of a taxpayer at any time in respect of a business of the taxpayer means the amount determined by the formula

$$(A + B + C + D + D.1) - (E + F)$$

where

A   is $3/4$ of the total of all eligible capital expenditures in respect of the business made or incurred by the taxpayer before that time and after the taxpayer's adjustment time,

---

Pending Amendment

Non-Resident Trusts, Foreign Investment Entities, and Technical Amendments (July 18, 2005)

The description of A in the definition "cumulative eligible capital" in subsection 14(5) of the Act is replaced by the following:

A   is the amount, if any, by which $3/4$ of the total of all eligible capital expenditures in respect of the business made or incurred by the taxpayer after the taxpayer's adjustment time and before that time exceeds the total of all amounts each of which is determined by the formula

$$1/2 \times (A.1 - A.2) \times (A.3/A.4)$$

where

A.1 is the amount required, because of paragraph $(1)(b)$ or $38(a)$, to be included in the income of a person or partnership (in this definition referred to as the "transferor") not dealing at arm's length with the taxpayer in respect of the disposition after December 20, 2002 of a property that was an eligible capital property acquired by the taxpayer directly or indirectly, in any manner whatever, from the transferor and not disposed of by the taxpayer before that time,

A.2 is the total of all amounts that can reasonably be considered to have been claimed as deductions under section 110.6 by the transferor in respect of that disposition,

A.3 is the transferor's proceeds from that disposition, and

A.4 is the transferor's total proceeds of disposition of eligible capital property in the taxation year of the transferor in which the property described in A.1 was disposed of,

Applicable: To taxation years that end after February 27, 2000, except that the expression "disposition after December 20, 2002 of a property that was an eligible capital property" in the description of A.1 in the description of A in the definition "cumulative eligible capital" in subsection 14(5) of the Act is to be read as the expression "disposition after 2003 of a property that was an eligible capital property" if

(a) the taxpayer referred to in that description of A.1 acquired the property referred to in that description from the transferor referred to in that description;

(b) the property was so acquired under an agreement in writing made before December 21, 2002, between the transferor, or a particular person that controlled the transferor, and another person who dealt at an arm's length with the transferor and the particular person; and

(c) no clause in the agreement or any other arrangement allows an obligation of any party to the agreement to be changed, reduced or waived in the event of a change to, or an adverse assessment under, the Act.

Explanatory Note:

Definition of Cumulative Eligible Capital

The definition "cumulative eligible capital" in subsection 14(5) of the Act provides for the calculation of a taxpayer's cumulative eligible capital property pool for the purpose of determining the taxpayer's allowable deduction in respect of eligible capital property (ECP) for the year.

Variable A in the definition "cumulative eligible capital" represents $^3/_4$ of the eligible capital expenditures of a taxpayer as the result of the acquisition of an eligible capital property after the taxpayer's "adjustment time" (generally since 1987). Variable A is amended to ensure that the taxpayer's pool includes only the taxable portion of the gain realized by the non-arm's length transferor on the disposition after December 20, 2002 of eligible capital property.

Variable A is generally reduced by $^1/_2$ of the gain of the transferor in respect of the property under paragraph 14(1)(b) or 38(a) of the Act. (Where the transferor has claimed a capital gains exemption in respect of the transfer under subsection 110.6 of the Act, subsection 14(3) of the Act reduces the taxpayer's eligible capital expenditure accordingly. The reduction in Variable A will therefore not include $^1/_2$ of the amount of that claim.) Where the transferor has realized such a gain in a taxation year in respect of more than one property, the amount of the gain of the transferor for the purposes of this calculation is that proportion of the gain that the proceeds of disposition of the eligible capital property acquired by the taxpayer is of the total proceeds of disposition of all such property disposed of in the transferor's taxation year.

The reduction to Variable A does not apply where the eligible capital property has previously been disposed of by the taxpayer or was acquired on or before December 20, 2002.

Example 1

Mr. X purchased a farm production quota several years ago for $300,000 and claimed no cumulative eligible capital amounts, such that his cumulative eligible capital at the end of his previous taxation year was $225,000. This year he sold the production quota to his sister, Mrs. Y, for its fair market value of $1,200,000. Mr. X reported income of $450,000 under paragraph 14(1)(b) of the Act, and did not claim a capital gains exemption under section 110.6 of the Act. (Alternatively, Mr. X could have made an election under subsection 14(1.01) of the Act to report a taxable capital gain under paragraph 38(a) of the Act.)

Because Mrs. Y purchased the production quota in a non-arm's length transaction, the amount included in Variable A of her cumulative eligible capital balance at the end of the year of acquisition would be $675,000 (i.e. $^3/_4$ of $1,200,000, less $^1/_2$ of the taxable gain of Mr. X of $450,000). This result may also be illustrated as the total of the taxable gain of Mr. X of $450,000 and $^3/_4$ of his eligible capital expenditure of $300,000.

Example 2

Assume the same facts as Example 1, except that Mr. X claimed a capital gains exemption of $250,000 in respect of his $450,000 taxable gain under paragraph 14(1)(b) of the Act.

Mrs. Y's eligible capital expenditure under subsection 14(3) of the Act is deemed to be $700,000, calculated as $^4/_3$ of the excess of

- $^3/_4$ of the actual proceeds of disposition of $1,200,000 (i.e. $900,000)

over

- $^3/_2$ of the $250,000 capital gains exemption claimed by Mr. X (i.e. $375,000)

The amount included in Variable A of Mrs. Y's cumulative eligible capital balance is calculated as follows:

● $^3/_4$ of her deemed eligible capital expenditure of $700,000		$525,000
less $^1/_2$ of the amount by which		
● the taxable gain of Mr. X exceeds	$450,000	
● the capital gains exemption claimed by Mr. X	250,000	
	200,000	
	$\times\ ^1/_2$	
		100,000
Amount included in Variable A		$425,000

The calculation of "cumulative eligible capital" is designed so that the pool cannot be negative immediately after the end of the year. In this regard, variable F in the calculation generally reduces the pool by the total amount of ECP deductions claimed in prior years (generally, variable P), net of amounts included in income in prior years (variable R) under subsection 14(1) of the Act as recapture of ECP deductions or as deemed capital gains.

Variable R in the definition "cumulative eligible capital" is amended to ensure that amounts included in the income of a corporation under former paragraph 14(1)(*b*) of the Act (as it applied to taxation years that ended before February 28, 2000) continue to be included in the calculation of variable F.

The amendments generally apply to taxation years that end after February 27, 2000.

B   is the total of

(*a*) $^3/_2$ of all amounts included under paragraph (1)(*b*) in computing the taxpayer's income from the business for taxation years that ended before that time and after October 17, 2000,

(*b*) $^9/_8$ of all amounts included under paragraph (1)(*b*) in computing the taxpayer's income from the business for taxation years that ended

(i) before that time, and

(ii) after February 27, 2000 and before October 18, 2000,

(*c*) all amounts included under paragraph (1)(*b*) in computing the taxpayer's income from the business for taxation years that ended

(i) before the earlier of that time and February 28, 2000, and

(ii) after the taxpayer's adjustment time,

(*d*) all amounts each of which is the amount that would have been included under subparagraph (1)(*a*)(v) (as that subparagraph applied for taxation years that ended before February 28, 2000) in computing the taxpayer's income from the business, if the amount

¶1400

determined for D in that subparagraph for the year were nil, for taxation years that ended

(i) before the earlier of that time and February 28, 2000, and

(ii) after February 22, 1994, and

(e) all taxable capital gains included, because of the application of subparagraph $(1)(a)(v)$ (as that subparagraph applied for taxation years that ended before February 28, 2000) to the taxpayer in respect of the business, in computing the taxpayer's income for taxation years that began before February 23, 1994,

C   is $^3/_2$ of the amount, if any, of the taxpayer's cumulative eligible capital in respect of the business at the taxpayer's adjustment time,

D   is the amount, if any, by which

(a) the total of all amounts deducted under paragraph $20(1)(b)$ in computing the taxpayer's income from the business for taxation years ending before the taxpayer's adjustment time

exceeds

(b) the total of all amounts included under subsection (1) in computing the taxpayer's income from the business for taxation years ending before the taxpayer's adjustment time,

D.1 is, where the amount determined by B exceeds zero, $^1/_2$ of the amount determined for Q in respect of the business

E   is the total of all amounts each of which is $^3/_4$ of the amount, if any, by which

(a) an amount which, as a result of a disposition occurring after the taxpayer's adjustment time and before that time, the taxpayer has or may become entitled to receive, in respect of the business carried on or formerly carried on by the taxpayer where the consideration given by the taxpayer therefor was such that, if any payment had been made by the taxpayer after 1971 for that consideration, the payment would have been an eligible capital expenditure of the taxpayer in respect of the business

exceeds

(b) all outlays and expenses to the extent that they were not otherwise deductible in computing the taxpayer's income and were made or incurred by the taxpayer for the purpose of giving that consideration, and

F   is the amount determined by the formula

$$(P + P.1 + Q) - R$$

where

P   is the total of all amounts deducted under paragraph $20(1)(b)$ in computing the taxpayer's income from the busi-

¶1400

ness for taxation years ending before that time and after the taxpayer's adjustment time,

P.1　is the total of all amounts each of which is an amount by which the cumulative eligible capital of the taxpayer in respect of the business is required to be reduced at or before that time because of subsection 80(7);

Q　is the amount, if any, by which

　　(a)　the total of all amounts deducted under paragraph $20(1)(b)$ in computing the taxpayer's income from the business for taxation years ending before the taxpayer's adjustment time

exceeds

　　(b)　the total of all amounts included under subsection (1) in computing the taxpayer's income for taxation years ending before the taxpayer's adjustment time, and

R　is the total of all amounts included, in computing the taxpayer's income from the business for taxation years that ended before that time and after the taxpayer's adjustment time, under subparagraph $(1)(a)$(iv) in respect of taxation years that ended before February 28, 2000 and under paragraph $(1)(a)$ in respect of taxation years that end after February 27, 2000;

Pending Amendment

Non-Resident Trusts, Foreign Investment Entities, and Technical Amendments (July 18, 2005)

The description of R in the definition "cumulative eligible capital" in subsection 14(5) of the Act is replaced by the following:

R　is the total of all amounts each of which is an amount included, in computing the taxpayer's income from the business for a taxation year that ended before that time and after the taxpayer's adjustment time

　　(a)　in the case of a taxation year that ends after February 27, 2000, under paragraph $(1)(a)$, or

　　(b)　in the case of a taxation year that ended before February 28, 2000,

　　　　(i)　under subparagraph $(1)(a)$(iv), as that subparagraph applied in respect of that taxation year, or

¶1400

(ii) under paragraph (1)(*b*), as that paragraph applied in respect of that taxation year, to the extent that the amount so included is in respect of an amount included in the amount determined for P;

Applicable: To taxation years that end after February 27, 2000.

Explanatory Note: [See the Explanatory Note following the amendment to the description of A in the definition "cumulative eligible capital" in subsection 14(5).]

[¶1401]

"eligible capital expenditure" — "eligible capital expenditure" of a taxpayer in respect of a business means the portion of any outlay or expense made or incurred by the taxpayer, as a result of a transaction occurring after 1971, on account of capital for the purpose of gaining or producing income from the business, other than any such outlay or expense

(*a*) in respect of which any amount is or would be, but for any provision of this Act limiting the quantum of any deduction, deductible (otherwise than under paragraph 20(1)(*b*)) in computing the taxpayer's income from the business, or in respect of which any amount is, by virtue of any provision of this Act other than paragraph 18(1)(*b*), not deductible in computing that income,

(*b*) made or incurred for the purpose of gaining or producing income that is exempt income, or

(*c*) that is the cost of, or any part of the cost of,

(i) tangible property of the taxpayer,

(ii) intangible property that is depreciable property of the taxpayer,

(iii) property in respect of which any deduction (otherwise than under paragraph 20(1)(*b*)) is permitted in computing the taxpayer's income from the business or would be so permitted if the taxpayer's income from the business were sufficient for the purpose, or

(iv) an interest in, or right to acquire, any property described in any of subparagraphs (i) to (iii)

Pending Amendment

Non-Resident Trusts, Foreign Investment Entities, and Technical Amendments (July 18, 2005)

Paragraph (*c*) of the definition "eligible capital expenditure" in subsection 14(5) of the Act is replaced by the following:

(*c*) that is the cost of, or any part of the cost of,

(i) tangible property, or for civil law corporeal property, of the taxpayer,

(ii) intangible property, or for civil law incorporeal property, that is depreciable property of the taxpayer,

(iii) property in respect of which any deduction (otherwise than under paragraph 20(1)(*b*)) is permitted in computing the taxpayer's income from the business or would be so permitted if the taxpayer's income from the business were sufficient for the purpose, or

(iv) an interest in, or for civil law a right in, or a right to acquire any property described in any of subparagraphs (i) to (iii)

Applicable: Royal Assent.

Explanatory Note: [See the Explanatory Note re amendments related to bijuralism following the amendment to subsection 13(5.2).]

but, for greater certainty and without restricting the generality of the foregoing, does not include any portion of

(d) any amount paid or payable to any creditor of the taxpayer as, on account or in lieu of payment of any debt or as or on account of the redemption, cancellation or purchase of any bond or debenture,

(e) where the taxpayer is a corporation, any amount paid or payable to a person as a shareholder of the corporation, or

(f) any amount that is the cost of, or any part of the cost of,

(i) an interest in a trust,

(ii) an interest in a partnership,

(iii) a share, bond, debenture, mortgage, hypothecary claim, note, bill or other similar property, or

(iv) an interest in, or right to acquire, any property described in any of subparagraphs (i) to (iii).

Pending Amendment

Non-Resident Trusts, Foreign Investment Entities, and Technical Amendments (July 18, 2005)

Subparagraph (f)(iv) of the definition "eligible capital expenditure" in subsection 14(5) of the Act is replaced by the following:

(iv) an interest in, or for civil law a right in, or a right to acquire any property described in any of subparagraphs (i) to (iii).

Applicable: Royal Assent.

Explanatory Note: [See the Explanatory Note re amendments related to bijuralism following the amendment to subsection 13(5.2).]

[¶1402]

"exempt gains balance" — "exempt gains balance" of an individual in respect of a business of the individual for a taxation year means the amount determined by the formula

$$A - B$$

where

A　is the lesser of

　　(a) the amount by which

　　　　(i) the amount that would have been the individual's taxable cap-
　　　　ital gain determined under paragraph 110.6(19)(b) in respect of
　　　　the business if

　　　　　　(A) the amount designated in an election under subsection
　　　　　　110.6(19) in respect of the business were equal to the fair
　　　　　　market value at the end of February 22, 1994 of all the eligible
　　　　　　capital property owned by the elector at that time in respect
　　　　　　of the business, and

　　　　　　(B) this Act were read without reference to subsection
　　　　　　110.6(20)

　　　exceeds

　　　　(ii) the amount determined by the formula

$$0.75(C - 1.1D)$$

　　　where

　　　　C　is the amount designated in the election that was made
　　　　　　under subsection 110.6(19) in respect of the business, and

　　　　D　is the fair market value at the end of February 22, 1994 of
　　　　　　the property referred to in clause (i)(A), and

　　(b) the individual's taxable capital gain determined under para-
　　graph 110.6(19)(b) in respect of the business, and

B　is the total of all amounts each of which is the amount determined
　　for D in subparagraph (1)(a)(v) in respect of the business for a
　　preceding taxation year that ended before February 28, 2000 or the
　　amount determined for D in paragraph (1)(b) for a preceding taxa-
　　tion year that ended after February 27, 2000.

Pending Amendment

**Non-Resident Trusts, Foreign Investment Entities, and Technical
Amendments (July 18, 2005)**

　　**Section 14 of the Act is amended by adding the following after
subsection (5):**

　　(5.1) Restrictive covenant amount. The description of E in the definition
"cumulative eligible capital" in subsection (5) does not apply to an amount that is

¶1402

received or receivable by a taxpayer in a taxation year if that amount is required to be included in the taxpayer's income because of subsection 56.4(2).

Applicable: After October 7, 2003.

Explanatory Note:

Restrictive Covenant Amount

New subsection 14(5.1) of the Act provides that the description E of the definition "cumulative eligible capital" in subsection 14(5) does not apply to an amount if the amount is required to be included in the taxpayer's income because of subsection 56.4(2). However, subsection 56.4(2) does not apply to an amount if paragraph 56.4(3)(b) applies to the amount, in which case the amount may be a cumulative eligible capital receipt for the purposes of applying section 14. As well, if new subparagraphs 56.4(7)(d)(i) or (ii) apply, consideration that could reasonably be regarded as being for the restrictive covenant granted by a taxpayer for nil proceeds may be — depending on the circumstances — a goodwill amount (as defined by new subsection 56.4(1)) that is to be included in computing the cumulative eligible capital of the taxpayer, or the taxpayer's eligible corporation (as defined by new subsection 56.4(1)). New section 56.4 is more fully described below in the notes accompanying that provision.

New subsection 14(5.1) is consequential to the rules for restrictive covenant amounts as set out in new section 56.4, and applies after October 7, 2003.

[¶1403]

(6) Exchange of property. Where in a taxation year (in this subsection referred to as the "initial year") a taxpayer disposes of an eligible capital property (in this section referred to as the taxpayer's "former property") and the taxpayer so elects under this subsection in the taxpayer's return of income for the year in which the taxpayer acquires an eligible capital property that is a replacement property for the taxpayer's former property, such amount, not exceeding the amount that would otherwise be included in the amount determined for E in the definition "cumulative eligible capital" in subsection (5) (if the description of E in that definition were read without reference to "³/₄ of") in respect of a business, as has been used by the taxpayer before the end of the first taxation year after the initial year to acquire the replacement property

---

Pending Amendment

Non-Resident Trusts, Foreign Investment Entities, and Technical Amendments (July 18, 2005)

The portion of subsection 14(6) of the Act before paragraph (a) is replaced by the following:

(6) Exchange of property. If in a taxation year (in this subsection referred to as the "initial year") a taxpayer disposes of an eligible capital property (in this section referred to as the taxpayer's "former property") and the taxpayer so elects under this subsection in the taxpayer's return of income for the year in which the taxpayer acquires an eligible capital property that is a replacement property for the taxpayer's former property, the amount, not exceeding the amount that would otherwise be included in the amount determined for E in the definition "cumulative eligible capital" in subsection (5) (if the description of E in that definition were read without reference to "3/4 of") in respect of a business, that has been used by the taxpayer to acquire the replacement property before the later of the end of the first taxation year after the initial year and 12 months after the end of the initial year

Applicable: In respect of dispositions that occur in taxation years that end on or after December 20, 2001.

Explanatory Note:

Exchange of Property

Where a taxpayer has disposed of an eligible capital property in a taxation year and has acquired a replacement eligible capital property before the end of the subsequent taxation year, subsection 14(6) of the Act allows the taxpayer to elect to defer the inclusion of an amount in income under subsection 14(1) of the Act that would normally result from a negative balance in the taxpayer's cumulative eligible capital account at the end of the year of disposition.

Subsection 14(6) is amended to accommodate taxation years that are shorter than 12 months, by providing that the period for acquiring a replacement property ends at the later of the end of the subsequent taxation year and the time that is 12 months after the end of the taxation year in which the property was disposed of. This amendment applies in respect of dispositions of eligible capital property that occur in taxation years that end on or after December 20, 2001.

(a) shall, subject to paragraph (b), not be included in the amount determined for E in that definition for the purpose of determining the cumulative eligible capital of the taxpayer in respect of the business; and

(b) shall, to the extent of $\frac{3}{4}$ thereof, be included in the amount determined for E in that definition for the purpose of determining the cumulative eligible capital of the taxpayer in respect of the business at a time that is the later of

(i) the time the replacement property was acquired by the taxpayer, and

(ii) the time the former property was disposed of by the taxpayer.

[¶1404]

(7) Replacement property. For the purposes of subsection (6), a particular eligible capital property of a taxpayer is a replacement property for a former property of the taxpayer if

(a) it is reasonable to conclude that the property was acquired by the taxpayer to replace the former property;

(a.1) it was acquired by the taxpayer for a use that is the same as or similar to the use to which the taxpayer put the former property;

(b) it was acquired for the purpose of gaining or producing income from the same or a similar business as that in which the former property was used; and

(c) where the former property was used by the taxpayer in a business carried on in Canada, the particular property was acquired for use by the taxpayer in a business carried on by the taxpayer in Canada.

[¶1405]

(8) Deemed residence in Canada.   Where an individual was resident in Canada at any time in a particular taxation year and throughout

(a) the preceding taxation year, or

(b) the following taxation year,

for the purpose of paragraph $(1)(a)$, the individual shall be deemed to have been resident in Canada throughout the particular year.

[¶1406]

(9) Effect of election under subsection 110.6(19).   Where an individual elects under subsection 110.6(19) in respect of a business, the individual shall be deemed to have received proceeds of a disposition on February 23, 1994 of eligible capital property in respect of the business equal to the amount determined by the formula

$$(A - B)\ \frac{4}{3}$$

where

A   is the amount determined in respect of the business under subparagraph (a)(ii) of the description of A in the definition "exempt gains balance" in subsection (5), and

B   is the amount determined in respect of the business under subparagraph (a)(i) of the description of A in the definition "exempt gains balance" in subsection (5).

[¶1407]

(10) Deemed eligible capital expenditure.   For the purposes of this Act, where a taxpayer received or is entitled to receive assistance from a government, municipality or other public authority in respect of, or for the acquisition of, property the cost of which is an eligible capital expenditure of the taxpayer in respect of a business, whether as a grant, subsidy, forgivable loan, deduction from tax, investment allowance or as any other form of assistance, that eligible capital expenditure shall at any time be deemed to be the amount, if any, by which the total of

(a) that eligible capital expenditure, determined without reference to this subsection, and

(b) such part, if any, of the assistance as the taxpayer repaid before

(i) the taxpayer ceased to carry on the business, and

(ii) that time

under a legal obligation to pay all or any part of the assistance

exceeds

(c) the amount of the assistance the taxpayer received or is entitled to receive before the earlier of that time and the time the taxpayer ceases to carry on the business.

[¶1408]

(11) Receipt of public assistance. For the purpose of subsection (10), where at any time a taxpayer who is a beneficiary under a trust or a member of a partnership received or is entitled to receive assistance from a government, municipality or other public authority, whether as a grant, subsidy, forgivable loan, deduction from tax, investment allowance or as any other form of assistance, the amount of the assistance that can reasonably be considered to be in respect of, or for the acquisition of, property the cost of which was an eligible capital expenditure of the trust or partnership shall be deemed to have been received at that time by the trust or partnership, as the case may be, as assistance from the government, municipality or other public authority for the acquisition of such property.

[¶1409]

(12) Loss on certain transfers.   Where

(a) a corporation, trust or partnership (in this subsection referred to as the "transferor") disposes at any time in a taxation year of a particular eligible capital property in respect of a business of the transferor in respect of which it would, but for this subsection, be permitted a deduction under paragraph 24(1)(a) as a consequence of the disposition, and

(b) during the period that begins 30 days before and ends 30 days after the disposition, the transferor or a person affiliated with the transferor acquires a property (in this subsection referred to as the "substituted property") that is, or is identical to, the particular property and, at the end of that period, a person or partnership that is either the transferor or a person or partnership affiliated with the transferor owns the substituted property,

the transferor is deemed, for the purposes of this section and sections 20 and 24, to continue to own eligible capital property in respect of the business, and not to have ceased to carry on the business, until the time that is immediately before the first time, after the disposition,

(c) at which a 30-day period begins throughout which neither the transferor nor a person affiliated with the transferor owns

(i) the substituted property, or

(ii) a property that is identical to the substituted property and that was acquired after the day that is 31 days before the period begins,

(d) at which the substituted property is not eligible capital property in respect of a business carried on by the transferor or a person affiliated with the transferor,

(e) at which the substituted property would, if it were owned by the transferor, be deemed by section 128.1 or subsection 149(10) to have been disposed of by the transferor,

(f) that is immediately before control of the transferor is acquired by a person or group of persons, where the transferor is a corporation, or

(g) at which the winding-up of the transferor begins (other than a winding-up to which subsection 88(1) applies), where the transferor is a corporation.

[¶1410]

(13) Deemed identical property. For the purpose of subsection (12),

(a) a right to acquire a property (other than a right, as security only, derived from a mortgage, hypothec, agreement for sale or similar obligation) is deemed to be a property that is identical to the property; and

(b) where a partnership otherwise ceases to exist at any time after the disposition, the partnership is deemed not to have ceased to exist and each person who, immediately before the partnership would, but for this paragraph, have ceased to exist, was a member of the partnership is deemed to remain a member of the partnership, until the time that is immediately after the first time described in paragraphs (12)(c) to (g).

[¶1411]

(14) Ceasing to use property in Canadian business. If at a particular time a non-resident taxpayer ceases to use, in connection with a business or part of a business carried on by the taxpayer in Canada immediately before the particular time, a property that was immediately before the particular time eligible capital property of the taxpayer (other than a property that was disposed of by the taxpayer at the particular time), the taxpayer is deemed to have disposed of the property immediately before the particular time for proceeds of disposition equal to the amount determined by the formula

$$A - B$$

where

A   is the fair market value of the property immediately before the particular time, and

B   is

(a) where at a previous time before the particular time the taxpayer ceased to use the property in connection with a business or part of a business carried on by the taxpayer outside Canada and began to use it in connection with a business or part of a business carried on by the taxpayer in Canada, the amount, if any, by which the fair market value of the property at the previous time exceeded its cost to the taxpayer at the previous time, and

(b) in any other case, nil.

[¶1412]

(15) Beginning to use property in Canadian business. If at a particular time a non-resident taxpayer ceases to use, in connection with a business or part of a business carried on by the taxpayer outside Canada immediately before the particular time, and begins to use, in connection with a business or part of a business carried on by the taxpayer in Canada, a property that is an eligible capital property of the taxpayer, the taxpayer is deemed to have disposed of the property immediately before the particular time and to have reacquired the property at the particular time for consideration equal to the lesser of the cost to the taxpayer of the property immediately before the particular time and its fair market value immediately before the particular time.

[¶1413]

SECTION 16.1:

(1) Leasing properties. Where a taxpayer (in this section referred to as the "lessee") leases tangible property (other than prescribed property) that would, if the lessee acquired the property, be depreciable property of the lessee, from a person resident in Canada other than a person whose taxable income is exempt from tax under this Part, or from a non-resident person who holds the lease in the course of carrying on a business through a permanent establishment in Canada, as defined by regulation, any income from which is subject to tax under this Part, who owns the property and with whom the lessee was dealing at arm's length (in this section referred to as the "lessor") for a term of more than one year, if the lessee and the lessor jointly elect in prescribed form filed with their returns of income for their respective taxation years that include the particular time when the lease began, the following rules apply for the purpose of computing the income of the lessee for the taxation year that includes the particular time and for all subsequent taxation years:

Pending Amendment

Non-Resident Trusts, Foreign Investment Entities, and Technical Amendments (July 18, 2005)

The portion of subsection 16.1(1) of the Act before paragraph (a) is replaced by the following: _____

SECTION 16.1:

(1) Leasing properties. Where a taxpayer (in this section referred to as the "lessee") leases tangible property, or for civil law corporeal property, that is not prescribed property and that would, if the lessee acquired the property, be depreciable property of the lessee, from a person resident in Canada other than a person whose taxable income is exempt from tax under this Part, or from a non-resident person who holds the lease in the course of carrying on a business through a permanent establishment in Canada, as defined by regulation, any income from which is subject to tax under this Part, who owns the property and with whom the lessee was dealing at arm's length (in this section referred to as the "lessor") for a term of more than one year, if the lessee and the lessor jointly elect in prescribed form filed with their returns of income

---

for their respective taxation years that include the particular time when the lease began, the following rules apply for the purpose of computing the income of the lessee for the taxation year that includes the particular time and for all subsequent taxation years:

Applicable: Royal Assent.

Explanatory Note: [See the Explanatory Note re amendments related to bijuralism following the amendment to subsection 13(5.2).]

(a) in respect of amounts paid or payable for the use of, or for the right to use, the property, the lease shall be deemed not to be a lease;

(b) the lessee shall be deemed to have acquired the property from the lessor at the particular time at a cost equal to its fair market value at that time;

(c) the lessee shall be deemed to have borrowed money from the lessor at the particular time, for the purpose of acquiring the property, in a principal amount equal to the fair market value of the property at that time;

(d) interest shall be deemed to accrue on the principal amount of the borrowed money outstanding from time to time, compounded semi-annually, not in advance, at the prescribed rate in effect

(i) at the earlier of

(A) the time, if any, before the particular time, at which the lessee last entered into an agreement to lease the property, and

(B) the particular time, or

(ii) where the lease provides that the amount payable by the lessee for the use of, or the right to use, the property varies according to prevailing interest rates in effect from time to time, and the lessee so elects, in respect of all of the property that is subject to the lease, in the lessee's return of income under this Part for the taxation year of the lessee in which the lease began, at the beginning of the period for which the interest is being calculated;

(e) all amounts paid or payable by or on behalf of the lessee for the use of, or the right to use, the property in the year shall be deemed to be blended payments, paid or payable by the lessee, of principal and interest on the borrowed money outstanding from time to time, calculated in accordance with paragraph (d), applied firstly on account of interest on principal, secondly on account of interest on unpaid interest and thirdly on account of unpaid principal, if any, and the amount, if any, by which any such payment exceeds the total of those amounts shall be deemed to be paid or payable on account of interest, and any amount deemed by reason of this paragraph to be a payment of interest shall be deemed to have been an amount paid or payable, as the case may be, pursuant to a legal obligation to pay interest in respect of the year on the borrowed money;

¶1413

(*f*) at the time of the expiration or cancellation of the lease, the assignment of the lease or the sublease of the property by the lessee, the lessee shall (except where subsection (4) applies) be deemed to have disposed of the property at that time for proceeds of disposition equal to the amount, if any, by which

(i) the total of

(A) the amount referred to in paragraph (*c*), and

(B) all amounts received or receivable by the lessee in respect of the cancellation or assignment of the lease or the sublease of the property

exceeds

(ii) the total of

(A) all amounts deemed under paragraph (*e*) to have been paid or payable, as the case may be, by the lessee on account of the principal amount of the borrowed money, and

(B) all amounts paid or payable by or on behalf of the lessee in respect of the cancellation or assignment of the lease or the sublease of the property;

(*g*) for the purposes of subsections 13(5.2) and (5.3), each amount paid or payable by or on behalf of the lessee that would, but for this subsection, have been an amount paid or payable for the use of, or the right to use, the property shall be deemed to have been deducted in computing the lessee's income as an amount paid or payable by the lessee for the use of, or the right to use, the property after the particular time;

(*h*) any amount paid or payable by or on behalf of the lessee in respect of the granting or assignment of the lease or the sublease of the property that would, but for this paragraph, be the capital cost to the lessee of a leasehold interest in the property shall be deemed to be an amount paid or payable, as the case may be, by the lessee for the use of, or the right to use, the property for the remaining term of the lease; and

(*i*) where the lessee elects under this subsection in respect of a property and, at any time after the lease was entered into, the owner of the property is a non-resident person who does not hold the lease in the course of carrying on a business through a permanent establishment in Canada, as defined by regulation, any income from which is subject to tax under this Part, for the purposes of this subsection the lease shall be deemed to have been cancelled at that time.

[¶1414]

(2) Assignments and subleases. Subject to subsections (3) and (4), where at any particular time a lessee who has made an election under subsection (1) in respect of a leased property assigns the lease or subleases the property to another person (in this section referred to as the "assignee"),

(a) subsection (1) shall not apply in computing the income of the lessee in respect of the lease for any period after the particular time; and

(b) if the lessee and the assignee jointly elect in prescribed form filed with their returns of income under this Part for their respective taxation years that include the particular time, subsection (1) shall apply to the assignee as if

(i) the assignee leased the property at the particular time from the owner of the property for a term of more than one year, and

(ii) the assignee and the owner of the property jointly elected under subsection (1) in respect of the property with their returns of income under this Part for their respective taxation years that include the particular time.

[¶1415]

(3) Idem.   Subject to subsection (4), where at any particular time a lessee who has made an election under subsection (1) in respect of a leased property assigns the lease or subleases the property to another person with whom the lessee is not dealing at arm's length, the other person shall, for the purposes of subsection (1) and for the purposes of computing that person's income in respect of the lease for any period after the particular time, be deemed to be the same person as, and a continuation of, the lessee, except that, notwithstanding paragraph (1)(b), that other person shall be deemed to have acquired the property from the lessee at the time that it was acquired by the lessee at a cost equal to the amount that would be the lessee's proceeds of disposition of the property determined under paragraph (1)(f) if that amount were determined without reference to clauses (1)(f)(i)(B) and (ii)(B).

[¶1416]

(4) Amalgamations and windings-up.   Notwithstanding subsection (2), where at any time a particular corporation that has made an election under subsection (1) in respect of a lease assigns the lease

(a) by reason of an amalgamation (within the meaning assigned by subsection 87(1)), or

(b) in the course of the winding-up of a Canadian corporation in respect of which subsection 88(1) applies,

to another corporation with which it does not deal at arm's length, the other corporation shall, for the purposes of subsection (1) and for the purposes of computing its income in respect of the lease after that time, be deemed to be the same person as, and a continuation of, the particular corporation.

[¶1417]

(5) Replacement property.   For the purposes of subsection (1), where at any time a property (in this subsection referred to as a "replacement property") is provided by a lessor to a lessee as a replacement for a similar property of the lessor (in this subsection referred to as the "original property") that was leased by the lessor to the lessee, and the amount payable by

¶1415

the lessee for the use of, or the right to use, the replacement property is the same as the amount that was so payable in respect of the original property, the replacement property shall be deemed to be the same property as the original property.

[¶1418]

(6) Additional property. For the purposes of subsection (1), where at any particular time

(a) an addition or alteration (in this subsection referred to as "additional property") is made by a lessor to a property (in this subsection referred to as the "original property") of the lessor that is the subject of a lease,

(b) the lessor and the lessee of the original property have jointly elected under subsection (1) in respect of the original property, and

(c) as a consequence of the addition or alteration, the total amount payable by the lessee for the use of, or the right to use, the original property and the additional property exceeds the amount so payable in respect of the original property,

the following rules apply:

(d) the lessee shall be deemed to have leased the additional property from the lessor at the particular time,

(e) the term of the lease of the additional property shall be deemed to be greater than one year,

(f) the lessor and the lessee shall be deemed to have jointly elected under subsection (1) in respect of the additional property,

(g) the prescribed rate in effect at the particular time in respect of the additional property shall be deemed to be equal to the prescribed rate in effect in respect of the original property at the particular time,

(h) the additional property shall be deemed not to be prescribed property, and

(i) the excess referred to in paragraph (c) shall be deemed to be an amount payable by the lessee for the use of, or the right to use, the additional property.

[¶1419]

(7) Renegotiation of lease. For the purposes of subsection (1), where at any time

(a) a lease (in this subsection referred to as the "original lease") of property is renegotiated in the course of a *bona fide* renegotiation, and

(b) as a result of the renegotiation, the amount payable by the lessee of the property for the use of, or the right to use, the property is altered in respect of a period after that time (otherwise than because of an addition or alteration to which subsection (6) applies), the original lease shall be deemed to have expired and the renegotiated lease shall be deemed to be a new lease of the property entered into at that time.

[¶1420]

SECTION 18:

(1) General limitations. In computing the income of a taxpayer from a business or property no deduction shall be made in respect of

Editorial Note: Subsection 18(1) expressly disallows the deduction of certain amounts that might otherwise be deductible under general principles. The rest of section 18 similarly sets out restrictions on the deductibility of amounts that might otherwise be deductible.

[¶1421]

(a) General limitation — an outlay or expense except to the extent that it was made or incurred by the taxpayer for the purpose of gaining or producing income from the business or property;

[¶1422]

(b) Capital outlay or loss — an outlay, loss or replacement of capital, a payment on account of capital or an allowance in respect of depreciation, obsolescence or depletion except as expressly permitted by this Part;

Editorial Note: The deduction (depreciation) of the cost of depreciable property is provided under the capital cost allowance provisions of paragraph $20(1)(a)$ and the regulations thereunder. The costs of certain intangible capital expenses are deductible under specific provisions (for example, financing costs and similar amounts under paragraphs $20(1)(c)$ through (f)). Most other intangible capital expenses fall into the "catch-all" category of eligible capital expenditure and are deducted (amortized) under paragraph $20(1)(b)$.

* * *

[¶1426]

SECTION 20:

(1) Deductions permitted in computing income from business or property. Notwithstanding paragraphs $18(1)(a)$, (b) and (h), in computing a taxpayer's income for a taxation year from a business or property, there may be deducted such of the following amounts as are wholly applicable to that source or such part of the following amounts as may reasonably be regarded as applicable thereto:

[¶1427]

(a) Capital cost of property — such part of the capital cost to the taxpayer of property, or such amount in respect of the capital cost to the taxpayer of property, if any, as is allowed by regulation;

[¶1428]

(b) Cumulative eligible capital amount — such amount as the taxpayer claims in respect of a business, not exceeding 7% of the taxpayer's cumulative eligible capital in respect of the business at the end of the year except that, where the year is less than 12 months, the

amount allowed as a deduction under this paragraph shall not exceed that proportion of the maximum amount otherwise allowable that the number of days in the taxation year is of 365;

* * *

[¶1430]

*(v.*1) *Resource allowance* — such amount as is allowed to the taxpayer for the year by regulation in respect of natural accumulations of petroleum or natural gas in Canada, oil or gas wells in Canada or mineral resources in Canada;

Editorial Note: S. 20(1)(*v.*1) is repealed for taxation years beginning after 2006. Transition rules are in effect for taxation years ending after 2002 and beginning before 2007.

* * *

[¶1432]

(cc) Expenses of representation — an amount paid by the taxpayer in the year as or on account of expenses incurred by the taxpayer in making any representation relating to a business carried on by the taxpayer,

(i) to the government of a country, province or state or to a municipal or public body performing a function of government in Canada, or

(ii) to an agency of a government or of a municipal or public body referred to in subparagraph (i) that had authority to make rules, regulations or by-laws relating to the business carried on by the taxpayer,

including any representation for the purpose of obtaining a licence, permit, franchise or trade-mark relating to the business carried on by the taxpayer;

* * *

[¶1433]

(4) Bad debts from dispositions of depreciable property.   Where an amount that is owing to a taxpayer as or on account of the proceeds of disposition of depreciable property (other than a timber resource property or a passenger vehicle having a cost to the taxpayer in excess of $20,000 or such other amount as may be prescribed) of the taxpayer of a prescribed class is established by the taxpayer to have become a bad debt in a taxation year, there may be deducted in computing the taxpayer's income for the year the lesser of

(*a*) the amount so owing to the taxpayer, and

(*b*) the amount, if any, by which the capital cost to the taxpayer of that property exceeds the total of the amounts, if any, realized by the taxpayer on account of the proceeds of disposition.

[¶1434]

(4.1) Idem.   Where an amount that is owing to a taxpayer as or on account of the proceeds of disposition of a timber resource property of the taxpayer is established by the taxpayer to have become a bad debt in a taxation year, the amount so owing to the taxpayer may be deducted in computing the taxpayer's income for the year.

[¶1436]

(4.2) Bad debts re eligible capital property.   Where, in respect of one or more dispositions of eligible capital property by a taxpayer, an amount that is described in paragraph (a) of the description of E in the definition "cumulative eligible capital" in subsection 14(5) in respect of the taxpayer is established by the taxpayer to have become a bad debt in a taxation year, there shall be deducted in computing the taxpayer's income for the year the amount determined by the formula

$$(A + B) - (C + D + E + F + G + H)$$

where

A   is the lesser of

   (a) $\frac{1}{2}$ of the total of all amounts each of which is such an amount that was so established to have become a bad debt in the year or a preceding taxation year, and

   (b) the amount that is

   (i) where the year ended after February 27, 2000, the amount, if any, that would be the total of all amounts determined by the formula in paragraph 14(1)(b) (if that formula were read without reference to the description of D) for the year, or for a preceding taxation year that ended after February 27, 2000, and

   (ii) where the year ended before February 28, 2000, nil;

B   is the amount, if any, by which

   (a) $\frac{3}{4}$ of the total of all amounts each of which is such an amount that was so established to be a bad debt in the year or a preceding taxation year

   exceeds the total of

   (b) $\frac{3}{2}$ of the amount by which

   (i) the value of A exceeds

   (ii) the amount included in the value of A because of subparagraph (b)(i) of the description of A in respect of taxation years that ended after February 27, 2000 and before October 18, 2000, and

   (c) $\frac{9}{8}$ of the amount included in the value of A because of subparagraph (b)(i) of the description of A in respect of taxation years that ended after February 27, 2000 and before October 18, 2000;

¶1436

C   is the total of all amounts each of which is an amount determined under subsection 14(1) or (1.1) for the year, or a preceding taxation year, that ends after October 17, 2000 and in respect of which a deduction can reasonably be considered to have been claimed under section 110.6 by the taxpayer;

D   is the total of all amounts each of which is an amount determined under subsection 14(1) or (1.1) for the year, or a preceding taxation year, that ended after February 27, 2000 and before October 18, 2000 and in respect of which a deduction can reasonably be considered to have been claimed under section 110.6 by the taxpayer;

E   is the total of all amounts each of which is an amount determined under subsection 14(1) or (1.1) for a preceding taxation year that ended before February 28, 2000 and in respect of which a deduction can reasonably be considered to have been claimed under section 110.6 by the taxpayer;

F   is the total of

(a) $\frac{2}{3}$ of the total of all amounts each of which is the value determined in respect of the taxpayer for D in the formula in paragraph 14(1)(b) for the year, or a preceding taxation year, that ends after October 17, 2000, and

(b) $\frac{8}{9}$ of the total of all amounts each of which is the value determined in respect of the taxpayer for D in the formula in paragraph 14(1)(b) for the year, or a preceding taxation year, that ended after February 27, 2000 and before October 18, 2000;

G   is the total of all amounts each of which is the value determined in respect of the taxpayer for D in the formula in subparagraph 14(1)(a)(v) (as that subparagraph applied for taxation years that ended before February 28, 2000) for a preceding taxation year; and

H   is the total of all amounts deducted by the taxpayer under this subsection for preceding taxation years.

[¶1438]

(4.3) Deemed allowable capital loss. Where, in respect of one or more dispositions of eligible capital property by a taxpayer, an amount that is described in paragraph (a) of the description of E in the definition "cumulative eligible capital" in subsection 14(5) in respect of the taxpayer is established by the taxpayer to have become a bad debt in a taxation year, the taxpayer is deemed to have an allowable capital loss from a disposition of capital property in the year equal to the lesser of

(a) the total of the value determined for A and $\frac{2}{3}$ of the value determined for B in the formula in subsection (4.2) in respect of the taxpayer for the year; and

(b) the total of all amounts each of which is

(i) the value determined for C or paragraph (a) of the description of F in the formula in subsection (4.2) in respect of the taxpayer for the year,

(ii) $3/4$ of the value determined for D or paragraph (b) of the description of F in the formula in subsection (4.2) in respect of the taxpayer for the year, or

(iii) $2/3$ of the value determined for E or G in the formula in subsection (4.2) in respect of the taxpayer for the year.

[¶1440]

(5) Sale of agreement for sale, mortgage or hypothecary claim included in proceeds of disposition. Where depreciable property, other than a timber resource property, of a taxpayer has, in a taxation year, been disposed of to a person with whom the taxpayer was dealing at arm's length, and the proceeds of disposition include an agreement for the sale of, or a mortgage or hypothecary claim on, land that the taxpayer has, in a subsequent taxation year, sold to a person with whom the taxpayer was dealing at arm's length, there may be deducted in computing the income of the taxpayer for the subsequent year an amount equal to the lesser of

(a) the amount, if any, by which the principal amount of the agreement for sale, mortgage or hypothecary claim outstanding at the time of the sale exceeds the consideration paid by the purchaser to the taxpayer for the agreement for sale, mortgage or hypothecary claim, and

(b) the amount determined under paragraph (a) less the amount, if any, by which the proceeds of disposition of the depreciable property exceed the capital cost to the taxpayer of that property.

[¶1444]

(5.1) Sale of agreement for sale, mortgage or hypothecary claim included in proceeds of disposition. Where a timber resource property of a taxpayer has, in a taxation year, been disposed of to a person with whom the taxpayer was dealing at arm's length, and the proceeds of disposition include an agreement for sale of, or a mortgage or hypothecary claim on, land that the taxpayer has, in a subsequent taxation year, sold to a person with whom the taxpayer was dealing at arm's length, there may be deducted in computing the income of the taxpayer for the subsequent year the amount, if any, by which the principal amount of the agreement for sale, mortgage or hypothecary claim outstanding at the time of the sale exceeds the consideration paid by the purchaser to the taxpayer for the agreement for sale, mortgage or hypothecary claim.

* * *

[¶1450]

(9) Application of para. (1)(cc). In lieu of making any deduction of an amount permitted by paragraph (1)(cc) in computing a taxpayer's income for a taxation year from a business, the taxpayer may, if the taxpayer so elects in prescribed manner, make a deduction of $^1/_{10}$ of that amount in computing the taxpayer's income for that taxation year and a like deduction in computing the taxpayer's income for each of the 9 immediately following taxation years.

* * *

[¶1458]

(16) Terminal loss. Notwithstanding paragraphs 18(1)(a), (b) and (h), where at the end of a taxation year,

(a) the total of all amounts used to determine A to D in the definition "undepreciated capital cost" in subsection 13(21) in respect of a taxpayer's depreciable property of a particular class exceeds the total of all amounts used to determine E to J in that definition in respect of that property, and

---

Pending Amendment

Non-Resident Trusts, Foreign Investment Entities, and Technical Amendments (July 18, 2005)

Paragraph 20(16)(a) of the Act is replaced by the following:

(a) the total of all amounts used to determine A to D.1 in the definition "undepreciated capital cost" in subsection 13(21) in respect of a taxpayer's depreciable property of a particular class exceeds the total of all amounts used to determine E to K in that definition in respect of that property, and

Applicable:　To taxation years that end after February 23, 1998.

Explanatory Note:

Terminal Loss

Subsection 20(16) of the Act permits a taxpayer to deduct, in computing the taxpayer's income for a year, the terminal loss of the taxpayer in respect of a class of depreciable property at the end of the year. That subsection is amended to add a reference to new descriptions D.1 and K of the definition "undepreciated capital cost" in subsection 13(21) of the Act. For information about those new descriptions, see the commentary to subsection 13(1).

This amendment applies to taxation years that end after February 23, 1998, and corrects a technical deficiency.

(b) the taxpayer no longer owns any property of that class,

in computing the taxpayer's income for the year

(c) there shall be deducted the amount of the excess determined under paragraph (a), and

(d) no amount shall be deducted for the year under paragraph (1)(a) in respect of property of that class.

[¶1460]

(16.1) Idem. Subsection (16) does not apply in respect of a passenger vehicle of a taxpayer that has a cost to the taxpayer in excess of $20,000 or such other amount as is prescribed.

Pending Amendment

Non-Resident Trusts, Foreign Investment Entities, and Technical Amendments (July 18, 2005)

Subsection 20(16.1) of the Act is replaced by the following:

(16.1) Non-application of s. (16). Subsection (16) does not apply

(a) in respect of a passenger vehicle of a taxpayer that has a cost to the taxpayer in excess of $20,000 or any other amount that is prescribed; and

(b) in respect of a taxation year in respect of a property that was a former property deemed by paragraph 13(4.3)(a) or (b) to be owned by the taxpayer, if

(i) within 24 months after the taxpayer last owned the former property, the taxpayer or a person not dealing at arm's length with the taxpayer acquires a similar property in respect of the same fixed place to which the former property applied, and

(ii) at the end of the taxation year, the taxpayer or the person owns the similar property or another similar property in respect of the same fixed place to which the former property applied.

Applicable: In respect of taxation years that end after December 20, 2002.

Explanatory Note:

Non-Application of Subsection (16)

Subsection 20(16.1) of the Act provides that a terminal loss under subsection 20(16) in respect of a depreciable property that is a "passenger vehicle" costing more than a prescribed amount (currently set at $30,000) is not deductible in computing income. That rule is renumbered as paragraph 20(16.1)(a) and new paragraph 20(16.1)(b) is added, applicable to taxation years that end after December 20, 2002. These amendments are made concurrently with the addition of subsections 13(4.2) and (4.3) of the Act and with the amendment of the definition "former business property" in subsection 248(1) of the Act.

New paragraph 20(16.1)(b) provides that a terminal loss is not available in respect of another person's former business property that was deemed under paragraphs 13(4.3)(a) or (b) (as the result of a joint election under subsection 13(4.2) by the taxpayer and the other person) to be owned by the taxpayer. For further information, refer to the commentary to subsections 13(4.2) and (4.3).

* * *

¶1460

[¶1466]

SECTION 21:

(1) Cost of borrowed money. Where in a taxation year a taxpayer has acquired depreciable property, if the taxpayer elects under this subsection in the taxpayer's return of income under this Part for the year,

(a) in computing the taxpayer's income for the year and for such of the 3 immediately preceding taxation years as the taxpayer had, paragraphs $20(1)(c)$, (d), (e) and $(e.1)$ do not apply to the amount or to the part of the amount specified in the taxpayer's election that, but for an election under this subsection in respect thereof, would be deductible in computing the taxpayer's income (other than exempt income) for any such year in respect of borrowed money used to acquire the depreciable property or the amount payable for the depreciable property; and

(b) the amount or the part of the amount, as the case may be, described in paragraph (a) shall be added to the capital cost to the taxpayer of the depreciable property so acquired by the taxpayer.

[¶1470]

(2) Borrowed money used for exploration or development. Where in a taxation year a taxpayer has used borrowed money for the purpose of exploration, development or the acquisition of property and the expenses incurred by the taxpayer in respect of those activities are Canadian exploration and development expenses, Canadian exploration expenses, Canadian development expenses, Canadian oil and gas property expenses, foreign resource expenses in respect of a country, or foreign exploration and development expenses, as the case may be, if the taxpayer so elects under this subsection in the taxpayer's return of income for the year,

(a) in computing the taxpayer's income for the year and for such of the three immediately preceding taxation years as the taxpayer had, paragraphs $20(1)(c)$, (d), (e) and $(e.1)$ do not apply to the amount or to the part of the amount specified in the taxpayer's election that, but for that election, would be deductible in computing the taxpayer's income (other than exempt income or income that is exempt from tax under this Part) for any such year in respect of the borrowed money used for the exploration, development or acquisition of property, as the case may be; and

(b) the amount or the part of the amount, as the case may be, described in paragraph (a) is deemed to be Canadian exploration and development expenses, Canadian exploration expenses, Canadian development expenses, Canadian oil and gas property expenses, foreign resource expenses in respect of a country, or foreign exploration and development expenses, as the case may be, incurred by the taxpayer in the year.

[¶1474]

(3) Borrowing for depreciable property. In computing the income of a taxpayer for a particular taxation year, where the taxpayer

(a) in any preceding taxation year

(i) made an election under subsection (1) in respect of borrowed money used to acquire depreciable property or an amount payable for depreciable property acquired by the taxpayer, or

(ii) was, by virtue of subsection 18(3.1), required to include an amount in respect of the construction of a depreciable property in computing the capital cost to the taxpayer of the depreciable property, and

(b) in each taxation year, if any, after that preceding taxation year and before the particular year, made an election under this subsection covering the total amount that, but for an election under this subsection in respect thereof, would have been deductible in computing the taxpayer's income (other than exempt income) for each such year in respect of the borrowed money used to acquire the depreciable property or the amount payable for the depreciable property acquired by the taxpayer,

if an election under this subsection is made in the taxpayer's return of income under this Part for the particular year, paragraphs 20(1)(c), (d), (e) and (e.1) do not apply to the amount or to the part of the amount specified in the election that, but for an election under this subsection in respect thereof, would be deductible in computing the taxpayer's income (other than exempt income) for the particular year in respect of the borrowed money used to acquire the depreciable property or the amount payable for the depreciable property acquired by the taxpayer, and the amount or part of the amount, as the case may be, shall be added to the capital cost to the taxpayer of the depreciable property.

[¶1478]

(4) Borrowing for exploration, etc. In computing the income of a taxpayer for a particular taxation year, where the taxpayer

(a) in any preceding taxation year made an election under subsection (2) in respect of borrowed money used for the purpose of exploration, development or acquisition of property,

(b) in each taxation year, if any, after that preceding taxation year and before the particular year, made an election under this subsection covering the total amount that, but for that election, would have been deductible in computing the taxpayer's income (other than exempt income or income that is exempt from tax under this Part) for each such year in respect of the borrowed money used for the exploration, development or acquisition of property, as the case may be, and

(c) so elects in the taxpayer's return of income for the particular year,

the following rules apply:

(d) paragraphs 20(1)(c), (d), (e) and (e.1) do not apply to the amount or to the part of the amount specified in the election that, but for the election, would be deductible in computing the taxpayer's income (other than exempt income or income that is exempt from tax under this Part) for the particular year in respect of the borrowed money used for the exploration, development or acquisition of property, and

(e) the amount or part of the amount, as the case may be, is deemed to be Canadian exploration and development expenses, Canadian exploration expenses, Canadian development expenses, Canadian oil and gas property expenses, foreign resource expenses in respect of a country, or foreign exploration and development expenses, as the case may be, incurred by the taxpayer in the particular year.

[¶1482]

(5) Reassessments. Notwithstanding any other provision of this Act, where a taxpayer has made an election in accordance with the provisions of subsection (1) or (2), such reassessments of tax, interest or penalties shall be made as are necessary to give effect thereto.

* * *

[¶1488]

SECTION 24:

(1) Ceasing to carry on business. Notwithstanding paragraph 18(1)(b), where at any time after a taxpayer ceases to carry on a business the taxpayer no longer owns any property that was eligible capital property in respect of the business and that has value, in computing the taxpayer's income for taxation years ending after that time,

(a) there shall be deducted, for the first such taxation year, the amount of the taxpayer's cumulative eligible capital in respect of the business at that time;

(b) no amount may be deducted under paragraph 20(1)(b) in respect of the business;

(c) for the purposes of determining the value of P in the definition "cumulative eligible capital" in subsection 14(5), the amount deducted by the taxpayer under paragraph (a) shall be deemed to be an amount deducted under paragraph 20(1)(b) in computing the taxpayer's income from the business for the taxation year that included that time; and

(d) for the purposes of subsection 14(1), section 14 shall be read without reference to subsection 14(4).

[¶1490]

(2) Business carried on by spouse or controlled corporation. Notwithstanding subsection (1), where at any time an individual ceases to carry on a business and thereafter the individual's spouse or common-law partner, or a corporation controlled directly or indirectly in any manner whatever by the individual, carries on the business and acquires all of the property that was eligible capital property in respect of the business owned by the individual before that time and that had value at that time,

(a) in computing the individual's income for the individual's first taxation year ending after that time, subsection (1) shall be read without reference to paragraph $(1)(a)$ and the reference in paragraph $(1)(c)$ to "the amount deducted by the taxpayer under paragraph (a)" shall be read as a reference to "an amount equal to the taxpayer's cumulative eligible capital in respect of the business immediately before that time";

(b) in computing the cumulative eligible capital of the spouse or common-law partner or the corporation, as the case may be, in respect of the business, the spouse or common-law partner or corporation shall be deemed to have acquired an eligible capital property and to have made an eligible capital expenditure at that time at a cost equal to $^4/_3$ of the total of

(i) the cumulative eligible capital of the taxpayer in respect of the business immediately before that time, and

(ii) the amount, if any, determined for F in the definition "cumulative eligible capital" in subsection 14(5) in respect of the business of the individual at that time;

(c) for the purposes of determining the cumulative eligible capital in respect of the business of the spouse or common-law partner or corporation after that time, an amount equal to the amount determined under subparagraph (b)(ii) shall be added to the amount otherwise determined in respect thereof for P in the definition "cumulative eligible capital" in subsection 14(5); and

(d) for the purpose of determining after that time the amount required to be included under paragraph $14(1)(b)$ in computing the income of the spouse, the common-law partner or the corporation in respect of any subsequent disposition of property of the business, there shall be added to the amount otherwise determined for Q in the definition "cumulative eligible capital" in subsection 14(5) the amount, if any, determined for Q in that definition in respect of the business of the individual immediately before the individual ceased to carry on business.

[¶1491]

(3) Where partnership has ceased to exist. Notwithstanding subsection (1), where at any time a partnership ceases to exist in circumstances to which neither subsection 98(3) nor subsection 98(5) applies, there may be deducted, in computing the income for the first taxation year beginning after that time of a taxpayer who was a member of the partnership immediately before that time, an amount determined by the formula

$$A \times \frac{B}{C}$$

¶1491

where

A　is the amount that would, had the partnership continued to exist, have been deductible under subsection (1) in computing its income;

B　is the fair market value of the taxpayer's interest in the partnership immediately before that time; and

C　is the fair market value of all interests in the partnership immediately before that time.

* * *

[¶1496]

SECTION 36: Railway companies. Where any amount in respect of an expenditure incurred by a taxpayer on or in respect of the repair, replacement, alteration or renovation of depreciable property of the taxpayer of a prescribed class is, under a uniform classification and system of accounts and returns prescribed by the National Transportation Agency pursuant to the *Railway Act*, required to be entered in the books of the taxpayer otherwise than as an expense,

　　(a) no deduction may be made in respect of that expenditure in computing the income of the taxpayer for a taxation year; and

　　(b) for the purposes of section 13 and regulations made under paragraph 20(1)(a), the taxpayer shall be deemed to have acquired, at the time the expenditure was incurred, depreciable property of a class prescribed by regulation at a capital cost equal to that amount.

[¶1500]

SECTION 37:

　(1) Scientific research and experimental development. Where a taxpayer carried on a business in Canada in a taxation year, there may be deducted in computing the taxpayer's income from the business for the year such amount as the taxpayer claims not exceeding the amount, if any, by which the total of

　　(a) the total of all amounts each of which is an expenditure of a current nature made by the taxpayer in the year or in a preceding taxation year ending after 1973

　　　(i) on scientific research and experimental development carried on in Canada, directly undertaken by or on behalf of the taxpayer, and related to a business of the taxpayer,

　　　(i.1) by payments to a corporation resident in Canada to be used for scientific research and experimental development carried on in Canada that is related to a business of the taxpayer, but only where the taxpayer is entitled to exploit the results of that scientific research and experimental development,

　　　(ii) by payments to

¶1500

(A) an approved association that undertakes scientific research and experimental development,

(B) an approved university, college, research institute or other similar institution,

(C) a corporation resident in Canada and exempt from tax under paragraph $149(1)(j)$, or

(D) [Repealed by S.C. 1996, c. 21, s. 9(4).]

(E) an approved organization that makes payments to an association, institution or corporation described in any of clauses (A) to (C)

to be used for scientific research and experimental development carried on in Canada that is related to a business of the taxpayer, but only where the taxpayer is entitled to exploit the results of that scientific research and experimental development, or

(iii) where the taxpayer is a corporation, by payments to a corporation resident in Canada and exempt from tax because of paragraph $149(1)(j)$, for scientific research and experimental development that is basic research or applied research carried on in Canada

(A) the primary purpose of which is the use of results therefrom by the taxpayer in conjunction with other scientific research and experimental development activities undertaken or to be undertaken by or on behalf of the taxpayer that relate to a business of the taxpayer, and

(B) that has the technological potential for application to other businesses of a type unrelated to that carried on by the taxpayer

(b) the lesser of

(i) the total of all amounts each of which is an expenditure of a capital nature made by the taxpayer (in respect of property acquired that would be depreciable property of the taxpayer if this section were not applicable in respect of the property, other than land or a leasehold interest in land) in the year or in a preceding taxation year ending after 1958 on scientific research and experimental development carried on in Canada, directly undertaken by or on behalf of the taxpayer, and related to a business of the taxpayer, and

(ii) the undepreciated capital cost to the taxpayer of the property so acquired as of the end of the taxation year (before making any deduction under this paragraph in computing the income of the taxpayer for the taxation year),

(c) the total of all amounts each of which is an expenditure made by the taxpayer in the year or in a preceding taxation year ending after 1973 by way of repayment of amounts described in paragraph (d),

(c.1) all amounts included by virtue of paragraph $12(1)(v)$, in computing the taxpayer's income for any previous taxation year, and

¶1500

(c.2) all amounts added because of subsection 127(27), (29) or (34) to the taxpayer's tax otherwise payable under this Part for any preceding taxation year, and

(c.3) in the case of a partnership, all amounts each of which is an excess referred to in subsection 127(30) in respect of the partnership for any preceding fiscal period,

exceeds the total of

(d) the total of all amounts each of which is the amount of any government assistance or non-government assistance (within the meanings assigned to those expressions by subsection 127(9)) in respect of an expenditure described in paragraph (a) or (b) that, at the taxpayer's filing-due date for the year, the taxpayer has received, is entitled to receive or can reasonably be expected to receive,

(d.1) the total of all amounts each of which is the super-allowance benefit amount (within the meaning assigned by subsection 127(9)) for the year or for a preceding taxation year in respect of the taxpayer in respect of a province,

(e) that part of the total of all amounts each of which is an amount deducted under subsection 127(5) in computing the tax payable under this Part by the taxpayer for a preceding taxation year where the amount can reasonably be attributed to

(i) a prescribed proxy amount for a preceding taxation year,

(ii) an expenditure of a current nature incurred in a preceding taxation year that was a qualified expenditure incurred in that preceding year in respect of scientific research and experimental development for the purposes of section 127, or

(iii) an amount included because of paragraph 127(13)(e) in the taxpayer's SR&ED qualified expenditure pool at the end of a preceding taxation year within the meaning assigned by subsection 127(9),

(f) the total of all amounts each of which is an amount deducted under this subsection in computing the taxpayer's income for a preceding taxation year, except amounts described in subsection (6),

(f.1) the total of all amounts each of which is the lesser of

(i) the amount deducted under section 61.3 in computing the taxpayer's income for a preceding taxation year, and

(ii) the amount, if any, by which the amount that was deductible under this subsection in computing the taxpayer's income for that preceding year exceeds the amount claimed under this subsection in computing the taxpayer's income for that preceding year,

(g) the total of all amounts each of which is an amount equal to twice the amount claimed under subparagraph 194(2)(a)(ii) by the taxpayer for the year or any preceding taxation year, and

¶1500

(h) where the taxpayer is a corporation control of which has been acquired by a person or group of persons before the end of the year, the amount determined for the year under subsection (6.1) with respect to the corporation.

[¶1502]

(1.1) Business of related corporations.   Notwithstanding paragraph (8)(c), for the purposes of subsection (1), where a taxpayer is a corporation, scientific research and experimental development, related to a business carried on by another corporation to which the taxpayer is related (otherwise than by reason of a right referred to in paragraph 251(5)(b)) and in which that other corporation is actively engaged, at the time at which an expenditure or payment in respect of the scientific research and experimental development is made by the taxpayer, shall be considered to be related to a business of the taxpayer at that time.

[¶1504]

(1.2) Deemed time of capital expenditure.   For the purposes of paragraph (1)(b), an expenditure made by a taxpayer in respect of property shall be deemed not to have been made before the property is considered to have become available for use by the taxpayer.

[¶1506]

(1.3) SR&ED in the exclusive economic zone.   For the purposes of this section and section 127 of this Act and Part XXIX of the Income Tax Regulations, an expenditure is deemed to have been made by a taxpayer in Canada if the expenditure is

(a) made by the taxpayer in the course of a business carried on by the taxpayer in Canada; and

(b) made for the prosecution of scientific research and experimental development in the exclusive economic zone of Canada, within the meaning of the *Oceans Act*, or in the airspace above that zone or the seabed or subsoil below that zone.

[¶1508]

(2) Research outside Canada.   In computing the income of a taxpayer for a taxation year from a business of the taxpayer, there may be deducted expenditures of a current nature made by the taxpayer in the year

(a) on scientific research and experimental development carried on outside Canada, directly undertaken by or on behalf of the taxpayer, and related to the business; or

(b) by payments to an approved association, university, college, research institute or other similar institution to be used for scientific research and experimental development carried on outside Canada related to the business provided that the taxpayer is entitled to exploit the results of that scientific research and experimental development.

[¶1512]

(3) Minister may obtain advice. The Minister may obtain the advice of the Department of Industry, the National Research Council of Canada, the Defence Research Board or any other agency or department of the Government of Canada carrying on activities in the field of scientific research as to whether any particular activity constitutes scientific research and experimental development.

[¶1516]

(4) Where no deduction allowed under section. No deduction may be made under this section in respect of an expenditure made to acquire rights in, or arising out of, scientific research and experimental development.

[¶1520]

(5) Where no deduction allowed under ss. 110.1 and 118.1. Where, in respect of an expenditure on scientific research and experimental development made by a taxpayer in a taxation year, an amount is otherwise deductible under this section and under section 110.1 or 118.1, no deduction may be made in respect of the expenditure under section 110.1 or 118.1 in computing the taxable income of, or the tax payable by, the taxpayer for any taxation year.

[¶1524]

(6) Expenditures of a capital nature. An amount claimed under subsection (1) that may reasonably be considered to be in respect of a property described in paragraph $(1)(b)$ shall, for the purpose of section 13, be deemed to be an amount allowed to the taxpayer in respect of the property under regulations made under paragraph $20(1)(a)$, and for that purpose the property shall be deemed to be of a separate prescribed class.

[¶1528]

(6.1) Amount referred to in para. (1)(h). Where a taxpayer is a corporation control of which was last acquired by a person or group of persons at any time (in this subsection referred to as "that time") before the end of a taxation year of the corporation, the amount determined for the purposes of paragraph $(1)(h)$ for the year with respect to the corporation in respect of a business is the amount, if any, by which

(a) the amount, if any, by which

(i) the total of all amounts each of which is

(A) an expenditure described in paragraph $(1)(a)$ or (c) that was made by the corporation before that time,

(B) the lesser of the amounts determined in respect of the corporation under subparagraphs $(1)(b)(i)$ and (ii) immediately before that time, or

(C) an amount determined in respect of the corporation under paragraph $(1)(c.1)$ for its taxation year ending immediately before that time

exceeds the total of all amounts each of which is

(ii) the total of all amounts determined in respect of the corporation under paragraphs $(1)(d)$ to (g) for its taxation year ending immediately before that time, or

(iii) the amount deducted by virtue of subsection (1) in computing the corporation's income for its taxation year ending immediately before that time

exceeds

(b) the total of

(i) where the business to which the amounts described in clause $(a)(i)(A)$, (B) or (C) may reasonably be considered to have been related was carried on by the corporation for profit or with a reasonable expectation of profit throughout the year, the total of

(A) the corporation's income for the year from the business before making any deduction under subsection (1), and

(B) where properties were sold, leased, rented or developed, or services were rendered, in the course of carrying on the business before that time, the corporation's income for the year, before making any deduction under subsection (1), from any other business substantially all the income of which was derived from the sale, leasing, rental or development, as the case may be, of similar properties or the rendering of similar services, and

(ii) the total of all amounts each of which is an amount determined in respect of a preceding taxation year of the corporation that ended after that time equal to the lesser of

(A) the amount determined under subparagraph (i) with respect to the corporation in respect of the business for that preceding year, and

(B) the amount in respect of the business deducted by virtue of subsection (1) in computing the corporation's income for that preceding year.

[¶1532]

(7) Definitions.   In this section,

"approved" — "approved" means approved by the Minister after the Minister has, if the Minister considers it necessary, obtained the advice of the Department of Industry or the National Research Council of Canada.

¶1532

[¶1536]

(8) Interpretation. In this section,

(a) references to expenditures on or in respect of scientific research and experimental development

(i) where the references occur in subsection (2), include only

(A) expenditures each of which was an expenditure incurred for and all or substantially all of which was attributable to the prosecution of scientific research and experimental development, and

(B) expenditures of a current nature that were directly attributable, as determined by regulation, to the prosecution of scientific research and experimental development, and

(ii) where the references occur other than in subsection (2), include only

(A) expenditures incurred by a taxpayer in a taxation year (other than a taxation year for which the taxpayer has elected under clause (B)), each of which is

(I) an expenditure of a current nature all or substantially all of which was attributable to the prosecution, or to the provision of premises, facilities or equipment for the prosecution, of scientific research and experimental development in Canada,

(II) an expenditure of a current nature directly attributable, as determined by regulation, to the prosecution, or to the provision of premises, facilities or equipment for the prosecution, of scientific research and experimental development in Canada, or

(III) an expenditure of a capital nature that at the time it was incurred was for the provision of premises, facilities or equipment, where at that time it was intended

1. that it would be used during all or substantially all of its operating time in its expected useful life for, or

2. that all or substantially all of its value would be consumed in,

the prosecution of scientific research and experimental development in Canada, and

(B) where a taxpayer has elected in prescribed form and in accordance with subsection (10) for a taxation year, expenditures incurred by the taxpayer in the year each of which is

(I) an expenditure of a current nature for, and all or substantially all of which was attributable to, the lease of premises, facilities or equipment for the prosecution of scientific research and experimental development in Canada, other than an expenditure in respect of general purpose office equipment or furniture,

(II) an expenditure in respect of the prosecution of scientific research and experimental development in Canada directly undertaken on behalf of the taxpayer,

(III) an expenditure described in subclause (A)(III), other than an expenditure in respect of general purpose office equipment or furniture,

(IV) that portion of an expenditure made in respect of an expense incurred in the year for salary or wages of an employee who is directly engaged in scientific research and experimental development in Canada that can reasonably be considered to relate to such work having regard to the time spent by the employee thereon, and, for this purpose, where that portion is all or substantially all of the expenditure, that portion shall be deemed to be the amount of the expenditure,

(V) the cost of materials consumed in the prosecution of scientific research and experimental development in Canada, or

---

Pending Amendment

Non-Resident Trusts, Foreign Investment Entities, and Technical Amendments (July 18, 2005)

Subclause 37(8)(a)(ii)(B)(V) of the Act is replaced by the following:

> (V) the cost of materials consumed or transformed in the prosecution of scientific research and experimental development in Canada, or

Applicable: To costs incurred after February 23, 1998.

Explanatory Note: Paragraph 37(8)(a) of the Act provides rules for interpreting the expression "expenditures on or in respect of scientific research and experimental development" which is used in subsections 37(1), (2) and (5).

Clauses 37(8)(a)(ii)(B) provides for the alternative "proxy" method for determining SR&ED expenditures. Subclause 37(8)(a)(ii)(B)(V) provides that, in the context of the proxy method for determining SR&ED expenditures, the references to expenditures on or in respect of SR&ED (other than in subsection 37(2)) include only, among things listed in clause (8)(a)(ii)(B), the cost of "materials consumed" in the prosecution of SR&ED in Canada.

Subclause 37(8)(a)(ii)(B)(V) is amended for costs incurred after February 23, 1998 in two respects. First, the phrase "materials consumed" is changed to "materials consumed or transformed".

(VI) $\frac{1}{2}$ of any other expenditure of a current nature in respect of the lease of premises, facilities or equipment used primarily for the prosecution of scientific research and experimental development in Canada, other than an expenditure in respect of general purpose office equipment or furniture;

(b) for greater certainty, references to scientific research and experimental development related to a business include any scientific

¶1536

research and experimental development that may lead to or facilitate an extension of that business;

(*c*) except in the case of a taxpayer who derives all or substantially all of the taxpayer's revenue from the prosecution of scientific research and experimental development (including the sale of rights arising out of scientific research and experimental development carried on by the taxpayer), the prosecution of scientific research and experimental development shall not be considered to be a business of the taxpayer to which scientific research and experimental development is related; and

(*d*) notwithstanding paragraph (*a*), references to expenditures on or in respect of scientific research and experimental development shall not include

(i) any capital expenditure made in respect of the acquisition of a building, other than a prescribed special-purpose building, including a leasehold interest therein,

(ii) any outlay or expense made or incurred for the use of, or the right to use, a building other than a prescribed special-purpose building, and

(iii) payments made by a taxpayer to

(A) a corporation resident in Canada and exempt from tax under paragraph 149(1)(*j*), an approved research institute or an approved association, with which the taxpayer does not deal at arm's length,

(B) a corporation other than a corporation referred to in clause (A), or

(C) an approved university, college or organization

to be used for scientific research and experimental development

(D) in the case of such a payment to a person described in clause (A) or (B), to the extent that the amount of the payment may reasonably be considered to have been made to enable the recipient to acquire a building or a leasehold interest in a building or to pay an amount in respect of the rental expense in respect of a building, and

(E) in the case of a payment to a person described in clause (C), to the extent that the amount of the payment may reasonably be considered to have been made to enable the recipient to acquire a building, or a leasehold interest in a building, in which the taxpayer has, or may reasonably be expected to acquire, an interest.

¶1536

Pending Amendment

Non-Resident Trusts, Foreign Investment Entities, and Technical Amendments (July 18, 2005)

Clause 37(8)(d)(iii)(E) of the English version of the Act is replaced by the following:

> (E) in the case of a payment to a person described in clause (C), to the extent that the amount of the payment may reasonably be considered to have been made to enable the recipient to acquire a building, or a leasehold interest in a building, in which the taxpayer has, or may reasonably be expected to acquire, an interest or, for civil law, a right.

Applicable: Royal Assent.

Explanatory Note: [See the Explanatory Note re amendments related to bijuralism following the amendment to subsection 13(5.2).]

[¶1538]

(9) Salary or wages.   For the purposes of clauses $(8)(a)(\text{ii})(A)$ and (B), an expenditure of a taxpayer does not include remuneration based on profits or a bonus, where the remuneration or bonus, as the case may be, is in respect of a specified employee of the taxpayer.

[¶1540]

(9.1) Limitation re specified employees.   For the purposes of clauses $(8)(a)(\text{ii})(A)$ and (B), expenditures incurred by a taxpayer in a taxation year do not include expenses incurred in the year in respect of salary or wages of a specified employee of the taxpayer to the extent that those expenses exceed the amount determined by the formula

$$A \times B/365$$

where

A   is 5 times the Year's Maximum Pensionable Earnings (as determined under section 18 of the *Canada Pension Plan*) for the calendar year in which the taxation year ends; and

B   is the number of days in the taxation year on which the employee is a specified employee of the taxpayer.

[¶1542]

(9.2) Associated corporations.   Where

(a) in a taxation year of a corporation that ends in a calendar year, the corporation employs an individual who is a specified employee of the corporation,

(b) the corporation is associated with another corporation (in this subsection and subsection (9.3) referred to as the "associated corporation") in a taxation year of the associated corporation that ends in the calendar year, and

(c) the individual is a specified employee of the associated corporation in the taxation year of the associated corporation that ends in the calendar year,

for the purposes of clauses $(8)(a)(ii)(A)$ and (B), the expenditures incurred by the corporation in its taxation year or years that end in the calendar year and by each associated corporation in its taxation year or years that end in the calendar year do not include expenses incurred in those taxation years in respect of salary or wages of the specified employee unless the corporation and all of the associated corporations have filed with the Minister an agreement referred to in subsection (9.3) in respect of those years.

[¶1544]

(9.3) Agreement among associated corporations. Where all of the members of a group of associated corporations of which an individual is a specified employee file, in respect of their taxation years that end in a particular calendar year, an agreement with the Minister in which they allocate an amount in respect of the individual to one or more of them for those years and the amount so allocated or the total of the amounts so allocated, as the case may be, does not exceed the amount determined by the formula

$$A \times B/365$$

where

A is 5 times the Year's Maximum Pensionable Earnings (as determined under section 18 of the *Canada Pension Plan*) for the particular calendar year, and

B is the lesser of 365 and the number of days in those taxation years on which the individual was a specified employee of one or more of the corporations,

the maximum amount that may be claimed in respect of salary or wages of the individual for the purposes of clauses $(8)(a)(ii)(A)$ and (B) by each of the corporations for each of those years is the amount so allocated to it for each of those years.

[¶1546]

(9.4) Filing. An agreement referred to in subsection (9.3) is deemed not to have been filed by a taxpayer unless

(a) it is in prescribed form; and

(b) where the taxpayer is a corporation, it is accompanied by

(i) where its directors are legally entitled to administer its affairs, a certified copy of their resolution authorizing the agreement to be made, and

(ii) where its directors are not legally entitled to administer its affairs, a certified copy of the document by which the person legally entitled to administer its affairs authorized the agreement to be made.

[¶1548]

(9.5) Deemed corporation. For the purposes of subsections (9.2) and (9.3) and this subsection, each

(a) individual related to a particular corporation,

(b) partnership of which a majority interest partner is

(i) an individual related to a particular corporation, or

(ii) a corporation associated with a particular corporation, and

(c) limited partnership of which a member whose liability as a member is not limited is

(i) an individual related to a particular corporation, or

(ii) a corporation associated with a particular corporation,

is deemed to be a corporation associated with the particular corporation.

[¶1550]

(10) Time for election. Any election made under clause $(8)(a)(ii)(B)$ for a taxation year by a taxpayer shall be filed by the taxpayer on the day on which the taxpayer first files a prescribed form referred to in subsection (11) for the year.

[¶1551]

(11) Filing requirement. Subject to subsection (12), no amount in respect of an expenditure that would be incurred by a taxpayer in a taxation year that begins after 1995 if this Act were read without reference to subsection 78(4) may be deducted under subsection (1) unless the taxpayer files with the Minister a prescribed form containing prescribed information in respect of the expenditure on or before the day that is 12 months after the taxpayer's filing-due date for the year.

[¶1552]

(12) Misclassified expenditures. If a taxpayer has not filed a prescribed form in respect of an expenditure in accordance with subsection (11), for the purposes of this Act, the expenditure is deemed not to be an expenditure on or in respect of scientific research and experimental development.

[¶1553]

(13) Non-arm's length contract — linked work. For the purposes of this section and sections 127 and 127.1, where

(a) work is performed by a taxpayer for a person or partnership at a time when the person or partnership does not deal at arm's length with the taxpayer, and

(b) the work would be scientific research and experimental development if it were performed by the person or partnership, the work is deemed to be scientific research and experimental development.

* * *

[¶1554]

SECTION 65:

(1) **Allowance for oil or gas well, mine or timber limit.** There may be deducted in computing a taxpayer's income for a taxation year such amount as an allowance, if any, in respect of

(a) a natural accumulation of petroleum or natural gas, oil or gas well, mineral resource or timber limit,

(b) the processing of ore (other than iron ore or tar sands) from a mineral resource to any stage that is not beyond the prime metal stage or its equivalent,

(c) the processing of iron ore from a mineral resource to any stage that is not beyond the pellet stage or its equivalent, or

(d) the processing of tar sands from a mineral resource to any stage that is not beyond the crude oil stage or its equivalent

as is allowed to the taxpayer by regulation.

[¶1555]

(2) **Regulations.** For greater certainty it is hereby declared that, in the case of a regulation made under subsection (1) allowing to a taxpayer an amount in respect of a natural accumulation of petroleum or natural gas, an oil or gas well or a mineral resource or in respect of the processing of ore,

(a) there may be allowed to the taxpayer by that regulation an amount in respect of any or all

(i) natural accumulations of petroleum or natural gas, oil or gas wells or mineral resources in which the taxpayer has any interest, or

---

Pending Amendment

Non-Resident Trusts, Foreign Investment Entities, and Technical Amendments (July 18, 2005)

Subparagraph 65(2)(a)(i) of the Act is replaced by the following:

(i) natural accumulations of petroleum or natural gas, oil or gas wells or mineral resources in which the taxpayer has any interest or, for civil law, right, or

Applicable: Royal Assent.

Explanatory Note: [See the Explanatory Note re amendments related to bijuralism following the amendment to subsection 13(5.2).]

(ii) processing operations described in any of paragraphs (1)(*b*), (*c*) and (*d*) that are carried on by the taxpayer; and

(*b*) notwithstanding any other provision contained in this Act, the Governor in Council may prescribe the formula by which the amount that may be allowed to the taxpayer by that regulation shall be determined.

[¶1556]

(3) Lessee's share of allowance.   Where a deduction is allowed under subsection (1) in respect of a coal mine operated by a lessee, the lessor and lessee may agree as to what portion of the allowance each may deduct and, in the event that they cannot agree, the Minister may fix the portions.

[¶1557]

SECTION 67.3:   Limitation re cost of leasing passenger vehicle.   Notwithstanding any other section of this Act, where

(*a*) in a taxation year all or part of the actual lease charges in respect of a passenger vehicle are paid or payable, directly or indirectly, by a taxpayer, and

(*b*) in computing the taxpayer's income for the year an amount may be deducted in respect of those charges,

in determining the amount that may be so deducted, the total of those charges shall be deemed not to exceed the lesser of

(*c*) the amount determined by the formula

$$\frac{(A \times B)}{30} - C - D - E$$

where

A   is $600 or such other amount as is prescribed,

B   is the number of days in the period commencing at the beginning of the term of the lease and ending at the earlier of the end of the year and the end of the lease,

C   is the total of all amounts deducted in computing the taxpayer's income for preceding taxation years in respect of the actual lease charges in respect of the vehicle,

D   is the amount of interest that would be earned on the part of the total of all refundable amounts in respect of the lease that exceeds $1,000 if interest were

(i) payable on the refundable amounts at the prescribed rate, and

(ii) computed for the period before the end of the year during which the refundable amounts were outstanding, and

E　is the total of all reimbursements that became receivable before the end of the year by the taxpayer in respect of the lease, and

(d) the amount determined by the formula

$$\frac{(A \times B)}{.85C} - D - E$$

where

A　is the total of the actual lease charges in respect of the lease incurred in respect of the year or the total of the actual lease charges in respect of the lease paid in the year (depending on the method regularly followed by the taxpayer in computing income),

B　is $20,000 or such other amount as is prescribed,

C　is the greater of $23,529 (or such other amount as is prescribed) and the manufacturer's list price for the vehicle,

D　is the amount of interest that would be earned on that part of the total of all refundable amounts paid in respect of the lease that exceeds $1,000 if interest were

(i) payable on the refundable amounts at the prescribed rate, and

(ii) computed for the period in the year during which the refundable amounts are outstanding, and

E　is the total of all reimbursements that became receivable during the year by the taxpayer in respect of the lease.

* * *

[¶1560]

SECTION 69:

(1) Inadequate considerations.　Except as expressly otherwise provided in this Act,

(a) where a taxpayer has acquired anything from a person with whom the taxpayer was not dealing at arm's length at an amount in excess of the fair market value thereof at the time the taxpayer so acquired it, the taxpayer shall be deemed to have acquired it at that fair market value;

(b) where a taxpayer has disposed of anything

(i) to a person with whom the taxpayer was not dealing at arm's length for no proceeds or for proceeds less than the fair market value thereof at the time the taxpayer so disposed of it,

(ii) to any person by way of gift *inter vivos*, or

(iii) to a trust because of a disposition of a property that does not result in a change in the beneficial ownership of the property; and

---

Pending Amendment

Non-Resident Trusts, Foreign Investment Entities, and Technical Amendments (July 18, 2005)

Paragraph 69(1)(*b*) of the English version of the Act is amended by striking out the word "and" at the end of subparagraph (iii).

Applicable: To dispositions that occur after December 23, 1998.

Explanatory Note: Subsection 69(1) of the Act provides rules that deal with gifts and non-arm's length dispositions of property, except where such transactions are expressly covered by other provisions in the Act that apply to the gift or other disposition. The English version of subparagraph 69(1)(*b*)(iii) is amended to correct an editorial error, by deleting the word "and" at the end of the subparagraph.

This amendment applies to dispositions that occur after December 23, 1998.

---

the taxpayer shall be deemed to have received proceeds of disposition therefor equal to that fair market value; and

(*c*) where a taxpayer acquires a property by way of gift, bequest or inheritance or because of a disposition that does not result in a change in the beneficial ownership of the property, the taxpayer is deemed to acquire the property at its fair market value.

[¶1562]

(1.1) Idem, where s. 70(3) applies.   Where a taxpayer has acquired property that is a right or thing to which subsection 70(3) applies, the following rules apply:

(*a*) paragraph (1)(*c*) is not applicable to that property; and

(*b*) the taxpayer shall be deemed to have acquired the property at a cost equal to the total of

(i) such part, if any, of the cost thereof to the taxpayer who has died as had not been deducted by the taxpayer in computing the taxpayer's income for any year, and

(ii) any expenditures made or incurred by the taxpayer to acquire the property.

* * *

[¶1568]

SECTION 70:

* * *

(5) Capital property of a deceased taxpayer. Where in a taxation year a taxpayer dies,

(a) the taxpayer shall be deemed to have, immediately before the taxpayer's death, disposed of each capital property of the taxpayer and received proceeds of disposition therefor equal to the fair market value of the property immediately before the death;

(b) any person who as a consequence of the taxpayer's death acquires any property that is deemed by paragraph (a) to have been disposed of by the taxpayer shall be deemed to have acquired it at the time of the death at a cost equal to its fair market value immediately before the death;

(c) where any depreciable property of the taxpayer of a prescribed class that is deemed by paragraph (a) to have been disposed of is acquired by any person as a consequence of the taxpayer's death (other than where the taxpayer's proceeds of disposition of the property under paragraph (a) are redetermined under subsection 13(21.1)) and the amount that was the capital cost to the taxpayer of the property exceeds the amount determined under paragraph (b) to be the cost to the person thereof, for the purposes of sections 13 and 20 and any regulations made for the purpose of paragraph 20(1)(a),

(i) the capital cost to the person of the property shall be deemed to be the amount that was the capital cost to the taxpayer of the property, and

(ii) the excess shall be deemed to have been allowed to the person in respect of the property under regulations made for the purpose of paragraph 20(1)(a) in computing income for taxation years that ended before the person acquired the property; and

(d) where a property of the taxpayer that was deemed by paragraph (a) to have been disposed of is acquired by any person as a consequence of the taxpayer's death and the taxpayer's proceeds of disposition of the property under paragraph (a) are redetermined under subsection 13(21.1), notwithstanding paragraph (b),

(i) where the property was depreciable property of a prescribed class and the amount that was the capital cost to the taxpayer of the property exceeds the amount so redetermined under subsection 13(21.1), for the purposes of sections 13 and 20 and any regulations made for the purpose of paragraph 20(1)(a),

(A) its capital cost to the person shall be deemed to be the amount that was its capital cost to the taxpayer, and

(B) the excess shall be deemed to have been allowed to the person in respect of the property under regulations made for the purpose of paragraph $20(1)(a)$ in computing income for taxation years that ended before the person acquired the property, and

(ii) where the property is land (other than land to which subparagraph (i) applies), its cost to the person shall be deemed to be the amount that was the taxpayer's proceeds of disposition of the land as redetermined under subsection 13(21.1).

[¶1570]

(5.1) Eligible capital property of deceased.   Notwithstanding subsection 24(1), where at any time a taxpayer dies and any person (in this subsection referred to as the beneficiary), as a consequence of the taxpayer's death, acquires an eligible capital property of the taxpayer in respect of a business carried on by the taxpayer immediately before that time (otherwise than by way of a distribution of property by a trust that claimed a deduction under paragraph $20(1)(b)$ in respect of the property or in circumstances to which subsection 24(2) applies),

(a) the taxpayer shall be deemed to have disposed of the property, immediately before the taxpayer's death, for proceeds equal to $4/3$ of that proportion of the cumulative eligible capital of the taxpayer in respect of the business that the fair market value immediately before that time of the property is of the fair market value immediately before that time of all of the eligible capital property of the taxpayer in respect of the business;

(b) subject to paragraph (c), the beneficiary shall be deemed to have acquired a capital property at the time of the taxpayer's death at a cost equal to the proceeds referred to in paragraph (a);

(c) where the beneficiary continues to carry on the business previously carried on by the taxpayer, the beneficiary shall be deemed to have, at the time of the taxpayer's death, acquired an eligible capital property and made an eligible capital expenditure at a cost equal to the total of

(i) the proceeds referred to in paragraph (a), and

(ii) $4/3$ of that proportion of the amount, if any, determined for F in the definition "cumulative eligible capital" in subsection 14(5) in respect of the business of the taxpayer at that time that the fair market value immediately before that time of the particular property is of the fair market value immediately before that time of all eligible capital property of the taxpayer in respect of the business,

and, for the purposes of determining at any time the beneficiary's cumulative eligible capital in respect of the business, an amount equal to $3/4$ of the amount determined under subparagraph (ii) shall be added to the amount otherwise determined, in respect of the business, for P in the definition "cumulative eligible capital" in subsection 14(5); and

(d) for the purpose of determining, after that time, the amount required by paragraph $14(1)(b)$ to be included in computing the income of the beneficiary in respect of any subsequent disposition of the property of the business, there shall be added to the amount determined for Q in the definition "cumulative eligible capital" in subsection 14(5) the amount determined by the formula

$$A \times \frac{B}{C}$$

where

A   is the amount, if any, determined for Q in that definition in respect of the business of the taxpayer immediately before that time,

B   is the fair market value immediately before that time of the particular property, and

C   is the fair market value immediately before that time of all eligible capital property of the taxpayer in respect of the business.

* * *

[¶1574]

(9) Transfer of farm property to child.   If any land in Canada or depreciable property in Canada of a prescribed class of a taxpayer to which subsection (5) would otherwise apply was, before the taxpayer's death, used principally in a farming business in which the taxpayer, the taxpayer's spouse or common-law partner or any of the taxpayer's children was actively engaged on a regular and continuous basis (or, in the case of property used in the operation of a woodlot, was engaged to the extent required by a prescribed forest management plan in respect of that woodlot), the property is, as a consequence of the death, transferred or distributed to a child of the taxpayer who was resident in Canada immediately before the death and it can be shown, within the period ending 36 months after the death or, if written application that this subsection apply has been made to the Minister by the taxpayer's legal representative within that period, within any longer period that the Minister considers reasonable in the circumstances, that the property has vested indefeasibly in the child,

(a) paragraphs (5)(a) and (b) do not apply in respect of the property,

(b) the taxpayer shall be deemed to have, immediately before the taxpayer's death, disposed of the property and received proceeds of disposition therefor equal to

(i) where the property was depreciable property of a prescribed class, the lesser of the capital cost and the cost amount to the taxpayer of the property immediately before the death, and

(ii) where the property is land (other than land to which subparagraph (i) applies), its adjusted cost base to the taxpayer immediately before the death,

and the child shall be deemed to have acquired the property at the time of the death at a cost equal to those proceeds, and

(c) where the property was depreciable property of a prescribed class, paragraphs (5)(c) and (d) apply as if the references therein to "paragraph (a)" and "paragraph (b)" were read as "paragraph (9)(b)",

except that, where the taxpayer's legal representative so elects in the taxpayer's return of income under this Part for the year in which the taxpayer died, paragraph (b) shall be read as follows:

"(b) the taxpayer shall be deemed to have, immediately before the taxpayer's death, disposed of the property and received proceeds of disposition therefor equal to such amount as the legal representative elects in the taxpayer's return of income under this Part for the year in which the taxpayer died, not greater than the greater of nor less than the lesser of

(i) where the property was depreciable property of a prescribed class,

(A) its fair market value immediately before the death, and

(B) the lesser of the capital cost and the cost amount to the taxpayer of the property immediately before the death, and

(ii) where the property is land (other than land to which subparagraph (i) applies),

(A) its fair market value immediately before the death, and

(B) its adjusted cost base to the taxpayer immediately before the death,

and the child shall be deemed to have acquired the property at the time of the death at a cost equal to those proceeds, except that for the purpose of this paragraph, where the elected amount exceeds the greater of the amounts determined under clauses (i)(A) and (B) or (ii)(A) and (B), as the case may be, it shall be deemed to be equal to the greater thereof, and where the elected amount is less than the lesser of the amounts determined under clauses (i)(A) and (B) or (ii)(A) and (B), as the case may be, it shall be deemed to be equal to the lesser thereof, and".

[¶1576]

(9.1) Transfer of farm property from trust to settlor's children. Where any property in Canada of a taxpayer that is land or depreciable property of a prescribed class has been transferred or distributed to a trust described in subsection (6) or 73(1) (as that subsection applied to transfers before 2000) or a trust to which subparagraph 73(1.01)(c)(i) applies and the property or a replacement property for that property in respect of which the trust has made an election under subsection 13(4) or 44(1) was, immediately before the death of the taxpayer's spouse or common-law partner who was a beneficiary under the trust, used in the business of farming and has, on the death of the spouse or common-law partner and as a consequence of the death, been transferred or distributed to and vested indefeasibly in an individual who was a child of the taxpayer and who was resident in Canada immediately before the death of the spouse or common-law partner, the following rules apply:

(*a*) subsections 104(4) and (5) do not apply to the trust in respect of the property,

(*b*) the trust shall be deemed to have, immediately before the spouse's or common-law partner's death, disposed of the property and received proceeds of disposition therefor equal to

(i) where the property was depreciable property of a prescribed class, the lesser of the capital cost and the cost amount to the trust of the property immediately before the death, and

(ii) where the property is land (other than land to which subparagraph (i) applies), its adjusted cost base to the trust immediately before the death,

and the child shall be deemed to have acquired the property at the time of the death at a cost equal to those proceeds,

(*c*) where any depreciable property of a prescribed class that is deemed by paragraph (*b*) to have been disposed of by the trust is acquired by a child of the taxpayer as a consequence of the spouse's or common-law partner's death (other than where the trust's proceeds of disposition of the property under paragraph (*b*) are redetermined under subsection 13(21.1)) and the amount that was the capital cost to the trust of the property exceeds the amount determined under paragraph (*b*) to be the cost to the child of the property, for the purposes of sections 13 and 20 and any regulations made for the purpose of paragraph 20(1)(*a*),

(i) its capital cost to the child shall be deemed to be the amount that was its capital cost to the trust, and

(ii) the excess shall be deemed to have been allowed to the child in respect of the property under regulations made for the purpose of paragraph 20(1)(*a*) in computing income for taxation years that ended before the child acquired the property, and

(*d*) where the property of the trust that is deemed by paragraph (*b*) to have been disposed of is acquired by a child of the taxpayer as a consequence of the spouse's or common-law partner's death and the trust's proceeds of disposition of the property under paragraph (*b*) are redetermined under subsection 13(21.1), notwithstanding paragraph (*b*),

(i) where the property was depreciable property of a prescribed class and the amount that was its capital cost to the trust exceeds the amount so redetermined under subsection 13(21.1), for the purposes of sections 13 and 20 and any regulations made for the purpose of paragraph 20(1)(*a*),

(A) its capital cost to the child shall be deemed to be the amount that was its capital cost to the trust, and

¶1576

(B) the excess shall be deemed to have been allowed to the child in respect of the property under regulations made for the purpose of paragraph $20(1)(a)$ in computing income for taxation years that ended before the child acquired the property, and

(ii) where the property is land (other than land to which subparagraph (i) applies), its cost to the child shall be deemed to be the amount that was the trust's proceeds of disposition as redetermined under subsection 13(21.1),

except that, where the trust so elects in its return of income under this Part for its taxation year in which the spouse or common-law partner died, paragraph (b) shall be read as follows:

" (b) the trust shall be deemed to have, immediately before the spouse's or common-law partner's death, disposed of the property and received proceeds of disposition therefor equal to such amount as the trust elects in its return of income under this Part for the year in which the spouse or common-law partner died, not greater than the greater of nor less than the lesser of

(i) where the property was depreciable property of a prescribed class,

(A) its fair market value immediately before the death, and

(B) the lesser of the capital cost and the cost amount to the trust of the property immediately before the death, and

(ii) where the property is land (other than land to which subparagraph (i) applies),

(A) its fair market value immediately before the death, and

(B) its adjusted cost base to the trust immediately before the death,

and the child shall be deemed to have acquired the property at the time of the death at a cost equal to those proceeds, except that for the purpose of this paragraph, where the elected amount exceeds the greater of the amounts determined under clauses (i)(A) and (B) or (ii)(A) and (B), as the case may be, it shall be deemed to be equal to the greater thereof, and where the elected amount is less than the lesser of the amounts determined under clauses (i)(A) and (B) or (ii)(A) and (B), as the case may be, it shall be deemed to be equal to the lesser thereof, ".

* * *

[¶1580]

(10) Definitions. In this section,

[¶1581]

"child" — "child" of a taxpayer includes

(a) a child of the taxpayer's child,

(*b*) a child of the taxpayer's child's child, and

(*c*) a person who, at any time before the person attained the age of 19 years, was wholly dependent on the taxpayer for support and of whom the taxpayer had, at that time, in law or in fact, the custody and control;

[¶1582]

"interest in a family farm partnership" — "interest in a family farm partnership" of a person at a particular time means an interest owned by the person at that time in a partnership where, at that time, all or substantially all of the fair market value of the property of the partnership was attributable to

(*a*) property that has been used by

(i) the partnership,

(ii) the person,

(iii) a spouse, common-law partner, child or parent of the person, or

(iv) a corporation a share of the capital stock of which was a share of the capital stock of a family farm corporation of the person or of a spouse, common-law partner, child or parent of the person,

principally in the course of carrying on a farming business in Canada in which the person or a spouse, common-law partner, child or parent of the person was actively engaged on a regular and continuous basis (or, in the case of property used in the operation of a woodlot, was engaged to the extent required by a prescribed forest management plan in respect of that woodlot),

(*b*) shares of the capital stock or indebtedness of one or more corporations all or substantially all of the fair market value of the property of which was attributable to property described in paragraph (*c*), or

(*c*) properties described in paragraph (*a*) or (*b*).

[¶1583]

"share of the capital stock of a family farm corporation" — "share of the capital stock of a family farm corporation" of a person at a particular time means a share of the capital stock of a corporation owned by the person at that time where, at that time, all or substantially all of the fair market value of the property owned by the corporation was attributable to

(*a*) property that has been used by

(i) the corporation or any other corporation, a share of the capital stock of which was a share of the capital stock of a family farm corporation of the person or of a spouse, common-law partner, child or parent of the person,

(i.1) a corporation controlled by a corporation referred to in subparagraph (i),

(ii) the person,

(iii) a spouse, common-law partner, child or parent of the person, or

(iv) a partnership, an interest in which was an interest in a family farm partnership of the person or of a spouse, common-law partner, child or parent of the person,

principally in the course of carrying on a farming business in Canada in which the person or a spouse, common-law partner, child or parent of the person was actively engaged on a regular and continuous basis (or, in the case of property used in the operation of a woodlot, was engaged to the extent required by a prescribed forest management plan in respect of that woodlot),

(b) shares of the capital stock or indebtedness of one or more corporations all or substantially all of the fair market value of the property of which was attributable to property described in paragraph (c), or

(c) properties described in paragraph (a) or (b).

* * *

[¶1584]

SECTION 73:

(1) *Inter vivos* transfers by individuals. For the purposes of this Part, where at any time any particular capital property of an individual (other than a trust) has been transferred in circumstances to which subsection (1.01) applies and both the individual and the transferee are resident in Canada at that time, unless the individual elects in the individual's return of income under this Part for the taxation year in which the property was transferred that the provisions of this subsection not apply, the particular property is deemed

---

Pending Amendment

Non-Resident Trusts, Foreign Investment Entities, and Technical Amendments (July 18, 2005)

The portion of subsection 73(1) of the Act before paragraph (a) is replaced by the following:

SECTION 73:

(1) *Inter vivos* transfers by individuals. For the purposes of this Part, where at any time any particular capital property (other than a specified participating interest) of an individual (other than a trust) has been transferred in circumstances to which subsection (1.01) applies and both the individual and the transferee are resident in Canada at that time, unless the individual elects in the individual's return of income under this Part for the taxation year in which the property was transferred that the provisions of this subsection not apply, the particular property is deemed

Applicable: To transfers that occur in taxation years that begin after 2002.

Explanatory Note: Subsection 73(1) of the Act generally provides for a tax-deferred disposition of capital property by an individual (other than a trust) where it is transferred by the individual in circumstances where subsection 73(1.01) applies and a number of other conditions are met.

Subsection 73(1) is amended so that it does not apply to a transfer of property that is a specified participating interest. The concept of a specified participating interest is generally relevant in the context of the foreign investment entity rules in sections 94.1 to 94.4. For more information on the definition "specified participating interest" in subsection 248(1), see the commentary on that definition.

This amendment applies to transfers that occur in taxation years that begin after 2002.

(a) to have been disposed of at that time by the individual for proceeds equal to,

(i) where the particular property is depreciable property of a prescribed class, that proportion of the undepreciated capital cost to the individual immediately before that time of all property of that class that the fair market value immediately before that time of the particular property is of the fair market value immediately before that time of all of that property of that class, and

(ii) in any other case, the adjusted cost base to the individual of the particular property immediately before that time; and

(b) to have been acquired at that time by the transferee for an amount equal to those proceeds.

Pending Amendment

Non-Resident Trusts, Foreign Investment Entities, and Technical Amendments (July 18, 2005)

Paragraph 53(2)(a) of the *Income Tax Amendments Act, 2000* [S.C. 2001, c. 17] is replaced by the following:

(a) in respect of transfers that occur in 2000, 2001 or 2002, for the purpose of subsection 73(1) of the Act, as enacted by subsection (1), the residence of a transferee trust shall be determined without reference to section 94 of the Act, as it reads in its application to taxation years that began before 2003;

Applicable: Deemed to have come into force on June 14, 2001.

Explanatory Note: Technical Amendments to the *Income Tax Amendments Act, 2000* (S.C. 2001, c. 17, 53(2)(a))

Subsection 73(1) of the *Income Tax Act* generally provides for a tax-free disposition of capital property if it is transferred by an individual to the individual's spouse, common-law partner or a trust for the exclusive benefit of the spouse or common-law partner during the lifetime of the spouse or common-law partner. For subsection 73(1) to apply, the transferor and transferee must both be resident in Canada at the time of the transfer. Where the transferee is a trust, in respect of transfers that occur in 2000 or

¶1584

2001, the residency requirement is determined without reference to subsection 94(1) as it read before 2002.

This amendment to the *Income Tax Amendments Act, 2000*, ensures that, in applying subsection 73(1) in respect of transfers that occur in 2000, 2001 or 2002, the residence of a transferee will be determined without reference to section 94 of the Act, as it reads in its application to taxation years that began before 2003.

This amendment is deemed to come into force on June 14, 2001.

[¶1586]

(1.01) Qualifying transfers. Subject to subsection (1.02), property is transferred by an individual in circumstances to which this subsection applies where it is transferred to

(*a*) the individual's spouse or common-law partner;

(*b*) a former spouse or common-law partner of the individual in settlement of rights arising out of their marriage or common-law partnership; or

(*c*) a trust created by the individual under which

(i) the individual's spouse or common-law partner is entitled to receive all of the income of the trust that arises before the spouse's or common-law partner's death and no person except the spouse or common-law partner may, before the spouse's or common-law partner's death, receive or otherwise obtain the use of any of the income or capital of the trust,

(ii) the individual is entitled to receive all of the income of the trust that arises before the individual's death and no person except the individual may, before the individual's death, receive or otherwise obtain the use of any of the income or capital of the trust, or

(iii) either

(A) the individual or the individual's spouse is, in combination with the other, entitled to receive all of the income of the trust that arises before the later of the death of the individual and the death of the spouse and no other person may, before the later of those deaths, receive or otherwise obtain the use of any of the income or capital of the trust, or

(B) the individual or the individual's common-law partner is, in combination with the other, entitled to receive all of the income of the trust that arises before the later of the death of the individual and the death of the common-law partner and no other person may, before the later of those deaths, receive or otherwise obtain the use of any of the income or capital of the trust.

[¶1588]

(1.02) Exception for transfers. Subsection (1.01) applies to a transfer of property by an individual to a trust the terms of which satisfy the conditions in subparagraph (1.01)(*c*)(ii) or (iii) only where

(a) the trust was created after 1999;

(b) either

(i) the individual had attained 65 years of age at the time the trust was created, or

(ii) the transfer does not result in a change in beneficial ownership of the property and there is immediately after the transfer no absolute or contingent right of a person (other than the individual) or partnership as a beneficiary (determined with reference to subsection 104(1.1)) under the trust; and

(c) in the case of a trust the terms of which satisfy the conditions in subparagraph (1.01)(*c*)(ii), the trust does not make an election under subparagraph 104(4)(*a*)(ii.1).

[¶1590]

(1.1) Interpretation. For greater certainty, a property is, for the purposes of subsections (1) and (1.01), deemed to be property of the individual referred to in subsection (1) that has been transferred to a particular transferee where,

(a) under the laws of a province or because of a decree, order or judgment of a competent tribunal made in accordance with those laws, the property

(i) is acquired or is deemed to have been acquired by the particular transferee,

(ii) is deemed or declared to be property of, or is awarded to, the particular transferee, or

(iii) has vested in the particular transferee; and

(b) the property was or would, but for those laws, have been a capital property of the individual referred to in subsection (1).

[¶1596]

(2) Capital cost and amount deemed allowed to spouse, etc., or trust. Where a transferee is deemed by subsection (1) to have acquired any particular depreciable property of a prescribed class of a taxpayer for an amount determined under paragraph (1)(*e*) and the capital cost to the taxpayer of the particular property exceeds the amount determined under that paragraph, for the purposes of sections 13 and 20 and any regulations made under paragraph 20(1)(*a*)

(a) the capital cost to the transferee of the particular property shall be deemed to be the amount that was the capital cost to the taxpayer thereof; and

(b) the excess shall be deemed to have been allowed to the transferee in respect of the particular property under regulations made under paragraph $20(1)(a)$ in computing income for taxation years before the acquisition thereof.

Pending Amendment

Non-Resident Trusts, Foreign Investment Entities, and Technical Amendments (July 18, 2005)

Subsection 73(2) of the Act is replaced by the following:

(2) Capital cost and amount deemed allowed to spouse, etc., or trust. If a transferee is deemed by subsection (1) to have acquired any particular depreciable property of a prescribed class of a taxpayer for an amount determined under paragraph $(1)(b)$ and the capital cost to the taxpayer of the particular property exceeds the amount determined under that paragraph, in applying sections 13 and 20 and any regulations made under paragraph $20(1)(a)$

(a) the capital cost to the transferee of the particular property is deemed to be the amount that was the capital cost to the taxpayer of the particular property; and

(b) the excess is deemed to have been allowed to the transferee in respect of the particular property under regulations made under paragraph $20(1)(a)$ in computing income for taxation years before the acquisition of the particular property.

Applicable: To transfers that occur after 1999.

Explanatory Note:

Capital Cost and Amount Deemed Allowed

Subsection 73(2) of the Act applies where a person ("transferor") transfers depreciable capital property ("DCP") of a prescribed class to a taxpayer ("transferee") in circumstances in which subsection 73(1) applies. If the capital cost to the transferor of the DCP is greater than the amount at which the transferee is deemed under subsection 73(1) to have acquired the DCP, subsection 73(2) ensures that the proper amount of capital cost allowance allowed to the transferor is available for recapture on a subsequent disposition of the DCP by the transferee.

Subsection 73(2) of the Act is amended to replace the reference to paragraph $73(1)(e)$ with a reference to paragraph $73(1)(b)$. Paragraph $73(1)(b)$ now provides for the amount at which the transferee is deemed to acquire property on a transfer to which subsection 73(1) applies.

This amendment applies to transfers that occur after 1999.

[¶1600]

(3) *Inter vivos* transfer of farm property to child.   For the purposes of this Part, if at any time any land in Canada or depreciable property in Canada of a prescribed class of a taxpayer or any eligible capital property in respect of a business carried on in Canada by a taxpayer is transferred by the taxpayer to a child of the taxpayer who was resident in Canada immediately before the transfer, and the property was, before the transfer, used principally in a farming business in which the taxpayer, the taxpayer's spouse or common-law partner or any of the taxpayer's children was actively engaged on a regular and continuous basis (or, in the case of property used in the operation of a woodlot, was engaged to the extent required by a prescribed forest management plan in respect of that woodlot),

(a) where the property transferred was depreciable property of a prescribed class, the taxpayer shall be deemed to have disposed of the property at the time of the transfer for proceeds of disposition equal to,

(i) in any case to which neither subparagraph (ii) nor (iii) applies, the proceeds of disposition otherwise determined,

(ii) if the proceeds of disposition otherwise determined exceeded the greater of

(A) the fair market value of the property immediately before the time of the transfer, and

(B) that proportion of the undepreciated capital cost to the taxpayer immediately before the time of the transfer of all of the depreciable property of the taxpayer of that class that the fair market value at that time of the property so transferred was of the fair market value at that time of all of the depreciable property of the taxpayer of that class,

the greater of the amounts referred to in clauses (A) and (B), or

(iii) if the proceeds of disposition otherwise determined were less than the lesser of the amounts referred to in clauses (ii)(A) and (B), the lesser of those amounts;

(b) where the property transferred was land, the taxpayer shall be deemed to have disposed of the property at the time of the transfer for proceeds of disposition equal to,

(i) in any case to which neither subparagraph (ii) nor (iii) applies, the proceeds of disposition otherwise determined,

(ii) if the proceeds of disposition otherwise determined exceeded the greater of

(A) the fair market value of the land immediately before the time of the transfer, and

(B) the adjusted cost base to the taxpayer of the land immediately before the time of the transfer,

the greater of the amounts referred to in clauses (A) and (B), or

(iii) if the proceeds of disposition otherwise determined were less than the lesser of the amounts referred to in clauses (ii)(A) and (B), the lesser of those amounts;

¶1600

(b.1) where the property transferred was eligible capital property, the taxpayer shall be deemed to have disposed of the property at the time of the transfer for proceeds of disposition equal to,

(i) in any case to which neither subparagraph (ii) nor (iii) applies, the proceeds of disposition otherwise determined,

(ii) if the proceeds of disposition otherwise determined exceeded the greater of

(A) the fair market value of the property immediately before the time of the transfer, and

(B) the amount determined by the formula

$$\frac{4}{3} \; (A \times \frac{B}{C})$$

where

A   is the cumulative eligible capital of the taxpayer in respect of the business,

B   is the fair market value of the property immediately before the transfer, and

C   is the fair market value immediately before that time of all eligible capital property of the taxpayer in respect of the business,

the greater of the amounts referred to in clauses (A) and (B), or

(iii) if the proceeds of disposition otherwise determined were less than the lesser of the amounts referred to in clauses (ii)(A) and (B), the lesser of those amounts;

(c) section 69 does not apply in determining the proceeds of disposition of the depreciable property, the land or the eligible capital property;

Pending Amendment

Non-Resident Trusts, Foreign Investment Entities, and Technical Amendments (July 18, 2005)

Paragraph 73(3)(c) of the Act is replaced by the following:

(c) subsection 69(1) does not apply in determining the proceeds of disposition of the depreciable property, the land or the eligible capital property;

Applicable: To dispositions that occur after December 20, 2002.

Explanatory Note:

Inter Vivos Transfer of Farm Property

Subsection 73(3) of the Act provides a tax-deferral for an *inter vivos* transfer of farm property by a taxpayer to a child of the taxpayer.

For dispositions made after December 20, 2002, paragraph 73(3)(c) is amended to clarify that subsection 73(3) does not apply if the anti-avoidance rule in subsection

¶1600

69(11) of the Act applies. When applicable, subsection 69(11) denies the benefit of the rollover by treating the vendor's proceeds of disposition to be equal to the fair market value of the transferred property notwithstanding any other provision of the Act.

(d) the child shall be deemed to have acquired the depreciable property or the land, as the case may be, for an amount equal to the proceeds of disposition determined under paragraph (a) or (b), respectively;

(d.1) where the property transferred was eligible capital property of the taxpayer, the child shall be deemed to have acquired a capital property, immediately after the transfer, at a cost equal to the proceeds of disposition determined under paragraph (b.1), except that, where the child continues to carry on the business previously carried on by the taxpayer, the taxpayer's spouse or common-law partner or any of the taxpayer's children, the taxpayer shall be deemed to have acquired an eligible capital property and to have made an eligible capital expenditure at a cost equal to the total of

---

Pending Amendment

Non-Resident Trusts, Foreign Investment Entities, and Technical Amendments (July 18, 2005)

The portion of paragraph 73(3)(d.1) of the English version of the Act before subparagraph (i) is replaced by the following:

(d.1) where the property transferred was eligible capital property of the taxpayer, the child is deemed to have acquired a capital property, immediately after the transfer, at a cost equal to the proceeds of disposition determined under paragraph (b.1), except that, where the child continues to carry on the business previously carried on by the taxpayer, the taxpayer's spouse or common-law partner or any of the taxpayer's children, the child is deemed to have acquired an eligible capital property and to have made an eligible capital expenditure at a cost equal to the total of

Applicable: Royal Assent.

Explanatory Note: Paragraph 73(3)(d.1) is amended, applicable on Royal Assent, to clarify its application in respect of an eligible capital property acquired by the child of the taxpayer.

(i) the proceeds of disposition referred to in paragraph (b.1), and

(ii) $\frac{4}{3}$ of the amount determined by the formula

$$(A \times \frac{B}{C}) - D$$

where

A   is the amount, if any, determined for F in the definition "cumulative eligible capital" in subsection 14(5) in respect of the business of the taxpayer immediately before the time of the transfer,

B   is the fair market value of the property immediately before that time,

¶1600

C is the fair market value immediately before that time of all eligible capital property of the taxpayer in respect of the business, and

D is the amount, if any, included under subparagraph $14(1)(a)(iv)$ in computing the income of the taxpayer as a result of the disposition,

and, for the purpose of determining at any subsequent time the child's cumulative eligible capital in respect of the business, an amount equal to $3/4$ of the amount determined under subparagraph (ii) shall be added to the amount otherwise determined in respect thereof for P in the definition "cumulative eligible capital" in subsection 14(5);

$(d.2)$ for the purposes of determining after the time of the transfer

(i) the amount deemed by subparagraph $14(1)(a)(v)$ to be the child's taxable capital gain, and

(ii) the amount to be included under subparagraph $14(1)(a)(v)$ or paragraph $14(1)(b)$ in computing the child's income

in respect of any subsequent disposition of the property of the business, there shall be added to the amount otherwise determined for Q in the definition "cumulative eligible capital" in subsection 14(5) the amount determined by the formula

$$A \times \frac{B}{C}$$

where

A is the amount, if any, determined for Q in that definition in respect of the business of the taxpayer immediately before the time of the transfer,

B is the fair market value immediately before that time of the property transferred, and

C is the fair market value immediately before that time of all eligible capital property of the taxpayer in respect of the business; and

(e) where the child is deemed to have acquired depreciable property of a prescribed class of the taxpayer for an amount determined under paragraph (d) and the capital cost to the taxpayer of the property exceeds the amount determined under that paragraph, for the purposes of sections 13 and 20 and any regulations made under paragraph $20(1)(a)$,

(i) the capital cost to the child of the property shall be deemed to be the amount that was the capital cost to the taxpayer thereof, and

(ii) the excess shall be deemed to have been allowed to the child in respect of the property under regulations made under paragraph $20(1)(a)$ in computing income for taxation years before the acquisition thereof.

¶1600

[¶1604]

(4) *Inter vivos* **transfer of family farm corporations and partnerships.** For the purposes of this Part, where at any particular time after April 10, 1978 a taxpayer has transferred property to a child of the taxpayer who was resident in Canada immediately before the transfer, and the property was, immediately before the transfer, a share of the capital stock of a family farm corporation of the taxpayer or an interest in a family farm partnership of the taxpayer (within the meaning assigned by subsection 70(10)), the following rules apply:

(a) the taxpayer shall be deemed to have disposed of the property at the time of the transfer for proceeds of disposition equal to,

   (i) in any case to which neither subparagraph (ii) nor (iii) applies, the proceeds of disposition otherwise determined,

   (ii) if the proceeds of disposition otherwise determined exceeded the greater of

   (A) the fair market value of the property immediately before the time of the transfer, and

   (B) the adjusted cost base to the taxpayer of the property immediately before the time of the transfer,

   the greater of the amounts referred to in clauses (A) and (B), or

   (iii) if the proceeds of disposition otherwise determined were less than the lesser of the amounts referred to in clauses (ii)(A) and (B), the lesser of those amounts;

(b) section 69 does not apply in determining the proceeds of disposition of the property; and

---

Pending Amendment

Non-Resident Trusts, Foreign Investment Entities, and Technical Amendments (July 18, 2005)

Paragraph 73(4)(b) of the Act is replaced by the following:

   (b) subsection 69(1) does not apply in determining the proceeds of disposition of the property; and

Applicable: To dispositions that occur after December 20, 2002.

Explanatory Note: Subsection 73(4) of the Act provides a tax-deferral for an *inter vivos* transfer of shares of a family farm corporation or an interest in a family farm partnership by a taxpayer to a child of the taxpayer.

For dispositions made after December 20, 2002, paragraph 73(4)(b) is amended to clarify that subsection 73(4) does not apply if the anti-avoidance rule in subsection 69(11) of the Act applies. When applicable, subsection 69(11) denies the benefit of the rollover by treating the vendor's proceeds of disposition to be equal to the fair market value of the transferred property notwithstanding any other provision of the Act.

¶1604

(c) the child shall be deemed to have acquired the property for an amount equal to the proceeds of disposition determined under paragraph (a).

[¶1606]

(5) Disposition of a NISA. Where at any time a taxpayer disposes of an interest in the taxpayer's NISA Fund No. 2, an amount equal to the balance in the fund so disposed of shall be deemed to have been paid out of the fund at that time to the taxpayer except that,

(a) where the interest is disposed of to the taxpayer's spouse or common-law partner, former spouse or common-law partner or an individual referred to in paragraph $(1)(d)$ (as it applies to transfers of property that occurred before 1993) in settlement of rights arising out of their marriage or common-law partnership, on or after the breakdown of the marriage or common-law partnership, that amount shall not be deemed to have been paid to the taxpayer if

(i) the disposition is made under a decree, order or judgment of a competent tribunal or, in the case of a spouse or common-law partner or former spouse or common-law partner, a written separation agreement, and

(ii) the taxpayer elects in the taxpayer's return of income under this Part for the taxation year in which the property was disposed of to have this paragraph apply to the disposition; and

(b) where the interest is disposed of to a taxable Canadian corporation in a transaction in respect of which an election is made under section 85, an amount equal to the proceeds of disposition in respect of that interest shall be deemed to be paid, at that time, to the taxpayer out of the taxpayer's NISA Fund No. 2.

[¶1608]

(6) Application of s. 70(10). The definitions in subsection 70(10) apply to this section.

* * *

[¶1622]

SECTION 85:

(1) Transfer of property to corporation by shareholders. Where a taxpayer has, in a taxation year, disposed of any of the taxpayer's property that was eligible property to a taxable Canadian corporation for consideration that includes shares of the capital stock of the corporation, if the taxpayer and the corporation have jointly elected in prescribed form and in accordance with subsection (6), the following rules apply:

(a) the amount that the taxpayer and the corporation have agreed on in their election in respect of the property shall be deemed to be the taxpayer's proceeds of disposition of the property and the corporation's cost of the property;

(b) subject to paragraph (c), where the amount that the taxpayer and the corporation have agreed on in their election in respect of the property is less than the fair market value, at the time of the disposition, of the consideration therefor (other than any shares of the capital stock of the corporation or a right to receive any such shares) received by the taxpayer, the amount so agreed on shall, irrespective of the amount actually so agreed on by them, be deemed to be an amount equal to that fair market value;

(c) where the amount that the taxpayer and the corporation have agreed on in their election in respect of the property is greater than the fair market value, at the time of the disposition, of the property so disposed of, the amount so agreed on shall, irrespective of the amount actually so agreed on, be deemed to be an amount equal to that fair market value;

(c.1) where the property was inventory, capital property (other than depreciable property of a prescribed class), a NISA Fund No. 2 or a property that is eligible property because of paragraph (1.1)(g) or (g.1), and the amount that the taxpayer and corporation have agreed on in their election in respect of the property is less than the lesser of

(i) the fair market value of the property at the time of the disposition, and

(ii) the cost amount to the taxpayer of the property at the time of the disposition,

the amount so agreed on shall, irrespective of the amount actually so agreed on by them, be deemed to be an amount equal to the lesser of the amounts described in subparagraphs (i) and (ii);

(c.2) subject to paragraphs (b) and (c) and notwithstanding paragraph (c.1), where the taxpayer carries on a farming business the income from which is computed in accordance with the cash method and the property was inventory owned in connection with that business immediately before the particular time the property was disposed of to the corporation,

(i) the amount that the taxpayer and the corporation agreed on in their election in respect of inventory purchased by the taxpayer shall be deemed to be equal to the amount determined by the formula

$$(A \times \frac{B}{C}) + D$$

where

A   is the amount that would be included because of paragraph 28(1)(c) in computing the taxpayer's income for the taxpayer's last taxation year beginning before the particular time if that year had ended immediately before the particular time,

¶1622

B is the value (determined in accordance with subsection 28(1.2)) to the taxpayer immediately before the particular time of the purchased inventory in respect of which the election is made,

C is the value (determined in accordance with subsection 28(1.2)) of all of the inventory purchased by the taxpayer that was owned by the taxpayer in connection with that business immediately before the particular time, and

D is such additional amount as the taxpayer and the corporation designate in respect of the property,

(ii) for the purpose of subparagraph 28(1)(*a*)(i), the disposition of the property and the receipt of proceeds of disposition therefor shall be deemed to have occurred at the particular time and in the course of carrying on the business, and

(iii) where the property is owned by the corporation in connection with a farming business and the income from that business is computed in accordance with the cash method, for the purposes of section 28,

(A) an amount equal to the cost to the corporation of the property shall be deemed to have been paid by the corporation, and

(B) the corporation shall be deemed to have purchased the property for an amount equal to that cost,

at the particular time and in the course of carrying on that business;

(*d*) where the property was eligible capital property in respect of a business of the taxpayer and the amount that, but for this paragraph, would be the proceeds of disposition of the property is less than the least of

(i) $4/3$ of the taxpayer's cumulative eligible capital in respect of the business immediately before the disposition,

(ii) the cost to the taxpayer of the property, and

(iii) the fair market value of the property at the time of the disposition,

the amount agreed on by the taxpayer and the corporation in their election in respect of the property shall, irrespective of the amount actually so agreed on by them, be deemed to be the least of the amounts described in subparagraphs (i) to (iii);

(*d*.1) for the purpose of determining after the time of the disposition the amount to be included under paragraph 14(1)(*b*) in computing the corporation's income, there shall be added to the amount otherwise determined for Q in the definition "cumulative eligible capital" in subsection 14(5) the amount determined by the formula

$$(A \times \frac{B}{C}) - 2(D - E)$$

where

¶1622

A   is the amount, if any, determined for Q in that definition in respect of the taxpayer's business immediately before the time of the disposition,

---

Pending Amendment

Non-Resident Trusts, Foreign Investment Entities, and Technical Amendments (July 18, 2005)

The portion of paragraph 85(1)(d.1) of the Act before the description of B is replaced by the following:

(d.1) for the purpose of determining after the time of the disposition the amount to be included under paragraph 14(1)(b) in computing the corporation's income, there shall be added to the amount otherwise determined for C in that paragraph the amount determined by the formula

$$\tfrac{1}{2} \times [(A \times B/C) - 2(D - E)]$$

where

A   is the amount, if any, determined for Q in the definition "cumulative eligible capital" in subsection 14(5) in respect of the taxpayer's business immediately before the time of the disposition,

Applicable: In respect of dispositions that occur after December 20, 2002.

Explanatory Note:

Transfer of Property to a Corporation By Shareholders

Subsection 85(1) of the Act provides a tax deferral for the transfer of various types of property by a taxpayer to a taxable Canadian corporation for consideration that includes shares of the corporation's capital stock. In general, tax deferral may be achieved if the taxpayer and the corporation jointly elect that the proceeds of disposition of the taxpayer and the eligible capital expenditure of, or cost to, the corporation are deemed to be less than the fair market value of the property transferred.

Paragraph 85(1)(d.1) generally reduces, for the corporation that has acquired an eligible capital property (ECP), the gain that would be included in income under paragraph 14(1)(b) of the Act on a subsequent disposition of the property. Paragraph 85(1)(d.1) adjusts the gain, in order to take into account the 1988 change of the rate of income inclusion and expenditure deductibility from $\tfrac{1}{2}$ to $\tfrac{3}{4}$, by adjusting the calculation of variable Q in the definition "cumulative eligible capital" in subsection 14(5) of the Act. Variable Q generally represents, for the period prior to the taxpayer's "adjustment time", the difference between ECP deductions claimed under paragraph 20(1)(b) of the Act and the total of recapture and gains from prior dispositions of eligible capital property by the taxpayer. Paragraph 85(1)(d.1) adjusts variable Q only for the purposes of calculating the amount to be included in a corporation's income under paragraph 14(1)(b), but not for the purpose of calculating the corporation's cumulative eligible capital balance for other purposes, such as the claiming of ECP deductions. Specifically, the adjustment of variable Q adjusts the value of variables A, B and C in the formula in paragraph 14(1)(b). Variables A and B are affected indirectly, since variable Q affects variable F in the calculation of the cumulative eligible capital balance.

Paragraph 85(1)(d.1) is amended concurrently with the addition of new paragraph 85(1)(d.11) of the Act. New paragraph 85(1)(d.11) generally applies to ensure that an amount that would have been recaptured ECP deductions to the taxpayer under subsection 14(1), if the taxpayer had disposed of the eligible capital property for an amount greater than the taxpayer's cumulative eligible capital at the time of the disposition, is subject to recapture in the hands of the corporation upon a subsequent sale of the property. This result is achieved by adding an allocation of the potential recapture to the taxpayer (i.e., variable F of the taxpayer) simultaneously to the corporation's eli-

¶1622

gible capital expenditures and aggregate ECP deductions (i.e., variables A and F respectively in the definition "cumulative eligible capital" of the corporation). This adjustment applies only for the purpose of calculating the amount to be included in income of the corporation under subsection 14(1) upon the subsequent disposition of eligible capital property. In this regard, variable F of the taxpayer is determined at the beginning of the taxpayer's following taxation year if the taxpayer's taxation year that included the transfer had ended immediately after the disposition time, determined without reference to new paragraph $(d.12)$. Variable F of the taxpayer is apportioned to the corporation in the same proportion as the fair market value of the property transferred is to the fair market value of total eligible capital property of the taxpayer immediately before the transfer.

Because new paragraph $85(1)(d.11)$ now accommodates variable F of the corporation, paragraph $85(1)(d.1)$ is amended to add $\frac{1}{2}$ of the taxpayer's variable Q amount directly to the corporation's variable C amount in paragraph $14(1)(b)$, rather than adjusting variable Q of the corporation (and thus variable F as well).

New paragraph $85(1)(d.12)$ of the Act is added, concurrently with new paragraph $85(1)(d.11)$, to ensure that a subsequent disposition of other ECP by the taxpayer does not result in recapture of depreciation under paragraph $14(1)(a)$ when the resulting gain from that disposition should have been taxed at a lower rate under paragraph $14(1)(b)$. This could happen, for instance, if the taxpayer were to defer all of the recapture to the corporation, such that the taxpayer's cumulative eligible capital balance at the end of the taxation year that includes the rollover is nil. In this case, if in the next taxation year the taxpayer were to make another disposition of ECP, paragraph $85(1)(d.12)$ would reduce to nil the amounts that would be determined for the taxpayer by subparagraph $14(1)(a)$ and variable B of paragraph $14(1)(b)$.

These amendments apply in respect of dispositions that occur after December 20, 2002.

Example of 85(1)(d.1) and (d.11)

Mr. X purchased an eligible capital property in 1984 (when the income inclusion rate for eligible capital property was one half) at a cost of $300,000. This was the first and only eligible capital property held in respect of his business. Mr. X claimed deductions of $40,650 under paragraph $20(1)(b)$ of the Act before his "adjustment time" (in the case of Mr. X, January 1, 1988), and of $11,482 subsequent to that time. Mr. X now transfers the property to a corporation in circumstances to which subsection 85(1) applies. Immediately before the time of the transfer, the fair market value of the property is $500,000. Mr. X and the corporation agree that the proceeds of disposition to Mr. X will be $203,391, which is $\frac{4}{3}$ of the cumulative eligible capital balance of $152,543. The balance is calculated as follows:

Eligible capital expenditure	$ 300,000
Rate applicable in 1984	50%
	150,000
Depreciation before 1988	<40,650>
Cumulative eligible capital at adjustment time	109,350
"C" amount: 3/2 of 109,350	164,025
"D" amount: depreciation before 1988	40,650
"P" amount: depreciation after 1987	<11,482>
"Q" amount: depreciation before 1988	<40,650>
Cumulative eligible capital of Mr. X	$ 152,543

Upon the subsequent sale of the property by the corporation for actual proceeds of disposition of $500,000, the amount included in the corporation's income under subsection 14(1) is calculated as follows:

Agreed amount of eligible capital expenditure ($\frac{4}{3}$ of $152,543)	$203,391
Eligible capital expenditure rate	75%

¶1622

"A" amount in cumulative eligible capital balance of corporation		152,543
$14(1)(a)$ calculation for corporation:		
Proceeds	$500,000	
Rate applicable	75%	
"E" amount in cumulative eligible capital balance of corporation		375,000
Excess		222,457
"F" for corporation: bumped by $85(1)(d.11)$ ($40,650 + $11,482)		52,132
$14(1)(a)$ income: lesser of "F" and excess		$ 52,132
$14(1)(b)$ calculation for corporation:		
Excess (as above)	$222,457	
Less: "B" amount: amount "F", as bumped by $85(1)(d.11)$	<52,132>	
"C" amount: $\frac{1}{2}$ of "Q" (above), as bumped by $85(1)(d.1)$	<20,325>	
Net	150,000	
Multiply by $\frac{2}{3}$	2/3	
$14(1)(b)$ income		$100,000
Total 14(1) income inclusion to corporation		$152,132

B   is the fair market value immediately before that time of the eligible capital property disposed of to the corporation by the taxpayer,

C   is the fair market value immediately before that time of all eligible capital property of the taxpayer in respect of the business,

D   is the amount, if any, that would be included under subsection 14(1) in computing the taxpayer's income as a result of the disposition if the values determined for C and D in paragraph $14(1)(b)$ were zero, and

E   is the amount, if any, that would be included under subsection 14(1) in computing the taxpayer's income as a result of the disposition if the value determined for D in paragraph $14(1)(b)$ were zero;

Pending Amendment

Non-Resident Trusts, Foreign Investment Entities, and Technical Amendments (July 18, 2005)

Subsection 85(1) of the Act is amended by adding the following after paragraph ($d.1$):

($d.11$) for the purpose of determining after the time of the disposition (referred to in this paragraph and in paragraph ($d.12$) as the "disposition time") the amount to be included under paragraph $14(1)(a)$ or (b) in computing the corporation's income, there shall be added to the amount otherwise determined for each of A and F in the definition "cumulative eligible capital" in subsection 14(5) the amount, if any, determined by the formula

$$A \times B/C$$

¶1622

where

A   is the amount, if any, that would be determined for F in that definition in respect of the taxpayer's business at the beginning of the taxpayer's following taxation year if the taxpayer's taxation year that includes the disposition time had ended immediately after the disposition time and if, in respect of the disposition, this Act were read without reference to paragraph $(d.12)$,

B   is the fair market value immediately before the disposition time of the eligible capital property disposed of to the corporation by the taxpayer, and

C   is the fair market value immediately before the disposition time of all eligible capital property of the taxpayer in respect of the business;

$(d.12)$ for the purpose of determining after the disposition time the amount to be included under paragraph $14(1)(a)$ or (b) in computing the taxpayer's income, the amount, if any, determined by the formula in paragraph $(d.11)$ in respect of the disposition is to be deducted from each of the amounts otherwise determined

(i) by subparagraph $14(1)(a)(ii)$, and

(ii) for the description of B in paragraph $14(1)(b)$;

Applicable: In respect of dispositions that occur after December 20, 2002.

Explanatory Note: [See the Explanatory Note following the amendment to paragraph $85(1)(d.1)$.]

(e) where the property was depreciable property of a prescribed class of the taxpayer and the amount that, but for this paragraph, would be the proceeds of disposition thereof is less than the least of

(i) the undepreciated capital cost to the taxpayer of all property of that class immediately before the disposition,

(ii) the cost to the taxpayer of the property, and

(iii) the fair market value of the property at the time of the disposition,

the amount agreed on by the taxpayer and the corporation in their election in respect of the property shall, irrespective of the amount actually so agreed on by them, be deemed to be the least of the amounts described in subparagraphs (i) to (iii);

$(e.1)$ where two or more properties, each of which is a property described in paragraph (d) or each of which is a property described in paragraph (e), are disposed of at the same time, paragraph (d) or (e), as the case may be, applies as if each property so disposed of had been separately disposed of in the order designated by the taxpayer before the time referred to in subsection (6) for the filing of an election in respect of those properties or, if the taxpayer does not so designate any such order, in the order designated by the Minister;

$(e.2)$ where the fair market value of the property immediately before the disposition exceeds the greater of

(i) the fair market value, immediately after the disposition, of the consideration received by the taxpayer for the property disposed of by the taxpayer, and

¶1622

(ii) the amount that the taxpayer and the corporation have agreed on in their election in respect of the property, determined without reference to this paragraph,

and it is reasonable to regard any part of the excess as a benefit that the taxpayer desired to have conferred on a person related to the taxpayer (other than a corporation that was a wholly owned corporation of the taxpayer immediately after the disposition), the amount that the taxpayer and the corporation agreed on in their election in respect of the property shall, regardless of the amount actually so agreed on by them, be deemed (except for the purposes of paragraphs (g) and (h)) to be an amount equal to the total of the amount referred to in subparagraph (ii) and that part of the excess;

$(e.3)$ where, under any of paragraphs $(c.1)$, (d) and (e), the amount that the taxpayer and the corporation have agreed on in their election in respect of the property (in this paragraph referred to as "the elected amount") would be deemed to be an amount that is greater or less than the amount that would be deemed, subject to paragraph (c), to be the elected amount under paragraph (b), the elected amount shall be deemed to be the greater of

(i) the amount deemed by paragraph $(c.1)$, (d) or (e), as the case may be, to be the elected amount, and

(ii) the amount deemed by paragraph (b) to be the elected amount;

$(e.4)$ where

(i) the property is depreciable property of a prescribed class of the taxpayer and is a passenger vehicle the cost to the taxpayer of which was more than $20,000 or such other amount as may be prescribed, and

(ii) the taxpayer and the corporation do not deal at arm's length,

the amount that the taxpayer and the corporation have agreed on in their election in respect of the property shall be deemed to be an amount equal to the undepreciated capital cost to the taxpayer of the class immediately before the disposition, except that, for the purposes of subsection 6(2), the cost to the corporation of the vehicle shall be deemed to be an amount equal to its fair market value immediately before the disposition;

(f) the cost to the taxpayer of any particular property (other than shares of the capital stock of the corporation or a right to receive any such shares) received by the taxpayer as consideration for the disposition shall be deemed to be an amount equal to the lesser of

(i) the fair market value of the particular property at the time of the disposition, and

(ii) that proportion of the fair market value, at the time of the disposition, of the property disposed of by the taxpayer to the corporation that

(A) the amount determined under subparagraph (i)

is of

(B) the fair market value, at the time of the disposition, of all properties (other than shares of the capital stock of the corporation or a right to receive any such shares) received by the taxpayer as consideration for the disposition;

(g) the cost to the taxpayer of any preferred shares of any class of the capital stock of the corporation receivable by the taxpayer as consideration for the disposition shall be deemed to be the lesser of the fair market value of those shares immediately after the disposition and that proportion of the amount, if any, by which the proceeds of the disposition exceed the fair market value of the consideration (other than shares of the capital stock of the corporation or a right to receive any such shares) received by the taxpayer for the disposition, that

(i) the fair market value, immediately after the disposition, of those preferred shares of that class,

is of

(ii) the fair market value, immediately after the disposition, of all preferred shares of the capital stock of the corporation receivable by the taxpayer as consideration for the disposition;

(h) the cost to the taxpayer of any common shares of any class of the capital stock of the corporation receivable by the taxpayer as consideration for the disposition shall be deemed to be that proportion of the amount, if any, by which the proceeds of the disposition exceed the total of the fair market value, at the time of the disposition, of the consideration (other than shares of the capital stock of the corporation or a right to receive any such shares) received by the taxpayer for the disposition and the cost to the taxpayer of all preferred shares of the capital stock of the corporation receivable by the taxpayer as consideration for the disposition, that

(i) the fair market value, immediately after the disposition, of those common shares of that class,

is of

(ii) the fair market value, immediately after the disposition, of all common shares of the capital stock of the corporation receivable by the taxpayer as consideration for the disposition; and

(i) where the property so disposed of is taxable Canadian property of the taxpayer, all of the shares of the capital stock of the Canadian corporation received by the taxpayer as consideration for the property shall be deemed to be taxable Canadian property of the taxpayer.

[¶1624]

(1.1) Definition of "eligible property".   For the purposes of subsection (1), "eligible property" means

(a) a capital property (other than real property, or an interest in or an option in respect of real property, owned by a non-resident person);

(b) a capital property that is real property, or an interest in or an option in respect of real property, owned by a non-resident insurer where that property and the property received as consideration for that property are designated insurance property for the year;

Pending Amendment

Non-Resident Trusts, Foreign Investment Entities, and Technical Amendments (July 18, 2005)

Paragraphs 85(1.1)(a) and (b) of the Act are replaced by the following:

(a) a capital property (other than real or immovable property, an option in respect of such property, or an interest in real property or a real right in an immovable, owned by a non-resident person);

(b) a capital property that is real or immovable property, an option in respect of such property, or an interest in real property or a real right in an immovable, owned by a non-resident insurer where that property and the property received as consideration for that property are designated insurance property for the year;

Applicable: Royal Assent.

Explanatory Note: [See the Explanatory Note re amendments related to bijuralism following the amendment to subsection 13(5.2).]

(c) a Canadian resource property;

(d) a foreign resource property;

(e) an eligible capital property;

(f) an inventory (other than real property, an interest in real property or an option in respect of real property);

Pending Amendment

Non-Resident Trusts, Foreign Investment Entities, and Technical Amendments (July 18, 2005)

Paragraph 85(1.1)(f) of the Act is replaced by the following:

(f) an inventory (other than real or immovable property, an option in respect of such property, or an interest in real property or a real right in an immovable);

Applicable: Royal Assent.

Explanatory Note: [See the Explanatory Note re amendments related to bijuralism following the amendment to subsection 13(5.2).]

(g) a property that is a security or debt obligation used by the taxpayer in the year in, or held by it in the year in the course of, carrying on the business of insurance or lending money, other than

¶1624

(i) a capital property,

(ii) inventory, or

(iii) where the taxpayer is a financial institution in the year, a mark-to-market property for the year;

(g.1) where the taxpayer is a financial institution in the year, a specified debt obligation (other than a mark-to-market property of the taxpayer for the year);

(h) a capital property that is real property, an interest in real property or an option in respect of real property, owned by a non-resident person (other than a non-resident insurer) and used in the year in a business carried on in Canada by that person; or

---

Pending Amendment

Non-Resident Trusts, Foreign Investment Entities, and Technical Amendments (July 18, 2005)

Paragraph 85(1.1)(h) of the Act is replaced by the following:

(h) a capital property that is real or immovable property, an option in respect of such property, or an interest in real property or a real right in an immovable, owned by a non-resident person (other than a non-resident insurer) and used in the year in a business carried on in Canada by that person; or

Applicable: Royal Assent.

Explanatory Note: [See the Explanatory Note re amendments related to bijuralism following the amendment to subsection 13(5.2).]

(i) a NISA Fund No. 2.

[¶1626]

(1.11) Exception. Notwithstanding subsection (1.1), a foreign resource property, or an interest in a partnership that derives all or part of its value from one or more foreign resource properties, is not an eligible property of a taxpayer in respect of a disposition by the taxpayer to a corporation where

(a) the taxpayer and the corporation do not deal with each other at arm's length; and

(b) it is reasonable to conclude that one of the purposes of the disposition, or a series of transactions or events of which the disposition is a part, is to increase the extent to which any person may claim a deduction under section 126.

—————————— **Pending Amendment** ——————————

Non-Resident Trusts, Foreign Investment Entities, and Technical Amendments (July 18, 2005)

Subsection 85(1.11) of the Act is replaced by the following:

(1.11) Exception. Notwithstanding subsection (1.1), the following property is not an eligible property of a taxpayer in respect of a disposition of the property in a taxation year by the taxpayer to a corporation:

(a) a foreign resource property, or an interest in a partnership that derives all or part of its value from one or more foreign resource properties, if

(i) the taxpayer and the corporation do not deal with each other at arm's length, and

(ii) it is reasonable to conclude that one of the purposes of the disposition, or a series of transactions or events of which the disposition is a part, is to increase the extent to which any person may claim a deduction under section 126; and

(b) a specified participating interest.

Applicable: To taxation years that begin after 2002.

Explanatory Note: Subsection 85(1.1) of the Act describes the types of property (referred to as "eligible property") that may be transferred to a corporation under subsection 85(1). Subsection 85(1.11) provides that certain foreign resource property (or an interest in a partnership that derives all or part of its value from one or more foreign resource properties) is not an "eligible property" of a taxpayer in respect of a transfer to a corporation.

Subsection 85(1.11) is amended to provide that a specified participating interest is not an eligible property of a taxpayer in respect of a transfer to a corporation. The concept of a specified participating interest is generally relevant in the context of the foreign investment entity rules in sections 94.1 to 94.4. For more information on the definition "specified participating interest" in subsection 248(1), see the commentary on that definition.

This amendment applies to taxation years that begin after 2002.

[¶1627]

(1.2) Application of subsection (1). Subsection (1) does not apply to a disposition by a taxpayer to a corporation of a property referred to in paragraph $(1.1)(h)$ unless

(a) immediately after the disposition, the corporation is controlled by the taxpayer, a person or persons related (otherwise than because of a right referred to in paragraph $251(5)(b)$) to the taxpayer or the taxpayer and a person or persons so related to the taxpayer;

(b) the disposition is part of a transaction or series of transactions in which all or substantially all of the property used in the business referred to in paragraph $(1.1)(h)$ is disposed of by the taxpayer to the corporation; and

(c) the disposition is not part of a series of transactions that result in control of the corporation being acquired by a person or group of persons after the time that is immediately after the disposition.

[¶1628]

(1.3) Meaning of "wholly owned corporation". For the purposes of this subsection and paragraph $(1)(e.2)$, "wholly owned corporation" of a taxpayer means a corporation all the issued and outstanding shares of the capital stock of which (except directors' qualifying shares) belong to

(a) the taxpayer;

(b) a corporation that is a wholly owned corporation of the taxpayer; or

(c) any combination of persons described in paragraph (a) or (b).

[¶1629]

(1.4) Definitions. For the purpose of subsection (1.1), "financial institution", "mark-to-market property" and "specified debt obligation" have the meanings assigned by subsection 142.2(1).

[¶1630]

(2) Transfer of property to corporation from partnership. Where

(a) a partnership has disposed, to a taxable Canadian corporation for consideration that includes shares of the corporation's capital stock, of any partnership property that was

(i) a capital property (other than real property, or an interest in or an option in respect of real property, where the partnership was not a Canadian partnership at the time of the disposition),

---

Pending Amendment

Non-Resident Trusts, Foreign Investment Entities, and Technical Amendments (July 18, 2005)

Subparagraph $85(2)(a)(i)$ of the Act is replaced by the following:

(i) a capital property (other than real or immovable property, an option in respect of such property, or an interest in real property or a real right in an immovable, where the partnership was not a Canadian partnership at the time of the disposition),

Applicable: Royal Assent.

Explanatory Note: [See the Explanatory Note re amendments related to bijuralism following the amendment to subsection 13(5.2).]

(ii) a property described in any of paragraphs $(1.1)(c)$ to (f), or

(iii) a property that would be described in paragraph $(1.1)(g)$ or $(g.1)$ if the references in those paragraphs to "taxpayer" were read as "partnership", and

(b) the corporation and all the members of the partnership have jointly so elected, in prescribed form and within the time referred to in subsection (6), paragraphs $(1)(a)$ to (i) are applicable, with such modifications as the circumstances require, in respect of the disposition as if the partnership were a taxpayer resident in Canada who had disposed of the property to the corporation.

* * *

[¶1634]

(5) Rules on transfers of depreciable property.   Where subsection (1) or (2) has applied to a disposition at any time of depreciable property to a person (in this subsection referred to as the "transferee") and the capital cost to the transferor of the property exceeds the transferor's proceeds of disposition of the property, for the purposes of sections 13 and 20 and any regulations made for the purpose of paragraph $20(1)(a)$,

   (a) the capital cost to the transferee of the property is deemed to be the amount that was its capital cost to the transferor; and

   (b) the excess is deemed to have been deducted by the transferee under paragraph $20(1)(a)$ in respect of the property in computing income for taxation years that ended before that time.

[¶1640]

(5.1) Acquisition of apprentice tools, re capital cost and deemed depreciation.   If subsection (1) has applied in respect of the acquisition at any particular time of any depreciable property by a corporation from an individual, the cost of the property to the individual was included in computing an amount under paragraph $8(1)(r)$ in respect of the individual, and the amount that would be the cost of the property to the individual immediately before the transfer if this Act were read without reference to subsection 8(7) (which amount is in this subsection referred to as the "individual's original cost") exceeds the individual's proceeds of disposition of the property,

   (a) the capital cost to the corporation of the property is deemed to be equal to the individual's original cost; and

   (b) the amount by which the individual's original cost exceeds the individual's proceeds of disposition in respect of the property is deemed to have been deducted by the corporation under paragraph $20(1)(a)$ in respect of the property in computing income for taxation years that ended before that particular time.

* * *

[¶1646]

SECTION 87:

(1) **Amalgamations.** In this section, an amalgamation means a merger of two or more corporations each of which was, immediately before the merger, a taxable Canadian corporation (each of which corporations is referred to in this section as a "predecessor corporation") to form one corporate entity (in this section referred to as the "new corporation") in such a manner that

(a) all of the property (except amounts receivable from any predecessor corporation or shares of the capital stock of any predecessor corporation) of the predecessor corporations immediately before the merger becomes property of the new corporation by virtue of the merger,

(b) all of the liabilities (except amounts payable to any predecessor corporation) of the predecessor corporations immediately before the merger become liabilities of the new corporation by virtue of the merger, and

(c) all of the shareholders (except any predecessor corporation), who owned shares of the capital stock of any predecessor corporation immediately before the merger, receive shares of the capital stock of the new corporation because of the merger,

otherwise than as a result of the acquisition of property of one corporation by another corporation, pursuant to the purchase of that property by the other corporation or as a result of the distribution of that property to the other corporation on the winding-up of the corporation.

* * *

[¶1650]

(2) **Rules applicable.** Where there has been an amalgamation of two or more corporations after 1971 the following rules apply:

(a) *Taxation year* — for the purposes of this Act, the corporate entity formed as a result of the amalgamation shall be deemed to be a new corporation the first taxation year of which shall be deemed to have commenced at the time of the amalgamation, and a taxation year of a predecessor corporation that would otherwise have ended after the amalgamation shall be deemed to have ended immediately before the amalgamation;

(b) *Inventory* — for the purpose of computing the income of the new corporation, where the property described in the inventory, if any, of the new corporation at the beginning of its first taxation year includes property that was described in the inventory of a predecessor corporation at the end of the taxation year of the predecessor corporation that ended immediately before the amalgamation (which taxation year of a predecessor corporation is referred to in this section as its "last taxation year"), the property so included shall be deemed to have been acquired by the new corporation at the beginning of its first taxation year for an amount determined in accordance with section 10 as the value thereof for the purpose of computing the income of the predecessor corporation for its last taxation year, except that where the income of the predecessor corporation for its last taxation year from a farming business was computed in accordance with the cash method, the amount so determined in respect of inventory owned in connection with that business shall be deemed to be the total of all amounts each of which is an amount included because of paragraph 28(1)(*b*) or (*c*) in computing that income for that year and, where the income of the new corporation from a farming business is computed in accordance with the cash method, for the purpose of section 28,

(i) an amount equal to that total shall be deemed to have been paid by the new corporation, and

(ii) the new corporation shall be deemed to have purchased the property for an amount equal to that total,

in its first taxation year and in the course of carrying on that business;

(c) Method adopted for computing income — in computing the income of the new corporation for a taxation year from a business or property

(i) there shall be included any amount received or receivable (depending on the method followed by the new corporation in computing its income for that year) by it in that year that would, if it had been received or receivable (depending on the method followed by the predecessor corporation in computing its income for its last taxation year) by the predecessor corporation in its last taxation year, have been included in computing the income of the predecessor corporation for that year, and

(ii) there may be deducted any amount paid or payable (depending on the method followed by the new corporation in computing its income for that year) by it in that year that would, if it had been paid or payable (depending on the method followed by the predecessor corporation in computing its income for its last taxation year) by the predecessor corporation in its last taxation year, have been deductible in computing the income of the predecessor corporation for that year;

(d) Depreciable property — for the purposes of sections 13 and 20 and any regulations made under paragraph 20(1)(*a*),

(i) where depreciable property of a prescribed class has been acquired by the new corporation from a predecessor corporation, the capital cost of the property to the new corporation shall be deemed to be the amount that was the capital cost of the property to the predecessor corporation, and

(ii) in determining the undepreciated capital cost to the new corporation of depreciable property of a prescribed class at any time,

(A) there shall be added to the capital cost to the new corporation of depreciable property of the class acquired before that time the cost amount, immediately before the amalgamation, to a predecessor corporation of each property included in that class by the new corporation,

(B) there shall be subtracted from the capital cost to the new corporation of depreciable property of that class acquired before that time the capital cost to the new corporation of property of that class acquired by virtue of the amalgamation,

(C) a reference in subparagraph 13(5)(*b*)(ii) to amounts that would have been deducted in respect of property in computing a taxpayer's income shall be construed as including a reference to amounts that would have been deducted in respect of that property in computing a predecessor corporation's income, and

(D) where depreciable property that is deemed by subsection 37(6) to be a separate prescribed class has been acquired by the new corporation from a predecessor corporation, the property shall continue to be deemed to be of that same separate prescribed class;

(d.1) Depreciable property acquired from predecessor corporation — for the purposes of this Act, where depreciable property (other than property of a prescribed class) has been acquired by the new corporation from a predecessor corporation, the new corporation shall be deemed to have acquired the property before 1972 at an actual cost equal to the actual cost of the property to the predecessor corporation, and the new corporation shall be deemed to have been allowed the total of all amounts allowed to the predecessor corporation in respect of the property, under regulations made under paragraph 20(1)(*a*), in computing the income of the predecessor corporation;

(e) Capital property — subject to paragraph *(e.4)* and subsection 142.6(5), where a capital property (other than depreciable property or an interest in a partnership) has been acquired by the new corporation from a predecessor corporation, the cost of the property to the new corporation shall be deemed to be the amount that was the adjusted cost base of the property to the predecessor corporation immediately before the amalgamation;

(e.1) Partnership interest — where a partnership interest that is capital property has been acquired from a predecessor corporation to which the new corporation was related, for the purposes of this Act, the cost of that partnership interest to the new corporation shall be deemed to be the amount that was the cost of that interest to the predecessor corporation and, in respect of that partnership interest, the new corporation shall be deemed to be the same corporation as and a continuation of the predecessor corporation;

(e.2) Security or debt obligation — subject to paragraphs *(e.3)* and *(e.4)* and subsection 142.6(5), where a property that is a security or debt obligation (other than a capital property or an inventory) of a

¶1650

predecessor corporation used by it in the year in, or held by it in the year in the course of, carrying on the business of insurance or lending money in the taxation year ending immediately before the amalgamation has been acquired by the new corporation from the predecessor corporation, the cost of the property to the new corporation shall be deemed to be the amount that was the cost amount of the property to the predecessor corporation immediately before the amalgamation;

(e.3) *Financial institutions — specified debt obligation —* where the new corporation is a financial institution in its first taxation year, it shall be deemed, in respect of a specified debt obligation (other than a mark-to-market property) acquired from a predecessor corporation that was a financial institution in its last taxation year, to be the same corporation as, and a continuation of, the predecessor corporation;

(e.4) *Financial institutions — mark-to-market property —* where

(i) the new corporation is a financial institution in its first taxation year and a property acquired by the new corporation from a predecessor corporation is a mark-to-market property of the new corporation for the year, or

(ii) a predecessor corporation was a financial institution in its last taxation year and a property acquired by the new corporation from the predecessor corporation was a mark-to-market property of the predecessor corporation for the year,

the cost of the property to the new corporation shall be deemed to be the amount that was the fair market value of the property immediately before the amalgamation;

(e.5) *Financial institutions — mark-to-market property —* for the purposes of subsections 112(5) to (5.2) and (5.4) and the definition "mark-to-market property" in subsection 142.2(1), the new corporation shall be deemed to be the same corporation as, and a continuation of, each predecessor corporation;

(f) *Eligible capital property —* for the purposes of determining under this Act any amount relating to cumulative eligible capital, an eligible capital amount, an eligible capital expenditure or eligible capital property, the new corporation shall be deemed to be the same corporation as, and a continuation of, each predecessor corporation;

(f.1) *Idem —* [Repealed by S.C. 1994, c. 7, Sched. VIII, s. 37(3).]

(g) *Reserves —* for the purpose of computing the income of the new corporation for a taxation year,

(i) any amount that has been deducted as a reserve in computing the income of a predecessor corporation for its last taxation year shall be deemed to have been deducted as a reserve in computing the income of the new corporation for a taxation year immediately preceding its first taxation year, and

¶1650

(ii) any amount deducted under paragraph $20(1)(p)$ in computing the income of a predecessor corporation for its last taxation year or a previous taxation year shall be deemed to have been deducted under that paragraph in computing the income of the new corporation for a taxation year immediately preceding its first taxation year;

(g.1) Continuation — for the purposes of sections 12.3 and 12.4, subsection 20(26) and section 26, the new corporation shall be deemed to be the same corporation as, and a continuation of, each predecessor corporation;

(g.2) Financial institution rules — for the purposes of paragraphs $142.4(4)(c)$ and (d) and subsections 142.5(5) and (7) and 142.6(1), the new corporation shall be deemed to be the same corporation as, and a continuation of, each predecessor corporation;

(g.3) Superficial losses — for the purposes of applying subsections 13(21.2), 14(12), 18(15) and 40(3.4) to any property that was disposed of by a predecessor corporation before the amalgamation, the new corporation is deemed to be the same corporation as, and a continuation of, each predecessor corporation;

(g.4) Superficial losses — capital property — for the purpose of applying paragraph $40(3.5)(c)$ in respect of any share that was acquired by a predecessor corporation, the new corporation is deemed to be the same corporation as, and a continuation of, each predecessor corporation;

Pending Amendment

Non-Resident Trusts, Foreign Investment Entities, and Technical Amendments (July 18, 2005)

Subsection 87(2) of the Act is amended by adding the following after paragraph (*g*.4):

(g.5) Patronage dividends — for the purpose of section 135, the new corporation is deemed to be the same corporation as, and a continuation of, each predecessor corporation;

Applicable: To amalgamations that occur, and to windings-up that begin, after 1997.

Explanatory Note:

Patronage Dividends

New paragraph 87(2)(*g*.5) of the Act deems a new corporation formed on an amalgamation to be the same corporation as and a continuation of each of the predecessor corporations for the purpose of section 135 of the Act. This paragraph, which applies to amalgamations that occur after 1997, ensures that the rules in section 135 concerning the deduction for and inclusion in income of patronage dividends continue to apply where a cooperative corporation or a customer of a cooperative corporation amalgamates with one or more other corporations between the time a cooperative corporation makes an allocation in proportion to patronage and the time that the patronage dividend is paid. This amendment ensures that payments made under subsection 135(1) by the new corporation in satisfaction of allocations made by a predecessor corporation will be deductible by the new corporation. In addition, new paragraph 87(2)(*g*.5) ensures that the deductibility of an amount paid to a new corporation formed on the amalgamation of

---

¶1650

the cooperative corporation's customer and another corporation will not be affected by the amalgamation.

(h) Debts — for the purpose of computing a deduction from the income of the new corporation for a taxation year under paragraph $20(1)(l)$, $(l.1)$ or (p)

(i) any debt owing to a predecessor corporation that was included in computing the income of the predecessor corporation for its last taxation year or a preceding taxation year,

(ii) where a predecessor corporation was an insurer or a corporation the ordinary business of which included the lending of money, any loan or lending asset made or acquired by the predecessor corporation in the ordinary course of its business of insurance or the lending of money, or

(iii) where a predecessor corporation was an insurer or a corporation the ordinary business of which included the lending of money, any instrument or commitment described in paragraph $20(1)(l.1)$ that was issued, made or assumed by the predecessor corporation in the ordinary course of its business of insurance or the lending of money,

and that by reason of the amalgamation, has been acquired by the new corporation, shall be deemed to be a debt owing to the new corporation that was included in computing its income for a preceding taxation year, a loan or lending asset made or acquired or an instrument or commitment that was issued, made or assumed by the new corporation in a preceding taxation year in the ordinary course of its business of insurance or the lending of money, as the case may be;

(h.1) Debts — for the purposes of section 61.4, the description of F in subsection 79(3), the definition "forgiven amount" in subsection 80(1), subsection 80.03(7) and section 80.04, the new corporation shall be deemed to be the same corporation as, and a continuation of, each predecessor corporation;

(i) Special reserve — for the purpose of computing a deduction from the income of the new corporation for a taxation year under paragraph $20(1)(n)$, any amount included in computing the income of a predecessor corporation from a business for its last taxation year or a previous taxation year in respect of property sold in the course of the business shall be deemed to have been included in computing the income of the new corporation from the business for a previous year in respect of that property;

(j) Special reserves — for the purposes of paragraphs $20(1)(m)$, $(m.1)$ and $(m.2)$, subsection 20(24) and section 34.2, the new corporation is deemed to be the same corporation as, and a continuation of, each predecessor corporation;

(j.1) Inventory adjustment — for the purposes of paragraph $20(1)(ii)$, an amount required by paragraph $12(1)(r)$ to be included in computing the income of a predecessor corporation for its last taxation year shall

¶1650

be deemed to be an amount required by paragraph $12(1)(r)$ to be included in computing the income of the new corporation for a taxation year immediately preceding its first taxation year;

(j.2) Prepaid expenses and matchable expenditures — for the purposes of subsections 18(9) and (9.01), section 18.1 and paragraph $20(1)(mm)$, the new corporation is deemed to be the same corporation as, and a continuation of, each predecessor corporation;

(j.3) Employee benefit plans, etc. — for the purposes of paragraphs $12(1)(n.1)$, $(n.2)$ and $(n.3)$ and $20(1)(r)$, (oo) and (pp), section 32.1, paragraph $104(13)(b)$ and Part XI.3, the new corporation shall be deemed to be the same corporation as, and a continuation of, each predecessor corporation;

(j.4) Accrual rules — for the purposes of subsections 12(3) and (9), section 12.2, subsection 20(19) and the definition "adjusted cost basis" in subsection 148(9) of this Act, and subsections 12(5) and (6) and paragraph $56(1)(d.1)$ of the *Income Tax Act*, chapter 148 of the Revised Statutes of Canada, 1952, the new corporation shall be deemed to be the same corporation as, and a continuation of, each predecessor corporation;

(j.5) Cancellation of lease — for the purposes of paragraphs $20(1)(z)$ and $(z.1)$, the new corporation shall be deemed to be the same corporation as, and a continuation of, each predecessor corporation;

(j.6) Continuing corporation — for the purposes of paragraphs $12(1)(t)$ and (x), subsections 12(2.2) and 13(7.1), (7.4) and (24), paragraphs $13(27)(b)$ and $(28)(c)$, subsections 13(29) and 18(9.1), paragraphs $20(1)(e)$, $(e.1)$ and (hh), sections 20.1 and 32, paragraph $37(1)(c)$, subsection 39(13), subparagraphs $53(2)(c)$(vi) and (h)(ii), paragraph $53(2)(s)$, subsections 53(2.1), 66(11.4) and 66.7(11), section 139.1, subsection 152(4.3), the determination of D in the definition "undepreciated capital cost" in subsection 13(21) and the determination of L in the definition "cumulative Canadian exploration expense" in subsection 66.1(6), the new corporation is deemed to be the same corporation as, and a continuation of, each predecessor corporation;

(j.7) Certain transfers and loans — for the purposes of sections 74.4 and 74.5, the new corporation shall be deemed to be the same corporation as, and a continuation of, each predecessor corporation;

(j.8) International banking centre business — for the purposes of section 33.1, the new corporation shall be deemed to be the same corporation as, and a continuation of, each predecessor corporation;

(j.9) Part VI and Part I.3 tax — for the purposes of determining the amount deductible by the new corporation for any taxation year under section 125.2 or 125.3, the new corporation shall be deemed to be the same corporation as, and a continuation of, each predecessor corporation;

¶1650

(j.91) Part I.3 and Part VI tax — for the purpose of determining the amount deductible under subsection 181.1(4) or 190.1(3) by the new corporation for any taxation year, the new corporation is deemed to be the same corporation as, and a continuation of, each predecessor corporation, except that this paragraph does not affect the determination of the fiscal period of any corporation or the tax payable by any predecessor corporation;

Pending Amendment

Non-Resident Trusts, Foreign Investment Entities, and Technical Amendments (July 18, 2005)

Paragraph 87(2)(j.91) of the Act is replaced by the following:

(j.91) Part I.3 and Part VI tax — for the purpose of determining the amount deductible under subsection 181.1(4) or 190.1(3) by the new corporation for any taxation year, the new corporation is deemed to be the same corporation as, and a continuation of, each predecessor corporation, except that this paragraph does not affect the determination of the fiscal period of any corporation or the tax payable by any corporation for any taxation year that ends before the amalgamation;

Applicable: To amalgamations that occur, and to windings-up that begin, after December 20, 2002.

Explanatory Note:

Part I.3 and Part VI Tax

Subsection 88(1) of the Act sets out rules relating to the winding-up of a subsidiary into a parent corporation that owns at least 90% of each class of shares of the subsidiary. A number of the rules that apply to amalgamations under subsection 87(2) of the Act also apply to windings-up under subsection 88(1).

Paragraph 87(2)(j.91) allows a new corporation, or, in the case of a winding-up under subsection 88(1), a parent corporation, to be considered as a continuation of its predecessors or subsidiary, as the case may be, for the purposes of determining an amount deductible under subsection 181.1(4) or 190.1(3) of the Act. Those provisions relate, respectively, to the deduction from a corporation's tax otherwise payable under Part I.3 of the Act of an amount in respect of its Canadian surtax, and the deduction from a financial institution's tax otherwise payable under Part VI of the Act of an amount in respect of its tax under Part I of the Act.

Paragraph 87(2)(j.91) is amended to clarify that it does not affect the fiscal period of, or tax payable by, any corporation for any taxation year that ends prior to an amalgamation, or, by virtue paragraph 88(1)(e.2), the commencement of a winding-up under subsection 88(1).

This amendment to paragraph 87(2)(j.91) applies to amalgamations that occur, and windings-up that begin, after December 20, 2002.

(j.92) Subsections 125(5.1) and 157.1(1) — for the purposes of subsection 125(5.1) and the definition "eligible corporation" in subsection 157.1(1), the new corporation is deemed to be the same corporation as, and a continuation of, each predecessor corporation;

(j.93) Mining reclamation trusts — for the purposes of paragraphs 12(1)(z.1) and (z.2) and 20(1)(ss) and (tt) and sections 107.3 and

127.41, the new corporation shall be deemed to be the same corporation as, and a continuation of, each predecessor corporation;

(j.94) Film or video productions — for the purposes of sections 125.4 and 125.5, the new corporation is deemed to be the same corporation as, and a continuation of, each predecessor corporation;

Pending Amendment

Non-Resident Trusts, Foreign Investment Entities, and Technical Amendments (July 18, 2005)

Subsection 87(2) of the Act is amended by adding the following after paragraph (j.94):

(j.95) Non-resident trusts and foreign investment entities — for the purposes of sections 94 to 94.4, the new corporation is deemed to be the same corporation as, and a continuation of, each predecessor corporation;

Applicable: To taxation years that begin after 2000.

Explanatory Note: Section 87 of the Act sets out rules that apply on the amalgamation of two or more taxable Canadian corporations. The amalgamated corporation is generally treated as a continuation of the predecessor corporations for the purposes of the Act.

New paragraph 87(2)(j.95) provides that, where there has been an amalgamation of two or more taxable Canadian corporations, the amalgamated corporation is deemed to be a continuation of its predecessor corporations for the purposes of sections 94 to 94.4, which relate to foreign trusts and foreign investment entities. Thus, for example, an amalgamated corporation will be considered to be a "contributor" (as defined in subsection 94(1)) to a trust if any predecessor corporation was a contributor to the trust. In addition, the new corporation's "deferral amount" (as defined in subsection 94.2(1)) in respect of an interest in a foreign investment entity will be determined in the same manner as a predecessor's "deferral amount" in respect of the same interest.

Because of the operation of paragraph 88(1)(e.2), new paragraph 87(2)(j.95) also applies to windings-up to which section 88 applies.

This amendment applies to taxation years that begin after 2000.

(k) Certain payments to employees — for the purpose of subsection 6(3), any amount received by a person from the new corporation that would, if received by the person from a predecessor corporation, be deemed for the purpose of section 5 to be remuneration for that person's services rendered as an officer or during a period of employment, shall be deemed for the purposes of section 5 to be remuneration for services so rendered by the person;

(l) Scientific research and experimental development — for the purposes of section 37 and Part VIII, the new corporation shall be deemed to be the same corporation as, and a continuation of, each predecessor corporation;

(l.1) Idem — for the purposes of this paragraph, paragraph *(l.2)* and section 37.1,

¶1650

(i) the base period for a particular taxation year of a new corporation that has fewer than 3 preceding taxation years shall be deemed to be the period

(A) commencing on the day that

(I) is the earliest of all days each of which is a day immediately before the commencement of a taxation year of a predecessor corporation in respect of the new corporation that ended after 1976, and

(II) is in the 3 year period ending on the day immediately before the commencement of the particular year, and

(B) ending immediately before the first day of the particular taxation year,

(ii) where subparagraph (i) applies,

(A) in determining the qualified expenditures made by the new corporation in its base period, there shall be included the total of all amounts each of which is the qualified expenditure made by a predecessor corporation in a taxation year that commenced in the base period of the new corporation, and

(B) in determining the total of the amounts paid to the new corporation by persons referred to in subparagraphs (b)(i) to (iii) of the definition "expenditure base" in subsection 37.1(5) in its base period, there shall be included the total of all such amounts paid to a predecessor corporation by a person referred to in those subparagraphs in a taxation year that commenced in the base period of the new corporation,

(iii) the capital cost to the new corporation of any property that was a research property of a predecessor corporation acquired by it from the predecessor corporation shall be deemed to be the capital cost thereof to the predecessor corporation and the property shall be deemed to be a research property of the new corporation, and

(iv) each amount determined in respect of the new corporation under subparagraph 37.1(3)(b)(i) or (iii), as the case may be, shall be deemed to be the total of the amount otherwise determined and the total of amounts each of which is the amount determined under subparagraph 37.1(3)(b)(i) or (iii), as the case may be, in respect of a predecessor corporation;

(l.2) Definition of "predecessor corporation" — for the purposes of this paragraph and paragraph *(l.1)*, "predecessor corporation" includes any corporation in respect of which a predecessor corporation was a new corporation;

(l.21) Forgiven amount — for the purposes of section 61.3, the definition "unrecognized loss" in subsection 80(1) and subsection 80.01(10), the new corporation is deemed to be the same corporation as, and a continuation of, each predecessor corporation;

(l.3) Replacement property — where before the amalgamation property of a predecessor corporation was unlawfully taken, lost, destroyed or taken under statutory authority, or was a former business property of the predecessor corporation, for the purposes of applying sections 13 and 44 and the definition "former business property" in subsection 248(1) to the new corporation in respect of the property and any replacement property acquired therefor, the new corporation shall be deemed to be the same corporation as, and a continuation of, the predecessor corporation;

Pending Amendment

Non-Resident Trusts, Foreign Investment Entities, and Technical Amendments (July 18, 2005)

Subsection 87(2) of the Act is amended by adding the following after paragraph (*l.3*):

(l.4) Subsection 13(4.2) election — for the purposes of subsection 13(4.3) and paragraph 20(16.1)(*b*), the new corporation is deemed to be the same corporation as, and a continuation of, each predecessor corporation;

Applicable: To amalgamations that occur, and to windings-up that begin, after December 20, 2002.

Explanatory Note:

Subsection 13(4.2) Election

New paragraph 87(2)(*l.4*) of the Act is added to provide that, for the purposes of the rules in new subsection 13(4.3) and paragraph 20(16.1)(*b*) of the Act in respect of which an election is made under new subsection 13(4.2), the new corporation is deemed to be the same corporation as, and a continuation of, each predecessor corporation. This new provision also applies in respect of the winding up of a corporation to which section 88 of the Act applies, as a result of the application of paragraph 88(1)(*e*.2). New paragraph 87(2)(*l.4*) applies to amalgamations that occur, and windings up that begin, after December 20, 2002.

(m) Reserves — for the purpose of computing the income of the new corporation for a taxation year, any amount claimed under subparagraph 40(1)(*a*)(iii) or 44(1)(*e*)(iii) in computing a predecessor corporation's gain for its last taxation year from the disposition of any property shall be deemed

(i) to have been claimed under subparagraph 40(1)(*a*)(iii) or 44(1)(*e*)(iii), as the case may be, in computing the new corporation's gain for a taxation year immediately preceding its first taxation year from the disposition of that property by it before its first taxation year, and

(ii) to be the amount determined under subparagraph 40(1)(*a*)(i) or 44(1)(*e*)(i), as the case may be, in respect of that property;

(m.1) Gift of non-qualifying security — for the purpose of computing the new corporation's gain under subsection 40(1.01) for any taxation year from the disposition of a property, the new corporation is deemed

¶1650

to be the same corporation as, and a continuation of, each predecessor corporation;

(n) Outlays made pursuant to warranty — for the purpose of section 42, any outlay or expense made or incurred by the new corporation in a taxation year, pursuant to or by virtue of an obligation described in that section incurred by a predecessor corporation, that would, if the outlay or expense had been made or incurred by the predecessor corporation in that year, have been deemed to be a loss of the predecessor corporation for that year from the disposition of a capital property shall be deemed to be a loss of the new corporation for that year from the disposition of a capital property;

(o) Expiration of options previously granted — for the purpose of subsection 49(2), any option granted by a predecessor corporation that expires after the amalgamation shall be deemed to have been granted by the new corporation, and any proceeds received by the predecessor corporation for the granting of the option shall be deemed to have been received by the new corporation therefor;

(p) Consideration for resource property disposition — for the purpose of computing a deduction from the income of the new corporation for a taxation year under section 64 of the *Income Tax Act*, chapter 148 of the Revised Statutes of Canada, 1952, any amount that has been included in computing the income of a predecessor corporation for its last taxation year or a previous taxation year by reason of subsection 59(1) or paragraph 59(3.2)(c) of this Act, of subsection 59(3) of the *Income Tax Act*, chapter 148 of the Revised Statutes of Canada, 1952, or of subsection 83A(5ba) or (5c) of that Act as it read in its application to a taxation year before the 1972 taxation year, shall be deemed to have been included in computing the income of the new corporation for a previous year by virtue thereof;

(q) Registered plans — for the purposes of sections 147, 147.1 and 147.2 and any regulations made under subsection 147.1(18), the new corporation shall be deemed to be the same corporation as, and a continuation of, each predecessor corporation;

Pending Amendment

Non-Resident Trusts, Foreign Investment Entities, and Technical Amendments (July 18, 2005)

Subsection 87(2) of the Act is amended by adding the following after paragraph (q):

¶1650

(r) Employees profit sharing plan — an election made under subsection 144(10) by a predecessor corporation is deemed to be an election made by the new corporation;

Applicable: To amalgamations that occur, and to windings-up that begin, after 1994.

Explanatory Note:

Employees Profit Sharing Plan

New paragraph $87(2)(r)$ of the Act preserves an election under subsection 144(10) in connection with an employees profit sharing plan that was made by a predecessor corporation before an amalgamation. Paragraph $88(1)(e.2)$ of the Act provides that this rule also applies, with appropriate modifications, for the purposes of the rules relating to the winding-up of a subsidiary corporation into its parent corporation.

This amendment applies to amalgamations that occur, and windings-up that begin, after 1994.

Pending Amendment

Additional 2005 Budget Measures (August 15, 2005)

Subsection 87(2) of the Act is amended by adding the following before paragraph (t):

(s) Tax deferred cooperative shares — for the purpose of section 135.1, if the new corporation is, at the beginning of its first taxation year, an agricultural cooperative corporation (within the meaning assigned by subsection 135.1(1)),

(i) the new corporation is deemed to be the same corporation as, and a continuation of, each predecessor corporation that was an agricultural cooperative corporation at the end of the predecessor corporation's last taxation year, and

(ii) if, on the amalgamation, the new corporation issues a share (in this subparagraph referred to as the "new share") that is described in all of paragraphs (b) to (d) of the definition "tax deferred cooperative share" in subsection 135.1(1) to a taxpayer in exchange for a share of a predecessor corporation (in this subparagraph referred to as the "old share") that was, at the end of the predecessor corporation's last taxation year, a tax deferred cooperative share within the meaning assigned by that definition, and the amount of paid-up capital, and the amount, if any, that the taxpayer is entitled to receive on a redemption, acquisition or cancellation, of the new share are equal to those amounts, respectively, in respect of the old share,

(A) the new share is deemed to have been issued at the time the old share was issued, and

(B) in applying subsection 135.1(2), the taxpayer is deemed to have disposed of the old share for nil proceeds;

Applicable: After 2005.

Explanatory Note: New paragraph $87(2)(s)$ of the Act is added as a consequence of the addition of the new rules in section 135.1 relating to the payment of tax-deferred patronage dividends by agricultural cooperative corporations. Paragraph $87(2)(s)$ provides that for the purpose of section 135.1, if the new corporation formed on an amalgamation is, at the beginning of its first taxation year, an agricultural cooperative corporation,

(i) the new corporation is deemed to be the same corporation as, and a continuation of each predecessor corporation that was an agricultural cooperative corporation and

¶1650

(ii) if, on the amalgamation, the new corporation issues a new share that is described in all of paragraphs (b) to (d) of the definition "tax deferred cooperative share" in subsection 135.1(1) in exchange for a tax deferred cooperative share ("old share") of a predecessor corporation and the amount of paid-up capital, and the amount that the taxpayer is entitled to receive on a redemption, acquisition or cancellation, of the new share are equal to those amounts, in respect of the old share, the new share is deemed to have been issued at the time the old share was issued, and in applying subsection 135.1(2), the taxpayer is deemed to have disposed of the old share for nil proceeds.

This amendment applies after 2005. It should be noted that as a result of existing paragraph 88(1)$(e.2)$ of the Act, the equivalent of new paragraph 87(2)(s) will in effect apply to windings-up under subsection 88(2).

(r) *1971 capital surplus on hand or paid-up capital deficiency* — [Repealed by 1977-78, c. 1, s. 42(2).]

(s) *Idem* — [Repealed by 1977-78, c. 1, s. 42(2).]

$(s.1)$ *Idem* — [Repealed by 1977-78, c. 1, s. 42(2).]

(t) *Pre-1972 capital surplus on hand* — for the purpose of subsection 88(2.1), any capital property owned by a predecessor corporation on December 31, 1971 that was acquired by the new corporation by virtue of the amalgamation shall be deemed to have been acquired by the new corporation before 1972 at an actual cost to it equal to the actual cost of the property to the predecessor corporation;

(u) *Shares of foreign affiliate* — where one or more shares of the capital stock of a foreign affiliate of a predecessor corporation have, by virtue of the amalgamation, been acquired by the new corporation and as a result of the acquisition the affiliate has become a foreign affiliate of the new corporation,

(i) for the purposes of subsection 91(5) and paragraph 92(1)(b), any amount required by section 92 to be added or deducted, as the case may be, in computing the adjusted cost base of any such share to the predecessor corporation before the amalgamation shall be deemed to have been so required to be added or deducted, as the case may be, in computing the adjusted cost base of the share to the new corporation, and

(ii) for the purposes of subsections 93(2) to (2.3), any exempt dividend received by the predecessor corporation on any such share is deemed to be an exempt dividend received by the new corporation on the share;

(v) *Gifts* — for the purposes of section 110.1, the new corporation shall be deemed to be the same corporation as, and a continuation of, each predecessor corporation with respect to gifts;

(w) *Losses* — [Repealed by 1983-84, c. 1, s. 38(3).]

(x) *Taxable dividends* — for the purposes of subsections 112(3) to (4.22),

¶1650

(i) any taxable dividend received on a share that was deductible from the predecessor corporation's income for a taxation year under section 112 or subsection 138(6) is deemed to be a taxable dividend received on the share by the new corporation that was deductible from the new corporation's income under section 112 or subsection 138(6), as the case may be,

(ii) any dividend (other than a taxable dividend) received on a share by the predecessor corporation is deemed to have been received on the share by the new corporation, and

(iii) a share acquired by the new corporation from a predecessor corporation is deemed to have been owned by the new corporation throughout any period of time throughout which it was owned by a predecessor corporation;

(y) Contributed surplus — for the purposes of subsections 84(1) and (10), the new corporation shall be deemed to be the same corporation as, and a continuation of, each predecessor corporation;

(y.1) Preferred-earnings amount — [Repealed by 1998, c. 19, s. 117(7).]

(z) Foreign tax carryover — for the purposes of determining the new corporation's unused foreign tax credit (within the meaning of subsection 126(7)) in respect of a country for any taxation year and determining the extent to which subsection 126(2.3) applies to reduce the amount that may be claimed by the new corporation under paragraph 126(2)(a) in respect of an unused foreign tax credit in respect of a country for a taxation year, the new corporation shall be deemed to be the same corporation as, and a continuation of, each predecessor corporation, except that this paragraph shall in no respect affect the determination of

(i) the fiscal period of the new corporation or any of its predecessor corporations, or

(ii) the tax payable under this Act by any predecessor corporation;

(z.1) Capital dividend account — for the purposes of computing the capital dividend account of the new corporation, it shall be deemed to be the same corporation as, and a continuation of, each predecessor corporation, other than a predecessor corporation to which subsection 83(2.1) would, if a dividend were paid immediately before the amalgamation and an election were made under subsection 83(2) in respect of the full amount of that dividend, apply to deem any portion of the dividend to be paid by the predecessor corporation as a taxable dividend;

(z.2) Application of Part III — for the purposes of Part III, the new corporation shall be deemed to be the same corporation as, and a continuation of, each predecessor corporation;

(aa) Refundable dividend tax on hand — where the new corporation was a private corporation immediately after the amalgamation, for the

¶1650

purpose of computing the refundable dividend tax on hand (within the meaning assigned by subsection 129(3)) of the new corporation at the end of its first taxation year there shall be added to the total determined under subsection 129(3) in respect of the new corporation for the year the total of all amounts each of which is the amount, if any, by which the refundable dividend tax on hand of a predecessor corporation at the end of its last taxation year exceeds its dividend refund (within the meaning assigned by subsection 129(1)) for its last taxation year, except that no amount shall be added under this paragraph in respect of a predecessor corporation

(i) that was not a private corporation at the end of its last taxation year, or

(ii) where subsection 129(1.2) would have applied to deem a dividend paid by the predecessor corporation immediately before the amalgamation not to be a taxable dividend for the purpose of subsection 129(1);

(bb) Mutual fund and investment corporations — where the new corporation is a mutual fund corporation or an investment corporation, there shall be added to

(i) the amount determined under each of paragraphs (*a*) and (*b*) of the definition "capital gains dividend account" in subsection 131(6), and

(ii) the values of A and B in the definition "refundable capital gains tax on hand" in that subsection

in respect of the new corporation at any time the amounts so determined and the values of those factors immediately before the amalgamation in respect of each predecessor corporation that was, immediately before the amalgamation, a mutual fund corporation or an investment corporation;

(bb.1) Flow-through entities — where a predecessor corporation was, immediately before the amalgamation, an investment corporation, a mortgage investment corporation or a mutual fund corporation and the new corporation is an investment corporation, a mortgage investment corporation or a mutual fund corporation, as the case may be, for the purpose of section 39.1, the new corporation is deemed to be the same corporation as, and a continuation of, the predecessor corporation;

(cc) Non-resident-owned investment corporation — in the case of a new corporation that is a non-resident-owned investment corporation,

(i) for the purpose of computing its allowable refundable tax on hand (within the meaning assigned by subsection 133(9)) at any time, where a predecessor corporation had allowable refundable tax on hand immediately before the amalgamation, the amount thereof shall be added to the total determined for A in the definition "allowable refundable tax on hand" in subsection 133(9),

¶1650

(ii) for the purpose of computing its capital gains dividend account (within the meaning assigned by subsection 133(8)) at any time, where a predecessor corporation had an amount in its capital gains dividend account immediately before the amalgamation, that amount shall be added to the amount determined under paragraph (a) of the description of A in the definition "capital gains dividend account" in subsection 133(8), and

(iii) for the purpose of computing its cumulative taxable income (within the meaning assigned by subsection 133(9)) at any time, where a predecessor corporation had cumulative taxable income immediately before the amalgamation, the amount thereof shall be added to the total determined for A in the definition "cumulative taxable income" in subsection 133(9);

(dd) Tax in respect of ineligible investments — [Repealed by 1973-74, c. 14, s. 26(3).]

(ee) Preferred-rate amount — [Repealed by 1984, c. 45, s. 27(5).]

(ff) Application of Part VII — [Repealed by 1977-78, c. 1, s. 42(5).]

(gg) Designated surplus — [Repealed by 1977-78, c. 1, s. 42(5).]

(hh) 1971 undistributed income on hand — [Repealed by 1977-78, c. 1, s. 42(5).]

(ii) Public corporation — where a predecessor corporation was a public corporation immediately before the amalgamation, the new corporation shall be deemed to have been a public corporation at the commencement of its first taxation year;

(jj) Interest on certain obligations — for the purposes of paragraph $81(1)(m)$, the new corporation shall be deemed to be the same corporation as, and a continuation of, each predecessor corporation;

(kk) Disposition of shares of controlled corporation — for the purposes of paragraph $40(2)(h)$,

(i) where a corporation was controlled, directly or indirectly in any manner whatever, by a predecessor corporation immediately before the amalgamation and has, by reason of the amalgamation, become controlled, directly or indirectly in any manner whatever, by the new corporation, the new corporation shall be deemed to have acquired control of the corporation so controlled at the time control thereof was acquired by the predecessor corporation, and

(ii) where a predecessor corporation was immediately before the amalgamation controlled, directly or indirectly in any manner whatever, by a corporation that, immediately after the amalgamation, controlled, directly or indirectly in any manner whatever, the new corporation, the new corporation shall be deemed to be the same corporation as, and a continuation of, each predecessor corporation;

(ll) Para. 20(1)(n) and subpara. 40(1)(a)(iii) amounts — notwithstanding any other provision of this Act, where any property was

¶1650

disposed of by a predecessor corporation, the new corporation shall, in computing

(i) the amount of any deduction under paragraph $20(1)(n)$ as a reserve in respect of the property sold in the course of business, and

(ii) the amount of its claim under subparagraph $40(1)(a)(iii)$ or $44(1)(e)(iii)$ in respect of the disposition of the property,

be deemed to be the same corporation as, and a continuation of, the predecessor corporation;

(mm) Idem — for the purposes of section 126.1, the new corporation shall be deemed to be the same corporation as, and a continuation of, each predecessor corporation;

Pending Amendment

Non-Resident Trusts, Foreign Investment Entities, and Technical Amendments (July 18, 2005)

Paragraph 87(2)(*mm*) of the Act is repealed.

(mm) Idem — [Repealed.]

Applicable: To amalgamations that occur, and to windings-up that begin, after March 20, 2003.

Explanatory Note:

UI Premium Tax Credit

Paragraph $87(2)(mm)$ of the Act ensures that an amalgamated corporation will be treated as a continuation of, and the same corporation as, each of its predecessor corporations for the purposes of the provisions relating to UI premium tax credit. That paragraph is repealed as a consequence of the repeal of the provisions relating to the UI premium tax credit. For additional information, see the commentary to section 126.1.

This change applies in respect of amalgamations that occur, and to windings-up that begin, after March 20, 2003.

(nn) Refundable Part VII tax on hand — for the purpose of computing the refundable Part VII tax on hand of the new corporation at the end of any taxation year, there shall be added to the total determined under paragraph $192(3)(a)$ the total of all amounts each of which is the amount, if any, by which

(i) a predecessor corporation's refundable Part VII tax on hand at the end of its last taxation year

exceeds

(ii) the predecessor corporation's Part VII refund for its last taxation year;

(oo) Investment tax credit — for the purpose of applying subsection $127(10.2)$ to any corporation, the new corporation is deemed to have had

¶1650

(i) a particular taxation year that

(A) where it was associated with another corporation in the new corporation's first taxation year, ended in the calendar year that precedes the calendar year in which that first year ends, and

(B) in any other case, immediately precedes that first year, and

(ii) taxable income for the particular year (determined before taking into consideration the specified future tax consequences for the particular year) equal to the total of all amounts each of which is a predecessor corporation's taxable income for its taxation year that ended immediately before the amalgamation (determined before taking into consideration the specified future tax consequences for that year);

(oo.1) Refundable investment tax credit and balance-due day — for the purpose of applying the definition "qualifying corporation" in subsection 127.1(2), and subparagraph (d)(i) of the definition "balance-due day" in subsection 248(1), to any corporation, the new corporation is deemed to have had

(i) a particular taxation year that

(A) where it was associated with another corporation in the new corporation's first taxation year, ended in the calendar year that precedes the calendar year in which that first year ends, and

(B) where clause (A) does not apply, immediately precedes that first year,

(ii) taxable income for the particular year (determined before taking into consideration the specified future tax consequences for the particular year) equal to the total of all amounts each of which is a predecessor corporation's taxable income for its taxation year that ended immediately before the amalgamation (determined before taking into consideration the specified future tax consequences for that year), and

(iii) a business limit for the particular year equal to the total of all amounts each of which is a predecessor corporation's business limit for its taxation year that ended immediately before the amalgamation;

(pp) Cumulative offset account computation — for the purpose of computing the cumulative offset account (within the meaning assigned by subsection 66.5(2)) of the new corporation at any time, there shall be added to the total otherwise determined under paragraph 66.5(2)(a) the total of all amounts each of which is the amount, if any, by which

(i) a predecessor corporation's cumulative offset account at the end of its last taxation year

exceeds

¶1650

(ii) the amount deducted under subsection 66.5(1) in computing the predecessor corporation's income for its last taxation year;

(qq) Continuation of corporation — for the purpose of computing the new corporation's investment tax credit at the end of any taxation year, the new corporation is deemed to be the same corporation as, and a continuation of, each predecessor corporation, except that this paragraph does not affect the determination of the fiscal period of any corporation or the tax payable by any predecessor corporation;

(rr) Tax on taxable preferred shares — for the purposes of subsections 112(2.9), 191(4), and 191.1(2) and (4), the new corporation shall be deemed to be the same corporation as, and a continuation of, each predecessor corporation;

(ss) Transferred liability for Part VI.1 tax — for the purposes of section 191.3, the new corporation shall be deemed to be the same corporation as, and a continuation of, each predecessor corporation;

(tt) Livestock — inclusion of deferred amount — for the purposes of subsections 80.3(3) and (5), the new corporation shall be deemed to be the same corporation as, and a continuation of, each predecessor corporation; and

(uu) Fuel tax rebates — for the purposes of paragraph 12(1)(x.1), the description of D.1 in the definition "non-capital loss" in subsection 111(8), and subsections 111(10) and (11), the new corporation is deemed to be the same corporation as, and a continuation of, each predecessor corporation.

* * *

[¶1662]

SECTION 88:

(1) Winding-up. Where a taxable Canadian corporation (in this subsection referred to as the "subsidiary") has been wound up after May 6, 1974 and not less than 90% of the issued shares of each class of the capital stock of the subsidiary were, immediately before the winding-up, owned by another taxable Canadian corporation (in this subsection referred to as the "parent") and all of the shares of the subsidiary that were not owned by the parent immediately before the winding-up were owned at that time by persons with whom the parent was dealing at arm's length, notwithstanding any other provision of this Act other than subsection 69(11), the following rules apply:

(a) subject to paragraphs *(a.1)* and *(a.3)*, each property (other than an interest in a partnership) of the subsidiary that was distributed to the parent on the winding-up shall be deemed to have been disposed of by the subsidiary for proceeds equal to

(i) in the case of a Canadian resource property, a foreign resource property or a right to receive production (as defined in subsection 18.1(1)) to which a matchable expenditure (as defined in subsection 18.1(1)) relates, nil, and

(ii) [Repealed by S.C. 1994, c. 7, Sched. VIII, s. 38(1).]

(iii) in the case of any other property, the cost amount to the subsidiary of the property immediately before the winding-up;

(a.1) each property of the subsidiary that was distributed to the parent on the winding-up shall, for the purpose of paragraph (2.1)(b) or (e), be deemed not to have been disposed of;

(a.2) each interest of the subsidiary in a partnership that was distributed to the parent on the winding-up shall, except for the purpose of paragraph 98(5)(g), be deemed not to have been disposed of by the subsidiary;

(a.3) where

(i) the subsidiary was a financial institution in its taxation year in which its assets were distributed to the parent on the winding up, and

(ii) the parent was a financial institution in its taxation year in which it received the assets of the subsidiary on the winding up,

each specified debt obligation (other than a mark-to-market property) of the subsidiary that was distributed to the parent on the winding-up shall, except for the purpose of subsection 69(11), be deemed not to have been disposed of, and for the purpose of this paragraph, "financial institution", "mark-to-market property" and "specified debt obligation" have the meanings assigned by subsection 142.2(1);

(b) the shares of the capital stock of the subsidiary owned by the parent immediately before the winding-up shall be deemed to have been disposed of by the parent on the winding-up for proceeds equal to the greater of

(i) the lesser of the paid-up capital in respect of those shares immediately before the winding-up and the amount determined under subparagraph (d)(i), and

(ii) the total of all amounts each of which is an amount in respect of any share of the capital stock of the subsidiary so disposed of by the parent on the winding-up, equal to the adjusted cost base to the parent of the share immediately before the winding-up;

(c) subject to paragraph 87(2)(e.3) (as modified by paragraph (e.2)), and notwithstanding paragraph 87(2)(e.1) (as modified by paragraph (e.2)), the cost to the parent of each property of the subsidiary distributed to the parent on the winding-up shall be deemed to be

(i) in the case of a property that is an interest in a partnership, the amount that but for this paragraph would be the cost to the parent of the property, and

(ii) in any other case, the amount, if any, by which

(A) the amount that would, but for subsection 69(11), be deemed by paragraph (a) to be the proceeds of disposition of the property

¶1662

exceeds

(B) any reduction of the cost amount to the subsidiary of the property made because of section 80 on the winding-up,

plus, where the property was a capital property (other than an ineligible property) of the subsidiary at the time that the parent last acquired control of the subsidiary and was owned by the subsidiary thereafter without interruption until such time as it was distributed to the parent on the winding-up, the amount determined under paragraph (d) in respect of the property and, for the purposes of this paragraph, "ineligible property" means

(iii) depreciable property,

(iv) property transferred to the parent on the winding-up where the transfer is part of a distribution (within the meaning assigned by subsection 55(1)) made in the course of a reorganization in which a dividend was received to which subsection 55(2) would, but for paragraph 55(3)(b), apply,

(v) property acquired by the subsidiary from the parent or from any person or partnership that was not (otherwise than because of a right referred to in paragraph 251(5)(b)) dealing at arm's length with the parent, or any other property acquired by the subsidiary in substitution for it, where the acquisition was part of the series of transactions or events in which the parent last acquired control of the subsidiary, and

(vi) property distributed to the parent on the winding-up where, as part of the series of transactions or events that includes the winding-up,

(A) the parent acquired control of the subsidiary, and

(B) any property distributed to the parent on the winding-up or any other property acquired by any person in substitution therefor is acquired by

(I) a particular person (other than a specified person) that, at any time during the course of the series and before control of the subsidiary was last acquired by the parent, was a specified shareholder of the subsidiary,

(II) 2 or more persons (other than specified persons), if a particular person would have been, at any time during the course of the series and before control of the subsidiary was last acquired by the parent, a specified shareholder of the subsidiary if all the shares that were then owned by those 2 or more persons were owned at that time by the particular person, or

(III) a corporation (other than a specified person or the subsidiary)

1. of which a particular person referred to in subclause (I) is, at any time during the course of the series and after control of

¶1662

the subsidiary was last acquired by the parent, a specified shareholder, or

2. of which a particular person would be, at any time during the course of the series and after control of the subsidiary was last acquired by the parent, a specified shareholder if all the shares then owned by persons (other than specified persons) referred to in subclause (II) and acquired by those persons as part of the series were owned at that time by the particular person;

$(c.1)$ for the purpose of determining after the winding-up the amount to be included under paragraph $14(1)(b)$ in computing the parent's income in respect of the business carried on by the subsidiary immediately before the winding-up, there shall be added to the amount otherwise determined for Q in the definition "cumulative eligible capital" in subsection 14(5) the amount, if any, determined for Q in that definition in respect of that business immediately before the disposition;

Pending Amendment

Non-Resident Trusts, Foreign Investment Entities, and Technical Amendments (July 18, 2005)

Paragraph 88(1)(*c*.1) of the Act is replaced by the following:

$(c.1)$ for the purpose of determining after the winding-up the amount to be included under subsection 14(1) in computing the parent's income in respect of the business carried on by the subsidiary immediately before the winding-up

(i) there shall be added to the amount otherwise determined for each of A and F in the definition "cumulative eligible capital" in subsection 14(5), the amount, if any, determined for the description of F in that definition in respect of that business immediately before the disposition, and

(ii) there shall be added to the amount determined for the description of C in the formula in paragraph $14(1)(b)$, one-half of the amount, if any, determined for the description of Q in that definition in respect of that business immediately before the disposition;

Applicable: In respect of dispositions that occur after December 20, 2002.

Explanatory Note: Subparagraph $88(1)(a)$(iii) of the Act generally provides that property of a subsidiary corporation is deemed to have been disposed of on its winding-up for proceeds of disposition equal to its cost amount to the subsidiary immediately before the winding-up. Under subparagraph $88(1)(c)$(ii) of the Act, the cost of such property to the parent corporation is equal to such proceeds of disposition. Paragraph $88(1)(c.1)$ of the Act ensures that an amount that would have been recaptured depreciation to the subsidiary under subsection 14(1) of the Act, if the subsidiary had instead disposed of the eligible capital property for fair market value proceeds, is subject to possible recapture in the hands of the parent upon a subsequent sale of the property.

Paragraph $88(1)(c.1)$ is renumbered as subparagraph $88(1)(c.1)$(ii) and remains unchanged. Paragraph $88(1)(c.1)$ is further amended by the addition of new subparagraph (i), which ensures that eligible capital property deductions claimed under paragraph $20(1)(b)$ of the Act by the subsidiary after its "adjustment time" (as defined in subsection 14(5) of the Act, i.e., generally the beginning of the first taxation year of the subsidiary that starts after June 30, 1988) are included in the amount subject to potential recapture.

¶1662

Paragraph $88(1)(c.1)$ applies to a parent corporation similarly to the application of paragraphs $85(1)(d.1)$ and $(d.11)$ of the Act to a transferee corporation. For additional information, refer to the commentary to those paragraphs for an example of that application.

Amended paragraph $88(1)(c.1)$ applies in respect of dispositions that occur after December 20, 2002.

$(c.2)$ for the purposes of this paragraph and subparagraph $(c)(vi)$,

(i) "specified person" at any time means the parent and each person that would, if this Act were read without reference to paragraph $251(5)(b)$, be related to the parent at that time and, for this purpose, a person shall be deemed not to be related to the parent where it can reasonably be considered that one of the main purposes of one or more transactions or events was to cause the person to be related to the parent so as to prevent a property that was distributed to the parent on the winding-up from being an ineligible property for the purpose of paragraph (c),

(ii) where at any time a property is owned or acquired by a partnership or a trust,

(A) the partnership or the trust, as the case may be, shall be deemed to be a person that is a corporation having one class of issued shares, which shares have full voting rights under all circumstances,

(B) each member of the partnership or beneficiary under the trust, as the case may be, shall be deemed to own at that time the proportion of the number of issued shares of the capital stock of the corporation that

(I) the fair market value at that time of that member's interest in the partnership or that beneficiary's interest in the trust, as the case may be,

is of

(II) the fair market value at that time of all the members' interests in the partnership or beneficiaries' interests in the trust, as the case may be, and

(C) the property shall be deemed to have been owned or acquired at that time by the corporation; and

(iii) in determining whether a person is a specified shareholder of a corporation,

(A) the reference in the definition "specified shareholder" in subsection 248(1) to "the issued shares of any class of the capital stock of the corporation or of any other corporation that is related to the corporation" shall be read as "the issued shares of any class (other than a specified class) of the capital stock of the corporation or of any other corporation that is related to the corporation

¶1662

and that has a significant direct or indirect interest in any issued shares of the capital stock of the corporation", and

(B) a corporation is deemed not to be a specified shareholder of itself;

(c.3) for the purpose of clause (c)(vi)(B), property acquired by any person in substitution for particular property or properties distributed to the parent on the winding-up includes

(i) property (other than a specified property) owned by the person at any time after the acquisition of control referred to in clause (c)(vi)(A) the fair market value of which is, at that time, wholly or partly attributable to the particular property or properties, and

(ii) property owned by the person at any time after the acquisition of control referred to in clause (c)(vi)(A) the fair market value of which is, at that time, determinable primarily by reference to the fair market value of, or to any proceeds from a disposition of, the particular property or properties

but does not include

(iii) money,

(iv) property that was not owned by the person at any time after the acquisition of control referred to in clause (c)(vi)(A), or

(v) property described in subparagraph (i) if the only reason the property is described in that subparagraph is because a specified property described in any of subparagraphs (c.4)(i) to (iv) was received as consideration for the acquisition of a share of the capital stock of the subsidiary in the circumstances described in subparagraphs (c.4)(i) to (iv);

Pending Amendment

Non-Resident Trusts, Foreign Investment Entities, and Technical Amendments (July 18, 2005)

Paragraph 88(1)(c.3) of the Act is amended by striking out the word "or" at the end of subparagraph (iv) and by adding the following after subparagraph (v):

(vi) a share of the capital stock of the subsidiary or a debt owing by it, if the share or debt, as the case may be, was owned by the parent immediately before the winding-up, or

(vii) a share of the capital stock of a corporation or a debt owing by a corporation, if the fair market value of the share or debt, as the case may be, was not, at any time after the beginning of the winding-up, wholly or partly attributable to property distributed to the parent on the winding-up;

Applicable: To windings-up that begin after 1997.

Explanatory Note: Paragraph $88(1)(c)$ of the Act generally provides that the cost to the parent of each property distributed to it on the winding-up of a subsidiary is equal to the subsidiary's proceeds of disposition plus, where the property is a capital property and is not an ineligible property, an amount determined under paragraph $88(1)(d)$ in respect of the property. "Ineligible property" is described in subparagraphs $88(1)(c)(iii)$ to (vi). Pursuant to subparagraph $88(1)(c)(vi)$, ineligible property includes any property distributed to the parent on the winding-up if, as part of the series of transactions or events that includes the winding-up, the property or property acquired in substitution for such property was acquired by a person or persons described in clause $88(1)(c)(vi)(B)$. Property acquired in substitution for property distributed on the winding-up ("substituted property") has its ordinary meaning and an extended meaning found in paragraph $88(1)(c.3)$ of the Act.

Paragraph $88(1)(c.3)$ of the Act provides that substituted property includes property described in subparagraphs $88(1)(c.3)(i)$ and (ii) but excludes property described in subparagraphs $88(1)(c.3)(iii)$ to (v). Subparagraph $88(1)(c.3)(i)$ provides that, for the purpose of clause $88(1)(c)(vi)(B)$, substituted property includes property (other than a "specified property") owned by a person after the acquisition of control of the subsidiary where the fair market value of the property is wholly or partly attributable to property distributed to the parent on the winding-up. Subparagraph $88(1)(c.3)(iv)$ ensures that property that would be substituted property under the ordinary meaning of the term will not be substituted property if it is not owned by the person after the acquisition of control.

Example 1 of the explanatory notes to the introduction of paragraph $88(1)(c.3)$ [see the explanatory notes to S.C. 1998, c.19 (formerly Bill C-28)] describes a scenario under the heading *Safe Income Crystallization* that illustrates the application of subparagraph $88(1)(c.3)(iv)$ to a situation involving a safe income crystallization prior to a takeover. In that example, Sco, a taxable Canadian corporation, owns 15% of Tco, a publicly traded taxable Canadian corporation. Another corporation ("Pco") makes a takeover offer for all the shares of Tco. In anticipation of the sale of the Tco shares, Sco incorporates Newco and transfers, on a tax-deferred basis under section 85 of the Act, all of its Tco shares to Newco in exchange for Newco shares. The adjusted cost base and the paid-up capital of the Newco shares are then increased by the amount equal to the so-called "safe income" attributable to the Tco shares. Immediately thereafter, Sco sells the Newco shares to Pco for cash and Newco is wound up into Pco.

In the example, subparagraph $88(1)(c.3)(iv)$ ensures that the Newco shares are not substituted property since Sco did not own the Newco shares after the acquisition of control of Newco by Pco. However, assuming that Tco is subsequently wound up into Pco, the non-depreciable capital property ("bump property") owned by Tco at the time of the acquisition of control of Tco would be ineligible property since, as part of the series of transactions or events that includes the winding up of Tco, property substituted for the bump property (i.e., the 15% of the Tco shares) would have been acquired by a specified shareholder of Tco (i.e., Newco) and would have been owned by Newco after the acquisition of control of Tco.

New subparagraphs $88(1)(c.3)(vi)$ and (vii) of the Act, which apply to windings-up that begin after 1997, are enacted to ensure that certain shares or debt will not be substituted property even if they are owned by a specified shareholder after the acquisition of control of the subsidiary. Subparagraph $88(1)(c.3)(vi)$ provides that shares or debt of the subsidiary will not be substituted property if such shares or debt are owned by the parent immediately before the winding-up of the subsidiary. Thus, in the example discussed above, the Tco shares, which are owned by Pco immediately before the winding-up of Tco, would not be substituted property.

Subparagraph $88(1)(c.3)(vii)$ provides that a share or debt of a corporation will not be substituted property if the fair market value of the share or debt is not attributable, at any time after the winding-up process begins, to property acquired by the parent on the winding-up. This exemption would apply, for example, if an individual ("Mr. S"),

¶1662

who is a specified shareholder of Tco, incorporates Newco in contemplation of the takeover of Tco and transfers the Tco shares to Newco. Mr. S then transfers the Newco shares to Sco. Immediately after the increase in the adjusted cost base of the shares of Newco (i.e., following the safe income crystallization) Sco sells the Newco shares to Pco. In this scenario, the Sco shares owned by Mr. S after the sale would not be substituted property by reason of new subparagraph $88(1)(c.3)(vii)$.

$(c.4)$ for the purposes of subparagraphs $(c.3)(i)$ and (v), a specified property is

(i) a share of the capital stock of the parent that was received as consideration for the acquisition of a share of the capital stock of the subsidiary by the parent or by a corporation that was a specified subsidiary corporation of the parent immediately before the acquisition,

---

Pending Amendment

Non-Resident Trusts, Foreign Investment Entities, and Technical Amendments (July 18, 2005)

Subparagraph $88(1)(c.4)(i)$ of the Act is replaced by the following:

(i) a share of the capital stock of the parent that was

(A) received as consideration for the acquisition of a share of the capital stock of the subsidiary by the parent or by a corporation that was a specified subsidiary corporation of the parent immediately before the acquisition, or

(B) issued for consideration that consists solely of money,

Applicable: To windings-up that begin after 1997.

Explanatory Note: Paragraph $88(1)(c.4)$ of the Act defines "specified property" for the purposes of subparagraphs $88(1)(c.3)(i)$ and (v) of the Act. Specified property is excluded from the extended meaning of a substituted property found in subparagraph $88(1)(c.3)(i)$. Subparagraph $88(1)(c.4)(i)$ is amended to include, within the definition "specified property", shares of the parent issued for consideration that consists solely of money. This amendment, which applies to windings-up that begin after 1997, ensures that a specified shareholder that participates in a takeover by acquiring shares of the parent for cash consideration will not be considered to have acquired substituted property within the meaning assigned by subparagraph $88(1)(c.3)(i)$.

(ii) an indebtedness that was issued by the parent as consideration for the acquisition of a share of the capital stock of the subsidiary by the parent,

(iii) a share of the capital stock of a taxable Canadian corporation that was received as consideration for the acquisition of a share of the capital stock of the subsidiary by the taxable Canadian corporation or by the parent where the parent was a specified subsidiary corporation of the taxable Canadian corporation immediately before the acquisition,

(iv) an indebtedness of a taxable Canadian corporation that was issued by it as consideration for the acquisition of a share of the capital

¶1662

stock of the subsidiary by the taxable Canadian corporation or by the parent where the parent was a specified subsidiary corporation of the taxable Canadian corporation immediately before the acquisition,

(v) where the subsidiary was formed on the amalgamation of 2 or more predecessor corporations at least one of which was a subsidiary wholly-owned corporation of the parent, a share of the capital stock of the subsidiary

(A) that was issued on the amalgamation in exchange for a share of the capital stock of a predecessor corporation, and

(B) that was, immediately after the amalgamation, redeemed, acquired or cancelled by the subsidiary for money, and

(vi) where the subsidiary was formed on the amalgamation of 2 or more predecessor corporations at least one of which was a subsidiary wholly-owned corporation of the parent, a share of the capital stock of the parent

(A) that was issued on the amalgamation in exchange for a share of the capital stock of a predecessor corporation, and

(B) that was, immediately after the amalgamation, redeemed, acquired or cancelled by the parent for money;

(c.5) for the purpose of paragraph (c.4), a corporation is a specified subsidiary corporation of another corporation, at any time, where the other corporation holds, at that time, shares of the corporation

(i) that give the shareholder 90% or more of the votes that could be cast under all circumstances at an annual meeting of shareholders of the corporation, and

(ii) having a fair market value of 90% or more of the fair market value of all the issued shares of the capital stock of the corporation;

(c.6) for the purpose of paragraph (c.3) and notwithstanding subsection 256(9), where control of a corporation is acquired by way of articles of arrangement, that control is deemed to have been acquired at the end of the day on which the arrangement becomes effective;

(c.7) for the purpose of subparagraph (c)(iii), a leasehold interest in a depreciable property and an option to acquire a depreciable property are depreciable properties;

(c.8) for the purpose of clause (c.2)(iii)(A), a specified class of the capital stock of a corporation is a class of shares of the capital stock of the corporation where

(i) the paid-up capital in respect of the class was not, at any time, less than the fair market value of the consideration for which the shares of that class then outstanding were issued,

(ii) the shares are non-voting in respect of the election of the board of directors of the corporation, except in the event of a failure or default under the terms or conditions of the shares,

¶1662

(iii) under neither the terms and conditions of the shares nor any agreement in respect of the shares are the shares convertible into or exchangeable for shares other than shares of a specified class of the capital stock of the corporation, and

(iv) under neither the terms and conditions of the shares nor any agreement in respect of the shares is any holder of the shares entitled to receive on the redemption, cancellation or acquisition of the shares by the corporation or by any person with whom the corporation does not deal at arm's length an amount (excluding any premium for early redemption) greater than the total of the fair market value of the consideration for which the shares were issued and the amount of any unpaid dividends on the shares;

(d) the amount determined under this paragraph in respect of each property of the subsidiary distributed to the parent on the winding-up is such portion of the amount, if any, by which the total determined under subparagraph (b)(ii) exceeds the total of

(i) the amount, if any, by which

(A) the total of all amounts each of which is an amount in respect of any property owned by the subsidiary immediately before the winding-up, equal to the cost amount to the subsidiary of the property immediately before the winding-up, plus the amount of any money of the subsidiary on hand immediately before the winding-up,

exceeds the total of

(B) all amounts each of which is the amount of any debt owing by the subsidiary, or of any other obligation of the subsidiary to pay any amount, that was outstanding immediately before the winding-up, and

(C) the amount of any reserve (other than a reserve referred to in paragraph $20(1)(n)$, subparagraph $40(1)(a)$(iii) or $44(1)(e)$(iii) of this Act or in subsection $64(1)$ or (1.1) of the *Income Tax Act*, chapter 148 of the Revised Statutes of Canada, 1952, as those two provisions read immediately before November 3, 1981) deducted in computing the subsidiary's income for its taxation year during which its assets were distributed to the parent on the winding-up, and

(i.1) the total of all amounts each of which is an amount in respect of any share of the capital stock of the subsidiary disposed of by the parent on the winding-up or in contemplation of the winding-up, equal to the total of all amounts received by the parent or by a corporation with which the parent was not dealing at arm's length (otherwise than because of a right referred to in paragraph $251(5)(b)$ in respect of the subsidiary) in respect of

(A) taxable dividends on the share or on any share (in this subparagraph referred to as a "replaced share") for which the share or a

¶1662

replaced share was substituted or exchanged to the extent that the amounts thereof were deductible from the recipient's income for any taxation year by virtue of section 112 or subsection 138(6) and were not amounts on which the recipient was required to pay tax under Part VII of the *Income Tax Act*, chapter 148 of the Revised Statutes of Canada, 1952, as it read on March 31, 1977, or

(B) capital dividends and life insurance capital dividends on the share or on any share (in this subparagraph referred to as a "replaced share") for which a share or a replaced share was substituted or exchanged,

as is designated by the parent in respect of that capital property in its return of income under this Part for its taxation year in which the subsidiary was so wound up, except that

(ii) in no case shall the amount so designated in respect of any such capital property exceed the amount, if any, by which the fair market value of the property at the time the parent last acquired control of the subsidiary exceeds the cost amount to the subsidiary of the property immediately before the winding-up, and

(iii) in no case shall the total of amounts so designated in respect of all such capital properties exceed the amount, if any, by which the total determined under subparagraph (b)(ii) exceeds the total of the amounts determined under subparagraphs (i) and (i.1),

$(d.1)$ subsection 84(2) and section 21 of the *Income Tax Application Rules* do not apply to the winding-up of the subsidiary, and subsections 13(21.2) and 14(12) do not apply to the winding-up of the subsidiary with respect to property acquired by the parent on the winding-up;

$(d.2)$ in determining, for the purposes of this paragraph and paragraphs (c) and (d), the time at which a person or group of persons (in this paragraph and paragraph $(d.3)$ referred to as the "acquirer") last acquired control of the subsidiary, where control of the subsidiary was acquired from another person or group of persons (in this paragraph referred to as the "vendor") with whom the acquirer was not (otherwise than solely because of a right referred to in paragraph 251(5)(b)) dealing at arm's length, the acquirer is deemed to have last acquired control of the subsidiary at the earlier of

(i) the time at which the vendor last acquired control (within the meaning that would be assigned by subsection 186(2) if the reference in that subsection to "another corporation" were read as "a person" and the references in that subsection to "the other corporation" were read as "the person") of the subsidiary, and

(ii) the time at which the vendor was deemed for the purpose of this paragraph to have last acquired control of the subsidiary;

$(d.3)$ for the purposes of paragraphs (c), (d) and $(d.2)$, where at any time control of a corporation is last acquired by an acquirer because of an acquisition of shares of the capital stock of the corporation as a

¶1662

consequence of the death of an individual, the acquirer is deemed to have last acquired control of the corporation immediately after the death from a person who dealt at arm's length with the acquirer;

Pending Amendment

Technical Amendments (February 27, 2004)

Subsection 88(1) of the Act is amended by adding the following after paragraph (d.3):

(d.4) for the purpose of subparagraph (d)(ii),

(i) if, at the time immediately before the winding-up, the subsidiary holds one or more shares of a foreign affiliate of the subsidiary, there shall be added to the cost amount, at that time, of each of those shares (referred to in this subparagraph as the "particular share") the amount determined by the formula

$$A \times B/C$$

where

A is the total of all amounts each of which is the amount, if any, by which

(A) the amount of a dividend received on any share of the foreign affiliate (or any other share of the foreign affiliate for which that share is substituted property) held by the subsidiary immediately before the winding-up, that was deductible under section 113 in computing the income of the subsidiary or of a corporation with which the subsidiary was not dealing at arm's length (otherwise than because of a right referred to in paragraph $251(5)(b)$ in respect of the foreign affiliate),

exceeds

(B) the portion of that dividend that may reasonably be considered to have reduced the foreign affiliate's exempt or taxable surplus in respect of the subsidiary that arose after the acquisition of control of the subsidiary by the parent (determined on the assumption that a dividend is paid out of the foreign affiliate's exempt or taxable surplus, as the case may be, in respect of the subsidiary, in the reverse order to that in which it was added to the foreign affiliate's exempt or taxable surplus in respect of the subsidiary),

B is the fair market value of the particular share immediately before the winding-up, and

C is the total of all amounts each of which is the fair market value of a share of the foreign affiliate held by the subsidiary immediately before the winding-up, and

(ii) if, at the time immediately before the winding-up, the subsidiary holds a partnership interest in a partnership (referred to in this subparagraph as a "holding partnership") which holds one or more shares of a foreign affiliate of the subsidiary, there shall be added to the cost amount, at that time, of the subsidiary's partnership interest in the holding partnership (referred to in this subparagraph as the "particular partnership interest"), the amount determined by the formula

$$D \times E/F$$

where

D is the total of all amounts each of which is the amount, if any, by which

(A) the amount of a dividend received on any share of the foreign affiliate (or any other share of the foreign affiliate for which that share is substituted property) held by the holding partnership immediately before the winding-up, that was deductible under section 113 in computing the income of the subsidiary or of a corporation with which the subsidiary was not dealing at arm's length (otherwise than because of a right referred to in paragraph 251(5)(b) in respect of the foreign affiliate),

exceeds

(B) the portion of that dividend that may reasonably be considered to have reduced the foreign affiliate's exempt or taxable surplus in respect of the subsidiary that arose after the acquisition of control of the subsidiary by the parent (determined on the assumption that a dividend is paid out of the foreign affiliate's exempt or taxable surplus, as the case may be, in respect of the subsidiary, in the reverse order to that in which it was added to the foreign affiliate's exempt or taxable surplus in respect of the subsidiary),

E　is the fair market value of the particular partnership interest immediately before the winding-up, and

F　is the total of all amounts each of which is the fair market value of a partnership interest in the holding partnership held by the subsidiary immediately before the winding-up;

Applicable: To amalgamations that occur, and to windings-up that begin, after February 27, 2004 and if the taxpayer so elects in writing and files the election with the Minister of National Revenue on or before the taxpayer's filing-due date for the taxpayer's taxation year that includes the day on which this Act is assented to, that subsection applies in respect of the taxpayer to all amalgamations that occur, and to all windings-up that begin, after December 20, 2002 and, notwithstanding subsections 152(4) to (5) of the Act, any assessment of the taxpayer's tax, interest and penalties payable under the Act for any taxation year that begins on or before February 27, 2004 shall be made that is necessary to take the election into account.

Explanatory Note: Subsection 88(1) of the Act provides rules that apply where a subsidiary has been wound up into its parent corporation where both corporations are taxable Canadian corporations and the parent owns at least 90% of the issued shares of each class of the capital stock of the subsidiary.

Subsection 88(1) is amended by adding proposed new paragraph (d.4) effective for amalgamations that occur after February 27, 2004 and to windings-up that begin after February 27, 2004. Taxpayers may elect to have the provision apply to all amalgamations that occur, and all windings-up that begin, after December 20, 2002.

In general terms, proposed new paragraph 88(1)(d.4) applies for the purpose of subparagraph 88(1)(d)(ii) and increases, in certain circumstances, the cost amount to the subsidiary of a share of a foreign affiliate of the subsidiary or the cost amount of a partnership interest in a partnership that holds such a share, thereby limiting the amount of a increase in cost base of a property to the parent that is the share or the interest in the partnership that might otherwise occur on an amalgamation or a winding up of the subsidiary.

New paragraph 88(1)(d.4) provides that

● if, at the time immediately before the winding-up, the subsidiary holds one or more shares of a foreign affiliate of the subsidiary, there shall be added to the cost amount, at that time, of each of those shares (referred to here as the "particular share") the amount determined by the formula

$$\frac{A \times B}{C}$$

¶1662

where

A is the total of all amounts each of which is the amount, if any, by which

(A) the amount of a dividend received on any share of the foreign affiliate (or any other share of the foreign affiliate for which that share is substituted property) held by the subsidiary immediately before the winding-up, that was deductible under section 113 in computing the income of the subsidiary or of a corporation with which the subsidiary was not dealing at arm's length (otherwise than because of a right referred to in paragraph 251(5)(*b*) in respect of the foreign affiliate),

exceeds

(B) the portion of that dividend that may reasonably be considered to have reduced the foreign affiliate's exempt or taxable surplus in respect of the subsidiary that arose after the acquisition of control of the subsidiary by the parent (determined on the assumption that a dividend is paid out of the foreign affiliate's exempt or taxable surplus, as the case may be, in respect of the subsidiary, in the reverse order to that in which it was added to the foreign affiliate's exempt or taxable surplus in respect of the subsidiary),

B is the fair market value of the particular share immediately before the winding-up, and

C is the total of all amounts each of which is the fair market value of a share of the foreign affiliate held by the subsidiary immediately before the winding-up, and

● if, at the time immediately before the winding-up, the subsidiary holds a partnership interest in a partnership (a "holding partnership") which holds one or more shares of a foreign affiliate of the subsidiary, there shall be added to the cost amount, at that time, of the subsidiary's partnership interest in the holding partnership (referred to as the "particular partnership interest"), the amount determined by the formula

$$\frac{D \times E}{F}$$

where

D is the total of all amounts each of which is the amount, if any, by which

(A) the amount of a dividend received on any share of the foreign affiliate (or any other share of the foreign affiliate for which that share is substituted property) held by a holding partnership immediately before the winding-up, that was deductible under section 113 in computing the income of the subsidiary or of a corporation with which the subsidiary was not dealing at arm's length (otherwise than because of a right referred to in paragraph 251(5)(*b*) in respect of the foreign affiliate),

exceeds

(B) the portion of that dividend that may reasonably be considered to have reduced the foreign affiliate's exempt or taxable surplus in respect of the subsidiary that arose after the acquisition of control of the subsidiary by the parent (determined on the assumption that a dividend is paid out of the foreign affiliate's exempt or taxable surplus, as the case may be, in respect of the subsidiary, in the reverse order to that in which it was added to the foreign affiliate's exempt or taxable surplus in respect of the subsidiary),

E is the fair market value of the particular partnership interest immediately before the winding-up, and

F is the total of all amounts each of which is the fair market value of a partnership interest in a holding partnership held by the subsidiary immediately before the winding-up.

¶1662

(e) [Repealed by 1977-78, c. 1, s. 43(8).]

(e.1) the subsidiary may, for the purposes of computing its income for its taxation year during which its assets were transferred to, and its obligations were assumed by, the parent on the winding-up, claim any reserve that would have been allowed under this Part if its assets had not been transferred to, or its obligations had not been assumed by, the parent on the winding-up and notwithstanding any other provision of this Part, no amount shall be included in respect of any reserve so claimed in computing the income of the subsidiary for its taxation year, if any, following the year in which its assets were transferred to or its obligations were assumed by the parent;

(e.2) paragraphs 87(2)(c), (d.1), (e.1), (e.3), (g) to (l), (l.3) to (u), (x), (z.1), (z.2), (aa), (cc), (ll), (nn), (pp), (rr), (tt) and (uu), subsection 87(6) and, subject to section 78, subsection 87(7) apply to the winding-up as if the references in those provisions to

(i) "amalgamation" were read as "winding-up",

(ii) "predecessor corporation" were read as "subsidiary",

(iii) "new corporation" were read as "parent",

(iv) "its first taxation year" were read as "its taxation year during which it received the assets of the subsidiary on the winding-up",

(v) "its last taxation year" were read as "its taxation year during which its assets were distributed to the parent on the winding-up",

(vi) "predecessor corporation's gain" were read as "subsidiary's gain",

(vii) "predecessor corporation's income" were read as "subsidiary's income",

(viii) "new corporation's income" were read as "parent's income",

(ix) [Repealed by 1984, c. 45, s. 28(2).]

(x) "any predecessor private corporation" were read as "the subsidiary (if it was a private corporation at the time of the winding-up)",

(xi) [Repealed by S.C. 1994, c. 7, Sched. II, s. 66(8).]

(xii) [Repealed by S.C. 1994, c. 7, Sched. II, s. 66(8).]

(xiii) "two or more corporations" were read as "a subsidiary",

(xiv) [Repealed by S.C. 1998, c. 19, s. 118(11).]

(xv) [Repealed by S.C. 1998, c. 19, s. 118(11).]

(xvi) "the life insurance capital dividend account of any predecessor corporation immediately before the amalgamation" were read as "the life insurance capital dividend account of the subsidiary at the time the subsidiary was wound-up",

(xvii) "predecessor corporation's refundable Part VII tax on hand" were read as "subsidiary's refundable Part VII tax on hand",

¶1662

(xviii) "predecessor corporation's Part VII refund" were read as "subsidiary's Part VII refund",

(xix) "predecessor corporation's refundable Part VIII tax on hand" were read as "subsidiary's refundable Part VIII tax on hand",

(xx) "predecessor corporation's Part VIII refund" were read as "subsidiary's Part VIII refund", and

(xxi) "predecessor corporation's cumulative offset account" were read as "subsidiary's cumulative offset account";

(*e*.3) for the purpose of computing the parent's investment tax credit at the end of any particular taxation year ending after the subsidiary was wound up,

(i) property acquired or expenditures made by the subsidiary or an amount included in the investment tax credit of the subsidiary by virtue of paragraph (*b*) of the definition "investment tax credit" in subsection 127(9) in a taxation year (in this paragraph referred to as the "expenditure year") shall be deemed to have been acquired, made or included, as the case may be, by the parent in its taxation year in which the expenditure year of the subsidiary ended, and

(ii) there shall be added to the amounts otherwise determined for the purposes of paragraphs (*f*) to (*k*) of the definition "investment tax credit" in subsection 127(9) in respect of the parent for the particular year

(A) the amounts that would have been determined in respect of the subsidiary for the purposes of paragraph (*f*) of the definition "investment tax credit" in subsection 127(9) for its taxation year in which it was wound up if the reference therein to "a preceding taxation year" were read as a reference to "the year or a preceding taxation year",

(B) the amounts determined in respect of the subsidiary for the purposes of paragraphs (*g*) to (*i*) and (*k*) of the definition "investment tax credit" in subsection 127(9) for its taxation year in which it was wound up, and

(C) the amount determined in respect of the subsidiary for the purposes of paragraph (*j*) of the definition "investment tax credit" in subsection 127(9) for its taxation year in which it was wound up except that, for the purpose of the calculation in this clause, where control of the subsidiary has been acquired by a person or group of persons (each of whom is referred to in this clause as the "purchaser") at any time (in this clause referred to as "that time") before the end of the taxation year in which the subsidiary was wound up, there may be added to the amount determined under subparagraph 127(9.1)(*d*)(i) in respect of the subsidiary the amount, if any, by which that proportion of the amount that, but for subsections 127(3) and (5) and sections 126,

¶1662

127.2 and 127.3, would be the parent's tax payable under this Part for the particular year, that,

(I) where the subsidiary carried on a particular business in the course of which a property was acquired, or an expenditure was made, before that time in respect of which an amount was included in computing the subsidiary's investment tax credit for its taxation year in which it was wound up, and the parent carried on the particular business throughout the particular year, the amount, if any, by which the total of all amounts each of which is the parent's income for the particular year from the particular business, or the parent's income for the particular year from any other business substantially all the income of which was derived from the sale, leasing, rental or development of properties or the rendering of services similar to the properties sold, leased, rented or developed, or the services rendered, as the case may be, by the subsidiary in carrying on the particular business before that time, exceeds the total of the amounts, if any, deducted for the particular year under paragraph $111(1)(a)$ or (d) by the parent in respect of a non-capital loss or a farm loss, as the case may be, for a taxation year in respect of the particular business

is of the greater of

(II) the amount determined under subclause (I), and

(III) the parent's taxable income for the particular year

exceeds the amount, if any, calculated under subparagraph $127(9.1)(d)(i)$ in respect of the particular business or the other business, as the case may be, in respect of the parent at the end of the particular year

to the extent that those amounts determined in respect of the subsidiary may reasonably be considered to have been included in computing the parent's investment tax credit at the end of the particular year by virtue of subparagraph (i);

and, for the purposes of the definitions "first term shared-use-equipment" and "second term shared-use-equipment" in subsection 127(9), the parent shall be deemed to be the same corporation as, and a continuation of, the subsidiary;

(e.4) for the purpose of computing the parent's employment tax credit at the end of any particular taxation year ending after the subsidiary was wound up,

(i) the subsidiary's taxpayer employment credits for any taxation year (in this paragraph referred to as the "employment year") and any amounts required to be added by virtue of subsection 127(15) of the *Income Tax Act*, chapter 148 of the Revised Statutes of Canada, 1952, in computing the subsidiary's employment tax credit at the end of the employment year shall be deemed to be taxpayer employment

¶1662

credits of the parent for, and amounts required to be added by virtue of that subsection in computing the parent's employment tax credit at the end of, its taxation year in which the employment year of the subsidiary ended, and

(ii) there shall be added to the amounts otherwise determined under paragraphs $127(16)(c)$ and (d) of the *Income Tax Act*, chapter 148 of the Revised Statutes of Canada, 1952, in respect of the parent for the particular taxation year, the amounts that would have been determined under those paragraphs in respect of the subsidiary for its taxation year in which it was wound-up if the reference in paragraph $127(16)(c)$ of that Act to "the five immediately preceding taxation years" were read as a reference to "that taxation year or the five immediately preceding taxation years" to the extent that those amounts determined in respect of the subsidiary may reasonably be considered to be in respect of a taxpayer employment credit or an amount required to be added by virtue of subsection $127(15)$ of that Act that is included in computing the parent's employment tax credit at the end of the particular year by virtue of subparagraph (i);

$(e.5)$ [Repealed by 1996, c. 21, s. 16(2).]

$(e.6)$ where a subsidiary has made a gift in a taxation year (in this section referred to as the "gift year"), for the purposes of computing the amount deductible under section 110.1 by the parent for its taxation years ending after the subsidiary was wound up, the parent shall be deemed to have made a gift in each of its taxation years in which a gift year of the subsidiary ended equal to the amount, if any, by which the total of all gifts made by the subsidiary in the gift year exceeds the total of all amounts deducted by the subsidiary under section 110.1 of this Act or paragraph $110(1)(a)$, (b) or $(b.1)$ of the *Income Tax Act*, chapter 148 of the Revised Statutes of Canada, 1952, in respect of those gifts;

Pending Amendment

Non-Resident Trusts, Foreign Investment Entities, and Technical Amendments (July 18, 2005)

Paragraph 88(1)(e.6) of the Act is replaced by the following:

$(e.6)$ if a subsidiary has made a gift in a taxation year (in this section referred to as the "gift year"), for the purposes of computing the amount deductible under section 110.1 by the parent for its taxation years that end after the subsidiary was wound up, the parent is deemed to have made a gift, in each of its taxation years in which a gift year of the subsidiary ended, equal to the amount, if any, by which the total of all amounts, each of which is the amount of a gift or, in the case of a gift made after December 20, 2002, the eligible amount of the gift, made by the subsidiary in the gift year exceeds the total of all amounts deducted under section 110.1 by the subsidiary in respect of those gifts;

Applicable: To windings-up that begin after December 20, 2002.

Explanatory Note: Paragraph 88(1)(*e*.6) of the Act permits a parent corporation to deduct the amount of a subsidiary's charitable gifts, gifts to Her Majesty, gifts to certain cultural institutions and ecological gifts, to the extent that they were not deducted by the subsidiary prior to the time of its winding-up. Paragraph 88(1)(*e*.6) is amended, consequential to the addition of new subsection 248(31) of the Act, to allow the parent to deduct the eligible amount of a gift made after December 20, 2002 that was not deducted by the subsidiary. For additional details, see the commentary to new subsection 248(31).

(*e*.61) the parent is deemed for the purpose of section 110.1 to have made any gift deemed by subsection 118.1(13) to have been made by the subsidiary after the subsidiary ceased to exist;

(*e*.7) for the purposes of

(i) determining the amount deductible by the parent under subsection 126(2) for any taxation year commencing after the commencement of the winding-up, and

(ii) determining the extent to which subsection 126(2.3) applies to reduce the amount that may be claimed by the parent under paragraph 126(2)(*a*),

any unused foreign tax credit (within the meaning of subsection 126(7)) of the subsidiary in respect of a country for a particular taxation year (in this section referred to as the "foreign tax year"), to the extent that it exceeds the total of all amounts each of which is claimed in respect thereof under paragraph 126(2)(*a*) in computing the tax payable by the subsidiary under this Part for any taxation year, shall be deemed to be an unused foreign tax credit of the parent for its taxation year in which the subsidiary's foreign tax year ended;

(*e*.8) for the purpose of applying subsection 127(10.2) to any corporation (other than the subsidiary)

(i) where the parent is associated with another corporation in a taxation year (in this paragraph referred to as the "current year") of the parent that begins after the parent received an asset of the subsidiary on the winding-up and that ends in a calendar year,

(A) the parent's taxable income for its last taxation year that ended in the preceding calendar year (determined before taking into consideration the specified future tax consequences for that last year) is deemed to be the total of

(I) its taxable income for that last year (determined before applying this paragraph to the winding-up and before taking into consideration the specified future tax consequences for that last year), and

(II) the total of the subsidiary's taxable incomes for its taxation years that ended in that preceding calendar year (determined

¶1662

without reference to clause (B) and before taking into consideration the specified future tax consequences for those years), and

(B) the subsidiary's taxable income for each of its taxation years that ends after the first time that the parent receives an asset of the subsidiary on the winding-up of the subsidiary is deemed to be nil, and

(ii) where the parent received an asset of the subsidiary on the winding-up before the current year and is not associated with any corporation in the current year, the parent's taxable income for its immediately preceding taxation year (determined before taking into consideration the specified future tax consequences for that preceding year) is deemed to be the total of

(A) its taxable income for that preceding taxation year (determined before applying this paragraph to the winding-up and before taking into consideration the specified future tax consequences for that preceding taxation year), and

(B) the total of the subsidiary's taxable incomes for its taxation years that ended in the calendar year in which that preceding taxation year ended (determined before taking into consideration the specified future tax consequences for those years);

(e.9) for the purpose of applying the definition "qualifying corporation" in subsection 127.1(2), and subparagraph (d)(i) of the definition "balance-due day" in subsection 248(1), to any corporation (other than the subsidiary)

(i) where the parent is associated with another corporation in a taxation year (in this paragraph referred to as the "current year") of the parent that begins after the parent received an asset of the subsidiary on the winding-up and ends in a calendar year,

(A) the parent's taxable income for its last taxation year that ended in the preceding calendar year (determined before taking into consideration the specified future tax consequences for that last year) is deemed to be the total of

(I) its taxable income for that last year (determined before applying this paragraph to the winding-up and before taking into consideration the specified future tax consequences for that last year), and

(II) the total of the subsidiary's taxable incomes for its taxation years that ended in that preceding calendar year (determined without reference to subparagraph (iii) and before taking into consideration the specified future tax consequences for those years), and

(B) the parent's business limit for that last year is deemed to be the total of

¶1662

(I) its business limit (determined before applying this paragraph to the winding-up) for that last year, and

(II) the total of the subsidiary's business limits (determined without reference to subparagraph (iii)) for its taxation years that ended in that preceding calendar year,

(ii) where the parent received an asset of the subsidiary on the winding-up before the current year and subparagraph (i) does not apply,

(A) the parent's taxable income for its immediately preceding taxation year (determined before taking into consideration the specified future tax consequences for that preceding year) is deemed to be the total of

(I) its taxable income for that preceding taxation year (determined before applying this paragraph to the winding-up and before taking into consideration the specified future tax consequences for that preceding taxation year), and

(II) the total of the subsidiary's taxable incomes for the subsidiary's taxation years that end in the calendar year in which that preceding taxation year ended (determined before taking into consideration the specified future tax consequences for those years), and

(B) the parent's business limit for that preceding taxation year is deemed to be the total of

(I) its business limit (determined before applying this paragraph to the winding-up) for that preceding taxation year, and

(II) the total of the subsidiary's business limits (determined without reference to subparagraph (iii)) for the subsidiary's taxation years that end in the calendar year in which that preceding taxation year ended, and

(iii) where the parent and the subsidiary are associated with each other in the current year, the subsidiary's taxable income and the subsidiary's business limit for each taxation year that ends after the first time that the parent receives an asset of the subsidiary on the winding-up are deemed to be nil;

(*f*) where property that was depreciable property of a prescribed class of the subsidiary has been distributed to the parent on the winding-up and the capital cost to the subsidiary of the property exceeds the amount deemed by paragraph (*a*) to be the subsidiary's proceeds of disposition of the property, for the purposes of sections 13 and 20 and any regulations made under paragraph 20(1)(*a*),

(i) notwithstanding paragraph (*c*), the capital cost to the parent of the property shall be deemed to be the amount that was the capital cost of the property to the subsidiary, and

¶1662

(ii) the excess shall be deemed to have been allowed to the parent in respect of the property under regulations made under paragraph $20(1)(a)$ in computing income for taxation years before the acquisition by the parent of the property;

(g) where the subsidiary was an insurance corporation,

(i) for the purposes of paragraphs $12(1)(d)$, (e), $(e.1)$, (i) and (s) and $20(1)(l)$, $(l.1)$, (p) and (jj) and $20(7)(c)$, subsection $20(22)$, sections 138, 138.1, 140, 142 and 148 and Part XII.3, the parent is deemed to be the same corporation as, and a continuation of, the subsidiary, and

(ii) for the purpose of determining the amount of the gross investment revenue required to be included under subsection $138(9)$ in the income of the subsidiary and the parent and the amount of gains and losses of the subsidiary and the parent from property used by them in the year or held by them in the year in the course of carrying on an insurance business in Canada

(A) the subsidiary and the parent shall, in addition to their normal taxation years, be deemed to have had a taxation year ending immediately before the time when the property of the subsidiary was transferred to, and the obligations of the subsidiary were assumed by, the parent on the winding-up, and

(B) for the taxation years of the subsidiary and the parent following the time referred to in clause (A), the property transferred to, and the obligations assumed by, the parent on the winding-up shall be deemed to have been transferred or assumed, as the case may be, on the last day of the taxation year ending immediately before that time and the parent shall be deemed to be the same corporation as and a continuation of the subsidiary with respect to that property, those obligations and the insurance businesses carried on by the subsidiary;

(h) for the purposes of subsections $112(5)$ to (5.2) and (5.4) and the definition "mark-to-market property" in subsection $142.2(1)$, the parent shall be deemed, in respect of each property distributed to it on the winding-up, to be the same corporation as, and a continuation of, the subsidiary; and

(i) for the purpose of subsection $142.5(2)$, the subsidiary's taxation year in which its assets were distributed to the parent on the winding-up shall be deemed to have ended immediately before the time when the assets were distributed.

*   *   *

¶1662

[¶1668]

SECTION 97:

(1) Contribution of property to partnership. Where at any time after 1971 a partnership has acquired property from a taxpayer who was, immediately after that time, a member of the partnership, the partnership shall be deemed to have acquired the property at an amount equal to its fair market value at that time and the taxpayer shall be deemed to have disposed of the property for proceeds equal to that fair market value.

[¶1674]

(2) Rules where election by partners. Notwithstanding any other provision of this Act other than subsection 13(21.2), where a taxpayer at any time disposes of any property that is a capital property, Canadian resource property, foreign resource property, eligible capital property or inventory of the taxpayer to a partnership that immediately after that time is a Canadian partnership of which the taxpayer is a member, if the taxpayer and all the other members of the partnership jointly so elect in prescribed form within the time referred to in subsection 96(4), the following rules apply:

Pending Amendment

Non-Resident Trusts, Foreign Investment Entities, and Technical Amendments (July 18, 2005)

The portion of subsection 97(2) of the Act before paragraph (*a*) is replaced by the following:

(2) Rules where election by partners. Notwithstanding any other provision of this Act other than subsection 13(21.2), where a taxpayer at any time in a taxation year disposes of any property (other than a specified participating interest) that is a capital property, Canadian resource property, foreign resource property, eligible capital property or inventory of the taxpayer to a partnership that immediately after that time is a Canadian partnership of which the taxpayer is a member, if the taxpayer and all the other members of the partnership jointly so elect in prescribed form within the time referred to in subsection 96(4),

Applicable: To dispositions that occur in taxation years that begin after 2002.

Explanatory Note: Subsection 97(2) of the Act provides rules that allow a person to transfer certain types of property on a tax-deferred "rollover" basis to a partnership.

Subsection 97(2) is amended so that it does not apply to a transfer of property that is a specified participating interest. The concept of a specified participating interest is generally relevant in the context of the foreign investment entity rules in sections 94.1 to 94.4. For more information on the definition "specified participating interest" in subsection 248(1), see the commentary on that definition.

This amendment applies to dispositions that occur in taxation years that begin after 2002.

(*a*) the provisions of paragraphs 85(1)(*a*) to (*f*) apply to the disposition as if

(i) the reference therein to "corporation's cost" were read as a reference to "partnership's cost",

(ii) the references therein to "other than any shares of the capital stock of the corporation or a right to receive any such shares" and to "other than shares of the capital stock of the corporation or a right to receive any such shares" were read as references to "other than an interest in the partnership",

(iii) the references therein to "shareholder of the corporation" were read as references to "member of the partnership",

(iv) the references therein to "the corporation" were read as references to "all the other members of the partnership", and

(v) the references therein to "to the corporation" were read as references to "to the partnership";

(b) in computing, at any time after the disposition, the adjusted cost base to the taxpayer of the taxpayer's interest in the partnership immediately after the disposition,

(i) there shall be added the amount, if any, by which the taxpayer's proceeds of disposition of the property exceed the fair market value, at the time of the disposition, of the consideration (other than an interest in the partnership) received by the taxpayer for the property, and

(ii) there shall be deducted the amount, if any, by which the fair market value, at the time of the disposition, of the consideration (other than an interest in the partnership) received by the taxpayer for the property so disposed of by the taxpayer exceeds the fair market value of the property at the time of the disposition; and

(c) where the property so disposed of by the taxpayer to the partnership is taxable Canadian property of the taxpayer, the interest in the partnership received by the taxpayer as consideration therefor shall be deemed to be taxable Canadian property of the taxpayer.

[¶1680]

(3) Where property acquired from majority interest partner. [Repealed by 1998, c. 19, s. 124(2).]

[¶1686]

(4) Where capital cost to partner exceeds proceeds of disposition.   Where subsection (2) has been applicable in respect of the acquisition of any depreciable property by a partnership from a taxpayer who was, immediately after the taxpayer disposed of the property, a member of the partnership and the capital cost to the taxpayer of the property exceeds the taxpayer's proceeds of the disposition, for the purposes of sections 13 and 20 and any regulations made under paragraph 20(1)(a)

¶1680

(a) the capital cost to the partnership of the property shall be deemed to be the amount that was the capital cost thereof to the taxpayer; and

(b) the excess shall be deemed to have been allowed to the partnership in respect of the property under regulations made under paragraph $20(1)(a)$ in computing income for taxation years before the acquisition by the partnership of the property.

[¶1688]

(5) Acquisition of apprentice tools, re capital cost and deemed depreciation. If subsection (2) has applied in respect of the acquisition at any particular time of any depreciable property by a partnership from an individual, the cost of the property to the individual was included in computing an amount under paragraph $8(1)(r)$ in respect of the individual, and the amount that would be the cost of the property to the individual immediately before the transfer if this Act were read without reference to subsection 8(7) (which amount is in this subsection referred to as the "individual's original cost") exceeds the individual's proceeds of disposition of the property,

(a) the capital cost to the partnership of the property is deemed to be equal to the individual's original cost; and

(b) the amount by which the individual's original cost exceeds the individual's proceeds of disposition in respect of the property is deemed to have been deducted by the partnership under paragraph $20(1)(a)$ in respect of the property in computing income for taxation years that ended before that particular time.

[¶1690]

SECTION 98:

(1) Disposition of partnership property. For the purposes of this Act, where, but for this subsection, at any time after 1971 a partnership would be regarded as having ceased to exist, the following rules apply:

(a) until such time as all the partnership property and any property substituted therefor has been distributed to the persons entitled by law to receive it, the partnership shall be deemed not to have ceased to exist, and each person who was a partner shall be deemed not to have ceased to be a partner,

(b) the right of each such person to share in that property shall be deemed to be an interest in the partnership, and

(c) notwithstanding subsection 40(3), where at the end of a fiscal period of the partnership, in respect of an interest in the partnership,

(i) the total of all amounts required by subsection 53(2) to be deducted in computing the adjusted cost base to the taxpayer of the interest at that time

exceeds

(ii) the total of the cost to the taxpayer of the interest determined for the purpose of computing the adjusted cost base to the taxpayer of that interest at that time and all amounts required by subsection 53(1) to be added to the cost to the taxpayer of the interest in computing the adjusted cost base to the taxpayer of that interest at that time,

the amount of the excess shall be deemed to be a gain of the taxpayer for the taxpayer's taxation year that includes that time from a disposition at that time of that interest.

[¶1692]

(2) Deemed proceeds. Subject to subsections (3) and (5) and 85(3), where at any time after 1971 a partnership has disposed of property to a taxpayer who was, immediately before that time, a member of the partnership, the partnership shall be deemed to have disposed of the property for proceeds equal to its fair market value at that time and the taxpayer shall be deemed to have acquired the property at an amount equal to that fair market value.

[¶1694]

(3) Rules applicable where partnership ceases to exist. Where at any particular time after 1971 a Canadian partnership has ceased to exist and all the partnership property has been distributed to persons who were members of the partnership immediately before that time so that immediately after that time each such person has, in each such property, an undivided interest that, when expressed as a percentage (in this subsection referred to as that person's "percentage") of all undivided interests in the property, is equal to the person's undivided interest, when so expressed, in each other such property, if each such person has jointly so elected in respect of the property in prescribed form and within the time referred to in subsection 96(4), the following rules apply:

Pending Amendment

Non-Resident Trusts, Foreign Investment Entities, and Technical Amendments (July 18, 2005)

The portion of subsection 98(3) of the Act before paragraph (*a*) is replaced by the following:

---

(3) Rules applicable where partnership ceases to exist. Where at any particular time after 1971 a Canadian partnership has ceased to exist and all the partnership property has been distributed to persons who were members of the partnership immediately before that time so that immediately after that time each such person has, in each such property, an undivided interest, or for civil law an undivided right, (which undivided interest or undivided right is referred to in this subsection as an "undivided interest or right", as the case may be) that, when expressed as a percentage (referred to in this subsection as that person's "percentage") of all undivided interests or rights in the property, is equal to the person's undivided interest or right, when so expressed, in each other such property, if each such person has jointly so elected in respect of the

---

property in prescribed form and within the time referred to in subsection 96(4), the following rules apply:

Applicable: Royal Assent.

Explanatory Note: [See the Explanatory Note re amendments related to bijuralism following the amendment to subsection 13(5.2).]

(a) each such person's proceeds of the disposition of the person's interest in the partnership shall be deemed to be an amount equal to the greater of

(i) the adjusted cost base to the person, immediately before the particular time, of the person's interest in the partnership, and

(ii) the amount of any money received by the person on the cessation of the partnership's existence, plus the person's percentage of the total of amounts each of which is the cost amount to the partnership of each such property immediately before its distribution;

(b) the cost to each such person of that person's undivided interest in each such property shall be deemed to be an amount equal to the total of

---

Pending Amendment

Non-Resident Trusts, Foreign Investment Entities, and Technical Amendments (July 18, 2005)

The portion of paragraph 98(3)(b) before subparagraph (i) of the Act is replaced by the following:

(b) the cost to each such person of that person's undivided interest or right in each such property shall be deemed to be an amount equal to the total of

Applicable: Royal Assent.

Explanatory Note: [See the Explanatory Note re amendments related to bijuralism following the amendment to subsection 13(5.2).]

(i) that person's percentage of the cost amount to the partnership of the property immediately before its distribution,

(i.1) where the property is eligible capital property, that person's percentage of $\frac{4}{3}$ of the amount, if any, determined for F in the definition "cumulative eligible capital" in subsection 14(5) in respect of the partnership's business immediately before the particular time, and

(ii) where the amount determined under subparagraph (a)(i) exceeds the amount determined under subparagraph (a)(ii), the amount determined under paragraph (c) in respect of the person's undivided interest in the property;

¶1694

Pending Amendment

Non-Resident Trusts, Foreign Investment Entities, and Technical Amendments (July 18, 2005)

Subparagraph 98(3)(*b*)(ii) of the Act is replaced by the following:

(ii) where the amount determined under subparagraph (*a*)(i) exceeds the amount determined under subparagraph (*a*)(ii), the amount determined under paragraph (*c*) in respect of the person's undivided interest or right in the property;

Applicable: Royal Assent.

Explanatory Note: [See the Explanatory Note re amendments related to bijuralism following the amendment to subsection 13(5.2).]

(*c*) the amount determined under this paragraph in respect of each such person's undivided interest in each such property that was a capital property (other than depreciable property) of the partnership is such portion of the excess, if any, described in subparagraph (*b*)(ii) as is designated by the person in respect of the property, except that

(i) in no case shall the amount so designated in respect of the person's undivided interest in any such property exceed the amount, if any, by which the person's percentage of the fair market value of the property immediately after its distribution exceeds the person's percentage of the cost amount to the partnership of the property immediately before its distribution, and

(ii) in no case shall the total of amounts so designated in respect of the person's undivided interests in all such capital properties (other than depreciable property) exceed the excess, if any, described in subparagraph (*b*)(ii);

Pending Amendment

Non-Resident Trusts, Foreign Investment Entities, and Technical Amendments (July 18, 2005)

Paragraph 98(3)(*c*) of the Act is replaced by the following:

(*c*) the amount determined under this paragraph in respect of each such person's undivided interest or right in each such property that was a capital property (other than depreciable property) of the partnership is such portion of the excess, if any, described in subparagraph (*b*)(ii) as is designated by the person in respect of the property, except that

(i) in no case shall the amount so designated in respect of the person's undivided interest or right in any such property exceed the amount, if any, by which the person's percentage of the fair market value of the property immediately after its distribution exceeds the person's percentage of the cost amount to the partnership of the property immediately before its distribution, and

(ii) in no case shall the total of amounts so designated in respect of the person's undivided interest or right in all such capital properties (other than depreciable property) exceed the excess, if any, described in subparagraph (b)(ii);

Applicable: Royal Assent.

Explanatory Note: [See the Explanatory Note re amendments related to bijuralism following the amendment to subsection 13(5.2).]

(d) [Repealed by 1986, c. 55, s. 26(2).]

(e) where the property so distributed by the partnership was depreciable property of the partnership of a prescribed class and any such person's percentage of the amount that was the capital cost to the partnership of that property exceeds the amount determined under paragraph (b) to be the cost to the person of the person's undivided interest in the property, for the purposes of sections 13 and 20 and any regulations made under paragraph $20(1)(a)$

(i) the capital cost to the person of the person's undivided interest in the property shall be deemed to be the person's percentage of the amount that was the capital cost to the partnership of the property, and

(ii) the excess shall be deemed to have been allowed to the person in respect of the property under regulations made under paragraph $20(1)(a)$ in computing income for taxation years before the acquisition by the person of the undivided interest;

Pending Amendment

Non-Resident Trusts, Foreign Investment Entities, and Technical Amendments (July 18, 2005)

Paragraph 98(3)(e) of the Act is replaced by the following:

(e) where the property so distributed by the partnership was depreciable property of the partnership of a prescribed class and any such person's percentage of the amount that was the capital cost to the partnership of that property exceeds the amount determined under paragraph (b) to be the cost to the person of the person's undivided interest or right in the property, for the purposes of sections 13 and 20 and any regulations made under paragraph $20(1)(a)$

(i) the capital cost to the person of the person's undivided interest or right in the property shall be deemed to be the person's percentage of the amount that was the capital cost to the partnership of the property, and

(ii) the excess shall be deemed to have been allowed to the person in respect of the property under regulations made under paragraph $20(1)(a)$ in computing

¶1694

income for taxation years before the acquisition by the person of the undivided interest or right;

Applicable: Royal Assent.

Explanatory Note: [See the Explanatory Note re amendments related to bijuralism following the amendment to subsection 13(5.2).]

(f) the partnership shall be deemed to have disposed of each such property for proceeds equal to the cost amount to the partnership of the property immediately before its distribution; and

(g) where the property so distributed by the partnership was eligible capital property in respect of the business,

(i) for the purposes of determining under this Act any amount relating to cumulative eligible capital, an eligible capital amount, an eligible capital expenditure or eligible capital property, each such person shall be deemed to have continued to carry on the business, in respect of which the property was eligible capital property and that was previously carried on by the partnership, until the time that the person disposes of the person's undivided interest in the property,

---

Pending Amendment

Non-Resident Trusts, Foreign Investment Entities, and Technical Amendments (July 18, 2005)

Subparagraph 98(3)(g)(i) of the Act is replaced by the following:

(i) for the purposes of determining under this Act any amount relating to cumulative eligible capital, an eligible capital amount, an eligible capital expenditure or eligible capital property, each such person shall be deemed to have continued to carry on the business, in respect of which the property was eligible capital property and that was previously carried on by the partnership, until the time that the person disposes of the person's undivided interest or right in the property,

Applicable: Royal Assent.

Explanatory Note: [See the Explanatory Note re amendments related to bijuralism following the amendment to subsection 13(5.2).]

(ii) for the purposes of determining the person's cumulative eligible capital in respect of the business, an amount equal to $3/4$ of the amount determined under subparagraph (b)(i.1) in respect of the business shall be added to the amount otherwise determined in respect thereof for P in the definition "cumulative eligible capital" in subsection 14(5), and

(iii) for the purpose of determining after the particular time the amount required by paragraph 14(1)(b) to be included in computing the person's income in respect of any subsequent disposition of property of the business, the value determined for Q in the definition "cumulative eligible capital" in subsection 14(5) is deemed to be the amount, if any, of that person's percentage of the value determined

¶1694

for Q in that definition in respect of the partnership's business immediately before the particular time.

[¶1698]

(4) Where s. (3) does not apply.　Subsection (3) is not applicable in any case in which subsection (5) or 85(3) is applicable.

[¶1702]

(5) Where partnership business carried on as sole proprietorship. Where at any particular time after 1971 a Canadian partnership has ceased to exist and within 3 months after the particular time one, but not more than one, of the persons who were, immediately before the particular time, members of the partnership (which person is in this subsection referred to as the "proprietor", whether an individual, a trust or a corporation) carries on alone the business that was the business of the partnership and continues to use, in the course of the business, any property that was, immediately before the particular time, partnership property and that was received by the proprietor as proceeds of disposition of the proprietor's interest in the partnership, the following rules apply:

(a) the proprietor's proceeds of disposition of the proprietor's interest in the partnership shall be deemed to be an amount equal to the greater of

(i) the total of the adjusted cost base to the proprietor, immediately before the particular time, of the proprietor's interest in the partnership, and the adjusted cost base to the proprietor of each other interest in the partnership deemed by paragraph (g) to have been acquired by the proprietor at the particular time, and

(ii) the total of

(A) the cost amount to the partnership, immediately before the particular time, of each such property so received by the proprietor, and

(B) the amount of any other proceeds of the disposition of the proprietor's interest in the partnership received by the proprietor;

(b) the cost to the proprietor of each such property shall be deemed to be an amount equal to the total of

(i) the cost amount to the partnership of the property immediately before that time,

(i.1) where the property is eligible capital property, $\frac{4}{3}$ of the amount, if any, determined for F in the definition "cumulative eligible capital" in subsection 14(5) in respect of the partnership's business immediately before the particular time, and

(ii) where the amount determined under subparagraph (a)(i) exceeds the amount determined under subparagraph (a)(ii), the amount determined under paragraph (c) in respect of the property;

(c) the amount determined under this paragraph in respect of each such property so received by the proprietor that is a capital property (other than depreciable property) of the proprietor is such portion of the excess, if any, described in subparagraph (b)(ii) as is designated by the proprietor in respect of the property, except that

(i) in no case shall the amount so designated in respect of any such property exceed the amount, if any, by which the fair market value of the property immediately after the particular time exceeds the cost amount to the partnership of the property immediately before that time, and

(ii) in no case shall the total of amounts so designated in respect of all such capital properties (other than depreciable property) exceed the excess, if any, described in subparagraph (b)(ii);

(d) [Repealed by 1986, c. 55, s. 26(4).]

(e) where any such property so received by the proprietor was depreciable property of a prescribed class of the partnership and the amount that was the capital cost to the partnership of that property exceeds the amount determined under paragraph (b) to be the cost to the proprietor of the property, for the purposes of sections 13 and 20 and any regulations made under paragraph 20(1)(a)

(i) the capital cost to the proprietor of the property shall be deemed to be the amount that was the capital cost to the partnership of the property, and

(ii) the excess shall be deemed to have been allowed to the proprietor in respect of the property under regulations made under paragraph 20(1)(a) in computing income for taxation years before the acquisition by the proprietor of the property;

(f) the partnership shall be deemed to have disposed of each such property for proceeds equal to the cost amount to the partnership of the property immediately before the particular time;

(g) where, at the particular time, all other persons who were members of the partnership immediately before that time have disposed of their interests in the partnership to the proprietor, the proprietor shall be deemed at that time to have acquired partnership interests from those other persons and not to have acquired any property that was property of the partnership; and

(h) where the property so received by the proprietor is eligible capital property in respect of the business,

(i) for the purpose of determining the proprietor's cumulative eligible capital in respect of the business, an amount equal to $3/4$ of the amount determined under subparagraph (b)(i.1) in respect of the business shall be added to the amount otherwise determined in respect thereof for P in the definition "cumulative eligible capital" in subsection 14(5), and

¶1702

(ii) for the purpose of determining after the particular time the amount required by paragraph $14(1)(b)$ to be included in computing the proprietor's income in respect of any subsequent disposition of property of the business, the value determined for Q in the definition "cumulative eligible capital" in subsection 14(5) is deemed to be the value, if any, determined for Q in that definition in respect of the partnership's business immediately before the particular time.

* * *

[¶1708]

SECTION 104:

* * *

(4) Deemed disposition by trust. Every trust is, at the end of each of the following days, deemed to have disposed of each property of the trust (other than exempt property) that was capital property (other than excluded property or depreciable property) or land included in the inventory of a business of the trust for proceeds equal to its fair market value (determined with reference to subsection 70(5.3)) at the end of that day and to have reacquired the property immediately after that day for an amount equal to that fair market value, and for the purposes of this Act those days are

(a) where the trust

(i) is a trust that was created by the will of a taxpayer who died after 1971 and that, at the time it was created, was a trust,

(i.1) is a trust that was created by the will of a taxpayer who died after 1971 to which property was transferred in circumstances to which paragraph $70(5.2)(b)$ or (d) or $(6)(d)$ applied and that, immediately after any such property vested indefeasibly in the trust as a consequence of the death of the taxpayer, was a trust,

---

Pending Amendment

Non-Resident Trusts, Foreign Investment Entities, and Technical Amendments (July 18, 2005)

Subparagraph 104(4)(a)(i.1) of the Act is replaced by the following:

(i.1) is a trust that was created by the will of a taxpayer who died after 1971 to which property was transferred in circumstances to which paragraph $70(5.2)(b)$ or (d) (as those paragraphs read in their application to taxation years that began before 2003), $(5.2)(c)$ or $(6)(d)$ applied and that, immediately after any such property vested indefeasibly in the trust as a consequence of the death of the taxpayer, was a trust,

---

Applicable: To trust taxation years that begin after 2002.

Explanatory Note: Subsection 104(4) of the Act sets out what is generally referred to as the "21-year deemed realization rule" for trusts. The purpose of subsection 104(4) is to prevent the use of trusts to defer indefinitely the recognition for tax purposes of gains accruing on capital property. Subsection 104(4) generally treats capital property of a trust (other than certain trusts for the benefit of a spouse or common-law partner) as having been disposed of and reacquired by the trust every 21 years at the property's fair market value.

Subparagraph $104(4)(a)(i.1)$ is amended to apply to a trust to which property is transferred in circumstances to which paragraph $70(5.2)(c)$ applied. It is also amended to ensure that it continues to apply to a trust to which property was transferred in circumstances to which paragraph $70(5.2)(b)$ or (d) applied as those paragraphs read in their application to taxation years that began before 2003.

Paragraph $104(4)(a.5)$ is introduced to provide for a deemed disposition day for a trust that is deemed by subsection 94(3) to be resident in Canada for a taxation year for the purpose of computing the trust's income for the year. The deemed disposition day is the day (in that taxation year) on which, because a "contributor" (as defined in subsection 94(1) of the Act) to the trust either ceases to be resident in Canada or ceases to be a contributor to the trust because of the application at any time of paragraph $94(2)(t)$, there is no resident contributor to the trust (or the only resident contributors to the trust are entities each of which is an entity the maximum amount recoverable from which under the provisions referred to in paragraph $94(3)(d)$ is limited to the entities' recovery limits determined under subsection 94(8)). However, no deemed disposition will occur under paragraph $104(4)(a.5)$ if subsection 94(5) applies in respect of the contributor ceasing on that day to be a resident contributor of the trust. For more information on section 94, see the commentary on that section.

Paragraph $104(4)(c)$ is amended so that there is not a deemed disposition day for a trust 21 years after any day determined under new paragraph $104(4)(a.5)$. In effect, the time from which 21 years is counted under paragraph $104(4)(c)$ is determined without regard to days determined without regard to days determined under any of paragraphs $104\ (4)(a)$ to $(a.5)$.

These amendments apply to trust taxation years that begin after 2002. They also apply to trust taxation years that begin after 2000, or after 2001, if the trust makes the appropriate election under the coming into-force provision for new section 94 of the Act.

(ii) is a trust that was created after June 17, 1971 by a taxpayer during the taxpayer's lifetime that, at any time after 1971, was a trust, or

(ii.1) is a trust (other than a trust the terms of which are described in clause (iv)(A) that elects in its return of income under this Part for its first taxation year that this subparagraph not apply) that was created after 1999 by a taxpayer during the taxpayer's lifetime and that, at any time after 1999, was a trust

under which

(iii) the taxpayer's spouse or common-law partner was entitled to receive all of the income of the trust that arose before the spouse's or common-law partner's death and no person except the spouse or common-law partner could, before the spouse's or common-law partner's death, receive or otherwise obtain the use of any of the income or capital of the trust, or

(iv) in the case of a trust described in subparagraph (ii.1) created by a taxpayer who had attained 65 years of age at the time the trust was created,

(A) the taxpayer was entitled to receive all of the income of the trust that arose before the taxpayer's death and no person except the taxpayer could, before the taxpayer's death, receive or otherwise obtain the use of any of the income or capital of the trust,

(B) the taxpayer or the taxpayer's spouse was, in combination with the spouse or the taxpayer, as the case may be, entitled to receive all of the income of the trust that arose before the later of the death of the taxpayer and the death of the spouse and no other person could, before the later of those deaths, receive or otherwise obtain the use of any of the income or capital of the trust, or

(C) the taxpayer or the taxpayer's common-law partner was, in combination with the common-law partner or the taxpayer, as the case may be, entitled to receive all of the income of the trust that arose before the later of the death of the taxpayer and the death of the common-law partner and no other person could, before the later of those deaths, receive or otherwise obtain the use of any of the income or capital of the trust,

the day on which the death or the later death, as the case may be, occurs;

(a.1) where the trust is a pre-1972 spousal trust on January 1, 1993 and the spouse or common-law partner referred to in the definition "pre-1972 spousal trust" in subsection 108(1) in respect of the trust was

(i) in the case of a trust created by the will of a taxpayer, alive on January 1, 1976, and

(ii) in the case of a trust created by a taxpayer during the taxpayer's lifetime, alive on May 26, 1976,

the day that is the later of

(iii) the day on which that spouse or common-law partner dies, and

(iv) January 1, 1993;

(a.2) where the trust makes a distribution to a beneficiary in respect of the beneficiary's capital interest in the trust, it is reasonable to conclude that the distribution was financed by a liability of the trust and one of the purposes of incurring the liability was to avoid taxes otherwise payable under this Part as a consequence of the death of any individual, the day on which the distribution is made (determined as if a day ends for the trust immediately after the time at which each distribution is made by the trust to a beneficiary in respect of the beneficiary's capital interest in the trust);

(a.3) where property (other than property described in any of subparagraphs 128.1(4)(b)(i) to (iii)) has been transferred by a taxpayer after December 17, 1999 to the trust in circumstances to which subsection 73(1) applied, it is reasonable to conclude that the property was so transferred in anticipation that the taxpayer would subsequently cease to reside in Canada and the taxpayer subsequently ceases to reside in Canada, the first day after that transfer during which the taxpayer ceases to reside in Canada (determined as if a day ends for the trust immediately after each time at which the taxpayer ceases to be resident in Canada);

(a.4) where the trust is a trust to which property was transferred by a taxpayer who is an individual (other than a trust) in circumstances in which section 73 or subsection 107.4(3) applied, the transfer did not result in a change in beneficial ownership of that property and no person (other than the taxpayer) or partnership has any absolute or contingent right as a beneficiary under the trust (determined with reference to subsection (1.1)), the day on which the death of the taxpayer occurs;

Pending Amendment

Non-Resident Trusts, Foreign Investment Entities, and Technical Amendments (July 18, 2005)

Subsection 104(4) of the Act is amended by adding the following after paragraph (a.4):

(a.5) where the trust is deemed by subsection 94(3) to be resident in Canada for a taxation year for the purpose of computing the trust's income for the taxation year, the day (in that taxation year) on which, because a contributor (in this paragraph, as defined by subsection 94(1)) either ceases to be resident in Canada or ceases to be a contributor to the trust because of the application at any time of paragraph 94(2)(t), there is no resident contributor (in this paragraph, as defined by subsection 94(1)) to the trust (or the only resident contributors to the trust are entities (in this paragraph, as defined by subsection 94(1)) each of which is an entity the maximum amount recoverable from which under the provisions referred to in paragraph 94(3)(d) is limited to the entities' recovery limits determined under subsection 94(8)), unless subsection 94(5) applies in respect of the contributor ceasing on the day to be a resident contributor to the trust;

Applicable: To trust taxation years that begin after 2002. [This amendment] also applies to trust taxation years that begin
  (a) after 2000, if the trust makes a valid election under paragraph [(a) of the application for new proposed section 94]; and
  (b) after 2001, if the trust makes a valid election under paragraph [(a) or (b) of the application for new proposed section 94].

Explanatory Note: [See the Explanatory Note following the amendment to subparagraph 104(4)(a)(i.1).]

(b) the day that is 21 years after the latest of

(i) January 1, 1972,

(ii) the day on which the trust was created, and

(iii) where applicable, the day determined under paragraph (a), (a.1) or (a.4) as those paragraphs applied from time to time after 1971; and

(c) the day that is 21 years after any day (other than a day determined under any of paragraphs (a) to (a.4)) that is, because of this subsec-

¶1708

tion, a day on which the trust is deemed to have disposed of each such property.

Pending Amendment

Non-Resident Trusts, Foreign Investment Entities, and Technical Amendments (July 18, 2005)

Paragraph 104(4)(c) of the Act is replaced by the following:

(c) the day that is 21 years after any day (other than a day determined under any of paragraphs (a) to (a.5)) that is, because of this subsection, a day on which the trust is deemed to have disposed of each such property.

Applicable: To trust taxation years that begin after 2002. [This amendment] also applies to trust taxation years that begin
  (a) after 2000, if the trust makes a valid election under paragraph [(a) of the application for new proposed section 94]; and
  (b) after 2001, if the trust makes a valid election under paragraph [(a) or (b) of the application for new proposed section 94].

Explanatory Note: [See the Explanatory Note following the amendment to subparagraph 104(4)(a)(i.1).]

Pending Amendment

Non-Resident Trusts, Foreign Investment Entities, and Technical Amendments (July 18, 2005)

Section 104 of the Act is amended by adding the following after subsection (4):

(4.1) Mark-to-market property. In determining whether property is capital property for the purpose of subsection (4), this Act is to be read without reference to subparagraph 39(1)(a)(ii.3).

Applicable: To trust taxation years that begin after 2002.

Explanatory Note: New subsection 104(4.1) of the Act provides that, for the purposes of the deemed disposition rule in subsection 104(4), a property's status as capital property is determined without reference to new subparagraph 39(1)(a)(ii.3). As a result, if subsection 94.2(3) applies for a taxation year to a taxpayer that is a trust in respect of a participating interest of the trust and the trust is deemed to have disposed of the interest because of the application of subsection 104(4), there is a recognition of the "deferral amount" in applying subsection 94.2(4).

This amendment applies to trust taxation years that begin after 2002.

[¶1712]

(5) Depreciable property. Every trust is, at the end of each day determined under subsection (4) in respect of the trust, deemed to have disposed of each property of the trust (other than exempt property) that was a depreciable property of a prescribed class of the trust for proceeds equal to its fair market value at the end of that day and to have reacquired the property immediately after that day at a capital cost (in this subsection referred to as the "deemed capital cost") equal to that fair market value, except that

(a) where the amount that was the capital cost to the trust of the property immediately before the end of the day (in this paragraph referred to as the "actual capital cost") exceeds the deemed capital cost to the trust of the property, for the purpose of sections 13 and 20 and any regulations made for the purpose of paragraph $20(1)(a)$ as they apply in respect of the property at any subsequent time,

(i) the capital cost to the trust of the property on its reacquisition shall be deemed to be the amount that was the actual capital cost to the trust of the property, and

(ii) the excess shall be deemed to have been allowed under paragraph $20(1)(a)$ to the trust in respect of the property in computing its income for taxation years that ended before the trust reacquired the property;

(b) for the purposes of this subsection, the reference to "at the end of a taxation year" in subsection 13(1) shall be read as a reference to "at the particular time a trust is deemed by subsection 104(5) to have disposed of depreciable property of a prescribed class"; and

(c) for the purpose of computing the excess, if any, referred to in subsection 13(1) at the end of the taxation year of a trust that included a day on which the trust is deemed by this subsection to have disposed of a depreciable property of a prescribed class, any amount that, on that day, was included in the trust's income for the year under subsection 13(1) as it reads because of paragraph (b), shall be deemed to be an amount included under section 13 in the trust's income for a preceding taxation year.

* * *

[¶1714]

SECTION 107:

* * *

(2) Distribution by personal trust. Subject to subsections (2.001), (2.002) and (4) to (5), where at any time a property of a personal trust or a prescribed trust is distributed by the trust to a taxpayer who was a beneficiary under the trust and there is a resulting disposition of all or any part of the taxpayer's capital interest in the trust,

(a) the trust shall be deemed to have disposed of the property for proceeds of disposition equal to its cost amount to the trust immediately before that time;

(b) subject to subsection (2.2), the taxpayer is deemed to have acquired the property at a cost equal to the total of its cost amount to the trust immediately before that time and the specified percentage of the amount, if any, by which

(i) the adjusted cost base to the taxpayer of the capital interest or part of it, as the case may be, immediately before that time (determined without reference to paragraph $(1)(a)$)

exceeds

(ii) the cost amount to the taxpayer of the capital interest or part of it, as the case may be, immediately before that time;

$(b.1)$ for the purpose of paragraph (b), the specified percentage is,

(i) where the property is capital property (other than depreciable property), 100%,

(ii) where the property is eligible capital property in respect of a business of the trust, 100%, and

(iii) in any other case, 75%;

Pending Amendment

Non-Resident Trusts, Foreign Investment Entities, and Technical Amendments (July 18, 2005)

Subparagraph 107(2)($b.1$)(iii) of the Act is replaced by following:

(iii) in any other case, 50%;

Applicable: To distributions made after December 20, 2002.

Explanatory Note:

Distribution by Personal Trust

Subsection 107(2) of the Act applies where a personal trust or a prescribed trust described in section 4800.1 of the Regulations distributes property to a beneficiary and there is a resulting disposition of part or all of the beneficiary's capital interest in the trust. Under paragraph $107(2)(a)$, the trust is deemed to have disposed of the property for proceeds of disposition equal to the property's cost amount. Under paragraph $107(2)(b)$, the property is deemed to have been acquired by the beneficiary for an amount equal to the total of the amount described in paragraph $107(2)(a)$ and a "bump" equal to the specified percentage of any excess of the adjusted cost base to the beneficiary of the capital interest over its cost amount (as defined by subsection 108(1) of the Act) to the beneficiary of the interest. Under subparagraph $107(2)(b.1)$(iii), the specified percentage for property (other than non-depreciable capital property and eligible capital property) is 75%. Where subsection 107(2) applies, paragraph $107(2)(c)$ provides that the beneficiary is deemed to have disposed of all or part, as the case may be, of the capital interest for proceeds equal to the amount determined under that paragraph.

Subparagraph $107(2)(b.1)$(iii) is amended to replace the reference to 75% with a reference to 50%, consistent with the current capital gains inclusion rate.

This amendment applies to distributions, from a trust, made after December 20, 2002.

Paragraph $107(2)(c)$ is amended to clarify that it applies to determine a taxpayer's proceeds of disposition of the capital interest in a trust (or of the part of it) disposed of by the taxpayer on a distribution, to which subsection 107(2) applies, of property by the trust.

This amendment applies to distributions, from a trust, made after 1999.

¶1714

Paragraph 107(2)(*d*.1) determines the tax consequences of the disposition of taxable Canadian property by a trust to a non-resident beneficiary before October 2, 1996. In the event that the property was explicitly deemed to have been taxable Canadian property under a number of specified provisions of the Act, paragraph 107(2)(*d*.1) ensures that it continues to be taxable Canadian property of the beneficiary.

Paragraph 107(2)(*d*.1) is amended by adding to the list of specified provisions, that explicitly deem property to be taxable Canadian property, a reference to subsection 85.1(5) of the Act.

This amendment applies in determining after October 1, 1996 whether property is taxable Canadian property.

(*c*) the taxpayer is deemed to have disposed of all or part, as the case may be, of the capital interest for proceeds equal to the amount, if any, by which

---

Pending Amendment

Non-Resident Trusts, Foreign Investment Entities, and Technical Amendments (July 18, 2005)

The portion of paragraph 107(2)(*c*) of the Act before subparagraph (i) is replaced by the following:

(*c*) the taxpayer's proceeds of disposition of the capital interest in the trust (or of the part of it) disposed of by the taxpayer on the distribution are deemed to be equal to the amount, if any, by which

Applicable: To distributions made after 1999.

Explanatory Note: [See the Explanatory Note following the amendment to subparagraph 107(2)(*b*.1)(iii).]

(i) the cost at which the taxpayer would be deemed by paragraph (*b*) to have acquired the property if the specified percentage referred to in that paragraph were 100%

exceeds

(ii) the total of all amounts each of which is an eligible offset at that time of the taxpayer in respect of the capital interest or the part of it;

(*d*) where the property so distributed was depreciable property of a prescribed class of the trust and the amount that was the capital cost to the trust of that property exceeds the cost at which the taxpayer is deemed by this section to have acquired the property, for the purposes of sections 13 and 20 and any regulations made under paragraph 20(1)(*a*)

(i) the capital cost to the taxpayer of the property shall be deemed to be the amount that was the capital cost of the property to the trust, and

(ii) the excess shall be deemed to have been allowed to the taxpayer in respect of the property under regulations made under paragraph

¶1714

20(1)(a) in computing income for taxation years before the acquisition by the taxpayer of the property;

(d.1) the property is deemed to be taxable Canadian property of the taxpayer where

(i) the taxpayer is non-resident at that time,

(ii) that time is before October 2, 1996, and

(iii) the property was deemed by paragraph 51(1)(f), 85(1)(i) or 85.1(1)(a), subsection 87(4) or (5) or paragraph 97(2)(c) to be taxable Canadian property of the trust; and

---

Pending Amendment

Non-Resident Trusts, Foreign Investment Entities, and Technical Amendments (July 18, 2005)

Subparagraph 107(2)(d.1)(iii) of the Act is replaced by the following:

(iii) the property was deemed by paragraph 51(1)(f), 85(1)(i) or 85.1(1)(a), subsection 85.1(5) or 87(4) or (5) or paragraph 97(2)(c) to be taxable Canadian property of the trust; and

---

Applicable: In determining after October 1, 1996 whether property is taxable Canadian property.

Explanatory Note: [See the Explanatory Note following the amendment to subparagraph 107(2)(b.1)(iii).]

(e) [Repealed by S.C. 1994, c. 7, Sched. VIII, s. 43(1).]

(f) where the property so distributed was eligible capital property of the trust in respect of a business of the trust,

(i) where the eligible capital expenditure of the trust in respect of the property exceeds the cost at which the taxpayer is deemed by this subsection to have acquired the property, for the purposes of sections 14, 20 and 24,

(A) the eligible capital expenditure of the taxpayer in respect of the property shall be deemed to be the amount that was the eligible capital expenditure of the trust in respect of the property, and

(B) ¾ of the excess shall be deemed to have been allowed under paragraph 20(1)(b) to the taxpayer in respect of the property in computing income for taxation years ending

(I) before the acquisition by the taxpayer of the property, and

(II) after the adjustment time of the taxpayer in respect of the business, and

(ii) for the purpose of determining after that time the amount required by paragraph 14(1)(b) to be included in computing the taxpayer's income in respect of any subsequent disposition of property of the business, there shall be added to the value otherwise determined for Q in the definition "cumulative eligible capital" in subsection 14(5) the amount determined by the formula

$$A \times \frac{B}{C}$$

where

A   is the amount, if any, determined for Q in that definition in respect of the business of the trust immediately before the distribution,

B   is the fair market value of the property so distributed immediately before the distribution, and

C   is the fair market value immediately before the distribution of all eligible capital property of the trust in respect of the business.

[¶1716]

(2.001) No rollover on election by a trust.   Where a trust makes a distribution of a property to a beneficiary of the trust in full or partial satisfaction of the beneficiary's capital interest in the trust and so elects in prescribed form filed with the Minister with the trust's return of income for its taxation year in which the distribution occurred, subsection (2) does not apply to the distribution if

(a) the trust is resident in Canada at the time of the distribution;

(b) the property is taxable Canadian property; or

(c) the property is capital property used in, eligible capital property in respect of, or property described in the inventory of, a business carried on by the trust through a permanent establishment (as defined by regulation) in Canada immediately before the time of the distribution.

[¶1718]

(2.002) No rollover on election by a beneficiary.   Where a non-resident trust makes a distribution of a property (other than a property described in paragraph (2.001)(b) or (c)) to a beneficiary of the trust in full or partial satisfaction of the beneficiary's capital interest in the trust and the beneficiary makes an election under this subsection in prescribed form filed with the Minister with the beneficiary's return of income for the beneficiary's taxation year in which the distribution occurred,

(a) subsection (2) does not apply to the distribution; and

(b) for the purpose of subparagraph (1)(a)(ii), the cost amount of the interest to the beneficiary is deemed to be nil.

[¶1720]

(2.01) Distribution of principal residence.   Where property that would, if a personal trust had designated the property under paragraph (c.1)

of the definition "principal residence" in section 54, be a principal residence (within the meaning of that definition) of the trust for a taxation year, is at any time (in this subsection referred to as "that time") distributed by the trust to a taxpayer in circumstances in which subsection (2) applies and the trust so elects in its return of income for the taxation year that includes that time,

(a) the trust shall be deemed to have disposed of the property immediately before the particular time that is immediately before that time for proceeds of disposition equal to the fair market value of the property at that time; and

(b) the trust shall be deemed to have reacquired the property at the particular time at a cost equal to that fair market value.

[¶1722]

(2.1) Other distributions.   Where at any time a property of a trust is distributed by the trust to a beneficiary under the trust, there would, if this Act were read without reference to paragraphs (h) and (i) of the definition "disposition" in subsection 248(1), be a resulting disposition of all or any part of the beneficiary's capital interest in the trust (which interest or part, as the case may be, is in this subsection referred to as the "former interest") and the rules in subsection (2) and section 132.2 do not apply in respect of the distribution,

(a) the trust is deemed to have disposed of the property for proceeds equal to its fair market value at that time;

(b) the beneficiary is deemed to have acquired the property at a cost equal to the proceeds determined under paragraph (a);

(c) subject to paragraph (e), the beneficiary's proceeds of disposition of the portion of the former interest disposed of by the beneficiary on the distribution are deemed to be equal to the amount, if any, by which

(i) the proceeds determined under paragraph (a) (other than the portion, if any, of the proceeds that is a payment to which paragraph (h) or (i) of the definition "disposition" in subsection 248(1) applies)

exceed the total of

(ii) where the property is not a Canadian resource property or foreign resource property, the amount, if any, by which

(A) the fair market value of the property at that time

exceeds the total of

(B) the cost amount to the trust of the property immediately before that time, and

(C) the portion, if any, of the excess that would be determined under this subparagraph if this subparagraph were read without reference to this clause that represents a payment to which paragraph (h) or (i) of the definition "disposition" in subsection 248(1) applies, and

(iii) all amounts each of which is an eligible offset at that time of the taxpayer in respect of the former interest;

(d) notwithstanding paragraphs (a) to (c), where the trust is non-resident at that time, the property is not described in paragraph $(2.001)(b)$ or (c) and, if this Act were read without reference to this paragraph, there would be no income, loss, taxable capital gain or allowable capital loss of a taxpayer in respect of the property because of the application of subsection 75(2) to the disposition at that time of the property,

(i) the trust is deemed to have disposed of the property for proceeds equal to the cost amount of the property,

(ii) the beneficiary is deemed to have acquired the property at a cost equal to the fair market value of the property, and

(iii) the beneficiary's proceeds of disposition of the portion of the former interest disposed of by the beneficiary on the distribution are deemed to be equal to the amount, if any, by which

(A) the fair market value of the property

exceeds the total of

(B) the portion, if any, of the amount of the distribution that is a payment to which paragraph (h) or (i) of the definition "disposition" in subsection 248(1) applies, and

(C) all amounts each of which is an eligible offset at that time of the taxpayer in respect of the former interest; and

(e) where the trust is a mutual fund trust, the distribution occurs in a taxation year of the trust before its 2003 taxation year, the trust has elected under subsection (2.11) in respect of the year and the trust so elects in respect of the distribution in prescribed form filed with the trust's return of income for the year,

(i) this subsection shall be read without reference to paragraph (c), and

(ii) the beneficiary's proceeds of disposition of the portion of the former interest disposed of by the beneficiary on the distribution are deemed to be equal to the amount determined under paragraph (a).

[¶1724]

(2.11) Gains not distributed to beneficiaries.   Where a trust makes one or more distributions of property in a taxation year in circumstances in which subsection (2.1) applies (or, in the case of property distributed after October 1, 1996 and before 2000, in circumstances in which subsection (5) applied)

(a) where the trust is resident in Canada at the time of each of those distributions and has so elected in prescribed form filed with the trust's return for the year or a preceding taxation year, the income of the trust for the year (determined without reference to subsection 104(6)) shall, for the purposes of subsections 104(6) and (13), be computed without regard to all of those distributions to non-resident persons (including a partnership other than a Canadian partnership); and

(b) where the trust is resident in Canada at the time of each of those distributions and has so elected in prescribed form filed with the trust's return for the year or a preceding taxation year, the income of the trust for the year (determined without reference to subsection 104(6)) shall, for the purposes of subsections 104(6) and (13), be computed without regard to all of those distributions.

[¶1726]

(2.12) Election — Subsection (2.11). An election made under subsection (2.11) by a mutual fund trust is deemed, for the trust's 2003 and subsequent taxation years, not to have been made if

(a) the election is made after December 20, 2000 and applies to any taxation year that ends before 2003; and

(b) the proceeds of disposition of a beneficiary's interest in the trust have been determined under paragraph (2.1)(e).

[¶1728]

(2.2) Flow-through entity. Where at any time before 2005 a beneficiary under a trust described in paragraph (h), (i) or (j) of the definition "flow-through entity" in subsection 39.1(1) received a distribution of property from the trust in satisfaction of all or a portion of the beneficiary's interests in the trust and the beneficiary files with the Minister on or before the beneficiary's filing-due date for the taxation year that includes that time an election in respect of the property in prescribed form, there shall be included in the cost to the beneficiary of a particular property (other than money) received by the beneficiary as part of the distribution of property the least of

(a) the amount, if any, by which the beneficiary's exempt capital gains balance (as defined in subsection 39.1(1)) in respect of the trust for the beneficiary's taxation year that includes that time exceeds the total of all amounts each of which is

(i) an amount by which a capital gain is reduced under section 39.1 in the year because of the beneficiary's exempt capital gains balance in respect of the trust,

(ii) twice an amount by which a taxable capital gain is reduced under section 39.1 in the year because of the beneficiary's exempt capital gains balance in respect of the trust, or

(iii) an amount included in the cost to the beneficiary of another property received by the beneficiary at or before that time in the year because of this subsection,

(b) the amount by which the fair market value of the particular property at that time exceeds the adjusted cost base to the trust of the particular property immediately before that time, and

(c) the amount designated in respect of the particular property in the election.

* * *

[¶1730]

SECTION 127:

* * *

(5) Investment tax credit. There may be deducted from the tax otherwise payable by a taxpayer under this Part for a taxation year an amount not exceeding the lesser of

(a) the total of

(i) the taxpayer's investment tax credit at the end of the year in respect of property acquired before the end of the year, of the taxpayer's flow-through mining expenditure for the year or a preceding taxation year, of the taxpayer's pre-production mining expenditure for the year or a preceding taxation year or of the taxpayer's SR&ED qualified expenditure pool at the end of the year or at the end of a preceding taxation year, and

(ii) the lesser of

(A) the taxpayer's investment tax credit at the end of the year in respect of property acquired in a subsequent taxation year, of the taxpayer's flow-through mining expenditure for a subsequent taxation year, of the taxpayer's pre-production mining expenditure for a subsequent taxation year or of the taxpayer's SR&ED qualified expenditure pool at the end of a subsequent taxation year to the extent that an investment tax credit was not deductible under this subsection for the subsequent year, and

(B) the amount, if any, by which the taxpayer's tax otherwise payable under this Part for the year exceeds the amount, if any, determined under subparagraph (i), and

(b) where Division E.1 applies to the taxpayer for the year, the amount, if any, by which

(i) the taxpayer's tax otherwise payable under this Part for the year

exceeds

(ii) the taxpayer's minimum amount for the year determined under section 127.51.

* * *

¶1730

[¶1731]

SECTION 248:

(1) Definitions. In this Act,

* * *

[¶1732]

"automobile" — "automobile" means

(a) a motor vehicle that is designed or adapted primarily to carry individuals on highways and streets and that has a seating capacity for not more than the driver and 8 passengers,

but does not include

(b) an ambulance,

(b.1) a clearly marked emergency-response vehicle that is used in connection with or in the course of an individual's office or employment with a fire department or the police;

(b.2) a clearly marked emergency medical response vehicle that is used, in connection with or in the course of an individual's office or employment with an emergency medical response or ambulance service, to carry emergency medical equipment together with one or more emergency medical attendants or paramedics,

(c) a motor vehicle acquired primarily for use as a taxi, a bus used in a business of transporting passengers or a hearse used in the course of a business of arranging or managing funerals,

(d) except for the purposes of section 6, a motor vehicle acquired to be sold, rented or leased in the course of carrying on a business of selling, renting or leasing motor vehicles or a motor vehicle used for the purpose of transporting passengers in the course of carrying on a business of arranging or managing funerals, and

(e) a motor vehicle

(i) of a type commonly called a van or pick-up truck, or a similar vehicle, that has a seating capacity for not more than the driver and two passengers and that, in the taxation year in which it is acquired or leased, is used primarily for the transportation of goods or equipment in the course of gaining or producing income,

(ii) of a type commonly called a van or pick-up truck, or a similar vehicle, the use of which, in the taxation year in which it is acquired or leased, is all or substantially all for the transportation of goods, equipment or passengers in the course of gaining or producing income, or

(iii) of a type commonly called a pick-up truck that is used in the taxation year in which it is acquired or leased primarily for the transportation of goods, equipment or passengers in the course of earning or producing income at one or more locations in Canada that are

(A) described, in respect of any of the occupants of the vehicle, in subparagraph $6(6)(a)$(i) or (ii), and

(B) at least 30 kilometres outside the nearest point on the boundary of the nearest urban area, as defined by the last census dictionary published by Statistics Canada before the year, that has a population of at least 40,000 individuals as determined in the last census published by Statistics Canada before the year.

* * *

[¶1733]

"disposition" — "disposition" of any property, except as expressly otherwise provided, includes

(a) any transaction or event entitling a taxpayer to proceeds of disposition of the property,

(b) any transaction or event by which,

(i) where the property is a share, bond, debenture, note, certificate, mortgage, agreement of sale or similar property, or an interest in it, the property is redeemed in whole or in part or is cancelled,

---

Pending Amendment

Non-Resident Trusts, Foreign Investment Entities, and Technical Amendments (July 18, 2005)

Subparagraph (b)(i) of the definition "disposition" in subsection 248(1) of the Act is replaced by the following:

(i) where the property is a share, bond, debenture, note, certificate, mortgage, hypothecary claim, agreement of sale or similar property, or an interest, or for civil law a right, in it, the property is in whole or in part redeemed, acquired or cancelled,

Applicable: To redemptions, acquisitions and cancellations that occur after December 23, 1998 and, where a particular redemption, acquisition or cancellation occurs before December 21, 2002, any assessment of a taxpayer's tax, interest and penalties payable under the Act for a taxation year that includes the time at which the particular redemption, acquisition or cancellation occurred shall, notwithstanding subsections 152(4) to (5) of the Act, be made that is necessary to take into account the application of [the amendment to subparagraph (b)(i) and the addition of paragraph (n) of the definition "disposition"].

Explanatory Note:

"disposition"

The expression "disposition" is used throughout the Act, particularly in provisions relating to transactions involving property.

The definition "disposition" was added to subsection 248(1) by S.C. 2001, chapter 17, ss. 188(5) [formerly Bill C-22]. In general, that definition is applicable to transactions and events that occur after December 23, 1998. The former definition "disposition" was

---

contained in section 54 of the Act, applicable to transactions and events that occurred before December 24, 1998.

Under the definition "disposition" in subsection 248(1), a "disposition" of any property includes a transaction or an event described in any of paragraphs (a) to (d) of that definition but does not include a transaction or an event described in any of paragraphs (e) to (m) of that definition.

Under subparagraph $(b)(i)$ of that definition, a disposition of a property includes any transaction or event by which, where the property is a share, bond, debenture, note, certificate, mortgage, agreement of sale or similar property, or an interest in it, the property "is redeemed in whole or in part or is cancelled".

The definition "disposition" in subsection 248(1) is amended in the following ways.

First, subparagraph $(b)(i)$ of the definition now provides that a disposition of property includes any transaction or event by which, where the property is a share, bond, debenture, note, certificate, mortgage, agreement of sale or similar property, or an interest in it, the property "is in whole or in part redeemed, acquired or cancelled". This amendment makes it clear that a disposition will also include a transaction or event by which the property is acquired.

Second, paragraph (n) is added to the definition. New paragraph (n) provides that a redemption, an acquisition or a cancellation of a share, or of a right to be issued a share, (which share or which right, as the case may be, is referred to as the "security") of the capital stock of a corporation (the "issuing corporation") held by another corporation (the "disposing corporation") is considered not to be a "disposition" in the case where

- the redemption, acquisition or cancellation occurs as part of a merger or combination of two or more corporations (including the issuing corporation and the disposing corporation) to form one corporate entity (referred to as the "new corporation"),

- the merger or combination is

  — an amalgamation (within the meaning assigned by subsection 87(1) of the Act) to which subsection 87(11) of the Act does not apply,

  — an amalgamation (within the meaning assigned by subsection 87(1)) to which subsection 87(11) applies, if the issuing corporation and the disposing corporation are described by subsection 87(11) as the parent and the subsidiary, respectively, or

  — foreign merger (within the meaning assigned by subsection 87(8.1) of the Act), and

- either

  — the disposing corporation receives no consideration for the security, or

  — in the case of a foreign merger (within the meaning assigned by subsection 87(8.1)), the disposing corporation receives no consideration for the security other than property that was, immediately before the foreign merger, owned by the issuing corporation and that, on the foreign merger, becomes property of the new corporation.

Both amendments apply to redemptions, acquisitions and cancellations that occur after December 23, 1998, and, where the redemption, acquisition or cancellation takes place before December 21, 2002, the Minister of National Revenue shall, notwithstanding subsections 152(4) to (5) of the Act, make any assessment of a taxpayer's tax, interest and penalties payable under the Act for any taxation years that include the time at which such a redemption, acquisition or cancellation occurred that is necessary to take into account the application of the amendments.

In connection with redemptions, acquisitions and cancellations that occur before December 24, 1998, see the commentary to new subsection 248(1.1) of the Act.

¶1733

Third, the definition "disposition" in subsection 248(1) is also amended by restricting the circumstances in which a transfer of property between trusts will not be treated as a disposition. In particular, paragraph (f) of the definition is amended so that a transfer of property from a trust to another trust will avoid, under that paragraph, characterization as a disposition only if both trusts are, at the time of the transfer, resident in Canada.

This amendment applies to transfers that occur after February 27, 2004.

(ii) where the property is a debt or any other right to receive an amount, the debt or other right is settled or cancelled,

(iii) where the property is a share, the share is converted because of an amalgamation or merger,

(iv) where the property is an option to acquire or dispose of property, the option expires, and

(v) a trust, that can reasonably be considered to act as agent for all the beneficiaries under the trust with respect to all dealings with all of the trust's property (unless the trust is described in any of paragraphs (a) to $(e.1)$ of the definition "trust" in subsection 108(1)), ceases to act as agent for a beneficiary under the trust with respect to any dealing with any of the trust's property,

(c) any transfer of the property to a trust or, where the property is property of a trust, any transfer of the property to any beneficiary under the trust, except as provided by paragraph (f) or (k), and

(d) where the property is, or is part of, a taxpayer's capital interest in a trust, except as provided by paragraph (h) or (i), a payment made after 1999 to the taxpayer from the trust that can reasonably be considered to have been made because of the taxpayer's capital interest in the trust,

but does not include

(e) any transfer of the property as a consequence of which there is no change in the beneficial ownership of the property, except where the transfer is

(i) from a person or a partnership to a trust for the benefit of the person or the partnership,

(ii) from a trust to a beneficiary under the trust, or

(iii) from one trust maintained for the benefit of one or more beneficiaries under the trust to another trust maintained for the benefit of the same beneficiaries,

(f) any transfer of the property as a consequence of which there is no change in the beneficial ownership of the property, where

(i) the transferor and the transferee are trusts,

(ii) the transfer is not by a trust resident in Canada to a non-resident trust,

¶1733

Pending Amendment

Non-Resident Trusts, Foreign Investment Entities, and Technical Amendments (July 18, 2005)

Subparagraphs *(f)*(i) and (ii) of the definition "disposition" in subsection 248(1) of the Act are replaced by the following:

(i) the transferor and the transferee are trusts that are, at the time of the transfer, resident in Canada,

(ii) [Repealed.]

Applicable: To transfers that occur after February 27, 2004.

Explanatory Note: [See the Explanatory Note following the amendment to subparagraph *(b)*(i) of the definition "disposition" in subsection 248(1).]

(iii) the transferee does not receive the property in satisfaction of the transferee's right as a beneficiary under the transferor trust,

(iv) the transferee held no property immediately before the transfer (other than property the cost of which is not included, for the purposes of this Act, in computing a balance of undeducted outlays, expenses or other amounts in respect of the transferee),

(v) the transferee does not file a written election with the Minister on or before the filing-due date for its taxation year in which the transfer is made (or on such later date as is acceptable to the Minister) that this paragraph not apply,

(vi) if the transferor is an amateur athlete trust, a cemetery care trust, an employee trust, an inter vivos trust deemed by subsection 143(1) to exist in respect of a congregation that is a constituent part of a religious organization, a related segregated fund trust (in this paragraph having the meaning assigned by section 138.1), a trust described in paragraph 149(1)*(o*.4) or a trust governed by an eligible funeral arrangement, an employees profit sharing plan, a registered education savings plan or a registered supplementary unemployment benefit plan, the transferee is the same type of trust, and

(vii) the transfer results, or is part of a series of transactions or events that results, in the transferor ceasing to exist and, immediately before the time of the transfer or the beginning of that series, as the case may be, the transferee never held any property or held only property having a nominal value,

(g) [Repealed.]

(h) where the property is part of a capital interest of a taxpayer in a trust (other than a personal trust or a trust prescribed for the purpose of subsection 107(2)) that is described by reference to units issued by the trust, a payment after 1999 from the trust in respect of the capital interest, where the number of units in the trust that are owned by the taxpayer is not reduced because of the payment,

¶1733

(i) where the property is a taxpayer's capital interest in a trust, a payment to the taxpayer after 1999 in respect of the capital interest to the extent that the payment

(i) is out of the income of the trust (determined without reference to subsection 104(6)) for a taxation year or out of the capital gains of the trust for the year, if the payment was made in the year or the right to the payment was acquired by the taxpayer in the year, or

(ii) is in respect of an amount designated in respect of the taxpayer by the trust under subsection 104(20),

(j) any transfer of the property for the purpose only of securing a debt or a loan, or any transfer by a creditor for the purpose only of returning property that had been used as security for a debt or a loan,

(k) any transfer of the property to a trust as a consequence of which there is no change in the beneficial ownership of the property, where the main purpose of the transfer is

(i) to effect payment under a debt or loan,

(ii) to provide assurance that an absolute or contingent obligation of the transferor will be satisfied, or

(iii) to facilitate either the provision of compensation or the enforcement of a penalty, in the event that an absolute or contingent obligation of the transferor is not satisfied,

(l) any issue of a bond, debenture, note, certificate, mortgage or hypothecary claim, and

(m) any issue by a corporation of a share of its capital stock, or any other transaction that, but for this paragraph, would be a disposition by a corporation of a share of its capital stock;

Pending Amendment

Non-Resident Trusts, Foreign Investment Entities, and Technical Amendments (July 18, 2005)

The definition "disposition" in subsection 248(1) of the Act is amended by striking out the word "and" at the end of paragraph (l), by adding the word "and" at the end of paragraph (m) and by adding the following after paragraph (m):

(n) a redemption, an acquisition or a cancellation of a share or of a right to acquire a share (which share or which right, as the case may be, is referred to in this paragraph as the "security") of the capital stock of a corporation (referred to in this paragraph as the "issuing corporation") held by another corporation (referred to in this paragraph as the "disposing corporation") if

(i) the redemption, acquisition or cancellation occurs as part of a merger or combination of two or more corporations (including the issuing corporation and the disposing corporation) to form one corporate entity (referred to in this paragraph as the "new corporation"),

(ii) the merger or combination is

¶1733

(A) an amalgamation (within the meaning assigned by subsection 87(1)) to which subsection 87(11) does not apply,

(B) an amalgamation (within the meaning assigned by subsection 87(1)) to which subsection 87(11) applies, if the issuing corporation and the disposing corporation are described by subsection 87(11) as the parent and the subsidiary, respectively, or

(C) a foreign merger (within the meaning assigned by subsection 87(8.1)), and

(iii) either

(A) the disposing corporation receives no consideration for the security, or

(B) in the case of a foreign merger (within the meaning assigned by subsection 87(8.1)), the disposing corporation receives no consideration for the security other than property that was, immediately before the foreign merger, owned by the issuing corporation and that, on the foreign merger, becomes property of the new corporation;

Applicable: To redemptions, acquisitions and cancellations that occur after December 23, 1998 and, where a particular redemption, acquisition or cancellation occurs before December 21, 2002, any assessment of a taxpayer's tax, interest and penalties payable under the Act for a taxation year that includes the time at which the particular redemption, acquisition or cancellation occurred shall, notwithstanding subsections 152(4) to (5) of the Act, be made that is necessary to take into account the application of [the amendment to subparagraph $(b)(i)$ and the addition of paragraph (n) of the definition "disposition"].

Explanatory Note: [See the Explanatory Note following the amendment to subparagraph $(b)(i)$ of the definition "disposition" in subsection 248(1).]

* * *

[¶1734]

"passenger vehicle" — *"*passenger vehicle*"* means an automobile acquired after June 17, 1987 (other than an automobile acquired after that date pursuant to an obligation in writing entered into before June 18, 1987) and an automobile leased under a lease entered into, extended or renewed after June 17, 1987;

* * *

[¶1735]

(16) Goods and services tax — input tax credit and rebate. For the purposes of this Act, other than this subsection and subsection 6(8), an amount claimed by a taxpayer as an input tax credit or rebate with respect to the goods and services tax in respect of a property or service shall be deemed to be assistance from a government in respect of the property or service that is received by the taxpayer

(a) where the amount was claimed by the taxpayer as an input tax credit in a return under Part IX of the *Excise Tax Act* for a reporting period under that Act,

(i) at the time the goods and services tax in respect of the input tax credit was paid or became payable, if the tax was paid or became payable in the reporting period, or

(ii) if no such tax was paid or became payable in respect of the input tax credit in the reporting period, at the end of the reporting period; or

(*b*) where the amount was claimed as a rebate with respect to the goods and services tax, at the time the amount was received or credited.

Pending Amendment

Non-Resident Trusts, Foreign Investment Entities, and Technical Amendments (July 18, 2005)

Subsection 248(16) of the Act is replaced by the following:

(16) Goods and services tax — input tax credit and rebate. For the purposes of this Act, other than this subsection and subsection 6(8), an amount claimed by a taxpayer as an input tax credit or rebate with respect to the goods and services tax in respect of a property or service is deemed to be assistance from a government in respect of the property or service that is received by the taxpayer

(*a*) where the amount was claimed by the taxpayer as an input tax credit in a return under Part IX of the *Excise Tax Act* for a reporting period under that Act,

(i) at the particular time that is the earlier of the time that the goods and services tax in respect of the input tax credit was paid and the time that it became payable,

(A) if the particular time is in the reporting period, or

(B) if,

(I) the taxpayer's threshold amount, determined in accordance with subsection 249(1) of the *Excise Tax Act*, is greater than $500,000 for the taxpayer's fiscal year (within the meaning assigned by that Act) that includes the particular time, and

(II) the taxpayer claimed the input tax credit at least 120 days before the end of the normal reassessment period, as determined under subsection 152(3.1), for the taxpayer in respect of the taxation year that includes the particular time,

(ii) at the end of the reporting period, if

(A) subparagraph (i) does not apply, and

(B) the taxpayer's threshold amount, determined in accordance with subsection 249(1) of the *Excise Tax Act*, is $500,000 or less for the fiscal year (within the meaning assigned by that Act) of the taxpayer that includes the particular time, and

(iii) in any other case, on the last day of the taxpayer's earliest taxation year

(A) that begins after the taxation year that includes the particular time, and

(B) for which the normal reassessment period, as determined under subsection 152(3.1), for the taxpayer ends at least 120 days after the time that the input tax credit was claimed; or

(*b*) where the amount was claimed as a rebate with respect to the goods and services tax, at the time the amount was received or credited.

Applicable: In respect of input tax credits that become eligible to be claimed in taxation years that begin after December 20, 2002.

¶1735

Explanatory Note:

Goods and Services Tax — Input Tax Credit and Rebate

Subsection 248(16) of the Act provides rules under which amounts received by, or credited to, a taxpayer as an input tax credit or rebate with respect to the goods and services tax (GST) are deemed to be assistance from a government received by a taxpayer. As a consequence, such amounts are either included in income or reduce the cost or capital cost of the related property, or the amount of the related expenditure or expenditure pool, for tax purposes.

Subsection 248(16) also specifies the time at which the receipt (or credit) of an input tax credit or rebate is deemed to be received as assistance. With respect to input tax credits, subparagraph $248(16)(a)$(i) provides that the assistance (i.e., the input tax credit) is considered to be received by a taxpayer at the time the GST in respect of the input tax credit was paid or became payable by the taxpayer if the GST was paid or became payable in the same reporting period under the *Excise Tax Act* in which the input tax credit was claimed. If a taxpayer does not claim the input tax credit in the same reporting period in which the GST was paid or became payable, subparagraph $248(16)(a)$(ii) includes the amount of assistance in the taxpayer's income for the taxation year that includes the end of the reporting period in which the taxpayer claimed the input tax credit.

Subsection 248(16) is amended in three respects for input tax credits that become eligible to be claimed in taxation years that begin after December 20, 2002.

First, subparagraph $248(16)(a)$(i) is amended to extend its application to cases where the input tax credit is claimed by a taxpayer in a reporting period that is subsequent to the period in which the related GST was paid or became payable if

- the taxpayer's threshold amount (as determined under subsection 249(1) of the *Excise Tax Act*) is greater than \$500,000 for the taxpayer's fiscal year (as defined by that Act) that includes the earlier of the time that the GST in respect of the input tax credit was paid and the time that it became payable, and

- the taxpayer claimed the input tax credit at least 120 days before the end of the normal reassessment period (as determined under subsection 152(3.1) of the *Income Tax Act*) for the taxpayer in respect of the taxation year that includes that earlier time.

In general, the change to this subparagraph means that an input tax credit of a taxpayer (who is a GST filer with a threshold amount greater than \$500,000 for GST purposes) is considered to have been received at the time the related GST was paid or became payable, even though the input tax credit is claimed in a later GST reporting period. However, this is the case only if the taxpayer claims the input tax credit at least 120 days before the taxation year in which the GST was paid or became payable becomes statute-barred for income tax purposes.

Second, subparagraph $248(16)(a)$(ii) is amended to provide that an input tax credit is considered to be received at the end of the reporting period in which it is claimed only if

- subparagraph $248(16)(a)$(i) does not apply, and

- the taxpayer's threshold amount (as determined under subsection 249(1) of the *Excise Tax Act*) is \$500,000 or less for the fiscal year of the taxpayer that includes the earlier of the time that the GST in respect of the input tax credit was paid or became payable.

Thus, subparagraph $248(16)(a)$(ii) does not apply if subparagraph $248(16)(a)$(i) applies. Where subparagraph $248(16)(a)$(i) does not apply, subparagraph $248(16)(a)$(ii) provides that the input tax credit is considered to have been received at the end of the reporting period in which it is claimed only if the taxpayer's threshold amount for GST purposes was $500,000 or less at the time the GST was paid or became payable.

Third, new subparagraph 248(16)(*a*)(iii) is added to apply in any other case. If applicable, that subparagraph provides that the input tax credit is considered to have been received on the last day of the taxpayer's earliest taxation year

- that begins after the taxation year that includes the earlier of the time that the GST in respect of the input tax credit was paid and the time that it became payable, and

- for which the normal reassessment period for the taxpayer ends at least 120 days after the time at which the input tax credit was claimed.

Reference should also made to the commentary to new subsection 248(17.1) of the *Income Tax Act* which provides a special rule in respect of the timing of a claim in respect of certain input tax credits assessed under the *Excise Tax Act*.

Pending Amendment

Non-Resident Trusts, Foreign Investment Entities, and Technical Amendments (July 18, 2005)

Section 248 of the Act is amended by adding the following after subsection (16):

(16.1) Quebec input tax refund and rebate. For the purpose of this Act, other than this subsection and subsection 6(8), an amount claimed by a taxpayer as an input tax refund or a rebate with respect to the Quebec sales tax in respect of a property or service is deemed to be assistance from a government in respect of the property or service that is received by the taxpayer

(*a*) where the amount was claimed by the taxpayer as an input tax refund in a return under *An Act respecting the Québec sales tax*, R.S.Q., c. T-0.1, for a reporting period under that Act,

(i) at the particular time that is the earlier of the time that the Quebec sales tax in respect of the input tax refund was paid and the time that it became payable,

(A) if the particular time is in the reporting period, or

(B) if,

(I) the taxpayer's threshold amount, determined in accordance with section 462 of that Act is greater than $500,000 for the taxpayer's fiscal year (within the meaning assigned by that Act) that includes the particular time, and

(II) the taxpayer claimed the input tax refund at least 120 days before the end of the normal reassessment period, as determined under subsection 152(3.1), for the taxpayer in respect of the taxation year that includes the particular time,

(ii) at the end of the reporting period, if

(A) subparagraph (i) does not apply, and

(B) the taxpayer's threshold amount, determined in accordance with section 462 of that Act is $500,000 or less for the fiscal year (within the meaning assigned by that Act) of the taxpayer that includes the particular time, and

(iii) in any other case, on the last day of the taxpayer's earliest taxation year

¶1735

(A) that begins after the taxation year that includes the particular time, and

(B) for which the normal reassessment period, as determined under subsection 152(3.1), for the taxpayer ends at least 120 days after the time that the input tax refund was claimed; or

(*b*) where the amount was claimed as a rebate with respect to the Quebec sales tax, at the time the amount was received or credited.

Applicable: In respect of input tax refunds and rebates that become eligible to be claimed in taxation years that begin after February 27, 2004.

Explanatory Note:

Quebec Sales Tax — Input Tax Refund and Rebate

New subsection 248(16.1) of the Act provides special rules for amounts received, or credited to, a taxpayer as an input tax refund or rebate in respect of Quebec sales tax. Such amounts are either included in a taxpayer's income or reduce the cost or capital cost of the related property, or the amount of the related expenditure or expenditure pool, for tax purposes.

In general, an input tax refund in respect of Quebec sales tax may — depending on the circumstances — have to be included in a taxpayer's income in the taxation year in which the taxpayer may first claim the refund, rather than the year in which it is received. A rebate of Quebec sales tax is included in income at the time the rebate is received or credited. For a more detailed explanation of the application of subsection 248(16.1), reference should be made to the commentary accompanying amendments to subsection 248(16), which provides analogous special rules in respect of the timing of the inclusion in income of certain input tax credits and rebates assessed under the *Excise Tax Act*.

Subsection 248(16.1) applies in respect of Quebec input tax refunds and rebates that become eligible to be claimed in taxation years that begin after February 27, 2004.

[¶1736]

(17) Application of s. (16) to passenger vehicles and aircraft. Where the input tax credit of a taxpayer under Part IX of the *Excise Tax Act* in respect of a passenger vehicle or aircraft is determined with reference to subsection 202(4) of the *Excise Tax Act*, subparagraphs (16)(*a*)(i) and (ii) shall, as they apply in respect of such property, be read as follows:

Pending Amendment

Non-Resident Trusts, Foreign Investment Entities, and Technical Amendments (July 18, 2005)

The portion of subsection 248(17) of the Act before the portion enclosed by quotation marks is replaced by the following:

(17) Application of subsection (16) to passenger vehicles and aircraft. If the input tax credit of a taxpayer under Part IX of the *Excise Tax Act* in respect of a passenger vehicle or aircraft is determined with reference to subsection 202(4) of that Act, subparagraphs (16)(*a*)(i) to (iii) are to be read as they apply in respect of the passenger vehicle or aircraft, as the case may be, as follows:

Applicable: In respect of input tax credits that become eligible to be claimed in taxation years that begin after December 20, 2002.

Explanatory Note:

Application of Subsection (16) to Passenger Vehicles and Aircraft

Subsection 248(17) of the Act applies in the case of an input tax credit in respect of a passenger vehicle or aircraft claimable by an individual or partnership where the credit is determined by reference to capital cost allowance in respect of the vehicle or aircraft (i.e., where there is less than exclusive use in commercial activity). Subsection 248(17) is amended to reflect the amendments made to subsection 248(16) as described in the commentary to that subsection.

The amendments to subsection 248(17) apply in respect of input tax credits that become eligible to be claimed in taxation years that begin after December 20, 2002.

" (i) at the beginning of the first taxation year or fiscal period of the taxpayer commencing after the end of the taxation year or fiscal period, as the case may be, in which the goods and services tax in respect of such property was considered for the purposes of determining the input tax credit to be payable, if the tax was considered for the purposes of determining the input tax credit to have become payable in the reporting period, or

(ii) if no such tax was considered for the purposes of determining the input tax credit to have become payable in the reporting period, at the end of the reporting period; or "

Pending Amendment

Non-Resident Trusts, Foreign Investment Entities, and Technical Amendments (July 18, 2005)

Section 248 of the Act is amended by adding the following after subsection (17):

(17.1) Application of subsection (16.1) to passenger vehicles and aircraft. If the input tax refund of a taxpayer under *An Act respecting the Québec sales tax*, R.S.Q., c. T-0.1, in respect of a passenger vehicle or aircraft is determined with reference to section 252 of that Act, subparagraphs (16.1)(a)(i) to (iii) are to be read as they apply in respect of the passenger vehicle or aircraft, as the case may be, as follows:

" (i) at the beginning of the first taxation year or fiscal period of the taxpayer that begins after the end of the taxation year or fiscal period, as the case may be, in which the Quebec sales tax in respect of such property was considered for the purposes of determining the input tax refund to be payable, if the tax was considered for the purposes of determining the input tax refund to have become payable in the reporting period, or

(ii) if no such tax was considered for the purposes of determining the input tax refund to have become payable in the reporting period, at the end of the reporting period; or ".

Applicable: In respect of input tax refunds and rebates that become eligible to be claimed in taxation years that begin after February 27, 2004.

(17.2) Input tax credit on assessment. An amount in respect of an input tax credit that is deemed by subsection 296(5) of the *Excise Tax Act* to have been claimed in a return or application filed under Part IX of that Act is deemed to have been so

¶1736

claimed for the reporting period under that Act that includes the time when the Minister makes the assessment referred to in that subsection.

Applicable: In respect of input tax credits that become eligible to be claimed in taxation years that begin after December 20, 2002.

(17.3) Quebec input tax refund on assessment. An amount in respect of an input tax refund that is deemed by section 30.5 of *An Act respecting the Ministère du Revenu*, R.S.Q., c. M-31, to have been claimed is deemed to have been so claimed for the reporting period under An Act respecting the Québec sales tax, R.S.Q., c. T- 0.1, that includes the day on which an assessment is issued to the taxpayer indicating that the refund has been allocated under that section 30.5.

Applicable: In respect of input tax refunds and rebates that become eligible to be claimed in taxation years that begin after February 27, 2004.

Explanatory Note:

Subsection 248(17.1) — Application of Subsection (16.1) to Passenger Vehicles and Aircraft

New subsection 248(17.1) of the Act applies in the case of an input tax refund of Quebec sales tax, in respect of a passenger vehicle or aircraft, claimable by an individual or partnership where the credit is determinable by reference to capital cost allowance in respect of the vehicle or aircraft (that is, where there is less than exclusive use in commercial activity). In general, this subsection defers the time the input tax refund is considered to be received for income tax purposes to the taxation year or fiscal period following that in which Quebec sales tax in respect of the property is considered as payable for the purposes of determining the input tax refund. This avoids circularity with subsection 248(16.1). The provision preserves the proper timing between the input tax refund entitlement and the adjustment to the capital cost. This change applies in respect of Quebec input tax refunds that become eligible to be claimed in taxation years that begin after February 27, 2004.

Subsection 248(17.2) — Input Tax Credit on Assessment

New subsection 248(17.2) of the Act determines, in respect of input tax credits that become eligible to be claimed in taxation years that begin after December 20, 2002, the time at which an input tax credit is considered to have been claimed in respect of certain input tax credit assessments made under the *Excise Tax Act* (ETA).

This subsection provides that, if an amount in respect of an input tax credit is deemed by subsection 296(5) of the ETA to have been claimed in a return or application filed under Part IX of that Act, the input tax credit is deemed to have been claimed for the GST reporting period that includes the time the Minister of National Revenue makes the GST assessment.

Accordingly, the rule in clause 248(16)(a)(i)(A) of the *Income Tax Act* (ITA) relating to the time at which an input tax credit is considered to have been received cannot apply to an input tax credit to which subsection 296(5) of the ETA applies. However, the other rules in paragraph 248(16)(a) of the ITA that determine the time at which an input tax credit is received are to be applied on the basis that an input tax credit (to which subsection 296(5) of the ETA applies) is not claimed by the taxpayer until the reporting period that includes the time at which the input tax credit is actually assessed — i.e., not the reporting period to which the assessment relates but the reporting period in which the input tax credit is deemed to be claimed for GST purposes.

Subsection 248(17.3) — Quebec Input Tax Credit on Assessment

New subsection 248(17.3) of the Act provides that an input tax refund of Quebec sales tax, that is deemed to be claimed by section 30.5 of *An Act respecting the Quebec Revenue Minister*, is deemed to be claimed for the reporting period under *An Act respecting Quebec Sales Tax* that includes the day on which an assessment is issued to

¶1736

the taxpayer indicating that the refund has been allocated to the taxpayer. This change applies in respect of Quebec input tax refunds and rebates that become eligible to be claimed in taxation years that begin after February 27, 2004.

[¶1738]

(18) Goods and services tax — repayment of input tax credit. For the purposes of this Act, where an amount is added at a particular time in determining the net tax of a taxpayer under Part IX of the *Excise Tax Act* in respect of an input tax credit relating to property or a service that had been previously deducted in determining the net tax of the taxpayer, that amount shall be deemed to be assistance repaid at the particular time in respect of the property or service pursuant to a legal obligation to repay all or part of that assistance.

Pending Amendment

Non-Resident Trusts, Foreign Investment Entities, and Technical Amendments (July 18, 2005)

Section 248 of the Act is amended by adding the following after subsection (18).

(18.1) Repayment of Quebec input tax refund. For the purposes of this Act, if an amount is added at a particular time in determining the net tax of a taxpayer under *An Act respecting the Québec sales tax*, R.S.Q., c. T-0.1, in respect of an input tax refund relating to property or service that had been previously deducted in determining the net tax of the taxpayer, that amount is deemed to be assistance repaid at the particular time in respect of the property or service under a legal obligation to repay all or part of that assistance.

Applicable: After February 27, 2004.

Explanatory Note:

Repayment of Quebec Input Tax Refund

New subsection 248(18.1) of the Act provides that an amount added in determining net tax of a taxpayer under *An Act respecting Quebec Sales Tax* in respect of an input tax refund relating to a property or service that had previously been deducted in computing such net tax is treated as assistance repaid under a legal obligation to repay that assistance. Such an amount could be so added under Quebec law pursuant to an assessment of Quebec sales tax. As a consequence, such an amount will either be deducted in computing income under paragraph 20(1)(*hh*) or will increase the cost or capital cost of the related property or the amount of the related expenditure or expenditure pool for tax purposes (as provided under subsection 13(7.1), paragraphs 37(1)(*c*) and 53(2)(*k*) and under the definitions "cumulative Canadian exploration expense" in subsection 66.1(6), "cumulative Canadian development expense" in subsection 66.2(5) and "cumulative Canadian oil and gas property expense" in subsection 66.4(5)). This change applies after February 27, 2004.

* * *

¶1738

CHAPTER 12

INCOME TAX APPLICATION RULES

Reproduced below are the relevant sections of the *Income Tax Application Rules* (ITARs) current to date of publication. The ITARs were enacted as part of the 1972 Tax Reform and provide transitional rules where assets are held continuously or through a series of non-arm's length transactions since 1971.

[¶1740]

SECTION 18:   General depreciation provisions.

(1) Where the capital cost to a taxpayer of any depreciable property that was acquired by the taxpayer before 1972 was required by any provision of the old law to be determined for the purpose of computing the amount of any deduction under any such provision in respect of that property, or would have been required by any provision of the old law to be determined for that purpose if any deduction under any such provision had been claimed by the taxpayer in respect of that property, the amount of the capital cost so required to be determined or that would have been so required to be determined, as the case may be, shall be deemed, for all purposes of the amended Act, to be the capital cost to the taxpayer of that property.

[¶1741]

(2) **Idem.**   Where a taxpayer acquired depreciable property before the beginning of the 1949 taxation year, for the purposes of section 13 of the amended Act and any regulations made under paragraph $20(1)(a)$ of that Act an amount equal to the total of

(a) all deductions allowed in computing the taxpayers income for the purpose of the *Income War Tax Act* as "special depreciation", "extra depreciation" or allowances in lieu of depreciation for property the taxpayer had at the beginning of the 1949 taxation year (except deductions allowed under subparagraph $6(1)(n)(ii)$ of that Act), and

(b) $\frac{1}{2}$ of all amounts allowed to the taxpayer under subparagraph $6(1)(n)(ii)$ of that Act for property that the taxpayer had at the beginning of the 1949 taxation year,

shall be deemed to have been allowed to the taxpayer under regulations made under paragraph $20(1)(a)$ of the amended Act in computing income for a taxation year before the 1949 taxation year.

[¶1742]

(3) Provisoes not applicable. The second and third provisoes to paragraph $6(1)(n)$ of the *Income War Tax Act* do not apply with respect to sales made after the beginning of the 1949 taxation year.

[¶1743]

(4) Reference to depreciation. Reference in this section to depreciation shall be deemed to include a reference to allowances in respect of depreciable property of a taxpayer made under paragraph $5(1)(a)$ of the *Income War Tax Act*.

[¶1744]

(5) Deduction deemed depreciation. An amount deducted under paragraph $5(1)(u)$ of the *Income War Tax Act* in respect of amounts of a capital nature shall, for the purpose of this section, be deemed to be depreciation taken into account in ascertaining the taxpayers income for the purpose of that Act or in ascertaining the taxpayers loss for the taxation year for which it was deducted.

[¶1745]

SECTION 20: Depreciable property.

(1) Where the capital cost to a taxpayer of any depreciable property acquired by the taxpayer before 1972 and owned by the taxpayer without interruption from December 31, 1971 until such time after 1971 as the taxpayer disposed of it is less than the fair market value of the property on valuation day and less than the proceeds of disposition thereof otherwise determined,

(a) for the purposes of section 13 of the amended Act, subdivision c of Division B of Part I of that Act and any regulations made under paragraph $20(1)(a)$ of that Act, the taxpayers proceeds of disposition of the property shall be deemed to be an amount equal to the total of its capital cost to the taxpayer and the amount, if any, by which the proceeds of disposition thereof otherwise determined exceed the fair market value of the property on valuation day,

(b) where the property has, by one or more transactions or events (other than the death of a taxpayer to which subsection 70(5) of the amended Act applies) between persons not dealing at arms length, become vested in another taxpayer

(i) for the purposes of the amended Act (other than, where paragraph $13(7)(e)$ of that Act applies in determining the capital cost to that other taxpayer of the property, for the purposes of paragraphs

$8(1)(j)$ and (p) and sections 13 and 20 of that Act), that other taxpayer shall be deemed to have acquired the property at a capital cost equal to the proceeds deemed to have been received for the property by the person from whom that other taxpayer acquired the property, and

(ii) for the purposes of this subsection, that other taxpayer shall be deemed to have acquired the property before 1972 at a capital cost equal to the capital cost of the property to the taxpayer who actually owned the property at the end of 1971, and to have owned it without interruption from December 31, 1971 until such time after 1971 as that other taxpayer disposed of it, and

(c) where the disposition occurred because of an election under subsection 110.6(19) of the amended Act,

(i) for the purposes of that Act (other than paragraphs $8(1)(j)$ and (p) and sections 13 and 20 of that Act), the taxpayer is deemed to have reacquired the property at a capital cost equal to

(A) where the amount designated in respect of the property in the election did not exceed 110% of the fair market value of the property at the end of February 22, 1994, the taxpayer's proceeds of disposition determined under paragraph (a) in respect of the disposition of the property that immediately preceded the reacquisition minus the amount, if any, by which the amount designated in respect of the property in the election exceeded that fair market value, and

(B) in any other case, the amount otherwise determined under subsection 110.6(19) of that Act to be the cost to the taxpayer of the property immediately after the reacquisition referred to in that subsection minus the amount by which the fair market value of the property on valuation day exceeded the capital cost of the property at the time it was last acquired before 1972, and

(ii) for the purposes of this subsection, the taxpayer's capital cost of the property after the reacquisition shall be deemed to be equal to the taxpayer's capital cost of the property before the reacquisition and the taxpayer shall be considered to have owned the property without interruption from December 31, 1971 until such time after February 22, 1994 as the taxpayer disposes of it.

[¶1746]

(1.1) Where depreciable property disposed of to spouse, trust or child. Subsection (1) does not apply in any case where

(a) subsection 70(6) or 73(1) of the amended Act applies in respect of the disposition by a taxpayer of any depreciable property of a prescribed class to the spouse, common-law partner, trust or transferee, as the case may be, referred to therein, and

(b) subsection 70(9) of the amended Act applies in respect of the disposition by a taxpayer of any depreciable property of a prescribed class to a child referred to therein,

except that where the spouse, common-law partner, trust, transferee or child, as the case may be, subsequently disposes of the property at any time, subsection (1) applies as if the spouse, common-law partner, trust, transferee or child, as the case may be, had acquired the property before 1972 and owned it without interruption from December 31, 1971 until that time.

[¶1747]

(1.11) Extended meaning of "child".   For the purposes of subsection (1.1), "child" of a taxpayer includes

(a) a child of the taxpayer's child;

(b) a child of the taxpayer's child's child; and

(c) a person who, at any time before attaining the age of 21 years, was wholly dependent on the taxpayer for support and of whom the taxpayer had, at that time, in law or in fact, the custody and control.

[¶1748]

(1.2) Other transfers of depreciable property.   Where, because of a transaction or an event in respect of which any of subsections 70(5), 85(1), (2) and (3), 87(2), section 88, subsections 97(2), 98(3) and (5) and 107(2) of the amended Act applies, a taxpayer has at any particular time after 1971 acquired any depreciable property of a prescribed class from a person who acquired the property before 1972 and owned it without interruption from December 31, 1971 until the particular time, for the purposes of subsection (1) the taxpayer shall be deemed to have acquired the property before 1972 and to have owned it without interruption from December 31, 1971 until such time after 1971 as the taxpayer disposed of it.

[¶1749]

(1.3) Transfers before 1972 not at arm's length.   Without restricting the generality of section 18, where any depreciable property has been transferred before 1972 in circumstances such that subsection 20(4) of the former Act would, if that provision applied to transfers of property made in the 1972 taxation year, apply, paragraph 69(1)(b) of the amended Act does not apply to the transfer and subsection 20(4) of the former Act applies thereto.

[¶1750]

(1.4) Depreciable property received as dividend in kind.   The capital cost to a taxpayer, as of any particular time after 1971, of any depreciable property (other than depreciable property referred to in subsection (1.3) or deemed by subparagraph (1)(b)(ii) to have been acquired by the taxpayer before 1972) acquired by the taxpayer before 1972 as, on account of, in lieu of payment of or in satisfaction of, a dividend payable in kind (other than a stock dividend) in respect of a share owned by the taxpayer of the capital stock of a corporation, shall be deemed to be the fair market value of that property at the time the property was so received.

[¶1751]

(2) Recapture of capital cost allowances.   In determining a taxpayer's income for a taxation year from farming or fishing, subsection 13(1) of the amended Act does not apply in respect of the disposition by the taxpayer of property acquired by the taxpayer before 1972 unless the taxpayer has elected to make a deduction for that or a preceding taxation year, in respect of the capital cost of property acquired by the taxpayer before 1972, under regulations made under paragraph $20(1)(a)$ of that Act other than a regulation providing solely for an allowance for computing income from farming or fishing.

[¶1752]

(3) Depreciable property of partnership of prescribed class. For the purposes of the amended Act, where a partnership had, on December 31, 1971, partnership property that was depreciable property of a prescribed class,

(a) the capital cost to the partnership of each property of that class shall be deemed to be an amount determined as follows:

(i) determine, for each person who, because of having been a member of the partnership on the later of June 18, 1971 and the day the partnership was created, and thereafter without interruption until December 31, 1971, can reasonably be regarded as having had an interest in the property of that class on December 31, 1971, the persons acquisition cost in respect of property of that class,

(ii) determine, for each such person, the amount that is that proportion of the person's acquisition cost in respect of property of that class that 100% is of the person's percentage in respect of property of that class,

(iii) select the amount determined under subparagraph (ii) for a person described therein that is not greater than any amount so determined for any other such person, and

(iv) determine that proportion of the amount selected under subparagraph (iii) (in this subsection referred to as the "capital cost of that class") that the fair market value on December 31, 1971 of that property is of the fair market value on that day of all property of that class,

and the amount determined under subparagraph (iv) is the capital cost to the partnership of that property;

(b) for the purposes of sections 13 and 20 of the amended Act and any regulations made under paragraph $20(1)(a)$ of that Act, the undepreciated capital cost to the partnership of property of that class as of any time after 1971 shall be computed as though the amount, if any, by which the capital cost of that class to the partnership exceeds the undepreciated cost to the partnership of that class had been allowed to the partnership in respect of property of that class under regulations made under paragraph $20(1)(a)$ of the amended Act in computing income for taxation years before that time;

(c) in computing the income for the 1972 and subsequent taxation years of each person who was a member of the partnership on June 18, 1971 and thereafter without interruption until December 31, 1971, there may be deducted such amount as the person claims for the year, not exceeding the amount, if any, by which the total of

(i) the lesser of

(A) the amount, if any, by which the amount that was the capital cost to the person of all property of that class exceeds the percentage, equal to the person's percentage in respect of property of that class, of the capital cost of that class to the partnership, and

(B) the amount that was the undepreciated capital cost to the person of property of that class as of December 31, 1971, and

(ii) the amount, if any, by which

(A) the undepreciated capital cost to the person of property of that class as of December 31, 1971, less the amount, if any, determined under subparagraph (i) in respect of property of that class,

exceeds

(B) the percentage, equal to the person's percentage in respect of property of that class, of the undepreciated cost to the partnership of that class,

exceeds the total of all amounts deducted under this paragraph in computing the persons income for preceding taxation years, and, for the purposes of section 3 of the amended Act, the amount so claimed shall be deemed to be a deduction permitted by subdivision e of Division B of Part I of that Act; and

(*d*) notwithstanding paragraph (*c*), a person who became a member of the partnership after June 18, 1971 and who was a member of the partnership thereafter without interruption until December 31, 1971 shall be deemed to be a person described in paragraph (*c*) and the amount that may be claimed thereunder as a deduction in computing the person's income for any taxation year shall not exceed 10% of the total of the amounts determined under subparagraphs (*c*)(i) and (ii).

[¶1753]

(4) Definitions.   In subsection (3),

[¶1754]

"acquisition cost" — "acquisition cost" of a person who was a member of a partnership on December 31, 1971 in respect of depreciable property of a prescribed class that was partnership property of the partnership on December 31, 1971 means the total of the undepreciated capital cost to the person of property of that class as of December 31, 1971 and the total depreciation allowed to the person before 1972 in respect of property of that class;

[¶1755]

"percentage" — "percentage" of a member of a partnership in respect of any depreciable property of a prescribed class that was partnership property of the partnership on December 31, 1971 means the interest of the member of the partnership in property of that class, expressed as a percentage of the total of the interests of all members of the partnership in property of that class on that day;

[¶1756]

"undepreciated cost to the partnership" — "undepreciated cost to the partnership" of any class of depreciable property means an amount determined as follows:

(*a*) determine, for each person who, because of having been a member of the partnership on the later of June 18, 1971 and the day the partnership was created, and thereafter without interruption until December 31, 1971, can reasonably be regarded as having had an interest in property of that class on December 31, 1971, the amount, if any, by which the undepreciated capital cost to the person of property of that class as of December 31, 1971 exceeds the amount, if any, determined under subparagraph $(3)(c)(i)$ for the person in respect of property of that class,

(b) determine, for each such person, the amount that is that proportion of the amount determined under paragraph (a) that 100% is of the person's percentage in respect of property of that class, and

(c) select the amount determined under paragraph (b) for a person described therein that is not greater than any amount so determined for any other such person,

and the amount selected under paragraph (c) is the undepreciated cost to the partnership of that class.

[¶1757]

(5) Other depreciable property of partnership. For the purposes of the amended Act, where a partnership had, on December 31, 1971, any particular partnership property that was depreciable property other than depreciable property of a prescribed class,

(a) the cost to the partnership of the particular property shall be deemed to be the amount that would be determined under paragraph $(3)(a)$ to be the capital cost thereof if

   (i) the particular property constituted a prescribed class of property, and

   (ii) the acquisition cost of each person described therein in respect of the particular property were its actual cost to the person or the amount at which the person was deemed by subsection 20(6) of the former Act to have acquired it, as the case may be;

(b) for the purposes of sections 13 and 20 of the amended Act and any regulations made under paragraph $20(1)(a)$ of that Act, the undepreciated capital cost of property of any class as of any particular time after 1971 shall be computed as if the amount, if any, by which

   (i) the amount determined under paragraph (a) to have been the cost to the partnership of the particular property,

exceeds

   (ii) the amount that would be determined under the definition "undepreciated cost to the partnership" in subsection (4) to be the undepreciated cost to the partnership of any class of depreciable property comprising the particular property if

      (A) paragraph (a) of that definition were read without reference to the words "the later of June 18, 1971 and the day the partnership was created, and thereafter without interruption until",

      (B) the amount determined under subparagraph $(3)(c)(i)$ for any person in respect of that class were nil, and

      (C) the undepreciated capital cost to each person described in the definition "acquisition cost" in subsection (4) of the particular property as of December 31, 1971 were the amount, if any, by which the amount assumed by subparagraph (a)(ii) to have been the acquisition cost of the person in respect of the property exceeds the total of all allowed to the person in respect of the property under regulations made under paragraph $11(1)(a)$ of the former Act in computing income for taxation years ending before 1972,

had been allowed to the partnership in respect of the particular property under regulations made under paragraph $20(1)(a)$ of the amended Act in computing income for taxation years ending before the particular time; and

(c) in computing the income for the 1972 and subsequent taxation years of each person who was, on December 31, 1971, a member of the partnership, there may be deducted such amount as the person claims for the year, not exceeding the amount, if any, by which

(i) the amount by which

(A) the amount assumed by clause (b)(ii)(C) to have been the undepreciated capital cost to the person of the particular property as of December 31, 1971

exceeds

(B) a percentage of the amount determined under subparagraph (b)(ii) in respect of the particular property, equal to the percentage that would be the person's percentage (within the meaning assigned by subsection (4)) in respect of the particular property if that property constituted a prescribed class,

exceeds

(ii) the total of all amounts deducted under this paragraph in computing the person's income for preceding taxation years,

and for the purposes of section 3 of the amended Act the amount so claimed shall be deemed to be a deduction permitted by subdivision e of Division B of Part I of that Act.

[¶1758]

SECTION 21: Goodwill and other nothings.

(1) Where as a result of a disposition occurring after 1971 a taxpayer has or may become entitled to receive an amount (in this section referred to as the "actual amount") in respect of a business carried on by the taxpayer throughout the period beginning January 1, 1972 and ending immediately after the disposition occurred, for the purposes of section 14 of the amended Act the amount that the taxpayer has or may become entitled to receive shall be deemed to be the total of

(a) an amount equal to a percentage, equal to 40% plus the percentage (not exceeding 60%) obtained when 5% is multiplied by the number of full calendar years ending in the period and before the transaction occurred, of the amount, if any, by which the actual amount exceeds the portion thereof referred to in subparagraph (b)(i), and

(b) an amount equal to the lesser of

(i) the percentage, described in paragraph (a), of such portion, if any, of the actual amount as may reasonably be considered as being the consideration received by the taxpayer for the disposition of, or for allowing the expiration of, a government right, and

(ii) the amount, if any, by which the portion described in subparagraph (i) exceeds the greater of

(A) the total of all amounts each of which is an outlay or expenditure made or incurred by the taxpayer as a result of a transaction that occurred before 1972 for the purpose of acquiring the government right, or the taxpayer's original right in respect of the government right, to the extent that the outlay or expenditure was not otherwise deducted in computing the income of the taxpayer for any taxation year and would, if made or incurred by the taxpayer as a result of a transaction that occurred after 1971, be an eligible capital expenditure of the taxpayer, and

(B) the fair market value to the taxpayer as at December 31, 1971 of the taxpayers specified right in respect of the government right, if no outlay or expenditure was made or incurred by the taxpayer for the purpose of acquiring the right or, if an outlay or expenditure was made or incurred, if that outlay or expenditure would have been an eligible capital expenditure of the taxpayer if it had been made or incurred as a result of a transaction that occurred after 1971.

[¶1759]

(2) Idem. Where the taxpayer and the person by whom the actual amount has become payable to the taxpayer were not dealing with each other at arm's length, for the purposes of computing the income of that person the portion of the actual amount in excess of the amount deemed by subsection (1) to be the amount that has become payable to the taxpayer shall be deemed not to have been an outlay, expense or cost, as the case may be, of that person.

[¶1760]

(2.1) Idem. Where after 1971 a taxpayer has acquired a particular government right referred to in subsection (1)

(*a*) from a person with whom the taxpayer was not dealing at arm's length, or

(*b*) under an agreement with a person with whom the taxpayer was not dealing at arm's length, if under the terms of the agreement that person allowed the right to expire so that the taxpayer could acquire a substantially similar right from the authority that had issued the right to that person,

and an actual amount subsequently becomes payable to the taxpayer as consideration for the disposition by the taxpayer of, or for the taxpayer allowing the expiration of, the particular government right or any other government right acquired by the taxpayer for the purpose of effecting the continuation, without interruption, of rights that are substantially similar to the rights that the taxpayer had under the particular government right, for the purpose of section 14 of the amended Act, the amount that has so become payable to the taxpayer shall be deemed to be the amount that would, if that person and the taxpayer had at all times been the same person, be determined under subsection (1) to be the amount that would have become so payable to the taxpayer.

[¶1761]

(2.2) Amalgamations. For the purposes of this section, an amalgamation (within the meaning of section 87 of the amended Act) of two or more Canadian corporations shall be deemed to be a transaction between persons not dealing at arm's length.

[¶1762]

(3) Definitions. In this section,

[¶1763]

"government right" — "government right" of a taxpayer means a right or licence

(a) that enables the taxpayer to carry on a business activity in accordance with a law of Canada or of a province or Canadian municipality, to an extent to which the taxpayer would otherwise be unable to carry it on in accordance therewith,

(b) that was granted or issued by Her Majesty in right of Canada or a province or a Canadian municipality, or by a department, board, agency or any other body authorized by or under a law of Canada, a province or a Canadian municipality to grant or issue such a right or licence, and

(c) that was acquired by the taxpayer

(i) as a result of a transaction that occurred before 1972, or

(ii) at a particular time for the purpose of affecting the continuation, without interruption, of rights that are substantially similar to the rights that the taxpayer had under a government right held by the taxpayer before the particular time;

[¶1764]

"original right" — "original right" of a taxpayer in respect of a government right means a right or licence

(a) described in the definition "government right" in this subsection, and

(b) acquired by the taxpayer as a result of a transaction that occurred before 1972 for a purpose other than the purpose described in subparagraph (c)(ii) of that definition,

if the government right was acquired by the taxpayer for the purpose of effecting the continuation, without interruption, of rights that are substantially similar to the rights that the taxpayer had under the right or licence;

[¶1765]

"specified right" — "specified right" of a taxpayer in respect of a government right means a right owned by a taxpayer on December 31, 1971 that was

(a) an original right, or

(b) a government right that was acquired by the taxpayer in substitution for the original right or that was one of a series of government rights acquired by the taxpayer for the purpose of effecting the continuation, without interruption, of rights that are substantially similar to the rights that the taxpayer had under the original right.

[¶1766]

SECTION 26:   Capital gains subject to tax.

*   *   *

(18) Transfer of farm land by a farmer to his child at death. Where

(a) a taxpayer owned, on December 31, 1971 and thereafter without interruption until the taxpayer's death, any land referred to in subsection 70(9) of the amended Act,

(b) the land has, on or after the death of the taxpayer and as a consequence thereof, been transferred or distributed to a child of the taxpayer who was resident in Canada immediately before the death of the taxpayer, and

(c) it can be shown, within the period ending 36 months after the death of the taxpayer or, where written application therefor has been made to the Minister by the legal representative of the taxpayer within that period, within such longer period as the Minister considers reasonable in the circumstances, that the land has become vested indefeasibly in the child,

the following rules apply:

(d) paragraph 70(9)(b) of the amended Act does not apply for the purpose of determining the cost to the child of the land or part thereof, as the case may be, and

(e) subsection (5) applies in respect of the transfer or distribution of the land to the child as if the references in that subsection to "June 18, 1971" were references to "December 31, 1971".

*   *   *

CHAPTER 13

INCOME TAX REGULATIONS

Reproduced below are the relevant sections of the Income Tax Regulations current to date of publication. Amendments pending at that time appear in boxes immediately below the provisions affected.

PART XI
Capital Cost Allowances

DIVISION I
DEDUCTIONS ALLOWED

[¶1780]

1100. **(1)** For the purposes of paragraphs $8(1)(j)$ and (p) and $20(1)(a)$ of the Act, the following deductions are allowed in computing a taxpayer's income for each taxation year:

Rates

(a) subject to subsection (2), such amount as he may claim in respect of property of each of the following classes in Schedule II not exceeding in respect of property

(i) of Class 1, 4 per cent,

(ii) of Class 2, 6 per cent,

(iii) of Class 3, 5 per cent,

(iv) of Class 4, 6 per cent,

(v) of Class 5, 10 per cent,

(vi) of Class 6, 10 per cent,

(vii) of Class 7, 15 per cent,

(viii) of Class 8, 20 per cent,

(ix) of Class 9, 25 per cent,

(x) of Class 10, 30 per cent,

(x.1) of Class 10.1, 30 per cent,

(xi) of Class 11, 35 per cent,

(xii) of Class 12, 100 per cent,

(xiii) of Class 16, 40 per cent,

(xiv) of Class 17, 8 per cent,

(xv) of Class 18, 60 per cent,

(xvi) of Class 22, 50 per cent,

(xvii) of Class 23, 100 per cent,

(xviii) of Class 25, 100 per cent,

(xix) of Class 26, 5 per cent,

(xx) of Class 28, 30 per cent,

(xxi) of Class 30, 40 per cent,

(xxii) of Class 31, 5 per cent,

(xxiii) of Class 32, 10 per cent,

(xxiv) of Class 33, 15 per cent,

(xxv) of Class 35, 7 per cent,

(xxvi) of Class 37, 15 per cent,

(xxvii) of Class 41, 25 per cent,

(xxviii) of Class 42, 12 per cent,

(xxix) of Class 43, 30 per cent,

(xxix.1) of Class 43.1, 30 per cent, and

(xxx) of Class 44, 25 per cent,

─────────── **Draft Regulation** ───────────

Capital Cost Allowance (July 9, 2005)

Paragraph 1100(1)(a) of the Income Tax Regulations is amended by striking out the word "and" at the end of subparagraph (xxix.1) and by adding the following after subparagraph (xxx):

(xxxi) of Class 45, 45 per cent, and

(xxxii) of Class 46, 30 per cent,

Applicable: Deemed to have come into force on March 23, 2004.

Explanatory Note:

Regulatory Impact Analysis Statement from July 9, 2005

Description

These amendments affect the capital cost allowance (CCA) rates applicable for the purposes of calculating depreciation of capital property for income tax purposes. A portion of the capital cost of a taxpayer's depreciable capital property is deductible as CCA each year in computing the taxpayer's income. The maximum CCA rate for each type of depreciable property is set out in the Income Tax Regulations (the Regulations). The useful lives of capital assets can change over time for several reasons, including technological obsolescence and changing market conditions. The Government's assessment of CCA rates is therefore an ongoing process to ensure that, in general, CCA rates reflect the useful life of depreciable assets and that the CCA rates do not impede the ability of Canadian firms to invest and compete.

As part of this review, the 2004 Budget announced certain adjustments to the CCA rates for computer equipment and data network infrastructure equipment.

In particular, these amendments

- provide for new Class 45 (45 percent CCA rate) applicable to certain computer equipment generally acquired after March 22, 2004;
- amend the definition of "exempt property" in paragraph 1100(1.13)(a) of the Regulations to exempt certain computer equipment from the specified leasing property rules;
- amend subsection 1101(5p) of the Regulations to remove a reference to Class 10 assets, to ensure that the separate class election provisions will not apply to computer equipment that is Class 45 property;
- provide for new Class 46 (30 percent CCA rate) applicable to data network infrastructure equipment acquired after March 22, 2004;
- add the definition of "data network infrastructure equipment" to subsection 1104(2) of the Regulations; and
- add, in paragraph 4600(2)(k) of the Regulations (investment tax credits for certain qualified properties acquired in Atlantic Canada), relieving references to new Classes 45 and 46 consequential to the introduction of those classes.

These amendments apply, in general, to property acquired after March 22, 2004. The tax policy rationale underlying these changes is discussed at pages 332 to 335 of Annex 9 of the *Budget Plan* of 2004. The amendments, except the change to paragraph 4600(2)(k) of the Regulations, were first released in draft form for public consultation on September 16, 2004 (see Appendix A of the *Legislative Proposals, Draft Regula-*

¶1780

tions and Explanatory Notes Relating to Income Tax concerning the 2004 Budget — Finance news release 2004-051).

Alternatives

These amendments are necessary to implement Budget 2004 proposals. These amendments ensure that the Regulations remain relevant in a rapidly changing economic and technological environment. No other alternatives were considered.

Benefits and costs

The Budget 2004 estimated the cost of these amendments to be $110 million in fiscal 2004–05 and $255 million during fiscal 2005–06. The costs and any revenue impacts arising in subsequent fiscal years have not been estimated. Since CCA deductions by taxpayers are discretionary in some cases and CCA rate changes only result in timing differences in revenue receipts, it is difficult to quantify the economic impact of these amendments.

Consultation

The CCA treatment accorded computer equipment and data network infrastructure equipment were the subject matter of a number of pre-budget submissions received by the Department of Finance from industry stakeholders. The Department of Finance held extensive consultation with officials of the Department of Industry and the Canada Customs and Revenue Agency during its pre-budget deliberations on this issue. These CCA changes are the outcome of those submissions and consultations. In addition, these amendments were released in draft form on September 16, 2004.

Strategic environmental assessment

These amendments are part of the Government's ongoing review of CCA rates, which is conducted to ensure that, in general, CCA rates reflect the useful life of depreciable assets and that the CCA rates do not impede the ability of Canadian firms to invest and compete. The CCA rates are changed, where appropriate, to provide for neutrality in the tax system. These CCA rate changes are not expected to change taxpayers' purchasing habits and, therefore, it is not likely that the amendments will have any significant environmental impact.

Compliance and enforcement

The *Income Tax Act* provides the necessary compliance mechanisms. These mechanisms allow the Minister of National Revenue to assess and reassess taxes payable, conduct audits and seize relevant records and documents.

Contact

Kerry Harnish, Tax Legislation Division, Department of Finance, L'Esplanade Laurier, 140 O'Connor Street, Ottawa, Ontario K1A 0G5, (613) 992-4385.

of the undepreciated capital cost to him as of the end of the taxation year (before making any deduction under this subsection for the taxation year) of property of the class;

[¶1782]

Class 13 — [Leasehold Interest]

(b) such amount as the taxpayer may claim in respect of the capital cost to the taxpayer of property of Class 13 in Schedule II, not exceeding

(i) where the capital cost of the property, other than property described in subparagraph $(2)(a)(v)$, (vi) or (vii), was incurred in the taxation year and after November 12, 1981, 50 per cent of the amount for the year calculated in accordance with Schedule III, and

(ii) in any other case, the amount for the year calculated in accordance with Schedule III, and, for the purposes of this paragraph and Schedule III, the capital cost to a taxpayer of a property shall be deemed to have been incurred at the time at which the property became available for use by the taxpayer;

[¶1784]

Class 14 — [Patent, Franchise, Concession or Licence]

(c) such amount as he may claim in respect of property of Class 14 in Schedule II not exceeding the lesser of

(i) the aggregate of the amounts for the year obtained by apportioning the capital cost to him of each property over the life of the property remaining at the time the cost was incurred, and

(ii) the undepreciated capital cost to him as of the end of the taxation year (before making any deduction under this subsection for the taxation year) of property of the class;

[¶1786]

In Lieu of Double Depreciation

(d) such additional amount as he may claim not exceeding in the case of property described in each of the classes in Schedule II, the lesser of

(i) one-half the amount that would have been allowed to him in respect of property of that class under subparagraph $6(n)$(ii) of the *Income War Tax Act* if that Act were applicable to the taxation year, and

(ii) the undepreciated capital cost to him as of the end of the taxation year (before making any deduction under this paragraph for the taxation year) of property of the class;

[¶1788]

Timber Limits and Cutting Rights

(e) such amount as he may claim not exceeding the amount calculated in accordance with Schedule VI in respect of the capital cost to him of a property, other than a timber resource property, that is a timber limit or a right to cut timber from a limit;

[¶1790]

Class 15 — [Woods Assets]

(f) such amount as he may claim not exceeding the amount calculated in accordance with Schedule IV in respect of the capital cost to him of property of Class 15 in Schedule II;

[¶1792]

Industrial Mineral Mines

(g) such amount as he may claim not exceeding the amount calculated in accordance with Schedule V in respect of the capital cost to him of a property that is an industrial mineral mine or a right to remove industrial minerals from an industrial mineral mine;

(h) [Revoked.]

[¶1794]

Additional Allowances — Fishing Vessels

(i) such additional amount as he may claim in the case of property of a separate class prescribed by subsection 1101(2) not exceeding the lesser of

(i) the amount by which the depreciation that could have been taken on the property, if the Orders in Council referred to in that subsection were applicable to the taxation year, exceeds the amount allowed under paragraph (a) in respect of the property, and

(ii) the undepreciated capital cost to him as of the end of the taxation year (before making any deduction under this paragraph for the taxation year) of property of the class.

(j) [Revoked.]

(k) [Revoked.]

[¶1800]

Additional Allowances — Certified Productions

(l) such additional amount as he may claim in respect of property for which a separate class is prescribed by subsection 1101(5k) not exceeding the lesser of

(i) the aggregate of his income for the year from that property and from property described in paragraph (n) of Class 12 in Schedule II, determined before making any deduction under this paragraph, and

(ii) the undepreciated capital cost to him of property of that separate class as of the end of the year before making any deduction under this paragraph for the year;

[¶1801]

Additional Allowance — Canadian Film or Video Production

(m) such additional amount as the taxpayer claims in respect of property for which a separate class is prescribed by subsection 1101(5k.1) not exceeding the lesser of

(i) the taxpayer's income for the year from the property, determined before making any deduction under this paragraph, and

(ii) the undepreciated capital cost to the taxpayer of the property of that separate class at the end of the year (before making any deduction under this paragraph for the year and computed without reference to subsection (2));

[¶1802]

Class 19 — [Accelerated Allowances]

(n) where the taxpayer is a corporation that had a degree of Canadian ownership in the taxation year, or is an individual who was resident in Canada in the taxation year for not less than 183 days, such amount as he may claim in respect of property of Class 19 in Schedule II that was acquired in a particular taxation year not exceeding the lesser of

(i) 50 per cent of the capital cost thereof to him, and

(ii) the amount by which the capital cost thereof to him exceeds the aggregate of the amounts deducted in respect thereof in computing his income for previous taxation years,

but the aggregate of amounts deductible for a taxation year in respect of property acquired in each of the particular taxation years, under this paragraph, shall not exceed the undepreciated capital cost to him as of the end of the taxation year (before making any deduction under this subsection for the taxation year) of property of the class;

(o) where the taxpayer is not entitled to make a deduction under paragraph (n) in computing his income for a taxation year, such amount as he may claim in respect of property of Class 19 in Schedule II not exceeding 20 per cent of the undepreciated capital cost to him as of the end of the taxation year (before making any deduction under this subsection for the taxation year) of property of the class;

[¶1806]

Class 20 — [Accelerated Allowances]

(p) such amount as he may claim in respect of property of Class 20 in Schedule II that was acquired in a particular taxation year not exceeding the lesser of

(i) 20 per cent of the capital cost thereof to him, and

(ii) the amount by which the capital cost thereof to him exceeds the aggregate of the amounts deducted in respect thereof in computing his income for previous taxation years,

but the aggregate of amounts deductible for a taxation year in respect of property acquired in each of the particular taxation years, under this paragraph, shall not exceed the undepreciated capital cost to him as of the end of the taxation year (before making any deduction under this subsection for the taxation year) of property of the class;

[¶1808]

Class 21 — [Accelerated Allowances]

(q) such amount as he may claim in respect of property of Class 21 in Schedule II that was acquired in a particular taxation year not exceeding the lesser of

(i) 50 per cent of the capital cost thereof to him, and

(ii) the amount by which the capital cost thereof to him exceeds the aggregate of the amounts deducted in respect thereof in computing his income for previous taxation years,

but the aggregate of amounts deductible for a taxation year in respect of property acquired in each of the particular taxation years, under this paragraph, shall not exceed the undepreciated capital cost to him as of the end of the taxation year (before making any deduction under this subsection for the taxation year) of property of the class;

(r)　[Revoked.]

(s)　[Revoked.]

(sa)　[Revoked.]

[¶1810]

[Additional Allowances — Grain Storage Facilities and
Grain Elevators]

(sb) such additional amount as he may claim in respect of property included in Class 3, 6 or 8 in Schedule II

(i) that is

(A) a grain elevator situated in that part of Canada that is defined in section 2 of the *Canada Grain Act* as the "Eastern Division" the principal use of which

(I) is the receiving of grain directly from producers for storage or forwarding or both,

(II) is the receiving and storing of grain for direct manufacture or processing into other products, or

(III) has been certified by the Minister of Agriculture to be the receiving of grain that has not been officially inspected or weighed,

(B) an addition to a grain elevator described in clause (A),

(C) fixed machinery installed in a grain elevator in respect of which, or in respect of an addition to which, an additional amount has been or may be claimed under this paragraph,

(D) fixed machinery, designed for the purpose of drying grain, installed in a grain elevator described in clause (A),

(E) machinery designed for the purpose of drying grain on a farm, or

(F) a building or other structure designed for the purpose of storing grain on a farm,

(ii) that was acquired by the taxpayer in the taxation year or in one of the three immediately preceding taxation years, at a time that was after April 1, 1972 but before August 1, 1974, and

(iii) that was not used for any purpose whatever before it was acquired by the taxpayer,

not exceeding the lesser of

(iv) where the property is included in Class 3, 22 per cent of the capital cost thereof, where the property is included in Class 6, 20 per cent of the capital cost thereof or where the property is included in Class 8,

(A) 14 per cent of the capital cost thereof in the case of property referred to in clause (i)(C), (D) or (F), and

(B) 14 per cent of the lesser of $15,000 and the capital cost thereof in the case of property described in clause (i)(E), and

(v) the undepreciated capital cost to him as of the end of the taxation year (before making any deduction under this paragraph for the taxation year) of property of the class;

[¶1812]

Classes 24, 27, 29 and 34

(*t*) for the taxation year that includes November 12, 1981, such amount as he may claim in respect of property of each of Classes 24, 27, 29 and 34 in Schedule II not exceeding the aggregate of

(i) 50 per cent of the lesser of

(A) the capital cost to him of all designated property of the class acquired by him in the year, and

(B) the undepreciated capital cost to him of property of the class as of the end of the year (computed as if no amount were included in respect of property, other than designated property of the class, acquired after November 12, 1981 and before making any deduction under this paragraph for the year),

(ii) the amount, if any, by which the amount determined under clause (i)(B) in respect of the class exceeds the amount determined under clause (i)(A) in respect of the class, and

(iii) the lesser of

(A) 25 per cent of the capital cost to him of all property, other than designated property, of the class acquired by him in the year and

(B) the undepreciated capital cost to him of property of the class as of the end of the year (before making any deduction under this paragraph for the year);

[¶1814]

[Classes 24, 27, 29 and 34 — Taxation Years
Commencing After November 12, 1981]

(*ta*) for taxation years commencing after November 12, 1981, such amount as he may claim in respect of property of each of Classes 24, 27, 29 and 34 in Schedule II not exceeding the aggregate of

(i) the aggregate of

(A) the lesser of

(I) 50 per cent of the capital cost to him of all designated property of the class acquired by him in the year, and

(II) the undepreciated capital cost to him of property of the class as of the end of the year (before making any deduction under this paragraph for the year and, where any of the property referred to in subclause (I) was acquired by virtue of a specified transaction, computed as if no amount were included in respect of property, other than designated property of the class acquired by him in the year), and

(B) 25 per cent of the lesser of

(I) the undepreciated capital cost to him of property of the class as of the end of the year (computed as if no amount were included in respect of designated property of the class acquired by him in the year and before making any deduction under this paragraph for the year), and

(II) the capital cost to him of all property, other than designated property, of the class acquired by him in the year, and

(ii) the lesser of

(A) the amount, if any, by which

¶1814

(I) the undepreciated capital cost to him of property of the class as of the end of the year (before making any deduction under this paragraph for the year)

exceeds

(II) the capital cost to him of all property of the class acquired by him in the year, and

(B) an amount equal to the aggregate of

(I) 50 per cent of the capital cost to him of all property of the class acquired by him in the immediately preceding taxation year, other than designated property of the class acquired in a specified transaction, and

(II) the amount, if any, by which the amount determined under clause (A) for the year with respect to the class exceeds the aggregate of 75 per cent of the capital cost to him of all property, other than designated property, of the class acquired by him in the immediately preceding taxation year and 50 per cent of the capital cost to him of designated property of the class acquired by him in the immediately preceding taxation year, other than designated property of the class acquired in a specified transaction,

and for the purposes of this paragraph and paragraph (t), "designated property" of a class means

(iii) property of the class acquired by him before November 13, 1981,

(iv) property deemed to be designated property of the class by virtue of paragraph $(2.1)(g)$ or $(2.2)(j)$, and

(v) property described in subparagraph $(2)(a)(v)$, (vi) or (vii),

and, for the purposes of this paragraph,

(vi) "specified transaction" means a transaction to which subsection 85(5), 87(1), 88(1), 97(4) or 98(3) or (5) of the Act applies, and

(vii) subject to paragraph $(2.2)(j)$, a property shall be deemed to have been acquired by a taxpayer at the time at which the property became available for use by the taxpayer;

(u) [Revoked.]

[¶1816]

Canadian Vessels

(v) such amount as the taxpayer may claim in respect of property that is

(i) a vessel described in subsection 1101(2a),

(ii) included in a separate prescribed class because of subsection 13(14) of the Act, or

(iii) a property that has been constituted a prescribed class by subsection 24(2) of Chapter 91 of the Statutes of Canada, 1966-67,

not exceeding the lesser of

(iv) where the property, other than property described in subparagraph $(2)(a)(v)$, (vi) or (vii), was acquired in the taxation year and after November 12, 1981, $16\frac{2}{3}$ per cent of the capital cost thereof to the taxpayer and, in any other case, $33\frac{1}{3}$ per cent of the capital cost thereof to the taxpayer, and

(v) the undepreciated capital cost to the taxpayer as of the end of the taxation year (before making any deduction under this paragraph for the taxation year) of property of the class,

and, for the purposes of subparagraph (iv), a property shall be deemed to have been acquired by a taxpayer at the time at which the property became available for use by the taxpayer for the purposes of the Act;

[¶1818]

Additional Allowances — Offshore Drilling Vessels

(va) such additional amount as he may claim in respect of property for which a separate class is prescribed by subsection 1101(2b) not exceeding 15 per cent of the undepreciated capital cost to him of property of that class as of the end of the taxation year (before making any deduction under this subsection for the taxation year);

[¶1820]

Additional Allowances — Class 28

(w) subject to section 1100A, such additional amount as he may claim in respect of property described in Class 28 acquired for the purpose of gaining or producing income from a mine or in respect of property acquired for the purpose of gaining or producing income from a mine and for which a separate class is prescribed by subsection 1101(4a), not exceeding the lesser of

(i) the taxpayer's income for the year from the mine, determined without reference to paragraph $12(1)(z.5)$ of the Act and before making any deduction under this paragraph, paragraph (x), (y) or (ya), paragraph $20(1)(v.1)$ of the Act, section 65, 66, 66.1, 66.2 or 66.7 of the Act or section 29 of the *Income Tax Application Rules*, and

---

Draft Regulation

Natural Resources (June 9, 2003)

Subparagraph $1100(1)(w)(i)$ **of the Income Tax Regulations is replaced by the following:**

(i) the taxpayer's income for the year from the mine, before making any deduction under this paragraph, paragraph (x), (y) or (ya), section 65, 66, 66.1, 66.2 or 66.7 of the Act or section 29 of the *Income Tax Application Rules*, and

---

Applicable: To taxation years that begin after 2006.

Explanatory Note:

Capital Cost Allowance — Mines

Paragraphs $1100(1)(w)$ to (ya) of the Regulations allow an accelerated capital cost allowance, up to the amount of specified income from one or more mines, with respect to certain mining assets. For this purpose, a taxpayer's income is computed without reference to a taxpayer's resource allowance, resource loss or certain resource deductions.

Paragraphs $1100(w)$ to (ya) are amended for taxation years that begin after 2006, to remove the reference to paragraphs $20(1)(v.1)$ (resource allowance) and $12(1)(z.5)$ (resource loss) of the Act, consequential upon the repeal of those paragraphs.

(ii) the undepreciated capital cost to him of property of that class as of the end of the taxation year (before making any deduction under this paragraph for the taxation year);

[¶1822]

[Additional Allowances — Class 28 — More Than One Mine]

(x) subject to section 1100A, such additional amount as he may claim in respect of property acquired for the purpose of gaining or producing income from more than one mine and for which a separate class is prescribed by subsection 1101(4b), not exceeding the lesser of

(i) the taxpayer's income for the year from the mines, determined without reference to paragraph $12(1)(z.5)$ of the Act and before making any deduction under this paragraph, paragraph (ya), paragraph $20(1)(v.1)$ of the Act, section 65, 66, 66.1, 66.2 or 66.7 of the Act or section 29 of the *Income Tax Application Rules*, and

---

Draft Regulation

Natural Resources (June 9, 2003)

Subparagraph $1100(1)(x)(i)$ of the Regulations is replaced by the following:

(i) the taxpayer's income for the year from the mines, before making any deduction under this paragraph, paragraph (ya), section 65, 66, 66.1, 66.2 or 66.7 of the Act or section 29 of the *Income Tax Application Rules*, and

Applicable: To taxation years that begin after 2006.

Explanatory Note: [Please see the Explanatory Note following the amendment to subparagraph $1100(1)(w)(i)$.]

(ii) the undepreciated capital cost to him of property of that class as of the end of the taxation year (before making any deduction under this paragraph for the taxation year);

[¶1824]

Additional Allowances — Class 41

(y) such additional amount as the taxpayer may claim in respect of property acquired for the purpose of gaining or producing income from a mine and for which a separate class is prescribed by subsection 1101(4c), not exceeding the lesser of

(i) the taxpayer's income for the year from the mine, determined without reference to paragraph $12(1)(z.5)$ of the Act and before making any deduction under this paragraph, paragraph (x) or (ya), paragraph $20(1)(v.1)$ of the Act, section 65, 66, 66.1, 66.2 or 66.7 of the Act or section 29 of the *Income Tax Application Rules*, and

---

Draft Regulation

Natural Resources (June 9, 2003)

Subparagraph $1100(1)(y)(i)$ of the Regulations is replaced by the following:

(i) the taxpayer's income for the year from the mine, before making any deduction under this paragraph, paragraph (x) or (ya), section 65, 66, 66.1, 66.2 or 66.7 of the Act or section 29 of the *Income Tax Application Rules*, and

Applicable: To taxation years that begin after 2006.

Explanatory Note: [Please see the Explanatory Note following the amendment to subparagraph $1100(1)(w)(i)$.]

(ii) the undepreciated capital cost to the taxpayer of property of that class as of the end of the taxation year (computed without reference to subsection (2) and before making any deduction under this paragraph for the taxation year);

[¶1826]

[Additional Allowances — Class 41 — More Than One Mine]

(ya) such additional amount as the taxpayer may claim in respect of property acquired for the purpose of gaining or producing income from more than one mine and for which a separate class is prescribed by subsection 1101(4d), not exceeding the lesser of

(i) the taxpayer's income for the year from the mines, determined without reference to paragraph 12(1)(z.5) of the Act and before making any deduction under this paragraph, paragraph 20(1)(v.1) of the Act, section 65, 66, 66.1, 66.2 or 66.7 of the Act or section 29 of the *Income Tax Application Rules*, and

---

Draft Regulation

Natural Resources (June 9, 2003)

Subparagraph 1100(1)(ya)(i) of the Regulations is replaced by the following:

(i) the taxpayer's income for the year from the mines, before making any deduction under this paragraph, section 65, 66, 66.1, 66.2 or 66.7 of the Act or section 29 of the *Income Tax Application Rules*, and

Applicable: To taxation years that begin after 2006.

Explanatory Note: [Please see the Explanatory Note following the amendment to subparagraph 1100(1)(w)(i).]

(ii) the undepreciated capital cost to the taxpayer of property of that class as of the end of the taxation year (computed without reference to subsection (2) and before making any deduction under this paragraph for the taxation year);

[¶1828]

Additional Allowances — Railway Cars

(z) such additional amount as the taxpayer may claim in respect of property for which a separate class is prescribed by paragraph 1101(5d)(c) not exceeding eight per cent of the undepreciated capital cost to the taxpayer of property of that class as of the end of the taxation year (before making any deduction under this subsection for the taxation year);

(z.1a) such additional amount as the taxpayer may claim in respect of property for which a separate class is prescribed by paragraph 1101(5d)(d), (e) or (f), not exceeding six per cent of the undepreciated capital cost to the taxpayer of property of that class as of the end of the taxation year (before making any deduction under this subsection for the taxation year);

(z.1b) where throughout the taxation year the taxpayer was a common carrier that owned and operated a railway, such additional amount as the taxpayer may claim in respect of property for which a separate class is prescribed by subsection 1101(5d.1), not exceeding three per cent of the undepreciated capital cost to the taxpayer of property of that class as of the end of the year (before making any deduction under this subsection for the year);

Draft Regulation

Capital Cost Allowance (March 16, 2001)

Subsection 1100(1) of the Income Tax Regulations is amended by adding the following after paragraph (z.1b):

(z.1c) where throughout the taxation year the taxpayer was a common carrier that owned and operated a railway, such additional amount as the taxpayer may claim in respect of property for which a separate class is prescribed by subsection 1101(5d.2), not exceeding 6% of the undepreciated capital cost to the taxpayer of property of that class as of the end of the year (before making any deduction under this subsection for the year);

Applicable: To property acquired after February 27, 2000.

Explanatory Note: New paragraph 1100(1)(z.1c) of the Income Tax Regulations (the "Regulations") provides an additional 6% capital cost allowance ("CCA") deduction for railway property of a common carrier that owns and operates a railway and that is included in a separate Class 35 (7% CCA rate) because of new subsection 1101(5d.2). This additional CCA allowance is consequential to changes to the CCA rate applicable to certain railway assets more fully described below in the commentary to new subsection 1103(2i) and amended Class 7 (15% CCA rate). This change applies to property acquired after February 27, 2000.

[¶1830]

Additional Allowances — Railway Track and Related Property

(za) such additional amount as he may claim in respect of property for which a separate class is prescribed by subsection 1101(5e) not exceeding 4% of the undepreciated capital cost to him of property of that class as of the end of the taxation year (before making any deduction under this subsection for the taxation year);

(za.1) where throughout the taxation year the taxpayer was a common carrier that owned and operated a railway, such additional amount as the taxpayer may claim in respect of property for which a separate class is prescribed by subsection 1101(5e.1), not exceeding six per cent of the undepreciated capital cost to the taxpayer of property of that class as of the end of the year (before making any deduction under this subsection for the year);

(za.2) where throughout the taxation year the taxpayer was a common carrier that owned and operated a railway, such additional amount as the taxpayer may claim in respect of property for which a separate class is prescribed by subsection 1101(5e.2), not exceeding five per cent of the undepreciated capital cost to the taxpayer of property of that class as of the end of the year (before making any deduction under this subsection for the year);

(*zb*) such additional amount as he may claim in respect of property for which a separate class is prescribed by subsection 1101(5f) not exceeding 3% of the undepreciated capital cost to him of property of that class as of the end of the taxation year (before making any deduction under this subsection for the taxation year);

[¶1834]

Additional Allowances — Railway Expansion and Modernization Property

(*zc*) where the taxpayer owns and operates a railway as a common carrier, such additional amount as he may claim in respect of property of a class in Schedule II (in this paragraph referred to as "designated property" of the class)

(i) that is

(A) included in Class 1 in Schedule II by virtue of paragraph (*h*) or (*i*) of that Class,

(B) a bridge, culvert, subway or tunnel included in Class 1 in Schedule II that is ancillary to railway track and grading,

(C) a trestle included in Class 3 in Schedule II that is ancillary to railway track and grading,

(D) included in Class 6 in Schedule II by virtue of paragraph (*j*) of that Class,

(E) machinery or equipment included in Class 8 in Schedule II that is ancillary to

(I) railway track and grading, or

(II) railway traffic control or signalling equipment, including switching, block signalling, interlocking, crossing protection, detection, speed control or retarding equipment, but not including property that is principally electronic equipment or systems software therefor,

(F) machinery or equipment included in Class 8 in Schedule II that

(I) was acquired principally for the purpose of maintaining or servicing, or

(II) is ancillary to and used as part of,

a railway locomotive or railway car,

(G) included in Class 10 in Schedule II by virtue of subparagraph (*m*)(i), (ii) or (iii) of that Class,

(H) included in Class 28 in Schedule II by virtue of subparagraph (d)(ii) of that Class (other than property referred to in subparagraph (m)(iv) of Class 10), or

(I) included in Class 35 in Schedule II,

(ii) that was acquired by him principally for use in or is situated in Canada,

(iii) that was acquired by him in respect of the railway in the taxation year or in one of the four immediately preceding taxation years, at a time that was after April 10, 1978 but before 1988, and

(iv) that was not used for any purpose whatever before it was acquired by him,

not exceeding the lesser of

(v) 6 per cent of the aggregate of the capital cost to him of the designated property of the class, and

(vi) the undepreciated capital cost to him as of the end of the taxation year (after making all deductions claimed by him under other provisions of this subsection for the taxation year but before making any deduction under this paragraph for the taxation year) of property of the class.

[¶1836]

Class 38

(zd) such amount as the taxpayer may claim in respect of property of Class 38 in Schedule II not exceeding that percentage which is the aggregate of

(i) that proportion of 40 per cent that the number of days in the taxation year that are in 1988 is of the number of days in the taxation year that are after 1987,

(ii) that proportion of 35 per cent that the number of days in the taxation year that are in 1989 is of the number of days in the taxation year, and

(iii) that proportion of 30 per cent that the number of days in the taxation year that are after 1989 is of the number of days in the taxation year

of the undepreciated capital cost to the taxpayer of property of that class as of the end of the taxation year (before making any deduction under this paragraph for the taxation year);

[¶1839]

Class 39

(*ze*) such amount as the taxpayer may claim in respect of property of Class 39 in Schedule II not exceeding that percentage which is the aggregate of

(i) that proportion of 40 per cent that the number of days in the taxation year that are in 1988 is of the number of days in the taxation year that are after 1987,

(ii) that proportion of 35 per cent that the number of days in the taxation year that are in 1989 is of the number of days in the taxation year,

(iii) that proportion of 30 per cent that the number of days in the taxation year that are in 1990 is of the number of days in the taxation year, and

(iv) that proportion of 25 per cent that the number of days in the taxation year that are after 1990 is of the number of days in the taxation year

of the undepreciated capital cost to the taxpayer of property of that class as of the end of the taxation year (before making any deduction under this paragraph for the taxation year);

[¶1840]

Class 40

(*zf*) such amount as the taxpayer may claim in respect of property of Class 40 in Schedule II not exceeding that percentage which is the aggregate of

(i) that proportion of 40 per cent that the number of days in the taxation year that are in 1988 is of the number of days in the taxation year that are after 1987,

(ii) that proportion of 35 per cent that the number of days in the taxation year that are in 1989 is of the number of days in the taxation year, and

(iii) that proportion of 30 per cent that the number of days in the taxation year that are in 1990 is of the number of days in the taxation year

of the undepreciated capital cost to the taxpayer of property of that class as of the end of the taxation year (before making any deduction under this paragraph for the taxation year).

[¶1841]

Additional Allowance — Year 2000 Computer Hardware and Systems Software

(zg) where the taxpayer

(i) has elected for the year in prescribed manner,

(ii) was not in the year a large corporation, as defined in subsection 225.1(8) of the Act, or a partnership any member of which was such a corporation in a taxation year that included any time that is in the partnership's year, and

(iii) acquired property included in paragraph (f) of Class 10 in Schedule II

(A) in the year,

(B) after 1997 and before November 1999, and

(C) for the purpose of replacing property that was acquired before 1998 that has a material risk of malfunctioning because of the change of the calendar year to 2000 and that is described in paragraph (f) of Class 10, or paragraph (o) of Class 12, in Schedule II,

such additional amount as the taxpayer claims in respect of all property described in subparagraph (iii) not exceeding the least of

(iv) the amount, if any, by which $50,000 exceeds the total of

(A) the total of all amounts each of which is an amount claimed by the taxpayer under this paragraph for a preceding taxation year,

(B) the total of all amounts each of which is an amount claimed by the taxpayer for the year or a preceding taxation year under paragraph (zh), and

(C) the total of all amounts each of which is an amount claimed under this paragraph or paragraph (zh) by a corporation for a taxation year in which it was associated with the taxpayer,

(v) 85% of the capital cost to the taxpayer of all property described in subparagraph (iii), and

(vi) the undepreciated capital cost to the taxpayer as of the end of the year (computed without reference to subsection (2) and after making all deductions claimed under other provisions of this subsection for the year but before making any deduction under this paragraph for the year) of property included in Class 10 in Schedule II; and

¶1841

[¶1842]

Additional Allowance — Year 2000 Computer Software

(zh) where the taxpayer

    (i) has elected for the year in prescribed manner,

    (ii) was not in the year a large corporation, as defined in subsection 225.1(8) of the Act, or a partnership any member of which was such a corporation in a taxation year that included any time that is in the partnership's year, and

    (iii) acquired property included in paragraph (o) of Class 12 in Schedule II

        (A) in the year,

        (B) after 1997 and before November 1999, and

        (C) for the purpose of replacing property that was acquired before 1998 that has a material risk of malfunctioning because of the change of the calendar year to 2000 and that is described in paragraph (f) of Class 10, or paragraph (o) of Class 12, in Schedule II,

such additional amount as the taxpayer claims in respect of all property described in subparagraph (iii) not exceeding the least of

    (iv) the amount, if any, by which $50,000 exceeds the total of

        (A) the total of all amounts each of which is an amount claimed by the taxpayer under this paragraph for a preceding taxation year,

        (B) the total of all amounts each of which is an amount claimed by the taxpayer for the year or a preceding taxation year under paragraph (zg), and

        (C) the total of all amounts each of which is an amount claimed under this paragraph or paragraph (zg) by a corporation for a taxation year in which it was associated with the taxpayer,

    (v) 50% of the capital cost to the taxpayer of all property described in subparagraph (iii), and

    (vi) the undepreciated capital cost to the taxpayer as of the end of the year (computed without reference to subsection (2) and after making all deductions claimed under other provisions of this subsection for the year but before making any deduction under this paragraph for the year) of property included in Class 12 in Schedule II.

[¶1843]

(1.1) Notwithstanding subsections (1) and (3), the amount deductible by a taxpayer for a taxation year in respect of a property that is a specified leasing property at the end of the year is the lesser of

(a) the amount, if any, by which the aggregate of

(i) all amounts that would be considered to be repayments in the year or a preceding year on account of the principal amount of a loan made by the taxpayer if

(A) the taxpayer had made the loan at the time that the property last became a specified leasing property and in a principal amount equal to the fair market value of the property at that time,

(B) interest had been charged on the principal amount of the loan outstanding from time to time at the rate, determined in accordance with section 4302, in effect at the earlier of

(I) the time, if any, before the time referred to in subclause (II), at which the taxpayer last entered into an agreement to lease the property, and

(II) the time that the property last became a specified leasing property

(or, where a particular lease provides that the amount paid or payable by the lessee of the property for the use of, or the right to use, the property varies according to prevailing interest rates in effect from time to time, and the taxpayer so elects, in respect of all of the property that is the subject of the particular lease, in the taxpayer's return of income under Part I of the Act for the taxation year of the taxpayer in which the particular lease was entered into, the rate determined in accordance with section 4302 that is in effect at the beginning of the period for which the interest is being calculated), compounded semi-annually not in advance, and

(C) the amounts that were received or receivable by the taxpayer before the end of the year for the use of, or the right to use, the property before the end of the year and after the time it last became a specified leasing property were blended payments of principal and interest, calculated in accordance with clause (B), on the loan applied firstly on account of interest on principal, secondly on account of interest on unpaid interest, and thirdly on account of principal, and

(ii) the amount that would have been deductible under this section for the taxation year (in this subparagraph referred to as the "particular year") that includes the time (in this subparagraph referred to as the "particular time") at which the property last became a specified leasing property of the taxpayer, if

(A) the property had been transferred to a separate prescribed class at the later of

(I) the beginning of the particular year, and

(II) the time at which the property was acquired by the taxpayer,

(B) the particular year had ended immediately before the particular time, and

¶1843

(C) where the property was not a specified leasing property immediately before the particular time, subsection (3) had applied,

exceeds

(iii) the aggregate of all amounts deducted by the taxpayer in respect of the property by reason of this subsection before the commencement of the year and after the time at which it last became a specified leasing property; and

(b) the amount, if any, by which,

(i) the aggregate of all amounts that would have been deducted by the taxpayer under this Part in respect of the property under paragraph $20(1)(a)$ of the Act in computing the income of the taxpayer for the year and all preceding taxation years had this subsection and subsections (11) and (15) not applied, and had the taxpayer, in each such year, deducted under paragraph $20(1)(a)$ of the Act the maximum amount allowed under this Part, read without reference to this subsection and subsections (11) and (15), in respect of the property,

exceeds

(ii) the total depreciation allowed to the taxpayer before the commencement of the year in respect of the property.

[¶1844]

(1.11) In this section and subsection 1101(5n), "specified leasing property" of a taxpayer at any time means depreciable property (other than exempt property) that is

(a) used at that time by the taxpayer or a person with whom the taxpayer does not deal at arm's length principally for the purpose of gaining or producing gross revenue that is rent or leasing revenue,

(b) the subject of a lease at that time to a person with whom the taxpayer deals at arm's length and that, at the time the lease was entered into, was a lease for a term of more than one year, and

(c) the subject of a lease of property where the tangible property, other than exempt property, that was the subject of the lease had, at the time the lease was entered into, an aggregate fair market value in excess of $25,000,

but, for greater certainty, does not include intangible property (including systems software and property referred to in paragraph (w) of Class 10 or paragraph (n) or (o) of Class 12 in Schedule II).

[¶1846]

(1.12) Notwithstanding subsections (1) and (1.1), where, in a taxation year, a taxpayer has acquired a property that was not used by the taxpayer for any purpose in that year and the first use of the property by the taxpayer is a lease of the property in respect of which subsection (1.1) applies, the amount allowed to the taxpayer under subsection (1) in respect of the property for the year shall be deemed to be nil.

[¶1848]

(1.13) For the purposes of this section,

(a) "exempt property" means

(i) general purpose office furniture or office equipment included in Class 8 in Schedule II (including for greater certainty, mobile office equipment such as cellular telephones and pagers) or general purpose electronic data processing equipment and ancillary data processing equipment, included in paragraph (*f*) of Class 10 in Schedule II, other than any individual piece thereof having a capital cost to the taxpayer in excess of $1,000,000,

---

Draft Regulation

Capital Cost Allowance (July 9, 2005)

Paragraph 1100(1.13)(*a*) of the Regulations is amended by adding the following after subparagraph (i):

(i.1) general-purpose electronic data processing equipment and ancillary data processing equipment, included in Class 45 in Schedule II, other than any individual item of that type of equipment having a capital cost to the taxpayer in excess of $1,000,000,

Applicable: Deemed to have come into force on March 23, 2004.

Explanatory Note: See the Regulatory Impact Analysis Statement following the addition of subparagraphs 1100(1)(*a*)(xxxi) and (xxxii).

(ii) furniture, appliances, television receivers, radio receivers, telephones, furnaces, hot-water heaters and other similar properties, designed for residential use,

(iii) a property that is a motor vehicle that is designed or adapted primarily to carry individuals on highways and streets and that has a seating capacity for not more than the driver and eight passengers, or a motor vehicle of a type commonly called a van or pick-up truck, or a similar vehicle,

(iv) a truck or tractor that is designed for hauling freight on highways,

(v) a trailer that is designed for hauling freight and to be hauled under normal operating conditions by a truck or tractor described in subparagraph (iv),

(vi) a building or part thereof included in Class 1, 3, 6, 20, 31 or 32 in Schedule II (including component parts such as electric wiring, plumbing, sprinkler systems, air-conditioning equipment, heating equipment, lighting fixtures, elevators and escalators) other than a building or part thereof leased primarily to a lessee that is

(A) a person who is exempt from tax by reason of section 149 of the Act,

(B) a person who uses the building in the course of carrying on a business the income from which is exempt from tax under Part I of the Act by reason of any provision of the Act, or

(C) a Canadian government, municipality or other Canadian public authority,

who owned the building or part thereof at any time before the commencement of the lease (other than at any time during a period ending not later than one year after the later of the date the construction of the building or part thereof was completed and the date the building or part thereof was acquired by the lessee),

(vii) vessel mooring space, and

(viii) property that is included in Class 35 in Schedule II,

and for the purposes of subparagraph (i), where a property is owned by two or more persons or partnerships, or any combination thereof, the capital cost of the property to each such person or partnership shall be deemed to be the total of all amounts each of which is the capital cost of the property to such a person or partnership;

(b) property shall be deemed to be the subject of a lease for a term of more than one year at any time where, at that time

(i) the property had been leased by the lessee thereunder, a person with whom the lessee does not deal at arm's length, or any combination thereof, for a period of more than one year ending at that time, or

(ii) it is reasonable, having regard to all the circumstances, to conclude that the lessor thereunder knew or ought to have known that the lessee thereunder, a person with whom the lessee does not deal at arm's length, or any combination thereof, would lease the property for more than one year; and

(c) for the purposes of paragraph (1.11)(c), where it is reasonable, having regard to all the circumstances, to conclude that one of the main reasons for the existence of two or more leases was to avoid the application of subsection (1.1) by reason of each such lease being a lease of property where the tangible property, other than exempt property, that was the subject of the lease had an aggregate fair market value, at the time the lease was entered into, not in excess of $25,000, each such lease shall be deemed to be a lease of tangible property that had, at the time the lease was entered into, an aggregate fair market value in excess of $25,000.

[¶1850]

(1.14) For the purposes of subsection (1.11) and notwithstanding subsection (1.13), where a taxpayer referred to in subsection (16) so elects in the taxpayer's return of income under Part I of the Act for a taxation year in respect of the year and all subsequent taxation years, all of the property of the taxpayer that is the subject of leases entered into in those years shall be deemed not to be exempt property for those years and the aggregate fair market value of all of the tangible property that is the subject of each such lease shall be deemed to have been, at the time the lease was entered into, in excess of $25,000.

[¶1852]

(1.15) Subject to subsection (1.16) and for the purposes of subsection (1.11), where at any time a taxpayer acquires property that is the subject of a lease with a remaining term at that time of more than one year from a person with whom the taxpayer was dealing at arm's length, the taxpayer shall be deemed to have entered into a lease of the property at that time for a term of more than one year.

[¶1854]

(1.16) Where, at any time, a taxpayer acquires from a person with whom the taxpayer is not dealing at arm's length, or by virtue of an amalgamation (within the meaning assigned by subsection 87(1) of the Act), property that was specified leasing property of the person from whom the taxpayer acquired it, the taxpayer shall, for the purposes of paragraph $(1.1)(a)$ and for the purpose of computing the income of the taxpayer in respect of the lease for any period after the particular time, be deemed to be the same person as, and a continuation of, that person.

[¶1856]

(1.17) For the purposes of subsections (1.1) and, (1.11), where at any particular time a property (in this subsection referred to as a "replacement property") is provided by a taxpayer to a lessee for the remaining term of a lease as a replacement for a similar property of the taxpayer (in this subsection referred to as the "original property") that was leased by the taxpayer to the lessee, and the amount payable by the lessee for the use of, or the right to use, the replacement property is the same as the amount that was so payable in respect of the original property, the following rules apply:

(a) the replacement property shall be deemed to have been leased by the taxpayer to the lessee at the same time and for the same term as the original property;

(b) the amount of the loan referred to in clause $(1.1)(a)(i)(A)$ shall be deemed to be equal to the amount of that loan determined in respect of the original property;

(c) the amount determined under subparagraph $(1.1)(a)(ii)$ in respect of the replacement property shall be deemed to be equal to the amount so determined in respect of the original property;

(d) all amounts received or receivable by the taxpayer for the use of, or the right to use, the original property before the particular time shall be deemed to have been received or receivable, as the case may be, by the taxpayer for the use of, or the right to use, the replacement property; and

(e) the original property shall be deemed to have ceased to be subject to the lease at the particular time.

[¶1858]

(1.18) For the purposes of subsection (1.1), where for any period of time any amount that would have been received or receivable by a taxpayer during that period in respect of the use of, or the right to use, a property of the taxpayer during that period is not received or receivable by the taxpayer as a consequence of a breakdown of the property during that period and before the lease of that property is terminated, that amount shall be deemed to have been received or receivable, as the case may be, by the taxpayer.

[¶1860]

(1.19) For the purposes of subsections (1.1) and (1.11), where at any particular time

(a) an addition or alteration (in this subsection referred to as "additional property") is made by a taxpayer to a property (in this subsection referred to as the "original property") of the taxpayer that is a specified leasing property at the particular time, and

(b) as a consequence of the addition or alteration, the aggregate amount receivable by the taxpayer after the particular time for the use of, or the right to use, the original property and the additional property exceeds the amount so receivable in respect of the original property,

the following rules apply:

(c) the taxpayer shall be deemed to have leased the additional property to the lessee at the particular time,

(d) the term of the lease of the additional property shall be deemed to be greater than one year,

(e) the prescribed rate in effect at the particular time in respect of the additional property shall be deemed to be equal to the prescribed rate in effect in respect of the lease of the original property at the particular time,

(f) subsection (1.11) shall be read without reference to paragraph (c) thereof in respect of the additional property, and

(g) the excess described in paragraph (b) shall be deemed to be an amount receivable by the taxpayer for the use of, or the right to use, the additional property.

[¶1862]

(1.2) For the purposes of subsections (1.1) and (1.11), where at any time

(a) a lease (in this subsection referred to as the "original lease") of property is renegotiated in the course of a *bona fide* renegotiation, and

(b) as a result of the renegotiation, the amount paid or payable by the lessee of the property for the use of, or the right to use, the property is altered in respect of a period after that time (otherwise than by reason of an addition or alteration to which subsection (1.19) applies),

the following rules apply:

(c) the original lease shall be deemed to have expired and the renegotiated lease shall be deemed to be a new lease of the property entered into at that time, and

(d) paragraph (1.13)(b) shall not apply in respect of any period before that time during which the property was leased by the lessee or a person with whom the lessee did not deal at arm's length.

[¶1864]

(1.3) For the purposes of subsections (1.1) and (1.11), where a taxpayer leases to another person a building or part thereof that is not exempt property, the references to "one year" in paragraphs (1.11)(b) and (1.13)(b), subsection (1.15) and paragraph (1.19)(d) shall in respect of that building or part thereof be read as references to "three years".

[¶1866]

Property Acquired in the Year

(2) Where at the end of a taxation year of a taxpayer

(a) the aggregate of all amounts, each of which is an amount added

(i) by reason of subparagraph 13(21)(f)(i) [subsection 13(21) "undepreciated capital cost", item A] of the Act in respect of a property acquired in the year or that became available for use by the taxpayer in the year, or

(ii) by reason of subparagraph 13(21)(f)(ii.1) or (ii.2) [subsection 13(21) "undepreciated capital cost", items C and D] of the Act in respect of an amount repaid in the year

to the undepreciated capital cost to the taxpayer of property of a class in Schedule II, other than

(iii) property included in paragraph (1)(v), paragraph (w) of Class 10 or any of paragraphs (a) to (c), (e) to (i), (k), (l) and (p) to (s) of Class 12,

(iv) property included in any of Classes 13, 14, 15, 23, 24, 27, 29 and 34,

(v) where the taxpayer was a corporation described in subsection (16) throughout the year, property that was specified leasing property of the taxpayer at that time,

(vi) property that was deemed to have been acquired by the taxpayer in a preceding taxation year by reason of the application of paragraph 16.1(1)(*b*) of the Act in respect of a lease to which the property was subject immediately before the time at which the taxpayer last acquired the property, and

(vii) property considered to have become available for use by the taxpayer in the year by reason of paragraph 13(27)(*b*) or (28)(*c*) of the Act

exceeds

(*b*) the aggregate of all amounts, each of which is an amount deducted

(i) by virtue of subparagraph 13(21)(*f*)(iv) or (v) [subsection 13(21) "undepreciated capital cost", items F and G] of the Act in respect of property disposed of in the year, or

(ii) by virtue of subparagraph 13(21)(*f*)(viii) [subsection 13(21) "undepreciated capital cost", item J] of the Act in respect of an amount the taxpayer received or was entitled to receive in the year

from the undepreciated capital cost to him of property of the class,

the amount that the taxpayer may deduct for the year under subsection (1) in respect of property of the class shall be determined as if the undepreciated capital cost to him as of the end of the year (before making any deduction under subsection (1) for the year) of property of the class were reduced by an amount equal to 50 per cent of the amount by which the aggregate determined under paragraph (*a*) exceeds the aggregate determined under paragraph (*b*).

[¶1868]

(**2.1**) Where a taxpayer has, after November 12, 1981 and before 1983, acquired or incurred a capital cost in respect of a property of a class in Schedule II and

(*a*) he was obligated to acquire the property under the terms of an agreement in writing entered into before November 13, 1981 (or, where the property is a property described in Class 31 in Schedule II, before 1982),

(*b*) he or a person with whom he was not dealing at arm's length commenced the construction, manufacture or production of the property before November 13, 1981 (or, where the property is a property described in Class 31 in Schedule II, before 1982),

(*c*) he or a person with whom he was not dealing at arm's length had made arrangements, evidenced in writing for the construction, manufacture or production of the property that were substantially advanced before November 13, 1981 and the construction, manufacture or production commenced before June 1, 1982, or

(*d*) he was obligated to acquire the property under the terms of an agreement in writing entered into before June 1, 1982 where arrangements, evidenced in writing, for the acquisition or leasing of the property were substantially advanced before November 13, 1981,

the following rules apply:

(e) no amount shall be included under paragraph $(2)(a)$ in respect of the property;

(f) where the property is a property to which paragraph $(1)(b)$ applies, that paragraph shall be read, in respect of the property, as "such amount, not exceeding the amount for the year calculated in accordance with Schedule III, as he may claim in respect of the capital cost to him of property of Class 13 in Schedule II";

(g) where the property is a property of a class to which paragraph $(1)(t)$ or (ta) applies, the property shall be deemed to be designated property of the class; and

(h) where the property is a property described in paragraph $(1)(v)$, subparagraph (iv) thereof shall be read, in respect of the property, as "33⅓ per cent of the capital cost thereof to him, and".

[¶1870]

(**2.2**) Where a property of a class in Schedule II is acquired by a taxpayer

(a) in the course of a reorganization in respect of which, if a dividend were received by a corporation in the course of the reorganization, subsection 55(2) of the Act would not be applicable to the dividend by reason of the application of paragraph $55(3)(b)$ of the Act, or

(b) [Revoked.]

(c) [Revoked.]

(d) [Revoked.]

(e) from a person with whom the taxpayer was not dealing at arm's length (otherwise than by virtue of a right referred to in paragraph $251(5)(b)$ of the Act) at the time the property was acquired,

and where

(f) the property was depreciable property of the person from whom it was acquired and was owned continuously by that person for the period from

(i) a day that was at least 364 days before the end of the taxation year of the taxpayer during which he acquired the property, or

(ii) November 12, 1981

to the day it was acquired by the taxpayer, or

(g) the rules provided in subsection (2.1) or this subsection applied in respect of the property for the purpose of determining the allowance under subsection (1) to which the person from whom the taxpayer acquired the property was entitled, the following rules apply:

(h) no amount shall be included under paragraph (2)(a) in respect of the property;

(i) where the property is a property to which paragraph (1)(b) applies, that paragraph shall be read, in respect of the property, as "such amount, not exceeding the amount for the year calculated in accordance with Schedule III, as he may claim in respect of the capital cost to him of property of Class 13 in Schedule II";

(j) where the property is a property of a class to which paragraph (1)(ta) applies,

(i) the property shall be deemed to be designated property of the class,

(ii) for the purposes of computing the amount determined under paragraph (1)(ta) for any taxation year of the taxpayer ending after the time the property was actually acquired by the taxpayer, the property shall be deemed, other than for the purposes of paragraph (f), to have been acquired by the taxpayer immediately after the commencement of the taxpayer's first taxation year that commenced after the time that is the earlier of

(A) the time the property was last acquired by the transferor of the property, and

(B) where the property was transferred in a series of transfers to which this subsection applies, the time the property was last acquired by the first transferor in that series,

unless

(C) where clause (A) applies, the property was acquired by the taxpayer before the end of the taxation year of the transferor of the property that includes the time at which that transferor acquired the property, or

(D) where clause (B) applies, the property was acquired by the taxpayer before the end of the taxation year of the first transferor that includes the time at which that transferor acquired the property,

(iii) where the taxpayer is a corporation that was incorporated or otherwise formed after the end of the transferor's, or where applicable, the first transferor's, taxation year in which the transferor last acquired the property, the taxpayer shall be deemed, for the purposes of subparagraph (ii),

(A) to have been in existence throughout the period commencing immediately before the end of that year and ending immediately after the taxpayer was incorporated or otherwise formed, and

¶1870

(B) to have had, throughout the period referred to in clause (A), fiscal periods ending on the day of the year on which the taxpayer's first fiscal period ended; and

(iv) the property shall be deemed to have become available for use by the taxpayer at the earlier of

(A) the time it became available for use by the taxpayer, and

(B) if applicable,

(I) the time it became available for use by the person from whom the taxpayer acquired the property, determined without reference to paragraphs $13(27)(c)$ and $(28)(d)$ of the Act, or

(II) the time it became available for use by the first transferor in a series of transfers of the same property to which this subsection applies, determined without reference to paragraphs $13(27)(c)$ and $(28)(d)$ of the Act; and

(k) where the property is a property described in paragraph $(1)(v)$, subparagraph (iv) thereof shall be read, in respect of the property, as "$33\frac{1}{3}$ per cent of the capital cost thereof to him, and".

[¶1872]

(2.21) Where a taxpayer is deemed by a provision of the Act to have disposed of and acquired or reacquired a property,

(a) for the purposes of paragraph $(2.2)(e)$ and subsections (19), 1101(1ad) and 1102(14) and (14.1), the acquisition or reacquisition shall be deemed to have been from a person with whom the taxpayer was not dealing at arm's length at the time of the acquisition or reacquisition; and

(b) for the purposes of paragraphs $(2.2)(f)$ and (g), the taxpayer shall be deemed to be the person from whom the taxpayer acquired or reacquired the property.

[¶1874]

(2.3) Where a taxpayer has disposed of a property and, by virtue of paragraph $(2.2)(h)$, no amount is required to be included under paragraph $(2)(a)$ in respect of the property by the person that acquired the property, no amount shall be included by the taxpayer under paragraph $(2)(b)$ in respect of the disposition of the property.

[¶1876]

(2.4) For the purposes of subsection (2), where a taxpayer has disposed of property described in Class 10 of Schedule II that would qualify as property described in paragraph (e) of Class 16 of Schedule II if the property had been acquired by the taxpayer after November 12, 1981, the proceeds of disposition of the property shall be deemed to be proceeds of disposition of property described in Class 16 of Schedule II and not of property described in Class 10 of Schedule II.

[¶1877]

(2.5) Where in a particular taxation year a taxpayer disposes of a property included in Class 10.1 in Schedule II that was owned by the taxpayer at the end of the immediately preceding taxation year,

    (*a*) the deduction allowed under subsection (1) in respect of the property in computing the taxpayer's income for the year shall be determined as if the property had not been disposed of in the particular year and the number of days in the particular year were one-half of the number of days in the particular year otherwise determined; and

    (*b*) no amount shall be deducted under subsection (1) in respect of the property in computing the taxpayer's income for any subsequent taxation year.

[¶1878]

Taxation Years Less Than 12 Months

(3) Where a taxation year is less than 12 months, the amount allowed as a deduction under this section, other than under any of paragraphs $(1)(c)$, (e), (f), (g), (1), (m), (w), (x), (y), (ya), (zg) and (zh), shall not exceed that proportion of the maximum amount otherwise allowable that the number of days in the taxation year is of 365.

(4) Reserved.

(5) [Revoked.]

(6) [Revoked.]

(7) Reserved.

[¶1886]

Railway Sidings

(8) Where a taxpayer, other than an operator of a railway system, has made a capital expenditure pursuant to a contract or arrangement with an operator of a railway system under which a railway siding that does not become the taxpayer's property is constructed to provide service to the taxpayer's place of business or to a property acquired by the taxpayer for the purpose of gaining or producing income, there is hereby allowed to the taxpayer, in computing income for the taxation year from the business or property, as the case may be, a deduction equal to such amount as he may claim not exceeding four per cent of the amount remaining, if any, after deducting from the capital expenditure the aggregate of all amounts previously allowed as deductions in respect of the expenditure.

[¶1888]

Patents

(9) Where a part or all of the cost of a patent is determined by reference to the use of the patent, in lieu of the deduction allowed under paragraph $(1)(c)$, a taxpayer, in computing his income for a taxation year from a business or property, as the case may be, may deduct such amount as he may claim in respect of property of Class 14 in Schedule II not exceeding the lesser of

(a) the aggregate of

(i) that part of the capital cost determined by reference to the use of the patent in the year, and

(ii) the amount that would be computed under subparagraph $(1)(c)(i)$ if the capital cost of the patent did not include the amounts determined by reference to the use of the patent in that year and previous years; and

(b) the undepreciated capital cost to him as of the end of the taxation year (before making any deduction under this subsection for the taxation year) of property of the class.

[¶1889]

(9.1) Where a part or all of the capital cost to a taxpayer of property that is a patent, or a right to use patented information, is determined by reference to the use of the property and that property is included in Class 44 in Schedule II, in lieu of the deduction allowed under paragraph $(1)(a)$, there may be deducted in computing the taxpayer's income for a taxation year from a business or property such amount as the taxpayer may claim in respect of property of the class not exceeding the lesser of

(a) the total of

(i) that part of the capital cost that is determined by reference to the use of the property in the year, and

(ii) the amount that would be deductible for the year by reason of paragraph $(1)(a)$ in respect of property of the class if the capital cost of property of the class did not include the amounts determined under subparagraph (i) for the year and preceding taxation years; and

(b) the undepreciated capital cost to the taxpayer as of the end of the taxation year (before making any deduction under this subsection for the taxation year) of property of the class.

(10) Reserved.

[¶1892]

Rental Properties

(11) Notwithstanding subsection (1), in no case shall the aggregate of deductions, each of which is a deduction in respect of property of a prescribed class owned by a taxpayer that includes rental property owned by him, otherwise allowed to the taxpayer by virtue of subsection (1) in computing his income for a taxation year, exceed the amount, if any, by which

(a) the aggregate of amounts each of which is

(i) his income for the year from renting or leasing a rental property owned by him, computed without regard to paragraph $20(1)(a)$ of the Act, or

(ii) the income of a partnership for the year from renting or leasing a rental property of the partnership, to the extent of the taxpayer's share of such income,

exceeds

(b) the aggregate of amounts each of which is

(i) his loss for the year from renting or leasing a rental property owned by him, computed without regard to paragraph $20(1)(a)$ of the Act, or

(ii) the loss of a partnership for the year from renting or leasing a rental property of the partnership, to the extent of the taxpayer's share of such loss.

[¶1894]

(12) Subject to subsection (13), subsection (11) does not apply in respect of a taxation year of a taxpayer that was, throughout the year,

(a) a life insurance corporation, or a corporation whose principal business was the leasing, rental, development or sale, or any combination thereof, of real property owned by it; or

(b) a partnership each member of which was a corporation described in paragraph (a).

[¶1896]

(13) For the purposes of subsection (11), where a taxpayer or partnership has a leasehold interest in a property that is property of Class 1, 3 or 6 in Schedule II by virtue of subsection 1102(5) and the property is leased by the taxpayer or the partnership to a person who owns the land, an interest therein or an option in respect thereof, on which the property is situated, this section shall be read without reference to subsection (12) with respect to that property.

[¶1898]

(14) In this section and section 1101, "rental property" of a taxpayer or a partnership means

(*a*) a building owned by the taxpayer or the partnership, whether owned jointly with another person or otherwise, or

(*b*) a leasehold interest in real property, if the leasehold interest is property of Class 1, 3, 6 or 13 in Schedule II and is owned by the taxpayer or the partnership,

if, in the taxation year in respect of which the expression is being applied, the property was used by the taxpayer or the partnership principally for the purpose of gaining or producing gross revenue that is rent, but, for greater certainty, does not include a property leased by the taxpayer or the partnership to a lessee, in the ordinary course of the taxpayer's or partnership's business of selling goods or rendering services, under an agreement by which the lessee undertakes to use the property to carry on the business of selling, or promoting the sale of, the taxpayer's or partnership's goods or services.

[¶1900]

(14.1) For the purposes of subsection (14), gross revenue derived in a taxation year from

(*a*) the right of a person or partnership, other than the owner of a property, to use or occupy the property or a part thereof, and

(*b*) services offered to a person or partnership that are ancillary to the use or occupation by the person or partnership of the property or the part thereof

shall be considered to be rent derived in that year from the property.

[¶1902]

(14.2) Subsection (14.1) does not apply in any particular taxation year to property owned by

(*a*) a corporation, where the property is used in a business carried on in the year by the corporation;

(*b*) an individual, where the property is used in a business carried on in the year by the individual in which he is personally active on a continuous basis throughout that portion of the year during which the business is ordinarily carried on; or

(*c*) a partnership, where the property is used in a business carried on in the year by the partnership if at least $2/3$ of the income or loss, as the case may be, of the partnership for the year is included in the determination of the income of

(i) members of the partnership who are individuals that are personally active in the business of the partnership on a continuous basis

¶1898

throughout that portion of the year during which the business is ordinarily carried on, and

(ii) members of the partnership that are corporations.

[¶1904]

Leasing Properties

(15) Notwithstanding subsection (1), in no case shall the aggregate of deductions, each of which is a deduction in respect of property of a prescribed class that is leasing property owned by a taxpayer, otherwise allowed to the taxpayer under subsection (1) in computing his income for a taxation year, exceed the amount, if any, by which

(a) the aggregate of amounts each of which is

(i) his income for the year from renting, leasing or earning royalties from, a leasing property or a property that would be a leasing property but for subsection (18), (19) or (20) where such property is owned by him, computed without regard to paragraph $20(1)(a)$ of the Act, or

(ii) the income of a partnership for the year from renting, leasing or earning royalties from, a leasing property or a property that would be a leasing property but for subsection (18), (19) or (20) where such property is owned by the partnership, to the extent of the taxpayer's share of such income,

exceeds

(b) the aggregate of amounts each of which is

(i) his loss for the year from renting, leasing or earning royalties from, a property referred to in subparagraph (a)(i), computed without regard to paragraph $20(1)(a)$ of the Act, or

(ii) the loss of a partnership for the year from renting, leasing or earning royalties from, a property referred to in subparagraph (a)(ii), to the extent of the taxpayer's share of such loss.

[¶1906]

(16) Subsection (15) does not apply in respect of a taxation year of a taxpayer that was, throughout the year,

(a) a corporation whose principal business was

(i) renting or leasing of leasing property or property that would be leasing property but for subsection (18), (19) or (20), or

(ii) renting or leasing of property referred to in subparagraph (i) combined with selling and servicing of property of the same general type and description,

¶1906

if the gross revenue of the corporation for the year from such principal business was not less than 90 per cent of the gross revenue of the corporation for the year from all sources; or

(*b*) a partnership each member of which was a corporation described in paragraph (*a*).

[¶1908]

(**17**) Subject to subsection (18), in this section and section 1101, "leasing property" of a taxpayer or a partnership means depreciable property other than

(*a*) rental property,

(*b*) computer software tax shelter property, or

(*c*) property referred to in paragraph (*w*) of Class 10 or in paragraph (*n*) of Class 12 in Schedule II,

where such property is owned by the taxpayer or the partnership, whether jointly with another person or otherwise, if, in the taxation year in respect of which the expression is being applied, the property was used by the taxpayer or the partnership principally for the purpose of gaining or producing gross revenue that is rent, royalty or leasing revenue, but for greater certainty, does not include a property leased by the taxpayer or the partnership to a lessee, in the ordinary course of the taxpayer's or partnership's business of selling goods or rendering services, under an agreement by which the lessee undertakes to use the property to carry on the business of selling, or promoting the sale of, the taxpayer's or partnership's goods or services.

[¶1910]

(**17.1**) For the purposes of subsection (17), where, in a taxation year, a taxpayer or a partnership has acquired a property

(*a*) that was not used for any purpose in that year, and

(*b*) the first use of the property by the taxpayer or the partnership was principally for the purpose of gaining or producing gross revenue that is rent, royalty or leasing revenue,

the property shall be deemed to have been used in the taxation year in which it was acquired principally for the purpose of gaining or producing gross revenue that is rent, royalty or leasing revenue.

[¶1912]

(**17.2**) For the purposes of subsections (1.11) and (17), gross revenue derived in a taxation year from

(*a*) the right of a person or partnership, other than the owner of a property, to use or occupy the property or a part thereof, and

(b) services offered to a person or partnership that are ancillary to the use or occupation by the person or partnership of the property or the part thereof

shall be considered to be rent derived in the year from the property.

[¶1914]

(17.3) Subsection (17.2) does not apply in any particular taxation year to property owned by

(a) a corporation, where the property is used in a business carried on in the year by the corporation;

(b) an individual, where the property is used in a business carried on in the year by the individual in which he is personally active on a continuous basis throughout that portion of the year during which the business is ordinarily carried on; or

(c) a partnership, where the property is used in a business carried on in the year by the partnership if at least $\frac{2}{3}$ of the income or loss, as the case may be, of the partnership for the year is included in the determination of the income of

(i) members of the partnership who are individuals that are personally active in the business of the partnership on a continuous basis throughout that portion of the year during which the business is ordinarily carried on, and

(ii) members of the partnership that are corporations.

[¶1916]

(18) Leasing property of a taxpayer or a partnership referred to in subsection (17) does not include

(a) property that the taxpayer or the partnership acquired before May 26, 1976 or was obligated to acquire under the terms of an agreement in writing entered into before May 26, 1976;

(b) property the construction, manufacture or production of which was commenced by the taxpayer or the partnership before May 26, 1976 or was commenced under an agreement in writing entered into by the taxpayer or the partnership before May 26, 1976; or

(c) property that the taxpayer or the partnership acquired on or before December 31, 1976 or was obligated to acquire under the terms of an agreement in writing entered into on or before December 31, 1976, if

(i) arrangements, evidenced by writing, respecting the acquisition, construction, manufacture or production of the property had been substantially advanced before May 26, 1976, and

(ii) the taxpayer or the partnership had before May 26, 1976 demonstrated a *bona fide* intention to acquire the property for the purpose of gaining or producing gross revenue that is rent, royalty or leasing revenue.

[¶1918]

(19) Notwithstanding subsection (17), a property acquired by a taxpayer

(a) in the course of a reorganization in respect of which, if a dividend were received by a corporation in the course of the reorganization, subsection 55(2) of the Act would not be applicable to the dividend by reason of the application of paragraph 55(3)(b) of the Act, or

(b) from a person with whom the taxpayer was not dealing at arm's length (otherwise than by virtue of a right referred to in paragraph 251(5)(b) of the Act) at the time the property was acquired,

that would otherwise be leasing property of the taxpayer, shall be deemed not to be leasing property of the taxpayer if immediately before it was so acquired by the taxpayer, it was, by virtue of subsection (18) or (20) or this subsection, not a leasing property of the person from whom the property was so acquired.

[¶1920]

(20) Notwithstanding subsection (17), a property acquired by a taxpayer or partnership that is a replacement property (within the meaning assigned by subsection 13(4) of the Act), that would otherwise be a leasing property of the taxpayer or partnership, shall be deemed not to be a leasing property of the taxpayer or partnership if the property replaced, referred to in paragraph 13(4)(a) or (b) of the Act, was, by reason of subsection (18) or (19) or this subsection, not a leasing property of the taxpayer or partnership immediately before it was disposed of by the taxpayer or partnership.

[¶1921]

Computer Software Tax Shelter Property

(20.1) The total of all amounts each of which is a deduction in respect of computer software tax shelter property allowed to the taxpayer under subsection (1) in computing a taxpayer's income for a taxation year shall not exceed the amount, if any, by which

(a) the total of all amounts each of which is

(i) the taxpayer's income for the year from a business in which computer software tax shelter property owned by the taxpayer is used, computed without reference to any deduction under subsection (1) in respect of such property, or

(ii) the income of a partnership from a business in which computer software tax shelter property owned by the partnership is used, to the extent of the taxpayer's share of such income that is included in computing the taxpayer's income for the year,

exceeds

(*b*) the total of all amounts each of which is

(i) a loss of the taxpayer from a business in which computer software tax shelter property is used, computed without reference to any deduction under subsection (1) in respect of such property, or

(ii) a loss of a partnership from a business in which computer software tax shelter property is used, to the extent of the taxpayer's share of such loss that is included in computing the taxpayer's income for the year.

[¶1922]

(**20.2**) For the purpose of this Part, computer software tax shelter property is computer software that is depreciable property of a prescribed class of a person or partnership where

(*a*) the person's or partnership's interest in the property is a tax shelter investment (as defined by subsection 143.2(1) of the Act) determined without reference to subsection (20.1); or

(*b*) an interest in the person or partnership is a tax shelter investment (as defined by subsection 143.2(1) of the Act) determined without reference to subsection (20.1).

[¶1923]

Certified Films and Video Tapes

(**21**) Notwithstanding subsection (1), where a taxpayer (in this subsection and subsection (22) referred to as the "investor") has acquired property of Class 10 or 12 in Schedule II that is a certified feature film or certified production (in this subsection and subsection (22) referred to as the "film or tape"), in no case shall the deduction in respect of property of that class otherwise allowed to the investor by virtue of subsection (1) in computing the investor's income for a particular taxation year exceed the amount that it would be if the capital cost to the investor of the film or tape were reduced by the aggregate of amounts, each of which is

(*a*) where the principal photography or taping of the film or tape is not completed before the end of the particular taxation year, the amount, if any, by which

(i) the capital cost to the investor of the film or tape as of the end of the year exceeds the aggregate of

(ii) where the principal photography or taping of the film or tape is completed within 60 days after the end of the year, the amount that may reasonably be considered to be the investor's proportionate share of the production costs incurred in respect of the film or tape before the end of the year,

(iii) where the principal photography or taping of the film or tape is not completed within 60 days after the end of the year, the amount that may reasonably be considered to be the investor's proportionate share of the lesser of

(A) the production costs incurred in respect of the film or tape before the end of the year, and

(B) the proportion of the production costs incurred to the date the principal photography or taping is completed that the percentage of the principal photography or taping completed as of the end of the year, as certified by the Minister of Communications, is of 100 per cent, and

(iv) the total of amounts determined under paragraphs (*b*) to (*e*) in respect of the film or tape as of the end of the year;

(*b*) where, at any time before the later of

(i) the date the principal photography or taping of the film or tape is completed, and

(ii) the date the investor acquired the film or tape,

a revenue guarantee (other than a revenue guarantee that is certified by the Minister of Communications to be a guarantee under which the person who agrees to provide the revenue is a licensed broadcaster or *bona fide* film or tape distributor) is entered into in respect of the film or tape whereby it may reasonably be considered certain, having regard to all the circumstances, that the investor will receive revenue under the terms of the revenue guarantee, the amount, if any, that may reasonably be considered to be the portion of the revenue that has not been included in the investor's income in the particular taxation year or a previous taxation year;

(*c*) where, at any time, a revenue guarantee, other than

(i) a revenue guarantee in respect of which paragraph (*b*) applies, or

(ii) a revenue guarantee under which the person (in this subsection referred to as the "guarantor") who agrees to provide the revenue under the terms of the guarantee is a person who does not deal at arm's length with either the investor or the person from whom the investor acquired the film or tape (in this subsection referred to as the "vendor") and in respect of which the Minister of Communications certifies that

(A) the guarantor is a licensed broadcaster or *bona fide* film or tape distributor, and

(B) the cost of the film or tape does not include any amount for or in respect of the guarantee,

is entered into in respect of the film or tape, the amount, if any, that may reasonably be considered to be the portion of the revenue that is to be received by the investor under the terms of the revenue guarantee that has not been included in the investor's income in the particular taxation year or a preceding taxation year, if

¶1923

(iii) the guarantor and the investor are not dealing at arm's length,

(iv) the vendor and the guarantor are not dealing at arm's length, or

(v) the vendor or a person not dealing at arm's length with the vendor undertakes in any way, directly or indirectly, to fulfill all or any part of the guarantor's obligations under the terms of the revenue guarantee;

(d) where, at any time, a revenue guarantee, other than a revenue guarantee in respect of which paragraph (b) or (c) applies, is entered into in respect of the film or tape, the amount, if any, that may reasonably be considered to be the portion of the revenue that is to be received by the investor under the terms of the revenue guarantee that

(i) is not due to the investor until a time that is more than four years after the first day on which the guarantor has the right to the use of the film or tape, and

(ii) has not been included in the investor's income in the particular taxation year or a previous taxation year; and

(e) the portion of any debt obligation of the investor outstanding at the end of the particular year that is convertible into an interest in the film or tape or in the investor.

[¶1924]

(21.1) Notwithstanding subsection (1), where a taxpayer has acquired property described in paragraph (s) of Class 10 in Schedule II, or in paragraph (m) of Class 12 of Schedule II, the deduction in respect of the property otherwise allowed to the taxpayer under subsection (1) in computing the taxpayer's income for a taxation year shall not exceed the amount that it would be if the capital cost to the taxpayer of the property were reduced by the portion of any debt obligation of the taxpayer outstanding at the end of the year that is convertible into an interest in the property or in the taxpayer.

[¶1925]

(22) Notwithstanding subsection (1), where an investor has acquired a film or tape after his 1977 taxation year and before 1979 and the principal photography or taping in respect of the film or tape is completed after a particular taxation year and not later than March 1, 1979, in no case shall the deduction in respect of property of Class 12 in Schedule II otherwise allowed to the investor by virtue of subsection (1) in computing his income for the particular taxation year exceed the amount, otherwise determined, if the capital cost to the investor of the film or tape were reduced by the amount, if any, by which

(a) the capital cost to the investor of the film or tape as of the end of the year

exceeds

(b) the amount that may reasonably be considered to be the investor's proportionate share of the production costs incurred in respect of the film or tape to March 1, 1979.

[¶1926]

(**23**) For the purposes of paragraph $(21)(a)$,

(a) in respect of a film or tape acquired in 1987, other than a film or tape in respect of which paragraph (b) applies, the references in paragraph $(21)(a)$ to "within 60 days after the end of the year" shall be read as references to "before July, 1988"; and

(b) in respect of a film or tape acquired in 1987 or 1988 that is included in paragraph (n) of Class 12 in Schedule II and that is part of a series of films or tapes that includes another property included in that paragraph, the references in paragraph $(21)(a)$ to "within 60 days after the end of the year" shall be read as references to "before 1989".

[¶1927]

Specified Energy Property

(**24**) Notwithstanding subsection (1), in no case shall the total of deductions, each of which is a deduction in respect of property of Class 34 or 43.1 in Schedule II that is specified energy property owned by a taxpayer, otherwise allowed to the taxpayer under subsection (1) in computing the taxpayer's income for a taxation year, exceed the amount, if any, by which

(a) the total of all amounts each of which is

  (i) the total of

    (A) the amount that would be the income of the taxpayer for the year from property described in Class 34 or 43.1 in Schedule II (other than specified energy property), or from the business of selling the product of the property, if that income were calculated after deducting the maximum amount allowable in respect of the property for the year under paragraph $20(1)(a)$ of the Act, and

    (B) the taxpayer's income for the year from specified energy property or from the business of selling the product of that property, computed without regard to paragraph $20(1)(a)$ of the Act, or

  (ii) the total of

    (A) the taxpayer's share of the amount that would be the income of a partnership for the year from property described in Class 34 or 43.1 in Schedule II (other than specified energy property), or from the business of selling the product of that property, if that income were calculated after deducting the maximum amount allowable in respect of the property for the year under paragraph $20(1)(a)$ of the Act, and

    (B) the income of a partnership for the year from specified energy property or from the business of selling the product of that property of the partnership, to the extent of the taxpayer's share of that income,

exceeds

(b) the total of all amounts each of which is

(i) the taxpayer's loss for the year from specified energy property or from the business of selling the product of that property, computed without regard to paragraph $20(1)(a)$ of the Act, or

(ii) the loss of a partnership for the year from specified energy property or from the business of selling the product of that property of the partnership, to the extent of the taxpayer's share of that loss.

Federal Budget Extract

Specified Energy Property Rules

[Reproduced below is an excerpt from the February 23, 2005 Federal Budget that sets out a proposal to apply the specified energy property rules to combustion turbines and electricity transmission and distribution assets.]

In addition to setting the appropriate CCA rate, rules are needed to protect the integrity of the CCA system. These include the specified energy property rules, which limit the amount of CCA deductions that may be used by passive investors in respect of specified energy property — generally property for which an incentive CCA rate is allowed under Class 34 or 43.1 — to the amount of income from such property. This prevents CCA deductions from being used by passive investors to shelter other sources of income.

This budget proposes that the specified energy property rules be extended to combustion turbines and electricity transmission and distribution assets that are eligible for the higher CCA rates proposed in this budget.

[¶1928]

(25) Subject to subsections (27) to (29), in this section and section 1101, "specified energy property" of a taxpayer or partnership (in this subsection referred to as "the owner") for a taxation year means property of Class 34 or 43.1 in Schedule II that was acquired by the owner after February 9, 1988 other than a particular property

(a) acquired to be used by the owner primarily for the purpose of gaining or producing income from a business carried on in Canada (other than the business of selling the product of the particular property) or from another property situated in Canada, or

(b) leased in the year, in the ordinary course of carrying on a business of the owner in Canada, to

(i) a person who can reasonably be expected to use the property primarily for the purpose of gaining or producing income from a business carried on in Canada (other than the business of selling the product of the particular property) or from another property situated in Canada, or

(ii) a corporation or partnership described in subsection (26), where the owner was

(iii) a corporation whose principal business was, throughout the year,

(A) the renting or leasing of leasing property or property that would be leasing property but for subsection (18), (19) or (20),

(B) the renting or leasing of property referred to in clause (A) combined with the selling and servicing of property of the same general type and description, or

(C) the manufacturing of property described in Class 34 or 43.1 in Schedule II that it sells or leases,

and the gross revenue of the corporation for the year from that principal business was not less than 90 per cent of the gross revenue of the corporation for the year from all sources, or

(iv) a partnership each member of which was a corporation described in subparagraph (iii) or paragraph (26)(*a*).

[¶1929]

(26) Subsection (24) does not apply to a taxation year of a taxpayer that was, throughout the year,

(*a*) a corporation whose principal business throughout the year was

(i) manufacturing or processing,

(ii) mining operations, or

(iii) the sale, distribution or production of electricity, natural gas, oil, steam, heat or any other form of energy or potential energy; or

(*b*) a partnership each member of which was a corporation described in paragraph (*a*).

[¶1930]

(27) Specified energy property of a person or partnership does not include property acquired by the person or partnership after February 9, 1988 and before 1990

(*a*) pursuant to an obligation in writing entered into by the person or partnership before February 10, 1988;

(*b*) pursuant to the terms of a prospectus, preliminary prospectus, registration statement or offering memorandum filed before February 10, 1988 with a public authority in Canada pursuant to and in accordance with the securities legislation of any province;

(*c*) pursuant to the terms of an offering memorandum distributed as part of an offering of securities where

(i) the offering memorandum contained a complete or substantially complete description of the securities contemplated in the offering as well as the terms and conditions of the offering of the securities,

(ii) the offering memorandum was distributed before February 10, 1988,

(iii) solicitations in respect of the sale of the securities contemplated by the offering memorandum were made before February 10, 1988, and

(iv) the sale of the securities was substantially in accordance with the offering memorandum; or

(d) as part of a project where, before February 10, 1988,

(i) some of the machinery or equipment to be used in the project had been acquired, or agreements in writing for the acquisition of that machinery or equipment had been entered into, by or on behalf of the person or partnership, and

(ii) an approval had been received by or on behalf of the person or partnership from a government environmental authority in respect of the location of the project.

[¶1932]

(28) A property acquired by a taxpayer

(a) in the course of a reorganization in respect of which, if a dividend were received by a corporation in the course of the reorganization, subsection 55(2) of the Act would not be applicable to the dividend by reason of the application of paragraph 55(3)(b) of the Act, or

(b) from a person with whom the taxpayer was not dealing at arm's length (otherwise than by virtue of a right referred to in paragraph 251(5)(b) of the Act) at the time the property was acquired

that would otherwise be specified energy property of the taxpayer shall be deemed not to be specified energy property of the taxpayer if, immediately before it was so acquired by the taxpayer, it was not, by virtue of subsection (27), this subsection or subsection (29), specified energy property of the person from whom the property was so acquired.

[¶1934]

(29) A property acquired by a taxpayer or partnership that is a replacement property (within the meaning assigned by subsection 13(4) of the Act), that would otherwise be specified energy property of the taxpayer or partnership, shall be deemed not to be specified energy property of the taxpayer or partnership if the property replaced, referred to in paragraph 13(4)(a) or (b) of the Act, was, by virtue of subsection (27), (28) or this subsection, not specified energy property of the taxpayer or partnership immediately before it was disposed of by the taxpayer or partnership.

EXEMPT MINING INCOME

[¶1938]

1100A.   (1) [Revoked.]

(2) Any election under subparagraph $13(21)(f)(vi)$ of the Act in respect of property of a prescribed class acquired by a corporation for the purpose of gaining or producing income from a mine shall be made by filing with the Minister, not later than the day on or before which the corporation is required to file a return of income pursuant to section 150 of the Act for its taxation year in which the exempt period in respect of the mine ended, one of the following documents in duplicate:

(a) where the directors of the corporation are legally entitled to administer the affairs of the corporation, a certified copy of their resolution authorizing the election to be made in respect of that class; and

(b) where the directors of the corporation are not legally entitled to administer the affairs of the corporation, a certified copy of the authorization of the making of the election in respect of that class by the person or persons legally entitled to administer the affairs of the corporation.

DIVISION II
SEPARATE CLASSES

[¶1940]

BUSINESSES AND PROPERTIES

1101.   (1) Where more than one property of a taxpayer is described in the same class in Schedule II and where

(a) one of the properties was acquired for the purpose of gaining or producing income from a business, and

(b) one of the properties was acquired for the purpose of gaining or producing income from another business or from the property,

a separate class is hereby prescribed for the properties that

(c) were acquired for the purpose of gaining or producing income from each business; and

(d) would otherwise be included in the class.

[¶1942]

(1a) For the purposes of subsection (1),

(a) a life insurance business, and

(b) an insurance business other than a life insurance business,

shall each be regarded as a separate business.

[¶1944]

(1ab) Where, at the end of 1971, more than one property of a taxpayer who was a member of a partnership at that time is described in the same class in Schedule II and where

(a) one of the properties can reasonably be regarded to be the interest of the taxpayer in a depreciable property that is partnership property of the partnership, and

(b) one of the properties is property other than property referred to in paragraph (a),

a separate class is hereby prescribed for all properties each of which

(c) is a property referred to in paragraph (a); and

(d) would otherwise be included in the class.

[¶1946]

(1ac) Subject to subsection (5h), where more than one property of a taxpayer is described in the same class in Schedule II, and one or more of the properties is a rental property of the taxpayer the capital cost of which to the taxpayer was not less than $50,000, a separate class is hereby prescribed for each such rental property of the taxpayer that would otherwise be included in the same class, other than a rental property that was acquired by the taxpayer before 1972 or that is

(a) a building or an interest therein, or

(b) a leasehold interest acquired by the taxpayer by reason of the fact that the taxpayer erected a building on leased land,

erection of which building was commenced by the taxpayer before 1972 or pursuant to an agreement in writing entered into by the taxpayer before 1972.

[¶1948]

(1ad) Notwithstanding subsection (1ac), a rental property acquired by a taxpayer

(a) in the course of a reorganization in respect of which, if a dividend were received by a corporation in the course of the reorganization, subsection 55(2) of the Act would not be applicable to the dividend by reason of the application of paragraph 55(3)(b) of the Act, or

(b) from a person with whom the taxpayer was not dealing at arm's length (otherwise than by virtue of a right referred to in paragraph 251(5)(b) of the Act) at the time the property was acquired,

that would otherwise be rental property of the taxpayer of a separate class prescribed under subsection (1ac), shall be deemed not to be property of a separate class prescribed under that subsection if, immediately before it was so acquired by the taxpayer, it was a rental property of the person from whom the property was so acquired of a prescribed class other than a separate class prescribed under that subsection.

[¶1950]

(1ae) Except in the case of a corporation or partnership described in subsection 1100(12), where more than one property of a taxpayer is described in the same class in Schedule II and where

> (*a*) one of the properties is a rental property other than a property of a separate class prescribed under subsection (1ac), and

> (*b*) one of the properties is a property other than rental property,

a separate class is hereby prescribed for properties that

> (*c*) are described in paragraph (*a*); and

> (*d*) would otherwise be included in the class.

[¶1951]

(1af) A separate class is hereby prescribed for each property included in Class 10.1 in Schedule II.

Draft Regulation

Limited Period Franchise, Concession or License (December 20, 2002)

[Consequential on the proposed addition of subsection 13(4.2) to the *Income Tax Act*], it is also proposed that section 1101 of the Regulations be amended, applicable after December 20, 2002, by adding the following after subsection (1af):

(1ag) If more than one property of a taxpayer is described in the same class in Schedule II, and one or more of the properties is a property in respect of which the taxpayer is a transferee that has elected under subsection 13(4.2) of the Act, a separate class is prescribed for each such property of the taxpayer that would otherwise be included in the same class.

Applicable: After December 20, 2002.

Explanatory Note: [Please see the explanatory notes following proposed subsections 13(4.2) and (4.3) of the *Income Tax Act*.]

[¶1952]

Fishing Vessels

(2) Where a property of a taxpayer that would otherwise be included in Class 7 in Schedule II is a property in respect of which a depreciation allowance could have been taken under Order in Council

> (*a*) P.C. 2798 of April 10, 1942,

(b) P.C. 7580 of August 26, 1942, as amended by P.C. 3297 of April 22, 1943, or

(c) P.C. 3979 of June 1, 1944,

if those Orders in Council were applicable to the taxation year, a separate class is hereby prescribed for each property, including the furniture, fittings and equipment attached thereto.

[¶1954]

Canadian Vessels

(2a) A separate class is hereby prescribed for each vessel of a taxpayer, including the furniture, fittings, radiocommunication equipment and other equipment attached thereto, that

(a) was constructed in Canada;

(b) is registered in Canada; and

(c) had not been used for any purpose whatever before it was acquired by the taxpayer.

[¶1956]

Offshore Drilling Vessels

(2b) A separate class is hereby prescribed for all vessels described in Class 7 in Schedule II, including the furniture, fittings, radiocommunication equipment and other equipment attached thereto, acquired by a taxpayer

(a) after May 25, 1976 and designed principally for the purpose of

(i) determining the existence, location, extent or quality of accumulations of petroleum or natural gas (other than mineral resources), or

(ii) drilling oil or gas wells; or

(b) after May 22, 1979 and designed principally for the purpose of determining the existence, location, extent or quality of mineral resources.

Draft Regulation

Capital Cost Allowance Vessels (December 20, 2002)

Section 1101 of the Income Tax Regulations is amended by adding the following after subsection (2b):

Vessels and a Structured Financing Facility

(2c) Subsections (2a) and (2b) do not apply to a vessel, nor to the furniture, fittings, radio communications equipment and other equipment attached to the vessel, if

¶1956

a structured financing facility relating to any such property has been agreed to by the Minister of Industry under the *Department of Industry Act.*

Applicable: Deemed to have come into force on November 7, 2001.

Explanatory Note: Section 1101 of the Income Tax Regulations provides separate classes in respect of certain property described in Schedule II to the Regulations.

In general, capital cost allowance Class 7 in Schedule II to the Regulations applies to vessels and attachments thereto (15% rate, declining balance method). However, an additional allowance is available under Regulations 1100(1)(*v*) and (*va*) in respect of certain vessels and their attachments. In particular, this is the case where a vessel and its attachments are included in a separate class because of subsection 1101(2a) or (2b) of the Regulations. As well, Class 41 (25% rate, plus an additional allowance) applies to vessels and attachments thereto if paragraph (*b*) of Class 41 applies.

Proposed new subsection 1101(2c) of the Regulations provides that the separate classes in subsections 1101(2a) and (2b) for vessels and attachments do not apply in cases where the Minister of Industry has agreed to a structured financing facility. This change is consequential to the creation of the Structured Financing Facility Program, which is administered by Industry Canada. In cases where a vessel or its attachments are financed with a benefit under the Structured Financing Facility Program, the maximum capital cost allowance rate applicable to the vessel and its attachments is 15% under Class 7.

For additional information, see the commentary to the amendment to Class 41.

This amendment applies after November 7, 2001.

[¶1958]

Timber Limits and Cutting Rights

(3) For the purposes of this Part and Schedules IV and VI, each property of a taxpayer that is

(*a*) a timber limit other than a timber resource property, or

(*b*) a right to cut timber from a limit other than a right that is a timber resource property,

is hereby prescribed to be a separate class of property.

[¶1960]

Industrial Mineral Mines

(4) For the purposes of this Part and Schedule V, where a taxpayer has

(*a*) more than one industrial mineral mine in respect of which he may claim an allowance under paragraph 1100(1)(*g*),

(*b*) more than one right to remove industrial minerals from an industrial mineral mine in respect of which he may claim an allowance under that paragraph, or

(*c*) both such a mine and a right,

each such industrial mineral mine and each such right to remove industrial minerals from an industrial mineral mine is hereby prescribed to be a separate class of property.

[¶1962]

New or Expanded Mines Properties

(4a) Where more than one property of a taxpayer is described in Class 28 in Schedule II and

(a) one of the properties was acquired for the purpose of gaining or producing income from only one mine, and

(b) one of the properties was acquired for the purpose of gaining or producing income from another mine,

a separate class is hereby prescribed for the properties that

(c) were acquired for the purpose of gaining or producing income from each mine;

(d) would otherwise be included in the class; and

(e) are not included in a separate class by virtue of subsection (4b).

[¶1964]

(4b) Where more than one property of a taxpayer is described in Class 28 in Schedule II and

(a) one of the properties was acquired for the purpose of gaining or producing income from particular mines, and

(b) one of the properties was acquired for the purpose of gaining or producing income from only one mine or more than one mine other than any of the particular mines,

a separate class is hereby prescribed for the properties that

(c) were acquired for the purpose of gaining or producing income from the particular mines; and

(d) would otherwise be included in the class.

[¶1966]

(4c) Where one or more properties of a taxpayer are described in paragraph (a), (a.1) or (a.2) of Class 41 in Schedule II and

(a) where all of the properties were acquired for the purpose of gaining or producing income from only one mine, or

(b) where

(i) one or more of the properties were acquired for the purpose of gaining or producing income from a particular mine, and

(ii) one or more of the properties were acquired for the purpose of gaining or producing income from another mine,

a separate class is hereby prescribed for the properties that

(c) were acquired for the purpose of gaining or producing income from each mine,

(d) would otherwise be included in the class, and

(e) are not included in a separate class by reason of subsection (4d).

[¶1968]

(4d) Where more than one property of a taxpayer is described in paragraph (a), (a.1) or (a.2) of Class 41 in Schedule II and

(a) one of the properties was acquired for the purpose of gaining or producing income from particular mines, and

(b) one of the properties was acquired for the purpose of gaining or producing income from only one mine or more than one mine other than any of the particular mines,

a separate class is hereby prescribed for the properties that

(c) were acquired for the purpose of gaining or producing income from the particular mines, and

(d) would otherwise be included in the class.

[¶1970]

Lease Option Agreements

(5) Where, by virtue of an agreement, contract or arrangement entered into on or after May 31, 1954, a taxpayer is deemed by section 18 of the *Income Tax Act*, as enacted by the Statutes of Canada, 1958, Chapter 32, subsection 8(1), to have acquired a property, a separate class is hereby prescribed for each such property and if the taxpayer subsequently actually acquires the property it shall be included in the same class.

[¶1972]

Telecommunication Spacecraft

(5a) For the purposes of this Part, each property of a taxpayer that is an unmanned telecommunication spacecraft described in paragraph (*f*.2) of Class 10 or in Class 30 in Schedule II is hereby prescribed to be a separate class of property.

[¶1974]

Multiple-Unit Residential Buildings

(5b) For the purposes of this Part, when any property of a taxpayer is a property of Class 31 or 32 in Schedule II and the capital cost of that property to the taxpayer was not less than $50,000, a separate class is hereby prescribed for each such property of the taxpayer that would otherwise be included in the same class.

[¶1976]

Leasing Properties

(5c) For the purposes of this Part, except in the case of a corporation or partnership described in subsection 1100(16), where more than one property of a taxpayer is described in the same class in Schedule II and where

(a) one of the properties is a leasing property, and

(b) one of the properties is a property other than a leasing property,

a separate class is hereby prescribed for properties that

(c) are described in paragraph (a); and

(d) would otherwise be included in the class.

[¶1978]

Railway Cars

(5d) Where more than one property of a taxpayer is a railway car included in Class 35 in Schedule II that was rented, leased or used by the taxpayer in Canada in the taxation year, other than a railway car owned by a corporation, or a partnership any member of which is a corporation, that

(a) was at any time in that taxation year a common carrier that owned or operated a railway, or

(b) rented or leased the railway cars at any time in that taxation year, by one or more transactions between persons not dealing at arm's length, to an associated corporation that was, at that time, a common carrier that owned or operated a railway,

a separate class is prescribed

(c) for all such properties acquired by the taxpayer before February 3, 1990 (other than such properties acquired for rent or lease to another person),

(d) for all such properties acquired by the taxpayer after February 2, 1990 (other than such properties acquired for rent or lease to another person),

(e) for all such properties acquired by the taxpayer before April 27, 1989 for rent or lease to another person, and

(f) for all such properties acquired by the taxpayer after April 26, 1989 for rent or lease to another person.

[¶1979]

(5d.1) A separate class is hereby prescribed for all property included in Class 35 in Schedule II acquired at a time after December 6, 1991 by a taxpayer that was at that time a common carrier that owned and operated a railway.

Draft Regulation

Capital Cost Allowance (March 16, 2001)

Subsection 1101(5d.1) of the Regulations is replaced by the following:

(5d.1) A separate class is hereby prescribed for all property included in Class 35 in Schedule II acquired at a time after December 6, 1991 and before February 28, 2000 by a taxpayer that was at that time a common carrier that owned and operated a railway.

(5d.2) A separate class is hereby prescribed for all property included in Class 35 in Schedule II acquired at a time after February 27, 2000 by a taxpayer that was at that time a common carrier that owned and operated a railway.

Applicable: To property acquired after February 27, 2000.

Explanatory Note: Section 1101 of the Regulations prescribes separate classes of property in certain cases.

Subsection 1101(5d.1) is replaced by new subsection 1101(5d.2), which prescribes a separate class for all property included in Class 35 (7% CCA rate) acquired after February 27, 2000 by a taxpayer that was at that time a common carrier that owned and operated a railway. The replacement of subsection 1101(5d.1) with subsection 1101(5d.2) is consequential to changes to the CCA rate applicable to certain railway assets more fully described below in the commentary to new subsection 1103(2i) and amended Class 7 (15% CCA rate).

Subsection 1101(5q) allows a taxpayer to elect to have a separate class for rapidly depreciating electronic equipment. Subsection 1101(5q) is amended consequential to new subsection 1101(5s), which is described below.

New subsection 1101(5s) prescribes a separate class for one or more properties acquired by a taxpayer in a taxation year where the property is described in paragraph (*a*) of Class 43, the property is acquired after February 27, 2000, the property has a cost of at least $1,000 and the taxpayer has elected under subsection (5q) that the separate class apply. It should also be noted that subsection 1103(2g) provides that the undepreciated capital cost ("UCC") in respect of each such separate class election that is remaining after five years is to be transferred to the general Class 43 UCC pool.

New subsection 1101(5t) prescribes a separate class election for one or more properties acquired by a taxpayer in a taxation year that is a new combustion turbine (including associated burners and compressors) that generates electricity and to which Class 17 (8% CCA rate) applies.

These amendments apply to property acquired after February 27, 2000.

¶1979

[¶1980]

Railway Track and Related Property

(5e) A separate class is hereby prescribed for all property included in Class 1 in Schedule II acquired by a taxpayer after March 31, 1977 and before 1988 that is

(*a*) railway track and grading, including components such as rails, ballast, ties and other track material;

(*b*) railway traffic control or signalling equipment, including switching, block signalling, interlocking, crossing protection, detection, speed control or retarding equipment, but not including property that is principally electronic equipment or systems software therefor; or

(*c*) a bridge, culvert, subway or tunnel that is ancillary to railway track and grading.

[¶1981]

(5e.1) A separate class is hereby prescribed for all property included in Class 1 in Schedule II acquired at a time after December 6, 1991 by a taxpayer that was at that time a common carrier that owned and operated a railway, where the property is

(*a*) railway track and grading, including components such as rails, ballast, ties and other track material;

(*b*) railway traffic control or signalling equipment, including switching, block signalling, interlocking, crossing protection, detection, speed control or retarding equipment, but not including property that is principally electronic equipment or systems software therefor; or

(*c*) a bridge, culvert, subway or tunnel that is ancillary to railway track and grading.

[¶1982]

(5e.2) A separate class is hereby prescribed for all trestles included in Class 3 in Schedule II acquired at a time after December 6, 1991 by a taxpayer that was at that time a common carrier that owned and operated a railway, where the trestles are ancillary to railway track and grading.

[¶1983]

(5f) A separate class is hereby prescribed for all trestles included in Class 3 in Schedule II acquired by a taxpayer after March 31, 1977 and before 1988 that are ancillary to railway track and grading.

[¶1984]

Deemed Depreciable Property

(5g) A separate class is hereby prescribed for each property of a taxpayer described in Class 36 in Schedule II.

[¶1986]

Leasehold Interest in Real Properties

(5h) For the purposes of this Part, where more than one property of a taxpayer is described in the same class in Schedule II and where

(a) one of the properties is a leasehold interest in real property described in subsection 1100(13), and

(b) one of the properties is a property other than a leasehold interest in real property described in subsection 1100(13),

a separate class is hereby prescribed for properties that

(c) are described in paragraph (a); and

(d) would otherwise be included in the class.

[¶1988]

Pipelines

(5i) A separate class is hereby prescribed for each property of a taxpayer described in Class 2 in Schedule II that is

(a) a pipeline the construction of which was commenced after 1984 and completed after September 1, 1985 and the capital cost of which to the taxpayer is not less than $10,000,000,

(b) a pipeline that has been extended or converted where the extension or conversion was completed after September 1, 1985 and the capital cost to the taxpayer of the extension or the cost to him of the conversion, as the case may be, is not less than $10,000,000, or

(c) a pipeline that has been extended and converted as part of a single program of extension and conversion of the pipeline where the program was completed after September 1, 1985 and the aggregate of the capital cost to the taxpayer of the extension and the cost to him of the conversion is not less than $10,000,000,

and in respect of which the taxpayer has, by letter attached to the return of his income filed with the Minister in accordance with section 150 of the Act for the taxation year in which the construction, extension, conversion or program, as the case may be, was completed, elected that this subsection apply.

¶1984

Federal Budget Extract

Transmission Pipelines and Related Equipment

[Reproduced below is an excerpt from the February 23, 2005 Federal Budget that sets out proposals for new capital cost allowance rates for transmission pipelines and related equipment]

Currently, hydrocarbon transmission pipelines are generally eligible for a 4-per-cent capital cost allowance (CCA) rate under Class 1 of Schedule II to the Income Tax Regulations. Because petroleum pumping equipment and natural gas compression equipment on such pipelines is not specifically included in any of the CCA classes, the sector has generally included such assets in Class 8 (20-per-cent CCA rate), the default class for property not included in any other class. However, court cases have called into question the classification of natural gas compression equipment, on such pipelines, that default into Class 8.

* * *

The budget proposes that the CCA rate for transmission pipelines (as contrasted with distribution lines) for petroleum, natural gas or related hydrocarbons be increased to 8 per cent from 4 per cent to better reflect the typical useful life of these assets. Included will be control and monitoring devices, valves and other ancillary equipment (other than pumping and compression equipment, discussed below). The proposed changes will not affect the existing treatment of gas or oil well equipment and pipelines for which the Minister of National Revenue, in consultation with the Minister of Natural Resources, is satisfied that the main source of supply is likely to be exhausted within 15 years of commencement of operation. Distribution pipelines that distribute gas to the ultimate consumers typically have a longer useful life than transmission pipelines. Accordingly, these properties will continue to be included in Class 1, eligible for a 4-per-cent CCA rate.

The budget also proposes changes to the treatment for pumping and compression equipment, and equipment ancillary to it, related to a transmission pipeline for petroleum, natural gas or related hydrocarbons. The tax treatment of such equipment is to be rationalized by establishing a uniform 15-per-cent CCA rate that better reflects the typical useful life of these assets. However, this change will not apply to gas or oil well equipment (which is already eligible for a 25-per-cent CCA rate) and buildings or other structures.

The useful life of a pipeline can, however, be shortened in cases where production from the associated resource ceases. Accordingly, the budget also proposes that a separate class election be introduced for transmission pipelines and related pumping and compression equipment. The separate class election, which must be made for the taxation year in which a property is acquired, allows taxpayers to place eligible property in a separate class for CCA purposes. Although the separate class election does not change the CCA rate specified for the class, it does provide that any remaining undepreciated balance in the class after the disposition of the property, can, for the year of disposition, be fully deducted as a terminal loss.

The new CCA rates for transmission pipelines will apply to equipment acquired on or after February 23, 2005 that has not been used or acquired for use before that date. The new CCA rates for pumping and compression equipment will apply to all such equipment acquired on or after February 23, 2005.

[¶1990]

(5j) An election under subsection (5i), (5l) or (5o) shall be effective from the first day of the taxation year in respect of which the election is made and shall continue to be effective for all subsequent taxation years.

[¶1992]

Certified Productions

(5k) A separate class is hereby prescribed for all property of a taxpayer included in Class 10 in Schedule II by reason of paragraph (w) thereof.

[¶1993]

Canadian Film or Video Production

(5k.1) A separate class is hereby prescribed for all property of a corporation included in Class 10 in Schedule II because of paragraph (x) of that Class that is property

(a) in respect of which the corporation is deemed under subsection 125.4(3) of the Act to have paid an amount on account of its tax payable under Part I of the Act for a taxation year; or

(b) acquired by the corporation from another corporation where

(i) the other corporation is deemed under subsection 125.4(3) of the Act to have paid an amount on account of its tax payable under Part I of the Act for a taxation year in respect of the property, and

(ii) the corporations were related to each other throughout the period that began when the other corporation first incurred a qualified labour expenditure (as defined in subsection 125.4(1) of the Act) in respect of the property and ended when the other corporation disposed of the property to the corporation.

[¶1994]

Class 38 — Property and Outdoor Advertising Signs

(5l) A separate class is hereby prescribed for each property of a taxpayer described in Class 38 in Schedule II or in paragraph (l) of Class 8 in Schedule II in respect of which the taxpayer has, by letter attached to the return of income of the taxpayer filed with the Minister in accordance with section 150 of the Act for the taxation year in which the property was acquired, elected that this subsection apply.

[¶1996]

Specified Energy Property

(5m) Where, for any taxation year, a property of a taxpayer or partnership is a specified energy property, a separate class is prescribed in respect of that property for that and subsequent taxation years.

[¶1998]

(5n) Notwithstanding subsection (5c), where at the end of any taxation year a property of a taxpayer is specified leasing property, a separate class is prescribed in respect of that property (including any additions or alterations to that property included in the same class in Schedule II) for that year and all subsequent taxation years.

[¶2000]

(5o) A separate class is prescribed for one or more properties of a class in Schedule II that are exempt properties, as defined in paragraph 1100(1.13)(a), of a taxpayer referred to in subsection 1100(16) in respect of which the taxpayer has, by letter attached to the return of income of the taxpayer filed with the Minister in accordance with section 150 of the Act for the taxation year in which the property or properties were acquired, elected that this subsection apply.

[¶2001]

Rapidly Depreciating Electronic Equipment

(5p) Subject to subsection (5q), a separate class is prescribed for one or more properties of a taxpayer acquired in a taxation year and included in the year in Class 8 in Schedule II, or for one or more properties of a taxpayer acquired in a taxation year and included in the year in Class 10 in Schedule II, where each of the properties has a capital cost to the taxpayer of at least $1,000 and is

(a) general-purpose electronic data processing equipment and systems software therefor, including ancillary data processing equipment, included in paragraph (f) of Class 10 in Schedule II;

(b) computer software;

(c) a photocopier; or

(d) office equipment that is electronic communications equipment, such as a facsimile transmission device or telephone equipment.

Draft Regulation

Capital Cost Allowance (July 9, 2005)

Subsection 1101(5p) of the Regulations is replaced by the following:

(5p) Subject to subsection (5q), a separate class is prescribed for one or more properties of a taxpayer acquired in a taxation year and included in the year in Class 8 in Schedule II, where each of the properties has a capital cost to the taxpayer of at least $1,000 and is

(a) computer software;

(b) a photocopier; or

(c) office equipment that is electronic communications equipment, such as a facsimile transmission device or telephone equipment.

Applicable: To property acquired after 2004.

Explanatory Note: See the Regulatory Impact Analysis Statement following the addition of subparagraphs $1100(1)(a)(xxxi)$ and $(xxxii)$.

[¶2002]

(5q) Subsection (5p) applies only in respect of a property or properties of a taxpayer in respect of which the taxpayer has (by letter attached to the return of income of the taxpayer filed with the Minister in accordance with section 150 of the Act for the taxation year in which the property or properties were acquired) elected that the subsection apply.

Draft Regulation

Capital Cost Allowance (March 16, 2001)

Subsection 1101(5q) of the Regulations is replaced by the following:

(5q) Each of subsections (5p) and (5s) applies to a property or properties of a taxpayer only if the taxpayer has (by letter attached to the taxpayer's return of income filed with the Minister in accordance with section 150 of the Act for the taxation year in which the property or properties were acquired) elected that the subsection apply to the property or properties, as the case may be.

Applicable: To property acquired after February 27, 2000.

Explanatory Note: Section 1101 of the Regulations prescribes separate classes of property in certain cases.

Subsection 1101(5d.1) is replaced by new subsection 1101(5d.2), which prescribes a separate class for all property included in Class 35 (7% CCA rate) acquired after February 27, 2000 by a taxpayer that was at that time a common carrier that owned and operated a railway. The replacement of subsection 1101(5d.1) with subsection 1101(5d.2) is consequential to changes to the CCA rate applicable to certain railway assets more fully described below in the commentary to new subsection 1103(2i) and amended Class 7 (15% CCA rate).

Subsection 1101(5q) allows a taxpayer to elect to have a separate class for rapidly depreciating electronic equipment. Subsection 1101(5q) is amended consequential to new subsection 1101(5s), which is described below.

New subsection 1101(5s) prescribes a separate class for one or more properties acquired by a taxpayer in a taxation year where the property is described in paragraph (a) of Class 43, the property is acquired after February 27, 2000, the property has a cost of at least $1,000 and the taxpayer has elected under subsection (5q) that the separate class apply. It should also be noted that subsection 1103(2g) provides that the undepreciated capital cost ("UCC") in respect of each such separate class election that is remaining after five years is to be transferred to the general Class 43 UCC pool.

New subsection 1101(5t) prescribes a separate class election for one or more properties acquired by a taxpayer in a taxation year that is a new combustion turbine (including associated burners and compressors) that generates electricity and to which Class 17 (8% CCA rate) applies.

These amendments apply to property acquired after February 27, 2000.

[¶2003]

Computer Software Tax Shelter Property

(5r) For the purpose of this Part, where

(a) more than one property of a taxpayer is described in the same class in Schedule II,

(b) one of the properties is computer software tax shelter property, and

(c) one of the properties is a property other than computer software tax shelter property,

for properties that are described in paragraph (b) and that would otherwise be included in the class, a separate class is prescribed.

Draft Regulation

Capital Cost Allowance (March 16, 2001)

Section 1101 of the Regulations is amended by adding the following after subsection (5r):

Manufacturing or Processing Property

(5s) Subject to subsection (5q), a separate class is prescribed for one or more properties of a taxpayer

(a) that were acquired in a taxation year and included in the year in Class 43 in Schedule II because of paragraph (a) of that Class; and

(b) that had a capital cost to the taxpayer of at least $1,000.

Combustion Turbines

(5t) A separate class is prescribed for one or more properties of a taxpayer that is a combustion turbine (including associated burners and compressors) included in Class 17 in Schedule II because of subparagraph (a.1)(i) of that Class if the taxpayer has (by letter attached to the taxpayer's return of income filed with the Minister in accordance with section 150 of the Act for the taxation year in which the property or properties were acquired) elected that this subsection apply to the property or properties.

Applicable: To property acquired after February 27, 2000, except that subsections 1101(5s) and (5t) of the Regulations apply in respect of property
(a) acquired by a taxpayer after February 27, 2000 and in a taxation year ending on or before the day of the publication of these Regulations in Part II of the *Canada Gazette*; and
(b) in respect of which the taxpayer has elected, in a letter filed with the Minister, before the end of the sixth calendar month beginning after the month in which these Regulations are so published.
For the purpose of subsection 1103(2g) of the Income Tax Regulations, an election that is in respect of property described in subsection 1101(5s) of the Regulations and that is made under paragraph (b) above is deemed to have been made in accordance with subsection 1105(5q) of the Income Tax Regulations.

Explanatory Note: Section 1101 of the Regulations prescribes separate classes of property in certain cases.

Subsection 1101(5d.1) is replaced by new subsection 1101(5d.2), which prescribes a separate class for all property included in Class 35 (7% CCA rate) acquired after February 27, 2000 by a taxpayer that was at that time a common carrier that owned and

¶2003

operated a railway. The replacement of subsection 1101(5d.1) with subsection 1101(5d.2) is consequential to changes to the CCA rate applicable to certain railway assets more fully described below in the commentary to new subsection 1103(2i) and amended Class 7 (15% CCA rate).

Subsection 1101(5q) allows a taxpayer to elect to have a separate class for rapidly depreciating electronic equipment. Subsection 1101(5q) is amended consequential to new subsection 1101(5s), which is described below.

New subsection 1101(5s) prescribes a separate class for one or more properties acquired by a taxpayer in a taxation year where the property is described in paragraph (a) of Class 43, the property is acquired after February 27, 2000, the property has a cost of at least $1,000 and the taxpayer has elected under subsection (5q) that the separate class apply. It should also be noted that subsection 1103(2g) provides that the undepreciated capital cost ("UCC") in respect of each such separate class election that is remaining after five years is to be transferred to the general Class 43 UCC pool.

New subsection 1101(5t) prescribes a separate class election for one or more properties acquired by a taxpayer in a taxation year that is a new combustion turbine (including associated burners and compressors) that generates electricity and to which Class 17 (8% CCA rate) applies.

These amendments apply to property acquired after February 27, 2000.

Federal Budget Extract

Combustion Turbines Generating Electricity

[Reproduced below is an excerpt from the February 23, 2005 Federal Budget that sets out a proposal to increase the capital cost allowance rate to 15% for combustion turbines that generate electricity and to apply the specified energy property rules to combustion turbines and electricity transmission and distribution assets.]

As a result of measures announced in the 2000 budget, combustion turbines that generate electricity are eligible for an 8-per-cent CCA rate [Class 17].

* * *

Available evidence associated with newer combustion turbines suggests that the current provisions do not reflect the useful life of these assets. The budget therefore proposes that the CCA rate for combustion turbines that generate electricity (including associated burners and compressors) be increased to 15 per cent. The 15-per-cent rate will apply to such property acquired on or after February 23, 2005, that has not been used or acquired for use before February 23, 2005.

Combustion turbines that generate electricity are currently eligible for a separate class election. The separate class election was provided in response to concerns that combustion turbines can have shorter useful lives than other electrical generating equipment.

Because the higher CCA rate proposed in this budget will better reflect the useful life of combustion turbines, it is proposed that the separate class election not be extended to combustion turbines eligible for the higher rate. To accommodate taxpayers who may have already planned purchases based on the availability of the separate class election, it is further proposed that taxpayers may elect to have combustion turbines acquired before 2006 that would otherwise be eligible for the 15-per-cent rate included in Class 17 and therefore eligible for the separate class election. The proposed election must be filed with the income tax return for the taxation year in which the property is acquired.

* * *

In addition to setting the appropriate CCA rate, rules are needed to protect the integrity of the CCA system. These include the specified energy property rules, which limit the amount of CCA deductions that may be used by passive investors in respect of

¶2003

specified energy property — generally property for which an incentive CCA rate is allowed under Class 34 or 43.1 — to the amount of income from such property. This prevents CCA deductions from being used by passive investors to shelter other sources of income.

This budget proposes that the specified energy property rules be extended to combustion turbines and electricity transmission and distribution assets that are eligible for the higher CCA rates proposed in this budget.

[¶2004]

Reference

(6) A reference in this Part to a class in Schedule II includes a reference to the corresponding separate classes prescribed by this section.

DIVISION III
PROPERTY RULES

[¶2005]

PROPERTY NOT INCLUDED

1102. (1) The classes of property described in this Part and in Schedule II shall be deemed not to include property

(a) the cost of which would be deductible in computing the taxpayer's income if the Act were read without reference to sections 66 to 66.4 of the Act;

(a.1) the cost of which is included in the taxpayer's Canadian renewable and conservation expense (within the meaning assigned by section 1219);

(b) that is described in the taxpayer's inventory;

(c) that was not acquired by the taxpayer for the purpose of gaining or producing income;

(d) that was acquired by an expenditure in respect of which the taxpayer is allowed a deduction in computing income under section 37 of the Act;

(e) that was acquired by the taxpayer after November 12, 1981, other than property acquired from a person with whom the taxpayer was not dealing at arm's length (otherwise than by virtue of a right referred to in paragraph 251(5)(b) of the Act) at the time the property was acquired if the property was acquired in circumstances where subsection (14) applies, and is

(i) a print, etching, drawing, painting, sculpture, or other similar work of art, the cost of which to the taxpayer was not less than $200,

(ii) a hand-woven tapestry or carpet or a handmade appliqué, the cost of which to the taxpayer was not less than $215 per square metre,

(iii) an engraving, etching, lithograph, woodcut, map or chart, made before 1900, or

(iv) antique furniture, or any other antique object, produced more than 100 years before the date it was acquired, the cost of which to the taxpayer was not less than $1,000,

other than any property described in subparagraph (i) or (ii) where the individual who created the property was a Canadian (within the meaning assigned by paragraph $1104(10)(a)$) at the time the property was created;

(f) that is property referred to in paragraph $18(1)(l)$ of the Act acquired after December 31, 1974, an outlay or expense for the use or maintenance of which is not deductible by virtue of that paragraph;

(g) in respect of which an allowance is claimed and permitted under Part XVII;

(h) that is a passenger automobile acquired after June 13, 1963 and before January 1, 1966, the cost to the taxpayer of which, minus the initial transportation charges and retail sales tax in respect thereof, exceeded $5,000, unless the automobile was acquired by a person before June 14, 1963 and has by one or more transactions between persons not dealing at arm's length become vested in the taxpayer;

(i) that was deemed by section 18 of the *Income Tax Act*, as enacted by the Statutes of Canada, 1958, Chapter 32, subsection 8(1), to have been acquired by the taxpayer and that did not vest in the taxpayer before the 1963 taxation year;

(j) of a life insurer, that is property used by it in, or held by it in the course of, carrying on an insurance business outside Canada; or

(k) that is linefill in a pipeline.

[¶2006]

Partnership Property

(1a) Where the taxpayer is a member of a partnership, the classes of property described in this Part and in Schedule II shall be deemed not to include any property that is an interest of the taxpayer in depreciable property that is partnership property of the partnership.

[¶2008]

Land

(2) The classes of property described in Schedule II shall be deemed not to include the land upon which a property described therein was constructed or is situated.

[¶2010]

Non-Residents

(3) Where the taxpayer is a non-resident person, the classes of property described in this Part and Schedule II shall, except for the purpose of determining the foreign accrual property income of the taxpayer for the purposes of subdivision i of Division B of Part I of the Act, be deemed not to include property that is situated outside Canada.

[¶2012]

Improvements or Alterations to Leased Properties

(4) Subject to subsection (5), "capital cost" for the purposes of paragraph 1100(1)(b) includes any amount expended by a taxpayer for or in respect of an improvement or alteration to a leased property.

[¶2014]

Buildings on Leased Properties

(5) Where the taxpayer has a leasehold interest in a property, a reference in Schedule II to a property that is a building or other structure shall include a reference to that leasehold interest to the extent that that interest

(a) was acquired by reason of the fact that the taxpayer

    (i) erected a building or structure on leased land,

    (ii) made an addition to a leased building or structure, or

    (iii) made alterations to a leased building or structure that substantially changed the nature of the property; or

(b) was acquired after 1975 or, in the case of any property of Class 31 or 32, after November 18, 1974, from a former lessee who had acquired it by reason of the fact that he or a lessee before him

    (i) erected a building or structure on leased land,

    (ii) made an addition to a leased building or structure, or

    (iii) made alterations to a leased building or structure that substantially changed the nature of the property.

[¶2015]

(5.1) Where a taxpayer has acquired a property that would, if the property had been acquired by a person with whom the taxpayer was not dealing at arm's length at the time the property was acquired by the taxpayer, be described in paragraph (5)(a) or (b) in respect of that person, a reference in Schedule II to a property that is a building or other structure shall, in respect of the taxpayer, include a reference to that property.

[¶2016]

Leasehold Interests Acquired Before 1949

(6) For the purposes of paragraphs $2(a)$ and (b) of Schedule III, where an item of capital cost has been incurred before the commencement of the taxpayer's 1949 taxation year, there shall be added to the capital cost of each item the amount that has been allowed in respect thereof as depreciation under the *Income War Tax Act* and has been deducted from the original cost to arrive at the capital cost of the item.

[¶2018]

River Improvements

(7) For the purposes of paragraph $1100(1)(f)$, capital cost includes an amount expended on river improvements by the taxpayer for the purpose of facilitating the removal of timber from a timber limit.

[¶2020]

Electrical Plant Used for Mining

(8) Where the generating or distributing equipment and plant (including structures) of a producer or distributor of electrical energy were acquired for the purpose of providing power to a consumer for use by the consumer in the operation in Canada of a mine, ore mill, smelter, metal refinery or any combination thereof and at least 80 per cent of the producer's or distributor's output of electrical energy

(a) for his 1948 and 1949 taxation years, or

(b) for his first two taxation years in which he sold power,

whichever period is later, was sold to the consumer for that purpose, the property shall be included in

(c) Class 10 in Schedule II if it is property acquired

(i) before 1988, or

(ii) before 1990

(A) pursuant to an obligation in writing entered into by the taxpayer before June 18, 1987,

(B) that was under construction by or on behalf of the taxpayer on June 18, 1987, or

(C) that is machinery or equipment that is a fixed and integral part of a building, structure, plant facility or other property that was under construction by or on behalf of the taxpayer on June 18, 1987, or

(d) Class 41 in Schedule II in any other case, except where the property would otherwise be included in Class 43.1 in Schedule II and the taxpayer has, by a letter filed with the return of income of the taxpayer filed with the Minister in accordance with section 150 of the Act for the taxation year in which the property was acquired, elected to include the property in Class 43.1.

[¶2022]

(9) Where a taxpayer has acquired generating or distributing equipment and plant (including structures) for the purpose of providing power for his own consumption in operating a mine, ore mill, smelter, metal refinery or any combination thereof and at least 80 per cent of the output of electrical energy was so used

(a) in his 1948 and 1949 taxation years, or

(b) in the first two taxation years in which he so produced power,

whichever period is the later, the property shall be included in

(c) Class 10 in Schedule II if it is property acquired

(i) before 1988, or

(ii) before 1990

(A) pursuant to an obligation in writing entered into by the taxpayer before June 18, 1987,

(B) that was under construction by or on behalf of the taxpayer on June 18, 1987, or

(C) that is machinery or equipment that is a fixed and integral part of a building, structure, plant facility or other property that was under construction by or on behalf of the taxpayer on June 18, 1987, or

(d) Class 41 in Schedule II in any other case, except where the property would otherwise be included in Class 43.1 in Schedule II and the taxpayer has, by a letter filed with the return of income of the taxpayer filed with the Minister in accordance with section 150 of the Act for the taxation year in which the property was acquired, elected to include the property in Class 43.1.

[¶2024]

(9.1) In their application to generating or distributing equipment and plant (including structures) that were acquired by the taxpayer before November 8, 1969, subsections (8) and (9) shall be read without reference to a "metal refinery".

[¶2026]

(9.2) Where a taxpayer acquires property after November 7, 1969 from a person with whom he was not dealing at arm's length that is property referred to in subsection (8) or (9), notwithstanding those subsections, that property shall not be included in Class 10 in Schedule II by the taxpayer unless the property had been included in that class by the person from whom it was acquired, by virtue of subsection (8) or (9) as it read in its application before November 8, 1969.

[¶2028]

Railway Companies

(10) For the purposes of section 36 of the Act, where a taxpayer is deemed to have acquired depreciable property of a prescribed class at the time a repair, replacement, alteration or renovation expenditure described therein was incurred,

(*a*) if the expenditure was incurred by the taxpayer before May 26, 1976, the class hereby prescribed is Class 4 in Schedule II; and

(*b*) if the expenditure was incurred by the taxpayer after May 25, 1976, the class hereby prescribed is the class in Schedule II in which the depreciable property that was repaired, replaced, altered or renovated would be included if such property had been acquired at the time the expenditure was incurred.

[¶2030]

Passenger Automobiles

(11) In paragraph (1)(*h*),

"*cost to the taxpayer*" of an automobile means, except as provided in subsections (12) and (13),

(*a*) except in any case coming under paragraph (*b*) or (*c*), the capital cost to the taxpayer of the automobile,

(*b*) except in any case coming under paragraph (*c*), where the automobile was acquired by a person (in this section referred to as the "original owner") after June 13, 1963, and has, by one or more transactions between persons not dealing at arm's length, become vested in the taxpayer, the greater of

(i) the actual cost to the taxpayer, and

(ii) the actual cost to the original owner, and

(*c*) where the automobile was acquired by the taxpayer outside Canada for use in connection with a permanent establishment, as defined for the purposes of Part IV or Part XXVI, outside Canada, the lesser of

(i) the actual cost to the taxpayer, and

(ii) the amount that such an automobile would ordinarily cost the taxpayer if he purchased it from a dealer in automobiles in Canada for use in Canada;

"initial transportation charges" in respect of an automobile means the costs incurred by a dealer in automobiles for transporting the automobile (before it had been used for any purpose whatever) from,

(*a*) in the case of an automobile manufactured in Canada, the manufacturer's plant, and

(*b*) in any other case, the place in Canada, if any, at which the automobile was received or stored by a wholesale distributor,

to the dealer's place of business;

"passenger automobile" means a vehicle, other than an ambulance or hearse, that was designed to carry not more than nine persons, and that is

(*a*) an automobile designed primarily for carrying persons on highways and streets, except an automobile that

(i) is designed to accommodate and is equipped with auxiliary folding seats installed between the front and the rear seats,

(ii) was acquired by a person carrying on the business of operating a taxi or automobile rental service, or arranging and managing funerals, for use in such business, and

(iii) is not a vehicle described in paragraph (*b*), or

(*b*) a station wagon or substantially similar vehicle;

"retail sales tax" in respect of an automobile means the aggregate of municipal and provincial retail sales taxes payable in respect of the purchase of the automobile by the taxpayer.

[¶2032]

(12) For the purposes of paragraph (1)(*h*), where an automobile is owned by two or more persons or by partners, a reference to "cost to the taxpayer" shall be deemed to be a reference to the aggregate of the cost, as defined in subsection (11), to each such person or partner.

[¶2034]

(13) In determining the cost to the taxpayer for the purposes of paragraph (1)(*h*), subsection 13(7) of the Act shall not apply unless the automobile was acquired by gift.

[¶2036]

Property Acquired by Transfer, Amalgamation or Winding-Up

(14) For the purposes of this Part and Schedule II, where a property is acquired by a taxpayer

(*a*) in the course of a reorganization in respect of which, if a dividend were received by a corporation in the course of the reorganization, subsection 55(2) of the Act would not be applicable to the dividend by reason of the application of paragraph 55(3)(*b*) of the Act, or

(*a*.1) [Revoked.]

(*b*) [Revoked.]

(*c*) [Revoked.]

(*d*) from a person with whom the taxpayer was not dealing at arm's length (otherwise than by virtue of a right referred to in paragraph 251(5)(*b*) of the Act) at the time the property was acquired, and

(*e*) [Revoked.]

the property, immediately before it was so acquired by the taxpayer, was property of a prescribed class or a separate prescribed class of the person from whom it was so acquired, the property shall be deemed to be property of that same prescribed class or separate prescribed class, as the case may be, of the taxpayer.

[¶2037]

(14.1) For the purposes of this Part and Schedule II, where a taxpayer has acquired, after May 25, 1976, property of a class in Schedule II (in this subsection referred to as the "present class") that had been previously owned before May 26, 1976 by the taxpayer or by a person with whom the taxpayer was not dealing at arm's length (otherwise than by virtue of a right referred to in paragraph 251(5)(*b*) of the Act) at the time the property was acquired, and at the time the property was previously so owned it was a property of a different class in Schedule II (in this subsection referred to as the "former class"), the property shall be deemed to be property of the former class and not property of the present class.

[¶2038]

Townsite Costs

(14.2) For the purpose of paragraph 13(7.5)(*a*) of the Act, a property is prescribed in respect of a taxpayer where the property would, if it had been acquired by the taxpayer, be property included in Class 10 in Schedule II because of paragraph (1) of that Class.

[¶2039]

Surface Construction and Bridges

(14.3) For the purpose of paragraph 13(7.5)(*b*) of the Act, prescribed property is any of

(*a*) a road (other than a specified temporary access road), sidewalk, airplane runway, parking area, storage area or similar surface construction;

(*b*) a bridge; and

(*c*) a property that is ancillary to any property described in paragraph (*a*) or (*b*).

[¶2040]

Manufacturing and Processing Enterprises

(**15**) For the purposes of subsection 13(10) of the Act,

(*a*) property is hereby prescribed that is

(i) a building included in Class 3 or 6 in Schedule II, or

(ii) machinery or equipment included in Class 8 in Schedule II,

except

(iii) property that may reasonably be regarded as having been acquired for the purpose of producing coal from a coal mine or oil, gas, metals or industrial minerals from a resource referred to in section 1201 as it read immediately before it was repealed by section 2 of Order in Council P.C. 1975-1323 of June 12, 1975, or

(iv) property acquired for use outside Canada; and

(*b*) a business carried on by the taxpayer is hereby prescribed as a manufacturing or processing business if,

(i) for the fiscal period in which the property was acquired, or

(ii) for the fiscal period in which a reasonable volume of business was first carried on,

whichever was later, the revenue received by the taxpayer, in the course of carrying on the business from

(iii) the sale of goods processed or manufactured by the taxpayer in Canada,

(iv) the leasing or renting of goods that were processed or manufactured by the taxpayer in Canada,

(v) advertisements in a newspaper or magazine that was produced by the taxpayer in Canada, and

(vi) construction carried on by the taxpayer in Canada,

was not less than $\frac{2}{3}$ of the revenue of the business for the period.

[¶2042]

(**16**) For the purposes of paragraph (15)(*b*), "revenue" means gross revenue minus the aggregate of

(*a*) amounts that were paid or credited in the period, to customers of the business, in relation to such revenue as a bonus, rebate or discount or for returned or damaged goods; and

(b) amounts included therein by virtue of section 13 or subsection 23(1) of the Act.

[¶2044]

Recreational Property

(17) Property referred to in paragraph (1)(f) does not include

(a) any property that the taxpayer was obligated to acquire under the terms of an agreement in writing entered into before November 13, 1974; or

(b) any property the construction of which was

(i) commenced by the taxpayer before November 13, 1974 or commenced under an agreement in writing entered into by the taxpayer before November 13, 1974, and

(ii) completed substantially according to plans and specifications agreed to by the taxpayer before November 13, 1974.

(18) [Repealed.]

[¶2048]

Additions and Alterations

(19) For the purposes of this Part and Schedule II, where

(a) a taxpayer acquired a property that is included in a class in Schedule II (in this subsection referred to as the "actual class"),

(b) the taxpayer acquires property that is an addition or alteration to the property referred to in paragraph (a),

(c) the property that is the addition or alteration referred to in paragraph (b) would have been property of the actual class if it had been acquired by the taxpayer at the time he acquired the property referred to in paragraph (a), and

(d) the property referred to in paragraph (a) would have been property of a class in Schedule II (in this subsection referred to as the "present class") that is different from the actual class if it had been acquired by the taxpayer at the time he acquired the addition or alteration referred to in paragraph (b),

the addition or alteration referred to in paragraph (b) shall, except as otherwise provided in this Part or in Schedule II, be deemed to be an acquisition by the taxpayer of property of the present class.

[¶2050]

Non-arm's Length Exception

(20) For the purposes of subsections 1100(2.2) and (19), 1101(1ad) and 1102(14) (in this subsection referred to as the "relevant subsections"), where, but for this subsection, a taxpayer would be considered to be dealing not at arm's length with another person as a result of a transaction or series of transactions the principal purpose of which may reasonably be considered to have been to cause one or more of the relevant subsections to apply in respect of the acquisition of a property, the taxpayer shall be considered to be dealing at arm's length with the other person in respect of the acquisition of that property.

[¶2051]

(21) Where a taxpayer has acquired a property described in Class 43.1 of Schedule II in circumstances in which clauses $(b)(iii)(A)$ and (B) or $(e)(iii)(A)$ and (B) of that class apply,

(a) the portion of the property, determined by reference to capital cost, that is equal to or less than the capital cost of the property to the person from whom the property was acquired, is included in that class; and

(b) the portion of the property, if any, determined by reference to capital cost, that is in excess of the capital cost of the property to the person from whom it was acquired, shall not be included in that class.

DIVISION IV
INCLUSIONS IN AND TRANSFERS BETWEEN CLASSES

[¶2052]

ELECTIONS TO INCLUDE PROPERTIES IN CLASS 1

1103. **(1)** In respect of properties otherwise included in any of Classes 2 to 10, 11 and 12 in Schedule II, a taxpayer may elect to include in Class 1 in Schedule II all such properties acquired for the purpose of gaining or producing income from the same business.

[¶2054]

Elections to Include Properties in Class 2, 4 or 17

(2) Where the chief depreciable properties of a taxpayer are included in Class 2, 4 or 17 in Schedule II, the taxpayer may elect to include in Class 2, 4 or 17 in Schedule II, as the case may be, a property that would otherwise be included in another class in Schedule II and that was acquired by him before May 26, 1976 for the purpose of gaining or producing income from the same business as that for which those properties otherwise included in the said Class 2, 4 or 17 were acquired.

[¶2056]

Elections to Include Properties in Class 8

(2a) In respect of properties otherwise included in Class 19 or 21 in Schedule II, a taxpayer may, by letter attached to the return of his income for a taxation year filed with the Minister in accordance with section 150 of the Act, elect to include in Class 8 in Schedule II all properties of the said Class 19 or all properties of the said Class 21, as the case may be, owned by him at the commencement of the year.

[¶2058]

Elections to Include Properties in Class 37

(2b) In respect of properties that would have been included in Class 37 in Schedule II had they been acquired after the date on which Class 37 became effective, a taxpayer may, by letter attached to the return of his income for a taxation year filed with the Minister in accordance with section 150 of the Act, elect to include in Class 37 all such properties acquired by the taxpayer before that date.

[¶2060]

Elections to Make Certain Transfers

(2c) Where a taxpayer has acquired, after May 25, 1976, all or any part of a property of a class in Schedule II (in this subsection referred to as the "present class") and the property or part thereof, if it had been acquired before May 26, 1976, would have been property of a different class in Schedule II (in this subsection referred to as the "former class") and

(*a*) he was obligated to acquire the property under the terms of an agreement in writing entered into before May 26, 1976,

(*b*) he commenced the construction, manufacture or production of the property before May 26, 1976 or the construction, manufacture or production of the property was commenced under an agreement in writing entered into by him before May 26, 1976, or

(*c*) he acquired the property on or before December 31, 1976 or he was obligated to acquire the property under the terms of an agreement in writing entered into on or before December 31, 1976, if

(i) arrangements, evidenced by writing, respecting the acquisition, construction, manufacture or production of the property had been substantially advanced before May 26, 1976, and

(ii) he had, before May 26, 1976, demonstrated a *bona fide* intention to acquire the property,

the taxpayer may, by letter attached to the return of his income filed with the Minister in accordance with section 150 of the Act, for the taxation year in which the property was acquired or for the immediately following taxation year, elect to transfer in the year of acquisition

(d) the property or the part thereof, acquired after May 25, 1976, from the present class to the former class; or

(e) the part of the property acquired before May 26, 1976, from the former class to the present class.

[¶2062]

(**2d**) Where a taxpayer has

(a) disposed of a property (in this subsection referred to as the "former property") of a class in Schedule II (in this subsection referred to as the "former class"), and

(b) before the end of the taxation year in which the former property was disposed of, acquired property (in this subsection referred to as the "new property") of a class in Schedule II (in this subsection referred to as the "present class") and the present class is neither

(i) the former class, nor

(ii) a separate class described in section 1101, other than subsection 1101(5d),

such that

(c) if the former property had been acquired at the time that the new property was acquired and from the person from whom the new property was acquired, the former property would have been included in the present class, and

(d) if the new property had been acquired at the time that the former property was acquired and from the person from whom the former property was acquired, the new property would have been included in the former class,

the taxpayer may, by letter attached to the return of income of the taxpayer filed with the Minister in accordance with section 150 of the Act in respect of the taxation year in which the former property was disposed of, elect to transfer the former property from the former class to the present class in the year of its disposition and, for greater certainty, the transfer shall be considered to have been made before the disposition of the property.

[¶2064]

Transfers from Class 40 to Class 10

(**2e**) For the purposes of this Part and Schedule II, where property of a taxpayer would otherwise be included in Class 40 in Schedule II, all such properties owned by the taxpayer shall be transferred from Class 40 to Class 10 immediately after the commencement of the first taxation year of the taxpayer commencing after 1989.

[¶2066]

Elections to Include Properties in Class 1, 3 or 6

(2f) In respect of properties otherwise included in Class 20 in Schedule II, a taxpayer may, by letter attached to the return of income of the taxpayer for a taxation year filed with the Minister in accordance with section 150 of the Act, elect to include in Class 1, 3 or 6 in Schedule II, as specified in the letter, all properties of Class 20 in Schedule II owned by the taxpayer at the commencement of the year.

[¶2067]

Transfers to Class 8 or Class 10

Draft Regulation

Capital Cost Allowance (March 16, 2001)

The heading before subsection 1103(2g) of the Regulations is replaced by the following:

Transfers to Class 8, Class 10 or Class 43

Applicable: To property acquired after February 27, 2000.
   For the purpose of subsection 1103(2g) of the Income Tax Regulations, an election that is in respect of property described in subsection 1101(5s) of the Regulations is deemed to have been made in accordance with subsection 1105(5q) of the Income Tax Regulations.

(2g) For the purposes of this Part and Schedule II, where one or more properties of a taxpayer are included in a separate class pursuant to an election filed by the taxpayer in accordance with subsection 1101(5q), all the properties in that class immediately after the beginning of the taxpayer's fifth taxation year beginning after the end of the first taxation year in which a property of the class became available for use by the taxpayer for the purposes of subsection 13(26) of the Act shall be transferred immediately after the beginning of that fifth taxation year from the separate class to the class in which the property would, but for the election, have been included.

[¶2068]

Elections Not to Include Properties in Class 44

(2h) A taxpayer may, by letter attached to the taxpayer's return of income filed with the Minister in accordance with section 150 of the Act for the taxation year in which a property was acquired, elect not to include the property in Class 44 in Schedule II.

Draft Regulation

Capital Cost Allowance (March 16, 2001)

Section 1103 of the Regulations is amended by adding the following after subsection (2h):

Election to Include Properties in Class 35

(2i) In respect of any property otherwise included in Class 7 in Schedule II because of paragraph (*h*) of that Class and to which paragraph 1100(1)(*z*.1a) and subsection 1101(5d), or paragraph 1100(1)(*z*.1c) and subsection 1101(5d.2), would apply if Class 35 of that Schedule applied to the property, the taxpayer may (by letter attached to the taxpayer's return of income filed with the Minister in accordance with section 150 of the Act for the taxation year in which the property is acquired) elect to include the property in Class 35 rather than in Class 7.

Applicable: Subject to section 13, to property acquired after February 27, 2000.

Explanatory Note: New subsection 1103(2i) is consequential to new paragraph (*h*) of Class 7 (15% CCA rate) and provides an election under which a taxpayer may include certain railway assets in Class 35 (7% CCA rate) rather than in Class 7. This election may be made only in respect of railway cars and railway suspension devices described in paragraph (*h*) of Class 7 that are acquired after February 27, 2000. Further, such property only qualifies to be placed in Class 35 under this election if the property would have been eligible for an additional 6% CCA allowance under paragraph 1100(1)(*z*.1a) and subsection 1101(5d), or paragraph 1100(1)(*z*.1c) and subsection 1101(5d.2), if Class 35 had applied to the property. While property to which subsection 1103(2i) applies is eligible for a combined CCA rate of 13% (7% + 6%) rather than the 15% CCA rate available to Class 7 property, such property is "exempt property" for the purposes of the specified leasing property rules in subsection 1100(1.13) of the Regulations.

[¶2069]

Election Rules

(3) To be effective in respect of a taxation year, an election under this section must be made not later than the last day on which the taxpayer may file a return of his income for the taxation year in accordance with section 150 of the Act.

[¶2070]

(4) An election under paragraph 1102(8)(*d*) or (9)(*d*) or this section shall be effective from the first day of the taxation year in respect of which the election is made and shall continue to be effective for all subsequent taxation years.

[¶2072]

(5) An election under subsection (1) or (2) shall be made by registered letter addressed to the District Office at which the taxpayer customarily files the returns required by section 150 of the Act.

DIVISION V
INTERPRETATION

[¶2076]

DEFINITIONS

1104. **(1)** Where the taxpayer is an individual and his income for the taxation year includes income from a business the fiscal period of which does not coincide with the calendar year, in respect of the depreciable properties acquired for the purpose of gaining or producing income from the business, a reference in this Part to

"end of the taxation year" shall be deemed to be a reference to the end of the fiscal period of the business; and

"taxation year" shall be deemed to be a reference to the fiscal period of the business.

[¶2078]

(2) In this Part and in Schedule II,

"certified feature film" means a motion picture film certified by the Minister of Communications to be a film of not less than 75 minutes running time in respect of which all photography or art work specifically required for the production thereof and all film editing therefor were commenced after November 18, 1974, and either the film was completed before May 26, 1976, or the photography or art work was commenced before May 26, 1976, and certified by him to be

(a) a film the production of which is contemplated in a coproduction agreement entered into between Canada and another country, or

(b) a film in respect of which

(i) the person who performed the duties of producer was a Canadian,

(ii) no fewer than $^2/_3$ in number of all the persons each of whom

(A) was a person who performed the duties of director, screenwriter, music composer, art director, picture editor or director of photography, or

(B) was the individual in respect of whose services as an actor or actress in respect of the film the highest remuneration or the second highest remuneration was paid or payable,

were Canadians,

(iii) not less than 75 per cent of the aggregate of the remuneration paid or payable to persons for services provided in respect of the film (other than remuneration paid or payable to or in respect of the persons referred to in subparagraphs (i) and (ii) or remuneration paid or payable for processing and final preparation of the film) was paid or payable to Canadians,

(iv) not less than 75 per cent of the aggregate of costs incurred for processing and final preparation of the film including laboratory work, sound recording, sound editing and picture editing (other than remuneration paid or payable to or in respect of persons referred to in subparagraphs (i), (ii) and (iii)), was incurred in respect of services rendered in Canada, and

(v) the copyright protecting its use in Canada is beneficially owned

(A) by a person who is either a Canadian or a corporation incorporated under the laws of Canada or a province, or

(B) jointly or otherwise by two or more persons described in clause (A),

other than a film

(c) acquired after the day that is the earlier of

(i) the day of its first commercial use, and

(ii) 12 months after the day the principal photography thereof is completed, or

(d) in respect of which certification under this definition has been revoked by the Minister of Communications as provided in paragraph (10)(b);

"*certified production*", in respect of a particular taxation year, means a motion picture film or video tape certified by the Minister of Communications to be a film or tape in respect of which all photography, taping or art work required specifically for the production thereof and all film or tape editing therefor were commenced after May 25, 1976, certified by him to be a film or tape in respect of which the principal photography or taping thereof was commenced before the end of the particular taxation year or was completed no later than 60 days after the end of that year and certified by him to be

(a) a film or tape the production of which is contemplated in a coproduction agreement entered into between Canada and another country, or

(b) a film or tape in respect of which

(i) the individual who performed the duties of producer was a Canadian,

(ii) the Minister of Communications has allotted not less than an aggregate of six units of production, not less than two of which were allotted by virtue of clause (A) or (B) and not less than one of which was allotted by virtue of clause (C) or (D), for individuals who provided services in respect of the film or tape, in the following manner:

(A) for the director, two units of production,

¶2078

(B) for the screenwriter, two units of production,

(C) for the actor or actress in respect of whose services for the film or tape the highest remuneration was paid or payable (unless in the opinion of the Minister of Communications the individual did not perform a major role in the film or tape), one unit of production,

(D) for the actor or actress in respect of whose services for the film or tape the second highest remuneration was paid or payable (unless in the opinion of the Minister of Communications the individual did not perform a major role in the film or tape), one unit of production,

(E) for the art director, one unit of production,

(F) for the director of photography, one unit of production,

(G) for the music composer, one unit of production, and

(H) for the picture editor, one unit of production,

shall be allotted, provided the individual in respect of such allotment was a Canadian,

(iii) not less than 75 per cent of the aggregate of all costs (other than costs determined by reference to the amount of income from the film or tape) paid or payable to persons for services provided in respect of producing the film or tape (other than remuneration paid or payable to, or in respect of, individuals referred to in subparagraph (i) or (ii), costs referred to in subparagraph (iv) incurred for processing and final preparation of the film or tape, and amounts paid or payable in respect of insurance, financing, brokerage, legal and accounting fees and similar amounts) was paid or payable to, or in respect of services provided by, Canadians, and

(iv) not less than 75 per cent of the aggregate of all costs (other than costs determined by reference to the amount of income from the film or tape) incurred for processing and final preparation of the film or tape, including laboratory work, sound re-recording, sound editing and picture editing (other than remuneration paid or payable to, or in respect of, individuals referred to in subparagraph (i) or (ii)) was incurred in respect of services provided in Canada,

other than a film or tape

(*c*) acquired after the day that is the earlier of

(i) the day of its first commercial use, and

(ii) 12 months after the day the principal photography or taping thereof is completed,

(*d*) acquired by a taxpayer who has not paid in cash, as of the end of the particular taxation year, to the person from whom he acquired the film or tape, at least 5 per cent of the capital cost to the taxpayer of the film or tape as of the end of the year,

¶2078

(*e*) acquired by a taxpayer who has issued in payment or part payment thereof, a bond, debenture, bill, note, mortgage or similar obligation in respect of which an amount is not due until a time that is more than four years after the end of the taxation year in which the taxpayer acquired the film or tape,

(*f*) acquired from a non-resident, or

(*g*) in respect of which certification under this definition has been revoked by the Minister of Communications as provided in paragraph (10)(*b*),

and, for the purposes of the application of this definition,

(*h*) in respect of a film or tape acquired in 1987, other than a film or tape in respect of which paragraph (*i*) applies, the reference in this definition to "commenced before the end of the particular taxation year or was completed no later than 60 days after the end of that year" shall be read as a reference to "commenced before the end of 1987 or was completed before July, 1988", and

(*i*) in respect of a film or tape acquired in 1987 or 1988 that is included in paragraph (*n*) of Class 12 in Schedule II and that is part of a series of films or tapes that includes another property included in that paragraph, the reference in this definition to "commenced before the end of the particular taxation year or was completed no later then 60 days after the end of that year" shall be read as a reference to "completed before 1989";

"*computer software*" includes systems software and a right or licence to use computer software;

Draft Regulation

Capital Cost Allowance (July 9, 2005)

Subsection 1104(2) of the Regulations is amended by adding the following in alphabetical order:

"*data network infrastructure equipment*" means network infrastructure equipment that controls, transfers, modulates or directs data, and that operates in support of telecommunications applications such as e-mail, instant messaging, audio- and video-over-Internet Protocol or Web browsing, Web searching and Web hosting, including data switches, multiplexers, routers, remote access servers, hubs, domain name servers, and modems, but does not include

(*a*) network equipment (other than radio network equipment) that operates in support of telecommunications applications, if the bandwidth made available by that equipment to a single end-user of the network is 64 kilobits per second or less in either direction,

(*b*) radio network equipment that operates in support of wireless telecommunications applications unless the equipment supports digital transmission on a radio channel,

(*c*) network equipment that operates in support of broadcast telecommunications applications and that is unidirectional,

¶2078

(*d*) network equipment that is end-user equipment, including telephone sets, personal digital assistants and facsimile transmission devices,

(*e*) equipment that is described in paragraph (*f*.2) or (v) of Class 10 or in Class 45,

(*f*) wires or cables, or similar property, and

(*g*) structures;

Applicable: Deemed to have come into force on March 23, 2004.

Explanatory Note: See the Regulatory Impact Analysis Statement following the addition of subparagraphs 1100(1)(*a*)(xxxi) and (xxxii).

"designated overburden removal cost" of a taxpayer means any cost incurred by him in respect of clearing or removing overburden from a mine in Canada owned or operated by him where the cost

(*a*) was incurred after November 16, 1978 and before 1988,

(*b*) was incurred after the mine came into production in reasonable commercial quantities,

(*c*) as of the end of the taxation year in which the cost was incurred, has not been deducted by the taxpayer in computing his income, and

(*d*) is not deductible, in whole or in part, by the taxpayer in computing his income for a taxation year subsequent to the taxation year in which the cost was incurred, other than by virtue of paragraph 20(1)(*a*) of the Act;

"designated underground storage cost" of a taxpayer means any cost incurred by him after December 11, 1979 in respect of developing a well, mine or other similar underground property for the storage in Canada of petroleum, natural gas or other related hydrocarbons;

"gas or oil well equipment" includes

(*a*) equipment, structures and pipelines, other than a well casing, acquired to be used in a gas or oil field in the production therefrom of natural gas or crude oil, and

(*b*) a pipeline acquired to be used solely for transmitting gas to a natural gas processing plant,

but does not include

(*c*) equipment or structures acquired for the refining of oil or the processing of natural gas including the separation therefrom of liquid hydrocarbons, sulphur or other joint products or by-products, or

(*d*) a pipeline for removal or for collection for immediate removal of natural gas or crude oil from a gas or oil field except a pipeline referred to in paragraph (*b*);

"general-purpose electronic data processing equipment" means electronic equipment that, in its operation, requires an internally stored computer program that

¶2078

(*a*) is executed by the equipment,

(*b*) can be altered by the user of the equipment,

(*c*) instructs the equipment to read and select, alter or store data from an external medium such as a card, disk or tape, and

(*d*) depends upon the characteristics of the data being processed to determine the sequence of its execution;

"*ore*" includes ore from a mineral resource that has been processed to any stage that is prior to the prime metal stage or its equivalent;

"*railway system*" includes a railway owned or operated by a common carrier, together with all buildings, rolling stock, equipment and other properties pertaining thereto, but does not include a tramway;

"*specified temporary access road*" means

(*a*) a temporary access road to an oil or gas well in Canada, and

(*b*) a temporary access road the cost of which would, if the definition "Canadian exploration expense" in subsection 66.1(6) of the Act were read without reference to paragraph (*l*) of that definition, be a Canadian exploration expense because of paragraph (*f*) or (*g*) of that definition;

"*systems software*" means a combination of computer programs and associated procedures, related technical documentation and data that

(*a*) performs compilation, assembly, mapping, management or processing of other programs,

(*b*) facilitates the functioning of a computer system by other programs,

(*c*) provides service or utility functions such as media conversion, sorting, merging, system accounting, performance measurement, system diagnostics or programming aids,

(*d*) provides general support functions such as data management, report generation or security control, or

(*e*) provides general capability to meet widespread categories of problem solving or processing requirements where the specific attributes of the work to be performed are introduced mainly in the form of parameters, constants or descriptors rather than in program logic,

and includes a right or licence to use such a combination of computer programs and associated procedures, related technical documentation and data;

"*tar sands ore*" means ore extracted from a deposit of bituminous sands or oil shales;

"*telegraph system*" includes the buildings, structures, general plant and communication and other equipment pertaining thereto;

¶2078

"telephone system" includes the buildings, structures, general plant and communication and other equipment pertaining thereto;

"television commercial message" means a commercial message as defined in the Television Broadcasting Regulations, 1987 made under the *Broadcasting Act*;

"tramway or trolley bus system" includes the buildings, structures, rolling stock, general plant and equipment pertaining thereto and where buses other than trolley buses are operated in connection therewith includes the properties pertaining to those bus operations.

[¶2080]

(3) Except as otherwise provided in subsection (6), in this Part and in Schedules II and V,

"industrial mineral mine" includes a peat bog or deposit of peat but does not include a mineral resource;

"mineral" includes peat;

"mining" includes the harvesting of peat.

(4) [Revoked.]

[¶2084]

Mining

(5) For the purposes of paragraphs $1100(1)(w)$ to (ya), subsections 1101 (4a) to (4d) and Classes 10, 28 and 41 in Schedule II, a taxpayer's "income from a mine", or any expression referring to a taxpayer's income from a mine, includes income reasonably attributable to

(a) the processing by the taxpayer of

(i) ore (other than iron ore or tar sands ore) all or substantially all of which is from a mineral resource owned by the taxpayer to any stage that is not beyond the prime metal stage or its equivalent,

(ii) iron ore all or substantially all of which is from a mineral resource owned by the taxpayer to any stage that is not beyond the pellet stage or its equivalent,

(iii) tar sands ore all or substantially all of which is from a mineral resource owned by the taxpayer to any stage that is not beyond the crude oil stage or its equivalent, or

(iv) material extracted by a well, all or substantially all of which is from a deposit of bituminous sands or oil shales owned by the taxpayer, to any stage that is not beyond the crude oil stage or its equivalent;

(b) the production by the taxpayer of material from a deposit of bituminous sands or oil shales; and

(c) the transportation by the taxpayer of

(i) output, other than iron ore or tar sands ore, from a mineral resource owned by the taxpayer that has been processed by him to any stage that is not beyond the prime metal stage or its equivalent,

(ii) iron ore from a mineral resource owned by the taxpayer that has been processed by him to any stage that is not beyond the pellet stage or its equivalent, or

(iii) tar sands ore from a mineral resource owned by the taxpayer that has been processed by him to any stage that is not beyond the crude oil stage or its equivalent,

to the extent that such transportation is effected through the use of property of the taxpayer that is included in Class 10 in Schedule II because of paragraph (m) thereof or that would be so included if that paragraph were read without reference to subparagraph (v) thereof and if Class 41 in Schedule II were read without the reference therein to that paragraph.

[¶2085]

(5.1) For the purpose of Class 41 in Schedule II, a taxpayer's "gross revenue from a mine" includes

(a) revenue reasonably attributable to the processing by the taxpayer of

(i) ore (other than iron ore or tar sands ore) from a mineral resource owned by the taxpayer to any stage that is not beyond the prime metal stage or its equivalent,

(ii) iron ore from a mineral resource owned by the taxpayer to any stage that is not beyond the pellet stage or its equivalent,

(iii) tar sands ore from a mineral resource owned by the taxpayer to any stage that is not beyond the crude oil stage or its equivalent, and

(iv) material extracted by a well from a mineral resource owned by the taxpayer that is a deposit of bituminous sands or oil shales to any stage that is not beyond the crude oil stage or its equivalent;

(b) the amount, if any, by which any revenue reasonably attributable to the processing by the taxpayer of

(i) ore (other than iron ore or tar sands ore) from a mineral resource not owned by the taxpayer, to any stage that is not beyond the prime metal stage or its equivalent,

(ii) iron ore from a mineral resource not owned by the taxpayer to any stage that is not beyond the pellet stage or its equivalent,

(iii) tar sands ore from a mineral resource not owned by the taxpayer to any stage that is not beyond the crude oil stage or its equivalent, and

(iv) material extracted by a well from a mineral resource not owned by the taxpayer that is a deposit of bituminous sands or oil shales to any stage that is not beyond the crude oil stage or its equivalent exceeds the cost to the taxpayer of the ore or material processed; and

(c) revenue reasonably attributable to the production by the taxpayer of material from a deposit of bituminous sands or oil shales.

[¶2086]

(5.2) For the purpose of subsection (5.1), "gross revenue from a mine" does not include revenue reasonably attributable to the addition of diluent, for the purpose of transportation, to material extracted from a deposit of bituminous sands or oil shales.

[¶2087]

(6) For the purposes of Class 10 in Schedule II,

(a) "income from a mine" includes income reasonably attributable to the processing of

(i) ore, other than iron ore or tar sands ore, from a mineral resource not owned by the taxpayer to any stage that is not beyond the prime metal stage or its equivalent,

(ii) iron ore from a mineral resource not owned by the taxpayer to any stage that is not beyond the pellet stage or its equivalent,

(iii) tar sands ore from a mineral resource not owned by the taxpayer to any stage that is not beyond the crude oil stage or its equivalent; and

(iv) material extracted by a well from a mineral resource not owned by the taxpayer that is a deposit of bituminous sands or oil shales to any stage that is not beyond the crude oil stage or its equivalent; and

(b) "mine" includes a well for the extraction of material from a deposit of bituminous sands or oil shales or from a deposit of calcium chloride, halite or sylvite.

[¶2088]

(7) For the purposes of paragraphs 1100(1)(w) to (ya), subsections 1101(4a) to (4d) and 1102(8) and (9), section 1107 and Classes 12, 28 and 41 in Schedule II,

(a) "mine" includes

(i) a well for the extraction of material from a deposit of bituminous sands or oil shales or from a deposit of calcium chloride, halite or sylvite, and

(ii) a pit for the extraction of kaolin or tar sands ore,

but does not include

(iii) an oil or gas well, or

(iv) a sand pit, gravel pit, clay pit, shale pit, peat bog, deposit of peat or a stone quarry (other than a kaolin pit or a deposit of bituminous sands or oil shales);

(b) all wells of a taxpayer for the extraction of material from one or more deposits of calcium chloride, halite or sylvite, the material produced from which is sent to the same plant for processing, are deemed to be one mine of the taxpayer; and

(c) all wells of a taxpayer for the extraction of material from a deposit of bituminous sands or oil shales that the Minister, in consultation with the Minister of Natural Resources, determines constitutes one project, are deemed to be one mine of the taxpayer.

[¶2090]

(8) For the purposes of subsection (7), "stone quarry" includes a mine producing dimension stone or crushed rock for use as aggregates or for other construction purposes.

Draft Regulation

Natural Resources (June 9, 2003)

Section 1104 of the Regulations is amended by adding the following after subsection (8):

(8.1) For greater certainty, for the purposes of paragraphs (c) and (e) of Class 28 and paragraph (a) of Class 41 in Schedule II, production means production in reasonable commercial quantities.

Applicable: To property acquired after 1987.

Explanatory Note: Section 1104 of the Regulations provides interpretive rules for the purposes of the rules related to capital cost allowance in Part XI of the Regulations.

New subsection 1104(8) of the Regulations is added to confirm, for greater certainty, for property acquired after 1987, that the references to production from a mine in paragraphs (c) and (e) of Class 28 and paragraph (a) of Class 41, each of which deal with mining assets, are a reference back to production in reasonable commercial quantities in paragraph (b) of Class 28.

[¶2092]

Manufacturing or Processing

(9) For the purposes of subsection 1100(26) and Class 29 in Schedule II, "manufacturing or processing" does not include

(a) farming or fishing;

(b) logging;

(c) construction;

(d) operating an oil or gas well or extracting petroleum or natural gas from a natural accumulation thereof;

(e) extracting minerals from a mineral resource;

(f) processing of

(i) ore, other than iron ore or tar sands ore, from a mineral resource to any stage that is not beyond the prime metal stage or its equivalent,

(ii) iron ore from a mineral resource to any stage that is not beyond the pellet stage or its equivalent, or

(iii) tar sands ore from a mineral resource to any stage that is not beyond the crude oil stage or its equivalent;

(g) producing industrial minerals;

(h) producing or processing electrical energy or steam, for sale;

(i) processing natural gas as part of the business of selling or distributing gas in the course of operating a public utility;

(j) processing heavy crude oil recovered from a natural reservoir in Canada to a stage that is not beyond the crude oil stage or its equivalent; or

(k) Canadian field processing.

[¶2094]

Certified Films and Video Tapes

(10) For the purposes of subsection 1100(21) and the definitions "certified feature film" and "certified production" in subsection (2),

(a) "Canadian" means an individual who was, at all relevant times,

(i) a Canadian citizen as defined in the *Citizenship Act*, or

(ii) a permanent resident within the meaning of the *Immigration Act, 1976*;

(b) a motion picture film or video tape that has been certified by

(i) the Secretary of State, or

(ii) the Minister of Communications

as a certified feature film or certified production, as the case may be, may have its certification revoked by the Minister of Communications where an incorrect statement was made in the furnishing of information for the purpose of obtaining that certification and a certification that has been so revoked is void from the time of its issue;

(c) "remuneration" does not include an amount determined by reference to the amount of income from a motion picture film or video tape;

(c.1) "revenue guarantee" means a contract or other arrangement under the terms of which a taxpayer has a right to receive a minimum rental revenue or other fixed revenue in respect of a right to the use, in any manner whatever, of a certified feature film or certified production;

¶2094

(c.2) a screenwriter shall be deemed to be an individual who is a Canadian where

(i) each individual involved in the preparation of the screenplay is a Canadian, or

(ii) the principal screenwriter is an individual who is a Canadian and

(A) the screenplay for the motion picture film or video tape is based upon a work authored by a Canadian,

(B) copyright in the work subsists in Canada, and

(C) the work is published in Canada;

(d) "unit of production" means a measure used by the Minister of Communications in determining the weight to be given for each individual Canadian referred to in subparagraph (b)(ii) of the definition "certified production" in subsection (2) who provides services in respect of a motion picture film or video tape; and

(e) where each individual who performed a service in respect of a motion picture film or video tape as the

(i) director,

(ii) screenwriter,

(iii) actor or actress in respect of whose services for the film or tape the highest remuneration was paid or payable,

(iv) actor or actress in respect of whose services for the film or tape the second highest remuneration was paid or payable,

(v) art director,

(vi) director of photography,

(vii) music composer, or

(viii) picture editor

was a Canadian, the Minister of Communications shall be deemed to have allotted six units of production in respect of the film or tape for the purposes of the definition "certified production" in subsection (2).

[¶2096]

Certified Class 34 Properties

(11) For the purposes of paragraph (h) of Class 34 in Schedule II, a certificate issued under

(a) subparagraph (d)(i) of that class may be revoked by the Minister of Industry, Trade and Commerce, or

(b) subparagraph (d)(ii) or paragraph (g) of that class, as the case may be, may be revoked by the Minister of Energy, Mines and Resources

where

(c) an incorrect statement was made in the furnishing of information for the purpose of obtaining the certificate, or

(d) the taxpayer does not conform to the plan described in subparagraph (d)(i) or (d)(ii) of that class, as the case may be,

and a certificate that has been so revoked shall be void from the time of its issue.

[¶2097]

Amusement Parks

(12) For the purposes of Class 37 in Schedule II, "amusement park" means a park open to the public where amusements, rides and audio-visual attractions are permanently situated.

[¶2098]

Class 43.1 — Energy Conservation Property

(13) The definitions in this subsection apply for the purposes of this subsection and subsection (14) and Class 43.1 in Schedule II.

Draft Regulation

Capital Cost Allowance — Energy Conservation Equipment and Alternative Energy Sources (December 18, 2004)

Subsection 1104(13) of the Regulations is amended by adding the following in alphabetical order:

"*basic oxygen furnace gas*" means the gas that is produced intermittently in a basic oxygen furnace of a steel mill by the chemical reaction of carbon in molten steel and pure oxygen.

Applicable: In respect of property that is acquired after 2000.

"*bio-oil*" means liquid fuel that is created from wood waste or plant residues using a thermo-chemical conversion process that takes place in the absence of oxygen.

Applicable: In respect of property that is acquired after February 18, 2003.

"*blast furnace gas*" means the gas produced in a blast furnace of a steel mill, by the chemical reaction of carbon (in the form of coke, coal or natural gas), the oxygen in air and iron ore.

Applicable: In respect of property that is acquired after 2000.

Explanatory Note: Please see the Regulatory Impact Analysis Statement following paragraph (d) of Class 43.1 of Schedule II.

"*digester gas*" means a mixture of gases that are produced from the decomposition of organic waste in a digester and that are execrated from an eligible sewage treatment facility for that organic waste.

¶2097

"distribution equipment" means equipment (other than transmission equipment) used to distribute electrical energy generated by electrical generating equipment.

"eligible landfill site" means a landfill site that is situated in Canada, or a former landfill site that is situated in Canada, and, if a permit or licence in respect of the site is or was required under any law of Canada or of a province, for which the permit or licence has been issued.

"eligible sewage treatment facility" means a sewage treatment facility that is situated in Canada and for which a permit or licence is issued under any law of Canada or of a province.

"eligible waste management facility" means a waste management facility that is situated in Canada and for which a permit or licence is issued under any law of Canada or of a province.

"enhanced combined cycle system" means an electrical generating system in which thermal waste from one or more natural gas compressor systems is recovered and used to contribute at least 20 per cent of the energy input of a combined cycle process in order to enhance the generation of electricity), but does not include the natural gas compressor systems.

"fossil fuel" means a fuel that is petroleum, natural gas or related hydrocarbons, coal, coal gas, coke, lignite or peat.

Draft Regulation

Capital Cost Allowance — Energy Conservation Equipment and Alternative Energy Sources (December 18, 2004)

The definition "fossil fuel" in subsection 1104(13) of the Income Tax Regulations is replaced by the following:

"fossil fuel" means a fuel that is petroleum, natural gas or related hydrocarbons, basic oxygen furnace gas, blast furnace gas, coal, coke gas, coke, lignite or peat.

Applicable: In respect of property that is acquired after 2000.

Explanatory Note: Please see the Regulatory Impact Analysis Statement following paragraph (*d*) of Class 43.1 of Schedule II.

"landfill gas" means a mixture of gases that are produced from the decomposition of organic waste and that are extracted from an eligible landfill site.

"municipal waste" means the combustible portion of waste material (other than waste material that is considered to be toxic or hazardous waste pursuant to any law of Canada or of a province) that is generated in Canada and that is accepted at an eligible landfill site or an eligible waste management facility and that, when burned to generate energy, emits only those fluids or other emissions that are in compliance with the law of Canada or of a province.

¶2098

Draft Regulation

Capital Cost Allowance — Energy Conservation Equipment and Alternative Energy Sources (December 18, 2004)

Subsection 1104(13) of the Regulations is amended by adding the following in alphabetical order:

"plant residue" means the residue of plants that would, but for its use in a system to convert biomass into bio-oil, be waste material, but does not include wood waste or waste that no longer has the chemical properties of the plants of which it is a residue.

Applicable: In respect of property that is acquired after February 18, 2003.

Explanatory Note: Please see the Regulatory Impact Analysis Statement following paragraph (*d*) of Class 43.1 of Schedule II.

"solution gas" means a fossil fuel that is gas that would otherwise be flared and has been extracted from a solution of gas and produced oil.

"thermal waste" means heat energy extracted from a distinct point of rejection in an industrial process.

"transmission equipment" means equipment used to transmit more than 75 per cent of the annual electrical energy generated by electrical generating equipment, but does not include a building.

"wood waste" includes scrap wood, sawdust, wood chips, bark, limbs, saw-ends and hog fuel, but does not include residuals (known as "black liquor") from wood pulp operations and any waste that no longer has the physical or chemical properties of wood.

[¶2099]

(14) Where property of a taxpayer is not operating in the manner required by paragraph (*c*) of Class 43.1 in Schedule II solely because of a deficiency, failing or shutdown — that is beyond the control of the taxpayer — of the system of which it is part and that previously operated in the manner required by that paragraph, that property is deemed, for the purpose of that paragraph, to be operating in the manner required under that paragraph during the period of the deficiency, failing or shutdown, if the taxpayer makes all reasonable efforts to rectify the circumstances within a reasonable time.

Draft Regulation

Capital Cost Allowance (March 16, 2001)

Section 1104 of the Regulations is amended by adding the following after subsection (14):

(15) For the purpose of subsection (14), a taxpayer's system referred to in that subsection that has at any particular time operated in the manner required by paragraph (*c*) of Class 43.1 in Schedule II includes at any time after the particular time a property of another person or partnership if

---

(a) the property, if it were owned by the taxpayer, would reasonably be considered to be part of the taxpayer's system;

(b) the property utilizes steam obtained from the taxpayer's system primarily in an industrial process (other than the generation of electrical energy);

(c) the operation of the property is necessary for the taxpayer's system to operate in the manner required by paragraph (c) of Class 43.1; and

(d) at the time that the taxpayer's system first became operational, the deficiency, failing or shutdown in the operation of the property could not reasonably have been anticipated by the taxpayer to occur within five years after that time.

Applicable:　To property acquired after February 21,1994.

Explanatory Note:　Generally, subsection 1104(14) of the Regulations provides that certain property (which is part of a system that was operated at a time within the parameters set out in paragraph (c) of Class 43.1 (30% CCA rate)) will continue to be considered to so operate during a period of a deficiency, failing or shutdown of the system that is beyond the control of the taxpayer. In such circumstances, the taxpayer is required to make all reasonable efforts to rectify the difficulty causing the deficiency, failing or shutdown within a reasonable period of time.

Concern has been expressed that the reference in subsection 1104(14) to a taxpayer's "system" does not include property of another taxpayer that provides a steam host, which is necessary for the taxpayer's system to operate in the manner required by Class 43.1. Thus, in cases where a taxpayer's system is not operating in the manner required under Class 43.1 because of a deficiency, failing or shutdown of the steam host's operation, subsection 1104(14) does not apply even if the taxpayer makes all reasonable efforts to have the deficiency rectified within a reasonable time.

New subsection 1104(15) provides that the reference in subsection 1104(14) to a taxpayer's system that was previously operated in the manner required by paragraph (c) of Class 43.1 includes the related property of another person or partnership if

- the property, if it were owned by the taxpayer, would reasonably be considered to be part of the taxpayer's system,

- the property utilizes steam obtained from the taxpayer's system primarily in an industrial process (other than the generation of electrical energy),

- the operation of the property is necessary for the taxpayer's system to operate in the manner required by paragraph (c) of Class 43.1, and

- at the time that the taxpayer's system first became operational, the deficiency, failing or shutdown in the operation of the property could not reasonably have been anticipated by the taxpayer to occur within five years after that time.

This relieving amendment applies to property acquired after February 21, 1994.

¶2099

DIVISION VI
CLASSES PRESCRIBED

[¶2100]

1105.   The classes of property provided in this Part and in Schedule II are hereby prescribed for the purposes of the Act.

DIVISION VII
CERTIFICATES ISSUED BY THE MINISTER OF CANADIAN HERITAGE

[¶2102]

INTERPRETATION

1106.   **(1)** The following definitions apply in this Division and in paragraph (x) of Class 10 in Schedule II.

"application for a certificate of completion", in respect of a film or video production, means an application by a prescribed taxable Canadian corporation in respect of the production, filed with the minister of Canadian Heritage before the day (in this Division referred to as "the production's application deadline") that is the later of

(a) the day that is 24 months after the end of the corporation's taxation year in which the production's principal photography began, or

(b) the day that is 18 months after the day referred to in paragraph (a), if the corporation has filed, with the Canada Customs and Revenue Agency, and provided to the minister of Canadian Heritage a copy of, a waiver described in subparagraph $152(4)(a)(ii)$ of the Act, within the normal reassessment period for the corporation in respect of the first and second taxation years ending after the production's principal photography began.

"Canadian" means a person that is

(a) an individual who is

   (i) a citizen, as defined in subsection $2(1)$ of the *Citizenship Act*, of Canada, or

   (ii) a permanent resident, as defined in subsection $2(1)$ of the *Immigration and Refugee Protection Act*, or

(b) a corporation that is a Canadian-controlled entity, as determined under sections 26 to 28 of the *Investment Canada Act*.

"Canadian government film agency" means a federal or provincial government agency whose mandate is related to the provision of assistance to film productions in Canada.

"certificate of completion", in respect of a film or video production of a corporation, means a certificate certifying that the production has been

completed, issued by the Minister of Canadian Heritage before the day (in this Division referred to as "the production's certification deadline") that is six months after the production's application deadline.

"excluded production" means a film or video production, of a particular corporation that is a prescribed taxable Canadian corporation,

(a) in respect of which

(i) the particular corporation has not filed an application for a certificate of completion before the production's application deadline,

(ii) a certificate of completion has not been issued before the production's certification deadline,

(iii) where the production is not a treaty co-production, neither the particular corporation nor another prescribed taxable Canadian corporation related to the particular corporation

(A) is, except to the extent of an interest in the production held by a prescribed taxable Canadian corporation as a co-producer of the production or by a prescribed person, the exclusive worldwide copyright owner in the production for all commercial exploitation purposes for the 25-year period that begins at the earliest time after the production was completed that it is commercially exploitable, and

(B) controls the initial licensing of commercial exploitation,

(iv) there is not an agreement in writing, for consideration at fair market value, to have the production shown in Canada within the 2-year period that begins at the earliest time after the production was completed that it is commercially exploitable,

(A) with a corporation that is a Canadian and is a distributor of film or video productions, or

(B) with a corporation that holds a broadcasting license issued by the Canadian Radio-television and Telecommunications Commission for television markets, or

(v) distribution is made in Canada within the 2-year period that begins at the earliest time after the production was completed that it is commercially exploitable by a person that is not a Canadian, or

(b) that is

(i) news, current events or public affairs programming, or a programme that includes weather or market reports,

(ii) a talk show,

(iii) a production in respect of a game, questionnaire or contest (other than a production directed primarily at minors),

(iv) a sports event or activity,

(v) a gala presentation or an awards show,

¶2102

(vi) a production that solicits funds,

(vii) reality television,

(viii) pornography,

(ix) advertising,

(x) a production produced primarily for industrial, corporate or institutional purposes, or

(xi) a production, other than a documentary, all or substantially all of which consists of stock footage.

"producer" means a producer of a film or video production, except that it does not include a person unless the person is the individual who

(a) controls and is the central decision maker in respect of the production;

(b) is directly responsible for the acquisition of the production story or screenplay and the development, creative and financial control and exploitation of the production; and

(c) is identified in the production as being the producer of the production.

"remuneration" means remuneration other than an amount determined by reference to profits or revenues.

"twinning arrangement" means the pairing of two distinct film or video productions, one of which is a Canadian film or video production and the other of which is a foreign film or video production.

[¶2104]

Prescribed Taxable Canadian Corporation

(2) For the purposes of section 125.4 of the Act and this Division, "prescribed taxable Canadian corporation" means a taxable Canadian corporation that is a Canadian, other than a corporation that is

(a) controlled directly or indirectly in any manner whatever by one or more persons all or part of whose taxable income is exempt from tax under Part I of the Act; or

(b) a prescribed labour-sponsored venture capital corporation, as defined in section 6701.

[¶2106]

Treaty Co-production

(3) For the purpose of this Division, "treaty co-production" means a film or video production whose production is contemplated under any of the following instruments, and to which the instrument applies:

¶2104

(a) a co-production treaty entered into between Canada and another State;

(b) the Memorandum of Understanding between the Government of Canada and the Government of the Hong Kong Special Administrative Region of the People's Republic of China on Film and Television Co-Production;

(c) the Common Statement of Policy on Film, Television and Video Co-Productions between Japan and Canada;

(d) the Memorandum of Understanding between the Government of Canada and the Government of the Republic of Korea on Television Co-Production; and

(e) the Memorandum of Understanding between the Government of Canada and the Government of the Republic of Malta on Audio-Visual Relations.

[¶2110]

Canadian Film or Video Production

(4) Subject to subsections (6) to (9), for the purposes of section 125.4 of the Act, this Part and Schedule II, "Canadian film or video production" means a film or video production, other than an excluded production, of a prescribed taxable Canadian corporation in respect of which the Minister of Canadian Heritage has issued a certificate (other than a certificate that has been revoked under subsection 125.4(6) of the Act) and that is

(a) a treaty co-production; or

(b) a film or video production

    (i) whose producer is a Canadian at all times during its production,

    (ii) in respect of which the Minister of Canadian Heritage has allotted not less than six points in accordance with subsection (5),

    (iii) in respect of which not less than 75% of the total of all costs for services provided in respect of producing the production (other than excluded costs) was payable in respect of services provided to or by individuals who are Canadians, and for the purpose of this subparagraph, excluded costs are

        (A) costs determined by reference to the amount of income from the production,

        (B) remuneration payable to, or in respect of, the producer or individuals described in any of subparagraphs (5)(a)(i) to (viii) and (b)(i) to (vi) and paragraph (5)(c) (including any individuals that would be described in paragraph (5)(c) if they were Canadians),

        (C) amounts payable in respect of insurance, financing, brokerage, legal and accounting fees, and similar amounts, and

        (D) costs described in subparagraph (iv), and

(iv) in respect of which not less than 75% of the total of all costs incurred for the post-production of the production, including laboratory work, sound re-recording, sound editing and picture editing, (other than costs that are determined by reference to the amount of income from the production and remuneration that is payable to, or in respect of, the producer or individuals described in any of subparagraphs $(5)(a)(i)$ to (viii) and $(b)(i)$ to (vi) and paragraph $(5)(c)$, including any individuals that would be described in paragraph $(5)(c)$ if they were Canadians) was incurred in respect of services provided in Canada.

*   *   *

PART XII

Resource and Processing Allowances

[¶2140]

1200. For the purposes of section 65 of the Act, there may be deducted in computing the income of a taxpayer for a taxation year such of the amounts determined in accordance with sections 1201 to 1209 and 1212 as are applicable.

[¶2200]

CANADIAN RENEWABLE AND CONSERVATION EXPENSE

1219. **(1)** Subject to subsections (2) to (4), for the purpose of subsection 66.1(6) of the Act, "Canadian renewable and conservation expense" means an expense incurred by a taxpayer, and payable to a person or partnership with whom the taxpayer is dealing at arm's length, in respect of the development of a project for which it is reasonable to expect that at least 50% of the capital cost of the depreciable property to be used in the project would be the capital cost of any property that is described in Class 43.1 of Schedule II or that would be such property but for this subsection, and includes such an expense incurred by the taxpayer

(a) for the purpose of making a service connection to the project for the transmission of electricity to a purchaser of the electricity, to the extent that the expense so incurred was not incurred to acquire property of the taxpayer;

(b) for the construction of a temporary access road to the project site;

(c) for a right of access to the project site before the earliest time at which a property described in Class 43.1 of Schedule II is used in the project for the purpose of earning income;

(d) for clearing land to the extent necessary to complete the project;

(e) for process engineering for the project, including

(i) collection and analysis of site data,

(ii) calculation of energy, mass, water, or air balances,

(iii) simulation and analysis of the performance and cost of process design options, and

(iv) selection of the optimum process design;

(f) for the drilling or completion of a well for the project; or

(g) for a test wind turbine that is part of a wind farm project of the taxpayer.

[¶2204]

(**2**) A Canadian renewable and conservation expense does not include any expense that

(a) is described in paragraphs 20(1)(c), (d), (e) or (e.l) of the Act; or

(b) is incurred by a taxpayer directly or indirectly and is

(i) for the acquisition of, or the use of or the right to use, land, except as provided by paragraph (1)(b), (c) or (d),

(ii) for grading or levelling land or for landscaping, except as provided by paragraph (1)(b),

(iii) payable to a non-resident person or a partnership other than a Canadian partnership (other than an expense described in paragraph (l)(g)),

(iv) included in the capital cost of property that, but for this section, would be depreciable property, except as provided by paragraph (1)(b), (d), (e), (f) or (g),

(v) an expenditure that, but for this section, would be an eligible capital expenditure, except as provided by any of paragraphs (l)(a) to (e),

(vi) included in the cost of inventory of the taxpayer,

(vii) an expenditure on or in respect of scientific research and experimental development,

(viii) a Canadian development expense or a Canadian oil and gas property expense,

(ix) incurred, for a project, in respect of any time at or after the earliest time at which a property described in Class 43.1 of Schedule II was used in the project for the purpose of earning income,

(x) incurred in respect of the administration or management of a business of the taxpayer, or

(xi) a cost attributable to the period of the construction, renovation or alteration of depreciable property, other than property described in Class 43.1 of Schedule II, that relates to

(A) the construction, renovation or alteration of the property, except as provided by paragraph $(1)(b)$, (f), or (g), or

(B) the ownership of land during the period, except as provided by paragraph $(1)(b)$, (c) or (d).

[¶2208]

(3) For the purpose of paragraph $(1)(g)$, "test wind turbine" means a fixed location device that is a wind energy conversion system that would, but for this section, be property included in Class 43.1 of Schedule II because of subparagraph $(d)(v)$ thereof, and in respect of which the Minister, in consultation with the Minister of Natural Resources, determines that

(a) the device is installed as part of a wind farm project of the taxpayer at which the electrical energy produced from wind by the device, and by all other test wind turbines that are part of the project, does not exceed

(i) one third of the project's planned nameplate capacity if

(A) in the opinion of the minister of Natural Resources, the project's planned nameplate capacity is limited from an engineering or scientific perspective, and

(B) the project's planned nameplate capacity does not exceed six megawatts, or

(ii) 20% of the project's planned nameplate capacity, in any other case;

(b) the project does not share with any other project a point of interconnection to an electrical energy transmission or distribution system;

(c) if the project does not have a point of interconnection to an electrical energy transmission or distribution system, the project has a point of interconnection to an electrical system

(i) of the taxpayer

(A) which system is more than 10 kilometres from any transmission system and from any distribution system, and

(B) from which system at least 90% of the electrical energy produced by the project is used in a business carried on by the taxpayer, or

(ii) of another person or partnership that deals at arm's length with the taxpayer

(A) which system is more than 10 kilometres from any transmission system and from any distribution system, and

(B) from which system at least 90% of the electrical energy produced by the project is used in a business carried on by the other person or partnership;

¶2208

(*d*) the primary purpose for installing the device is to test the level of electrical energy produced by the device from wind at the place of installation;

(*e*) no other test wind turbine is installed within 1500 metres of the device; and

(*f*) no other wind energy conversion system is installed within 1500 metres of the device until the level of electrical energy produced from wind by the device has been tested for at least 120 calendar days.

[¶2212]

(**4**) For greater certainty, a Canadian Renewable and Conservation Expense includes an expense incurred by a taxpayer to acquire a fixed location device that is a wind energy conversion system only if the device is described in paragraph $(1)(g)$.

PART XVII

Capital Cost Allowances, Farming and Fishing

DIVISION I
DEDUCTIONS ALLOWED

[¶2310]

RATES

1700. (**1**) For the purposes of paragraph $20(1)(a)$ of the Act, there is hereby allowed to a taxpayer, in computing his income from farming or fishing, as the case may be, a deduction for each taxation year in respect of each property that was used for the purpose of gaining or producing income from farming or fishing equal to such amount as he may claim, not exceeding in the case of

(*a*) a building or other structure, not described elsewhere in this subsection, including component parts such as electric wiring, plumbing, sprinkler systems, air-conditioning equipment, heating equipment, lighting fixtures, elevators and escalators, $2\frac{1}{2}$ per cent,

(*b*) a building or other structure of

(i) frame,

(ii) log,

(iii) stucco on frame,

(iv) galvanized iron, or

(v) corrugated iron,

construction including component parts such as electric wiring, plumbing, sprinkler systems, air-conditioning equipment, heating equipment, lighting fixtures, elevators and escalators, 5 per cent,

(c) a fence, 5 per cent,

(d) a scow or a vessel, including furniture, fittings or equipment attached thereto, but not including radiocommunication equipment, $7\frac{1}{2}$ per cent,

(e) nonautomotive equipment and machinery, 10 per cent,

(f) automotive equipment, a sleigh or a wagon, 15 per cent,

(g) radiocommunication equipment, 15 per cent,

(h) tile drainage acquired before the 1965 taxation year, 10 per cent,

(i) a water storage tank, 5 per cent,

(j) a gas well that is part of the equipment of a farm and from which the gas produced is not sold, 10 per cent, and

(k) a tool costing less than \$100, 100 per cent,

of the depreciable cost to the taxpayer of the property.

[¶2312]

Taxation Years Less Than 12 Months

(2) Where a taxation year is less than 12 months, the amount allowed as a deduction under subsection (1) shall not exceed that proportion of the maximum amount otherwise allowable that the number of days in the taxation year is of 365.

[¶2314]

Property Disposed of During Year

(3) Where a taxpayer has disposed of a property before the end of a taxation year, the amount allowed as a deduction under subsection (1) in respect of that property for the year shall not exceed that proportion of the maximum amount otherwise allowable that the number of months in the taxation year during which the property was owned by the taxpayer is of 12.

[¶2316]

Leasehold Interests

(4) Where a taxpayer has property that was used for the purpose of gaining or producing income from farming or fishing and that would be included in Class 13 in Schedule II if he had claimed an allowance under Part XI, he may deduct, in computing his income from farming or fishing for a taxation year, an amount not exceeding the amount he could have deducted in respect of that property for the year under paragraph 1100(1)(b).

DIVISION II
MAXIMUM DEDUCTIONS

[¶2318]

1701. **(1)** The amount allowed as a deduction under section 1700 in respect of a property shall not exceed the amount by which the capital cost of the property to the taxpayer exceeds the aggregate of the deductions from income allowed under this Part in respect of the property for previous taxation years.

[¶2320]

(2) In respect of the 1972 and subsequent taxation years, where subsection 20(5) of the *Income Tax Application Rules* applies to a particular property, notwithstanding subsection (1), the amount allowed as a deduction under section 1700 in respect of the property shall not exceed the amount by which

(a) the amount determined to be the undepreciated capital cost of the property, under paragraph 20(5)(b) of the *Income Tax Application Rules, 1971,*

exceeds

(b) the aggregate of the deductions from income allowed under this Part in respect of the property for previous taxation years ending after 1971.

DIVISION III
PROPERTY NOT INCLUDED

[¶2322]

1702. **(1)** Nothing in this Part shall be construed as allowing a deduction in respect of a property

(a) the cost of which is deductible in computing the taxpayer's income;

(b) that is described in the taxpayer's inventory;

(c) that was acquired by an expenditure in respect of which the taxpayer is allowed a deduction from income under section 37 of the Act;

(d) that has been constituted a prescribed class by subsection 24(2) of chapter 91, S.C. 1966-67;

(e) that is included in a separate prescribed class established under subsection 13(14) of the Act;

(f) that was not used in the business during the year;

(g) that is

(i) an animal, or

(ii) a tree, shrub, herb or similar growing thing;

¶2322

(h) that was not acquired by the taxpayer for the purpose of gaining or producing income from farming or fishing;

(i) that has been included at any time by the taxpayer in a class prescribed under Part XI;

(j) that is a passenger automobile acquired after June 13, 1963, and before January 1, 1966, the cost to the taxpayer of which, minus the initial transportation charges and retail sales tax in respect thereof, exceeded $5,000, unless the automobile was acquired by a person before June 14, 1963 and has, by one or more transactions between persons not dealing at arm's length, become vested in the taxpayer; or

(k) that was acquired by the taxpayer after 1971.

[¶2324]

(2) Where a taxpayer is a member of a partnership, the properties referred to in this Part shall be deemed not to include any property that is an interest of the taxpayer in depreciable property that is partnership property of the partnership.

[¶2326]

(3) The properties referred to in section 1700 shall be deemed not to include the land upon which a property described therein was constructed or is situated.

[¶2328]

(4) Where the taxpayer is a non-resident person, the properties referred to in section 1700 shall be deemed not to include property that is situated outside Canada.

[¶2330]

(5) The provisions of subsections 1102(11), (12) and (13) are applicable *mutatis mutandis* to paragraph (1)(j).

DIVISION IV
INTERPRETATION

[¶2332]

TAXATION YEARS FOR INDIVIDUALS IN BUSINESS

1703. **(1)** Where a taxpayer is an individual and his income for the taxation year includes income from a business the fiscal period of which does not coincide with the calendar year, in respect of depreciable properties acquired for the purpose of gaining or producing income from the business, a reference in this Part to

(a) "the taxation year" shall be deemed to be a reference to the fiscal period of the business; and (*b*) "the end of the taxation year" shall be deemed to be a reference to the end of the fiscal period of the business.

[¶2334]

Depreciable Cost

(**2**) In this Part, "depreciable cost" to a taxpayer of property means, except as otherwise provided, the actual cost of the property to the taxpayer or the amount at which he is deemed under subsection 13(7) of the Act to have acquired the property, as the case may be.

[¶2336]

(**3**) Notwithstanding the other provisions of this section, in the case of property the cost of which to a partnership has been determined under paragraph 20(5)(*a*) of the *Income Tax Application Rules, 1971*, the depreciable cost to the taxpayer of the property for the purposes of this Part shall be deemed to be an amount equal to the cost to the partnership of the particular property as determined under that paragraph.

[¶2338]

Personal Use of Property

(**4**) Where a taxpayer has, in a taxation year, regularly used a property in part for the purpose of gaining or producing income from farming or fishing and in part for a purpose other than gaining or producing income, the depreciable cost to the taxpayer of the property for the purposes of this Part is the proportion of the amount that would otherwise be the depreciable cost that the use regularly made of the property for the purpose of gaining or producing income from farming or fishing is of the whole use regularly made of the property.

[¶2340]

Grants, Subsidies or Other Government Assistance

(**5**) Where a taxpayer has received or is entitled to receive a grant, subsidy or other assistance from a government, municipality or other public authority in respect of or for the acquisition of property, the depreciable cost to the taxpayer of the property for the purposes of this Part is the amount that would otherwise be the depreciable cost minus the amount of the grant, subsidy or other assistance.

[¶2342]

Transactions Not at Arm's Length

(**6**) Where property did belong to a person (in this subsection referred to as the "original owner") and has, by one or more transactions between persons not dealing at arm's length, become vested in a taxpayer, the depreciable cost to the taxpayer of the property for the purposes of this Part is the lesser of

(a) the actual capital cost of the property to the taxpayer; and

(b) the amount by which the actual capital cost of the property to the original owner exceeds the aggregate of

(i) the total amount of depreciation for the property that, since the commencement of 1917, has been or should have been taken into account in accordance with the practice of the Department of National Revenue in ascertaining the income of the original owner and all intervening owners for the purposes of the *Income War Tax Act* or in ascertaining a loss for a year when there was no income under that Act,

(ii) any accumulated depreciation reserves that the original owner or an intervening owner had for the property at the commencement of 1917 and that were recognized by the Minister for the purposes of the *Income War Tax Act*, and

(iii) the aggregate of the deductions, if any, allowed under this Part in respect of the property to the original owner and all intervening owners.

[¶2344]

Property Acquired From a Parent

(7) Notwithstanding subsection (6), where depreciable property has been acquired by a taxpayer under such circumstances that the provisions of section 85H of the Act as it read in its application to the 1971 and prior taxation years are applicable for the determination of the capital cost of the property, the depreciable cost to the taxpayer of the property for the purposes of this Part is the capital cost as determined under that section.

[¶2346]

Property Acquired by Gift

(8) Subsection (6) does not apply in respect of property which a taxpayer has acquired by gift.

DIVISION V
APPLICATION OF THIS PART

[¶2348]

1704. This Part shall apply only to a taxpayer who, in computing his income, has never claimed an allowance under Part XI in respect of a property at a time when an allowance could have been claimed under this Part in respect of that property, other than an allowance claimed by the taxpayer under Part XI that may be claimed in respect of a property described in

(a) paragraph $1100(1)(r)$ as enacted by Order in Council P.C. 1965-1118 of June 18, 1965 and as amended by Order in Council P.C. 1965-2320 of December 29, 1965;

(b) paragraph $1100(1)(sa)$ as enacted by Order in Council P.C. 1968-2261 of December 10, 1968;

(c) paragraph $1100(1)(v)$; or

(d) Class 20 in Schedule II.

PART XXIX

Scientific Research and Experimental Development

[¶2370]

INTERPRETATION

2900. **(1)** [Repealed.]

(2) For the purposes of clause $37(8)(a)(i)(B)$ and subclause $37(8)(a)(ii)(A)(II)$ of the Act, the following expenditures are directly attributable to the prosecution of scientific research and experimental development:

(a) the cost of materials consumed or transformed in such prosecution;

(b) where an employee directly undertakes, supervises or supports such prosecution, the portion of the amount incurred for salary or wages of the employee that can reasonably be considered to be in respect of such prosecution; and

(c) other expenditures, or those portions of other expenditures, that are directly related to such prosecution and that would not have been incurred if such prosecution had not occurred.

[¶2372]

(3) For the purposes of subclause $37(8)(a)(ii)(A)(II)$ of the Act, the following expenditures are directly attributable to the provision of premises, facilities or equipment for the prosecution of scientific research and experimental development:

(a) the cost of the maintenance and upkeep of such premises, facilities or equipment; and

(b) other expenditures, or those portions of other expenditures, that are directly related to that provision and that would not have been incurred if those premises or facilities or that equipment had not existed.

[¶2373]

(4) For the purposes of the definition "qualified expenditure" in subsection 127(9) of the Act, the prescribed proxy amount of a taxpayer for a taxation year, in respect of a business, in respect of which the taxpayer elects under clause $37(8)(a)(ii)(B)$ of the Act is 65% of the total of all amounts each of which is that portion of the amount incurred in the year by the taxpayer in respect of salary or wages of an employee of the taxpayer who is directly engaged in scientific research and experimental development carried on in Canada that can reasonably be considered to relate to the scientific research and experimental development having regard to the time spent by the employee on the scientific research and experimental development.

[¶2374]

(5) Subject to subsections (6) to (8), where in subsection (4) the portion of an expenditure is all or substantially all of the expenditure, that portion shall be replaced by the amount of the expenditure.

[¶2375]

(6) The amount determined under subsection (4) as the prescribed proxy amount of a taxpayer for a taxation year in respect of a business shall not exceed the amount, if any, by which

(a) the total of all amounts deducted in computing the taxpayer's income for the year from the business,

exceeds the total of all amounts each of which is

(b) an amount deducted in computing the income of the taxpayer for the year from the business under any of sections 20, 24, 26, 30, 32, 37, 66 to 66.8 and 104 of the Act, or

(c) an amount incurred by the taxpayer in the year in respect of any outlay or expense made or incurred for the use of, or the right to use, a building other than a special-purpose building.

[¶2376]

(7) In determining the prescribed proxy amount of a taxpayer for a taxation year, the portion of the amount incurred in the year by the taxpayer in respect of salary or wages of a specified employee of the taxpayer that is included in computing the total described in subsection (4) shall not exceed the lesser of

(a) 75% of the amount incurred by the taxpayer in the year in respect of salary or wages of the employee, and

(b) the amount determined by the formula

$$2.5 \times A \times B/365$$

where

A   is the Year's Maximum Pensionable Earnings (as determined under section 18 of the *Canada Pension Plan*) for the calendar year in which the taxation year ends, and

B   is the number of days in the taxation year in which the employee is an employee of the taxpayer.

[¶2377]

(8) Where

(*a*) a taxpayer is a corporation,

(*b*) the taxpayer employs in a taxation year ending in a calendar year an individual who is a specified employee of the taxpayer,

(*c*) the taxpayer is associated with another corporation (referred to as the "associated corporation") in a taxation year of the associated corporation ending in the calendar year, and

(*d*) the individual is an employee of the associated corporation in the taxation year of the associated corporation ending in the calendar year,

the total of all amounts that may be included in computing the total described in subsection (4) in respect of salaries or wages of the individual by the taxpayer in its taxation year ending in the calendar year and by all associated corporations in their taxation years ending in the calendar year shall not exceed the amount that is 2.5 times the Year's Maximum Pensionable Earnings (as determined under section 18 of the *Canada Pension Plan*) for the calendar year.

[¶2378]

(9) For the purposes of subsections (4) and (7), an amount incurred in respect of salary or wages of an employee in a taxation year does not include

(*a*) an amount described in section 6 or 7 of the Act;

(*b*) an amount deemed under subsection 78(4) of the Act to have been incurred;

(*c*) bonuses; or

(*d*) remuneration based on profits.

[¶2379]

(10) For the purpose of subsection (8),

(*a*) an individual related to a particular corporation, and

(*b*) a partnership any member of which is an individual related to a particular corporation or is a corporation associated with a particular corporation,

shall be deemed to be a corporation associated with the particular corporation.

[¶2380]

(11) The depreciable property of a taxpayer that is prescribed for the purposes of the definition "first term shared-use-equipment" in subsection 127(9) of the Act is

(*a*) a building of the taxpayer;

(b) a leasehold interest of the taxpayer in a building;

(c) a property of the taxpayer if, at the time it was acquired by the taxpayer, the taxpayer or a person related to the taxpayer intended that it would be used in the prosecution of scientific research and experimental development during the assembly, construction or commissioning of a facility, plant or line for commercial manufacturing, commercial processing or other commercial purposes (other than scientific research and experimental development) and intended

(i) that it would be used during its operating time in its expected useful life primarily for purposes other than scientific research and experimental development, or

(ii) that its value would be consumed primarily in activities other than scientific research and experimental development; and

(d) part of a property of the taxpayer if, at the time the part was acquired by the taxpayer, the taxpayer or a person related to the taxpayer intended that the part would be used in the prosecution of scientific research and experimental development during the assembly, construction or commissioning of a facility, plant or line for commercial manufacturing, commercial processing or other commercial purposes (other than scientific research and experimental development), and intended

(i) that it would be used during its operating time in its expected useful life primarily for purposes other than scientific research and experimental development, or

(ii) that its value would be consumed primarily in activities other than scientific research and experimental development.

[¶2382]

Prescribed Expenditures

2901.   For the purposes of paragraph 37.1(5)(c) [Repealed by S.C. 1998, c. 19, s. 87(1).] of the Act, a prescribed expenditure is

(a) an expenditure of a current nature incurred by a corporation in respect of

(i) the general administration or management of a business, including

(A) administrative salary or wages and related benefits in respect of a person whose duties are not all or substantially all directed to the prosecution of scientific research and experimental development, except to the extent that such expenditure is described in subsection 2900(2) or (3),

(B) a legal or accounting fee,

(C) an amount described in any of paragraphs 20(1)(c) to (g) of the Act,

(D) an entertainment expense,

(E) an advertising or selling expense,

(F) a convention expense,

(G) a due or fee in respect of membership in a scientific or technical society or organization, and

(H) a fine or penalty, or

(ii) the maintenance and upkeep of premises, facilities or equipment to the extent that such expenditure is not attributable to the prosecution of scientific research and experimental development,

except any such expenditure incurred by a corporation that derives all or substantially all of its revenue from the prosecution of scientific research or the sale of rights in or arising out of scientific research carried on by it;

(b) an expenditure of a capital nature incurred by a corporation in respect of

(i) the acquisition of property, except any such expenditure that was incurred for and was all or substantially all attributable to the prosecution, or to the provision of premises, facilities or equipment for the prosecution, of scientific research and experimental development, or

(ii) the acquisition of property that is qualified property within the meaning assigned by subsection 127(9) of the Act;

(c) an expenditure made to acquire rights in, or arising out of, scientific research and experimental development; or

(d) an expenditure on scientific research and experimental development in respect of which an amount is deductible under section 110 of the Act.

[¶2384]

2902. For the purposes of the definition "qualified expenditure" in subsection 127(9) of the Act, a prescribed expenditure is

(a) an expenditure of a current nature incurred by a taxpayer in respect of

(i) the general administration or management of a business, including

(A) an administrative salary or wages and related benefits in respect of a person whose duties are not all or substantially all directed to the prosecution of scientific research and experimental development, except to the extent that such expenditure is described in subsection 2900(2) or (3),

(B) a legal or accounting fee,

(C) an amount described in any of paragraphs 20(1)(c) to (g) of the Act,

(D) an entertainment expense,

(E) an advertising or selling expense,

(F) a conference or convention expense,

(G) a due or fee in respect of membership in a scientific or technical society or organization, and

(H) a fine or penalty, or

(ii) the maintenance and upkeep of premises, facilities or equipment to the extent that such expenditure is not attributable to the prosecution of scientific research, and experimental development,

(b) an expenditure of a capital nature incurred by a taxpayer in respect of

(i) the acquisition of property, except any such expenditure that at the time it was incurred

(A) was for first term shared-use-equipment or second term shared-use-equipment, or

(B) was for the provision of premises, facilities or equipment if, at the time of the acquisition of the premises, facilities or equipment, it was intended

(I) that the premises, facilities or equipment would be used during all or substantially all of the operating time of the premises, facilities or equipment in the expected useful life of the premises, facilities or equipment for the prosecution of scientific research and experimental development in Canada, or

(II) that all or substantially all of the value of the premises, facilities or equipment would be consumed in the prosecution of scientific research and experimental development in Canada,

(ii) the acquisition of property that is qualified property within the meaning assigned by subsection 127(9) of the Act, or

(iii) the acquisition of property that has been used or acquired for use or lease, for any purpose whatever before it was acquired by the taxpayer;

(c) an expenditure made to acquire rights in, or arising out of, scientific research and experimental development;

(d) an expenditure on scientific research and experimental development in respect of which an amount is deductible under section 110.1 or section 118.1 of the Act; or

(e) an expenditure of a current or capital nature, to the extent that the taxpayer has received or is entitled to receive a reimbursement in respect thereof from

¶2384

Draft Regulation

Scientific Research & Experimental Development (October 27, 1998)

The portion of paragraph 2902(e) before subparagraph (i) is replaced by the following:

(e) for the purpose of sections 194 and 195 of the Act, an expenditure of a current or capital nature, to the extent that the taxpayer has received or is entitled to receive a reimbursement in respect of the expenditure from

Applicable: To amounts that become receivable after December 20, 1991.

Explanatory Note: Section 2902 defines a prescribed expenditure for the purposes of subsection 127(9) of the *Income Tax Act*. Prescribed expenditures are not eligible for investment tax credits.

Paragraph 2902(e) of the Income Tax Regulations is amended consequential on the amendments to the definition "contract payment" in subsection 127(9) of the Act. Those amendments provided that a contract payment included certain payments for scientific research and experimental development that is performed for or on behalf of a person entitled to a deduction in respect of the amount because of subparagraph 37(1)(a)(i) or (i.1) of the Act. Contract payments received reduce the base upon which a taxpayer's ITC in respect of SR&ED is calculated. Those amendments were effective for amounts that became payable after December 20, 1991. In view of the amended definition of "contract payment" applicable to ITCs in respect of SR&ED, the provisions of paragraph 2902(e) became redundant for ITC purposes. However, paragraph 2902(e) of the Regulations is still relevant in respect of claims for refunds of Part VIII Refundable Tax on Corporations in Respect of the Scientific Research and Experimental Development Tax Credit. Regulation 2902(e) is, therefore, amended to apply only for the purposes of the Part VIII Refundable Tax. This amendment applies to amounts that become receivable after December 20, 1991.

(i) a person resident in Canada, other than

(A) Her Majesty in right of Canada or a province,

(B) an agent of Her Majesty in right of Canada or a province,

(C) a corporation, commission or association that is controlled, directly or indirectly in any manner whatever, by Her Majesty in right of Canada or a province or by an agent of her Majesty in right of Canada or a province, or

(D) a municipality in Canada or a municipal or public body performing a function of government in Canada, or

(ii) a person not resident in Canada to the extent that the said reimbursement is deductible by the person in computing his taxable income earned in Canada for any taxation year.

¶2384

PART XL

Borrowed Money Costs

[¶2390]

INTEREST ON INSURANCE POLICY LOANS

4001. For the purposes of subsection 20(2.1) of the Act, the amount of interest to be verified by the insurer in respect of a taxpayer shall be verified in prescribed form no later than the last day on which the taxpayer is required to file his return of income under section 150 of the Act for the taxation year in respect of which the interest was paid.

PART XLI

Representation Expenses

[¶2392]

4100. For the purposes of subsection 20(9) of the Act, an election shall be made by filing with the Minister the following documents in duplicate:

(a) a letter from the taxpayer specifying the amount in respect of which the election is being made; and

(b) where the taxpayer is a corporation, a certified copy of the resolution of the directors authorizing the election to be made.

PART XLIII

Interest Rates

[¶2394]

4302. Notwithstanding section 4301, for the purposes of paragraph $16.1(1)(d)$ of the Act and subsection 1100(1.1), the interest rate in effect during any month is the rate that is one percentage point greater than the rate that was, during the month before the immediately preceding month, the average yield, expressed as a percentage per year rounded to two decimal points, prevailing on all outstanding domestic Canadian-dollar Government of Canada bonds on the last Wednesday of that month with a remaining term to maturity of over 10 years, as first published by the Bank of Canada.

PART LXXIII

Prescribed Amounts and Areas

[¶2396]

7307. **(1)** For the purposes of subsection 13(2), paragraph $13(7)(g)$, subparagraph $13(7)(h)$(iii), subsections 20(4) and (16.1), the description of B in paragraph $67.3(d)$ and subparagraph $85(1)(e.4)(i)$ of the Act, the amount prescribed is

(a) with respect to an automobile acquired, or leased under a lease entered into, after August 1989 and before 1991, \$24,000; and

(b) with respect to an automobile acquired, or leased under a lease entered into, after 1990, the amount determined by the formula

$$A + B$$

where

A is, with respect to an automobile acquired, or leased under a lease entered into,

(i) before 1997, \$24,000,

(ii) in 1997, \$25,000,

(iii) in 1998 or 1999, \$26,000,

(iv) in 2000, \$27,000, or

(v) after 2000, \$30,000, and

B is the sum that would have been payable in respect of federal and provincial sales taxes on the acquisition of the automobile if it had been acquired, at a cost equal to A before the application of the federal and provincial sales taxes, if the automobile

(i) was acquired, at the time of the acquisition, or

(ii) was leased, at the time the lease was entered into.

Department of Finance Press Release

2005 Automobile Deduction Limits and Expense Benefit Rates for Business

[Reproduced below is an excerpt from Department of Finance News Release No. 2004-081, dated December 17, 2004, which states that the maximum allowable cost of a passenger vehicle purchased in 2005 remains at \$30,000, unchanged from the level for 2003 and 2004.]

Minister of Finance Ralph Goodale announced today the automobile expense deduction limits and the prescribed rates for the automobile operating expense benefit that will apply in 2005. Specifically:

● The ceiling on the capital cost of passenger vehicles for capital cost allowance (CCA) purposes will remain at \$30,000 (plus applicable federal and provincial sales taxes) for purchases after 2004. This ceiling restricts the cost of a vehicle on which CCA may be claimed for business purposes.

* * *

[¶2398]

(2) For the purpose of the description of A in section 67.2 of the Act, the amount prescribed in respect of an automobile that is acquired either after August 1989 and before 1997 or after 2000 is \$300.

Department of Finance Press Release

2005 Automobile Deduction Limits and Expense Benefit Rates for Business

[Reproduced below is an excerpt from Department of Finance News Release No. 2004-081, dated December 17, 2004, which states that the maximum allowable interest deduction on amounts borrowed to purchase a passenger vehicle in 2005 remains at $300, unchanged from the level for 2003 and 2004.]

Minister of Finance Ralph Goodale announced today the automobile expense deduction limits and the prescribed rates for the automobile operating expense benefit that will apply in 2005. Specifically:

* * *

- The maximum allowable interest deduction for amounts borrowed to purchase an automobile will remain at $300 per month for loans related to vehicles acquired after 2004. This limit reflects the reasonable cost of financing a vehicle for business purposes.

* * *

[¶2400]

(3) For the purpose of the description of A in paragraph 67.3(c) of the Act, the amount prescribed in respect of a taxation year of a lessee is, with respect to an automobile leased under a lease entered into

(a) after August 1989 and before 1991, $650; and

(b) after 1990, the amount determined by the formula

$$A + B$$

where

A   is

(i) for leases entered into after 1990 but before 1997, $650,

(ii) for leases entered into in 1997, $550,

(iii) for leases entered into in 1998 or 1999, $650,

(iv) for leases entered into in 2000, $700, and

(v) for leases entered into after 2000, $800, and

B   is the sum of the federal and provincial sales taxes that would have been payable on a monthly payment under the lease in the taxation year of the lessee if, before those taxes, the lease had required monthly payments equal to A.

Department of Finance Press Release

2005 Automobile Deduction Limits and Expense Benefit Rates for Business

[Reproduced below is an excerpt from Department of Finance News Release No. 2004-081, dated December 17, 2004, which states that the maximum deductible monthly leasing cost for passenger vehicles leased in 2005 remains at $800, unchanged from the level for 2003 and 2004.]

Minister of Finance Ralph Goodale announced today the automobile expense deduction limits and the prescribed rates for the automobile operating expense benefit that will apply in 2005. Specifically:

* * *

● The limit on deductible leasing costs will remain at $800 per month (plus applicable federal and provincial sales taxes) for leases entered into after 2004. This limit, which ensures that the level of deductions for leased and purchased vehicles is consistent, is one of two restrictions on the deduction of automobile lease payments. A separate restriction prorates deductible lease costs where the value of the vehicle exceeds the capital cost ceiling.

* * *

[¶2402]

(4) For the purpose of the description of C in paragraph $67.3(d)$ of the Act, the amount prescribed in respect of an automobile leased under a lease entered into after August 1989 is the amount equal to $^{100}/_{85}$ of the amount determined in accordance with subsection (1) in respect of the automobile.

PART LXXXII

Prescribed Properties and Permanent Establishments

[¶2410]

PRESCRIBED PROPERTIES

8200. For the purposes of subsection 16.1(1) of the Act, "prescribed property" means

(a) exempt property, within the meaning assigned by paragraph $1100(1.13)(a)$, other than property leased on or before February 2, 1990 that is

(i) a truck or tractor that is designed for use on highways and has a "gross vehicle weight rating" (within the meaning assigned that expression by the Motor Vehicle Safety Regulations) of 11,778 kilograms or more,

(ii) a trailer that is designed for use on highways and is of a type designed to be hauled under normal operating conditions by a truck or tractor described in subparagraph (i), or

(iii) a railway car,

(b) property that is the subject of a lease where the tangible property, other than exempt property (within the meaning assigned by paragraph $1100(1.13)(a)$), that was the subject of the lease had, at the time the lease was entered into, an aggregate fair market value not in excess of $25,000, and

(c) intangible property.

[¶2414]

8200.1. For the purposes of subsection 13(18.1) and subparagraph 241(4)(d)(vi.1) of the Act, prescribed energy conservation property means property described in Class 43.1 in Schedule II.

SCHEDULE II

Capital Cost Allowances

[¶2420]

CLASS 1

(4 per cent)

Property not included in any other class that is

(a) a bridge;

(b) a canal;

(c) a culvert;

(d) a dam;

(e) a jetty acquired before May 26, 1976;

(f) a mole acquired before May 26, 1976;

(g) a road, sidewalk, airplane runway, parking area, storage area or similar surface construction, acquired before May 26, 1976;

(h) railway track and grading, including components such as rails, ballast, ties and other track material,

   (i) that is not part of a railway system, or

   (ii) that was acquired after May 25, 1976;

(i) railway traffic control or signalling equipment, acquired after May 25, 1976, including switching, block signalling, interlocking, crossing protection, detection, speed control or retarding equipment, but not including property that is principally electronic equipment or systems software therefor;

(j) a subway or tunnel, acquired after May 25, 1976;

(k) electrical generating equipment (except as specified elsewhere in this Schedule);

(l) a pipeline, other than gas or oil well equipment, unless, in the case of a pipeline for oil or natural gas, the Minister, in consultation with the Minister of Energy, Mines and Resources, is or has been satisfied that the main source of supply for the pipeline is or was likely to be exhausted within 15 years after the date on which operation of the pipeline commenced;

(m) the generating or distributing equipment and plant (including structures) of a producer or distributor of electrical energy;

(n) manufacturing and distributing equipment and plant (including structures) acquired primarily for the production or distribution of gas, except

(i) a property acquired for the purpose of producing or distributing gas that is normally distributed in portable containers,

(ii) a property acquired for the purpose of processing natural gas, before the delivery of such gas to a distribution system, or

(iii) a property acquired for the purpose of producing oxygen or nitrogen;

(o) the distributing equipment and plant (including structures) of a distributor of water;

(p) the production and distributing equipment and plant (including structures) of a distributor of heat; or

(q) a building or other structure, or part thereof, including component parts such as electric wiring, plumbing, sprinkler systems, air-conditioning equipment, heating equipment, lighting fixtures, elevators and escalators.

Federal Budget Extract

Transmission Pipelines and Related Equipment

[Reproduced below is an excerpt from the February 23, 2005 Federal Budget that sets out proposals for new capital cost allowance rates for transmission pipelines and related equipment]

Currently, hydrocarbon transmission pipelines are generally eligible for a 4-per-cent capital cost allowance (CCA) rate under Class 1 of Schedule II to the Income Tax Regulations. Because petroleum pumping equipment and natural gas compression equipment on such pipelines is not specifically included in any of the CCA classes, the sector has generally included such assets in Class 8 (20-per-cent CCA rate), the default class for property not included in any other class. However, court cases have called into question the classification of natural gas compression equipment, on such pipelines, that default into Class 8.

* * *

The budget proposes that the CCA rate for transmission pipelines (as contrasted with distribution lines) for petroleum, natural gas or related hydrocarbons be increased to 8 per cent from 4 per cent to better reflect the typical useful life of these assets. Included will be control and monitoring devices, valves and other ancillary equipment (other than pumping and compression equipment, discussed below). The proposed changes will not affect the existing treatment of gas or oil well equipment and pipelines for which the Minister of National Revenue, in consultation with the Minister of Natural Resources, is satisfied that the main source of supply is likely to be exhausted within 15 years of commencement of operation. Distribution pipelines that distribute gas to the ultimate consumers typically have a longer useful life than transmission pipelines. Accordingly, these properties will continue to be included in Class 1, eligible for a 4-percent CCA rate.

The budget also proposes changes to the treatment for pumping and compression equipment, and equipment ancillary to it, related to a transmission pipeline for petroleum, natural gas or related hydrocarbons. The tax treatment of such equipment is to be

¶2420

rationalized by establishing a uniform 15-per-cent CCA rate that better reflects the typical useful life of these assets. However, this change will not apply to gas or oil well equipment (which is already eligible for a 25-per-cent CCA rate) and buildings or other structures.

The useful life of a pipeline can, however, be shortened in cases where production from the associated resource ceases. Accordingly, the budget also proposes that a separate class election be introduced for transmission pipelines and related pumping and compression equipment. The separate class election, which must be made for the taxation year in which a property is acquired, allows taxpayers to place eligible property in a separate class for CCA purposes. Although the separate class election does not change the CCA rate specified for the class, it does provide that any remaining undepreciated balance in the class after the disposition of the property, can, for the year of disposition, be fully deducted as a terminal loss.

The new CCA rates for transmission pipelines will apply to equipment acquired on or after February 23, 2005 that has not been used or acquired for use before that date. The new CCA rates for pumping and compression equipment will apply to all such equipment acquired on or after February 23, 2005.

Federal Budget Extract

Electricity Transmission and Distribution Assets

[Reproduced below is an excerpt from the February 23, 2005 Federal Budget that sets out a proposal to increase the capital cost allowance rate for electricity transmission and distribution assets currently described in paragraph (*m*) of Class 1 and to apply the specified energy property rules to combustion turbines and electricity transmission and distribution assets.]

Currently, electricity transmission and distribution assets (e.g., power lines, transformers and substation equipment) are eligible for a 4-per-cent CCA rate.

*   *   *

Available evidence associated with transmission and distribution equipment suggests that the current provisions do not reflect the useful life of these assets. The budget therefore proposes that the CCA rate for transmission and distribution equipment and structures (but not including buildings) of a distributor of electrical energy be increased to 8 per cent. This rate will better reflect the estimated useful life of these assets.

The 8-per-cent rate will apply to assets acquired on or after February 23, 2005 that have not been used or acquired for use before February 23, 2005.

*   *   *

In addition to setting the appropriate CCA rate, rules are needed to protect the integrity of the CCA system. These include the specified energy property rules, which limit the amount of CCA deductions that may be used by passive investors in respect of specified energy property — generally property for which an incentive CCA rate is allowed under Class 34 or 43.1 — to the amount of income from such property. This prevents CCA deductions from being used by passive investors to shelter other sources of income.

This budget proposes that the specified energy property rules be extended to combustion turbines and electricity transmission and distribution assets that are eligible for the higher CCA rates proposed in this budget.

¶2420

Draft Regulation

Capital Cost Allowance (March 16, 2001)

Paragraph (q) of Class 1 in Schedule II to the Regulations is replaced by the following:

(q) a building or other structure, or a part of it, including any component parts such as electric wiring, plumbing, sprinkler systems, air-conditioning equipment, heating equipment, lighting fixtures, elevators and escalators (except property described in any of paragraphs (k) and (m) to (p) or in any of paragraphs (a) to (e) of Class 8).

Applicable: To property acquired after 1987.

Explanatory Note: Paragraph (q) of Class 1 in Schedule II to the Regulations (4% CCA rate) applies to a building or structure, or component parts thereof.

Concern has been expressed that Class 8 (20% CCA rate) may not apply to certain buildings, structures, or component parts — described in paragraphs (a) to (e) of Class 8 — if Class 1 applies to such property because of paragraph (q) of that Class. To clarify that paragraph (q) of Class 1 does not apply to a property if any of paragraphs (a) to (e) of Class 8 apply to the property, paragraph (q) of Class 1 is amended to exclude structures, buildings or equipment referred to in paragraphs (a) to (e) of Class 8. Consequential to this change, paragraph (q) of Class 1 is also amended to exclude from its application property described in certain other paragraphs of Class 1. This relieving amendment is applicable to property acquired after 1987.

[¶2422]

CLASS 2

(6 per cent)

Property that is

(a) electrical generating equipment (except as specified elsewhere in this Schedule);

(b) a pipeline, other than gas or oil well equipment, unless, in the case of a pipeline for oil or natural gas, the Minister in consultation with the Minister of Energy, Mines and Resources, is or has been satisfied that the main source of supply for the pipeline is or was likely to be exhausted within 15 years from the date on which operation of the pipeline commenced;

(c) the generating or distributing equipment and plant (including structures) of a producer or distributor of electrical energy, except a property included in Class 10, 13, 14, 26 or 28;

(d) manufacturing and distributing equipment and plant (including structures) acquired primarily for the production or distribution of gas, except

(i) a property included in Class 10, 13 or 14,

(ii) a property acquired for the purpose of producing or distributing gas that is normally distributed in portable containers,

(iii) a property acquired for the purpose of processing natural gas, before delivery of such a gas to a distribution system,

(iv) a property acquired for the purpose of producing oxygen or nitrogen;

(e) the distributing equipment and plant (including structures) of a distributor of water, except a property included in Class 10, 13 or 14; or

(f) the production and distributing equipment and plant (including structures) of a distributor of heat, except a property included in Class 10, 13 or 14;

acquired by the taxpayer

(g) before 1988, or

(h) before 1990

(i) pursuant to an obligation in writing entered into by the taxpayer before June 18, 1987,

(ii) that was under construction by or on behalf of the taxpayer on June 18, 1987, or

(iii) that is machinery or equipment that is a fixed and integral part of a building, structure, plant facility or other property that was under construction by or on behalf of the taxpayer on June 18, 1987.

[¶2424]

CLASS 3

(5 per cent)

Property not included in any other class that is

(a) a building or other structure, or part thereof, including component parts such as electric wiring, plumbing, sprinkler systems, air-conditioning equipment, heating equipment, lighting fixtures, elevators and escalators, acquired by the taxpayer

(i) before 1988, or

(ii) before 1990

(A) pursuant to an obligation in writing entered into by the taxpayer before June 18, 1987,

(B) that was under construction by or on behalf of the taxpayer on June 18, 1987, or

(C) that is a component part of a building that was under construction by or on behalf of the taxpayer on June 18, 1987;

(b) a breakwater;

(c) a dock;

(d) a trestle;

¶2424

(e) a windmill;

(f) a wharf;

(g) an addition or alteration, made during the period that is after March 31, 1967 and before 1988, to a building that would have been included in this class during that period but for the fact that it was included in Class 20;

(h) a jetty acquired after May 25, 1976;

(i) a mole acquired after May 25, 1976;

(j) telephone, telegraph or data communication equipment, acquired after May 25, 1976, that is a wire or cable;

(k) an addition or alteration, other than an addition or alteration described in paragraph (k) of Class 6, made after 1987, to a building included, in whole or in part,

(i) in this class,

(ii) in Class 6 by virtue of subparagraph (a)(viii) thereof, or

(iii) in Class 20,

to the extent that the aggregate cost of all such additions or alterations to the building does not exceed that lesser of

(iv) $500,000, and

(v) 25 per cent of the aggregate of the amounts that would, but for this paragraph, be the capital cost of the building and any additions or alterations thereto included in this class or Class 6 or 20; or

(l) ancillary to a wire or cable referred to in paragraph (j) or Class 42 and that is supporting equipment such as a pole, mast, tower, conduit, brace, crossarm, guy or insulator.

Federal Budget Extract

Cable for Telecommunications Infrastructure

[Reproduced below is an excerpt from the February 23, 2005 Federal Budget that sets out a proposal to increase the capital cost allowance rate to 12% for telecommunications cable that is not fibre-optic cable.]

Currently, wire and cable used for telephone, telegraph or data communication, other than fibre-optic cable, is eligible for a 5-per-cent CCA rate [Class 3]. Fibre-optic cable is eligible for a 12-per-cent CCA rate.

* * *

A review of the CCA rate for wire and cable used for telephone, telegraph or data communication that is not fibre-optic cable indicates that a higher CCA rate would better reflect the useful life of these assets. The budget proposes that the CCA rate for wire or cable used for telephone, telegraph or data communication not included in any other class be increased to 12 per cent. This rate will better reflect the estimated useful life of these assets.

The 12-per-cent CCA rate will apply to assets acquired on or after February 23, 2005 that have not been used or acquired for use before February 23, 2005.

¶2424

[¶2426]

CLASS 4

(6 per cent)

Property that would otherwise be included in another class in this Schedule that is

(a) a railway system or a part thereof, except automotive equipment not designed to run on rails or tracks, that was acquired after the end of the taxpayer's 1958 taxation year and before May 26, 1976; or

(b) a tramway or trolley bus system or a part thereof, except property included in Class 10, 13 or 14.

[¶2428]

CLASS 5

(10 per cent)

Property that is

(a) a chemical pulp mill or ground wood pulp mill, including buildings, machinery and equipment, but not including hydro-electric power plants and their equipment, or

(b) an integrated mill producing chemical pulp or ground wood pulp and manufacturing therefrom paper, paper board or pulp board, including buildings, machinery and equipment, but not including hydro-electric power plants and their equipment,

but not including any property that was acquired after the end of the taxpayer's 1962 taxation year.

[¶2430]

CLASS 6

(10 per cent)

Property not included in any other class that is

(a) a building of

  (i) frame,

  (ii) log,

  (iii) stucco on frame,

  (iv) galvanized iron, or

  (v) corrugated metal

construction, including component parts such as electric wiring, plumbing, sprinkler systems, air-conditioning equipment, heating equipment, lighting fixtures, elevators and escalators, if the building

(vi) is used by the taxpayer for the purpose of gaining or producing income from farming or fishing,

(vii) has no footings or any other base support below ground level,

(viii) was acquired by the taxpayer before 1979 and is not a building described in subparagraph (vi) or (vii),

(ix) was acquired by the taxpayer after 1978 under circumstances such that

(A) he was obligated to acquire the building under the terms of an agreement in writing entered into before 1979, and

(B) the installation of footings or any other base support of the building was commenced before 1979, or

(x) was acquired by the taxpayer after 1978 under circumstances such that

(A) he commenced construction of the building before 1979, or

(B) the construction of the building was commenced under the terms of an agreement in writing entered into by him before 1979, and

the installation of footings or any other base support of the building was commenced before 1979;

(b) a wooden breakwater;

(c) a fence;

(d) a greenhouse;

(e) an oil or water storage tank;

(f) a railway tank car acquired before May 26, 1976;

(g) a wooden wharf;

(h) an aeroplane hangar acquired after the end of the taxpayer's 1958 taxation year;

(i) an addition or alteration, made

(A) during the period that is after March 31, 1967 and before 1979, or

(B) after 1978 if the taxpayer was obligated to have it made under the terms of an agreement in writing entered into before 1979,

to a building that would have been included in this class during that period but for the fact that it was included in Class 20;

(j) a railway locomotive acquired after May 25, 1976, but not including an automotive railway car; or

(k) an addition or alteration, made after 1978 to a building included in this class by virtue of subparagraph (a)(viii), to the extent that the

¶2430

aggregate cost of all such additions and alterations to the building does not exceed $100,000.

[¶2452]

CLASS 7

(15 per cent)

Property that is

(a) a canoe or rowboat;

(b) a scow;

(c) a vessel, but not including a vessel

    (i) of a separate class prescribed by subsection 1101(2a), or

    (ii) included in Class 41;

(d) furniture, fittings or equipment attached to a property included in this class, but not including radiocommunication equipment;

(e) a spare engine for a property included in this class;

(f) a marine railway; or

(g) a vessel under construction, other than a vessel included in Class 41.

Draft Regulation

Capital Cost Allowance (March 16, 2001)

Class 7 in Schedule II to the Regulations is amended by striking out the word "or" at the end of paragraph (f) and by adding the following after paragraph (g):

    (h) subject to an election made under subsection 1103(2i), property acquired after February 27, 2000 that is

        (i) a rail suspension device designed to carry trailers that are designed to be hauled on both highways and railway tracks, or

        (ii) a railway car; or

    (i) property acquired after February 27, 2000 that is a railway locomotive, but not including an automotive railway car.

Applicable: To property acquired after February 27, 2000.

Explanatory Note: Class 7 (15% CCA rate) is amended to apply to certain railway property acquired after February 27, 2000. Generally, Class 7 will apply to property that is a railway car, a railway locomotive (other than an automotive railway car) or a railway suspension device designed to carry trailers that are designed to be hauled on both highways and railway tracks. In certain cases, a taxpayer may be eligible to elect under new subsection 1103(2i) to include certain leased railway cars and railway suspension devices in Class 35 (7% CCA rate). Such taxpayers may be eligible to deduct an additional allowance of 6% in respect of such railway property and not have the specified leasing property rules apply to the railway property. New subsection 1103(2i) is more fully described in the commentary accompanying that change.

¶2452

[¶2454]

CLASS 8

(20 per cent)

Property not included in Class 1, 2, 7, 9, 11 or 30 that is

Draft Regulation

Capital Cost Allowance (March 16, 2001)

The portion of Class 8 in Schedule II to the Regulations before paragraph (*a*) is replaced by the following:

CLASS 8

Property not included in Class 1, 2, 7, 9, 11, 17 or 30 that is

Applicable: To property acquired after February 27, 2000.

Explanatory Note: Class 8 (20% CCA rate) is amended to exclude from its application Class 17 property. This amendment is consequential to the inclusion in Class 17 of certain property more fully described below in the commentary accompanying that change.

(*a*) a structure that is manufacturing or processing machinery or equipment;

(*b*) tangible property attached to a building and acquired solely for the purpose of

(i) servicing, supporting or providing access to or egress from, machinery or equipment,

(ii) manufacturing or processing, or

(iii) any combination of the functions described in subparagraphs (i) and (ii);

(*c*) a building that is a kiln, tank or vat, acquired for the purpose of manufacturing or processing;

(*d*) a building or other structure, acquired after February 19, 1973, that is designed for the purpose of preserving ensilage on a farm;

(*e*) a building or other structure, acquired after February 19, 1973, that is

(i) designed to store fresh fruits or fresh vegetables at a controlled level of temperature and humidity, and

(ii) to be used principally for the purpose of storing fresh fruits or fresh vegetables by or for the person or persons by whom they were grown;

(*f*) electrical generating equipment acquired after May 25, 1976, if

¶2454

(i) the taxpayer is not a person whose business is the production for the use of or distribution to others of electrical energy,

(ii) the equipment is auxiliary to the taxpayer's main power supply, and

(iii) the equipment is not used regularly as a source of supply;

(g) electrical generating equipment, acquired after May 25, 1976, that has a maximum load capacity of not more than 15 kilowatts;

(h) portable electrical generating equipment acquired after May 25, 1976;

(i) a tangible capital property that is not included in another class in this Schedule except

(i) land or any part thereof or any interest therein,

(ii) an animal,

(iii) a tree, shrub, herb or similar growing thing,

(iv) an oil or gas well,

(v) a mine,

(vi) a specified temporary access road of the taxpayer,

(vii) radium,

(viii) a right of way,

(ix) a timber limit,

(x) a tramway track, or

(xi) property of a separate class prescribed by subsection 1101(2a);

(j) property not included in any other class that is radio-communication equipment acquired after May 25, 1976;

(k) a rapid transit car that is used for the purpose of public transportation within a metropolitan area and is not part of a railway system;

(l) an outdoor advertising poster panel or bulletin board; or

(m) a greenhouse constructed of a rigid frame and a replaceable, flexible plastic cover.

Federal Budget Extract

Transmission Pipelines and Related Equipment

[Reproduced below is an excerpt from the February 23, 2005 Federal Budget that sets out proposals for new capital cost allowance rates for transmission pipelines and related equipment]

Currently, hydrocarbon transmission pipelines are generally eligible for a 4-per-cent capital cost allowance (CCA) rate under Class 1 of Schedule II to the Income Tax Regulations. Because petroleum pumping equipment and natural gas compression equipment on such pipelines is not specifically included in any of the CCA classes, the sector has generally included such assets in Class 8 (20-per-cent CCA rate), the default class for property not included in any other class. However, court cases have called into question the classification of natural gas compression equipment, on such pipelines, that default into Class 8.

*   *   *

The budget proposes that the CCA rate for transmission pipelines (as contrasted with distribution lines) for petroleum, natural gas or related hydrocarbons be increased to 8 per cent from 4 per cent to better reflect the typical useful life of these assets. Included will be control and monitoring devices, valves and other ancillary equipment (other than pumping and compression equipment, discussed below). The proposed changes will not affect the existing treatment of gas or oil well equipment and pipelines for which the Minister of National Revenue, in consultation with the Minister of Natural Resources, is satisfied that the main source of supply is likely to be exhausted within 15 years of commencement of operation. Distribution pipelines that distribute gas to the ultimate consumers typically have a longer useful life than transmission pipelines. Accordingly, these properties will continue to be included in Class 1, eligible for a 4-per-cent CCA rate.

The budget also proposes changes to the treatment for pumping and compression equipment, and equipment ancillary to it, related to a transmission pipeline for petroleum, natural gas or related hydrocarbons. The tax treatment of such equipment is to be rationalized by establishing a uniform 15-per-cent CCA rate that better reflects the typical useful life of these assets. However, this change will not apply to gas or oil well equipment (which is already eligible for a 25-per-cent CCA rate) and buildings or other structures.

The useful life of a pipeline can, however, be shortened in cases where production from the associated resource ceases. Accordingly, the budget also proposes that a separate class election be introduced for transmission pipelines and related pumping and compression equipment. The separate class election, which must be made for the taxation year in which a property is acquired, allows taxpayers to place eligible property in a separate class for CCA purposes. Although the separate class election does not change the CCA rate specified for the class, it does provide that any remaining undepreciated balance in the class after the disposition of the property, can, for the year of disposition, be fully deducted as a terminal loss.

The new CCA rates for transmission pipelines will apply to equipment acquired on or after February 23, 2005 that has not been used or acquired for use before that date. The new CCA rates for pumping and compression equipment will apply to all such equipment acquired on or after February 23, 2005.

[¶2456]

Class 9

(25 per cent)

Property acquired before May 26, 1976, other than property included in Class 30, that is

(*a*) electrical generating equipment, if

     (i) the taxpayer is not a person whose business is the production for the use of or distribution to others of electrical energy,

     (ii) the equipment is auxiliary to the taxpayer's main power supply, and

     (iii) the equipment is not used regularly as a source of supply,

(*b*) radar equipment,

(c) radio transmission equipment,

(d) radio receiving equipment,

(e) electrical generating equipment that has a maximum load capacity of not more than 15 kilowatts, or

(f) portable electrical generating equipment,

and property acquired after May 25, 1976 that is

(g) an aircraft;

(h) furniture, fittings or equipment attached to an aircraft; or

(i) a spare part for an aircraft, or for furniture, fittings or equipment attached to an aircraft.

[¶2458]

CLASS 10

(30 per cent)

Property not included in any other class that is

(a) automotive equipment, including a trolley bus, but not including

(i) an automotive railway car acquired after May 25, 1976,

(ii) a railway locomotive, or

(iii) a tramcar,

(b) a portable tool acquired after May 25, 1976 for the purpose of earning rental income for short terms, such as hourly, daily, weekly or monthly, except a property described in Class 12,

(c) harness or stable equipment,

(d) a sleigh or wagon,

(e) a trailer, including a trailer designed to be hauled on both highways and railway tracks,

(f) general-purpose electronic data processing equipment and systems software therefor, including ancillary data processing equipment, acquired after May 25, 1976, but not including property that is principally or is used principally as

---

Draft Regulation

Capital Cost Allowance (July 9, 2005)

The portion of paragraph (f) of Class 10 in Schedule II to the Regulations before subparagraph (i) is replaced by the following:

(f) general-purpose electronic data processing equipment and systems software for that equipment, including ancillary data processing equipment, acquired after May 25, 1976 and before March 23, 2004 (or after March 22, 2004 and before 2005

¶2458

if an election in respect of the property is made under subsection 1101(5q)), but not including property that is principally or is used principally as

Applicable: Deemed to have come into force on March 23, 2004.

Explanatory Note: See the Regulatory Impact Analysis Statement following the addition of subparagraphs 1100(1)(a)(xxxi) and (xxxii).

(i) electronic process control or monitor equipment,

(ii) electronic communications control equipment,

(iii) systems software for a property referred to in subparagraph (i) or (ii), or

(iv) data handling equipment unless it is ancillary to general-purpose electronic data processing equipment,

(f.1) a designated underground storage cost, or

(f.2) an unmanned telecommunication spacecraft designed to orbit above the earth,

and property (other than property included in Class 41 or property included in Class 43 that is described in paragraph (b) of that Class) that would otherwise be included in another Class in this Schedule, that is

(g) a building or other structure (other than property described in paragraph (l) or (m)) that would otherwise be included in Class 1, 3 or 6 and that was acquired for the purpose of gaining or producing income from a mine, except

(i) a property included in Class 28,

(ii) a property acquired principally for the purpose of gaining or producing income from the processing of ore from a mineral resource that is not owned by the taxpayer,

(iii) an office building not situated on the mine property, or

(iv) a refinery that was acquired by the taxpayer

(A) before November 8, 1969, or

(B) after November 7, 1969 and that had been used before November 8, 1969 by any person with whom the taxpayer was not dealing at arm's length;

(h) contractor's movable equipment, including portable camp buildings, acquired for use in a construction business or for lease to another taxpayer for use in that other taxpayer's construction business, except a property included in

(i) this Class by virtue of paragraph (t),

(ii) a separate class prescribed by subsection 1101(2b), or

(iii) Class 22 or 38;

¶2458

(i) a floor of a roller skating rink;

(j) gas or oil well equipment;

(k) property (other than property included in Class 28 or property described in paragraph (l) or (m)) that was acquired for the purpose of gaining or producing income from a mine and that is

(i) a structure that would otherwise be included in Class 8, or

(ii) machinery or equipment,

except a property acquired before May 9, 1972 for the purpose of gaining or producing income from the processing of ore after extraction from a mineral resource that is not owned by the taxpayer;

(l) property acquired after the 1971 taxation year for the purpose of gaining or producing income from a mine and providing services to the mine or to a community where a substantial proportion of the persons who ordinarily work at the mine reside, if such property is

(i) an airport, dam, dock, fire hall, hospital, house, natural gas pipeline, power line, recreational facility, school, sewage disposal plant, sewer, street lighting system, town hall, water pipeline, water pumping station, water system, wharf or similar property,

(ii) a road, sidewalk, airplane runway, parking area, storage area or similar surface construction, or

(iii) machinery or equipment ancillary to any of the property described in subparagraph (i) or (ii),

but is not

(iv) a property included in Class 28, or

(v) a railway not situated on the mine property;

(m) property acquired after March 31, 1977, principally for the purpose of gaining or producing income from a mine, if such property is

(i) railway track and grading including components such as rails, ballast, ties and other track material,

(ii) property ancillary to the track referred to in subparagraph (i) that is

(A) railway traffic control or signalling equipment, including switching, block signalling, interlocking, crossing protection, detection, speed control or retarding equipment, or

(B) a bridge, culvert, subway, trestle or tunnel,

(iii) machinery or equipment ancillary to any of the property referred to in subparagraph (i) or (ii), or

(iv) conveying, loading, unloading or storing machinery or equipment, including a structure, acquired for the purpose of shipping output from the mine by means of the track referred to in subparagraph (i),

¶2458

but is not

(v) property included in Class 28, or

(vi) for greater certainty, rolling stock,

(n) property that was acquired for the purpose of cutting and removing merchantable timber from a timber limit and that will be of no further use to the taxpayer after all merchantable timber that the taxpayer is entitled to cut and remove from the limit has been cut and removed, unless the taxpayer has elected to include another property of this kind in another class in this Schedule;

(o) mechanical equipment acquired for logging operations, except a property included in Class 7;

(p) an access road or trails for the protection of standing timber against fire, insects or disease;

(q) property acquired for a motion picture drive-in theatre;

(r) property included in this class by virtue of subsection 1102(8) or (9), except a property included in Class 28;

(s) a motion picture film or video tape acquired after May 25, 1976, except a property included in paragraph (w) or (x) or in Class 12;

(t) a property acquired after May 22, 1979 that is designed principally for the purpose of

(i) determining the existence, location, extent or quality of accumulations of petroleum or natural gas,

(ii) drilling oil or gas wells, or

(iii) determining the existence, location, extent or quality of mineral resources,

except a property included in a separate class prescribed by subsection 1101(2b);

(u) property acquired after 1980 to be used primarily in the processing in Canada of heavy crude oil recovered from a natural reservoir in Canada to a stage that is not beyond the crude oil stage or its equivalent that is

(i) property that would otherwise be included in Class 8 except railway rolling stock or a property described in paragraph (j) of Class 8,

(ii) an oil or water storage tank,

(iii) a powered industrial lift truck that would otherwise be included in paragraph (a),

(iv) property that would otherwise be included in paragraph (f), or

(v) property acquired after August 31, 1984 that is equipment used for the purpose of effecting an interface between a cable distribution

¶2458

system and electronic products used by consumers of that system and that is designed primarily

(i) to augment the channel capacity of a television receiver or radio,

(ii) to decode pay television or other signals provided on a discretionary basis, or

(iii) to achieve any combination of functions described in subparagraphs (i) and (ii),

(w) a certified production acquired after 1987 and before March 1996; or

(x) a Canadian film or video production.

[¶2460]

CLASS 10.1

(30 per cent)

Property that would otherwise be included in Class 10 that is a passenger vehicle, the cost of which to the taxpayer exceeds $20,000 or such other amount as may be prescribed for the purposes of subsection 13(2) of the Act.

[¶2462]

CLASS 11

(35 per cent)

Property not included in any other class that is used to earn rental income and that is

(a) an electrical advertising sign owned by the manufacturer thereof, acquired before May 26, 1976; or

(b) an outdoor advertising poster panel or bulletin board acquired by the taxpayer

(i) before 1988, or

(ii) before 1990

(A) pursuant to an obligation in writing entered into by the taxpayer before June 18, 1987, or

(B) that was under construction by or on behalf of the taxpayer on June 18, 1987.

[¶2464]

CLASS 12

(100 per cent)

Property not included in any other class that is

(a) a book that is part of a lending library;

(b) chinaware, cutlery or other tableware;

(c) a kitchen utensil costing less than

    (i) $100, if acquired before May 26, 1976, or

    (ii) $200, if acquired after May 25, 1976;

(d) a die, jig, pattern, mould or last;

(e) a medical or dental instrument costing less than

    (i) $100, if acquired before May 26, 1976, or

    (ii) $200, if acquired after May 25, 1976;

(f) a mine shaft, main haulage way or similar underground work designed for continuing use, or any extension thereof, sunk or constructed after the mine came into production, to the extent that the property was acquired before 1988;

(g) linen;

(h) a tool costing less than

    (i) $100, if acquired before May 26, 1976, or

    (ii) $200, if acquired after May 25, 1976;

(i) a uniform;

(j) the cutting or shaping part in a machine;

(k) apparel or costume, including accessories used therewith, used for the purpose of earning rental income;

(l) a video tape acquired before May 26, 1976;

(m) a motion picture film or video tape that is a television commercial message;

(n) a certified feature film or certified production;

(o) computer software acquired after May 25, 1976, but not including systems software or property acquired after August 8, 1989 and before 1993 that is described in paragraph (s);

(p) a metric scale or a scale designed for ready conversion to metric weighing, acquired after March 31, 1977 and before 1984 for use in a retail business and having a maximum weighing capacity of 100 kilograms;

(q) a designated overburden removal cost; or

(r) a video-cassette, a video-laser disk or a digital video disk, that is acquired for the purpose of renting and that is not expected to be rented to any one person for more than 7 days in any 30-day period;

and property that would otherwise be included in another class in this Schedule that is

¶2464

(s) acquired by the taxpayer after August 8, 1989 and before 1993, for use in a business of selling goods or providing services to consumers that is carried on in Canada, or for lease to another taxpayer for use by that other taxpayer in such a business, and that is

(i) electronic bar code scanning equipment designed to read bar codes applied to goods held for sale in the ordinary course of the business,

(ii) a cash register or similar sales recording device designed with the capability of calculating and recording sales tax imposed by more than one jurisdiction in respect of the same sale,

(iii) equipment or computer software that is designed to convert a cash register or similar sales recording device to one having the capability of calculating and recording sales tax imposed by more than one jurisdiction in respect of the same sale, or

(iv) electronic equipment or computer software that is ancillary to property described in subparagraph (i), (ii) or (iii) and all or substantially all the use of which is in conjunction with that property.

[¶2466]

Class 13

Property that is a leasehold interest and property acquired by a taxpayer that would, if that property had been acquired by a person with whom the taxpayer was not dealing at arm's length at the time the property was acquired by the taxpayer, be a leasehold interest of that person, except

(a) an interest in minerals, petroleum, natural gas, other related hydrocarbons or timber and property relating thereto or in respect of a right to explore for, drill for, take or remove minerals, petroleum, natural gas, other related hydrocarbons or timber;

(b) that part of the leasehold interest that is included in another class in this Schedule by reason of subsection 1102(5) or (5.1); or

(c) a property included in Class 23.

[¶2468]

Class 14

Property that is a patent, franchise, concession or licence for a limited period in respect of property, except

(a) a franchise, concession or licence in respect of minerals, petroleum, natural gas, other related hydrocarbons or timber and property relating thereto (except a franchise for distributing gas to consumers or a licence to export gas from Canada or from a province) or in respect of a right to explore for, drill for, take or remove minerals, petroleum, natural gas, other related hydrocarbons or timber;

(b) a leasehold interest;

(c) a property included in Class 23;

(d) a licence to use computer software; or

(e) a property that is included in Class 44.

[¶2470]

CLASS 15

Property that would otherwise be included in another class in this Schedule and that

(a) was acquired for the purpose of cutting and removing merchantable timber from a timber limit, and

(b) will be of no further use to the taxpayer after all merchantable timber that the taxpayer is entitled to cut and remove from the limit has been cut and removed,

except

(c) property that the taxpayer has, in the taxation year or a preceding taxation year, elected not to include in this class, or

(d) a timber resource property.

[¶2472]

CLASS 16

(40 per cent)

Property acquired before May 26, 1976 that is

(a) an aircraft,

(b) furniture, fittings or equipment attached to an aircraft, or

(c) a spare part for a property included in this class,

property acquired after May 25, 1976 that is

(d) a taxicab,

property acquired after November 12, 1981 that is

(e) a motor vehicle that

(i) would be an automobile as that term is defined in subsection 248(1) of the Act, if that definition were read without reference to paragraph (d) thereof,

(ii) was acquired for the purpose of renting or leasing, and

(iii) is not expected to be rented or leased to any person for more than 30 days in any 12 month period,

property acquired after February 15, 1984 that is

(f) a coin-operated video game or pinball machine,

and property acquired after December 6, 1991 that is

(g) a truck or tractor designed for hauling freight, and that is primarily so used by the taxpayer or a person with whom the taxpayer does not deal at arm's length in a business that includes hauling freight, and that has a "gross vehicle weight rating" (as that term is defined in subsection 2(1) of the Motor Vehicle Safety Regulations) in excess of 11,788 kg.

[¶2474]

CLASS 17

(8 per cent)

Property that would otherwise be included in another class in this Schedule that is

(a) a telephone system, telegraph system, or a part thereof, acquired before May 26, 1976, except

(i) radiocommunication equipment, or

(ii) a property included in Class 10, 13, 14 or 28,

Draft Regulation

Capital Cost Allowance (March 16, 2001)

Class 17 in Schedule II to the Regulations is amended by adding the word "or" at the end of paragraph (a) and by adding the following after paragraph (a):

(a.1) property (other than a building or other structure) acquired after February 27, 2000 that has not been used for any purpose whatever before it was acquired by the taxpayer and that is

(i) electrical generating equipment (other than electrical generating equipment described in any of paragraphs (f) to (h) of Class 8), or

(ii) production and distribution equipment of a distributor of water or steam used for heating or cooling (including, for this purpose, pipe used to collect or distribute an energy transfer medium but not including equipment or pipe used to distribute water that is for consumption, disposal or treatment),

Applicable: To property acquired after February 27, 2000.

Explanatory Note: Class 17 (8% CCA rate) is amended to apply to property (other than a building or other structure) acquired after February 27, 2000 that has not been used for any purpose whatever before it was acquired by the taxpayer and that is

● electrical generating equipment (other than electrical generating equipment described in any of paragraphs (f) to (h) of Class 8), or

● production and distribution equipment of a distributor of water or steam used for heating or cooling (including, for this purpose, pipe used to collect or distribute an energy transfer medium but not including equipment or pipe used to distribute water that is for consumption, disposal or treatment).

---

and property not included in any other class, acquired after May 25, 1976, that is

¶2474

(b) telephone, telegraph or data communication switching equipment, except

(i) equipment installed on customers' premises, or

(ii) property that is principally electronic equipment or systems software therefor; or

(c) a road (other than a specified temporary access road of the taxpayer), sidewalk, airplane runway, parking area, storage area or similar surface construction.

Federal Budget Extract

Combustion Turbines Generating Electricity

[Reproduced below is an excerpt from the February 23, 2005 Federal Budget that sets out a proposal to increase the capital cost allowance rate to 15% for combustion turbines that generate electricity and to apply the specified energy property rules to combustion turbines and electricity transmission and distribution assets.]

As a result of measures announced in the 2000 budget, combustion turbines that generate electricity are eligible for an 8-per-cent CCA rate [Class 17].

* * *

Available evidence associated with newer combustion turbines suggests that the current provisions do not reflect the useful life of these assets. The budget therefore proposes that the CCA rate for combustion turbines that generate electricity (including associated burners and compressors) be increased to 15 per cent. The 15-per-cent rate will apply to such property acquired on or after February 23, 2005, that has not been used or acquired for use before February 23, 2005.

Combustion turbines that generate electricity are currently eligible for a separate class election. The separate class election was provided in response to concerns that combustion turbines can have shorter useful lives than other electrical generating equipment.

Because the higher CCA rate proposed in this budget will better reflect the useful life of combustion turbines, it is proposed that the separate class election not be extended to combustion turbines eligible for the higher rate. To accommodate taxpayers who may have already planned purchases based on the availability of the separate class election, it is further proposed that taxpayers may elect to have combustion turbines acquired before 2006 that would otherwise be eligible for the 15-per-cent rate included in Class 17 and therefore eligible for the separate class election. The proposed election must be filed with the income tax return for the taxation year in which the property is acquired.

* * *

In addition to setting the appropriate CCA rate, rules are needed to protect the integrity of the CCA system. These include the specified energy property rules, which limit the amount of CCA deductions that may be used by passive investors in respect of specified energy property — generally property for which an incentive CCA rate is allowed under Class 34 or 43.1 — to the amount of income from such property. This prevents CCA deductions from being used by passive investors to shelter other sources of income.

This budget proposes that the specified energy property rules be extended to combustion turbines and electricity transmission and distribution assets that are eligible for the higher CCA rates proposed in this budget.

¶2474

[¶2476]

CLASS 18

(60 per cent)

Property that is a motion picture film acquired before May 26, 1976, except

(*a*) a television commercial message; or

(*b*) a certified feature film.

[¶2478]

CLASS 19

Property acquired by the taxpayer after June 13, 1963 and before January 1, 1967 that would otherwise be included in Class 8 if,

(*a*) in the taxation year in which the property was acquired,

(i) the taxpayer was an individual who was resident in Canada for not less than 183 days, or

(ii) the taxpayer was a corporation that had a degree of Canadian ownership;

(*b*) the property was acquired for use in Canada in a business carried on by the taxpayer that,

(i) for the fiscal period in which the property was acquired, or

(ii) for the fiscal period in which the business first commenced selling goods in reasonable commercial quantities,

whichever was later, was a business in which the aggregate of

(iii) its net sales, as they would be determined under paragraphs 71A(2)(*d*) and (*f*) of the former Act (within the meaning assigned by paragraph 8(*b*) of the *Income Tax Application Rules, 1971*), from the sale of goods processed or manufactured in Canada by the business,

(iv) an amount equal to that part of its gross revenue that is rent from goods processed or manufactured in Canada in the course of the business, and

(v) its gross revenue from advertisements in a newspaper or magazine produced by the business,

was not less than $2/3$ of the amount by which the gross revenue from the business for the period exceeded the aggregate of each amount paid or credited in the period to a customer of the business as a bonus, rebate or discount or for returned or damaged goods, and was not a business that was principally

(vi) operating a gas or oil well,

(vii) logging,

(viii) mining,

(ix) construction, or

(x) a combination of two or more of the activities referred to in subparagraphs (vi) to (ix); and

(*c*) the property had not been used for any purpose whatever before it was acquired by the taxpayer.

[¶2480]

CLASS 20

Property that would otherwise be included in Class 3 or 6

(*a*) that was acquired after December 5, 1963 and before April 1, 1967 that is

(i) a building,

(ii) an extension to a building, outside the previously existing walls or roof of the building, if the aggregate cost of the extensions added in the aforementioned period exceeded the lesser of

(A) $100,000, and

(B) 25 per cent of the capital cost to the taxpayer of the building on December 5, 1963, or

(iii) an addition or alteration to a property described in subparagraph (i) or (ii),

and that has been certified by the Minister of Industry, upon application by the taxpayer in such form as may be prescribed by the Minister of Industry,

(iv) to be situated in an area that was a designated area, as determined for the purposes of section 71A of the former Act (within the meaning assigned by paragraph 8(*b*) of the *Income Tax Application Rules, 1971*),

(A) at the time the property was acquired,

(B) in a case where the property was built by the taxpayer, at the time construction was commenced, or

(C) in a case where the property was built for the taxpayer pursuant to a contract entered into by the taxpayer, at the time the contract was entered into, and

(v) to have not been used for any purpose whatever before it was acquired by the taxpayer; or

(*b*) the capital cost of which was included in the approved capital costs as defined in the *Area Development Incentives Act* upon which approved capital cost the Minister of Industry has based the amount of a development grant authorized under that Act.

[¶2482]

CLASS 21

Property that would otherwise be included in Class 8 or Class 19

(a) that was acquired after December 5, 1963 and before April 1, 1967 and that

(i) was acquired for use in a business carried on by the taxpayer that has been certified by the Minister of Industry, for the purposes of section 71A of the former Act (within the meaning assigned by paragraph 8(b) of the *Income Tax Application Rules, 1971*), to be a new manufacturing or processing business in a designated area for the fiscal period in which the property was acquired or for a subsequent fiscal period, and

(ii) had not been used for any purpose whatever before it was acquired by the taxpayer; or

(b) the capital cost of which was included in the approved capital costs as defined in the *Area Development Incentives Act* upon which approved capital cost the Minister of Industry has based the amount of a development grant authorized under that Act.

[¶2484]

CLASS 22

Property acquired by the taxpayer after March 16, 1964 and

(a) before 1988, or

(b) before 1990

(i) pursuant to an obligation in writing entered into by the taxpayer before June 18, 1987, or

(ii) that was under construction by or on behalf of the taxpayer on June 18, 1987

that is power-operated movable equipment designed for the purpose of excavating, moving, placing or compacting earth, rock, concrete or asphalt, except a property included in Class 7.

[¶2486]

CLASS 23

(100 per cent)

Property that is

(a) a leasehold interest or a concession in respect of land granted under or pursuant to an agreement in writing with the Canadian Corporation for the 1967 World Exhibition where such leasehold interest or concession is to expire not later than June 15, 1968;

(b) a building or other structure, including component parts, erected on land that is the subject matter of a leasehold interest or concession described in paragraph (a) where such building or other structure, including component parts, is of a temporary nature and is required by the agreement to be removed not later than June 15, 1968;

(c) a leasehold interest or licence in respect of land granted under or pursuant to an agreement in writing with the Expo 86 Corporation where such leasehold interest or licence is to expire not later than January 31, 1987; or

(d) a building or other structure, including component parts, erected on land that is the subject matter of a leasehold interest or licence described in paragraph (c) where such building or other structure, including component parts, is of a temporary nature and is required by the agreement to be removed not later than January 31, 1987.

[¶2488]

CLASS 24

Property acquired after April 26, 1965 and before 1971

(a) that would otherwise be included in Class 2, 3, 6 or 8 and that

(i) was acquired primarily for the purpose of preventing, reducing or eliminating pollution of

(A) any of the inland, coastal or boundary waters of Canada, or

(B) any lake, river, stream, watercourse, pond, swamp or well in Canada,

by industrial waste, refuse or sewage created by operations in the course of carrying on a business by the taxpayer or that would be created by such operations if the property had not been acquired and used, and

(ii) had not been used for any purpose whatever before it was acquired by the taxpayer,

but not including property acquired for use in the production of by-products or the recovery of materials unless the by-products are produced from, or the materials are recovered from, materials that after April 26, 1965,

(iii) were being discarded as waste by the taxpayer, or

(iv) were commonly being discarded as waste by other taxpayers who carried on operations of a type similar to the operations carried on by the taxpayer,

and property acquired before 1999

(b) that would otherwise be included in another class in this Schedule

(i) that has not been included by the taxpayer in any other class,

(ii) that had not been used for any purpose whatever before it was acquired by the taxpayer,

(iii) that was acquired by the taxpayer after 1970 primarily for the purpose of preventing, reducing or eliminating pollution of

(A) any of the inland, coastal or boundary waters of Canada, or

(B) any lake, river, stream, watercourse, pond, swamp or well in Canada,

that is caused, or that, if the property had not been acquired and used, would be caused by

(C) operations carried on by the taxpayer at a site in Canada at which operations have been carried on by him from a time that is before 1974,

(D) the operation in Canada of a building or plant by the taxpayer, the construction of which was either commenced before 1974 or commenced under an agreement in writing entered into by him before 1974, or

(E) the operation of transportation or other movable equipment that has been operated by the taxpayer in Canada (including any of the inland, coastal or boundary waters of Canada) from a time that is before 1974,

or that was acquired by him after May 8, 1972, that would otherwise have been property referred to in this subparagraph except that

(F) it was acquired

(I) for the purpose of gaining or producing income from a business by a taxpayer whose business includes the preventing, reducing or eliminating of pollution of a kind referred to in this subparagraph that is caused or that otherwise would be caused primarily by operations referred to in clause (C), (D) or (E) carried on by other taxpayers (not including persons referred to in section 149 of the Act), and

(II) to be used in a business referred to in subclause (I) in the preventing, reducing or eliminating of pollution of a kind referred to in this subparagraph, or

(G) it was acquired

(I) for the purpose of gaining or producing income from a property by a corporation whose principal business is the purchasing of conditional sales contracts, accounts receivable, bills of sale, chattel mortgages, bills of exchange or other obligations representing part or all of the sale price of merchandise or services, the lending of money, or the leasing of property, or any combination thereof, and

¶2488

(II) to be leased to a taxpayer (other than a person referred to in section 149 of the Act) to be used by him, in an operation referred to in clause (C), (D), (E) or (F), in the preventing, reducing or eliminating of pollution of a kind referred to in this subparagraph, and

(iv) that has, upon application by the taxpayer to the Minister of the Environment, been accepted by that Minister as property the primary use of which is to be the preventing, reducing or eliminating of pollution of a kind referred to in subparagraph (iii)

and for the purposes of paragraphs (*a*) and (*b*)

(*c*) where a corporation (in this paragraph referred to as the "predecessor corporation") has, as a result of an amalgamation within the meaning assigned by subsection 87(1) of the Act, merged at any time after 1973 with one or more other corporations to form one corporate entity (in this paragraph referred to as the "new corporation"), the new corporation shall be deemed to be the same corporation as, and a continuation of, the predecessor corporation;

(*d*) where a corporation (in this paragraph referred to as the "subsidiary") has been wound up at any time after 1973 in circumstances to which subsection 88(1) of the Act applies, the parent (within the meaning assigned by that subsection) shall be deemed to be the same corporation as, and a continuation of, the subsidiary; and

(*e*) this class shall be read without reference to subparagraph (*b*)(i) where paragraph (*c*) or (*d*) applies to the taxpayer and the property was acquired before 1992.

[¶2490]

CLASS 25

(100 per cent)

Property that would otherwise be included in another class in this Schedule that is property acquired by the taxpayer

(*a*) before October 23, 1968, or

(*b*) after October 22, 1968 and before 1974, where the acquisition of the property may reasonably be regarded as having been in fulfilment of an obligation undertaken in an agreement made in writing before October 23, 1968 and ratified, confirmed or adopted by the legislature of a province by a statute that came into force before that date,

if the taxpayer was, on October 22, 1968, a corporation, commission or association to which, on the assumption that October 22, 1968 was in its 1969 taxation year, paragraph 62(1)(*c*) of the former Act (within the meaning assigned by paragraph 8(*b*) of the *Income Tax Application Rules, 1971*),

(*c*) would not apply; and

¶2490

(d) would have applied but for subparagraph (i) or (ii) of that paragraph.

[¶2492]

CLASS 26

(*5 per cent*)

Property that is

(a) a catalyst; or

(b) deuterium enriched water (commonly known as "heavy water") acquired after May 22, 1979.

[¶2494]

CLASS 27

Property acquired before 1999 that would otherwise be included in another Class in this Schedule

(a) that has not been included by the taxpayer in any other class;

(b) that had not been used for any purpose whatever before it was acquired by the taxpayer;

(c) that was acquired by the taxpayer after March 12, 1970 primarily for the purpose of preventing, reducing or eliminating air pollution by

(i) removing particulate, toxic or injurious materials from smoke or gas, or

(ii) preventing the discharge of part or all of the smoke, gas or other air pollutant,

that is discharged or that, if the property had not been acquired and used, would be discharged into the atmosphere as a result of

(iii) operations carried on by the taxpayer at a site in Canada at which operations have been carried on by him from a time that is before 1974,

(iv) the operation in Canada of a building or plant by the taxpayer, the construction of which was either commenced before 1974 or commenced under an agreement in writing entered into by him before 1974, or

(v) the operation of transportation or other movable equipment that has been operated by the taxpayer in Canada (including any of the inland, coastal or boundary waters of Canada) from a time that is before 1974,

or that was acquired by him after May 8, 1972, that would otherwise have been property referred to in this paragraph except that

(vi) it was acquired

(A) for the purpose of gaining or producing income from a business by a taxpayer whose business includes the preventing, reducing or eliminating of air pollution that is caused or that otherwise would be caused primarily by operations referred to in subparagraph (iii), (iv) or (v) carried on by other taxpayers (not including persons referred to in section 149 of the Act), and

(B) to be used in a business referred to in clause (A) in the preventing, reducing or eliminating of air pollution in a manner referred to in this paragraph, or

(vii) it was acquired

(A) for the purpose of gaining or producing income from a property by a corporation whose principal business is the purchasing of conditional sales contracts, accounts receivable, bills of sale, chattel mortgages, bills of exchange or other obligations representing part or all of the sale price of merchandise or services, the lending of money, or the leasing of property, or any combination thereof, and

(B) to be leased to a taxpayer (other than a person referred to in section 149 of the Act) to be used by him, in an operation referred to in subparagraph (iii), (iv), (v) or (vi), in the preventing, reducing or eliminating of air pollution in a manner referred to in this paragraph; and

(d) that has, upon application by the taxpayer to the Minister of the Environment, been accepted by that Minister as property the primary use of which is to be the preventing, reducing or eliminating of air pollution in a manner referred to in paragraph (c)

and for the purposes of paragraphs (a) to (d),

(e) where a corporation (in this paragraph referred to as the "predecessor corporation") has, as a result of an amalgamation within the meaning assigned by subsection 87(1) of the Act, merged at any time after 1973 with one or more other corporations to form one corporate entity (in this paragraph referred to as the "new corporation"), the new corporation shall be deemed to be the same corporation as, and a continuation of, the predecessor corporation;

(f) where a corporation (in this paragraph referred to as the "subsidiary") has been wound up at any time after 1973 in circumstances to which subsection 88(1) of the Act applies, the parent (within the meaning assigned by that subsection) shall be deemed to be the same corporation as, and a continuation of, the subsidiary; and

(g) this class shall be read without reference to paragraph (a) where paragraph (e) or (f) applies to the taxpayer and the property was acquired before 1992.

¶2494

[¶2496]

CLASS 28

(30 per cent)

Property situated in Canada that would otherwise be included in another class in this Schedule that

(*a*) was acquired by the taxpayer

(i) before 1988, or

(ii) before 1990

(A) pursuant to an obligation in writing entered into by the taxpayer before June 18, 1987,

(B) that was under construction by or on behalf of the taxpayer on June 18, 1987, or

(C) that is machinery or equipment that is a fixed and integral part of a building, structure, plant facility or other property that was under construction by or on behalf of the taxpayer on June 18, 1987,

and that

(*b*) was acquired by the taxpayer principally for the purpose of gaining or producing income from one or more mines operated by the taxpayer and situated in Canada and each of which

(i) came into production in reasonable commercial quantities after November 7, 1969, or

(ii) was the subject of a major expansion after November 7, 1969

(A) whereby the greatest designed capacity, measured in weight of input of ore, of the mill that processed the ore from the mine was not less than 25% greater in the year following the expansion than it was in the year preceding the expansion, or

(B) where in the one year period preceding the expansion

(I) the Minister, in consultation with the Minister of Natural Resources, determines that the greatest designed capacity of the mine, measured in weight of output of ore, immediately after the expansion was not less than 25% greater than the greatest designed capacity of the mine immediately before the expansion, and

(II) either

1. no mill processed the ore from the mine at any time, or

2. the mill that processed the ore from the mine processed other ore,

(*c*) was acquired by the taxpayer

¶2496

(i) after November 7, 1969,

(ii) before the coming into production of the mine or the completion of the expansion of the mine referred to in subparagraph $(b)(i)$ or (ii), as the case may be, and

(iii) in the case of a mine that was the subject of a major expansion described in subparagraph $(b)(ii)$, in the course of and principally for the purposes of the expansion,

(d) had not, before it was acquired by the taxpayer, been used for any purpose whatever by any person with whom the taxpayer was not dealing at arm's length, and

(e) is any of the following, namely,

(i) property that was acquired before the mine came into production and that would, but for this class, be included in Class 10 by virtue of paragraph (g), (k), (l) or (r) of that class or would have been so included in that class if it had been acquired after the 1971 taxation year,

(ii) property that was acquired before the mine came into production and that would, but for this class, be included in Class 10 by virtue of paragraph (m) of that class, or

(iii) property that was acquired after the mine came into production and that would, but for this class, be included in Class 10 by virtue of paragraph (g), (k), (l) or (r) of that class,

or that would be described in paragraphs (b) to (e) if in those paragraphs each reference to a "mine" were read as a reference to a "mine that is a location in a bituminous sands deposit, oil sands deposit or oil shale deposit from which material is extracted", and each reference to "after November 7, 1969" were read as "before November 8, 1969".

[¶2498]

CLASS 29

Property not included in Class 41 because of paragraph (c) or (d) of that Class that would otherwise be included in another class in this Schedule

(a) that is property manufactured by the taxpayer, the manufacture of which was completed by him after May 8, 1972, or other property acquired by the taxpayer after May 8, 1972,

(i) to be used directly or indirectly by him in Canada primarily in the manufacturing or processing of goods for sale or lease, or

(ii) to be leased, in the ordinary course of carrying on a business in Canada of the taxpayer, to a lessee who can reasonably be expected to use, directly or indirectly, the property in Canada primarily in Canadian field processing carried on by the lessee or in the manufacturing or processing by the lessee of goods for sale or lease, if the taxpayer is a corporation whose principal business is

(A) leasing property,

(B) manufacturing property that it sells or leases,

(C) the lending of money,

(D) the purchasing of conditional sales contracts, accounts receivable, bills of sale, chattel mortgages, bills of exchange or other obligations representing part or all of the sale price of merchandise or services, or

(E) selling or servicing a type of property that it also leases,

or any combination thereof, unless use of the property by the lessee commenced before May 9, 1972;

(b) that is

(i) property that, but for this class, would be included in Class 8, except railway rolling stock or a property described in paragraph (j) of Class 8,

(ii) an oil or water storage tank,

(iii) a powered industrial lift truck,

(iv) electrical generating equipment described in Class 9, or

(v) property described in paragraph (b) or (f) of Class 10; and

(c) that is property acquired by the taxpayer

(i) before 1988, or

(ii) before 1990

(A) pursuant to an obligation in writing entered into by the taxpayer before June 18, 1987,

(B) that was under construction by or on behalf of the taxpayer on June 18, 1987, or

(C) that is machinery or equipment that is a fixed and integral part of a building, structure, plant facility or other property that was under construction by or on behalf of the taxpayer on June 18, 1987.

[¶2500]

CLASS 30

Property that is an unmanned telecommunication spacecraft designed to orbit above the earth and acquired by the taxpayer

(a) before 1988, or

(b) before 1990

(i) pursuant to an obligation in writing entered into by the taxpayer before June 18, 1987, or

(ii) that was under construction by or on behalf of the taxpayer on June 18, 1987.

[¶2502]

CLASS 31

(5 per cent)

Property that is a multiple-unit residential building in Canada that would otherwise be included in Class 3 or Class 6 and in respect of which

(a) a certificate has been issued by Canada Mortgage and Housing Corporation certifying

(i) in respect of a building that would otherwise be included in Class 3, that the installation of footings or any other base support of the building was commenced

(A) after November 18, 1974 and before 1980, or

(B) after October 28, 1980 and before 1982,

as the case may be, and

(ii) in respect of a building that would otherwise be included in Class 6, that the installation of footings or any other base support of the building was commenced after December 31, 1977 and before 1979,

and that, according to plans and specifications for the building, not less than 80 per cent of the floor space will be used in providing self-contained domestic establishments and related parking, recreation, service and storage areas;

(b) not more than 20 per cent of the floor space is used for any purpose other than the purposes referred to in paragraph (a);

(c) the certificate referred to in paragraph (a) was issued on or before the later of

(i) December 31, 1981, and

(ii) the day that is 18 months after the day on which the installation of footings or other base support of the building was commenced; and

(d) the construction of the building proceeds, after 1982, without undue delay, taking into consideration acts of God, labour disputes, fire, accidents or unusual delay by common carriers or suppliers of materials or equipment

and that was acquired by the taxpayer

(e) before June 18, 1987, or

(f) after June 17, 1987 pursuant to

(i) an obligation in writing entered into by the taxpayer before June 18, 1987, or

(ii) the terms of a prospectus, preliminary prospectus, registration statement, offering memorandum or notice required to be filed with a public authority in Canada and filed before June 18, 1987 with that public authority.

[¶2504]

CLASS 32

(10 per cent)

Property that is a multiple-unit residential building in Canada that would otherwise be included in Class 6 if the reference to "1979" in subparagraph (a)(viii) of that Class were read as a reference to "1980", and in respect of which

(a) a certificate has been issued by Central Mortgage and Housing Corporation certifying

(i) that the installation of footings or any other base support of the building was commenced after November 18, 1974 and before 1978, and

(ii) that, according to plans and specifications for the building, not less than 80 per cent of the floor space will be used in providing self-contained domestic establishments and related parking, recreation, service and storage areas; and

(b) not more than 20 per cent of the floor space is used for any purpose other than the purposes referred to in subparagraph (a)(ii).

[¶2506]

CLASS 33

(15 per cent)

Property that is a timber resource property.

[¶2508]

CLASS 34

Property that would otherwise be included in Class 1, 2 or 8

(a) that is

(i) electrical generating equipment,

(ii) production equipment and pipelines of a distributor of heat,

(iii) steam generating equipment that was acquired by the taxpayer primarily for the purpose of producing steam to operate property described in subparagraph (i), or

(iv) an addition to a property described in subparagraph (i), (ii) or (iii),

but not including buildings or other structures,

(b) that was acquired by the taxpayer after May 25, 1976,

(c) that

(i) was acquired by the taxpayer for use by him in a business carried on in Canada, or

(ii) is to be leased by the taxpayer to a lessee for use by the lessee in Canada, and

(d) that is property in respect of which a certificate has been issued

(i) before December 11, 1979 by the Minister of Industry, Trade and Commerce certifying that the property is part of a plan designed to

(A) produce heat derived primarily from the consumption of wood wastes or municipal wastes,

(B) produce electrical energy by the utilization of fuel that is petroleum, natural gas or related hydrocarbons, coal, coal gas, coke, lignite or peat (in this clause referred to as "fossil fuel"), wood wastes or municipal wastes, or any combination thereof, if the consumption of fossil fuel (expressed as the high heat value of the fossil fuel), if any, chargeable to electrical energy on an annual basis in respect of the property is no greater than 7,000 British Thermal Units per kilowatt-hour of electrical energy produced, or

(C) recover heat that is a by-product of an industrial process, or

(ii) after December 10, 1979, by the Minister of Energy, Mines and Resources certifying that the property is part of a plan designed to

(A) produce heat derived primarily from the consumption of natural gas, coal, coal gas, lignite, peat, wood wastes or municipal wastes, or any combination thereof,

(B) produce electrical energy by the utilization of fuel that is petroleum, natural gas or related hydrocarbons, coal, coal gas, coke, lignite or peat (in this clause referred to as "fossil fuel"), wood wastes or municipal wastes, or any combination thereof, if the consumption of fossil fuel (expressed as the high heat value of the fossil fuel), if any, chargeable to electrical energy on an annual basis in respect of the property is no greater than 7,000 British Thermal Units per kilowatt-hour of electrical energy produced, or

(C) recover heat that is a by-product of an industrial process,

and property that was acquired by the taxpayer after December 10, 1979 (other than property described in paragraph (a)) and would otherwise be included in another Class in this Schedule

(e) that is

(i) active solar heating equipment including solar collectors, solar energy conversion equipment, storage equipment, control equipment, equipment designed to interface solar heating equipment with other heating equipment, and solar water heaters, used to

¶2508

(A) heat a liquid or air to be used directly in the course of manufacturing or processing,

(B) provide space heating when installed in a new building or other new structure at the time of its original construction where that construction commenced after December 10, 1979, or

(C) heat water for a use other than a use described in clause (A) or (B),

(ii) a hydro electric installation of a producer of hydro electric energy with a planned maximum generating capacity not exceeding 15 megawatts upon completion of site development that is the generating equipment and plant (including structures) of that producer including a canal, a dam, a dyke, an overflow spillway, a penstock, a powerhouse complete with generating equipment and other equipment ancillary thereto, control equipment, fishways or fish bypasses and transmission equipment, except distribution equipment and a property included in Class 10 or 17,

(iii) heat recovery equipment that is designed to conserve energy or reduce the requirement to acquire energy by extracting and reusing heat from thermal waste including condensers, heat exchange equipment, steam compressors used to upgrade low pressure steam, waste heat boilers and ancillary equipment such as control panels, fans, instruments or pumps,

(iv) an addition or alteration to a hydro electric installation described in subparagraph (ii) that results in a change in generating capacity if the new maximum generating capacity at the hydro electric installation does not exceed 15 megawatts, or

(v) a fixed location device acquired after February 25, 1986, that is a wind energy conversion system designed to produce electrical energy, consisting of a wind-driven turbine, generating equipment and related equipment, including control and conditioning equipment, support structures, a powerhouse complete with equipment ancillary thereto, and transmission equipment, but not including distribution equipment, equipment designed to store electrical energy or property included in Class 10 or 17,

(*f*) that

(i) was acquired by the taxpayer for use by him for the purpose of gaining or producing income from a business carried on in Canada or from property situated in Canada, or

(ii) is to be leased by the taxpayer to a lessee for use by the lessee in Canada, and

(*g*) that is property in respect of which a certificate has been issued by the Minister of Energy, Mines and Resources,

but not including

¶2508

(h) property in respect of which a certificate issued under paragraph (d) or (g) has been revoked pursuant to subsection 1104(11),

(i) property that had been used before it was acquired by the taxpayer unless the property had previously been included in Class 34 for the purpose of computing the income of the person from whom it was acquired.

(j) property acquired by the taxpayer after February 21, 1994 other than

(i) property acquired by the taxpayer

(A) pursuant to an agreement of purchase and sale in writing entered into by the taxpayer before February 22, 1994,

(B) in order to satisfy a legally binding obligation entered into by the taxpayer in writing before February 22, 1994 to sell electricity to a public power utility in Canada,

(C) that was under construction by or on behalf of the taxpayer on February 22, 1994, or

(D) that is machinery or equipment that is a fixed and integral part of a building, structure or other property that was under construction by or on behalf of the taxpayer on February 22, 1994, and

(ii) property acquired by the taxpayer before 1996

(A) pursuant to an agreement of purchase and sale in writing entered into before 1995 to acquire the property from a person or partnership in circumstances where

(I) the property was part of a project that was under construction by the person or partnership on February 22, 1994, and

(II) it is reasonable to conclude, having regard to all of the circumstances, that the person or partnership constructed the project with the intention of transferring all or part of the project to another taxpayer after completion, or

(B) pursuant to an agreement in writing entered into before 1995 by the taxpayer with a person or partnership where the taxpayer agrees to assume a legally binding obligation entered into by the person or partnership before February 22, 1994 to sell electricity to a public power utility in Canada, or

(k) property in respect of which a certificate has not been issued under paragraph (d) or (g) before the time that is the later of

(i) the end of 1995, and

(ii) 2 years after the property is acquired by the taxpayer or, where the property is property acquired in circumstances to which paragraph (j) applies, 2 years after substantial completion of the property.

¶2508

[¶2510]

Class 35

(7 per cent)

Property not included in any other class that is

(*a*) a railway car acquired after May 25, 1976; or

(*b*) a rail suspension device designed to carry trailers that are designed to be hauled on both highways and railway tracks.

[¶2512]

Class 36

Property acquired after December 11, 1979 that is deemed to be depreciable property by virtue of paragraph 13(5.2)(*c*) of the Act.

[¶2514]

Class 37

(15 per cent)

Property that would otherwise be included in another class in this Schedule that is property used in connection with an amusement park, including

(*a*) land improvements (other than landscaping) for or in support of park activities, including

(i) roads, sidewalks, parking areas, storage areas, or similar surface constructions, and

(ii) canals,

(*b*) buildings (other than warehouses, administration buildings, hotels or motels), structures and equipment (other than automotive equipment), including

(i) rides, attractions and appurtenances associated with a ride or attraction, ticket booths and facades,

(ii) equipment, furniture and fixtures, in or attached to a building included in this class,

(iii) bridges, and

(iv) fences or similar perimeter structures, and

(*c*) automotive equipment (other than automotive equipment designed for use on highways or streets),

and property not included in another class in this Schedule that is a waterway or a land improvement (other than landscaping, clearing or levelling land) used in connection with an amusement park.

[¶2516]

CLASS 38

Property not included in Class 22 but that would otherwise be included in that class if that class were read without reference to paragraphs (a) and (b) thereof.

[¶2518]

CLASS 39

Property acquired after 1987 and before February 26, 1992 that is not included in Class 29, but that would otherwise be included in that Class if that Class were read without reference to subparagraphs (b)(iii) and (v) and paragraph (c) thereof.

[¶2520]

CLASS 40

Property acquired after 1987 and before 1990 that is a powered industrial lift truck or property described in paragraph (b) or (f) of Class 10 and that is property not included in Class 29 but that would otherwise be included in that class if that class were read without reference to paragraph (c) thereof.

[¶2522]

CLASS 41

(25 per cent)

Property

(a) not included in Class 28 that would otherwise be included in that Class if that Class were read without reference to paragraph (a) of that Class and if subparagraphs (e)(i) to (iii) of that Class were read as follows:

　" (i) property that was acquired before the mine came into production and that would, but for this Class, be included in Class 10 because of paragraph (g), (k), (l) or (r) of that Class or would have been so included in that Class if it had been acquired after the 1971 taxation year, and property that would, but for this Class, be included in Class 41 because of subsection 1102(8) or (9),

　(ii) property that was acquired before the mine came into production and that would, but for this Class, be included in Class 10 because of paragraph (m) of that Class, or

　(iii) property that was acquired after the mine came into production and that would, but for this Class, be included in Class 10 because of paragraph (g), (k), (l) or (r) of that Class, and property that would, but for this Class, be included in Class 41 because of subsection 1102(8) or (9);"

(a.1) that is the portion, expressed as a percentage determined by reference to capital cost, of property that

(i) would, but for this Class, be included in Class 10 because of paragraph (g), (k) or (l) of that Class, or that is included in this Class because of subsection 1102(8) or (9),

(ii) is not described in paragraph (a) or (a.2),

(iii) was acquired by the taxpayer principally for the purpose of gaining or producing income from one or more mines that are operated by the taxpayer and situated in Canada, and that became available for use for the purpose of subsection 13(26) of the Act in a taxation year, and

(iv) had not, before it was acquired by the taxpayer, been used for any purpose by any person or partnership with whom the taxpayer was not dealing at arm's length,

where that percentage is determined by the formula

$$100 \times \frac{[\,A - (B \times 365/C)\,]}{A}$$

where

A   is the total of all amounts each of which is the capital cost of a property of the taxpayer that became available for use for the purpose of subsection 13(26) of the Act in the year and that is described in subparagraphs (i) to (iv) in respect of the mine or mines, as the case may be,

B   is 5% of the taxpayer's gross revenue from the mine or mines, as the case may be, for the year, and

C   is the number of days in the year;

(a.2) that

(i) is property that would, but for this Class, be included in Class 10 because of paragraph (g), (k) or (l) of that Class or that is included in his Class because of subsection 1102(8) or (9),

(ii) was acquired by the taxpayer in a taxation year principally for the purpose of gaining or producing income from one or more mines each of which

(A) is one or more wells operated by the taxpayer for the extraction of material from a deposit of bituminous sands or oil shales, operated by the taxpayer and situated in Canada.

(B) was the subject of a major expansion after March 6, 1996, and

(C) is a mine in respect of which the Minister, in consultation with the Minister of Natural Resources, determines that the greatest designed capacity of the mine, measured in volume of oil that is not beyond the crude oil stage or its equivalent, immediately after

¶2522

the expansion was not less than 25% greater than the greatest designed capacity of the mine immediately before the expansion,

(iii) was acquired by the taxpayer

(A) after March 6, 1996,

(B) before the completion of the expansion, and

(C) in the course of and principally for the purposes of the expansion, and

(iv) had not, before it was acquired by the taxpayer, been used for any purpose by any person or partnership with whom the taxpayer was not dealing at arm's length;

$(a.3)$ that is property included in this Class because of subsection 1102(8) or (9), other than property described in paragraph (a) or $(a.2)$ or the portion of property described in paragraph $(a.1)$;

(b) that is property

Draft Regulation

Capital Cost Allowance Vessels (December 20, 2002)

The portion of paragraph (b) of Class 41 in Schedule II to the Regulations before subparagraph (i) is replaced by the following:

(b) that is property, other than property described in subsection 1101(2c),

Applicable: Deemed to have come into force on November 7, 2001.

Explanatory Note: Capital cost allowance Class 41 in Schedule II to the Regulations is amended to exclude from paragraph (b) property described in subsection 1101(2c) of the Regulations. This amendment is consequential to new subsection 1101(2c), and the Structured Financing Facility Program for new Canadian built vessels administered by Industry Canada.

This amendment applies after November 7, 2001.

(i) described in paragraph $(f.1)$, (g), (j), (k), (l), (m), (r), (t) or (u) of Class 10 that would be included in that Class if this Schedule were read without reference to this paragraph; or

(ii) that is a vessel, including the furniture, fittings, radio communication equipment and other equipment attached thereto, that is designed principally for the purpose of

(A) determining the existence, location, extent or quality of accumulations of petroleum, natural gas or mineral resources, or

(B) drilling oil or gas wells,

and that was acquired by the taxpayer after 1987 other than property that was acquired before 1990

¶2522

(iii) pursuant to an obligation in writing entered into by the taxpayer before June 18, 1987,

(iv) that was under construction by or on behalf of the taxpayer on June 18, 1987, or

(v) that is machinery and equipment that is a fixed and integral part of property that was under construction by or on behalf of the taxpayer on June 18, 1987.

(c) acquired by the taxpayer after May 8, 1972, to be used directly or indirectly by the taxpayer in Canada primarily in Canadian field processing, where the property would be included in Class 29 if

(i) Class 29 were read without reference to subparagraphs (b)(iii) and (v) and paragraph (c) of that Class,

(ii) subsection 1104(9) were read without reference to paragraph (k) of that subsection, and

(iii) this Schedule were read without reference to this Class, Class 39 and Class 43; or

(d) acquired by the taxpayer after December 5, 1996 (otherwise than pursuant to an agreement in writing made before December 6, 1996) to be leased, in the ordinary course of carrying on a business in Canada of the taxpayer, to a lessee who can reasonably be expected to use, directly or indirectly, the property in Canada primarily in Canadian field processing carried on by the lessee, where the property would be included in Class 29 if

(i) Class 29 were read without reference to subparagraphs (b)(iii) and (v) and paragraph (c) of that Class, and

(ii) this Schedule were read without reference to this Class, Class 39 and Class 43.

[¶2524]

CLASS 42

(12 per cent)

Property that is fibre-optic cable.

[¶2526]

CLASS 43

(30 per cent)

Property acquired after February 25, 1992 that

(a) is not included in Class 29, but that would otherwise be included in that Class if that Class were read without reference to subparagraphs (b)(iii) and (v) and paragraph (c) thereof; or

(b) is property

(i) that is described in paragraph (k) of Class 10 and that would be included in that Class if this Schedule were read without reference to this paragraph and paragraph (b) of Class 41, and

(ii) that, at the time of its acquisition, can reasonably be expected to be used entirely in Canada and primarily for the purpose of processing ore extracted from a mineral resource located in a country other than Canada.

[¶2528]

CLASS 43.1

(30 per cent)

Property, other than reconditioned or remanufactured equipment, that would otherwise be included in Class 1, 2 or 8

Draft Regulation

Capital Cost Allowance (March 16, 2001)

The portion of Class 43.1 in Schedule II to the Regulations before paragraph (a) is replaced by the following:

CLASS 43.1

Property, other than reconditioned or remanufactured equipment, that would otherwise be included in Class 1, 2 or 8 or in Class 17 because of subparagraph (a.1)(i) of that Class

Applicable: To property acquired after February 27, 2000.

Explanatory Note: Class 43.1 (30% CCA rate) is amended to allow it to apply to qualifying electrical generating equipment that would otherwise be Class 17 property because of subparagraph (a.1)(i) of Class 17. This amendment is consequential to the inclusion in Class 17 of certain property more fully described in the commentary accompanying that change.

(a) that is

(i) electrical generating equipment, including any heat generating equipment used primarily for the purpose of producing heat energy to operate the electrical generating equipment,

(ii) equipment that generates both electrical and heat energy,

---

Draft Regulation

Capital Cost Allowance — Energy Conservation Equipment and Alternative Energy Sources (December 18, 2004)

Subparagraph (a)(ii) of Class 43.1 in Schedule II to the Regulations is replaced by the following:

(ii) equipment that generates both electrical and heat energy other than, for greater certainty, fuel cell equipment,

---

(ii.1) fixed location fuel cell equipment that has a peak capacity of not less than 3 kilowatts of electrical output and uses hydrogen generated only from ancillary fuel reformation equipment,

Applicable: To property that is acquired after February 18, 2003.

Explanatory Note: Please see the Regulatory Impact Analysis Statement following paragraph (*d*) of Class 43.1 of Schedule II.

(iii) heat recovery equipment used primarily for the purpose of conserving energy, or reducing the requirement to acquire energy, by

(A) extracting thermal waste that is generated by equipment referred to in subparagraph (i) or (ii), and

(B) reusing the thermal waste to generate electrical energy from equipment referred to in subparagraph (i) or (ii),

(iv) control, feedwater and condensate systems and other equipment, where that property is ancillary to equipment described in subparagraph (i), (ii) or (iii), or

---

Draft Regulation

Capital Cost Allowance — Energy Conservation Equipment and Alternative Energy Sources (December 18, 2004)

Subparagraph (*a*)(iv) of Class 43.1 in Schedule II to the Regulations is replaced by the following:

(iv) control, feedwater and condensate systems and other equipment, if that property is ancillary to equipment described in any of subparagraphs (i) to (iii), or

Applicable: To property that is acquired after February 18, 2003.

Explanatory Note: Please see the Regulatory Impact Analysis Statement following paragraph (*d*) of Class 43.1 of Schedule II.

(v) an addition to a property described in any of subparagraphs (i) to (iv),

other than buildings or other structures, heat rejection equipment (such as condensers and cooling water systems), transmission equipment, distribution equipment, fuel storage facilities and fuel handling equipment,

(*b*) that

(i) is situated in Canada,

(ii) is

(A) acquired by the taxpayer for use by the taxpayer for the purpose of gaining or producing income from a business carried on in Canada or from property situated in Canada, or

¶2528

(B) leased by the taxpayer to a lessee for the use by the lessee for the purpose of gaining or producing income from a business carried on in Canada or from property situated in Canada, and

(iii) has not been used for any purpose before it was acquired by the taxpayer unless

(A) the property was depreciable property that

(I) was included in Class 34 or 43.1 of the person from whom it was acquired, or

(II) that would have been included in Class 34 or 43.1 of the person from whom it was acquired had the person made a valid election to include the property in Class 43.1 pursuant to paragraph $1102(8)(d)$ or $1102(9)(d)$, and

(B) the property was acquired by the taxpayer not more than five years after the time it is considered to have become available for use, for the purpose of subsection 13(26) of the Act, by the person from whom it was acquired and remains at the same site in Canada as that at which that person used the property, and

(c) that is

(i) part of a system (other than an enhanced combined cycle system) that

(A) is used by the taxpayer, or by a lessee of the taxpayer, to generate electrical energy, or both electrical and heat energy, using only fuel that is fossil fuel, wood waste, municipal waste, landfill gas or digester gas, or any combination of those fuels, and

---

Draft Regulation

Capital Cost Allowance — Energy Conservation Equipment and Alternative Energy Sources (December 18, 2004)

Clause $(c)(i)(A)$ of Class 43.1 in Schedule II to the Regulations is replaced by the following:

(A) is used by the taxpayer, or by a lessee of the taxpayer, to generate electrical energy, or both electrical and heat energy, using only fuel that is fossil fuel, wood waste, municipal waste, landfill gas, digester gas or bio-oil, or any combination of those fuels, and

Applicable: To property that is acquired after February 18, 2003.

Explanatory Note: Please see the Regulatory Impact Analysis Statement following paragraph (d) of Class 43.1 of Schedule II.

(B) has a heat rate attributable to fossil fuel (other than solution gas) not exceeding 6,000 Btu per kilowatt-hour of electrical energy generated by the system, which heat rate is calculated as the fossil fuel (expressed as the high heat value of the fossil fuel) used by

¶2528

the system that is chargeable to gross electrical energy output on an annual basis, or

(ii) part of an enhanced combined cycle system that

(A) is used by the taxpayer, or by a lessee of the taxpayer, to generate electrical energy using only a combination of natural gas and waste heat from one or more natural gas compressor systems located on a natural gas pipeline,

(B) has an incremental heat rate not exceeding 6,700 Btu per kilowatt-hour of electricity generated by the system, which heat rate is calculated as the natural gas (expressed as its high heat value) used by the system that is chargeable to gross electrical energy output on an annual basis, and

(C) does not have economically viable access to a steam host,

and property (other than property described in paragraph (a)) that would otherwise be included in another class in this Schedule

(d) that is

(i) active solar heating equipment used by the taxpayer, or by a lessee of the taxpayer, primarily for the purpose of heating a liquid or gas used directly in an industrial process, including such equipment that consists of solar collectors, solar energy conversion equipment, solar water heaters, energy storage equipment, control equipment and equipment designed to interface solar heating equipment with other heating equipment, but not including buildings,

---

Draft Regulation

Capital Cost Allowance — Energy Conservation Equipment and Alternative Energy Sources (December 18, 2004)

Subparagraph (d)(i) of Class 43.1 in Schedule II to the Regulations is replaced by the following:

(i) active solar heating equipment used by the taxpayer, or by a lessee of the taxpayer, primarily for the purpose of heating a liquid or gas used directly in an industrial process or in a greenhouse, including such equipment that consists of solar collectors, solar energy conversion equipment, solar water heaters, energy storage equipment, control equipment and equipment designed to interface solar heating equipment with other heating equipment, but not including buildings,

Applicable: To property that is acquired after February 18, 2003.

Explanatory Note: Please see the Regulatory Impact Analysis Statement following paragraph (d) of Class 43.1 of Schedule II.

(ii) a hydro-electric installation of a producer of hydro-electric energy, where that installation

(A) has an annual average generating capacity not exceeding 15 megawatts upon completion of site development, and

¶2528

Draft Regulation

Capital Cost Allowance — Energy Conservation Equipment and Alternative Energy Sources (December 18, 2004)

Clause (d)(ii)(A) of Class 43.1 in Schedule II to the Regulations is replaced by the following:

(A) has, if acquired after February 21, 1994 and before December 11, 2001, an annual average generating capacity not exceeding 15 megawatts upon completion of the site development, or, if acquired after December 10, 2001, a rated capacity at the hydro-electric installation site that does not exceed 50 megawatts, and

---

Applicable: After December 10, 2001.

Explanatory Note: Please see the Regulatory Impact Analysis Statement following paragraph (d) of Class 43.1 of Schedule II.

(B) is the electrical generating equipment and plant (including structures) of that producer including a canal, a dam, a dyke, an overflow spillway, a penstock, a powerhouse (complete with electrical generating equipment and other ancillary equipment), control equipment, fishways or fish bypasses, and transmission equipment,

other than distribution equipment and property otherwise included in Class 10 or 17,

(iii) an addition or alteration to a hydro-electric installation described in subparagraph (ii) that results in an increase in generating capacity, if the resulting annual average generating capacity of the hydro-electric installation does not exceed 15 megawatts,

---

Draft Regulation

Capital Cost Allowance — Energy Conservation Equipment and Alternative Energy Sources (December 18, 2004)

Subparagraph (d)(iii) of Class 43.1 in Schedule II to the Regulations is replaced by the following:

(iii) an addition or alteration, which is acquired after February 21, 1994 and before December 11, 2001, to a hydro-electric installation that is described in subparagraph (ii) or that would be so described if that installation were acquired by the taxpayer after February 21, 1994, and which results in an increase in generating capacity, if the resulting annual average generating capacity of the hydro-electric installation does not exceed 15 megawatts,

(iii.1) an addition or alteration, which is acquired after December 10, 2001, to a hydro-electric installation that is described in subparagraph (ii) or that would be so described if that installation were acquired by the taxpayer after February 21, 1994, and which results in an increase in generating capacity, if the

¶2528

resulting rated capacity at the hydro-electric installation site does not exceed 50 megawatts,

Applicable: After December 10, 2001.

Explanatory Note: Please see the Regulatory Impact Analysis Statement following paragraph (d) of Class 43.1 of Schedule II.

(iv) heat recovery equipment used by the taxpayer, or by a lessee of the taxpayer, primarily for the purpose of conserving energy, or reducing the requirement to acquire energy, by

(A) extracting thermal waste that is generated directly in an industrial process (other than in an industrial process that generates or processes electrical energy), and

(B) reusing the thermal waste directly in an industrial process (other than in an industrial process that generates or processes electrical energy),

including such equipment that consists of heat exchange equipment, compressors used to upgrade low pressure steam, vapour or gas, waste heat boilers and other ancillary equipment such as control panels, fans, instruments or pumps, but not including buildings,

(v) a fixed location device that is a wind energy conversion system that

(A) is used by the taxpayer, or by a lessee of the taxpayer, primarily for the purpose of generating electrical energy, and

(B) consists of wind-driven turbine, electrical generating equipment and related equipment, including

(I) control, conditioning and battery storage equipment,

(II) support structures,

(III) powerhouse complete with other ancillary equipment, and

(IV) transmission equipment,

other than distribution equipment, auxiliary electrical generating equipment or property otherwise included in Class 10 or 17,

(vi) fixed location photovoltaic equipment that

(A) is used by the taxpayer, or by a lessee of the taxpayer, primarily for the purpose of generating electrical energy from solar energy,

(B) has a peak capacity of not less than 3 kilowatts of electrical output, and

(C) consists of solar cells or modules and related equipment including

(I) control, conditioning and battery storage equipment.

(II) support structures, and

¶2528

(III) transmission equipment,

other than buildings, distribution equipment, auxiliary electrical generating equipment and property otherwise included in Class 10 or 17,

(vii) above-ground equipment used by the taxpayer, or by a lessee of the taxpayer, primarily for the purpose of generating electrical energy solely from geothermal energy, including such equipment that consists of pumps, heat exchangers, steam separators, electrical generating equipment and ancillary equipment used to collect the geothermal heat, but not including buildings, transmission equipment, distribution equipment, equipment designed to store electrical energy and property otherwise included in Class 10 or 17,

(viii) above-ground equipment used by the taxpayer, or by a lessee of the taxpayer, primarily for the purpose of collecting landfill gas or digester gas, including such equipment that consists of fans, compressors, storage tanks, heat exchangers and other ancillary equipment used to collect the gas, to remove non-combustibles and contaminants from the gas or to store the gas, but not including buildings or property otherwise included in Class 10 or 17,

(ix) equipment used by the taxpayer, or by a lessee of the taxpayer, primarily for the purpose of generating heat energy from the consumption of wood waste, municipal waste, landfill gas or digester gas, if the heat energy is used directly in an industrial process carried on by the taxpayer or lessee, including such equipment that consists of fuel handling equipment used to upgrade the combustible portion of the fuel and control, feedwater and condensate systems, and other ancillary equipment, but not including buildings or other structures, property otherwise included in Class 10 or 17, heat rejection equipment (such as condensers and cooling water systems), fuel storage facilities, fuel handling equipment and electrical generating equipment, or

---

Draft Regulation

Capital Cost Allowance — Energy Conservation Equipment and Alternative Energy Sources (December 18, 2004)

Subparagraph (*d*)(ix) of Class 43.1 in Schedule II to the Regulations is replaced by the following:

(ix) equipment used by the taxpayer, or by a lessee of the taxpayer, primarily for the purpose of generating heat energy from the consumption of wood waste, municipal waste, landfill gas, digester gas or bio-oil, if the heat energy is used directly in an industrial process, or in a greenhouse, of the taxpayer or lessee, including such equipment that consists of fuel handling equipment used to upgrade the combustible portion of the fuel and control, feedwater and condensate systems, and other ancillary equipment, but not including buildings or other structures, heat rejection equipment (such as condensers and cooling

¶2528

water systems), fuel storage facilities, other fuel handling equipment and electrical generating equipment, and property otherwise included in Class 10 or 17,

Applicable: To property that is acquired after February 18, 2003.

Explanatory Note: Please see the Regulatory Impact Analysis Statement following paragraph (*d*) of Class 43.1 of Schedule II.

(x) an expansion engine with one or more turbines, or cylinders, that convert the compression energy in pressurized natural gas into shaft power that generates electricity, including the related electrical generating equipment and ancillary controls, where the expansion engine

(A) is part of a system that is installed

(I) on a distribution line of a distributor of natural gas, or

(II) on a branch distribution line of a taxpayer primarily engaged in the manufacturing or processing of goods for sale or lease if the branch line is used to deliver natural gas directly to the taxpayer's manufacturing or processing facility, and

(B) is used instead of a pressure reducing valve, and

Draft Regulation

Capital Cost Allowance — Energy Conservation Equipment and Alternative Energy Sources (December 18, 2004)

Paragraph (*d*) of Class 43.1 in Schedule II to the Regulations is amended by striking out the word "and" at the end of subparagraph (x) and by adding the following after that subparagraph:

(xi) equipment used in a system of the taxpayer that converts wood waste or plant residue into bio-oil, if that bio-oil is used by the taxpayer, or by a lessee of the taxpayer, primarily for the purpose of generating electricity, or electricity and heat, other than equipment used for the collection, storage or transportation of wood waste or plant residue, buildings or other structures and property otherwise included in Class 10 or 17, or

(xii) fixed location fuel cell equipment used by the taxpayer, or by a lessee of the taxpayer, that has a peak capacity of not less than 3 kilowatts of electrical output and uses hydrogen generated only from ancillary electrolysis equipment that uses electricity generated by photovoltaic, wind energy conversion or hydro-electric equipment, of the taxpayer or the lessee, and equipment ancillary to the fuel cell equipment other than buildings or other structures, transmission equipment, distribution equipment, auxiliary electrical generating equipment and property otherwise included in Class 10 or 17, and

Applicable: To property that is acquired after February 18, 2003.

Explanatory Note:

Regulatory Impact Analysis Statement from December 18, 2004

These amendments implement measures proposed in the 2001 and 2003 Budgets to broaden the application of Class 43.1 in Schedule II to the Income Tax Regulations (the "Regulations"). Class 43.1 provides taxpayers with an accelerated capital cost allowance to encourage more efficient use of fossil fuels and the use of renewable or alternative

¶2528

energy sources. By virtue of Class 43.1, qualifying assets of a taxpayer are eligible for a capital cost allowance rate of 30 percent, computed on a declining balance basis. Included in the class are wind energy equipment, small hydro equipment, geothermal electricity equipment, certain types of efficient cogeneration equipment, photovoltaic equipment and other types of renewable or alternative energy production equipment.

These amendments

● add "basic oxygen furnace gas" and "blast furnace gas" to the definition of "fossil fuel" in subsection 1104(13) of the Regulations. Only certain types of fuel (including fossil fuel) may be used by certain properties described in Class 43.1. These changes apply to property acquired after 2000 that uses such fuel.

● increase the upper limit on the size of a small hydroelectric project that qualifies for Class 43.1 treatment to a maximum rated capacity of 50 megawatts (MW), from the current limit of an annual average generating capacity of 15 MW. This change applies to property acquired after December 10, 2001.

● add "bio-oil" to the list of fuels one or more of which must be the only type of fuel used by certain property described in Class 43.1 and, subject to certain conditions, provide that equipment used to generate electricity using bio-oil is also eligible for Class 43.1 treatment. This change applies to any property acquired after February 18, 2003, that uses such fuel.

● extend Class 43.1 treatment to certain fixed-location fuel cells that use hydrogen generated from either fuel reformation equipment or ancillary electrolysis equipment, if acquired after February 18, 2003.

● extend Class 43.1 treatment to certain active solar heating equipment that is used for the purpose of heating a liquid or gas used directly in a greenhouse, as well as to certain equipment that generates heat energy from the consumption of certain waste fuels, if the heat energy is used directly in a greenhouse. These changes apply to equipment acquired after February 18, 2003.

The measures concerning "blast furnace gas" and small hydroelectric projects are discussed in detail at page 223 of Annex 7 to The Budget Plan of 2001. As well, these proposals were first released in draft form by the Department of Finance on February 5, 2002 (Finance News Release 2002-013). Subsequent to that release, the Department of Finance agreed to recommend to the Minister of Finance that "basic oxygen furnace gas" be treated in the same manner as blast furnace gas.

The measures concerning bio-oil, fixed location fuel cells and certain equipment used in greenhouses are discussed in detail at pages 338 and 339 of Annex 9 to The Budget Plan of 2003 [reproduced at the end of Class 43.1]. No draft of the amendments to the Regulations concerning these measures have been previously released for consultation.

[The Department of Finance contact for these draft regulations is Gurinder Grewal at (613) 992-1862.]

(e) that

    (i) is situated in Canada,

    (ii) is

        (A) acquired by the taxpayer for use by the taxpayer for the purpose of gaining or producing income from a business carried on in Canada or from property situated in Canada, or

        (B) leased by the taxpayer to a lessee for the use by the lessee for the purpose of gaining or producing income from a business carried on in Canada or from property situated in Canada, and

¶2528

(iii) has not been used for any purpose before it was acquired by the taxpayer unless

(A) the property was depreciable property that

(I) was included in Class 34 or 43.1 of the person from whom it was acquired, or

(II) would have been included in Class 34 or 43.1 of the person from whom it was acquired had the person made a valid election to include the property in Class 43.1 pursuant to paragraph $1102(8)(d)$ or $1102(9)(d)$, and

(B) the property was acquired by the taxpayer not more than five years after the time it is considered to have become available for use, for the purpose of subsection 13(26) of the Act, by the person from whom it was acquired and remains at the same site in Canada as that at which that person used the property.

Federal Budget Extract

Efficient and Renewable Energy Generation Equipment

[Reproduced below is an excerpt from the February 23, 2005 Federal Budget that sets out proposals to include additional types of energy generation and distribution equipment in Class 43.]

An accelerated capital cost allowance (CCA) rate of 30 per cent is provided under Class 43.1 in Schedule II to the Income Tax Regulations for investments in equipment that, in general, produces heat for an industrial process, or electricity, by using fossil fuel efficiently or renewable energy sources. This accelerated rate is an explicit exception to the practice of setting CCA rates to reflect the useful life of assets.

Where the majority of the tangible property acquired for use in a project is included in Class 43.1, certain start-up expenses (mostly intangible) for the project are treated as Canadian Renewable and Conservation Expenses. These expenses may be deducted in full in the year incurred, carried forward indefinitely for use in future years, or transferred to investors under flow-through share agreements.

* * *

High-Efficiency and Renewable Energy Generation Equipment

The budget proposes to include certain highly fossil-fuel-efficient and renewable energy generation equipment — which is currently eligible for the 30-per-cent CCA rate under Class 43.1 — in a new class eligible for a 50-per-cent CCA rate. The increased rate will apply to such equipment acquired on or after February 23, 2005 and before 2012. As is currently the case with Class 43.1, the specified energy property rules will be extended to apply to this new Class.

High-Efficiency Cogeneration Systems

Cogeneration systems (also called combined heat and power or CHP systems) produce heat and power simultaneously by capturing the waste heat from the electrical generation process and using it for another purpose, such as manufacturing or space heating.

Cogeneration equipment is currently eligible for Class 43.1 treatment if it converts approximately 57 per cent or more of the energy value of the input fossil fuel into electricity and usable heat. In formal terms, this requires a system to use no more than 6000 British Thermal Units (BTUs) of fossil fuel per kilowatt-hour of electricity produced on an annual basis. The energy content of specified waste fuels, such as wood

¶2528

waste, municipal waste, bio-oil and biogas, is not counted for the purposes of this "heat rate" calculation.

The budget proposes that cogeneration equipment that would otherwise be included in Class 43.1 will be included in the new class entitled to a 50-per-cent CCA rate if the equipment is part of a high-efficiency cogeneration system with an annual heat rate from fossil fuel that does not exceed 4750 BTUs per kilowatt-hour of electricity production. This corresponds to a total system efficiency of approximately 72 per cent. To be eligible for the new class, the equipment must be acquired on or after February 23, 2005 and before 2012. Systems eligible for Class 43.1 treatment that exceed the 4750 BTU threshold will still qualify for the current 30-per-cent CCA rate.

Renewable Energy Generation Systems

Class 43.1 also includes a range of renewable energy generation equipment, including wind turbines, small hydroelectric facilities, active solar heating equipment, fixed location photovoltaic equipment and geothermal energy equipment.

The budget proposes that such equipment that would otherwise be included in Class 43.1 will be eligible for the new 50-per-cent CCA rate class. To be eligible for the new Class, the equipment must be acquired on or after February 23, 2005 and before 2012.

Extending Incentives for Investment in Efficient and Renewable Energy Generation

The Government continues to review Class 43.1 on an ongoing basis to ensure inclusion of appropriate energy generation technologies that have the potential to contribute to energy efficiency and the use of alternative energy sources. Frequent additions have been made to the class since its inception in 1994. The budget proposes two further additions to Class 43.1: distribution equipment used in district energy systems that rely on efficient cogeneration; and biogas production equipment.

Distribution Equipment of a District Energy System

District or community energy systems transfer heat between a central generation plant and a group or district of buildings by continuously circulating steam, hot water or cold water through a system of underground pipes. As noted, Class 43.1 currently includes fossil-fuel efficient cogeneration equipment. District energy is an ideal application for cogeneration, since it provides a productive use for low-grade heat created in the process of generating electricity, thereby enabling the system to achieve a high level of energy efficiency.

The budget proposes to extend eligibility for Class 43.1 to specified distribution equipment of a taxpayer that is part of a district energy system used by the taxpayer (or a lessee) primarily to provide district heating or cooling through the use of heat produced by electrical cogeneration equipment that meets the requirements of Class 43.1, including the heat rate requirements. Eligible components of a taxpayer's system will be pipes, pumps, chillers, meters and control equipment and heat exchangers attached to the main distribution line of the district energy system. Assets forming part of the internal heat and cooling system of the host building will not be eligible.

This change will apply to eligible equipment acquired on or after February 23, 2005. Where the distribution assets are acquired on or after February 23, 2005 and before 2012, and they carry heat produced by cogeneration equipment acquired during that period that qualifies for the new 50-per-cent CCA rate Class, the distribution assets will also qualify for the new Class.

Biogas Production Equipment

Class 43.1 currently includes above-ground equipment used primarily to collect landfill gas and digester gas from a licensed sewage treatment facility. Capture and use of these greenhouse gases contributes to climate change objectives, utilizes energy that would otherwise be wasted, and diversifies Canada's energy supply mix.

¶2528

To encourage further capture and use of biogas, the budget proposes to extend eligibility for Class 43.1 to equipment used to produce biogas (which is primarily methane) from the anaerobic digestion of manure. Eligible equipment will be property of a taxpayer that is part of a system that is used by the taxpayer (or a lessee) primarily to produce, store and use biogas primarily for the production by the taxpayer (or the lessee) of heat for use in an industrial process, or electricity, and that is an anaerobic digester reactor, a buffer tank, biogas piping, a biogas storage tank, biogas scrubbing equipment, or generation equipment. Collection equipment, buildings and other structures, and equipment used to process the residue after digestion or to treat recovered liquids, will not be included.

This change will apply to eligible equipment acquired on or after February 23, 2005. Further, such eligible equipment acquired before 2012 will be included in the new 50-per-cent CCA rate Class.

Federal Budget Extract

Capital Cost Allowance Class 43.1 (Renewable and Alternative Energy)

[Reproduced below is an excerpt from the February 18, 2003 Federal Budget that sets out proposals concerning Class 43.1. These measures have been implemented with draft regulations, dated December 18, 2004. This Budget extract concerning the amendments is referred to in the regulatory impact analysis statement for these draft regulations that is reproduced following the amendment to add subparagraphs (xi) and (xii) to paragraph (*d*) of Class 43.1.]

Under the capital cost allowance (CCA) regime in the income tax system, Class 43.1 provides tax incentives in defined circumstances to encourage a more efficient use of fossil fuels and the use of renewable and alternative energy sources. Eligible assets qualify for an accelerated CCA rate of 30 per cent. Since the introduction of Class 43.1 in the 1994 budget, the Government has expanded eligibility for this class.

The 2001 budget announced consultations with industry to determine whether additional improvements were required for Class 43.1. As a result of the consultations and submissions received, this budget proposes to further broaden eligibility for Class 43.1. These changes will apply to property acquired after February 18, 2003.

Fuel cells use hydrogen to generate electricity, or electricity and heat. This budget proposes that certain fixed-location fuel cells and ancillary fuel reformation and electrolysis equipment will now be eligible for Class 43.1 treatment. In order to qualify:

- the fuel cells must have a peak capacity of not less than 3 kilowatts of electrical output;

- the fuel cells must be part of a system that includes fuel reformation equipment or electrolysis equipment;

- where the fuel cells use hydrogen generated from ancillary fuel reformation equipment that uses fossil fuel, the fuel cell system will be required to satisfy the existing 6000-BTU-per-Kwh heat rate calculation; and

- where the fuel cells of a taxpayer use hydrogen generated by ancillary electrolysis equipment, the electrolysis equipment must use solar energy, wind energy conversion or hydroelectric energy equipment of the taxpayer.

This change will help make fuel cells more cost-competitive with both conventional power sources and other new technologies already in Class 43.1.

This budget also proposes changes to provide incentives for the use of bio-oil. Bio-oil is created through a thermo-chemical conversion process that uses biomass that is wood waste or other plant residues. Equipment of a taxpayer that is used in a system to convert biomass into bio-oil will now be eligible for Class 43.1 if this bio-oil is used by the taxpayer (or a lessee) primarily to generate electricity or electricity and heat. Bio-oil is considered to be a neutral energy source with respect to greenhouse gases. This change will provide other environmental benefits and further encourage the efficient use of forestry and agricultural residues.

¶2528

The budget also proposes changes to extend eligibility for Class 43.1 to certain equipment used primarily to generate heat energy for use in a taxpayer's greenhouse operation. Qualifying equipment will include active solar heating equipment and equipment used to generate heat energy from the consumption of wood waste, municipal waste, landfill gas or digester gas. This measure will help promote the use of renewable and alternative energy in the Canadian greenhouse industry.

[¶2530]

CLASS 44

(25 per cent)

Property that is a patent, or a right to use patented information for a limited or unlimited period.

Draft Regulation

Capital Cost Allowance (July 9, 2005)

Schedule II to the Regulations is amended by adding the following after Class 44:

CLASS 45

Property acquired after March 22, 2004 (other than property acquired before 2005 in respect of which an election is made under subsection 1101(5q)) that is general-purpose electronic data processing equipment and systems software for that equipment, including ancillary data processing equipment, but not including property that is principally or is used principally as

(a) electronic process control or monitor equipment;

(b) electronic communications control equipment;

(c) systems software for equipment referred to in paragraph (a) or (b); or

(d) data handling equipment (other than data handling equipment that is ancillary to general-purpose electronic data processing equipment).

CLASS 46

Property acquired after March 22, 2004 that is data network infrastructure equipment, and systems software for that equipment, that would, but for this Class, be included in Class 8 because of paragraph (i) of that Class.

Applicable: Deemed to have come into force on March 23, 2004.

Explanatory Note: See the Regulatory Impact Analysis Statement following the addition of subparagraphs 1100(1)(a)(xxxi) and (xxxii).

SCHEDULE III

Capital Cost Allowances, Class 13

[¶2534]

1.   For the purposes of paragraph $1100(1)(b)$, the amount that may be deducted in computing the income of a taxpayer for a taxation year in respect of the capital cost of property of Class 13 in Schedule II is the lesser of

(a) the aggregate of each amount determined in accordance with section 2 of this Schedule that is a prorated portion of the part of the capital cost to him, incurred in a particular taxation year, of a particular leasehold interest; and

(b) the undepreciated capital cost to the taxpayer as of the end of the taxation year (before making any deduction under section 1100) of property of the class.

[¶2536]

2.   Subject to section 3 of this Schedule, the prorated portion for the year of the part of the capital cost, incurred in a particular taxation year, of a particular leasehold interest is the lesser of

(a) $\frac{1}{5}$ of that part of the capital cost; and

(b) the amount determined by dividing that part of the capital cost by the number of 12-month periods (not exceeding 40 such periods) falling within the period commencing with the beginning of the particular taxation year in which the capital cost was incurred and ending with the day the lease is to terminate.

[¶2538]

3.   For the purpose of determining, under section 2 of this Schedule, the prorated portion for the year of the part of the capital cost, incurred in a particular taxation year, of a particular leasehold interest, the following rules apply:

(a) where an item of the capital cost of a leasehold interest was incurred before the taxation year in which the interest was acquired, it shall be deemed to have been incurred in the taxation year in which the interest was acquired;

(b) where, under a lease, a tenant has a right to renew the lease for an additional term, or for more than one additional term, after the term that includes the end of the particular taxation year in which the capital cost was incurred, the lease shall be deemed to terminate on the day on which the term next succeeding the term in which the capital cost was incurred is to terminate;

(c) the prorated portion for the year of the part of the capital cost, incurred in a particular taxation year, of a particular leasehold interest shall not exceed the amount, if any, remaining after deducting from

¶2534

that part of the capital cost the aggregate of the amounts claimed and deductible in previous years in respect thereof;

(d) where, at the end of a taxation year, the aggregate of

(i) the amounts claimed and deductible in previous taxation years in respect of a particular leasehold interest, and

(ii) the proceeds of disposition, if any, of part or all of that interest

equals or exceeds the capital cost as of that time of the interest, the prorated portion of any part of that capital cost shall, for all subsequent years, be deemed to be nil; and

(e) where, at the end of a taxation year, the undepreciated capital cost to the taxpayer of property of Class 13 in Schedule II is nil, the prorated portion of any part of the capital cost as of that time shall, for all subsequent years, be deemed to be nil.

[¶2540]

4.   Where a taxpayer has acquired a property that would, if the property had been acquired by a person with whom the taxpayer was not dealing at arm's length at the time the property was acquired, be a leasehold interest of that person, a reference in this Schedule to a leasehold interest shall, in respect of the taxpayer, include a reference to that property, and the terms and conditions of the leasehold interest of that property in respect of the taxpayer shall be deemed to be the same as those that would have applied in respect of that person had that person acquired the property.

SCHEDULE IV

Capital Cost Allowances, Class 15

[¶2544]

1.   For the purposes of paragraph 1100(1)(f), the amount that may be deducted in computing the income of a taxpayer for a taxation year in respect of property described in Class 15 in Schedule II is the lesser of

(a) an amount computed on the basis of a rate per cord, board foot or cubic metre cut in the taxation year; and

(b) the undepreciated capital cost to the taxpayer as of the end of the taxation year (before making any deduction under section 1100 for the taxation year) of property of that class.

[¶2546]

2.   Where all the property of the class is used in connection with one timber limit or section thereof, the rate per cord, board foot or cubic metre is the amount determined by dividing

(a) the undepreciated capital cost to the taxpayer as of the end of the taxation year (before making any deduction under section 1100 for the taxation year) of the property

by

(b) the number of cords, board feet or cubic metres of timber in the limit or section thereof as of the commencement of the taxation year, obtained by deducting the quantity cut up to that time from the amount shown by the latest cruise.

[¶2548]

3. Where a part of the property of the class is used in connection with one timber limit or a section thereof and a part is used in connection with another limit or section thereof, a separate rate shall be computed for each part of the property, in the manner provided in section 2 of this Schedule, as though each part of the property were the taxpayer's only property of that class.

SCHEDULE V

Capital Cost Allowances, Industrial Mineral Mines

[¶2554]

1. For the purposes of paragraph 1100(1)(g), the amount that may be deducted in computing the income of a taxpayer for a taxation year in respect of a property described in that paragraph that is an industrial mineral mine or a right to remove industrial minerals from an industrial mineral mine is the lesser of

(a) an amount computed on the basis of a rate (computed under section 2 or 3 of this Schedule, as the case may be) per unit of mineral mined in the taxation year; and

(b) the undepreciated capital cost to the taxpayer as of the end of the taxation year (before making any deduction under section 1100) of the mine or right.

[¶2556]

2. Where the taxpayer has not been granted an allowance in respect of the mine or right for a previous taxation year, the rate for a taxation year is an amount determined by dividing the capital cost of the mine or right to the taxpayer minus the residual value, if any, by

(a) in any case where the taxpayer has acquired a right to remove only a specified number of units, the specified number of units of material that he acquired a right to remove; and

(b) in any other case, the number of units of commercially mineable material estimated as being in the mine when the mine or right was acquired.

[¶2558]

3.   Where the taxpayer has been granted an allowance in respect of the mine or right in a previous taxation year, the rate for the taxation year is

(a) where paragraph (b) does not apply, the rate employed to determine the allowance for the most recent year for which an allowance was granted; and

(b) where it has been established that the number of units of material remaining to be mined in the previous taxation year was in fact different from the quantity that was employed in determining the rate for the previous year referred to in paragraph (a), or where it has been established that the capital cost of the mine or right is substantially different from the amount that was employed in determining the rate for that previous year, a rate determined by dividing the undepreciated capital cost to the taxpayer of the mine or right as of the commencement of the year minus the residual value, if any, by

(i) in any case where the taxpayer has acquired a right to remove only a specified number of units, the number of units of commercially mineable material that, at the commencement of the year, he had a right to remove, and

(ii) in any other case, the number of units of commercially mineable material estimated as remaining in the mine at the commencement of the year.

[¶2560]

4.   In lieu of the aggregate of deductions otherwise allowable under this Schedule, a taxpayer may elect that the deduction for the taxation year be the lesser of

(a) $100; and

(b) the amount received by him in the taxation year from the sale of mineral.

[¶2562]

5.   In this Schedule, "residual value" means the estimated value of the property if all commercially mineable material were removed.

SCHEDULE VI

Capital Cost Allowances, Timber Limits and Cutting Rights

[¶2570]

1.   For the purposes of paragraph 1100(1)(e), the amount that may be deducted in computing the income of a taxpayer for a taxation year in respect

of the capital cost to him of a property, other than a timber resource property, that is a timber limit or a right to cut timber from a limit is the lesser of

(a) the aggregate of

(i) an amount computed on the basis of a rate (determined under section 2 or 3 of this Schedule) per cord, board foot or cubic metre cut in the year, and

(ii) the lesser of

(A) $1/10$ of the amount expended by the taxpayer after the commencement of his 1949 taxation year that is included in the capital cost to him of the timber limit or right, for surveys, cruises or preparation of prints, maps or plans for the purpose of obtaining a licence or right to cut timber, and

(B) the amount expended as described in clause (A) minus the aggregate of amounts deducted under this subparagraph in computing the income of the taxpayer in previous years; and

(b) the undepreciated capital cost to the taxpayer as of the end of the year (before making any deduction under section 1100 for the year) of the timber limit or right.

[¶2572]

2. If the taxpayer has not been granted an allowance in respect of the limit or right for a previous taxation year, the rate for a taxation year is an amount determined by dividing

(a) the capital cost of the limit or right to the taxpayer, minus the aggregate of the residual value of the timber limit and any amount expended by the taxpayer after the commencement of his 1949 taxation year that is included in the capital cost to him of the timber limit or right, for surveys, cruises or preparation of prints, maps or plans for the purpose of obtaining a licence or right to cut timber,

by

(b) the quantity of timber in the limit or the quantity of timber the taxpayer has obtained a right to cut, as the case may be, (expressed in cords, board feet or cubic metres) as shown by a cruise.

[¶2576]

3. If the taxpayer has been granted an allowance in respect of the limit or right in a previous taxation year, the rate for a taxation year is

(a) where paragraph (b) does not apply, the rate employed to determine the allowance for the most recent year for which an allowance was granted; and

(b) where it has been established that the quantity of timber that was in the limit or that the taxpayer had a right to cut was in fact substantially different from the quantity that was employed in determining the rate for the previous year referred to in paragraph (a), or where it has been established that the capital cost of the limit or right is substantially different from the amount that was employed in determining the rate for that previous year, a rate determined by dividing

(i) the undepreciated capital cost to the taxpayer of the limit or right as of the commencement of the year, minus the residual value,

by

(ii) the estimated remaining quantity of timber that is in the limit or that the taxpayer has a right to cut, as the case may be, (expressed in cords, board feet or cubic metres) at the commencement of the year.

[¶2578]

4.   In lieu of the deduction otherwise determined under this Schedule, a taxpayer may elect that the deduction for a taxation year be the lesser of

(a) $100; and

(b) the amount received by him in the taxation year from the sale of timber.

[¶2580]

5.   In this Schedule, "residual value" means the estimated value of the property if the merchantable timber were removed.

CHAPTER 14

INTERPRETATION BULLETINS

Please note that, while all Interpretation Bulletins reproduced below were the versions current at time of publication of this book, some may not reflect the most recent amendments to the law and regulations. Reference should also be made to the text of the law and regulations when consulting a Bulletin.

[3105]   Interpretation Bulletin IT-79R3:   Capital Cost Allowance — Buildings or Other Structures

[Interpretation Bulletin IT-79R3 is dated May 24, 1991.]

Reference: Paragraph $20(1)(a)$ and Classes 1, 3, 6 and 8 in Schedule II to the Regulations (also subsections 1102(5) and (19) of the Regulations)

Application

This bulletin cancels and replaces Interpretation Bulletin IT-79R2 issued on January 10, 1980 and the Special Release dated January 29, 1982.

Summary

This bulletin deals with buildings and structures for capital cost allowance purposes. Generally, buildings or other structures acquired after 1987 are included in Class 1 (4%) instead of Class 3 (5%). This bulletin defines "building" and "structure" and deals with Classes 1, 3, 6, and 8 in Schedule II of the Regulations to the extent those classes pertain to buildings and structures. It also discusses component parts of buildings or other structures.

Discussion and Interpretation

Meaning of "Building" and "Structure"

1. "Building" is a term of wide range covering any structure with walls and a roof affording protection and shelter. The word "structure" includes anything of substantial size that is built up from component parts and intended to remain permanently on a permanent foundation. This definition of "structure" was considered by the Supreme Court of Canada in *British Columbia Forest Products Ltd v. Minister of National Revenue*, 71 DTC 5178 — [1971] CTC 270 which also concluded that the word "structure" when used in the context of "building or other structure" does not mean only a struc-

¶3105

ture in the nature of a building. Bridges or hydro-electric transmission towers, for example, while clearly not buildings, are structures.

2. Portable shelters such as housing, office and other service units are regarded as buildings if they are installed and intended to remain in a particular location. Such things as tents, canvas marquees and air-supported fabric domes that are not part of a rigid structure are not considered to be buildings or structures.

3. A building or other structure erected on leased land is, by reason of subsection 1102(5) of the Regulations, included in the class that describes the structure and not in Class 13 as a leasehold interest. For example, a bridge built on leased land would fall within Class 1. Subsection 1102(5) of the Regulations is considered to apply to any property referred to in Schedule II of the Regulations which is either a "building" or a "structure", and not just to a "building or other structure" as referred to in Classes 1, 3, and 8.

Class 1 (4%)

4. Ordinarily, buildings or other structures, or parts thereof, acquired after 1987 (except to the extent included in Class 3 where 6(a), (b) or (c) below apply) are included in Class 1 for capital cost allowance purposes. Exceptions to this general rule are structures and buildings specifically included in other classes such as a structure that is manufacturing or processing machinery or equipment (Class 8), a building of frame construction that has no footings or other base support below ground level (Class 6), certain buildings acquired for use in a resource industry (Class 41) or portable camp buildings (Class 10).

5. An addition or alteration to a building is to be included in Class 1 if it is

(a) an addition or alteration to a building included in Class 1, or

(b) an addition or alteration to a building of another class made after 1987 where subsection 1102(19) of the Regulations applies.

Generally, subsection 1102(19) applies to an addition or alteration made to a property that would have been in a different class if the property had been acquired at the time the addition or alteration was made. For

example, an addition or alteration made after 1987 to a Class 3 building is included in Class 1 where the building would have been included in Class 1 if it had been acquired at the time of the addition or alteration. However, subsection 1102(19) of the Regulations does not apply to the extent that an addition or alteration is subject to a specific provision in Schedule II of the Regulations such as those described in 7(c) and 9(d) below. Also, see the example in 10 below.

Class 3 (5%)

6. A building or other structure, or part thereof, that is not specifically included in another class is included in Class 3 if acquired (see the current version of IT-50) by the taxpayer before 1988, or before 1990

(a) pursuant to an obligation in writing entered into by the taxpayer before June 18, 1987,

(b) that was under construction by or on behalf of the taxpayer on June 18, 1987, or

(c) that is a component part of a building that was under construction by or on behalf of the taxpayer on June 18, 1987.

7. An addition or alteration to a building is to be included in Class 3 if it is:

(a) an addition or alteration to a building that was included in Class 20 and that would otherwise have been included in Class 3, made during the period that is after March 31, 1967 and before 1988,

(b) an addition or alteration to a building of another class made after December 26, 1978 and before 1988 where subsection 1102(19) of the Regulations applies (see 5 above),

(c) an addition or alteration made after 1987 to a building included, in whole or in part, in

    (i) Class 3,

    (ii) Class 6 by virtue of subparagraph (a)(viii) of Class 6, or

    (iii) Class 20.

The amount included in Class 3 in (c) above is restricted to the total cost of all such additions or alterations to the building (except to the extent included in paragraph

(k) of Class 6 (see 9(d) below)) that does not exceed the lesser of

(d) $500,000, and

(e) 25 per cent of the capital cost of the building and any addition or alterations made thereto prior to 1988 included in Class 3, 6 or 20.

Any amount that exceeds the lesser of (d) and (e) above falls within Class 1 (see 5(b) above and the example in 10 below).

Class 6 (10%)

8. A building of frame, log, stucco on frame or galvanized or corrugated iron construction is included in Class 6, provided the building meets one of the following criteria:

(a) it was acquired by the taxpayer before 1979,

(b) it is used by the taxpayer for the purpose of gaining or producing income from farming or fishing,

(c) it has no footings or any other base support below ground level,

(d) it was acquired by the taxpayer after 1978 under circumstances where

(i) the taxpayer was obligated to acquire the building under the terms of an agreement in writing entered into before 1979, and

(ii) the installation of footings or any other base support of the building was commenced before 1979, or

(e) it was acquired by the taxpayer after 1978 under circumstances where

(i) the taxpayer commenced construction of the building before 1979 and the installation of footings or any other base support of the building was commenced before 1979, or

(ii) the construction of the building was commenced under the terms of an agreement in writing entered into by the taxpayer before 1979 and the installation of footings or any other base support of the building was commenced before 1979.

9. An addition or alteration to a building of frame, log, stucco on frame or galvanized or corrugated iron construction as described in paragraph (a) of Class 6 is included in Class 6 if it is an addition or alteration

(a) made before 1979,

(b) to a building used by the taxpayer for the purpose of gaining or producing income from farming or fishing,

(c) to a building that has no footings or any other base support below ground level, or

(d) made after 1978 to a building described in paragraph (a) of Class 6 (other than to a building described in (b) or (c) above) acquired before 1979 to the extent that the aggregate cost of all such additions or alterations to the building does not exceed $100,000 (see the example in 10 below).

If an addition or alteration was made in part in 1978 and in part after that year, the costs incurred after 1978 will not be considered to be made before 1979 for purposes of (a) above. The year that costs will be considered to form part of the cost of the building is discussed in the current version of IT-50.

With regard to the requirements in (d) above, where the cost of an addition or alteration, or the aggregate of costs of additions or alterations to a building exceeds $100,000, the amount that qualifies for inclusion in Class 6 is $100,000. The $100,000 aggregate is the total for all years and is not an annual amount. Where the addition or alteration is made prior to 1988, any amount exceeding $100,000 is included in Class 3 (see 7(b) above). Where an addition or alteration is made after 1987, any amount exceeding $100,000 is included in Class 3, to the extent permitted by paragraph (k) of Class 3 (see 7(c) above) and any amount not included in either Class 6 or Class 3 is included in Class 1 (see 5(b) above).

10. The application of 9(d), 7(c) and 5(b) above is illustrated in the following example:

In 1978 a taxpayer purchased a building of frame construction with base support below ground level for $250,000. The building is used by the taxpayer to earn income from a business that is not farming or fishing. Alter-

¶3105

ations costing $60,000 were made to the building in 1983. In 1988, an addition costing $150,000 was made to the building.

1978

Class 6

Capital cost of building (see 8(a) above) $250,000

1983

Class 6

Alteration to building that falls within paragraph (k) of Class 6 (see 9(d) above) . . . . $ 60,000

1988

Class 6

Portion of addition to building that falls within paragraph (k) of Class 6 (see 9(d) above):

Maximum of total additions and alterations that falls within Class 6 . . . . $100,000

Less: alteration made in 1983 . . . .   60,000 $ 40,000

Class 3

Portion of addition to building that falls within paragraph (k) of Class 3 (see 7(c) above):

Total cost of addition $150,000

Less: cost allocated to Class 6   40,000

Cost of addition available for Class 3 . . . . $110,000

The cost of the addition available may only be included in Class 3 to the extent it does not exceed the lesser of

(a) $500,000, and

(b) 25% $\times$ $350,000 ($250,000 + 60,000 + 40,000) . . . $ 87,500

Class 1

Portion of addition to building that falls within Class 1 (see 5(b) above):

Total cost of addition $150,000

Less: Cost allocated to Class 6 . . . . $40,000

Cost allocated to Class 3   87,500   127,500 $ 22,500

11. An addition or alteration to a building that is included in Class 20 and that would otherwise have been included in Class 6, made

(a) during the period that is after March 31, 1967 and before 1979 or

(b) after 1978 if the taxpayer was obligated to have it made under the terms of an agreement in writing entered into before 1979

is also to be included in Class 6 by virtue of paragraph (i) of Class 6.

¶3105

12. A building that has a basic or main supporting structure of wood or wooden timbers is regarded as a building of frame construction. This is so whether its outer sheathing is brick veneer, shingles, clapboard, featheredge, asbestos shingles, aluminum siding, plywood, fiberglass, prefabricated panelling, galvanized, painted or corrugated iron or steel, and whether these materials form the outer walls alone or in combination with insulation and an inner wall, provided that the sheathing material does not form the basic structural support of the building.

13. A building made of logs is considered to be a building of logs regardless of its framework (if any).

14. A building of galvanized iron or corrugated iron construction is one whose exterior construction, including the roof, consists chiefly of galvanized or corrugated iron or steel. Such a building may have a framework of steel girders, be lined with insulation or have interior walls and still qualify. The terms galvanized iron and corrugated iron do not include galvanized or corrugated panels made of any material other than iron or steel; in particular they do not include corrugated aluminum nor do they include a composite type of panel even though it is faced with a thin covering of corrugated steel.

Component Parts

15. For greater certainty, Classes 1, 3 and 6 of Schedule II specify that buildings or other structures that fall into those classes also include component parts such as electric wiring, plumbing, sprinkler systems, air-conditioning equipment, heating equipment, lighting fixtures, elevators and escalators. The particular items cited, however, are not regarded as being an all-inclusive description of component parts of a building. There are other component parts of a building that ordinarily go with the building when it is bought or sold, or that may be purchased separately from the building, but which relate to the functioning of a building. Examples are storm doors and windows, automatic stokers, sump pumps, combination heating and cooling units, and complex fire alarm systems. Such items are included

in Class 1, 3 or 6, depending on the type of building and the date of acquisition. Other properties which may be component parts and which are specifically included in other classes, such as certain electrical generating equipment (also see comments in 18 below) fall within the class in which they are specifically included.

16. The term "component parts" as used in Classes 1, 3 and 6 should be interpreted as referring only to those component parts owned by the taxpayer who is the owner of the building of which they are part. It is common practice for one taxpayer to lease to another items which, when installed, become component parts of a building or other structure owned by the lessee but with the lease providing that the leased property remains the property of the lessor. Where this situation exists, the lessor ordinarily is permitted to claim capital cost allowance for the leased property on its own merits (in most cases, under Class 8), rather than as component parts. Where the purported lease of component parts is considered to be a sale, (see the current version of IT-233), component parts are considered to be owned by the lessee and are included in the same class as the building or other structure.

Class 8 (20%)

17. Tanks, vats and hoppers when located outside a plant building but erected on a steel framework or other permanent foundation, although structures, are included in Class 8 if acquired for use in manufacturing or processing. Similarly, the housing and framework for outdoor conveyor systems acquired for use in manufacturing or processing operations are included in Class 8.

18. Property that is attached to a building, however firmly, is included in Class 8 if it is acquired exclusively for those purposes stated in Class 8. For example, concrete footings, foundations and structural steel exclusively for the support of machinery are regarded as Class 8 assets. Stairs and platforms, the sole purpose of which is to provide access to machinery, also fall within Class 8, whether they are attached to the building or the machinery.

¶3105

[3107]   Interpretation Bulletin IT-102R2:   Conversion of Property, Other than Real Property, From or To Inventory

[*Interpretation Bulletin IT-102R2 is dated July 22, 1985.*]

Reference: Section 9 (also section 45, subsections 13(7) and 248(1), and paragraphs 13(21)(*c*) and 54(*a*), 54(*b*) and 54(*c*))

The comments in this bulletin apply for taxation years commencing after its issue date. Proposals contained in the Notices of Ways and Means Motions of May 9 and May 23, 1985 are not considered in this release.

1. This bulletin deals with conversions of business property, other than real property either from inventory to capital property or from capital property to inventory, without a change in ownership thereof. The bulletin does not deal with the rules in section 45 concerning the determination of capital gains or losses or with the rules in subsection 13(7) concerning capital cost allowance and its recapture. See IT-218 for the Department's views on profit on the sale of real property other than a principal residence.

2. Inventory is defined in subsection 248(1) as being "a description of property the cost or value of which is relevant in computing a taxpayer's income from a business for a taxation year". Capital property is defined in paragraph 54(*b*) as being "any depreciable property of the taxpayer, and any property (other than depreciable property), any gain or loss from the disposition of which would, if the property were disposed of, be a capital gain or a capital loss, as the case may be, of the taxpayer".

3. Capital property, whether or not depreciable property of a prescribed class, that is used for the purpose of earning income from a business or property is not, as a general rule, converted to inventory simply because it is put on the market for sale. Accordingly, where capital property is sold, the sales proceeds will ordinarily be treated as proceeds of disposition of capital property for all purposes of the Act. It is, however, the Department's position that exceptions to this general rule will occur.

4. Where a taxpayer both sells and either rents or leases property of the same kind, it is the Department's position that all proceeds from the sale of property that has been rented or leased constitutes income of the taxpayer from the sale of inventory unless

(a) the taxpayer operates a separate and clearly distinguishable leasing division, including the keeping of separate records,

(b) specific property is set aside by the taxpayer for either renting or leasing and is factually so used, and

(c) properties that are so rented or leased are normally sold for an amount that is less than their cost to the taxpayer.

Where the conditions in (a) to (c) above are complied with, the ultimate disposal of property used for renting or leasing will be treated as the disposal of capital property.

5. It is recognized that a taxpayer whose business consists only of the renting or leasing of property is, from time to time, required to renew such property by selling it after it has been rented or leased for a period of time, and purchasing new property. In these circumstances, where the proceeds from the disposal of each individual property normally exceed the taxpayer's cost thereof, the proceeds from the sale of all of the taxpayer's property that has been rented or leased will be considered to be received by the taxpayer on account of income rather than capital.

6. Notwithstanding 4 and 5 above, where, at any time, a particular property is leased

(a) without option to purchase,

(b) for a sufficiently long period of time so that the anticipated sales price of the particular property at the time of expiry of the lease will not ordinarily exceed its cost to the lessor, and

(c) the particular property is not ordinarily replaced by other property during the currency of the lease,

the lessor may, from that time, treat the particular property as capital property rather than inventory for all purposes of the Act.

7. The facts of each case will determine whether or not a conversion of property, as described in 1 above has occurred. For

¶3107

example, a conversion is generally not considered to have taken place where

(a) property that was purchased primarily for resale is temporarily withdrawn from inventory and used in a business to earn income, for example demonstrator or courtesy vehicles by a car dealer, salesmen's samples or the use of equipment by employees in carrying out their business responsibilities, or

(b) the cost of property was incorrectly classified in the accounts of a business and has been reclassified to reflect the use made of the property, as capital property or inventory, as the case may be, since it was acquired.

Capital Property Converted to Inventory

8.   Where capital property is converted to inventory, the action of conversion does not constitute a disposition within the meaning of paragraphs $13(21)(c)$ and $54(c)$. It is, however, recognized that the ultimate disposition of a property that was so converted may give rise to a gain or loss on capital account, a gain or loss on income account or a gain or loss that is partly capital and partly income. Accordingly, with respect to capital property that has been converted to inventory, taxpayers may calculate capital gains or losses, if any, on the basis that a notional disposition of such property occurred on the date of conversion. The amount of such a notionally determined capital gain or loss in respect of a property will be the difference between its adjusted cost base, as defined in paragraph $54(a)$, (subject to the ITAR rules for property held on December 31, 1971) and its fair market value on the date of conversion. These notionally determined capital

gains or losses will be considered to give rise to taxable capital gains or allowable capital losses for the taxation year during which the actual disposition of the relevant property occurs and will be required to be so reported in that same year. The amount of any income gain or loss arising on actual disposition of the converted property will be determined in accordance with generally accepted accounting principles on the basis that its initial inventory value is its fair market value on the date of conversion.

Inventory Converted to Capital Property

9.   Where at any time a taxpayer finds it necessary to convert a particular property from inventory to capital property, its capital cost for all purposes of the Act will be its inventory value at that time. Such a conversion might occur, for example, where a particular property in inventory

(a) is required for lease in the leasing division of a taxpayer described in 4 above,

(b) has been leased by any taxpayer under the conditions described in 6 above, or

(c) is otherwise used by the taxpayer as a fixed asset of the business.

10.   The conversion of a unit of merchandise from inventory to capital property, as envisaged by 9 above, is not considered to be either a disposition or an acquisition. Therefore, on such a conversion, the application of the half-rate capital cost allowance rules in the first year of ownership will be based on the actual date of acquisition rather than the date of conversion.

[3111]   Interpretation Bulletin IT-123R6:   Transactions Involving Eligible Capital Property

[Interpretation Bulletin IT-123R6 is dated June 1, 1997.]

Reference: Section 14   (also sections 102 and 110.6; the definition of "eligible capital property" in section 54; subsections 20(4.2), 24(1), 39.1(5), 96(1), 104(21) and 104(21.2); the definition of "capital dividend account" in subsection 89(1), the definition of "exempt capital gains balance" in subsection 39.1(1) and the definitions of "Canadian partnership" and "individual" in subsection 248(1); paragraphs $20(1)(b)$, $20(1)(n)$ and $20(1)(p)$; and

¶3111

subparagraph 39(1)(*b*)(ii) of the Act; and section 21 of the *Income Tax Application Rules, 1971* (ITAR))

Application

This bulletin cancels and replaces Interpretation Bulletin IT-123R5, dated October 30, 1992. Generally, the rules dealt with in this bulletin (the new system) are applicable to corporations with taxation years commencing on or after July 1, 1988, and to other taxpayers with fiscal periods commencing on or after January 1, 1988. For a discussion of the relevant provisions for prior periods (the old system), see Interpretation Bulletin IT-123R4 dated May 30, 1985. Certain transitional provisions discussed in this bulletin affect the rules under both the new system and the old system.

Summary

This bulletin discusses transactions involving eligible capital property for a particular business of a taxpayer. Eligible capital property may be broadly described as intangible capital property, such as goodwill and other "nothings", the cost of which neither qualifies for capital cost allowance nor is deductible in the year of its acquisition as a current expense.

A portion of each expenditure to acquire eligible capital property is added into a pool, and a portion of the proceeds from each disposition of eligible capital property reduces the pool. A deduction may be claimed, in computing the taxpayer's income from the business for a particular year, of up to 7% of any positive balance in the pool at the end of that year. Generally, if the pool has a negative balance at the end of the year, an amount will be required to be included in computing the taxpayer's income. In certain circumstances, a portion of the negative balance is eligible for a capital gains deduction.

An election can be made to defer all or a portion of a negative balance in the pool resulting from a disposition of eligible capital property, if a replacement property is acquired in the immediately following year. This bulletin also discusses other topics in connection with eligible capital property, including the transition from the old system to the new system.

Discussion and Interpretation

1. The cumulative eligible capital (cumulative EC) for a business is, in effect, an expenditure pool (the pool) relating to eligible capital property (EC property). EC property may be broadly described as intangible capital property, such as goodwill and other "nothings", the cost of which neither qualifies for capital cost allowance nor is deductible in the year of its acquisition as a current expense. As discussed more fully below, the pool is increased by a portion of each eligible capital expenditure (EC expenditure) made to acquire EC property and is decreased by each eligible capital amount (EC amount) resulting from a disposition of EC property. Generally, depending on whether the balance in the pool at the end of a particular taxation year is positive or negative, a deduction may be claimed or an amount must be included in income for the year.

2. The cumulative EC (i.e., the pool), as well as any EC expenditure or EC amount taken into account in calculating the balance of the pool, must be determined "in respect of a [particular] business". If a taxpayer has more than one business (see the current version of IT-206), these items must be determined separately for each business. For purposes of discussion in this bulletin, it is assumed that the taxpayer has only one business.

3. According to its definition in section 54, "EC property" is basically any property which, if disposed of by the taxpayer, would result in an EC amount. An "EC amount", which according to subsection 14(1) is an amount determined under variable E in the subsection 14(5) definition of "cumulative EC" (the method of calculation is discussed in ¶9 below), is essentially an amount resulting from a disposition of property where, if any payment had been made after 1971 by the taxpayer for that property, such payment would have qualified as an EC expenditure for the business. This test in variable E in the definition of "cumulative EC" is often referred to as the "mirror image test", which is discussed more fully in the current version of IT-386. The combined effect of the above-mentioned provisions is that an EC property is basically any property the cost of which would qualify as an EC expenditure of the taxpayer. For a discussion of what qualifies as an "EC expenditure", which is defined under subsection 14(5), see the current version of IT-143.

¶3111

4. Unless specifically stated to the contrary, the reference in this bulletin to a "year" means a "taxation year" and, in the case of an individual, both "taxation year" and "year" mean the fiscal period of the business which ends in the taxation year.

5. The provisions regarding EC property as amended by S.C. 1988, c. 55 (formerly Bill C-139) or by subsequent amending statutes are referred to in this bulletin as the provisions under the "new system". The new system commenced at the taxpayer's "adjustment time", which is defined in subsection 14(5) as follows:

(a) in the case of a corporation formed as a result of an amalgamation occurring after June 30, 1988 — immediately before the amalgamation;

(b) in the case of any other corporation — immediately after the beginning of its first taxation year that commenced after June 30, 1988; and

(c) for any other taxpayer — immediately after the beginning of the first fiscal period of the business that commenced after 1987.

The system of provisions applying prior to the taxpayer's adjustment time is referred to in this bulletin as the "old system", which is dealt with (although not described as such) in IT-123R4. A comparison of the old and new systems is contained in Schedule A at the end of this bulletin.

The New System

6. Although the definition of "cumulative EC" in subsection 14(5) provides for a determination of the balance in the pool of cumulative EC at any particular time, in actual practice taxpayers usually prepare a schedule of cumulative EC for each year, carrying forward the final balance in the pool at the end of one year as the opening balance for the next year. The balance in the pool at the beginning of the first year under the new system is simply $3/2$ of (or $1\frac{1}{2}$ times) the balance at the taxpayer's adjustment time, i.e., $3/2$ of the balance (if any) at the end of the last year under the old system. The increases and decreases to the pool that occur under the new system are discussed in ¶s 7 to 26 below and are illustrated in Schedule B at the end of this bulletin.

7. The pool is increased in a particular year by $3/4$ (the inclusion rate) of each EC expenditure made or incurred in the year. For a discussion of what qualifies as an EC expenditure, see the current version of IT-143.

8. The taxpayer may receive assistance from a government, municipality or other public authority in respect of, or for the acquisition of, EC property of a business. By virtue of subsection 14(10), the EC expenditure for the property is reduced by, or the pool is decreased by $3/4$ of, the amount of such assistance that the taxpayer receives or is entitled to receive after February 21, 1994.

Example 1

The taxpayer acquires an EC property for $100,000 and receives government assistance of $50,000 towards the purchase of that property. The pool is increased by $3/4$ of ($100,000 − $50,000) = $37,500.

Example 2

The taxpayer acquires an EC property for $100,000 in year 1. In year 2, the taxpayer becomes entitled to receive government assistance of $50,000 in respect of the property. In year 1, the pool is increased by $3/4$ of $100,000 = $75,000. In year 2, the pool is decreased by $3/4$ of $50,000 = $37,500. Therefore, as of year 2, the pool has been increased by a net amount of $75,000 − $37,500 = $37,500.

Subsection 14(10) can apply to assistance in the form of a grant, subsidy, forgivable loan, deduction from tax, investment allowance or any other form of assistance. The subsection does not apply, however, to assistance that the taxpayer receives or becomes entitled to receive after ceasing to carry on the business. If subsection 14(10) does apply and the taxpayer has reduced the EC pool by $3/4$ of (or reduced the EC expenditure by) the amount of the assistance, the subsection allows the taxpayer to increase the pool by $3/4$ of (or increase the EC expenditure by) any amount of the assistance that the taxpayer has repaid under a legal obligation to do so. This rule does not apply, however, if the taxpayer makes the repayment after ceasing to carry on the business (instead, the taxpayer claims a deduction under paragraph 20(1)(*hh*.1) as described in the current version of IT-313). By virtue of subsection 14(11), the above rules in subsection 14(10) can apply to the EC property (and thus to the EC pool) of a business carried on by a trust or partnership where a beneficiary

¶3111

of the trust or a member of the partnership, as the case may be, is the person that receives or becomes entitled to receive the assistance.

9. The pool is decreased in a particular year by each EC amount for the year. An EC amount results from a disposition of EC property. Examples of situations in which an EC amount can occur are given in the current version of IT-386. When an EC property has been disposed of, the resulting EC amount for the year of disposition is calculated by multiplying $3/4$ (the inclusion rate) times what is referred to in this bulletin as the "base for the EC amount", which is simply the excess (if any) of

(a) the taxpayer's total proceeds of disposition, i.e., the total of all amounts which the taxpayer has received or may become entitled to receive in the year of the disposition or subsequent years, over

(b) all outlays and expenses made or incurred by the taxpayer in connection with the disposition, to the extent that such outlays and expenses were not otherwise deductible in computing the taxpayer's income.

10. The pool is decreased by any amount by which it is required to be reduced by virtue of the operation of subsection 80(7). If an amount is forgiven on the settlement of a "commercial obligation" (as defined in subsection 80(1)) issued by the taxpayer, subsection 80(7) provides that $3/4$ of the remaining unapplied portion of the forgiven amount (as determined under the rules in section 80) shall be applied (to the extent designated in prescribed form filed with the taxpayer's return for the taxation year in which the debt is settled) to reduce the taxpayer's EC pool.

11. If at the end of a taxation year there is a positive balance in the pool, paragraph $20(1)(b)$ provides for a deduction (the paragraph $20(1)(b)$ deduction), in computing the taxpayer's income from the business for that year, of up to 7% of such positive balance. The pool is then decreased by the amount so deducted.

12. If, on the other hand, there is a negative balance in the pool at the end of the year, subsection 14(1) usually requires that an amount be included in computing the

taxpayer's income for the year. The rules for this income inclusion under subsection 14(1) vary for two different categories of taxpayers, as discussed below.

Taxpayers in the First Category

13. An individual resident in Canada throughout the taxation year (i.e., the year at the end of which the negative balance in the pool occurs) is included in the first category of taxpayers if the business for which the negative balance in the pool occurs is

(a) the individual's business, or

(b) the business of a partnership which is a Canadian partnership throughout the year (i.e., the partner's fiscal period at the end of which the negative balance in the pool occurs) and the individual is a member of that Canadian partnership at some time in that year (such membership can be either direct or indirect through another Canadian partnership or series of Canadian partnerships).

For purposes of the above discussion, an "individual" as defined in subsection 248(1) includes a trust. A "Canadian partnership" is defined by section 102 as a partnership all of the members of which are resident in Canada at all relevant times (which, for purposes of subsection 14(1), would be throughout the partnership's entire taxation year for which the negative balance in the pool occurs). It should also be noted that an individual is not excluded from the first category of taxpayers if another member of any partnership mentioned in (b) above is a corporation, a corporate partnership or a tiered corporate partnership as described in ¶21(c) below. By virtue of subsection 14(8), an individual that became or ceased to be resident in Canada during a particular taxation year is deemed to be resident in Canada throughout that year, for purposes of being included in the first category of taxpayers, as long as the individual was resident in Canada throughout the previous or the subsequent year.

14. If the taxpayer is in the first category, there is an income inclusion under subparagraph $14(1)(a)(iv)$ (the subparagraph $14(1)(a)(iv)$ recapture income inclusion), which is equal to the lesser of two amounts:

(a) the negative balance in the pool at the end of the year; and

(b) the total net recapturable amount (as referred to in this bulletin), which is calculated as A + B + B.1 − C (this net amount cannot be less than zero).

The variables in this formula are as follows:

A is the sum of all paragraph $20(1)(b)$ deductions for prior years under the new system.

B is the net of all paragraph $20(1)(b)$ deductions less income inclusions for prior years under the old system (note that under the old system no distinction was made as to whether an income inclusion represented a recapture of paragraph $20(1)(b)$ deductions or otherwise, and also note that this net amount for B cannot be less than zero).

B.1 is the total of all amounts by which the pool is to be reduced because of subsection 80(7) (see ¶10 above).

C is the sum of all subparagraph $14(1)(a)(iv)$ recapture income inclusions for prior years under the new system.

The amount of the subparagraph $14(1)(a)(iv)$ recapture income inclusion for the year, as determined above

(c) is then added back to the pool (the reason for this is explained in ¶s 16 and 17 below); and

(d) will be included in amount C in the formula above when determining the total net recapturable amount in a subsequent year.

15. If the negative balance in the pool at the end of the year (i.e., the amount in ¶14(a) above) is greater than the total net recapturable amount (as determined by the formula described in ¶14(b) above),

- the total net recapturable amount (if any) is fully recaptured by means of the subparagraph $14(1)(a)(iv)$ recapture income inclusion for the year; and

- subparagraph $14(1)(a)(v)$ then applies.

The rules in subparagraph $14(1)(a)(v)$ differ for fiscal periods ending before February 23, 1994 (see ¶16 below) and fiscal periods ending after February 22, 1994 (see ¶17 below).

16. Generally, for each fiscal period ending before February 23, 1994, in addition to a subparagraph $14(1)(a)(iv)$ recapture income inclusion, there is a deemed taxable capital gain under subparagraph $14(1)(a)(v)$. A subparagraph $14(1)(a)(v)$ deemed taxable capital gain is calculated as the excess (if any) of

(a) the negative balance in the pool at the end of the year (i.e., the amount in ¶14(a) above), over

(b) the sum of

- the subparagraph $14(1)(a)(iv)$ recapture income inclusion for the year (which, as just mentioned, is the full recapture of the total net recapturable amount), and

- ½ of variable B in the formula in ¶14(b) above.

A subparagraph $14(1)(a)(v)$ deemed taxable capital gain calculated under the above formula cannot be less than zero. When a subparagraph $14(1)(a)(v)$ deemed taxable capital gain occurs, the following rules apply:

- The subparagraph $14(1)(a)(v)$ deemed taxable capital gain for the year enters into the calculation of the taxpayer's income for the year under paragraph $3(b)$ and qualifies, subject to the limitations in section 110.6, for a capital gains deduction by the taxpayer.

- In addition to the amount of the subparagraph $14(1)(a)(iv)$ recapture income inclusion for the year being added back to the pool (see ¶14(c) above), also added back to the pool are

— the amount of the subparagraph $14(1)(a)(v)$ deemed taxable capital gain for the year, and

— ½ of variable B in the formula in ¶14(b) above.

All of these add-backs to the pool bring the pool balance back to nil. In other words, these add-backs ensure that no portion of the negative balance at the end of the year can be subject to taxation in a subsequent year. This principle is illustrated in the example in Schedule B (see the 1990 taxation year). Note that the subparagraph

¶3111

$14(1)(a)(v)$ deemed taxable capital gain for the year should not be included in amount C in the formula in ¶14(b) above when determining the total net recapturable amount in a subsequent year.

17. Generally, for each fiscal period ending after February 22, 1994, in addition to a subparagraph $14(1)(a)(iv)$ recapture income inclusion, there is an income inclusion under subparagraph $14(1)(a)(v)$. A subparagraph $14(1)(a)(v)$ income inclusion is determined by the following formula:

$$A - B - C - D$$

A subparagraph $14(1)(a)(v)$ income inclusion calculated under the above formula cannot be less than zero. The variables in the formula are as follows:

A   is the negative balance in the pool at the end of the year (i.e., the amount in ¶14(a) above).

B   is the total net recapturable amount as of the end of the year as determined in ¶14(b) above.

C   is ½ of variable B in the formula in ¶14(b) above.

D   is the amount that the taxpayer claims out of the taxpayer's "exempt gains balance" (as defined in subsection 14(5)) in respect of the business for the year.

With regard to variable D above, the taxpayer will have created an exempt gains balance if the taxpayer was an individual (other than a trust) or a personal trust and the taxpayer made an election to have paragraph $110.6(19)(b)$ apply in respect of a business carried on by the taxpayer on February 22, 1994 (otherwise than as a member of a partnership). Subsection 110.6(19) was added to the Act to allow taxpayers to recognize capital gains accrued to February 22, 1994, because of the elimination of the $100,000 capital gains exemption for dispositions of property after that date. Paragraph $110.6(19)(b)$ provides for the creation of a deemed taxable capital gain equal to the amount of the subparagraph $14(1)(a)(v)$ deemed taxable capital gain (if any) that would have resulted under the rules for fiscal periods ending before February 23, 1994 (as discussed in ¶16 above) if

- the taxpayer's taxation year had ended on February 22, 1994, and

- the taxpayer had disposed of all the EC property of the business for an amount of proceeds designated by the taxpayer.

The taxpayer will then have included the paragraph $110.6(19)(b)$ deemed taxable capital gain in income for the taxation year that included February 22, 1994 and it will have qualified for a capital gains deduction (subject to the limitations in section 110.6 in force as of February 22, 1994). Note that this is so regardless of whether or not the taxpayer's paragraph $110.6(19)(b)$ designated proceeds were equal to the fair market value of all the taxpayer's EC property for the business as of February 22, 1994 (for the sake of brevity, the latter amount is hereafter referred to simply as the "fair market value"). Note also that since the deemed taxable capital gain will have occurred under paragraph $110.6(19)(b)$ rather than under subparagraph $14(1)(a)(v)$, the taxpayer's paragraph $110.6(19)(b)$ designated proceeds will not have resulted in an EC amount that reduced the EC pool at that time. If the taxpayer's paragraph $110.6(19)(b)$ designated proceeds were equal to or less than the fair market value, the taxpayer's exempt gains balance will have started out at an amount equal to the taxpayer's deemed taxable capital gain. (If the taxpayer's paragraph $110.6(19)(b)$ designated proceeds were more than the fair market value, less favourable results will have occurred. For further particulars, see paragraph $110.6(19)(b)$ and also subsection 14(9).) The taxpayer may claim all or a portion of the exempt gains balance as variable D in the above formula in order to reduce a subparagraph $14(1)(a)(v)$ income inclusion resulting, for example, from an EC amount pertaining to an actual disposition of an EC property for which a paragraph $110.6(19)(b)$ election had previously been made.

The taxpayer's exempt gains balance for a particular taxation year is reduced by any amount claimed as variable D above for a previous year.

When a subparagraph $14(1)(a)(v)$ income inclusion occurs, the following rules apply:

- The subparagraph $14(1)(a)(v)$ income inclusion for the year is included in the taxpayer's income from the business for the year. How-

¶3111

ever, if some or all of the subparagraph $14(1)(a)(v)$ income inclusion can reasonably be attributed to a disposition of "qualified farm property" as defined in subsection $110.6(1)$, some or all of that income inclusion may qualify for a capital gains deduction by the taxpayer. (Although, as mentioned earlier, the $100,000 capital gains exemption was eliminated for dispositions of property occurring after February 22, 1994, there was no such elimination of the $500,000 capital gains exemption for dispositions of qualified farm property.) The rules in section 14 should be consulted in conjunction with those in section 110.6 to determine the amount of capital gains deduction that may be claimed for the subparagraph $14(1)(a)(v)$ income inclusion.

● In addition to the amount of the subparagraph $14(1)(a)(iv)$ recapture income inclusion for the year being added back to the pool (see ¶14(c) above), also added back to the pool are

— the amount of the subparagraph $14(1)(a)(v)$ income inclusion for the year,

— the amount of variable D for the year in the above formula, and

— ½ of variable B in the formula in ¶14(b) above.

All of these "add-backs" to the pool bring the pool balance back to nil. In other words, these add-backs ensure that no portion of the negative balance at the end of the year can be subject to taxation in a subsequent year.

Note that the subparagraph $14(1)(a)(v)$ income inclusion for the year should not be included in amount C in the formula in ¶14(b) above when determining the total net recapturable amount in a subsequent year.

18. Although subparagraph $14(1)(a)(v)$ can apply in the manner described in ¶s 15 to 17 above to a trust resident in Canada throughout the year (i.e., because such a trust can be included in the first category of taxpayers see ¶13 above), a capital gains deduction is generally not available to a trust under section 110.6. However, it may be possible in some cases for a beneficiary (of the trust) who is an individual resident in Canada throughout the year (see ¶13 above) to claim a capital gains deduction in respect of the trust's subparagraph $14(1)(a)(v)$ amount by means of the flow-through provisions in subsections $104(21)$ and (21.2) in conjunction with section 110.6, subject to the requirements contained in all of these provisions. Subsections $104(21)$ and (21.2) are discussed in the current version of IT-381.

19. Subparagraph $14(1)(a)(v)$ can apply in the manner described in ¶s 15 to 17 above where the business is carried on by a Canadian partnership (i.e., if the first category of taxpayers applies — see ¶13(b) above). By virtue of subsection $96(1)$, the subparagraph $14(1)(a)(v)$ amount is calculated at the partnership level but flows through to the partnership's members (see the current version of IT-138. It may be possible in some cases for a member of the Canadian partnership who is an individual resident in Canada throughout the year (see ¶13 above) to claim a section 110.6 capital gains deduction with respect to his or her share of the subparagraph $14(1)(a)(v)$ amount, subject to the requirements contained in all of the above-mentioned provisions. In the case of a member of the Canadian partnership which is a corporation, its share of the subparagraph $14(1)(a)(v)$ amount will not qualify for a capital gains deduction. In the case of a member of the Canadian partnership which is a trust, see ¶18 above.

20. If

● an individual is a member of a partnership,

● a subsection $110.6(19)$ election has been made in respect of the individual's interest in the partnership, and

● the partnership has a subparagraph $14(1)(a)(v)$ amount, a share of which flows through the partnership to the individual (see ¶19 above), the individual's share of the subparagraph $14(1)(a)(v)$ amount may be able to be reduced by means of subsection $39.1(5)$. For further particulars, see subsection $39.1(5)$ and the calculation of an individual's "exempt capital gains balance" as determined under subsection $39.1(1)$.

¶3111

Taxpayers in the Second Category

21. The second category of taxpayers includes the following:

(a) any taxpayer (e.g., an individual, including a trust, or a corporation) not resident in Canada throughout the taxation year (see ¶13 above);

(b) any taxpayer (e.g., an individual, including a trust, or a corporation), if the business for which the negative balance in the pool occurs is that of a partnership which is not a Canadian partnership (as described in ¶13 above) throughout the year (i.e., the partner's fiscal period at the end of which the negative balance in the pool occurs) and the taxpayer is a member of that partnership in that year either directly or indirectly through another partnership or series of partnerships; and

(c) any corporation, if the business is that of the corporation itself or of a corporate partnership or tiered corporate partnership of which the corporation is a member in the year either directly or indirectly through another partnership or series of partnerships. For purposes of this discussion, a "corporate partnership" means a partnership all the members of which are corporations. A "tiered corporate partnership" means a partnership all the members of which ultimately are corporations, i.e., each corporation's membership in the partnership is either direct or is indirect through another partnership or series of partnerships.

22. If the taxpayer is in the second category and there is a negative balance in the pool at the end of the year, there may be an income inclusion (i.e., in the income from the taxpayer's business) under paragraph $14(1)(b)$. The income inclusion is calculated as the excess (if any) of

(a) the negative balance in the pool at the end of the year over

(b) $\frac{1}{2}$ of the net amount of all paragraph $20(1)(b)$ deductions under the old system less income inclusions under the old system (this net amount cannot be less than zero).

The amount of the paragraph $14(1)(b)$ income inclusion for the year is then added back to the pool. Also added back to the pool

is amount (b) above (i.e., $\frac{1}{2}$ of the net amount of all paragraph $20(1)(b)$ deductions under the old system less income inclusions under the old system). These two add-backs to the pool bring the pool balance back to nil. In other words, these add-backs ensure that no portion of the negative balance at the end of the year can be subject to taxation in a subsequent year.

Non-Arm's Length Transfers

23. Where a person (e.g., a corporation or an individual, including a trust) or a partnership (either of which is hereafter referred to as the "transferee") acquires, directly or indirectly, in any manner whatever, an EC property from a non-arm's length person or partnership (either of which is hereafter referred to as the "transferor"), subsection 14(3) can sometimes reduce the transferee's EC expenditure. In addition to the requirement that the transferor and transferee must not be dealing at arm's length, subsection 14(3) can apply only if the property was first an EC property for the transferor's business and is then acquired as an EC property for the transferee's business. The subsection does not apply, however, to property acquired by the transferee as a consequence of the death of the transferor. Where subsection 14(3) applies, the transferee's EC expenditure is "deemed" (determined) to be $\frac{4}{3}$ of

(a) the amount determined by the transferor as the EC amount from the disposition of the property minus

(b) the total of all amounts that may reasonably be considered to have been claimed as a section 110.6 capital gains deduction by the transferor or any other person with whom the transferee was not dealing at arm's length in connection with the transferor's disposition of the property to the transferee or in connection with any previous disposition of the same property.

Example

Mr. A acquires an EC property for his business. The purchase price for the property is $100 and thus he adds $75 to the EC property pool for the business. The balance in the pool at the end of the year is $75 and Mr. A claims a paragraph $20(1)(b)$ deduction of $5, reducing the pool balance to $70. In the following year, Mr. A sells the EC property to A Jr., his son, for $200 (the fair market value at that time). Mr. A's EC amount from the disposition is $150 (assume that there are no costs for the disposition), which causes a negative balance of $80 in his EC pool at the end of that year. Under subparagraph 14(1)(*a*)(iv), $5 of that negative balance is included in Mr. A's income as a recapture of the prior year's paragraph 20(1)(*b*) deduction (see the rules discussed in ¶14 above). The remaining $75 is included in Mr. A's income under subsection 14(1)(*a*)(v) and he claims a corresponding capital gains deduction of $75 in respect of the disposition of the property (see the rules discussed in ¶s 16 and 17 above). Under subsection 14(3), A Jr.'s EC expenditure for the EC property acquired for his business is determined to be ⁴⁄₃ of his father's $150 EC amount minus ⁴⁄₃ of his father's $75 capital gains deduction. A Jr.'s EC expenditure is therefore $100 instead of the $200 he actually paid, and $75 rather than $150 is added to the pool for his business.

Finally, it should be noted that the above reduction to the transferee's EC expenditure can be reversed to the extent that the transferee receives proceeds, in a subsequent disposition of the property, in excess of the transferee's EC expenditure (as initially determined under the subsection 14(3) formula given above). However, if the subsequent disposition is to a person or partnership (the subsequent transferee) that does not deal at arm's length with a person who has claimed a section 110.6 capital gains deduction in connection with the property, the subsequent transferee's EC expenditure could be reduced by virtue of subsection 14(3) — see (b) in the subsection 14(3) formula above.

24. Subparagraph 110.6(19)(*b*)(ii) contains a rule that pertains to the reduction, under subsection 14(3) as described in ¶23(b) above, to a non-arm's length transferee's EC expenditure for EC property. Under the rule in subparagraph 110.6(19)(*b*)(ii), if the non-arm's length transferor made an election for the EC property under paragraph 110.6(19)(*b*) (see ¶17 above) before it was acquired by the transferee, the transferor's paragraph 110.6(19)(*b*) deemed taxable capital gain is deemed to have been claimed as a section 110.6 capital gains deduction by the transferor or by any other person with whom the transferee was not dealing at arm's length in connection with a disposition of the EC property on February 22, 1994. In

other words, the transferee's EC expenditure for the EC property would be reduced by ⁴⁄₃ of the transferor's paragraph 110.6(19)(*b*) deemed taxable capital gain in respect of the property.

Replacement Properties

25. Where a taxpayer disposes of an EC property (the former property) in a particular taxation year (the first year) and in the immediately following year (the second year) acquires another EC property to replace the former property, subsection 14(6) can be used to prevent the reduction of a positive balance (or the creation of a negative balance) in the pool at the end of the first year which might otherwise result from the disposition. In such a situation, the taxpayer can elect under subsection 14(6) to exclude from the calculation of the base for the EC amount that would otherwise occur for the first year, such part (not exceeding the total) of that base as is used by the taxpayer in the second year to acquire the replacement property. Thus, where all of the base for the EC amount is so used, the disposition of the former property cannot result in any EC amount in the first year or cause a negative balance in the pool at the end of the first year. The amount excluded in this manner from the calculation of the base for the EC amount that would otherwise occur for the first year then becomes the base for an EC amount for the second year. The resulting deferred EC amount, which is calculated by multiplying that base by the inclusion rate of ³⁄₄, decreases the pool in the second year but is offset by the increase to the pool in the same year of ³⁄₄ of the EC expenditure for the replacement property.

Subsection 14(7) contains requirements that must be satisfied in order for a property to qualify as a replacement property for a former property. See also the current version of IT-259.

26. An election under subsection 14(6) is to be filed with the taxpayer's return for the year in which the replacement property is acquired. In the situation described in ¶25 above, i.e., where the former property is disposed of in the first year and the replacement property is not acquired until the second year, the taxpayer should initially file the return for the first year without the benefit of the subsection 14(6) election. Then, when the election is filed with the return for the second year, the taxpayer may

¶3111

request a reassessment of the tax for the first year. Further particulars may be found in the current version of IT-259.

Transitional Provisions

27. As indicated in Schedule A, the inclusion rate under the new system is $3/4$, whereas it was $1/2$ under the old system. Also, the taxpayer's total proceeds from the disposition of EC property are used in the base for the EC amount for the year of disposition under the new system, whereas only the portion of the total proceeds becoming payable to the taxpayer in any particular year was used in the base for the EC amount for that particular year under the old system. The coming-into-force rules for the new system, as described below, permit the transition from the old system to the new system while taking into account these differences.

28. Where a disposition of an EC property occurred in a year that was under the old system (i.e., before the taxpayer's adjustment time) either

(a) on or before June 17, 1987, or

(b) after June 17, 1987, but pursuant to the terms of an obligation entered into in writing on or before June 17, 1987,

an EC amount from the disposition can still occur in a later year under the new system (i.e., after the taxpayer's adjustment time) where a portion of the proceeds from the disposition does not become payable until that later year. In calculating the EC amount for that later year under the new system, only the portion of the total proceeds from the disposition that becomes payable to the taxpayer in that year will be used in the base for the EC amount. The inclusion rate is $3/4$. Note that, in most cases, the disposition has resulted in an EC amount for an earlier year under the old system (because a portion of the proceeds became payable to the taxpayer in that earlier year) and thus the outlays and expenses made or incurred in connection with the disposition have already been taken into account in the base for the EC amount for that earlier year.

29. Where a disposition of an EC property occurred under the old system (i.e., before the taxpayer's adjustment time) but after June 17, 1987, otherwise than pursuant to the terms of an obligation entered into in writing before June 18, 1987, in calculating the EC amount for the year of dis-

position under the old system the taxpayer's total proceeds from the disposition must be used in the base for the EC amount (thus, there cannot be any further EC amount from the disposition in a later year under the new system). The inclusion rate is $1/2$.

30. Where a disposition of an EC property occurs in a year under the new system (i.e., after the taxpayer's adjustment time) but pursuant to the terms of an obligation entered into in writing on or before June 17, 1987, an EC amount occurs under the new system for each year in which any portion of the proceeds from the disposition becomes payable to the taxpayer. In calculating the EC amount for each of these years, the inclusion rate is $3/4$ and the portion of the proceeds from the disposition that becomes payable to the taxpayer in that year is taken into account in the base for the EC amount. In the first of these years (which may or may not be the year of the disposition), outlays and expenses made or incurred by the taxpayer in connection with the disposition are also taken into account in the base for the EC amount, to the extent that such outlays and expenses were not otherwise deductible in computing the taxpayer's income.

31. Subsection 14(3), as described in ¶23 above, applies to acquisitions of EC property by a transferee from a non-arm's length transferor that occur after 1987. However, if such an acquisition occurred after 1987 but before the transferee's adjustment time, i.e., while the old system was still in effect for the transferee, a factor of 2 rather than $1/3$ is used in the formula in ¶23 above when determining the transferee's EC expenditure for the property. $1/2$, rather than $3/4$, of that EC expenditure is then added to the transferee's pool under the old system.

32. Where the taxpayer has disposed of a former property in the last year under the old system and acquired a replacement property in the first year under the new system, a subsection 14(6) election can be made in essentially the same manner as described in ¶s 25 and 26 above. It should be noted, however, that whether the taxpayer should use

(a) the taxpayer's total proceeds from the disposition of the former property, or

(b) only the portion of such proceeds that became payable to the taxpayer in the year of the disposition

¶3111

for purposes of determining the base for the EC amount that would otherwise occur in the year of the disposition (which is under the old system) depends on the date of the disposition (or the date of any written obligation entered into for the disposition). In this connection, see the transitional rules described in ¶s 28 and 29 above. For purposes of calculating, in the year of the acquisition of the replacement property (which is under the new system), both the deferred EC amount to be deducted from the pool for the former property and the amount to be added to the pool in connection with the EC expenditure for the replacement property, an inclusion rate of ¾ is used.

33. In determining what portion of the total proceeds from a disposition becomes payable to a taxpayer in any particular year for purposes of applying the transitional provisions described above, the comments in IT-123R4 should be considered, including those regarding section 21 of the *Income Tax Application Rules, 1971* (ITAR). As indicated in those comments, subsection 21(1) of the ITAR (as it read for years under the old system) reduced the amount payable to the taxpayer for any particular year to a percentage that was less than 100% of that amount payable only if the disposition occurred before the 1984 calendar year. However, the terms of a disposition before 1984 may have called for periodic payments one or more of which would become payable, as it turns out, some time after the taxpayer's adjustment time, i.e., in a year or years under the new system. In such a case, the transitional provision described in ¶28 above applies, but is modified by subsection 21(1) of the ITAR as it read in the year of the disposition. That is, an amount payable in a year under the new system is reduced to the percentage of that amount payable as determined in the year of the disposition which occurred before 1984.

Government Rights

34. In addition to the percentage limitation rule described in ¶33 above (which applies to amounts payable from all dispositions of EC property occurring before 1984), subsection 21(1) of the ITAR contains further limitations on the calculation of an EC amount resulting from the disposition of, or allowing the expiration of, a government right. If the disposition or expiration of the government right occurred before June 18, 1987 (or pursuant to the terms of an obliga-

tion entered into in writing before June 18, 1987), see the limitation rules discussed in ¶13 of IT-123R4. It should be noted that, even though the disposition or expiration occurred in a year that was under the old system, these rules in ¶13 of IT-123R4 can still apply for the purpose of determining an amount that becomes payable in a year that is under the new system, i.e., for the purpose of applying the transitional provision described in ¶28 above. If the disposition or expiration of the government right has occurred after June 17, 1987 (otherwise than pursuant to the terms of an obligation entered into in writing before June 18, 1987), subsection 21(1) of the ITAR applies, in the year of such disposition or expiration, with respect to the taxpayer's total proceeds rather than with respect to the portion of such proceeds payable to the taxpayer. The total proceeds from the disposition or expiration of the government right are calculated as the actual total proceeds minus the greater of two amounts:

(a) the cost of the "government right" or the taxpayer's "original right" in respect of the government right (as defined in subsection 21(3) of the ITAR) incurred prior to 1972 to the extent that such cost was not otherwise deducted in computing the income of the taxpayer for any taxation year, and

(b) the fair market value of the taxpayer's "specified right" in respect of the government right (as defined in subsection 21(3) of the ITAR) as at December 31, 1971.

Capital Dividend Account

35. An amount relating to a corporation's gain on the disposition of an EC property is included in its "capital dividend account" by virtue of its definition in subsection 89(1). For further particulars on this topic, see the current version of IT-66.

Bad Debts from Sale of EC Property

36. Subsection 20(4.2) provides for a deduction for a bad debt arising on a disposition of EC property occurring after June 17, 1987 (other than on a disposition pursuant to the terms of an obligation entered into in writing before June 18, 1987). Further particulars regarding subsection 20(4.2) are contained in the current version of IT-442. For a bad debt arising on a disposition of EC property occurring before

¶3111

June 18, 1987 (or on a disposition pursuant to the terms of an obligation entered into in writing before June 18, 1987), paragraph $20(1)(p)$ may still apply — see paragraph 19 of IT-123R4.

Amount Not Due Until Later Year

37. Where a sale of an EC property results in an income inclusion in the year of disposition under subsection 14(1) as described above, but some part of the sale price is not due until a later year, a reserve under paragraph $20(1)(n)$ is not permitted. This is because the sale of an EC property is not considered to be a sale of property "in the course of the business" as required by paragraph $20(1)(n)$.

Terminal Allowance

38. Section 24 contains a rule allowing, under certain conditions, a taxpayer who has ceased to carry on a business to deduct the full amount of any positive balance in the cumulative EC pool for the business. An exception to this rule occurs where there is a "rollover" of the taxpayer's positive balance in the pool to the taxpayer's spouse or corporation. For further discussion of this topic, see the current version of IT-313. It should also be noted that subparagraph $39(1)(b)(ii)$ precludes claims for capital losses on the disposition of EC property whether or not the business to which it relates has ceased.

Eligible Capital Property of a Deceased Taxpayer

39. The rules regarding EC property that apply as a result of the death of a taxpayer, including those pertaining to the acquisition of EC property of a deceased taxpayer by another person, are discussed in the current version of IT-313.

Related Bulletins

The titles of the interpretation bulletins referred to above are as follows:

- IT-66 — *Capital Dividends*

- IT-138 — *Computation and Flow-Through of Partnership Income*

- IT-143 — *Meaning of Eligible Capital Expenditure*

- IT-206 — *Separate Businesses*

- IT-259R3 — *Exchanges of Property*

- IT-313R2 — *Eligible Capital Property — Rules Where a Taxpayer Has Ceased Carrying on a Business or Has Died*

- IT-381 — *Trusts — Capital Gains and Losses and the Flow-Through of Taxable Capital Gains to Beneficiaries*

- IT-386 — *Eligible Capital Amounts*

- IT-442 — *Bad Debts and Reserves for Doubtful Debts*

Schedule A
Comparison of Old and New Systems

Transaction or Item		*Treatment under*	
	Old System	*New System*	
	All Taxpayers	*First Category[1]*	*Second Category[2]*
Balance in pool at end of immediately preceding year under the old system	Becomes opening balance in pool in current year.	3/2 of balance becomes opening balance in pool in current year (first year under new system). See 6 of this bulletin.	3/2 of balance becomes opening balance in pool in current year (first year under new system). See 6 of this bulletin.
Balance in pool at end of immediately preceding year under the new system	N/A	Becomes opening balance in pool in current year. See 6 of this bulletin.	Becomes opening balance in pool in current year. See 6 of this bulletin.

¶3111

	All Taxpayers	*First Category*[1]	*Second Category*[2]
EC expenditure	Increase pool by 1/2 of EC expenditure.	Increase pool by 3/4 of EC expenditure. See 7 of this bulletin.	Increase pool by 3/4 of EC expenditure. See 7 of this bulletin.
Disposition of EC property	Decrease pool by EC amount=1/2 × (proceeds payable to the taxpayer less outlays and expenses).	Decrease pool by EC amount=3/4×(taxpayer's total proceeds less outlays and expenses). See 9 of this bulletin.	Decrease pool by EC amount=3/4×(taxpayer's total proceeds less outlays and expenses). See 9 of this bulletin.
Positive balance in pool at end of the year	May deduct up to 10% of positive balance for purposes of computing income for year. Decrease pool by amount deducted.	May deduct up to 7% of positive balance for purposes of computing income for year. Decrease pool by amount deducted. See 11 of this bulletin.	May deduct up to 7% of positive balance for purposes of computing income for year. Decrease pool by amount deducted. See 11 of this bulletin.
Negative balance in pool at end of the year	Income inclusion occurs equal to full amount of negative balance. Increase pool by the income inclusion to bring balance back to nil.	A subparagraph $14(1)(a)(\text{iv})$ recapture income inclusion occurs if deductions previously claimed. There may also be • a subparagraph $14(1)(a)(\text{v})$ deemed taxable capital gain (which may qualify for a capital gains deduction) if the fiscal period ends before February 23, 1994[3], or • a subparagraph $14(1)(a)(\text{v})$ income inclusion (which may qualify for a capital gains deduction for qualified farm property) if the fiscal period ends after February 22, 1994[3], either of which is reduced by an adjustment (if there were old system deductions). A sub-paragraph $14(1)(a)(\text{v})$ income inclusion may also be reduced by means of the "exempt gains balance." Increase pool by all these amounts (i.e., the subparagraph $14(1)(a)(\text{iv})$ recapture income inclusion, the subparagraph $14(1)(a)(\text{v})$ deemed taxable capital gain or subparagraph $14(1)(a)(\text{v})$ income inclusion, the adjustment, and the amount of exempt gains balance used) to bring pool balance back to nil. See 14 to 17 of this bulletin.	Income inclusion is equal to the negative balance less an adjustment (which occurs if there were old system deductions). Increase pool by both amounts (i.e., the income inclusion and the adjustment) to bring balance back to nil. See 22 of this bulletin.

[1] For a determination of which taxpayers are included in the first category, see 13 of this bulletin.

[2] For a determination of which taxpayers are included in the second category, see 21 of this bulletin.

[3] An individual partner's share of a partnership's subparagraph $14(1)(a)(\text{v})$ amount may also be able to be reduced by means of the partner's "exempt capital gain balance" — see 20 of this bulletin.

¶3111

Schedule B
The Cumulative Eligible Capital Pool
Example of Calculation under the New System

Assumptions:

1) The taxpayer is an individual whose business has a fiscal year end of December 31.
2) The balance in the pool at the end of the 1987 taxation year under the old system was $100,000.
3) The total net amount of paragraph $20(1)(b)$ deductions less subsection $14(1)$ income inclusions under the old system was $15,000.
4) The acquisitions and dispositions of EC property, resulting in EC expenditures and EC amounts, respectively, are as indicated below under the transactions for each year.
5) The EC property which is purchased in 1993 replaces the EC property sold in 1992. The taxpayer therefore makes a subsection $14(6)$ election when filing the 1993 return and requests that the EC amount for the 1992 sale be adjusted in accordance with that election.
6) The EC property which the taxpayer purchases in 1994 for $100,000 is from a non-arm's length vendor who incurs no selling expenses.

   The transaction results in a subparagraph $14(1)(a)(v)$ income inclusion of $60,000 for the vendor. However, the EC property is a qualified farm property and all of the $60,000 is sheltered from taxation in the vendor's hands by means of a section 110.6 capital gains deduction.

Transaction or Item		Variable in 14(5) definition of "cumulative EC"	Increase	Decrease	Balance
1988 Taxation Year					
Opening balance: 3/2 × $100,000 (see assumption 2)		Variable C			$ 150,000
EC expenditure for $50,000:					
Add to pool 3/4 of EC expenditure		Variable A	$37,500		187,500
Deduct from pool paragraph $20(1)(b)$ deduction @ 7%		Variable P		$13,125	174,375
1989 Taxation Year					
Deduct from pool paragraph $20(1)(b)$ deduction @ 7%		Variable P		12,206	162,169
1990 Taxation Year					
Sale of EC property:					
Sale proceeds	$410,000				
Less selling expenses	10,000				
Base for the EC amount	$400,000				
Deduct from pool EC amount = 3/4 of base		Variable E		300,000	$(137,831)^1$
Subparagraph $14(1)(a)(iv)$ recapture income inclusion, which is limited to total net recapturable amount:					
Old system (see assumption 3)	$15,000				
New system:					
Previous paragraph $20(1)(b)$ deductions:					
1988	$13,125				
1989	12,206				
	25,331				
Less previous income inclusions	N/A	25,331			
Subparagraph $14(1)(a)(iv)$ recapture income inclusion — add this amount back to the pool	$40,331	Variable R	$40,331^2$		

¶3111

Transaction or Item		*Variable in 14(5) definition of "cumulative EC"*	*Increase*	*Decrease*	*Balance*
Subparagraph $14(1)(a)(v)$ deemed taxable capital gain:					
Negative balance in the pool at the end of the year (see above)	$137,831				
Less the sum of					
Subparagraph $14(1)(a)(iv)$ recapture income inclusion for the year (see above)	$40,331				
1/2 of the $15,000 portion of the net recapturable amount that originates from the old system (see assumption 3)	7,500 47,831				
Subparagraph $14(1)(a)(v)$ deemed taxable capital gain — add this amount back to the pool	$ 90,000	Variable B	$90,000^2$		
Add back to pool 1/2 of the $15,000 portion of the net recapturable amount that originates from the old system (see calculation of deemed taxable capital gain immediately above)		Variable D.1	$7,500^2$		NIL^2
1991 Taxation Year					
EC expenditure for $100,000:					
Add to pool 3/4 of EC expenditure		Variable A	75,000		75,000
Deduct from pool paragraph $20(1)(b)$ deduction @ 7%		Variable P		5,250	69,750
1992 Taxation Year					
Sale of EC property:					
Sale proceeds	$210,000				
Less selling expenses	10,000				
Base for EC amount as otherwise determined	200,000				
Less amount excluded under subsection 14(6) election filed with the 1993 return (see assumption 5)	200,000				
Revised base for EC amount	$ NIL				

¶3111

Transaction or Item	Variable in 14(5) definition of "cumulative EC"	Increase	Decrease	Balance
Deduct from pool EC amount = 3/4 of revised base	Variable E		NIL	69,750
Deduct from pool paragraph 20(1)(b) deduction @ 7%	Variable P		4,883	64,867
1993 Taxation Year				
Base for the EC amount = the $200,000 excluded from base for EC amount for 1992 under subsection 14(6) election filed with this year's return (see assumption 5):				
Deduct from pool EC amount = 3/4 of that base	Variable E		150,000	(85,133)
EC expenditure for $240,000 to replace EC property sold in 1992 (see assumption 5):				
Add to pool 3/4 of EC expenditure	Variable A	180,000		94,867
Deduct from pool paragraph 20(1)(b) deduction @ 7%	Variable P		6,641	88,226
1994 Taxation Year				
Purchase of EC property for $100,000 — subsection 14(3) calculation of EC expenditure (see assumption 6):				

Vendor's EC amount	$75,000
Less vendor's capital gains deduction	60,000
Difference	$15,000
Purchaser's EC expenditure = 4/3 of difference	$20,000

Transaction or Item	Variable	Increase	Decrease	Balance
Add to pool 3/4 of purchaser's EC expenditure	Variable A	15,000		103,226
Deduct from pool paragraph 20(1)(b) deduction @ 7%	Variable P		7,226	96,000
1995 Taxation Year				
Deduct from pool paragraph 20(1)(b) deduction @ 7%	Variable P		6,720	89,280
1996 Taxation Year				
Deduct from pool paragraph 20(1)(b) deduction @ 7%	Variable P		6,250	83,030

[1] This is the negative balance of the end of the 1990 taxation year.
[2] The three "add backs" bring the pool balance from $(137,831) back to nil.

Explanation of Changes

Introduction

The purpose of the Explanation of Changes is to give the reasons for the revisions to an interpretation bulletin. It outlines revisions that we have made as a result of changes to the law, as well as changes reflecting new or revised departmental interpretations.

Reasons for the Revision

This bulletin has been revised to reflect amendments to the *Income Tax Act* enacted under the 5th Supplement to the Revised Statutes of Canada, 1985; S.C. 1994, c. 21 (formerly Bill C-27); S.C. 1995, c. 3 (formerly Bill C-59); and S.C. 1995, c. 21 (formerly Bill C-70). The bulletin is not affected

¶3111

by any proposed legislation released as of May 30, 1997.

Legislative and Other Changes

Effective for taxation years ending after November 1991, the following structural amendments to the Act were made:

- The definitions of "cumulative eligible capital" (cumulative EC), "eligible capital expenditure" (EC expenditure) and "adjustment time" were removed from paragraphs $14(5)(a)$, (b) and (c) of the Act, respectively, and instead placed in alphabetical order in subsection $14(5)$.

- The definition of "eligible capital property" (EC property) was removed from paragraph $54(d)$ of the Act and instead placed in alphabetical order (with other definitions) in section 54.

- The definition of "capital dividend account" was removed from paragraph $89(1)(b)$ of the Act and instead placed in alphabetical order (with other definitions) in subsection $89(1)$.

- The definitions of "government right", "original right" and "specified right" were removed from paragraphs $21(3)(a)$, (b) and (c) of the *Income Tax Application Rules, 1971* (ITAR) and instead placed in alphabetical order in subsection $21(3)$ of the ITAR.

- The above-mentioned definition for "cumulative eligible capital" was changed in form to a mathematical formula.

These structural amendments to the Act are reflected in ¶s 3, 5, 6, 34 (formerly ¶29) and ¶35 (formerly ¶30) and Schedule B of the bulletin.

¶8 is new. It has been added to the bulletin in order to discuss the effect of the rules in subsections 14(10) and (11). These subsections apply to assistance from a government, municipality or other public authority that a taxpayer receives or becomes entitled to receive after February 21, 1994 and to repayments of such assistance.

¶10 is new. It has been added to the bulletin in order to discuss the effect of an amendment to section 14 that applies to taxation years ending after February 21, 1994. The amendment relates to subsection 80(7) and the forgiveness of debt.

A new part has been added at the end of ¶13 (formerly ¶11) in order to discuss the deemed residence rule in subsection 14(8). Although subsection 14(8) was added to the Act since this bulletin was last issued, it applies for the 1988 and subsequent taxation years.

¶14 (formerly ¶12) has been revised in order to reflect an amendment to section 14 that applies to taxation years ending after February 21, 1994. This amendment is shown in ¶14 as variable B.1 and it is related to the amendment covered in new ¶10 with respect to subsection 80(7) and the forgiveness of debt (see explanation above). Also in ¶14, we now use the term "subparagraph $14(1)(a)(iv)$ recapture income inclusion" rather than "income inclusion under subsection 14(1)" in order to distinguish this income inclusion from the "subparagraph $14(1)(a)(v)$ income inclusion" described in ¶17.

¶s 15 to 17 replace former ¶13. ¶17 reflects amendments to section 14 that generally apply to fiscal periods ending after February 22, 1994. These amendments to section 14 relate to the elimination of the $100,000 capital gains exemption in section 110.6, which applies for dispositions of property after February 22, 1994, as well as related amendments to section 110.6 permitting the recognition of capital gains accrued to February 22, 1994. The amendments to section 14 include what we refer to in the bulletin as the "subparagraph $14(1)(a)(v)$ income inclusion", the "exempt gains balance" and related amendments.

¶18 (formerly ¶14), which refers to a beneficiary of a trust in connection with the application of subparagraph $14(1)(a)(v)$ to the trust, is revised as a consequence of the revisions to the rules described in ¶s 15 to 17 (formerly ¶13).

¶19 (formerly ¶15), which refers to a member of a Canadian partnership in connection with the application of subparagraph $14(1)(a)(v)$ to the partnership's business, is revised as a consequence of the revisions to

¶3111

the rules described in ¶s 15 to 17 (formerly ¶13).

¶20 is new. It has been added to the bulletin to make a reference to subsection 39.1(5) and the definition of "exempt capital gains balance" in subsection 39.1(1), both of which were added to the Act for the 1994 and subsequent taxation years.

The last part of ¶23 (formerly ¶18) has been revised in order to clarify that the subsequent disposition of the property need not be at arm's length in order for the reversal of the subsection 14(3) reduction to the transferee's EC expenditure to occur, but that the subsequent transferee could then be subject to the subsection 14(3) reduction.

¶24 is new. It has been added to the bulletin in order to discuss the rule in subparagraph $110.6(19)(b)(ii)$, which applies to EC property acquired by a non-arm's length transferee after February 22, 1994.

In Schedule A of the bulletin, the last item under the heading "First Category" has been revised because of the amendments to the law that are reflected in ¶s 15 to 17 (formerly ¶13).

Assumption 6 of Schedule B has been revised. This revision refers to a subparagraph $14(1)(a)(v)$ income inclusion (which is discussed in ¶17 under the rules for fiscal periods ending after February 22, 1994).

Other changes to the bulletin include

- clarification changes; and

- the removal of the detailed discussion of topics considered outside the scope of the new bulletin.

[3115] Interpretation Bulletin IT-128R: Capital Cost Allowance — Depreciable Property

[*Interpretation Bulletin IT-128R is dated May 21, 1985.*]

Reference: Paragraphs $20(1)(a)$ and $13(21)(b)$ of the Act (also 1102(1) of the Income Tax Regulations)

This bulletin replaces and cancels Interpretation Bulletin IT-128 issued on October 29, 1973.

1. The classes of property described in Part XI of the Regulations and in Schedule II in respect of which capital cost allowances are deductible under paragraph $20(1)(a)$ in computing income do not include property that was not in fact acquired by the taxpayer or property listed in Regulation 1102(1), a partial list of which includes

(a) property the cost of which is deductible in computing the taxpayer's income;

(b) property that is described in the taxpayer's inventory;

(c) property that was not acquired for the purpose of gaining or producing income;

(d) property that was acquired by an expenditure in respect of which the taxpayer is allowed a deduction under section 37;

(e) property that was acquired after November 12, 1981 that is

(i) a print, etching, drawing, painting, sculpture, or other similar work of art, the cost of which to the taxpayer was not less than $200,

(ii) a hand-woven tapestry or carpet or a handmade appliqué, the cost of which to the taxpayer was not less than $215 per square metre,

(iii) an engraving, etching, lithograph, woodcut, map or chart, made before 1900, or

(iv) antique furniture, or any other antique object, produced more than 100 years before the date it was acquired, the cost of which to the taxpayer was not less than $1,000,

other than property that was acquired from a person with whom the taxpayer was not dealing at arm's length (otherwise than by virtue of a right referred to in paragraph $251(5)(b)$) at the time the property was acquired if the property was acquired in circumstances where the provisions of Regulation 1102(14) were applicable, and other than property described in (i) or (ii) above that

¶3115

was created by an individual who was a Canadian, as defined by Regulation 1104(10)(*a*), at the time the property was created;

(f) property that is a camp, yacht, lodge or golf course or facility acquired after December 31, 1974 (subject to the transitional rules in Regulation 1102(17)) if any outlay or expense for the use or maintenance of that property is not deductible by virtue of paragraph 18(1)(*l*) (also see IT-148R3);

(g) property in respect of which a capital cost allowance for the purposes of paragraph 20(1)(*a*) is claimed and permitted under Part XVII of the Regulations by a farmer or fisherman.

Ownership

2. Capital cost allowance may only be claimed in respect of capital expenditures made in respect of property owned by the taxpayer or in which the taxpayer has a leasehold interest. In this connection it is important to note that in computing the income of a partnership, subsection 96(1) and Regulations 1102(1*a*) require that partnership property (including depreciable property) be accounted for as if it were owned at the partnership level.

3. In most instances, where a taxpayer incurs a cost in respect of a capital asset, ownership of or a lease to that asset will be obtained either at the time the cost was incurred or at a later date. However, there may be circumstances in which neither a freehold nor a leasehold interest in the property is acquired. If a taxpayer constructs and incurs the cost of a structure on land owned by another person, or otherwise incorporates an asset into property owned by another as an integral part thereof, and does not have a leasehold interest in or ownership of the asset, capital cost allowance may not be claimed in respect of such property. This will be the case where a road providing access to a taxpayer's plant is built at the taxpayer's expense on land owned by a municipality. Also, capital expenditures for architectural and engineering services in preparing plans and estimates for new plants, or for additions to existing plants or other construction work of a capital nature, are not subject to capital cost allowance if the work for which the plans and estimates were prepared is not carried out. However, an expenditure of this nature may be an eli-

gible capital expenditure (defined in paragraph 14(5)(*b*)) for which an allowance is permitted by virtue of paragraph 20(1)(*b*) of the Act (see IT-143R2).

Capital Expenditures on Depreciable Property Versus Current Expenditures on Repairs and Maintenance

4. The following guidelines may be used in determining whether an expenditure is capital in nature because depreciable property was acquired or improved, or whether it is currently deductible because it is in respect of the maintenance or repair of a property:

(a) *Enduring Benefit* — Decisions of the courts indicate that when an expenditure on a tangible depreciable property is made "with a view to bringing into existence an asset or advantage for the enduring benefit of a trade", then that expenditure normally is looked upon as being of a capital nature. Where, however, it is likely that there will be recurring expenditures for replacement or renewal of a specific item because its useful life will not exceed a relatively short time, this fact is one indication that the expenditures are of a current nature.

(b) *Maintenance or Betterment* — Where an expenditure made in respect of a property serves only to restore it to its original condition, that fact is one indication that the expenditure is of a current nature. This is often the case where a floor or a roof is replaced. Where, however, the result of the expenditure is to materially improve the property beyond its original condition, such as when a new floor or a new roof clearly is of better quality and greater durability than the replaced one, then the expenditure is regarded as capital in nature. Whether or not the market value of the property is increased as a result of the expenditure is not a major factor in reaching a decision. In the event that the expenditure includes both current and capital elements and these can be identified, an appropriate allocation of the expenditure is necessary. Where only a minor part of the expenditure is of a capital nature, the Department is prepared to treat the whole as being of a current nature.

¶3115

(c) *Integral Part or Separate Asset* — Another point that may have to be considered is whether the expenditure is to repair a part of a property or whether it is to acquire a property that is itself a separate asset. In the former case the expenditure is likely to be a current expense and in the latter case it is likely to be a capital outlay. For example, the cost of replacing the rudder or propeller of a ship is regarded as a current expense because it is an integral part of the ship and there is no betterment; but the cost of replacing a lathe in a factory is regarded as a capital expenditure because the lathe is not an integral part of the factory but is a separate marketable asset. Between such clear-cut cases there are others where a replaced item may be an essential part of a whole property yet not an integral part of it. Where this is so, other factors such as relative values must be taken into account.

(d) *Relative Value* — The amount of the expenditure in relation to the value of the whole property or in relation to previous average maintenance and repair costs often may have to be weighed. This is particularly so when the replacement itself could be regarded as a separate, marketable asset. While a spark plug in an engine may be such an asset, one would never regard the cost of replacing it as anything but an expense; but where the engine itself is replaced, the expenditure not only is for a separate marketable asset but also is apt to be very substantial in relation to the total value of the property of which the engine forms a part, and, if so, the expenditure likely would be regarded as capital in nature. On the other hand, the relationship of the amount of the expenditure to the value of the whole property is not, in itself, necessarily decisive in other circumstances, particularly where a major repair job is done which is an accumulation of lesser jobs that would have been classified as current expense if each had been done at the time the need for it first arose; the fact that they were not done earlier does not change the nature of the work

when it is done, regardless of its total cost.

(e) *Acquisition of Used Property* — Where used property is acquired by a taxpayer and at the time of acquisition it requires repairs or replacements to put it in suitable condition for use, the cost of such work is regarded as capital in nature even though, in other circumstances, it would be treated as current expense.

(f) *Anticipation of Sale* — Repairs made in anticipation of the sale of a property or as a condition of the sale are regarded as capital in nature. On the other hand, where the repairs would have been made in any event and the sale was negotiated during the course of the repairs, or after their completion, the cost should be classified as though no sale was contemplated.

Depreciable Assets versus Inventory Assets

5. The Department's practice with respect to a taxpayer who deals in a particular kind of property and who also uses that kind of property for some other purpose is discussed in IT-102R2.

Buildings Incidentally Acquired on Obtaining a Site

6. Where a taxpayer purchases real estate including a building and the building is torn down within a relatively short time after purchase, the question arises as to whether the building should be classed as depreciable property. If the building is demolished by the purchaser without having been used to earn income, the building cannot be regarded as depreciable property. Also, where the building is used to earn income for only a short time prior to demolition, it is not regarded as depreciable property unless the taxpayer can clearly establish that the prime intention on acquiring the building was for the purpose of gaining or producing income. The Department's practice with respect to the costs of demolishing a building incidentally acquired on obtaining a site is discussed in IT-485.

¶3115

[3120]　Interpretation Bulletin IT-143R3:　Meaning of Eligible Capital Expenditure

[Interpretation Bulletin IT-143R3 is dated August 29, 2002.]

Reference: The definition of "eligible capital expenditure" in subsection 14(5) (also sections 68 and 69, the definition of "eligible capital property" in section 54, the definition of "cumulative eligible capital" in subsection 14(5), and paragraphs 13(7.5)(*b*), 13(7.5)(*c*) and 13(7.5)(*d*) of the *Income Tax Act*; and Class 14 of Schedule II to the Income Tax Regulations.

Contents

Application

This bulletin cancels and replaces IT-143R2 dated August 10, 1983, as revised by Special Release dated October 30, 1992.

Summary

An eligible capital expenditure in respect of a business is, in the simplest terms, a capital expenditure (i.e., an expenditure that results in an enduring benefit) that does not come within any of the capital cost allowance classes but rather goes into an eligible capital property pool. A percentage of the balance of the pool at the end of the year may be claimed as a deduction for the year.

An "eligible capital expenditure" is a defined term in the *Income Tax Act*. The major part of the definition lists exclusions, i.e., expenditures that do not qualify as an eligible capital expenditure. One of the most fundamental of these exclusions is the cost of any tangible property. However, not every intangible property qualifies as an eligible capital expenditure.

This bulletin covers the details of the definition of an "eligible capital expenditure" and then discusses a number of specific types of expenditures for purposes of determining whether or not they fall within that definition. For the most part, this discussion contains general positions with respect to this question, and does not deal with exceptional cases.

Discussion and Interpretation

Introduction

1. Many expenditures commonly called "nothings", of which the cost of goodwill is the most notable, were not deductible from income under the provisions of the pre-1972 Act either as an expense or by way of capital cost allowances. Certain "nothings" are given special treatment in the current Act as "eligible capital expenditures". A discussion of this special treatment is contained in the

current version of IT-123, *Transactions Involving Eligible Capital Property.*

2. An "eligible capital expenditure", which is defined in subsection 14(5), may be broadly described as an outlay or expense made or incurred by a taxpayer:

(a) in respect of a business;

(b) as a result of a transaction occurring after 1971;

(c) on account of capital; and

(d) for the purpose of gaining or producing income from the business (whether or not income from the business was actually produced by such outlay or expense).

Where a taxpayer carries on more than one business, the eligible capital expenditure arising from an outlay or expense will form part of the "cumulative eligible capital", as defined in subsection 14(5), only of that business to which it relates. An outlay or expense made or incurred with respect to income from property (e.g., non-business rental or investment income) or with respect to a capital gain or a capital loss, will not be an eligible capital expenditure since it does not meet the purpose stated in (d) above. Many expenditures, however, can meet these broad requirements but still will fall within the specific exclusions found in paragraphs (*a*) to (*f*) of the definition of "eligible capital expenditure", which are dealt with in ¶3.

Specific Exclusions

3. The following are not eligible capital expenditures:

(a) amounts which, in the computation of income are:

(i) not deductible in the current period because of some quantum restriction (e.g., the portion, if any, of cumulative Canadian exploration expense not deductible in the year under paragraph 66.1(2)(*a*) because of the limitation contained in paragraph 66.1(2)(*b*)),

(ii) not deductible by virtue of a specific provision in the Act, other than paragraph 18(1)(*b*), (e.g., a personal or living expense as contemplated by paragraph 18(1)(*h*)), or

(iii) specifically deductible from income by virtue of any provision of the Act (e.g., expenditures for which a deduction is permitted by virtue of section 20);

(b) all or any part of the cost of:

(i) tangible property, including all tangible depreciable property (e.g., buildings) and non-depreciable tangible capital property (e.g., land),

(ii) intangible property that is depreciable property (for examples of such property, see ¶11 and ¶29, or see intangible property to which paragraph 13(7.5)(*c*) applies),

(iii) any other intangible but non-depreciable property which is deductible, or would be deductible, if the related income were sufficiently large (e.g., a right owned by a mining company that is a Canadian resource property that is deductible under subsection 66.2(2)), and

(iv) an interest in, or a right to acquire, any property included in (b)(i), (ii) and (iii) above;

(c) an amount paid or payable to any creditor on any debt or on the redemption, cancellation or purchase of any bond or debenture (e.g., payments made in connection with the redemption of bonds or debentures before maturity and also any excess of redemption price over issue price where the bonds were issued at a discount and redeemed at par value or issued at par value and redeemed at a premium). A bonus or premium paid by a mortgagor to a mortgagee in consideration for the mortgagee's consent to an early redemption of the mortgage is considered to constitute an amount paid to a creditor on account or in lieu of payment of any debt and consequently this premium or bonus cannot qualify as an "eligible capital expenditure";

(d) amounts paid or payable by a corporation to a person in his or her capacity as a shareholder. The amounts referred to by this exclusion are limited to dividend payments, distributions on the reduction, in any manner whatever, of share capital and any payment or appropriation of property referred to in subsection 15(1);

(e) the cost of, or any part of the cost of, an interest in either a trust or partnership, a share, bond, debenture, mortgage, hypothecary claim, note, bill or other similar property or an interest in, or right to acquire, any such property; and

(f) expenditures made to produce "exempt income" as defined in subsection 248(1).

4. An expenditure must meet the conditions of ¶2 and not be excluded by ¶3 before it qualifies as an eligible capital expenditure. The application of these tests to specific expenditures is outlined in the following paragraphs.

Goodwill

5. The Courts have referred to several definitions of goodwill, two of which are:

(a) "Goodwill is the whole advantage, whatever it may be, of the reputation and connection of the firm which may have been built up by years of honest work or gained by lavish expenditures of money".

(b) It is "the privilege, granted by the seller of a business to the purchaser, of trading as his recognized successor; the possession of a ready-formed 'connection' of customers, considered as an element in the saleable value of a business, additional to the value of the plant, stock-in-trade, book debts, etc.".

6. Goodwill cannot be divorced from the business itself. It follows the business and may be sold with the business, but it cannot be sold separately. Generally, goodwill arises as a recognizable asset only when a business is acquired at a price in excess of the value, as a going concern, of its net assets.

7. Where goodwill, as a recognizable asset, is acquired by the purchaser of a business in the circumstances described in ¶6, the consideration given for the goodwill, as well as any legal and accounting fees that can be directly associated with the purchase of the goodwill, will qualify as an eligible capital expenditure. If the portion of the total consideration for the business that is allocated to the goodwill is unreasonable, or

if the goodwill has a value which the vendor and purchaser have not specified, the Canada Customs and Revenue Agency (CCRA) can apply the provisions of section 68 to deem what may reasonably be regarded as the amount for the goodwill. This amount would then be applied uniformly to both the vendor and the purchaser. If section 68 is applied for this purpose, the CCRA will take into account all the relevant facts and circumstances of the particular case (see the findings of the Federal Court of Appeal in *George Golden v. The Queen*, 83 DTC 5138, (1983) C.T.C. 112, which were upheld by the Supreme Court of Canada — 86 DTC 6138, (1986) 1 C.T.C. 274). Such relevant facts and circumstances include the relative positions of the vendor and the purchaser and the relative fair market values of all the assets of the business that are acquired. Where the vendor and purchaser are dealing at arm's length, their agreement as to the allocation of the total price for the business amongst its various assets is given considerable weight as evidence of the reasonableness of the amount so allocated to the goodwill. The reasonableness of the allocation is further supported where there is evidence that it has resulted from hard bargaining between the parties. In a non-arm's length transaction, section 68 could apply where the total purchase price of the assets of the business equals the total of their fair market values but the allocation of that total purchase price amongst those assets, including the goodwill, is not considered to be reasonable. However, where the total purchase price of the business assets in a non-arm's length transaction does not equal the total of their fair market values, the provisions of section 69 will apply.

Customer Lists and Ledger Accounts

8. Where a taxpayer acquires lists or ledger accounts of clients, customers or subscribers, it is necessary to determine whether the cost of acquisition is a capital expenditure or an expense of the year. The current version of IT-187, *Customer Lists and Ledger Accounts*, describes the general guidelines applicable to this determination. Generally, the cost of a list bringing an enduring benefit to the business of the purchaser is a capital outlay and is an eligible capital expenditure.

¶3120

Trademarks, Patents, Franchises and Licences in Mortmain

9. The costs of obtaining a trademark registration to protect a trade name, design or product are allowable as deductions in computing income. This includes the designing, legal and registration costs, and also any payment made to some other person to refrain from contesting the registration.

10. Where, on the other hand, a taxpayer buys a trademark from another person who has developed a trademark of enduring value, the amount paid for it is a capital expenditure not subject to capital cost allowance. However, it is an "eligible capital expenditure", assuming it meets all the other requirements of that definition in subsection 14(5).

11. An outlay or expense made or incurred to acquire, or in an attempt to acquire, a patent, franchise, concession or licence for use in a business qualifies as an eligible capital expenditure provided that the outlay or expense did not result in the acquisition of a depreciable property of Class 14 of Schedule II of the Income Tax Regulations or a property that is described as an exception in paragraphs (*a*), (*b*), (*c*), (*d*) or (*e*) of Class 14. See the current version of IT-477, *Capital Cost Allowance — Patents, Franchises, Concessions and Licences*, for comments regarding properties that qualify as Class 14. An amount paid by a taxpayer, either separately or as part of the purchase price paid for the acquisition of the assets or business of another person, for the right to stand in the place of that other person in making an application for a patent, franchise, concession or licence or a renewal thereof, may also qualify as an eligible capital expenditure.

12. Amounts expended by corporations to acquire or renew licences in mortmain are not regarded as outlays for gaining income and are not eligible capital expenditures.

Expenses of Incorporation, Reorganization or Amalgamation

13. Incorporation expenses include all the expenses necessarily incurred by the incorporators to bring a corporation into existence, including:

(a) fees required by the appropriate government agency (federal or provincial);

(b) cost of affidavits;

(c) advertising expenses in those jurisdictions where applicants are required to give notice of their intention to apply for a charter;

(d) legal fees;

(e) costs of preparation of articles of incorporation and of bylaws;

(f) expenses incurred by applicants in attending preliminary meetings; and

(g) accountant's fees associated with the incorporation.

14. The CCRA considers that incorporation expenses and similar expenses incurred in the setting up of a new corporation or in connection with an amalgamation of two or more corporations, as well as expenses incurred in connection with the reorganization of the affairs of a corporation (including the costs of supplementary letters patent), are "eligible capital expenditures" if they meet the requirements of that definition in subsection 14(5) as explained in ¶2.

Fines, Penalties and Legal Damages

15. If a fine or penalty was paid or incurred in connection with the acquisition of an eligible capital property, the cost of the fine or penalty would be added to the eligible capital expenditure pertaining to that property. For more information, see the current version of IT-104, *Deductibility of Fines or Penalties*.

16. If damages were paid or incurred in connection with the acquisition of an eligible capital property, the cost of the damages would be added to the eligible capital expenditure pertaining to that property. For more information, see the current version of IT-467, *Damages, Settlements and Similar Payments*.

Political Contributions

17. Contributions by a taxpayer to a political party or other political organizations or to the campaign funds of a candidate for public office, whether or not allowed as a deduction under subsection 127(3), are not eligible capital expenditures.

Expenses of Issuing Shares or Borrowing Money

18. Paragraph $20(1)(e)$ provides for the deduction (subject to the limitations indicated therein) of an expense, including a commission, fee or other amount, paid or payable after November 16, 1978 by a taxpayer for or on account of services rendered by a person as a salesperson, agent or dealer in securities, incurred in the course of issuing or selling shares of the taxpayer or in the course of borrowing money. See the current version of IT-341, *Expenses of Issuing or Selling Shares, Units in a Trust, Interests in a Partnership or Syndicate and Expenses of Borrowing Money*, for more information on the application of paragraph $20(1)(e)$. Prior to November 17, 1978 these expenses were not deductible from income under paragraph $20(1)(e)$ but qualified as "eligible capital expenditures" provided they met the requirements of that definition in subsection 14(5).

Brokerage Fees on Purchase of Shares, Debentures, etc.

19. Brokerage fees incurred on the acquisition of a share, bond, debenture, mortgage, hypothecary claim, note, bill or other similar property are generally considered to form part of the cost of such property, and do not therefore qualify as "eligible capital expenditures" by virtue of subparagraph (f)(iii) of that definition in subsection 14(5).

Appraisal Costs

20. A taxpayer's reasonable costs, incurred after 1984, of surveying or valuing (appraising) a capital property for the purpose of its acquisition or disposition are, by virtue of paragraph $53(1)(n)$, added to the adjusted cost base of that property to the extent that such costs are not deducted by the taxpayer in computing income for any taxation year or attributable to any other property.

However, where a taxpayer incurs the cost of surveying or valuing (appraising) a capital property (e.g., a building) in anticipation of its purchase for use in earning income from a business but the purchase does not actually occur (e.g., the purchase is aborted), such cost would qualify as an eligible capital expenditure. An exception to this result would occur if the surveying or appraisal cost was incurred after March 6, 1996 and the aborted purchase was in

respect of a property described in subsection 1102(14.3) of the Income Tax Regulations (e.g., a parking area), since the surveying or appraisal cost would then become the cost of depreciable property (typically Class 1) by virtue of paragraphs $13(7.5)(b)$, (c) and (d) of the Act.

The cost of valuing a property, which is itself an eligible capital property (e.g., a government right) held by and used in the business of a taxpayer, qualifies as an eligible capital property for that business.

21. An outlay or expense made or incurred by a taxpayer to obtain an appraisal for a purpose other than gaining or producing income from a business does not qualify as an eligible capital expenditure. Examples of outlays or expenses of this kind are:

(a) the cost of an appraisal of property held on December 31, 1971 for the purpose of establishing its Valuation Day value;

(b) the cost of an appraisal of capital property owned by the taxpayer;

(c) the cost of an appraisal of a rental property owned by the taxpayer where the rental thereof is not part of a business of that taxpayer; and

(d) the cost of an appraisal which constitutes either part or all of the cost of acquisition, or an expense of disposition, of a property described in ¶3(b).

22. The cost of an appraisal incurred for the purpose of gaining or producing income from a business and not on account of capital is deductible in computing a taxpayer's income for the taxation year in which it is incurred. For example, the cost of an appraisal of a property for insurance purposes, the cost of an appraisal of assets of a public utility necessary to support an application for a rate increase and the cost of an appraisal of assets that are the inventory of a business would be deductible from income to the extent that each is reasonable in the circumstances.

Legal and Accounting Fees

23. Since an outlay or expense is an eligible capital expenditure only if it is incurred for the purpose of gaining or producing income from a business, legal and accounting fees incurred in an abortive

¶3120

attempt to acquire shares of a corporation would normally not qualify. Where, however, the taxpayer can demonstrate that he or she proposed to make the business of the corporation part of a similar business which the taxpayer already operated, the fees may qualify as eligible capital expenditures. For the CCRA's interpretation of "similar business" see the current version of IT-259, *Exchanges of Property*. Legal and accounting fees incurred by a taxpayer in connection with the purchase or sale of shares held by the taxpayer as capital property are included as a component of the adjusted cost base of the shares or deducted from the sale proceeds as disposal costs, as applicable. Expenses incurred in connection with the issue of shares of the capital stock of a corporation are discussed in ¶18. Legal and accounting fees incurred to oppose a bid to take over control of a corporation are not eligible capital expenditures. For more information, see the current version of IT-99, *Legal and Accounting Fees.*

Milk Quotas and Other Government Rights or Licences

24. Milk quotas issued by provincial milk marketing boards are generally issued at no cost to the producer. However, transfers of quotas for value may generally be made, subject to the terms and approval of the board. The cost of a milk quota purchased after 1971 is an eligible capital expenditure. Similarly, a quota exchange fee (e.g., to increase an existing quota) paid to a milk marketing board is an eligible capital expenditure.

The cost of other similar rights or licences issued under governmental authority is also an eligible capital expenditure.

Stock Exchange Seats and Memberships

25. The cost of a seat on a Canadian stock exchange or a stock exchange outside Canada that carries with it certain rights and privileges similar to those attaching to a share of a corporation is excluded from the definition of an "eligible capital expenditure" by subparagraph (*f*)(iii) of that definition in subsection 14(5) and such a seat is considered to be a capital property. Generally, these rights and privileges are outlined in the bylaws of the exchange and are as follows:

(a) The number of seats on the exchange is restricted.

(b) The seats may be acquired by purchase either from the exchange itself or on the open market.

(c) The amount received by the exchange on the sale of a seat is treated as a receipt of capital.

(d) The exchange differentiates between the "seat" and the "membership" in the exchange. Even if the ownership of a seat (or the right to use it) is a necessary qualification for membership, it does not, in or by itself, entitle one to become a member. A prospective member must still obtain the approval of the other members and pay an entrance or initiation fee.

26. Where the rights and privileges conferred on seat holders of Canadian or foreign exchanges are different than those set out in ¶25, the CCRA will review those rights and privileges upon request to determine whether the particular stock exchange seat to which those rights and privileges attach is a capital property.

Initiation or Admission Fees

27. The entrance or initiation fees paid to a stock exchange are eligible capital expenditures.

28. Initiation or admission fees paid to an organization (e.g. for call to the bar or for membership in a professional accounting institute) are eligible capital expenditures where it can be shown that the annual membership fees of the organization are allowable deductions in computing income of a business.

Easements

29. An amount paid by a taxpayer for the right of access to or the right of way over, upon or through land owned by another person may qualify as an eligible capital expenditure.

Such an amount would not qualify as an eligible capital expenditure, however, if it was incurred after March 6, 1996 and was for the right to use, or in respect of, property described in subsection 1102(14.3) of the Income Tax Regulations (e.g., a road described therein). In that case, the cost incurred would become the cost of depreciable property (typically Class 1) by virtue of paragraphs 13(7.5)(*b*), (*c*) and (*d*) of the Act.

¶3120

Capital Expenditures in Respect of Another Person's Property

30. An outlay or expense incurred after March 6, 1996 by a taxpayer, for the purpose of increasing the operational efficiency of a business by means of improving the property owned by some other person, would be the taxpayer's cost of depreciable property (typically Class 1) by virtue of paragraphs 13(7.5)(*b*), (*c*) and (*d*) of the Act, if the other person's property is property described in subsection 1102(14.3) of the Income Tax Regulations. This would be the case, for example, for the taxpayer's cost of improvements to city-owned streets, intersections, sidewalks, street lighting, etc. surrounding the taxpayer's shopping centre.

If, on the other hand, the other person's property was not a property described in Regulation 1102(14.3) or, in any event, if the taxpayer's cost was incurred before March 7, 1996, such cost to the taxpayer would generally be a non-deductible, non-depreciable capital outlay that qualifies as an eligible capital expenditure. An exceptional case may occur where the particular facts and circumstances lead to the conclusion that such a cost was a current expense, as was found by the Federal Court–Trial Division in the case of *Oxford Shopping Centres Ltd. v. The Queen*, 79 DTC 5458, [1980] C.T.C. 7 (which decision was upheld by the Federal Court of Appeal — 81 DTC 5065, (1981) C.T.C. 128). See the current version of IT-417, *Prepaid Expenses and Deferred Charges*, for a discussion on running expenses.

Forfeited Deposits

31. A forfeited deposit is not an eligible capital expenditure. See the current version of IT-461, *Forfeited Deposits*, for information on the treatment of forfeited deposits.

Non-Competition Payment

32. An amount paid by a taxpayer to another person with whom the taxpayer deals at arm's length, to obtain that other person's covenant not to engage in any business within a designated geographical area during a specified period of time, that is the same as or is similar to the business carried on by the taxpayer, may qualify as an eligible capital expenditure.

Other Bulletins

33. The current version of each Interpretation Bulletin listed below also makes reference to and contains limited discussion on the qualification of certain expenditures as eligible capital expenditures:

- IT-128, *Capital Cost Allowance — Depreciable Property*

- IT-211, *Membership Dues — Associations and Societies*

- IT-330, *Dispositions of Capital Property Subject to Warranty, Covenant, or Other Conditional or Contingent Obligations*

- IT-350, *Investigation of Site*

- IT-359, *Premiums and Other Amounts With Respect to Leases*

- IT-364, *Commencement of Business Operations*

- IT-386, *Eligible Capital Amounts*

- IT-425, *Miscellaneous Farm Income*

- IT-475, *Expenditures on Research and for Business Expansion*

- IT-501, *Capital Cost Allowance — Logging Assets*

Explanation of Changes

Introduction

The purpose of the *Explanation of Changes* is to give the reasons for the revisions to an interpretation bulletin. It outlines revisions that we have made as a result of changes to the law, as well as changes reflecting new or revised interpretations of the CCRA.

Reasons for the Revision

This bulletin has been revised to reflect changes in the law.

Legislative and Other Changes

¶2 and subsequent paragraphs have been revised to reflect that the definition of "eligible capital expenditure" is no longer contained in paragraph 14(5)(*b*) but rather is found in alphabetical order in subsection 14(5).

¶3120

¶2 has been revised to reflect that the definition of "cumulative eligible capital" is no longer contained in paragraphs 14(5)(a) but rather is found in alphabetical order in subsection 14(5).

¶3(a)(i) and ¶3(b)(ii) have been revised to reflect more current examples.

¶3(b)(ii) now makes reference to a property to which paragraph 13(7.5)(c) applies, as an intangible property that is depreciable property. Subsection 13(7.5) was added to the Act since the issuance of the former bulletin.

¶3(e) and ¶19 have been revised to reflect that the word "hypothec" is no longer contained in subparagraph (f)(iii) of the definition of "eligible capital expenditure" in subsection 14(5), but that the words "hypothecary claim" were added to that subparagraph as of June 14, 2001.

¶11 has been revised to reflect the addition of paragraph (e) (which refers to Class 44) to the exceptions listed under Class 14 of Schedule II of the Income Tax Regulations.

¶15 has been revised because of revisions in the current version of IT-104, *Deductibility of Fines or Penalties.*

¶16 has been revised because of revisions in the current version of IT-467, *Damages, Settlements and Similar Payments.*

¶20, 29 and 30 have been revised to reflect the effect of paragraphs 13(7.5)(b), (c) and (d). Subsection 13(7.5) was added to the Act since the issuance of the former bulletin.

¶23 now contains a statement, essentially the same as already contained in the current version of IT-99, *Legal and Accounting Fees*, with respect to legal and accounting fees incurred to oppose a bid to take over control of a corporation.

¶24 now contains a statement that a quota exchange fee (e.g., to increase an existing quota) paid to a milk marketing board is an eligible capital expenditure.

¶32 of the former bulletin has been discontinued, as it was rendered inaccurate by the addition to the Act of subsection 80(7). That provision is outside the scope of this bulletin, but is discussed in the current version IT-123, *Transactions Involving Eligible Capital Property.*

Other changes throughout the bulletin have been made only for purposes of clarification or readability.

[3125]   Interpretation Bulletin IT-147R3:   Capital Cost Allowance — Accelerated Write-Off of Manufacturing and Processing Machinery and Equipment

[*Interpretation Bulletin IT-147R3 is dated September 14, 1992.*]

Reference: Paragraph 20(1)(a) (also subsections 1100(3), 1100(15), 1102(14), 1102(14.1), 1103(2d), 1103(2e) and 1104(9) and paragraphs 1100(1)(ta), 1100(1)(ze) and 1100(1)(zf) of the Income Tax Regulations, and Classes 29, 39 and 40 of Schedule II to the Regulations)

Application

This bulletin cancels and replaces Interpretation Bulletin IT-147R2, dated June 19, 1985. Minor amendments were made on April 20, 2001.

Summary

This bulletin discusses manufacturing and processing machinery and equipment eligible to be included in Class 29 of Schedule II, if acquired before 1988, and in either Class 39 or Class 40, if acquired after 1987. The bulletin also explains the method of calculating the maximum capital cost allowance available under the appropriate class,

the requirements that must be met for property to be included in these classes, and the conditions that must be met to be eligible to claim capital cost allowance under Classes 29, 39 or 40. These classes provide write-offs at a higher rate and in a shorter time period than would otherwise be available. In addition, the bulletin explains the meaning of terms such as "primarily", "used directly or indirectly", "principal business" and "the activities of manufacturing goods for sale or lease". Subject to transitional rules, Class 29 includes only property acquired before 1988. Classes 39 and 40 have been established to contain property acquired after 1987, which would formerly have been included in

¶3125

Class 29. Capital cost allowance rates for Classes 39 and 40 are subject to a phased-in annual reduction from 40 per cent in 1988 to 25 per cent after 1990 for Class 39, and from 40 per cent in 1988 to 30 per cent after 1989 for Class 40. Subsection 1103(2e) of the Regulations provides that all property in Class 40 is transferred to Class 10 at the beginning of the taxpayer's first taxation year commencing after 1989, effectively eliminating Class 40 at that time.

When a Class 29 property has been disposed of in a taxation year and in any taxation year before the end of that taxation year a Class 39 or Class 40 property has been acquired, subsection 1103(2d) of the Regulations may permit a taxpayer to elect to have transferred the Class 29 property to the new class before its disposition. This bulletin explains the election and its consequences.

Discussion and Interpretation

1. Class 29 provides for a capital cost allowance rate of 50 per cent on a straight line basis. The introduction of Classes 39 and 40 (calculated on a declining balance) effectively reduces the capital cost allowance available on Class 29 property. Subject to transitional rules described below, property acquired after 1987, which would have been included in Class 29 if acquired before 1988, will be included either in Class 39 or in Class 40. Class 39 will contain all such property except powered industrial lift trucks, portable tools described in paragraph (b) of Class 10, and property described in paragraph (f) of Class 10 that is general-purpose electronic data processing equipment and related systems software. The property so excluded from Class 39 will, when acquired before 1990, be included in Class 40 and when acquired after 1989 be included in Class 10. Subsection 1103(2e) of the Regulations provides that all property in Class 40 is transferred to Class 10 immediately after the beginning of the first taxation year commencing after 1989, effectively eliminating this Class at that time.

2. Capital cost allowance for 1988, 1989 and 1990 years for Class 40 is calculated under paragraph 1100(1)(zf) on the declining balance, and the rate is 40 per cent for 1988, 35 per cent for 1989 and 30 per cent for 1990. These same rates apply to Class 39 under paragraph 1100(1)(ze) for the years 1988 to 1990, but after 1990 the

rate drops to 25 per cent and remains at that level. If the taxpayer's fiscal period (taxation year) does not coincide with the calendar year, the relevant annual rates of capital cost allowance are prorated based on the number of days in the taxation year that are in each calendar year.

Note: Under amendments proposed in the Federal Budget of February 25, 1992, the capital cost allowance rate for eligible manufacturing and processing machinery and equipment acquired after February 25, 1992 will be increased from 25 per cent to 30 per cent.

Property Eligible for Accelerated Write-Off

3. For property to be eligible for inclusion in Class 39 or Class 40 (or Class 29 for acquisitions prior to 1988), the taxpayer must acquire or manufacture the property to be

(a) used directly or indirectly by the taxpayer in Canada primarily in the manufacturing or processing of goods for sale or lease, or

(b) leased by certain corporations (see 15 below) to a lessee who can reasonably be expected to use, directly or indirectly, the property in Canada primarily in the manufacturing or processing of goods for sale or lease.

4. The property described in 3 above must be

(a) property that would otherwise be included in Class 8 (such as factory machinery and equipment), other than radiocommunication equipment or railway rolling stock,

(b) an oil or water storage tank,

(c) a powered industrial lift truck,

(d) electrical generating equipment described in Class 9,

(e) a portable tool described in paragraph (b) of Class 10, or

(f) general-purpose electronic data processing equipment and systems software described in paragraph (f) of Class 10.

Any property described above that is acquired after 1987 will be included in Class

¶3125

39 or 40, or Class 10 as discussed in 1 and 2 above.

5. When a taxpayer acquires a property, subsection 1102(14) of the Regulations generally requires the taxpayer to place the property in the same prescribed class or separate prescribed class as that of the vendor of the property provided

(a) the property is acquired by the taxpayer after June 17, 1987 in the course of a qualifying butterfly reorganization, as described in paragraph 55(3)(b), or

(b) the taxpayer and the vendor were not dealing at arm's length (otherwise than by a paragraph 251(5)(b) right for acquisitions after December 15, 1987) at the time the property was acquired.

Where subsection 1102(14) of the Regulations applies, property that otherwise would qualify for Class 29, of the taxpayer acquiring it, is deemed to be Class 8 property if, immediately before it was acquired, it belonged to Class 8 of the person from whom it was acquired. Anti-avoidance rules for subsection 1102(14) of the Regulations are provided in subsection 1102(20).

6. For acquisitions before June 18, 1987, subsection 1102(14) of the Regulations provides that when a property is acquired by a taxpayer from a person

(a) in a transaction for which an election was made under subsection 85(1) or (2), 97(2) or 98(3), or section 115.1 (for taxation years beginning after 1984),

(b) in a transaction to which subsection 85(5.1) or 98(5) applies,

(c) by virtue of an amalgamation (within the meaning assigned by subsection 87(1)),

(d) as the result of the winding-up of a Canadian corporation under subsection 88(1),

(e) with whom the taxpayer was not dealing at arm's length at the time the property was acquired, or

(f) for rent or lease to the person from whom the property was acquired or to another person who, at the time the property was acquired, was not dealing at arm's length with the person from whom the property was acquired,

and that property was property of a prescribed class or separate prescribed class of the person from whom it was acquired, the property was deemed to be property of the same prescribed class or separate prescribed class of the taxpayer.

7. Subsection 1102(14.1) of the Regulations provides that when a taxpayer has acquired property of a class (say Class 29) that had been previously owned before May 26, 1976 by either the taxpayer or a person with whom the taxpayer did not deal at arm's length at the time of the acquisition, and at the time that it was previously owned it was property of a different class (say Class 8), the property is deemed to be property of the original class (i.e., Class 8). The above rule is subject to the exception, generally applicable to acquisitions after December 15, 1987, that the non-arm's length relationship was not solely as a result of a right referred to in paragraph 251(5)(b) of the Act. Unlike subsection 1102(14) of the Regulations, subsection 1102(14.1) only applies to property previously owned before May 26, 1976.

Election to Transfer Property

8. Subsection 1103(2d) of the Regulations provides for an election to allow taxpayers to transfer property from one class (the old class) to another (the new class). The election may be useful when, in a taxation year, a Class 29 property has been disposed of and before the end of that taxation year a new Class 39 (or Class 40) property has been acquired. The effect of the election is that the old property is transferred to the new class before the disposition of the property. This election may allow a taxpayer

(a) to defer a recapture of capital cost allowance, or

(b) to increase the amount of capital cost allowance available in the year when subsection 1100(2) (the half-year rule) would otherwise have restricted the amount claimed (see the current version of IT-285, *Capital Cost Allowance — General Comments*, for an explanation of the half-year rule).

The election is made by letter in the tax return for the year of disposition. It must be made by the deadline for filing returns under section 150 of the Act.

¶3125

Meaning of Terms

9. The term *to be used (to use) directly or indirectly* in 3 above refers to property acquired by the taxpayer for the purpose of being an integral and essential part of the taxpayer's or lessee's manufacturing or processing activities, as well as any ancillary equipment such as furniture and fixtures, repair and maintenance equipment and fire extinguishing equipment, which is acquired for use in those activities. Although such equipment is generally located in the manufacturing or processing plant, it may also qualify if located elsewhere. Furniture and equipment acquired by the taxpayer for use by the taxpayer or lessee primarily in activities such as selling, distribution, and administration, which are not manufacturing or processing, are not eligible for the accelerated write-off. Direct or indirect use of a computer in manufacturing or processing is considered to include direct manufacturing and processing applications, and ancillary activities such as maintaining inventory records, production scheduling, engineering design, and production control, but does not include the maintenance of financial and accounting information such as accounts receivable and payable records, general ledger accounts, payroll records, customer lists, and sales invoices and analyses.

10. When a taxpayer includes a property in Class 29, 39 or 40, the property will be accepted as having been manufactured or acquired by the taxpayer for the purpose outlined in 3 above if it is actually used for that purpose after manufacture, acquisition or after leasing, as the case may be, and provided there has not been an unreasonable delay before the property is put into use. Also, it will generally be accepted that the property was manufactured or acquired for use as described in 3 above if the property was not put to any use for an extended period of time after manufacture or acquisition, and if there are sound business reasons as to why it is not being used as originally intended (e.g., if it would be economically unsound to carry out the original intention because of unforeseen or changed circumstances).

11. The term *"primarily"* means *"principally"* or *"chiefly"*. In establishing whether or not a particular property is used primarily in manufacturing or processing activities, generally the determining factor is the proportion of time that it is used in these activities. Property which is used more than 50 per cent of the time in manufacturing or processing activities will qualify to be included in Class 29, 39 or 40, as the case may be.

12. The manufacturing or processing activities referred to in 3 above must be carried out on goods for sale or lease, however, the manufacturer or processor of the goods does not necessarily have to be the vendor of the goods.

13. In some cases, it may be difficult to determine the amount of time that a particular piece of equipment is used in the manufacturing or processing of those goods that are for sale or lease, and those that are not for sale or lease. In such circumstances, any reasonable method of determining the primary use of the equipment will be accepted. For example, when equipment is used in two operations, an analysis of gross revenue from each operation may be helpful in determining the primary use of that equipment.

14. Subsection 1104(9) of the Regulations provides that, for purposes of Classes 29 and 39, "manufacturing or processing" does not include farming, fishing, logging, construction, and specified resource activities. The current version of IT-145, *Canadian Manufacturing and Processing Profits — Reduced Rate of Corporate Tax*, outlines some of the specifically excluded activities as well as explains various activities which are considered to be "manufacturing or processing" within the ordinary meaning of the term.

Persons Eligible for Accelerated Write-Off

15. All taxpayers are eligible to claim the accelerated write-off under Class 29, 39 or 40 on property which they manufacture or acquire for use by them in Canada primarily in manufacturing or processing of goods for sale or lease. When property is manufactured or acquired by a corporation that is leasing that property in the ordinary course of carrying on business in Canada to other taxpayers who are expected to use it as described in 3(b) above, in order for the property to qualify to be included in Class 29, 39 or 40, the corporation's principal business must be

(a) leasing property,

¶3125

(b) manufacturing property that it sells or leases,

(c) lending money,

(d) purchasing conditional sale contracts, accounts receivable, bills of sale, chattel mortgages, bills of exchange or other obligations representing part or all of the sale price of merchandise or services, or

(e) selling or servicing a type of property that it also leases,

or any combination of these businesses.

16. In determining the nature of a taxpayer's principal business, the following factors will be considered:

(a) the number of employees engaged in each branch or phase of a company's operations;

(b) the amount of gross revenue from each phase of operations; and

(c) the amount of capital employed in each phase of operations.

Ordinarily, the above factors will be considered in relation only to a specific year. However, when a company's normal activities have ceased or substantially decreased, the pattern of operations over several years may be considered in deciding whether there has been only a temporary break in the normal activities of the company or an actual change in the principal business.

Other Issues

17. Generally, for acquisitions before 1988, paragraph $1100(1)(ta)$ of the Regulations provided that the maximum capital cost allowance that may be claimed was 25 per cent of the capital cost in the year of acquisition, 50 per cent in the next following year, and 25 per cent in the third year. In addition to the percentage of capital cost allowed in the second and third year, the taxpayer may claim, for those years, any unused portion from the preceding years. Any undepreciated capital cost for such property remaining after 1987 can continue to be claimed in this manner. As required by subsection 1100(3), when a taxation year is less than 12 months, the amount deductible under paragraph $1100(1)(ta)$ cannot exceed the proportion of the maximum amount otherwise allowable that the number of days in the taxation year is of 365. The treatment of property acquired after 1987 is set out in 1 and 2 above. In some circumstances, subsection 1100(15) may restrict the maximum capital cost allowance otherwise determined under paragraph $1100(1)(ta)$. For a discussion of subsection 1100(15) see the current version of IT-443 and Special Release, *Leasing Property — Capital Cost Allowance Restrictions.*

[3130]   Interpretation Bulletin IT-170R: Sale of Property — When Included in Income Computation

[*Interpretation Bulletin IT-170R is dated August 25, 1980.*]

Reference: Paragraphs $12(1)(b)$, $13(21)(c)$ and subparagraph $54(c)(i)$ (also section 79 and subparagraphs $13(21)(d)(i)$, $54(c)(v)$ and $54(h)(i)$)

This bulletin cancels and replaces IT-170 dated August 6, 1974.

1. The comments contained in this bulletin are specifically directed to transactions that are sales of property and do not necessarily have application in other situations. The comments are inapplicable where subsection 44(2) of the Act is applicable which specifically provides a time for the inclusion of property sales in the income computation.

2. When the words of subparagraph $54(c)(i)$ are read in conjunction with subparagraph $54(h)(i)$, it is evident that the date of disposition of capital property sold occurs at the time that the vendor is "entitled to . . . the sale price". Since the corresponding provisions in paragraph $13(21)(c)$ and subparagraph $13(21)(d)(i)$ contain these identical words, the same conclusion follows in respect of depreciable property sold. In this manner the date of disposition is given a somewhat restricted meaning when a disposition of capital property involves a sale.

3. Where property is sold, paragraph $12(1)(b)$ requires an amount to be included in the computation of a taxpayer's income from a business at the time that the amount

becomes "receivable by the taxpayer" (unless the taxpayer is permitted to use the "cash basis" of reporting). Since the amount that becomes receivable in respect of property sold is the sale price, the taxable event under paragraph $12(1)(b)$ in respect of the sale of property can be stated as occurring on the date that the sale price becomes receivable to the vendor.

4. Subparagraph $54(c)(v)$ makes it clear for the purposes of subdivision c of Division B of Part I that the Act is interested only in dispositions that involve a change in beneficial ownership (unless the contrary is expressly stated). This is also the Department's view in respect of dispositions of depreciable property described in paragraph $13(21)(c)$ and the sale of trading assets under paragraph $12(1)(b)$. A transaction that can be described as a "sale" is therefore disregarded for purposes of this bulletin if there is no concurrent change in beneficial ownership. Such transactions will usually involve a "purchaser" who can be described as an agent, nominee, trustee or prête-nom corporation of a "vendor" who basically retains the right to deal with the property as though it were his own. (See Ruling TR-22 for an example.)

Time of Entitlement

5. Despite the absence of terminology in paragraph $12(1)(b)$ identical to that found in section 54 and subsection 13(21) (see 2 and 3 above), it is the Department's view that the sale price of any property sold is brought into account for income tax purposes when the vendor has an absolute but not necessarily immediate right to be paid. As long as a "condition precedent" remains unsatisfied, a vendor does not have an absolute right to be paid. However, the fact that an event subsequent to the completion of a sale restores the ownership of the property involved to the vendor or adjusts the sale price does not alter the fact that the vendor was at a particular time entitled to the sale price and therefore disposed of the property for tax purposes at that time. Similarly, the fact that a contract of sale is subject to ratification is of no consequence in determining a date of disposition unless it is made a condition precedent of the agreement.

6. A "condition precedent" is an event (beyond the direct control of the vendor) that suspends completion of the contract until the condition is met or waived and that

could cancel the contract *ab initio* if it is not met or waived. Two examples of conditions precedent are

(a) a condition in a contract for the sale of a hotel business that provides that the transfer of ownership is not to take place until the purchaser obtains a liquor licence, and

(b) a condition in a contract for the sale of land that suspends completion until the purchaser's solicitor has approved the vendor's title to the property.

7. Formal agreements of purchase and sale are frequently explicit as to the date of exchange and, unless circumstances indicate that a specified date was changed or was not the true intent of both parties, the date so specified is presumed to be the date of entitlement. Where the date of exchange is not expressly agreed between the parties, the time that the attributes of ownership pass from the vendor to the purchaser is presumed to be the date of entitlement. Since this test is the same test that is applied to determine the date of acquisition of depreciable property by a purchaser, the comments contained in IT-50R are equally valid in determining a vendor's date of disposition in these cases.

8. Since possession, use and risk are the primary attributes of beneficial ownership, registration of legal title alone is of little significance in determining the date of disposition. Factors that are strong indicators of the passing of ownership include:

(a) physical or constructive possession (refer to IT-50R),

(b) entitlement to income from the property,

(c) assumption of responsibility for insurance coverage, and

(d) commencement of liability for interest on purchaser's debt that forms a part of the sale price.

Real Property Sales

9. In the case of sales of real property (as well as sales of other property where the contract could be specifically enforced by the courts), a purchaser acquires an equitable interest in the property upon execution of a binding agreement for sale or an accepted offer to purchase. Although it may

¶3130

be correct to say that the property has been "sold" at that time, there is not necessarily a disposition at that time for the purposes of paragraphs $13(21)(c)$ and $54(c)$ because of the restricted meaning given in respect of a disposition that involves a sale (see 2 above). It is equally clear that a vendor will not necessarily have an "amount receivable" under paragraph $12(1)(b)$ at that time. There will be no effect for income tax purposes unless and until the vendor becomes entitled to the sale price.

10. Many agreements involving the sale of real property propose a "closing date" for the completion of the sale. This is normally the date that beneficial ownership is intended to pass from the vendor to the purchaser and the time that the vendor is entitled to the sale price but the facts of a particular situation must support that the expressed intent was in fact carried out. In cases where the "closing date" is to occur "on or before" a specified date, the actual date of closing must be determined by the particular facts such as

(a) the date funds required to be paid on closing were actually paid,

(b) the date that the title was conveyed,

(c) the date of adjustments of insurance premiums, rentals, mortgage interest, realty taxes etc., and

(d) the date of possession by the purchaser.

Sale of Shares

11. The date of disposition of shares sold in stock exchange transactions is discussed in IT-133.

12. A shareholder who deposits a share with a depository pursuant to a "take-over bid" (as defined and regulated by provincial or federal statutes) is entitled to the sale price on the earlier of

(a) the date that the offerer takes up the share, and

(b) the date upon which all conditions of the offer have been satisfied or waived.

13. Shares are considered to be "taken up" at the time of payment if this occurs before the period of acceptance expires and there is no indication that the offeror acquired the usual ownership rights before that time. Although an offeror usually

reserves a short period of time after the expiry date of the offer to effect payment for shares taken up, a shareholder is nevertheless entitled to payment at the time that the offeror's obligation to pay is unconditional.

14. Most take-over bids provide the offeror with the right to withdraw his offer at any time up to a specified date following the period of acceptance if the directors of the corporation (the subject of the take-over bid) take any action that materially changes the undertaking, assets or capital of the corporation. As long as such a right remains in effect and is not waived, a shareholder is not entitled to the sale price. Another condition frequently found in takeover bids is the right of the offeror to withdraw the offer if less than a specified percentage of the outstanding shares is on deposit at the end of the period of acceptance. Although it may be argued that (in the absence of other unsatisfied conditions) a shareholder is entitled to the sale price when the specified percentage of shares has been achieved, it is the Department's view that entitlement normally occurs only after the expiry of the period of acceptance (unless payment is made before that time).

15. A trustee or escrow agent is frequently appointed to retain physical possession of shares for the period of time during which their selling price is not fully paid. An agreement setting out the duties of such a trustee or agent usually contains provisions that effectively modify the ownership rights of the vendor and purchaser during the transitional period. In such cases, the time that beneficial ownership passes from the vendor to the purchaser can be difficult to ascertain. Although each case can only be judged in the light of all of the relevant facts and circumstances, the Department's views on the significance of modifications to some of the usual attributes of share ownership are outlined in 16 to 18 below.

16. Suspension of a purchaser's right to transfer shares to a third party before the vendor has been fully paid is not regarded as a significant factor in determining beneficial ownership.

17. A purchaser's right to dividends, voting rights and right to a return of capital in the event of the corporation's dissolution are considered to be important factors in determining beneficial ownership. The potential reversion of these rights to a

vendor in the event of a specified default situation is not regarded as an indication that beneficial ownership has not passed. Registration on the records of the corporation is of no significance where the agreement between the vendor, purchaser and trustee or agent validly assigns a particular right to a person who is not the registered owner. For example, a vendor may actually receive a dividend because he is the registered shareholder of shares sold which have been endorsed in blank and deposited with a trustee under an agreement that compels him to remit the dividend to the purchaser.

18. Where a sale of shares involves a change in effective control of the subject corporation, restrictions on dividends and voting rights are frequently imposed upon the purchaser while any portion of the sale price remains unpaid. As long as such restrictions can reasonably be regarded as being for the protection of the vendor's right to collect the sale price, they are not consid-

ered significant in determining beneficial ownership.

Reacquisition of Property Sold

19. Many agreements contemplate the reacquisition by the vendor of property that has been sold upon the happening of a specified event, the failure of a specified event to occur or a specified default of the purchaser. Where a reacquisition of beneficial ownership occurs by reason of the purchaser's failure to pay all or any part of an amount owing, section 79 provides rules to determine the tax consequences for both vendor and purchaser. Although the Act provides no specific rules where reacquisition occurs in situations to which section 79 does not apply, it is clear that such an occurrence does not retroactively nullify the effects of the original disposition for income tax purposes even if the agreement restores the vendor and purchaser to their relative positions before the sale took place.

[3145]   Interpretation Bulletin IT-190R2:   Capital Cost Allowance — Transferred and Misclassified Property

[Interpretation Bulletin IT-190R2 is dated December 29, 1989.]

Reference: Subsections 13(5) and 13(6) (also section 1103 of the Income Tax Regulations)

Application

This bulletin cancels and replaces Interpretation Bulletin IT-190R dated February 20, 1980. The comments herein on subsection 13(5) apply to taxation years and fiscal periods commencing after June 17, 1987 that end after 1987. Where it is necessary to apply subsection 13(5) for a prior year or period, please refer to the law itself.

Summary

This bulletin deals with the rules for computing the undepreciated capital cost of property of a prescribed class that has been transferred from one class to another class. It also deals with the direction the Minister may make where property has not been properly classified by a taxpayer.

Discussion and Interpretation

1. Subsection 13(5) contains the rules for computing the undepreciated capital cost of property of a prescribed class that has been transferred from one class to another. Generally, the rules in 13(5) apply where:

(a) a transfer between two classes is necessary because of an amendment to the Act or Regulations,

(b) misclassified property is transferred to its proper class pursuant to subsection 13(6) (see 6 to 8 below),

(c) a taxpayer makes an election under section 1103 of the Regulations to include all depreciable property in a particular class or to transfer certain depreciable property between classes, or

(d) property that has been properly included in a class is subsequently transferred to another class because of a change of its use in the income earning process.

See the current version of IT-464 for a discussion on subsection 13(5.1) where a taxpayer, who has a leasehold interest in a property, acquires ownership of that property.

2. Paragraph 13(5)(a) deems the transferred property to be depreciable property of

¶3145

the class to which the property is transferred (hereinafter referred to as the "other class") and not depreciable property of the class in which the transferred property formerly was included (hereinafter referred to as the "former class"). This provides for the transfer of the capital cost of the property to the other class.

3. Under paragraph 13(5)(b) an amount is determined that is then excluded in computing the total depreciation allowed to a taxpayer for property of the former class and is included in computing the total depreciation allowed to the taxpayer for property of the other class. The amount calculated is usually the total of all capital cost allowance claimed by the taxpayer on the transferred property before the year of transfer (see 4 below). However, in order to prevent a recapture from occurring in the former class, where the excess of the original capital cost of the transferred property over the undepreciated capital cost of the former class immediately before the transfer is greater than the amount calculated in the previous sentence, then this excess is used instead.

4. In the calculation of the depreciation previously claimed on the transferred property, the rate to be used, pursuant to 13(5)(b)(ii), is the effective rate deducted in respect of the former class in a particular year. Where, for example, in one taxation year a taxpayer claimed and was allowed, on a class having a 20 per cent maximum rate, only $125 on an undepreciated capital cost of $1,000, the effective rate deducted was 12.5 per cent. It is this rate of 12.5 per cent that is used in determining the amount of depreciation allowed in that year on property later transferred to another class.

5. The rules in subsection 13(5) concerning transfers of property apply only to the property that is in the taxpayer's possession on the date as of which the transfer is to be made. For example, subsection 13(5) would not apply to a property in Class 8 disposed of in a taxation year prior to the

taxation year in respect of which the Minister has made a direction under subsection 13(6) (see 6 below) concerning the property. Accordingly, proceeds from disposition of property that was in an incorrect class at the time it was disposed of, remain as a credit to that class.

6. Where a taxpayer has misclassified depreciable property or should have reclassified it pursuant to a change in the Act or the Regulations or because of a change in its use in the income earning process, and has claimed and been allowed capital cost allowance in the incorrect class, the Department may reassess the years involved to correct the misclassification and the capital cost allowance in the incorrect class. However, if such a correction has not been made, the Minister may make a direction in respect of a taxation year under subsection 13(6) to deem the property to be of the incorrect class for the years prior to the year for which direction is made and to be transferred to the correct class beginning in the year for which the direction is made. Only property that was still on hand at the beginning of the year in respect of which a direction is made is transferred.

7. If a taxpayer requests that a correction be made beginning with the first year in which the misclassified property was acquired or became misclassified and subsection 152(4) does not prevent reassessment of any years involved, reassessments will ordinarily be made to correct the capital cost allowances claimed in those years and no direction will be required under subsection 13(6). Also, see the current version of Information Circular 84-1 where a taxpayer acquired a property of one class which after "certification" qualifies for inclusion in another class.

8. The Director-Taxation in a District Taxation Office may exercise the power of the Minister under subsection 13(6) pursuant to subsection 900(2) of the Income Tax Regulations.

[3147] Interpretation Bulletin IT-195R4: Rental Property — Capital Cost Allowance Restrictions

[*Interpretation Bulletin IT-195R4 is dated September 6, 1991.*]

Reference: Subsections 1100(11) through 1100(14.2) of the Income Tax Regulations (also subsections 1100(15), 1100(17), 1101(1ae) and 1102(5) of the Regulations, Classes 1,

3, 6, 13, 31 and 32 of Schedule II of the Regulations and subsection 20(16) and paragraph $20(1)(a)$ of the Act)

Application

This bulletin cancels and replaces IT-195R3 dated April 27, 1981. Note that CCA claims in respect of rental or leasing property may also be restricted by the proposed "available for use" and "specified leasing property" rules. Other bulletins will discuss the latter rules in more detail.

Summary

This bulletin discusses the restriction on claims for capital cost allowance (CCA) that would otherwise be deductible in respect of rental properties. With certain exceptions, this restriction prevents a taxpayer or partnership from creating or increasing the amount of a loss for income tax purposes by claiming CCA on rental properties. It thereby prevents the taxpayer from using such losses to shelter or reduce other income subject to tax. In this bulletin, references to subsections and paragraphs are to subsections and paragraphs of the Regulations, except where indicated.

Discussion and Interpretation

General — Operation of the CCA Restriction

1. Subsection 1100(11) restricts the amount of CCA that may be claimed on rental properties of a taxpayer, or of a partnership of which the taxpayer is a member. This restriction is referred to in this bulletin as the "CCA restriction". Subsection 1100(11) applies where a taxpayer owns property of a class prescribed for CCA purposes and that class includes rental property owned by the taxpayer. With respect to all such classes of properties owned by the taxpayer, the taxpayer's total claim for CCA that would otherwise be allowed in computing income for a taxation year may not exceed the amount, if any, by which

(a) the taxpayer's income for the year from renting or leasing rental property which the taxpayer owns (computed before any claims for CCA that would otherwise be deductible under paragraph $20(1)(a)$ of the Act)

and

(b) the income of a partnership for the year from renting or leasing rental

property of the partnership, to the extent of the taxpayer's share of such income

exceeds

(c) the taxpayer's loss for the year from renting or leasing rental property owned by the taxpayer (computed before any claims for CCA that would otherwise be deductible under paragraph $20(1)(a)$ of the Act)

and

(d) the loss of a partnership for the year from renting or leasing rental property of the partnership, to the extent of the taxpayer's share of such loss.

2. Accordingly, if a taxpayer has more than one class of rental properties, the CCA restriction is not applied to the individual classes of rental properties but rather to the total CCA that may be claimed against all the taxpayer's rental properties. The entire CCA claim for all the properties must not exceed the total of the rental income from all properties less the total of the rental losses from the properties. Any recapture of CCA is included in computing these totals. In computing the amount of CCA allowable where a terminal loss has occurred, it will be necessary to deduct the terminal loss first and then to claim ordinary CCA to the extent, if any, of the remaining net rental income from all properties.

Definition of Rental Property

3. For the purposes of the CCA restriction, a "rental property" of a taxpayer or partnership is defined in subsection 1100(14) to mean

(a) a building (other than a MURB as noted in 14 below) owned by the taxpayer or partnership, whether jointly with another person or otherwise, or

(b) a leasehold interest in real property if the leasehold interest is property of Class 1, 3, 6 or 13 (or, for taxation years before 1988, Class 3, 6 or 13) and is owned by the taxpayer or partnership.

To be a rental property, the property must be used in the year by the taxpayer or partnership principally for the purposes of

¶3147

gaining or producing gross revenue that is rent. Rental property does not include a property leased by a taxpayer or partnership (the lessor) in the ordinary course of the lessor's business of selling goods or rendering services, where this is done under an agreement by which the lessee undertakes to use the property to carry on the sale or promotion of the sale of the lessor's goods or services. For example, a building leased by an oil company to a dealer for the operation of a service station in order to display and sell the oil company's goods is not a rental property of the oil company.

Meaning of "Principally"

4. As used in the definition of rental property in subsection 1100(14), the word "principally" means "primarily" or "chiefly". In establishing whether a property is used principally for a given purpose, one of the main factors to be considered is the proportion of time that the property is used for that purpose. If the property is used more than 50 percent of the time for the purposes of gaining or producing gross revenue that is rent, that pattern of use is a good indication that the property is used principally for that purpose. Another important factor to be considered is the proportion of the amount of space rented in relation to the total area of the building. Again, if more than 50 percent of the total area is rented, that is an indication that the property is being used principally for producing rental revenue. See the current version of IT-331, *Investment Tax Credit*, for additional comments on the meaning of the word "principally".

Taxpayers Not Subject to the CCA Restriction

5. Subsection 1100(12) provides that the CCA restriction does not apply to a taxpayer if that taxpayer was throughout the year

(a) a life insurance corporation,

(b) a corporation whose principal business was the leasing, rental, development or sale (or any combination thereof) of real property owned by it, or

(c) a partnership each member of which was a corporation described in (a) or (b) above.

However, subsection 1100(13) limits the application of subsection 1100(12). As a result, the CCA restriction will remain applicable to most situations (specifically, those described in subsection 1102(5)) in which any of the entities in (a) to (c) above has a leasehold interest in a building on leased land and the building is leased back to the owner of the land, or to a person who owns an interest in or option on the land. See the current version of IT-371, *Rental Property — Meaning of Principal Business*, for comments concerning subsection 1100(12).

Meaning of "Rent"

6. For the purposes of the definition of rental property in subsection 1100(14), (see 3 above), in determining whether a property was used principally for gaining or producing gross revenue that is rent, subsection 1100(14.1) is applicable. The latter subsection provides that for 1986 and subsequent years, gross revenue derived in a taxation year from

(a) the right of a person or partnership, other than the owner of a property, to use or occupy the property or a part thereof, and

(b) services offered to a person or partnership that are ancillary to (i.e. subordinate to or dependant upon) the use or occupation by the person or partnership of the property or the part thereof,

shall be considered to be rent derived in that year from the property. The coming-into-force provisions with respect to subsection 1100(14.1) are very extensive, with variations that depend upon the nature of the property acquired and the timing of the acquisition. Reference should be made to these provisions for more precise details. Thus, unless one of the exceptions set out in the coming-into-force provisions or 7 below applies, gross revenue that is rent will include revenue derived from a property such as a hotel, motel or nursing home operation, where it is established that such revenue is ancillary to the use or occupation of the property. On the other hand, if the services offered (for example, medical care in a nursing home) are such that they go beyond being merely ancillary to the use and occupation of the property, gross revenue derived from such services is not considered to be rent derived from the property.

Exceptions

7. Subsection 1100(14.2) sets out certain exceptions to the application of subsection

¶3147

1100(14.1). As a result, the comments in 6 above do not apply in any particular taxation year to a property owned by

(a) a corporation, where the property is used in a business carried on in the year by the corporation,

(b) an individual, where the property is used in a business carried on in the year by the individual and the individual is personally active in that business on a continuous basis throughout that portion of the year during which the business is ordinarily carried on, or

(c) a partnership, where the property is used in a business carried on in the year by the partnership if at least $\frac{2}{3}$ of the income or loss, as the case may be, of the partnership for the year is included in the determination of the income of

(i) members of the partnership who are individuals that are personally active in the business of the partnership on a continuous basis throughout that portion of the year during which the business is ordinarily carried on, and

(ii) members of the partnership that are corporations.

Whether or not an individual is "personally active on a continuous basis throughout that portion of the year during which the business is ordinarily carried on" is a question of fact. In making such a determination, consideration will be given to the nature of the business and the individual's involvement in the day-to-day operation of that business. For example, if the business consists of operating a nursing home, the simple periodic review of operating results or the occasional recommendation of the home to potential clientele by the individual will not be sufficient to establish that the individual is "personally active on a continuous basis". On the other hand, the CCA restriction will not normally apply if the individual participates on a full-time basis in management decisions, occupant services, staffing and locating clientele.

Separate Classes for Rental and Non-Rental Properties

8. Subsection 1101(1ae) provides that rental properties of a taxpayer which would otherwise be placed in the same class as other non-rental properties of the taxpayer

are required to be placed in a separate class. However, this requirement does not apply to a rental property of a taxpayer exempted under subsection 1100(12) from the CCA restriction (see 5 above). Where the conditions of subsection 1100(12) are met throughout one year but not throughout another year, it will be necessary to transfer the rental property into or out of the separate class prescribed by subsection 1101(1ae).

Property Converted from Business to Rental Use During the Year

9. CCA may be restricted in the following circumstances:

(a) a taxpayer or partnership ceases to carry on business activities part way through the taxation year,

(b) at that time, the taxpayer or partnership commences to use depreciable property that is a building or leasehold interest described in 3(a) or (b) above to generate gross revenue that is rent or leasing revenue, and

(c) this property is used principally for rental purposes as determined in 4 above.

The CCA claim for a taxation year with respect to such properties which then qualify as rental property is restricted to the net rental or leasing income generated for that year from the property after its conversion from business use.

Rental Property of Members of Partnerships

10. A partnership that is subject to the CCA restriction calculates the amount of CCA it can claim and allocates the resulting net rental income or loss among the members of the partnership. Where such a member also holds rental property as a proprietor, the comments in 1 and 2 above will apply in a similar manner to the member's own rental properties. The share of partnership rental income or loss allocated to the member will be combined with the total rental income or loss after expenses, but before CCA, from the member's own rental properties. CCA may be claimed on the member's rental properties (subject to prescribed rates) only to the extent of that combined rental income, if any.

¶3147

Furniture, Fixtures and Appliances

11. Furniture, fixtures and appliances acquired for a rental building represent "leasing properties" as defined in subsection 1100(17). The CCA on such assets is restricted under subsection 1100(15) in a manner that generally parallels the rules for rental real estate previously discussed. Where a landlord charges a flat rental fee for an apartment inclusive of furniture, fixtures and appliances, the guidelines outlined in the current version of IT-443, *Leasing Property — Capital Cost Allowance Restrictions*, should be referred to in order to determine if an allocation of income between the rental and leasing properties is necessary.

Allocation of Income and Expenses Between Leasing and Rental Properties

12. Where an allocation of income between leasing and rental properties is necessary (see 11 above), the CCA is treated separately for each type of property and cannot be aggregated and claimed against total rental income. Also, for the purposes of subsections 1100(11) and (15), rental fees and expenses must be apportioned on a reasonable basis between the rental and leasing properties.

13. Where an allocation of income between rental and leasing properties is not necessary, the restrictions in 12 above do not apply. However, the total CCA claimed in respect of both properties cannot exceed the combined income from both properties.

Multiple-Unit Residential Buildings

14. As it applies to taxation years before 1994, paragraph 1100(14)(a) provides that multiple-unit residential buildings (MURBs) which qualify as property of Class 31 or 32

are excluded from the definition of rental property. This exclusion will cease for the 1994 and subsequent taxation years. Likewise, paragraph 1100(17)(b) provides that for taxation years prior to 1994 only, such MURBs and the furniture, fixtures or equipment located within and ancillary thereto are excluded from the definition of leasing property. Where parking, recreation, service and storage facilities are not located within the qualified MURB, an allocation of revenue and deductions to rental as opposed to leasing activities will be necessary only if such facilities are used in a rental operation separate and unrelated to the rental of the units contained in the MURB.

15. Notwithstanding the comments in 14 above, if a MURB is acquired after June 17, 1987 it will be considered a rental property and will be subject to the CCA restriction. However, should such a MURB be acquired pursuant to

(a) an obligation in writing entered into by the taxpayer before June 18, 1987, or

(b) the terms of a prospectus, preliminary prospectus, registration statement, offering memorandum or notice required to be filed with a public authority in Canada and filed before June 18, 1987 with such public authority,

it will not be considered a rental property and will not be subject to the CCA restriction.

For additional comments on MURBs which qualify as property of Class 31 or 32, see the current version of IT-367, *Capital Cost Allowance — Multiple-Unit Residential Buildings*.

[3155] Interpretation Bulletin IT-220R2: Capital Cost Allowance — Proceeds of Disposition of Depreciable Property

[*Interpretation Bulletin IT-220R2 is dated May 25, 1990.*]

Reference: Subsection 13(21) and 13(21.1) (also section 68, subsections 20(4), 39(1), 50(1) and 248(1) definition of "cost amount" and paragraphs 12(1)(i), 40(1)(b) and 54(c) and 54(h) of the Act, paragraph 1102(1)(c) of the Income Tax Regulations and paragraph 20(1)(a) of the *Income Tax Application Rules, 1971* (ITAR))

Application

This bulletin cancels and replaces Interpretation Bulletin IT-220R dated Sep-

tember 8, 1980 and the Special Release thereto dated June 5, 1984.

¶3155

Summary

This bulletin discusses the tax implications inherent in the disposition of depreciable property from the perspective of both the recapture of capital cost allowance and capital gains. The results of a disposition for proceeds in excess of the capital cost of a depreciable property are explained, as is the meaning of the terms "disposition of property" and "proceeds of disposition of property" and the effect thereon of various related deeming provisions of the Act. Also explained are the results that occur when a related debt becomes bad, the application of section 68 when a sale involves depreciable properties of two different classes or depreciable properties and something else with the total consideration expressed in one lump sum, and the deeming provisions of subsection 13(21.1) where a building is disposed of at a loss.

Discussion and Interpretation

1. A disposition of depreciable property made after December 31, 1971 is subject to the provisions of the Act dealing with capital gains and losses. Where any depreciable property is disposed of for proceeds in excess of the capital cost to the taxpayer, that disposition may give rise to a capital gain as determined by paragraph $39(1)(a)$ subject to the special transitional rules provided by section 20 of the ITAR. However, any loss on the disposition of depreciable property is specifically excluded from a taxpayer's capital loss by paragraph $39(1)(b)$ and as a result no deduction is permitted for such losses.

2. The terms "disposition of property" and "proceeds of disposition of property" are defined by subsection 13(21) for purposes of sections 13 and 20 and the regulations made under paragraph $20(1)(a)$ applicable to provisions dealing with depreciable property, and by section 54 for the purpose of subdivision c of Division B of Part I of the Act applicable to the disposition of capital property (including depreciable property). In both cases, a disposition includes any transaction or event entitling a taxpayer to proceeds of disposition of property. These provisions, which are not all-inclusive, do not exclude the possibility that there may be other circumstances in which a disposition takes place, nor do they exclude the possibility that there may be other forms of pro-

ceeds of disposition. In certain circumstances, the disposition or the proceeds of disposition of depreciable property may be determined by special provisions in the Act. The Appendix lists some of these provisions and the interpretation bulletins issued at this date that provide details of their application.

Bad Debts

*3. Subsection 20(4) may apply where a taxpayer has disposed of depreciable property (other than a timber resource property or a passenger vehicle that cost more than $20,000 or such other prescribed amount) and the proceeds of disposition have, according to section 13, been credited to the relevant class. In the event that part or all of those proceeds is established by the taxpayer to have become a bad debt in the year, subsection 20(4) provides for a deduction in computing income for the year. In such cases, the taxpayer may deduct the lesser of

(a) the amount of the bad debt owing to the taxpayer, and

(b) the amount, if any, by which the taxpayer's capital cost of the property exceeds any amounts actually realized by the taxpayer on account of the proceeds of disposition.

In addition, the bad debt itself is deemed by subsection 50(1) to have been disposed of at the end of the year and to have been reacquired immediately thereafter at a cost of nil. To the extent that the loss from the deemed disposition of the bad debt, calculated in accordance with the provisions of paragraph $40(1)(b)$, has not been deducted under subsection 20(4), that loss may constitute a capital loss. Where the debt arose from a non-arm's length disposition, see the current version of IT-159, *Capital Debts Established to be Bad Debts.* The provisions of subsection 20(4) apply only where an amount is uncollectible, not where it is merely a doubtful account. Where there is a later recovery of part or all of the bad debt for the former proceeds of disposition of the depreciable property, paragraph $12(1)(i)$ includes the amount so recovered in the taxpayer's income to the extent that this amount has been deducted under subsection 20(4) in computing the taxpayer's income for a preceding taxation year. Furthermore, the amount recovered constitutes

---

* As amended by Special Release, February 11, 1994.

¶3155

a gain on a disposition of property having a nil cost base and, to the extent that the amount is not required to be included in income by paragraph $12(1)(i)$, it is a capital gain subject to the provisions of the Act dealing with such gains.

Combined Consideration

4. The provisions of section 68, as it affects depreciable property, can apply to consideration for,

(a) both depreciable and non-depreciable property,

(b) depreciable properties included in two or more prescribed classes, or

(c) depreciable property and something other than property, such as services.

This section commonly applies where the whole consideration is set forth in an agreement as a lump sum, or where part of the consideration is allocated in a lump sum to cover two or more things (property or services).

5. Even where a value is specified in an agreement for each class or kind of property or service and the total consideration for the whole sale is reasonable, a re-allocation of the consideration between the various kinds or classes of property or services, may, nevertheless, be made by the Department if some or all of the values specified are considered unreasonable. Where, however, the parties to the agreement are dealing at arm's length, the agreement is *prima facie* evidence of the reasonableness of the allocation specified therein. A taxpayer's allocation is further supported where there is evidence of hard bargaining between the parties involved in arriving at that allocation. However, see 9 to 16 below for comments on the application of subsection 13(21.1).

6. The prime requirements for a determination under section 68 are, therefore, that it

(a) be reasonable in relation to the relative positions of the two parties to the transaction,

(b) be based on the facts of the particular case, and

(c) have regard to the fair market value of the properties or services involved.

7. In making a determination under section 68, the matter is to be considered from the viewpoint of both the vendor and the purchaser. For example, where land and a building are sold for a lump sum, the fact that the purchaser demolished the building shortly after the sale is taken into account. However, the demolition alone is not regarded as conclusive evidence that the sale price was solely in consideration of land. Where this situation exists and the total sale price is not in excess of the fair market value of comparable land, it may be reasonable to conclude that the sale was essentially one of land and that the price was in consideration only of land, even though the building was still usable and may have had some value to the vendor. Where such a demolition took place and the total selling price exceeded the fair market value of comparable land because the purchaser had a special reason for wanting that particular property, it may be reasonable to conclude that the vendor received for the building an amount equal to the excess over the fair market value of the land alone, and that the purchaser is deemed to have paid that amount for the building. If in these circumstances the purchaser demolished the building without using it for the purpose of gaining or producing income, it is not depreciable property in the purchaser's hands by reason of paragraph $1102(1)(c)$ of the Regulations and the purchaser is not entitled to capital cost allowance nor a terminal loss in respect of it. In these latter circumstances, the demolition of the building is considered a disposition and may result in a capital loss in the purchaser's hands. See also the comments in the current version of IT-128.

8. Where the buildings are not demolished shortly after the purchase, again the facts of each case will determine whether any part of the price was in respect of those buildings and whether the property was depreciable property. In this connection, the Department will consider various factors including

(a) length of time prior to demolition and whether the building was income producing,

(b) repairs and maintenance to the buildings,

(c) amount of income earned,

¶3155

(d) renewal of leases, if any, and the length of the renewal, and

(e) costs of breaking leases, if any.

Deemed Proceeds of Disposition of a Building

*9. When a building is sold for proceeds that are less than its proportionate share of the undepreciated capital cost of its class, subsection 13(21.1) provides special rules to allocate proceeds of disposition between land and buildings, to restrict the potential terminal loss and possibly recapture capital cost allowances previously taken. Where the proceeds from the building (including proceeds determined by the application of section 68) are less than the lesser of the "cost amount" (see 11 below) and the capital cost to the taxpayer of the building immediately before its disposition, the rules in paragraph 13(21.1)(a) or (b) apply. However, these rules do not apply where the land on which the building is situated has always been owned by a person dealing at arm's length with the owner of the building.

10. The special rule under paragraph 13(21.1)(a) applies where both the disposition of the building and the land subjacent to, or immediately contiguous to and necessary for the use of the building (the "related land"), takes place in the same taxation year, although not necessarily simultaneously. Where the related land is disposed of by a person not dealing at arm's length with the building owner, this rule applies when the disposition occurs within a period coinciding with the duration of the building owner's taxation year that encompasses the time of disposition of the building. Under this rule, combined proceeds are compulsorily allocated between land and building, primarily to ensure that no loss will be claimed in respect of the disposition of the building unless it is determined that no gain is reported on the land component.

*11. In applying this rule, it is first necessary to calculate the cost amount of both the land and the building. Cost amount is defined in subsection 248(1). In the case of land, the cost amount is its adjusted cost base. In the case of a building, the cost amount is the building's proportionate share of the undepreciated capital cost of the class that the capital cost of the building is of the capital cost of all property of that class that

had not been previously disposed of. In calculating this proportionate amount, certain limitations on capital cost in subsection 13(7), which normally apply in determining the capital cost of a building, do not apply and the capital cost of a building will reflect its acquisition (or partial acquisition) at fair market value. (Normally, paragraphs 13(7)(b), (d) and (e) provide that the capital cost can be limited to an amount that is less than fair market value in cases where a non-income producing depreciable property begins to be used for producing income, where the income producing use of a depreciable property increases and where there is a non-arm's length acquisition of a depreciable property.)

12. The proceeds of disposition of the related land are then deemed to be the amount by which the combined proceeds of disposition of the land and building exceed the deemed proceeds of disposition of the building (as computed in 13 or 14 below). The cost to the purchaser of the land is determined without reference to subsection 13(21.1).

13. With respect to dispositions before May 10, 1985 (including a disposition at any time made pursuant to the terms of an agreement in writing entered into before that date), the proceeds of disposition of the building, calculated immediately prior to the disposition, are deemed to be the lesser of

(a) the combined proceeds of land and building as otherwise determined, reduced by the lesser of

(i) the cost amount of the land to the vendor, and

(ii) the fair market value of the land, and

(b) the greater of

(i) the fair market value of the building, and

(ii) the cost amount of the building.

14. With respect to dispositions occurring at a particular time after May 9, 1985 the proceeds of disposition of the building are deemed to be the lesser of

(a) the amount, if any, by which

(i) the aggregate of

---

* As amended by Special Release, February 11, 1994.

¶3155

(A) the fair market value of the building at the particular time, and

(B) the fair market value of the land immediately before its disposition

exceeds

(ii) the lesser of

(A) the fair market value of the land immediately before its disposition, and

(B) the cost amount otherwise determined less capital gains arising upon dispositions of the land within the three preceding years between the taxpayer and non-arm's length parties, and

(b) the greater of

(i) the fair market value of the building at the particular time, and

(ii) the lesser of

(A) the cost amount of the building, and

(B) the capital cost to the taxpayer of the building immediately before its disposition.

15. Where the land area disposed of exceeds that necessary for the use of the building, paragraph $13(21.1)(a)$ is considered to apply only in respect of the portion that is necessary for the use of the building.

In such cases, a reasonable allocation of the total proceeds and the total cost for tax purposes of the land between the necessary and the superfluous portions of the land is required for the calculations described above.

16. Where the related land is not disposed of in the same taxation year as the building but was owned at any time before the disposition of the building by the taxpayer or by a person with whom the taxpayer was not dealing at arm's length, paragraph $13(21.1)(b)$ provides a second rule. In this case, where the taxpayer is an individual, the deemed proceeds of disposition of the building for purposes of determining the remaining undepreciated capital cost of the class (or the terminal loss if the building is the last property in the class) are the proceeds otherwise determined plus one-quarter (one-half for fiscal periods ending before 1988 and one-third for fiscal periods ending in 1988 and 1989) of the excess of the cost amount (see 11 above) of the building (or its fair market value, if that is greater) over the proceeds otherwise determined. Where the taxpayer is a corporation, the coming-into-force provisions of 1988, c. 55, s. 6(19) for subparagraph $13(21.1)(b)(ii)$ should be referred to in order to determine the deemed proceeds of disposition of the building for the purposes of the second rule mentioned above. The proceeds of disposition of the land are not reduced under this rule.

APPENDIX

Reference to the Income Tax Act	Description	Interpretation Bulletin
$3(b)$	Capital Gains and Losses on Disposition of Business Property by an Individual	IT-134
$13(21)(c)$	Compensation for Loss of Business Income or of Property Used in a Business.	IT-182
$13(21)(c)$	Disposition — Absence of Consideration	IT-460
$13(21)(f)$	Conversion of Property from or to Inventory	IT-102
$13(21)(f)$	Conversion of Property, Other than Real Property, from or to Inventory	IT-102
$20(1)(a)$	Capital Cost Allowance — Date of Acquisition of Depreciable Property.	IT-50
$20(1)(a)$	Capital Cost Allowance — Depreciable Property . .	IT-128
$20(1)(a)$	Capital Cost Allowance — Taxation Year of Individuals	IT-172
$20(5)$	Sale of Mortgage Included in Proceeds of Disposition of Depreciable Property.	IT-323
42	Dispositions of Capital Property Subject to Warranty, Covenant, etc.	IT-330

¶3155

Reference to the Income Tax Act	Description	Interpretation Bulletin
43	Part Dispositions	IT-264
43	Capital Cost Allowance — Partial Dispositions of Property	IT-418
44	Exchanges of Property	IT-259
45	Principal Residence	IT-120
50(1)	Capital Debts Established to be Bad Debts	IT-159
54(*h*)	Expropriations — Time and Proceeds of Disposition	IT-271
70	*Inter Vivos* Transfer of Farm Property to Child	IT-268
70	Intergenerational Transfers of Farm Property on Death	IT-349
70	Buy-Sell Agreements	IT-140
74.1(1)	Interspousal Transfers and Loans of Property Made after May 22, 1985	IT-511
74.1(2)	Transfers and Loans of Property Made after May 22, 1985 to a Related Minor	IT-510
79	Mortgage Foreclosures and Conditional Sales Repossessions	IT-505
85	Transfer of Property to a Corporation under Subsection 85(1)	IT-291
125(1)	The Small Business Deduction — Income from an Active Business, a Specified Investment Business and a Personal Services Business	IT-73
ITAR 20(1)	Capital Property Owned on December 31, 1971 — Depreciable Property	IT-217

[3158]   Interpretation Bulletin IT-259R4:   Exchange of Property

[Interpretation Bulletin IT-259R4 is dated September 23, 2003.]

Reference: Section 44, subsections 13(4), 13(4.1), 14(6) and 14(7) (also sections 70 and 128.1, paragraphs 87(2)(*l*.3), 88(1)(*a*) and 96(1)(*a*) and subparagraph 40(1)(*a*)(iii) and the definition of "proceeds of disposition" in section 54 and subsection 13(21))

At the Canada Customs and Revenue Agency (CCRA), we issue income tax interpretation bulletins (ITs) in order to provide technical interpretations and positions regarding certain provisions contained in income tax law. Due to their technical nature, ITs are used primarily by our staff, tax specialists, and other individuals who have an interest in tax matters. For those readers who prefer a less technical explanation of the law, we offer other publications, such as tax guides and pamphlets.

While the comments in a particular paragraph in an IT may relate to provisions of the law in force at the time they were made, such comments are not a substitute for the law. The reader should, therefore, consider such comments in light of the relevant provisions of the law in force for the particular taxation year being considered, taking into

account the effect of any relevant amendments to those provisions or relevant court decisions occurring after the date on which the comments were made.

Subject to the above, an interpretation or position contained in an IT generally applies as of the date on which it was published, unless otherwise specified. If there is a subsequent change in that interpretation or position and the change is beneficial to taxpayers, it is usually effective for future assessments and reassessments. If, on the other hand, the change is not favourable to taxpayers, it will normally be effective for the current and subsequent taxation years or for transactions entered into after the date on which the change is published.

Most of our publications are available on our Web site at: **www.ccra.gc.ca**

¶3158

If you have any comments regarding matters discussed in an IT, please send them to:

Manager, Technical Publications and Projects Section
Income Tax Rulings Directorate
Policy and Legislation Branch
Canada Customs and Revenue Agency
Ottawa ON K1A 0L5
or by email at the following address:
bulletins@ccra.gc.ca

Contents

	Paragraphs
Application	
Summary	
Discussion and Interpretation	
General	1-6
Election to Use Subsections 44(1), 13(4) and 14(6)	7-8
Replacement Property — General	9-14
Replace the Former Property	15
Same or a Similar Use	16-17
Same or a Similar Business . . .	18-21
Amalgamations and Wind-Ups	22
Partnerships	23
Non-Residents and Deceased Taxpayers	24-25
Adjustment Resulting from the Replacement of the Former Property — Examples	26-29
Explanation of Changes	

Application

This bulletin cancels and replaces Interpretation Bulletin IT-259R3, dated August 4, 1998. The effective date of a particular legislative provision discussed in the bulletin may be indicated in the *Explanation of Changes* section (or, in some cases, in the *Discussion and Interpretation* section) of the bulletin. However, where the bulletin is silent with respect to the effective date of a particular provision, such date can be obtained from the legislation itself. Unless otherwise stated, all statutory references throughout the bulletin are to the Act.

Please note that this bulletin has not been revised to reflect the legislative proposals announced December 20, 2002.

Summary

Subsections 13(4) and 44(1) permit a taxpayer to elect to defer the recognition of income or capital gains where a "former property" is involuntarily disposed of, or a former property that is a "former business property" is voluntarily disposed of, and a "replacement property" is acquired. Subsection 14(6) provides similar treatment in respect of eligible capital property that is "former property" voluntarily or involuntarily disposed of where "replacement property" is acquired. Where all the applicable conditions are met, these rules allow taxpayers that have disposed of property to defer the resulting tax consequences and relocate businesses without incurring immediate tax consequences. Where the former property (other than eligible capital property) has been involuntarily disposed of, for example, stolen, destroyed or taken under statutory authority, the replacement property must be acquired within two years of the end of the taxation year in which the disposition of the property is deemed to have occurred and proceeds to have become receivable. Where the property is former business property and the disposition is voluntary, or eligible capital property, the replacement property must be acquired within one year of the end of the taxation year in which the disposition occurred (for depreciable property of a prescribed class or eligible capital property) or when an amount becomes receivable as proceeds of disposition (for capital property). The replacement property must be acquired to replace the former property, have the same or similar use as the former property and, if the former property was used for the purpose of gaining or producing income from a business, the replacement property must be acquired for the purpose of gaining or producing income from the same or a similar business.

Discussion and Interpretation

General

1. Subsection 44(1) provides for the deferral of all or part of a capital gain on the disposition of a capital property, other than a share of the capital stock of a corporation, where the property is either:

(a) a property the "proceeds of disposition" of which include compensation for property unlawfully taken (for example, stolen), destroyed or taken under statutory authority (for example, expropriated), insurance proceeds payable for property lost or destroyed, or the sale price of property sold to a person who gave notice of an intention to take it under statutory authority, as described in paragraph (*b*), (*c*) or (*d*) of the definition of "proceeds of disposition" in section 54 or paragraph (*b*), (*c*) or (*d*) of the definition of "proceeds of disposition" in subsection 13(21); or

(b) a property that was immediately before the disposition a former business property of the taxpayer (see below).

Unless otherwise specified, a reference in this bulletin to a former property includes either of the situations described in (a) and (b).

(Dispositions described in (a) above are commonly referred to as "involuntary dispositions" while those in (b) above are commonly referred to as "voluntary dispositions.")

In addition, all or part of the recapture of capital cost allowance on the disposition of a property described above that is depreciable property of a prescribed class may be deferred by virtue of subsection 13(4), and inclusion of all or part of the proceeds of disposition of an eligible capital property in the computation of cumulative eligible capital may be deferred under subsection 14(6), where a replacement property is acquired (see the current version of IT-123, *Transactions Involving Eligible Capital Property*).

A "former business property" as defined in subsection 248(1) is capital property that is real property or an interest therein that is used by the taxpayer or a person related to the taxpayer primarily for the purpose of gaining or producing income from a business but generally does not include rental property. (For additional information, see the current version of IT-491, *Former Business Property*).

2. In order for the provisions of subsection 44(1), 13(4) or 14(6) to apply, the following requirements must be met:

(a) The taxpayer must dispose of, and acquire a replacement property which is in the case of

(i) subsection 44(1), a capital property,

(ii) subsection 13(4), a depreciable property of a prescribed class, and

(iii) subsection 14(6), an eligible capital property.

Refer to the comments in ¶s 9 to 21 as to what constitutes a replacement property.

(b) For involuntary dispositions of former property (depreciable property of a prescribed class or any other capital property but excluding eligible capital property), the replacement property must be acquired before the end of the second taxation year following the year in which subsection 44(2) deems the disposition of the former property to occur and the proceeds of that disposition to be receivable. The subsection deems the disposition to occur and the proceeds to be receivable in the year in which the earliest of the following events occurs:

(i) the taxpayer agrees on the full amount of compensation for the property;

(ii) the tribunals or courts make the final determination of compensation for the property;

(iii) two years elapse after the loss, destruction or taking of the property if no proceeding before a tribunal or court has been taken before that time;

(iv) the taxpayer dies or ceases to be a resident in Canada which results in the deemed disposition of the property; and

(v) a corporate taxpayer that is not a subsidiary corporation, referred to in subsection 88(1), is wound up.

Where such a former property was taken under statutory authority, the replacement property can be acquired at any time after a taxpayer receives notice of an intention to take the property under statutory authority and before the end of the time period noted above. For example, where a taxpayer received notice of an intention to expropriate in 1997 and the property was expropriated in that year, but pursuant to subsection 44(2) the disposition of that property does not occur until the 1999 taxation year, the taxpayer can acquire the replacement property at any time after the time of notice

¶3158

of an intention to expropriate in 1997 and before the end of the 2001 taxation year.

(c) If the property is described in ¶1(b), the replacement property must be acquired before the end of the first taxation year following the taxation year in which

(i) an amount becomes receivable as proceeds of disposition of the former property, in the case of subsection 44(1), or

(ii) the disposition occurred, in the case of subsection 13(4).

For the disposition of an eligible capital property, the replacement property must be acquired within one year after the end of the taxation year in which the former property is disposed.

(d) The replacement property cannot be disposed of prior to the date of disposition of the former property. In the example in (b) above, a property acquired in 1997 and disposed of in 1998 could not be a replacement property.

(e) Except where the property is described in ¶1(a), the property disposed of must be a former business property or an eligible capital property.

(f) A valid election must be made (see ¶7).

There is no requirement in the Act that the replacement property be acquired after the former property is disposed of, but the property must nevertheless qualify as a replacement property. For further comments where there is an amalgamation or a winding-up, see ¶22.

3. A taxpayer is required to report any recaptured capital cost allowance, taxable capital gain or amount determined under subsection 14(1) arising from the disposition of a former property in the year of disposition where the replacement property is acquired in a subsequent taxation year. However, provided a replacement property is acquired within the specified time limits, the taxpayer may request that the income tax return for the year of disposition of the former property be reassessed to generate a refund in respect of the income taxes paid on income arising on that disposition. In order to alleviate the financial burden that

might ensue from this situation, acceptable security may be provided in lieu of payment of taxes owing until the time for the final determination of taxes is made or the time period for acquiring the replacement property has expired. Where this practice is followed, the full cost of providing such security is borne by the taxpayer and the interest on the unpaid taxes will continue to accrue at the appropriate prescribed rates subject to being reduced by interest credited on any subsequent reassessment giving effect to the deferral.

4. Where more than one capital property has been disposed of in circumstances where subsection 44(1) is applicable, the provisions of that subsection apply to each such property and its replacement property individually. In the case of land and buildings thereon, this term is considered to refer to land and each individual building thereon separately and, for purposes of this subsection, the capital gain on each of these properties should be calculated separately. However, under subsection 44(6) a taxpayer may be permitted to reallocate the proceeds of disposition of a former business property composed of land and one or more buildings between the land component and the building component. The amount eligible for reallocation is limited to the excess of proceeds of disposition otherwise determined of one or the other of the components over its adjusted cost base. If, for instance, the proceeds of disposition of land determined without reference to subsection 44(6) exceed its adjusted cost base, a taxpayer can elect to treat all or a portion of the excess as being proceeds of disposition of the building component of the former business property and thereby defer recognition of all or a portion of the accrued capital gain with respect to the land. See ¶29 for an example of the operation of subsection 44(6). The election to change the allocation between land and building must be filed in an income tax return of the taxpayer for the year in which the replacement property is acquired. "Land," for the purposes of subsection 44(6), is "the land (or an interest therein) subjacent to, or immediately contiguous to and necessary for the use of, the building."

5. When a taxpayer calculates a capital gain under subsection 44(1) for a particular taxation year, a reserve provided by subparagraph 40(1)(a)(iii) may not be claimed. However, subparagraph 44(1)(e)(iii) pro-

¶3158

vides that a reasonable reserve in respect of proceeds of disposition that are payable after the end of the year is available in most instances, based on the capital gain as reduced under subsection 44(1). Where promissory notes are included as proceeds, see the current version of IT-436, *Reserves — Where Promissory Notes Are Included in Disposal Proceeds*. Pursuant to subsection 44(7), no such reserve is allowed where the taxpayer, at the end of the year or at any time in the immediately following year, is not resident in Canada or is exempt from tax under Part I of the Act, or where the person that acquires the former property of the taxpayer is a controlled or controlling corporation as described in paragraph 44(7)(*b*).

6. Other restrictions on allowable reserves are provided by subparagraph 44(1)(*e*)(iii) which limit reserves in order that at least one fifth of a gain is recognized in the year of disposition of the property and in each of the four following years. Gains in respect of certain transfers to children are eligible for a deferral extending over a ten-year period rather than the five-year period referred to above. This exception is provided in subsection 44(1.1) and applies only to dispositions from a parent to a child of family farm land and buildings where the rules in subsection 73(3) also apply. An individual (other than a trust) who is claiming a reserve under subparagraph 44(1)(*e*)(iii) should use the prescribed form, T1030, *Election to Claim a Capital Gains Reserve for Individuals (other than trusts) When Calculating the Amount of a Capital Gain Using the Replacement Property Rules*, while other taxpayers may claim the reserve in their income tax returns.

Election to Use Subsections 44(1), 13(4) and 14(6)

7. A taxpayer must elect to have the provisions of subsections 44(1), 13(4) and 14(6) apply. The election should be made as follows:

(a) If the disposition and replacement take place in the same year, the taxpayer's calculation (in the income tax return for that year) of the recaptured capital cost allowance, the amount under subsection 14(5) by reason of subsection 14(6) (that is, for purposes of determining the balance in the pool of eligible capital property — see the current version of IT-123), or the cap-

ital gain by virtue of subsection 44(1) will be considered to constitute an election.

(b) If the property is not replaced until a subsequent year, the election should take the form of a letter attached to the income tax return for the year the replacement property is acquired. The letter should include a description of the replacement property and the former property, a request for an adjustment to the recapture of capital cost allowance, the taxable capital gain reported, or the amount included in income by virtue of subsection 14(1) in a prior year, and a calculation of the revised recapture, taxable capital gain or cumulative eligible capital.

(c) If the replacement property is acquired prior to the year of disposition of the property, the election to apply subsections 13(4), 44(1) and 14(6) should take the form of a letter attached to the income tax return for the year in which the replacement property is acquired and the letter should include descriptions of the replacement property and the property that is to be replaced. If the taxpayer late?files such an election, it will be accepted if it is filed in the income tax return for the year in which the former property is disposed of, provided it is evident that the new property qualifies as a replacement property.

If a former property is depreciable property, subsection 44(4) provides that if a taxpayer elects on that property under subsection 44(1), the taxpayer is deemed to have elected also under subsection 13(4), and if the taxpayer elects under subsection 13(4), the taxpayer is deemed to have elected under subsection 44(1) as well.

8. Under the combined provisions of subsection 220(3.2) of the Act and Part VI of the Regulations, depending on the circumstances,

(a) a late or amended election under subsection 13(4), 14(6), 44(1) or 44(6); or

(b) a request to revoke such an election;

may be accepted.

For further particulars, see the current version of Information Circular 92-1, *Guide-*

¶3158

lines for Accepting Late, Amended or Revoked Elections.

Replacement Property — General

9. A taxpayer is considered to have acquired replacement property at the time the acquisition would ordinarily be considered to have been made under the provisions of the Act and the general principles of law. See the current version of IT-285, *Capital Cost Allowance — General Comments*, for a discussion of the time of acquisition of depreciable property. Where a replacement property can be considered to have been acquired, it is not necessary that the total acquisition cost be paid in cash. For example, where a qualifying replacement property has been acquired at a cost of $100,000 with $20,000 paid in cash, and the balance covered by a mortgage, the total cost of $100,000 qualifies for purposes of the subsection 44(1), 13(4) or 14(6) election. On the other hand, where, at a given time, an amount has been paid, for example in the form of the deposit on a replacement property, and that property has not been acquired, the amount expended does not so qualify.

10. In some situations, it may be necessary to purchase more than one property to replace another. In such situations, each of the properties purchased will be considered a replacement property provided each qualifies as a replacement of the original property. Conversely, the replacement of two or more capital properties with one property may also be accepted. See illustrations in ¶s 27 and 28.

11. The fact that the specific funds received for the former property are used to acquire another property in no way bears on the determination of whether or not the acquired property constitutes a replacement. It also follows that where a taxpayer temporarily invests such funds pending a decision on the acquisition of a replacement property, the temporary investment would normally not itself constitute the replacement.

12. Where a taxpayer reacquires a former property within the time period described in paragraph ¶2(b) as a result of, for example, the abandonment of the property by the expropriating authority, the taxpayer is considered to have acquired the property as a replacement.

13. If a taxpayer exchanges one property for another, the new property will qualify as a replacement property provided it is in fact a replacement property and the other requirements of subsection 44(1) are met. Examples of such exchanges are as follows:

(a) An expropriating authority exchanges properties with a taxpayer.

(b) Taxpayer A exchanges farm lands with taxpayer B.

14. By virtue of subsections 13(4.1), 14(7) and 44(5), a particular property acquired by the taxpayer will qualify as a replacement property for the former property owned by the taxpayer (for purposes of the rules in subsection 13(4) for depreciable property, subsection 14(6) for eligible capital property and section 44 for capital property, respectively) if it meets each one of the following conditions that is applicable:

(a) for eligible capital property

(i) it must be reasonable to conclude that the property was acquired by the taxpayer to replace the former property;

(ii) it must be acquired by the taxpayer for a use that is the same as or similar to the use to which the taxpayer put the former property;

(iii) it must be acquired for the purpose of gaining or producing income from the same or a similar business as that in which the former property was used; and

(iv) where the former property was used by the taxpayer in a business carried on in Canada, it must be acquired for use by the taxpayer in a business carried on by the taxpayer in Canada.

(b) for depreciable property of a prescribed class and other capital property

(i) it must be reasonable to conclude that the property was acquired by the taxpayer to replace the former property;

(ii) it must be acquired by the taxpayer and used by the taxpayer or a person related to the taxpayer for a use that is the same as or similar to the use to which the taxpayer or a person

¶3158

related to the taxpayer put the former property;

(iii) where the former property was used by the taxpayer or a person related to the taxpayer for the purpose of gaining or producing income from a business, it must be acquired for the purpose of gaining or producing income from that or a similar business or for the use by a person related to the taxpayer for such a purpose;

(iv) where the former property was taxable Canadian property, the particular depreciable or capital property is also a taxable Canadian property of the taxpayer; and

(v) where the former property was a taxable Canadian property of the taxpayer that is not a treaty-protected property, the particular depreciable or capital property is also a taxable Canadian property of the taxpayer that is not a treaty-protected property.

Replace the Former Property

15. To satisfy the requirement in paragraph $14(7)(a)$ and in paragraphs $13(4.1)(a)$ and $44(5)(a)$ (as described in ¶s 14(a)(i) and 14(b)(i)), it must be reasonable to conclude that the property was acquired to replace the former property. In this regard, there must be some correlation or direct substitution, that is, a causal relationship between the disposition of a former property and the acquisition of the new property or properties. Where it cannot readily be determined whether one property is actually being replaced by another, the newly acquired property will not be considered a replacement property for the former property. For example, consider the situation where a taxpayer has a number of retail locations some of which are in the process of commencing operations while others are scheduled for closing. A new location probably would not be considered a replacement property for an old location if the business operations at the two locations are carried on simultaneously (other than for a brief transitional period, for example, while the inventory at the old location is liquidated). Generally, the geographical location of the "replacement property" is not determinative when considering whether one property is a replacement for another.

Same or a Similar Use

16. Where a former property described in ¶1(a) was not used for the purpose of gaining or producing income from a business, the following comments apply in determining whether a replacement property is acquired for "the same or a similar use" as required by paragraphs $13(4.1)(a.1)$ and $44(5)(a.1)$ (as described in ¶14(b)(ii)).

(a) This requirement is met where the use of the property is the same or similar to the use to which the taxpayer or a person related to the taxpayer put the former property. Since the former property must have been used, land that has never been used by the taxpayer or a related person cannot qualify as a former property. Land (or any other capital property) that has been used for non-income earning purposes can qualify as a former property (for example, a personal-use cottage that is expropriated). Land that is acquired for resale cannot qualify because it is not a capital property.

(b) Although the property generally will bear the same physical description as the former property, for example, land replaced by land or a building by a building (but see ¶4), there may be cases where a different type of property provides the same use or function as the former property. For example, where shares of a cooperative corporation which carry rights to accommodation in an office building are acquired to replace an expropriated office building of the taxpayer, the shares could constitute a replacement property.

17. Where the former property was used for the purpose of gaining or producing income from a business, another property will usually be considered to be a property acquired for the "same or a similar use" if it is acquired to gain or produce income from the same or a similar business and if it generally bears the same physical description as the former property. For example, a taxpayer may replace a warehouse with a manufacturing building used in the same or a similar business because both properties are buildings and the two uses are "similar" in that they are both part of the overall process of providing products from the same or a similar business to the consumer. It must be kept in mind, however, that the "same or a

¶3158

similar use" test referred to in ¶s 14(a)(ii) and (b)(ii) is still a separate test from, and is not overridden by, the "same or a similar business" test referred to in ¶s 14(a)(iii) and (b)(iii) and discussed in ¶s 18 to 21. Thus, for example, if a company owned a residential property used to house its employees, a building used to carry on the company's day-to-day operations would generally not be considered as having the "same or a similar use" even though both properties are real property and are used in the same business. Also, a property normally will not be a replacement property acquired for the same or a similar use when it is acquired to replace a former property and at the same time provide substantial other uses. An insignificant secondary use of a new replacement property is not a concern. A former business property cannot be replaced with a rental property.

Same or a Similar Business

18. The term "similar business" as used in the phrase "the same or a similar business" or "from that or a similar business" in paragraphs 13(4.1)(b), 14(7)(b) and 44(5)(b) (see ¶s 14(a)(iii) and (b)(iii)) are interpreted in a reasonably broad manner. In this respect, two businesses will be considered to be "similar" if they both fall within the same one of the following categories:

(a) merchandising — retailing and wholesaling;

(b) farming;

(c) fishing;

(d) forestry and forest products;

(e) extractive industries, including refining;

(f) financial services;

(g) communications;

(h) transportation;

(i) construction, including subcontracting; and

(j) manufacturing and processing.

19. With regard to the categories referred to in ¶18, where a business falls into more than one, a similar business will be one that falls into any one of these categories for which the business qualifies; for example, a plywood plant qualifies under

category (d) — forestry and forest products, and under category (j) — manufacturing and processing. As a result, if the plywood plant is sold, any business that falls in category (d) or category (j) will be considered a "similar business."

20. A taxpayer who changes from one business category to another but continues to deal in the same product will normally be considered to be in a "similar business." For example, a taxpayer involved in the merchandising of a product may change to the manufacture and production of the same product and still be considered to be in a "similar" business. On the other hand, where a taxpayer carries on a number of separate businesses (see the current version of IT-206, *Separate Businesses*) and the same products are not involved, these businesses will not be considered to be similar businesses. For example, a taxpayer who operates a hotel business and a manufacturing business as separate businesses cannot be considered to have similar businesses.

21. Service industries, such as hotels, restaurants, repairs, professional services, barbershops, funeral parlours, laundries, real estate agencies, tourism, and entertainment, are not included in the categories referred to in ¶18, because most of these industries are too varied and different to permit categorization. Where there is a question of whether two businesses in a service industry or in any other industry not included in the categories in ¶18 are "similar businesses," the determination will have to be made on the facts of the case. For such cases, "similar business" will be interpreted in a reasonably broad manner.

Amalgamations and Wind-Ups

22. In a situation where, before a section 87 amalgamation occurs, property of a predecessor corporation

(a) has been lost, stolen, destroyed or expropriated, or

(b) was a "former business property" of the predecessor corporation,

paragraph 87(2)(l.3) prevents the deferral rules in sections 13 and 44 from being lost. Paragraph 87(2)(l.3) does this by deeming, for purposes of applying those sections and the definition of "former business property" in subsection 248(1) to the new corporation with respect to the former property and any replacement property acquired for the former property, that the new corporation is the same corporation as, and is a continuation of, the predecessor corporation. Paragraph $88(1)(e.2)$ similarly prevents the loss of such a deferral in a winding-up to which subsection 88(1) applies. Also, since properties distributed to a parent by a subsidiary in a winding-up are deemed by paragraph $88(1)(a)$ to have been disposed of by the subsidiary and are thus considered to have been acquired by the parent, a property acquired upon winding up may serve as a replacement property for purposes of subsections 13(4.1), 14(7) and 44(5) in respect of the disposition of a "former property" by the parent corporation if all of the other requirements of the relevant subsection are satisfied. While paragraphs $87(2)(l.3)$ and $88(1)(e.2)$ prevent the deferral rules from being lost, it may not be reasonable to conclude that property acquired by a corporation prior to an amalgamation or acquired by the parent corporation as a consequence of the winding-up of a subsidiary corporation is a replacement property for property disposed of by the amalgamated corporation, by a predecessor corporation that is included in the amalgamation, or by the parent corporation where a subsidiary has been wound up. Each situation must be considered on its facts to determine whether it is reasonable to conclude that the acquired property is a replacement property for the former property or former business property.

Partnerships

23. Subsections 44(1), 14(6) and 13(4) apply to a partnership if the requirements outlined in ¶2 are met. Section 44 and subsection 13(4) would also apply to a member of a partnership who acquires a replacement property for a personally owned former business property which is or was being used in the partnership business. These provisions would not apply however to a situation where the partnership disposes of a former business property and a partner (or partners) acquires the replacement property because, pursuant to paragraph $96(1)(a)$, the partnership is considered to be a person separate from its partners for purposes of income and loss computations under subdivision j.

Non-Residents and Deceased Taxpayers

24. The provisions of subsections 44(1) and 13(4) can apply to a non-resident who has disposed of taxable Canadian property and who acquires a qualifying replacement property that is also taxable Canadian property. See also ¶s 14(a)(iv) and 14(b)(iv).

25. Where a taxpayer dies or ceases to be resident in Canada and is deemed pursuant to section 70 or paragraph $128.1(4)(b)$ respectively to have disposed of a capital property, the provisions of subsections 13(4) and 44(1) do not apply. However, where a taxpayer dies, subsection 72(2) will, in certain circumstances, permit an election so that a reserve under subsection 44(1) may be claimed in respect of the deceased person.

Adjustment Resulting from the Replacement of the Former Property — Examples

26. Where a replacement property has been acquired, and the taxpayer complies with the requirements noted in ¶2, subsections 44(1) and 13(4) provide certain rules that affect the gain resulting from the disposition of the former property and also the ultimate disposition of the replacement property. The following examples illustrate the application of these provisions to the expropriation of a property, which constituted depreciable property of a prescribed class to the former owner:

Example

Assume:

(1)	Original capital cost of the former property (acquired in the 1980 taxation year)	$100,000
(2)	Date of expropriation	June 30, 1997
(3)	Year-end of the taxpayer	December 31
(4)	Date replacement property acquired	June 30, 1999
(5)	Original capital cost of the replacement property	$130,000
(6)	Day on which the former property is deemed to have been disposed of pursuant to subsection 44(2)	June 30, 2000
(7)	Proceeds of disposition determined as of the day in (6) above	$175,000

¶3158

		Replacement Property in a DIFFERENT CCA Class than Former Property		Replacement Property in the SAME CCA Class as Former Property	

Application of Subsection 44(1)

(1) **Gain on Disposition of Former Property determined under paragraph 44(1)(e) (year ending December 31, 2000)**

Lesser of:

(a) Gain otherwise determined:

Proceeds of disposition		$175,000		$175,000	
In excess of capital cost		100,000	$ 75,000	100,000	$ 75,000

(b) Amount by which:

Proceeds of disposition		$175,000		$175,000	
Exceed the cost of the replacement property		130,000	$ 45,000	130,000	$ 45,000
Gain on disposal			$ 45,000		$ 45,000

(2) **Capital Cost of Replacement Property determined under paragraph 44(1)(f) after June 30, 2000**

Original cost....................		$130,000		$130,000	
Less: Amount by which (1)(a) above..........................	$75,000				
Exceeds (1)(b) above	45,000	30,000	$100,000	30,000	$100,000

	Replacement Property in a DIFFERENT CCA Class than Former Property		Replacement Property in the SAME CCA Class as Former Property
	Class A (Former Property)	Class B (Replacement Property)	Class A (Both Properties)

Undepreciated Capital Cost (UCC) at December 31, 2000

(3) **Subsection 13(21)**

Capital cost of former property (**A** of the definition of UCC in subsection 13(21))	$100,000		$100,000
Capital cost of replacement property (**A** of the definition of UCC in subsection 13(21)) adjusted by paragraph 44(1)(f))	N/A	$100,000	$100,000
	$100,000	$100,000	$200,000
Less: Capital cost allowance claimed (assumed) (**E** of the definition of UCC in subsection 13(21))	90,000	5,000	95,000
	$ 10,000	$ 95,000	$105,000

¶3158

Less: Disposition of former property determined under paragraph 13(4)(c) (Note 1)	10,000	N/A	10,000
Less: Disposition of a depreciable property determined under paragraph 13(4)(d) (Note 2)	N/A	90,000	90,000
UCC at the end of the year	NIL	$ 5,000	$ 5,000

Note 1

	Replacement Property in a DIFFERENT CCA Class than Former Property		Replacement Property in the SAME CCA Class as Former Property	
Disposition of former property determined under paragraph 13(4)(c):				
Amount otherwise determined under **F** of the definition of UCC in subsection 13(21)		$100,000		$100,000
Deduct: lesser of:				
(i) amount otherwise determined under **F** of the definition of UCC in subsection 13(21)	$100,000		$100,000	
Deduct: UCC immediately before the time the former property was disposed of	10,000		10,000	
	$ 90,000	90,000	$ 90,000	90,000
(ii) acquisition cost of replacement property . .	$130,000		$130,000	
		$ 10,000		$ 10,000

Note 2

Pursuant to paragraph 13(4)(d), the reduction determined under paragraph 13(4)(c) of $90,000 in both cases is deemed to be proceeds of disposition of a depreciable property that had a capital cost equal to that amount and that was property of the same class as the replacement property.

27. Where two or more capital properties of the taxpayer are replaced by one replacement property, for example, two expropriated buildings are replaced by one building, for the purpose of subsections 13(4) and 44(1), that portion of the cost of the replacement that can be considered to be a replacement for a particular former property can be allocated by the taxpayer on a reasonable basis to the particular former property. (Normally the allocation should be based on the proportion that the original cost of a former property is to the total cost of all former properties.) To illustrate:

¶3158

Example

	Former Properties		Replacement Property
	A	B	C

Assume:

1. Cost of former properties and .... Capital Cost Allowance class .... — $200,000 (Class 3) — $100,000 (Class 6)
2. Proceeds of disposition of former properties .... — $300,000 — $200,000
3. Original cost of replacement property and ...... Capital Cost Allowance class .... — $450,000 (Class 6)

Application of subsection 44(1)

(1) **Gain on Disposition of Former Property under paragraph 44(1)(e)**

Lesser of:

(a) Gain otherwise determined .... — $100,000 — $100,000

(b) Amount by which:
Proceeds of disposition exceed the cost of the replacement property attributable to each former property .... — $300,000 — $200,000

$\dfrac{\$200,000}{\$300,000} \times \$450,000$ $300,000

$\dfrac{\$100,000}{\$300,000} \times \$450,000$ 150,000

                                               NIL $ 50,000

Gain on disposal .... — NIL — $ 50,000

(2) **Cost of Replacement Property under paragraph 44(1)(f)**

Original Cost $450,000

Less: Amount by which (1)(a) above .... — $100,000 — $100,000

      Exceeds (1)(b) above .... — NIL — 50,000

                                      $100,000 $ 50,000   150,000

Cost of replacement property $300,000

	Class 3 Former Property A	Class 6 Former Property B and Replacement Property
(3) **Undepreciated Capital Cost**		
Capital Cost of Former Properties ..	$200,000	$100,000
Less: Capital Cost Allowance claimed (assumed)	150,000	75,000
UCC immediately before disposition	$ 50,000	$ 25,000
Addition of Replacement property — capital cost adjusted by paragraph 44(1)(f)	N/A	300,000
	$ 50,000	$325,000
Less: Disposition of former property determined under paragraph 13(4)(c) (Note 1) ...	50,000	25,000
Less: Disposition of a depreciable property determined under paragraph 13(4)(d) (Note 2) ...	N/A	225,000
UCC after above adjustments	NIL	$ 75,000

¶3158

Note 1

Disposition of former properties under paragraph 13(4)(c):

	Former Property A		Former Property B	
Amount otherwise determined under **F** of the definition of UCC in subsection 13(21)		$200,000		$100,000
Deduct: lesser of:				
(i) amount otherwise determined under **F** of the definition of UCC in subsection 13(21)	$200,000		$100,000	
Deduct: UCC immediately before the time the property was disposed of	50,000		25,000	
	$150,000	150,000	$ 75,000	75,000
(ii) acquisition cost of replacement property attributable to each former property (see (1) above)	$300,000		$150,000	
		$ 50,000		$ 25,000

Note 2

Pursuant to paragraph 13(4)(d), the reductions determined under paragraph 13(4)(c) of $150,000 for former property A and $75,000 for former property B are deemed to be proceeds of disposition of a depreciable property that had a capital cost equal to that amount and that was property of the same class as the replacement property.

28. Where, in the reverse situation, one property is replaced by two or more replacement properties for the purpose of subsection 44(1), the cost of each replacement property can be aggregated in determining the amount of the gain from the former property. In situations, such as where the replacement properties constitute properties of different prescribed classes or where one such property is acquired prior to the disposition of the former property and the other within the allowable period after the disposition of the former property, it may be necessary to make a reasonable apportionment of the proceeds of disposition determined under paragraph 13(4) and of the cost of replacement properties determined under paragraph 44(1)(f). (Normally the allocation should be based on the proportion that the original cost of a replacement property is to the total costs of all replacement properties.)

Example

	Former Property	Replacement Properties	
	A	B	C
Assume:			
(1) Cost of former property and	$300,000		
Capital Cost Allowance class	(Class 3)		
(2) Proceeds of disposition of former property . . .	$500,000		
(3) Original cost of replacement properties and . .		$300,000	$150,000
Capital Cost Allowance class		(Class 3)	(Class 6)

¶3158

Application of subsection 44(1)

(1) **Gain on Disposition of Former Property —
paragraph 44(1)(e)**

Lesser of:

(a) Gain otherwise determined $200,000

(b) Amount by which:
    Proceeds of disposition $500,000
    Exceed the cost of the replacement
property.   450,000
                                                                      $ 50,000

Gain on disposal . . . . $ 50,000

	Replacement Properties	
	B	C

(2) **Cost of Replacement Properties — paragraph 44(1)(f)**

		B	C
Original Cost		$300,000	$150,000

Less: Amount by which (1)(a) above $200,000

Exceeds (1)(b) above.   50,000

                                                                      $150,000

Deduct: Amount of $150,000 above to be allocated to
property B

$$\frac{\$300,000}{\$450,000} \times \$150,000$$ 100,000

Deduct: Amount of $150,000 above to be allocated to
property C

$$\frac{\$150,000}{\$450,000} \times \$150,000$$ 50,000

Cost of replacement properties $200,000 $100,000

	Class 3	Class 6
	Former Property A and Replacement Property B	Replacement Property C

(3) **Undepreciated Capital Cost**

Capital Cost of Former Properties. $300,000

Less: Capital Cost Allowance claimed
(assumed)   100,000

UCC immediately before disposition $200,000

Plus: Addition of Replacement property
    — capital cost adjusted by paragraph
44(1)(f) 200,000 $100,000
                                                                      $400,000 $100,000

Less: Disposition of former property
    determined under paragraph 13(4)(c)
    (Note 1).   200,000

Less: Disposition of a depreciable property
    determined under paragraph 13(4)(d)
    (Note 2). . . . .

$$\frac{\$300,000}{\$450,000} \times \$100,000$$ 66,667

$$\frac{\$150,000}{\$450,000} \times \$100,000$$ 33,333

UCC after adjustments . . . . $133,333 $ 66,667

¶3158

Note 1

Disposition of former properties under paragraph 13(4)(*c*):

Amount otherwise determined under **F** of the definition UCC in subsection 13(21)..............			$300,000
Deduct: lesser of:			
(i) amount otherwise determined under **F** of the definition in subsection 13(21)......	$300,000		
Deduct: UCC immediately before the time the property was disposed of...........................	200,000	$100,000	
(ii) acquisition cost of replacement properties ($300,000 + $150,000)		$450,000	100,000
			$200,000

Note 2

Pursuant to paragraph 13(4)(*d*), the reductions determined under paragraph 13(4)(*c*) of $100,000 is deemed to be proceeds of disposition of a depreciable property that had a capital cost equal to that amount and that was property of the same class as the replacement property. Because the replacement property was included in two classes, the amount determined under paragraph 13(4)(*d*) has been apportioned between the two classes.

29. Subsection 44(6) provides a mechanism for a taxpayer who disposes of a former business property consisting of, for example, a building of low value and land of high value to permit the allocation of part of the proceeds of disposition of the land to the building. The reallocated proceeds can then be used in the application of subsection 44(1). The applications of subsections 44(6), 44(1) and 13(4) and the computation under subsection 13(21) are illustrated in the following example:

Example

Assume:

(1)	Cost of former land	$ 10,000
(2)	Capital cost of former building	$ 90,000
(3)	UCC of class of former building at March 31, 2000	$ 15,000
(4)	Date of disposition of former business property and acquisition of replacement property...	March 31, 2000
(5)	Proceeds from sale of former land...............................	$100,000
(6)	Proceeds from sale of former building	$ 25,000
(7)	Cost of replacement land..	$ 40,000
(8)	Cost of replacement building of different class from former building	$ 60,000

(1)	**Reallocation of Proceeds under subsection 44(6)**	
	(a) Land	
	● Proceeds..	$100,000
	● Less: Adjusted cost base (cost)	10,000
	Amount available	$ 90,000
	(b) Building	
	● Proceeds..	$ 25,000
	● Less: Adjusted cost base (capital cost)	90,000
	Amount available	NIL

¶3158

For illustration purposes, computations are made reallocating (A) $90,000, (B) $60,000 and (C) $35,000 as elected amounts from the proceeds of disposition of the land to the proceeds of disposition of the building:

(c) Reallocated proceeds are:

	(A)	(B)	(C)
(i) Land	$ 10,000	$ 40,000	$ 65,000
(ii) Building	115,000	85,000	60,000
Combined proceeds...................	$125,000	$125,000	$125,000

(2) **Application of subsection 44(1)**

(a) Gain on disposition of land:

	(A)	(B)	(C)
(i) Reallocated Proceeds	$ 10,000	$ 40,000	$ 65,000
Less: Adjusted cost base (cost).............	10,000	10,000	10,000
Gain under clause $44(1)(e)(i)(A)$	NIL	$ 30,000	$ 55,000
(ii) Reallocated proceeds	$ 10,000	$ 40,000	$ 65,000
Less: Cost of replacement land	40,000	40,000	40,000
Gain under clause $44(1)(e)(i)(B)$	NIL	NIL	$ 25,000
Gain under subparagraph $44(1)(e)(i)$ is the lesser of (i) and (ii)	NIL	NIL	$ 25,000

(b) Gain on disposition of building:

	(A)	(B)	(C)
(i) Reallocated proceeds	$115,000	$ 85,000	$ 60,000
Less: Lesser of (A) original proceeds ($25,000) and (B) adjusted cost base $90,000)	25,000	25,000	25,000
Gain under clause $44(1)(e)(i)(A)$	$ 90,000	$ 60,000	$ 35,000
(ii) Reallocated proceeds	$115,000	$ 85,000	$ 60,000
Less: Cost of replacement building	60,000	60,000	60,000
Gain under clause $44(1)(e)(i)(B)$	$ 55,000	$ 25,000	NIL
Gain on disposition of building is the lesser of (i) and (ii)	$ 55,000	$ 25,000	NIL

(c) Cost of replacement land:

	(A)	(B)	(C)
Cost otherwise determined	$ 40,000	$ 40,000	$ 40,000
Less: the amount by which (a)(i) above	NIL	$ 30,000	$ 55,000
exceeds (a)(ii) above	NIL	NIL	25,000
	NIL	$ 30,000	$ 30,000
Cost of replacement land	$ 40,000	$ 10,000	$ 10,000

(d) Capital cost of replacement building:

	(A)	(B)	(C)
Capital cost otherwise determined.............	$ 60,000	$ 60,000	$ 60,000
Less: the amount by which (b)(i) above	$ 90,000	$ 60,000	$ 35,000
exceeds (b)(ii) above.....................	55,000	25,000	NIL
	$ 35,000	$ 35,000	$ 35,000
Capital cost of replacement building............	$ 25,000	$ 25,000	$ 25,000

(3) **Application of subsection 13(4)**

	(A)(B)(C)
(a) Building proceeds under **F** of the definition of UCC in subsection 13(21)	
(i) Otherwise determined (subsection 44(6) not applicable)........	$25,000
Less: UCC of class	15,000
Amount under subparagraph $13(4)(c)(i)$	$10,000
(ii) Amount used to acquire replacement	$60,000

¶3158

(iii) Proceeds otherwise determined................................ $25,000
Less: lesser of (i) and (ii).. 10,000
Proceeds under **F** of the definition of UCC in
subsection 13(21) $15,000

(b) Deemed proceeds in replacement class
Amount of reduction in (a)(iii) above $10,000

(4) **Computation of UCC under subsection 13(21) at March 31, 2000**

	Former Property Class	Replacement Property Class
(a) Capital cost	$90,000	$25,000
(b) Depreciation allowed............................	(75,000)	NIL
(c) Proceeds	(15,000)	(10,000)
	NIL	$15,000

(5) **Comparison of Tax Results**

	No Election[1]	Election (A)	Election (B)	Election (C)
(a) Capital gain				
(i) Land	$90,000	NIL	NIL	$25,000
(ii) Building	NIL	$55,000	$25,000	NIL
(b) Cost of replacement land......	$40,000	$40,000	$10,000	$10,000
(c) Capital cost of replacement building	$60,000	$25,000	$25,000	$25,000
(d) Recapture of CCA	$10,000	NIL	NIL	NIL
(e) UCC				
(i) Former property class....	NIL	NIL	NIL	NIL
(ii) Replacement property class....................	$60,000	$15,000	$15,000	$15,000

[1] The column shows the results that would occur if there were neither an election under subsection 13(4) and 44(1) nor subsection 44(6).

Explanation of Changes

Introduction

The purpose of the *Explanation of Changes* is to give the reasons for the revisions to an interpretation bulletin. It outlines revisions that we have made as a result of changes to the law, as well as changes reflecting new or revised departmental interpretations.

Reasons for the Revision

We have revised the bulletin to reflect changes to the *Income Tax Act* resulting from S.C. 1999, c. 22 (formerly Bill C-72) and S.C. 2001, c. 17 (formerly Bill C-22).

Legislative and Other Changes

¶1 was revised to reflect the amendment to subsection 44(1) that the replacement property provisions do not apply to shares of the capital stock of a corporation. These amendments apply to shares disposed of after April 15, 1999, subject to transitional relief for shares disposed of after that day as a consequence of a public takeover bid or offer filed with a public authority before April 16, 1999. A comment was also added to

reflect that a reference in the bulletin to former property includes a former business property.

¶2(c) was revised to add specific comments regarding the period in which a replacement property must be acquired for a former property that is eligible capital property.

¶5 was revised to remove comments regarding the application of subparagraph 44(1)(e)(iii) for taxation years ending before February 21, 1994.

¶14 was revised to reflect the amendments to paragraphs 44(5)(c) and 13(4.1)(c). New paragraphs 44(5)(c) and 13(4.1)(c) reproduce the effect of the existing paragraphs and new paragraphs 44(5)(d) and 13(4.1)(d) add a new requirement that where the former property was a taxable Canadian property other than treaty-protected property, the replacement property must be as well. This amendment is applicable to dispositions that occur in taxation years ending after 1997.

¶15 discusses the requirement in paragraphs 13(4.1)(a), 14(7)(a) and

¶3158

$44(5)(a)$ that it be reasonable to conclude that the acquired property was acquired to replace the former property. As announced at the 2002 Canadian Tax Foundation (CTF) Conference, this paragraph is being amended to emphasize that there must be a correlation or causal relationship between the acquisition of the new property and the disposition of the old property. As a result, the statement regarding business expan-

sions has been removed and the example has been clarified. A complete copy of our comments at the 2002 CTF Conference has been published in *Income Tax Technical News No. 25.*

Throughout the bulletin, we have made minor changes for clarification or readability purposes.

[3160] Interpretation Bulletin IT-267R2: Capital Cost Allowance — Vessels

[*Interpretation Bulletin IT-267R2 is dated February 28, 1995.*]

Reference: Paragraph $20(1)(a)$ (also subsections 13(1), 13(4), 13(14), 13(16) and 13(17) and the definitions of "conversion," "conversion cost" and "vessel" in subsection 13(21)) of the *Income Tax Act* and subsections 1100(16), 1101(2a), 1101(2b), 1102(14), 1102(14.1) and 1102(20), paragraphs 1100(1)(v) and 1100(1)(va), and Classes 7 and 41 of Schedule II of the Income Tax Regulations)

Application

This bulletin cancels and replaces Interpretation Bulletin IT-267R dated December 31, 1979, and the Special Release dated March 14, 1985.

Summary

This bulletin outlines the capital cost allowance provisions that apply to vessels and includes a discussion on the classification of various types of vessels and the corresponding rates of capital cost allowance, as well as the recapture of depreciation for vessels.

Discussion and Interpretation

General

1. "Vessel" is defined in subsection 13(21) to mean a vessel as defined in the *Canada Shipping Act*. The *Canada Shipping Act* states that a "vessel" includes any ship or boat or any other vessel used, or designed to be used, in navigation. For example, the following are considered vessels, if used or designed to be used in navigation:

(a) dredges, barges or lighters, even if they are rudderless or not self-propelled;

(b) dracones; and

(c) floating cranes.

2. Vessels, other than "Canadian vessels" (see 5 and 6 below) and most "offshore

drilling vessels" (see 7 to 10 below), are included in Class 7 in Schedule II of the Regulations. The furniture, fittings and equipment (other than radiocommunication equipment) attached to, and spare engines for, such vessels are also included in Class 7. The maximum annual rate of capital cost allowance ("CCA") for Class 7 property is 15% applied to the undepreciated capital cost of the class and the maximum CCA claim is subject to the "50% rule" for property acquired in a year. See the current version of Interpretation Bulletin IT-285, *Capital Cost Allowance — General Comments*, for a discussion of the "50% rule." In addition, if a vessel (or a vessel under construction, see 3 below) is acquired and is not considered available for use, the CCA claim will be restricted until the time that it is available for use. The "available for use" rules are contained in subsections 13(26) to (31).

3. A vessel under construction is included in Class 7 even though the vessel may qualify to be included in a separate class when construction is completed (see 5, 8 and 10 below). However, a vessel under construction that is described in Class 41 (see 9 below) is included in Class 41.

Accelerated Capital Cost Allowance

4. A "Canadian vessel" or an "offshore drilling vessel" may have all or part of its cost qualify as a separate prescribed class having a CCA rate designed to create an incentive for the acquisition, construction or

¶3160

conversion of the vessel. These vessels are outlined in 5 to 10 below.

Canadian Vessels

5. Under paragraph $1100(1)(v)$ of the Regulations, accelerated CCA on a straight-line basis at a maximum annual rate of $33\frac{1}{3}\%$ of the capital cost of the property ($16\frac{2}{3}\%$ for the year of acquisition, see 6 below) is available for the following properties ("Canadian vessels"):

(a) a vessel described in subsection 1101(2a) of the Regulations (including the furniture, fittings, radiocommunication equipment and other attached equipment) that:

(i) was constructed in Canada;

(ii) is registered in Canada; and

(iii) had not been used for any purpose whatever before it was acquired by the taxpayer;

(b) a "conversion cost" (defined in subsection 13(21) as the cost of a conversion for a vessel; and "conversion", also defined in subsection 13(21), for a vessel, means a conversion or major alteration in Canada by a taxpayer); and

(c) a vessel, or a conversion cost for a vessel, established as a separate prescribed class under the *Canadian Vessel Construction Assistance Act* that was repealed on March 23, 1967.

Each vessel is established as a separate prescribed class under subsection 1101(2a) of the Regulations and each conversion cost for a vessel is established as a separate prescribed class under subsection 13(14) of the Act. These properties will not be considered to have been acquired for purposes of calculating the accelerated CCA claim until they are available for use.

6. The maximum CCA rate is limited to $16\frac{2}{3}\%$ for the year of acquisition for properties described in 5 above, other than:

(a) specified leasing property of a corporation that was throughout the year a corporation described in subsection 1100(16) of the Regulations;

(b) property acquired by a taxpayer when a lease of the property terminates and the "50% rule" had already applied to the taxpayer for the property in a pre-

vious year because the taxpayer had made an election, under section 16.1, to be considered as having acquired the leased property; and

(c) property for which CCA claims were deferred under the available for use rules but which are considered to be available for use under the "rolling-start" rule in paragraph $13(27)(b)$ or $(28)(c)$.

Offshore Drilling Vessels

7. The term "offshore drilling vessel" refers to:

(a) floating drillships, stabilized by dynamic positioning and, where possible, by anchoring; and

(b) semi-submergible rigs stabilized by submerging pontoons to a more stable depth and by anchoring. An offshore drilling platform of the "jack-up" type that stands on the seabed is not considered to be a vessel. For a discussion of CCA for drilling rigs that are not vessels, see the current version of Interpretation Bulletin IT-476, *Capital Cost Allowance — Gas and Oil Exploration and Production Equipment.*

8. Depending on the circumstances, an "offshore drilling vessel" could be included in any one of the following classes:

(a) Class 7 (see 2 above), if it is not a vessel described in (b), (c) or (d);

(b) a separate class established for each qualifying vessel by subsection 1101(2a) of the Regulations, if the vessel meets the requirements of that Regulation (i.e., it is a "Canadian vessel" — see 5 above);

(c) Class 41, when the vessel so qualifies both as to principal design and acquisition dates (see 9 below), if it is not a vessel described in (b); or

(d) a separate class for vessels meeting the requirements of subsection 1101(2b) of the Regulations both as to principal design and acquisition dates (see 10 below), if it is not a vessel described in (b).

9. A vessel (including the furniture, fittings, radiocommunication equipment and other equipment attached thereto) acquired

¶3160

after 1987 will generally be included in Class 41 if it is designed principally for the purpose of:

(a) determining the existence, location, extent or quality of accumulations of petroleum, natural gas or mineral resources; or

(b) drilling oil or gas wells.

The maximum annual rate of CCA for Class 41 property is 25% applied to the undepreciated capital cost of the class, subject to the "50% rule" and the "available for use" rules, as noted in 2 above.

However, a vessel will not be included in Class 41 if it was acquired before 1990 and:

(i) pursuant to a written obligation entered into by the taxpayer before June 18, 1987;

(ii) was under construction by or on behalf of the taxpayer on June 18, 1987; or

(iii) is machinery and equipment that is a fixed and integral part of property that was under construction by or on behalf of the taxpayer on June 18, 1987.

In addition, as discussed in 8 above, a vessel will not be included in Class 41 if it is a "Canadian vessel."

10. For offshore drilling vessels that otherwise qualify for the maximum annual CCA rate of 15% under Class 7, paragraph 1100(1)(va) of the Regulations permits the deduction of an additional maximum annual CCA of 15%. These vessels are in a separate prescribed class under subsection 1101(2b) of the Regulations. The combined maximum annual CCA rate is, in effect, 30% for this separate class of vessels, subject to the "50% rule" and the available for use rules, as noted in 2 above. Under subsection 1101(2b) of the Regulations, a separate class is prescribed for all vessels described in Class 7 in Schedule II, rather than a separate class for each vessel. Vessels, including the furniture, fittings, radiocommunication equipment and other equipment attached thereto, will so qualify for the separate prescribed class if they are acquired by a taxpayer:

(a) after May 25, 1976, and are designed principally for the purpose of:

(i) determining the existence, location, extent or quality of accumulations of petroleum or natural gas (other than mineral resources); or

(ii) drilling oil or gas wells; or

(b) after May 22, 1979, and designed principally for the purpose of determining the existence, location, extent or quality of mineral resources.

Most offshore drilling vessels acquired after 1987 will be included in Class 41 and not a separate prescribed class under subsection 1101(2b) of the Regulations. In addition, as discussed in 8 above, a vessel will not be included in a separate prescribed class under subsection 1101(2b) of the Regulations if it is a "Canadian vessel."

Property Acquired by Transfer, Amalgamation or Winding-Up

11. When a taxpayer acquires a property, subsection 1102(14) of the Regulations generally requires the taxpayer to place the property in the same prescribed class or separate prescribed class as that of the vendor of the property provided:

(a) the property is acquired by the taxpayer after June 17, 1987 in the course of a qualifying butterfly reorganization, as described in paragraph 55(3)(b); or

(b) the taxpayer and the vendor were not dealing at arm's length (otherwise than by a paragraph 251(5)(b) right for acquisitions after December 15, 1987) at the time the property was acquired.

In determining whether the parties are not dealing at arm's length for this purpose, the anti-avoidance rule in subsection 1102(20) of the Regulations should be consulted for property acquired after December 15, 1987.

Subsection 1102(14.1) of the Regulations provides that when a taxpayer has acquired property of a class that had been previously owned before May 26, 1976, by either the taxpayer or a person with whom the taxpayer did not deal at arm's length at the time of the acquisition, and at the time that the property was previously owned it was property of a different class, the property is deemed to be property of the original class. This rule is subject to the exception, generally applicable to acquisitions after

¶3160

December 15, 1987, that the non-arm's length relationship was not solely as a result of a right referred to in paragraph 251(5)(*b*). Unlike subsection 1102(14) of the Regulations, subsection 1102(14.1) only applies to property previously owned before May 26, 1976.

Recaptured Depreciation

12. The disposition of a vessel may give rise to the recapture of CCA in the usual manner under subsection 13(1) (see the current version of Interpretation Bulletin IT-478, *Capital Cost Allowance — Recapture and Terminal Loss*). Relief may be available by deferring the recapture of CCA under the replacement property rules described in subsection 13(4) (see the current version of Interpretation Bulletin IT-259, *Exchanges of Property*) or under subsection 13(16) (see 13 below).

13. A taxpayer may, under subsection 13(16), elect to defer the recognition of the recapture of CCA on the disposition of a vessel. Under the election, the proceeds of disposition from a vessel that would have been included in the taxpayer's income for that year are treated as proceeds of disposition of property of another prescribed class that includes a vessel owned by the taxpayer. The election must be made before the time prescribed for the filing of the taxpayer's income tax return for the year in which the vessel was disposed.

14. When a vessel is acquired in or as a result of a transaction to which subsection 1102(14) or 1102(14.1) of the Regulations applies (see 11 above), the fact that the former owner had a choice as to the income tax treatment of the proceeds of disposition, under subsection 13(16), will not disqualify the vessel from continuing to be property of that same prescribed class or separate prescribed class to the purchaser. Consequently, the purchaser will be eligible to claim CCA for that vessel at the same rate that the former owner was entitled to.

15. When a separate prescribed class has been constituted by virtue of the conversion of a vessel (see 5(b) and (c) above), and the vessel is disposed of by the owner, subsection 13(17) deems that class to have been transferred to the class in which the vessel was included immediately before its disposition. In dealing with the proceeds of disposition, a taxpayer to whom subsection 13(17) applies may also elect under subsection

13(16) (see 13 above). When a converted vessel is acquired in or as a result of a transaction to which subsection 1102(14) or 1102(14.1) of the Regulations applies (see 11 above), it is considered that, although the provisions of subsections 13(16) and 13(17) apply and continue to apply to the taxpayer who disposed of the vessel, the taxpayer acquiring the converted vessel is allowed to include the conversion cost in the separate prescribed class in which the cost had been included by the transferor before the transfer. Consequently, the taxpayer acquiring the converted vessel will be entitled to claim accelerated CCA for the conversion cost at the rate permitted by paragraph 1100(1)(*v*) of the Regulations (as described in 5 above).

Explanation of Changes

Introduction

The purpose of the *Explanation of Changes* is to give the reasons for the revisions to an interpretation bulletin. It outlines revisions that we have made as a result of changes to the law, as well as changes reflecting new or revised departmental interpretations.

Overview

This bulletin updates Interpretation Bulletin IT-267R, and its March 14, 1985 Special Release, which explain the capital cost allowance provisions for vessels. We revised the bulletin to delete the references to the requirement for certificates to be obtained from the Minister of Regional Industrial Expansion (or its successors) regarding the certification of vessels for accelerated capital cost allowance purposes. Such certificates are not required for property acquired after July 13, 1990. The amendments to the Act and Regulations have been enacted by S.C. 1991, c. 49 (former Bill C-18) and P.C. 1994-139, SOR/91-196, January 25, 1994, respectively. The revised bulletin also deals with vessels that may be Class 41 property.

The contents of this bulletin are not affected by any draft legislation released prior to January 1, 1995.

Legislative and Other Changes

¶1 (portions of former ¶s 4 and 16) contains the definition of "vessel." We have deleted a portion of former ¶4 because it referred to the *Maritime Code Act* that has

¶3160

not yet been proclaimed into force. We have also deleted a portion of former ¶16 because it dealt with the now repealed requirement for the certification of vessels.

¶2 (former ¶1) outlines the general operation of the capital cost allowance ("CCA") system for vessels. ¶2 now also refers to the possible application of the "50% rule" for property acquisitions in a year and the "available for use" rules (which were introduced in Bill C-18).

We have added new ¶3 to state that vessels under construction (except for Class 41 vessels) are property that is included in Class 7.

We have revised ¶5 (former ¶6) to remove the requirement for vessels (and conversion plans for vessels) to be certified, and to refer to the impact of the "available for use" rules on the acquisition date of vessels for purposes of the accelerated CCA provisions under paragraph $1100(1)(v)$ of the Regulations.

We have added new ¶6 to indicate the types of properties to which the "50% rule" for property acquired in a year does not apply for purposes of paragraph $1100(1)(v)$ of the Regulations.

We have amended ¶8 to provide for the classification of vessels in Class 41 and to delete references to the certification requirement.

New ¶9 outlines the vessels to be included in Class 41, and the CCA rate that applies to that class.

We have revised ¶11 (former ¶13) because of amendments to subsection 1102(14) of the Regulations, and the addition of subsections 1102(14.1) and 1102(20) to the Regulations. In addition, we have deleted the references to the certification requirement.

We have revised ¶12 (former ¶10) to delete information relating to special depreciation taken before 1949, and to subsection 13(15), because such information is dated and is only relevant for a small number of taxpayers.

We have deleted former ¶s 2 and 5 because they dealt with dated information that applies to few taxpayers. Former ¶2 described acquisitions of property before 1972, and former ¶5 outlined the CCA provisions that applies to certain vessels constructed or converted in the 1940s.

We have deleted former ¶s 14, 15 and 18 of IT-267R because they outlined the now obsolete certification requirements and procedures.

We have deleted former ¶17 because it refers to government assistance, a topic which is more fully covered in the current version of Interpretation Bulletin IT-273, *Government Assistance — General Comments.*

We have made a number of other changes to improve the overall clarity and readability of the bulletin.

[3165] Interpretation Bulletin IT-274R: Rental Properties — Capital Cost of $50,000 or More

[*Interpretation Bulletin IT-274R is dated April 9, 1990.*]

Reference: Subsection 1101(1ac) of the Income Tax Regulations (also subsections 1100(11) and 1100(14), 1101(1ad) and 1101(5b) and 1103(1) of the Income Tax Regulations)

Application

This bulletin replaces and cancels Interpretation Bulletin IT-274 dated December 22, 1975.

Summary

This bulletin deals with the requirement to include in a separate capital cost allowance class each rental property acquired at a capital cost of $50,000 or more.

Discussion and Interpretation

1. Subsection 1101(1ac) of the Regulations prescribes a separate class for each rental property (as defined by subsection 1100(14) of the Regulations) that a taxpayer has acquired after 1971 at a capital cost of $50,000 or more, other than a building the erection of which commenced or was agreed to in writing before 1972. These provisions also apply to all deemed acquisitions of

¶3165

rental property under the Act but do not apply to acquisitions in the specific circumstances outlined in subsection 1101(1ad) of the Regulations. Also excepted are properties that are leasehold interests in real property described in subsection 1100(13) of the Regulations which are required to be included in a separate class for all such leasehold interests by virtue of subsection 1101(5h) of the Regulations.

2. In determining the capital cost of a rental property only the portion of the total purchase price that would be allocable to Class 1, 3, 6 or 13 is considered in deciding whether the rental property should be in a separate class. For example, the proper portion of the total purchase price of a furnished apartment building is allocated to land, furniture and building (the rental property).

3. In the case of a condominium building or row-housing structure where a taxpayer has acquired one or more units, the cost of the unit or the aggregate cost of all the units within the same building or structure will constitute one separate class if this cost or aggregate cost is $50,000 or more. If a taxpayer owns units in different buildings or structures, the separate class provisions of subsection 1101(1ac) of the Regulations apply to any individual building or structure that has an aggregate cost to the taxpayer of $50,000 or more. Where the cost of the unit includes a share in the common property, the proper portion should be allocated to land and other classes of property held in common to determine the cost of the rental property itself.

4. Ordinarily additions made after 1971 to a rental property acquired before 1972 do not put it in a separate class under subsection 1101(1ac) of the Regulations even though the capital cost of the additions may be $50,000 or more. Each rental property acquired after 1971 for less than $50,000 must be put in a separate class if subsequent additions increase its capital cost to at least $50,000. Subsection 13(5) of the Act outlines the procedure for transferring the property into the separate class (see the current version of IT-190).

5. A separate class is not prescribed for a share in a rental property acquired by a taxpayer for less than $50,000 under a tenancy in common or joint tenancy even though the total capital cost of the property is $50,000 or more. However, a separate class is prescribed for each rental property, having a total capital cost of $50,000 or more, that is partnership property even if one or more partners' interest in the partnership is less than $50,000.

6. For taxation years prior to 1994, multiple-unit residential buildings (MURBs) under Classes 31 and 32 of Schedule II are excluded from the definition of rental property pursuant to paragraph 1100(14)(a) of the Regulations. Thus MURBs are not subject to the rental loss restrictions on capital cost allowances in subsection 1100(11) of the Regulations until taxation years after 1993. However, by virtue of subsection 1101(5b) of the Regulations, where a property of Class 31 or 32 of Schedule II has a capital cost to the taxpayer of $50,000 or more, a separate class for it is prescribed; therefore, the principles regarding separate classes for rental properties with capital costs of $50,000 or more which are discussed in this bulletin will apply in the case of Class 31 or 32 buildings. For further information on MURBs, refer to the current version of IT-367.

7. Subsection 1101(1ac) of the Regulations applies whether the rental income from the rental property is income from a business or property. Where the income is from a business, a taxpayer may elect under subsection 1103(1) of the Regulations (see the current version of IT-327) to transfer to Class 1 all properties (including rental properties) otherwise included in Classes 2 to 12 inclusive and acquired for the purpose of gaining or producing income from the same business. When the election is made, each rental property acquired after 1971 with a capital cost of $50,000 or more transferred to Class 1 must be put in a separate Class 1.

¶3165

[3175] Interpretation Bulletin IT-285R2: Capital Cost Allowance — General Comments

[*Interpretation Bulletin IT-285R2 is dated March 31, 1994.*]

Reference: Paragraph $20(1)(a)$ (also paragraph $18(1)(b)$ and Part XI of the Income Tax Regulations)

Application

This bulletin cancels and replaces Interpretation Bulletin IT-285R dated October 11, 1985 and the Special Release to IT-285R dated March 31, 1987, as well as the following bulletins (relevant commentary has been incorporated into this bulletin):

IT-50R *Capital Cost Allowances — Date of Acquisition of Depreciable Property*

IT-174R *Capital Cost Allowance — Meaning of "Capital Cost of Property"*

IT-205 *Capital Cost Allowance — Capital Cost of Property in a Foreign Country*

Summary

This bulletin discusses the capital cost allowance system in general terms. Capital cost allowance (CCA) replaces accounting depreciation for income tax purposes. The term "capital cost" generally means the actual cost of a depreciable property; however, there are many sections of the *Income Tax Act* that can change the capital cost, some of which are discussed in this bulletin. A listing of other bulletins that discuss the determination of capital cost can be found at the end of this bulletin. This bulletin also discusses the date a depreciable property is considered to have been acquired and makes reference to the possible application of the "available for use rules". These rules may delay a CCA claim for up to two years if a depreciable property is acquired but is not considered to be "available for use". The "50% rule", which may restrict capital cost allowance in the year an asset is acquired, is also discussed. A reference to depreciable property in this bulletin does not include farming or fishing assets acquired before January 1, 1972, and classified for depreciation purposes under Part XVII of the Regulations. Certain types of assets and the classes into which they fall for capital cost allowance purposes are discussed in other interpretation bulletins listed at the end of this bulletin. The issues in this bulletin are discussed under the following headings and under the paragraphs noted:

	Paragraphs
General	1-2
Classes of Depreciable Property	3-7
Capital Cost of Property	6-12
Reduction of Capital Cost — Assistance or Inducements . .	13-14
Ownership	15-22
"50% Rule" — Property Acquired in the Year	23-25
Short Fiscal Period	26
Other Interpretation Bulletins	27-28

Discussion and Interpretation

General

1. In computing income from a business or property, paragraph $18(1)(b)$ prohibits the deduction of any outlay, loss or replacement of capital, payment on account of capital or any allowance for depreciation, obsolescence or depletion, unless specifically allowed in Part I of the Act. Paragraph $20(1)(a)$ allows a deduction, in computing the income from a business or property, of any amount allowed by Regulation in respect of the capital cost of a property. The amount that is allowed by Regulation is referred to as "capital cost allowance" (CCA).

2. Under Part XI of the Regulations, depreciable property is grouped into prescribed classes that are described in Schedule II of the Regulations. The maximum rate of CCA allowed is prescribed for each class in subsection 1100(1) of the Regulations. In most cases, CCA is calculated on a diminishing balance and expressed as a percentage of the undepreciated capital cost of the class at year-end. In general terms, "undepreciated capital cost" (UCC) is defined as the total capital cost of all the property in the class (whether or not still owned), less the total CCA previously claimed for all years and the net proceeds (or capital cost if less) from dispositions before that time of property that was included in the class. Most CCA rates are set out in paragraph 1100(1)(a) of the Regulations, while the remaining paragraphs of subsection 1100(1) of the Regulations set

¶3175

out a number of special rates applicable to specific types of property and certain additional accelerated allowances. In addition to the classes set out in Schedule II, certain separate classes are prescribed by section 1101 of the Regulations. In general, a taxpayer may deduct any amount up to the maximum available for the year taking into consideration any restrictions such as those mentioned in 12, 15 and 23 to 26 below or restrictions on certain types of property such as rental or leasing property (subsections 1100(11) to (20) of the Regulations) or specified leasing property (subsections 1100(1.1) to (1.3) of the Regulations). CCA that is available but not claimed in a year is not "carried forward" to the next year. However, any available CCA not claimed in a year remains as part of the UCC balance for CCA claims in future years.

Classes of Depreciable Property

3. A property is not depreciable property and CCA cannot be claimed for it unless it fits within the description of a class in Schedule II or Part XI of the Regulations. A tangible capital property not specifically covered in any other class may not be placed in what appears to be the most appropriate class; rather, it is included in Class 8 of Schedule II, unless it is excluded by the specific exceptions therein or is excluded by section 1102 of the Regulations. Property that is excluded is not depreciable property and no CCA is available for that property. Some of the exclusions under section 1102 of the Regulations are discussed in the current version of IT-128, *Capital Cost Allowance — Depreciable Property.*

4. Certain words used in the Regulations to describe properties may have wider meanings than those ordinarily attributed to them. For example, "automotive equipment" in Class 10 of Schedule II includes outboard motors and air cushion vehicles popularly known as "hovercraft". Other examples appear in other interpretation bulletins on the subject of capital cost allowance (see 27 below).

5. The descriptive phrase "property that would otherwise be included in" appears in several classes in Schedule II, which could lead to uncertainty as to the class in which a particular property may belong. If a property is described in more than one class and the descriptive phrase mentioned above appears in only one of those classes, the property

must be included in the class in which the phrase appears. If, however, the descriptive phrase appears in more than one of those classes in which the property is described, the taxpayer may choose from among those in which the phrase appears, providing that the other requirements of the chosen class are met. For example, a taxpayer may choose to include air pollution equipment acquired in connection with mining activities in Class 27 rather than Class 41. Although ordinarily in such circumstances the property is included in the class allowing the greater CCA, the taxpayer may choose to place it in another class to avoid immediate recapture of CCA on the disposition of other property of that class.

6. The descriptive phrase, "not included in any other class", appears frequently in Schedule II. A property may be included in a class in which such phrase appears only if it is not described in another class within Schedule II or any separate class established under Part XI of the Regulations. If the descriptive phrase appears in all classes in which a property is described, the taxpayer may choose from among them.

7. Section 1103 of the Regulations contains elections that, under certain conditions, permit a taxpayer to transfer property otherwise included in one class to another class. For details on these elections see the current version of IT-327, *Capital Cost Allowance — Elections* under Regulation 1103.

Capital Cost of Property

8. The term "capital cost of property" generally means the full cost to the taxpayer of acquiring the property and includes:

(a) legal, accounting, engineering or other fees incurred to acquire the property; and

(b) in the case of a property a taxpayer manufactures for the taxpayer's own use, it includes material, labour and overhead costs reasonably attributable to the property, but nothing for any profit which might have been earned had the asset been sold.

In addition, by virtue of subsections 18(3.1) to 18(3.7), the capital cost of a building includes certain outlays or expenses (commonly referred to as "soft costs") that are costs attributable to the period of, and

¶3175

relating to, the construction, renovation or alteration of the building or such costs related to the ownership, during that period, of land subjacent to the building, or land contiguous to the land subjacent to the building that is used (or intended to be used) for a parking area, driveway, yard, garden or any similar use and is necessary for the use (or intended use) of the building.

Note: If the draft legislation released by the Minister of Finance on August 30, 1993 is enacted into law as currently proposed, new subsection 13(33) will provide that, for greater certainty, where a person acquires a depreciable property (the acquired property) for consideration that includes a transfer of property (for example, a trade-in), the portion of the cost to the person of the acquired property attributable to the transfer shall not exceed the fair market value of the transferred property. This new subsection will apply to depreciable property acquired after November 1992.

9. If a property is acquired in a transaction requiring payment in a foreign currency, including property situated in a foreign country and used to earn income, the historical cost of the property should be expressed in Canadian dollars. Generally, the rate of exchange in effect on the date of acquisition should be used to convert the amount to Canadian dollars. However, payments on account of the purchase price of the property made before the date of acquisition should be converted to Canadian dollars using the exchange rate on the dates of such payments. Foreign exchange gains and losses on payments made after the date of acquisition do not form part of the capital cost of the property.

10. In cases where a taxpayer becomes a resident of Canada and owns depreciable property in a foreign country, which is property that was and continues to be used to earn income in that foreign country, the capital cost of that depreciable property for CCA purposes is the historical cost of the property converted to Canadian dollars in the manner explained in 9 above. The capital cost will not be reduced by any depreciation allowances recognized by that foreign country.

Note: If the draft legislation released by the Minister of Finance on August 30, 1993 is enacted into law as currently pro-

posed, the capital cost of such depreciable property for CCA purposes will, by virtue of proposed paragraphs 128.1(1)(b) and (c), be the fair market value of the property immediately before the time immediately before the taxpayer becomes a resident of Canada. This results from the fact that subsection 128.1(1) will apply for purposes of the Act, while subsection 48(3) (repealed by the draft legislation) applied for purposes of subdivision c of division B. It should also be noted that under proposed paragraph 128.1(1)(a), where a taxpayer is a corporation or a trust, the taxpayer's taxation year shall be deemed to have ended immediately before becoming a resident of Canada and a new taxation year shall be deemed to have commenced at the time the taxpayer becomes resident. These amendments will apply after 1992; however, they may apply earlier in respect of a corporation electing to be subject to proposed new subsection 250(5.1) (in which case, they will apply from the corporation's time of continuation).

11. If an old building used by a taxpayer for a long time to earn income is demolished to build a new one, the cost of demolition is not considered to be part of the capital cost of the new building (unless the taxpayer so desires), but may be deducted as an expense in the year. The tax treatment of the costs of demolishing a building incidentally acquired on obtaining a site is discussed in the current versions of IT-128, *Capital Cost Allowance — Depreciable Property* and IT-485, *Cost of Clearing or Levelling Land.*

12. Where a building or other structure is being erected by or for a taxpayer on land owned by the taxpayer or where a taxpayer erects, makes an addition or makes alterations to a building or other structure to which paragraph 1102(5)(a) of the Regulations applies, the taxpayer is considered to have acquired a building or other structure, at any particular time, to the extent of:

(a) the construction costs incurred by the taxpayer to that time, including the cost to the taxpayer of materials that have been put in place, but not including holdbacks that constitute a conditional liability (for example, a holdback which requires that the work be approved by the taxpayer's architect or engineer before payment), or

¶3175

(b) progress billings received by the taxpayer to that time, net of any holdbacks that constitute a conditional liability.

However, a building (or part thereof) that is under construction may be considered not to be available for use and, as a result, CCA may be restricted by the "available for use rules" in subsections 13(26) and 13(28).

Reduction of Capital Cost — Assistance or Inducements

13. Generally, the capital cost of property is incurred by a taxpayer if the expenditures or outlays for the acquisition of the property are met by the taxpayer. On occasion, however, a taxpayer in question may receive or be entitled to receive some form of assistance for the acquisition. If any form of assistance is received, the capital cost of the property for which it was received may have to be reduced or the amount of the assistance included in income. See the current version of IT-273, *Government Assistance — General Comments*, if any form of assistance has been received.

14. Where a taxpayer acquires depreciable property and at a later date the vendor agrees to reduce the amount owing under a negotiated adjustment of the purchase price, the capital cost of the property is reduced by the amount of the reduction at the beginning of the taxation year in which the price adjustment takes place. As a result of the reduction to the capital cost of the property, the undepreciated capital cost of the class of the property is reduced by the same amount and at the same time. If the adjustment can be established to be a true forgiveness of debt, rather than a reduction in the purchase price, the rules in section 80 will apply.

Ownership

15. CCA may be claimed only for property owned by the taxpayer (however, see 22 below) or property in which the taxpayer has a leasehold interest. However, a taxpayer who acquires or holds property as an agent or nominee for another cannot claim CCA on such property. It should be noted that, in calculating the income of a partnership, subsection 96(1) of the Act and subsection 1102(1a) of the Regulations require that partnership property (including depreciable property) be accounted for as if it were owned at the partnership level. If the

depreciable property acquired is not considered "available for use", the CCA may be restricted until such a time as it is available for use. The "available for use rules" are in subsections 13(26) to (31) of the Act.

16. If a taxpayer's year-end intervenes between the date the taxpayer ordered a depreciable property and the date it was delivered to the taxpayer in usable condition, it sometimes becomes necessary to determine whether, for CCA purposes, the taxpayer "acquired" the property before the end of the taxation year.

17. Generally, a taxpayer will be considered to have acquired a depreciable property at the earlier of:

(a) the date on which title to it is obtained, and

(b) the date on which the taxpayer has all the incidents of ownership such as possession, use, and risk, even though legal title remains in the vendor as security for the purchase price (as is commercial practice under a conditional sale agreement).

In order that the cost of an asset may fall within a specified class, the purchaser must have a current ownership right in the asset itself and not merely rights under a contract, of which the asset is the subject, to acquire it in the future.

18. In determining whether or not depreciable property is acquired by a taxpayer, the legal relationship between the vendor and the purchaser of the property should be reviewed. For example, where chattels are being acquired, the relevant sale of goods legislation would be applicable. Each of the provinces (other than Quebec) has a *Sale of Goods Act* pertaining to sales of chattels laying down substantially the same rules for the ownership rights to assets bought and sold. The basic rule is that property in respect of specific assets passes, and is therefore acquired by the purchaser, at the time when the parties to the contract intend it to pass as evidenced by the terms of the contract, the conduct of the parties and any other circumstances.

19. If, however, the intention of the parties is not evidenced as discussed above, the following rules apply to determine when property is to pass:

¶3175

(a) if there is an unconditional contract for the sale of a specific asset in a deliverable state, property will pass to the purchaser when the contract is made, and it is immaterial whether the time of payment or delivery or both are postponed;

(b) if there is a contract for the sale of a specific asset and:

(i) the seller is bound to do something to the asset to put it into a deliverable state, or

(ii) the asset is in a deliverable state, but the seller must weigh, measure, test or do some other act or thing to ascertain the price,

then property does not pass until the seller has satisfied those conditions and the purchaser has notice thereof.

20. For the purpose of 18 and 19 above, property can pass and acquisition take place only if the asset is in existence and, even then, only if it is a "specific" asset, i.e., one that can be identified as the object of the contract. For example, this requirement is not met by a contract for the purchase of machinery which is described simply as being of a certain make and model, but it is met if the machinery is further identified by its serial number, since only one particular machine can be so described. It should be noted here that it is customary in some industries, for example, the automotive and other heavy equipment manufacturing industry, to issue contracts that describe the property being purchased as being of a certain make, model and even serial number at a time when the property does not exist but is scheduled for production. Under this type of contract, the purchaser acquires the property when the property has been produced and the purchaser has knowledge that it is in a deliverable state.

21. In most cases, where a taxpayer incurs a cost for a capital asset, the ownership of, or a lease to, that asset will be obtained either at the time the cost was incurred or at a later date. However, there may be circumstances in which neither a freehold nor a leasehold interest in the property is acquired. If a taxpayer constructs and incurs the cost of a structure on land owned by another person, or otherwise incorporates an asset into property owned by another as an integral part thereof, and does not have a leasehold interest in or ownership of the asset, CCA may not be claimed for the property. This will be the case where a road providing access to a taxpayer's plant is built at the taxpayer's expense on land owned by a municipality. Also, capital expenditures for architectural and engineering services in preparing plans and estimates for new plants, or for additions to existing plants or other construction work of a capital nature, are not subject to CCA if the work for which the plans and estimates were prepared is not carried out. However, an expenditure of this nature may be an eligible capital expenditure (defined in paragraph $14(5)(b)$) for which an allowance is permitted under paragraph $20(1)(b)$ (see the current version of IT-143, *Meaning of Eligible Capital Expenditure*).

22. Where by joint election subsection 16.1(1) applies to leased tangible property, the lessee is deemed to have acquired the property, at the particular time the lease commenced, at a cost equal to its fair market value at that time. Consequently, the lessee may be eligible to claim CCA on the property, although the lessee does not own the property.

"50% Rule" — Property Acquired in the Year

23. Subsection 1100(2) of the Regulations limits CCA claims in the taxation year of acquisition of most depreciable property to the amount otherwise available less one-half of the CCA attributable to "net acquisitions" in the year, determined on a class by class basis. The term "net acquisitions" refers to cost of acquisitions in the year in excess of net proceeds of disposition (or capital cost if less) in that year. Thus, where the lesser of net proceeds of disposition and capital cost of property of a particular class in a taxation year exceeds the costs of any additions to the same class in that year, the rule has no effect.

24. The following properties are exempt from the application of the 50% rule:

(a) Class 12 property (thus preserving the availability of 100% write off in the year of acquisition) except:

(i) a motion picture film or video tape that is a television commercial message,

¶3175

(ii) Class 12(o) computer software (i.e., not systems software or certain property described in Class 12(s)),

(iii) a certified production acquired before 1988 and a certified feature film,

(iv) a videotape cassette acquired after February 15, 1984 for the purpose of renting and that is not expected to be rented to any one person for more than 7 days in any 30 day period,

(v) a die, jig, pattern, mould or last, and

(vi) the cutting or shaping part in a machine;

(b) such patents, franchises, concessions or licences as are included in Class 14;

(c) property acquired for the purpose of cutting and removing merchantable timber included in Class 15;

(d) the following properties to which special 50% rules apply:

(i) property of Classes 24, 27, 29 and 34 to which paragraphs 1100(1)(t) and (ta) of the Regulations apply (see the current versions of IT-147, *Capital Cost Allowance — Accelerated Write-Off of Manufacturing and Processing Machinery and Equipment* and IT-336, *Capital Cost Allowance — Pollution Control Property*), and

(ii) property of Class 13 to which paragraph 1100(1)(b) of the Regulations applies (see the current version of IT-464, *CCA — Leasehold Interests*);

(e) Class 23 property (in connection with Expo 86) acquired after 1983 for which a 100% write off is available in the year of acquisition;

(f) a certified production acquired after 1987;

(g) vessels and other costs to which paragraph 1100(1)(v) of the Regulations applies (see the current version of IT-267, *Capital Cost Allowance — Vessels*);

(h) specified leasing property of a corporation that was throughout the year a

corporation described in subsection 1100(16) of the Regulations;

(i) property that was deemed to have been acquired in a preceding taxation year under paragraph 16.1(1)(b) (see 22 above) in respect of a lease to which the property was subject immediately before the taxpayer last acquired the property; and

(j) property considered to have become available for use by the taxpayer in the year by reason of paragraph 13(27)(b) or 13(28)(c).

25. Application of the 50% rule described in 23 above is also subject to exemptions for the acquisition of property in a non-arm's length transaction (except where paragraph 251(5)(b) applies) and in the course of certain corporate reorganizations. These exemptions, contained in subsection 1100(2.2) of the Regulations, are applicable only if:

(a) the property was depreciable property of the transferor, and was owned continuously by that person, either from November 12, 1981 or from a date that was at least 364 days before the end of the transferee's taxation year in which the property was acquired (by the transferee), to the date of acquisition; or

(b) the property was exempted from the 50% rule because of the application of subsection 1100(2.1) or 1100(2.2) of the Regulations to the transferor.

Example: Mr. A is the controlling shareholder of a corporation which has a taxation year ending on December 31. On November 1, 1991, Mr. A sold to the corporation depreciable property which he had owned since December 15, 1990. The property would be excluded from the 50% rule because Mr. A had owned it continuously from a date (December 15, 1990) that was at least 364 days before the end of the corporation's taxation year in which the corporation acquired the property (December 31, 1991), until it was acquired by the corporation. Even if Mr. A had only acquired the property on June 30, 1991 but he had acquired it from his father, both Mr. A and the corporation would be exempted from the application of the 50% rule on their acquisitions, provided

¶3175

the property was depreciable property of the father and the father acquired it at least 364 days before the end of Mr. A's 1991 taxation year and owned it continuously until it was acquired by Mr. A.

Short Fiscal Period

26. If a taxpayer's fiscal period is less than 12 months, subsection 1100(3) of the Regulations restricts CCA claims to that portion of the maximum amount otherwise allowable that the number of days in the fiscal period is of 365 (see the current version of IT-172, *Capital Cost Allowance — Taxation Year of Individuals*). This applies to all of the CCA provisions in subsection 1100(1) of the Regulations except for Classes 14 and 15, and paragraphs 1100(1)(e) (Timber Limits and Cutting Rights), 1100(1)(g) (Industrial Mineral Mines), 1100(1)(l) (Additional Allowances — Certified Productions), 1100(1)(w) (Additional Allowances — Class 28), 1100(1)(x) (Mines) and 1100(1)(y) and (ya) (Additional Allowances — Class 41) of the Regulations. The provisions of subsection 1100(3) of the Regulations apply in addition to the 50% rule, i.e., if an asset is acquired in a taxation year of six month's duration, in effect, only one-quarter (approximately) of the maximum annual rate of CCA that would normally be available for that asset will be allowed in that taxation year.

Other Interpretation Bulletins

27. Refer to the current version of the following bulletins (listed alphabetically by subject) for information on CCA claims regarding particular types of property:

Building IT-79
Certified Feature Productions and
Certified Short Productions IT-441

Class 8 property IT-472
"Construction" — Meaning of Con-
dominiums IT-411 IT-304
Contractor's moveable equipment . . IT-306
Disposition of depreciable property IT-220
Earth-moving equipment IT-469
Elections under Regulation 1103 . . IT-327
Emphyteutic lease IT-324
Gas and oil exploration and pro-
duction equipment IT-476
Industrial mineral mines IT-492
Leasehold interests IT-464
Leasing property IT-443
Logging assets IT-501
Manufacturing and processing
machinery and equipment IT-147
Multi-unit residential buildings IT-367
Partial disposition of property IT-418
Patents, franchises, concessions
and licences IT-477
Pipelines IT-482
Pollution control property IT-336
Radio and television equipment . . . IT-317
Recapture and terminal loss IT-478
Rental properties — $50,000 or
more IT-274
Rental properties — restrictions . . . IT-195
Taxation year of individuals IT-172
Transferred and misclassified prop-
erty IT-190
Vessels IT-267
Video tapes, films, computer
software and master recording
tapes IT-283

28. In certain circumstances, the capital cost of depreciable property may be determined or altered by special provisions in the Act. The following list indicates some of these provisions and the interpretation bulletins currently issued that provide details of their application:

The Act	*Description of provision discussed in bulletin*	*Bulletin*
13(5),(6)	Transferred property or misclassified property	IT-190
13(7)	Passenger vehicle cost in excess of $20,000	IT-521
13(7.1)	Receipt of inducements or other forms of assistance	IT-273
13(12)	Expenses of representation	IT-99
13(21)(b)	Capital cost allowance — depreciable property	IT-128
13(21)(c)	Conversion of property to and from inventory	IT-102
20(1)(a), (aa)	Cost of clearing or levelling land	IT-485
20(1)(a), 21(1)	Election to capitalize cost of borrowed money	IT-121
44	Replacement property, expropriation of property	IT-259
69(1)	Property acquired in "non-arm's length" transaction	IT-169
69(1)	Property acquired as a gift or from inheritance	IT-209
80	Debtors gain on settlement of debt	IT-293

¶3175

The Act	*Description of provision discussed in bulletin*	*Bulletin*
85	Transfer of property to a corporation	IT-291
98(3)	Distribution of property on cessation of partnership	IT-471
107(2)	Property distributed by trust to a capital beneficiary	IT-209
127(5)	Investment tax credit	IT-331

Explanation of Changes

Introduction

The purpose of the *Explanation of Changes* is to give the reasons for the revisions to an interpretation bulletin. It outlines revisions that we have made as a result of changes to the law, as well as changes reflecting new or revised departmental interpretations.

Overview

This bulletin discusses the capital cost allowance system in general terms and some of the sections of the *Income Tax Act* that can change the capital cost of a property. It also discusses the date a depreciable property is considered to have been acquired, the "50% rule" (which may restrict capital cost allowance in the year of acquisition) and refers to the possible application of the "available for use rules". The bulletin also lists other bulletins which discuss certain types of assets and the classes into which they fall for capital cost allowance purposes, and bulletins which discuss the determination of capital cost.

The bulletin has been revised to incorporate and cancel the Special Release to IT-285R, as well as the following bulletins:

IT-50R *Capital Cost Allowances — Date of Acquisition of Depreciable Property*

IT-174R *Capital Cost Allowance — Meaning of "Capital Cost of Property"*

IT-205 *Capital Cost Allowance — Capital Cost of Property in a Foreign Country*

These bulletins have been consolidated for simplification purposes, by having all general comments regarding the capital cost allowance system in one bulletin. The revised bulletin also reflects various amendments which have been made to the *Income Tax Act* and to the Income Tax Regulations. The proposed amendments in the August 30, 1993 draft legislation which affect this bulletin have been reflected in italics where applicable (a Bill for this legislation will likely be introduced in the House of Com-

mons in the current session of Parliament). The contents of this bulletin are not affected by the draft Regulations in April 26, 1993 Federal Budget or by the proposed changes in Bill C-9 (this bill received first reading in the House of Commons on February 4, 1994).

The bulletin does not reflect the 5th Supplement to the Revised Statutes of Canada, 1985 or any changes which may result from the February 22, 1994 Federal Budget.

Legislative and Other Changes

Throughout the bulletin, we have made minor changes for clarification or readability purposes. New ¶7 has been added to refer to the elections under section 1103 of the Regulations that, under certain conditions, are available to taxpayers.

New ¶8 replaces former ¶s 1 and 2 of IT-174R. The new paragraph also includes a reference to the "soft costs" which, by virtue of subsections 18(3.1) to 18(3.7), are included in the capital cost of a building.

The note at the end of new ¶8 reflects proposed new subsection 13(33) in the August 30, 1993 draft legislation. This new provision will apply in determining the cost of a depreciable property which a person acquires for consideration that includes a transfer of property (for example, a trade-in).

New ¶9 replaces former ¶3 of IT-174R. An explanation has been added, for clarification purposes, with respect to the exchange rate to use where payments (in foreign currency) are made before the date of acquisition of a property.

New ¶10 replaces former ¶3 of IT-205 and has been updated for the same reasons as new ¶9 explained above.

The note at the end of new ¶10 has been added to reflect proposed new paragraphs 128.1(1)(*b*) and (*c*) in the August 30, 1993 draft legislation. These provisions will apply in determining the capital cost of a depreciable property for capital cost allowance

¶3175

(CCA) purposes, where a taxpayer becomes a resident of Canada and owns the property in a foreign country, which is property that was and continues to be used to earn income in that country.

New ¶11 replaces former ¶4 of IT-174R.

New ¶12 is former ¶7 of IT-50R, except that 12(a) and (b) have been revised to indicate that the costs incurred and the progress billings received should not include holdbacks that constitute a conditional liability. This revision reflects the decision in *Newfoundland Light & Power Co. Ltd. v. The Queen*, 90 DTC 6166, [1990] 1 CTC 229. A reference to the CCA restrictions under the "available for use rules" has also been added.

New ¶13 replaces former ¶s 5 and 7 of IT-174R. The new paragraph does not discuss assistance and inducements in detail. Instead, it refers to the current version of IT-273, *Government Assistance — General Comments*, which discusses this topic.

New ¶14 replaces former ¶6 of IT-174R.

New ¶15 has been added for clarification purposes. The comments in this paragraph are consistent with ¶2 of IT-128R, *Capital Cost Allowance — Depreciable Property*. The new paragraph also refers to the restrictions that apply when a taxpayer acquires or holds property as an agent or nominee for another. This agrees with the decision in *Garness v. M.N.R.*, 82 DTC 1663, [1982] CTC 2647. A reference to the CCA restrictions under the "available for use rules" has also been added.

New ¶s 16 to 20 contain the same information as ¶s 1 to 6 of IT-50R.

New ¶21 has been added to explain the restrictions that apply, with respect to CCA, where a taxpayer incorporates an asset into property owned by another as an integral part thereof, and the taxpayer does not have a leasehold interest in, or ownership of, the asset. The new paragraph also explains the treatment of architectural and engineering services for certain plans and estimates, where the work for which the plans and estimates were prepared is not carried out. This paragraph reflects the position set out in ¶3 of IT-128R.

New ¶22 has been added to explain that, where subsection 16.1(1) applies to leased tangible property, CCA may be claimed by a lessee although he or she does not own the property.

New ¶24 (former ¶10 of IT-285R) reflects amendments to subsection 1100(2) of the Regulations dated December 27, 1988, December 14, 1989, September 27, 1990, March 14, 1991 and January 27, 1994. These amendments added more exceptions to the "50% rule".

New ¶25 (former ¶11 of IT-285R) reflects amendments to subsection 1100(2.2) of the Regulations, dated December 14, 1989. These amendments relate to the situations where the subsection applies. In addition, the dates in the example of the new paragraph have been updated to more current dates and the sale of the property to the corporation, in this example, is no longer on the day of the corporation's year-end. This is to clarify that the property must be owned by the transferor from a day that is at least 364 days before the end of the transferee's taxation year, in which the transferee acquired the property, to the date of acquisition by the transferee.

New ¶26 (former ¶13 of IT-285R) reflects amendments to subsection 1100(3) of the Regulations which are applicable to the 1986 and subsequent taxation years.

Former ¶8 of IT-174R has been updated and divided into new ¶s 27 and 28. ¶27 refers to bulletins that give information regarding CCA claims for particular types of property, and ¶28 refers to certain provisions that determine or alter capital cost, with a reference to the relevant interpretation bulletins.

¶12 of IT-285R has been deleted since that paragraph applied to years which are now statute-barred.

¶8 of IT-50R, which dealt with motion picture films, has been deleted since this topic is discussed in the current version of IT-441, *Capital Cost Allowance — Certified Feature Productions and Certified Short Productions*.

¶s 1 and 2 of IT-205 have been deleted since the topics previously discussed in these paragraphs are now discussed in new ¶s 8 to 10.

¶3175

[3180]　Interpretation Bulletin IT-304R2:　Condominiums

[Interpretation Bulletin IT-304R2 is dated June 2, 2000.]

Reference:　Paragraphs $20(1)(a)$, $149(1)(l)$ and $150(1)(a)$ of the *Income Tax Act* (also paragraph $20(1)(aa)$ of the Act, Class 1 of Schedule II of the Income Tax Regulations and subsections $1100(11)$, $1100(14)$, $1101(1ac)$ and $1100(1ae)$ of the Regulations)

Application

This bulletin cancels and replaces Interpretation Bulletin IT-304R, dated May 13, 1991, formerly called *Capital Cost Allowance — Condominiums.*

Summary

This bulletin provides a brief overview of the condominium system of ownership in Canada. It explains, in general terms, the purpose and function of a condominium corporation created under provincial or territorial legislation. Also, it indicates the type of returns that a condominium corporation has to file for federal income tax purposes.

The bulletin also comments on the classification, for capital cost allowance and other purposes, of the costs incurred in the acquisition of a condominium unit. It comments on the tax treatment of the taxpayer's share of the costs incurred in maintaining the common property of a condominium development. These comments are pertinent in calculating the income or loss from the use of the condominium in the course of earning income from a business or property, but do not apply to an individual who owns and occupies the unit as a personal or vacation residence.

Discussion and Interpretation

Legal Basis of the Condominium

1. Each of Canada's ten provinces and three territories have statutes which recognize the condominium system of ownership, that is, the separate ownership of a condominium unit combined with shared ownership of common property within the condominium development. In this bulletin, we refer to terms used in the Condominium Acts of Ontario and British Columbia, which are representative of the terminology likely to be encountered in most other provincial and territorial legislation. (However, refer to ¶9 for the situation in the Province of Quebec.)

2. A condominium combines two distinct types of property ownership. A unit owner normally owns the unit in fee simple and shares ownership of the common areas of the condominium property with all the other unit owners. A condominium is legally created by the acceptance and registration of a "declaration" and "description" or a "strata plan" in the appropriate land registry or land titles office. Generally, the legal consequences of such registration are as follows:

(a) A condominium corporation, as discussed in ¶3, comes into existence and its members become the owners of the "units" or "strata lots" so created as a result of the incorporation (collectively referred to as units in this bulletin).

(b) Units may be dealt with and regarded as real property and are held in fee simple by the owner. A unit is either the separate unit structure or that portion of a multi-unit structure which consists of all the space between the partitions, floors and ceilings separating it from other units and from the common elements or common property.

(c) Each such owner shares ownership of the "common elements" or "common property," which is all that part of the land and buildings not included within any units. Such common elements or property include parking lots, landscaped areas, laundry rooms, hallways, elevators, and stairwells. The proportional interest in the common elements or property is established in the documents filed in the land registry or land titles office.

Although the term condominium is usually associated with a residential development, a condominium may also be a commercial, industrial, resort or mixed-use development. The purpose and type of any condominium development will be set out in its declaration, by-laws and rules.

Condominium Corporation

3. A condominium corporation created under Canadian provincial or territorial legislation is a corporation without share cap-

¶3180

ital whose members are the owners. The objects of such a corporation include, among other things, the management of the real property and any other assets of the corporation. The corporation also has a duty to control, manage and administer the common elements and assets of the corporation, and to ensure that the unit owners comply with the corporation's registered condominium documents, its by-laws and the provisions of the relevant condominium legislation. Provided that they are not contrary to relevant condominium legislation or the registered condominium documents, the board of the corporation may pass by-laws to govern, among other things:

- the management of the property;

- the maintenance of the common elements;

- the use and management of the assets of the corporation; and

- the assessment and collection of condominium fees and contributions towards the common expenses.

Generally, the expenditures of such a corporation are met by its members on a proportionate basis. Any excess of the members' condominium fees and contributions over the corporation's expenditures for the year is not considered to be income of the corporation. Income from other sources or activities, such as interest earned on the corporation's operating or reserve funds or rental and other incidental income is income of the corporation (however, see ¶4 for comments on the status of a residential condominium corporation as a non-profit corporation). If a condominium corporation carries on a business, any profits from that business must be included in its income and it will not be considered a non-profit corporation.

Paragraph 150(1)(a) requires all corporations, including condominium corporations, to file an income tax return each year, even if they are exempt from paying tax under Part I. A residential condominium corporation that qualifies as a non-profit organization under paragraph 149(1)(l) is exempt from Part I tax on its taxable income but is required to file Form T1044, *Non-Profit Organization (NPO) Information Return*, with its T2 tax return. Although it is a question of fact whether a particular condominium corporation qualifies for an exemption under paragraph 149(1)(l), most

residential condominium corporations qualify as non-profit organizations within the meaning of this paragraph. For information on the conditions necessary to qualify as a tax-exempt non-profit organization, see the current version of IT-496, *Non-Profit Organizations*.

Condominium Unit Used to Earn Business or Rental Income

General

5. The following comments apply when a condominium unit is used in a business or is rented to other persons, but do not apply when it is used primarily as a personal residence (either as a principal residence or a vacation residence) of the owner. When a condominium is rented to others during the time it is not used personally by the owner, the comments which follow are only applicable if the owner has a reasonable expectation of profit from the rental of the condominium.

Capital Cost Allowance

6. For capital cost allowance (CCA) purposes, when a unit includes land, the usual allocation of cost between land and building must be made (see the current version of IT-220, *Capital Cost Allowance — Proceeds of Disposition of Depreciable Property*). This allocation is necessary, for example, where a ground floor apartment unit includes an outdoor patio, or where a detached single-family condominium unit includes a front or back yard which is not part of the common elements. As indicated in ¶2(c), when a unit is purchased the purchaser also acquires a proportionate interest in the common elements pertaining to the unit. An allocation between land, building and other depreciable property (such as a parking lot) is also required in respect of the costs attributable to the common elements. As a result, the capital cost of a unit includes the cost of acquisition and capital expenditures related to the building portion of the unit as well as any costs attributable to the unit holder's proportionate interest in the common elements of any depreciable property held by the corporation. For units acquired after 1987, the capital cost of a condominium unit (building portion) is generally included in Class 1 of Schedule II to the Regulations for CCA purposes. However, if the unit was acquired before 1988, it may have qualified for inclusion in Class 3, Class

6, Class 31 or Class 32. For more details see the current version of IT-79, *Capital Cost Allowance — Buildings or Other Structures*.

CCA Restriction and Separate Class Rule

7. Subsection 1100(11) of the Regulations restricts the amount of CCA that may be claimed on rental properties. A condominium unit which meets the definition of "rental property" in subsection 1100(14) is subject to this restriction with the result that a unit owner cannot create or increase a net loss from the rental of property. In addition, subsection 1101(1ac) of the Regulations requires the establishment of a separate class for each rental property with a capital cost of at least $50,000. However, if the taxpayer owns two or more units or lots in the same building with an aggregate capital cost of at least $50,000, all such units or lots in the same building are considered to be a single rental property in a separate prescribed class.

Repairs and Renovations

8. Usually, a part of the condominium fee paid by the unit owner goes into the condominium corporation's reserve fund for maintenance, repairs, improvements or additions to the common elements. Furthermore, a unit owner may be charged an extraordinary levy by the condominium corporation for a portion of the costs relating to repairs or renovations required to be made to the common elements. In either case, no deduction or capitalization of the expense is permitted until the amount is laid out to earn income by the condominium corporation. This is because prepaid expenses, or expenses which are paid before they are actually incurred, are not deductible as explained in the current version of IT-417, *Prepaid Expenses and Deferred Charges*. Whether the unit owner deducts the amount as a current expense or capitalizes it depends on the nature of the work done. Refer to the current version of IT-128, *Capital Cost Allowance — Depreciable Property* for further details on how such costs are classified. Certain capital expenditures incurred for disability-related devices or modifications to a building to accommodate disabled individuals are deductible under paragraph $20(1)(qq)$ or $20(1)(rr)$ in the year the expense is paid. The devices and modifications which qualify under these provisions are listed in sections 8800 and 8801

of the Regulations. Capital expenditures incurred in respect of the land do not form part of the capital cost of the building portion of the unit and are not deductible in computing income except as specifically provided for in the Act. The cost of landscaping, for example, may be deductible under paragraph $20(1)(aa)$.

Quebec

9. In the province of Quebec, the condominium system of ownership is recognized in the *Civil Code of Quebec*. It contains articles dealing with the "divided co-ownership of immovables" which are analogous to the condominium legislation in effect in the other provinces and territories. These provisions provide for the direct ownership of condominium units (called "fractions"). Each fraction includes a portion of the land and building which is the property of a specific co-owner and is reserved for the sole use of that co-owner (called "les parties privatives") and an undivided interest in the common areas of the land and building (called "les parties communes"). When a declaration of co-ownership is published, a syndicate is established as a legal person responsible for protecting the rights of the co-owners and managing and maintaining the common portions of the condominium. For income tax purposes, such a syndicate is considered to be a corporation. Allowing for these differences, the comments in this bulletin apply equally to condominiums established under the *Civil Code of Quebec*.

Explanation of Changes

Introduction

The purpose of the Explanation of Changes is to give the reasons for the revisions to an interpretation bulletin. It outlines the revisions we have made as a result of changes to the law, as well as changes reflecting new or revised interpretations.

Reason for the Revision

This revision was undertaken as a result of a change in the Canada Customs and Revenue Agency's position with respect to condominium corporations as announced in the last article of Income Tax Technical News No. 4, dated February 20, 1995. The bulletin explains, in general terms, the purpose and function of a condominium corporation (a syndicate in Quebec) and describes the types of returns which must be filed by the

¶3180

condominium corporation for income tax purposes. It also discusses the unit owner's deduction of certain expenses, including CCA, applicable when a condominium unit is used to earn income from a business or from the rental of the unit. The bulletin was also modified to reflect changes to the *Income Tax Act* resulting from S.C. 1994, c. 7 Sch. VIII (1993, c. 24) and to the CCA classes for buildings. Comments concerning multiple unit residential buildings (MURBs) have been deleted because the tax incentives applicable to such buildings are no longer available.

Legislative and Other Changes

The Summary has been expanded and the reference to Information Circular 79-7, *The Condominium Corporation and Its Members*, was deleted because this circular was cancelled (see Income Tax Technical News No. 4, dated February 20, 1995).

¶2 was revised to indicate that condominiums may be created for other than residential purposes and lists the other types of condominium developments.

New ¶3 was added to explain in general terms the purpose and function of a condominium corporation. It also provides examples of the types of income a condominium corporation may earn.

New ¶4 explains that all condominium corporations, whether or not they are taxable, are required to file an income tax return each year. It also indicates that a residential condominium corporation can qualify as a tax-exempt non-profit organization and, if so, it may have to file a non-profit information return as well as an income tax return.

New ¶6 brings forward the information contained in former ¶3 and ¶4. It has been expanded to indicate that for capital cost allowance purposes the building portion of a condominium unit that was purchased after 1987 is included in Class 1. A reference to the current version of IT-79, *Capital Cost Allowance — Buildings or Other Structures*, was added because it explains Class 1, Class 3 and Class 6 of Schedule II of the Income Tax Regulations in more detail.

¶7 was revised to add a reference to subsections 1100(11) and 1100(14) of the Regulations, which prevent the creation or increase of a rental loss by claiming CCA on a condominium unit that is a rental property.

¶8 was revised to reflect the addition of subsections $20(1)(qq)$ and $20(1)(rr)$ as a result of S.C. 1994, c. 7 Sch VIII (1993, c. 24).

¶9 was revised to reflect certain changes concerning condominium developments in Quebec that were incorporated into the *Civil Code of Quebec*, which came into effect on January 1, 1994.

Former ¶5 indicated that two or more condominium units owned by a taxpayer in the same building are considered to have a single capital cost for the purpose of the addition to Class 6, 31 or 32 of Schedule II of the Regulations. The comments in former ¶5 are no longer applicable because a condominium unit acquired after 1987 falls within Class 1 or 3. Unlike the description of Classes 6, 31 and 32, the description of Class 1 and Class 3 includes property which is an interest in a building.

Former ¶6 was eliminated because the tax incentives relating to MURBs are no longer available. That is, after 1993, CCA on a Class 31 or 32 property cannot create or increase a rental loss.

Throughout the bulletin, we have made minor changes for clarification or readability purposes.

¶3180

[3185]   Interpretation Bulletin IT-306R2:   Capital Cost Allowance — Contractor's Movable Equipment

[*Interpretation Bulletin IT-306R2 is dated March 25, 1994.*]

Reference: Paragraph $20(1)(a)$ of the *Income Tax Act* and paragraph (h) of Class 10 of Schedule II to the Income Tax Regulations

Application

This bulletin replaces and cancels Interpretation Bulletin IT-306R dated June 25, 1982.

Summary

This bulletin describes some types of contractor's movable equipment that qualify for inclusion in Class 10. (Capital cost allowance may be claimed on Class 10 assets at the rate of 30% of the undepreciated capital cost of the class as of the end of the taxation year.)

Discussion and Interpretation

1. Portable camp buildings (bunkhouses, cookhouses and similar buildings) are specifically included in paragraph (h) of Class 10 of Schedule II to the Income Tax Regulations (Class $10(h)$) as contractor's movable equipment.

2. For contractor's movable equipment acquired after December 23, 1991 (except acquisitions described in 3 below), Class $10(h)$ specifically requires the equipment to have been acquired for use in a construction business or for lease to another taxpayer for use in that other taxpayer's construction business.

3. For contractor's movable equipment acquired before December 24, 1991, or acquired before 1993

(a) pursuant to an agreement in writing entered into by the taxpayer before December 24, 1991, or

(b) that was under construction by or on behalf of the taxpayer on December 23, 1991,

there was no specific requirement in Class $10(h)$ that the equipment was to have been acquired for use in a construction business or for lease to another taxpayer for use in that other taxpayer's construction business. For such equipment, the Department accepts the conclusion of the Tax Court of Canada that "contractor" is not restricted to a construction contractor (see *Laidlaw*

Waste Systems Ltd. v. Minister of National Revenue, 89 DTC 259, [1989] 1 CTC 2375). That is, for such equipment, "contractor" has a sufficiently wide meaning to include construction contractors, waste disposal contractors, cleaning contractors and other similar contractors. However, "contractor" is not broad enough to include retail merchants.

4. The term "contractor's movable equipment" refers to the kind of equipment that normally is moved from place to place in the course of a contractor's business activities. Equipment leased by a contractor that would qualify as contractor's movable equipment if owned by the contractor qualifies as Class 10 property of the lessor (i.e., the owner). The term "contractor's movable equipment" is wide enough to include movable equipment owned by a contractor, even though such equipment would not normally be regarded as contractor's movable equipment if owned by a person who is not a contractor. For example, welding equipment owned by an operator of a garage or welding shop is Class 8 property but is Class 10 property if owned and moved from place to place by a person engaged in construction work. The properties described in 6 and 7 below are specifically excluded from contractor's movable equipment.

5. Whether or not a large piece of equipment is movable may depend on its particular use. Part of a job that ordinarily is done at a fixed plant sometimes is done elsewhere such as at a construction site. As a result, a contractor may have at the construction or other site a portable machine that qualifies as "contractor's movable equipment" even though it is otherwise the same type of machine as one in the contractor's fixed plant. For example, a stone crusher of relatively large size that can be partly dismantled and moved from place to place may be used at construction sites and thus may be included in Class 10, whereas the same type of crusher, or even a smaller one, that is installed at a fixed plant would be included in another class.

¶3185

6. Contractor's movable equipment that is power-operated and designed for the purpose of excavating, moving, placing or compacting earth, rock, concrete or asphalt is included in Class 22 or 38 rather than Class 10. (See the current version of IT-469, *Capital Cost Allowance — Earth-Moving Equipment.*)

7. Vessels designed principally for natural resource exploration or the drilling of oil or gas wells as described in subsection 1101(2b) of the Regulations, other property acquired after May 22, 1979 that also is designed principally for natural resource exploration or the drilling of oil or gas wells that qualifies as Class 10 property by virtue of paragraph (t) of Class 10 and property included in Class 41 are not considered to be contractor's movable equipment. (See the current versions of IT-267, *Capital Cost Allowance — Vessels* and IT-476, *Capital Cost Allowance — Gas and Oil Exploration and Production Equipment.*)

Explanation of Changes

Introduction

The purpose of the *Explanation of Changes* is to give the reasons for the revisions to an interpretation bulletin. It outlines revisions we have made as a result of changes to the law, as well as changes reflecting new or revised departmental interpretations.

Overview

This bulletin discusses the subject of what properties qualify as "contractor's movable equipment" in Class 10(h) (capital cost allowance rate 30%). We have revised the bulletin primarily as a result of an amendment to the Regulations (Class 10(h)), and also to reflect the Department's interpretation for pre-amendment (including "grandfathered") acquisitions which has changed as a result of a court decision.

Legislative and Other Changes

Renumbering of opening paragraphs: We have moved the information in ¶1 of the old bulletin to the "Summary" statement in the new bulletin. Old ¶2 has accordingly become new ¶1.

New ¶2 and ¶3: The Department's interpretation in old ¶3 and ¶4 was that the word "contractor" was restricted to construction contractor. However, in the *Laidlaw Waste Systems* decision (89 DTC 259, [1989] 1 CTC 2375), the Tax Court of Canada concluded that "contractor's movable equipment" was not restricted to construction contractors and was wide enough to also include waste disposal contractors, but was not broad enough to include retail merchants. As a result of this decision, the Regulations have recently been amended so that "contractor's movable equipment" in Class 10(h) is specifically restricted to equipment acquired for use in a construction business or for lease to another taxpayer for use in that other taxpayer's construction business. The amendment generally applies for equipment acquired after December 23, 1991. For acquisitions before December 24, 1991, or within a grandfathering period, the Department follows the *Laidlaw* case.

New ¶4 and ¶5: The discussion in these paragraphs is essentially the same as in old ¶3 and ¶4 except that, again because of the *Laidlaw* decision (which applies only to pre-amendment or grandfathered acquisitions), references to "construction" contractors, work or sites are now given only as examples of the principles discussed in those paragraphs. At the end of new ¶5, it is now indicated that a stone crusher that is installed at a fixed plant (and thus does not qualify as Class 10 "contractor's movable equipment") would be included in "another class" (rather than "Class 8" as stated at the end of old ¶4). (When IT-306R was written in 1982, such an asset could only have been included in Class 8. Since that time, however, such an asset could possibly have been included in any one of a number of different classes depending on the date the taxpayer acquired the asset and how it was used.)

New ¶6 and ¶7: These paragraphs, which are essentially the same as old ¶5 and ¶6, discuss the properties that are specifically excluded from Class 10(h). Now referred to in these exclusions are assets in Class 38 and Class 41, both of which came into being under the Tax Reform Measures.

Clarification changes: Throughout the bulletin, we have changed some of the wording and the order of some sentences to clarify the bulletin and improve its cohesiveness without changing the substance of what was said in the old bulletin.

¶3185

[3215] Interpretation Bulletin IT-371: Rental Property — Meaning of "Principal Business"

[Interpretation Bulletin IT-371 is dated April 25, 1977.]

Reference: 1100(12) of the Income Tax Regulations (also paragraph $20(1)(a)$ of the Act)

1. Interpretation Bulletin IT-195R4, "Rental Property — Capital Cost Allowance Restrictions", describes the effect of Regulation 1100(11) upon the amount of capital cost allowance claimed by a taxpayer on "rental property" as defined by Regulation 1100(14). This bulletin is concerned with the provisions of Regulation 1100(12) which excepts certain corporations and partnerships from those restrictions.

2. Regulation 1100(12) provides that the capital cost allowance restriction prescribed by Regulation 1100(11) does not apply to a taxpayer that was throughout the year a life insurance corporation, a corporation whose principal business was the leasing, rental development or sale, or any combination thereof, of real property owned by it, or a partnership each member of which was a corporation described above. This provision applies as well to non-residents as to residents.

3. A partnership qualifies within Regulation 1100(12) only if each of its members is a corporation described therein. That is, each corporate member must have been throughout the year, a life insurance corporation or a corporation whose principal business was the leasing, rental, development or sale, or any combination thereof, of real property owned by it, if the partnership is to qualify.

4. A partnership having a partnership as a member at any time in the year cannot qualify under Regulation 1100(12) even though that member qualified because all of its members were, throughout the year, qualified corporations.

Principal Business

5. Whether or not a business is a "principal" business is a matter of significance only where the taxpayer carries on more than one business in the taxation year. The phrase "principal business" is not defined by the Act or the Regulations and accordingly the words must be given their usual meaning and the identity of a taxpayer's principal

business determined from the facts of the particular case.

6. Regulation 1100(12) requires that the business be the taxpayer's principal business "throughout the year". In this respect it is similar to subsection 18(8) of the Act but it is unlike other references to "principal business" in the Act (for example, subsection 66(2) and subparagraph $133(8)(d)(iv)$) which only require the particular business to have been a principal business in the taxation year. Nevertheless it is the Department's view that the criteria for identifying a principal business for the purposes of Regulation 1100(12) are not different from those set out in Interpretation Bulletin IT-290, "Non-Resident-Owned Investment Corporation — Meaning of Principal Business".

7. There is no standard set of criteria that may be looked to where the nature of each of a taxpayer's businesses is known but it must be determined which of them is his principal business; the significant factors of each case must be searched out and evaluated. In the Department's view the following are among the factors which may be relevant:

(a) the profits realized by each of the businesses;

(b) the volume and the value of the gross sales or transactions of each business;

(c) the value of the assets of each business;

(d) the capital employed in each business; and

(e) the time, attention and effort expended by the employees, agents or officers in each business.

8. Although the determination of which of a taxpayer's businesses is the principal business is made in respect of a particular taxation year, it is often necessary to consider patterns over several years. Thus, if a particular business has been the principal business and in a particular year (evaluated

in isolation from preceding and succeeding years) it fails to satisfy many of the tests, it does not necessarily follow that another business has become the principal business in that year. For example it may be that, because of economic conditions and not because of a change in management's policies, there has been in a particular year a reduction in the level of activities of the business which was the principal business, so that another business appears to have assumed that role. If this condition continues only in the short run and thereafter the business again satisfies the tests of being the principal business, the Department's view is that the principal business may not have changed during that period. Whether this is so in any particular case can only be determined by a review of the circumstances of that case.

9. Interpretation Bulletin IT-72R2, *Meaning of "Active Business"* indicates the

Department's view that a corporation which derives income from rentals is in the rentals business and thus satisfies one of the criteria of Regulation 1100(12). If it has no other businesses or if it has other businesses but the rentals business is its principal business, then the requirements of the Regulation are met, although the business may not satisfy the tests of being an active business.

10. In the Department's view a person who operates a hotel is in the business of providing services and not in the rental business. Thus a corporation in that business does not qualify under Regulation 1100(12) no matter that it is its principal business.

11. "Real property" in the context of Regulation 1100(12) includes a reference to buildings which are depreciable property of the taxpayer whether situated on land owned by him or in which he has a leasehold interest.

[3220]   **Interpretation Bulletin IT-418:   Capital Cost Allowance — Partial Dispositions of Property**

[*Interpretation Bulletin IT-418 is dated June 26, 1978.*]

Reference: Subsection 13(21) (also section 43, subsection 13(1) and subparagraph $54(a)(i)$)

1. Section 43 of the Act provides that, for the purpose of computing the gain or loss from the disposition of part of a property, the adjusted cost base (ACB) of the whole property immediately prior to the disposition must be apportioned on a reasonable basis between the part disposed of and the part retained. A disposition of part of a property may refer either to the disposition of a physical part of the property or to the disposition of an undivided interest therein. Where the property is depreciable property, subparagraph $54(a)(i)$ defines the adjusted cost base to mean the capital cost of the property but makes no provision for adjustments thereto under section 53. Subsection 248(1) indicates that the definition in subparagraph $54(a)(i)$ applies for all purposes of the Act. The determination of capital cost in various circumstances is explained in IT-174 *Capital Cost Allowance — Meaning of "Capital Cost of Property"*.

2. Where a taxpayer disposes of only part of a depreciable property of a prescribed class (other than a timber resource property as defined in paragraph $13(21)(d.1)$), the capital cost of the part disposed of must be

determined for the purpose of clause $13(21)(f)(iv)(B)$, in order to determine the amount of any recaptured depreciation under subsection 13(1) and the undepreciated capital cost of the property remaining in the class under paragraph $13(21)(f)$. To accomplish this, it is the Department's view that the apportionment rule in section 43 should be used. However, no reduction of the capital cost referred to in subparagraph $13(21)(f)(i)$ will be required as a result of a partial disposition, since that paragraph refers to the capital cost of all depreciable property in a prescribed class that has been acquired before the time the undepreciated capital cost is calculated. This would include property that has previously been disposed of in whole or in part.

3. The following illustrates the application of the principles in 2 above in a situation where the taxpayer disposes of a physical part of a depreciable property (other than a timber resource property) and the capital cost of the part disposed of and of the part retained is ascertainable with accuracy.

¶3220

Example:

Assume a taxpayer with a fiscal period ending May 31, has a depreciable property which is the sole property of its class. The capital cost allowance schedule as of May 31, 1977, shows:

Capital cost of property in the class, acquired after December 31, 1971 .... $ 15,000

less: Total depreciation allowed ....   ($ 10,000)

Undepreciated capital cost of the class .... $ 5,000

(a) On June 1, 1977, the taxpayer sells one-half of the property for $17,000. The capital cost of the part disposed of is known to be 50% of the capital cost of the whole property immediately before the sale.

The capital gain on the date of sale and the undepreciated capital cost as well as any recaptured depreciation at the year end would be calculated as follows:

(i) **Calculation of Capital Gain**

Proceeds of disposition, June 1, 1977.......... $17,000

less:

Capital cost of part sold immediately before disposition (Section 43) .... $ 7,500

Selling expenses   1,000   8,500

Capital gain (paragraph 39(1)(a))   8,500

(ii) **Calculation of recaptured depreciation and U.C.C. as at May 31, 1978**

Capital cost of all property in class (13(21)(f)(i)) $15,000

Recaptured depreciation in previous taxation years (13(21)(f)(ii)) ....   NIL

$15,000

less:

Total depreciation allowed prior to year end (13(21)(f)(iii)) $10,000

Proceeds of all dispositions prior to year end ($17,000 − $1,000) $16,000

Capital cost of part of property sold (Section 43)....................................... $ 7,500

The lesser of the two (13(21)(f)(iv)) .... $ 7,500 $17,500

Recaptured depreciation (13(1)) ....   ($2,500)

U.C.C. of class (13(21)(f)) ....   NIL

(b) On July 1, 1978, the taxpayer sells the remaining one-half of the property for $18,000. The capital cost of the remaining part, per (a) above, is 50% of the capital cost of the whole property.

The capital gain on the date of sale and the undepreciated capital cost as well as any recaptured depreciation at the year end would be calculated as follows:

¶3220

(i) **Calculation of Capital Gain**

Proceeds of disposition, July 1, 1978		$18,000
less:		
Capital cost of part sold immediately before disposition (Section 43)	7,500	
Selling expenses	$ 1,200	$ 8,700
Capital gain (paragraph 39(1)(*a*))		$ 9,300

(ii) **Calculation of recaptured depreciation and U.C.C. as at May 31, 1979**

Capital cost of all property in class (13(21)(*f*)(i))		$15,000
Recaptured depreciation in previous taxation years (13(21)(*f*)(ii))		$ 2,500
		$17,500
less:		
Total depreciation allowed prior to year end (13(21)(*f*)(iii))	$10,000	
Proceeds of all dispositions prior to year end ($35,000 less total of selling expenses ($2,200)	$32,800	
Capital cost of both parts sold (Section 43)	$15,000	
The lesser of the two (13(21)(*f*)(iv))	$15,000	$25,000
Recaptured depreciation (13(1))		$(7,500)
U.C.C. of class (13(21)(*f*))		NIL

4. In the following paragraphs, the application of the principles in 2 above is considered for situations where the taxpayer disposes of part of a depreciable property (other than a timber resource property) and the capital cost of the part disposed of cannot be ascertained with accuracy. Where this is so, section 43 merely requires that the attribution of a portion of the capital cost of the whole property to the part sold must be reasonable.

5. Where the value of different parts of the same property can be ascertained, one method that could be used to determine the capital cost of the part sold is to take that proportion of the capital cost of the whole property that the amount or value of the consideration for the part disposed of (before the deduction of selling expenses) is of the amount above plus the fair market value at the date of disposition of the part retained.

Example:

A taxpayer disposed of a part of a depreciable property acquired after December 31, 1971, for $18,000. The capital cost of the whole property immediately before the disposition was $42,000. A valuation was made of the part of the property retained on the date of disposition of the other part. The part retained was valued at $66,000. Accordingly, the capital cost of the part disposed of for purposes of clause 13(21)(*f*)(iv)(B) was $9,000, calculated as follows:

$$\frac{\$18,000}{\$18,000 + \$66,000} \times \$42,000 = \$9,000$$

6. The formula outlined in the preceding paragraph for the *pro rata* apportionment of the capital cost of a depreciable property would not be reasonable in all circumstances. Where, for instance, the value of different parts of the same property cannot be ascertained, it will be a question of fact as to what is a reasonable allocation of the capital cost of the whole property to the part disposed of and the part retained. Further, where the taxpayer, before the disposition, had incurred an expenditure that was wholly attributable to one specific part of the property, it would be unreasonable to make the *pro rata* apportionment on the disposition of part of the property, without first excluding the amount of that expenditure from the capital cost. Having made the apportionment, the amount of the expenditure would then be added back to the capital

¶3220

cost of the part disposed of or retained, as the case may be.

Timber Resource Properties

7. Where a taxpayer disposes of only a part of a timber resource property (as defined in paragraph $13(21)(d.1)$), it will not be necessary to apply the apportionment rule of section 43. Any gain within the meaning of paragraph $40(1)(a)$ which may arise from such a disposition is not a capital gain by reason of subparagraph $39(1)(a)(iv)$, but is subject to recapture

under subsection 13(1) by virtue of subparagraph $13(21)(f)(v)$.

8. Subparagraph $13(21)(f)(v)$ requires the amount of the proceeds, less selling expenses, of each disposition of a timber resource property or part thereof to be deducted from the capital cost of the property in the class. It follows that any negative balance in the class resulting from the calculation under paragraph $13(21)(f)$ will be included in the taxpayer's income for the year pursuant to subsection 13(1).

[3225] Interpretation Bulletin IT-422: Definition of Tools

[Interpretation Bulletin IT-422 is dated August 30, 1978.]

Reference: Paragraph $20(1)(a)$ of the Act (also Schedule B of the Income Tax Regulations)

This bulletin had minor amendments made on April 20, 2001.

1. The purpose of this bulletin is to outline the Department's position regarding the definition of the word "tools" for purposes of paragraph (h) of Class 12 of the Regulations.

2. It is the Department's view that a tool is an instrument of manual operation, that is, it is an instrument to be used and managed by hand instead of being moved and controlled by machinery. In order for an asset to be a tool it must be designed to create a physical change in something or to be used as an instrument of measurement or manipulation. Examples are hammers, saws, squares, screwdrivers and hand-held power tools.

3. The fact that an object can be moved or set up by hand does not, in itself, make it

a tool for Class 12 purposes. Thus, pallets that are moved by lift trucks when loaded with goods, or scaffolding which is assembled by hand and moved by and but not "manually used" are not Class 12 items. However, shopping carts, metal trays used for carrying bread by hand, milk crates and returnable softdrink cases are Class 12 assets when they are capitalized.

4. An asset can be a tool in a general sense but its predominating character may be that of machinery and equipment. Thus, an item such as a typewriter which might be considered a tool, is properly regarded as machinery and is placed in Class 8.

5. The current version of Interpretation Bulletin IT-165, *Returnable Containers*, discusses alternate tax treatments of the cost of "returnable containers."

[3232] Interpretation Bulletin IT-443: Leasing Property — Capital Cost Allowance Restrictions

[Interpretation Bulletin IT-443 is dated March 14, 1980.]

Reference: 1100(15) of the Income Tax Regulations (also 1100(16) to 1100(20) and 1101(5c) of the Income Tax Regulations)

1. Regulation 1100(15) limits the amount of capital cost allowance (CCA) that can be claimed on leasing property owned by a taxpayer, other than a taxpayer described in 8 below, so as to prevent him from creating or increasing a loss to shelter non-leasing income. Any comment in this bulletin with reference to leasing property of a taxpayer

also applies to leasing property of a partnership.

Leasing Property

2. The term "leasing property" is defined in Regulation 1100(17). Certain properties commented on in paragraphs 11 to 15 below

are specifically excluded from the definition of leasing property. Leasing property of a taxpayer is depreciable property of a prescribed class other than

  (a) rental property as defined in Regulation 1100(14) (See also IT-195R4),

  (b) multiple-unit residential buildings of Class 31 or 32 and furniture, fixtures or equipment located within and ancillary to them, or

  (c) Class $12(n)$ property, e.g., a certified feature film.

The depreciable property must be used principally for the purpose of gaining or producing gross revenue that is rent, royalty or leasing revenue. Leasing property does not include a property leased in the ordinary course of selling goods or rendering services under an agreement by which the lessee undertakes to use the property to carry on the business of selling or promoting the sale of the taxpayer's goods or services (e.g., display equipment leased by a manufacturer to a dealer for promoting the sale of the manufacturer's goods is not leasing property). *Paragraph 1100(17.1) of the Regulations was added effective March 10, 1982 to provide that property is leasing property in the year acquired, even though it is not used for any purpose in that year, if the first use of that property was principally for the purpose of gaining or producing gross revenue that is rent, royalty or leasing revenue.

3. The word "principally" in the definition of leasing property in Regulation 1100(17) means "primarily" or "chiefly". In establishing whether a depreciable property is used principally for a given purpose, the determining factor is the proportion of time that the property is used for that purpose. Property used more than 50% of the time for the purpose of gaining or producing gross revenue that is rent, royalty or leasing revenue is considered to be used principally for that purpose. Such revenue includes charter fees and other revenue for the use of a vessel leased to an operator on a "bare-boat" basis.

Separate Class

4. Leasing properties which would otherwise be described in the same class as non-leasing properties are required to be included in a separate class by virtue of Regulation 1101(5c). Regulation 1101(5c) does not apply however to leasing property of a taxpayer exempted from the CCA limitation under Regulation 1100(16). Where the conditions of Regulation 1100(16) are met throughout one year but not in another year it will be necessary to transfer the leasing property into or out of the separate class.

**5. The restriction in Regulation 1100(15) does not apply to individual classes of leasing properties if a taxpayer has more than one class, but to the total CCA that may be claimed against all the leasing properties. In determining the maximum CCA that may be claimed on leasing properties, the taxpayer is required to compute separately the aggregate of his income and the aggregate of his losses for the year from renting, leasing or earning royalties from leasing properties and properties that would be leasing properties were it not for Regulations 1100(18) to (20). Such aggregates are computed without regard to paragraph $20(1)(a)$ so that any recapture of CCA from such properties is included but terminal losses are excluded. The maximum CCA that may be claimed on all the leasing properties cannot exceed the amount by which the aggregate of such income exceeds the aggregate of such losses.

6. A partnership that is subject to the provisions of Regulation 1100(15) calculates the amount of CCA that it can claim under the above rules and allocates the resulting net leasing income or loss among the partners. Where one of the partners also holds leasing property as a proprietor, the CCA limitation will apply in a similar way to his own leasing property. His total income or loss (after expenses but before CCA) on his own leasing property will be combined with his share of partnership leasing income or loss. The partner may then claim CCA on his own leasing properties to the extent of the "combined" leasing income (net of losses), if any.

7. Where a taxpayer acquires a rental property as defined in Regulation 1100(14) and leasing property that is located within or is ancillary to the rental property (e.g., furniture and fixtures or appliances in units of a rental property) for purposes of calculating the amount of CCA limitations

---

* Added by Correction Sheet No. 1, April 15, 1983.

** As amended by Special Release, December 27, 1985.

under Regulations 1100(15) and (11), an allocation of income between leasing and rental property is necessary where:

(a) there are separate and significant rental charges for the use of the leasing property in the lease or rental agreement,

(b) the rent charged to tenants using the leasing property is markedly higher than that charged to other tenants not using such property, or

(c) the capital cost of the leasing property is significant in relation to the capital cost of the rental property.

Generally an allocation of income is not necessary for a tenant's use of kitchen appliances included in all units of a rental property, other appliances or facilities provided for the common use of all tenants, or indoor or outdoor parking areas. Where a flat amount is charged for the use of rental property and leasing property combined, and no allocation of income is considered necessary, CCA may be claimed in respect of either or both properties provided the aggregate CCA claimed does not exceed the combined rental and leasing income.

Principal Business

8. Regulation 1100(15) does not apply, by virtue of Regulation 1100(16), to certain corporations whose principal businesses are renting or leasing of leasing property including property that would be leasing property were it not excluded under Regulation 1100(18), (19) or (20), or the renting or leasing of such property combined with the sale and service of property of the same general type and description. Such a corporation will qualify for exclusion if its gross revenue for the year from such a principal business was not less than 90% of its gross revenue from all sources. The above also applies to a partnership each member of which was a corporation, provided each such partner can meet the above criteria. Interpretation Bulletin IT-371 provides some comments on the meaning of principal business.

9. A corporation or each partner of a corporate partnership must meet the requirements of Regulation 1100(16) for each taxation year in respect of which it claims to be exempted from the CCA limitation. Moreover, these requirements must be met

throughout a taxation year and not merely during part of that year.

10. The term "gross revenue" is defined in subsection 248(1). The Department considers that for purposes of Regulation 1100(16)(*a*) "gross revenue" from the principal business referred to therein includes:

(a) gross revenue from renting or leasing of property described in that Regulation or from the servicing of property of the same general type and description as well as royalty income from all such property;

(b) proceeds from the sale of property described in that Regulation or property of the same general type and description;

(c) interest and other financing charges incidental to the taxpayer's activities set out in (a) and (b) above, other than a money-lending business, and earned in the course of selling or leasing property.

For purposes of the gross revenue test of a corporation where the corporation has an interest in a partnership, it is considered that the gross revenue of the partnership, to the extent of the corporation's profit sharing percentage thereof, flows through to the gross revenue of the corporation. Therefore, the gross revenue of the partnership from a particular source will be included in the gross revenue of the corporation from that source to the extent of the profit sharing ratio.

Property excluded from Leasing Property

11. Property that meets the requirements of Regulation 1100(18), (19) or (20) is excluded from leasing property. Regulation 1100(18) provides the transitional rules since the concept of leasing property and CCA limitation thereon became law on May 26, 1976. It should be noted that Regulation 1100(18) does not apply, however, to property acquired after May 25, 1976 that is an addition or improvement to property excluded from leasing property by virtue of Regulation 1100(18), so that the addition itself may be leasing property.

12. Regulations 1100(19) and (20) deem depreciable property acquired after May 25, 1976 which would otherwise be leasing

¶3232

property not to be leasing property under certain conditions. Regulation 1100(19) deems property not to be leasing property if the property was acquired by "rollover" in the following circumstances:

(a) property disposed of to a Canadian corporation by a shareholder under subsection 85(1) or by a partnership under subsection 85(2),

(b) property transferred under subsection 97(2) to a Canadian partnership by a partner (see Interpretation Bulletin IT-413 entitled "Partnership as 'Person' or 'Taxpayer' for subsection 97(2)") or property distributed under subsection 98(3) to partners on the dissolution of a Canadian partnership;

(c) property acquired by amalgamation under section 87; or

*(d) property acquired under subsection 88(1) by a Canadian corporation on the winding-up of its wholly-owned Canadian subsidiary corporation and the property acquired was, by virtue of Regulation 1100(18), (19) or (20), not a leasing property of the vendor.

13. Regulation 1100(20) deems property not to be leasing property if it is a "replace-

ment property" for property that is lost, destroyed or expropriated or that was a former business property as referred to in paragraphs $13(4)(a)$ and (b) of the Act and the property replaced was, by virtue of Regulation 1100(18) or (19), not a leasing property.

14. Technically the exemptions provided for in Regulations 1100(19) and (20) are limited to a first "rollover" and a first acquisition of "replacement property". Administratively, however, it is the Department's practice to accept the application of Regulations 1100(19) and (20) to a second and subsequent "rollover" or second and subsequent acquisition of "replacement property"provided all other requirements are met.

**15. It is the Department's view that Regulation 1100(18) only applies to property that meets the criteria of a leasing property under Regulation 1100(17). In other words, Regulation 1100(18) can only operate to exclude a property from being a leasing property if the property is, in fact, a leasing property under Regulation 1100(17). It follows therefore, that Regulations 1100(19) and (20) can also only apply with respect to a property that meets the criteria of a leasing property under Regulation 1100(17).

[3237] Interpretation Bulletin IT-460: Dispositions — Absence of Consideration

[*Interpretation Bulletin IT-460 is dated October 6, 1980.*]

Reference: Paragraphs $13(21)(c)$ and $54(c)$ (also paragraphs $13(21)(d)$ and $54(h)$)

1. A disposition can generally be regarded as an event or transaction where possession, control and all other aspects of property ownership are relinquished. Although there is usually a corresponding acquisition of the property by another person and consideration flowing to the person disposing of the property, it is the Department's view that neither of these characteristics need always be present for the purposes of paragraphs $13(21)(c)$ and $54(c)$. It is clear that there need not be a corresponding acquisition of property in all cases when a person disposing of property is entitled to receive proceeds as described in paragraphs $13(21)(d)$ and $54(h)$, but the

application of the law is less certain when no proceeds are involved.

2. Where the Department is satisfied that a disposition has taken place under the general meaning of the term as described in 1 above and there are no actual or deemed proceeds involved, an amount of zero may be used as proceeds of disposition in subparagraph $40(1)(b)(i)$ for purposes of computing a loss from the disposition.

3. The following are examples of events that the Department considers to be dispositions even though no actual proceeds are involved:

---

* As amended by Correction Sheet No. 1, April 15, 1983.

** As amended by Special Release, December 27, 1985.

(a) a capital property is stolen or destroyed and there is no entitlement or right to compensation (insurance proceeds, salvage, etc.) and none is forthcoming;

(b) a capital property is lost or abandoned and beyond reasonable expectation of recovery;

(c) a corporation, in which a taxpayer holds shares of a particular class as a capital property, surrenders (or has cancelled or withdrawn) its articles of incorporation and there are no assets to which the shareholders of that class are or could become entitled (but see 6 below);

(d) a capital property is confiscated or expropriated without compensation by a government;

(e) a partnership, in which a taxpayer has a partnership interest (a capital property), is dissolved and the taxpayer is not entitled to and does not receive any share of the partnership's net assets (if any);

(f) a capital property is transferred by way of gift or donation.

*4. The following occurrences do not constitute a disposition (within the meaning of paragraph 54(c)) of a share of a corporation:

(a) the corporation's shares are delisted from a stock exchange,

(b) a regulatory authority issues a "cease trading" order in respect of the corporation's shares,

(c) the corporation goes into receivership (but see 5 below), or

(d) the corporation becomes bankrupt (but see 5 below).

*5. For 1978 and subsequent taxation years, a shareholder of a corporation that has become bankrupt (including a corporation against which a receiving order has been issued by a Court) during a particular taxation year is deemed by subsection 50(1) to have disposed of his shareholdings for no proceeds at the end of that year (unless the shares were acquired as consideration for the disposition of personal-use property).

6. Corporate legislation in various jurisdictions frequently provides for the restoration of corporations that have previously been formally dissolved, as in 3(c) above. Such a restoration will not nullify the disposition of a class of shares by its shareholders that took place upon dissolution provided that

(a) the corporation had no assets at the time of dissolution to which the shareholders of that particular class of shares were or could have become entitled, and

(b) there was no reason to believe at the time of dissolution that the corporation would be restored.

In other cases a careful examination of the applicable facts is necessary to establish that a *bona fide* disposition did occur upon dissolution.

[3240]   Interpretation Bulletin IT-464R: Capital Cost Allowance — Leasehold Interests

[*Interpretation Bulletin IT-464R is dated October 25, 1985.*]

Reference: Paragraph 20(1)(a) and subsections 13(5.1) and 20(16) of the Act (also subsections 1100(2.1), 1102(4) and 1102(5), paragraph 1100(1)(b) and Schedule III of the Income Tax Regulations)

This bulletin replaces and cancels IT-464 dated December 8, 1980. Minor amendments were made on April 20, 2001.

1. Subject to paragraphs 1100(2.1)(f) (see 2 below) and 1100(2.2)(i) (see IT-285R2), paragraph 1100(1)(b) of the

Regulations provides that a taxpayer may claim in a taxation year an amount of capital cost allowance in respect of properties in Class 13 of Schedule II that does not exceed the aggregate of

---

* As amended by Correction Sheet No. 1, April 15, 1983.

(a) 50% of the amount calculated in accordance with Schedule III where the capital costs of the properties were incurred in the particular taxation year and after November 12, 1981, and

(b) the amount calculated in accordance with Schedule III (see 12 below) in all other cases.

The property included in Class 13 is property that is a leasehold interest except

(c) an interest in minerals, petroleum, natural gas, other related hydrocarbons or timber and property relating thereto or in respect of a right to explore for, drill for, take or remove minerals, petroleum, natural gas, other related hydrocarbons or timber,

(d) that part of the leasehold interest that is included in another class by reason of subsection 1102(5) of the Regulations (see 20 below), or

(e) a property that is included in Class 23.

2. The 50% rule in 1(a) above is not applicable to a leasehold interest the capital cost of which was acquired or incurred after November 12, 1981 and before 1983 if any of the following conditions apply:

(a) The taxpayer was obligated to acquire the leasehold interest under terms of an agreement in writing entered into before November 13, 1981.

(b) The taxpayer or a non-arm's length person commenced the construction, manufacture or production of leasehold improvements before November 13, 1981.

(c) The taxpayer or a non-arm's length person had made arrangements evidenced in writing for the construction, manufacture or production of leasehold improvements that were substantially advanced before November 13, 1981 and the construction, manufacture or production commenced before June 1, 1982.

(d) The taxpayer was obligated to acquire the leasehold interest under the terms of an agreement in writing entered into before June 1, 1982 where arrangements, evidenced in writing, for leasing the property or the acquisition of leasehold improvements (as the case may be) were substantially advanced before November 13, 1981.

Acquisition of a Leasehold Interest

3. A leasehold interest is the interest of a tenant in any leased tangible property. A tenant who leases property acquires a leasehold interest in that property regardless of whether or not any capital cost is incurred in respect of that interest. However, a depreciable property is not considered to have been acquired until a capital cost has been incurred in respect of that property. It is necessary to determine with regard to certain apparent leasing agreements, whether these agreements are in substance leasing agreements or agreements either for the purchase of the property or for loans. IT-233R comments on these latter types of agreements.

4. A tenant who has acquired

(a) an assignment of a leased property or a part of a leased property, or

(b) a sublease on a leased property,

is considered to have acquired a leasehold interest.

Capital Cost of a Leasehold Interest

5. The capital cost of a leasehold interest of Class 13 property includes

(a) an amount that a tenant expends in respect of improvements or alterations to a leased property that are capital in nature, other than improvements or alterations that are included as a building or structure pursuant to subsection 1102(5) (see 20 below), and

(b) an amount that a tenant expends to obtain or extend a lease or sublease or pays to the landlord to permit the sublease of the property.

6. Certain amounts paid by a tenant in respect of a lease are not considered to form part of the capital cost of a leasehold interest. Examples of these are as follows:

(a) an amount paid by a tenant to cancel a lease (see IT-359R2), and

(b) an amount paid by a tenant in lieu of rent or as a prepayment of rent (see IT-261R).

¶3240

7. A leasehold interest does not include the cost of alterations or improvements made by the landlord of a property at the request of the tenant. Such costs are either expenses of the landlord or subject to capital cost allowance depending on whether they constitute a current expense or a capital expenditure.

8. When a tenant makes improvements and alterations to leased property and subsequently abandons them, they are not considered to have been acquired by the landlord as a gift, bequest or inheritance under paragraph 69(1)(c). The landlord is, therefore, not entitled to claim capital cost allowance in respect of such property.

Disposition of a Leasehold Interest

9. The time of disposition of a leasehold interest by a tenant includes

(a) the time of expiration of a lease if it is not renewed, except where the taxpayer continues to occupy the premises on a periodic tenancy or other continuing basis,

(b) the time of cancellation of a lease if it is prior to the expiration date,

(c) the time of an assignment by the tenant of a lease but not including the subletting of a leased property (the subletting of a leased property is considered to be a partial disposition of a lease), and

(d) the time of a conversion of a leasehold interest to a freehold interest.

10. Where a leasehold interest is disposed of and proceeds of disposition, if any, are less than the undepreciated capital cost at the end of the year in Class 13, a terminal loss under subsection 20(16) is deductible provided the lessee disposes of all leasehold interests in Class 13 by the end of that year and does not acquire depreciable property that is a leasehold interest before the end of the year.

11. Where a tenant, who has a leasehold interest in a property, acquires ownership of that property after March 31, 1977, subsection 13(5.1) provides that

(a) the leasehold interest is deemed to have been disposed of by the taxpayer at the time of the acquisition of the property for proceeds equal to the capital cost of the leasehold interest minus the capital cost allowance allowed in respect thereof before that time,

(b) the property acquired is deemed to be depreciable property of a prescribed class of the taxpayer acquired at that time, and to the cost of that property is to be added the capital cost of the leasehold interest immediately before the deemed disposition of it, and

(c) the aggregate capital cost allowance allowed to the taxpayer before that disposition in respect of the leasehold interest is to be added to the capital cost allowance allowed to the taxpayer before that time in respect of the class to which the acquired property belongs.

CCA Computed Under Schedule III

12. Section 2 of Schedule III requires that a calculation of one or more "prorated portions" be made (see 13 below) in respect of each leasehold interest of a taxpayer. Section 1 of Schedule III limits the capital cost allowance for a taxation year to the lesser of

(a) the sum of the prorated portions calculated in accordance with the rules and limitations described in 13 to 17 below, and

(b) the undepreciated capital cost of the whole of Class 13 before any allowance for that year is deducted.

To reflect the limitation imposed by subparagraph 1100(1)(b)(i), (a) above should be read as 50% of the amount otherwise calculated with respect to an expenditure incurred after November 12, 1981 (if not subject to the transitional rules described in 2 above nor the rule contained in paragraph 1100(2.2)(i) of the Regulations) for the year in which the expenditure is incurred.

13. Section 2 of Schedule III provides that for purposes of determining the "prorated portion", the capital cost incurred by the taxpayer in a particular taxation year in respect of any particular leasehold interest owned by the taxpayer is treated separately and each such segment of capital cost is referred to in this bulletin as a "unit of capital cost". A "prorated portion" in respect of a unit of capital cost is determined as the lesser of

¶3240

(a) one-fifth of the unit of capital cost, and

(b) the amount determined by dividing the unit of capital cost by the number of 12-month periods (not exceeding 40 such periods) falling within the period commencing with the beginning of the particular taxation year in which the capital cost was incurred and ending with the day the lease is to terminate.

Although section 3 sets out further rules affecting the computation of prorated portions as discussed in 14 to 17 below, the actual computation of the prorated portion of a particular unit of capital cost is made only once. Capital costs incurred in a subsequent taxation year in respect of the same leasehold interest will constitute another unit of capital cost requiring computation of another prorated portion. Similarly, a separate computation is required for capital costs incurred in the same taxation year for each leasehold interest.

14. By reason of paragraph 3(a) of Schedule III and for the purposes of section 2 only, capital costs incurred in respect of a particular leasehold interest in a taxation year preceding the one in which the interest was acquired are deemed to have been incurred in the latter year and will be included in the same unit of capital cost as any costs actually incurred in that latter year in respect of that interest. "The taxation year in which the interest was acquired" should be read as referring to the taxation year in which the taxpayer entered into possession of the property in accordance with the terms of the lease but not, for example, to a preceding year in which the taxpayer acquired an option to lease the property or was allowed to do work on it prior to commencement of the actual leasehold period. The tenant of a property rented and occupied without the benefit of a written lease who makes capital expenditures on the property is regarded as having a leasehold interest in that property on an oral basis; proration of those expenditures therefore will be made over 5 years.

15. For the purpose of computing the number of 12-month periods referred to in paragraph 2(b) of Schedule III, it is provided in paragraph 3(b) of Schedule III that where the tenant has under the lease a right to renew the lease, there shall be taken into account not only the term of the lease itself

but also the term of the first possible renewal thereof. Paragraph 2(b), however, limits the total number of 12-month periods that will be used to 40. In the application of paragraph 3(b), it is necessary to determine that the terms for the possible renewal period are established in the lease and that the tenant does not have merely the right to negotiate the lease. If the latter is the case, it is considered that a new lease is to be negotiated rather than that the existing lease is to be renewed, and any period specified therein will not be taken into account for the purposes of paragraph 2(b). Uncertainty as to the precise dollar amount of future rentals is not in itself cause to ignore the initial lease renewal term providing the lease contains a firm commitment by the landlord to renew at a future "fair market value" rent which is to be established between the parties.

16. Paragraph 3(c) of Schedule III assures that the total deductions allowable in respect of a unit of capital cost will never exceed the total capital cost of that unit. Paragraph 3(d) contains a similar limitation regarding the capital costs incurred in respect of an entire leasehold interest, which makes it unnecessary to attempt to allocate the proceeds of disposition of part or all of a leasehold interest between two or more units of capital cost. In the case of paragraph 3(d), where at the end of a taxation year the aggregate of the allowances claimed in previous taxation years in respect of a particular leasehold interest and any proceeds of disposition from that interest equals or exceeds the capital cost as of that time of that interest, the prorated portion is for all subsequent years deemed to be nil. This does not prohibit allowances for capital costs incurred in a subsequent taxation year in respect of that same interest. It should be noted that neither paragraph contains a provision to deny claims in respect of a leasehold interest that has expired or has been otherwise disposed of. Thus, if the rules of paragraph (d) or (e) (see 17 below) are not applicable, the 50% that a taxpayer was unable to claim in the first year in respect of a unit of capital cost (see 12 above) may be claimed in the year following the end of the amortization period determined under 13 above, even though the related leasehold interest does not exist at that time.

17. Paragraph 3(e) of Schedule III provides that, where the undepreciated capital

¶3240

cost of the whole of Class 13 is nil at the end of a taxation year, no further allowances will be given for capital costs incurred up to that time. Reduction of the undepreciated capital cost to nil during a taxation year will not have this effect, however, if capital costs in respect of either an existing or a new leasehold interest are incurred after that time before the end of the year in an amount sufficient to re-establish a debit balance in the class.

18. Except when separate capital cost allowance classes are prescribed pursuant to section 1101 of the Regulations, all leasehold interests of a taxpayer that fall within Class 13 form a single class of property, despite the separate calculations required by Schedule III in respect of each leasehold interest.

19. Appendix I provides an example of the computation of capital cost allowance of Class 13 property under Schedule III.

Buildings or Structures

20. The capital cost of a leasehold interest that qualifies for inclusion in Class 13 does not include that part of a leasehold interest that is included in another class by reason of subsection 1102(5). This subsection provides that a reference to a property that is a "building or structure" in Schedule II of the Regulations includes a leasehold interest to the extent that the interest

(a) was acquired by reason of the fact that the taxpayer

    (i) erected a building or structure on leased land,

    (ii) made an addition to a leased building or structure, or

    (iii) made alterations to a leased building or structure that substantially changed the nature of the property, or

(b) was acquired after 1975 or, in the case of any property of Class 31 or 32, after November 18, 1974, from a former lessee and that lessee or a predecessor lessee had acquired the interest by

    (i) erecting a building or structure on leased land,

    (ii) making an addition to a leased building or structure, or

    (iii) making alterations to a leased building or structure that substantially changed the nature of the property.

The net effect of this requirement is that property described in subsection 1102(5) is included in another class of Schedule II, usually Class 3.

21. It is difficult to provide general rules as to what alterations to a leased building or structure have "substantially changed the nature of the property" and this is really a question of fact that depends on the degree and the extent of the alterations. The following may serve as a guide:

(a) the conversion by a tenant of one room into an office, or of one room into two rooms, is not such a change;

(b) a new store front, in itself, is not such a change; but

(c) the conversion by a tenant of a house into a duplex, apartment, offices or stores is such a change.

22. As a result of the requirements of subsection 1102(5) of the Regulations, it may be necessary in some situations to divide the capital cost of a leasehold interest into more than one prescribed class. For example, where a taxpayer expends an amount to obtain a leasehold interest in land and constructs a building that falls into Class 3, the capital cost of acquiring the lease will be included in Class 13 and the capital cost of the building will be included in Class 3. An allocation of the proceeds of disposition, if any, of such a leasehold interest will also be necessary and this should be done on a reasonable basis.

APPENDIX I

Illustration of the Application of Schedule III

As an illustration of the application of Schedule III, assume that a taxpayer, whose business taxation year is the calendar year, has had no leasehold interests, but in 1978 agrees to rent two adjoining vacant stores (X and Y) for use in the business, this being leasehold interest "A". The lease runs for 5 years from January 1, 1979 and contains rights to renew, on stated terms, for two further 5-year terms. In December 1978, the taxpayer is allowed to make certain altera-

¶3240

tions, costing $4,000, to store X, and immediately after getting possession on January 1, 1979, makes additional alterations to it at a cost of $11,000. In 1979, also, another store is rented (leasehold interest "B") for a term of 4 years from October 1 and at once alterations costing $6,000 are made. In 1980, the taxpayer expends $3,600 on alterations to store Y. In 1981, the taxpayer no longer needs store Y and is able to sell the part of

leasehold interest "A" relating to it for $2,900. In 1983 the taxpayer rents another store (leasehold interest "C") for a 5-year term and makes alterations in that year costing $10,000. Also, in 1983, the taxpayer disposes of the remainder of leasehold interest "A" for $9,400. Again in 1983, the taxpayer pays $1,800 to extend lease B for a further 6 years and in 1984 makes alterations costing $7,500.

	Leasehold Interest "A"			*Leasehold Interest "B"*		*Leasehold Interest "C"*	*Class Total*
	Store X	*Store Y*	*Total*	*Original*	*Extension*		
	$	$	$	$	$	$	$
1978 Capital expenditure	4,000		4,000				4,000
1979 Capital expenditure	11,000		11,000	6,000			17,000
	15,000(A)		15,000	6,000			21,000
1979 CCA	(1,500)(B)		(1,500)	(1,200)			(2,700)
1979 UCC at year end	13,500		13,500	4,800			18,300
1980 Capital expenditure		3,600	3,600				3,600
	13,500	3,600	17,100	4,800			21,900
1980 CCA	(1,500)	(400)(C)	(1,900)	(1,200)			(3,100)
1980 UCC at year end	12,000	3,200	15,200	3,600			18,800
1981 Disposal		(2,900)	(2,900)				(2,900)
	12,000	300	12,300	3,600			15,900
1981 CCA	(1,500)	(400)(D)	(1,900)	(1,200)			(3,100)
1981 UCC at year end	10,500	(100)	10,400	2,400			12,800
1982 CCA	(1,500)	(400)(D)	(1,900)	(1,200)			(3,100)
1982 UCC at year end	9,000	(500)	8,500	1,200			9,700
1983 Capital expenditure					1,800	10,000	11,800
1983 Disposal	(9,400)		(9,400)				(9,400)
	(400)	(500)	(900)	1,200	1,800	10,000	12,100
1983 CCA	(1,500)	(400)	(1,900)	(1,200)	(150)(E)	(1,000)(E)	(4,250)
1983 UCC at year end	(1,900)	(900)	(2,800)	0	1,650	9,000	7,850
1984 Improvements	—	—			7,500		7,500
1983 UCC at	(1,900)	(900)	(2,800)	0	9,150	9,000	15,350
1984 CCA	—	—	—(F)		(1,050)(G)	(2,000)	(3,050)
1984 UCC at year end	(1,900)	(900)	(2,800)	0	8,100	7,000	12,300
1985 CCA	—	—	—	—	(1,800)	(2,000)	(3,800)
1985 UCC at year end	(1,900)	(900)	(2,800)	0	6,300	5,000	8,500
1986 CCA	—	—	—	—	(1,800)	(2,000)	(3,800)
1986 UCC at year end	(1,900)	(900)	(2,800)	0	4,500	3,000	4,700
1987 CCA	—	—	—	—	(1,800)	(2,000)	(3,800)
1987 UCC at year end	(1,900)	(900)	(2,800)	0	2,700	1,000	900
1988 CCA:							
— per paragraph 1(*a*) of Schedule III					(1,800)	(1,000)(H)	(2,800)
— reduction required by paragraph 1(*b*)					$1,900(I)*		1,900
					2,800		
1988 UCC at year end	(1,900)	(900)	(2,800)	NIL			NIL

¶3240

	Leasehold Interest "A"			*Leasehold Interest "B"*		*Leasehold Interest "C"*	*Class Total*
	Store X	*Store Y*	*Total*	*Original*	*Extension*		
	$	$	$	$	$	$	$

Footnotes:

(A) By reason of paragraph 3(a) of Schedule III, the 1978 expenditure is deemed to have been made in 1979 and the 1979 unit of capital cost for leasehold interest "A" therefore is $15,000.

(B) Because of paragraph 3(b), the number of 12-month periods to be used for the purposes of section 2 is 10 (original lease plus first succeeding renewal) and the prorated portion for each year will be $1,500.

(C) The 1980 unit of capital cost for store Y ($3,600) must be apportioned over only 9 years, since this is the number of 12-month periods still remaining in the lease and first renewal when those costs were incurred; and the prorated portion thus will be $400.

(D) Since there is an undepreciated capital cost for leasehold interest "A", the taxpayer remains entitled to an annual allowance of $400 in respect of the unit of capital cost relating to store Y.

(E) The allowance for leasehold interest "C" is restricted to $1,000 and the extension to leasehold interest "B" to $150 by virtue of Regulation 1100(1)(b)(i),

being 1/2 of the $2,000 and $300 otherwise deductible under Schedule III.

(F) Paragraph 3(d) prohibits any allowances in respect of this interest in the 1984 and subsequent taxation years since no balance remains for the interest.

(G) The 1984 allowance for the improvements to leasehold interest "B" is restricted to 50% of the prorated amount of $1,500.

(H) Although leasehold interest "C" has expired by the end of 1988 an additional $1,000 is available in 1988 being the amount denied by the application of the 50% rule in 1983.

(I) In 1988 the balance in the class before taking CCA for that year is less than the CCA amounts available for leasehold interests "B" and "C". In these circumstances, paragraph 1(b) of Schedule III restricts the allowance for the year to the balance in the class. Finally, as that allowance reduces the undepreciated capital cost of the class to nil, no further allowances can be made in subsequent years, by reasons of paragraph 3(e), in respect of any of the capital expenditures referred to in the foregoing.

[3245] Interpretation Bulletin IT-469R: Capital Cost Allowance — Earth-Moving Equipment

[Interpretation Bulletin IT-469R is dated September 28, 1990.]

Reference: Paragraph 20(1)(a) of the Act (also subsections 1100(2), 1101(3) and 1101(5l), 1103(2d), 1104(5) and 1104(6) and Classes 22 and 38 of Schedule II of the Income Tax Regulations)

Application

This bulletin replaces and cancels Interpretation Bulletin IT-469 dated February 16, 1981.

Summary

This bulletin outlines the criteria in determining whether or not certain equipment qualifies to be included in Class 22 or 38 of Schedule II of the Income Tax Regulations as "power-operated movable equipment designed for the purpose of excavating,

moving, placing or compacting earth, rock, concrete or asphalt" (referred to in this bulletin as "qualifying equipment"). It also deals with the rates applicable to the two classes and the elections available to create a separate class for Class 38 property and to transfer property from Class 22 to 38.

Discussion and Interpretation

1. Subject to 7 below, Class 22 applies to qualifying equipment acquired after

¶3245

March 16, 1964 and before 1988, or before 1990 if it was

(a) acquired pursuant to an obligation in writing entered into by the taxpayer before June 18, 1987, or

(b) under construction by or on behalf of the taxpayer on June 18, 1987.

The maximum capital cost allowance in a taxation year for property included in Class 22 is 50% of the undepreciated capital cost of the class at the end of the taxation year.

2. Subject to 7 below, Class 38 applies to qualifying equipment acquired after 1987 unless acquired in 1988 or 1989 and 1(a) or (b) above applies. The maximum capital cost allowance in a taxation year for property included in Class 38 is 40%, 35% and 30% of the undepreciated capital cost of the class at the end of the taxation year for the 1988, 1989 and 1990 and subsequent calendar years, respectively. For taxation years which include a part of two calendar years with different rates, the rate applicable to the class for a calendar year is prorated based on the number of days of the taxation year in each applicable calendar year. The aggregate of the resulting rates determines the maximum rate of capital cost allowance for the taxation year. For example, the maximum rate for a taxpayer with a taxation year commencing on October 1, 1988 and ending on September 30, 1989 is established as follows:

$$\frac{40\% \text{ (rate for 1988)} \times 92 \text{ (days of taxation year in 1988)}}{365 \text{ (days in the taxation year)}} = 10.08\%$$

$$\frac{35\% \text{ (rate for 1989)} \times 273 \text{ (days of taxation year in 1989)}}{365 \text{ (days in the taxation year)}} = 26.17\%$$

Maximum rate for the taxation year   36.25%

3. Subsection 1101(5l) of the Regulations provides for an election to classify a property described in Class 38 in a separate class. The election must be made by letter in the tax return for the taxation year in which the taxpayer acquired the property. The election must be made no later than the last day on which the taxpayer may file a tax return for the taxation year in accordance with section 150 of the Act. The separate class election would allow a terminal loss to be realized if the property in the separate class is disposed of by abandonment or otherwise and there is an undepreciated capital

cost for that separate class at the end of the taxation year.

4. Subsection 1100(2) of the Regulations limits capital cost allowance claims in the taxation year of acquisition of Class 22 or 38 property to the amount otherwise available less one-half of the capital cost allowance attributable to "net acquisitions" in the year, determined on a class by class basis. The term "net acquisitions" generally refers to the cost of acquisitions in the year in excess of the net proceeds of dispositions in that year. Where a taxpayer has disposed of a Class 22 property in a particular taxation year and has acquired a Class 38 property before the end of the particular taxation year that is not included in a separate class (see 3 above), subsection 1103(2d) of the Regulations provides for an election to transfer the Class 22 property, before its disposition, to Class 38. This will have the effect of reducing or eliminating the capital cost allowance attributable to "net acquisitions" in a year. The use of this election also allows a taxpayer, in certain circumstances, to defer recapture of capital cost allowance by treating the Class 22 property as if it were included in Class 38. The election must be made by letter in the tax return for the taxation year in which the Class 22 property was disposed of. The election must be made no later than the last day on which the taxpayer may file a tax return for the taxation year in accordance with section 150 of the Act.

5. The phrase "power-operated" in Class 22 means a piece of equipment that is driven or handled either by its own motor or by a separate but closely associated source of power, such as a tractor in the case of earth-moving equipment or an air-compressor in the case of a rock drill. Where the separate source of power is portable and is designed to be particularly suitable for the operation of equipment described in Class 22 or 38 it may be included in that same class if it is used primarily for the operation of such equipment. Horse-powered or hand-operated equipment does not come within the scope of Class 22 or 38.

6. "Movable" equipment includes a machine that is designed to be moved, as the work requires, on its own wheels, treads or skids, or to be carried (e.g., certain compressed air drills). Immovable or semi-portable equipment is excluded from

¶3245

Class 22 or 38. For example, a machine for manufacturing cement blocks, which is used for the purpose of compacting concrete but is not movable, is excluded.

7. The following properties are not included in Class 22 or 38, even though they may fit the description of qualifying equipment:

(a) Vessels (including dredges), equipment forming part of a marine railway, and any other property included in Class 7,

(b) Property forming part of a railway, included in Class 4,

(c) Logging equipment included in Class 10 by virtue of paragraphs (n) or (o) of that class,

(d) Mining equipment and other property used in connection with a mine included in Class 28 or 41 or in Class 10 by virtue of paragraph (k), (l), (m) or (r) of that class,

(e) Power-operated movable equipment designed principally for natural resource exploration and included in Class 10 by virtue of paragraph (t) of that class or Class 41 by virtue of subparagraph $(b)(i)$ of that class.

8. For equipment to qualify under Class 22 or 38, the key requirement is that it be designed to be used for one or more of the purposes of excavating, moving, placing or compacting earth, rock, concrete or asphalt. Generally, the actual use by a taxpayer of a property that meets the foregoing qualifications is not a factor in determining whether or not it qualifies for inclusion in Class 22 or 38 unless its use is such that it would bring the asset into another class which would override Class 22 or 38. For example, if an asset is used in mining or logging, that use would indicate that it was acquired for such purpose and therefore is required to be included in Class 10, 28 or 41 rather than Class 22 or 38. Class 22 or 38 may also apply to equipment acquired after March 16, 1964 which has been leased to other persons for use by them.

9. Automotive equipment described in paragraph (a) of Class 10 may qualify for inclusion in Class 22 or 38, because the provisions of Class 22 or 38 override that paragraph of Class 10. However, where the automotive equipment is also described in one of

paragraphs (k) to (o), (r) or (t) of Class 10 or in Class 41, as well as Class 22 or 38, it is included in Class 10 or 41 since those paragraphs override Class 22 or 38.

Logging Road Equipment

10. The phrase "mechanical equipment acquired for logging operations" in paragraph (o) of Class 10 is considered to include power-operated, movable, road-building equipment acquired to construct roads to or within a timber limit. In accordance with the Federal Court of Appeal decision in the case of *Lor-Wes Contracting Ltd. v. The Queen*, [1985] 2 CTC 79 — 85 DTC 5310, the phrase applies to mechanical equipment acquired by a subcontractor of such roads. Such equipment is not included in Class 22 or 38.

Mining and Processing Equipment

11. Whether or not such equipment is owned by the owner of a mineral resource, the extended definition of "income from a mine" provided by subsections 1104(5) and (6) of the Regulations prevents the inclusion in Class 22 or 38 of equipment used in any stage of mineral production to the prime metal, pellet or crude oil stage or its equivalent. For example, trucks owned and operated by a processor of ore to the prime metal stage and used to haul ore from a mine to the refinery may not be included in Class 22 or 38.

Industrial Mineral Mining Equipment

12. An industrial mineral mine is a "mine" for purposes of Part XI of the Regulations. Subsections 1104(5) and (6) of the Regulations only extend the meaning of the term "mine" for the purposes stated. Accordingly, equipment acquired in relation to an industrial mineral mine that would otherwise qualify for inclusion in Class 22 or 38 is included in Class 10 by virtue of paragraph (k), (l) or (m) of that class or in Class 41 by virtue of paragraph (b) of that class. Examples of such equipment are shovels and loaders used in and around a gravel pit prior to processing activities and trucks used to transport the gravel to a processing plant.

Contractor's Movable Equipment

13. Property which is contractor's movable equipment except property qualified for inclusion in paragraph (t) of Class 10, in paragraph (b) of Class 41 or in a separate class prescribed by subsection 1101(2b) of

¶3245

the Regulations, is to be included in Class 10 by virtue of paragraph (h) of that class. However, if such property would also qualify for inclusion in Class 22 or 38, it is included in Class 22 or 38 and not Class 10 because of the specific exclusion in subparagraph (h)(iii) of Class 10.

14. Generally cranes or hoists used in lifting or placing objects or material do not qualify for inclusion in Class 22 or 38. If such equipment is designed, modified or acquired with special accessories to enable it to be used for the purposes of excavating, moving, placing or compacting earth, rock, concrete or asphalt, such equipment may be included in Class 22 or 38.

15. Equipment that handles one or more of the items specified in Class 22 (i.e., earth, rock, concrete or asphalt) but does so for some purpose other than excavating, moving, placing or compacting as referred to in that class would not qualify for inclusion

in that class or in Class 38. Examples of such equipment are

(a) an asphalt batching plant,

(b) crushing, washing and screening equipment, and

(c) a cement mixer not designed for the direct placing of concrete. On the other hand, a truck-mounted cement mixer is included in Class 22 or 38 because it is designed to allow its contents to be put directly into place.

16. The following are items, frequently used by contractors and others, that do not meet the requirements for inclusion in Class 22 or 38:

(a) pile drivers and related equipment,

(b) truck weigh scales, and

(c) equipment transporters.

[3250] Interpretation Bulletin IT-472: Capital Cost Allowance — Class 8 Property

[Interpretation Bulletin IT-472 is dated February 16, 1981.]

Reference: Paragraph $20(1)(a)$ (also Part XI of the Income Tax Regulations and Class 8 of Schedule II).

1. Paragraph $13(21)(b)$ of the Act defines depreciable property as property in respect of which the taxpayer has been allowed, or is entitled to, a deduction in computing income as permitted by the Regulations made under paragraph $20(1)(a)$. Class 8 property is one of the classes of property prescribed in Schedule II of the Regulations. However, unlike other classes in Schedule II, paragraph (i) of Class 8 provides that a tangible capital property that is not specifically included in any other class comes within Class 8, provided that it is not specifically excluded by the exceptions in that paragraph or by Regulation 1102. For this reason, Class 8 is sometimes referred to as the "catch-all" class. This bulletin comments on Class 8 property with emphasis on property that is to be included in this class by reason of paragraph (i).

*2. Class 8 was originally designed to cover tangible capital assets that were not included in another class in Schedule II. However, its scope has subsequently been enlarged and now, in addition to the original

"catch-all" provision of paragraph (i), Class 8 contains provisions for a number of inclusions and exclusions, which may be summarized as follows:

(a) Paragraphs (a) to (h) describe specific properties which fall in Class 8, provided that they are not otherwise included in Class 2, 7, 9, 11 or 30 (see 4 to 6 below).

(b) A tangible capital property that is not included in any other class qualifies, by reason of the "catch-all" provision in paragraph (i), for inclusion in Class 8. It should be noted that to qualify for the inclusion it must be a *tangible* property and not be subject to the specific exclusions in subparagraphs (i) to (xi) of paragraph (i) (see 7 below).

(c) Paragraph (j) contains a general provision qualifying for inclusion in Class 8 all radiocommunication equipment acquired after May 25, 1976, that is not included in any other class.

---

* As amended by Special Release, September 6, 1991.

¶3250

(d) Paragraph (k) provides for the inclusion of a rapid transit car that is used for public transportation within a metropolitan area and is not part of a railway system.

(e) Paragraph (l) provides for the inclusion of an outdoor advertising poster panel or bulletin board.

Certain property that would otherwise be included in Class 8 must be included in one of the following classes where the property meets the description of that particular class: Class 4, 10(g) to (w), 15, 17(a), 19, 21, 24(a), 25, 28, 29, 34, 37, 39 or 41. Under certain circumstances specified in Regulation 1103(2) a property which would otherwise be included in Class 8 that was acquired before May 26, 1976, to produce income from a particular business may, if the taxpayer so elects, be included in Class 2, 4 or 17 with other property acquired for that business. In addition, property which would otherwise be included in Class 8 may be included in Class 1, if the taxpayer elects under Regulation 1103(1) to include in Class 1 that property and all other properties otherwise included in Classes 2 to 12 that were acquired to produce income from the same business. Finally, a taxpayer with certain property which would otherwise be included in Class 8 may choose instead to include that property in Class 24(b) or in Class 27, if it meets the description in that class. On the other hand, a taxpayer with property which would otherwise be included in Class 19 or Class 21 may elect under Regulation 1103(2a) to include in Class 8 all the properties of either of these classes owned by him at the beginning of a taxation year.

3. Subject to the above comments, the remainder of this bulletin deals with those properties specifically included in or excluded from Class 8 and provides examples of assets which, in the Department's view, qualify for inclusion in Class 8.

4.

(a) A structure that is manufacturing or processing machinery or equipment is included in Class 8 under paragraph (a). Other machinery or equipment of any kind that is not specifically included in any other class may also fall in Class 8 by reason of paragraph (i);

(b) Tangible property attached to a building is not included in the same class as the building but in Class 8 under paragraph (b), if it is acquired solely for

   (i) servicing, supporting, or providing access to machinery or equipment,

   (ii) manufacturing or processing, or

   (iii) a combination of functions in (i) and (ii).

Common examples of such property are: hoppers located outside a plant building but erected on a steel framework or other permanent foundation, as well as the housing and framework for outdoor elevators and conveyor systems, acquired for use in manufacturing or processing operations; concrete footings, foundations and structural steel used exclusively for the support of machinery or equipment; stairs and platforms used solely to provide access to machinery or equipment. It is not necessary that the building, to which this property is attached, be owned by the taxpayer to qualify for the inclusion of that property in Class 8.

*5. Class 8 includes under paragraphs (c) to (e) and (l) the following buildings or structures:

(a) A building that is a kiln, tank or vat acquired for manufacturing or processing operations; this includes a building that is a tobacco bulk curing kiln;

(b) a building or other structure, acquired after February 19, 1973, that is designed for the purpose of preserving ensilage on a farm;

(c) a building or other storage facility, acquired after February 19, 1973, that is designed to provide storage at a controlled level of temperature and humidity for fresh fruits and vegetables if these facilities are used principally for such storage by the grower of such fruits and vegetables.

(d) An outdoor advertising poster panel or bulletin board acquired after 1987, other than property acquired before 1990 that was acquired pursuant to a

---

* As amended by Special Release, September 6, 1991.

¶3250

written obligation entered into before June 18, 1987 or was under construction on June 18, 1987. Such property when used to earn rental income was previously included in Class 11. A special election, discussed in 11 below, is available for this property under Regulation 1103(2d).

6. Electrical generating equipment acquired after May 25, 1976 is included in Class 8 under paragraphs (f) to (h) if:

(a) the taxpayer's business is not the production for the use of or distribution to others of electrical energy, the equipment is auxiliary to the taxpayer's main power supply, and it is not used regularly as a source of supply,

(b) the equipment has a maximum load capacity of not more than 15 kilowatts, or

(c) the equipment is portable.

7. It should be noted that tangible property that is specifically excluded from Class 8 by virtue of subparagraphs (i) to (xi) of paragraph (i) may qualify for capital cost allowance under other provisions, e.g., a mine is excluded from Class 8 by reason of subparagraph (v), but may qualify under Regulation 1100(1)(g) and Schedule V as an industrial mineral mine.

Property Included in Class 8 under Paragraph (i)

*8. Various types of tangible capital property that are not included in any other class in Schedule II come within Class 8 by reason of the provision of paragraph (i). The Department considers the following property to be so included in Class 8:

(a) Libraries of taxpayers practising a profession. This includes reference libraries, data banks, land surveyor's field notes, credit bureau dockets, archives of a notary public or reference material purchased by a taxpayer;

(b) Bowling alleys, since such alleys are not regarded as a component part of the building in which they are located;

(c) An advertising sign (e.g., poster panel, bulletin board) or electrical advertising sign (e.g., neon sign) not

qualifying for inclusion in Class 11 and not otherwise qualifying for inclusion in Class 8 by virtue of paragraph (l) thereof. A sign attached to the exterior of rented premises otherwise qualifying as Class 8 property will be included in Class 13, when the sign was purchased by a tenant and must be left behind upon the expiration of the lease. This includes a removable store front door, doorway or show window;

(d) A mannequin or a dummy for merchandise display;

(e) Grain handling equipment of line and terminal grain elevators, such as:

(i) driers and related heating equipment;

(ii) scales;

(iii) cleaning equipment;

(iv) elevator legs, conveyors and spouting;

(v) car dumpers and shovels;

(vi) dust control systems;

(f) Storage and refrigeration equipment of a cold storage warehouse; refrigeration machinery and lockers of a frozen food locker plant; and refrigerating units used in walk-in refrigeration rooms;

(g) Cobalt 60;

(h) A filtration system, including the pump, for an outdoor swimming pool; also underwater lights and the wiring therefor, ladders, diving boards, slides, etc. are included in Class 8, unless the taxpayer includes them in Class 6 as component parts of the pool;

(i) Mattresses, pillows, eiderdowns, electric sheets, electric blankets and other bedding used by hotels and motels and not included in "linen" under Class 12;

(j) Pumping equipment of a gas or oil pipeline carrier, including engines, motors, pumps, special foundations therefor and the costs of installation, such as heavy wiring, transformers, etc. (but not including buildings or building foundations as such);

---

* As amended by Special Release, September 6, 1991.

¶3250

(k) A pipeline for oil or natural gas not included in Class 2 where the Minister has been satisfied that the main source of supply is likely to be exhausted within 15 years;

(l) Rugs and carpets initially installed to furnish a new or renovated hotel, theatre, store or similar establishment;

(m) A so-called "building" made of air-supported fabric which is not a building or other structure within the ordinary meaning of these words;

(n) Water well equipment such as casing, cribwork, piping, etc. However, the cost of drilling the well is a deductible expense;

(o) A storage tank designed for all-purpose storage of liquid products, but not an oil or water storage tank (which must be included in Class 6(e)). On the other hand, a building that is a tank acquired for the purpose of manufacturing or processing, although a Class 8 property, is included in that class by virtue of paragraph (c) (see 5 above);

(p) Sheet music, scores, transcriptions, phonograph records and the like acquired by a self-employed professional musician or an orchestra;

(q) A master audio-tape or a master disc used in the phonograph record industry. However, a master die (stamper) for processing records is a Class 12 property;

*(r) Returnable containers if treated by the taxpayer (vendor) as depreciable property. This includes pallets, cable reels, paper cores and other shipping or cargo containers in, or by which, goods are delivered and are normally returned for use (For further comments see IT-165.);

(s) [Deleted by Special Release, September 6, 1991.]

(t) Artificial snow making equipment (compressor, spray gun, piping);

(u) Auto-refractor eye-testing equipment;

(v) Tile drainage if installed by the owner of land, provided that the cost thereof was not deducted in computing income from a farming business under section 30. Where land is purchased with tile drainage already installed, the full purchase price is considered to relate to the land and, therefore, no part of it is subject to capital cost allowance;

(w) A kitchen utensil, medical or dental instrument, or a tool not specifically included in Class 12 (costing $200 or more);

(x) A greenhouse steam plant, except where it is located in or immediately adjacent to the greenhouse (or a combined greenhouse and storage or shipping building) and its steam output is used primarily to heat only that one greenhouse (or combined building). In that case, the steam plant should be regarded as a component part of the greenhouse and subject to capital cost allowance at the Class 6 rate;

(y) Utility systems such as water pipes, electrical wiring or sewer lines connecting individual units of a mobile home or trailer park on land owned by the taxpayer, except property included in Class 2;

(z) A filmstrip (if it is acquired and used together with a motion picture film, it may be included in Class 10, 12 or 18), see IT-283R2;

(aa) Telephone switching equipment acquired after May 25, 1976, and installed on the premises of a customer of the owner of such equipment.

*9. The above list of properties is not intended to be complete. It is only representative of various types of property which qualify for inclusion in Class 8 under the present legislation. IT-79R3 entitled "Capital Cost Allowance — Buildings or Other Structures" has additional comments on Class 8 property described in 4, 5(a) and 8(o) of this bulletin. Comments on computer and systems software that is Class 8 property will be found in IT-283R2 "Capital Cost Allowance — Video Tapes, Films, Computer Software and Master Recording Tapes".

*10. For property acquired after 1987 subsection 1101(5l) of the Regulations provides for an election to classify a property

---

* As amended by Special Release, September 6, 1991.

¶3250

described in paragraph (l) of Class 8 into a separate class. The election must be made by letter in the tax return for the taxation year in which the taxpayer acquired the property. Subject to coming into force rules, the election must be made no later than the last day on which the taxpayer may file a tax return for the year in accordance with section 150 of the Act. The separate class election would allow a terminal loss to be claimed if the property in the separate class is disposed of or abandoned for proceeds which are less than the undepreciated capital cost remaining in the separate class. The election is effective from the first day of the taxation year for which the election is made and remains effective for all subsequent years (Regulation 1101(5j)).

**11. Subsection 1103(2d) of the Regulations provides an election which allows taxpayers to transfer property from one class (the old class) to another (the new class). The effect of the election is that the property is transferred to the new class before its disposition. The election can be made when, in the same year,

(a) a property (new property) is acquired in the new class,

(b) a property of the old class is disposed of,

(c) property of the old class would have been in the same class as the new property if it were acquired at the same time and from the same person as the new property, and vice versa for the property of the new class, and

(d) the new class is not a separate class described in Regulation 1101.

This election may allow a taxpayer to defer a recapture of capital cost allowance, or increase the amount of capital cost allowance available in the year where regulation 1100(2) (the 50% rule) would otherwise have restricted the amount claimed. (See the current version of IT-285, *Capital Cost Allowance — General Comments* for an explanation of the 50% rule.)

The election is made by letter in the tax return for the year of disposition. It must be made by the deadline for filing returns under section 150 of the Act.

[3255] Interpretation Bulletin IT-476: Capital Cost Allowance — Gas and Oil Exploration and Production Equipment

[*Interpretation Bulletin IT-476 is dated April 30, 1981.*]

Reference: Paragraph 20(1)(a) of the Act (also subsection 1104(2) and Class 10 of Schedule II of the Income Tax Regulations)

1. The comments in this bulletin pertain to the classification for capital cost allowance purposes of depreciable equipment acquired for exploring and producing gas and oil. They do not extend to exploration and development expenses referred to in sections 66, 66.1 or 66.2, or to manufacturing and distributing equipment used in connection with the refining of oil or processing of natural gas.

2. Where capital equipment, other than well casing, is acquired for drilling or exploration purposes, its cost is not a "Canadian exploration and development expense" referred to in paragraph 66(15)(b), nor is it a Canadian exploration expense or a Canadian development expense referred to in paragraphs 66.1(6)(a) or 66.2(5)(a). Such equipment may, however, qualify for inclu-

sion in a prescribed class under Part XI of the Regulations.

3. Drilling rigs (other than rigs that qualify as vessels under Class 7), whether owned by an oil or gas company or by a contract driller, are included in Class 10. For a discussion of capital cost allowance in respect of offshore drilling rigs, see IT-267R2, "Capital Cost Allowance — Vessels."

4. By virtue of the exclusions in paragraphs (i)(iv) and (i)(vi) of Class 8, capital cost allowance is not available in respect of an oil or gas well as such. However, equipment located below the well head including tubing (but not well casing), in-ground pumping equipment, and other ancillary in-ground equipment is "gas or oil

---

** Added by Special Release, September 6, 1991.

¶3255

well equipment" included in Class 10, by virtue of paragraph (j), thereof. Also, the well head and equipment above it, e.g., the casing head, tubing head, Christmas tree or, in the case of a low pressure oil well requiring pumping, the pumping unit, is also "gas or oil well equipment".

5. Gas or oil well equipment is defined in subsection 1104(2) of the Regulations. It includes, in addition to the equipment referred to in 4 above, only such equipment, pipelines or structures as are necessary in a gas or oil field for the production of natural gas or crude oil. It is the Department's view that, in respect of an oil well or field, operations up to and including the primary field separator and field storage facilities are production operations. Similarly, in a gas field, operations involving a primary separation of the well effluent in the field together with any necessary storage operation in the field are also production operations. Consequently all equipment (including measuring and testing equipment), pipelines and structures used in such operations are gas or oil well equipment.

6. By virtue of the definition in subsection 1104(2) of the Regulations oil well equipment does not include pipelines used to remove crude oil or natural gas from the field after primary separation and storage or

equipment or structures used for the refining of oil or the processing of natural gas. However, a pipeline used solely for transmitting gas to a natural gas processing plant is included by definition in gas or oil well equipment. A field gathering system used solely to feed such a gas pipeline will also be included.

*7. A natural gas compressor station located in the gas field that is used to enhance the recovery of gas from a reservoir either by the creation of a pressure differential within the gathering system in order to expedite the flow from the gas reservoir or as part of a secondary recovery program, is gas or oil well equipment. A natural gas compressor station used in conjunction with a gathering system to either stabilize the varying field pressures for transmission of the gas to a gas processing plant or to compress the gas to a pressure required for its transmission to a gas processing plant is gas or oil well equipment. Equipment, structures and connecting lines for the purpose of disposing of waste substances produced from a gas or oil well, for the purpose of injecting gas or liquids into a gas or oil formation to facilitate production therefrom or for the purpose of enhancing the recovery from a gas or oil well will also qualify as gas or oil well equipment.

[3260]   Interpretation Bulletin IT-477:   Capital Cost Allowance — Patents, Franchises, Concessions and Licences [Consolidated]

[Interpretation Bulletin IT-477 is dated April 30, 1981 — consolidated October 2001.]

Reference: Paragraph $20(1)(a)$ of the Act (also Class 14 of Schedule II, paragraph $1100(1)(c)$ and subsection 1100(9) of the Income Tax Regulations)

Application

This bulletin is a consolidation of the following:

- IT-477 dated April 30, 1981; and

- subsequent amendments thereto.

For further particulars, see the "Bulletin Revisions" section near the end of this bulletin.

Summary

This bulletin deals with paragraph $20(1)(a)$ of the *Income Tax Act* (the Act) and paragraph $1100(1)(c)$ of the Income Tax Regulations (the Regulations) which allow a taxpayer to claim capital cost allowance in respect of property in Class 14 of Schedule II of the Regulations.

---

* As amended by Correction Sheet No. 3, June 6, 1983.

¶3260

Discussion and Interpretation

General

1. Class 14 property is prescribed to be property that is a patent, franchise, concession or licence for a limited period in respect of property but not including

(a) a franchise, concession or licence in respect of minerals, petroleum, natural gas, other related hydrocarbons or timber and property relating thereto (except a franchise for distributing gas to consumers or a licence to export gas from Canada or from a province) or in respect of a right to explore for, drill for, take or remove minerals, petroleum, natural gas, other related hydrocarbons or timber,

(b) a leasehold interest, or

(c) a property that is included in Class 23.

(d) a licence to use computer software (applicable in respect of property acquired after May 25, 1976).

2. The general rules regarding capital cost allowance are not discussed in detail in this bulletin but it should be kept in mind that a property is not included in Class 14 (or any other class of property described in Part XI and Schedule II of the Regulations) if it is a property described in subsection 1102(1) of the Regulations.

Calculation of Maximum Allowance

3. Pursuant to paragraph $1100(1)(c)$ of the Regulations, the maximum capital cost allowance available to a taxpayer in any year in respect of Class 14 property is the lesser of:

(a) the aggregate of the amounts obtained by apportioning the capital cost of each property over the life of the property remaining at the time the cost was incurred, or

(b) the undepreciated capital cost to him as of the end of the taxation year of property of that class.

4. It is the CCRA's view that the life of the property referred to in ¶3(a) generally refers to the maximum period that the property may be used for the purposes of earning income. That is, the apportionment of the capital cost of a Class 14 property should generally be made equally over the remaining life of the property. However, the CCRA accepts that the capital cost of a Class 14 property may be apportioned on another basis where, based on the legal agreements and other relevant factors, the taxpayer can clearly demonstrate that it is reasonable. For example, where a 3 year licence provides that a television program may be broadcast three times in year 1, and once in each of years 2 and 3, it would generally be appropriate to allocate $\frac{3}{5}$ of the capital cost to year 1 and $\frac{1}{5}$ to each of years 2 and 3.

5. Where less than the maximum allowance is claimed in a taxation year, the difference between the amount claimed and the maximum allowance for that year can be deducted only as a terminal loss under subsection 20(16) in a taxation year at the end of which the taxpayer owns no Class 14 property. For example, assume that a taxpayer with a December 31 year-end acquires, on January 1, 2000, a licence expiring on December 31, 2004, which represents the taxpayer's only asset in Class 14. Assume further that the asset was acquired at a cost of $1,000 and that, based on the life of the licence, the taxpayer is entitled to an allowance of up to $200 per year. If only $1 is claimed in 2000, the maximum allowance continues to be $200 in subsequent years and the $199 not claimed in 2000 would become deductible as a terminal loss in 2004, if no Class 14 property is owned by the taxpayer at the end of 2004.

6. Subsection 1100(3) of the Regulations which, in certain instances, requires capital cost allowance to be prorated over a short taxation year, does not apply to Class 14 property.

Election in Case of Patent

7. Where the cost of a patent is determined wholly or partly by reference to the use of the patent, capital cost allowance may be claimed under subsection 1100(9) of the Regulations rather than under paragraph $1100(1)(c)$. Under this subsection, the taxpayer is permitted to deduct an amount, not exceeding the undepreciated capital cost of the property in Class 14, of up to the aggregate of

(a) the part of the capital cost of the patent determined by reference to the use of the patent in the year, and

¶3260

(b) the part of the capital cost of the Class 14 property apportioned to the year under 3(a) above after excluding from capital cost any amounts determined by reference to the use of the patent in that year or previous years.

8. It should be noted that subsection 1100(9) of the Regulations applies to patents only and not to any other Class 14 property. For instance, a licence to use a patent will, if it is for a limited period, qualify as Class 14 property but will not be eligible for the elective treatment under this subsection.

Definitions

9. In Canada, a patent is defined in the *Patent Act* as letters patent for an invention. Accordingly, no patent exists under that Act until the date the letters patent are granted and issued as noted on the face of the patent, and capital cost allowance is not available in respect of the cost of acquiring a patent while a patent is pending. The life of a patent in Canada is 17 years from the date the letters patent are granted and issued.

10. Foreign patents, that is those granted by a foreign government, may qualify as depreciable property in the same way as other foreign property. Reference is made to IT-205 in this regard. The relevant foreign law would govern in determining when the patent comes into existence, whether or not the patent is "for a limited term" and the "life of the property remaining at the time the cost was incurred" for the purposes of claiming capital cost allowance.

11. The words "franchise, concession or licence", are not capable of easy definition. Generally, they must be given the meaning or sense in which they are normally employed by businessmen on this continent and they extend, not only to certain kinds of rights, privileges or monopolies conferred by or pursuant to legislation or by governmental authority, but also to analogous rights, privileges or authorities created by contract between private parties. Again, generally, these words are used to refer to some right, privilege or monopoly that enables the holder to carry on his business or earn income from property, or that facilitates the carrying on of his business or the earning of income from property. These words do not extend to a contract under which a person is entitled to remuneration for the performance of specified services,

nor to a covenant not to compete for a limited period.

12. A trademark does not qualify as a Class 14 property. (See IT-143R.)

Expectation of Class 14 Property

13. A payment made to obtain a patent, franchise, concession or licence is included in the capital cost of the property whether made to the actual grantor or to a holder of such property in order that he will relinquish it in favour of the payer. Where, however, a taxpayer pays an amount, either separately or as part of a payment to acquire the business or assets of another person, for which he does not obtain an existing patent, franchise, concession or licence but only the right to stand in place of that other person in applying for such a property or for a renewal thereof, no part of that amount is paid for property of Class 14; such amount may, however, qualify as an eligible capital expenditure for the purposes of section 14. An example would be where a taxpayer pays an amount to a vendor for a licensed taxicab where the licence is not transferable but he fully expects that the licensing authority will issue a new licence to him. Such amount would not be depreciable as the taxpayer is paying for a mere expectation of being granted a licence.

"Life of the Property" and "Limited Period"

14. Property that is a patent, franchise, concession or licence qualifies under Class 14 only if it is for a "limited period", and its cost is depreciable, pursuant to paragraph $1100(1)(c)$ of the Regulations, "over the life of the property remaining at the time the cost was incurred". That is, it must be for a period capable of being ascertained at the time the cost was incurred. For example, under the *Copyright Act*, copyright in a work generally subsists for the life of the author and fifty years after his death. As the period during which the author may live is not ascertainable during his lifetime, a taxpayer may only include in Class 14 a copyright acquired after the death of the author. On the other hand, a licence for a limited term of up to 50 years under a copyright granted before the author's death would be depreciable.

15. The provisions of a franchise, concession or licence concerning renewals or

¶3260

extensions following the original term are relevant in determining the life of the property and whether or not the property is for a limited period. Where such renewals or extensions are automatic or within the control of the taxpayer, that is they do not require any further negotiation with or the concurrence or consent of the grantor, the life of the property includes such additional periods. For instance, where a franchise with an initial term of 5 years can be renewed at the option of the franchisee for one further 3-year period, the life of the franchise is 8 years. On the other hand, where the concurrence of the franchiser is required, the life of the property does not include any renewal period. Where the taxpayer has an option to renew or extend the term only if certain conditions are met, for instance meeting certain performance or sales criteria, the circumstances of the particular case must be examined to determine whether or not, when he acquired the property, it was reasonably certain that these conditions would be met. If so, the additional periods are included in the life of the property.

16. Where renewal or extension periods are considered part of the life of the property under the criteria set out in 15 above, and where the number of such renewals or extensions is indefinite, the property is not for a limited period and does not qualify as a Class 14 property. Where the number of such renewals or extensions is definite, for example, where a licence is for an initial term of 5 years and the licensee has options to renew the licence for two further 3-year periods, the property is for a limited term, in this example 11 years. The number of renewals or extensions may, in fact, be limited in certain circumstances even if the relevant agreement does not expressly provide such limits. For instance, a licence under a Canadian patent under which the licensee has unlimited rights of renewal has a limited life because the life of the patent is itself limited to 17 years.

17. Provisions, including *force majeure* and contingency termination clauses, which may result in an early termination of the life of a property are not considered relevant in determining the life of the property and whether or not the property is for a limited period. For example, a franchise with an initial term of 5 years containing an option exercisable by the franchisee to renew for one further period of 5 years is for a limited

period, namely 10 years, notwithstanding that the franchiser may become entitled to terminate the franchise agreement upon giving 60 days notice.

Industrial Designs

18. Under the *Industrial Design Act*, an industrial design is protected for a period of 5 years from the date of registration subject to renewal for a further period of up to 5 years. A registered industrial design is considered to be a franchise for a limited period and the life of the property on initial registration is 10 years.

Capital Cost

19. The capital cost of a Class 14 property includes the purchase price, if any, and any legal fees and disbursements, registration fees and representation expenses laid out to acquire the property. Expenses paid in a year in making a representation, relating to a business being carried on by a taxpayer, to a government, government agency or other body referred to in paragraph $20(1)(cc)$, including any representation for the purpose of obtaining a licence, permit, franchise or patent, are deductible under paragraph $20(1)(cc)$ (or, if an election is made, under subsection $20(9)$). However, if the representation expense was laid out to acquire a Class 14 property, it will also form part of the capital cost thereof. To avoid a further deduction under paragraph $20(1)(a)$ in respect of the same amount and to permit recapture of the expenditure, subsection $13(12)$ deems the amount deducted under paragraph $20(1)(cc)$ (or in respect of which an election has been made under subsection $20(9)$), to the extent that it forms part of the capital cost of the property, to have been allowed as capital cost allowance.

20. Where expenses related to the acquisition of a Class 14 property are incurred in a year prior to the year in which the property is acquired, they will be added to the capital cost of the property in the year of its acquisition. No claim for capital cost allowance may be made in a year prior to the year of the actual acquisition of the relevant property.

21. The capital cost to the original owner of a patent or industrial design includes research and development expenses incurred in discovering, designing or developing the property to the extent that such expenses have not already been deducted as

¶3260

scientific research expenditures or ordinary operating expenses in the computation of income.

22. Once the invention or design has been developed to the point where a patent or an industrial design registration can be obtained, subsequent expenses for the purpose of turning the property to account would not form part of its capital cost.

Bulletin Revisions

Since the issuance of IT-477 on April 30, 1981, there have been no revisions to ¶s 2 and 3 or ¶s 6 to 22.

The first sentence of the original ¶1 is now the Summary of the consolidated bulletin.

¶4 was modified to reflect the CCRA's revised interpretative position regarding the apportionment of the cost of a Class 14 property.

The example given in ¶5 was updated so as not to contradict the revised interpretative position set out in ¶4.

[3265] Interpretation Bulletin IT-478R2: Capital Cost Allowance — Recapture and Terminal Loss

[Interpretation Bulletin IT-478R2 is dated September 17, 1999.]

Reference: Subsections 13(1) and 20(16) (also subsections 8(2), 13(2), 13(3), 13(7.1), 13(7.4), 13(8), 13(9), 20(16.1), 20(16.2), 20(16.3) and 25(3); the definition of "total depreciation" and "undepreciated capital cost" in subsection 13(21); and paragraphs 8(1)(*j*), 8(1)(*p*) and 13(7)(*a*) of the *Income Tax Act*; and sections 1103 and 7307 of the Income Tax Regulations)

On November 1, 1999, Revenue Canada will begin operations as the Canada Customs and Revenue Agency.

Application

This bulletin replaces and cancels IT-478R, dated March 9, 1992. The effective date of a particular legislative provision discussed in this bulletin may be indicated in the Explanation of Changes section (or, in some cases, in the Discussion and Interpretation section). However, where the bulletin is silent with respect to the effective date of a particular provision, such date can be obtained from the legislation itself.

Summary

This bulletin discusses recaptures of capital cost allowance and terminal losses, which are based on the undepreciated capital cost of depreciable property of a prescribed class. Generally, if the total of all the decreases exceeds the total of all the increases to the undepreciated capital cost of a particular class as of the end of a taxation year, a recapture of that excess is included in the taxpayer's income. Recaptures are usually caused by dispositions of depreciable property, although they can also result from delayed receipts of government assistance.

If the total of all the increases exceeds the total of all the decreases to the undepreciated capital cost of the class as of the end of the year and there are no properties remaining in the class, a terminal loss is deducted in computing the taxpayer's income. If a business is discontinued, a terminal loss for a particular class of depreciable property used in the business is not available unless and until all the property in that class is disposed of.

This bulletin also discusses provisions that can alter the amount of recapture or terminal loss or affect the taxation year in which a recapture or terminal loss will occur. Rules pertaining to non-residents are also discussed, as well as other miscellaneous matters.

Discussion and Interpretation

Calculation of Undepreciated Capital Cost

1. The undepreciated capital cost (UCC) of depreciable property of a prescribed class is used as the base for claiming a deduction for capital cost allowance (CCA) for that class. The system of provisions under which UCC is calculated is also used for determining the amount that is to be included in income under subsection 13(1) as a recap-

¶3265

ture of CCA or the amount to be deducted from income under subsection 20(16) as a terminal loss. According to the definition of "undepreciated capital cost" in subsection 13(21), the UCC to a taxpayer of depreciable property of a particular class as of a particular time is equal to the amount, if any, by which the total of the increases to the UCC of the class exceeds the total of the decreases to the UCC of the class.

2. The increases to the taxpayer's UCC of a particular class are as follows (each reference to a "property" means a "depreciable property of the class"):

(a) the capital cost to the taxpayer of each property acquired before the time of the UCC calculation;

(b) each amount of CCA recapture for the class included, by virtue of section 13, in the taxpayer's income for any taxation year ending before the time of the UCC calculation;

(c) the amount of each repayment (pursuant to a legal obligation) by the taxpayer, after the taxpayer's disposition of a particular property (and before the time of the UCC calculation), of any assistance from a government, municipality or other public authority as described in subsection 13(7.1), if the repayment would have increased the capital cost of the property by virtue of paragraph 13(7.1)(*d*) had it occurred before the property's disposition;

(d) the amount of each repayment (pursuant to a legal obligation) by the taxpayer, after the taxpayer's disposition of a particular property (and before the time of the UCC calculation), of any inducement, assistance or other amount received and described in paragraph 12(1)(*x*), if such amount received previously reduced the capital cost of the property pursuant to an election under subsection 13(7.4) and the repayment would then have increased the capital cost of the property by virtue of paragraph 13(7.4)(*b*) had it occurred before the property's disposition; and

(e) each amount payable after February 23, 1998 and paid by the taxpayer before the time of the UCC calculation as or on account of a proposed or existing countervailing or anti-dumping duty on a particular property.

3. The decreases to the taxpayer's UCC of a particular class are as follows (each reference to a "property" means a "depreciable property of the class"):

(a) the total depreciation (i.e., CCA) allowed to the taxpayer for the class before the time of the UCC calculation;

(b) any amount by which the taxpayer's UCC for the class is required (otherwise than because of a reduction in the taxpayer's capital cost of depreciable property) to be reduced at or before the time of the UCC calculation because of subsection 80(5), under what is commonly known as the "debt forgiveness rules";

(c) for each disposition of a property of the taxpayer (other than a timber resource property) that has occurred before the time of the UCC calculation, the lesser of the following two amounts:

● the proceeds of the property's disposition minus any disposition costs of the taxpayer, and

● the taxpayer's capital cost of the property;

(d) for each disposition of a timber resource property of the taxpayer that has occurred before the time of the UCC calculation, the proceeds of the property's disposition minus any disposition costs of the taxpayer;

(e) each amount of investment tax credit allowed to the taxpayer on a property for a taxation year which has ended before the UCC calculation and after the taxpayer's disposition of the property (note: if the UCC calculation is made prior to the 1988 taxation year, also include any investment tax credit allowed to the taxpayer for the current year before the time of the UCC calculation and after the taxpayer's disposition of the property);

(f) each amount of assistance from a government, municipality or other public authority as described in subsection 13(7.1), which the taxpayer received (or which the taxpayer was entitled to receive) after the taxpayer's disposition of a property and before the UCC calculation, in respect of or for the (previous) acquisition of the property, if

¶3265

such assistance would have decreased the capital cost of the property by virtue of paragraph 13(7.1)(*f*) had it been received before the property's disposition;

(g) with respect to a Class 28 mining property of the taxpayer (as a mine operator), the amount of income from the mine that was exempt from tax under ITAR 28, as it read prior to October 29, 1985, if the taxpayer elected under section 1100A of the Income Tax Regulations to claim accelerated CCA on that class; and

(h) each amount received by the taxpayer after February 23, 1998 and before the time of the UCC calculation in respect of a refund of an amount described in 2(e) added to the UCC of the class.

4. Although the definition of "undepreciated capital cost" in subsection 13(21) provides that the UCC of a class as of a particular time is calculated as the excess (if any) of all the increases over all the decreases to that UCC which have occurred since the inception of the class, in actual practice most taxpayers carry forward the UCC at the end of the previous taxation year as the UCC at the beginning of the current year. If this is done, the taxpayer then needs only to add and subtract the increases and decreases for the current year for purposes of calculating the UCC at the end of the current year.

Recapture of Capital Cost Allowance

5. If the total of all the decreases exceeds the total of all the increases to the UCC of a class as of the end of a taxation year, subsection 13(1) provides that this excess shall be included in computing the taxpayer's income for the year. This "CCA recapture" then becomes an increase for purposes of ¶2(b) when calculating the UCC of the class in a subsequent year, thus ensuring that such recapture will not be included in income again. A CCA recapture can occur in a number of different situations, as in the following examples:

(a) The proceeds (net of costs) of a property disposition in the current taxation year exceed the UCC of its class as of the end of the preceding year, which was relatively low because of CCA claims and/or previous dispositions to

that point. If there are no (or insufficient) increases (e.g., property acquisitions) to the UCC of the class in the current year to offset this excess, a recapture occurs. It should be noted that a recapture can occur from a property disposition whether or not other property remains in the class at the end of the current year and also, in a case where the property disposed of was used in a business, whether or not the business ceased prior to the current year.

(b) None of the property remaining in a class is disposed of in the current taxation year. However, an amount of government assistance is received in the year with respect to a property of the class disposed of in a previous year. The amount so received exceeds the UCC of the class as of the end of the preceding year, which was relatively low for the same reason or reasons given in (a). If there are no (or insufficient) increases to the UCC of the class in the current year to offset this excess, a recapture occurs.

(c) In the preceding year, all of the property of a class was disposed of and a terminal loss occurred, after which the UCC of the class was nil (see ¶7). An amount of government assistance is received in the current year with respect to a property previously disposed of. Since the amount so received exceeds the nil UCC, if there are no (or insufficient) increases to the UCC of the class in the current year to offset this excess, a recapture occurs.

6. If a recapture of CCA results from the disposition of property in a particular year and full payment of the proceeds of the disposition is not received in that year, the taxpayer

(a) must nevertheless include the entire amount of the CCA recapture in income for that year, and

(b) is not entitled to any reserve on the recaptured amount.

Terminal Loss

7. If, at the end of a particular taxation year,

(a) the total of all the increases exceeds the total of all the decreases to the UCC of a prescribed class, and

(b) the taxpayer no longer owns any property in that class,

subsection 20(16) provides that this excess shall be deducted in computing the taxpayer's income for the year. This is commonly referred to as claiming a "terminal loss." Subsection 20(16) also provides that no CCA may be claimed under paragraph $20(1)(a)$ for that class for the year. A terminal loss that is deducted under subsection 20(16) is then included in the "total depreciation" allowed (as defined in subsection 13(21)) and thus it becomes part of the UCC decrease described in ¶$3(a)$. This occurs in order to bring the UCC balance (after the terminal loss is claimed) to nil, thus preventing the terminal loss from being subsequently claimed again.

A taxpayer disposing of the remaining property of a class after ceasing a business in which the property was used, may qualify for a terminal loss even though income is no longer earned from the business at the time of the disposition.

To the extent that a terminal loss cannot be absorbed by income otherwise determined for the particular taxation year, it creates or increases a non-capital loss that can be carried forward or back to other years in accordance with section 111. For further comments on section 111, see the current version of IT-232, *Losses — Their Deductibility in the Loss Year or in Other Years*.

In the case of depreciable property for which CCA was claimed in computing income from an office or employment (see paragraphs $8(1)(j)$ and (p) of the Act), a terminal loss cannot be claimed. This is because subsection 8(2) restricts the deductions that can be claimed in computing income from an office or employment to those permitted by section 8, and a deduction for a terminal loss is not permitted by that section — paragraphs $8(1)(j)$ and (p) provide for the deduction of such part of the capital cost of certain types of depreciable property "as is allowed by regulation," but a terminal loss is not allowed by means of the Income Tax Regulations.

Depreciable Property Not Disposed of After Ceasing to Carry on a Business

8. If a business is discontinued, the taxpayer is not entitled to claim a terminal loss for the UCC of a particular class of depreciable property that was used in the business unless and until all the assets in the class are disposed of (see the requirement in ¶7(b)). Thus, for example, if the taxpayer retains property of the class without using it for any other purpose, no terminal loss in respect of the class can be claimed. Furthermore, the taxpayer is not entitled to claim CCA on the property in any subsequent year unless it is used in that year to earn income from a business or property as required for purposes of a deduction under paragraph $20(1)(a)$ of the Act and subsection 1100(1) of the Income Tax Regulations. If, on the other hand, the taxpayer commences to use the property for a non-income-producing purpose, there is a deemed disposition of the property at that time at its fair market value pursuant to paragraph $13(7)(a)$. Such a deemed disposition could result in a CCA recapture or possibly in a terminal loss (the latter would require that no other property remain in the class).

Passenger Vehicles Costing More Than the Prescribed Amount

9. Applicable to taxation years and fiscal periods commencing after June 17, 1987 and ending after 1987, subsection 13(2) provides that an excess of the UCC decreases over the increases as of the end of a taxation year, as referred to in ¶5, shall not be included in income (i.e., recaptured) if it is in respect of a "passenger vehicle" (as defined in subsection 248(1)) having a cost in excess of $20,000 or such other amount as may be prescribed (see ¶10). To prevent the recapture of such excess in a subsequent year, it is deemed to have been included in income and thus is included in the UCC increase described in ¶2(b) when calculating UCC at the end of that subsequent year.

10. Applicable to taxation years and fiscal periods commencing after June 17, 1987 and ending after 1987, subsection 20(16.1) provides that an excess of the UCC increases over the decreases as of the end of

¶3265

a taxation year, as referred to in ¶7, is not deductible as a terminal loss if it is in respect of a "passenger vehicle" (as defined in subsection 248(1)) having a cost in excess of $20,000 or such other amount as may be prescribed. The terminal loss so denied is nevertheless then included in the "total depreciation" allowed (as defined in subsection 13(21)) and thus it becomes part of the UCC decrease described in ¶3(a). This occurs in order to reduce the UCC balance to nil.

Subsection 7307(1) of the Income Tax Regulations provides that the amount prescribed for purposes of subsection 13(2) (see ¶9) and subsection 20(16.1) is as follows:

- for a passenger vehicle acquired after August 1989 and before 1991 — the amount is $24,000;

- for a passenger vehicle acquired after 1990 — the amount is $24,000 plus the applicable federal and provincial sales taxes on that amount (see, however, the note immediately below).

Note: In Finance Canada's News Release 96-103, dated December 23, 1996, it was announced that for a passenger vehicle acquired in 1997, the amount would be $25,000 plus the applicable federal and provincial sales taxes on that amount. In Finance Canada's News Release 97-112, dated December 4, 1997, it was announced that for a passenger vehicle acquired in 1998, the amount would be $26,000 plus the applicable federal and provincial sales taxes on that amount. In Finance Canada's News Release 98-127, dated December 16, 1998, it was announced that for a passenger vehicle acquired in 1999, the amount would remain at $26,000 plus the applicable federal and provincial sales taxes on that amount.

For purposes of the above rules, "federal and provincial sales taxes" include the goods and services tax (GST) and the harmonized sales tax (HST).

Transfer of Depreciable Property From One Class to Another

11.   Section 1103 of the Income Tax Regulations provides for elections that under prescribed conditions permit certain properties otherwise included in one class to be transferred to another class for CCA purposes. Normally, such a transfer is made to defer either immediate recapture or a terminal loss. For further comments on this provision, see the current version of IT-327, *Capital Cost Allowance — Elections Under Regulation 1103.*

Rules Regarding Fiscal Period of an Individual's Business

12.   Subsection 249(1) of the Act provides that an individual's taxation year is the calendar year. If an individual has a business, paragraph 249.1(1)(*b*) requires — with certain exceptions, the most notable of which is for a business not carried on in Canada — that the fiscal period of the business must coincide with the calendar year. However, an individual usually can file an election under subsection 249.1(4) not to have paragraph 249.1(1)(*b*) apply, in order that the individual's business can have a fiscal period that does not coincide with the calendar year.

If an individual's business has a fiscal period which does not coincide with the calendar year (i.e., because of a subsection 249.1(4) election or because the business is otherwise exempted from the application of paragraph 249.1(1)(*b*)), the individual's income from the business for a taxation year is, by virtue of subsection 11(1), such income for the fiscal period ending in the calendar year. However, subsection 11(1) is subject to the rules in sections 34.1 and 34.2. If the fiscal period for the individual's business does not coincide with the calendar year because of a subsection 249.1(4) election, section 34.1 contains rules the effect of which is that the income from the business is nevertheless essentially reported on a calendar year basis (using an estimated amount of such income for the calendar year). If the application of section 34.1 (or paragraph 249.1(1)(*b*)) has resulted in income from the business for periods totalling more than 12 months being included in the individual's income for the 1995 taxation year, section 34.2 provides, under certain circumstances, for a reserve mechanism that spreads this additional income effect over a ten-year period.

If an individual's business has a fiscal period which does not coincide with the calendar year and there is a disposition (other than a disposition occurring after the discontinuance of the business) of depreciable

¶3265

property which was acquired for the purpose of gaining or producing income from the business, the above-mentioned rule in subsection 11(1) — again, subject to the above-mentioned rules in sections 34.1 and 34.2 — applies:

- for purposes of reporting a recapture or applying the passenger vehicle rule discussed in ¶9 — this occurs by virtue of subsection 13(3), or

- for purposes of claiming a terminal loss or applying the passenger vehicle rule discussed in ¶10 — this occurs by virtue of subsection 20(16.2).

In a case where the business is discontinued and the individual later disposes of depreciable property which was acquired for the purpose of gaining or producing income from the business and which the individual has not subsequently used for another purpose,

(a) any resulting recapture is included, by virtue of subsection 13(8), in computing the individual's income for the calendar year in which the property disposition occurs;

(b) any resulting terminal loss is claimed, by virtue of subsection 20(16.3), in computing the individual's income for that calendar year; and

(c) the passenger vehicle rules discussed in ¶s 9 and 10 are applied, by virtue of subsections 13(8) and 20(16.3), respectively, in computing the individual's income for that calendar year.

13. If an individual has a business with a fiscal period that does not coincide with the calendar year — other than by means of an election under subsection 249.1(4) (see ¶12) — and if the individual has disposed of the business during a fiscal period of the business, the individual may elect under subsection 25(1) that the fiscal period of the business be deemed to have ended on the date that it ordinarily would have ended if the business had not been disposed of. (In order for the subsection 25(1) election to be valid, subsection 25(2) requires that the individual be a resident of Canada at the end of the intended deemed fiscal period-end.) If the individual can and does elect under subsection 25(1), subsection 25(3) provides that subsection 13(8) (see ¶12) is not applicable. As a result, a recapture or the pas-

senger vehicle rule discussed in ¶9 will apply in computing the individual's income for the calendar year in which the subsection 25(1) deemed fiscal period ends, which may in some cases be different from the calendar year in which the property disposition has occurred.

Statute-Barred Years

14. The reference in ¶3(a) to "total depreciation allowed" is considered to be a reference to the amount of CCA actually deducted and allowed in computing the taxpayer's income. (This position is based on an extension of the reasoning of the decision rendered by the Federal Court of Appeal in *The Dominion of Canada General Insurance Company v. The Queen*, 86 DTC 6154, [1986] 1 CTC 423. In that case, the taxpayer claimed and was allowed a particular amount as a policy reserve for the 1968 taxation year. It was subsequently determined that the taxpayer had not been entitled to the reserve; however, the Minister was by that time statute-barred from reassessing the 1968 year to disallow it. Since the taxpayer had actually deducted and been allowed the reserve for the 1968 year, the taxpayer was required to include the amount of the reserve in income for the 1969 year.) If a revision is to be made to the capital cost of a depreciable property (e.g., because of a reallocation of the total purchase price of a piece of real estate between the land and the building) acquired during a taxation year that is now statute-barred, the amount of CCA actually deducted in respect of the depreciable property in any statute-barred year will not be adjusted. Instead, the Department will recalculate the UCC as of the beginning of the first non-statute-barred year by using the revised capital cost (rather than the original capital cost) of the property for purposes of the increase described in ¶2(a) while continuing to use the actual CCA deducted in each statute-barred year for purposes of the decrease described in ¶3(a).

If this recalculation results in a reduced UCC as of the beginning of the first non-statute-barred year (i.e., because of a downward revision to the property's capital cost), the Department will make the necessary downward revisions to the CCA claimed in that first non-statute-barred year and all subsequent non-statute-barred years. If, on the other hand, the recalculation results in

¶3265

an increased UCC as of the beginning of the first non-statute-barred year (i.e., because of an upward revision to the property's capital cost), the Department will consider a written request from the taxpayer to make upward changes to the CCA claimed for that year and/or any subsequent non-statute-barred year, subject to the limitations set out in the current version of Information Circular 84-1, *Revision of Capital Cost Allowance Claims and Other Permissive Deductions*.

If the revision to the property's capital cost causes the UCC decreases to exceed the UCC increases as of the end of a year now statute-barred, the recapture of that excess amount under subsection 13(1) will not be added into the taxpayer's income for that year or a subsequent year. (However, as indicated above, CCA claimed in non-statute-barred years will be disallowed to the extent necessary.) If an excess of UCC decreases over increases arises in a non-statute-barred year, the resulting recapture will be included in the taxpayer's income for that year and all CCA claimed in that year, and in subsequent non-statute-barred years, will be reassessed accordingly.

Recapture and Terminal Loss of a Person Not Resident in Canada

15. If a taxpayer has acquired depreciable property for the purpose of gaining or producing income and commences at a later time to use it for some other purpose, paragraph 13(7)(*a*) provides for a deemed disposition of the property at fair market value. In applying paragraph 13(7)(*a*) in respect of a person not resident in Canada, subsection 13(9) provides that a reference to "gaining or producing income" in relation to a business is to be read as a reference to "gaining or producing income from a business wholly carried on in Canada or such part of a business as is wholly carried on in Canada." As a result of the application of paragraph 13(7)(*a*) and subsection 13(9), if a person not resident in Canada changes the use of property from a use in a business, or part of a business, wholly carried on in Canada to a use for some other purpose, there is a deemed disposition of the property at its fair market value at the time of the change. Thus, paragraph 13(7)(*a*) applies to a person who is not resident in Canada when, for example, the person carries on a business both in Canada and in another country

and transfers to the other country a property used in the part of the business wholly carried on in Canada, or when, for example, the person becomes a non-resident and subsequently transfers to another country a property used in a business wholly carried on in Canada. A property that is used in both the part of a business carried on wholly in Canada and the part carried on wholly in another country, such as could be the case for transportation equipment, will normally not be considered to be property to which subsection 13(9) applies.

16. If a disposition of property (including a deemed disposition under subsection 13(7)) of a person not resident in Canada results in a recapture of CCA, the recapture is included in the non-resident's income by virtue of subparagraph 115(1)(*a*)(ii) or 115(1)(*a*)(iii.2). A section 115.1 election may affect the amount to be included in income. Section 115.1 is discussed in the current version of the following bulletins: IT-270, *Foreign Tax Credit*; IT-173, *Capital Gains Derived in Canada by Residents of the United States*; and IT-420, *Non-Residents — Income Earned in Canada*.

17. If a disposition of property (including a deemed disposition under subsection 13(7)) results in a terminal loss that pertains to income included in a non-resident's taxable income earned in Canada under subparagraph 115(1)(*a*)(ii) (i.e., from a business carried on by the non-resident in Canada), the terminal loss may be deducted by the non-resident in determining taxable income earned in Canada under subsection 115(1). If a "non-capital loss" (this term is defined in subsection 111(8) and modified by subsection 111(9) for non-residents of Canada) results in this situation, see the current version of IT-262, *Losses of Non-Residents and Part-Year Residents*. A non-resident who files an election under section 216 is entitled to claim a terminal loss if applicable. However, by virtue of paragraph 216(1)(*c*), such a person is not entitled to deduct a non-capital loss. The section 216 election is discussed in the current version of IT-393, *Election re Tax on Rents and Timber Royalties — Non-Residents*.

Deemed Disposition on Ceasing to be Resident in Canada

18. If a taxpayer ceases to be resident in Canada and has a deemed disposition of a

¶3265

depreciable property in accordance with subsection 128.1(4), a recapture of CCA or a terminal loss may result from such deemed disposition, either of which would be reported under paragraph 114(*a*).

Miscellaneous

19. A terminal loss that would otherwise occur for a particular taxation year may be eliminated for that year by a provision in the Act which modifies the amount of the proceeds of disposition of a depreciable property in certain circumstances, such as, for example, subsection 13(21.1) (see the current version of IT-220, *Capital Cost Allowance — Proceeds of Disposition of Depreciable Property*, for comments on that provision) or subsection 13(21.2).

20. If the "restricted farm loss" provisions of section 31 apply to restrict the amount of loss that a taxpayer may deduct in a particular taxation year in respect of a farming business, and in the same year the taxpayer has a terminal loss from the disposition of depreciable property used in that business, the terminal loss forms part of the loss for the year that is subject to those restricted farm loss provisions. The current versions of IT-232, *Losses — Their Deductibility in the Loss Year or in Other Years*, and IT-322, *Farm Losses*, discuss the restricted farm loss provisions.

Explanation of Changes

Reasons for the Revision

This bulletin is being revised to reflect legislative amendments enacted under the 5th Supplement to the Revised Statutes of Canada, 1985; S.C. 1994, c. 21; S.C. 1995, c. 21; S.C. 1996, c. 21; S.C. 1998, c. 19; and S.C. 1999, c. 22.

Legislative and Other Changes

The definitions of "total depreciation" and "undepreciated capital cost" are no longer contained in paragraphs 13(21)(*e*) and (*f*) of the *Income Tax Act*, respectively, but rather are arranged alphabetically in subsection 13(21). These amendments, which are only structural changes in the Act, are reflected in the revised bulletin.

¶2(c) discusses the increase to the UCC of a class that is made for the repayment, after the disposition of a depreciable property in the class, of assistance described in subsection 13(7.1) that was previously

received with respect to the property. When discussing such repayment in the former bulletin, we included the words "where the assistance has previously reduced the capital cost of the property by virtue of paragraph 13(7.1)(*f*)." We have removed these words in the revised bulletin because ¶2(c) also includes any repayment of assistance that, instead of previously reducing the capital cost of the property by virtue of paragraph 13(7.1)(*f*), previously reduced the UCC of the class (as described in ¶3(e) of the former bulletin and ¶3(f) of the revised bulletin).

¶2(e) has been added to the bulletin to describe a UCC increase that was added to the definition of "undepreciated capital cost" for amounts payable after February 23, 1998. ¶3(b) now describes a UCC decrease that was added to the definition of "undepreciated capital cost" for taxation years ending after February 21, 1994. (Because the description of this UCC decrease has been included in ¶3(b) of the revised bulletin, former ¶s 3(b) to (f) have been renumbered as ¶s 3(c) to (g) in the revised bulletin.)

¶3(h) has been added to the bulletin to describe a UCC decrease that was added to the definition of "undepreciated capital cost" for amounts received after February 23, 1998. The last part of ¶7 now states that a terminal loss cannot be claimed in computing income from an office or employment. This statement has been added to the bulletin for purposes of providing additional information, rather than as a result of any change in the legislation or in a departmental position. An italicized note has been added near the end of ¶10 to discuss rules pertaining to passenger vehicles that were announced in News Releases issued by Finance Canada.

¶12 now discusses rules in paragraph 249.1(1)(*b*) and subsection 249.1(4), which took effect for fiscal periods beginning after 1994.

¶12 now indicates that subsection 11(1) is subject to the rules in sections 34.1 and 34.2. This occurred by means of an amendment to subsection 11(1) that took effect for the 1995 and subsequent taxation years. (The addition of sections 34.1 and 34.2 to the Act took effect after 1994. Subsequent amendments to sections 34.1 and 34.2 are outside the scope of this bulletin.)

¶3265

¶12 has been revised to reflect certain amendments to the Act which were structural in nature. Under these amendments, the rules previously contained in subsection 13(3) are now contained partly in that subsection and partly in subsection 20(16.2), and the rules previously contained in subsection 13(8) are now contained partly in that subsection and partly in subsection 20(16.3).

¶13 now indicates that, in order for an individual to make an election under subsection 25(1) in respect of a business, subsection 249.1(4) cannot apply in respect of the business. This restriction on the operation of subsection 25(1) took effect for fiscal periods beginning after 1994.

¶13 now reflects the interaction of subsection 25(3) (which has not been amended) with subsection 13(8) as the latter currently reads in the Act after the structural amendment mentioned above.

¶17 has been revised to reflect a structural change in the Act whereby the definition of "non capital loss" was moved from paragraph 111(8)(b) and arranged alphabetically with other definitions in subsection 111(8).

¶18 now reflects the repeal of section 48 and the addition to the Act of section 128.1. These amendments generally took effect after 1992. It should be noted that unlike former section 48, which only pertained to capital gains and losses, section 128.1 applies also for purposes of recaptures and terminal losses. It should also be noted that, in the former bulletin, ¶18 was the last paragraph under the heading "Recapture and Terminal Loss of a Person Not Resident in Canada." In view of the fact that the recapture or terminal loss discussed in 18 actually occurs while the taxpayer is still a resident, the paragraph has been given a new heading of its own.

¶19 now makes a reference to subsection 13(21.2), which was added to the Act — replacing subsection 85(5.1) (which was repealed) — effective for dispositions of property occurring after April 26, 1995 (with certain transitional rules).

Changes in the revised bulletin not specifically mentioned above are changes that have been made for purposes of clarification or for purposes of providing additional information, rather than as the result of a change in the law or in a departmental position.

[3270]   Interpretation Bulletin IT-481:   Timber Resource Property and Timber Limits [Consolidated]

[*Interpretation Bulletin IT-481 is dated November 27, 1981 — consolidated January 2004.*]

Reference: The definition of "timber resource property" in subsection 13(21) of the *Income Tax Act* (the "Act"); and subsection 1101(3), paragraph 1100(1)(e), Class 33 of Schedule II and Schedule VI of the Income Tax Regulations (the "Regulations") (also the definition of "undepreciated capital cost" in subsection 13(21), paragraph 20(1)(a) and paragraph 39(1)(a) of the Act; and subsection 1102(14) and subparagraph 1100(1)(a)(xxiv) of the Regulations)

Latest Revisions — Reference section and ¶s 2, 7 and 8

At the Canada Customs and Revenue Agency (CCRA), we issue income tax interpretation bulletins (ITs) in order to provide technical interpretations and positions regarding certain provisions contained in income tax law. Due to their technical nature, ITs are used primarily by our staff, tax specialists, and other individuals who have an interest in tax matters. For those readers who prefer a less technical explanation of the law, we offer other publications, such as tax guides and pamphlets.

While the comments in a particular paragraph in an IT may relate to provisions of the law in force at the time they were made, such comments are not a substitute for the law. The reader should, therefore, consider such comments in light of the relevant provisions of the law in force for the particular taxation year being considered, taking into account the effect of any relevant amendments to those provisions or relevant court decisions occurring after the date on which the comments were made.

Subject to the above, an interpretation or position contained in an IT generally applies as of the date on which it was published, unless otherwise specified. If there is a subsequent change in that interpretation or position and the change is beneficial to taxpayers, it is usually effective for future assessments and reassessments. If, on the other hand, the change is not favourable to taxpayers, it will normally be effective for the current and subsequent taxation years or for transactions entered into after the date on which the change is published.

Most of our publications are available on our Web site at: **www.ccra.gc.ca**

If you have any comments regarding matters discussed in an IT, please send them to:

Income Tax Rulings Directorate
Policy and Legislation Branch
Canada Customs and Revenue Agency
Ottawa ON K1A 0L5
or by email at the following address:
bulletins@ccra.gc.ca

Contents

	Paragraphs
Application	
Summary	
Discussion and Interpretation	
Timber Resource Property....	1-2
Timber Limits and Cutting Rights	3-6
General	7-8
Bulletin Revisions	

Application

This bulletin is a consolidation of the following:

- Interpretation Bulletin IT-481 dated November 27, 1981; and

- subsequent amendments thereto.

For further particulars, see the "Bulletin Revisions" section near the end of this bulletin.

Unless otherwise noted, all statutory references throughout the bulletin are to the Act.

Summary

This bulletin discusses the differences between the tax treatment of "timber resource properties" (as defined in subsection 13(21)) and "timber limits" (referred to in paragraph 1100(1)(*e*) of the Regula-

tions). The cost of acquisition of the former is included in Class 33 (which has a 15% rate of capital cost allowance ("CCA")), and a disposition of such property generally results in an income inclusion rather than a capital gain. A deduction in respect of the capital cost of a timber limit or a right to cut timber from a limit other than a timber resource property is calculated in accordance with Schedule VI of the Regulations and the disposition of such property may result in a capital gain.

Discussion and Interpretation

Timber Resource Property

1. A timber resource property is defined as a right or license to cut or remove timber from a limit or area in Canada (an "original right") if that original right was acquired by the taxpayer after May 6, 1974 and, at the time of acquisition of the original right, the taxpayer may be reasonably regarded as having acquired, directly or indirectly, the right to

(a) extend or renew that original right, or

(b) acquire another such right or license in substitution therefor, or the taxpayer may reasonably expect, at the time of acquisition of the original right, to be able to extend or renew that right or to acquire another right or license in substitution therefor in the normal course of events. Any right or license acquired after May 6, 1974 as an extension, renewal or substitution, or as one of a series of extensions, renewals or substitutions, for the original right, is also timber resource property even if the original right or license was acquired before May 7, 1974. In determining whether a particular right is a timber resource property, it will therefore be necessary to determine whether the right is extendable, renewable or can be substituted for. To do so may involve examining the issuing documents or applicable provincial legislation or even determining provincial practice where the documents and legislation are silent.

2. A timber resource property is depreciable capital property and is included in Class 33 of Schedule II of the Regulations. It is distinguishable from other capital property in that its disposition for proceeds in

¶3270

excess of its capital cost does not result in a capital gain by virtue of the exclusion provided by subparagraph $39(1)(a)(iv)$. Any excess of proceeds of disposition, net of costs of disposition over the undepreciated capital cost of all of the timber resource properties in Class 33, is included in income by virtue of variable G in the definition of "undepreciated capital cost" in subsection 13(21) and subsection 13(1). There is no requirement that timber resource properties be included in separate classes.

Timber Limits and Cutting Rights

3. Paragraph $20(1)(a)$ and paragraph $1100(1)(e)$ of the Regulations provide for a deduction in respect of the capital cost of a timber limit or right to cut timber from a limit, other than a timber resource property. The amount claimed may not exceed the amount calculated in accordance with Schedule VI of the Regulations. Each property that is a timber limit is prescribed by subsection 1101(3) of the Regulations to be a separate class of property. Paragraph $1100(1)(e)$, subsection 1101(3) and Schedule VI of the Regulations specifically exclude timber resource properties from their application. Rather than deduct an amount calculated pursuant to section 1 and section 2 or section 3 of Schedule VI of the Regulations, a taxpayer may elect to deduct the lesser of $100 and the amount of his timber sales in the year in accordance with section 4 of Schedule VI of the Regulations.

4. A timber limit or cutting right may be acquired with or without title to the land on which the timber stands. Unlike land on which is located a property which qualifies for inclusion in one of the classes in Schedule II of the Regulations, land which is acquired as a part of a timber limit is depreciable under Schedule VI of the Regulations and does not exist as a separate property for purposes of the Act. Accordingly, any proceeds received from the sale of such land (up to the cost of the whole property) must be credited to the class and will result in a recapture of capital cost allowance if the credit exceeds the undepreciated capital cost of the timber limit prior to the sale.

5. The sale of a timber limit or cutting right, unlike the sale of a timber resource property, may, depending on all of the facts, result in a capital gain where the proceeds of disposition exceed the capital cost. Paragraph $39(1)(a)$ does not exclude timber limits from capital gains treatment as it does timber resource properties. A capital gain will not result, of course, if the facts indicate that the sale transaction is of an income nature.

6. Although paragraph $65(1)(a)$ provides for the deduction of an amount as an allowance in respect of a timber limit as may be allowed by regulation, this provision does not have any effect, because Part XII of the Regulations, the prescribed regulation, does not provide for any allowance in respect of a timber limit.

General

7. A timber resource property is defined in subsection 13(21), while a timber limit is not defined in the Act. A property that would be a timber resource property except for the fact that it was acquired before May 7, 1974 is a timber limit. Where a taxpayer purchases a right to cut timber from a limit from a province, whether that right is a timber resource property or a timber limit depends on all of the characteristics of the arrangement with the province. If a taxpayer acquires land on which there is standing timber (for example, freehold timberlands), such property is a timber limit.

8. Timber limits that are owned by a corporation and acquired by a taxpayer in the course of a reorganization or from a non-arm's length party described in paragraphs $1102(14)(a)$ and (d) of the Regulations, respectively, are also timber limits to the taxpayer acquiring the property. This is so despite the fact that, at the time of the reorganization or transfer from a non-arm's length party, the property may otherwise qualify as a timber resource property. It should be noted that, in determining whether the parties are not dealing at arm's length for this purpose, the anti-avoidance rule in subsection 1102(20) of the Regulations should be consulted. For a discussion of the meaning of "arm's length", see the current version of IT-419, *Meaning of Arm's Length*.

Bulletin Revisions

Since the issuance of IT-481 on November 27, 1981, there have been no significant revisions to ¶s 1 and 3 to 6 (formerly ¶s 2 and 4 to 7). [January 13, 2004]

In the Reference section, certain provisions of the Act and Regulations have been

¶3270

moved from being a secondary reference to a primary reference and certain minor references have been deleted. [January 13, 2004]

The Reference section and ¶s 2 (former ¶3) and 7 (former ¶8) have been updated to reflect the formatting changes of certain definitions contained in subsection 13(21) following the adoption of chapter 1 of R.S.C. 1985 (5th Supplement). [January 13, 2004]

"Content", "Application" and "Summary" sections have been added to the bulletin. [January 13, 2004]

¶1 of IT-481 is now contained in the Summary of the consolidated bulletin. Consequently, ¶s 2 to 9 of IT-481 have been renumbered as ¶s 1 to 8, respectively. [January 13, 2004]

In ¶7, the first and part of the second sentence of former ¶8 have been deleted in order to eliminate superfluous wording. [January 13, 2004]

¶8 (former ¶9) has been revised to reflect the repeal of paragraphs (b) and (c) of subsection 1102(14) of the Regulations and now refers to paragraphs (a) and (d) of the Regulations that apply to property acquired in the course of a reorganization or from a non-arm's length party, respectively. [January 13, 2004]

Throughout the bulletin, we have made minor changes for clarification or readability purposes. [January 13, 2004]

[3275] Interpretation Bulletin IT-482R: Pipelines

[Interpretation Bulletin IT-482R is dated September 2, 2003.]

Reference: Classes 1, 8, 17, 41, 43 and 43.1 of Schedule II to the Income Tax Regulations (the "Regulations") (also subsection 10(1), the definition of "eligible capital expenditure" in subsection 14(5) and paragraph 20(1)(ee) of the *Income Tax Act* (the "Act"))

Contents

Application

Summary

Discussion and Interpretation

Meaning of Pipeline	1-2
Capital Cost of a Pipeline	3-4
CCA Classes	
Class 1	5
Other Classes	6-8
Land Developers	9
Utilities Service Connections . .	10

Explanation of Changes

Application

This bulletin replaces and cancels Interpretation Bulletin IT-482 dated November 30, 1981 entitled *Capital Cost Allowance — Pipelines* and the Special Release to that bulletin dated February 28, 1986. While some of the comments are applicable to pipelines in general, regardless of the type of liquid or gas being conveyed, the current version of Interpretation Bulletin IT-476, *Capital Cost Allowance — Equipment Used in Petroleum and Natural Gas Activities*, should be referred to for information on the capital cost allowance (CCA) classification of pipelines and attachments

thereto used in petroleum and natural gas activities.

The effective date of a particular legislative provision discussed in the bulletin may be indicated in the *Discussion and Interpretation* section of the bulletin. However, where the bulletin is silent with respect to the effective date of a particular provision, such date can be obtained from the legislation itself. Unless otherwise stated, all statutory references throughout the bulletin are to the Act.

Summary

This bulletin outlines the various income tax treatments that may be applicable to pipelines and attachments thereto except, as noted above, for those dealt with in the current version of Interpretation Bulletin IT-476, *Capital Cost Allowance — Equipment Used in Petroleum and Natural Gas Activities*. It also discusses the types of costs that are included in the capital cost of a pipeline.

Generally, pipelines and certain attachments thereto that are depreciable property of a taxpayer are included in Class 1(l). However, in some cases, such property may qualify for inclusion in other classes. Pipes

¶3275

that are a component part of a building, structure or equipment will usually be included in the same CCA class as that of the building, structure or equipment. Attachments to a pipeline that are **not** considered to be an integral part of the pipeline are included in another class — such as Class 1(n), (o), or (p); or Class 8(i).

In addition, comments on the tax treatment of the cost of

a) sewers and water mains for land developers, and

b) utilities service connections made by a taxpayer have been also included.

Discussion and Interpretation

Meaning of Pipeline

1. Although the word "pipeline" is not defined in the Act, it is considered to mean the physical facilities through which liquids (e.g., water and slurry) or gases (e.g., natural gas, nitrogen, oxygen and carbon dioxide) are conveyed. This would include the pipe, valves, control devices and other attachments to the pipe that are considered to be an integral and component part of the pipeline (e.g., its branches, extensions and racks).

2. Where an attachment to a pipeline is not an integral and component part of the pipeline, it is considered to be separate equipment from that of the pipeline (a "pipeline appendage"). This position is based on the decisions in the court cases *British Columbia Forest Products Limited*, 71 DTC 5178, [1971] CTC 270 (S.C.C.); *Northern and Central Gas Corporation Limited*, 87 DTC 5439, [1987] 2 CTC 241 (F.C.A.); *Nova, an Alberta Corporation*, 88 DTC 6386, [1988] 2 CTC 167 (F.C.A.); and *Pacific Northern Gas Limited*, 91 DTC 5287, [1991] 1 CTC 469 (F.C.A.). Pipeline appendages generally include equipment such as compressor stations, regulating stations, liquefying and storage facilities, meters, metering stations, hydrants, pumping equipment (e.g., engines, motors, pumps and costs of installation, such as wiring, transformers and special foundations) and pumping stations.

Capital Cost of a Pipeline

3. The capital cost of a pipeline will include the cost to the taxpayer of the pipe-

line itself (including the attachments thereto referred to in ¶1), as well as the costs of

- clearing, filling and levelling rights of way, and

- excavating and back-filling trenches for the installation of the pipe.

Paragraph (k) of subsection 1102(1) of the Regulations deems that linefill contained in a pipeline cannot be included in any class of depreciable property.

4. When a pipeline is to be constructed on land owned by another person, it is often necessary to obtain an easement or right of way from the owner of the land, in order to obtain right of access. The cost incurred by a taxpayer to acquire such an easement or right of way will qualify as an "eligible capital expenditure" if the requirements of that definition in subsection 14(5) are met (see the current version of Interpretation Bulletin IT-143, *Meaning of Eligible Capital Expenditure*). A lump sum one-time payment for damages to crops or property is generally considered to be part of the capital cost of a pipeline.

CCA Classes

Class 1

5. Subject to the comments in ¶6–8, a pipeline that is depreciable property of a taxpayer is generally included in Class 1 by virtue of paragraph (l) thereof. Attachments to a pipeline referred to in ¶1 will be included in the same CCA class as that of the pipeline.

Pipeline appendages (see ¶2) that are part of the distributing equipment and plant of a distributor of water are included in Class 1(o), whereas those that are part of the production and distributing equipment and plant of a distributor of heat are included in Class 1(p). Pipeline appendages that are part of manufacturing and distributing equipment and plant acquired primarily for the production and distribution of gas will be in Class 1(n) except if they are part of manufacturing and distributing equipment and plant acquired for the purpose of

- producing oxygen or nitrogen, or

¶3275

- producing or distributing gas that is normally distributed in portable containers.

Pipeline appendages that are **not** included in Classes $1(n)$ to (p) will be included in another class — such as Class 8 under paragraph (i) thereof, or Class 43 — manufacturing and processing equipment — (if the requirements of that class are met). However, property that qualifies for inclusion in Class 1 cannot be included in Class 43.

Other Classes

6. Because the preamble of Class 43.1 specifically includes property that would otherwise be included in Class 1 (see ¶5), such property that is used in renewable energy and energy conservation activities may be included in Class 43.1 as long as it meets the other requirements of that class.

7. Subparagraph $(l)(i)$ of Class 10 describes certain property including water pipelines, water pumping stations, water systems, sewers and natural gas pipelines that are acquired for the purpose of gaining or producing income from a mine and providing services to the mine or to a community where a substantial proportion of the persons who ordinarily work at the mine reside. Such property acquired after 1987 will be included in Class 41 rather than Class 10. However, other pipelines acquired for the purpose of gaining or producing income from a mine will be included in Class $1(l)$ (subject to the comments in ¶8).

8. Pipes for plumbing, heating and air-conditioning equipment which are integral and component parts of a building are included with the cost of the building as property of the same CCA class as that of the building. Similarly, short lines of pipe which form an integral and component part of a structure will be included in the same CCA class as that of the structure (i.e., Class $1(q)$, 41, 43, 43.1 or 8). In addition, provided that they may reasonably be considered an integral and component part of the equipment, short lines of pipes running between pieces of equipment may be capitalized as part of the cost of the particular equipment. As a result, these short pipes will qualify for inclusion in the same CCA class as that of the equipment. Examples of possible CCA classes that equipment (including short pipes) may qualify for inclusion in, depending on whether the requirements of the class are met, are: Class 41, 43, 43.1 or 8.

Pipelines installed and owned by a taxpayer that run from a building to the boundary of the taxpayer's property, or pipelines which are **not** an integral part of a building, structure, machinery or equipment, will (subject to the comments in ¶6 and 7) usually be included in Class $1(l)$. However, where the costs of such lines are insignificant, the CCRA will accept their inclusion as component parts of the building.

For a discussion of the CCA classes applicable to buildings including component parts thereof, refer to the current version of Interpretation Bulletin IT-79, *Capital Cost Allowance — Buildings or Other Structures*.

Note: Appendix C of the Explanatory Notes Relating to Income Tax *issued by the Department of Finance with the* Notice of Ways and Means Motion *tabled in the House of Commons on March 16, 2001 proposes to add a new paragraph (a.1) to Class 17. If this addition is enacted as proposed, production and distribution equipment (other than buildings and other structures) of a distributor of water or steam used for heating or cooling will be included in Class 17 (8% CCA rate) rather than in Class 1 (4% CCA rate). Such equipment includes pipe used to collect or distribute an energy transfer medium, but excludes equipment or pipe used to distribute water that is for consumption, disposal or treatment. The new paragraph will apply to equipment acquired after February 27, 2000 that has not been used or acquired for use prior that date. It is also proposed that a consequential amendment will be made to the preamble in Class 8 to exclude property included in Class 17.*

Land Developers

9. For land developers, the costs of sewers and water mains constitute a component of the cost of the inventory of land for the purposes of subsection 10(1) (see the current version of Interpretation Bulletin IT-153, *Land Developers — Subdivision and Developments Costs and Carrying Charges on Land*).

Utilities Service Connections

10. An amount paid by a taxpayer for pipes that will supply gas, water or sewers to the taxpayer's place of business may be a

¶3275

deduction from the taxpayer's income from a business under paragraph 20(1)(ee), depreciable property included in Class 1(l), or an "eligible capital expenditure", as the case may be.

Paragraph 20(1)(ee) cannot apply if a taxpayer owns or will own the pipe that is used in making the service connection. Title to the pipe sometimes vests in the taxpayer if it is within the boundaries of the taxpayer's property and, if this is the case, the pipe will usually be included in Class 1(l) as depreciable property (see ¶8). Where a service connection is made and title to part of it passes to the taxpayer, for example — where a service connection is laid both inside and outside the boundaries of the taxpayer's land and the taxpayer has title only to that part of the pipe which is within the boundaries of the taxpayer's land, a reasonable apportionment of the cost is required and only the portion attributable to the part of the pipe for which title has not passed will be deductible under paragraph 20(1)(ee) (if the other requirements of that provision are met).

Where a taxpayer owns a rental property to which service connections are made, it is a question of fact whether the rental income can be considered to be income from property or income from business (see the current version of Interpretation Bulletin IT-434, *Rental of Real Property by Individual*). Only if the income is from a business will the costs of the service connection qualify for a deduction under paragraph 20(1)(ee) (if the other requirements of that provision are met).

In addition, the amount paid for a service connection must be made to a person with whom the taxpayer deals at arm's length and that person must also supply the goods or services for which the service connection has been made (although no amount is deductible under paragraph 20(1)(ee) for the cost of supplying those goods or services). Where the cost of a service connection does not qualify for a deduction under paragraph 20(1)(ee), or as depreciable property or inventory (see ¶9), the cost may qualify as an "eligible capital expenditure". For further information, see the current version of Interpretation Bulletin IT-143, *Meaning of Eligible Capital Expenditure*.

Explanation of Changes

Introduction

The purpose of the *Explanation of Changes* is to give the reasons for the revisions to an interpretation bulletin. It outlines revisions that we have made as a result of changes to the law, as well as changes reflecting new or revised interpretations.

Reasons for the Revision

We have revised the bulletin to reflect various amendments to Classes 1, 2, 10, 24 and 28 that have been enacted since the date of the last bulletin and before the date of this bulletin, as well as to include the new Classes 41, 43 and 43.1 and new paragraph (k) in subsection 1102(1) of the Regulations. The proposed addition of paragraph (a.1) to Class 17 as announced by the Department of Finance on March 16, 2001 is also indicated.

Legislative and Other Changes

Since the bulletin has been expanded to discuss various tax treatments that may be applicable to pipelines, its title has been changed accordingly.

Classes 2, 10, and 28 referred to in the former bulletin have been updated to reflect the current applicable CCA classes. Comments in ¶2, 5, 6, and 8 of the former bulletin dealing with the CCA classification of pipelines and pipeline appendages used in petroleum and natural gas activities have been deleted as they are discussed in the current version of Interpretation Bulletin IT-476, *Capital Cost Allowance — Equipment Used in Petroleum and Natural Gas Activities*.

An Index, Application Section (part of former ¶1) and Summary Section (part of former ¶1) have been added to the bulletin.

In ¶2 (part of former ¶3), references to court cases have been added which support the position that an attachment to a pipeline that is not an integral and component part of the pipeline will be considered as separate equipment from that of the pipeline.

¶3 (formerly ¶4 and 7) has been changed to indicate that, because of a legislative

¶3275

amendment, linefill in a pipeline can no longer be treated as depreciable property.

New ¶4 contains comments on the tax treatment of payments made to obtain an easement or right of way on land owned by another person.

In ¶5 (parts of former ¶2 and 3), a discussion has been added on the inclusion of pipeline appendages in Classes 1(n), (o) and (p), and on property that can and cannot be included in Class 43.

New ¶6 indicates that property which qualifies for inclusion in Class 1 may be included in Class 43.1 if the other requirements of that class are met.

¶8 (parts of former ¶3 and 9) no longer includes the CCA classes for buildings, but instead refers the reader to Interpretation Bulletin IT-79, *Capital Cost Allowance — Buildings or Other Structures* for that information. The treatment of pipes forming a component part of a building and equipment has been extended to pipes forming a component part of a structure. The proposed addition of paragraph (a.1) to Class 17 is indicated in the italicized note below ¶8.

New ¶10 provides a discussion on the tax treatment of pipes that are used to provide utility service connections.

Throughout the bulletin, we have made minor changes for clarification or readability purposes and deleted comments that are no longer applicable.

[3280] Interpretation Bulletin IT-485: Cost of Clearing or Levelling Land

[Interpretation Bulletin IT-485 is dated April 19, 1982.]

Reference: Paragraph $20(1)(a)$ and $20(1)(aa)$ and section 30

1. In order to be able to erect a building or other structure or to make a road, a parking area or other surface construction, a taxpayer may find it necessary to clear or level the surface of the land on which that depreciable property is to be built.

2. In the above circumstances, the cost of clearing or levelling ordinarily will be accepted as part of the depreciable cost of the property built on the land rather than as part of the cost of the land itself.

3. The term "clearing" as used in this bulletin may involve the removal of trees, stumps, shrubbery or boulders, while "levelling" may involve either filling low-lying or uneven land or the removal of solid rock, mounds or even hills. In addition, any one of these may be accompanied by drainage of the land or the diversion of a spring or stream.

4. Where depreciable property of more than one class is built on cleared or levelled land or where part of the land is either used for extensive landscaping or is not put to any use, a reasonable division of the clearing or levelling costs should be made so that each depreciable property and the land itself will bear an appropriate part of the costs. The portion applicable to land will be deductible under paragraph $20(1)(aa)$ to the extent that it constitutes landscaping. For a complete discussion on this subject see IT-296 "Landscaping of Grounds".

5. The cost of clearing or levelling will be allocable to the depreciable cost of depreciable property only if the taxpayer commences to build the depreciable property thereon without undue delay. Otherwise the costs must be considered as an integral part of the cost of the land. Normally it is expected that work on the construction of the depreciable property would have begun in the same taxation year unless the clearing or levelling was done near the end of that year, in which case it should begin early in the next following year. Cognisance will be taken of weather conditions (e.g., it may be necessary to wait for the following spring to commence actual construction) and of particular and unexpected difficulties encountered, such as a strike or delays beyond the taxpayer's control in obtaining a building permit. Otherwise the clearing or levelling and the actual construction should form one continuous operation.

Building Incidentally Acquired on Obtaining a Site

6. In some cases a taxpayer may buy a piece of real estate, including a building with the intention of tearing down the

building. Where the taxpayer has not used the building to earn income, it would seem clear that the purchase price was paid for the land and might even have been greater if the building had not been on it. In these circumstances, the cost of demolishing the existing structure, less the amount of any salvage, will form a part of the cost of the land.

Where a building has been acquired in the circumstances outlined above but has been rented for a short period before demolition, the above rule applies, but the net rental income therefrom may be applied in reduction of the cost of the land.

Golf Courses

*7. Where the clearing or levelling and preparation of the soil is for the purpose of laying out a golf course, by far the greatest part of that work would be to prepare a base for greens, tees and fairways. Since these do not constitute depreciable property, the cost of that part of the work will not be depreciable but will form part of the cost of the land. If a club house, pro shop or parking area is erected on part of the cleared or levelled land, however, that part will be recognized in accordance with 5 above.

Farmers Clearing and Levelling Land or Laying Tile Drainage

8. Where a taxpayer is carrying on the business of farming, whether as owner or tenant of a farm, section 30 allows him to deduct, in computing his income from that business, amounts paid by him for clearing or levelling land or laying tile drainage for the purpose of carrying on such business. Where an amount is so deductible, paragraph $1102(1)(a)$ and subsection $1702(1)$ of the Regulations operate to exclude that amount from the cost of depreciable property so that capital cost allowance cannot be claimed thereon. Clearing or levelling land for this purpose includes brushing and breaking land, i.e., clearing the land of brush, trees, roots, stones etc. and the initial ploughing for the purpose of putting the land into productive use.

9. Where expenditures were made voluntarily by a tenant farmer prior to 1965 for clearing land or for tile drainage and the cost formed part of his leasehold interest subject to capital cost allowance under Class 13, such allowances can continue to be made in accordance with the terms of that Class.

[3285] Interpretation Bulletin IT-492: Capital Cost Allowance — Industrial Mineral Mines

[Interpretation Bulletin IT-492 is dated November 8, 1982.]

Reference: Paragraph $20(1)(a)$ of the Act (also $1100(1)(g)$, $1101(4)$ and 1104 and Schedule V of the Income Tax Regulations)

1. This bulletin discusses the type of industrial mineral mine in respect of which capital cost allowance under Part XI of the Regulations is available, and the method of calculating the amount of capital cost allowance that may be claimed.

2. Capital cost allowance is available to a taxpayer pursuant to paragraph $20(1)(a)$, Regulation $1100(1)(g)$ and Schedule V to the Regulations, in respect of the capital cost to him of

  (a) an industrial mineral mine, or

  (b) a right to remove industrial minerals from an industrial mineral mine,

except where, in either case, the industrial mineral mine is a "mineral resource"

defined in subsection $248(1)$. Provision is made in Part XII of the Regulations for an allowance in respect of a mineral resource.

3. The term "industrial mineral" means a non-metallic mineral capable of being used in industry, and the word mineral has its ordinary meaning of any chemical or compound occurring naturally as a product of inorganic processes. Some of the most common industrial minerals are:

Asbestos	Sulphur
Barite	Sand
Gypsum	Silica
Potash (sylvite)	Phosphate
Salt (halite)	Quartz
Gravel	Feldspar
Clay	Flourspar

---

* Please refer to Technical News 20 for revisions to this paragraph.

¶3285

Stone	Graphite
Limestone	Mica
Bentonite	Nepheline Syenite
Talc	

However, their classification as minerals from an "industrial mineral mine" may be altered as a result of the definition of a "mineral resource" in subsection 248(1) which includes a mineral deposit in respect of which

(a) the Minister of Energy, Mines and Resources has certified that the principal mineral extracted is an industrial mineral contained in a non-bedded deposit,

(b) the principal mineral extracted is sylvite, halite or gypsum, or

(c) the principal mineral extracted is silica extracted from sandstone or quartzite.

As a result, only minerals contained in bedded deposits will qualify as minerals from an industrial mineral mine unless the taxpayer has failed to obtain certification from the Minister of Energy, Mines and Resources in respect of a non-bedded deposit. Gravel, clay, stone, limestone, sand and feldspar usually occur in bedded deposits. On the other hand, asbestos, barite, flourspar, graphite, mica, nepheline syenite and talc usually occur in non-bedded deposits.

4. Although peat is not a mineral, for purposes of Part XI of the Regulations and Schedules II and V to the Regulations an industrial mineral mine includes a peat bog or deposit of peat, a mineral includes peat, and mining includes the harvesting of peat, by virtue of Regulation 1104(3).

5. Where the taxpayer has not been granted an allowance for a previous taxation year, the rate of the allowance in accordance with Schedule V to the Regulations is determined by dividing the capital cost of the mine or right to the taxpayer minus the residual value thereof, if any, by

(a) in any case where the taxpayer acquired a right to remove only a specified number of units, the specified number of units that he acquired a right to remove, and

(b) in any other case, the number of units of commercially mineable material esti-

mated as being in the mine when the mine or right was acquired.

Residual value refers to the estimated value of the property if all commercially mineable material were removed. Once established, the above rate continues to apply from year to year unless a recalculation is required to be made in circumstances set out in 6 below.

6. The rate established in accordance with 5 above is required to be recalculated in any year that it is determined that

(a) the capital cost of the mine or right is in fact substantially different from the previous capital cost amount used, or

(b) the number of units of commercially mineable material contained in the mine was, at the commencement of the year in which the last recalculation of the rate occurred or at the date of acquisition of the mine or right where no recalculation has occurred, different from the number of units used in the last recalculation or the initial calculation where no recalculation has yet occurred.

The new rate is then recalculated by dividing the undepreciated capital cost of the mine or right as of the commencement of the year, determined in accordance with paragraph $13(21)(f)$ using the corrected capital cost where appropriate, less any residual value, by

(a) in any case where the taxpayer had acquired a right only to remove a specified number of units, the number of units of commercially mineable material at the commencement of the year that he had a right to remove, and

(b) in any other case, the number of units of commercially mineable material estimated as remaining in the mine at the commencement of that year.

7. The maximum capital cost allowance that may be claimed in respect of a particular mine or right is the lesser of

(a) the amount computed by applying the rate established in accordance with 5 or 6 above to the number of units actually mined during the fiscal period under consideration, and

¶3285

(b) the undepreciated capital cost of the mine or right.

A taxpayer may, in lieu of claiming capital cost allowance as determined above for all his industrial mineral mines or rights, claim an amount not exceeding the lesser of

(a) $100, or

(b) the amount received by him in the taxation year from the sale of mineral.

In such case, the taxpayer, if he has more than one mine or right, may allocate the amount deducted among his mines and rights. It should be noted that no adjustment of the rate is provided for when a taxpayer fails to claim the maximum capital cost allowance in any year.

8. Capital cost allowance under Part XI is limited to the capital cost of the mine or right and a disposition of the mine or right may give rise to a capital gain, recapture or terminal allowance. It should be noted in this regard that Regulation 1101(4) deems each mine or right in respect of which capital cost allowance may be claimed pursuant to Regulation 1100(1)(g) to be a separate prescribed class.

9. Where land acquired as an industrial mineral mine is disposed of, the entire consideration received therefor is proceeds of disposition of depreciable property, namely, the industrial mineral mine, and is included in the calculation of the undepreciated capital cost of the class in which the mine is included under paragraph 13(21)(f). This is so even if the mine is exhausted prior to such disposition, or the taxpayer reserves the right to remove the industrial minerals, or has already, in a separate transaction, dis-

posed of that right. A terminal allowance cannot arise as long as any part of the land or the right to remove the minerals therefrom is retained by the taxpayer.

10. Expenditures made for surveying, testing or developing an industrial mineral mine or right for the purpose of determining whether it should be acquired are current operating expenses provided the taxpayer is in the mining business; otherwise, they are not deductible. As to whether a taxpayer is carrying on business at the time, see IT-364. Such expenditures made after the decision to acquire the property but prior to actual acquisition will be included in the capital cost of the industrial mineral mine or right unless the property is not in fact acquired, in which case these costs would be eligible capital property provided the taxpayer is in the mining business or a related business. If the taxpayer is not carrying on such business at the time of incurrence, the expenditures will not be deductible. Where, however, the property in respect of which the expenditures were incurred is acquired, the expenditures form part of the capital cost of that property. If such costs are incurred after the acquisition of the property or right, they are deductible as expenses of the year in which they were incurred, unless they are classed as a "designated overburden removal cost" as defined in Regulation 1104(2), in which case they will be included in Class 12. However, by virtue of Regulation 1104(7), a mine for purposes of Class 12 does not include a sand pit, gravel pit, clay pit, shale pit, peat bog, deposit of peat or a stone quarry, thus eliminating most industrial mineral mines from receiving Class 12 application.

[3290] Interpretation Bulletin IT-501: Capital Cost Allowance — Logging Assets

[*Interpretation Bulletin IT-501 is dated September 4, 1984.*]

Reference: Paragraph 20(1)(a) of the Act (also Classes 10 and 15 of Schedule II and Schedule IV of the Income Tax Regulations)

1. This bulletin discusses the classification, for capital cost allowance purposes, of various assets used in the logging industry. The classification and determination of the maximum capital cost allowance rates for timber resource properties and timber limits are discussed in IT-481.

*2. Logging operations are generally considered to encompass any of the following:

(a) cutting or "felling" trees in the woods,

(b) trimming off branches and tops,

(c) "bucking" into desired log lengths,

---

* As amended by Special Release, December 30, 1987.

¶3290

(d) transporting logs to tidewater, or some other central gathering point, e.g., dry land sort, and

(e) booming, rafting, or loading onto barges for towing to the mill.

Where a taxpayer is engaged not only in logging but also in a manufacturing enterprise such as the operation of a sawmill or pulp and paper mill, assets used in the processing of logs into the final product are not logging assets. For example, wood-handling equipment in the mill yards of a pulp and paper company is not a logging asset since it is used in the first stage of the manufacturing process. In addition, where operations described in (d) or (e) above are carried out by a contractor who neither owns the limit or cutting rights nor carries out the operations described in (a) to (c), the contractor does not carry on a logging operation.

Immovable Woods Assets

3. The expression "immovable woods assets" as used in this bulletin refers to immovable property acquired for the purpose of cutting and removing merchantable timber from a timber limit, which property will be of no further use to the taxpayer after all merchantable timber has been removed from the limit. Examples of logging assets of this kind that are most commonly in use are camp and depot buildings (including water, sewer and electrical systems), roads, bridges, canals, culverts, railway track and grading, dams, telephone lines, fire protection towers, docks and wharves for loading logs and for loading or unloading supplies, and flumes and chutes. Vessels located in land-locked waters, in circumstances where they cannot be removed or sold, are also considered to be assets of this kind.

4. Immovable woods assets which have a useful life of three years or less by reason of the fact that all merchantable timber will have been removed in that time from the particular area serviced by those assets may be written off as current expenses in the year in which they are incurred. However, a taxpayer may choose to treat these costs as costs of acquisition of immovable woods assets, and must treat them as immovable woods assets if the useful life will exceed three years.

Classification — Schedule II

5. Although specific assets may be property described in various other classes, immovable woods assets may, at the option of the taxpayer, be classified in the year acquired as property to be included in paragraph (n) of Class 10 or in Class 15. Classification as property described in paragraph (n) of Class 10, however, is contingent upon all property that qualifies therein being classified thereunder and not merely some of it. On the other hand, a taxpayer may classify some or all immovable woods assets as property of Class 15 or of any other classes in which they are described, other than paragraph (n) of Class 10. It should be noted that river improvements made to facilitate the removal of timber from a particular limit qualify for inclusion in Class 15 by virtue of Regulation 1102(7), but are not otherwise depreciable property, i.e. may not be included in Class 10 or in any other prescribed class.

6. By virtue of Regulation 1100(1)(f) and Schedule IV to the Regulations, a taxpayer with property in Class 15 is entitled to claim capital cost allowance based on a rate per cord or board foot of production in the year, rather than at an amount not exceeding a fixed percentage rate applied to the undepreciated capital cost of the class. If all the property in Class 15 was used for the one limit or section thereof, the rate per cord or board foot is determined by dividing the undepreciated capital cost of the property by the number of cords or board feet of timber in the limit or section thereof as at the commencement of the taxation year. Where different parts of the class were used in connection with different timber limits or sections thereof, separate rates are computed for each part of the class as though each part of the class were the taxpayer's only property of that class. The same rate will continue from year to year unless there is a cruise which indicates a change in the quantity of timber recoverable from the limit or there are additions to or deletions from the capital cost of the class.

Roads

7. The cost of constructing any road on land in which the taxpayer has no beneficial ownership interest is not a capital cost of

¶3290

depreciable property, although it may be an eligible capital expenditure (see IT-128). However, permits and other rights granted by landowners in respect of roads usually confer significant incidents of land ownership on the grantee in which case road construction costs can be property included in depreciable property classes. A road that is expected to have a useful life beyond the life of the timber limit it is servicing should be included in Class 1 or 17 (depending on the date of its acquisition) if not included in Class 10(p). Access roads or trails for the protection of standing timber against fire, insects and disease qualify for inclusion in Class 10(p). Roads which meet the description of immovable woods assets in 3 above may be included in Class 1, Class 17, Class 10(n), Class 10(p) or Class 15. Notwithstanding any of the preceding comments, a taxpayer may, as an alternative, treat expenditures which relate to a spur road or trail branching off from another road for access to a specific timber stand or area from which all merchantable timber will be removed within three years as expenses of the year in which they are incurred. Nevertheless, the cost of an "addendum road" (a road in respect of which the costs are recoverable from the crown, usually by a reduction in "stumpage" charges) is simply an account receivable and is neither deductible nor depreciable.

Logging Equipment

8. Certain equipment, acquired for logging operations but not covered by Class 10(n), ordinarily will also fall within the scope of one of the following paragraphs of Class 10:

10(a) — automotive equipment.

10(c), (d) or (e) — harness or stable equipment, sleighs, wagons or trailers.

10(o) — mechanical equipment, not including property described in Class 7 (see Boats, below).

Electrical generating equipment, radiocommunication equipment, and miscellaneous equipment which is not specifically described in another class, may be property to be included under paragraph (f), (j) or (i) respectively of Class 8. Any of the above noted equipment that was acquired for use in respect of one timber limit only and will

be of no further use after all the merchantable timber has been removed from that limit may be classified under Class 15 for allowances based on the production from the limit. As discussed in 5 above, the classification of equipment acquired for use at one timber limit as property of any class other than Class 10 will prevent the classification of any other property of the taxpayer under paragraph (n) of Class 10. Also, logging equipment is excluded from Class 29 by virtue of Regulation 1104(9)(b).

*9. Examples of specialized logging equipment which may be included in Class 10 are as follows:

(a) *Automotive equipment* — trucks, tractors, skidders, "tree harvesters" and self-propelled cranes.

(b) *Mechanical equipment (when acquired for logging operations)* — yarders, sulkies, logging arches, slashers, barkers, loaders, unloaders, hoists, winches, garage equipment, machine shop equipment, blacksmith shop equipment, railway locomotives and rolling stock and power-operated, movable, road-building equipment acquired to construct roads to or within a timber limit.

Boats

10. Canoes, rowboats, scows, tugboats and other vessels and their fittings may not be classified as mechanical equipment acquired for logging operations under paragraph (o) of Class 10. Normally they are included as property of Class 7 (see IT-267R2). Where a boat is acquired for use in respect of one timber limit only and will be abandoned when all the merchantable timber has been removed from that limit, it may be classified as property to be included in paragraph (n) of Class 10 or in Class 15 (see 5 above).

Boomchains

11. Boomchains represent supplies to be accounted for as inventory of the taxpayer.

Power Saws

12. The Department is prepared to allow a taxpayer who is required by a contract of employment to supply a power saw to deduct from income the cost of the power

---

* As amended by Special Release, December 30, 1987.

¶3290

saw in the year of purchase. The Department's practice is set out in Information Circular 74-6R, "Power Saw Expenses".

Leased Logging Equipment

13. Leasing equipment acquired by a taxpayer and subsequently leased to a person carrying on a logging operation is normally not considered to have been acquired by the lessor for logging operations. Instead, it is considered to have been acquired for the purpose of leasing. Accordingly, such property is included in the class in which it is otherwise described, and not in paragraph (o) of Class 10. However, the lessor may be considered to have acquired the property for

logging operations in the following circumstances:

(a) where the property acquired is specialized logging equipment and cannot conveniently be used for purposes other than logging, or

(b) where the property, although it is capable of being used for purposes other than logging, is acquired specifically to be leased out to a person to be used in that person's logging operations.

In either case, the lessor may include the property in Class 10 by virtue of paragraph (o) thereof.

[3295] Interpretation Bulletin IT-521R: Motor Vehicle Expenses Claimed by Self-Employed Individuals

[Interpretation Bulletin IT-521R is dated December 16, 1996.]

Reference: Paragraph $18(1)(a)$ (also sections 67, 67.2, 67.3 and 67.4, subsections 13(2), 20(16.1), and the definitions of "passenger vehicle", "automobile" and "motor vehicle" in subsection 248(1), and paragraphs $13(7)(g)$, $13(7)(h)$, $18(1)(h)$ and $85(1)(e.4)$ of the *Income Tax Act*; and section 7307, subsections 1100(2), 1100(2.5) and $1101(1af)$, subparagraph $1100(1)(a)(x.1)$ and Class 10.1 of Schedule II of the Income Tax Regulations).

Application

This bulletin cancels and replaces Interpretation Bulletin IT-521 dated August 25, 1989.

Summary

Subsection 9(1) provides that a taxpayer's income from a business or property is the profit from that business or property subject to the rules in Part I of the *Income Tax Act*. Section 18 contains several limitations concerning the deductions permitted. The purpose of paragraph $18(1)(a)$ is to deny a deduction for all outlays and expenses except to the extent that the outlays or expenses are made for the purpose of gaining or producing income from a business or property. The deduction for specific outlays and expenses is discussed in other provisions of the Act. Section 67 limits an otherwise deductible amount to an amount that is reasonable in the circumstances.

The purpose of this bulletin is to provide guidelines to a self-employed individual who is eligible to deduct expenses of operating a vehicle in computing income from a business or property. The commentary below discusses the meaning given to various words and expressions, the types of expenses that are deductible and the procedures for appor-

tioning those expenses (including capital cost allowance) between personal and business use. Also discussed are the restrictions that apply to the deductibility of lease payments, interest and capital cost allowance, as well as the types of use which constitute personal use rather than business use.

Business and Professional Income, a supplementary income tax guide, contains discussion and examples that may be helpful to users of this bulletin.

References in this bulletin to an "individual" should be read as a reference to an individual other than a trust.

Discussion and Interpretation

1. The terms "passenger vehicle", "automobile" and "motor vehicle" used throughout this bulletin have particular significance. They are defined in subsection 248(1) and can be described as follows:

(a) a "passenger vehicle" is an automobile (see b below) acquired after June 17, 1987 or leased under a lease entered into, extended or renewed after that date;

(b) an "automobile" is

¶3295

(i) a motor vehicle (see (c) below) that is designed or adapted primarily to carry individuals on highways and streets and that has a seating capacity for not more than the driver and eight passengers, but does not include

(ii) an ambulance,

(iii) a motor vehicle acquired primarily for use as a taxi, a bus used in a business of transporting passengers or a hearse used in the course of a business of arranging or managing funerals,

(iv) except for the purpose of section 6, a motor vehicle acquired to be sold, rented or leased in the course of carrying on a business of selling, renting or leasing motor vehicles or a motor vehicle used for the purpose of transporting passengers in the course of carrying on a business of arranging or managing funerals, and

(v) a motor vehicle of a type commonly called a van or pick-up truck or a similar vehicle

● that has a seating capacity for not more than the driver and 2 passengers and that, in the taxation year in which it is acquired, is used primarily for the transportation of goods or equipment in the course of gaining or producing income, or

● the use of which, in the taxation year in which it is acquired, is all or substantially all for the transportation of goods, equipment or passengers in the course of gaining or producing income; and

(c) a "motor vehicle" is an automotive vehicle designed or adapted to be used on highways and streets but does not include

(i) a trolley bus, or

(ii) a vehicle designed or adapted to be operated exclusively on rails.

Whether or not a vehicle is "acquired primarily" for the stated use will be decided based on the facts of the particular case. Generally, the Department considers that the "used primarily" test will be met where

more than 50% of the distance travelled by the vehicle is for the stated purpose.

2. The comments in this bulletin are directed to

(a) a self-employed individual who owns or leases a "motor vehicle" used by the individual or an employee of the individual to earn income from a business (including a profession) of the individual, and

(b) an individual who is a member of a partnership and personally owns or leases a "motor vehicle" to earn income from the business of the partnership and who is not fully reimbursed by the partnership for all the vehicle's expenses that pertain to the business.

Motor Vehicle Expenses

3. Where a "motor vehicle" is used by an individual in a taxation year partly to earn business income and partly for personal use, the deductible amount is normally that proportion of the aggregate of the

(a) total operating expenses (see ¶5 below) of the vehicle incurred by the individual in the year,

(b) capital cost allowance (see ¶s 13 to 20 below), and

(c) interest (see ¶21 below)

that the distance travelled by the vehicle to earn the business income is of the total distance travelled by the vehicle for the year. For example, where the aggregate of (a), (b) and (c) as described above for a year is $8,000 and the total distance travelled for the year is 32,000 kilometres of which 24,000 represent business use, the deductible amount is $6,000 determined as follows:

$$\frac{24,000}{32,000} \times \$8,000 = \$6,000$$

4. Should an individual own or lease two or more "motor vehicles" used partly for business purposes and partly for personal purposes, the above calculation may be applied separately for each vehicle or, for convenience, the calculation may be applied for both or all the vehicles taken together. That is, the operating expenses, capital cost allowance and interest (see ¶s 5, 13 to 20 and 21 below) for each "motor vehicle" may

¶3295

be combined and the deductible amount determined on the basis of the ratio of combined distance travelled for business purposes to combined total distance travelled, provided the result so determined is reasonable and not materially different from that where the determination is made for each vehicle.

5. The term "operating expenses" referred to in ¶3(a) above includes the cost of fuel, maintenance (for example, car washes, grease, oil and servicing charges), repairs (other than accident repairs — see ¶7 below), licences, insurance and, except as noted in ¶6 below, "eligible" leasing costs (see ¶s 9 to 12 below), less the aggregate of all rebates or other amounts (except where used to calculate the "eligible" leasing cost) received or receivable by the individual for the expenses and not included in the individual's income.

6. Where an individual, who leases a "motor vehicle" on a long-term basis but is not entitled to claim capital cost allowance on it, makes frequent use of the vehicle during normal work hours for business purposes, but the distance travelled for that purpose is comparatively low, the "eligible" leasing cost (see ¶s 9 to 12 below) for that vehicle may be excluded from the operating expenses if the individual so requests and the circumstances warrant it. The "eligible" leasing cost is then apportioned on the basis of a reasonable combination of distance travelled and time the "motor vehicle" was used for business purposes. For example, if a "motor vehicle" were used for business purposes five days out of seven in a normal work week, it might indicate that (allowing for personal use in the evening, usual holidays, time off for sickness, etc.) it was used 65% of the time for business purposes. If, on a distance-travelled basis, the vehicle were used only 25% for business purposes, combining the two factors might suggest that 45% of the "eligible" leasing cost should be attributed to business use. However, where a "motor vehicle" is used infrequently for business purposes, the apportionment must be on the distance-travelled basis alone, even though the vehicle is available at all times for business purposes.

7. Accident repair expenses, whether incurred to repair damages resulting from the accident to a "motor vehicle" driven by the individual or to the property of others, are deductible in full if the vehicle was being used for business purposes at the time of the accident. Any amount deductible is net after recoveries through insurance or damage claims. No portion of such expenses is deductible if the vehicle was being used for personal purposes at the time of the accident.

8. To be deductible, "motor vehicle" expenses must be reasonable in the circumstances and supportable by vouchers. (The vouchers need not be filed with the individual's income tax return; however, they must be retained for examination on request.) A claim by an individual for "motor vehicle" expenses calculated on a cents-per-kilometre (mile) basis is not acceptable. To support a claim where a "motor vehicle" is used in part for business purposes and in part for personal purposes, a record should be kept of total distance travelled and distance travelled for business purposes in a year. The record should contain at least the date, destination and distance travelled for each trip.

Eligible Leasing Cost

9. Other than as discussed in ¶10 below for a "passenger vehicle", the "eligible" leasing cost (referred to in ¶s 5 and 6 above) of a "motor vehicle" for a taxation year is the cost to the individual of leasing the vehicle in the year.

10. Section 67.3 provides that the "eligible" leasing cost, referred to in ¶9 above, of a "passenger vehicle" for a taxation year shall not exceed the lesser of

(a) the amount determined by the formula

$$\frac{(A \times B)}{30} - C - D - E$$

and

(b) the amount determined by the formula

$$\frac{(A \times B)}{.85\ C} - D - E$$

where in the formula in (a) above

A   is $600 or such other amount as is prescribed,

B   is the number of days in the period commencing at the beginning of the term of the lease and ending at the earlier of the end of the year and the end of the lease,

¶3295

C is the total of all amounts deducted in computing the individual's income for preceding taxation years for the actual lease charges for the vehicle,

D is the amount of interest that would be earned on the part of the total of all refundable amounts for the lease that exceeds $1,000, if interest were

    (i) payable on the refundable amounts at the prescribed rate, and

    (ii) computed for the period before the end of the year during which the refundable amounts were outstanding, and

E is the total of all reimbursements that became receivable before the end of the year by the individual in connection with the lease, and

where in the formula in (b) above

A is the total of the actual lease charges for the lease incurred for the year or the total of the actual lease charges for the lease paid in the year (depending on the method regularly followed by the individual in computing income),

B is $20,000 or such other amount as is prescribed,

C is the greater of $23,529 (or such other amount as is prescribed) and the manufacturer's list price for the vehicle,

D is the amount of interest, that would be earned on that part of the total of all refundable amounts paid on the lease that exceeds $1,000 if interest were

    (i) payable on the refundable amounts at the prescribed rate, and

    (ii) computed for the period in the year during which the refundable amounts are outstanding, and

E is the total of all reimbursements that became receivable during the year by the individual in connection with the lease.

Subsection 7307(3) of the Regulations prescribed the amount for A in the formula (a) above as $650 for the period after August 1989 and before 1991, and after 1990 the prescribed amount is equal to the total of $650 and the greatest amount of the Goods and Services Tax (GST) and Provincial Sales Tax (PST) that would have been

payable on a monthly payment under the lease in the taxation year of the lessee, if the lease had required monthly payments, before those taxes, of $650.

Subsection 7307(1) of the Regulations prescribes the amount for B in the formula (b) above as $24,000 for an automobile acquired or leased under an agreement entered into after August 1989 and before 1991, and where the automobile is acquired or leased, under an agreement entered into after 1990, the prescribed amount is $24,000 plus GST and PST payable had the automobile been acquired for $24,000. Pursuant to subsection 7307(4) of the Regulations, C in the formula (b) is the amount prescribed for an automobile leased under a lease entered into after August 1989 that is the amount equal to 100/85 of the amount determined for B in this formula.

The prescribed rate of interest for the relevant period is described in section 4301 of the Regulations. The rate is determined quarterly and can be obtained from any Revenue Canada tax services office.

For the purposes of D in the above formulas, a "refundable amount" includes any amount that the individual is entitled to receive from the lessor at some time under the lease. It would include an amount loaned to the lessor by the individual to effect a reduction of the lease payments.

The amount determined by the above formulas for a particular taxation year for a "passenger vehicle" may generally be described as the lesser of

    (c) the amount by which $600 (or such other amount as is prescribed) times the number of "months" the vehicle was leased since the beginning of the lease, less any amounts deducted in prior years for the lease exceeds the deemed interest and receivable reimbursements referred to in D and E, respectively, of the above formulas, and

    (d) the proportion (not exceeding one) of actual lease payments made during the year that $20,000 (or such other amount as is prescribed) is of 85% of the amount described for C of the formula in (b) above, less the deemed interest and receivable reimbursements referred to in D and E, respectively, of the above formulas. (This computation

¶3295

is designed to provide a restriction for a leased "passenger vehicle" similar to the capital cost allowance restriction discussed in ¶13 below for a purchased "passenger vehicle".)

11. Where an individual computes income from a farming or fishing business using the "cash method" described in section 28 and the total amount paid in a particular year on a lease (entered into before April 27, 1995) is greater than the amount deductible for the year as determined under the above formulas, the individual may be permitted to claim all or part of that greater amount subject to the following limitation. The individual will be permitted to deduct the amount paid in the year to the extent that the aggregate of that amount and all other amounts deducted in preceding years on the lease does not exceed the aggregate of all amounts on the lease that would be deductible over the term of the lease if such amounts were required to be paid in equal monthly payments. For example, assume that such an individual leases a passenger vehicle for three years commencing on January 1, 1993 and makes a payment of $3,000 on that date and makes 36 equal monthly payments of $400 thereafter. If we further assume that no refundable amounts in excess of $1,000 or reimbursements receivable are involved, the total amount payable under the lease ($17,400) would be deductible if paid by way of 36 equal payments of $483.33, because the application of the above formulas in such a case would not reduce the amount deductible. Thus, the individual would be allowed to deduct in 1993 the $7,800 paid in that year. In 1994 and 1995, the individual would deduct the $4,800 paid in each of those years.

Note: In a Ways and Means Motion released by the Minister of Finance on June 20, 1996 it is proposed that paragraph 28(1)(e) be amended to provide that payments (other than for inventory) that reduce cash-basis income of a farming or fishing business for a year will not include prepaid expenses relating to a taxation year of the business that is two or more taxation years after the year of payment. It is further proposed that paragraph 28(1)(e.1) will provide a deduction in a taxation year of a taxpayer for amounts paid in a previous year by the taxpayer where the amounts would be deductible in computing income for the

current taxation year from the taxpayer's business of farming or fishing if that income were not computed in accordance with the cash method. To be deductible by a taxpayer the amount will be required to have been paid in a preceding taxation year in the course of carrying on the business of farming or fishing and not be deductible in computing the income of the business for any other taxation year. The amendments, if enacted as proposed, will apply to amounts paid after April 26, 1995, except for amounts paid pursuant to written agreements entered into by the payer before April 27, 1995.

If paragraphs 28(1)(e) and (e.1) are enacted as proposed, the following is an example of the application of those paragraphs.

Assume that an individual computes income from a farming or fishing business using the "cash method" described in section 28 and on January 1, 1996, the individual leases a passenger vehicle for three years, makes a payment of $3,000 on that date and agrees to pay $600 per month for 1996, 1997 and 1998.

The application of paragraphs 28(1)(e) and (e.1) would produce the following amounts:

1996 — $9,200 [($600 × 12 months) + $2,000]

1997 — $7,200 [$600 × 12 months]

1998 — $8,200 [($600 × 12 months) + $1,000]

Section 67.3 would then be applied to the above amounts to determine the "eligible" leasing cost for each year.

Example — Computation of "Eligible" Leasing Cost

12. The following is an example of a computation of the "eligible" leasing cost for a lease entered into after 1990 for a "passenger vehicle" using the formulas in ¶10 above for a taxpayer on the accrual basis of reporting income.

Assume the following set of facts:

(a) Lease charges payable for the year for the vehicle ($750 per month) $9,000

(b) Days in the year that the vehicle was leased under the particular lease 365

(c) Days in the previous year that the vehicle was leased under the particular lease 184

(d) Amount deducted in the previous year for the vehicle based on the application of the formulas in ¶10 above for that year $3,545

(e) Manufacturer's list price for the vehicle $30,000

(f) Refundable amount .... $12,000[(1)]

(g) Prescribed rate under section 4301 of the Regulations .... 10%[(2)]

(h) Reimbursements receivable for the year in connection with the lease of the vehicle $800

(i) Reimbursements receivable for the year and for previous years in connection with the lease of the vehicle $1,200

Based on the above, D of the formula in 10(a) above is $1,655; that is, 549/365 × [($12,000 − $1000) × .10], and D of the formula in 10(b) is $1,100; that is, ($12,000 − $1,000) × .10

Computation

The "eligible" leasing cost is the lesser of

(i) $\frac{\$748^{(3)} \times 549}{30} - \$3,545 - 1,655 - 1,200 = \$7,288$

and

(ii) $\frac{\$9,000 \times \$27,600^{(4)}}{.85 \times \$32,470^{(5)}} - \$1,100 - 800 = \$7,100$

or $7,100

[(1)] The refundable amount of $12,000 represents an interest free loan made to the lessor by the individual at the beginning of the lease and that is to be paid back by the lessor at the end of the lease.

[(2)] To simplify the example, the rate for the full 18 months is assumed to be 10%. The prescribed rate is subject to adjustment for each quarter of a particular year.

[(3)] $650 plus GST and PST.

[(4)] $24,000 plus GST and PST.

[(5)] Greater of $27,600 × 100/85 and $30,000

Capital Cost Allowance

13. Where an "automobile" owned by an individual is a "passenger vehicle" costing more than $20,000 (or such other amount as may be prescribed), the amount of capital cost allowance that may be claimed on the vehicle is restricted by limiting the amount of the capital cost and the undepreciated capital cost of the relevant class (see ¶s 14 and 15 below).

14. Paragraphs 13(7)(g) and (h), respectively, provide that the capital cost of a "passenger vehicle" to an individual is to be determined as follows:

(a) where the cost of the "passenger vehicle" exceeds $20,000, or such other amount as is prescribed, the capital cost of the vehicle shall be deemed to be $20,000 or that other prescribed amount, as the case may be; and

(b) notwithstanding (a), where the "passenger vehicle" is acquired by the individual at any time from a person with whom the individual does not deal at arm's length, the capital cost of the vehicle at that time shall be deemed to be the least of

(i) the fair market value of the vehicle at that time,

(ii) the amount that immediately before that time was the "cost amount" (as defined in subsection 248(1)) to that person of the vehicle, and

(iii) $20,000 or such other amount as is prescribed.

Subsection 7307(1) of the Regulations, described in ¶10 above, prescribes the amounts for the purposes of paragraphs 13(7)(g) and (h).

15. Under subparagraph 1100(1)(a)(x.1) of the Regulations each "passenger vehicle" having a cost of more than $20,000 (or such other amount as may be prescribed for the purposes of subsection 13(2)) owned by an individual and used to earn income is included in Class 10.1 depreciable at the rate of 30% on a declining balance basis. Subsection 1101(1af) of the Regulations prescribes a separate class for each such vehicle. The capital cost of the vehicle in each separate

class is determined in the manner set out in ¶14 above. "Passenger vehicles" costing less than $20,000 (or such other amount as may be prescribed) and motor vehicles such as vans and pick-up trucks are placed in Class 10 and the balance in the class is subject to capital cost allowance at a rate of 30% on a declining balance basis. Certain other motor vehicles, such as taxi cabs are included in Class 16 and are subject to capital cost allowance at the rate of 40% on the declining balance. Subsection 7307(1) of the Regulations, described in ¶10 above, prescribes the amounts for subsection 13(2).

16. Subsection 1100(2) of the Regulations limits the capital cost allowance to one-half the normal amount in the year a "motor vehicle" is acquired or became available for use. However, subsection 1100(2.5) of the Regulations permits an individual to claim, in the year of disposition of a "passenger vehicle" that was included in Class 10.1 and that was owned by the individual at the end of the preceding taxation year, one-half the amount that the individual would have been permitted to claim as capital cost allowance had the vehicle not been disposed of.

17. Where an individual is entitled to claim capital cost allowance in computing total "motor vehicle" expenses, the capital cost allowance claim may be calculated by either of the following methods:

(a) by determining the amount of interest, operating expenses and capital cost allowance, apportioning them on the basis discussed in ¶3 above and entering the business portion on the appropriate lines on Form T2124, *Statement of Business Activities*, which is provided with the *Business and Professional Income* booklet (a supplementary income tax guide). Alternatively, where there is frequent business use of the vehicle during normal work hours but the distance travelled for that purpose is comparatively low, the capital cost allowance may be excluded from the total amount to be apportioned on the basis discussed in ¶3 above and instead be apportioned separately on the basis discussed in ¶6 above; that is, on the basis of a reasonable combination of distance travelled and time the vehicle was used for business purposes; or

(b) subject to (i) and (ii) below, by calculating capital cost allowance on that proportion of the capital cost (see ¶14 above concerning the $20,000 limitation) of the vehicle that the business use is of the total use and claiming the allowance separately from other expenses. This alternative method is acceptable only if

(i) the proportion of the capital cost on which the allowance is calculated is approximately equal to what the proportion for business use would be on the distance-travelled basis, or on the combined distance-travelled and time-used basis discussed in (a) above, and

(ii) an appropriate adjustment under paragraph 13(7)(*d*) is made concerning any change in the use regularly made of the vehicle for business and personal purposes.

18. Where a "motor vehicle" is used solely for business purposes for part of a year and solely for personal purposes for the other part, appropriate adjustments under paragraphs 13(7)(*a*) and (*b*) must be made to capital cost allowance schedules that may, subject to the comments in ¶19 below, result in a recapture of capital cost allowance or a terminal loss. An example of where the foregoing procedure would apply is where an individual practises a profession or carries on a business (such as that of a commission agent) for only part of the year.

19. By virtue of subsection 13(2), there will not be included in an individual's income any recaptured capital cost allowance on a Class 10.1 "passenger vehicle". Any amount not included in income by virtue of subsection 13(2) is deemed to be included in the individual's income for the purpose of B of the definition of "undepreciated capital cost" in subsection 13(21) thus ensuring that the result of the computation under the definition "undepreciated capital cost" in subsection 13(21) of the particular class will be nil.

Also, by virtue of subsection 20(16.1), an individual may not claim a terminal loss for a Class 10.1 "passenger vehicle".

20. For the purposes of the Act and the Regulations governing capital cost allowance, recapture of capital cost allowance

¶3295

and terminal losses, the definition of "total depreciation" in subsection 13(21) defines that amount as the aggregate of amounts deducted for capital cost allowance and terminal losses. The definition includes in "total depreciation" amounts that would have been deducted as a terminal loss but for subsection 20(16.1), as discussed in ¶19 above.

Interest

21. Where an amount of interest is paid or payable by an individual on borrowed money used to acquire a "passenger vehicle", or on an amount paid or payable for the acquisition thereof, section 67.2 limits the amount deductible to a maximum of $250 for each 30 days in the period for which the interest was paid or payable. Thus, the interest referred to in ¶3(c) above for a "passenger vehicle" is the lesser of the relevant interest paid or payable (depending on the method of computing income) in the period and the amount determined by the formula

$$\frac{A \times B}{30}$$

where

A is $250 or such other amount as may be prescribed, and

B is the number of days in the period for which the interest was paid or payable, as the case may be.

Pursuant to subsection 7307(2) of the Regulations, for the purposes of A the amount prescribed for an automobile acquired after August 1989 is $300.

The comments in the second sentence of ¶17(a) above regarding the alternative method of apportioning capital cost allowance also apply to apportioning interest.

Joint Owners or Lessees

22. Where an individual owns or leases a "passenger vehicle" jointly with one or more other persons, section 67.4 provides that the amounts of $600, $23,529, $20,000 and $250 (or such other amounts replacing them as may be prescribed) referred to in 10, 13, 14 and 21 above shall be apportioned among them on the basis of the fair market value of their respective interests in the vehicle. For example, if an individual owned an interest valued at $9,000 in a "passenger vehicle" valued at $27,000, the $300 limit referred to

in ¶21 above for that individual would be $100 (that is, $9,000/$27,000 × $300) for each relevant 30 days ($3.33 per day).

Section 85 Rollover

23. Where an individual disposes of a "passenger vehicle" (having an actual cost to the individual of more than $20,000 or such other amount as may be prescribed) to a non-arm's length taxable Canadian corporation pursuant to the provisions of subsection 85(1), paragraph 85(1)(e.4) provides that the amount the individual and the corporation have agreed on in their election shall be deemed to be equal to the undepreciated capital cost of the vehicle to the individual immediately before the disposition. This ensures that the cost amount referred to in ¶14 above will be maintained in non-arm's length transfers that are subject to subsection 85(1). See the current version of IT-419, *Meaning of Arm's Length* for comments on whether an individual is at non-arm's length with a corporation. Subsection 7307(1) of the Regulations, described in ¶10 above, prescribes the amounts for paragraph 85(1)(e.4).

General Remarks

24. Although expenses incurred in travelling between different premises of the same business are deductible by an individual who otherwise qualifies, expenses incurred by the individual for the purpose of travelling between the individual's home and place of business are not, unless it is established that the home is the base of business operations. If the individual has an office or other fixed place of business located elsewhere, the home is normally regarded as not being the base of business operations. The fact that all services are rendered at some other person's place of business does not necessarily make that place the individual's base of business operations. The individual's home may be the base of business operations even though a room therein is not set aside and used solely for the purpose of earning income. The following are examples of homes that may be regarded as the base of business operations:

(a) the home of a specialist in anaesthesia who performs all office functions of the practice at home, takes emergency calls there, renders all services to patients at one or more hospitals and has no office or other accommodation at the hospital or at any other place other than the home;

(b) the home of an independent real estate agent who has an office there, has no business accommodation elsewhere and renders services to clients at their homes or at the sites of real properties; and

(c) the home of a plumber, electrician or painter whose office is at home where all supplies are kept, who has no other place of business and who renders all services to customers at whatever places are necessary to fulfill contractual obligations.

25. Travelling "in the course of" carrying on a business does not include travelling from a place where one business is carried on to another place where an entirely different business is carried on. For observations on "Travelling to Rental Properties", please see the current version of *Rental Income*, a supplementary income tax guide.

26. By virtue of section 67, "motor vehicle" expenses are not deductible to the extent they are unreasonable.

Appendix

Assumptions:

- Dr. Lethe is a self-employed anaesthetist who practices at the General Hospital. She does not have an office where she sees her patients but rather sees them in the hospital after they have been admitted.

- Dr. Lethe has an office in her home where she does all of the administration work in connection with her practice.

- Dr. Lethe's fiscal period ends on December 31.

- On November 1, 1993, Dr. Lethe traded-in the automobile that she had purchased for $28,000 plus GST and PST in 1990. She was allowed $15,000 as the fair market value of trade-in. The new automobile cost $55,000 plus GST and PST.

- Dr. Lethe paid interest of $800 in 1993 and $3,200 in 1994 on the money she borrowed to buy the automobile. She paid no interest in 1993

on the automobile that she purchased in 1990.

For the years 1993 and 1994, Dr. Lethe's log on the use of her automobile reveals that approximately 20% of the mileage driven was involved in going to and from the hospital. The log also reveals that approximately 70% of the time when her automobile was away from her home it was in use going to or from the hospital or sitting at the hospital.

Analysis:

The automobile that Dr. Lethe purchased in 1990 was placed in Class 10.1 of Schedule II of the Regulations (see ¶15 above) since the prescribed amount for passenger vehicles purchased in 1990 was $24,000 (see the discussion of subsection 7307(1) in ¶10 above). Pursuant to subsection 1100(2.5) of the Regulations (see ¶16 above), Dr. Lethe can include capital cost allowance of $1,499[(1)] in calculating the amount of automobile expenses that she can deduct in 1993 for this automobile. (While the proceeds of disposition in 1993 exceeded the 1992 undepreciated capital cost, pursuant to subsection 13(2) (see ¶19 above), there is no recapture of capital cost allowance on Class 10.1 property.) The automobile that Dr. Lethe purchased in 1993 was placed in Class 10.1 of Schedule II of the Regulations (see ¶15 above) since the prescribed amount for passenger vehicles purchased in 1993 was $24,000 plus GST and PST on $24,000 (see the discussion of subsection 7307(1) in ¶10 above). The amount of $24,000 plus GST and PST was $28,080 in the province where Dr. Lethe lived. Dr. Lethe can include $4,212[(2)] in 1993 and $7,160[(3)] in 1994 in capital cost allowance in calculating the amount of automobile expenses that she can deduct for those years for this automobile.

Dr. Lethe can include interest of $610 in 1993 and $3,200 in 1994 in calculating the amount of motor vehicle expenses that she can deduct in those years. The interest limit discussed in ¶21 above is $300/30 × 61 = $610 in 1993 and $300/30 × 365 = $3,650 in 1994.

Generally, the personal use of an automobile includes travelling between a person's home and place of business. However, since Dr. Lethe performs the administrative functions of her profession at home and does not have an office somewhere else, her home can be regarded as her base of business operations. Therefore, travelling between her home and the hospital does not constitute the personal use of her automobile (see ¶24 above).

Dr. Lethe may deduct approximately 20% of her motor vehicle expenses if she apportions them on the basis of the distance travelled to earn business income to the total distance travelled (as described in ¶3 above) or approximately 45% [$\frac{1}{2}$(20% + 70%)] if she apportions them on the basis of distance and time used in the business (as described in ¶17(a) above).

While Dr. Lethe includes the various amounts of capital cost allowance and interest noted above in calculating the amount of motor vehicle expenses for the year she must reduce those amounts to reflect her personal use of the automobile to determine the amount that she can deduct in calculating her income.

(1)　CCA on the Class 10.1 property purchased in 1990 is calculated as follows:

1990 cost of acquisition as determined under paragraph 13(7)(g) (see ¶14 above)	$24,000
1990 CCA (30% × $24,000 × 1/2$^{(i)}$)	3,600
1990 UCC	20,400
1991 CCA (30% × $20,400)	6,120
1991 UCC	14,280
1992 CCA (30% × $14,280)	4,284
1992 UCC	9,996
1993 CCA (30% × $9,996 × 1/2$^{(ii)}$)	$1,499

CCA on the Class 10.1$^{(iii)}$ property purchased in 1993 is calculated as follows:

1993 cost of acquisition as determined under paragraphs 13(7)(g) (see ¶14 above)	$28,080
(2)　1993 CCA (30% × $28,080 × 1/2$^{(i)}$)	4,212
1993 UCC	23,868
(3)　1994 CCA (30% × $23,868)	$7,160

(i)　Pursuant to subsection 1100(2) of the Regulations, CCA is reduced to one half of the normal amount in the year a motor vehicle is acquired or becomes available for use (see ¶16 above).

(ii)　Pursuant to subsection 1100(2.5) of the Regulations, CCA is reduced to one half of the normal amount in the year a Class 10.1 motor vehicle is disposed of (see ¶16 above).

(iii)　Subsection 1101(1af) of the Regulations prescribes a separate Class 10.1 for each passenger vehicle (see ¶15 above).

Explanation of Changes

Introduction

The purpose of the Explanation of Changes is to explain the reasons for the revisions to an interpretation bulletin. It outlines revisions that we have made as a result of changes to the law, as well as changes reflecting new or revised departmental interpretations.

Reasons for the Revision

The bulletin has been revised to reflect amendments to the *Income Tax Act* resulting from S.C. 1994, c. 7 Schedule II (S.C. 1991, c. 49 — formerly Bill C-18) which generally apply after 1987, the Ways and Means Motion Amending the *Income Tax Act* and Related Acts issued by the Minister of Finance on June 20, 1996 and to make incidental changes.

In a Press Release dated December 12, 1995, the Parliamentary Secretary to the Minister of Finance referred to subsections 7307(1) to (4) of the Regulations (as described in ¶s 10 and 21 of the bulletin) and announced that the subsections would not be changed for 1996.

Except as described in the Note at the end of ¶11, the comments in the bulletin are not affected by proposed legislation that has been released as of October 30, 1996.

Legislative and Other Changes

¶1 reflects the amended definition of "automobile". Generally, the amendment removes from the definition of "automobile", buses, vans, pick-up trucks and motor vehicles used for transporting passengers in the business of arranging or managing funerals. The amendment applies to taxation years and fiscal periods commencing after June 17, 1987 that end after 1987.

¶10 has been revised as follows:

¶3295

- to reflect an amendment to section 67.3. The amendment deletes the reference to provincial sales tax and permits taxpayers using the cash basis method of calculating income to deduct amounts paid in connection with the cost of leasing a passenger vehicle;

- to describe the relevant prescribed amounts; and

- to delete a position that relates to individuals who compute income under section 28 and, as a result of a prepayment under a lease, pay an amount in a year that exceeds the amount deductible in the year under section 67.3. The comments were moved to ¶11.

The amendment to section 67.3 applies to taxation years and fiscal periods commencing after June 17, 1987 that end after 1987, except that, with respect to amounts paid or payable as a reimbursement in respect of a lease expense, it is applicable to taxation years that end after July 13, 1990.

¶11 is part of former 10. A note has been added at the end of the paragraph to reflect an amendment proposed in the Ways and Means Motion Amending the *Income Tax Act* and Related Acts released by the Minister of Finance on June 20, 1996. The proposed amendment provides that certain payments that reduce the cash-basis income of a taxpayer in a farming or fishing business may not be deducted in the year of payment but may be deducted in a later year. The administrative position described in 11 will only apply to leases entered into before April 27, 1995 since the Ways and Means

Motion of June 20, 1996 amend section 28 to effectively produce a statutory requirement relating to the accounting for prepaid expenses.

¶12 (former ¶28) gives an example of the application of section 67.3, including the changes described in ¶10, and reflects the amounts presently prescribed in section 7307 of the Regulations.

¶17(a) (former ¶15(a)) reflects revisions made to Form T2124, *Statement of Business Activities*.

¶21 (former ¶19) reflects an amendment to section 67.2. The amendment eliminates unintended results for taxpayers who use the cash basis method of calculating income when interest is paid on the acquisition of a passenger vehicle. The amendment applies to taxation years and fiscal periods commencing after June 17, 1987 that end after 1987.

In former ¶13 the comments concerning the transfer of vehicles from Class 10 to Class 10.1 have not been carried forward as they are no longer relevant.

Formers ¶s 22 to 24 have not been carried forward as the topics discussed in those paragraphs are fully described in *Rental Income*, a supplementary income tax guide.

An appendix was added to illustrate some of the provisions discussed in the bulletin.

Throughout the bulletin we have deleted observations which are no longer relevant and we have revised some of the wording to improve readability without altering the substance.

[3300] Interpretation Bulletin IT-522R: Vehicle, Travel and Sales Expenses of Employees

[*Interpretation Bulletin IT-522R is dated March 29, 1996.*]

Reference: Paragraphs $8(1)(f)$, $8(1)(h)$, $8(1)(h.1)$ and $8(1)(j)$ (also sections 67.1, 67.2, 67.3 and 67.4, subsections $6(6)$, $8(4)$, $8(9)$, $8(10)$, $13(2)$, $13(7)$, $13(11)$, $20(16)$, $20(16.1)$, $70(5)$, $70(6)$, $81(3.1)$ and the definitions of "passenger vehicle", "automobile" and "motor vehicle" in subsection 248(1), and paragraphs $6(1)(b)$, and $85(1)(e.4)$ of the *Income Tax Act*; and section 7307, subsections $1100(2)$, $1100(2.5)$ and $1101(1af)$, subparagraph$1100(1)(a)(x.1)$ and Class 10.1 of Schedule II of the Income Tax Regulations)

Application

This bulletin replaces and cancels Interpretation Bulletin IT-522 dated August 25, 1989.

Summary

An employee may only deduct those reasonable outlays and expenses related to employment income which are specifically

¶3300

permitted under section 8 in determining employment income.

The bulletin describes:

- the rules concerning the deduction of sales, motor vehicle and travel expenses incurred in earning income from an office or employment;

- the limitations on expenses for passenger vehicles whether leased or owned by the employee;

- the definitions of "passenger vehicle", "automobile" and "motor vehicle";

- the inclusion in, and exclusions from, income of allowances received by an employee in connection with sales, motor vehicle and travel expenses.

Employment Expenses, a supplementary income tax guide, contains a discussion and examples that may be helpful in determining the expenses that may be deducted by employees earning commission income as well as employees earning a salary.

The topics are discussed under the following headings:

Discussion and Interpretation

Meaning of the Terms *Passenger Vehicle, Automobile* and *Motor Vehicle*

1. The terms "passenger vehicle", "automobile" and "motor vehicle" used throughout this bulletin have particular significance. They are defined in subsection 248(1) and can be described as follows:

(a) a "passenger vehicle" is an automobile (see (b) below) acquired after June 17, 1987 or leased under a lease entered into, extended or renewed after that date;

(b) an "automobile" is

(i) a motor vehicle (see (c) below) that is designed or adapted primarily to carry individuals on highways and streets and that has a seating capacity for not more than the driver and eight passengers, but does not include

(ii) an ambulance,

(iii) a motor vehicle acquired primarily for use as a taxi, a bus used in a business of transporting passengers or a hearse used in the course of a business of arranging or managing funerals,

(iv) except for the purpose of section 6, a motor vehicle acquired to be sold, rented or leased in the course of carrying on a business of selling, renting or leasing motor vehicles or a motor vehicle used for the purpose of transporting passengers in the course of carrying on a business of arranging or managing funerals, and

(v) a motor vehicle of a type commonly called a van or pick-up truck or a similar vehicle

- that has a seating capacity for not more than the driver and two passengers and that, in the taxation year in which it is acquired, is used primarily for the transportation of goods or equipment in the course of gaining or producing income, or

- the use of which, in the taxation year in which it is acquired, is all or substantially all for the transportation of goods, equipment or passengers in the course of gaining or producing income; and

¶3300

(c) a "motor vehicle" is an automotive vehicle designed or adapted to be used on highways and streets but does not include

(i) a trolley bus, or

(ii) a vehicle designed or adapted to be operated exclusively on rails.

Whether or not a vehicle is "acquired primarily" for the stated use will be decided based on the facts of the particular case. Generally, the Department considers that the "used primarily" test will be met where more than 50% of the distance travelled by the vehicle is for the stated purpose.

2. The comments in this bulletin are directed to an employee who

(a) owns or leases a "motor vehicle" or aircraft (that is, not to one who has the use of a "motor vehicle" or aircraft provided by the employer), and

(b) is entitled to deduct "motor vehicle" or aircraft expenses under paragraph $8(1)(f)$, (h) or $(h.1)$ (and thus entitled to deduct applicable interest and capital cost allowance under paragraph $8(1)(j)$) in computing income from an office or employment. (¶35 below describes who is entitled to deduct expenses under paragraph $8(1)(f)$ while ¶31 below describes who is entitled to make deductions under paragraphs $8(1)(h)$ and $(h.1)$.)

"Motor Vehicle" Expenses

3. Where a "motor vehicle" is used by an employee in a taxation year partly to earn income from an office or employment and partly for personal purposes, the deductible amount is normally that proportion of the aggregate of the

(a) total operating expenses (see ¶5 below) of the vehicle incurred by the employee in the year,

(b) capital cost allowance (see ¶15 to ¶19 below), and

(c) interest (see ¶28 below)

that the distance travelled by the vehicle to earn the employment income is of the total distance travelled by the vehicle for the year, less the total of all rebates, allowances or reimbursements (other than reimbursements deducted in computing the "eligible" leasing cost referred to in ¶5 and ¶9 below) received by the employee in the year concerning the above aggregate and not

required to be included in the employee's income.

For example, where

● the aggregate of (a), (b) and (c) as described above for a year is $8,000 and the employee receives no reimbursement for such expenses, and

● the total distance travelled for the year is 32,000 kilometres of which 24,000 represents employment use, the deductible amount is $6,000 determined as follows:

$$\frac{24,000}{32,000} \times \$8,000 = \$6,000$$

If the employee has been reimbursed $2,000 and no portion of that reimbursement was deducted in computing the "eligible" leasing cost, the deductible amount would be $4,000 (that is, $6,000 − $2,000).

4. Should an employee own or lease two or more "motor vehicles" used partly for earning income from an office or employment and partly for personal purposes, the calculation in ¶3 above may be applied separately for each vehicle or, for convenience, the calculation may be applied for all the vehicles taken together. That is, the operating expenses, capital cost allowance and interest (see ¶5, ¶15 to ¶19 and ¶28 below) for each "motor vehicle" may be combined and the deductible amount determined on the basis of the ratio of combined distance travelled to earn income from an office or employment to combined total distance travelled, provided the result so determined is reasonable and not materially different from that where the determination is made for each vehicle.

5. The term "operating expenses" referred to in ¶3(a) above includes the cost of fuel, maintenance (for example, car washes, oil, grease and servicing charges), repairs (other than accident repairs — see ¶7 below), licences, insurance and, except as noted in ¶6 below, the "eligible" leasing cost (see ¶8 and ¶9 below).

6. Where an employee, who leases a "motor vehicle" on a long-term basis but is not entitled to claim capital cost allowance (see ¶15 to ¶19 below) on it, makes frequent use of the vehicle during the normal work hours in the course of earning income from an office or employment, but the distance travelled for that purpose is comparatively low, the "eligible" leasing cost for that vehicle may be excluded from the operating expenses if the employee so requests and the circumstances warrant it. The "eligible"

leasing cost is then apportioned on the basis of a reasonable combination of distance travelled and time the "motor vehicle" was used in the course of earning income from the office or employment.

For example, if a "motor vehicle" were used in the course of earning income from an office or employment five days out of seven in a normal work week, it might indicate that (allowing for personal use in the evening, usual holidays, time off for sickness, etc.) it was used 65% of the time for employment purposes. If, on a distance-travelled basis, the vehicle were used only 25% for employment purposes, combining the two factors might suggest that 45% of the "eligible" leasing cost should be attributed to employment use. However, where a "motor vehicle" is used infrequently in the course of earning income from an office or employment, the apportionment must be on the distance-travelled basis alone, even though the vehicle is available at all times for employment purposes.

7. Accident repair expenses, whether incurred to repair damages resulting from the accident to a "motor vehicle" driven by the employee or to the property of others, are deductible in full if the vehicle was being used to earn income from an office or employment at the time of the accident. Any amount deductible is net after recoveries through insurance or damage claims. No portion of such expenses is deductible if the vehicle was being used for personal purposes at the time of the accident.

8. Other than as discussed in ¶9 below for a "passenger vehicle", the "eligible" leasing cost referred to in ¶5 above of a "motor vehicle" for a taxation year is the amount paid in the year by the employee for leasing the vehicle.

9. Section 67.3 provides that the "eligible" leasing cost, referred to in ¶8 above, of a "passenger vehicle" for a taxation year shall not exceed the lesser of

(a) the amount determined by the formula

$$\frac{(A \times B)}{30} - C - D - E$$

and

(b) the amount determined by the formula

$$\frac{(A \times B)}{.85\ C} - D - E$$

where in the formula in (a) above

A is $600 or such other amount as is prescribed,

B is the number of days in the period commencing at the beginning of the term of the lease and ending at the earlier of the end of the year and the end of the lease,

C is the total of all amounts deducted in computing the employee's income for preceding taxation years for the actual lease charges for the vehicle,

D is the amount of interest that would be earned on the part of the total of all refundable amounts for the lease that exceeds $1,000, if interest were

(i) payable on the refundable amounts at the prescribed rate, and

(ii) computed for the period before the end of the year during which the refundable amounts were outstanding, and

E is the total of all reimbursements that became receivable before the end of the year by the employee in connection with the lease, and

where in the formula in (b) above

A is the total of the actual lease charges for the lease paid in the year,

B is $20,000 or such other amount as is prescribed,

C is the greater of $23,529 (or such other amount as is prescribed) and the manufacturer's list price for the vehicle,

D is the amount of interest, that would be earned on that part of the total of all refundable amounts paid on the lease that exceeds $1,000 if interest were

(i) payable on the refundable amounts at the prescribed rate, and

(ii) computed for the period in the year during which the refundable amounts are outstanding, and

E is the total of all reimbursements that became receivable during the year by the employee in connection with the lease.

Subsection 7307(3) of the Regulations prescribed the amount for A in the formula (a) above as $650 for the period after August 1989 and before 1991, and after 1990 the prescribed amount is equal to the total of $650 and the greatest amount of the Goods and Services Tax (GST) and Provincial Sales Tax (PST) that would have been payable on a monthly payment under the lease in the taxation year of the lessee, if the lease had required monthly payments, before those taxes, of $650.

¶3300

Subsection 7307(1) of the Regulations prescribes the amount for B in the formula (b) above as $24,000 for an automobile acquired or leased under an agreement entered into after August 1989 and before 1991, and where the automobile is acquired or leased, under an agreement entered into after 1990, the prescribed amount is $24,000 plus GST and PST payable had the automobile been acquired for $24,000.

Pursuant to subsection 7307(4) of the Regulations, C in the formula (b) is the amount prescribed for an automobile leased under a lease entered into after August 1989 that is the amount equal to 100/85 of the amount determined for B in this formula.

The prescribed rate of interest for the relevant period is described in section 4301 of the Regulations. The rate is determined quarterly and can be obtained from any Revenue Canada Tax Services Office.

For the purposes of D in the above formulas, a "refundable amount" includes any amount that the employee is entitled to receive from the lessor at some time with respect to the lease. It would include an amount loaned to the lessor by the employee to effect a reduction of the lease payments.

Where the total amount paid in a particular year on a lease is greater than the amount as determined under the above formulas, the employee may be permitted to claim all or part of that greater amount subject to the following limitation. The employee will be permitted to claim the amount paid in the year to the extent that the aggregate of that amount and all other amounts deducted in preceding years on the lease does not exceed the aggregate of all amounts on the lease that would be deductible over the term of the lease if such amounts were required to be paid in equal monthly payments. For example, assume that an employee leases a passenger vehicle for three years commencing on January 1, 1993 and makes a payment of $3,000 on that date and makes 36 equal monthly payments of $400 thereafter. If we further assume that no refundable amounts in excess of $1,000 or reimbursements receivable are involved, the total amount payable under the lease ($17,400) would be deductible if paid by way of 36 equal payments of $483.33, because the application of the above formulas in such a case would not reduce the amount deductible. Thus, the employee would be allowed to deduct in 1993 the $7,800 paid in that year. In 1994 and 1995, the employee would deduct the $4,800 paid in each of those years.

The amount determined by the above formulas for a particular taxation year for a "passenger vehicle" may generally be described as the lesser of

(c) the amount by which $600 (or such other amount as is prescribed) times the number of "months" the vehicle was leased since the beginning of the lease, less any amounts deducted in prior years for the lease, exceeds the deemed interest and receivable reimbursements referred to in D and E, respectively, of the above formulas, and

(d) the proportion (not exceeding one) of actual lease payments made during the year that $20,000 (or such other amount as is prescribed) is of 85% of the amount described for C of the formula in (b) above, less the deemed interest and receivable reimbursements referred to in D and E, respectively, of the above formulas. (This computation is designed to provide a restriction for a leased "passenger vehicle" similar to the capital cost allowance restriction discussed in ¶16 below for a purchased "passenger vehicle".)

Example — Computation of "Eligible" Leasing Cost

10. The following is an example of a computation of the "eligible" leasing cost for a lease entered into after 1990 for a "passenger vehicle" using the formulas in ¶9 above.

Assume the following set of facts:

(a) Lease charges paid in the year for the vehicle ($750 per month) ....$ 9,000

(b) Days in the year that the vehicle was leased under the particular lease...... 365

(c) Days in the previous year that the vehicle was leased under the particular lease 184

(d) Amount claimed in the previous year for the vehicle based on the application of the formulas in ¶9 above for that year ....$ 3,109

(e) Manufacturer's list price for the vehicle $36,000

(f) Refundable amount......$12,000[(1)]

(g) Prescribed rate under section 4301 of the Regulations .... 10%[(2)]

¶3300

(h) Reimbursements receivable for the year on the lease of the vehicle . . . . . . $ 800

(i) Reimbursements receivable for the year and for previous years on the lease of the vehicle . . . . . . $ 1,200

Based on the above, D of the formula in ¶9(a) above is $1,655; that is, 549/365 × [($12,000 − $1,000) × .10], and D of the formula in 9(b) above is $1,100; that is, ($12,000 − $1,000) × .10.

Computation

The "eligible" leasing cost is the lesser of

(i) $\dfrac{\$748^{(3)} \times 549}{30}$

$- \ \$3,109 \ - \ 1,655 \ - \ 1,200 \ = \ \$7,724$

and

(ii) $\dfrac{\$9,000 \ \times \ \$27,600^{(4)}}{.85 \ \times \ \$36,000}$

$- \ \$1,100 \ - \ 800 \ = \ \$6,218$

or $6,218

$^{(1)}$ The refundable amount of $12,000 represents an interest free loan made to the lessor by the employee at the beginning of the lease and that is to be paid back to the employee at the end of the lease.

$^{(2)}$ Although the prescribed rate is subject to adjustment for each quarter in a particular year, to simplify the example, the rate for the full 18 months is assumed to be 10%.

$^{(3)}$ $650 plus GST and PST.

$^{(4)}$ $24,000 plus GST and PST.

Aircraft Expenses

11. Subject to the comments in ¶12 and ¶30 below, where an aircraft is used by an employee partly to earn income from an office or employment and partly for personal purposes, the deductible amount is normally that proportion of the total operating expenses of the aircraft incurred by the employee in the year (plus capital cost allowance and interest where applicable) that the hours flown to earn income from an office or employment are of the total flying hours for the year. Thus, the portion of the operating expenses of an aircraft that is deductible from income from an office or employment is calculated as follows:

$$\frac{\text{hours flown to earn income from an office or employment}}{\text{total flying hours}} \times \frac{\text{operating}}{\text{expenses}} = \frac{\text{deductible portion of operating expenses}}$$

12. The comments in ¶4, ¶6 and ¶7 above discuss variations under which the deductible portion of a "motor vehicle's" operating expenses may be calculated. Those comments have equal application to a situation where an aircraft is used to earn income from an office or employment and, in this respect, a reference to distance travelled should be read as a reference to hours flown.

Records to be Kept

13. To be deductible, "motor vehicle" or aircraft expenses must be reasonable in the circumstances and supportable by vouchers. (The vouchers need not be filed with the employee's income tax return; however, they must be retained for examination on request.) A claim by an employee for "motor vehicle" expenses calculated on a cents-per-kilometre (mile) basis or for aircraft expenses calculated on a dollars-per-flying hour basis is not acceptable. To support a claim where a "motor vehicle" is used in part to earn income from an office or employment and in part for personal purposes, a record should be kept of total distance travelled and distance travelled in the year to earn the income. Similarly, where an aircraft is used in part to earn income from an office or employment and in part for personal purposes, a record should be kept of the total flying hours and hours flown in the course of earning the income. The record of distance travelled or hours flown to earn the income should contain at least the date, destination and distance travelled or hours flown for each trip.

14. Travelling between the employee's home and the place of employment is personal travel and the portion of the expenses relating to this travel is not deductible.

Capital Cost Allowance — "Motor Vehicle" and Aircraft

15. Where an employee, who is entitled to deduct expenses under either paragraph 8(1)(f) or (h.1) and satisfies the requirements of subsection 8(10) (see ¶58 below), owns a "motor vehicle" used in the performance of the duties of the office or employment, capital cost allowance on it may be deducted by virtue of paragraph 8(1)(j).

16. Where an "automobile" owned by an employee is a "passenger vehicle", paragraphs 13(7)(g) and (h), respectively, provide that the capital cost of the vehicle to the employee is to be determined as follows:

¶3300

(a) where the cost of the "passenger vehicle" exceeds $20,000 or such other amount as is prescribed, the capital cost thereof shall be deemed to be $20,000 or that other prescribed amount, as the case may be; and

(b) notwithstanding (a), where the "passenger vehicle" is acquired by the employee at any time from a person with whom the employee does not deal at arm's length, the capital cost of the vehicle at that time shall be deemed to be the least of

(i) the fair market value of the vehicle at that time,

(ii) the amount that immediately before that time was the "cost amount" (as defined in subsection 248(1)) to that person of the vehicle, and

(iii) $20,000 or such other amount as is prescribed.

Subsection 7307(1) of the Regulations, described in ¶9 above, prescribes the amounts for the purposes of paragraphs 13(7)(g) and (h).

17. Under subparagraph 1100(1)(a)(x.1) of the Regulations each "passenger vehicle" having a cost of more than $20,000 (or such other amount as may be prescribed for the purposes of subsection 13(2)) owned by an employee and used to earn income from an office or employment will be included in Class 10.1 depreciable at the rate of 30% on a declining balance basis. Subsection 1101(1af) of the Regulations prescribes a separate class for each such vehicle. The capital cost of the vehicle in each separate class will be determined in the manner set out in ¶16 above. "Passenger vehicles" costing less than $20,000 (or such other amount as may be prescribed) are placed in Class 10 and the balance in the class is depreciable at a rate of 30% on a declining balance basis. Subsection 7307(1) of the Regulations, described in ¶9 above, prescribes the amounts for subsection 13(2).

18. By virtue of subsection 13(2), there will not be included in an employee's income from an office or employment any recaptured capital cost allowance on a Class 10.1 "passenger vehicle". Any amount not included in income by virtue of subsection 13(2) is deemed to be included in the employee's income for the purpose of B of the definition "undepreciated capital cost" in subsection 13(21), thus ensuring that the result of the computation under the definition "undepreciated capital cost" in subsection 13(21) of the particular class will be nil.

19. Where an "automobile" owned by an employee is a "passenger vehicle" having a cost to the employee of more than $20,000, or such other amount as may be prescribed, and the employee disposes of the vehicle to a non-arm's length taxable Canadian corporation pursuant to the provisions of subsection 85(1), paragraph 85(1)(e.4) provides that the amount the employee and the corporation have agreed on in their election shall be deemed to be an amount equal to the undepreciated capital cost of the vehicle to the employee immediately before the disposition. This ensures that the cost amount referred to in ¶16 above will be maintained in non-arm's length transfers that are subject to subsection 85(1). If the corporation subsequently makes the automobile available to any employee or a person related to any employee, pursuant to paragraph 85(1)(e.4), the cost of the automobile, for the purpose of determining the standby charge under subsection 6(2), is its fair market value immediately before the disposition to the corporation. See the current version of IT-419, *Meaning of Arm's Length*, for comments on whether an employee is at non-arm's length with a corporation. Subsection 7307(1) of the Regulations, described in ¶9 above, prescribes the amounts for paragraph 85(1)(e.4).

20. By virtue of paragraph 8(1)(j), an employee who meets the conditions of either paragraph 8(1)(f) or (h) and satisfies the requirement of subsection 8(10) (see ¶58 below) may deduct capital cost allowance on the cost of an aircraft that is required for use in the performance of the employee's duties of an office or employment. To be "required for use", an aircraft must be necessary for the satisfactory performance of the employee's duties. However, this does not necessarily imply that the employer must order the employee to use this means of transportation. Furthermore, subsection 8(9) (see ¶30 below) will limit the amount deductible, including capital cost allowance, to an amount that is reasonable having regard to the relative cost and availability of other modes of transportation.

21. An aircraft (including furniture, fittings, equipment and small parts) that was acquired after May 25, 1976 or that has not been used continuously since that date to earn income from an office or employment is a Class 9 asset (depreciable at the rate of 25% on a declining balance basis).

22. "Aircraft" means any machine used or designed for travelling in the air but does not include a machine designed to derive support in the atmosphere from reactions

¶3300

against the earth's surface of air expelled from the machine (for example, a hover-craft).

23. Where an employee is entitled to claim capital cost allowance in computing total "motor vehicle" or aircraft expenses, the capital cost allowance claim may be calculated by either of the following methods:

(a) by entering the full amount of interest and operating expenses (before reduction by the portion relating to personal use) on Form T777, *Statement of Employment Expenses*, which is provided with the *Employment Expenses* booklet (a supplementary income tax guide), and then including the full capital cost allowance in the total amount to be apportioned on the basis discussed in ¶3 and ¶11 above. Alternatively, where there is frequent use of the "motor vehicle" or aircraft during normal work hours to earn income from an office or employment but the distances travelled or hours flown for that purpose are comparatively low, the capital cost allowance may be excluded from the total amount to be apportioned on the basis discussed in ¶3 and ¶11 above and be apportioned on the basis discussed in ¶6 and referred to in ¶12 above; that is, on the basis of a reasonable combination of distance travelled or hours flown and time the vehicle or aircraft was used in the course of earning income from the office or employment; or

(b) subject to (i) and (ii) below, by calculating capital cost allowance on that proportion of the capital cost of the "motor vehicle" (see ¶16 above concerning the capital cost limitation) or aircraft that the employment use is of the total use and claiming the allowance separate from other expenses. This alternative method is acceptable only if

(i) the proportion of the capital cost on which the allowance is calculated is approximately equal to what the proportion for employment use would be on the distance-travelled or hours-flown basis, or on the combined distance-travelled (or hours-flown) and time-used basis discussed in (a) above, and

(ii) an appropriate adjustment under paragraph 13(7)(*d*) is made concerning any change in the use regularly made of the vehicle or aircraft for employment and personal purposes.

24. If an employee is still using a "motor vehicle" or aircraft at the end of the year to earn income from an office or employment, generally, the capital cost allowance for the full year is deductible even though the employment commenced part-way through the year. Subsection 1100(2) of the Regulations limits the capital cost allowance to one-half the normal amount in the year a "motor vehicle" or aircraft is acquired or became available for use. However, subsection 1100(2.5) of the Regulations permits an employee to claim, in the year of disposition of a "passenger vehicle" that was included in Class 10.1 and that was owned by the employee at the end of the preceding year, one-half the amount that the employee would have been permitted to claim as capital cost allowance had the vehicle not been disposed of. Where an amount remains in Class 10.1 after the disposition of the passenger vehicle that was owned by an employee, the employee is not entitled to deduct a terminal loss under subsection 20(16). Where an amount remains in Class 10 after the disposition of a "motor vehicle" that was owned by an employee and there is no property in the class at the end of the year, the employee is not entitled to deduct a terminal loss under subsection 20(16). Pursuant to paragraph 8(1)(*j*) an employee may deduct such part of the capital cost of a motor vehicle that is used in the performance of the duties of the office or employment as is allowed by regulation. A terminal loss is not allowed by regulation.

25. Subsection 70(5) or 70(6), as the case may be, provides that all depreciable property of a prescribed class is deemed to have been disposed of immediately before death.

26. Where, before the end of a particular year, an employee

(a) disposes of an aircraft or "motor vehicle" previously used to perform the duties of an office or employment and does not replace it with a similar property,

(b) is deemed under subsection 13(7) to have disposed of an aircraft or "motor vehicle" as a result of ceasing to use it to perform the duties of an office or employment, or

(c) is deemed to have disposed of an aircraft or "motor vehicle" immediately before death as discussed in ¶25 above, and a balance remains in the particular class at the end of the year, capital cost allowance (except as noted in ¶24 above) is not deductible in that year. However, subsection 13(11) provides

¶3300

the authority for recapturing the capital cost allowance previously allowed on an employee's aircraft or "motor vehicle" except where subsection 13(2) provides an exemption for the vehicle (see ¶18 above). For the purpose of (b) above, an employee is not considered to have ceased to use an aircraft or vehicle to perform the duties of employment if such cessation is only temporary, provided the nature of the employment has not changed in such a manner that the use of the aircraft or vehicle is no longer required in the performance of those duties.

Interest on Borrowed Money Used to Acquire a "Motor Vehicle" or Aircraft

27. Where an employee who is entitled to deduct expenses under paragraph 8(1)(f), (h) or (h.1) incurs debt to acquire an aircraft or "motor vehicle" used in the performance of the duties of an office or employment, paragraph 8(1)(j) provides for a deduction of a portion of the interest paid in the year on the debt. The deductible portion of the interest may be determined on the basis discussed in ¶3 and ¶11 above or, where there is frequent use of the aircraft or vehicle during the normal work hours in the course of earning income from an office or employment but the hours flown or distance travelled for that purpose is comparatively low, on the basis discussed in ¶6 above and referred to in ¶12 above. The amount of the interest to be so apportioned is subject to the limitation discussed in ¶28 below for a "passenger vehicle" and in ¶30 below for an aircraft. No interest is deductible where the requirements of subsection 8(10) are not met — see ¶58 below.

28. Where an aircraft or a "motor vehicle" other than a "passenger vehicle" is involved, the interest referred to in ¶3(c) above is that determined under paragraph 8(1)(j) as discussed in ¶27 above. Where the vehicle is a "passenger vehicle", section 67.2 limits the amount deductible to a maximum of $250 or such other amount as may be prescribed for each 30 days in the period for which the interest was paid. Thus, the interest referred to in ¶3(c) above for a "passenger vehicle" is the lesser of the relevant interest paid in the period and the amount determined by the formula

$$\frac{A}{30} \times B$$

where

A   is $250 or such other amount as may be prescribed, and

B   is the number of days in the period for which the interest was paid.

Pursuant to subsection 7307(2) of the Regulations for the purposes of A the amount prescribed for an automobile acquired after August 1989 is $300.

Joint Owners or Lessees

29. Where an employee owns or leases a "passenger vehicle" jointly with one or more other persons, section 67.4 provides that the amounts of $600, $23,529, $20,000 and $250 (or such other amounts replacing them as may be prescribed) referred to in ¶9, ¶16 and ¶28 above shall be apportioned among them on the basis of the fair market value of their respective interests in the vehicle. For example, if an employee owned an interest valued at $9,000 in a "passenger vehicle" valued at $27,000, the $300 limit referred to in ¶28 above for that employee would be $100 (that is, $9,000 ÷ $27,000 × $300) for each relevant 30 days ($3.33 per day).

Aircraft Expenses — Limitation

30. For the purposes of ¶11, ¶20 and ¶27 above, subsection 8(9) limits the amount an employee may claim in the operation of an aircraft, owned or leased, to an amount that is reasonable having regard to the relative cost and availability of other modes of transportation. For example, where an employee's territory is inaccessible or it is impractical to travel to it other than by private aircraft, the Department will consider the costs of operating the aircraft (including capital cost allowance and interest where applicable) that are attributable to earning income from an office or employment to be reasonable, provided the conditions set out in paragraphs 8(1)(f) and (j) or paragraphs 8(1)(h) and (j), as the case may be, are met and the conditions of subsection 8(10) are satisfied (see ¶58 below). However, where other modes of transportation are available to the employee but the use of a private aircraft is chosen instead, the employee must be prepared to justify that the expenses associated with the use of the aircraft are reasonable; otherwise, the claim will be reduced to the reasonable costs of the alternate transportation.

Employees in General

31. Provided the requirement in subsection 8(10) is satisfied (see ¶58 below), an employee is entitled to deduct under paragraph 8(1)(h) or (h.1) amounts spent in the year for travelling provided the amounts are

reasonable in the circumstances and all of the following conditions are met:

(a) the employee is ordinarily required to carry on the duties of the office or employment away from the employer's place of business or in different places (see ¶32 below);

(b) under the contract of employment, the employee is required to pay travel expenses incurred in the performance of the duties of the office or employment (see ¶33 below); and

(c) where the expense is deducted under paragraph 8(1)(h)

(i) the employee is not in receipt of an allowance for travel expenses that was excluded from income by virtue of subparagraph 6(1)(b)(v), (vi), or (vii) (see ¶40 to ¶49 below), and

(ii) the employee has not claimed any deduction for the year under paragraph 8(1)(e) (expenses of certain railway company employees away from their ordinary residence or home terminal), 8(1)(f) (salesperson's expenses) or 8(1)(g) (transport employee's expenses); or

(d) where the expense is deducted under paragraph 8(1)(h.1)

(i) the employee is not in receipt of an allowance for motor vehicle expenses that was excluded from income by virtue of paragraph 6(1)(b), and

(ii) the employee has not claimed any deduction for the year under paragraph 8(1)(f) (salesperson's expenses).

32. Concerning ¶31(a) above,

(a) "ordinarily" means "customarily" or "habitually" rather than "continually", but there should be some degree of regularity in the travelling that the employee is required to do,

(b) "required" means that the travelling is necessary to the satisfactory performance of the employee's duties (it does not necessarily imply that the employer must order the employee to travel),

(c) "place of business" generally is considered to have reference to a permanent establishment of the employer such as an office, factory, warehouse, branch or store, or to a field office at a large construction job, and

(d) "in different places" generally refers to the situation where the employer does not have a single or fixed place of business. For example, a school inspector who has a number of schools to supervise and is required to travel from school to school meets this requirement. Similarly, an employee who is required to travel from building to building within the boundaries of the employer's property meets this requirement if the employer's property is very large and the distance between buildings is sufficient to justify the use of a "motor vehicle". On the other hand, where the employee is employed on a ship, the ship is the employer's place of business where the employee is ordinarily required to carry on the duties, and the fact that the ship may travel to different places is insufficient to meet this requirement.

33. Concerning ¶31(b) above, the requirement will be met where the following conditions are satisfied:

(a) the employer must clearly indicate on the required form T2200 (see ¶58 below) that the employee is required to pay travel expenses incurred in the performance of duties; and

(b) the employee's reasonable travel costs must not be fully reimbursed by the employer. In determining the reasonableness of the amount claimed by the employee for travel costs, consideration will be given to the mode of transportation used by the employee versus the mode of transportation that could be used to satisfy the requirement to travel.

34. Concerning the requirement in ¶31(c)(i) and ¶31(d)(i) above,

(a) where for one type of travel expense, an employee receives an allowance that is excluded from income by virtue of paragraph 6(1)(b), but the employee must pay a second type of travel expense for which no allowance or reimbursement is received, the second type of travel expense will not be disallowed provided it is otherwise deductible under paragraph 8(1)(h) or (h.1). For example, where an employee while on an out-of-town business trip receives a daily meal allowance that is excluded from income by virtue of subparagraph 6(1)(b)(vii) and the employee must bear the cost of "motor vehicle"

¶3300

expenses, the employee will not be prevented from claiming the vehicle expenses if they are otherwise allowable under paragraph $8(1)(h.1)$, and

(b) where an employee receives an allowance for travel expenses that must be included in income, the employee may claim actual expenses under paragraph $8(1)(h)$ or $(h.1)$ (and capital cost allowance and interest under paragraph $8(1)(j)$) if the other requirements of paragraph $8(1)(h)$ or $(h.1)$, and the requirement of subsection 8(10) as discussed in ¶58 below, are met.

Salespersons

35. Provided the requirement in subsection 8(10) is met (see ¶58 below) and subject to the limitation discussed in ¶37 below, amounts expended by an employee to earn employment income are deductible under paragraph $8(1)(f)$ where the employee is employed in the year in connection with the selling of property or negotiating of contracts, and

(a) the contract of employment required the employee to pay the expenses so incurred,

(b) the employee was ordinarily required to carry on the duties of employment away from the employer's place of business,

(c) the employee was remunerated in whole or in part by commissions or other similar amounts fixed by reference to the volume of the sales made or the contracts negotiated, and

(d) the employee was not in receipt of an allowance for travel expenses that was excluded from income by virtue of subparagraph $6(1)(b)(v)$ (see ¶45 below), to the extent that such amounts were not

(e) outlays, losses or replacements of capital or payments on account of capital, except capital cost allowance and interest deductible under paragraph $8(1)(j)$ as discussed in ¶15, ¶27 and ¶28 above,

(f) outlays or expenses made or incurred for club dues or the use of recreational facilities that would, by virtue of paragraph $18(1)(l)$, not be deductible if the employment were a business carried on by the salesperson. The paragraph $18(1)(l)$ restrictions are discussed in the current version of IT-148, *Recreational Properties and Club Dues*, or

(g) payments which reduced the amount of the standby charge that was required to be included in income in the year. See the current version of IT-352, *Employee's Expenses, Including Work Space in Home Expenses*, where an employee who is entitled to deduct expenses under paragraph $8(1)(f)$ has an office in the home.

36. Although expenses deductible under paragraph $8(1)(f)$ may include expenses other than travel expenses, the comments in ¶32, ¶33 and ¶34 above, which apply to employees in general, are applicable where relevant to any expenses claimed by a salesperson under paragraph $8(1)(f)$. In this regard and with reference to ¶34(a) above, the only expenses disallowed solely because the requirement in ¶35(d) above is not met will be those that relate to the particular travel allowance excluded from income by virtue of subparagraph $6(1)(b)(v)$.

37. The amount deductible under paragraph $8(1)(f)$ is limited to the amount of the commissions or other similar amounts referred to above in ¶35(c). This limitation does not apply, however, to amounts deducted under paragraph $8(1)(j)$ for capital cost allowance (see ¶15 above) or interest (see ¶27 and ¶28 above). Where the deduction under paragraph $8(1)(j)$, together with the deduction available under paragraph $8(1)(f)$, exceeds the employee's commission income, the excess may be applied against other income. Any excess not applicable in this manner will represent a non-capital loss of the employee.

38. Where a salesperson, who receives both a travel allowance that is excluded from income under subparagraph $6(1)(b)(vii)$ (for example, the meal allowance referred to in ¶34(a) above) and a "motor vehicle" allowance that is required to be included in income, includes both allowances in income and claims related expenses otherwise allowable under paragraph $8(1)(f)$, the Department will not challenge such reporting. However, it may be advantageous for a salesperson who meets the conditions set out in paragraph $8(1)(h.1)$ to only deduct motor vehicle expenses under that paragraph rather than include the allowance under subparagraph $6(1)(b)(vii)$ and deduct expenses under paragraph $8(1)(f)$.

Clergy

39. The requirement in ¶31(a) above will normally be met where a member of the clergy is ministering to a diocese, parish or congregation and is required to travel to dif-

¶3300

ferent places in the course of performing the related duties.

Allowances for Travel Expenses — General

40. In this bulletin, the word "allowance" means any periodic or other payment that an employee receives from an employer, in addition to salary or wages, without having to account for its use. It may be computed by reference to distance or time (for example, a "motor vehicle" expense allowance based on the distance driven or a travel expense allowance based on the number of days away) or on some other basis. An allowance is subject to tax unless it falls within the exceptions listed in subparagraphs $6(1)(b)(i)$ to (ix) or subsection $81(3.1)$ (see ¶54 below), or unless it is excluded from income under subsection $6(6)$ (see ¶53 below). See ¶50 below for a discussion on the meaning of "reimbursement" and "accountable advance".

41. If the Department considers that an allowance, which is claimed to be non-taxable under subparagraph $6(1)(b)(v)$, (vi), (vii) or (vii.1), is unreasonably high, the employee is required to provide vouchers or other acceptable evidence to show that the allowance is not in excess of a reasonable amount. Where the employee is unable to show that the allowance is reasonable, the whole amount of the allowance is included under paragraph $6(1)(b)$ in computing the employee's income and, if the employee qualifies, an amount may be deducted under paragraph $8(1)(f)$, (h), $(h.1)$ or (j), depending on the circumstances, as discussed in ¶31 through ¶38 above. An allowance for travel expenses is not considered unreasonable merely because the employee's total expenses for business travel exceed the total travel allowances received in the year.

42. Subparagraphs $6(1)(b)(x)$ and (xi) deem an allowance received in a taxation year by an employee for the use of a "motor vehicle" in connection with or in the course of an office or employment not to be a reasonable amount for the purposes of subparagraphs $6(1)(b)(v)$, (vi) and (vii.1) where

(a) the allowance is not calculated solely by reference to the number of kilometres for which the vehicle was so used in the year, or

(b) the employee receives an allowance for use of the vehicle and is reimbursed in whole or in part for expenses for the use of the vehicle in the year in connection with the office or employment except where, for the 1993 and later

taxation years, the reimbursement is for supplementary business insurance or toll or ferry charges and the amount of the allowance is determined without reference to those reimbursed expenses.

Where the allowance is not a reasonable amount the whole amount of the allowance is included under paragraph $6(1)(b)$ in computing the employee's income and, if the employee qualifies, an appropriate amount may be deducted under paragraph $8(1)(f)$, (h), $(h.1)$ or (j), depending on the circumstances, as discussed in ¶31 through ¶38 above.

43. In addition to the requirements in ¶42 above, in order to be excluded from income by virtue of paragraphs $6(1)(b)(v)$, (vi) or (vii.1), the allowance for a motor vehicle must be reasonable. Under section 7306 of the Regulations a payer will be limited to a deduction based on 31 cents for the first 5,000 kilometres and 25 cents for the remaining kilometres (or 35 cents and 29 cents, respectively, where the kilometres are driven in the Yukon or Northwest Territories). Although the reasonableness of an allowance is normally decided based on the facts of the particular case, the Department will, as a general rule, accept as reasonable an allowance based on 31 cents (or 35 cents in the Yukon or Northwest Territories) for the first 5,000 kilometres and 25 cents (or 29 cents in the Yukon or Northwest Territories) for the remaining kilometres, or such other amounts as may be prescribed, where such allowance is not materially different from that which would otherwise be considered reasonable.

Note: In a Press Release dated December 12, 1995, the Parliamentary Secretary to the Minister of Finance announced that for 1996 the limit for tax-exempt allowances paid by employers to employees will be increased from 31 cents to 33 cents for the first 5,000 kilometres driven, and from 25 cents to 27 cents per kilometre for each additional kilometre driven (except for the Yukon and Northwest Territories, where the tax-exempt allowance will be 37 cents for the first 5,000 kilometres driven, and 31 cents for each additional kilometre).

44. Where an employee receives a set periodic (monthly, weekly, etc.) amount from the employer, and the amount is calculated solely by reference to the number of kilometres for which the automobile was used in the year in an office or employment the periodic amount may constitute an

¶3300

advance rather than an allowance. It will constitute an advance where all of the following attributes are present:

(a) there is a beginning-of-the-year agreement between the employer and employee that the employee will receive a stated amount for each kilometre travelled by the employee's vehicle in connection with or in the course of the office or employment;

(b) there is a year-end accounting. That is, at the end of the year (or, where the employee ceases to be employed during the year, at the time the employment ceases), the total of the periodic advances received in the year is compared with the result obtained when the stated amount per kilometre is multiplied by the kilometres travelled by the vehicle in the year in connection with or in the course of the office or employment. If the total of the advances exceeds the result so obtained, the employee must reimburse the employer for the amount of the difference and vice-versa. Simply reporting any excess on the employee's T4 supplementary is not acceptable; and

(c) the per-kilometre amount, the amount of each monthly advance and the projected annual kilometrage are reasonable.

For further information on advances, see ¶50 to ¶52 below under the caption Reimbursements and Accountable Advances.

Allowance for Travel Expenses — Salespersons and Clergy

45. Subject to the comments in ¶42 above, a reasonable allowance for travel expenses is non-taxable by reason of subparagraph $6(1)(b)(v)$ provided it was for a period when the employee was employed in connection with the selling of property or negotiating of contracts for the employer. Consequently, the subparagraph does not apply to bill-collectors, maintenance or servicepersons, or to salespersons when engaged in any duties other than selling.

46. Subject to the comments in ¶42 above, a reasonable allowance received by a member of the clergy is non-taxable by reason of subparagraph $6(1)(b)(vi)$ provided that

(a) the member was in charge of or ministering to a diocese, parish or congregation, and

(b) the allowance was for transportation expenses incident to the discharge of the duties of the office or employment.

47. Where an employee referred to in subparagraph $6(1)(b)(v)$, (vi), (vii) or (vii.1) receives an allowance for travel expenses which is unreasonably low, the allowance is technically required to be included in income. However, the Department will not insist upon its inclusion provided that no amount is claimed for travel expenses by the employee under paragraph $8(1)(h)$ or $(h.1)$.

Allowance For Travel Expenses — Other Employees

48. An allowance (other than for the use of a "motor vehicle") received by an employee (other than one employed in connection with the selling of property or negotiating of contracts for the employer) for travel expenses is taxable under paragraph $6(1)(b)$ except where the conditions of subparagraph $6(1)(b)(vii)$ are satisfied; that is,

(a) the allowance is a reasonable amount,

(b) the allowance is received for travelling away from the municipality and the metropolitan area where the employer's establishment, at which the employee ordinarily worked or to which the employee made reports, was located, and

(c) the travelling is done in the performance of the duties of the office or employment.

49. An allowance received by an employee (other than one employed in connection with the selling of property or negotiating of contracts for the employer) for the use of a "motor vehicle" is taxable under paragraph $6(1)(b)$ except where the conditions of subparagraphs $6(1)(b)(vii.1)$, are satisfied; that is,

(a) the allowance is a reasonable amount (see ¶42 above), and

(b) the allowance is received for travelling in the performance of the duties of the office or employment.

Travelling to the place where a person works generally does not qualify as "travelling in the performance of the duties of the office or employment". For example, an employee described in ¶57(a) below would not be "travelling in the performance of the duties of the office or employment" when the

¶3300

employee is travelling from his or her residence to the employer's place of business where he or she reports for instruction or work assignment but the same employee would be "travelling in the performance of the duties of the office or employment" when the employee is travelling between the employer's place of business where the instructions or work assignments are received and where the employer is carrying out the contract.

Reimbursements and Accountable Advances

50. In this bulletin, "reimbursement" and "accountable advance" have the following meanings:

(a) a reimbursement means a payment by an employer to an employee to repay the employee for amounts spent by the employee on the employer's business. Where an employee receives a reasonable allowance to cover particular "motor vehicle" expenses and for other "motor vehicle" expenses the employee charges the cost to the employer (for example, the employee uses the employer's credit card), the amount charged to the employer does not represent a reimbursement. Where subparagraphs 6(1)(b)(x) and (xi) do not apply (see ¶42 above) and the conditions in subparagraph 6(1)(b)(vii.1) are satisfied (see ¶49 above), the allowance is excluded from income under subparagraph 6(1)(b)(vii.1); and

(b) an accountable advance means an amount given by an employer to an employee for expenses to be incurred by the employee on the employer's business and to be accounted for by the production of vouchers and the return of any amount not so spent.

51. Usually a reimbursement or an accountable advance for travel expenses is not income in the hands of the employee receiving it, unless it represents payment of the employee's personal expenses. For example, a reimbursement or accountable advance for expenses incurred in travelling between home and the employer's place of business at which the employee ordinarily reports for work is included in income.

52. Where a spouse accompanies an employee on a business trip, the payment or reimbursement by the employer of the spouse's travel expenses is a taxable benefit to the employee, unless the spouse was, in fact, engaged primarily in business activities on behalf of the employer during the trip.

Employment at Special Work Site

53. An allowance, accountable advance or reimbursement received by an employee for board and lodging or certain transportation expenses is excluded from income under subsection 6(6) provided that all the requirements of that subsection are met. In general, this subsection applies to an employee who is required to work at a location some distance from home, either because the duties there are of a temporary nature or because the remoteness of the location is such that the employee could not reasonably be expected to establish a home there. In order to qualify, among other things, the duties of employment must require the employee to be away from home for a period of at least 36 hours. Detailed comments on the requirements of subsection 6(6) are contained in the current version of IT-91, *Employment at Special or Remote Work Sites*.

Part-time Employees

54. The cost of getting to and from the place of employment is a personal or living expense of the employee. Subsection 81(3.1) provides that, to the extent it does not exceed a reasonable amount, an allowance or reimbursement of travel expenses paid by an employer to a part-time employee for travelling to and from the employee's part-time employment shall not be included in computing the employee's income provided that

(a) the part-time employee and the employer were dealing at arm's length,

(b) throughout the period that the expenses were incurred, the employee had other employment or was carrying on a business,

(c) the allowance or reimbursement was paid on account of travel expenses incurred by the employee in respect of part-time employment, other than expenses incurred in the performance of the duties of the part-time employment, and

(d) the duties of the part-time employment were performed at a location not less than 80 kilometres from both the ordinary place of residence and the principal place of employment or business of the employee.

Meals

55. Except where the employee is required to be away from home for a period of at least twelve hours from the munici-

¶3300

pality and the metropolitan area in which the employer's establishment is located, subsection 8(4) provides that the employee may not deduct under paragraph 8(1)(*f*) or (*h*) the cost of meals consumed while away from home in the course of performing the duties of employment. This means that the employee usually cannot be allowed a deduction for meals unless they are consumed during a trip that requires an overnight stay away from home. Where the employee is entitled to deduct an amount for the cost of a meal, the amount deductible is limited under subsection 67.1(1) to 50% (80% for expenses incurred before February 22, 1994 for food and beverages consumed before March 1994) of the lesser of

(a) the amount paid for the meal, and

(b) a reasonable amount for the meal.

The limitation on the cost of meals is discussed in the current version of IT-518, *Food, Beverages and Entertainment Expenses*. For further information, see the current version of Information Circular 73-21, *Away-from-Home Expenses*.

56. The employer's establishment referred to in subsection 8(4) is the one to which the employee ordinarily reports for work. It includes an employer's place of business (see ¶32(c) above) and may also include any place where the employer is carrying out a contract. Where the employer has more than one place of business to which an employee ordinarily reports on a continuing basis, the establishment referred to in subsection 8(4) is the one to which the employee reports most frequently. Where more than one of the employer's places of business is located within the same municipality or metropolitan area, all such places of business will be viewed as a single establishment for the purpose of subsection 8(4).

57. In determining whether subsection 8(4) applies to an employee who is working at a place where the employer is carrying out a contract, a distinction must be made between two groups of employees.

(a) The first group consists of employees (for example, supervisory engineers) who are employed on a more-or-less permanent basis. Where such an employee is required to report for instruction or a new assignment at a place of business of the employer but spends most of the time away from it working at places where the employer is carrying out contracts, subsection 8(4) does not prevent the employee from deducting the cost of meals (subject to the percentage limitation discussed in

¶55 above) consumed while away for the required 12 hours from the municipality and metropolitan area in which that place of business is located. However, subsection 8(4) will apply if the employee is not so away.

(b) The second group consists of temporary employees; for example, employees hired to work on a particular project of the employer and who may or may not be kept on the payroll when that project is completed. Where such an employee is hired to work solely at a place where the employer is carrying out a contract and the employee's responsibility is to report to that place for work and to receive instructions from a person who is in charge there (that is, the employee does not ordinarily report to any other establishment of the employer), the place where the contract is being carried out is regarded as the employer's particular establishment to which the employee ordinarily reports for work. By reason of subsection 8(4), amounts spent on meals consumed while working at that place are not deductible in computing the employee's income. However, where the employer requires the employee to work somewhere else on a temporary basis so that the employee is away for at least twelve hours from the municipality and metropolitan area in which the particular establishment is located, the employee is entitled to a deduction for the cost of meals, subject to the percentage limitation discussed in ¶55 above.

The comments in (b) above generally are also applicable in the case of any employee who is hired at a series of places at which the employer is carrying out a contract or contracts, each such place in turn being looked upon as the establishment to which the employee is ordinarily required to report for work during the time worked there. The deduction entitlement referred to in the last sentence of (b) above is unlikely to have any application to such an employee.

General Remarks

58. Subsection 8(10) provides that no amount may be deducted under paragraph 8(1)(*f*), (*h*) or (*h*.1) for a year unless the employee obtains a form T2200, *Declaration of Conditions of Employment* signed by the employer certifying that the conditions set out in paragraph 8(1)(*f*), (*h*) or (*h*.1) were met for that year. The T2200 should be kept with the taxpayer's records for examination on request.

¶3300

59. Travel expenses, to be allowable, must be incurred by the employee exclusively for travelling in the course of employment. Amounts paid for business promotion (for example, costs of entertainment of customers or suppliers) are not travel expenses, even though laid out for business reasons while the employee is travelling in the course of employment and even though the employer may provide for such expenses in any travelling allowance made to the employee. Although they are not travel expenses, costs of entertainment may qualify under paragraph 8(1)(f) as a deduction from income where the requirements of that paragraph are met (see ¶35 and ¶36 above). Where an employee is entitled to deduct an amount for the cost of entertainment, the amount deductible is limited under subsection 67.1(1) to 50% (80% for expenses incurred before February 22, 1994 for entertainment enjoyed before March 1994) of the lesser of

(a) the amount paid for the entertainment, and

(b) an amount for the entertainment that would be reasonable in the circumstances. The limitation for the cost of entertainment is discussed in the current version of IT-518, *Food, Beverages and Entertainment Expenses.*

60. To the extent that travel expenses are unreasonable, they are not deductible by virtue of section 67.

61. Pursuant to subsection 6(8), an employee who

(a) deducts an expense under section 8 or

(b) includes an amount in the capital cost of a motor vehicle that is used, or an aircraft that is required for use, in the performance of the employee's duties of an office or employment and the employee receives a rebate for any GST for the expense or for the capital cost of the motor vehicle or aircraft, the amount of the rebate in the year of receipt

(c) is included in income from an office or employment to the extent the rebate relates to the expense, or

(d) reduces the capital cost of the motor vehicle or aircraft to the extent that the rebate relates to that property.

Preparation of T4 Slips by Employer

62. If an employer is providing its employees with allowances, reimbursements

or accountable advances for travel expenses, reference should be made to ¶40 through ¶52 above when preparing T4 slips.

Appendix

Assumptions:

● Mr. Sammy Runz is a travelling salesperson who receives a commission on his sales. He is required to pay his automobile expenses but receives an allowance of $.22 per kilometre plus a reimbursement of up to $50 per month for petroleum products.

● In 1993, Mr. Runz sold an automobile for $4,000 which he had used in his employment from the time of its acquisition in 1990. Mr. Runz paid $20,000 including PST and GST for this automobile. (Prior to the acquisition of this car, Mr. Runz used automobiles supplied by his employer.) Mr. Runz claims the maximum amount of capital cost allowance to which he is entitled.

● On September 1, 1993, Mr. Runz purchased a new automobile at a cost of $28,000 plus GST and PST (which amounted to $4,200). To assist in purchasing this automobile he borrowed some money and paid interest of $800 on the debt. Mr. Runz retired this debt on December 31, 1993.

● In 1994, Mr. Runz's employer decided to resume supplying its salespersons with automobiles and on June 30, 1994 Mr. Runz sold the automobile that he had purchased in 1993 to his employer for the fair market value at June 30, 1994.

Analysis:

While a reasonable allowance for travel expenses of a person engaged in selling property or negotiating contracts for an employer need not be included in income by virtue of subparagraph 6(1)(b)(v) (see ¶45 above) the amount that Mr. Runz received is deemed by subparagraph 6(1)(b)(xi) not to be a reasonable allowance since he received both an allowance and a reimbursement of expenses (see ¶42 above).

If Mr. Runz's employer provides him with a form T2200, *Declaration of Conditions of Employment* (see ¶58 above) and certifies that the conditions set out in paragraph 8(1)(f) are met (see ¶35 above) Mr. Runz will be able to claim capital cost allowance and interest expense under paragraph

¶3300

$8(1)(j)$ for the automobiles used by him in his employment (see ¶15 and ¶27 above).

The automobile that Mr. Runz acquired in 1990 was placed in Class 10 of Schedule II of the Regulations (see ¶17 above) since the prescribed amount for passenger vehicles purchased in 1990 was $24,000 (see the discussion of subsection 7307(1) of the Regulations in ¶9 above). Mr. Runz may include capital cost allowance of $3,000 in 1990, $5,100 in 1991 and $3,570 in 1992$^{(1)}$ in calculating the amount of automobile expenses that he can deduct in those years. He is not entitled to include either capital cost allowance or a terminal loss in calculating his income for 1993 for the automobile that he purchased in 1990.

The automobile that Mr. Runz acquired in 1993 was placed in Class 10.1 of Schedule II of the Regulations (see ¶17 above) since the prescribed amount for passenger vehicles purchased after 1990 is $24,000 plus the GST and PST on $24,000 (see the discussion of subsection 7307(1) of the Regulations in ¶9 above). The amount of $24,000 plus GST and PST thereon was $27,600 in the province where Mr. Runz lived. Mr. Runz can include $4,140$^{(2)}$ in 1993 and $3,519$^{(3)}$ in 1994 of capital cost allowance on this vehicle in calculating the amount of automobile expenses that he can deduct in those years. There can be neither a recapture of capital cost allowance nor a terminal loss on the disposition of a Class 10.1 property (see ¶18 and ¶24 above).

Mr. Runz can include the interest of $800 in calculating the amount of motor vehicle expenses that he can deduct in 1993. The interest limit discussed in ¶28 above is $300 $\div$ 30 $\times$ 122 = $1,220.

While Mr. Runz includes the various amounts of capital cost allowance and interest noted above in calculating the amount of motor vehicle expenses for the year he must reduce those amounts to reflect his personal use of the automobile to determine the amount that he can deduct in calculating his income.

$^{(1)}$ The capital cost allowance is calculated as:

1990 cost of acquisition	$20,000
1990 CCA (30% $\times$ 20,000 $\times$ ½*)	3,000
1990 Undepreciated capital cost	$17,000
1991 CCA (30% $\times$ 17,000)	5,100
1991 Undepreciated capital cost	$11,900
1992 CCA (30% $\times$ 11,900)	3,570
1992 Undepreciated capital cost	$ 8,330
1993 Proceeds of disposition	4,000
	$ 4,330

$^{(2)}$ Capital cost allowance for 1993 is calculated as:

1993 cost of acquisition as determined under paragraph 13(7)(g) (see ¶16 above)	$27,600
1993 CCA (30% $\times$ 27,600 $\times$ ½*)	4,140
1993 Undepreciated capital cost	$23,460

$^{(3)}$ Capital cost allowance for 1994 is calculated as:

Undepreciated capital cost at the end of 1993	$23,460
1994 CCA (30% $\times$ 23,460 $\times$ ½**)	$ 3,519

*Pursuant to subsection 1100(2) of the Regulations, CCA is reduced to one half of the normal amount in the year a motor vehicle is acquired or becomes available for use (see ¶24 above).

**Pursuant to subsection 1100(2.5) of the Regulations, CCA is reduced to one half of the normal amount in the year a Class 10.1 motor vehicle is disposed of (see ¶24 above).

Explanation of Changes

Introduction

The purpose of the Explanation of Changes is to explain the reasons for the revisions to an interpretation bulletin. It outlines revisions that we have made as a result of changes to the law, as well as changes reflecting new or revised departmental interpretations.

Overview

The bulletin describes the taxability of allowances for travelling expenses that an employee may receive in connection with an office or employment and the sales and travel expenses that an employee may deduct in computing income from such a source.

The bulletin reflects amendments to the *Income Tax Act* resulting from S.C. 1994, c.7 Schedule II (S.C. 1991, c.49 — formerly Bill C-18), S.C. 1994, c.21 (formerly Bill C-27), and S.C. 1995, c.3 (formerly Bill C-59). In a Press Release dated December 12, 1995, the Parliamentary Secretary to the Minister of Finance referred to subsections 7307(1)–(4) of the Regulations (as described in paragraphs 9 and 28 of the bulletin) and announced that the subsections would not be changed for 1996. Except as described in the note following ¶43, the comments in the bulletin are not otherwise affected by proposed legislation that has been released as of February 16, 1996.

¶3300

Legislative and Other Changes

¶1 reflects the amended definition of "automobile" contained in Bill C-18. Generally, the amendment removes from the definition of "automobile", buses, vans, pick-up trucks and motor vehicles used for transporting passengers in the business of arranging or managing funerals.

¶9 reflects the amendment to section 67.3 contained in Bill C-18. The amendment deletes the reference to provincial sales tax and permits taxpayers using the cash basis method of calculating income to deduct amounts paid in connection with the cost of leasing a passenger vehicle. A description of the relevant prescribed amounts was also added.

¶10 gives an example of the application of section 67.3, including the changes described in ¶9, and reflects the amounts presently prescribed in section 7307 of the Regulations. ¶31 reflects an amendment to paragraph $8(1)(h)$ and the addition of paragraph $8(1)(h.1)$ by Bill C-18. Paragraph $8(1)(h)$ is no longer concerned with motor vehicle travel expenses which are now dealt with in paragraph $8(1)(h.1)$.

¶35 (former ¶36) reflects the amendment in Bill C-18 to paragraph $8(1)(f)$. This amendment clarifies the limits of the deduction provided for under paragraph $8(1)(f)$ by stating that no deduction is permitted for a payment which results in a reduction of the standby charge that would otherwise be included in the employee's income.

¶38 (former ¶39) was revised to incorporate observations from former ¶34 and to describe that it may be advantageous for a salesperson who is in receipt of two travel allowances (only one of which is excluded from income) and who is entitled to deduct motor vehicle expenses under paragraph $8(1)(h.1)$ to only deduct expenses under that paragraph rather than include both allowances in income and deduct expenses under paragraph $8(1)(f)$.

¶42 (former ¶43) reflects the amendments in Bill C-18 and Bill C-27 to subparagraphs $6(1)(b)(x)$ and (xi). It is now provided that an allowance under subparagraph $6(1)(b)(v)$, (vi) or (vii.1) is deemed not to be a reasonable amount and must therefore be included in income if the employee is also reimbursed in whole or in part for expenses other than supplementary business insurance, toll or ferry charges, or if the allowance is not based solely on the number of kilometres the vehicle is used for employment purposes.

¶43 (former ¶45) reflects the regulations as promulgated. A note has been added following the paragraph to describe a Press Release dated December 12, 1995 which, for 1996, increased the tax-exempt allowances paid by employers to employees by 2 cents per kilometre.

¶49 (former ¶51) was expanded to provide an example of an employee travelling in the performance of the duties of an office or employment.

¶55 (former ¶58) reflects the Bill C-59 amendment to subsection 67.1 which reduced the portion of the cost of food and beverages that an employee could deduct to 50% from 80%.

¶59 (former ¶61) reflects the Bill C-59 amendment to subsection 67.1 which reduced the portion of the cost of entertainment that an employee could deduct to 50% from 80%.

¶62 was added to reflect subsection 6(8). The provision applies to an employee who in certain circumstances receives a rebate of the goods and services tax.

Former ¶46 was not carried forward as the comments are no longer relevant.

Former ¶52 was not carried forward as subparagraphs $6(1)(b)(vii)$ and (vii.1) were amended by Bill C-18 to permit allowances that are not reasonable to be included in income rather than only those in excess of a reasonable amount.

An Appendix was added to illustrate some of the provisions discussed in the bulletin.

Throughout the bulletin we have deleted observations which are no longer relevant and we have revised some of the wording to improve readability without altering the substance.

¶3300

CHAPTER 15

INFORMATION CIRCULARS

Please note that, while all Information Circulars reproduced below were the versions current at time of publication of this book, some may not reflect the most recent amendments to the law and regulations. Reference should also be made to the text of the law and regulations when consulting a Circular.

[3500] Information Circular No. 84-1: Revision of Capital Cost Allowance Claims and Other Permissive Deductions

[Interpretation Bulletin 84-1 is dated July 9, 1984.]

The guidelines in cancelled IT-112R are now incorporated in this Information Circular. There has been no change in the Department's practice set out in cancelled IT-112R in respect to claims for capital cost allowance or other permissive deductions. The practice is continued without interruption.

1. From time to time, the Department receives requests from taxpayers to permit a revision of capital cost allowance claims for previous taxation years. As well, the situation often arises where a revision results from a reassessment by the Department. The following comments outline the types of revisions that generally occur and the circumstances under which requests for a revision will be accepted by the Department. These comments apply equally to other permissive deductions, such as special mortgage reserves calculated under section 33, scientific research expenditures of a capital nature calculated under paragraph $37(1)(b)$, or taxable capital gains reserves calculated under subparagraph $40(1)(a)(iii)$.

2. A reference to the words "reassessment of tax" or "taxes payable" in this circular includes, in the case of a self-employed individual, a reference to contributions required under the *Canada Pension Plan Act*.

3. Under paragraph $20(1)(a)$ of the *Income Tax Act* a taxpayer has the right to deduct, in computing income for tax purposes, such amounts of capital cost allowance (up to the maximum allowed by regulation) as are desired. Any revision to an amount previously deducted, which the Department may make, as described in 4, 5, 6, 8, 9 and 10 below, will not be made unless the taxpayer makes the request in writing.

Reassessments

4. Where a taxpayer has charged to expense in a year the cost of property which should have been capitalized, that expense will be disallowed to the taxpayer by virtue of paragraph 18(1)(b). In such cases the taxpayer will be allowed, if so desired, to make a revised capital cost allowance claim for the year in order to claim capital cost allowance on the cost of the property that should have been capitalized.

5. Where an upward reassessment of tax is made in a year through adjustments other than those outlined in 4 above, and a taxpayer has not claimed maximum capital cost allowances in all classes in that year, the taxpayer will be advised of the circumstances and allowed, if so desired, to make a revised claim for that year.

6. Where a taxpayer has claimed more capital cost allowance than is permissible for one class of property and less than the maximum allowed for another class, the Department would ordinarily be required to reassess tax on the excess allowance claimed over the maximum for the former class. In these circumstances the taxpayer will be allowed, if so desired, to have some part of the excessive allowance transferred to the latter class.

Errors in Classification

7. Where there is a misclassification of depreciable property by a taxpayer, revision of the capital cost allowance schedules will ordinarily be made for all years that can be reassessed within the limitations imposed by subsection 152(4). It should be noted, however, that where depreciable property has been misclassified by a taxpayer or should have, but has not, been reclassified by a taxpayer pursuant to a change in the Act or Regulations, and an allowance in respect of the capital cost of that property has been claimed and allowed under the incorrect class, subsection 13(6) provides that the Minister of National Revenue may direct that, for years prior to the year specified in the direction, the misclassified property be deemed to have been property of the class in which it was originally classified, and then be deemed to have been transferred to its proper class at the beginning of the specified year. Subsection 13(5) sets out the mechanics under which transfers of misclassified property are dealt with in such circumstances and is explained in detail in

Interpretation Bulletin IT-190R2, "Capital Cost Allowance — Transferred and Misclassified Property."

Property Subject to "Certification"

8. A taxpayer may acquire depreciable property of one class which after "certification" or "acceptance" by a designated Minister or other body then qualifies for inclusion in another class providing for a faster write-off. For example, a motion picture film otherwise property of class $10(q)$ becomes property of class $12(n)$ after certification as a certified feature film. Where this is the case and the taxpayer's year-end intervenes between the date of acquisition of the property and the date "certification" or "acceptance" in respect of that property is given, it is the Department's policy to allow the taxpayer, after the date of certification or acceptance, to treat the property as property of the class providing for the faster write-off, effective from the date of acquisition. The taxpayer may then make revised claims for additional capital cost allowance for all prior taxation years affected that are not statute barred to reassessment, unless the comments in 10 below with regard to statute-barred years apply.

Revisions Requested in Taxable Years

9. If a taxpayer requests a revision of capital cost allowance claimed in a year that was assessable to tax, such requests will be acceded to only if the time has not expired for filing a notice of objection in respect of that year (i.e., 90 days from the day of mailing of the notice of assessment or reassessment for that year) unless the comments in 8 above apply. If, however, circumstances are such that the request for revision of capital cost allowance claimed in a year accompanies a request for an offsetting change in some other "permissive" deduction, the result of which is that no change occurs in the assessed tax for that year (or any other year for which the 90 day time-limit has expired), such requests will ordinarily be acceded to.

Revisions Requested in Non-Taxable Years

10. Where a taxpayer requests a revision of capital cost allowance claimed in a taxation year for which a notification that no tax is payable had been issued (e.g., because of a non-capital loss in that year, the application of a non-capital loss of another year, or the

¶3500

fact that income was exempt from tax in that year), such request will be allowed provided there is no change in the tax payable for the year or any other year filed, including one that is statute barred, for which the time has expired for filing a notice of objection. Such request will not be allowed, however, where after February 24, 1977 the Minister has issued a notice of determination pursuant to subsection 152(1.1). A taxpayer who wishes to revise the capital cost allowance in a year for which a notice of determination has been issued should do so within 90 days from the day of mailing the notice of determination for that year.

Requests for Revision

11. Where a taxpayer wishes to request a revision of prior years' capital cost allowance claims within the limits described above, a letter should be forwarded to the director of the district taxation office in which the taxpayer files income tax returns. This letter should set out the pertinent information concerning the requested revisions along with amended capital cost allowance schedules and any other schedules which are affected by the revision.

Future Position of the Department

12. In view of the changes to the *Income Tax Act* by S.C. 1983-84, Chapter 1, the Department will be reviewing the above positions and may announce changes at a later date.

¶3500

REFERENCE TABLES

Income Tax Act

Interpretation Bulletins

Information Circulars

INDEX

Ded

Eli

Oil

Tax

Tax